INTRODUCTION TO
Physical Anthropology

FIFTEENTH EDITION

Robert Jurmain
Professor Emeritus, San Jose State University

Lynn Kilgore
University of Colorado, Boulder

Wenda Trevathan
Professor Emerita, New Mexico State University

Russell L. Ciochon
University of Iowa

Eric J. Bartelink
Associate Professor, California State University, Chico

CENGAGE
Learning®

Australia • Brazil • Mexico • Singapore • United Kingdom • United States

**Introduction to Physical Anthropology,
Fifteenth Edition**
Robert Jurmain, Lynn Kilgore,
Wenda Trevathan, Eric J. Bartelink

Product Director: Marta Lee-Perriard

Product Manager: Nedah Rose

Content Developer: Kate Scheinman

Content Development Manager:
Trudy Brown

Product Assistant: Timothy A. Kappler

Content Project Manager: Rita Jaramillo

Art Director: Michael Cook

Manufacturing Planner: Judy Inouye

Production Service/Compositor:
MPS Limited

Text Designer: Diane Beasley

Cover Designer: Michael Cook

Cover Images: Chimp: David Tipling/Getty;
DNA: Titima Ongkantong/Shutterstock;
Skull: Russell L. Ciochon

For product information and technology assistance, contact us at
Cengage Learning Customer & Sales Support, 1-800-354-9706.
For permission to use material from this text or product,
submit all requests online at www.cengage.com/permissions.
Further permissions questions can be e-mailed to
permissionrequest@cengage.com.

Library of Congress Control Number: 2016947229

Student Edition:
ISBN: 978-1-337-09982-0

Loose-leaf Edition:
ISBN: 978-1-337-11569-8

Cengage Learning
20 Channel Center Street
Boston, MA 02210
USA

Cengage Learning is a leading provider of customized learning solutions with
employees residing in nearly 40 different countries and sales in more than
125 countries around the world. Find your local representative at **www.cengage.com.**

Cengage Learning products are represented in Canada by Nelson Education, Ltd.

To learn more about Cengage Learning Solutions, visit **www.cengage.com.**

Purchase any of our products at your local college store or at our preferred online
store **www.cengagebrain.com.**

Printed in the United States of America

ARCTIC OCEAN

75°N

Circle

NORWAY

SWEDEN   FINLAND

60°N

RUSSIA

Sungir

ESTONIA
LATVIA
DENMARK   LITHUANIA
Neander   BELARUS
Valley
Spy
Heidelberg (Mauer)   Okladnikov Cave/Denisova Cave
Mladeč, Předmosti, Dolní Věstonice
KAZAKHSTAN   MONGOLIA
45°N
Krapina   Oase
UZBEKISTAN
Arago   Dmanisi   Jinniushan   NORTH KOREA
Ceprano   Teshik-Tash   Zhoukoudian
Petralona   Ordos   Dali   SOUTH KOREA
TURKEY   CHINA   JAPAN
Tighenif   Lantian
30°N
Amud   IRAN   Hexian
Jebel   Shanidar
Skhul/Tabun   Qafzeh   PAKISTAN   PACIFIC
LIBYA   Liujiang   Maba
EGYPT   NEPAL   BHUTAN   Tropic of Cancer
TAIWAN
SAUDI ARABIA   INDIA   MYANMAR   HONG KONG
MACAU
Toros-Menalla   OMAN   OCEAN   15°N
CHAD   SUDAN   YEMEN   BANGLADESH
LAOS
NIGER   THAILAND   VIETNAM   PHILIPPINES   NORTHERN
MARIANA
ISLANDS
Hadar   DJIBOUTI   KAMPUCHEA   REPUBLIC OF THE
Middle Awash (Aramis, Bouri,   MARSHALL ISLANDS
Bodo   Herto, Dikika)   SRI LANKA
ETHIOPIA   MALDIVES   FEDERATED STATES
Omo   SOMALIA   BRUNEI   OF MICRONESIA
East and West Turkana   Niah Cave   Equator
UGANDA   KENYA   MALAYSIA   BORNEO
Kanapoi   SINGAPORE
Tugen Hills   RWANDA
Olduvai/Laetoli   BURUNDI   INDIAN   PAPUA
TANZANIA   Ngandong   NEW GUINEA   SOLOMON ISLANDS
SEYCHELLES   Sangiran   INDONESIA   TUVALU
COMOROS ISLANDS   Trinil   Flores
15°S
ZAMBIA   MAURITIUS   VANUATU
Kabwe   MADAGASCAR   OCEAN   NEW CALEDONIA   FIJI
ZIMBABWE
NAMIBIA   BOTSWANA   MOZAMBIQUE   AUSTRALIA   Tropic of Capricorn
MALAWI
WALVIS BAY   Sterkfontein/Swartkrans/Drimolen/Malapa
(status to be   Lake Mungo   30°S
determined)   Taung   SWAZILAND
Florisbad   Border Cave   Kow Swamp
LESOTHO
SOUTH AFRICA   NEW ZEALAND
Klasies River Mouth   45°S

1. SLOVENIA
2. CROATIA
3. BOSNIA AND HERZEGOVINA
4. ALBANIA
5. MACEDONIA
6. SERBIA AND MONTENEGRO

60°S

75°S

30°E   60°E   90°E   120°E   150°E

Brief Contents

CHAPTER 1 Introduction to Physical Anthropology   3

Heredity and Evolution

CHAPTER 2 The Development of Evolutionary Theory   25

CHAPTER 3 The Biological Basis of Life   49

CHAPTER 4 Heredity and Evolution   81

CHAPTER 5 Macroevolution: Processes of Vertebrate and Mammalian Evolution   113

Primates

CHAPTER 6 Survey of the Living Primates   143

CHAPTER 7 Primate Behavior   185

CHAPTER 8 Overview of the Fossil Primates   225

Hominin Evolution

CHAPTER 9 Paleoanthropology: Reconstructing Early Hominin Behavior and Ecology   263

CHAPTER 10 Hominin Origins in Africa   287

CHAPTER 11 The First Dispersal of the Genus *Homo: Homo erectus* and Contemporaries   319

CHAPTER 12 Premodern Humans   347

CHAPTER 13 The Origin and Dispersal of Modern Humans   383

Contemporary Human Evolution

CHAPTER 14 Modern Human Biology: Patterns of Variation   411

CHAPTER 15 Modern Human Biology: Patterns of Adaptation   437

CHAPTER 16 Legacies of Human Evolutionary History: Effects on the Life Course   467

CHAPTER 17 The Human Disconnection   491

Appendix A: Atlas of Primate Skeletal Anatomy   507

Appendix B: Sexing and Aging the Skeleton   515

Glossary   520

References   531

Index   557

Contents

Preface   xi
Acknowledgments   xv
Supplements   xvii

CHAPTER 1

Introduction to Physical Anthropology   3

The Human Connection   6
Biocultural Evolution   6
What Is Anthropology?   10

Cultural Anthropology   11
Linguistic Anthropology   11
Archaeology   12
Physical Anthropology   12
Applied Anthropology   18
Physical Anthropology and the Scientific Method   19
The Anthropological Perspective   21
A Closer Look   Forensic Anthropology in Practice   22
Summary of Main Topics   23
Critical Thinking Questions   23

Heredity and Evolution

CHAPTER 2

The Development of Evolutionary Theory   25

A Brief History of Evolutionary Thought   26
    The Scientific Revolution   28
    Precursors of the Theory of Evolution   29
    The Discovery of Natural Selection   33
    In Darwin's Shadow   38
Natural Selection   39
    Natural Selection in Action   39
    Natural Selection and Reproductive Success   41
Constraints on Nineteenth-Century Evolutionary Theory   42
Opposition to Evolution Today   43
    A Brief History of Opposition to Evolution in the United States   44
At a Glance   The Mechanism of Natural Selection   45
How Do We Know?   46

Summary of Main Topics   47
Critical Thinking Questions   47

CHAPTER 3

The Biological Basis of Life   49

Cells   50
From DNA to Protein   52
    DNA Structure   52
A Closer Look   Rosalind Franklin: The Fourth (but Invisible) Member of the Double Helix Team   53
    DNA Replication   53
    Protein Synthesis   54
What Is a Gene?   57
A Closer Look   Noncoding DNA—Not Junk After All   59
Regulatory Genes   60
At a Glance   Coding and Noncoding DNA   61
Mutation: When Genes Change   62

Cell Division   64
  Chromosomes   64
  Karyotyping Chromosomes   66
  Mitosis   67
  Meiosis   69
New Frontiers   72
How Do We Know?   77
Summary of Main Topics   78
Critical Thinking Questions   78

CHAPTER 4

Heredity and Evolution   81

The Genetic Principles Discovered by Mendel   83
  Segregation   84
  Dominance and Recessiveness   85
  Independent Assortment   86
Mendelian Inheritance in Humans   87
  Misconceptions about Dominance
  and Recessiveness   89
  Patterns of Mendelian Inheritance   90
Non-Mendelian Inheritance   94
  Polygenic Inheritance   94
At a Glance   Mendelian vs. Polygenic Traits   96
  Mitochondrial Inheritance   97
  Pleiotropy   97
Genetic and Environmental Factors   98
Modern Evolutionary Theory   98
  The Modern Synthesis   98
  A Current Definition of Evolution   99
Factors That Produce and Redistribute
Variation   100
  Mutation   100
  Gene Flow   100
  Genetic Drift and Founder Effect   102
Natural Selection Is Directional and Acts on
Variation   105
Review of Genetics and Evolutionary Factors   108
How Do We Know?   109
Summary of Main Topics   109
Critical Thinking Questions   110

CHAPTER 5

Macroevolution: Processes
of Vertebrate and Mammalian
Evolution   113

How We Connect: Discovering the Place of Humans
in the Natural World   114
  Principles of Classification   116
Making Connections: Constructing Classifications
and Interpreting Evolutionary Relationships   117
  Comparing Evolutionary Systematics
  with Cladistics   117
A Closer Look   Evo-Devo: The Evolution
Revolution   118
  An Example of Cladistic Analysis: The Evolutionary
  History of Cars and Trucks   120
  Using Cladistics to Interpret Organisms   121
Definition of Species   123
At a Glance   Comparing Two Approaches to
Interpretation of Evolutionary Relationships   124
  Interpreting Species and Other Groups
  in the Fossil Record   126
  Recognition of Fossil Species   126
  Recognition of Fossil Genera   127
What Are Fossils and How Do They Form?   128
Humans Are Vertebrates: Distant Connections
through Geological Time   130
A Closer Look   Deep Time   132
Humans Are Also Mammals:
Closer Connections   134
Processes of Macroevolution   136
  Adaptive Radiation   136
  Generalized and Specialized Characteristics   137
  Working Together: Microevolution
  and Macroevolution   138
How Do We Know?   138
Summary of Main Topics   139
Critical Thinking Questions   140

Primates

CHAPTER 6

Survey of the Living Primates   143

Primate Characteristics   144

    Limbs and Locomotion   146

    Dentition and Diet   146

    The Senses and the Brain   146

    Maturation, Learning, and Behavior   147

A Closer Look Primate Cranial Anatomy   148

Primate Adaptations   148

    Evolutionary Factors   149

    Geographical Distribution and Habitats   150

    Diet and Teeth   150

    Locomotion   151

Primate Classification   155

A Survey of the Living Nonhuman Primates   157

    Lemurs and Lorises   157

    Tarsiers   159

    Anthropoids: Monkeys, Apes, and Humans   160

    Hominoids: Apes and Humans   166

Endangered Primates   174

A Closer Look Aye-Ayes: Victims of Derived Traits and Superstition   175

    The Bushmeat Trade   179

How Do We Know?   181

Summary of Main Topics   182

Critical Thinking Questions   182

CHAPTER 7

Primate Behavior   185

The Evolution of Behavior   186

    Some Factors That Influence Social Structure   188

A Closer Look Types of Nonhuman Primate Social Groups   190

Why Be Social?   191

Primate Social Behavior   192

    Dominance   192

At a Glance Primate Social Strategies   193

    Communication   194

    Aggressive and Affiliative Behaviors within Groups   196

Reproduction and Reproductive Behaviors   198

    Reproductive Strategies   198

    Sexual Selection   199

    Is Infanticide a Reproductive Strategy?   200

    Mothers, Fathers, and Infants   201

Nonhuman Primate Models for the Evolution of Human Behavior   203

    Brain and Body Size   204

Language   206

    The Evolution of Language   209

Primate Cultural Behavior   211

At a Glance Evolution of Human Language   212

    Conflict between Groups   216

Prosocial Behaviors: Affiliation, Altruism, and Cooperation   218

    Altruism   219

The Primate Continuum   221

How Do We Know?   222

Summary of Main Topics   222

Critical Thinking Questions   223

CHAPTER 8

Overview of the Fossil Primates   225

Background to Primate Evolution: Late Mesozoic   226

    Primate Origins   227

A Closer Look Building Family Trees from Genes   228

Made to Order: Archaic Primates   229

Eocene Euprimates   231

    Lemur Connections? The Adapoids   233

    Closer Connections to Living Primates: The Evolution of True Lemurs and Lorises   234

At a Glance Key Early Primate Names   234

    Tarsier Connections? The Omomyoids   236

    Evolution of True Tarsiers   237

    Eocene and Oligocene Early Anthropoids   237

A Closer Look Primate Diversity in the Fayum   239

Oligocene Primates   240

    True Anthropoids   240

Early Platyrrhines: New World Anthropoids   242

A Closer Look Island Hopping and Primate Evolution   244

Miocene Primates   245

Monkeying Around   245

Aping Monkeys   248

At a Glance Key Early Anthropoid Names   250

True Apes   253

At a Glance Key Fossil Ape Names   253

Evolution of Extant Hominoids   258

Hylobatids: The Lesser Apes   258

The African Great Apes   258

Asia's Lone Great Ape   259

How Do We Know?   260

Summary of Main Topics   261

Critical Thinking Questions   261

Hominin Evolution

CHAPTER **9**

Paleoanthropology: Reconstructing Early Hominin Behavior and Ecology   263

Understanding Our Direct Evolutionary Connections: What's a Hominin?   264

What's in a Name?   265

Biocultural Evolution: The Human Capacity for Culture   266

Discovering Human Evolution: The Science of Paleoanthropology   267

A Closer Look What Were Early Hominins Doing, and How Do We Know?   268

Connecting the Dots through Time: Paleoanthropological Dating Methods   272

A Closer Look Chronometric Dating Estimates   275

Experimental Archaeology   276

Stone Tool (Lithic) Technology   277

Analysis of Bone   278

Reconstruction of Early Hominin Environments and Behavior   279

Why Did Hominins Become Bipedal?   279

How Do We Know?   283

Summary of Main Topics   284

Critical Thinking Questions   284

CHAPTER **10**

Hominin Origins in Africa   287

Walking the Walk: The Bipedal Adaptation   288

The Mechanics of Walking on Two Legs   288

A Closer Look Major Features of Bipedal Locomotion   290

Digging for Connections: Early Hominins from Africa   293

Pre-Australopiths (6.0+ to 4.4 mya)   293

Australopiths (4.2 to 1.2 mya)   297

At a Glance Key Pre-Australopith Discoveries   298

A Closer Look Cranial Capacity   302

A Contemporaneous and *Very* Different Kind of Hominin   303

Later More Derived Australopiths (3.0 to 1.2 mya)   304

New Connections: A Transitional Australopith?   307

Closer Connections: Early *Homo* (2.0 to 1.4 mya)   310

Interpretations: What Does It All Mean?   311

Seeing the Big Picture: Adaptive Patterns of Early African Hominins   313

How Do We Know?   315

Summary of Main Topics   316

Critical Thinking Questions   316

CHAPTER **11**

The First Dispersal of the Genus *Homo: Homo erectus* and Contemporaries   319

A New Kind of Hominin   320

The Morphology of *Homo erectus*   321

Body Size   321

Brain Size   321

Cranial Shape   324

The Geographic Range of *Homo erectus* 325

    The First *Homo erectus: Homo erectus* from Africa 325

At a Glance Key *Homo erectus* Discoveries from Africa 327

    A New Hominin Discovery in South Africa 327

    Who Were the Earliest African Emigrants? 328

    Homo erectus from Indonesia 330

    Homo erectus from China 331

A Closer Look In Search of Ancient Human Ancestors—and a Little Shade 332

A Closer Look Dragon Bone Hill: Cave Home or Hyena Den? 336

    Asian and African *Homo erectus*: A Comparison 336

At a Glance Key *Homo erectus* Discoveries from Asia 338

    Later *Homo erectus* from Europe 338

At a Glance Key *Homo erectus* and Contemporaneous Discoveries from Europe and Western Asia 340

Technological Trends During the Time of *Homo erectus* 340

Seeing the Connections: Interpretations of *Homo erectus* 341

Something New and Different: The "Little People" 342

How Do We Know? 344

Summary of Main Topics 345

Critical Thinking Questions 345

CHAPTER 12

Premodern Humans 347

When, Where, and What 348

    The Pleistocene 348

    Dispersal of Middle Pleistocene Hominins 349

    Middle Pleistocene Hominins: Terminology 350

Premodern Humans of the Middle Pleistocene 351

    Africa 351

At a Glance Key Premodern Human (*H. heidelbergensis*) Fossils from Africa 352

    Europe 352

    Asia 353

At a Glance Key Premodern Human (*H. heidelbergensis*) Fossils from Europe 353

    A Review of Middle Pleistocene Evolution 356

At a Glance Key Premodern Human (*H. heidelbergensis*) Fossils from Asia 356

Middle Pleistocene Culture 357

Neandertals: Premodern Humans of the Late Pleistocene 358

    Western Europe 360

    Central Europe 363

    Western Asia 365

    Central Asia 366

    Surprising Connections: Another Contemporary Hominin? 366

At a Glance Key Neandertal Fossil Discoveries 367

Culture of Neandertals 367

    Technology 368

    Subsistence 368

    Speech and Symbolic Behavior 369

A Closer Look The Evolution of Language 370

    Burials 370

Molecular Connections: The Genetic Evidence 372

    Neandertal DNA 373

A Closer Look Are They Human? 374

Seeing Close Human Connections: Understanding Diversity among Premodern Humans 376

How Do We Know? 379

Summary of Main Topics 379

Critical Thinking Questions 380

CHAPTER 13

The Origin and Dispersal of Modern Humans 383

Approaches to Understanding Modern Human Origins 385

    The Regional Continuity Model: Multiregional Evolution 385

    Replacement Models 385

At a Glance Scenarios of Modern Human Origins 387

At a Glance Genetic Relationships among Modern Humans, Denisovans, and Neandertals 388

The Earliest Discoveries of Modern Humans 389

    Africa 389

    The Near East 392

At a Glance Key Early Modern *Homo sapiens* Discoveries from Africa and the Near East 394

    Asia 394

    Australia 396

    Central Europe 396

    Western Europe 397

At a Glance Key Early Modern *Homo sapiens* Discoveries from Europe and Asia 400

Technology and Art in the Upper Paleolithic 400

    Europe 400

    Africa 405

A Closer Look Maybe You *Can* Take It with You 406

Summary of Upper Paleolithic Culture 407

How Do We Know? 408

Summary of Main Topics 409

Critical Thinking Questions 409

Contemporary Human Evolution

CHAPTER 14

Modern Human Biology: Patterns of Variation 411

Historical Views of Human Variation 412

The Concept of Race 413

A Closer Look Racial Purity: A False and Dangerous Ideology 414

Contemporary Interpretations of Human Variation 418

    Human Polymorphisms 419

    Polymorphisms at the DNA Level 421

At a Glance Genetic Polymorphisms Used to Study Human Variation 421

A Closer Look What DNA Tells Us about Ancient Human Migrations 422

Population Genetics 425

At a Glance Population Genetics Research 427

    Calculating Allele Frequencies 428

A Closer Look Calculating Allele Frequencies: PTC Tasting in a Hypothetical Population 429

    Evolution in Action: Modern Human Populations 430

Human Biocultural Evolution 431

How Do We Know? 434

Summary of Main Topics 435

Critical Thinking Questions 435

CHAPTER 15

Modern Human Biology: Patterns of Adaptation 437

The Adaptive Significance of Human Variation 438

    Solar Radiation and Skin Color 439

    The Thermal Environment 444

A Closer Look Skin Cancer and UV Radiation 446

    High Altitude 449

Infectious Disease 451

At a Glance Zoonoses and Human Infectious Disease 452

The Continuing Impact of Infectious Disease 454

Human Skeletal Biology: What Bones Can Tell Us about Ancient Diseases, Trauma, and Lifestyles 458

    Evidence of Prehistoric Diseases 458

    Reconstruction of Prehistoric Behavioral Patterns 461

How Do We Know? 463

Summary of Main Topics 463

Critical Thinking Questions 464

CHAPTER 16

Legacies of Human Evolutionary History: Effects on the Life Course 467

Evolved Biology and Contemporary Lifestyles—Is There a Mismatch? 468

Biocultural Evolution and the Life Course   469

Diet and Nutrition through the Life Course   469

Too Much and Too Little   472

At a Glance Diet, Lifestyle, and Consequences   473

Other Factors Influencing Growth
and Development: Genes, Environment,
and Hormones   475

Life History Theory and the Human Life Course   477

Pregnancy, Birth, Infancy, and Childhood   478

Onset of Reproductive Function in Humans   481

Decline in Reproductive Function   482

Aging and Longevity   483

Are We Still Evolving?   487

How Do We Know?   488

Summary of Main Topics   488

Critical Thinking Questions   489

CHAPTER 17

The Human Disconnection   491

Human Impacts on the Planet and on Other
Life-Forms   492

Humans and the Impact of Culture   493

Global Climate Change   494

Public Perceptions of Climate Change   495

Earth's Shrinking Polar Ice   496

Impact on Biodiversity   500

Acceleration of Evolutionary Processes   502

Looking for Solutions   503

Is There Any Good News?   505

How Do We Know?   506

Summary of Main Topics   506

Critical Thinking Questions   506

APPENDIX A

Atlas of Primate Skeletal Anatomy   507

APPENDIX B

Sexing and Aging the Skeleton   515

Glossary   520

References   531

Index   557

Preface

This textbook is about where we come from and the scientific ways we can explore our beginnings. Our species, like all species on earth, evolved from earlier life-forms. As a result of this long shared ancestry, we and all other life are *connected* in a variety of ways: genetically, anatomically, physiologically, and even behaviorally. These connections are the main focus of the book and are highlighted in every chapter.

Physical anthropology, also called "biological anthropology," is the study of human adaptation, variability, and evolution as well as of our living and fossil relatives from a biological perspective. Consequently, throughout this text, you will encounter topics that emphasize basic biological concepts. This broad biological framework allows us to connect our evolutionary history with that of other life-forms in order to better understand the evolutionary pressures that shaped our species.

In the last few years scientific knowledge in many fields has accumulated amazingly fast. What's more, the biological sciences are certainly among the most rapidly expanding areas of knowledge as information increases dramatically every year—indeed, every month. This edition has been updated to reflect these changes and to provide the most current information available.

But, in reality, our presentation is just a beginning for students new to this field of study. It is our goal to give students a strong foundation relating to the key aspects of evolutionary biology, which includes physical anthropology. Our aim is to provide fundamental information which will allow you to better understand some of the dramatic scientific advances that almost surely will directly affect you in coming years. The addition of Eric Bartelink as a coauthor for the fifteenth edition also brings a fresh perspective to this text. To provide even greater assistance than in previous editions, we have added new photos and have expanded the scope of the text. All these changes reflect our long-term commitment to our textbook as an effective teaching and learning instrument.

Because genetic mechanisms lie at the heart of understanding evolution, in the early chapters (2 though 5) we address the basic aspects of life, cells, DNA, and the ways species change. In Chapters 6 and 7, we turn to an exploration of our evolutionary cousins, the nonhuman primates, and show how they are closely connected to us genetically, physically, and behaviorally. In Chapters 8 through 13, we first discuss the evolutionary history of early primates and how they relate to living nonhuman primates and our own earliest ancestors (Chapter 8). In Chapters 9 through 13, we turn to a more detailed exploration of our specific human evolutionary history over the past 6 million years. This evolutionary journey begins with our small-brained, apelike ancestors in Africa and follows the development of their descendants through time and over an expanding geographical range into Asia and Europe, and much later into Australia and the Americas.

In the last section of this book (Chapters 14–17), we cover the most recent part of our evolutionary journey with a discussion of modern human biology, and we trace the ongoing evolution of our species. Major topics include the nature of human variation (including an anthropological discussion of the social construct of "race"), patterns of adaptation in recent human populations, and the developmental changes experienced by humans through the course of their lives. In the concluding chapter, "The Human Disconnection," we discuss how contemporary humans are severely altering the planet. We compare these recent and sudden developments with our species' long evolutionary past, when humans were not so numerous or so dependent on nonrenewable resources.

New in the Fifteenth Edition

First, as previously mentioned, we have maintained the unifying concept of our "connection" to all life as the framework for presenting material throughout the text. To further reinforce this central focus, each chapter opens with a visual aid that clearly shows students the biological connections as they are organized within and between chapters. At the start of every chapter, we have provided student learning objectives (linked to the main chapter headings) and a short chapter outline; these tools provide a preview of the upcoming chapter content. Toward the end of each chapter, we have expanded the "How Do We Know?" text boxes, which summarize the basic scientific information that allows physical anthropologists and other biologists to draw accurate conclusions regarding our evolutionary history. We have also incorporated a "What Do You Think?" activity that allows students to decide what to do next.

In Chapter 2, we have expanded the discussion of creationism, and have contextualized recent public debate on evolutionary theory between scientists and creationists. We also provide additional examples of natural selection in action.

As genetic technology continues to grow at an unprecedented pace, it is our task to present the most relevant new discoveries in as simple a manner as possible. In addition to discussing the newly developed synthetic bacterial cell in Chapter 3, we discuss the basis for genetic typing of biological materials used in forensic science. In Chapter 4, we provide additional examples of genetic disorders, and in Chapter 5, we have added additional information on classifying fossils and as well as a discussion of how and why fossils form.

Primatologists are regularly reporting on new discoveries about our closest relatives, the nonhuman primates, clarifying our continuity with them. Since many of our primate cousins are unfamiliar to our readers, we've updated several photos to provide new examples of primates in the wild or to highlight specific behaviors. In Chapter 6, we add a discussion of the genetic relationship between humans and our closest living relatives, the chimpanzees. Today, most nonhuman primates are endangered, and we hope to raise awareness of them among students who read this book. We've significantly updated the statistics on threatened primate species and provide a discussion of recent efforts in primate conservation. Chapter 7 provides an expanded discussion of evidence of culture among nonhuman primates.

Chapter 8 has been updated to include new discoveries as well as ongoing reinterpretations of fossil primates. These changes include an expanded section on the evolution of the platyrrhine lineage as well as the recent announcement of the discovery of a skull and partial skeleton of a new small-bodied ape, *Pliobates*, found in Catalonia, Spain. In addition, a discussion of another fossil ape, *Khoratpithecus*, has been added. This fossil appears to show a closer evolutionary relationship to the orangutan. The chapter includes new photographs of more recently discovered fossil primates.

Remarkable new discoveries of fossil hominins and evidence of their behavior are discussed in Chapters 9 through 13. In Chapter 9, we discuss evidence for the earliest known stone tools (tentatively dated to 3.3 million years ago) and provide a discussion of the scars of human evolution that result from being a bipedal primate.

Chapter 10 includes a discussion of a possible new hominin species discovered in Ethiopia (dated to 3.4 million years ago), expands the discussion of *Australopithecus sediba* based on the most recent research, and provides a heads-to-toe perspective on bipedal anatomy.

In Chapter 11, we have made the most extensive and critical updates to the book. We have included a discussion of a possible new hominin species, *Homo naledi*, recently discovered in the Rising Star Cave complex in South Africa. Although dates of these fossils are forthcoming, this discovery provides the most extensive assemblage of early hominin remains from Africa, and includes individuals of all age groups. Another very significant discovery is the remains of *Homo floresiensis* at a second locale (Mata Menge) on the island of Flores. This new discovery, dated to the Middle Pleistocene, indicates that *Homo floresiensis* underwent insular dwarfism very early on, supporting the notion that this lineage descended from a *Homo erectus* population. Further, new chronometric dates from Liang Bua Cave (the original Flores locale) indicate the fossils are actually much older than originally thought (between 100,000 and 60,000 years old). Due to these new discoveries, the entire discussion of *Homo floresiensis* has been shifted completely to Chapter 11. The chapter also has updates relating to the study of *Homo erectus* growth rates and estimation of body size, a new *Homo erectus* discovery from Dmanisi, Georgia, that represents the most complete skull of an early hominin, the earliest probable evidence for the systematic use of fire based on studies from Wonderwerk Cave in South Africa, new dating on a *Homo erectus* fossil from China, and an expanded discussion of the role of meat consumption in hominin evolution.

Chapter 12 has been extensively revised to include an expanded discussion of the most recent genetic discoveries on Middle Pleistocene premodern humans, Neandertals, and Denisovans. These molecular discoveries show that Neandertals and Denisovans interbred with modern humans, and their genes can still be found in many contemporary human populations. A new discussion of Neandertal diets is provided based on analyses of stable isotopes of Neandertal bones and plant starch grains from dental calculus. In addition, we provide a discussion of a recent reanalysis of hominin cranial remains from the Upper Awash region of Ethiopia. These remains suggest the presence of *Homo heidelbergensis* around 850,000 years ago, thus providing the earliest potential evidence for this species in Africa. Finally, we have expanded on the discussion of the 300,000-year-old fossilized wooden spears recovered from Schöningen, Germany, based on several new studies and interpretations of these fascinating artifacts.

Chapter 13 expands on the origins of modern human populations, and highlights new genetic findings regarding Late Pleistocene migration events. We have updated the chapter to discuss early evidence for complex behaviors and artistic representations among early modern humans from South Africa and Indonesia. We have also added a section on the history of the molecular clock as a tool to study the origin of modern humans. Updated art and "At a Glance" features provide exciting visuals for students to compare different models for the origins of modern humans as well as the genetic relationships between different hominin populations during the Late Pleistocene.

In Chapters 14 through 16, our focus turns to modern human biology. We have updated information on the global issues of HIV and tuberculosis infection, the reemergence of infectious diseases due to the overuse of antibiotics and the anti-vaccination movement, and perspectives on human variation used in forensic anthropology.

One theme that we emphasize throughout the book is that we are the result of not only biological but also cultural evolutionary factors. In other words, we are a *biocultural* species. In Chapter 16, now titled "Legacies of Human Evolutionary History: Effects on the Life Course," we focus on ways in which biology and culture act on the human life course from conception, through reproduction, to the end of life. There are a number of ways in which our biology, resulting from millions of years of evolution, seems to be mismatched with the lives we lead today, leading in some cases to compromised health. For example, the biology of women may not be well suited to the highly frequent menstrual cycling that results from the use of modern forms of birth control. Some health disorders that we are dealing with today may stem from the dramatic differences between the diets of our ancestors and the foods we eat today. In this chapter, there's a new discussion of recent research on the human gut microbiome, human brain growth rates, infant dependency, menopause, pleiotropic genes, factors influencing cancer risk, and the Paleolithic diet trend.

Finally, in concluding Chapter 17 ("The Human Disconnection"), we focus on another theme that runs through the book—why it is so crucial that we know and understand human evolutionary history, its impact on the world today, and how we have distanced ourselves from other living species with which we share so many connections. We humans and the consequences of our activities are probably the most important influences on evolution today, causing the extinction or near extinction of thousands of other life-forms and threatening the very planet on which we live. Our disconnection from other species and from our own evolutionary past poses the biggest challenges our species has ever faced. Only by understanding how we got to this point can we begin to respond to the challenges that are in our future and the futures of our children and grandchildren.

We also expanded our treatment of climate change in Chapter 17, including revised figures. The discussion provides current information from the National Snow and Ice Data Center showing that in September 2015, the Arctic sea ice extent was 1.94 million square miles, significantly lower than the average extent from 1982 to 2010. We point out that there has been a steady decline in Arctic sea ice since the year 2000, and we briefly deal with the likely consequences of continued melting.

Four appendices are available as learning aids for the textbook. Appendix A provides an atlas of primate skeletal anatomy, including labeled diagrams of the skeleton of a human, a chimpanzee, and a macaque, as well as more detailed diagrams of the anatomical regions of the human skeleton. Appendix B is a guide to sex and age determination of human skeletal remains. Appendices C and D are available online in MindTap. Appendix C is a summary of the early hominin fossil record from Africa, and includes sketches and background information on various key discoveries. Appendix D provides additional information and population genetics examples that demonstrate microevolution in action.

In-Chapter Learning Aids

Connections graphic at the beginning of each chapter shows the biological relationships emphasized in the chapter in the context of topics in other chapters.

Student Learning Objectives, corresponding to the main headings within the chapter, are listed on the opening page of each chapter.

A Closer Look boxes are high-interest features found throughout the book. They supplement chapter material and include more in-depth discussion of selected stimulating topics.

A running glossary in the margins provides definitions of terms immediately adjacent to the text where the term is first introduced. A full glossary is provided at the back of the book.

At a Glance boxes found throughout the book briefly summarize complex or controversial material in a visually simple fashion.

Figures, including numerous photographs, line drawings, and maps, most in full color, are carefully selected to clarify text materials and directly support the discussion in the text.

How Do We Know? chapter concluding sections (with "What Do You Think?" scenarios) summarize the basic scientific information used in drawing accurate conclusions about our evolutionary history.

Critical Thinking Questions at the end of each chapter reinforce key concepts and encourage students to think critically about what they have read.

Full bibliographical citations throughout the book provide sources from which the materials are drawn. This type of documentation guides students to published, peer-reviewed source materials and illustrates for students the proper use of references. All cited sources are listed in the comprehensive list of *References* at the back of the book.

Acknowledgments

Over the years, many friends and colleagues have assisted us with our books. For this edition we are especially grateful to the reviewers who so carefully commented on the manuscript and made such helpful suggestions: Sheela Athreya, Texas A&M University; Rory Becker, Eastern Oregon University; Graciela Cabana, University of Tennessee; Susan Cachel, Rutgers University; Autumn Cahoon, Sierra College; Tamara Cheshire, Sacramento City College; Martin Cohen, Los Angeles City Community Colleges; Denise Cucurny, California State University, Long Beach; Darryl de Ruiter, Texas A&M University; Joanne Devlin, University of Tennessee; John Doershuk, Cornell College and University of Iowa; Gerrell Drawhorn, California State University, Sacramento; Diana Durand, University of Arkansas; Dicken Everson, Mt. San Jacinto College; Julie Farnum Montclair State, University; Peter Fashing, California State University, Fullerton; Robyn Fayko, Sacramento City College; Christina Fojas, University of Tennessee; Frances Forrest, Queens College–City University of New York; Alexis Gray, Norco College; Gillian Grebler, East Los Angeles College and Santa Monica College; Sharon Gursky, Texas A&M University; Catherine Haradon, Santa Monica College; Dale Hoffman, Folsom Lake College/American River College; David Jacobsen, Fullerton College; Ellen Kapsalis, University of Maimi; Andrew Kindon, West Valley College; Alice Kingsnorth, Sierra College; John Krigbaum, University of Florida; Paul Langenwalter, Biola University; Kevin Langergraber, Arizona State University; Rich Lawler, James Madison University; April Mejia, Norco College; Ellen Miller, Wake Forest University; Bahram Mobasher, University of California, Riverside; Jennifer Molina-Stidger, Sierra College; Amy Mundorff, University of Tennessee; Theresa Murray, Las Positas College; John Nadolski, Sierra College; Endre Nyerges, Centre College; John Patton, California State University, Fullerton; Michael Pietrusewsky, University of Hawaii at Manoa; Jennifer Price, Mendocino College; David Raichlen, University of Arizona; Tim Raposa, Folsom Lake College; John Reeves, The University of Akron; Shannen Robson, Eastern Oregon University; Lisa Salvi, Coastline College; Stephen Schlecht, University of Michigan; Nancy Shlaes, Governors State University; Noah Simons, University of Oregon; Matthew Sponheimer, University of Colorado, Boulder; Vincent Stefan, Lehman College–City University of New York; Linda Taylor, University of Miami; Allison Tripp, Chaffey College; Larry Ulibarri, University of Oregon; Julie Vazquez College of the Canyons; Patricia Vinyard, University of Akron; Erin Waxenbaum, Northwestern University; Darcy Wiewall, Antelope Valley College; Scott Williams, New York University; and Brita Wynn, Sierra College/Sacramento City College.

We wish to thank the team at Cengage Learning: Nedah Rose, Kate Scheinman, and Rita Jaramillo. Moreover, for their unflagging expertise and patience, we are grateful to our copy editor, Larry Goldberg, our project manager, Jill Traut, and her skilled staff at MPS Limited.

To the many friends and colleagues who have generously provided photographs, support, or advice, we are greatly appreciative: David Alba, Zeresenay Alemsegel, Otto Bader, Nanette Barkey, Amy Bartelink, Malia Bartelink, Melanie Beasley, Chris Beard, David Begun, Brenda Benefit, Lee Berger, Jonathan Bloch, Doug Boyer, C. K. Brain, Günter Bräuer, David Brill, Peter Brown, Ray Carson, Yaowalak Chaimanee, Desmond Clark, Ron Clarke, Bill Clemens, Raymond Dart, Henri de Lumley, Louis de Bonis, Didier Descouens, Michael Donnenberg, Duke Lemur Center, John Fleagle, Diane France, Robert Franciscus, David Frayer, Kathleen Galvin, Kenneth Garrett, Philip Gingerich, Danielle Gregory, Gregg Gunnell, David Haring, Terry Harrison, John Hawks, John Hodgkiss, Almut Hoffman, Pat Holroyd, Ellen Ingmanson, Fred Jacobs, Don Johanson, Peter Jones, Krista Latham, Mushtaq Kahn, John Kappelman, Richard Kay, William Kimbel, Charles Knowles, Arlene Kruse, Yutaku Kunimatsu, Tamara Leher, Julie Lesnik, Linda Levitch, Thomas J. Loebel, David Lordkipanidze, Carles Lalueza-Fox, Giorgio Manzi, Tetsuro Matsuzawa, Monte McCrossin, Colleen Milligan, Corinna Most, Jackie Murad, the late Turhon Murad, National Museums of Kenya, Gerald Newlands, Xijum Ni, James O'Connell, John Oates, Bonnie Pedersen, Alexandra Perrone, David Pilbeam, Gul Reyman, Charlotte Roberts, Duane Rumbaugh, Sastrohamijoyo Sartono, Peter Schmid, Rose Sevick, Beth Shook, the late Elwyn Simons, Meredith Small, Fred Smith, Thierry Smith, Kirstin Sterner, Masanaru Takai, Nelson Ting, Phillip Tobias,

Erik Trinkaus, William Turnbaugh, Bence Viola, Alan Walker, Carol Ward, Wally Wecker, Dietrich Wegner, James Westgate, Randy White, Tim White, P. Willey, Milford Wolpoff, Xinzhi Wu, João Zilhão, Bernhard Zipfel.

Over the years, many students have pledged their time and expertise to help improve Chapter 8. We would especially like to thank Kiran Patel for her invaluable help in researching and editing Chapter 8. In addition, we thank K. Lindsay Hunter for her efforts with earlier editions of Chapter 8. We thank Chloe Daniel for her comments on Chapter 8, Toby Avalos for his help researching Chinese apes, and Mike Hussey for help with photographs.

For the current and past four editions, John Fleagle has made anatomical diagrams available that were originally used in his book, *Primate Adaptation and Evolution* (Academic Press, 1999). Others who have assisted in forming the concepts that we have put into written form include David Begun, Eric Delson, John Fleagle, Gregg Gunnell, Terry Harrison, Pat Holroyd, Andrew Kitchen, Philip Rightmire, Kirstin Sterner, Nelson Ting, Tim White, and Iyad Zalmout.

Robert Jurmain
Lynn Kilgore
Wenda Trevathan
Russell Ciochon
Eric Bartelink

August 2016

Dedication
In memory of Elwyn Simons (1930–2016).

Supplements

Introduction to Physical Anthropology, Fifteenth Edition, comes with an outstanding supplements program to help instructors create an effective learning environment so that students can more easily master the latest discoveries and interpretations in the field of physical anthropology.

Supplements for the Instructor

Online Instructor's Manual for *Introduction to Physical Anthropology*, Fifteenth Edition
This online resource includes a sample syllabus showing how to integrate MindTap with the text, as well as chapter outlines, learning objectives, key terms and concepts, lecture suggestions, and enrichment topics.

Online Test Bank for *Introduction to Physical Anthropology*, Fifteenth Edition
Organize your course and capture your students' attention with the resources found in the test bank, including multiple-choice, true/false, short-answer, and essay questions—most with answers and page references for each chapter of the text.

Online PowerPoints for *Introduction to Physical Anthropology*, Fifteenth Edition
These vibrant Microsoft PowerPoint lecture slides for each chapter assist you with your lecture by providing concept coverage using images, figures, and tables directly from the textbook.

Cengage Learning Testing Powered by Cognero
This is a flexible, online system that allows you to:
- Import, edit, and manipulate test bank content from the *Introduction to Physical Anthropology* test bank or elsewhere, including your own favorite test questions.
- Create multiple test versions in an instant.
- Deliver tests from your LMS, your classroom, or wherever you want.

Supplements for the Student

MindTap for *Introduction to Physical Anthropology*, Fifteenth Edition
MindTap engages and empowers students to produce their best work—consistently. By seamlessly integrating course material with activities, apps, and much more, MindTap creates a unique learning path that fosters increased comprehension and efficiency.

For students:
- MindTap delivers real-world relevance with activities and assignments that help students build critical thinking and analytical skills that will transfer to other courses and their professional lives.
- MindTap helps students stay organized and efficient with a single destination that reflects what's important to the instructor, along with the tools students need to master the content.
- MindTap empowers and motivates students with information that shows where they stand at all times—both individually and compared with the highest performers in class.

Additionally, for instructors, MindTap allows you to:
- Control what content students see and when they see it with a learning path that can be used as is or matched to your syllabus exactly.
- Create a unique learning path of relevant readings and multimedia and activities that move students up the learning taxonomy from basic knowledge and comprehension to analysis, application, and critical thinking.
- Integrate your own content into the MindTap Reader using your own documents or pulling from sources like RSS feeds, YouTube videos, websites, Googledocs, and more.
- Use powerful analytics and reports that provide a snapshot of class progress, time in course, engagement, and completion.

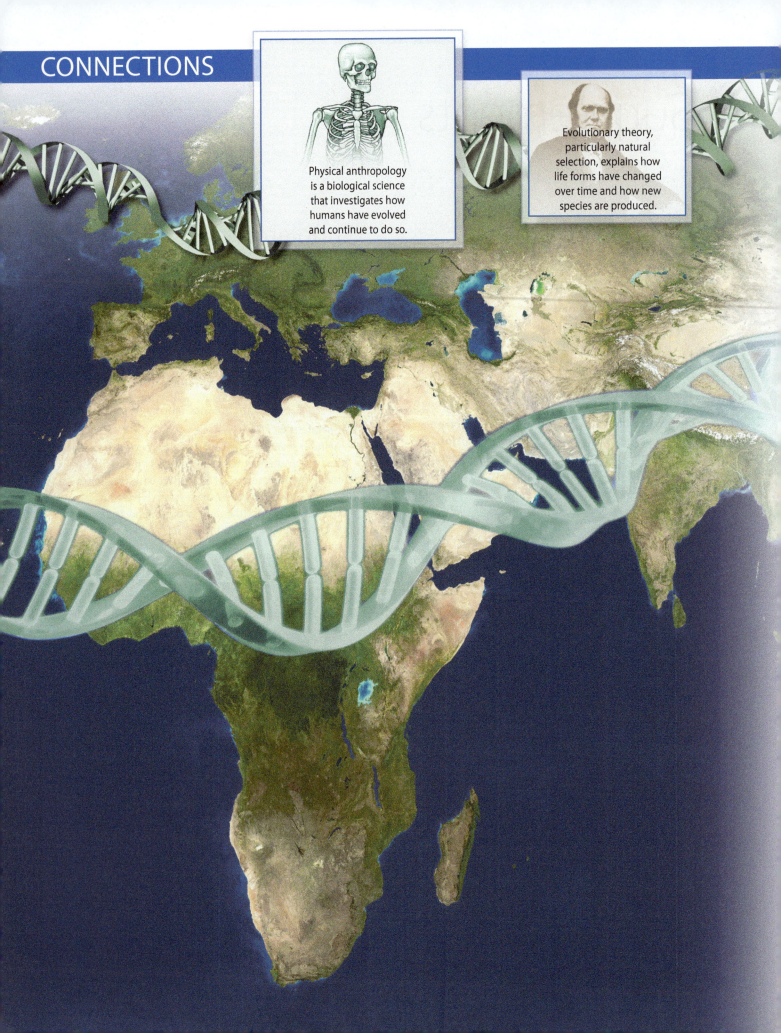

CONNECTIONS

Physical anthropology is a biological science that investigates how humans have evolved and continue to do so.

Evolutionary theory, particularly natural selection, explains how life forms have changed over time and how new species are produced.

Introduction to Physical Anthropology

The Human Connection

Biocultural Evolution

What Is Anthropology?

Cultural Anthropology

Linguistic Anthropology

Archaeology

Physical Anthropology

Applied Anthropology

Physical Anthropology and the Scientific Method

The Anthropological Perspective

Student Learning Objectives   After studying the material in this chapter, you should be able to:

▶ Describe how all life-forms are interconnected through evolution.

▶ Define biocultural evolution and explain its relevance to human evolution.

▶ Describe the discipline of anthropology as it is practiced in the United States, including its four subfields.

▶ Articulate the fundamentals of the scientific method and the importance of hypothesis testing within physical anthropology.

▶ Explain how an anthropological perspective provides a holistic view of the human experience.

One day, perhaps during the rainy season some 3.7 million years ago, two or three animals walked across a grassland **savanna** in what is now northern Tanzania, in East Africa. These individuals were early **hominins**, members of the same evolutionary lineage that includes our own **species**, *Homo sapiens*. Fortunately for us, a record of their passage on that long-forgotten day remains in the form of fossilized footprints, preserved in hardened volcanic deposits. As chance would have it, shortly after heels and toes were pressed into the damp soil, a nearby volcano erupted. The ensuing ashfall blanketed everything on the ground. In time, the ash layer hardened into a deposit that remarkably preserved the tracks of numerous animals, including those early hominins, for nearly 4 million years (Fig. 1-1).

This illustration emphasizes the fact that all-life forms on earth, including humans, are ultimately connected by DNA.

Peter Jones

▲ **Figure 1-1**

Early hominin footprints at Laetoli, Tanzania. The tracks to the left were made by one individual, while those to the right appear to have been made by two individuals, the second stepping in the tracks of the first.

savanna (also spelled savannah) A large flat grassland with scattered trees and shrubs. Savannas are found in many regions of the world with dry and warm-to-hot climates.

hominins Colloquial term for members of the evolutionary group that includes modern humans and all extinct bipedal relatives.

species A group of organisms that can interbreed to produce fertile offspring. Members of one species are reproductively isolated from members of all other species (i.e., they cannot mate with them to produce fertile offspring).

These now famous prints indicate that two individuals, one smaller than the other, perhaps walking side by side, left parallel sets of tracks. But because the larger individual's prints are obscured, possibly by those of a third, it's unclear how many actually made that journey so long ago. What is clear is that the prints were made by an animal that habitually walked **bipedally** (on two feet), and that fact tells us that those ancient travelers were hominins.

In addition to the footprints, scientists working at this site (called Laetoli) and at other locations have discovered many fossilized parts of skeletons of an animal we call *Australopithecus afarensis*. Because the remains have been extensively studied, we know that these hominins were anatomically similar to ourselves, although their brains were only about one-third the size of ours. They may have used stones and sticks as simple tools, but there is no evidence that they actually made stone tools. In fact, they were very much at the mercy of nature's whims. They certainly could not outrun most predators, and their canine teeth were fairly small, so compared to many other animals, they were pretty much defenseless.

We've asked numerous questions about the Laetoli hominins, but we will never be able to answer them all. These early human ancestors left a fossilized trail for us to follow, and their journey ended so long ago that we cannot really grasp how much time has passed since that day. But it remains for us to learn as much as we can about them, and as we continue to do this, their greater journey continues.

On July 20, 1969, a television audience numbering in the hundreds of millions watched as two human beings stepped out of a spacecraft onto the surface of the moon. People born after that date have always lived in an age of space exploration, and many may now take that first moon landing more or less for granted. But the significance of that first moonwalk can't be overstated, because it represents humankind's presumed mastery over the natural forces that govern our presence on earth. For the first time ever, people actually walked upon the surface of a celestial body that, as far as we know, has never had biological life.

As the astronauts gathered geological specimens and frolicked in near weightlessness, they left traces of their fleeting presence in the form of footprints in the lunar dust (Fig. 1-2). On the surface of the moon, where no rain falls and no wind blows, the footprints remain undisturbed to this day. They survive as silent testimony to a brief visit by a medium-sized, big-brained creature that presumed to challenge the very forces that created it.

You may wonder why anyone would care about early hominin footprints and how they can possibly be relevant to your life. You may also wonder why a physical **anthropology** textbook would begin by discussing two such seemingly unrelated events as ancient hominins walking across an African savanna and a moonwalk. But the fact is, these two events are very closely connected.

Physical (or biological) anthropology is a scientific discipline concerned with the biological and behavioral characteristics of human beings, as well as those of our closest relatives, the nonhuman **primates** (apes, monkeys, tarsiers, lemurs, and lorises), and our ancestors. This kind of research helps us explain what it means to be human and how we came to be the way we are. This is an ambitious goal and it probably isn't fully attainable, but it's certainly worth pursuing. We're the only species to ponder our own existence and question how we fit into the spectrum of life on earth. Most people view humanity as quite separate from the rest of the animal kingdom. But at the same time, many are curious about the similarities we share with other species. Maybe, as a child, you looked at your dog and tried to figure out how her front legs might correspond to your arms. Or perhaps during a visit to the zoo, you recognized the similarities between a chimpanzee's hands or facial expressions and your own. Maybe you wondered if he also shared your thoughts and feelings. If you've ever had thoughts and questions like these, then you've indeed been curious about humankind's place in nature.

▲ **Figure 1-2**
Human footprints left on the lunar surface during the *Apollo* mission.

How did *Homo sapiens*, a result of the same evolutionary forces that produced all other forms of life on this planet, gain the power to control the flow of rivers and even alter the climate on a global scale? As tropical animals, how were we able to leave the tropics and eventually occupy most of the earth's land surfaces? How did we adjust to different environmental conditions as we dispersed? How could our species, which numbered fewer than 1 billion until the mid-nineteenth century, come to number more than 7.3 billion worldwide today and, as we now do, add another billion people approximately every 12 or 13 years?

These are some of the many questions that physical anthropologists try to answer through the study of human **evolution**, variation, and **adaptation**. These issues, and many others, are covered in this textbook, because physical anthropology is, in large part, human biology seen from an evolutionary perspective. On hearing the term *evolution*, most people think of the appearance of new species. Certainly new species are one important consequence of evolution, but not the only one. Evolution is an ongoing biological process with more than one outcome. Simply stated, evolution is a change in the **genetic** makeup of a population from one generation to the next, and it can be defined and studied at two levels. Over time, some genetic changes in populations do result in the appearance of a new species (or *speciation*), especially when those populations are isolated from one another. Change at this level is called *macroevolution*. At the other level, there are genetic alterations *within* populations; and though this type of change may not lead to speciation, it does cause populations of a species to differ from one another in the frequency of certain traits. Evolution at this level is referred to as *microevolution*. Evolution at both these levels will be discussed in this book.

bipedally On two feet; walking habitually on two legs.

anthropology The field of inquiry that studies human culture and evolutionary aspects of human biology; includes cultural anthropology, archaeology, linguistics, and physical, or biological, anthropology.

primates Members of the mammalian order Primates (pronounced "pry-may´-tees"), which includes lemurs, lorises, tarsiers, monkeys, apes, and humans.

evolution A change in the genetic structure of a population. The term is also frequently used to refer to the appearance of a new species.

adaptation An anatomical, physiological, or behavioral response of organisms or populations to the environment. Adaptations result from evolutionary change (specifically as a result of natural selection).

genetic Having to do with the study of gene structure and action, and the patterns of inheritance of traits from parent to offspring. Genetic mechanisms are the foundation of evolutionary change.

The Human Connection

The unifying theme of this textbook is how human beings are linked to all other life on earth. We are all connected to other organisms in countless ways, as you will learn throughout this book. For example, our DNA is structurally identical to that of every living thing. Indeed, we share genes that are involved in the most fundamental life processes with even the simplest of animals, such as sponges. These genes have changed very little over the course of several hundred million years of evolution. With few exceptions, our cells have the same structure and work the same way as in all life forms. Anatomically, we have the same muscles and bones as other animals. What's more, many aspects of our **behavior** have direct connections to nonhuman species, especially other primates.

The countless connections we share with other organisms show that humans are a product of the same evolutionary forces that produced all living things. But clearly we aren't identical to any other species. In fact, all species are unique in some ways. Humans are one contemporary component of a vast biological **continuum** at a particular point in time; and in this regard, we aren't really all that special. Stating that humans are part of a continuum doesn't imply that we're at the peak of development on that continuum. Depending on the criteria used, humans can be seen to exist at one end of the spectrum or the other, or somewhere in between, but we don't occupy a position of inherent superiority over other species (Fig. 1-3).

However, human beings are unquestionably unique regarding one highly significant characteristic, and that is intellect. After all, humans are the only species, born of earth, to stir the lunar dust. We're the only species to develop language and complex culture as a means of buffering nature's challenges, and by doing so we have gained the power to shape the planet's very destiny.

Biocultural Evolution

Biological anthropologists don't just study physiological and biological systems. When these topics are considered within the broader context of human evolution, another factor must be considered, and that is **culture**. Culture is an extremely important concept, not only as it relates to modern humans but also because of its critical role in human evolution. Quite simply, and in a very broad sense, culture can be seen as the strategy by which humans adapt to the natural environment. In fact, culture has so altered and dominated our world that it has become the environment in which we live. Culture includes technologies ranging from stone tools to computers; subsistence patterns, from hunting and gathering to global agribusiness; housing types, from thatched huts to skyscrapers; and clothing, from animal skins to high-tech synthetic fibers (Fig. 1-4). Technology, religion, values, social organization, language, kinship, marriage rules, gender roles, dietary practices, inheritance of property, and so on are all aspects of culture. Each culture shapes people's perceptions of the external environment, or their **worldview**, in particular ways that distinguish a particular society from all others.

One important point to remember is that culture isn't genetically passed from one generation to the next. We aren't born with innate knowledge that leads us to behave in ways appropriate to our own culture. Culture is transmitted from generation to generation through the process of *learning*, a process that begins, quite literally, at birth. We are all products of the culture in which we are raised, and since most human behavior is learned, it follows that most human behaviors, perceptions, values, and reactions are shaped by culture.

behavior Anything organisms do that involves action in response to internal or external stimuli; the response of an individual, group, or species to its environment. Such responses may or may not be deliberate, and they aren't necessarily the result of conscious decision making (which is absent in single-celled organisms, insects, and many other species).

continuum A set of relationships in which all components fall along a single integrated spectrum (e.g., color). All life reflects a single biological continuum.

culture Behavioral aspects of human adaptation, including technology, traditions, language, religion, marriage patterns, and social roles. Culture is a set of learned behaviors transmitted from one generation to the next by nonbiological (i.e., nongenetic) means.

worldview General cultural orientation or perspective shared by the members of a society.

▶ **Figure 1-3**

Traditional and recent technologies. (**a**) An early stone tool from East Africa. This artifact represents one of the oldest types of stone tools found anywhere. (**b**) The Hubble Space Telescope, a late twentieth-century tool, orbits the earth every 96 minutes at an altitude of 360 miles. Because it is above the earth's atmosphere, it provides distortion-free images of objects in deep space. (**c**) A cuneiform tablet. Cuneiform, the earliest form of writing, involved pressing symbols into clay tablets. It originated in southern Iraq some 5,000 years ago. (**d**) Text messaging, a fairly recent innovation in satellite communication, has generated a new language of sorts. Today, more than 500 million text messages are sent every day worldwide. (**e**) A Samburu woman in East Africa building a traditional but complicated dwelling of stems, small branches, and mud. (**f**) These Hong Kong skyscrapers are typical of cities in industrialized countries today.

CONNECTIONS

▶ Figure 1-4
Humans are biologically connected to all forms of life. This central theme will be addressed in every chapter of this textbook as shown in this figure.

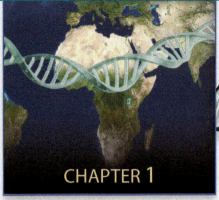

CHAPTER 1

Physical anthropology is a biological science that investigates how humans have evolved and continue to do so.

NASA

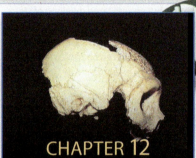

CHAPTER 2

Evolutionary theory, particularly natural selection, explains how life forms have changed over time and how new species are produced.

Bettmann/Corbis

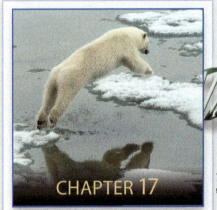

CHAPTER 17

Humans have recently become disconnected from other life and are rapidly altering the planet.

Keenpress/Getty Images

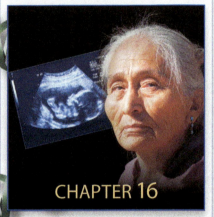

CHAPTER 16

Human development and adaptation is best understood from an evolutionary perspective.

David P. Smith/Shutterstock.com

CHAPTER 12

The immediate predecessors of modern humans, including the Neandertals, were much like us, but had some anatomical and behavioral differences. Human development and adaptation is best understood from an evolutionary perspective.

Fred Smith

CHAPTER 15

Through natural selection, humans have and continue to adapt to environmental factors including solar radiation, cold, altitude, and, most importantly, infectious disease.

Robert Jurmain

CHAPTER 14

Modern human variation is best understood by examining similarities and differences in DNA among populations.

Guido Cozzi/Terra/Atlantide Phototravel/Corbis

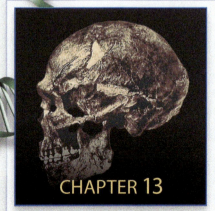

CHAPTER 13

Modern humans first evolved in Africa and later spread to other areas of the world, where they occasionally interbred with Neandertals and other premodern humans.

Harry Nelson

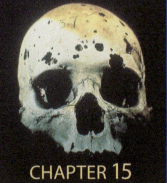

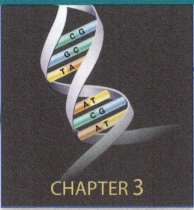

CHAPTER 3

The DNA molecule is the basis of all life.

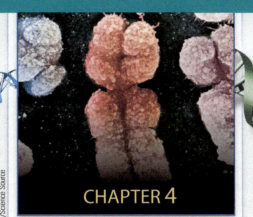

CHAPTER 4

Evolution occurs when DNA changes and genetic variation is further influenced by natural selection and other factors.

Biophoto Associates/Science Source

CHAPTER 5

Humans are both vertebrates and mammals, and their evolutionary history over many millions of years explains our early roots.

Russell L. Ciochon

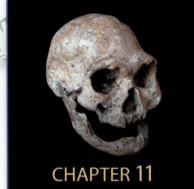

CHAPTER 11

Hominins began to disperse out of Africa around 2 million years ago, and during the next 1 million years inhabited much of Eurasia.

David Lordkipanidze

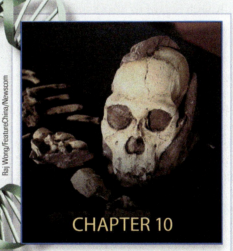

CHAPTER 10

The first more human-like animals (hominins) appeared in Africa around 6 mya ago and evolved into a variety of different species.

Raj Wong/FeatureChina/Newscom

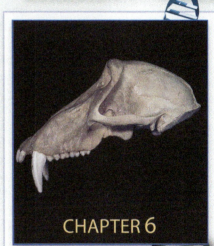

CHAPTER 6

Humans are primates and share many biological characteristics with other primates.

Lynn Kilgore

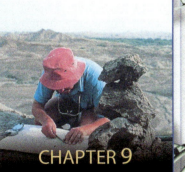

CHAPTER 9

Paleoanthropology, which includes physical anthropology, archaeology, and geology, provides the scientific basis to understand hominin evolution.

Institute of Human Origins, photo by Nanci Kahn

CHAPTER 8

Fossil evidence indicates our primate origins date to at least 65 million years ago.

Russell L. Ciochon

CHAPTER 7

Partly because of common evolutionary history, many human behaviors are also seen in other primates.

Anup Shah/Getty Images

It's important to emphasize that even though culture isn't genetically determined, the human predisposition to assimilate culture and function within it is very much influenced by biological factors. Most nonhuman animals rely to varying degrees on learned behavior. This is especially true of the great apes (gorillas, chimpanzees, bonobos, and orangutans), which exhibit several aspects of culture.

The predisposition for culture is perhaps the most critical component of human evolutionary history, and it was inherited from our early hominin or even prehominin ancestors. In fact, the common ancestor we share with chimpanzees may have had this predisposition. But during the course of human evolution, the role of culture became increasingly important. Over time, as you will see, culture influenced many aspects of our biological makeup; in turn, aspects of biology influenced cultural practices. For this reason, humans are the result of long-term interactions between biology and culture. We call these interactions **biocultural evolution**, and in this respect, humans are unique.

Biocultural interactions have resulted in many anatomical, biological, and behavioral changes during the course of human evolution. Alterations in the shape of the pelvis, increased brain size, reorganization of neurological structures, smaller teeth, and the development of language are some of the results of the evolutionary process in our lineage. Today biocultural interactions are as important as ever, especially with regard to health and disease. Air pollution and exposure to dangerous chemicals have increased the prevalence of respiratory disease and cancer. While air travel makes it possible for people to travel thousands of miles in just a few hours, we aren't the only species that can do this. Millions of disease-causing organisms travel on airplanes with their human hosts, making it possible for infectious diseases to spread within hours across the globe. A recent example is the 2014 Ebola virus epidemic, which spread into the United States by affected travelers from West Africa.

Many human activities have changed the patterns of such infectious diseases as tuberculosis, influenza, and malaria. After the domestication of nonhuman animals, close contact with chickens, pigs, and cattle greatly increased human exposure to some of the diseases these animals carry. Through this contact we've also changed the genetic makeup of disease-causing microorganisms. For example, the H1N1 "swine flu" virus that caused the 2009 pandemic actually contains genetic material derived from viruses that infect three different species: humans, birds, and pigs. As it turned out, that pandemic wasn't as serious as had originally been feared, but the next one could be. Because we have overused antibiotics, we've made many bacteria resistant to treatment and many are even deadly. Likewise, although we're making progress in treating malaria, the microorganism that causes it has developed resistance to some treatments and preventive medications. We've also increased the geographical distribution of malaria- carrying mosquitoes through agricultural practices and global climate change. While it's clear that humans have influenced the development and spread of infectious disease, we still don't know the many ways that changes in infectious disease patterns are affecting human biology and behavior. Anthropological research in this one area alone is extremely relevant to all of us, and there are many other critical topics that biological anthropologists explore.

biocultural evolution The mutual interactive evolution of human biology and culture; the concept that biology (anatomy, neurological attributes, etc.) makes culture possible and that developing culture further influences the direction of biological evolution; this is a basic concept in understanding the unique components of human evolution.

What Is Anthropology?

Many anthropology students contemplate this question when their parents or friends ask, "What are you studying?" The answer is often followed by a blank stare or a comment about dinosaurs. So, what is anthropology, and how is it different from several related disciplines?

Like physical anthropologists, biologists investigate human adaptation and evolution. Similarly, historians and sociologists also study aspects of human societies past and present. But when biological or social research also considers the interactions between evolutionary and cultural factors, it's included in the discipline of anthropology.

In the United States, anthropology is divided into four main subfields: cultural, or social, anthropology; linguistic anthropology; archaeology; and physical, or biological, anthropology. Each of these, in turn, is divided into several specialized areas of interest. This four-field approach concerns all aspects of humanity across space and time. Each subdiscipline emphasizes different aspects of the human experience, but together they offer a means of explaining variation in human biological and behavioral adaptations. In addition, each of these subfields has practical applications, and many anthropologists pursue careers outside the university environment. This kind of anthropology is called **applied anthropology**, and it's extremely important today.

Cultural Anthropology

Cultural, or social, anthropology is the study of patterns of belief and behavior found in modern and historical cultures. The origins of cultural anthropology can be traced to the nineteenth century, when travel and exploration brought Europeans into contact (and sometimes conflict) with various cultures in Africa, Asia, Oceania, and the New World.

This contact sparked an interest in "traditional" societies and led many early anthropologists to study and record lifestyles that are now mostly extinct. These studies produced many descriptive **ethnographies** that covered a range of topics, such as religion, ritual, myth, the use of symbols, diet, technology, gender roles, and child-rearing practices. Ethnographic accounts, in turn, formed the basis for comparative studies of numerous cultures. By examining the similarities and differences among cultures, cultural anthropologists have been able to formulate many hypotheses regarding fundamental aspects of human behavior.

The focus of cultural anthropology shifted over the course of the twentieth century. Cultural anthropologists still work in remote areas, but increasingly they've turned their focus toward their own cultures and the people around them. Thus, ethnographic techniques have been applied to the study of diverse subcultures and their interactions with one another in contemporary metropolitan areas (urban anthropology). The population of any city is composed of many subgroups defined by economic status, religion, ethnic background, profession, age, level of education, and so on. Even the student body of your own college or university is made up of many subcultures, and as you walk across campus, you see students of many nationalities and diverse religious and ethnic backgrounds.

Linguistic Anthropology

Linguistic anthropology focuses on the relationship between human speech and language and different aspects of culture, such as the role of symbols in society, social identity, and cultural beliefs and ideologies. In a broader sense, the field explores the origins of language in general as well as specific languages. By examining similarities between contemporary languages, linguists have been able to trace historical ties between particular languages and groups of languages, thus facilitating the identification of language families and perhaps past relationships between human populations.

Because the spontaneous acquisition and use of language is a uniquely human characteristic, it's an important topic for linguistic anthropologists, who, along

applied anthropology The practical application of anthropological and archaeological theories and techniques. For example, many biological anthropologists work in the public health sector.

ethnographies Detailed descriptive studies of human societies. In cultural anthropology, an ethnography is traditionally the study of a non-Western society.

with specialists in other fields, study the process of language acquisition in infants. Because insights into the process may well have implications for the development of language in human evolution, as well as in growing children, it's also an important subject to physical anthropologists.

Archaeology

Archaeology is the study of earlier cultures by anthropologists who specialize in the scientific recovery, analysis, and interpretation of the material remains of past societies. Archaeologists obtain information from **artifacts** and structures left behind by earlier cultures. The remains of earlier societies, in the form of tools, structures, art, eating implements, fragments of writing, food refuse, and so on, provide a great deal of information about many important aspects of a society, such as religion, social structure, and subsistence practices.

Unlike in the past, sites aren't excavated simply for the artifacts or "treasures" they may contain. Rather, they're excavated to gain information about human behavior. For example, patterns of behavior are reflected in the dispersal of human settlements across a landscape and in the distribution of cultural remains within them. Archaeological research may focus on specific localities or peoples and attempt to identify, for example, various aspects of social organization, subsistence practices, or factors that led to the collapse of a civilization. Alternatively, inquiry may reflect an interest in broader issues relating to human culture in general, such as the development of agriculture or the rise of cities.

Physical Anthropology

As we've already said, *physical anthropology* is the study of human biology within the framework of evolution with an emphasis on the interaction between biology and culture. This subdiscipline is also referred to as *biological anthropology*, and you'll find the terms used interchangeably. *Physical anthropology* is the original term, and it reflects the initial interests anthropologists had in describing human physical variation. The American Association of Physical Anthropologists, its journal (*American Journal of Physical Anthropology*), many college courses, and numerous publications retain this term. The designation *biological anthropology* reflects the shift in emphasis to more biologically oriented topics, such as genetics, evolutionary biology, nutrition, physiological adaptation, and growth and development. This shift occurred largely because of advances in the field of genetics and molecular biology since the late 1950s. Although we've continued to use the traditional term in the title of this textbook, you'll find that all of the major topics we discuss pertain to biological issues.

The origins of biological anthropology can be traced to two principal areas of interest among nineteenth-century European and American scholars: the ancestry of modern species, including humans, and human variation. Although most of these scholars held religious convictions, they were beginning to doubt the literal interpretation of the biblical account of creation and to support explanations that emphasized natural processes rather than supernatural phenomena. Eventually, the sparks of interest in biological change over time were fanned into flames by the publication of Charles Darwin's *On the Origin of Species* in 1859.

Today, **paleoanthropology**, the study of anatomical and behavioral evolution as revealed in the human fossil record, is a major subfield of physical anthropology (Fig. 1-5). Thousands of fossilized remains of early primates, including human ancestors, are now kept in research collections. Taken together, these fossils span at least 7 million years of human prehistory. Although most of these fossils are incomplete, they provide us with a significant wealth of knowledge that

artifacts Objects or materials made or modified for use by hominins. The earliest artifacts are usually tools made of stone or occasionally bone.

paleoanthropology The interdisciplinary approach to the study of earlier hominins—their chronology, physical structure, archaeological remains, habitats, and so on.

▲ **Figure 1-5**

(**a**) Paleoanthropologists excavating at the Drimolen site, South Africa. (**b**) Primate paleontologist Russell L. Ciochon holding a fossil jaw of Gigantopithecus. *Gigantopithecus* is the name given to the largest apes that have ever lived.

increases each year. It's the ultimate goal of paleoanthropological research to identify the various early human and human-like species, establish a chronological sequence of relationships among them, and gain insights into their adaptation and behavior. Only then will we have a clear picture of how and when modern humans came into being.

To some extent, **primate paleontology** can be viewed as a subset of paleoanthropology. Primate paleontology is the study of the primate fossil record, which extends back to the beginning of primate evolution some 65 million years ago (mya). Virtually every year, fossil-bearing geological beds around the world yield important new discoveries. By studying fossil primates and comparing them with anatomically similar living species, primate paleontologists are learning a great deal about factors such as diet or locomotion in earlier forms. They can also try to identify aspects of behavior in some extinct primates and attempt to clarify what we know about evolutionary relationships between extinct and modern species, including ourselves.

Visible physical variation was the other major area of interest for early physical anthropologists. Enormous effort was spent in measuring, describing, and explaining visible differences between various human populations, with particular attention being focused on skin color, body proportions, and the shape of the head and face. Although some of these early approaches were misguided and even racist, they gave birth to many body measurements that are sometimes still used. They've been used to design everything from wheelchairs to office furniture. They have also been used to determine the absolute minimum amount of leg room a person needs in order to remain sane during a 3-hour flight on a commercial airliner. Lastly, they are also very important to the study of skeletal remains from archaeological sites (Fig. 1-6).

Today, physical anthropologists are concerned with human variation because of its possible *adaptive significance* and because they want to identify the factors that have produced not only visible physical variation but genetic variation as well. In

primate paleontology The study of fossil primates, especially those that lived before the appearance of hominins.

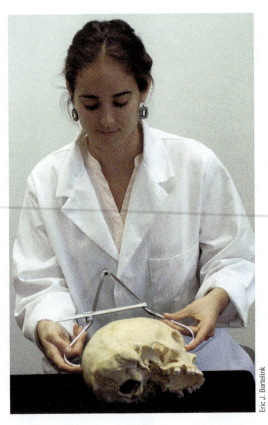

Eric J. Bartelink

▲ **Figure 1-6**
Anthropologist Alexandra Perrone using spreading calipers to measure the length of a human cranium.

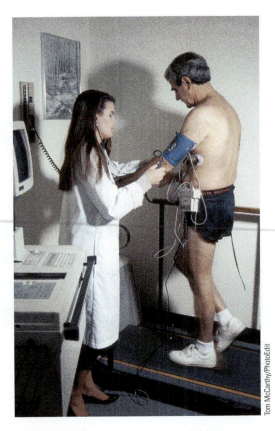

Tom McCarthy/PhotoEdit

▲ **Figure 1-7**
This researcher is using a treadmill test to assess a subject's heart rate, blood pressure, and oxygen consumption.

other words, many traits that typify certain populations evolved as biological adaptations, or adjustments, to local environmental conditions such as sunlight, altitude, or infectious disease. Other characteristics may be the result of geographical isolation or the descent of populations from small founding groups.

Since the early 1990s, the focus of human variation studies has shifted completely away from the visible differences we see in people to the underlying genetic factors that influence these and many other traits. This shift occurred partly because the examination of genetic variation between populations and individuals of any species helps to explain biological change over time, which is precisely what the evolutionary process is all about.

Modern population studies also examine other important aspects of human variation, including how different groups respond physiologically to different kinds of environmentally induced stress (Fig. 1-7). Such stresses may include high altitude, cold, or heat. *Nutritional anthropologists* study the relationships between various dietary components, cultural practices, physiology, and certain aspects of health and disease (Fig. 1-8). Investigations of human fertility, growth, and development are also closely related to the topic of nutrition. These fields of inquiry, which are fundamental to studies of adaptation in modern human populations, can also provide insights into hominin evolution.

It would be impossible to study evolutionary processes without some knowledge of how traits are inherited. For this reason and others, genetics is a crucial area of study within physical anthropology. Modern physical anthropology wouldn't exist as an evolutionary science if it weren't for advances in the understanding of genetic mechanisms.

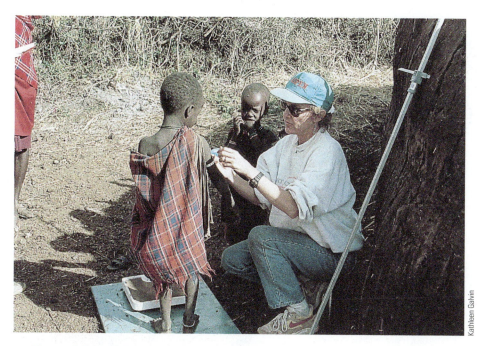

▲ **Figure 1-8**

Dr. Kathleen Galvin measures the upper arm circumference of a young Maasai boy in Tanzania. Data derived from various body measurements, including height and weight, were used in a health and nutrition study of groups of Maasai cattle herders.

Molecular anthropologists use cutting-edge technologies to investigate evolutionary relationships between human populations as well as between humans and nonhuman primates. To do this, they examine similarities and differences in **DNA** sequences between individuals, populations, and species. What's more, by extracting DNA from certain fossils (for example, Neandertals), these researchers have contributed to our understanding of evolutionary relationships between extinct and living species. As genetic technologies continue to be developed, molecular anthropologists will play a key role in explaining human evolution, adaptation, and our biological relationships with other species (Fig. 1-9).

DNA (deoxyribonucleic acid) The double-stranded molecule that contains the genetic code. DNA is a main component of chromosomes.

▲ **Figure 1-9**

(a) Molecular anthropologist Dr. Beth Shook extracting ancient DNA from a human skeleton.

(b) Molecular anthropologist Nelson Ting collecting red colobus fecal samples for a study of genetic variation in small groups of monkeys isolated from one another by agricultural clearing.

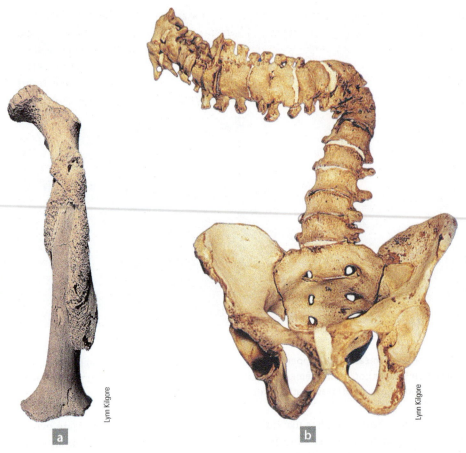

▶ **Figure 1-10**

Two examples of pathological conditions in human skeletal remains from the Nubian site of Kulubnarti in Sudan. These remains are approximately 1,000 years old. (**a**) A partially healed fracture of a child's left femur (thigh bone). This child died around the age of 6, probably of an infection that resulted from this injury. (**b**) Very severe congenital scoliosis in an adult male. The curves are due to developmental defects in individual vertebrae. (This is not the most common form of scoliosis.)

Lynn Kilgore

Lynn Kilgore

osteology The study of skeletal material. Human osteology focuses on the interpretation of skeletal remains from archaeological sites, skeletal anatomy, bone physiology, and growth and development. Some of the same techniques are used in paleoanthropology to study early hominins.

bioarchaeology The study of skeletal remains and their archaeological context.

paleopathology The branch of osteology that studies the evidence of disease and injury in human skeletal (or, occasionally, mummified) remains from archaeological sites.

forensic anthropology An applied anthropological approach focused on the application of osteology and archaeology to legal matters. Forensic anthropologists work with coroners and others in identifying and analyzing human remains.

However, before genetic and molecular techniques became widespread, **osteology**, the study of the skeleton, was the only way that anthropologists could study our immediate ancestors. In fact, a thorough knowledge of skeletal structure and function is still critical to the interpretation of fossil material today. For this reason, osteology has long been viewed as central to physical anthropology. In fact, it's so important that when many people think of biological anthropology, the first thing that comes to mind is bones!

Bone biology and physiology are of major importance to many other aspects of physical anthropology besides human evolution. Many osteologists specialize in the measurement of skeletal elements, essential for identifying stature and growth and development patterns in archaeological populations. In the last 30 years or so, the reconstruction of past human behavior through the study of human skeletal remains from archaeological contexts has often been called **bioarchaeology**. Bioarchaeologists study human remains and their archaeological context to make interpretations about diet, skeletal and dental health, activity patterns, nutritional stress, social status, and relationships between earlier human populations.

Paleopathology, the study of disease and trauma in ancient skeletal populations, is a major component of bioarchaeology. Paleopathologists investigate the prevalence of trauma, certain infectious diseases (such as syphilis and tuberculosis), nutritional deficiencies, and numerous other conditions that may leave evidence in bones and teeth (Fig. 1-10). This research can tell us a great deal about the lives of individuals and populations in the past. Paleopathology also yields information regarding the history of certain disease processes, and for this reason it's of interest to scientists in biomedical fields.

Forensic anthropology is directly related to osteology and paleopathology and has become of increasing interest to the public because of TV shows like *Bones* (based on a character created by practicing forensic anthropologist Kathy Reichs) and *Crime Scene Investigation*. Technically, this approach is the application of anthropological (usually osteological and often archaeological) techniques to legal issues, such as personal identification of human remains and the analysis of skeletal trauma for law enforcement agencies. Forensic anthropologists help identify skeletal remains for law enforcement agencies, as well as in mass disasters or genocide investigations. They've been involved in numerous cases having important legal, historical, and human consequences (Fig. 1-11). They were instrumental in

Eric Bartelink

◀ **Figure 1-11**

(**a**) Anthropologists conducting a forensic excavation of the skeletal remains of a homicide victim. The recovery, analysis, and identification of homicide victims provides closure to families and contributes to resolving medicolegal cases for law enforcement. (**b**) These forensic anthropologists, working in a lab near Baghdad, are examining the skeletal remains of Kurdish victims of genocide. They cataloged the injuries of 114 individuals buried in a mass grave, and some of their evidence was used against Saddam Hussein during his trial in 2006.

U.S. Army Corps of Engineers, and the Regime Crime Liaison Office

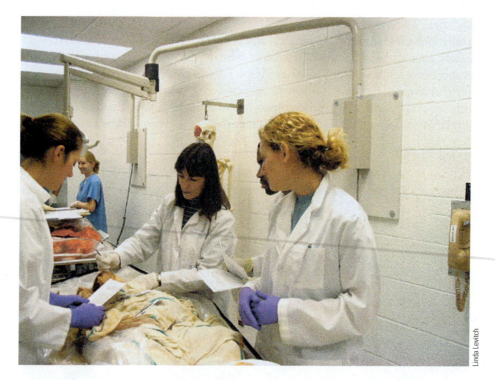

▶ Figure 1-12
Dr. Linda Levitch teaching a human anatomy class at the University of North Carolina School of Medicine.

identifying the skeletons of most of the Russian imperial family, executed in 1918, and many participated in the overwhelming task of trying to identify the remains of victims of the September 11, 2001, terrorist attacks in the United States.

Anatomy is yet another important area of interest for physical anthropologists. In living organisms, bones and teeth are intimately linked to the soft tissues that surround and act on them. Consequently a thorough knowledge of soft tissue anatomy is essential to understanding the biomechanical relationships involved in movement. Such relationships are important in assessing the structure and function of limbs and other components of fossilized remains. For these reasons and others, many physical anthropologists specialize in anatomical studies. In fact, several physical anthropologists are professors in anatomy departments at universities and medical schools (Fig. 1-12).

Given our evolutionary focus and the fact that we ourselves are primates, it's natural that **primatology**, the study of the living nonhuman primates, has become increasingly important since the late 1950s (Fig. 1-13). Today, dozens of nonhuman primate species have been and are being studied. Because nonhuman primates are our closest living relatives, identifying the underlying factors related to their social behavior, communication, infant care, reproductive behavior, and so on helps us develop a better understanding of the natural forces that have shaped so many aspects of modern human behavior. Nonhuman primates are also important to study in their own right. This is particularly true today because the majority of primate species are threatened or seriously endangered. For this reason many primatologists have become actively involved in primate conservation. Only through study will scientists be able to recommend policies that can better ensure the survival of many nonhuman primates as well as thousands of other species.

Applied Anthropology

Applied anthropology is the practical use of anthropological theories and methods outside the academic setting, but applied and academic anthropology aren't mutually exclusive approaches. In fact, applied anthropology relies on the research and

primatology The study of the biology and behavior of nonhuman primates (lemurs, lorises, tarsiers, monkeys, and apes).

▲ **Figure 1-13**

(**a**) Primatologist Corinna Most studying mother-infant interactions among a troop of wild olive baboons at the Uaso Ngiro Baboon Project (UNBP) in Kenya. (**b**) Primatologist Jill Pruetz follows a chimpanzee in Senegal, West Africa.

theories of academic anthropologists and at the same time has much to contribute to theory and techniques. Hence, many anthropologists contribute their expertise to both academic and applied research.

Within biological anthropology, forensic anthropology is a good example of the applied approach. However, the practical application of the techniques of physical anthropology isn't new. During World War II, for example, physical anthropologists were extensively involved in designing gun turrets and airplane cockpits. Since then, many physical anthropologists have pursued careers in genetic and biomedical research, public health, evolutionary medicine, medical anthropology, and the conservation of nonhuman primates, and many hold positions in museums and zoos. In fact, a background in physical anthropology is excellent preparation for almost any career in the medical and biological fields (Fig. 1-14).

Physical Anthropology and the Scientific Method

Science is a method of explaining natural phenomena. It involves observing phenomena, developing **hypotheses** to explain what has been observed, and developing a research design or series of experiments to test these hypotheses. This is an

science A body of knowledge gained through observation and experimentation; from the Latin *scientia*, meaning "knowledge."

hypotheses (*sing.*, hypothesis) Provisional explanations of phenomenon. Hypotheses require verification or falsification through testing.

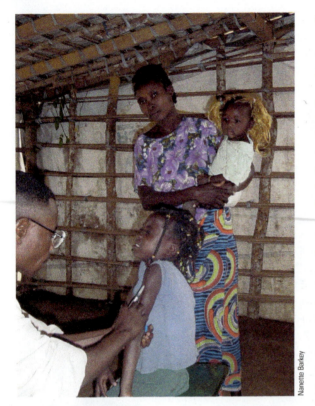

Nanette Barkey

▲ **Figure 1-14**

Nanette Barkey, a medical anthropologist involved in a repatriation project in Angola, photographed this little girl being vaccinated at a refugee transit camp. Vaccinations were being administered to Angolan refugees returning home in 2004 from the Democratic Republic of Congo, where they had fled to escape warfare in their own country.

empirical Relying on experiment or observation; from the Latin *empiricus*, meaning "experienced."

scientific method An approach to research whereby a problem is identified, a hypothesis (provisional explanation) is stated, and that hypothesis is tested by collecting and analyzing data.

data (*sing.*, datum) Facts from which conclusions can be drawn; scientific information.

quantitatively Pertaining to measurements of quantity and including such properties as size, number, and capacity. When data are quantified, they're expressed numerically and can be tested statistically.

empirical approach to gaining information. Because biological anthropologists are engaged in scientific research, they adhere to the principles of the **scientific method** by identifying a research problem and then gathering information to solve it.

Once a question or problem has been identified, the first step is usually to explore the existing literature (books and journals) to determine what other people have done to resolve the issue. Based on this preliminary research and other observations, one or even several tentative explanations (hypotheses) are then proposed. The next step is to develop a research design or methodology to test the hypothesis. These methods involve collecting information, or **data**, that can then be studied and analyzed. Data can be analyzed in many ways, most of the time involving various statistical tests or mathematical modeling. During the data collection and analysis phase, it's important for scientists to use a strictly controlled approach so that they can precisely describe their techniques and results. This precision is critical because it enables others to repeat the experiments and allows scientists to make comparisons between their study and the work of others.

For example, when scientists collect data on tooth size in hominin fossils, they must specify which teeth are measured, how they're measured, and the results of the measurements (expressed numerically, or **quantitatively**). Then, by analyzing the data, the investigators try to draw conclusions about the meaning and significance of their measurements. This body of information then becomes the basis of future studies, often by other researchers, who can compare their own results with those already obtained.

Hypothesis testing is the very core of the scientific method, and although it may seem contradictory at first, it's based on the potential to *falsify* the hypothesis. Falsification doesn't mean that the entire hypothesis is untrue, but it does indicate that the hypothesis may need to be refined and subjected to further testing.

Eventually, if a hypothesis stands up to repeated testing, it may become part of a **theory** or perhaps a theory itself. There's a popular misconception that a theory is nothing more than conjecture, or a "hunch." But in science, theories are proposed explanations of robust relationships between natural phenomena. Theories usually concern broader, more universal views than hypotheses, which have a narrower focus and deal with more specific relationships between phenomena. But like hypotheses, theories aren't facts. *They are tested explanations of facts.* For example, it's a fact that when you drop an object, it falls to the ground. The explanation for this fact is the theory of gravity. But, like hypotheses, theories can be altered over time with further experimentation and by using newly developed technologies in testing. The theory of gravity has been tested many times and qualified by experiments showing how the mass of objects affects how they're attracted to one another. So far, the theory has held up.

Scientific testing of hypotheses may take several years (or longer) and may involve researchers who weren't part of the original work. What's more, new methods may permit different kinds of testing that weren't previously possible; this is a strength, not a weakness, of scientific research. For example, since the 1970s, primatologists have reported that male nonhuman primates (as well as males of many other species) sometimes kill infants. One hypothesis has been that infanticidal males only kill the offspring of other males and not their own. But many scientists have objected to this hypothesis and have proposed several alternatives. For one thing, there was no way to know for certain that the males weren't killing their own offspring; if they were, this would argue against the hypothesis. However, in more recent research, scientists have collected DNA samples from dead infants and the males who killed them. The evidence showed that most of the time, the males were not related to their victims. This result doesn't prove that the original hypothesis is accurate but it does strengthen it. This study is described in more detail in Chapter 7, but we mention it here to emphasize that science is an ongoing process that builds on previous work and benefits from newly developed techniques (in this case, DNA testing) in ways that constantly expand our knowledge.

Throughout this book we present several examples of how different approaches to research and new technologies (especially in the field of genetics) have helped support or alter numerous hypotheses. Scientific research is frequently ridiculed and/or dismissed by the general public, politicians, and some members of the press. (Particularly good current examples of this relate to climate change research and evolution.) These antiscience positions have been quite successful because the majority of people don't understand the nature or goals of scientific research.

There's one more extremely important fact about hypotheses and theories: *Any proposition that is stated as absolute or does not allow the possibility of falsification is not a scientific hypothesis and should never be considered as such.* For a statement to be considered a scientific hypothesis, there must be a way to evaluate its validity. A statement such as "ghosts exist" may be true but there is no rational, empirical means (based on experience or experiment) of testing it. Therefore acceptance of such a view is based on faith rather than scientific verification. *The purpose of scientific research is not to establish absolute truths; rather, it is to generate ever more accurate and consistent explanations of phenomena in our universe based on observation and testing.* At its very heart, scientific methodology is an exercise in rational thought and critical thinking.

The development of critical thinking skills is an extremely important benefit of a college education. Such skills enable people to evaluate, compare, analyze, critique, and synthesize information so that they won't accept everything they hear at face value. Critical thinking skills are perhaps most needed when it comes to advertising and politics. People spend billions of dollars every year on "natural" dietary supplements based on marketing claims that may not have even been tested. So when a salesperson tells you that, for example, echinacea helps prevent colds, you should ask if that statement has been scientifically tested, how it was tested, when, by whom, and where the results were published. Similarly, when politicians make claims in 30-second sound bites, check those claims before you accept them as truth. Be skeptical, and if you do check the validity of advertising and political statements, you'll find that frequently they're either misleading or just plain wrong.

The Anthropological Perspective

Perhaps the most important benefit you'll receive from this textbook and this course is a wider appreciation of the human experience. To understand human beings and how our species came to be, we must broaden our viewpoint through both time and space. All branches of anthropology fundamentally seek to do this in what we call the *anthropological perspective.*

Physical anthropologists, for example, are interested in how humans both differ from and are similar to other animals, especially nonhuman primates. For example, we've defined *hominins* as bipedal primates, but what are the major anatomical components of bipedal locomotion and how do they differ from, say, those in a **quadrupedal** ape? To answer these questions, biological anthropologists have studied the anatomical structures involved in human locomotion (muscles, hips, legs, and feet) and compared them with the same structures in various nonhuman primates.

Through a perspective that is broad in space and time, we can begin to grasp the diversity of the human experience within the context of biological and behavioral

theory A broad statement of scientific relationships or underlying principles that has been substantially verified through the testing of hypotheses.

scientific testing The precise repetition of an experiment or expansion of observed data to provide verification; the procedure by which hypotheses and theories are verified, modified, or discarded.

quadrupedal Using all four limbs to support the body during locomotion; the basic mammalian (and primate) form of locomotion.

A Closer Look Forensic Anthropology in Practice

Forensic anthropology is the application of the principles of physical anthropology and archaeology to the legal system, especially as they relate to the study of the human skeleton. Forensic anthropologists are often called on to assist local law enforcement with crime scene recovery and analysis of human remains. Because of their specialized knowledge and training in physical anthropology, archaeology, and forensic science, they are ideally suited to assist with cases involving badly decomposed or skeletonized remains. Although many forensic anthropologists are employed by universities, there is a growing number who work in medical examiner's offices, museums, state and federal law enforcement agencies, human rights organizations, and for mass disaster agencies (Fig. 1).

The first step in a potential forensic investigation is to determine if the remains are human or nonhuman, and the second step is to determine if they are of recent or ancient origin. A skeletal analysis initially begins with establishing a *biological profile* of the person whose remains are under investigation. This involves the estimation of the person's sex, age at death, ancestry, and living height (*stature*). These characteristics aid in narrowing down the pool of missing persons to consider for comparison. A positive identification of an unknown individual can be made through comparisons of antemortem (conditions that affected the skeleton during life) records, such as medical and dental X-rays, with unique biological characteristics observed on the skeleton. These may include genetic anomalies, such as unusual or atypical skeletal or dental features, or pathological conditions, such as bone infections or healed fractures. Multiple points of similarity between antemortem and postmortem records (i.e., information collected on the deceased individual) can then help to establish identity. Finally, an analysis involves a comprehensive assessment of skeletal trauma, usually classified as blunt-force, sharp-force, or projectile trauma. Forensic anthropologists carefully document trauma that occurred at or around the time of death (*perimortem trauma*) to provide investigators with information regarding the circumstances of death. They also study postmortem alterations, such as damage to bone caused by exposure to the sun or by scavenging animals. It is critical to be able to differentiate this damage from trauma caused by interpersonal violence.

Ultimately, forensic anthropologists provide services that may help to resolve a case and provide closure to families. They are sometimes called into court as expert witnesses to testify regarding the identity of an individual and to describe traumatic injuries identified on skeletal remains that may pertain to the cause and manner of death. It is strongly recommended that people who wish to practice forensic anthropology receive a doctorate in physical anthropology and undergo certification through the American Board of Forensic Anthropology (see www.theabfa.org). As of 2016, there are 79 active board-certified forensic anthropologists in North America.

Eric Bartelink

▲ **Figure 1**
Forensic anthropologist Dr. Colleen Milligan examines a fire scene where human remains were discovered.

connections with other species. In this way, we may better understand the limits and potentials of humankind. By extending our knowledge to include cultures other than our own, we may hope to avoid the **ethnocentric** pitfalls inherent in a more limited view of humanity.

This **relativistic** view of culture is perhaps more important now than ever before because, in our interdependent global community, it allows us to understand other people's concerns and to view our own culture from a broader perspective. Likewise, by examining our species as part of a wide spectrum of life, we realize that we can't judge other species using only human criteria. Each species is unique, with needs and a behavioral repertoire not exactly like that of any other. By recognizing that we share many similarities (both biological and behavioral) with other animals,

ethnocentric Viewing other cultures from the inherently biased perspective of one's own culture. Ethnocentrism often causes other cultures to be seen as inferior to one's own.

relativistic Viewing entities as they relate to something else. Cultural relativism is the view that cultures have merits within their own historical and environmental contexts.

perhaps we may come to recognize that they have a place in nature just as surely as we ourselves do.

We hope that after reading the following pages, you will have an increased understanding not only of the similarities we share with other biological organisms but also of the processes that have shaped the traits that make us unique. We live in what may well be the most crucial time for our planet in the past 65 million years. We are members of the one species that, through the very agency of culture, has wrought such devastating changes in ecological systems that we must now alter our technologies or face potentially unspeakable consequences. In such a time, it's vital that we attempt to gain the best possible understanding of what it means to be human. We believe that the study of physical anthropology is one endeavor that aids in this attempt, and that is indeed the goal of this textbook.

Summary of Main Topics

- Humans are connected to all other life-forms on earth and exist as part of a biological continuum.
- Biocultural evolution serves as an integrative framework from which to study the dual effects of biology and culture on the evolution of the human lineage.
- The major subfields of anthropology are cultural anthropology, linguistic anthropology, archaeology, and physical anthropology.
- Physical anthropology is a discipline that seeks to explain how and when human beings evolved. This requires a detailed examination of the primate and particularly the hominin fossil record. Another major topic of physical anthropology is human biological variation, its genetic basis,

and its adaptive significance. In addition, physical anthropologists study the behavior and biology of nonhuman primates, partly as a method of understanding humans but also because nonhuman primates are important in their own right.

- Because physical anthropology is a scientific approach to the investigation of all aspects of human evolution, variation, and adaptation, research in this field is based on the scientific method. The scientific method is a system of inquiry that involves the development of hypotheses to explain phenomena. To determine the validity of hypotheses, scientists develop research designs aimed at collecting information (data) and testing the data to

see if they support the hypothesis. If the hypothesis is not supported by the data, it may be rejected or modified and retested. If it is supported, it may also be modified or refined over time and further tested. These additional tests frequently use new technologies that have been developed since the original hypothesis was proposed. If a hypothesis stands up to repeated testing, it may eventually be accepted as a theory or part of a theory.

- The anthropological perspective involves bringing together all four of the subfields of anthropology to provide a more holistic view of humans and their place in nature.

Critical Thinking Questions

1. Given that you've only just been introduced to the field of physical anthropology, why do you think subjects such as skeletal anatomy, genetics, nonhuman primate behavior, and human evolution are integrated into a discussion of what it means to be human?

2. Do you see a connection between hominin footprints that are almost 4 million years old and human footprints left on the moon in 1969? If so, do you think this relationship is important? What does the fact that there are human footprints on the moon

say about human adaptation? (Consider both biological and cultural adaptation.)

3. Can you identify some areas of overlap between the subfields of anthropology? Why is it important to understand humankind from a holistic perspective?

CONNECTIONS

Physical anthropology investigates how humans have evolved.

Evolutionary theory, particularly natural selection, explains how life forms have changed over time.

DNA molecule is the basis of all life.

The Development of Evolutionary Theory

A Brief History of Evolutionary Thought

The Scientific Revolution

Precursors of the Theory of Evolution

The Discovery of Natural Selection

In Darwin's Shadow

Natural Selection

Natural Selection in Action

Natural Selection and Reproductive Success

Constraints on Nineteenth-Century Evolutionary Theory

Opposition to Evolution Today

A Brief History of Opposition to Evolution in the United States

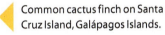

Common cactus finch on Santa Cruz Island, Galápagos Islands.
Minden Pictures/Superstock; Top Middle Image: Bettmann/Corbis

Student Learning Objectives After studying the material in this chapter, you should be able to:

▶ Trace the major developments in scientific thinking that led to the discovery of evolutionary processes.

▶ Describe how natural selection operates on biological variation in species to cause evolutionary change over time.

▶ Explain some of the limitations and gaps in evolutionary theory at the end of the nineteenth century.

▶ Discuss the history of opposition to the teaching of evolution in the United States.

Has anyone ever asked you, "If humans evolved from monkeys, why do we still have monkeys?" Or maybe, "If evolution happens, why don't we ever see new species?" These are the kinds of questions people sometimes ask if they don't understand evolutionary processes or if they don't believe that evolution occurs. Evolution is one of the most fundamental of all biological processes and one of the most misunderstood. The explanation for this misunderstanding is simple: Evolution is not taught in most primary and secondary schools in the United States. In fact, it's frequently avoided. Even in colleges and universities, it receives the most detailed treatment in biological anthropology. If you're not an anthropology or biology major and you're taking a class in biological anthropology mainly to fulfill a science requirement, there is a good chance you'll probably never study evolution again.

By the end of this course, you will know the answers to the questions in the preceding paragraph. Briefly, no one who understands evolution would ever say that humans evolved from monkeys, because we didn't. We didn't evolve from chimpanzees either. The earliest human ancestors evolved from a species that lived some 6 to 8 million years ago (mya). That ancestral species was the *last common ancestor* we share with chimpanzees. In turn, the lineage that eventually gave rise to apes and humans separated from a monkey-like ancestor some 20 mya. Monkeys are still around because as early primate lineages diverged from one another, each went its separate way, with some populations evolving into apes (one of which later evolved into the earliest human ancestor) and other populations remaining as monkeys. Over millions of years, some of these groups became extinct while others evolved into the species we know today. Thus all living species are the current results of processes that go back millions of years. The evolution of new species takes time, often on the order of hundreds of thousands to millions of years, which is why we don't witness the appearance of new species except microorganisms. We can, however, observe *microevolutionary* changes in many species, including humans.

The subject of evolution is controversial, especially in the United States, because some views hold that evolutionary statements run counter to religious teachings. In fact, as you're probably aware, there is strong opposition in the United States to the teaching of evolution in public schools. Opponents of teaching evolution often say, "It's just a theory," meaning that evolution is just an idea or hunch. As we pointed out in Chapter 1, scientific theories aren't just ideas, although that's how the word *theory* is commonly used in everyday conversation. However, when dealing with scientific issues, referring to a concept as "theory" means it has robust support. Theories have been tested and subjected to verification through multiple accumulated lines of evidence (for example, repeated hypothesis testing), and they have not been disproved, despite decades of rigorous experimentation. It is absolutely true that evolution is a theory, one supported by a mounting body of genetic and fossil evidence that grows daily. It's a theory that explains how biological change occurs in species over time, and it has stood the test of time. Today, evolutionary theory stands as the most fundamental unifying force in biological science, and evolutionary biologists can explain many evolutionary processes in ways that were impossible even a decade ago.

Because physical anthropology is concerned with all aspects of how humans came to be and how we adapt physiologically and behaviorally to the external environment, the details of the evolutionary process are crucial to the field. Given the central importance of evolution to biological anthropology, it is helpful to know how the mechanics of the process came to be discovered. Also, if we want to understand and make critical assessments of the controversy that surrounds the issue today, we need to explore the social and political events that influenced the discovery of evolutionary principles.

A Brief History of Evolutionary Thought

The discovery of evolutionary principles first took place in western Europe and was made possible by advances in scientific thinking that date back to the sixteenth century. Having said this, we must recognize that Western science borrowed many of its ideas from other cultures, especially the Arabs, Indians, and Chinese. In fact, intellectuals in these cultures and in ancient Greece had developed notions of biological evolution centuries before Charles Darwin did (Teresi, 2002), but they never formulated them into a cohesive theory.

Charles Darwin was the first person to explain the basic mechanics of the evolutionary process. But while he was developing his theory of **natural selection**, a Scottish naturalist named Alfred Russel Wallace independently reached the same conclusion. That natural selection, the single most important force of evolutionary change, was proposed at more or less the same time by two British men in the mid-nineteenth century may seem like a strange coincidence. But actually if Darwin and Wallace hadn't made their simultaneous discoveries, someone else soon would have, and that someone would probably have been British or French. That's because the groundwork had already been laid in Britain and France, and many scientists there were prepared to accept explanations of biological change that would have been unacceptable even 25 years before.

In science as in other human endeavors, knowledge is usually gained through a series of small steps rather than giant leaps. Just as technological change is based on past achievements, scientific knowledge builds on previously developed theories. Therefore, it's informative to examine the development of ideas that led Darwin and Wallace to independently arrive at the theory of evolution by natural selection.

Throughout the Middle Ages, one predominant feature of the European worldview was that all aspects of nature, including all forms of life and their relationships to one another, never changed. This view was partly shaped by a feudal society that was itself a rigid class system that had barely changed for centuries. But the most important influence was an extremely powerful religious system in which the teachings of Christianity were held to be the only "truth." Consequently it was generally accepted that all life on earth had been created by God exactly as it existed in the present and the belief that life-forms could not and did not change, came to be known as **fixity of species**. Anyone who questioned these notions of fixity, especially in the fifteenth and sixteenth centuries, could be accused of challenging God's perfection, which was heresy. Generally it was a good idea to avoid being accused of heresy because this was a crime punishable by trial by fire (a nasty, fiery death) (Fig. 2-1).

natural selection The most critical mechanism of evolutionary change, first described by Charles Darwin; the term refers to genetic change or changes in the frequencies of certain traits in populations due to differential reproductive success between individuals.

fixity of species The notion that species, once created, can never change is diametrically opposed to theories of biological evolution.

Savonarola Being Burnt at the Stake, Piazza della Signoria, Florence (oil on panel), Italian School, (16th century)/Museo di San Marco dell'Angelico, Florence, Italy/Bridgeman Images

◀ **Figure 2-1**

Portion of a Renaissance painting that depicts the execution of Father Girolamo Savonarola in 1498 in Florence, Italy (artist unknown). Savonarola wasn't promoting scientific arguments, but he did run afoul of church leaders. His execution by burning was a common punishment for those, including many scientists and philosophers, who promoted scientific explanations of natural phenomena.

The plan of the entire universe was viewed as God's design. In what is called the "argument from design," anatomical structures were held to have been engineered to meet their intended purpose. Limbs, internal organs, and eyes all fit the functions they performed; and they, along with the rest of nature, were part of the Grand Designer's deliberate plan. Also, the Grand Designer was thought to have completed his works as recently as 4004 B.C. The prevailing belief in the earth's brief existence, together with fixity of species, was a virtually insurmountable obstacle to the development of evolutionary theory. The idea of immense geological time, which today we take for granted, simply didn't exist. In fact, until the concepts of fixity and time were fundamentally altered, it was simply not possible to conceive of evolution by means of natural selection.

The Scientific Revolution

So what transformed this centuries-old belief in a rigid, static universe into a view of worlds in continuous motion? How did the earth's brief history become an immense expanse of incomprehensible time? How did the scientific method as we know it today develop? These are important questions, but we could also ask why it took so long for Europe to break away from traditional beliefs. After all, scholars in India and the Arab world had developed concepts of planetary motion, for example, centuries earlier.

The development of evolutionary theory came about as a result of a series of discoveries that led to major **paradigm shifts**. For example, the discovery of the New World and circumnavigation of the globe in the fifteenth century overturned some very basic European ideas about the planet. Among other things, the earth could no longer be thought of as flat. Also, as Europeans began to explore the New World, encountering plants and animals they'd never seen before, their awareness of biological diversity expanded.

There were other attacks on traditional beliefs. In 1514, a Polish mathematician named Copernicus challenged a notion proposed more than 1,500 years earlier, in the fourth-century B.C., by the Greek philosopher Aristotle. Aristotle had taught that the sun and planets existed in a series of concentric spheres that revolved around the earth (Fig. 2-2), a system that was, in turn, surrounded by the stars. Thus it came to be accepted that the earth was the center of the solar system. In fact, scholars in India had figured out that the earth orbited the sun long before Copernicus did; but Copernicus is generally credited with changing the idea that earth was the center of the universe.

Copernicus' theory was discussed in intellectual circles, but it didn't attract much attention from the Catholic Church. (Catholicism was the only form of Christianity until the 1520s.) Nevertheless, the theory did contradict a major premise of church doctrine, which at that time wholeheartedly embraced the teachings of Aristotle. By the 1300s, the church had accepted these teachings as dogma because they reinforced the notion that the earth, and the humans on it, were the central focus of God's creation and must therefore have a central position in the solar system.

However, in the early 1600s, an Italian mathematician named Galileo Galilei restated Copernicus' views, using logic and mathematics to support his claim. To his misfortune, Galileo was eventually confronted by the highest-ranking officials of the Catholic Church (including his former friend, Pope Urban VIII), and had to face the Roman Inquisition (the court of justice associated with the church). He spent the last nine years of his life under house arrest, but continued to publish scientific works (outside of Italy) that were far less controversial. Nevertheless, in intellectual circles there had been a paradigm shift. The solar system had changed; the sun was now at its center, and the earth and other planets revolved around it as the entire system journeyed through space.

paradigm shift A transition from one conceptual framework or prevailing and widely accepted viewpoint to another. The acceptance of the discovery that the sun is the center of our solar system is an example of a paradigm shift.

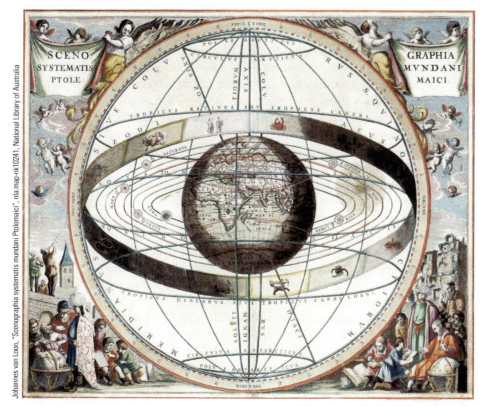

Johannes van Loon, "Scenographia systematis mundani Ptolemaici", nla.map-nk10241, National Library of Australia

◀ **Figure 2-2**
This beautifully illustrated seventeenth-century map shows the earth at the center of the solar system. Around it are seven concentric circles depicting the orbits of the moon, the sun, and the five planets that were known at the time. (Note also the signs of the zodiac.)

Throughout the sixteenth and seventeenth centuries, European scientists developed other methods and theories that revolutionized scientific thought. The seventeenth century, in particular, saw the discovery of the principles of physics (such as motion and gravity), and the invention of numerous scientific instruments, including the microscope. These advances made it possible to investigate many previously misunderstood natural phenomena. Even with these advances, the idea that living forms could change over time simply didn't occur to people.

Precursors of the Theory of Evolution

Before early naturalists could begin to understand the many forms of organic life, they had to list and describe them. As research progressed, scholars became increasingly impressed with the amount of biological diversity they observed.

The concept of species, as we think of them today, wasn't proposed until the seventeenth century, when John Ray, a minister educated at the University of Cambridge, developed it. He recognized that groups of plants and animals could be differentiated from other groups by their ability to mate with one another and produce fertile offspring. He placed such groups of **reproductively isolated** organisms into categories, which he called species (*sing.,* species). Thus, by the late 1600s, the biological criterion of reproduction was used to define species, much as it is today (Young, 1992). Ray also recognized that species frequently share similarities with other species, and he grouped these together in a second level of classification he called the genus (*pl.,* genera). He was the first to use the labels *genus* and *species* in this way, and these terms are still in use today.

Carolus Linnaeus (1707–1778) was a Swedish naturalist who developed a method of classifying plants and animals. In his famous work *Systema Naturae* (System of Nature), first published in 1735, he standardized Ray's use of genus and species terminology and established the system of **binomial nomenclature**. He also added

reproductively isolated   Pertaining to groups of organisms that, mainly because of genetic differences, are prevented from mating and producing offspring with members of other such groups. For example, dogs cannot mate and produce offspring with cats.

binomial nomenclature   (*binomial,* meaning "two names") In taxonomy, the convention established by Carolus Linnaeus whereby genus and species names are used to refer to living things. For example, *Homo sapiens* refers to human beings.

two more categories: class and order. Linnaeus' four-level system became the basis for **taxonomy**, the system of classification we still use today.

Linnaeus also included humans in his classification of animals, placing them in the genus *Homo* and species *sapiens*. (Genus and species names are always italicized or underlined.) Including humans in this scheme was controversial because it defied contemporary thought that humans, made in God's image, should be considered unique and separate from the rest of the animal kingdom. Unfortunately for other species, most people still have this view, in spite of all the research that has demonstrated biological and behavioral continuity among all animals including ourselves. Linnaeus also originally classified whales as fish; however, he later changed his mind and reclassified them as mammals based on their anatomical features (a controversial idea at the time).

For all his progressive tendencies, Linnaeus still believed in fixity of species, although in later years, faced with mounting evidence to the contrary, he came to question it. Indeed, fixity was being challenged on many fronts, especially in France, where voices were being raised in favor of a universe based on change and, more to the point, in favor of a biological relationship between similar species based on descent from a common ancestor.

Georges-Louis Comte Leclerc de Buffon (1707–1788), a French naturalist, recognized the dynamic relationship between the external environment and living forms. In his 36-volume *Histoire Naturelle* (*Natural History*), first published in 1749, he recognized that different regions have unique plants and animals. He also stressed that animals had come from a "center of origin," but he never discussed the diversification of life over time. Even so, Buffon recognized that alterations of the external environment, including the climate, were agents of change in species. For this reason, the twentieth-century evolutionary biologist Ernst Mayr said of him: "He was not an evolutionist, yet he was the father of evolutionism" (Mayr, 1981, p. 330).

Today, Erasmus Darwin (1731–1802) is best known as Charles Darwin's grandfather. But he was also a physician, poet, and leading member of an important intellectual community in England (known as the Lunar Society of Birmingham). In fact, Darwin counted among his friends some of the most important figures of the industrial revolution—a time of rapid technological and social change. In his most famous poem, Darwin expressed the view that life had originated in the seas and that all species had descended from a common ancestor. Thus he introduced many of the ideas that his grandson would propose 56 years later. These concepts include vast expanses of time for life to evolve, competition for resources, and the importance of the environment in evolutionary processes. From letters and other sources, we know that Charles Darwin read his grandfather's writings, but we don't know how much they influenced him.

Neither Buffon nor Erasmus Darwin attempted to *explain* the evolutionary process, but a French naturalist named Jean-Baptiste Lamarck (1744–1829) did. Lamarck (Fig. 2-3) suggested a dynamic relationship between species and the environment such that if the external environment changed, an animal's activity patterns would also change to accommodate the new circumstances. This would result in the increased or decreased use of certain body parts (that is, "use it or lose it"); consequently those body parts would be modified. According to Lamarck, the parts that weren't used would disappear over time. However, the parts that continued to be used, perhaps in different ways, would change. Such physical changes would occur in response to bodily "needs," so that if a particular part of the body felt a certain need, "fluids and forces" would be directed to that point, and the structure would be modified. Because the alteration would make the animal better suited to its habitat, the new trait would be passed on to offspring. This theory is known as the *inheritance of acquired characteristics*, or the *use-disuse* theory.

▲ **Figure 2-3**

Portrait of Jean-Baptiste Lamarck. Lamarck believed that species change was influenced by environmental change. He is best known for his theory of the inheritance of acquired characteristics.

Portrait of Jean-Baptiste de Monet (1744-1829) Chevalier de Lamarck, 1802-03 (oil on canvas), Thevenin, Charles (1764-1838)/ Private Collection/Bridgeman Images

taxonomy The branch of science concerned with the rules of classifying organisms on the basis of evolutionary relationships.

One of the most frequently given hypothetical examples of Lamarck's theory is the giraffe, which, having stripped all the leaves from the lower branches of a tree (environmental change), tries to reach the leaves on upper branches. As "vital forces" move to tissues of the neck, it becomes slightly longer and the giraffe can reach higher. The longer neck is then transmitted to offspring, with the eventual result that all giraffes have longer necks than did their predecessors (Fig. 2-4). So, according to this theory, *a trait acquired by an animal during its lifetime can be passed on to offspring.* Today we know that this explanation is wrong because only those traits that are influenced by genetic information contained within sex cells (eggs and sperm) can be inherited (see Chapter 3).

Because Lamarck's explanation of species change was incorrect on a genetic level, he is frequently scorned even today. But in fact Lamarck deserves a great deal of credit because he emphasized the importance of interactions between organisms and the external environment in the evolutionary process. He also coined the term *biology* to refer to the study of living organisms, and a central feature of this new discipline was the idea of species change.

Lamarck's most vehement opponent was a French vertebrate paleontologist named Georges Cuvier (1769–1832). Cuvier introduced the concept of extinction to explain the disappearance of animals represented by fossils; this concept was

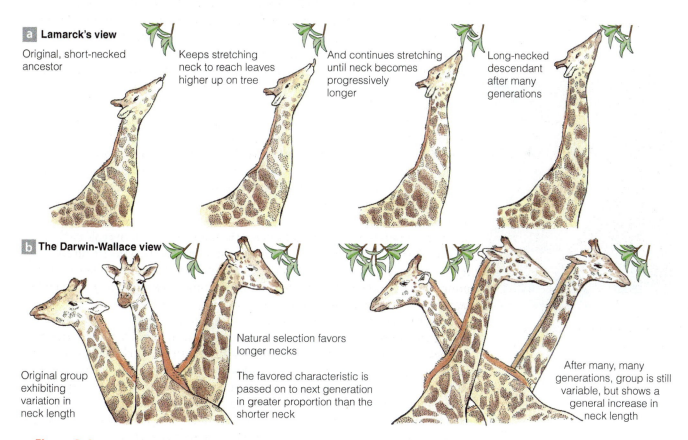

a **Lamarck's view**

Original, short-necked ancestor

Keeps stretching neck to reach leaves higher up on tree

And continues stretching until neck becomes progressively longer

Long-necked descendant after many generations

b **The Darwin-Wallace view**

Original group exhibiting variation in neck length

Natural selection favors longer necks

The favored characteristic is passed on to next generation in greater proportion than the shorter neck

After many, many generations, group is still variable, but shows a general increase in neck length

▲ **Figure 2-4**

Contrasting ideas about the mechanism of evolution. (**a**) Lamarck's theory held that acquired characteristics can be passed to offspring. Short-necked giraffes stretched to reach higher into trees for food; therefore their necks grew longer as a result. According to Lamarck, this acquired trait was then passed on to offspring, who were born with longer necks. (**b**) The Darwin-Wallace theory of natural selection states that there is variation in neck length among giraffes. If having a longer neck provides an advantage for feeding, the trait will be passed on to a greater number of offspring, leading to an overall increase in the length of giraffe necks over many generations.

elaborated in his 1813 publication *Essay on the Theory of the Earth*. Cuvier was a brilliant anatomist, but he never grasped the dynamic concept of nature and continued to insist on the fixity of species. So, rather than assuming that similarities between fossil forms and living species indicate evolutionary relationships, Cuvier proposed a variation of a doctrine known as **catastrophism**.

Catastrophism was the belief that the earth's geological features are the results of sudden, worldwide cataclysmic events. Cuvier's version of catastrophism suggested that a series of regional disasters had destroyed most or all of the local plant and animal life in many places. These areas were then restocked with new, similar forms that migrated in from unaffected regions. In order to be consistent with emerging fossil evidence, which indicated that organisms had become more complex over time, Cuvier proposed that after each disaster, the incoming migrants were more similar to living species because they had been produced by more recent creation events. In this way, Cuvier's explanation of increased complexity over time avoided any notion of evolution, but it still managed to account for the evidence of change so well preserved in the fossil record.

In 1798, an English economist named Thomas Malthus (1766–1834) wrote *An Essay on the Principle of Population*. This important essay inspired both Charles Darwin and Alfred Russel Wallace in their separate discoveries of natural selection. It's interesting that, although Malthus had an enormous influence on these two men, he wasn't interested in species change at all. Instead, he was arguing for limits to human population growth. He pointed out that in nature, there is a tendency for animal populations to increase in size, but the amount of resources (food and water) remains relatively the same. Therefore population size is held in check by resource availability. Even though humans can reduce constraints on population size by producing more food, Malthus argued that the lack of sufficient food and water would always be a constant source of "misery" and famine for humankind if our numbers continued to increase. Unfortunately we are now testing Malthus' hypothesis, as the number of humans on earth reached 7.4 billion in 2016!

Both Darwin and Wallace extended Malthus' principles to all organisms, not just humans. Moreover, they recognized the important fact that when population size is limited by resource availability, there is constant competition. This is a crucial point, because competition among individuals is the ultimate key to understanding natural selection.

Charles Lyell (1797–1875) is considered the founder of modern geology (Fig. 2-5). He was a lawyer, a geologist, and, for many years, Charles Darwin's friend and mentor. Before meeting Darwin in 1836, Lyell had earned acceptance in Europe's most prestigious scientific circles, thanks to his highly praised *Principles of Geology*, first published during the years 1830–1833.

In this extremely important work, Lyell argued that the geological processes we see today are the same as those that existed in the past. This theory, called geological **uniformitarianism**, didn't originate entirely with Lyell, having been proposed by James Hutton in the late 1700s. Even so, it was Lyell who demonstrated that forces such as wind, water erosion, local flooding, frost, decomposition of vegetable matter, volcanoes, earthquakes, and glacial movements had all contributed in the past to produce the geological landscape that we see today. What's more, these processes were ongoing, indicating that geological change was still happening and that the forces driving such change were consistent, or *uniform*, over time. In other words, various aspects of the earth's surface (mountain ranges, rivers, the position of continents, and so forth) vary through time, but the *underlying processes* that influence them are constant.

Lyell also emphasized the obvious: namely, that for such slowly acting forces to produce momentous change, the earth must be far older than anyone had previously suspected. By providing an immense time scale and thereby changing

▲ **Figure 2-5**
Portrait of Charles Lyell.

catastrophism The view that the earth's geological landscape is the result of violent cataclysmic events. Cuvier promoted this view, especially in opposition to Lamarck.

uniformitarianism The theory that the earth's features are the result of long-term processes that continue to operate in the present just as they did in the past. Elaborated on by Lyell, this theory opposed catastrophism and greatly contributed to the concept of deep geological time.

Hutton-Deutsch Collection/Corbis

◀ Figure 2-6
(**a**) These limestone cliffs in southern France were formed around 300 million years ago from shells and the skeletal remains of countless sea creatures. (**b**) Stone cut from the same limestone containing fossilized shells.

perceptions of the earth's history from a few thousand to many millions of years, Lyell changed the framework within which scientists viewed the geological past. Thus the concept of "deep time" (Gould, 1987) remains one of Lyell's most significant contributions to the discovery of evolutionary principles, because the immensity of geological time permitted the necessary time depth for the inherently slow process of evolutionary change (Fig. 2-6).

As you can see, the roots of evolutionary theory are deeply embedded in the late eighteenth and early nineteenth centuries. During that time, many lesser-known but very important people also contributed to this intellectual movement. One such person was Mary Anning (1799–1847), who lived in the town of Lyme Regis, on the south coast of England.

Anning's father died when she was 11 years old, leaving his wife and two children destitute. Fortunately, he had taught Mary to recognize marine fossils embedded in the cliffs near the town. Thus, she began to earn a living by collecting and selling fossils to collectors who were becoming increasingly interested in the remains of creatures that many people believed had been killed in the Noah flood.

After Anning's discovery of the first *complete* fossil of *Ichthyosaurus*, a large marine reptile, and the first *Plesiosaurus* fossil (another ocean-dwelling reptile), some of the most famous scientists in England repeatedly visited her home. Eventually she became known as one of the world's leading "fossilists." By sharing her extensive knowledge of fossil species with many of the leading scientists of the day, she contributed to the understanding of the evolution of marine life, which spanned over 200 million years. But because she was a woman and of low social position, Anning wasn't acknowledged in the numerous scientific publications she facilitated. In recent years, however, she has achieved the recognition she deserves; her portrait hangs prominently in the British Museum (Natural History) in London.

The Discovery of Natural Selection

Having already been introduced to Erasmus Darwin, you shouldn't be surprised to learn that his grandson Charles grew up in an educated family with ties to the intellectual circles of the time. Charles Darwin (1809–1882) was one of six children of

▲ **Figure 2-7**
Charles Darwin, photographed
five years before the publication of
On the Origin of Species.

Dr. Robert and Susannah Darwin (Fig. 2-7). Being the grandson not only of Erasmus Darwin but also of the wealthy Josiah Wedgwood (of Wedgwood China fame), Charles grew up enjoying the comfortable lifestyle of the landed gentry in rural England.

As a boy, Darwin had a keen interest in nature, but this interest did little to dispel the generally held view among family and friends that he was in no way remarkable. In fact, his performance at school was no more than ordinary.

After his mother's death when he was 8 years old, Darwin was raised by his father and older sisters. Because he showed little interest in anything except hunting, shooting, and perhaps science, his father sent him to Edinburgh University to study medicine. It was there that Darwin first became acquainted with the evolutionary theories of Lamarck and others.

During that time (the 1820s), notions of evolution were becoming feared in England and elsewhere. Anything identified with postrevolutionary France was viewed with suspicion by the established order in England, and Lamarck, partly because he was French, was especially vilified by British scientists.

It was also a time of growing political unrest in Britain. The Reform Movement, which sought to undo the many inequalities of the traditional class system, was under way, and like most social movements, it had a radical faction. Because many of the radicals were atheists and socialists who also supported Lamarck's ideas, many people came to associate evolution with atheism and political subversion. The growing fear of evolutionary ideas led many to believe that if these ideas were generally accepted, "the Church would crash, the moral fabric of society would be torn apart, and civilized man would return to savagery" (Desmond and Moore, 1991, p. 34). It's unfortunate that some of the most outspoken early proponents of species change were so vehemently anti-Christian, because their rhetoric helped to establish the entrenched suspicion and misunderstanding of evolutionary theory that persists today.

While at Edinburgh, Darwin studied with professors who were outspoken supporters of Lamarck. So, even though he disliked medicine and left Edinburgh after two years, his experience there was a formative period in his intellectual development.

Although Darwin was fairly indifferent to religion, he next went to Cambridge to study theology. It was during his Cambridge years that he cultivated interests in natural science and immersed himself in botany and geology. Following his graduation in 1831, he was invited to join a scientific expedition that would circle the globe. And so it was that Darwin set sail aboard HMS *Beagle* on December 17, 1831 (Fig. 2-8). The famous voyage of the *Beagle* would take almost five years and would forever change not only the course of Darwin's life but also the history of biological science (Fig. 2-9).

Darwin went aboard the *Beagle* believing in the fixity of species. But during the voyage he privately began to have doubts. For one thing, he came across fossils of ancient giant animals that, except for size, looked very much like species that still lived in the same vicinity. The similarities he saw caused him to speculate that the fossils represented ancestors of those living forms.

During the now famous stopover at the Galápagos Islands, off the coast of Ecuador, Darwin noticed that the vegetation and animals (especially birds) shared many similarities with those on the South American mainland. But they weren't identical to them. What's more, the birds varied from island to island. Darwin collected 13 varieties of Galápagos finches, and it was clear that they represented a closely related group; but some of their physical traits were

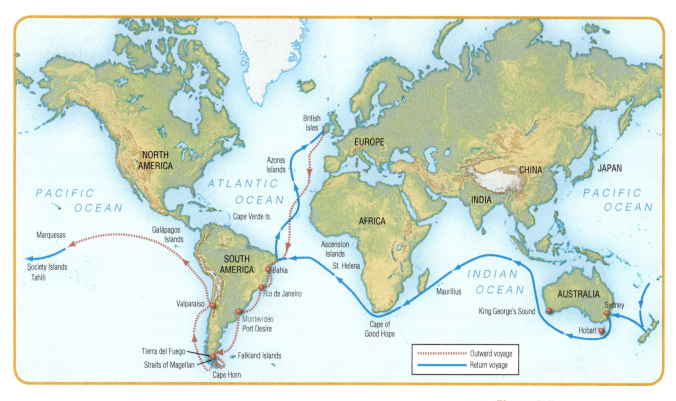

▲ **Figure 2-8**
The route of HMS *Beagle*.

different, particularly the shape and size of their beaks (Fig. 2-10). Darwin also collected finches from the mainland, and these appeared to represent only one group, or species.

The insight that Darwin gained from the finches is legendary. But, contrary to popular misconception, it wasn't until *after* he returned to England that he recognized the significance of the variation in beak structure. In fact, during the voyage, he had paid little attention to the finches. John Gould, a well-known British ornithologist

◀ **Figure 2-9**
A painting by John Chancellor of HMS *Beagle* sailing through the Galápagos Islands in 1835.

Gordon Chancellor

Ground finch	Tree finch	Tree finch (called woodpecker finch)	Ground finch (known as warbler finch)
Main food: seeds	Main food: leaves, buds, blossoms, fruits	Main food: insects	Main food: insects
Beak: heavy	Beak: thick, short	Beak: stout, straight	Beak: slender

▲ **Figure 2-10**
Beak variation in Darwin's Galápagos finches.

and colleague of Darwin, identified and classified the Galápagos finches, noting variation in their traits, including beak size. Darwin, recognizing a relationship between finch beak size and diet (for example, seed hardness), began to consider that traits reflected adaptations to specific environments. Further, Darwin eventually began to consider the factors that could lead to the modification of one species into many (Gould, 1985; Desmond and Moore, 1991). He realized that the various Galápagos finches had all descended from a common mainland ancestor and had been modified over time in response to different island habitats and dietary preferences.

Darwin returned to England in October 1836 and was immediately accepted into the most prestigious scientific circles. He married his cousin Emma Wedgwood and moved to the village of Down, near London, where he spent the rest of his life writing on topics ranging from fossils to orchids (Fig. 2-11). But the question of species change was his overriding passion.

At Down, Darwin began to develop his views on what he called *natural selection*. This concept was borrowed from animal breeders, who choose, or "select," as breeding stock those animals that possess certain traits that the breeders want to emphasize in offspring. Animals with undesirable traits are "selected against," or prevented from breeding. A dramatic example of the effects of selective

▶ **Figure 2-11**
Down House as seen from the rear. Darwin wrote *On the Origin of Species* and numerous other publications here.

breeding can be seen in the various domestic dog breeds shown in Fig. 2-12. Darwin applied his knowledge of domesticated species to naturally occurring ones, and he recognized that in undomesticated organisms, the selective agent was nature, not humans.

By the late 1830s, Darwin had realized that biological variation within a species (that is, differences among individuals) was crucial. Furthermore, he realized that sexual reproduction increased variation, although he didn't know why. Then, in 1838, he read Malthus' essay, and there he found the answer to the question of how new species came to be. He accepted Malthus' idea that populations increase at a faster rate than the food supply, and he recognized that in nonhuman animals, population size is always limited by the amount of available food and water. He also recognized that these two facts lead to a constant "struggle for existence," a phrase taken from Malthus' essay. The idea that in each generation more offspring are born than can survive to adulthood coupled with the notions of competition for resources and biological diversity was all Darwin needed to develop his theory of natural selection. He wrote: "It at once struck me that under these circumstances favourable variations would tend to be preserved, and unfavourable ones to be destroyed. The result of this would be the formation of a new species" (F. Darwin, 1950,

▼ **Figure 2-12**

All domestic dog breeds share a common ancestor, the wolf. The extreme variation exhibited by dog breeds today has been achieved in a relatively short time through artificial selection. In this situation, humans allow only certain dogs to breed in order to emphasize specific characteristics. (We should note that many traits desired by human breeders are detrimental to the dogs themselves.)

Great Dane: Eric Isselee/Shutterstock.com Chihuahua: iStockphoto.com/Mpikula Yorkshire Terrier: iStockphoto.com/Eriklam Wolf: Corbis RF/SuperStock
Dogs surrounding wolf: Lynn Kilgore and Lin Marshall

▲ Figure 2-13

Alfred Russel Wallace independently identified natural selection as the key to the evolutionary process.

Alfred Russel Wallace (oil on canvas), Evstafieff (19th century)/ Down House, Downe, Kent, UK/© Historic England/Bridgeman Images

pp. 53–54). Basically, this quotation summarizes the entire theory of natural selection.

By 1844, Darwin had written a short summary of his natural selection hypothesis but he didn't think he had enough data to support it, so he continued his research without publishing. He also had other reasons for not publishing what he knew would be a highly controversial work. He was deeply troubled that his wife, Emma, saw his ideas as running counter to her strong religious convictions (Keynes, 2002). Also, as a member of the established order, he knew that many of his friends and associates were concerned with threats to the status quo, and evolutionary theory was viewed as a very serious threat indeed.

In Darwin's Shadow

Unlike Darwin, Alfred Russel Wallace (1823–1913) was born into a family of modest means (Fig. 2-13). He went to work at the age of 14 and, with little formal education, moved from one job to the next. Eventually he became interested in collecting plants and animals and joined expeditions to the Amazon and Southeast Asia, where he acquired firsthand knowledge of many natural phenomena.

In 1855, Wallace published an article suggesting that current species were descended from other species and that the appearance of new ones was influenced by environmental factors (Trinkaus and Shipman, 1992). This article caused Lyell and others to urge Darwin to publish, but he continued to hesitate.

Then, in 1858, Wallace sent Darwin another paper, "On the Tendency of Varieties to Depart Indefinitely from the Original Type." In it, Wallace described evolution as a process driven by competition and natural selection. When he received Wallace's paper, Darwin realized that if he continued to wait, Wallace might get credit for a theory (natural selection) that he himself had developed. He quickly wrote a paper presenting his ideas, and both papers were read before the Linnean Society of London that same year to an audience of about 30 members. Neither author was present. Wallace was in Borneo conducting research and Darwin was mourning the recent death of his young son.

The papers received little notice at the time. But in December 1859, when Darwin completed and published his greatest work, *On the Origin of Species*,* the storm broke, and it still hasn't abated (Fig. 2-14). Although public opinion was negative, there was much scholarly praise for the book, and scientific opinion gradually came to Darwin's support. The question of species was now explained: Species could change, they weren't fixed, and they evolved from other species through the mechanism of natural selection.

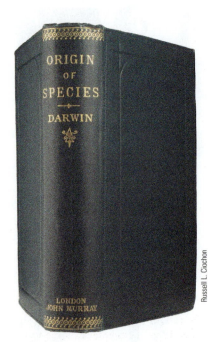

▲ Figure 2-14

Charles Darwin's *Origin of Species*, the book that revolutionized biological science.

———————

*The full title is *On the Origin of Species by Means of Natural Selection, or the Preservation of Favoured Races in the Struggle for Life.*

Natural Selection

Early in his research, Darwin had realized that natural selection was the key to evolution. With the help of Malthus' ideas, he saw *how* selection in nature could be explained. In the struggle for existence, those *individuals* with favorable variations would survive and reproduce, but those with unfavorable variations would not. For Darwin, the explanation of evolution was simple. The basic processes, as he understood them, are as follows:

1. All species are capable of producing offspring at a faster rate than food supplies increase.
2. There is biological variation in all species.
3. In each generation more offspring are produced than survive, and because of limited resources, there is competition among individuals.
4. Individuals who possess favorable variations or traits (for example, speed, resistance to disease, protective coloration) have an advantage over those who don't. In other words, they have greater **fitness**, because favorable traits increase the likelihood that they will survive to adulthood and reproduce.
5. The environmental context determines whether or not a trait is beneficial. What is favorable in one setting may be a liability in another. Consequently the traits that become most advantageous are the results of a natural process.
6. Traits are inherited and passed on to the next generation. Because individuals who possess favorable traits contribute more offspring to the next generation than do others, over time those favorable traits become more common in the population. Less favorable characteristics aren't passed as frequently, so they become less common over time and are "weeded out." Individuals who produce more offspring in comparison with others are said to have greater **reproductive success**, or fitness.
7. Over long periods of time, successful variations accumulate in a population, so that later generations may be distinct from their ancestors. Thus, over time, a new species may appear.
8. Geographical isolation also contributes to the formation of new species. As populations of a species become geographically isolated from one another, for whatever reasons (for example, distance or natural barriers such as mountain ranges and rivers), they begin to adapt to different environments. Over time, as populations continue to respond to different **selective pressures** (that is, different ecological circumstances), they may become distinct species. The 13 species of Galápagos finches are presumably all descended from a common ancestor that lived on the South American mainland. Thus, they illustrate the role of geographical isolation.

Before Darwin, individual members of species were not considered important, so they weren't the focus of research. But as we've seen, Darwin recognized the uniqueness of individuals and realized that variation among them could explain how selection occurs. Favorable variations are selected, or chosen, for survival by nature; unfavorable ones are eliminated. *Natural selection operates on individuals*, either favorably or unfavorably, but *it's the population that evolves*. It is important to emphasize that the unit of natural selection is the individual; the unit of evolution is the population. This is because individuals don't change genetically but, over time, populations do.

Natural Selection in Action

One of the most frequently cited examples of natural selection relates to changes in the coloration of a species of peppered moth. In the 1990s, the peppered moth

fitness Pertaining to natural selection, a measure of the relative reproductive success of individuals. Fitness can be measured by an individual's genetic contribution to the next generation compared with that of other individuals. The terms *genetic fitness, reproductive fitness*, and *differential net reproductive success* are also used.

reproductive success The number of offspring an individual produces and rears to reproductive age, or an individual's genetic contribution to the next generation.

selective pressures Forces in the environment that influence reproductive success in individuals.

story came under criticism, mainly due to issues with the original research design of the 1950s experiments. However, more recent investigations have found strong support for the original premise as an example of natural selection (Majerus, 2009; Cook et al., 2012). Thus, we use it here to illustrate how natural selection works.

Before the nineteenth century, the most common variety of the peppered moth in England was a mottled gray color. During the day, as the moths rested on lichen-covered tree trunks, their coloration provided camouflage (Fig. 2-15). There was also a dark gray variety of the same species, but because the dark moths were not as well camouflaged, they were more frequently eaten by birds; therefore they were less common. (In this example, the birds are the *selective agents*, and they apply *selective pressures* on the moths.) Yet by the end of the nineteenth century, the darker form had almost completely replaced the common gray one.

The cause of this change was the changing environment of industrialized nineteenth-century England. Coal dust from factories and fireplaces settled on the trees, turning them dark gray and killing the lichen. The moths continued to rest on the trees, but the light gray ones became more conspicuous as the trees became darker, and they were increasingly targeted by birds. Thus, the light gray moths began to contribute fewer genes to the next generation than the darker moths, and the proportion of lighter moths decreased while the dark moths became more common. A similar color shift also occurred in North America. But the introduction of clean air acts in both Britain and the United States reduced the amount of air pollution (at least from coal), and the predominant color of the peppered moth once again became the light mottled gray. This kind of evolutionary shift in response to environmental change is called *adaptation*. More recent genetic evidence supports these interpretations, and found that an unusual mutation introduced around 1819 resulted in the black peppered moth variant (van't Hof et al., 2016).

The medium ground finch of the Galápagos Islands provides another example of natural selection. In 1977, drought killed many of the plants that produced the smaller, softer seeds favored by these birds. This forced a population of finches on one of the islands to feed on larger, harder seeds. Even before 1977, some birds had smaller, less robust beaks than others (that is, there was variation). During the drought, because they were less able to process the larger seeds, more smaller-beaked birds died than larger-beaked birds. So, although overall population size declined, average beak thickness in the survivors and their offspring increased, simply because larger-beaked individuals were surviving in greater numbers and producing more offspring. In other words, they had greater reproductive success. But during heavy rains in 1982–1983, smaller seeds became more plentiful again and the pattern in beak size reversed itself, demonstrating again how reproductive success is related to environmental conditions (Boag and Grant, 1981; Ridley, 1993). Lamichhaney and colleagues (2016) recently identified a gene that strongly contributes to overall beak size and morphology in birds. They found

Perennou Nuridsany/Science Source

Michael Willmer Forbes Tweedie/Science Source

▲ **Figure 2-15**

Variation in the peppered moth. (**a**) The dark form is more visible on the light, lichen-covered tree. (**b**) On trees darkened by pollution, the lighter form is more visible.

evidence for a rapid genetic change in the medium ground finch during severe drought conditions in 2004 and 2005 on the Galápagos Islands. In this instance, the genetic change resulted in a significant decline in beak size during the drought due to higher mortality among larger-beaked birds.

The best illustration of natural selection, however—and certainly one with potentially grave consequences for humans—is the increase in resistant strains of disease-causing microorganisms. When antibiotics were first introduced in the 1940s, they were seen as the cure for bacterial disease. However, that optimistic view didn't take into account that bacteria, like other organisms, possess genetic variation. Consequently, though an antibiotic will kill most bacteria in an infected person, any bacterium with an inherited resistance to that particular treatment will survive. In turn, the survivors reproduce and pass their drug resistance to future generations, so that eventually, the population is mostly made up of bacteria that don't respond to treatment. What's more, because bacteria produce new generations every few hours, antibiotic-resistant strains are continuously appearing. As a result, many types of infection no longer respond to treatment. For example, tuberculosis was once thought to be well controlled, but there's been a resurgence of TB in recent years because some strains of the bacterium that causes it are resistant to most of the antibiotics used to treat it.

These examples (moths, finches, and bacteria) provide the following insights into the fundamentals of evolutionary change produced by natural selection:

1. *A trait must be inherited if natural selection is to act on it.* A characteristic that isn't hereditary (such as a temporary change in hair color produced by the hairdresser) won't be passed on to offspring. In finches, for example, beak size is a hereditary trait.

2. *Natural selection cannot occur without population variation in inherited characteristics.* If, for example, all the peppered moths had initially been light gray and the trees had become darker, the survival and reproduction of the moths could have been so low that the population might have become extinct. *Selection can work only with variation that already exists.*

3. *Fitness is a relative measure that changes as the environment changes.* Fitness is simply differential net reproductive success. In the initial stage, the lighter moths were more fit because they produced more offspring. But as the environment changed, the dark gray moths became more fit. Later, a further change reversed the pattern again. Likewise, the majority of Galápagos finches will have larger or smaller beaks, depending on external conditions. So it should be obvious that statements regarding the "most fit" don't mean anything without reference to specific environments.

4. *Natural selection can act only on traits that affect reproduction.* If a characteristic isn't expressed until later in life, after organisms have reproduced, natural selection can't influence it. This is because the trait's inherited components have already been passed on to offspring. Many forms of cancer and cardiovascular disease are influenced by hereditary factors, but because these diseases usually affect people after they've had children, natural selection can't act against them. By the same token, if a condition usually kills or compromises the individual before he or she reproduces, natural selection is able to act against it because the trait won't be passed on.

Natural Selection and Reproductive Success

So far, our examples have shown how different death rates influence natural selection (for example, moths or finches that die early leave fewer offspring). But mortality is only part of the picture. Another important aspect of natural selection is **fertility**, because an animal that gives birth to more young contributes more genes to the next

fertility The ability to conceive and produce healthy offspring.

generation than an animal that produces fewer. But fertility isn't the entire story either, because the crucial element is the number of young raised successfully to the point where they themselves reproduce. We call this *differential net reproductive success*. The way this mechanism works can be demonstrated through another example.

In swifts (small birds that resemble swallows), data show that producing more offspring doesn't necessarily guarantee that more young will be successfully raised. The number of eggs hatched in a breeding season is a measure of fertility. The number of birds that mature and are eventually able to leave the nest is a measure of net reproductive success, or successfully raised offspring. The following table shows the correlation between the number of eggs hatched (fertility) and the number of young that leave the nest (reproductive success), averaged over four breeding seasons (Lack, 1966):

Number of eggs hatched (fertility)	2 eggs	3 eggs	4 eggs
Average number of young raised (reproductive success)	1.92	2.54	1.76
Sample size (number of nests)	72	20	16

As you can see, the most efficient number of eggs is three, because that number yields the highest reproductive success. Raising two offspring is less beneficial to the parents, because the end result isn't as successful as with three eggs. Trying to raise more than three is actually detrimental, as the parents may not be able to provide enough nourishment for any of the offspring. Offspring that die before reaching reproductive age are, in evolutionary terms, equivalent to never being born. Moreover, an offspring that dies can be a minus to the parents, because before it dies it drains parental resources. It may even inhibit their ability to raise other offspring, thus reducing their reproductive success even further. Selection favors those genetic traits that yield the maximum net reproductive success. If the number of eggs laid is a genetic trait in birds (and it seems to be), natural selection in swifts should act to favor laying three eggs as opposed to two or four.

Constraints on Nineteenth-Century Evolutionary Theory

Darwin argued for the concept of evolution in general and the role of natural selection in particular. But he didn't understand the exact mechanisms of evolutionary change. As we've already seen, natural selection acts on *variation* within species; but what Darwin didn't understand was where the variation came from. In the nineteenth century, this remained an unanswered question, plus no one understood how offspring inherited traits from their parents. Almost without exception, nineteenth-century scientists believed inheritance to be a *blending* process in which parental characteristics were mixed together to produce intermediate expressions in offspring. Given this notion, we can see why the true nature of genes was unimaginable; and with no alternative explanation, Darwin accepted the blending theory of inheritance. As it turns out, a contemporary of Darwin's had actually worked out the rules of heredity. However, the work of this Augustinian monk, named Gregor Mendel (whom you'll meet in Chapter 4), wasn't recognized until the beginning of the twentieth century.

The first three decades of the twentieth century saw the merger of natural selection theory and Mendel's discoveries. This was a crucial development because until then, scientists thought these concepts were unrelated. Then, in 1953, the structure of DNA was discovered. This landmark achievement was followed by even more amazing advances in the field of genetics. The human **genome** was sequenced in 2003, followed by the chimpanzee genome in 2005. The genomes of many other species have also now been sequenced. By comparing the genomes of different species (a field called comparative genomics), scientists can examine how genetically similar or different they are. This can explain many aspects of how these species evolved. Also, since the early 1990s, several scientists have merged the fields of evolutionary and developmental biology into a new field called evolution of development, or simply "evo-devo." This approach, which compares the actions of different developmental genes and the factors that regulate them, is making it possible to explain evolution in ways that were impossible even 15 years ago. Scientists are truly on the threshold of revealing many secrets of the evolutionary process. If only Darwin could know what we know now!

Opposition to Evolution Today

More than a century and a half after the publication of *Origin of Species*, the debate over evolution is far from over, especially in the United States and, increasingly, in several Muslim countries. Among the biological community, evolution is indisputable. The genetic evidence for it is solid and accumulates daily. Anyone who appreciates and understands genetic mechanisms cannot avoid the conclusion that populations and species evolve. What's more, the majority of Christians don't believe that biblical depictions should be taken literally. But at the same time, some surveys show that roughly half of all Americans don't believe that evolution occurs. A recent Gallup Poll (May 8–11, 2014), in fact, showed that 42 percent of Americans believe in biblical creationism (Newport, 2014). There are a number of reasons for this.

The mechanisms of evolution are complex and do not lend themselves to simple explanations. Understanding them requires some familiarity with genetics and biology, a familiarity that most people don't have unless they've taken related courses in school. What is more, many people want definitive, clear-cut answers to complex questions. But as you learned in Chapter 1, science doesn't always provide definitive answers to questions; by design, it doesn't establish absolute truths; and it doesn't *prove* facts. Another thing to consider is that regardless of their culture, most people are raised in belief systems that don't emphasize **biological continuity** between species or offer scientific explanations for natural phenomena.

The relationship between science and religion has never been easy (remember Galileo), even though both serve in their own ways to explain natural phenomena. As you read in Chapter 1, scientific explanations are based on data analysis, hypothesis testing, and interpretation. Religions, meanwhile, are systems of faith-based beliefs. A major difference between science and religion is that religious explanations aren't amenable to scientific testing. Religion and science concern different aspects of the human experience, but they aren't inherently mutually exclusive approaches. That is, belief in God doesn't exclude the occurrence of biological evolution; and acknowledgment of evolutionary processes doesn't preclude the existence of God. What's more, evolutionary theories aren't rejected by all religions or by most forms of Christianity.

Some years ago, the Vatican hosted an international conference on human evolution; in 1996, Pope John Paul II issued a statement that "fresh knowledge leads to recognition of the theory of evolution as more than just a hypothesis." Today, the official position of the Catholic Church is that evolutionary processes do occur, but that the human soul is of divine creation and not subject to evolutionary processes. Likewise, mainstream Protestants don't generally see a conflict. Unfortunately those who believe in an absolutely literal interpretation of the Bible (called *fundamentalists*) accept no compromise.

genome The entire genetic makeup of an individual or species.

biological continuity A biological continuum. When expressions of a phenomenon continuously grade into one another so that there are no discrete categories, they exist on a continuum. Color is one such phenomenon, and life-forms are another.

A Brief History of Opposition to Evolution in the United States

Reacting to rapid cultural change after World War I, conservative Christians sought a revival of what they considered to be "traditional values." In their view, one way to achieve this was to prevent any mention of evolution in public schools. One result of this effort was a state law, passed in Tennessee in 1925, that banned the teaching of any theory (particularly evolution) that did not support the biblical version of the creation of humankind. To test the validity of this law, the American Civil Liberties Union persuaded a high school teacher named John Scopes to submit to being arrested and tried for teaching evolution (Fig. 2-16). The subsequent trial, called the "Scopes Monkey Trial," was a 1920s equivalent of current celebrity trials. In the end, Scopes was convicted and fined $100, though the conviction was later overturned. Although most states didn't actually forbid the teaching of evolution, Arkansas, Tennessee, and a few others continued to prohibit any mention of it until 1968, when the U.S. Supreme Court struck down the ban against teaching evolution in public schools. (One coauthor of this textbook remembers when her junior high school science teacher was fired for mentioning evolution in Little Rock, Arkansas.)

By the mid-1960s, coverage of evolution in textbooks had increased. As a result, **Christian fundamentalists** renewed their campaign to eliminate evolution from public school curricula and to introduce antievolutionary material into public school classes. The *creation science* movement was born out of this effort.

Proponents of creation science are called "creationists" because they explain the existence of the universe as the result of a sudden creation event that occurred over the course of six 24-hour days, as described in the book of Genesis. The premise of creation science is that the biblical account of the earth's origins and the story of Noah and the flood can be supported by scientific evidence.

Creationists have insisted that what they used to call "creation science" and now call "intelligent design" (ID) is a valid scientific explanation of the earth's origins. They've argued that in the interest of fairness, a balanced view should be offered in public schools: If evolution is taught as science, then creationism should also be taught as science. Sounds fair, doesn't it? But ID isn't science at all, for the simple reason that creationists insist that their view is absolute and infallible. Therefore creationism is not a hypothesis that can be tested, nor is it amenable to falsification.

Christian fundamentalists Adherents to a movement in American Protestantism that began in the early twentieth century. This group holds that the teachings of the Bible are infallible and should be taken literally.

▶ **Figure 2-16**
Photo taken at the "Scopes Monkey Trial." The well-known defense attorney Clarence Darrow is sitting on the edge of the table. John Scopes, wearing a white shirt, is sitting with his arms folded behind Darrow.

Bettmann/Corbis

Because hypothesis testing is the basis of all science, creationism by its very nature cannot be considered science.

Since the 1970s, creationists have become increasingly active on local school boards and in state legislatures, promoting laws that mandate the teaching of creationism in public schools. However, state and federal courts have consistently overruled these laws because they violate the "establishment clause" of the First Amendment of the U.S. Constitution, which states that "Congress shall make no law respecting an establishment of religion, or prohibiting the free exercise thereof." This statement guarantees the separation of church and state, and it means that the government can neither promote nor inhibit the practice of any religion. Therefore the use of public institutions (including schools), paid for by taxes, to promote any particular religion is unconstitutional. Of course this does not mean that individuals can't have private religious discussions or pray in publicly funded institutions; but it does mean that such places can't be used for organized religious events. This hasn't stopped creationists, who encourage teachers to claim "academic freedom" to teach creationism. To avoid objections based on the guarantee of separation of church and state, proponents of ID claim that they don't emphasize any particular religion. But this argument doesn't address the essential point that teaching *any* religious views in a way that promotes them in publicly funded schools is a violation of the U.S. Constitution. Several states have attempted to introduce ID into the school curriculum (for example, Missouri, Montana, Colorado, Oklahoma, and Indiana). In 2004, Kitzmiller et al. *v.* Dover Area School District (York, Pennsylvania) became the first legal challenge in federal court against the teaching of ID in the public school system. The ruling ultimately was made in favor of the plaintiffs, who argued that the teaching of ID in the biology curriculum represented a form of creationism and violated separation of church and state.

On February 4, 2014, science educator Bill Nye (of Bill Nye, the Science Guy) and creationist Ken Ham sparred in a debate centered on the question, "Is Creation a Viable Model of Origins?" Ham invited Nye to the debate, held at the Creation Museum he founded in Petersburg, Kentucky. The debate was widely publicized and promised to provide a philosophical discussion regarding the scientific evidence of

At a Glance   The Mechanism of Natural Selection

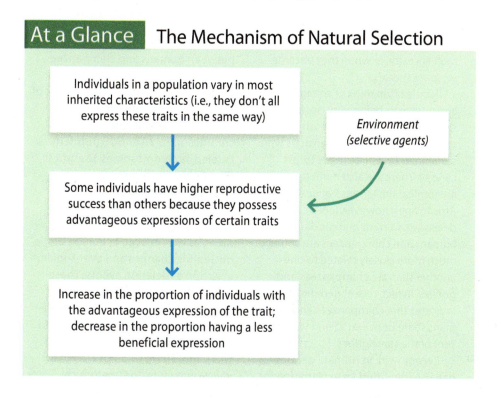

evolution versus evidence for young earth creationism. Although debates between evolutionists and creationists had occurred many times in the past, this one drew significant national attention and stimulated public discussion on the evidence for evolution. The live debate drew more than 3 million television viewers, and the video of the debate has been viewed several million times on various Internet websites. Predictably, each side attempted to discredit the other. Nye focused on the scientific support for evolutionary theory, including evidence that the earth is 4.5 billion years old, and that all life is interconnected based on DNA evidence and the fossil record. Ham claimed that evolution is a "historical science" based on speculation, in contrast with the more concrete "observational sciences," such as physics and chemistry. He included video segments from three scientists who do not accept evolution (to create the false perception that there is wide disagreement within the scientific community), and argued, like all young-earth creation scientists, that the earth is only 6,000 years old. Although most polls suggested that Bill Nye won the debate, many feel that the media publicity helped to raise greater awareness of the creationist agenda. While Nye was praised by some scientists, many others felt that engaging in public debate with creationists does little to sway opinions one way or the other, and may be counterproductive by giving creationism too much legitimacy.

It is curious that the biological process that has led to the appearance of millions of plants and animals on our planet should generate such controversy. Our current understanding of evolution is directly traceable to developments in intellectual thought over the past 400 years. Many people contributed to this shift in perspective; we've named only a few to provide a short historical view. It is quite likely that, in the next 20 years, scientists will identify many of the secrets of our evolutionary past through advances in genetic technologies and the continued discovery of fossil material. For evolutionary science, the early twenty-first century is indeed an exciting time.

How Do We Know?

During the last 150 years, biologists have gathered overwhelming evidence to support evolutionary theory. In this chapter we have emphasized the role of natural selection, which is demonstrated by studying the effects of human selective breeding on such species as domestic dogs. We can see how natural selection causes microevolutionary change by observing alterations over a few decades in many species. And evolutionary change, including speciation, can also be documented much faster (just a few weeks) in rapidly reproducing species such as bacteria. Within the past 25 years, scientists have developed many techniques that allow them to directly compare different species genetically. In fact, they can now provide reliable estimates as to when

two related species last shared a common ancestor, or when they became separate species.

People often think of chimpanzees and gorillas as being very closely related species and it's easy to see why. Both are knuckle-walking African apes who sometimes brachiate in the forest canopy. There are also numerous anatomical similarities between these African apes; however, looks can be deceiving. Current genetic data indicate humans and chimpanzees are actually much more closely related to one another than are chimpanzees and gorillas. In fact, recent genetic research indicates that chimpanzees and humans share between 95 and 98.5 percent of the same genes.

Recent work in primate genomics has also identified an explanation for

the difference in chromosome number between humans and chimpanzees. Genetic studies indicate that human chromosome number 2 is the result of the fusion of two ancestral chromosomes still found in chimpanzees, chromosomes 2A and 2B (formerly labeled as chromosomes 12 and 13) (The Chimpanzee Sequencing and Analysis Consortium, 2005). This research also found additional evidence of chromosomal rearrangement, as well as over 35 million single nucleotide changes and over 5 million insertion or deletion events. These new developments are revealing important clues regarding the divergence between the chimpanzee and human lineages around 7–8 million years ago. These findings may make you wonder why the anatomical differences between humans and chimpanzees seem so pronounced. Clearly, the genetic differences, however small, are significant and do indeed account for the anatomical differences between humans and chimpanzees. Ongoing work in primate genomics, especially research on *Hox* genes (that is, the genes that regulate the expression of certain traits such as body segmentation), will play an important role in understanding the transformation from quadrupedalism to bipedalism in the hominin lineage.

What Do You Think?

Do you agree with the idea of classifying humans and chimpanzees more closely together? Do you think more weight should be given to genetic data or to information derived from comparative anatomy? ◼

Summary of Main Topics

- Our current understanding of evolutionary processes is directly traceable to developments in intellectual thought in western Europe and the East over the past 400 years. Darwin and Wallace were able to discover the process of natural selection and evolution because of the discoveries of numerous scientists who had laid the groundwork for them. Among others, Galileo, Lyell, Lamarck, Linnaeus, and Malthus all contributed to a dramatic shift in how people viewed the planet and themselves as part of a system governed by natural processes.

- Charles Darwin and Alfred Russel Wallace recognized that there is variation among individuals in any population (human or nonhuman). Having come to understand how animal breeders selected for certain traits in cattle, pigeons, and other species, Darwin was able to formulate the theory of natural selection. Stated in the simplest terms, natural selection is a process whereby individuals who possess favorable traits (characteristics that permit them to survive and reproduce in a specific environment) will produce more offspring than individuals who have less favorable traits. Over time, the beneficial characteristics will become more frequent in the population, and the makeup of the population (or even a species) will change.

- As populations of a species become reproductively isolated from one another (perhaps because of distance or geographical barriers), they become increasingly different (at a genetic level) as each population adapts, by means of natural selection, to its own environment. Eventually, the populations may become distinct enough that they can no longer interbreed; at this point, they are considered separate species.

- In the United States, and increasingly in some Muslim countries, the teaching of evolutionary processes is denounced because they are seen as contradictory to certain religious views. In recent years, Christian fundamentalists in the United States have argued in favor of teaching "creation science" or "intelligent design" in public schools. So far, courts have ruled against various attempts to promote "creation science" because the U.S. Constitution provides for the separation of church and state.

Critical Thinking Questions

1. After having read this chapter, how would you respond to the question, "If humans evolved from monkeys, why do we still have monkeys?"

2. What key discoveries were crucial to Darwin and Wallace's development of the theory of evolution by natural selection?

3. We live in an age of unprecedented technological change that is rapidly altering almost all aspects of our lives. Can you think of a paradigm shift that has occurred because of technological innovations in the past 30 years or so?

4. Given what you've read about the scientific method in Chapter 1, how would you explain the differences between science and religion as methods of explaining natural phenomena? Do you personally see a conflict between evolutionary and religious explanations of how species came to be?

5. How does the peppered moth example demonstrate that evolution is not directional? In other words, explain how the environment influences whether a trait will be selected for or against.

CONNECTIONS

Evolutionary theory, particularly natural selection, explains how life forms have changed over time.

DNA is the basis of all life.

Heredity is based on the transmission of DNA from one generation to the next.

The Biological Basis of Life

Cells

From DNA to Protein

DNA Structure

DNA Replication

Protein Synthesis

What Is a Gene?

Regulatory Genes

Mutation: When Genes Change

Cell Division

Chromosomes

Karyotyping Chromosomes

Mitosis

Meiosis

New Frontiers

Student Learning Objectives After studying the material in this chapter, you should be able to:

▶ Describe the key components of a cell discussed in the text.

▶ Discuss the structure and function of DNA and indicate why DNA is the biological basis of life.

▶ Explain what genes do and why they are important to evolution.

▶ Explain why regulatory genes are important to the evolutionary process.

▶ Explain how evolution influenced the emergence of sickle-cell anemia.

▶ Describe the process of cell division for body cells and sex cells.

▶ Explain why the study of genetics is critical to physical anthropology today.

You've just gotten home after a rotten day, and you're watching the news on TV. The first story, after around 20 minutes of commercials, is about genetically modified foods, synthetic DNA, or the controversy over stem cell research. What do you do? Change the channel? Press the mute button? Go to sleep? Or do you follow the story? If you watch it, do you understand it, and do you think it's important to you personally? In fact, all of these topics are important to you because you live in an age when genetic discoveries and genetically based technologies are advancing daily, and one way or another, they're going to profoundly affect your life.

At some point, you or someone you love will probably need lifesaving medical treatment, perhaps

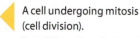

A cell undergoing mitosis (cell division).

for cancer, and this treatment will almost certainly be based on genetic research. Like it or not, you already eat genetically modified foods, and you may eventually take advantage of developing reproductive technologies. Sadly, you may also see the development of biological weapons based on genetically altered bacteria and viruses. But fortunately, you'll also live to see many of the secrets of evolution revealed through genetic research. So even if you haven't been particularly interested in genetic issues, you should be aware that they affect your life every day.

As you already know, this book is about human evolution, variation, and adaptation, all of which are ultimately linked to life processes that involve cells, the duplication and decoding of genetic information, and the transmission of this information between generations. So before we go any further, we must examine the basic principles of genetics. Genetics is the study of how genes work and how traits are passed from one generation to the next. Although most physical anthropologists don't specialize in this field, they're very familiar with it because the various subdisciplines of biological anthropology are ultimately connected by genetics.

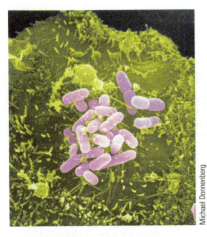

▲ **Figure 3-1**
Each one of these pink sausage-shaped structures is a single-celled bacterium.

Michael Donnenberg

proteins Three-dimensional molecules that serve a wide variety of functions through their ability to bind to other molecules.

nucleus A structure (organelle) found in all eukaryotic cells. The nucleus contains DNA and RNA, among other things.

molecules Structures made up of two or more atoms. Molecules can combine with other molecules to form more complex structures.

DNA (deoxyribonucleic acid) The double-stranded molecule that contains the genetic code. DNA is a main component of chromosomes.

RNA (ribonucleic acid) A single-stranded molecule similar in structure to DNA. Three forms of RNA are essential to protein synthesis: messenger RNA (mRNA), transfer RNA (tRNA), and ribosomal RNA (rRNA).

Cells

In order to discuss genetic and evolutionary principles, it's first necessary to understand the basic functions of cells. Cells are the fundamental units of life in all organisms. In some life-forms, such as bacteria, the entire organism consists of only a single cell (Fig. 3-1). However, more complex *multicellular* forms, such as plants and animals, are composed of billions of cells. In fact, an adult human body may be composed of as many as 1 trillion (1,000,000,000,000) cells, all functioning in complex ways that ultimately promote the survival of the individual.

Life on earth began more than 3.5 billion years ago in the form of single-celled organisms, represented today by bacteria and blue-green algae. Structurally more complex cells, called *eukaryotic* cells, appeared approximately 1.7 billion years ago, and because they are the kind of cell found in multicellular organisms, they will be the focus of this chapter. Despite the numerous differences among various forms of life, it's important to understand that the cells of all living organisms share many similarities because of their common evolutionary past. In this way, all living things are ultimately connected.

In general, a eukaryotic cell is a three-dimensional structure composed of carbohydrates, lipids (fats), nucleic acids, and **proteins**. It also contains several kinds of substructures called *organelles*, one of which is the **nucleus** (*pl.*, nuclei), a discrete unit surrounded by a thin membrane called the *nuclear membrane* (Fig. 3-2). Inside the nucleus are two kinds of **molecules** that contain the genetic information that controls the cell's functions. These two molecules are the nucleic acids **DNA (deoxyribonucleic acid)** and **RNA (ribonucleic acid)**.

The nucleus is surrounded by a gel-like substance called **cytoplasm**, which contains many other types of organelles involved in activities related to the function of the cell and organism. These activities include breaking down nutrients and converting them to other substances, storing and releasing energy, eliminating waste, and manufacturing proteins through a process called **protein synthesis**.

Two of these organelles, **mitochondria** (*sing.*, mitochondrion) and **ribosomes**, require further mention. Mitochondria (Fig. 3-3) produce energy and can be thought of as the cell's engines. Mitochondria are structures enclosed within a folded membrane and contain their own distinct DNA, called **mitochondrial DNA (mtDNA)**, which directs mitochondrial activities. Mitochondrial DNA has the same molecular structure and function as nuclear DNA (that is, DNA found in the nucleus), but it's organized somewhat differently. In recent years, mtDNA has attracted a lot of attention because of the traits it influences and because it can be used to study certain

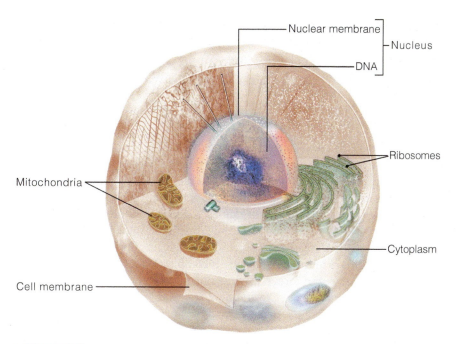

△ Figure 3-2

Structure of a generalized eukaryotic cell, illustrating its three-dimensional nature. Various organelles are shown; but for simplicity, only those we discuss are labeled.

evolutionary processes. For these reasons, we'll discuss mitochondrial inheritance in more detail later. Ribosomes, which will also be discussed later, are partly composed of RNA. They're important because they're essential to protein synthesis.

There are basically two types of cells: **somatic cells** and **gametes**. Somatic cells make up the body tissues, such as muscles, bones, organs, and the brain. Gametes, or sex cells, are specifically involved in reproduction and are not important as structural components of the body. There are two types of gametes: egg cells, produced in female ovaries, and sperm cells, which develop in male testes. The sole function of a sex cell is to unite with a gamete from another individual to form a **zygote**, which has the potential of developing into a new individual. In this way, gametes transmit genetic information from parent to offspring.

cytoplasm The semifluid, gel-like substance contained within the cell membrane. The nucleus and numerous structures involved with cell function are found within the cytoplasm.

protein synthesis The manufacture of proteins; that is, the assembly of chains of amino acids into functional protein molecules. Protein synthesis is directed by DNA.

mitochondria (*sing.*, mitochondrion) Structures contained within the cytoplasm of eukaryotic cells that convert energy, derived from nutrients, to a form that can be used by the cell.

ribosomes Structures composed of a form of RNA called ribosomal RNA (rRNA) and protein. Ribosomes are found in a cell's cytoplasm and are essential to the manufacture of proteins.

mitochondrial DNA (mtDNA) DNA found in the mitochondria. Mitochondrial DNA is inherited only from the mother.

somatic cells Basically, all the cells in the body except those involved with reproduction.

gametes Reproductive cells (eggs and sperm in animals) developed from precursor cells in ovaries and testes.

zygote A cell formed by the union of an egg cell and a sperm cell. It contains the full complement of chromosomes (in humans, 46) and has the potential of developing into an entire organism.

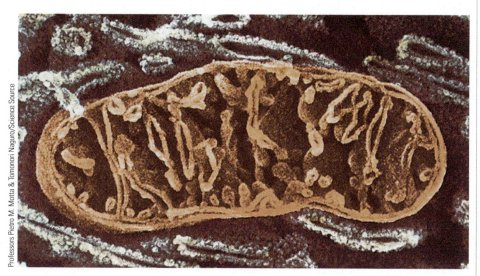

Professors Pietro M. Motta & Tomonori Naguro/Science Source

△ Figure 3-3

Scanning electron micrograph of a mitochondrion.

From DNA to Protein

To address the structure and function of DNA, this section describes DNA as the building blocks of all life forms, the process of DNA replication, and protein synthesis.

DNA Structure

DNA is the very basis of life because it directs all cellular activities. So if we want to understand these activities and how traits are inherited, we must know something about the structure and function of DNA. The exact physical and chemical properties of DNA were unknown until 1953, when, at the University of Cambridge, in England, an American researcher named James Watson and three British scientists, Francis Crick, Maurice Wilkins, and Rosalind Franklin, developed a structural and functional model of DNA (Watson and Crick, 1953a, b). It's impossible to overstate the importance of this achievement because it completely revolutionized the fields of biology and medicine and forever altered our understanding of biological and evolutionary mechanisms (see "A Closer Look: Rosalind Franklin: The Fourth [but Invisible] Member of the Double Helix Team").

The DNA molecule is composed of two chains of even smaller units called **nucleotides**. A nucleotide, in turn, is made up of three components: a sugar molecule (deoxyribose), a phosphate group (a molecule composed of phosphorus and oxygen), and one of four nitrogenous *bases* (Fig. 3-4). In DNA, nucleotides are stacked on top of one another to form a chain that is bonded by its bases to another nucleotide chain. Together the two chains twist to form a spiral, or helical shape. Thus, the DNA molecule is double-stranded and is described as forming a *double helix* that resembles a twisted ladder. If we follow the twisted ladder analogy, the sugars and phosphates represent the two sides while the bases and the bonds that join them form the rungs.

nucleotides Basic units of the DNA molecule, composed of a sugar, a phosphate, and one of four DNA bases.

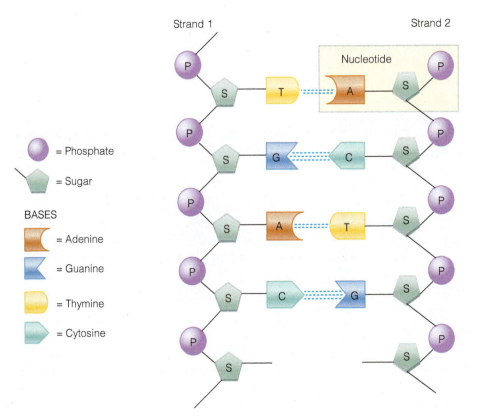

▶ **Figure 3-4**
Part of a DNA molecule. The illustration shows the two DNA strands with the sugar (green) and phosphate (purple) molecules forming the sides of the strands and the bases (labeled T, A, G, and C) joined together in the middle.

A Closer Look Rosalind Franklin: The Fourth (but Invisible) Member of the Double Helix Team

In 1962, three men, James Watson, Francis Crick, and Maurice Wilkins, won the Nobel Prize for medicine and physiology. They earned this most prestigious of all scientific honors for their discovery of the structure of the DNA molecule, which they had published in 1953. But due credit was not given to a fourth, equally deserving but unacknowledged person named Rosalind Franklin, who had died of ovarian cancer in 1958. But even if she had been acknowledged in 1962, Franklin still wouldn't have been a Nobel recipient because the Nobel Prize isn't awarded posthumously.

Franklin was a chemist who went to the University of Cambridge in 1951, after being invited to study the structure of DNA. Before that, she'd been in Paris using a technique called X-ray diffraction, a process that reveals the positions of atoms in crystalline structures. What Franklin didn't know was that a colleague in her Cambridge lab, Maurice Wilkins, was working on the same DNA project. To make matters worse, Wilkins hadn't been told what her position was, so he thought she'd been hired as his assistant. Needless to say, this was hardly a good way to begin a working relationship, and as you might expect, there were a few tense moments between them.

Franklin soon produced some excellent X-ray diffraction images of some DNA fibers that Wilkins had provided, and the images clearly showed that the structure was helical. Furthermore, she worked out that there were two strands, not one. Wilkins innocently (but without Franklin's knowledge) showed the images to Watson and Crick, who were working in another laboratory, also at Cambridge. Within two weeks, Watson and Crick had developed their now famous model of a double-stranded helix without Franklin's knowledge.

Desperately unhappy at Cambridge, Franklin took a position at King's College, London, in 1953. In April of that year, she and a student published an article in the journal *Nature* that dealt indirectly with the helical structure of DNA.

▲ **Figure 1**
Rosalind Franklin

The article by Watson and Crick was published in the same issue.

During her lifetime, Franklin gained recognition for her work in carbons, coal, and viruses, topics on which she published many articles; and she was happy with the reputation she achieved. After her death, Watson made many derogative comments about Rosalind Franklin, including several in print. Even so, it appears that they remained on friendly terms until she died at the age of 37 of ovarian cancer. She also remained friendly with Crick, but she never knew that their revolutionary discovery was partly made possible by her photographic images.

The four bases are the key to how DNA works. These bases are *adenine*, *guanine*, *thymine*, and *cytosine*, usually referred to by their initial letters: A, G, T, and C. When the double helix is formed, one type of base is able to pair, or bond, with only one other type: A can pair only with T, and G can pair only with C (Fig. 3-4). This specificity is absolutely essential to the DNA molecule's ability to **replicate**, or make an exact copy of itself.

DNA Replication

Cells multiply by dividing to make exact copies of themselves. This, in turn, enables organisms to grow and injured tissues to heal. There are two kinds of cell division. In the simpler form, a cell divides one time to produce two identical "daughter" cells,

replicate To duplicate. The DNA molecule is able to make copies of itself.

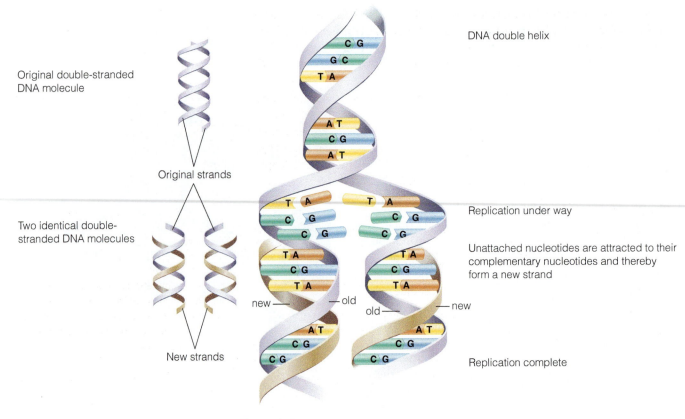

Original double-stranded DNA molecule

Original strands

Two identical double-stranded DNA molecules

New strands

DNA double helix

Replication under way

Unattached nucleotides are attracted to their complementary nucleotides and thereby form a new strand

new — old

old — new

Replication complete

▲ **Figure 3-5**

DNA replication. During DNA replication, the two strands of the DNA molecule (purple) are separated, and each strand serves as a template for the formation of a new strand (brown). When replication is complete, there are two DNA molecules, each consisting of one new strand and one original strand.

each of which receives a full set of genetic material. This is important, because a cell can't function properly without the right amount of DNA. But before a cell can divide, its DNA must replicate.

Replication begins when **enzymes** break the bonds between bases throughout the DNA molecule, separating the two previously joined strands of nucleotides and leaving their bases exposed (Fig. 3-5). These exposed bases then attract unattached DNA nucleotides that have been made by DNA elsewhere in the cell nucleus. Because each base can pair with only one other type of base, the attraction between bases occurs in a **complementary** way. This means that the two previously joined parental nucleotide chains serve as models, or templates, for forming new strands of nucleotides. As each new strand is formed, its bases are joined to the bases of an original strand. When the process is complete, there are two double-stranded DNA molecules exactly like the original one. Importantly, each newly formed molecule consists of one original nucleotide chain joined to a newly formed chain.

Protein Synthesis

One of the most important activities of DNA is to direct the assembly of proteins (protein synthesis) within cells. Proteins are complex three-dimensional molecules that function through their ability to bind to other molecules. For example, the protein **hemoglobin** (Fig. 3-6), found in red blood cells, is able to bind to oxygen, which it carries to cells throughout the body.

enzymes Specialized proteins that initiate and direct chemical reactions in the body.

complementary In genetics, referring to the fact that DNA bases form pairs (called base pairs) in a precise manner. For example, adenine can bond only to thymine. These two bases are said to be complementary because one requires the other to form a complete DNA base pair.

hemoglobin A protein molecule that occurs in red blood cells and binds to oxygen molecules.

Proteins function in countless ways. Some, such as collagen (the most common protein in the body), are structural components of tissues. Enzymes are also proteins, which regulate chemical reactions. For example, a digestive enzyme called *lactase* breaks down *lactose*, or milk sugar, into two simpler sugars. Another class of proteins includes many types of **hormones**. Hormones are produced by specialized cells and then released into the bloodstream to circulate to other parts of the body, where they produce specific effects in tissues and organs. For example, insulin—a hormone produced by cells in the pancreas—causes cells in the liver to absorb energy-producing glucose (sugar) from the blood. People whose pancreatic cells fail to produce sufficient amounts of insulin have one of the two types of diabetes. Lastly, many kinds of proteins can enter a cell's nucleus and attach directly to a cell's DNA. This is very important because when these proteins bind to the DNA, they can regulate its activity. From this brief description, you can see that proteins make us what we are. So protein synthesis must occur accurately, because if it doesn't, physiological development and cellular activities can be disrupted or even prevented.

Proteins are made up of chains of smaller molecules called **amino acids**. In all, there are 20 amino acids, 8 of which must be obtained from foods. These are known as *essential* amino acids (Chapter 16). The remaining 12 are produced in cells and are known as *nonessential* amino acids. These 20 amino acids are combined in different amounts and sequences to produce at least 90,000 different proteins. What makes proteins different from one another is the number and sequence of their amino acids.

In part, DNA is a recipe for making a protein, because it's the sequence of DNA bases that ultimately determines the order of amino acids in a protein. In the DNA instructions, a *triplet*, or group of three bases, specifies a particular amino acid. For example, if a triplet consists of the base sequence cytosine, guanine, and adenine (CGA), it specifies the amino acid arginine (Table 3-1). Therefore, a small portion of a DNA recipe might look like this (except that there would be no spaces between the triplets): AGA CGA ACA ACC TAC TTT TTC CTT AAG GTC.

Protein synthesis actually takes place outside the cell nucleus, in the cytoplasm at the ribosomes. But the DNA molecule can't leave the cell's nucleus. Therefore the first step in protein synthesis is to copy the DNA message into a form of RNA called **messenger RNA (mRNA)**, which can pass through the nuclear membrane into the cytoplasm. Although RNA is similar to DNA, it is different in some important ways:

1. It's single-stranded. (This is true for the forms we discuss here but not true for all forms of RNA.)
2. It contains a different type of sugar.
3. It contains the base uracil as a substitute for the DNA base thymine. (Uracil binds to adenine in the same way thymine does.)

The mRNA molecule forms on the DNA template in pretty much the same way that new DNA molecules do. As in DNA replication, the two DNA strands separate, but only partially, and one of these strands attracts free-floating RNA nucleotides (also produced in the cell), which are joined together on the DNA template. The formation of mRNA is called *transcription* because, in fact, the DNA code is being copied, or transcribed (Fig. 3-7 on p. 57). Transcription continues until a section of DNA called a terminator region (composed of one of three specific DNA triplets) is reached and the process stops (Table 3-1). At this point, the mRNA strand,

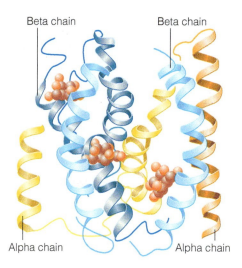

▲ Figure 3-6
Diagrammatic representation of a hemoglobin molecule. Hemoglobin molecules are composed of four chains of amino acids (two alpha chains and two beta chains).

hormones Substances (usually proteins) that are produced by specialized cells and that travel to other parts of the body, where they influence chemical reactions and regulate various cellular functions.

amino acids Small molecules that are the components of proteins.

messenger RNA (mRNA) A form of RNA that's assembled on a sequence of DNA bases. It carries the DNA code to the ribosome during protein synthesis.

Table 3-1 | The Genetic Code

Amino Acid Symbol	Amino Acid	mRNA Codon	DNA Triplet
Ala	Alanine	GCU, GCC, GCA, GCG	CGA, CGG, CGT, CGC
Arg	Arginine	CGU, CGC, CGA, CGG, AGA, AGG	GCA, GCG, GCT, GCC, TCT, TCC
Asn	Asparagine	AAU, AAC	TTA, TTG
Asp	Aspartic acid	GAU, GAC	CTA, CTG
Cys	Cysteine	UGU, UGC	ACA, ACG
Gln	Glutamine	CAA, CAG	GTT, GTC
Glu	Glutamic acid	GAA, GAG	CTT, CTC
Gly	Glycine	GGU, GGC, GGA, GGG	CCA, CCG, CCT, CCC
His	Histidine	CAU, CAC	GTA, GTG
Ile	Isoleucine	AUU, AUC, AUA	TAA, TAG, TAT
Leu	Leucine	UUA, UUG, CUU, CUC, CUA, CUG	AAT, AAC, GAA, GAG, GAT, GAC
Lys	Lysine	AAA, AAG	TTT, TTC
Met	Methionine	AUG	TAC
Phe	Phenylalanine	UUU, UUC	AAA, AAG
Pro	Proline	CCU, CCC, CCA, CCG	GGA, GGG, GGT, GGC
Ser	Serine	UCU, UCC, UCA, UCG, AGU, AGC	AGA, AGG, AGT, AGC, TCA, TCG
Thr	Threonine	ACU, ACC, ACA, ACG	TGA, TGG, TGT, TGC
Trp	Tryptophan	UGG	ACC
Tyr	Tyrosine	UAU, UAC	ATA, ATG
Val	Valine	GUU, GUC, GUA, GUG	CAA, CAG, CAT, CAC
Terminating triplets		UAA, UAG, UGA	ATT, ATC, ACT

codons Triplets of messenger RNA bases that code for specific amino acids during protein synthesis.

transfer RNA (tRNA) A type of RNA that binds to specific amino acids and transports them to the ribosome during protein synthesis.

mutation A change in DNA. The term can refer to changes in DNA bases (specifically called point mutations) as well as to changes in chromosome number and/or structure.

gene A sequence of DNA bases that specifies the order of amino acids in an entire protein, a portion of a protein, or any functional product, such as RNA. A gene may be composed of thousands of DNA bases.

comprising anywhere from 5,000 to perhaps as many as 200,000 nucleotides, peels away from the DNA model, and a portion of it travels through the nuclear membrane to the ribosome. Meanwhile, the bonds between the DNA bases are reestablished and the DNA molecule is once more intact.

As the mRNA strand arrives at the ribosome, its message is translated, or decoded (Fig. 3-8). Just as each DNA triplet specifies one amino acid, so do mRNA triplets, which are called **codons**. Therefore the mRNA strand is "read" in codons, or groups of three mRNA bases at a time (Table 3-1). Subsequently, another form of RNA, called **transfer RNA (tRNA)**, brings each amino acid to the ribosome. The ribosome then joins that amino acid to another amino acid in the order dictated by the sequence of mRNA codons (or, ultimately, DNA triplets). In this way, amino acids are linked together to form a molecule that will eventually be a protein or part of a protein. But it's important to mention that if a DNA base or sequence of bases is changed through **mutation**, some proteins may not be made or they may be defective. In this case, cells won't function properly, or they may not function at all.

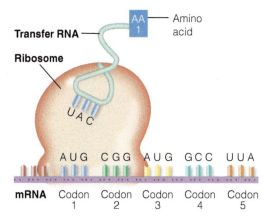

a As the ribosome binds to the mRNA, tRNA brings a particular amino acid, specified by the mRNA codon, to the ribosome.

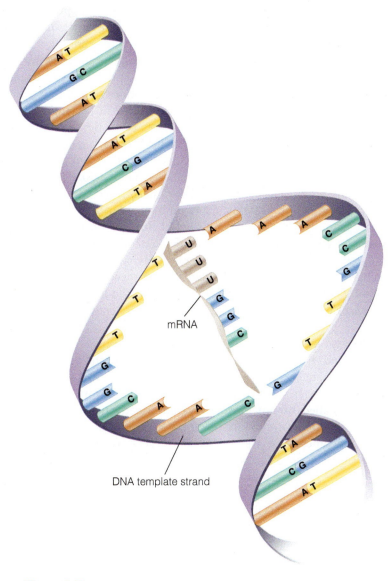

▲ Figure 3-7

Transcription. In this illustration, the two DNA strands have partly separated. Messenger RNA (mRNA) nucleotides have been drawn to the template strand and a strand of mRNA is being made. Note that the mRNA strand will exactly complement the DNA template strand except that uracil (U) replaces thymine (T).

b The tRNA binds to the first codon while a second tRNA–amino acid complex arrives at the ribosome.

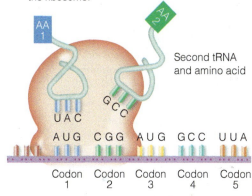

c The ribosome moves down the mRNA, allowing a third amino acid to be brought into position by another tRNA molecule. Note that the first two amino acids are now joined together.

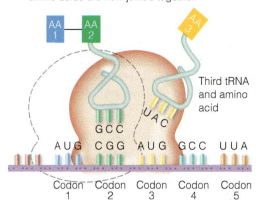

▲ Figure 3-8

Assembly of an amino acid chain in protein synthesis.

What Is a Gene?

The answer to this question is complicated, and the definition of the term **gene** is still the subject of some debate. In the past, textbooks compared genes to a string of beads, with each bead representing one gene on a chromosome. For 50 years or so, biologists considered a gene to be an uninterrupted sequence of DNA bases responsible for the manufacture of a protein or part of a protein. Or, put another way, a gene could be defined as *a segment of DNA that specifies the sequence of amino acids in a particular protein*. This definition, based on the concept of a one gene–one protein relationship, was a core principle in biology for decades, but it's been substantially modified, partly in recognition of the fact that DNA codes not only for proteins but also for RNA and other DNA nucleotides.

Moreover, when the human **genome** was sequenced in 2001, scientists concluded that humans have only about 25,000 genes, pretty much the same number as most other mammals (International Human Genome Sequencing Consortium, 2001; Venter et al., 2001). This number has now been revised down to approximately 21,000 genes (Pennisi, 2005). Yet we produce as many as 90,000 proteins! Furthermore, protein-coding genes (also called *coding sequences*), the DNA segments that are transcribed into proteins, make up only about 2 to 3 percent of the entire human genome! The rest is composed of **noncoding DNA**, or what used to be called "junk DNA" (see "A Closer Look: Noncoding DNA—Not Junk After All"). Thus gene action is much more complicated than previously believed and it's impossible for every protein to be coded for by a specific gene. This shift in perspective is a good example of something we discussed in Chapter 1, that hypotheses and theories can and do change over time as we continue to acquire new knowledge.

Geneticists have also learned that only some parts of genes, called **exons**, are actually transcribed into mRNA and thus code for specific amino acids. In fact, most of the nucleotide sequences in genes are not expressed during protein synthesis. (By *expressed* we mean that the DNA sequence is actually making a product.) Many sequences, called **introns**, are initially transcribed into mRNA and then clipped out (Fig. 3-9). Therefore introns aren't translated into amino acid sequences. Moreover, the intron segments that are snipped out of a gene aren't always the same ones. This means that the exons can be combined in different ways to make segments that code for more than one protein. That's how 21,000 coding sequences can make 90,000 proteins. Genes can also overlap one another, and there can be genes within genes. But they're still a part of the DNA molecule, and it's the combination of introns and exons, interspersed along a DNA strand, that makes up the unit we call a gene. So much for beads on a string.

genome The entire genetic makeup of an individual or species. In humans, it's estimated that the human genome comprises about 3 billion DNA bases.

noncoding DNA DNA that does not direct the production of proteins. However, such DNA segments produce thousands of molecules (e.g., RNA) that are involved in gene regulation. Thus the term noncoding DNA is misleading.

exons Segments of genes that are transcribed and are involved in protein synthesis. (The prefix *ex* denotes that these segments are expressed.)

introns Segments of genes that are initially transcribed and then deleted. Because introns are not expressed, they aren't involved in protein synthesis.

▶ **Figure 3-9**
Diagrammatic representation of how our views of gene function have changed. According to the traditional view, genes are discrete segments of DNA, each coding for a specific protein. (**a**) We now know that genes are composed of some DNA segments that are expressed (exons), and others that are not (introns). (**b**) Introns aren't expressed because they're deleted during the formation of mRNA. (**c**) The remaining exons can be rearranged to form several different coding sequences, each of which produces a different protein.

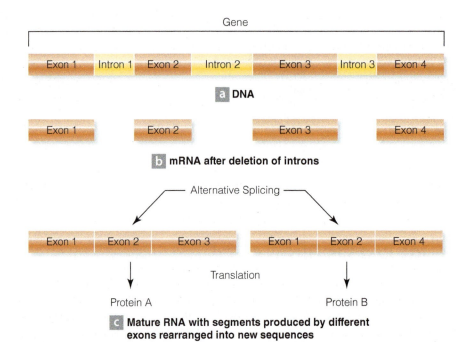

A Closer Look Noncoding DNA—Not Junk After All

In all fields of inquiry, important discoveries always raise new questions that eventually lead to further revelations. There's probably no statement that could be more appropriately applied to the field of genetics. For example, in 1977, geneticists recognized that during protein synthesis, the initially formed mRNA molecule contains many more nucleotides than are represented in the subsequently produced protein. This finding led to the discovery of *introns*, portions of genes that don't code for proteins. In the 1980s, geneticists learned that only about 2 percent of human DNA is contained within exons, the segments that actually provide the code for protein synthesis. We also know that a human gene can specify the production of as many as three different proteins by using different combinations of the exons interspersed within it (Pennisi, 2005).

As discussed earlier, with only 2 percent of the human genome directing protein synthesis, humans have more non-protein-coding DNA than any other species so far studied. Invertebrates and some vertebrates have only small amounts of noncoding sequences, and yet they're fully functional organisms. So just what does all this noncoding DNA (originally called "junk DNA") do in humans? Apparently much of it codes for different forms of RNA that act to regulate gene function, but it does not directly participate in protein synthesis (Pennisi, 2005; The ENCODE Project Consortium, 2012).

Almost half of all human DNA consists of noncoding segments that are repeated over and over and over. Depending on their length, these segments have been referred to as tandem repeats, satellites, or microsatellites, but now they're frequently lumped together and called copy number variants (CNVs). Microsatellites have an extremely high mutation rate and can gain or lose repeated segments and then return to their former length. But this tendency to mutate means that the number of repeats in a given microsatellite varies between individuals. And this tremendous variation has been the basis for DNA fingerprinting, a technique commonly used to provide evidence in criminal cases. Actually, anthropologists are now using microsatellite variation for all kinds of research, from tracing migrations of populations to paternity testing in nonhuman primates.

Some of the variations in microsatellite composition are associated with various disorders, so we can't help wondering why these variations exist. One answer is that some microsatellites influence the activities of protein-coding DNA sequences. Also, by losing or adding material, they can alter the sequences of bases in genes, thus becoming a source of mutation in functional genes. These mutations are a source of genetic variation.

Lastly, there are transposable elements (TEs), the so-called *jumping genes*. These are DNA sequences that can make thousands of copies of themselves, which are then scattered throughout the genome. One family of TEs, called Alu, is found only in primates. About 5 percent of the human genome is made up of Alu sequences, and although most of these are shared with other primates, about 7,000 are unique to humans (Chimpanzee Sequencing and Analysis Consortium, 2005).

TEs mainly code for proteins that enable them to move about, and because they can land right in the middle of coding sequences (exons), TEs cause mutations. Some of these mutations are harmful, and TEs have been associated with numerous disease conditions, including some forms of cancer (Deragon and Capy, 2000). At the same time, TEs essentially create new exons, thereby generating variations on which natural selection can act. Moreover, they also regulate the activities of many genes, including those involved in development. So rather than being junk, TEs are increasingly being recognized as serving extremely important functions in the evolutionary process, including the introduction of genetic changes that have led to the origin of new lineages.

Clearly, the answer to the question "What is a gene?" is complicated, and a completely accurate definition may be a long time coming. However, a proposed and more inclusive definition simply states that a gene is "a complete chromosomal segment responsible for making a functional product" (Snyder and Gerstein, 2003).

In spite of all the recently obtained information that has changed some of our views and expanded our knowledge of DNA, there is one fact that doesn't change. The genetic code is *universal*, and at least on earth, DNA is the molecule that governs the expression, inheritance, and evolution of biological traits in all forms of life. The DNA of all organisms, from bacteria to oak trees to fruit flies to human beings, is composed of the same molecules using the same kinds of instructions. The DNA triplet CGA, for example, specifies the amino acid alanine regardless of species. These similarities imply biological relationships between all forms of life—and a common ancestry as well. What makes fruit flies distinct from humans isn't differences in the DNA material itself, but differences in how that material is arranged and regulated.

Regulatory Genes

Some genes act solely to control the expression of other genes. Basically these **regulatory genes** make various kinds of RNA, proteins, and other molecules that switch other DNA segments (genes) on or off. Also, many regulatory genes diminish or enhance the expression of other genes. They play a fundamental role in embryological development, cellular function, and evolution. In fact, without them, life as we know it could not exist. The study of regulatory genes and their role in evolution is still in its infancy; but as information about them continues to accumulate, we will eventually be able to answer many of the questions we still have about the evolution of species.

DNA deactivation during embryonic development is one good example of how regulatory genes work. As you know, all somatic cells contain the same genetic information; but in any given cell, only a fraction of the DNA is actually involved in protein synthesis. For example, like the cells of the stomach lining, bone cells have DNA that codes for the production of digestive enzymes. But bone cells don't produce digestive enzymes. Instead, they make collagen, the main organic component of bone. This is because cells become specialized during embryonic development to perform only certain functions, and most of their DNA is permanently switched off by regulatory genes. In other words, they become specific types of cells, such as bone cells.

There are thousands of kinds of regulatory genes and one crucially important group is referred to as **homeobox genes**. The best known homeobox genes are the *Hox* genes, which direct the early segmentation of embryonic tissues. They also determine the identity of individual segments, by specifying what they will become, such as part of the head or thorax. *Hox* genes interact with other genes to determine the characteristics of developing body segments and structures but not their actual development. For example, they determine where, in a developing embryo, limb buds will appear; and they establish the number and overall pattern of the different types of vertebrae, the bones that make up the spine (Fig. 3-10).

regulatory genes Genes that influence the activity of other genes. Regulatory genes direct embryonic development and are involved in physiological processes throughout life. They are critically important to the evolutionary process.

homeobox genes An evolutionarily ancient family of regulatory genes that directs the development of the overall body plan and the segmentation of body tissues. There are at least 20 families of homeobox genes.

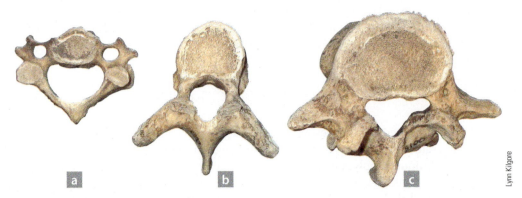

Lynn Kilgore

▲ **Figure 3-10**
The differences in these three vertebrae, from different regions of the spine, are caused by the action of *Hox* genes during embryonic development. (**a**) The cervical (neck) vertebrae have characteristics that differentiate them from (**b**) thoracic vertebrae, which are attached to the ribs, and also from (**c**) lumbar vertebrae of the lower back. *Hox* genes determine the overall pattern not only of each type of vertebra but also of each individual vertebra.

All homeobox genes are highly conserved, meaning that they've been maintained throughout much of evolutionary history. They're present in all invertebrates (such as worms and insects) and vertebrates, and they don't vary greatly from species to species. This type of conservation means not only that these genes are vitally important but also that they evolved from genes that were present in some of the earliest forms of life. Moreover, changes in the behavior of homeobox genes are responsible for various physical differences between closely related species or different breeds of domesticated animals. For these reasons, homeobox genes, and the many other kinds of regulatory genes, are now a critical area of research in evolutionary and developmental biology.

The finches of the Galápagos Islands provide an excellent example of how regulatory genes influence evolutionary change. In Chapter 2, we saw how Charles Darwin came to recognize that variation in these finches was an example of natural selection. Scientists have now explained the genetic basis for some of the finch variation by identifying two of the regulatory genes involved in the shape and size of bird beaks (Abzhanov et al., 2004, 2006). One of these genes (also involved in bone formation) is expressed to a greater degree during the embryonic development of wide-beaked ground finches than in that of finches with narrower beaks. Likewise, another gene is more active during beak development in finches that have longer, narrower beaks. Therefore the length and width of bird beaks are controlled by the activity of at least two different regulatory genes, allowing each aspect of beak size to evolve separately.

There are many other types of highly conserved genes as well. For example, recent sequencing of the sea sponge genome has shown that humans share many genes with sea sponges (Srivastava et al., 2010). This doesn't mean that sponges were ancestral to humans, but it does mean that we have genes that were already in existence some 600 mya. These genes ultimately laid the foundation for the evolution of complex animals, and they're crucial to many of the basic cellular processes that are fundamental to life today. These processes include cell growth, a cell's ability to recognize foreign cells (immunity), the development of specific cell types, and signaling between cells during growth and development.

We cannot overstate the importance of regulatory genes in evolution. The fact that these genes, with little modification, are present in all complex (as well as in some not so complex) organisms, including humans, is the basis of biological continuity, the connection between species. The "At a Glance" outlines the concepts we just discussed.

At a Glance   Coding and Noncoding DNA

Coding DNA	Noncoding DNA ("Junk" DNA)
Codes for sequences of amino acids (i.e., functional proteins) or RNA molecules	Function not well known; majority probably does not code for proteins; but regulatory genes, sometimes classed as noncoding DNA, do produce proteins; terminology may change
Comprises approximately 2% of human nuclear DNA	Comprises about 98% of human nuclear DNA
Includes exons within functional genes	Includes introns within functional genes and multiple repeated segments elsewhere on chromosomes

Mutation: When Genes Change

The best way to understand how genes function is to see what happens when they change, or mutate. Normal adult hemoglobin is made up of four amino acid chains (two *alpha* chains and two *beta* chains) that are the direct products of gene action. Each beta chain is in turn composed of 146 amino acids. There are several hemoglobin disorders with genetic origins, and perhaps the best known of these is **sickle-cell anemia**, which results from a defect in the beta chain. People with sickle-cell anemia inherit, from both parents, a mutated form of the gene that directs the formation of the beta chain. This mutation is caused by the substitution of one amino acid (*valine*) for the amino acid that's normally present (*glutamic acid*). This single amino acid substitution on the beta chain results in the production of a less efficient form of hemoglobin called hemoglobin S (Hb^S) instead of the normal form, which is called hemoglobin A (Hb^A). In situations where the availability of oxygen is reduced, such as at high altitude or when oxygen requirements are increased through exercise, red blood cells with Hb^S collapse and become sickle-shaped (Fig. 3-11). What follows is a cascade of events, all of which result in severe anemia and its consequences (Fig. 3-12). Briefly, these consequences include impaired circulation from blocked capillaries, red blood cell destruction, oxygen deprivation to vital organs (including the brain), and, without treatment, death.

People who inherit the altered form of the gene from only one parent don't have sickle-cell anemia, but they do have what's called *sickle-cell trait*. Fortunately for them, they're much less severely affected because only about 40 percent of their hemoglobin is abnormal.

The cause of sickle-cell anemia is a very slight change in the *Hb* gene. Remember that hemoglobin beta chains each have 146 amino acids. What's more, to emphasize the importance of a seemingly minor alteration, consider that triplets of DNA bases are required to specify amino acids. Therefore it takes 438 bases (146 × 3) to produce the chain of 146 amino acids that forms the adult hemoglobin beta chain. But a change in only one of these 438 bases produces the life-threatening complications seen in sickle-cell anemia. Figure 3-13 shows the DNA base sequence and the resulting amino acid products for both normal and sickling hemoglobin. As you can see, a single base substitution (from CTC to CAC) can result in an altered amino acid sequence, from

... proline—*glutamic acid*—glutamic acid ...
to
... proline—*valine*—glutamic acid ...

sickle-cell anemia A severe inherited hemoglobin disorder in which red blood cells collapse when deprived of oxygen. It results from inheriting two copies of a mutant allele. The type of mutation that produces the sickle-cell allele is a point mutation.

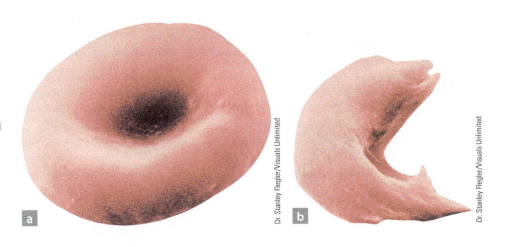

▶ **Figure 3-11**
Scanning electron micrographs of (**a**) a normal, fully oxygenated red blood cell and (**b**) a collapsed, sickle-shaped red blood cell that contains Hb^S.

Dr. Stanley Flegler/Visuals Unlimited

Dr. Stanley Flegler/Visuals Unlimited

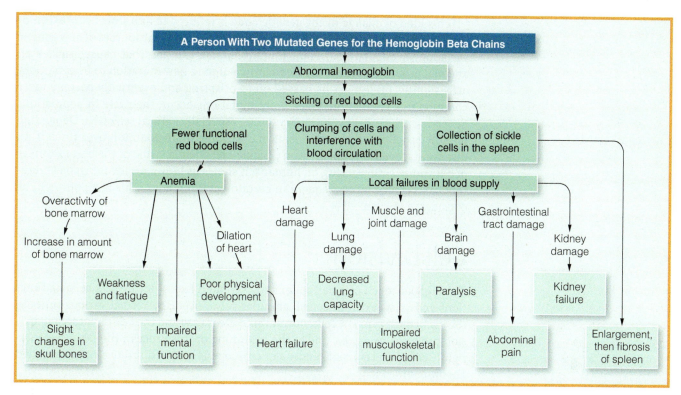

▲ Figure 3-12

Diagram showing the cascade of symptoms that can occur in people with sickle-cell anemia.

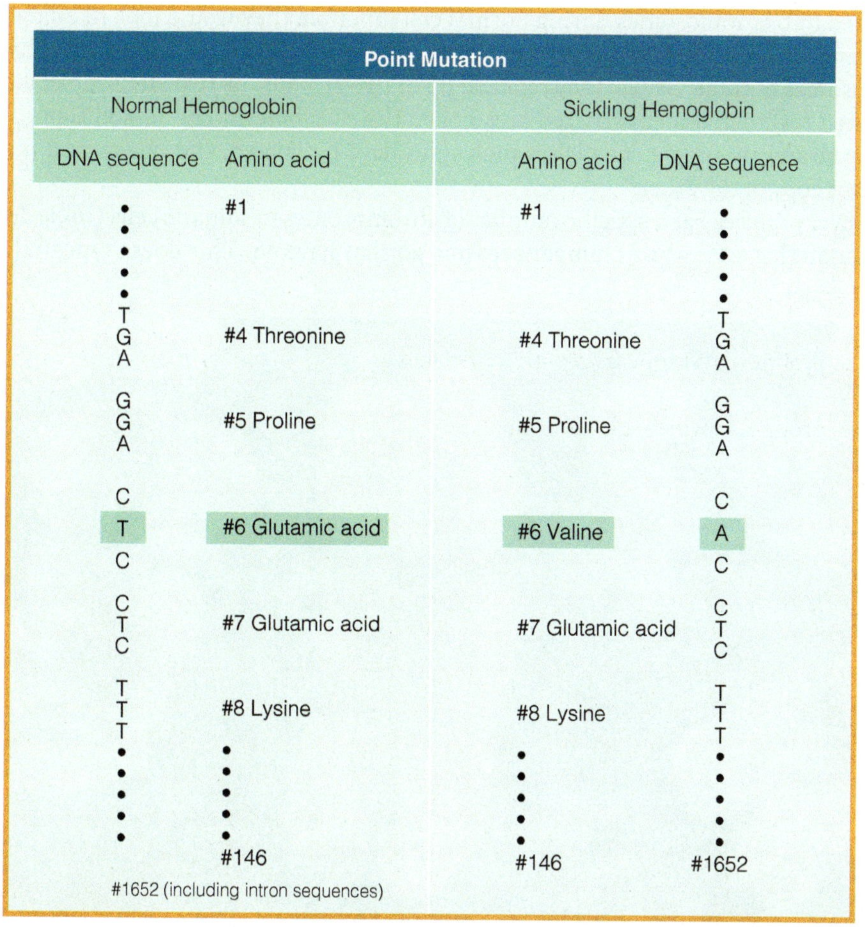

Point Mutation			
Normal Hemoglobin		Sickling Hemoglobin	
DNA sequence	Amino acid	Amino acid	DNA sequence
• • • • •	#1	#1	• • • • •
T G A	#4 Threonine	#4 Threonine	T G A
G G A	#5 Proline	#5 Proline	G G A
C			C
T	#6 Glutamic acid	#6 Valine	A
C			C
C T C	#7 Glutamic acid	#7 Glutamic acid	C T C
T T T	#8 Lysine	#8 Lysine	T T T
• • • •			• • • •
#1652 (including intron sequences)	#146	#146	#1652

◀ **Figure 3-13**

Substitution of one base at position 6 produces sickling hemoglobin.

This kind of change in the genetic code is referred to as a **point mutation** or *base substitution*. In evolution, these changes are important sources of new genetic variation in populations. Point mutations, like the one that causes sickle-cell anemia, probably occur fairly frequently. But for a new mutation to be evolutionarily significant, it must be passed on to offspring and eventually become more common in a population. Once point mutations occur, their fate in populations depends on the other evolutionary forces, especially natural selection. Depending on how beneficial a mutation is, it may become more common over time; if it's disadvantageous, it probably won't. Sickle-cell anemia is one of the best examples of natural selection acting on humans; it shows us how a disadvantageous mutation can become more frequent in certain environments. This last point will be considered in Chapter 4.

Cell Division

Throughout much of a cell's life, its DNA (all 6 feet of it!) directs cellular functions and exists as an uncoiled, granular substance. However, at various times in the life of most types of cells, normal activities cease and the cell divides. Cell division produces new cells, and at the beginning of this process, the DNA becomes tightly coiled and is visible under a microscope as a set of discrete structures called **chromosomes** (Fig. 3-14).

Chromosomes

Chromosomes are composed of DNA and protein (Fig. 3-15). If the DNA were organized into chromosomes during normal cell function, they would look like single-stranded structures. However, during the early stages of cell division when chromosomes become visible, they're made up of two strands, or two DNA molecules, joined together at a constricted area called the *centromere*. The reason there are two strands is simple: The DNA molecules have replicated, and one strand is an exact copy of the other.

Every species has a specific number of chromosomes in somatic cells (Table 3-2). Humans have 46, while chimpanzees and gorillas have 48. This doesn't mean that

point mutation A change in one of the four DNA bases.

chromosomes Discrete structures composed of DNA and proteins found only in the nuclei of cells. Chromosomes are visible under magnification only during certain phases of cell division.

▶ **Figure 3-14**
Colorized scanning electronmicrograph of human chromosomes.

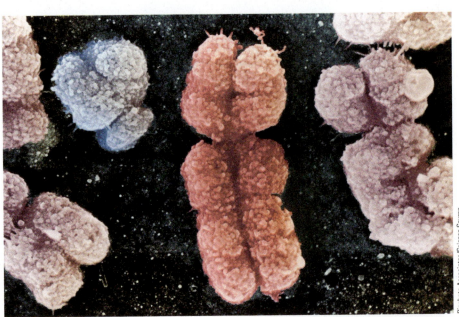

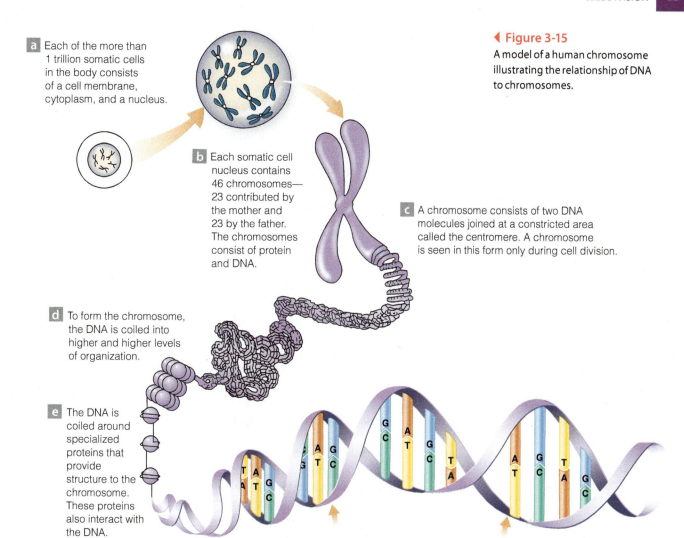

a Each of the more than 1 trillion somatic cells in the body consists of a cell membrane, cytoplasm, and a nucleus.

◀ **Figure 3-15**
A model of a human chromosome illustrating the relationship of DNA to chromosomes.

b Each somatic cell nucleus contains 46 chromosomes—23 contributed by the mother and 23 by the father. The chromosomes consist of protein and DNA.

c A chromosome consists of two DNA molecules joined at a constricted area called the centromere. A chromosome is seen in this form only during cell division.

d To form the chromosome, the DNA is coiled into higher and higher levels of organization.

e The DNA is coiled around specialized proteins that provide structure to the chromosome. These proteins also interact with the DNA.

f A specific sequence of nucleotide base pairs constitutes a gene.

Table 3-2	Standard Chromosomal Complement in Various Organisms	
Organism	**Chromosome Number in Somatic Cells**	**Chromosome Number in Gametes**
Human (*Homo sapiens*)	46	23
Chimpanzee (*Pan troglodytes*)	48	24
Gorilla (*Gorilla gorilla*)	48	24
Dog (*Canis familiaris*)	78	39
Chicken (*Gallus domesticus*)	78	39
Frog (*Rana pipiens*)	26	13
Housefly (*Musca domestica*)	12	6
Onion (*Allium cepa*)	16	8
Corn (*Zea mays*)	20	10
Tobacco (*Nicotiana tabacum*)	48	24

Source: Based on Cummings, 2000, p. 16.

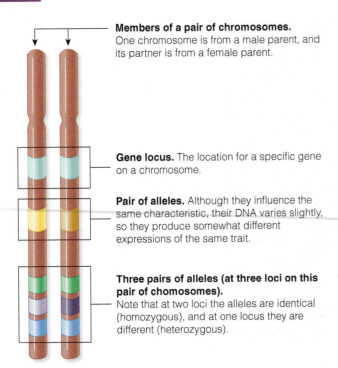

Members of a pair of chromosomes. One chromosome is from a male parent, and its partner is from a female parent.

Gene locus. The location for a specific gene on a chromosome.

Pair of alleles. Although they influence the same characteristic, their DNA varies slightly, so they produce somewhat different expressions of the same trait.

Three pairs of alleles (at three loci on this pair of chomosomes). Note that at two loci the alleles are identical (homozygous), and at one locus they are different (heterozygous).

▲ **Figure 3-16**
As this diagram illustrates, alleles are located at the same locus on paired chromosomes, but they aren't always identical.

autosomes All chromosomes except the sex chromosomes.

sex chromosomes In mammals, the X and Y chromosomes.

locus (*pl.*, loci) (lo'-kus, lo-sigh') The position or location on a chromosome where a given gene occurs. The term is sometimes used interchangeably with *gene*.

alleles Alternate forms of a gene. Alleles occur at the same locus on paired chromosomes and thus govern the same trait, but because they're different, their action may result in different expressions of that trait.

karyotype The chromosomes of an individual, or what is typical of a species, viewed microscopically and displayed in a photograph. The chromosomes are arranged in pairs and according to size and position of the centromere.

humans have less DNA than chimpanzees and gorillas. It just means that the DNA is packaged differently.

There are two basic types of chromosomes: **autosomes** and **sex chromosomes**. Autosomes carry information that governs all physical characteristics except primary sex determination. The two sex chromosomes are the X and Y chromosomes; in mammals, the Y chromosome is directly involved in determining maleness. Although the X chromosome is called a sex chromosome, it actually functions more like an autosome because it's not involved in primary sex determination and it influences several other traits. Among mammals, all genetically normal females have two X chromosomes (XX), and they're female only because they don't have a Y chromosome. (Female is the default setting.) All genetically normal males have one X and one Y chromosome (XY).

Chromosomes occur in pairs, so all normal human somatic cells have 22 pairs of autosomes and one pair of sex chromosomes (23 pairs in all). With few exceptions, abnormal numbers of autosomes are fatal—usually soon after conception. Although abnormal numbers of sex chromosomes aren't usually fatal, they may result in sterility and frequently have other consequences. So to function normally, it's essential for a human cell to possess both members of each chromosomal pair, or a total of 46 chromosomes.

Offspring inherit one member of each chromosomal pair from the father (the paternal chromosome) and one member from the mother (the maternal chromosome). Members of chromosomal pairs are alike in size and position of the centromere, and they carry genetic information governing the same traits. However, this doesn't mean that partner chromosomes are genetically identical; it just means that they influence the same traits. For example, on both copies of a person's ninth chromosome, there's a **locus**, or gene position, that determines which of the four ABO blood types (A, B, AB, or O) he or she will have. However, these two ninth chromosomes might not have identical DNA segments at the ABO locus. In other words, at numerous genetic loci, there may be more than one possible form of a gene, and these different forms are called **alleles** (Fig. 3-16).

Alleles are alternate forms of a gene that can direct the cell to produce slightly different forms of a product, and ultimately, different expressions of a trait—as in the hemoglobin S (Hb^S) example. At the ABO locus, there are three possible alleles: *A*, *B*, and *O*. However, since individuals have only two ninth chromosomes, only two alleles are present in any one person. And the variation in alleles at the ABO locus is what accounts for the variation among humans in ABO blood type.

Karyotyping Chromosomes

One method frequently used to examine chromosomes in an individual is to produce a karyotype. (An example of a human **karyotype** is shown in Fig. 3-17.) The chromosomes used in karyotypes are obtained from dividing cells. White blood cells can be cultured, chemically treated, and microscopically examined to identify the ones that are dividing. These cells are then photographed through a microscope to produce *photomicrographs* of intact, double-stranded chromosomes. Partner chromosomes are then matched up, and the entire set is arranged in descending order by size so that the largest chromosome appears first.

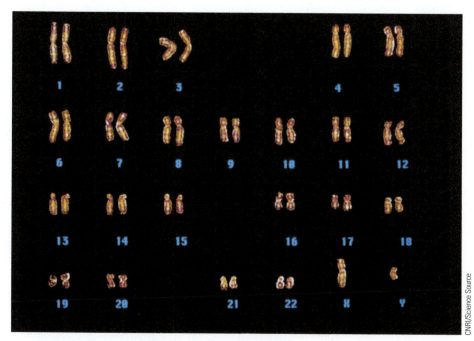

CNRI/Science Source

◀ **Figure 3-17**
A karyotype of a human male with the chromosomes arranged by size, position of the centromere, and banding patterns.

Karyotyping has had numerous practical applications. Physicians and genetic counselors use karyotypes to help diagnose chromosomal disorders in patients, and they're used in prenatal testing to identify chromosomal abnormalities in developing fetuses. Karyotype analysis has also revealed many chromosomal similarities shared by different species, including humans and nonhuman primates. But, now that scientists can directly compare the genomes of species, karyotyping probably won't continue being used for this or several other purposes.

Mitosis

As we mentioned earlier, normal cellular function is periodically interrupted so that the cell can divide. Cell division in somatic cells is called **mitosis**, and it's the way somatic cells reproduce. It occurs during growth and development, and it's the process that repairs injured tissues and replaces older cells with newer ones. But while mitosis produces new somatic cells, another type of cell division, called **meiosis**, may lead to the development of new individuals, since it produces reproductive cells, or gametes.

In the early stages of mitosis, a human somatic cell has 46 double-stranded chromosomes, and as the cell begins to divide, these chromosomes line up along its center and split apart so that the two strands separate (Fig. 3-18). Once the two strands are apart, they pull away from each other and move to opposite ends of the dividing cell. At this point, each strand is a distinct chromosome, *composed of one DNA molecule*. Following the separation of chromosome strands, the cell membrane pinches in and seals, so that there are two new cells, each with a full complement of DNA, or 46 chromosomes.

Mitosis is referred to as "simple cell division" because a somatic cell divides one time to produce two daughter cells that are genetically identical to each other and to the original cell. In mitosis, the original cell possesses 46 chromosomes, and each new daughter cell inherits an exact copy of all 46. This precision is made possible by the DNA molecule's ability to replicate. Therefore DNA replication ensures that the amount of genetic material remains constant from one generation of cells to the next.

mitosis Simple cell division; the process by which somatic cells divide to produce two identical daughter cells.

meiosis Cell division in specialized cells in ovaries and testes. Meiosis involves two divisions and results in four daughter cells, each containing only half the original number of chromosomes. These cells can develop into gametes.

a The cell is involved in metabolic activities. DNA replication occurs, but chromosomes are not visible.

b The nuclear membrane disappears, and double-stranded chromosomes are visible.

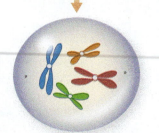
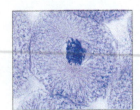

▶ **Figure 3-18**
Diagrammatic representation of mitosis. The blue images next to some of these illustrations are photomicrographs of actual chromosomes in a dividing cell.

c The chromosomes align themselves at the center of the cell.

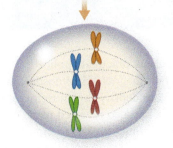
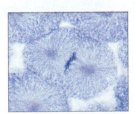

d The chromosomes split at the centromere, and the strands separate and move to opposite ends of the dividing cell.

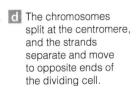

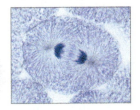

e The cell membrane pinches in as the cell continues to divide. The chromosomes begin to uncoil (not shown here).

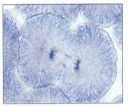

f After mitosis is complete, there are two identical daughter cells. The nuclear membrane is present, and chromosomes are no longer visible.

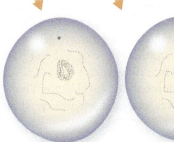

We should mention here that certain types of somatic cells don't divide. Red blood cells are produced continuously by specialized cells in bone marrow, but they can't divide because they have no nucleus and no nuclear DNA. Once the brain and nervous system are fully developed, brain and nerve cells (neurons) stop dividing, although there is some debate about this issue. Liver cells also do not divide after growth has stopped unless this vital organ is damaged through injury or disease. With these three exceptions (red blood cells, mature neurons, and liver cells), somatic cells are regularly duplicated through the process of mitosis.

Meiosis

While mitosis produces new cells, meiosis can lead to the development of a new organism because it produces reproductive cells (gametes). Although meiosis is similar to mitosis, it's more complicated. In meiosis, there are two divisions instead of one. Also, meiosis produces four daughter cells, not two, and each of these four cells contains only half the original number of chromosomes. While the process is similar in both males and females, only males produce four viable sperm cells at the end. Females, in contrast, produce one viable egg and three nonfunctioning cells known as *polar bodies.* Additionally, the process in females begins prior to birth, then ceases, and then resumes again during puberty, whereas the process in males begins during puberty.

During meiosis, specialized cells in male testes and female ovaries divide and eventually develop into sperm and egg cells. Initially, these cells contain the full complement of chromosomes (46 in humans); but after the first division (called *reduction division*), the number of chromosomes in the two daughter cells is 23, or half the original number (Fig. 3-19). This reduction of chromosome number is crucial because the resulting gamete, with its 23 chromosomes, may eventually unite with another gamete that also has 23 chromosomes. The product of this union is a *zygote*, or fertilized egg, in which the original number of chromosomes (46) has been restored. In other words, a zygote inherits the exact amount of DNA it needs (half from each parent) to develop and function normally. If it weren't for reduction division in meiosis, it wouldn't be possible to maintain the correct number of chromosomes from one generation to the next.

During the first division, partner chromosomes come together to form pairs of double-stranded chromosomes that line up along the cell's center. Pairing of partner chromosomes is essential because while they're together, members of pairs exchange genetic information in a process called **recombination**. Pairing is also important because it ensures that each new daughter cell receives only one member of each pair.

As the cell begins to divide, the chromosomes themselves remain intact (that is, double-stranded), but *members of pairs* pull apart and move to opposite ends of the cell. After the first division, there are two new daughter cells, but they aren't identical to each other or to the parental cell. They're different because each cell contains only one member of each chromosome pair (that is, only 23 chromosomes), each of which still has two strands. Also, because of recombination, each chromosome now contains some combinations of alleles it didn't have before.

The second meiotic division is similar to division in mitosis. (For a comparison of mitosis and meiosis, see Fig. 3-20 on p. 71.) In the two newly formed cells, the 23 double-stranded chromosomes line up at the cell's center and, as in mitosis, the strands of each chromosome separate and move apart. Once this second division is completed, there are four daughter cells, each with 23 single-stranded chromosomes, or 23 DNA molecules.

recombination The exchange of genetic material between paired chromosomes during meiosis; also called *crossing over.*

◀ **Figure 3-19**
Diagrammatic representation
of meiosis.

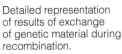

Detailed representation
of results of exchange
of genetic material during
recombination.

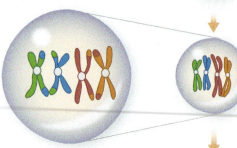

a Chromosomes are not visible
as DNA replication occurs in
a cell preparing to divide.

b Double-stranded chromosomes
become visible, and partner
chromosomes exchange genetic
material in a process called
recombination or crossing over.

c Chromosome pairs migrate to the center of the cell.

d **First Division** (reduction division)

Partner chromosomes separate, and members
of each pair move to opposite ends of the dividing
cell. This results in only half the original number
of chromosomes in each new daughter cell.

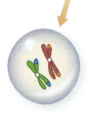

e After the first meiotic division,
there are two daughter cells, each
containing only one member of
each original chromosomal pair,
or 23 nonpartner chromosomes.

f **Second Division**

In this division, the chromosomes split at
the centromere, and the strands move to
opposite sides of the cell.

g After the second division,
meiosis results in four daughter
cells. These may mature to
become functional gametes,
containing only half the DNA
in the original cell.

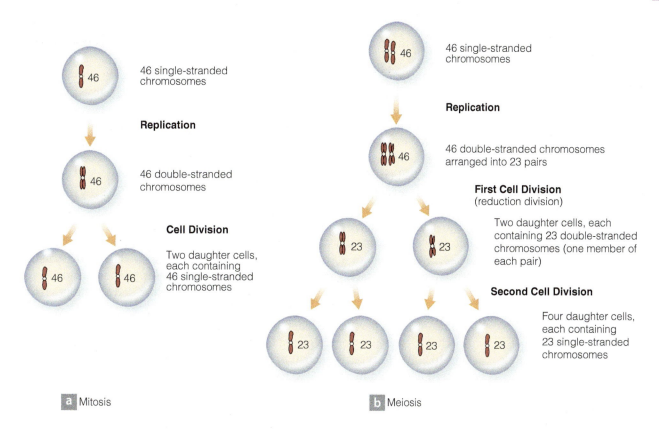

46 single-stranded chromosomes

Replication

46 double-stranded chromosomes

Cell Division

Two daughter cells, each containing 46 single-stranded chromosomes

46 single-stranded chromosomes

Replication

46 double-stranded chromosomes arranged into 23 pairs

First Cell Division
(reduction division)

Two daughter cells, each containing 23 double-stranded chromosomes (one member of each pair)

Second Cell Division

Four daughter cells, each containing 23 single-stranded chromosomes

a Mitosis

b Meiosis

The Evolutionary Significance of Meiosis Meiosis occurs in all sexually reproducing organisms and is an extremely important evolutionary innovation because it increases genetic variation in populations. Members of sexually reproducing species aren't genetically identical **clones** of other individuals because they receive genetic contributions from two parents. Just from the **random assortment** of chromosome pairs during the first division of meiosis, each parent can produce around 8 million genetically different gametes. In human matings, literally trillions of genetic combinations can result in the offspring of two parents. Consequently every individual represents a unique combination of genes that, in all likelihood, has never occurred before and will never occur again.

As you can see, genetic diversity is considerably enhanced by meiosis, and this diversity is essential if species are to adapt to changing selective pressures. As we mentioned in Chapter 2, natural selection acts on genetic variation in populations; thus if all individuals were genetically identical, natural selection would have nothing to act upon and evolution couldn't occur. In all species, *mutation* is the only source of new genetic variation because it produces new alleles. But sexually reproducing species have an additional advantage because recombination produces new *arrangements* of genetic information, potentially providing additional material for selection to act on. In fact, the influence of meiosis on genetic variation is the main advantage of sexual reproduction. Thus, sexual reproduction and meiosis are of major evolutionary importance because they contribute to the role of natural selection in populations.

Problems with Meiosis For fetal development to occur normally, the process of meiosis must be exact. If chromosomes or chromosome strands don't separate during either of the two divisions, serious problems can develop. This failure to separate is called *nondisjunction*, and when it happens, one of the daughter cells receives two copies of the affected chromosome while the other daughter cell receives none. If such an affected gamete unites with a normal gamete containing

▲ **Figure 3-20**
Mitosis and meiosis compared. In mitosis, one division produces two daughter cells, each of which contains 46 chromosomes. In meiosis, there are two divisions. After the first, there are two cells, each containing only 23 chromosomes (one member of each original chromosome pair). Each daughter cell divides again, so that the final result is four cells, each with only half the original number of chromosomes.

clones Organisms that are genetically identical to another organism. The term may also be used to refer to genetically identical DNA segments, molecules, or cells.

random assortment The chance distribution of chromosomes to daughter cells during meiosis. Along with recombination, random assortment is an important source of genetic variation (but not new alleles).

23 chromosomes, the resulting zygote will have either 45 or 47 chromosomes. If there are 47, then there will be three copies of one chromosome instead of two, a situation called *trisomy*.

You can appreciate the potential effects of an abnormal number of chromosomes if you remember that the zygote, by means of mitosis, ultimately gives rise to all the cells in the developing body. Consequently every one of those cells will inherit an incorrect number of chromosomes. And since most abnormal numbers of autosomes are lethal, the embryo is usually spontaneously aborted, frequently before the pregnancy is even recognized.

Trisomy 21 (also referred to as Down syndrome) is the only example of an incorrect number of autosomes that's compatible with life beyond the first few years after birth. Trisomy 21 is caused by the presence of three copies of chromosome 21. It occurs in approximately 1 out of every 1,000 live births and is associated with various developmental and health problems. These problems include congenital heart defects (seen in about 40 percent of affected newborns) as well as increased susceptibility to respiratory infections and leukemia. However, the most widely recognized effect is mental impairment, which is variably expressed and ranges from mild to severe.

Trisomy 21 is partly associated with advanced maternal age. For example, the risk of a 20-year-old woman giving birth to an affected infant is just 0.05 percent (5 in 10,000). However, 3 percent of babies born to mothers aged 45 and older are affected (a 60-fold increase). Actually, most affected infants are born to women under the age of 35, but that's because the majority of women who have babies are less than 35 years old. The increased prevalence of trisomy 21 with maternal age is thought to be related to the fact that meiosis actually begins in females during their own fetal development and then stops, only to be resumed and completed at ovulation. This means that a woman's gametes are as old as she is, and age-related changes in the chromosomes themselves appear to increase the risk of nondisjunction, at least for some chromosomes.

Nondisjunction also occurs in sex chromosomes (Table 3-3). For example, a man may have two X chromosomes and one Y chromosome (XXY) or one X chromosome and two Y chromosomes (XYY). Likewise, a woman may have only one X chromosome (X0), or she may have more than two (XXX). Although abnormal numbers of sex chromosomes don't always result in spontaneous abortion or death, they can cause sterility, some mental impairment, and other problems. And while it's possible to live without a Y chromosome (roughly half of all people do), it's impossible for an embryo to survive without an X chromosome. (Remember, X chromosomes carry genes that influence many traits.) Clearly normal development depends on having the correct number of chromosomes.

New Frontiers

Since the discovery of DNA structure and function in the 1950s, the field of genetics has revolutionized biological science and reshaped our understanding of inheritance, genetic disease, and evolutionary processes. For example, a technique developed in 1986, called **polymerase chain reaction (PCR)**, enables scientists to make thousands of copies of small samples of DNA, which can then be analyzed. In the past, DNA samples from crime scenes or ancient skeletal remains were usually too small to be studied. But PCR makes it possible to examine DNA sequences in, for example, Neandertal fossils and Egyptian mummies, and it has limitless potential for many disciplines, including forensic science, medicine, and paleoanthropology.

Another application of PCR allows scientists to identify *DNA fingerprints*, so called because they appear as patterns of repeated DNA sequences that are unique

polymerase chain reaction (PCR)
A method of producing thousands of copies of a DNA sample.

Table 3-3 | Examples of Nondisjunction in Sex Chromosomes

Chromosomal Complement	Condition	Estimated Incidence	Manifestations
XXX	Trisomy X	1 per 1,000 female births	Affected women are usually clinically normal, but there is a slight increase in sterility and mental impairment compared to the general population. In cases with more than three X chromosomes, mental impairment can be severe.
XYY	XYY syndrome	1 per 1,000 male births	Affected males are fertile and tend to be taller than average.
XO	Turner syndrome	1 per 10,000 female births	Affected females are short-statured, have broad chests and webbed necks, and are sterile. There is usually no mental impairment, but concepts relating to spatial relationships, including mathematics, can pose difficulties. Between 95 and 99% of affected fetuses die before birth.
XXY	Klinefelter syndrome	1 per 1,000 male births	Symptoms are noticeable by puberty: reduced testicular development, reduced facial and body hair, some breast development in about half of all cases, and reduced fertility or sterility. Some individuals exhibit lowered intelligence. Additional X chromosomes (XXXY) are associated with mental impairment.

to each individual (Fig. 3-21). For example, one person might have a segment of six bases such as ATTCTA repeated 3 times, while another person might have 20 copies of the same sequence. DNA fingerprinting is perhaps the most powerful tool available for human identification. Scientists have used it to identify scores of remains, including members of the Russian royal family murdered in 1918 and victims of the September 11, 2001, terrorist attacks. Moreover, the technique has been used to exonerate many innocent people wrongly convicted of crimes, in some cases decades after they were imprisoned.

Over the last two decades, scientists have used the techniques of *recombinant DNA technology* to transfer genes from the cells of one species into those of another. One common method has been to insert human genes that direct the production of various proteins into bacterial cells in laboratories. The altered bacteria can then produce human gene products, such as insulin. Until the early 1980s, people with type 1 diabetes relied on insulin derived from nonhuman animals. However, this insulin wasn't plentiful, and some patients became allergic to it. But since 1982, abundant supplies of human insulin, produced by bacteria, have been available, and insulin derived from bacteria doesn't cause allergic reactions.

In recent years, genetic manipulation has become increasingly controversial owing to questions related to product safety, environmental concerns, animal welfare, and concern over the experimental use of human embryos. For example, the insertion of bacterial DNA into certain crops has made them toxic to leaf-eating insects, thus reducing the need for pesticides. Cattle and pigs are commonly treated with antibiotics and genetically engineered growth hormone to increase growth rates. There's no concrete evidence that humans are susceptible to the insect-repelling bacterial DNA or harmed by consuming meat and dairy products from animals treated with growth hormone. But there are concerns over the unknown effects of long-term exposure.

Cloning has been one of the most controversial of all the new genetic technologies. However, cloning isn't as new as you might think. Anyone who has ever taken a cutting from a plant and rooted it to grow a new one has produced a clone. Many mammalian species have now been cloned, and researchers have even produced

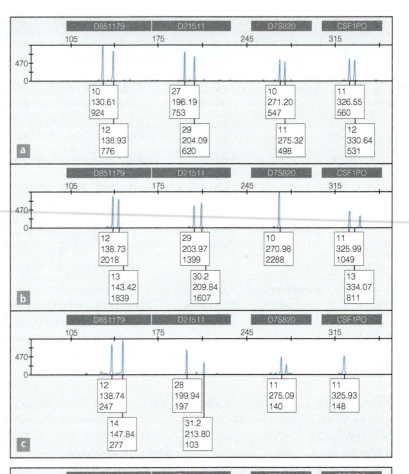

▶ **Figure 3-21**
Six partial DNA fingerprints, one of which represents blood from a crime scene (**a**). The other five (**b–f**) represent potential suspects. By comparing the STR alleles, you can determine who left their blood at the crime scene.

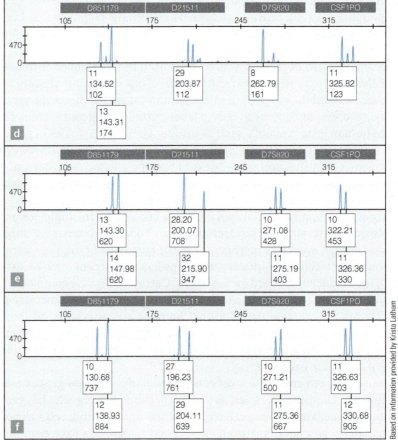

clones of dead mice that were frozen for as long as 16 years. This gives rise to hopes that eventually it may be possible to clone extinct animals, such as mammoths, from the frozen bodies of animals that died several thousand years ago (Wakayama et al., 2008). But don't count on visiting a *Jurassic Park* type zoo anytime soon.

As exciting as these innovations are, probably the single most important advance in genetics has been the progress made by the **Human Genome Project** (International Human Genome Sequencing Consortium, 2001; Venter et al., 2001). The goal of this international effort, begun in 1990, was to sequence the entire human genome, which consists of some 3 billion bases making up approximately 21,000 protein-coding genes. This extremely important project was completed in 2003. Since that time, the genomes of hundreds of species have been sequenced, including chimpanzees (Chimpanzee Sequencing and Analysis Consortium, 2005), western lowland gorillas (Scally et al., 2012), orangutans (Locke et al., 2011), bonobos (Prüfer et al., 2012), and rhesus macaques (Rhesus Macaque Genome Sequencing and Analysis Consortium, 2007). By comparing different primate genomes, including that of humans, molecular anthropologists are revealing more details regarding phylogenetic relationships among all primate species.

Since the publication of the human genome, DNA sequencing technologies have become increasingly inexpensive, more widely available, and much faster. In May 2010, researchers finished sequencing the entire Neandertal genome (Green et al., 2010). To date, the most exciting announcement stemming from this research is that modern Europeans and Asians (but not Africans) inherited 1 to 4 percent of their genes from ancient Neandertal ancestors. This finding sheds light on debates concerning whether or not early modern humans interbred with Neandertals. These debates have been ongoing in physical anthropology for more than 50 years, and while this new genetic evidence does not conclusively end the discussion, it strongly supports the argument that some interbreeding did indeed take place and that many of us carry a few Neandertal genes (see Chapter 13).

Eventually, comparative genome analysis should provide a thorough assessment of genetic similarities and differences, and thus the evolutionary relationships, between humans and other primates. What's more, we can already look at human variation in an entirely different light than we could even 15 years ago. Among other things, genetic comparisons between human groups can inform us about population movements in the past and what selective pressures may have been exerted on different populations to produce some of the variability we see.

Completion of the Neandertal genome sequence wasn't the only groundbreaking achievement in 2010. After 10 years of effort, scientists created a functional, synthetic bacterial genome (Gibson et al., 2010). This synthetic genome is the first life-form ever made by humans, and it has major implications for biotechnology. (Understandably, it has also raised many ethical concerns.) Basically, geneticists sequenced the 1 million bases in a bacterial chromosome. (Bacterial DNA is organized into a single ring-shaped chromosome.) They then produced an artificial chromosome by assembling DNA segments and splicing them together, interspersed with "noncoding" sequences they had invented. These noncoding sequences allowed them to distinguish the genome they had created from the natural one. The new synthetic DNA was then inserted into a bacterial cell of a different species. The original DNA of the recipient cell had been removed, and the cell began to follow the instructions of the new DNA. That is, it produced proteins characteristic of a different bacterial species! Moreover, the recipient cell replicated, and now there are laboratory colonies of the "new" bacterium (Fig. 3-22).

It's important to emphasize that this project did not create a completely new synthetic life-form because the genome had been transferred into an already existing cell. Nevertheless, the door has been opened for the development of artificial organisms. Though it may never be possible to create new species as complex as birds and

Human Genome Project An international effort aimed at sequencing and mapping the entire human genome, completed in 2003.

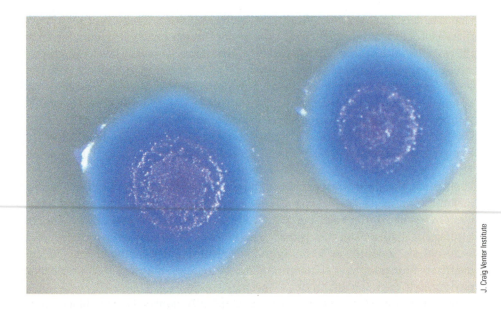

▶ **Figure 3-22**
Self-replicating synthetic bacteria.
Researchers inserted a gene into the
synthetic bacteria that makes this
colony appear blue. This was so they
could distinguish these cells from the
original bacteria (which aren't blue)
and therefore determine if the new
cells were indeed replicating.

mammals, we can almost certainly expect to see the production of artificial, single-celled organisms, many of which will have medical applications. But the potential for abuse, especially in the development of biological weapons, will obviously be of grave concern. Still, the human development of a self-replicating bacterium with altered DNA from another species is an extraordinary milestone in biology. It is not an exaggeration to say that this is the most exciting time in the history of evolutionary biology since Darwin published *On the Origin of Species.*

Equally exciting was the sequencing of the entire genome of another premodern human group called the Denisovans (Reich et al., 2010; Meyer et al., 2012). This group is dated to around 50,000 ya and the entire collection of Denisovan skeletal remains consists of a tiny finger bone and two teeth discovered in Siberia. Yet, in a feat that would have been unimaginable just 10 years ago, researchers have been able to obtain high quality DNA from the finger bone and sequence the entire genome of this population! The Denisovan genome has now been compared to that of their Neandertal cousins and to the genomes of modern human populations (see Chapter 12).

Eventually, comparative genome analysis should provide a thorough assessment of genetic similarities and differences and thus of the evolutionary relationships between humans and other primates. What's more, we can already look at human variation in an entirely different light than was possible just 10 years ago (see Chapter 15). Among other things, genetic comparisons between human groups can inform us about population movements in the past and what selective pressures may have been exerted on different populations to produce some of the variability we see.

The Encyclopedia of DNA Elements, or ENCODE, is a project initially conceived to follow up on the progress made by the Human Genome Project. This huge study, begun in 2003, now involves an international consortium of more than 400 researchers who, in September 2012, simultaneously published 30 articles in several scientific journals. Initially, the project set out to catalog the functional DNA sequences contained within the vast stretches of non-protein-coding DNA, determine what they do, and examine how the human genome is regulated (Pennisi, 2005; Maher, 2012; The ENCODE Project Consortium, 2012).

The current results of the ENCODE project are far too numerous to mention here. But some of the most important results include the discovery that as much as 80 percent of the human genome is involved in some form of biochemical function.

That estimate may be high and most of the biochemical functions have not been identified. In fact, some of them are probably not even important. But some of these activities include the manufacture of noncoding RNA (RNA that is not involved in protein synthesis but that regulates gene function), and binding sites where regulatory proteins attach. In short, some of what used to be called "junk DNA" is active in gene regulation. It is also of great interest that many regulatory factors have been shown to be involved in disease, including autoimmune conditions such as rheumatoid arthritis, Crohn's disease, and multiple sclerosis (Maurano et al., 2012). This discovery will radically alter future approaches to the diagnosis and treatment of genetically caused diseases.

The ENCODE project has determined that at least 9 percent (and probably much more) of the human genome has regulatory functions. It has also determined that the regulation of protein-coding genes is more complex and has evolved more quickly in humans than in most other species. Moreover, evolution occurs more rapidly in regulatory elements. These facts may partly explain the accelerated pace of evolutionary change in modern humans compared to that of other animals. Ultimately the detailed understanding of how gene regulation works will revolutionize how we view evolutionary processes. The focus of many genetic and evolutionary studies will shift away from protein-coding genes and toward regulatory elements. The factors that regulate gene activity in embryonic development are also the basis of evolutionary change. It follows that if we are going to reveal the secrets of our evolutionary past, we must first examine how DNA function is regulated in the present. Certainly the term "junk DNA" will be laid to rest.

How Do We Know?

DNA technology is commonly featured in fictional television shows, such as *Bones* and *CSI*. In addition, shows about forensic science and news programs routinely feature cases where DNA analysis has aided in solving crimes. From this chapter, we learned that DNA is the tie that binds all life-forms. Within our species, DNA between individuals is 99.9 percent identical! Based on this information, you may wonder how DNA can be used to solve crimes. The answer lies in the 0.1 percent difference between individuals. Forensic DNA specialists focus on regions of the genome that show high levels of variation between individuals. These variations occur as repeated sections of DNA in the noncoding regions of the genome, which tend to vary in length between individuals. Short tandem repeats (STRs), which occur as two to five repeating nucleotides, are used for DNA-based forensic identifications. The FBI requires a match at 13 STR locations to identify an individual as the source of a biological sample from a crime scene (for example, blood, semen, saliva), to establish paternity, or to identify a deceased person. When a sample matches an individual at all 13 regions, the likelihood of a false match is often one in several billion or trillion. DNA technology has been instrumental not only in solving recent crimes, but also in solving "cold cases" where biological evidence retained from past crimes can still be tested. DNA analysis has also been instrumental in large-scale identification efforts, such as in the terrorist attacks at the World Trade Center on September 11, 2001, and in the identification of victims of genocide from past conflicts, such as the Balkan Wars (1992–1995). Additionally, DNA testing on historic and prehistoric remains can be used to examine relationships between past populations or individuals and also between modern and ancient populations.

What Do You Think?

DNA technology has revolutionized our understanding of genetic variation and evolution, as well as our ability to solve criminal cases. Can you think of a recent example reported in the news that used DNA analysis to help solve a criminal case? What new advances in forensic DNA technology are likely to occur over the next decade? ■

Summary of Main Topics

- Cells are the fundamental units of life, and in multicellular organisms, there are basically two types. Somatic cells make up body tissues, while gametes (eggs and sperm) are reproductive cells that transmit genetic information from parents to offspring.

- Genetic information is contained in the DNA molecule, found in the nucleus of cells and in mitochondria. The DNA molecule is capable of replication, or making copies of itself. Replication makes it possible for daughter cells to receive a full complement of DNA (contained in chromosomes). DNA also controls protein synthesis by directing the cell to arrange amino acids in the proper sequence for each protein. Also involved in the process of protein synthesis is another, similar molecule called RNA.

- Genes are sequences of DNA bases that specify the order of amino acids in an entire protein, a portion of a protein, or any functional product. About 98 percent of our DNA doesn't actually code for protein production. Some noncoding sequences, called introns, are contained within genes. Introns are initially transcribed into mRNA but are then deleted before the mRNA leaves the cell nucleus. Genes are important to our understanding of evolution since they reflect biological relationships among organisms and are the tie that binds together all life forms.

- There are many genes that regulate the function of other genes. One class of regulatory genes, the homeobox genes, directs the development of the overall body plan. Other regulatory genes turn genes on and off. A high percentage of non-protein-coding DNA is involved in gene regulation. In fact, humans have more regulatory DNA than any other species so far studied.

- Sickle-cell anemia is an inherited genetic disorder. It results from a point mutation that causes a substitution of one amino acid for another. Its prevalence is influenced by natural selection, especially in certain environments where the mutation has an advantage.

- Cells multiply by dividing and when they do, the DNA within them is visible microscopically in the form of chromosomes. In humans, there are 46 chromosomes (23 pairs). If the full complement isn't precisely distributed to succeeding generations of cells, there can be serious consequences. Somatic cells divide during growth or tissue repair or to replace old worn-out cells. Somatic cell division is called mitosis. A cell divides one time to produce two daughter cells, each possessing a full and identical set of chromosomes. Sex cells are produced when specialized cells in the ovaries and testes divide during meiosis. Unlike mitosis, meiosis is characterized by two divisions that produce four nonidentical daughter cells, each containing only half the amount of DNA (23 chromosomes).

- The study of genetics is important in physical anthropology today because it provides a global perspective on modern human variation, allows us to understand past migration events and relationships among the world's populations, allows us to analyze DNA in fossil hominins, and helps to solve criminal cases.

Critical Thinking Questions

1. Before you read this chapter, were you aware that the DNA in your body is structurally the same as that in all other organisms? Do you see this fact as having potential to clarify some of the many questions we still have regarding biological evolution? Why?

2. Do you think proteins are exactly the same in all species? If not, how do you think they would differ in terms of their composition, and why might these differences be important to biological anthropologists?

3. How can regulatory genes, especially *Hox* genes, play an important role in biological evolution?

4. What are the major differences between somatic and sex cell division? Why are these processes so important?

Heredity and Evolution

The Genetic Principles Discovered by Mendel

Segregation

Dominance and Recessiveness

Independent Assortment

Mendelian Inheritance in Humans

Misconceptions about Dominance and Recessiveness

Patterns of Mendelian Inheritance

Non-Mendelian Inheritance

Polygenic Inheritance

Mitochondrial Inheritance

Pleiotropy

Genetic and Environmental Factors

Modern Evolutionary Theory

The Modern Synthesis

A Current Definition of Evolution

Factors That Produce and Redistribute Variation

Mutation

Gene Flow

Genetic Drift and Founder Effect

Natural Selection Is Directional and Acts on Variation

Review of Genetics and Evolutionary Factors

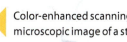

Color-enhanced scanning electron microscopic image of a stem cell.

3D4Medical/Science Source; Top Middle Image: Biophoto Associates/Science Source

Student Learning Objectives   After studying the material in this chapter, you should be able to:

▶ Explain the principles of inheritance, first discovered by Gregor Mendel.

▶ Describe how dominant and recessive traits are inherited, how these modes of inheritance differ from each another, and their relevance to the study of genetic disorders in humans.

▶ Describe the differences between polygenic inheritance, mitochondrial inheritance, and pleiotropy. Explain the relevance of each form of inheritance.

▶ Explain the interaction between environment and genotype in producing the phenotype.

▶ Summarize the modern theory of evolution (that is, the Modern Synthesis).

▶ Discuss how mutation, genetic drift, gene flow, and natural selection interact over time to produce evolutionary change in populations and species.

▶ Discuss how natural selection works and why there must be genetic variation in a population for natural selection to occur. You should also be able to provide some examples of natural selection in humans.

▶ Provide an example of multiple evolutionary processes working together to influence a genetic trait.

Have you ever had a cat with five, six, or even seven toes? Even if you haven't, you may have seen one, because extra toes are fairly common in cats. Or, maybe you've known someone with an extra finger or toe, because some people have extra digits too. Anne Boleyn, mother of England's Queen Elizabeth I and the first of Henry VIII's wives to lose her head, apparently had at least part of an extra little finger. (Of course, this had nothing to do with her early demise; that's another story.)

▶ Figure 4-1
(**a**) Hand of a person with polydactyly.
(**b**) Front foot of a polydactylous cat.

iStockphoto.com/Stocksnapper
Melanie Beasley

Having extra digits (fingers and toes) is called *polydactyly*, and it's pretty certain that one of Anne Boleyn's parents was also polydactylous (Fig. 4-1). It's also likely that any polydactylous cat has a parent with extra toes. But how do we know this? Actually, it's fairly simple. We know it because polydactyly is inherited in a predictable way. Its pattern of inheritance was discovered 150 years ago by a monk named Gregor Mendel, and thus referred to as a Mendelian trait (Fig. 4-2).

For at least 10,000 years, people have raised domesticated plants and animals. However, it wasn't until the twentieth century that scientists understood *how* **selective breeding** could increase the frequency of desirable characteristics. From the time when ancient Greek philosophers considered the question of how traits were inherited until well into the nineteenth century, the most common belief was that the traits seen in offspring resulted from the *blending* of parental traits. There were different explanations of how this happened, but numerous scholars, including Charles Darwin, accepted some aspects of this explanation focused on blending.

selective breeding A practice whereby animal or plant breeders choose which individual animals or plants will be allowed to mate based on the traits (such as coat color or body size) they hope to produce in the offspring. Animals or plants that don't have the desirable traits aren't allowed to breed.

akg-images/Newscom

▶ Figure 4-2
Portrait of Gregor Mendel.

The Genetic Principles Discovered by Mendel

It may seem strange that, after discussing recent discoveries about DNA, we now turn our attention to the middle of the nineteenth century, but that's when the science of genetics was born. By examining how the basic principles of inheritance were discovered, we can more easily understand them. It wasn't until Gregor Mendel (1822–1884) considered the question of heredity that it began to be resolved. Mendel was living in an abbey in what is now the Czech Republic. At the time he began his research, he'd already studied botany at the University of Vienna. He had also performed various experiments in the monastery gardens, and this background led him to investigate how physical traits, such as color or height, could be expressed in plant **hybrids**.

Mendel worked with garden peas (*Pisum sativum*), concentrating on seven different traits (Fig. 4-3). Mendel's selection of this self-pollinating plant species was fortuitous in that each trait could be expressed in one of two ways. You may think it's unusual to discuss peas in an anthropology book, but they provide a simple example of the basic rules of inheritance. The principles Mendel discovered apply to all biological organisms, including humans, another fact that illustrates biological connections among all living things.

Trait Studied	Dominant Form		Recessive Form	
Seed shape		round		wrinkled
Seed color		yellow		green
Pod shape		inflated		wrinkled
Pod color		green		yellow
Flower color		purple		white
Flower position		along stem		at tip
Stem length		tall		short

◀ **Figure 4-3**
The traits Mendel studied in peas.

hybrids Offspring of parents who differ from each other with regard to certain traits or certain aspects of genetic makeup; also known as heterozygotes.

Segregation

First, Mendel grew groups of pea plants that were different from one another with regard to at least one trait. For example, in one group all the plants were tall, while in another all were short. To see how the expression of height would change from one generation to the next, he crossed tall plants with short plants, calling them the *parental* generation. According to traditional views, all the hybrid offspring, which he called the *F₁ generation*, should have been intermediate in height. But they weren't. Instead they were all tall (Fig. 4-4).

Next, Mendel let the F₁ plants self-fertilize to produce a second generation (the F₂ generation). But this time, only about three quarters of the offspring were tall; the remaining one quarter were short. One expression (short) of the trait (height) had completely disappeared in the F₁ generation and then reappeared in the F₂ generation. Moreover, the expression that was present in all the F₁ plants was more common in the F₂ plants, occurring in a ratio of approximately 3:1 (three tall plants for every short one).

These results suggested that different expressions of a trait were controlled by discrete *units* (we would call them genes), which occur in pairs, and that offspring inherit one unit from each parent. Mendel realized that the members of a pair of units that control a trait somehow separate into different sex cells and are again united with another member during fertilization of the egg. This is Mendel's *first principle of inheritance,* known as the **principle of segregation**.

▶ **Figure 4-4**
Results of crosses when only one trait (height) at a time is considered.

principle of segregation Genes (alleles) occur in pairs because chromosomes occur in pairs. During gamete formation, the members of each pair of alleles separate, so that each gamete contains one member of each pair.

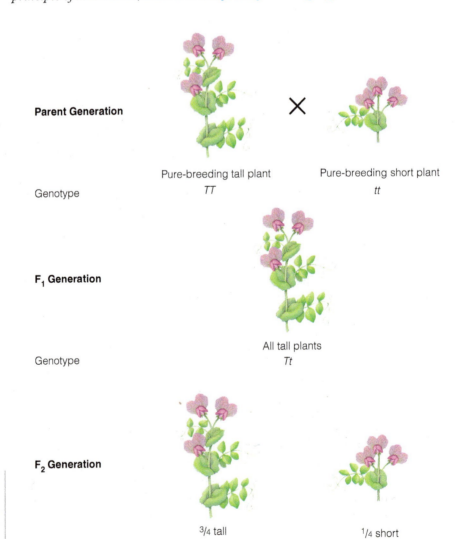

Parent Generation

Pure-breeding tall plant   Pure-breeding short plant
Genotype   *TT*   *tt*

F₁ Generation

All tall plants
Genotype   *Tt*

F₂ Generation

¾ tall   ¼ short
Genotypes   *TT* or *Tt*   *tt*

Today we know that meiosis explains Mendel's principle of segregation. During meiosis, paired chromosomes, and the genes they carry, separate from each other and end up in different gametes. However, in the zygote, the full complement of chromosomes is restored, and both members of each chromosome pair are present in the offspring.

Dominance and Recessiveness

Mendel also realized that the "unit" for the absent characteristic (shortness) in the F_1 plants hadn't actually disappeared. It was still there, but for some reason it wasn't expressed. Mendel described the expression that seemed to be lost as "**recessive**," and the expressed trait "**dominant**." Thus, the principles of *dominance* and *recessiveness* were developed, and they remain important concepts in genetics today.

As it turns out, height in garden peas is controlled by two different alleles at the same genetic locus; we'll call it the height locus. The allele that specifies tall is dominant to the allele for short. (It's worth mentioning that height isn't controlled this way in all plants.) In Mendel's experiments, all the parent plants had two copies of the same allele, either dominant or recessive, depending on whether they were tall or short. When two copies of the same allele are present, the individual is said to be **homozygous**. Thus all the tall parent plants were homozygous for the dominant allele and all the short parent plants were homozygous for the recessive allele. This explains why crossing tall plants with tall plants produced only tall offspring. Likewise, all the crosses between short plants produced only short offspring. All the plants in the parent generation had the same allele—that is, they lacked genetic variation at the height locus. However, all the F_1 plants (hybrids) inherited one allele from each parent plant: a tall allele from one parent and a short allele from the other. Therefore they all inherited two different alleles at the height locus. Individuals that have two different alleles at a locus are **heterozygous**.

Figure 4-5 illustrates the crosses that Mendel initially performed. By convention, letters that represent alleles or genes are italicized, with uppercase letters referring to dominant alleles (or dominant traits) and lowercase letters referring to recessive alleles (or recessive traits). Therefore,

T = the allele for tallness
t = the allele for shortness

The same symbols are combined to describe an individual's actual genetic makeup, or **genotype**. The term *genotype* usually refers to the alleles at a specific genetic locus in an organism. Thus the genotypes of the plants in Mendel's experiments were

TT = homozygous tall plants
Tt = heterozygous tall plants
tt = homozygous short plants

Figure 4-5 also shows the different ways alleles can be combined when the F_1 plants are self-fertilized to produce an F_2 generation. Therefore the figure shows all the *genotypes* that are possible in the F_2 generation and, statistically speaking, it shows that we would expect one quarter of the F_2 plants to be homozygous dominant (TT), half to be heterozygous (Tt), and the remaining one quarter to be homozygous recessive (tt).

You can also see the proportions of F_2 **phenotypes**, the observed physical manifestations of genes, illustrating why Mendel saw approximately three tall plants for every short plant in the F_2 generation. One quarter of the F_2 plants are tall because

recessive Describing a trait that isn't expressed in heterozygotes; it also refers to the allele that governs the trait. For a recessive allele to be expressed, an individual must have two copies of it (i.e., the individual must be homozygous).

dominant In genetics, describing a trait governed by an allele that's expressed in the presence of another allele (i.e., in heterozygotes). Dominant alleles prevent the expression of recessive alleles in heterozygotes. (This is the definition of *complete* dominance.)

homozygous Having the same allele at the same locus on both members of a pair of chromosomes.

heterozygous Having different alleles at the same locus on members of a pair of chromosomes.

genotype The genetic makeup of an individual. Genotype usually refers to an organism's genetic makeup (or alleles) at a particular locus.

phenotypes The observable or detectable physical characteristics of an organism; the detectable expressions of genotypes, frequently influenced by environmental factors.

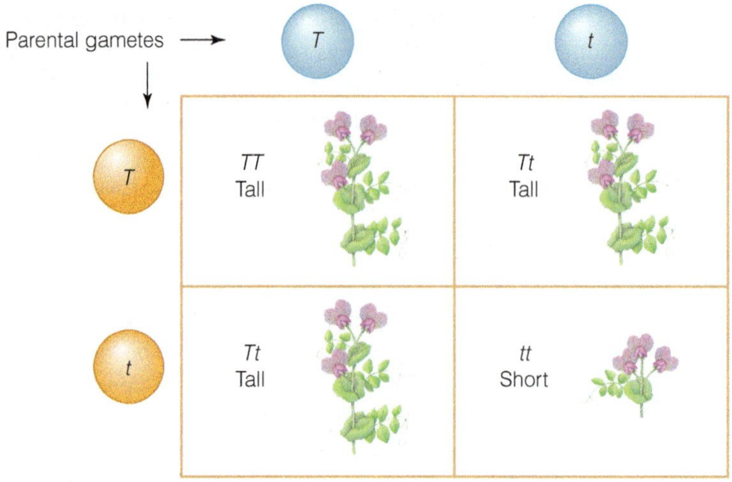

Parental gametes ⟶

▲ **Figure 4-5**

Punnett square representing possible genotypes and phenotypes and their proportions in the F$_2$ generation. The circles across the top and at the left of the Punnett square represent the gametes of the F$_1$ parents. Each square receives one allele from the gamete above it and another from the gamete to the left. Thus the square at the upper left has two dominant (*T*) alleles. Likewise the upper right square receives a recessive (*t*) allele from the blue gamete above it and a dominant (*T*) allele from the orange gamete to its left. In this way, the four squares illustrate that, statistically, one quarter of the F$_2$ plants can be expected to be homozygous tall (*TT*); another half of the plants can also be expected to be tall but will be heterozygous (*Tt*); and the remaining quarter can be expected to be short because they are homozygous for the recessive "short" allele (*tt*). Thus, three quarters of the plants can be expected to be tall and one quarter short.

they have the *TT* genotype. Furthermore, an additional half, which are heterozygous (*Tt*), are also tall because *T* is dominant to *t*, so it's expressed in the phenotype. The remaining one quarter are homozygous recessive (*tt*), and they're short because no dominant allele is present. It's important to understand that the *only* way a recessive allele can be expressed is if it occurs with another recessive allele—that is, if the individual is homozygous recessive at the particular locus in question.

Independent Assortment

Mendel also demonstrated that different characteristics aren't necessarily inherited together by showing that plant height and seed color are independent of each other. That is, any tall pea plant has a 50-50 chance of producing either yellow or green peas. Because of this fact, he developed the **principle of independent assortment**. According to this principle, the units (genes) that code for different traits (in this example, plant height and seed color) sort out independently of each other during gamete formation (Fig. 4-6). Today we know that this happens because the genes that control plant height and seed color are located on different, nonpartner chromosomes and, during meiosis, the chromosomes travel to newly forming cells independently of one another in a process called **random assortment**.

But if Mendel had used just *any* two traits, his results would have been different at least some of the time. This is because genes on the same chromosome aren't independent of each other, and they usually stay together during meiosis. Even though Mendel didn't know about chromosomes, he certainly knew that all characteristics weren't independent of one another. But because he wanted to emphasize independence, he reported only on those traits that illustrated independent assortment.

principle of independent assortment The distribution of one pair of alleles into gametes does not influence the distribution of another pair. The genes controlling different traits are inherited independently of one another.

random assortment The chance distribution of chromosomes to daughter cells during meiosis. Along with recombination, random assortment is an important source of genetic variation (but not new alleles).

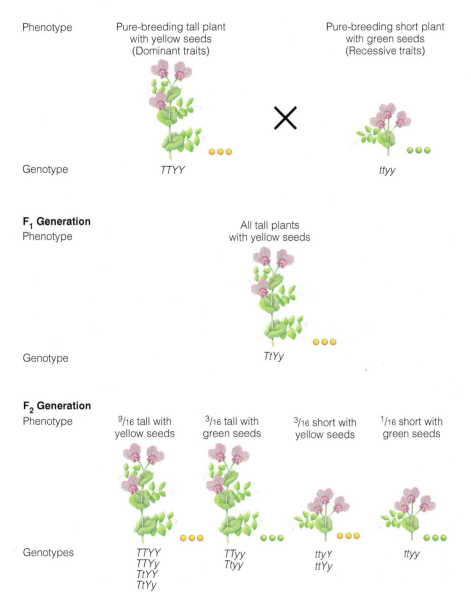

Phenotype — Pure-breeding tall plant with yellow seeds (Dominant traits) X Pure-breeding short plant with green seeds (Recessive traits)

Genotype — *TTYY*   *ttyy*

F₁ Generation
Phenotype — All tall plants with yellow seeds

Genotype — *TtYy*

F₂ Generation
Phenotype — ⁹/₁₆ tall with yellow seeds   ³/₁₆ tall with green seeds   ³/₁₆ short with yellow seeds   ¹/₁₆ short with green seeds

Genotypes —
TTYY
TTYy
TtYY
TtYy

TTyy
Ttyy

ttyY
ttYy

ttyy

◀ **Figure 4-6**
Results of a cross when two traits (height and seed color) are considered simultaneously. These two traits are independent of each other; that is, they aren't necessarily inherited together. Also shown are the genotypes associated with each phenotype. Notice that the ratio of tall plants to short plants is three quarters to one quarter, or 3:1, the same as in Figure 4-4. Likewise, the ratio of yellow seeds to green seeds is 3:1. Thus, the phenotypic ratio in the F₂ generation is 9:3:3:1.

In 1866, Mendel's results were published, but the methodology and statistical nature of the research were beyond the thinking of the time, and their significance was overlooked and unappreciated. But by the end of the nineteenth century, several investigators had made important contributions to the field of biology. For example, chromosomes had been discovered and cell division had been explained. In just 34 years, new discoveries and further hypothesis testing had revised many scientists' views of inheritance. Thus, by 1900, Mendel's work was generally accepted by biologists, who immediately recognized the importance of his research.

Mendelian Inheritance in Humans

Mendelian traits, also called *discrete traits*, are controlled by alleles at only one genetic locus (or, in some cases, two or more very closely linked loci). The most comprehensive listing of Mendelian traits in humans is available on the Internet. *Online Mendelian Inheritance in Man* (www.ncbi.nlm.nih.gov/omim/) currently lists more than 21,000 human characteristics that are inherited according to Mendelian principles.

Mendelian traits Characteristics that are influenced by alleles at only one genetic locus. Examples include many blood types, such as ABO. Many genetic disorders, including sickle-cell anemia and Tay-Sachs disease, are also Mendelian traits.

Although some Mendelian characteristics have readily visible phenotypic expressions (such as polydactyly), most don't. The majority of Mendelian traits are biochemical in nature, and many genetic disorders result from harmful alleles inherited in Mendelian fashion (Table 4-1). So if it seems as though textbooks overly emphasize genetic disease in discussions of Mendelian traits, it's because many of the known Mendelian characteristics result from harmful alleles.

A number of genetic disorders are caused by dominant alleles (see Table 4-1). This means that if a person inherits only one copy of a harmful dominant allele, the condition it causes will be present regardless of the presence of a different, recessive allele on the partner chromosome.

Table 4-1 | Some Mendelian Traits in Humans

Dominant Traits Condition	Manifestations	Recessive Traits Condition	Manifestations
Achondroplasia	Dwarfism due to growth defects involving the long bones of the arms and legs; trunk size usually normal; head enlarged, with a prominent forehead.	Cystic fibrosis	Among the most common genetic (Mendelian) disorders among European Americans; abnormal secretions of the exocrine glands, with pronounced involvement of the pancreas; most patients develop obstructive lung disease. Until the recent development of new treatments, only about half of all patients survived to early adulthood.
Brachydactyly	Shortened fingers and toes.		
Familial hyper-cholesterolemia	Elevated cholesterol levels and cholesterol plaque deposition; a leading cause of heart disease, with death frequently occurring by middle age.		
Neurofibromatosis	Symptoms range from the appearance of abnormal skin pigmentation to large tumors resulting in severe deformities; in extreme cases can lead to paralysis, blindness, and death.	Tay-Sachs disease	Most common among Ashkenazi Jews; degeneration of the nervous system beginning at about 6 months of age; lethal by age 2 or 3 years.
Marfan syndrome	The eyes and cardiovascular and skeletal systems are affected; symptoms include greater than average height, long arms and legs, eye problems, and enlargement of the aorta; death due to rupture of the aorta is common. Abraham Lincoln may have had Marfan syndrome.	Phenylketonuria (PKU)	Inability to metabolize the amino acid phenylalanine; results in mental impairment if left untreated during childhood; treatment involves strict dietary management and some supplementation.
Huntington disease	Progressive degeneration of the nervous system accompanied by dementia and seizures; age of onset variable but commonly between 30 and 40 years.	Albinism	Inability to produce normal amounts of the pigment melanin; results in very fair, untannable skin, light blond hair, and light eyes; may also be associated with vision problems. (There is more than one form of albinism.)
Camptodactyly	Malformation of the hands whereby the fingers, usually the little finger, is permanently contracted.	Sickle-cell anemia	Abnormal form of hemoglobin (Hb^S) that results in collapsed red blood cells, blockage of capillaries, reduced blood flow to organs, and, without treatment, death.
Hypodontia of upper lateral incisors	Upper lateral incisors are absent or only partially formed (peg-shaped). Pegged incisors are a partial expression of the allele.	Thalassemia	A group of disorders characterized by reduced or absent alpha or beta chains in the hemoglobin molecule; results in severe anemia and, in some forms, death.
Cleft chin	Dimple or depression in the middle of the chin; less prominent in females than in males.		
PTC tasting	The ability to taste the bitter substance phenylthiocarbamide (PTC). Tasting thresholds vary, suggesting that alleles at another locus may also exert an influence.	Absence of permanent dentition	Failure of the permanent dentition to form. The primary dentition is not affected.

Recessive conditions are commonly associated with the lack of a substance, usually an enzyme (see Table 4-1). For a person actually to have a recessive disorder, he or she must have two copies of the recessive allele causing it. People who have only one copy of a harmful recessive allele are unaffected. But even though they don't actually have the recessive condition, they can still pass the allele that causes it on to their children. For this reason they're frequently called *carriers*. (Remember, half their gametes will carry the recessive allele.) If such a person's mate is also a carrier, it's possible for them to have a child who will be homozygous for the allele, and that child will be affected. In fact, in a mating between two carriers, the risk of having an affected child is 25 percent (refer back to Fig. 4-5).

Blood groups, such as the ABO system, provide some of the best examples of Mendelian traits in humans. The ABO system is governed by three alleles, *A*, *B*, and *O*, found at the *ABO* locus on the ninth chromosome. These alleles determine a person's ABO blood type by coding for the production of molecules called **antigens** on the surface of red blood cells. If only antigen A is present, the blood type (phenotype) is A; if only B is present, the blood type is B; if both are present, the blood type is AB; and when neither is present, the blood type is O (Table 4-2).

The *O* allele is recessive to both *A* and *B*; therefore if a person has type O blood, he or she must have two copies of the *O* allele. However, since both *A* and *B* are dominant to *O*, an individual with blood type A can actually have one of two genotypes: *AA* or *AO*. The same is true of type B, which results from the genotypes *BB* and *BO* (see Table 4-2). However, type AB presents a slightly different situation, called **codominance**, where two different alleles are present and both are expressed. Therefore when both *A* and *B* alleles are present, both A and B antigens can be detected on the surface of red blood cells.

Misconceptions about Dominance and Recessiveness

Most people have the impression that dominance and recessiveness are all-or-nothing situations. This misconception especially pertains to recessive alleles. The general view is that when these alleles occur in carriers (heterozygotes), they have no effect on the phenotype; that is, they are completely inactivated by the presence of another (dominant) allele. Certainly this is how it appeared to Gregor Mendel.

However, various biochemical techniques available today show that many recessive alleles actually do have some effect on the phenotype, although these effects aren't usually detectable through simple observation. It turns out that in heterozygotes, the products of many recessive alleles are reduced but not completely eliminated. Therefore our perception of recessive alleles greatly depends on whether we examine them at the directly observable phenotypic level or the biochemical level.

There are also a number of misconceptions about dominant alleles. Many people think of dominant alleles as somehow "stronger" or "better," and there is always the

Table 4-2	ABO Genotypes and Associated Phenotypes	
Genotypes	**Antigens on Red Blood Cells**	**ABO Blood Type (Phenotype)**
AA, AO	A	A
BB, BO	B	B
AB	A and B	AB
OO	None	O

antigens Large molecules found on the surface of cells. Several different loci govern various antigens on red and white blood cells. (Foreign antigens provoke an immune response.)

codominance The expression of two alleles in heterozygotes. In this situation, neither allele is dominant or recessive, so they both influence the phenotype.

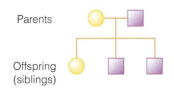

▲ Figure 4-7
Typical symbols used in pedigree charts. Circles and squares represent females and males respectively. Horizontal lines connecting two individuals indicate mating. Vertical lines connect generations.

▲ Figure 4-8
Ellie Simmonds, who has achondroplasia, won two gold medals for Great Britain in swimming events at both the 2008 and 2012 Paralympic Games. She inherited one copy of the dominant allele that causes achondroplasia by inhibiting bone growth during fetal development. As a result, her legs and arms are disproportionally short. People with achondroplasia are also unable to fully extend their arms—something that has not inhibited her swimming abilities.

pedigree chart A diagram showing family relationships. It's used to trace the hereditary pattern of particular genetic (usually Mendelian) traits.

mistaken notion that dominant alleles are more common in populations because natural selection favors them. These misconceptions undoubtedly stem from the label "dominant" and its connotations of power or control. But in genetic usage, this view is misleading. Just think about it. If dominant alleles were always more common, then a majority of people would have conditions such as achondroplasia and Marfan syndrome (see Table 4-1). But obviously that's not true.

Previously held views of dominance and recessiveness were influenced by available technologies, and as genetic technologies continue to change, new theories will emerge and our perceptions will be further altered. (This is another example of how new techniques and continued hypothesis testing can lead to a revision of hypotheses and theories.) In fact, although dominance and recessiveness will remain important factors in genetics, it's clear that the ways in which these concepts will be taught will be adapted to accommodate new discoveries.

Patterns of Mendelian Inheritance

It's important to be able to establish the pattern of inheritance of genetic traits, especially those that cause serious disease. Also, in families with a history of inherited disorders, it's important to determine an individual's risk of inheriting harmful alleles or expressing symptoms. The technique traditionally used to assess risk of genetic disease has been the construction of a **pedigree chart**, a diagram of matings and offspring in a family over the span of a few generations. Pedigree analysis helps researchers determine if a trait is Mendelian and also helps establish the mode of inheritance. By determining whether the gene that influences a particular trait is located on an autosome or sex chromosome and whether a particular allele is dominant or recessive, researchers have identified six different modes of Mendelian inheritance in humans: *autosomal dominant, autosomal recessive, X-linked recessive, X-linked dominant, Y-linked,* and *mitochondrial.* We'll discuss the first three in some detail.

Standardized symbols are used in pedigree charts. Squares and circles represent males and females, respectively. Horizontal lines connecting individuals indicate matings, and offspring are connected to horizontal mating lines by vertical lines. Siblings are joined by a horizontal line connected to a vertical line that descends from the parents (Fig. 4-7).

Autosomal Dominant Traits As the term implies, autosomal dominant traits are governed by dominant alleles located on autosomes (that is, any chromosome except X or Y). One example of an autosomal dominant trait is achondroplasia, a form of dwarfism characterized by a normal-sized trunk and head but shortened arms and legs (see Table 4-1 and Fig. 4-8). Achondroplasia occurs in approximately 1 out of every 10,000 live births. It is usually caused by a spontaneous point mutation in a gene that influences the development of cartilage and thus bone growth.

Because achondroplasia is caused by a dominant allele, anyone who inherits just one copy of it will have the trait. In this discussion, the symbol *A* refers to the dominant allele that causes the condition and *a* represents the recessive, normal allele. Since the allele is rare, virtually everyone who has achondroplasia is a heterozygote (*Aa*). Unaffected individuals (that is, almost everybody) are homozygous recessive (*aa*).

Figure 4-9 is a partial pedigree chart for achondroplasia. It's apparent from this pedigree that all affected members have at least one affected parent, so the condition doesn't skip generations. This pattern is true for all autosomal dominant traits. Another characteristic of autosomal dominant traits is that males and females are more or less equally affected. Also important regarding dominant

Gareth Copley/Getty Images

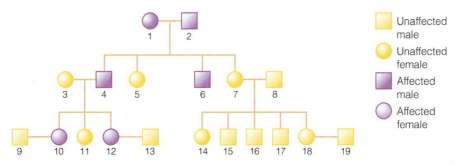

▲ Figure 4-9

Inheritance of an autosomal dominant trait as illustrated by a human pedigree for achondroplasia. How can individuals 5, 7, 11, 14, 15, 16, 17, and 18 be unaffected? What is the genotype of all affected individuals? (To answer the second question, let A = the dominant allele and a = the recessive allele.)

traits is that approximately half the offspring of affected parents are also affected (Fig. 4-10). This proportion is what we would predict for an autosomal dominant trait where only one parent is affected, because half of that parent's gametes will have the dominant but harmful allele.

Autosomal Recessive Traits   Autosomal recessive traits are also influenced by genes on autosomes, but they show a different pattern of inheritance. A good example is shown in Figure 4-11, a pedigree chart for albinism. The most common form of albinism is a metabolic disorder caused by an autosomal recessive allele that prevents the production of a pigment called melanin (see Chapter 15). Thus albinos have unusually light hair, skin, and eyes (Fig. 4-12). The frequency of this type of albinism varies widely among populations, with a prevalence of about 1 in 37,000 people of European ancestry; but approximately 1 in 200 Hopi Indians are affected.

Pedigrees for autosomal recessive traits show obvious differences from those for autosomal dominant characteristics. For one thing, an affected offspring can be

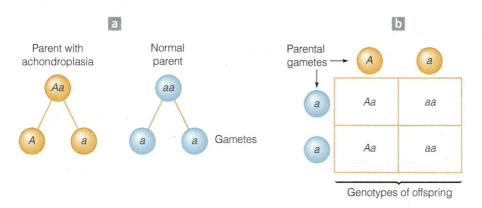

▲ Figure 4-10

The pattern of inheritance of autosomal dominant traits is the direct result of the distribution of chromosomes and the alleles they carry into gametes during meiosis. (**a**) A diagram of possible gametes produced by two parents, one with achondroplasia and another with normal development of the extremities. The achondroplastic individual can produce two types of gametes: half with the dominant allele (A) and half with the recessive allele (a). All gametes produced by the normal-height parent will carry the recessive allele. (**b**) A Punnett square depicting the possible genotypes in the offspring of one parent with achondroplasia (Aa) and one with normal extremities (aa). Statistically, we would expect half the offspring to have the Aa genotype and thus have achondroplasia. The other half would be homozygous recessive (aa) and their extremities would grow normally.

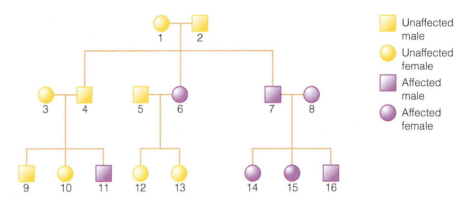

▲ **Figure 4-11**

Partial pedigree for albinism, an autosomal recessive trait. Why are some of the offspring of affected individuals unaffected? Individuals 6 and 7, children of unaffected parents, are affected. Why? Four individuals are definitely unaffected carriers. Which ones are they? Why is individual 11 affected when his parents aren't?

▲ **Figure 4-12**

(**a**) A Tanzanian woman with her young albino son. (**b**) This albino horse may be beautiful, but it should not be kept outdoors all the time. With virtually no pigmentation, it would be highly susceptible to sunburn and various forms of skin cancer, including melanoma.

produced by two phenotypically normal parents. In fact, most people who express recessive conditions have unaffected parents. In addition, the proportion of affected offspring from most matings is less than half. But when both parents have the trait, all their offspring will be affected. As in the pattern for autosomal dominant traits, males and females are equally affected.

The Mendelian principle of segregation explains the pattern of inheritance of autosomal recessive traits. In fact, this pattern is the very one Mendel first described in his pea experiments (look back at Fig. 4-5). Unaffected parents who produce an albino child *must both be carriers*, and their child will be homozygous for the recessive allele causing the abnormality. The Punnett square in Figure 4-13 shows how such a mating produces both unaffected and affected offspring in predictable proportions—the typical *phenotypic ratio* of 3:1.

Sex-Linked Traits Sex-linked traits are controlled by genes located on the X and Y chromosomes. Almost all of the more than 1,000 sex-linked traits listed in *Online Mendelian Inheritance in Man* are influenced by genes on the X chromosome (Table 4-3). Most of the coding sequences (that is, those segments that actually specify a protein) on the Y chromosome are involved in determining maleness and testis function.

Hemophilia, one of the best known of the X-linked traits, is caused by a recessive allele on the X chromosome. This allele prevents the formation of a clotting factor in the blood, and affected individuals suffer bleeding episodes and may actually bleed to death from injuries that most of us would consider trivial.

The most famous pedigree illustrating this condition is that of Queen Victoria (1820–1901) of England and her descendants (Fig. 4-14). The most striking feature shown by this pattern of inheritance is that almost all affected people are males, because males have only one X chromosome and therefore only one copy of X-linked genes. This means that *any allele*, even a recessive one, located on their X chromosome will be expressed, because there's no possibility of a dominant allele

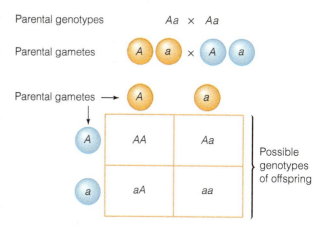

▲ **Figure 4-13**

A cross between two phenotypically normal parents, both carriers of the albinism allele. From a mating such as this between two carriers, statistically we would expect the following possible proportions of genotypes and phenotypes in the offspring: homozygous dominants (*AA*) with normal phenotype, 25 percent; heterozygotes, or carriers (*Aa*) with normal phenotype, 50 percent; and homozygous recessives (*aa*) with albinism, 25 percent. This yields the phenotypic ratio of three with normal pigmentation to one albino.

Table 4-3	Levels of Organization in the Evolutionary Process			
Evolutionary Factor	**Level**	**Evolutionary Process**	**Technique of Study**
Mutation	DNA	Storage of genetic information; ability to replicate; influences phenotype by production of proteins	Biochemistry, recombinant DNA
Mutation	Chromosomes	A vehicle for packaging and transmitting genetic material (DNA)	Light or electron microscope
Recombination (sex cells only)	Cell	The basic unit of life that contains the chromosomes and divides for growth and for production of sex cells	Light or electron microscope
Natural selection	Organism	The unit, composed of cells, that reproduces and that we observe for phenotypic traits	Visual study, biochemistry
Drift, gene flow	Population	A group of interbreeding organisms; changes in allele frequencies between generations; it's the population that evolves	Statistical analysis

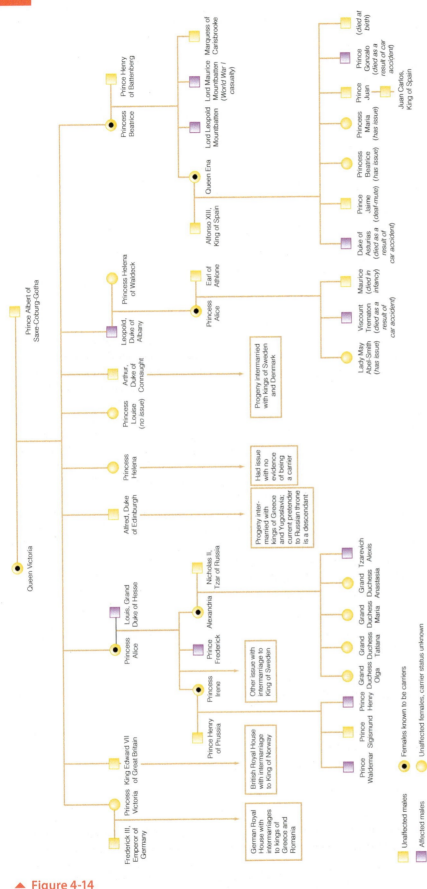

▲ Figure 4-14
Pedigree for Queen Victoria and some of her descendants, showing the inheritance of hemophilia, an X-linked recessive trait in humans.

on a partner chromosome to block it. Females, on the other hand, show the same pattern of expression of X-linked traits as for autosomal traits, because they have two X chromosomes. That is, just as with any other pair of chromosomes, the only way an X-linked recessive allele can be expressed in a female is if she has two copies of it. However, females who have one copy of the hemophilia allele are carriers, and they may have some tendency toward bleeding, even though they aren't severely affected.

Non-Mendelian Inheritance

In addition to discrete phenotypic traits that are inherited in a Mendelian (that is, dichotomous) manner, there are a number of traits that are inherited through other mechanisms. These include polygenic inheritance, mitochondrial inheritance, and pleiotropy.

Polygenic Inheritance

Mendelian traits are described as *discrete*, or *discontinuous*, because their phenotypic expressions don't overlap; instead, they fall into clearly defined categories (Fig. 4-15a). For example, in the ABO system, the four phenotypes are completely distinct from one another; that is, there is no intermediate form between type A and type B. In other words, Mendelian traits don't show *continuous* variation.

However, many traits do have a wide range of phenotypic expressions, which form a graded series. These are called **polygenic**, or *continuous*, traits (Fig. 4-15b and c). While Mendelian traits are governed by only one genetic locus, polygenic characteristics are governed by alleles at two or more loci, and each locus has some influence on the phenotype. Throughout the history of biological anthropology, the most frequently discussed examples of polygenic inheritance in humans have been skin, hair,

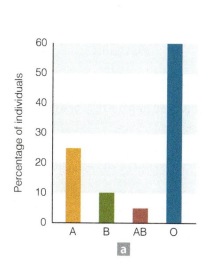

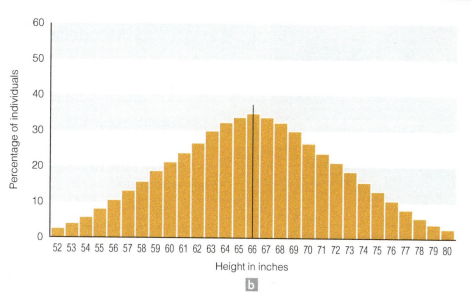

5′3″ 5′4″ 5′5″ 5′6″ 5′7″ 5′8″ 5′9″ 5′10″ 5′11″ 6′0″ 6′1″ 6′2″ 6′3″ 6′4″ 6′5″
Height (feet/inches)

c

Courtesy of Ray Carson, University of Florida News and Public Affairs

▲ **Figure 4-15**

(**a**) This bar graph shows the discontinuous distribution of a Mendelian trait (ABO blood type) in a hypothetical population. Expression of the trait is described in terms of frequencies. (**b**) This histogram represents the continuous expression of a polygenic trait (height) in a large group of people. Notice that the percentage of extremely short or tall individuals is low; most people are closer to the mean, or average height, represented by the vertical line at the center of the distribution. (**c**) A group of male students arranged according to height. The most common height is 70 inches, which is the mean, or average, for this group.

and eye color (Fig. 4-16). The "At a Glance" on page 96 outlines the main differences between Mendelian and polygenic traits.

Coloration is determined by melanin, a **pigment** produced by specialized cells called melanocytes (see Chapter 16), and the amount of melanin that is produced determines how dark or light a person's skin will be. Melanin production is influenced by interactions between several different loci that have now been identified. A study by Lamason and colleagues (2005) showed that one single, highly *conserved* gene (called *MC1R*) with two alleles makes a greater contribution to melanin production than some other melanin-producing genes. Moreover, geneticists know of at least four other pigmentation genes. This is very important because they can now examine the complex interactions between these genes and also how their functions are influenced by regulatory genes. So the story of melanin production is a complicated one, but it's exciting that many long-standing questions about variation in human skin color will be answered in the not too distant future.

polygenic Referring to traits influenced by genes at two or more loci. Examples include stature, skin color, eye color, and hair color. Many polygenic traits are influenced by environmental factors such as nutrition and exposure to sunlight.

pigment In this context, molecules that influence the color of skin, hair, and eyes.

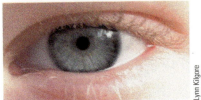

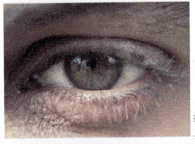

Lynn Kilgore

Robert Jurmain

▲ **Figure 4-16**

Eye color is a polygenic characteristic and is a good example of continuous variation.

At a Glance	Mendelian vs. Polygenic Traits

Mendelian Traits	**Polygenic Traits**
Influenced by one gene	Influenced by more than one gene
Expression not usually influenced by environment	Expression may be influenced by environment
Distribution of phenotypes into just a few discrete categories (e.g., in complete dominance with two alleles, there are just two phenotypes)	Distribution of phenotypes is continuous with no discrete categories (many phenotypes can be distinguished)

As we stated earlier, eye color is influenced by more than one gene, and some of the genes that influence skin color are also involved. However, a gene called *OCA2*, located on chromosome 15, is apparently the most important gene in the development of blue eyes (Fig. 4-16). *OCA2* is involved in pigmentation of the iris of the eye, and mutations in this gene lead to a form of albinism. Sturm and colleagues (2008) demonstrated that this gene accounts for 74 percent of the variation in human eye color in European populations. (Northern European populations and their descendants exhibit more variability in eye color than is seen in any other human populations, and they're the only ones in which significant numbers of people have blue eyes.) Moreover, specific variations of the *OCA2* gene were found in virtually 100 percent of blue-eyed people from Denmark, Turkey, and Jordan. In addition, point mutations in one of several genes that regulate *OCA2* are also "perfectly associated" with blue eyes (Eiberg et al., 2008). Thus when we examine any trait, we must look not only at the genes traditionally associated with it but *also at the DNA sequences that regulate it.* Indeed, it's looking more and more like genes don't really do much by themselves; they just follow orders, and if the orders vary, their effects will also vary.

Polygenic traits actually account for most of the readily observable phenotypic variation in humans, and they've traditionally served as a basis for racial classification. In addition to skin, hair, and eye color, there are many other polygenic characteristics—including stature, shape of the face, and fingerprint pattern—to name a few. Because they exhibit continuous variation, most polygenic traits can be measured on a scale composed of equal increments. For example, height (stature) is measured in feet and inches (or meters and centimeters). If we were to measure height in a large number of individuals, the distribution of measurements would continue uninterrupted from the shortest extreme to the tallest (see Fig. 4-15b and c). That's what is meant by the term *continuous traits.*

Because polygenic traits can usually be measured, physical anthropologists can analyze them using certain statistical tests. The use of simple summary statistics, such as the *mean* (average) or *standard deviation* (a measure of variation within a group), permits basic descriptions of populations and comparisons between them. For example, a physical anthropologist might be interested in average height in two different populations, whether or not differences between the two are statistically significant, and if so, why. (Incidentally, *all* physical traits measured and statistically treated in fossils are polygenic in nature.)

Mendelian traits can't be measured in the same way because they're either present or absent—expressed one way or another. But this doesn't mean that they provide less information about genetic processes. They can be described in terms of frequency within populations, which makes it possible to compare groups for differences in prevalence. For example, one population may have a high frequency of blood type A while type A may be almost completely absent in another group. Also, Mendelian traits can be analyzed for mode of inheritance (dominant or recessive).

Last, for many Mendelian traits, the approximate or exact positions of genetic loci are known, which makes it possible to examine the mechanisms and patterns of inheritance at these loci. This type of study isn't yet possible for polygenic traits because they're influenced by several genes that are only now being traced to specific loci.

Mitochondrial Inheritance

Another component of inheritance involves the organelles called *mitochondria* (see Chapter 3). All cells contain several hundred of these oval-shaped structures, which convert energy (derived from the breakdown of nutrients) to a form that can be used to perform cellular functions.

Each mitochondrion contains several copies of a ring-shaped DNA molecule, or chromosome. While *mitochondrial DNA (mtDNA)* is distinct from chromosomal DNA, its molecular structure and functions are the same. The entire molecule has been sequenced and is known to contain around 40 genes that direct the conversion of energy within the cell.

Like the DNA in a cell's nucleus, mtDNA is subject to mutations, some of which cause certain genetic disorders resulting from impaired energy conversion. Importantly, animals of both sexes inherit all their mtDNA, and thus the expression of all mitochondrial traits, from their mothers. Because mtDNA is inherited from only one parent, meiosis and recombination do not occur. This means that all the variation in mtDNA among individuals is caused by mutation, which makes mtDNA extremely useful for studying genetic change over time. So far, geneticists have used mutation rates in mtDNA to investigate evolutionary relationships between species, to trace ancestral relationships within the human lineage, and to study genetic variability among individuals and/or populations. While these techniques are still being refined, it's clear that we have a lot to learn from mtDNA.

Pleiotropy

While polygenic traits are governed by the actions of several genes, **pleiotropy** is a situation where a single gene influences more than one characteristic. Although this might seem unusual, pleiotropic effects are probably the rule rather than the exception.

The autosomal recessive disorder phenylketonuria (PKU) provides one example of pleiotropy (see Table 4-1). Individuals who are homozygous for the *PKU* allele don't produce the enzyme involved in the initial conversion of the amino acid *phenylalanine* to another amino acid, *tyrosine*. Because of this block in the metabolic pathway, phenylalanine breaks down into substances that accumulate in the central nervous system; without dietary management, these substances lead to mental deficiencies and several other consequences. Tyrosine is ultimately converted to several other substances, including the pigment melanin; therefore numerous other systems can also be affected. Thus another manifestation of PKU, owing to a diminished ability to produce melanin, is that affected people usually have blue eyes, fair skin, and light hair. There are many examples of pleiotropic genes, including the allele that causes sickle-cell anemia. Thus the action of one gene can influence a number of seemingly unrelated traits.

pleiotropy A situation where the action of one gene affects several different traits.

Genetic and Environmental Factors

By now you may have the impression that phenotypes are entirely the expressions of genotypes; but that's not true. (Here the terms *genotype* and *phenotype* are used in a broader sense to refer to an individual's *entire* genetic makeup and *all* observable or detectable characteristics.) Genotypes set limits and potentials for development, but they also interact with the environment, and many (but not all) aspects of the phenotype are influenced by this genetic-environmental interaction. For example, adult stature is influenced by both genes and the environment. Even though the maximum height a person can achieve is genetically determined, childhood nutrition and health status (both environmental factors) are also important. Other important environmental factors include exposure to sunlight, altitude, temperature, and both toxic waste and airborne pollutants, which unfortunately are increasing almost everywhere. These and many other factors contribute in complex ways to the continuous phenotypic variation seen in traits governed by several genetic loci. However, for many characteristics, it's not possible to identify the *specific* environmental components that influence the phenotype.

Mendelian traits are less likely to be influenced by environmental factors. For example, ABO blood type is determined at fertilization and remains fixed throughout an individual's lifetime, regardless of diet, exposure to ultraviolet radiation, temperature, and so forth.

Mendelian and polygenic inheritance show different patterns of phenotypic variation. In the former, variation occurs in discrete categories, while in the latter, it's continuous. However, it's important to understand that even for polygenic characteristics, Mendelian principles still apply at individual loci. In other words, if a trait is influenced by six loci, each one of those loci may have two or more alleles, with some perhaps being dominant to others. It's the combined action of the alleles at all six loci, interacting with the environment, that produces the phenotype.

Modern Evolutionary Theory

By the beginning of the twentieth century, the foundations for evolutionary theory had already been developed. Darwin and Wallace had described natural selection 40 years earlier, and the rediscovery of Mendelian genetics in 1900 contributed the other major component: a mechanism for inheritance. We might expect that these two basic contributions would have been combined into a consistent theory of evolution, but they weren't. For the first 30 years of the twentieth century, some scientists argued that mutation was the main factor in evolution, while others emphasized natural selection. What they really needed was a merger of the two views rather than an either-or situation, but this didn't happen until the mid-1930s.

The Modern Synthesis

In the late 1920s and early 1930s, biologists realized that mutation and natural selection weren't opposing processes: They *both* contributed to biological evolution. The two major foundations of the biological sciences were finally brought together in what is called the **Modern Synthesis**. From such a "modern" (that is, the middle of the twentieth century onward) perspective, evolution is defined as a two-stage process:

Modern Synthesis A synthesis of multiple lines of evidence to integrate Mendelian genetics and natural selection within evolutionary theory.

1. The production and redistribution of **variation** (inherited differences among organisms)
2. *Natural selection* acting on this variation, whereby inherited differences, or variations, among individuals differentially affect their ability to successfully reproduce

A Current Definition of Evolution

As we discussed in Chapter 2, Darwin saw evolution as the gradual unfolding of new varieties of life from preexisting ones. Certainly this is one result of the evolutionary process. But these long-term effects can come about only through the accumulation of many small genetic changes occurring over the generations. Today we can demonstrate how evolution works by examining some of the small genetic changes seen in populations and how they increase or decrease in frequency. From this perspective, we define evolution as *a change in* **allele frequency** *from one generation to the next.*

Allele frequencies are indicators of the genetic makeup of a **population**, the members of which share a common **gene pool**. To show how allele frequencies change, we'll use a simplified example of an inherited trait, again the ABO blood types. (*Note*: There are several blood groups, not just the ABO system, and they're all controlled by different genes.)

Let's assume that the students in your anthropology class represent a population and that we've determined everyone's ABO blood type. (To be considered a population, individuals must choose mates more often from *within* the group than from outside it. Obviously your class won't meet this requirement, but we'll overlook that.) The proportions of the *A*, *B*, and *O* alleles are the allele frequencies for this trait. If 50 percent of all the *ABO* alleles in your class are *A*, 40 percent are *B*, and 10 percent are *O*, the frequencies of these alleles are *A* = .50, *B* = .40, and *O* = .10.

Since the frequencies of these alleles represent proportions of a total, it's obvious that allele frequencies can refer only to groups of individuals, or populations. Individuals don't have allele frequencies; they have either *A*, *B*, or *O* in any combination of two. Also, from conception onward, a person's genetic makeup is fixed.* If you start out with blood type A, you will always have type A. Therefore only a population can evolve over time; individuals can't.

Assume that 20 years from now we calculate the frequencies of the *ABO* alleles for the offspring of our classroom population and find the following: *A* = .30, *B* = .40, and *O* = .30. We can see that the relative proportions have changed: *A* has decreased, *O* has increased, and *B* has remained the same. This would not be a big deal, but in a biological sense, minor changes such as this constitute evolution. Over the short span of just a few generations, changes in the frequencies of inherited traits may be very small; but if they continue to happen, and particularly if they go in one direction as a result of natural selection, they can produce new adaptations and even new species.

Whether we're talking about the short-term effects (as in our classroom population) from one generation to the next, which is sometimes called **microevolution**, or the long-term effects through time, called speciation or **macroevolution**, the basic evolutionary mechanisms are similar. But how do allele frequencies change? Or, to put it another way, what causes evolution? As we've already said, evolution is a two-stage process. Genetic variation must first be produced by mutation, so that natural selection can then act upon it.

---

*Although a person's genetic makeup is determined at conception, certain environmental factors, over time, can alter gene expression. However the nucleotide sequences themselves remain the same.

variation In genetics, inherited differences among individuals; the basis of all evolutionary change.

allele frequency In a population, the percentage of all the alleles at a locus accounted for by one specific allele.

population Within a species, a group of individuals where mates are usually found.

gene pool All of the genes shared by the reproductive members of a population.

microevolution Small changes occurring within species, such as changes in allele frequencies.

macroevolution Changes produced only after many generations, such as the appearance of a new species.

Factors That Produce and Redistribute Variation

Mutation

You've already learned that a mutation is a change in DNA. There are many kinds of mutations, but here we focus on point mutations, or substitutions of one DNA base for another. (Actually, alleles are the results of point mutations.) Point mutations must occur in sex cells if they're to have evolutionary consequences. This is because in order for evolutionary change to occur, the mutation must be passed from one generation to the next. If a mutation takes place in a person's somatic cells but not in gametes, it won't be passed on to offspring. If, however, a genetic change occurs in the sperm or egg of one of the students in our classroom (*A* mutates to *B*, for instance), the offspring's blood type will be different from that of the parent, causing a minute shift in the allele frequencies of the next generation.

Actually, except in microorganisms, it's rare for evolution to take place solely because of mutations. Mutation rates for any given trait are usually low, so we wouldn't really expect to see a mutation at the *ABO* locus in a population as small as your class. In larger populations, mutations might be observed in 1 individual out of 10,000, but by themselves they would have no impact on allele frequencies. However, when mutation is combined with natural selection, evolutionary changes can occur more rapidly.

It's important to remember that mutation is the basic creative force in evolution, since it's the *only* way to produce *new* genes (that is, variation). Its role as the ultimate source of all new genetic variation is key to the first stage of the evolutionary process.

In Chapter 3, we discussed the importance to the evolutionary process of mutations in regulatory genes. We also mentioned that many DNA sequences contain variable numbers of certain segments called *copy number variants* (CNVs) (see "A Closer Look: Noncoding DNA—Not Junk After All" in Chapter 3). Individuals and species have different numbers of certain segments within their genes, and these differences influence a gene's overall effect. When CNVs occur in regulatory genes, particularly those involved in development, they can cause dramatic phenotypic changes.

CNVs occur as a result of deletions or duplications of DNA segments within a gene. **Tandem repeats** are a type of duplication that has attracted a great deal of attention in recent years because they have much higher mutation rates than single alleles do and therefore could have a significant influence on rates of evolution. In one study, Fondon and Garner (2004) examined the relationship between tandem repeats in regulatory genes and phenotypic expression. Among other things, they showed how a tandem repeat in a regulatory gene involved in bone growth has dramatically influenced the shape of the cranium of bull terriers (Fig. 4-17).

The changes in bull terrier crania are the results of artificial selection for a specific trait (the long drooping snout), influenced by variation in a regulatory gene. While this is not speciation, it is dramatic evidence of how tandem repeats in protein-coding genes can produce significant phenotypic variation for natural selection to act on. Indeed, tandem repeats have played, and continue to play, a highly significant role in evolution.

tandem repeats Short, adjacent segments of DNA within a gene that are repeated several times.

gene flow Exchange of genes between populations.

Gene Flow

Gene flow is the exchange of genes between populations. The term *migration* is also sometimes used; but strictly speaking, *migration* refers to the movement of people. In contrast, *gene flow* refers to the exchange of genes between groups, which can

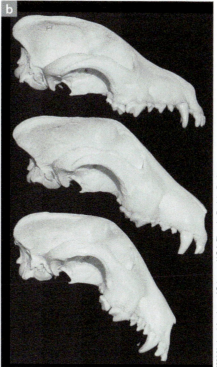

◀ **Figure 4-17**
(**a**) Selective breeding in bull terriers has produced dramatic changes in the shape of the head, resulting in a concave profile and downward-turning nose. (**b**) These three purebred bull terrier crania clearly illustrate how the shape of the head changed in this breed in just 35 years. The dates for the crania, from top to bottom, are 1931, 1950, and 1976. (The 1931 specimen, from a Swiss lab, provided DNA for use in comparisons with modern bull terriers DNA.)

happen only if the migrants interbreed. Also, even if individuals move temporarily and have offspring in the new population, they don't necessarily stay there. For example, the children of U.S. soldiers and Vietnamese women represent gene flow. Even though the fathers returned to the United States after the Vietnam War, some of their genes remained behind, although not in sufficient numbers to appreciably change allele frequencies.

In humans, mating patterns are mostly determined by social factors, and cultural anthropologists can work closely with biological anthropologists to isolate and measure this aspect of evolutionary change. Human population movements (particularly in the last 500 years) have reached previously unheard of proportions, and very few breeding isolates remain. But migration on a smaller scale has been a consistent feature of human evolution since the first dispersal of our genus, and gene flow between populations (even though sometimes limited) helps explain why speciation has been rare during the past million years or so.

An interesting example of how gene flow influences microevolutionary changes in modern human populations is seen in African Americans. African Americans are largely of West African descent, but there has also been considerable genetic admixture with European Americans. By measuring allele frequencies for specific genetic loci, we can estimate the amount of migration of European alleles into the African American gene pool. Data from northern and western U.S. cities (including New York, Detroit, and Oakland) have shown that the proportion of *non*-African genes in the African American gene pool is 20 to 25 percent (Cummings, 2000).

Gene flow occurs for reasons other than large-scale movements of populations. In fact, significant changes in allele frequencies can come about through long-term patterns of mate selection whereby members of a group traditionally obtain mates from certain other groups. This is especially true if mate exchange consistently occurs in one direction over a long period of time. For example, if group A chooses mates from group B but group B doesn't reciprocate, eventually group A will have an increased proportion of group B alleles. If, however, mate exchange

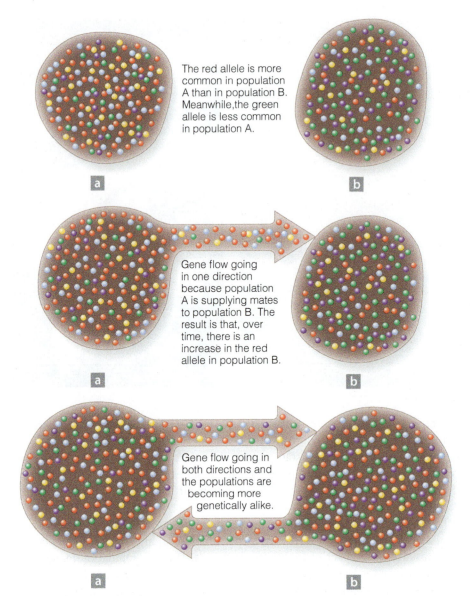

Gene flow. In this illustration, the colored dots represent different alleles and the circles that contain them represent two populations.

between groups is reciprocal, over time the two groups will become more alike genetically (Fig. 4-18).

Genetic Drift and Founder Effect

Genetic drift is the random factor in evolution, and it's a function of population size. *Drift occurs solely because the population is small*. If an allele is rare in a small population, it may disappear because, just by chance, it isn't passed on to offspring (Fig. 4-19a). Thus genetic drift reduces genetic variability in small populations.

One particular kind of genetic drift, called **founder effect**, is seen in many modern human and nonhuman populations. Founder effect can occur when a small band of "founders" leaves its parent group and forms a colony somewhere else. Over time, a new population will be established, and as long as mates are chosen only from within this population, all of its members will be descended from the small original group of founders. Therefore all the genes in the expanding group will have come from the original colonists. In such a case, an allele that was rare in the founders' parent

genetic drift Evolutionary changes, or changes in allele frequencies, produced by random factors in small populations. Genetic drift is a result of small population size.

founder effect A type of genetic drift in which allele frequencies are altered in small populations that are taken from larger populations or are remnants of the latter.

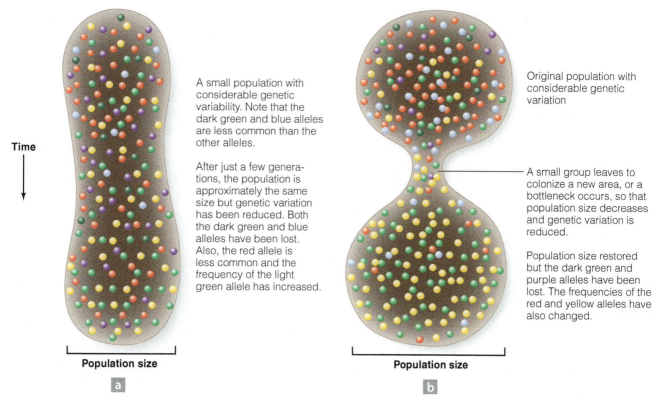

Time ↓

A small population with considerable genetic variability. Note that the dark green and blue alleles are less common than the other alleles.

After just a few generations, the population is approximately the same size but genetic variation has been reduced. Both the dark green and blue alleles have been lost. Also, the red allele is less common and the frequency of the light green allele has increased.

Original population with considerable genetic variation

A small group leaves to colonize a new area, or a bottleneck occurs, so that population size decreases and genetic variation is reduced.

Population size restored but the dark green and purple alleles have been lost. The frequencies of the red and yellow alleles have also changed.

Population size

a

Population size

b

▲ **Figure 4-19**

Small populations are subject to genetic drift, where rare alleles can be lost because, just by chance, they aren't passed to offspring. Also, although more common alleles may not be lost, their frequencies may change for the same reason. (**a**) This diagram represents six alleles (different-colored dots) that occur at one genetic locus in a small population. You can see that in a fairly short period of time (three or four generations), rare alleles can be lost and genetic diversity consequently reduced. (**b**) This diagram illustrates the founder effect, a form of genetic drift where diversity is lost because a large population is drastically reduced in size and consequently passes through a genetic "bottleneck." Founder effect also happens when a small group leaves the larger group and "founds" a new population elsewhere. (In this case, the group of founders is represented by the bottleneck.) Those individuals that survive (the founders) and the alleles they carry represent only a sample of the variation that was present in the original population. And future generations, all descended from the survivors, will therefore have less variability.

population but was carried by even one of the founders can eventually become common among the founders' descendants (Fig. 4-19b). This is because a high proportion of people in later generations will all be descended from that one founder.

Colonization isn't the only way founder effect can happen. Small founding groups may be the survivors of a larger group that was mostly wiped out by some type of disaster. But like the small group of colonists, the survivors possess only a sample of all the alleles that were present in the original population.

Therefore, just by chance alone, some alleles may be completely lost from a population's gene pool while others may become the only alleles at loci that previously had two or more. Whatever the cause, the outcome is a reduction in genetic diversity, and the allele frequencies of succeeding generations may be substantially different from those of the original, larger population. The loss of genetic diversity in this type of situation is called a *genetic bottleneck*, and the effects can be highly detrimental to a species.

There are many known examples (both human and nonhuman) of species or populations that have passed through genetic bottlenecks. (In fact, many

▲ **Figure 4-20**
Cheetahs, like many other species, have passed through a genetic bottle-neck. Consequently they have little genetic variation as a species.

species are going through genetic bottlenecks right now.) Genetically, cheetahs (Fig. 4-20) are an extremely uniform species, and biologists believe that at some point in the past these magnificent cats suffered a catastrophic decline in numbers. For unknown reasons related to the species-wide loss of numerous alleles, male cheetahs produce a high percentage of defective sperm compared with other cat species. Decreased reproductive potential, greatly reduced genetic diversity, and other factors (including human hunting) have combined to jeopardize the continued existence of this species. Other species that have passed through genetic bottlenecks include California elephant seals, sea otters, and condors. Indeed, humans are much more genetically uniform than chimpanzees, and it appears that all modern human populations are the descendants of a few small groups.

One human example of genetic drift is provided by a fatal recessive condition called Amish microcephaly, in which a mutation results in abnormally small brains and heads in fetuses. The disorder is found only in the Old Order Amish community of Lancaster County, Pennsylvania, where it occurs in approximately 1 in 500 births (Kelley et al., 2002; Rosenberg et al., 2002). Genealogical research showed that affected families have all been traced back nine generations to a single couple. One member of this couple carried the deleterious recessive allele that, because of customs promoting marriage within (what was then) a small group, has greatly increased in frequency with very serious consequences.

Another well-studied example of genetic drift and the founder effect comes from the same group of Old Order Amish. As mentioned above, these individuals only marry within the community, which has resulted in an unusually high number of genetic disorders, such as Ellis-van Creveld syndrome (a type of dwarfism often associated with cleft lip or palate, polydactyly, and dental abnormalities). This disorder can be traced to a couple who were part of the original founding population in 1744. As a result of the small breeding population and subsequent genetic drift, the disorder is now overrepresented among the Pennsylvania Amish (McKusick, 2000).

Much insight into the evolutionary factors that have acted in the past can be gained by understanding how such mechanisms continue to operate on human populations today. In small populations, drift plays an important evolutionary role because fairly sudden fluctuations in allele frequency occur solely because of small population size. Likewise, throughout a good deal of human evolution, at least the last 4 to 5 million years, hominins probably lived in small groups, and drift probably had a significant impact.

Additional insight concerning the relative influences of the different evolutionary factors has emerged in recent studies of the early dispersal of modern *Homo sapiens*. Evidence suggests that in the last 100,000 to 200,000 years, our species experienced a genetic bottleneck that considerably influenced the pattern of genetic variation seen in all human populations today.

As we've seen, both gene flow and genetic drift can produce some evolutionary changes by themselves. However, these changes are usually *microevolutionary* ones; that is, they produce changes within species over the short term. To produce the kind of evolutionary changes that ultimately result in new species (for example, the diversification of the first primates or the appearance of the earliest hominins), natural selection is necessary. But natural selection can't operate independently of the other evolutionary factors: mutation, gene flow, and genetic drift.

Table 4-4 | Levels of Organization in the Evolutionary Process

Evolutionary Factor	Level	Evolutionary Process	Technique of Study
Mutation	DNA	Storage of genetic information; ability to replicate; influences phenotype by production of proteins	Biochemistry, recombinant DNA
Mutation	Chromosomes	A vehicle for packaging and transmitting genetic material (DNA)	Light or electron microscope
Recombination (sex cells only)	Cell	The basic unit of life that contains the chromosomes and divides for growth and for production of sex cells	Light or electron microscope
Natural selection	Organism	The unit, composed of cells, that reproduces and that we observe for phenotypic traits	Visual study, biochemistry
Drift, gene flow	Population	A group of interbreeding organisms; changes in allele frequencies between generations; it's the population that evolves	Statistical analysis

Recombination   As we saw in Chapter 3, members of chromosome pairs exchange segments of DNA during meiosis. By itself, recombination doesn't change allele frequencies or cause evolution. However, when paired chromosomes exchange DNA, genes sometimes find themselves in different genetic environments. (It's as if they had moved to a new neighborhood.) This fact can be important because the functions of some genes can be influenced simply by the alleles they're close to. Thus recombination not only changes the composition of parts of chromosomes but can also affect how some genes act, and slight changes of gene function can become material for natural selection to act on. (The levels of organization in the evolutionary process are summarized in Table 4-4.)

Natural Selection Is Directional and Acts on Variation

The evolutionary factors just discussed (mutation, gene flow, genetic drift, and recombination) interact to produce variation and to distribute genes within and between populations. But there is no long-term *direction* to any of these factors, and for adaptation and evolution to occur, a population's gene pool must change in a specific direction. This means that some alleles must consistently become more common while others become less common, and natural selection is the one factor that can cause this kind of directional change in allele frequency *relative to specific environmental factors*. If the environment changes, selection pressures change and allele frequencies shift. Such shifts in allele frequencies are called *adaptation*. This is exactly what we described in the peppered-moth example in Chapter 2.

In humans, the best-documented example of natural selection involves hemoglobin S (*HbS*), an abnormal form of hemoglobin that results from a point mutation in the gene that produces part of the hemoglobin molecule. As you learned in Chapter 3, if an individual inherits the hemoglobin S (*HbS*) allele from both parents, he or she will have sickle-cell anemia. Worldwide, sickle-cell anemia causes an estimated 100,000 deaths each year; in the United States, approximately 40,000 to 50,000 people, mostly of African descent, have this disease (Ashley-Koch et al., 2000).

The *Hb^S* mutation (see Chapter 3) occurs occasionally in all human populations, but usually the allele is rare. However, in some populations, especially in western and central Africa, it's more common than elsewhere, with frequencies as high as 20 percent. The *Hb^S* allele is also fairly common in parts of Greece and India (Fig. 4-21). Given the devastating effects of hemoglobin S in homozygotes, you may wonder why it's so common in some populations. It seems as though natural selection would eliminate it, but it doesn't. In fact, natural selection has actually increased its frequency, and the explanation for this situation can be summed up in one word: malaria.

Malaria is an infectious disease caused by a single-celled parasitic organism known as *Plasmodium* (its genus name). It is transmitted to humans by mosquitoes, and it kills an estimated 1 to 3 million people worldwide every year. After an infected mosquito bite, plasmodial parasites invade red blood cells, where they obtain the oxygen they need for reproduction (Fig. 4-22). The consequences of this infection to the human host include fever, chills, headache, nausea, vomiting, and frequently death. In parts of western and central Africa, where malaria is always present, as many as 50 to 75 percent of 2- to 9-year-olds are afflicted.

In the mid-twentieth century, the geographical correlation between malaria and the distribution of the sickle-cell allele (*Hb^S*) was the only evidence of a biological relationship between the two (Fig. 4-23). But now we know that people (heterozygotes) with **sickle-cell trait** have greater resistance to malaria than people with

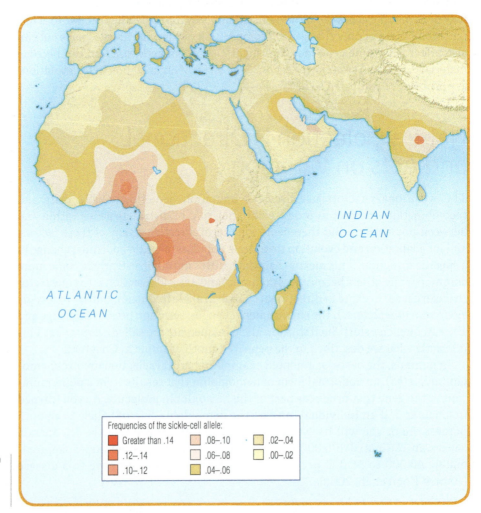

▶ **Figure 4-21**
The distribution of the sickle-cell allele in the Old World.

ATLANTIC OCEAN

INDIAN OCEAN

Frequencies of the sickle-cell allele:

Greater than .14	.08–.10	.02–.04
.12–.14	.06–.08	.00–.02
.10–.12	.04–.06	

sickle-cell trait Heterozygous condition where a person has one *Hb^A* allele and one *Hb^S* allele. Thus they have some normal hemoglobin.

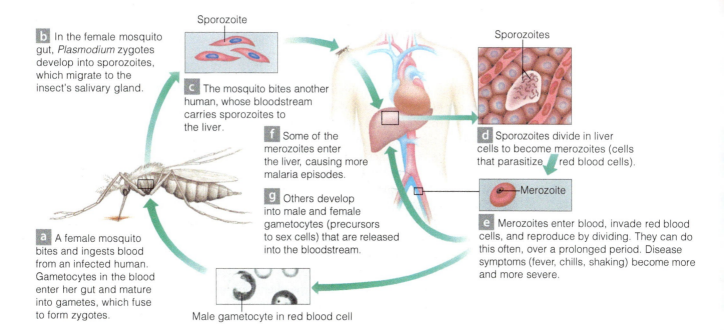

b In the female mosquito gut, *Plasmodium* zygotes develop into sporozoites, which migrate to the insect's salivary gland.

Sporozoite

c The mosquito bites another human, whose bloodstream carries sporozoites to the liver.

f Some of the merozoites enter the liver, causing more malaria episodes.

g Others develop into male and female gametocytes (precursors to sex cells) that are released into the bloodstream.

a A female mosquito bites and ingests blood from an infected human. Gametocytes in the blood enter her gut and mature into gametes, which fuse to form zygotes.

Male gametocyte in red blood cell

Sporozoites

d Sporozoites divide in liver cells to become merozoites (cells that parasitize red blood cells).

Merozoite

e Merozoites enter blood, invade red blood cells, and reproduce by dividing. They can do this often, over a prolonged period. Disease symptoms (fever, chills, shaking) become more and more severe.

▲ **Figure 4-22**
The life cycle of the parasite that causes malaria.

only normal hemoglobin. This is because people with sickle-cell trait have some red blood cells that contain hemoglobin S, and these cells don't provide a suitable environment for the malarial parasite. In other words, having some hemoglobin S is beneficial because it affords some protection from malaria. So in areas where malaria is present, it acts as a selective agent favoring the heterozygous phenotype because people with sickle-cell trait have higher net reproductive success than those with only normal hemoglobin, who often die of malaria. But selection for heterozygotes means that the Hb^s allele will be maintained in the population. Thus there will always be some people with sickle-cell anemia, and they, of course, will have the lowest reproductive success, since most, without treatment, will die before reaching adulthood.

INDIAN OCEAN

ATLANTIC OCEAN

Areas where malaria is present

◀ **Figure 4-23**
The distribution of malaria in the Old World.

Review of Genetics and Evolutionary Factors

In this chapter, discussion focused on how genetic information is passed from one generation to the next. We also reviewed evolutionary theory, emphasizing the crucial role of natural selection. The various levels (molecular, cellular, individual, and populational) are different components of the evolutionary process, and they're related to each other in a way that can eventually produce evolutionary change. A step-by-step example will make this clear.

Consider a population in which almost everyone has hemoglobin A. For all practical purposes, there's almost no variation regarding this trait, and without some source of new variation, evolution is not possible. However, in every generation, a few people carry a spontaneous mutation that changes just one DNA base in the Hb^A gene. This single point mutation, or base substitution, actually creates a new allele (Hb^S) in the DNA sequence, slightly altering the protein product (the hemoglobin molecule) and ultimately the phenotype of the individual. But for the mutated allele to have any evolutionary potential, it must be present in the gametes and transmitted to offspring.

Once a mutation has occurred, it will exist within a chromosome, which, along with other chromosomes, may be inherited by offspring. And if a person has the mutation on only one member of a pair of chromosomes, there's a 50-50 chance that the mutation will be passed on to each child he or she has.

But what does all this have to do with evolution? To repeat an earlier definition, evolution is based on a change in allele frequency in a population from one generation to the next. The key point here is that we are considering populations, because it's the populations that change over time.

We can determine if allele frequencies have changed in a population where sickle-cell hemoglobin is found by determining the percentage of individuals with the Hb^S allele versus those with the normal Hb^A allele. If the relative proportions of these alleles change with time, the population is evolving at the Hb^A locus. But in addition to knowing that evolution is occurring, it's important to know why, and there are several possible explanations. First, the only way the new Hb^S allele could have arisen is by mutation, and we've shown how this can happen in a single individual. But this isn't an evolutionary change, since the alteration of one person's genes in a relatively large population won't change the allele frequencies of the entire population. Somehow, this new allele must *spread* in the population; and in the case of Hb^S, the allele spread because it was favored by natural selection. And the reason it was favored is because it conferred some advantage in an environment where malaria was present.

As you learned earlier, genetic drift can also greatly alter the frequencies of alleles in small populations. Just by chance, some alleles may not be passed on, and after a few generations, they're completely lost. Other alleles, meanwhile, may end up being the only allele at a particular locus. This situation represents a loss of variation in the population.

In the course of human evolution, drift has probably played a significant role; it's important to remember that at this microevolutionary level, drift and/or gene flow can (and will) produce evolutionary change, even in the absence of natural selection. However, such change will be random because natural selection is the only factor that can cause allele frequencies to change in a particular direction.

The way natural selection has worked in the past and still operates today (as with sickle-cell hemoglobin) is through differential net reproductive success. That is, individuals who carry a particular allele or combination of alleles produce more offspring than other individuals with different alleles. Hence if a certain allele is beneficial in a particular environment, its frequency should increase slowly from generation to generation. Likewise alleles that are detrimental should become less common. When this process is compounded over hundreds of generations at numerous loci, the result is significant evolutionary change. The levels of organization in the evolutionary process are summarized in Table 4-3 on page 93.

How Do We Know?

As you learned on pages 87–94, many human disorders are caused by mutations in genes (alleles) at one locus. This has practical implications for many of us who may eventually have to make important life decisions due to a family history of genetic disease. Obviously, the more we know about Mendelian disorders, the better prepared we are to make such decisions.

In Table 4-1 we listed Tay-Sachs disease as an example of an autosomal recessive trait, most commonly seen in Ashkenazi Jews (Jews of eastern European descent). Tay-Sachs is actually a good example of why the inheritance and expression of dominant and recessive characteristics in populations is not as simple as textbooks (including this one) sometimes make it seem.

Tay-Sachs disease is a fatal disorder caused by the lack of an enzyme produced by the *HEXA* gene—an enzyme that breaks down lipids (molecules made of fats and other substances). In the absence of the enzyme, these substances accumulate in the brain. Resulting neurological symptoms usually appear by the age of 6 months and include blindness, deafness, paralysis,

and death, usually before 3 years of age. This description applies to the most common manifestation of the disease, infantile Tay-Sachs disease. The other two forms, juvenile and late onset, are much less common and are caused by other mutations in the *HEXA* gene. In fact there are more than 100 mutations in the gene; all of them affect how the enzyme functions (Kaback, 2000) and they cause different expressions of the disease. But scientists began to be aware of the many different mutations only in the 1970s, and more are still being discovered.

As we stated, infantile Tay-Sachs is most commonly seen in Ashkenazi Jews. But Cajun populations of southern Louisiana also exhibit Tay-Sachs in much higher frequencies than other populations. As it turns out, the cause is the same mutation in both populations. A different mutation causes higher than normal frequencies in French Canadians. In all three groups, founder effect is the principal explanation for the increased frequency of the mutations in the *HEXA* gene. Indeed, researchers have traced the Cajun mutation back to a single couple that lived in France in the eighteenth century (McDowell et al, 1992).

Likewise, French Canadians are mostly descendants of a small founder population. In addition, they tended to marry other French Canadians because they were isolated from the general population by geographic, language, and cultural differences.

As you can see from this one briefly described condition, patterns of genetic disease result from the interactions of several factors. In the case of Tay-Sachs, multiple recessive mutations in one gene have interacted with population movement and social factors to produce the distribution of Tay-Sachs disease we see today.

What Do You Think?

With modern technology, we have the ability to conduct prenatal testing of a fetus for Mendelian diseases, such as Tay-Sachs (tested in umbilical cord blood and amniotic fluid samples). Additionally, parents can be screened to determine the likelihood of having a child with a particular Mendelian disease. What are some of the ethical issues associated with this type of testing? ■

Summary of Main Topics

- In the mid-nineteenth century, a monk named Gregor Mendel discovered the principles of segregation, independent assortment, and dominance and recessiveness by doing experiments with pea plants. Although the field of genetics progressed exponentially during the twentieth century, the concepts first put forth by Mendel remain the basis of our current knowledge of how traits are inherited.
- Basic Mendelian principles are applied to the study of the various modes of inheritance we're familiar with today. The most important factor in all the Mendelian modes of inheritance is the role of segregation of chromosomes and the alleles they carry during meiosis. Mendel's research further provides the basis for our understanding of how and when dominant and recessive traits are expressed.

- Mendelian traits are known as discrete or discontinuous traits because their phenotypic expression does not overlap. Other traits show a wide range of phenotypic expression. Polygenic inheritance involves the action of two or more alleles contributing toward phenotypic expression. In contrast, pleiotropic genes involve a single allele influencing more than one trait. Finally, mitochondrial DNA is only passed down the maternal lineage, and provides a useful means for studying population lineages through time.

- Many phenotypic traits, such as adult stature and body size, reflect the interaction of both genes and environment. These are most commonly polygenic or pleiotropic traits, where environmental factors can play a role in phenotypic expression.

- Building on fundamental nineteenth-century contributions by Charles Darwin and the rediscovery of Mendel's work in 1900, advances in genetics throughout the twentieth century contributed to contemporary evolutionary thought. In particular, the combination of natural selection with Mendel's principles of inheritance and experimental evidence concerning the nature of mutation have all been synthesized into a modern understanding of evolutionary change. In this contemporary theory of evolution, evolutionary change is seen as a two-stage process. The first stage is the production and redistribution of variation. The second stage is the process whereby natural selection acts on the accumulated genetic variation.

- Mutation is crucial to all evolutionary change because it's the only source of completely new genetic material (that is, new alleles), which increases variation. In addition, recombination, genetic drift, and gene flow redistribute variation within individuals (recombination), within populations (genetic drift), and between populations (gene flow).

- Natural selection is the central determining factor influencing the long-term direction of evolutionary change. How natural selection works can best be explained as differential net reproductive success, or how successful individuals are compared to others, in leaving offspring to succeeding generations. The detailed history of the evolutionary spread of the sickle-cell allele provides the best-documented example of natural selection among recent human populations. It must be remembered that evolution is an integrated process, and this chapter concluded with a discussion of how the various evolutionary factors can be integrated into a single comprehensive view of evolutionary change.

- Certain alleles can be selected for or against in a population due to natural selection. Once a mutation is introduced, natural selection may select for *or* against it depending on whether it improves or reduces fitness. Many mutations are considered neutral because they are not under selective pressure.

Critical Thinking Questions

1. If two people with blood type A, both with the *AO* genotype, have children, what *proportion* of their children would be expected to have blood type O? Why? Can these two parents have a child with AB blood? Why or why not?

2. Why are the principles of segregation and independent assortment key to understanding inheritance? How do these principles differ from Darwin's belief in blending inheritance? Sickle-cell anemia is frequently described as affecting only Africans or people of African descent; it's considered a "racial" disease that doesn't affect other populations. How would you explain to someone that this view is wrong?

3. Give some examples of how selection, gene flow, genetic drift, and mutation have acted on populations or species in the past. Try to think of at least one human and one nonhuman example. Why do you think genetic drift might be important to endangered species today?

Evolution results from DNA changes and the action of other evolutionary factors.

Humans are both vertebrates and mammals, and we've shared evolutionary history for millions of years.

Humans are primates and share many biological characteristics with other primates.

Macroevolution: Processes of Vertebrate and Mammalian Evolution

5

How We Connect:
Discovering the Place of
Humans in the Natural World

Principles of Classification

Making Connections:
Constructing Classifications
and Interpreting
Evolutionary Relationships

Comparing Evolutionary
Systematics with Cladistics

An Example of Cladistic Analysis:
The Evolutionary History of Cars
and Trucks

Using Cladistics to Interpret
Organisms

Definition of Species

Interpreting Species and Other
Groups in the Fossil Record

Recognition of Fossil Species

Recognition of Fossil Genera

What Are Fossils
and How Do They Form?

Humans Are Vertebrates:
Distant Connections
through Geological Time

Humans Are Also Mammals:
Closer Connections

Processes of
Macroevolution

Adaptive Radiation

Generalized and Specialized
Characteristics

Working Together:
Microevolution and
Macroevolution

Paleontologists excavating a mammoth skeleton from North America.

Phil Degginger/Alamy; Top Images: Biophoto Associates/
Science Source; © Cengage Learning; Lynn Kilgore

Student Learning Objectives After studying the material in this chapter, you should be able to:

▶ Explain how humans are connected to other organisms through the Linnaean taxonomic system.

▶ Compare and contrast the more traditional classification approach (evolutionary systematics) with that of cladistics.

▶ Explain how species are defined by biologists and how they originate from prior species.

▶ Explain what a fossil is and describe how different kinds of fossils are formed.

▶ Outline the geological time scale for vertebrate evolution and discuss the role of continental drift in shaping the current configuration of species.

▶ Define the major characteristics of mammals, especially those of placental mammals.

▶ Compare macroevolution and microevolution and explain how they are similar and how they differ.

Many people think of paleontology as a pretty dreary subject of interest only to overly serious academics. But have you ever been to a natural history museum— or perhaps to one of the larger, more elaborate toy stores? If so, you may have seen a full-size mock-up of *Tyrannosaurus rex*, one that might even move its head and arms and scream threateningly. These displays are usually encircled by enthralled adults and flocks of noisy, excited children. These same onlookers, however, show almost no interest in the display cases containing fossils of early marine organisms. Yet every trace of early life has a fascinating story to tell.

The study of the history of life on earth is full of mystery and adventure. The bits and pieces of fossils are the remains of once living, breathing animals (some of them extremely large and dangerous). Searching for these fossils in remote corners of the globe—from the Gobi Desert in Mongolia, to the rocky outcrops of Madagascar, to the badlands of South Dakota—is not a task for the faint of heart. Piecing together the tiny clues and ultimately reconstructing what *Tyrannosaurus rex* or a small, 50-million-year-old primate looked like and how it might have behaved is really much like detective work. Sure, it can be serious; but it's also a lot of fun.

In this chapter, we review the evolution of vertebrates—more specifically, mammals. It's important to understand these more general aspects of evolutionary history so that we can place our own species in its proper biological context. *Homo sapiens* is only one of millions of species that have evolved. More than that, people have been around for just an instant in the vast expanse of time that life has existed, and we want to know where we fit in this long and complex story of life on earth. To discover the human connection to other organisms within this incredibly long story, we also discuss some contemporary issues relating to evolutionary theory. In particular, we emphasize concepts relating to large-scale evolutionary processes— that is, *macroevolution* (in contrast to the microevolutionary focus of Chapter 4). The fundamental perspectives reviewed here concern geological history, principles of classification, and the nature of evolutionary change. These perspectives will serve as a basis for topics covered throughout much of the remainder of this book.

How We Connect: Discovering the Place of Humans in the Natural World

There are millions of species living today; if we were to include microorganisms, the total would likely exceed tens of millions. And if we added in the multitudes of species that are now extinct, the total would be staggering—perhaps *hundreds* of millions! Where do we fit in, and what types of evidence do scientists use to answer this question?

Biologists need to deal scientifically with all this diversity. One way to do this is to use a system of **classification** that organizes diversity into categories and at the same time indicates evolutionary relationships.

Multicellular organisms that move about and ingest food are called animals (Fig. 5-1). Within the kingdom Animalia, there are more than 20 major groups called *phyla* (*sing.*, phylum). **Chordata** is one of these phyla; it includes all animals with a nerve cord, gill slits (at some stage of development), and a supporting cord along the back. In turn, most chordates are **vertebrates**—so called because they have a vertebral column. Vertebrates also have a developed brain and paired sensory structures for sight, smell, and balance.

The vertebrates themselves are subdivided into five classes: cartilaginous fishes, bony fishes, amphibians, reptiles/birds, and mammals. We'll discuss mammalian classification later in this chapter.

By putting organisms into increasingly narrow groupings, we organize diversity into categories and also make statements about evolutionary and genetic relationships between species and groups of species. Further dividing mammals into orders makes the statement that, for example, all carnivores (Carnivora) are more closely related to one another than they are to any species placed in another order. Consequently bears, dogs, and cats (Carnivora) are more closely related to one

classification In biology, the ordering of organisms into categories, such as orders, families, and genera, to show evolutionary relationships.

Chordata The phylum of the animal kingdom that includes vertebrates.

vertebrates Animals with segmented, bony spinal columns. Vertebrates include fishes, amphibians, reptiles (including birds), and mammals.

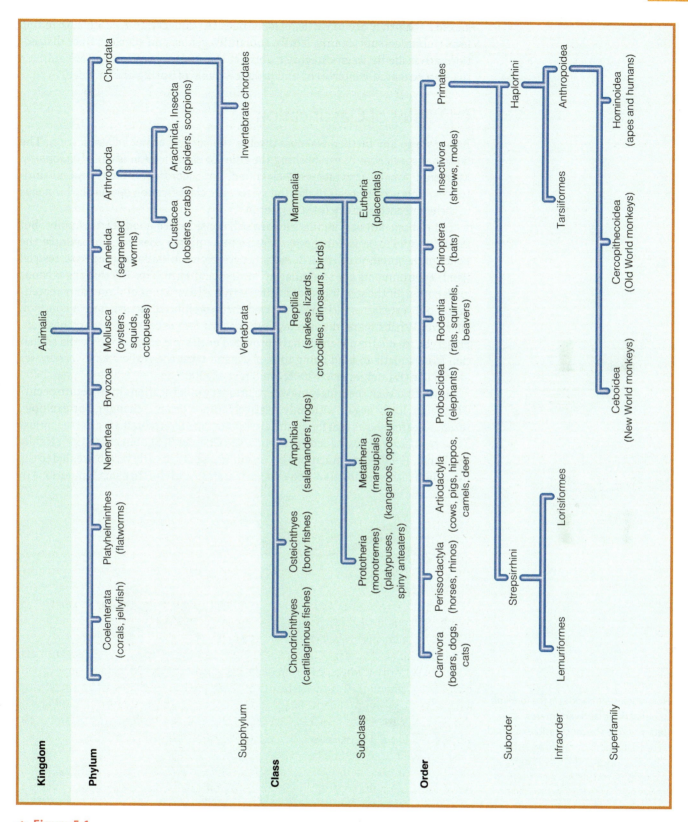

▲ **Figure 5-1**

In this classification chart, modified from Linnaeus, all animals are placed in certain categories based on structural similarities. Not all members of categories are shown; for example, there are up to 20 orders of placental mammals (8 are depicted). Chapter 6 presents a more comprehensive classification of the primate order.

another than they are to cattle, pigs, or deer (Artiodactyla). At each succeeding level (suborder, superfamily, family, subfamily, genus, and species), finer distinctions are made between categories until, at the species level, only those animals that can potentially interbreed and produce viable offspring are included.

Principles of Classification

Before we go any further, we must discuss the basis of animal classification. The field that specializes in establishing the rules of classification is called *taxonomy*. Most traditionally, organisms are classified first according to their physical similarities. This was the basis of the first systematic classification devised by Linnaeus in the eighteenth century (see Chapter 2).

Today, basic physical similarities are still considered a good starting point. But for similarities to be useful, they *must* reflect evolutionary descent. For example, the bones of the forelimb of all air-breathing vertebrates initially adapted to terrestrial (land) environments are so similar in number and form (Fig. 5-2) that the obvious explanation for the striking resemblance is that all four kinds of these "four-footed" (tetrapod) vertebrates ultimately derived their forelimb structure from a common ancestor. What's more, discoveries over the past two decades of remarkably well-preserved fossils from Canada have provided exciting evidence of how the transition from aquatic to land living took place and what the earliest land vertebrates looked like (Daeschler et al., 2006; Shubin et al., 2006).

How could such seemingly major evolutionary modifications in structure occur? They quite likely began with only relatively minor genetic changes. For example, recent research shows that forelimb development in all vertebrates is directed by just a few regulatory genes, called *Hox* genes (see Chapter 3; Shubin et al., 1997; Riddle and Tabin, 1999). A few mutations in certain *Hox* genes in early vertebrates led to the basic limb plan seen in all subsequent vertebrates. With further small mutations in

▶ **Figure 5-2**
Homologies. Similarities in the forelimb bones of these land vertebrates (tetrapods) can be most easily explained by descent from a common ancestor.

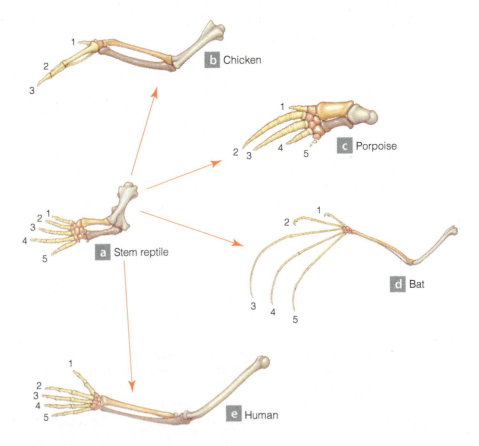

these genes or in the genes they regulate, the varied structures that make up the wing of a chicken, the flipper of a porpoise, or the upper limb of a human developed. You should recognize that *basic* genetic regulatory mechanisms are highly conserved in animals; that is, they've been maintained relatively unchanged for hundreds of millions of years. Like a musical score with a basic theme, small variations on the pattern can produce the various "tunes" that differentiate one organism from another. This is the essential genetic foundation for most macroevolutionary change; it is a crucial point, showing how we quite easily connect biologically with other life-forms and how our and their evolutionary histories are part of the same grand story of life on earth (see "A Closer Look: Evo-Devo: The Evolution Revolution" on pages 118–119).

Structures that are shared by species on the basis of descent from a common ancestor are called **homologies**. Homologies alone are reliable indicators of evolutionary relationship, but we have to be careful not to draw hasty conclusions from superficial similarities. For example, both birds and butterflies have wings, but they shouldn't be grouped together on the basis of this single characteristic; butterflies (as insects) differ dramatically from birds in several other, even more fundamental ways. (For example, birds have an internal skeleton, central nervous system, and four limbs; insects don't.)

Here's what's happened in evolutionary history: From quite distant ancestors, both butterflies and birds developed wings *independently*. So their (superficial) similarities are a product of separate evolutionary responses to roughly similar functional demands. Such similarities, based on independent functional adaptation and not on shared evolutionary descent, are called **analogies**. The process that leads to the development of analogies (also called analogous structures) such as wings in birds and butterflies is termed **homoplasy**.

Making Connections: Constructing Classifications and Interpreting Evolutionary Relationships

Evolutionary biologists typically use two major approaches, or "schools," when they interpret evolutionary relationships with the goal of producing classifications. The first approach, called **evolutionary systematics**, is the more traditional. The second approach, called **cladistics**, emerged primarily in the latter half of the twentieth century. Although aspects of both approaches are still used by most evolutionary biologists, in recent years cladistic methodologies have predominated among evolutionary biologists, including physical anthropologists. Indeed, one noted primate evolutionist commented that "virtually all current studies of primate phylogeny involve the methods and terminology" of cladistics (Fleagle, 1999, p. 1).

Comparing Evolutionary Systematics with Cladistics

Before we begin drawing distinctions between these two approaches, it's first helpful to note features shared by both evolutionary systematics and cladistics. First, both schools are interested in tracing evolutionary relationships and in constructing classifications that reflect these relationships. Second, both schools recognize that organisms must be compared using specific features (called *characters*) and that some of these characters are more informative than others. And third (deriving directly from the previous two points), both approaches focus exclusively on homologies.

But these approaches also have some significant differences—in how characters are chosen, which groups are compared, and how the results are interpreted and

homologies Similarities between organisms based on descent from a common ancestor.

analogies Similarities between organisms based strictly on common function, with no assumed common evolutionary descent.

homoplasy (*homo*, meaning "same," and *plasy*, meaning "growth") The separate evolutionary development of similar characteristics in different groups of organisms.

evolutionary systematics A traditional approach to classification (and evolutionary interpretation) in which presumed ancestors and descendants are traced in time by analysis of homologous characters.

cladistics An approach to classification that attempts to make rigorous evolutionary interpretations based solely on analysis of certain types of homologous characters (those considered to be derived characters).

A Closer Look Evo-Devo: The Evolution Revolution

In Chapter 4, you learned how, in the 1930s, scientists came to a better understanding of evolution once they realized that Mendel's principles and natural selection were both essential components of the process. This merger of ideas was a major step in evolutionary science, and with the discovery of the structure of DNA in 1953, the foundations of evolutionary biology were firmly established.

Almost half a century after the structure of the DNA molecule was revealed, another merger of disciplines occurred (Goodman and Coughlin, 2000). In 1999, the field of evolutionary developmental biology, or evo-devo, emerged through the unification of evolutionary biology with developmental biology. This combination resulted directly from research demonstrating that major evolutionary transformations involve changes in the very same regulatory genes that direct embryological development. The main goals of evo-devo are to discover how animals are put together and how the genes that control their development can, over time, produce new species.

Right now, there are millions of animal species (including insects and marine life), but they probably represent less than 1 percent of all the species that have ever existed on earth (Carroll et al., 2001). In spite of how diverse these species are, they share many anatomical similarities. They're all bilaterally symmetrical, meaning that one side is like the other except for certain aspects of internal organs. Also, and this is important, they all have a modular body plan made up of repeated segments. Arthropods (invertebrates with jointed feet, including all insects, spiders, and crustaceans) have segmented bodies and legs; and many have segmented wings, which are ultimately derived from leg-like appendages (Fig. 1).

Vertebrates also have segmented body parts, and this segmentation begins with the development of the head and vertebral column. Although the number of vertebrae and the number of each type of vertebra vary among species, the spine is made of repeated segments (Fig. 2).

Individual body parts are also modular. In humans, upper arms and thighs have one bone; forearms and lower legs have two; wrists and ankles have eight and seven, respectively; and hands and feet have five digits (see Fig. 5-2 and Appendix A). While snakes, whales, and dolphins don't have legs and feet, they're descended from animals that did. Moreover, some of these species, such as pythons and whales, have skeletal pelvic remnants.

We know that during embryonic development, bodies are formed according to a pattern that characterizes each species; and that pattern is dictated by a species' genome. Because of advances in comparative genomics, we also now know that the coding sequences of even distantly related species are very similar. For example, around 99 percent of mouse genes have a human counterpart (Mouse Genome Sequencing Consortium, 2002). So, what is it that makes us so different from mice?

Until about 25 years ago, biologists thought that changes in protein-coding genes were the key to evolutionary change, but now it's clear that changes in regulatory genes are the real answer to the question of how macroevolution occurs. DNA sequences of regulatory genes don't differ greatly among species; however (and this is key), these genes do differ when it comes to when, where, and how long they function. And these differences lead to major physical differences, because anatomical development depends on genes turning on and off at different times and in different places. There are many different kinds of regulatory genes, and they all instruct cells to make proteins (and different kinds of RNA) that in turn modulate the activity of yet other genes. Regulatory genes can be thought of as switches that turn other genes on or off at specific times in specific parts of the body (Carroll et al., 2008).

Many evolutionary biologists refer to the group of body-building regulatory genes as the *genetic tool kit*. It is highly conserved and is shared by all vertebrates and invertebrates. Through the roughly 600 million years of animal evolution, many of the genes that make up the tool kit have been somewhat changed by mutation and many have duplicated to produce families of genes. But given the amount of time and the huge array of descendant species, changes in the DNA sequences of tool kit genes have been extraordinarily minimal. Consequently, the roughly 10 percent of your genome that consists of regulatory genes has almost exactly

▼ **Figure 1**

The modular body plan of insects is clearly shown in this centipede and sow bug (also known as pill bug, wood louse, and roly poly). Their bodies, legs, and even antennae, are all composed of series of repeated segments.

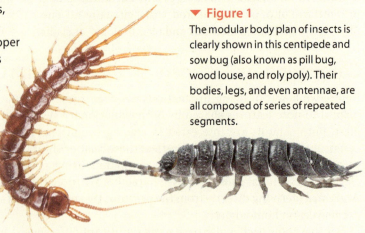

iStockphoto.com/Antagain

iStockphoto.com/Tomasz Zachariasz

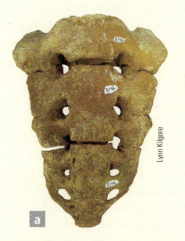

▲ **Figure 2**

Two examples of *Hox* transformations. (**a**) This sacrum, seen from the front, is composed of six vertebrae when there should be only five. This was caused by the malfunction of one of the *Hox* genes involved in the initial patterning of the sacral vertebrae. (**b**) Top view of a sixth lumbar vertebra, the presence of which, in itself, is the result of a *Hox* malfunction. In addition, the left side has the morphology of a first sacral vertebra, and the opening on the right side is typical only of cervical (neck) vertebrae.

the same DNA sequences as the regulatory genes of mice. It goes without saying that the tool kit genes serve as the best example of biological continuity among all animals, living and extinct. You should now be able to appreciate these most basic connections that link all animals, including us, with one another.

The genetic tool kit is composed of genes that make two basic kinds of proteins: *transcription factors* and *signaling molecules*. Here we're focusing on transcription factors, protein molecules that bind to specific DNA segments called *enhancers* or *promoters*. By binding to enhancers, transcription factors switch genes on and off, and they also determine how long those genes produce proteins.

Many transcription factors are produced by homeobox genes. These genes contain a highly conserved region of 180 nucleotides called the homeobox, and this sequence codes for the proteins that bind to enhancers. There are several families of genes that contain homeoboxes; the most familiar one is called *Hox* for short.

As we discussed in Chapter 3, *Hox* genes direct the early stages of embryonic development. Initially, they establish the identity of regions of the body and the pattern of structures along the main body axis that runs lengthwise through the embryo. These structures are actually early precursors to the head and vertebral column. Later in

development, these same genes establish where limb buds will form and also determine limb polarity (that is, front, back, and sides). Mutations in these genes cause the transformation of one body part to another; we've learned about the most famous of these transformations from experiments on fruit flies, in which induced mutations cause all sorts of bizarre phenotypes (such as legs where antennae should be).

Most invertebrates have 10 *Hox* genes, fruit flies have 8, but vertebrates have more. Mammals, for example, have 39, located on four different chromosomes. The reason vertebrates have more *Hox* genes than insects do is that, over time, the invertebrate versions have duplicated in vertebrates. From these observations, we can see that vertebrate *Hox* genes are descended from invertebrate *Hox* genes. Just to illustrate how conserved these genes are, many experiments have shown them to be interchangeable between species. For example, one study showed that fruit flies can function normally with *Hox* proteins derived from chick embryos (Lutz et al., 1996). This remarkable similarity indicates that these genes haven't changed much since fruit flies and chickens last shared a common ancestor some 600 million years ago (Ayala and Rzhetskydagger, 1998).

The science of evo-devo allows us, for the first time, to understand how morphological change and macroevolution can occur through the action of the genes that make up the genetic tool kit. This understanding has been made possible through the recently developed techniques of gene cloning and comparative genomics. By adding the evidence provided by evo-devo to comparative anatomy and fossil studies, scientists are on the threshold of demonstrating how evolution has worked to produce the spectacular biological diversity we see today. The key to this great puzzle is to understand that it all derives from simple beginnings with a set of genes that have been shared by all animals for hundreds of millions of years. As Charles Darwin said in the last paragraph of *Origin of Species*, "There is grandeur in this view of life . . . from so simple a beginning endless forms most beautiful and most wonderful have been, and are being evolved." This quotation has been a favorite of biologists and anthropologists, not only for its eloquence, but also because we've long known that over many millions of years, life-forms have become more complex. For 150 years, we've explained this increased complexity in terms of natural selection, and we still do. But now we have the tools we need to reveal the very mechanism that allowed complexity to develop in the first place.

eventually incorporated into evolutionary schemes and classifications. The primary difference is that cladistics more explicitly and rigorously defines the kinds of homologies that yield the most useful information. For example, at a very basic level, all life (except for some viruses) shares DNA as the molecule underlying all organic processes. However, beyond inferring that all life most likely derives from a single origin, the mere presence of DNA tells us nothing further regarding more specific relationships among different kinds of life-forms. To draw further conclusions, we must look at particular characters that certain groups share as the result of more recent ancestry.

This perspective emphasizes an important point: Some homologous characters are much more informative than others. We saw earlier that all terrestrial vertebrates share homologies in the number and basic arrangement of bones in the forelimb. Even though these similarities are broadly useful in showing that these large evolutionary groups (amphibians, reptiles, and mammals) are all related through a distant ancestor, they don't provide information we can use to distinguish one group from another (a reptile from a mammal, for example). These kinds of characters (also called traits) that are shared through such remote ancestry are said to be **ancestral**, or primitive. We prefer the term *ancestral* because it doesn't reflect negatively on the evolutionary value of the character in question. In biological anthropology, the term *primitive* or *ancestral* simply means that a character seen in two organisms is inherited in both of them from a distant ancestor.

In most cases, analyzing ancestral characters doesn't supply enough information to make accurate evolutionary interpretations of relationships between different groups. In fact, misinterpretation of ancestral characters can easily lead to quite inaccurate evolutionary conclusions. Cladistics focuses on traits that distinguish particular evolutionary lineages; such traits are far more informative than ancestral traits. Lineages that share a common ancestor are called a **clade**, giving the name *cladistics* to the field that seeks to identify and interpret these groups. It is perhaps the most fundamental point of cladistics that evolutionary groups (that is, clades) all share one common ancestor and are thus said to be **monophyletic**. If a proposed evolutionary grouping is found to have more than one ancestor (rather than a single one shared by *all* members), it is said to be **polyphyletic**, and it represents neither a well-defined clade nor an evolutionary group actually separate from other ones. We'll encounter problems of exactly this nature in Chapter 6, when we tackle the classification of a small primate called a tarsier as well as that of the great apes.

When we try to identify a clade, the characters of interest are said to be **derived**, or **modified** relative to their ancestral state. Thus, while the general ancestral bony pattern of the forelimb in land vertebrates doesn't allow us to distinguish among them, the further modification of this pattern in certain groups (as hooves, flippers, or wings, for instance) does.

An Example of Cladistic Analysis: The Evolutionary History of Cars and Trucks

A simplified example might help clarify the basic principles used in cladistic analysis. Figure 5-3a shows a hypothetical "lineage" of passenger vehicles. All of the "descendant" vehicles share a common ancestor, the prototype passenger vehicle. The first major division (I) differentiates passenger cars from trucks. The second split/diversification (II) is between luxury cars and sports cars (you could, of course, imagine many other subcategories). Derived characters that might distinguish trucks from cars could include type of frame, suspension, wheel size, and, in some forms, an open cargo bed. Derived characters that might distinguish sports cars from luxury cars could include engine size and type, wheel base size, and a decorative racing stripe.

---

ancestral Referring to characters inherited by a group of organisms from a remote ancestor and thus not diagnostic of groups (lineages) that diverged after the character first appeared; also called primitive.

clade A group of organisms sharing a common ancestor. The group includes the common ancestor and all descendants.

monophyletic Referring to an evolutionary group (clade) composed of descendants all sharing a common ancestor.

polyphyletic Referring to an evolutionary group composed of descendants with more than one common ancestor (and thus not a true clade).

derived (modified) Referring to characters that are modified from the ancestral condition and thus diagnostic of particular evolutionary lineages.

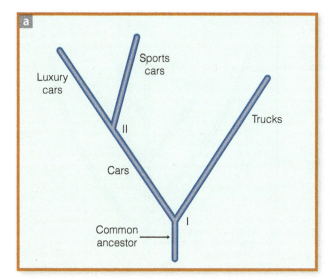
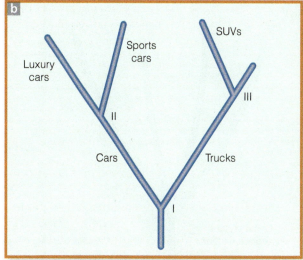

▲ **Figure 5-3**
Evolutionary "trees" showing the development of passenger vehicles.

Now let's assume that you're presented with an "unknown" vehicle (that is, one as yet unclassified). How do you decide what kind of vehicle it is? You might note such features as four wheels, a steering wheel, and a seat for the driver, but these are *ancestral* characters (found in the common ancestor) of all passenger vehicles. If, however, you note that the vehicle lacks a cargo bed and raised suspension (so it's not a truck) but has a racing stripe, you might conclude that it's a car, and more than that, a sports car (since it has a derived feature presumably of *only* that group).

All this seems fairly obvious, and you've probably noticed that this simple type of decision making characterizes much of human mental organization. Still, we frequently deal with complications that aren't so obvious. What if you're presented with a sports utility vehicle (SUV) with a racing stripe (Fig. 5-3b)? SUVs are basically trucks; the presence of the racing stripe could be seen as a homoplasy with sports cars. The lesson here is that we need to be careful, look at several traits, decide which are ancestral and which are derived, and finally try to recognize the complexity (and confusion) introduced by homoplasy.

Our example of passenger vehicles is useful up to a point. Because it concerns human inventions, the groupings possess characters that humans can add and delete in almost any combination. Naturally occurring organic systems are more limited in this respect. Any species can possess only those characters that have been inherited from its ancestor or that have been subsequently modified (derived) from those shared with the ancestor. So any modification in *any* species is constrained by that species' evolutionary legacy—that is, what the species starts out with.

Using Cladistics to Interpret Organisms

Another example, one drawn from paleontological (fossil) evidence of actual organisms, can help clarify these points. Most people know something about dinosaur evolution, and some of you may know about the recent controversies surrounding this topic. There are several intriguing issues concerning the evolutionary history of dinosaurs, and recent fossil discoveries have shed considerable light on them. Here we consider one of the more fascinating questions: the relationship of dinosaurs to birds.

Traditionally, it was thought that birds were a quite distinct group from reptiles and not especially closely related to any of them (including extinct forms, such as the dinosaurs; Fig. 5-4a). Still, the early origins of birds were clouded in mystery and have been much debated for more than a century. In fact, the first fossil evidence of

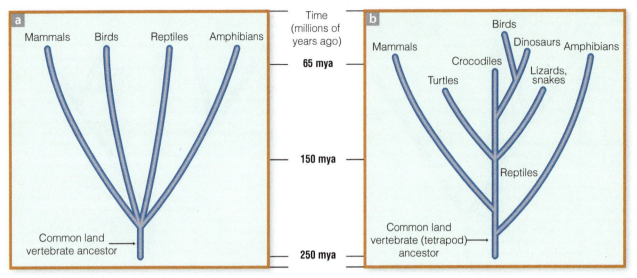

▲ **Figure 5-4**

Evolutionary relationships of birds and dinosaurs. (**a**) Traditional view, showing no close relationship. (**b**) Revised view, showing common ancestry of birds and dinosaurs.

a very primitive bird (now known to be about 150 million years old) was discovered in 1861, just two years following Darwin's publication of *Origin of Species*. Despite some initial and quite remarkably accurate interpretations linking these early birds to dinosaurs, most experts concluded that there was no close relationship. This view persisted through most of the twentieth century. But discoveries made in the last three decades have supported the hypothesis that birds *are* closely related to some dinosaurs. Two developments in particular have influenced this change of opinion: the remarkable discoveries in the 1990s from China, Madagascar, and elsewhere and the application of cladistic methods to the interpretation of these and other fossils. (Here's another example of how new discoveries as well as new approaches can become the basis for changing hypotheses.)

Recent finds from Madagascar of chicken-sized, primitive birds dated to 70–65 mya show an elongated second toe (similar, in fact, to that in the dinosaur *Velociraptor*, made infamous in the film *Jurassic Park*). Indeed, these primitive birds from Madagascar show many other similarities to *Velociraptor* and its close cousins, which together comprise a group of small-to medium-sized ground-living, carnivorous dinosaurs called **theropods**. Even more extraordinary finds have been unearthed recently in China, where the traces of what were once *feathers* have been found embossed in fossilized sediments! For many researchers, these new finds have finally solved the mystery of bird origins (Fig. 5-4b), leading them to conclude that "birds are not only *descended* from dinosaurs, they *are* dinosaurs (and reptiles)—just as humans are mammals, even though people are as different from other mammals as birds are from other reptiles" (Padian and Chiappe, 1998, p. 43).

There are some doubters who remain concerned that the presence of feathers in dinosaurs (145–125 mya) might simply be a homoplasy (that is, these creatures may have developed the trait independently from its appearance in birds). Certainly, the possibility of homoplasy must always be considered, as it can add considerably to the complexity of what seems like a straightforward evolutionary interpretation. Indeed, strict cladistic analysis assumes that homoplasy is not a common occurrence; if it were, perhaps no evolutionary interpretation could be very straightforward! In the case of the proposed relationship between some (theropod) dinosaurs and birds, the presence of feathers looks like an excellent example of a **shared derived** characteristic, which therefore *does* link these lineages. What's more, cladistic analysis emphasizes that several characteristics should be examined, since homoplasy might muddle an interpretation based on just one or two shared traits. In the bird/dinosaur case, several other characteristics further suggest their evolutionary relationship.

theropods Small- to medium-sized ground-living dinosaurs, dated to approximately 150 mya and thought to be related to birds.

shared derived Relating to specific character traits shared in common between two life-forms and considered the most useful for making evolutionary interpretations.

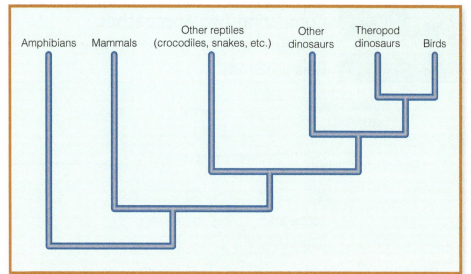

◀ Figure 5-5

This cladogram shows the relationships of birds, dinosaurs, and other terrestrial vertebrates. Notice that there's no time scale, and both living and fossil forms are shown along the same dimension—that is, ancestor-descendant relationships aren't indicated. The chart is slightly simplified, as there are other branches (not shown) within the reptiles (with birds slightly more closely related to crocodiles than to other reptiles, such as snakes and lizards).

One last point must be mentioned. Traditional evolutionary systematics illustrates the hypothesized evolutionary relationships using a *phylogeny*, more properly called a **phylogenetic tree**. Strict cladistic analysis, however, shows relationships in a **cladogram** (Fig. 5-5). If you examine the charts in Figures 5-4 and 5-5, you'll see some obvious differences. A phylogenetic tree incorporates the dimension of time, as shown in Figure 5-4 (you can find many other examples in this and upcoming chapters). A cladogram doesn't indicate time; all forms (fossil and modern) are shown along one dimension. Phylogenetic trees usually attempt to make some hypotheses regarding ancestor-descendant relationships (for example, theropods are ancestral to modern birds). Cladistic analysis (through cladograms) makes no attempt whatsoever to discern ancestor-descendant relationships. In fact, strict cladists are quite skeptical that the evidence really permits such specific evolutionary hypotheses to be scientifically confirmed (because there are many more extinct species than living ones). The "At a Glance" on page 124 compares these two evolutionary approaches to interpreting evolutionary relationships.

In practice, most physical anthropologists (and other evolutionary biologists) utilize cladistic analysis to identify and assess the utility of traits and to make testable hypotheses regarding the relationships between groups of organisms. They also frequently extend this basic cladistic methodology to further hypothesize likely ancestor-descendant relationships shown relative to a time scale (that is, in a phylogenetic tree). In this way, aspects of both traditional evolutionary systematics and cladistic analysis are combined to produce a more complete picture of evolutionary history.

Definition of Species

Whether biologists are doing a cladistic or more traditional phylogenetic analysis, they're comparing groups of organisms—that is, different species, genera (*sing.*, genus), families, orders, and so forth. Fundamental to all these levels of classification is the most basic, the species. It's appropriate, then, to ask how biologists define species. We addressed this issue briefly in Chapter 1, where we used the most common definition, one that emphasizes interbreeding and reproductive isolation. While it's not the only definition of species (others are discussed shortly), this view, called the **biological species concept** (Mayr, 1970), is the one preferred by most zoologists.

phylogenetic tree A chart showing evolutionary relationships as determined by evolutionary systematics. It contains a time component and implies ancestor-descendant relationships.

cladogram A chart showing evolutionary relationships as determined by cladistic analysis. It's based solely on interpretation of shared derived characters. It contains no time component and does not imply ancestor-descendant relationships.

biological species concept A depiction of a species as a group of individuals capable of fertile interbreeding but reproductively isolated from other such groups.

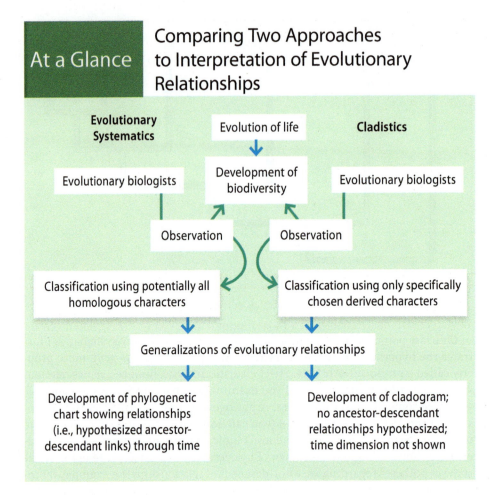

At a Glance

Comparing Two Approaches to Interpretation of Evolutionary Relationships

Evolutionary Systematics

Evolution of life

Cladistics

Evolutionary biologists

Development of biodiversity

Evolutionary biologists

Observation

Observation

Classification using potentially all homologous characters

Classification using only specifically chosen derived characters

Generalizations of evolutionary relationships

Development of phylogenetic chart showing relationships (i.e., hypothesized ancestor-descendant links) through time

Development of cladogram; no ancestor-descendant relationships hypothesized; time dimension not shown

To understand what species are, you might consider how they come about in the first place—what Darwin called the "origin of species." This most fundamental of macroevolutionary processes is called **speciation**. According to the biological species concept, the way new species are first produced involves some form of isolation. Picture a single species (baboons, for example) composed of several populations distributed over a wide geographical area. Gene exchange between populations (gene flow) will be limited if a geographical barrier, such as an ocean or a large river, effectively separates these populations. This extremely important form of isolating mechanism is called *geographical isolation*.

If one baboon population (A) is separated from another baboon population (B) by a river that has changed course, individual baboons of population A will not mate with individuals from B (Fig. 5-6). As time passes (perhaps hundreds or thousands of generations), genetic differences will accumulate in both populations. If population size is small, we can assume that genetic drift will also cause allele frequencies to change in both populations. And because drift is *random*, we wouldn't expect the effects to be the same. Consequently the two populations will begin to diverge genetically.

As long as gene exchange is limited, the populations can only become more genetically different over time. What's more, further difference can be expected if the baboon groups are occupying slightly different habitats. These additional genetic differences would be incorporated through the process of natural selection. Certain individuals in population A would be more reproductively fit in their own environment, but they would show less reproductive success in the environment occupied by population B. So allele frequencies will shift further, resulting in even greater divergence between the two groups.

speciation The process by which a new species evolves from an earlier species. Speciation is the most basic process in macroevolution.

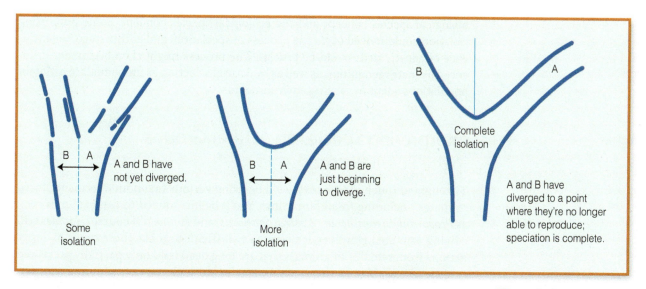

Figure 5-6

This speciation model illustrates branching evolution, or cladogenesis, which is caused by increasing reproductive isolation.

With the cumulative effects of genetic drift and natural selection acting over many generations, the result will be two populations that—even if they were to come back into geographical contact—could no longer interbreed. More than just geographical isolation might now apply. There may, for instance, be behavioral differences that interfere with courtship—what we call *behavioral isolation*. Using our *biological* definition of species, we would now recognize two distinct species where initially only one existed.

Another related process that can contribute to the further differentiation of populations into incipient species concerns mate recognition. This is sometimes called the **recognition species concept**, though the crucial process, again, concerns reproduction (that is, who's mating with whom; Ridley, 1993).

Assume, in our baboon example, that some isolation has already occurred and that phenotypic (and genotypic) differences are beginning to be established between two populations. In this situation, coloration patterns of faces or the size, location, coloration, or even smell of the female genital swelling might vary from group to group. If so, then a female from population A might not recognize a male from population B as an appropriate mate (and vice versa, of course). Natural selection would quickly favor such discrimination if hybrids were less reproductively successful than within-population crosses. Indeed, once such "selective breeding" became established, speciation would be accelerated considerably.

Another definition of species focuses primarily on natural selection and emphasizes that speciation is the result of influences of varied habitats. In this view, called the **ecological species concept**, a species is defined as a group of organisms exploiting a single niche. Also called an **ecological niche**, this is the physical as well as biological position of an organism within the biological world (that is, within the full ecosystem).

For each population, the ecological niche will vary slightly, and different phenotypes will be slightly more advantageous in each. For example, one population might be more arboreal and another more terrestrial; but there would not be an intermediate population equally successful on the ground and in the trees.

In recent years, the ecological species concept has attracted support from several evolutionary biologists, especially among physical anthropologists. While the biological species concept emphasizes gene flow and reproductive isolation, the ecological species concept stresses the role of natural selection. Clearly, our approach in this text has been to focus on the evolutionary contribution of natural selection; thus, the ecological species concept has much to offer here. Nevertheless, our understanding of species need not entail an either-or choice between the

recognition species concept A depiction of species in which the key aspect is the ability of individuals to identify members of their own species for purposes of mating (and to avoid mating with members of other species). In theory, this type of selective mating is a component of a species concept emphasizing mating and is therefore compatible with the biological species concept.

ecological species concept The concept that a species is a group of organisms exploiting a single niche. This view emphasizes the role of natural selection in separating species from one another.

ecological niche The position of a species within its physical and biological environments. A species' ecological niche is defined by such components as diet, terrain, vegetation, type of predators, relationships with other species, and activity patterns, and each niche is unique to a given species. Together, ecological niches make up an ecosystem.

biological species concept and the ecological species concept. Some population isolation could indeed *begin* the process of speciation, and at this stage, the influence of genetic drift could be crucial. The process might then be further influenced by mate recognition as well as by natural selection as individuals in different populations adapt to varying environments.

Interpreting Species and Other Groups in the Fossil Record

Throughout much of this text, we'll be using various taxonomic terms for fossil primates (including fossil hominins). You'll be introduced to genus names such as *Proconsul, Sivapithecus, Australopithecus*, and *Homo*. (Of course, *Homo* is still a living primate.) However, it's especially difficult to make these types of designations from remains of animals that are long dead (and only partially preserved as skeletal remains). In these contexts, what do such names mean in evolutionary terms?

Our goal in applying species, genus, or other taxonomic labels to groups of organisms is to make meaningful biological statements about the variation that's represented. As we look at populations of living or long-extinct animals, we are certainly going to see variation; this happens in *any* sexually reproducing organism due to recombination (see Chapter 3). As a result of recombination, each individual organism is a unique combination of genetic material, and the uniqueness is often reflected to some extent in the phenotype.

Besides such *individual variation*, we see other kinds of systematic variation in all biological populations. *Age changes* alter overall body size, as well as shape, in many mammals. One pertinent example for fossil human and ape studies is the change in number, size, and shape of teeth from deciduous teeth, also known as baby or milk teeth (only 20 teeth are present) to the permanent dentition (32 are present). It would be an obvious error to distinguish two fossil forms based solely on such age-dependent criteria. If one individual were represented just by milk teeth and another (seemingly very different) individual just by adult teeth, they could easily be different-aged individuals from the *same* population. Researchers dealing with fragmentary remains must be alert to variation of this sort. Otherwise, they could mistakenly think that pieces of a 2-year-old are from a different species than the mother!

Variation due to sex also plays an important role. Differences in physical characteristics between males and females of the same species, called **sexual dimorphism**, can result in marked variation in body size and proportions in adults of the same species (we'll discuss this important topic in more detail in Chapter 6).

Recognition of Fossil Species

Keeping in mind all the types of variation present within interbreeding groups of organisms, the minimum biological category we'd like to define in fossil primate samples is the *species*. As already defined (according to the biological species concept), a species is a group of interbreeding or potentially interbreeding organisms that is reproductively isolated from other such groups. In modern organisms, this concept is theoretically testable by observations of reproductive behavior. In animals long extinct, such observations are obviously impossible. Our only way, then, of getting a handle on the variation we see in fossil groups is to refer to living animals.

In studying a fossil group, we may observe obvious variation, such as some individuals being larger and with bigger teeth than others. The question then becomes: What's the biological significance of this variation? Two possibilities come to mind.

sexual dimorphism Differences in physical characteristics between males and females of the same species. For example, humans are slightly sexually dimorphic for body size, with males being taller, on average, than females of the same population. Sexual dimorphism is very pronounced in many species, such as gorillas.

Either the variation is accounted for by individual, age, and sex differences seen *within* every biological species (that is, it is **intraspecific**), or the variation represents differences *between* reproductively isolated groups (that is, it is **interspecific**). To decide which answer is correct, we have to look at contemporary species.

If the amount of variation we observe in fossil samples is comparable to that seen today *within species of closely related forms*, then we have little justification to "split" our sample into more than one species. We must, however, be careful in choosing modern analogues because rates of evolution vary among different groups of mammals. So, for example, in studying extinct fossil primates, we must compare them with well-known modern primate species. Even so, studies of living groups have shown that defining exactly where species boundaries begin and end is often difficult. In dealing with extinct species, the uncertainties are even greater. In addition to the overlapping patterns of variation *spatially* (over space), variation also occurs *temporally* (through time). In other words, even more variation will be seen in **paleospecies**, since individuals may be separated by thousands or even millions of years. Applying a strict Linnaean taxonomy to such a situation presents an unavoidable dilemma. Standard Linnaean classification, designed to take account of variation present at any given time, describes a static situation. But when we deal with paleospecies, the time frame is expanded and the situation can be dynamic (that is, later forms might differ from earlier forms). In such a dynamic situation, taxonomic decisions (where to draw species boundaries) are ultimately going to be somewhat arbitrary.

Because the task of interpreting paleospecies is so difficult, paleoanthropologists have sought various solutions. Most researchers today define species using clusters of derived traits (identified cladistically). But owing to the ambiguity of how many derived characters are required to identify a fully distinct species (as opposed to a subspecies), the frequent mixing of characters into novel combinations, and the always difficult problem of homoplasy, there continues to be disagreement. A good deal of the dispute is driven by philosophical orientation. Exactly how much diversity should one expect among fossil primates, especially among fossil hominins?

Some researchers, called "splitters," claim that speciation occurred frequently during hominin evolution, and they often identify numerous fossil hominin species in a sample being studied. As the nickname suggests, these scientists are inclined to split groups into many species. Others, called "lumpers," assume that speciation was less common and see much variation as being intraspecific. These scientists lump groups together, so that fewer hominin species are identified, named, and eventually plugged into evolutionary schemes. Sometimes researchers will use the phrase *sensu lato* (which means "in the broadest sense") to refer to a collection of fossils *lumped* into a group, and the phrase *sensu stricto* (which means "in the strictest sense") to refer to a collection of fossils that have been *split* into more specific groups. This is especially apparent with fossils within the genus *Homo*. As you'll see in the following chapters, debates of this sort are pervasive within paleoanthropology, perhaps more than in any other branch of evolutionary biology.

Recognition of Fossil Genera

The next and broader level of taxonomic classification, the **genus** (*pl.*, genera), presents another challenge for biologists. To have more than one genus, we obviously must have at least two species (reproductively isolated groups), and the species of one genus must differ in a basic way from the species of another genus. A genus is therefore defined as a group of species composed of members more closely related to one another than they are to species from any other genus.

Grouping species into genera can be quite subjective and is often much debated by biologists. One possible test for contemporary animals is to check for

intraspecific Within species; refers to variation seen within the same species.

interspecific Between species; refers to variation beyond that seen within the same species to include additional aspects seen between two different species.

paleospecies Species defined from fossil evidence, often covering a long time span.

genus (*pl.*, genera) A group of closely related species.

results of hybridization between individuals of different species—rare in nature but quite common in captivity. If members of two normally separate species interbreed and produce live (though not necessarily fertile) offspring, the two parental species are probably not too different genetically and should therefore be grouped in the same genus. A well-known example of such a cross is horses with donkeys (*Equus caballus* × *Equus asinus*), which normally produces live but sterile offspring (mules).

As previously mentioned, we can't perform breeding experiments with extinct animals, which is why another definition of genus is critical. Species that are members of the same genus share the same broad **adaptive zone**. An adaptive zone represents a general ecological lifestyle more basic than the narrower ecological niche characteristic of an individual species. This ecological definition of genus can be an immense aid in interpreting fossil primates. Teeth are the most frequently preserved parts, and they often can provide excellent general ecological inferences. Cladistic analysis also helps scientists to make judgments about evolutionary relationships. That is, members of the same genus should all share derived characters not seen in members of other genera.

As a final comment, we should stress that classification by genus is not always a straightforward decision. For instance, in emphasizing the very close genetic similarities between humans (*Homo sapiens*) and chimpanzees (*Pan troglodytes*), some current researchers (Wildman et al., 2003) place both in the same genus (*Homo sapiens, Homo troglodytes*). This philosophy has caused some to advocate for extension of basic human rights to great apes (as proposed by members of the Great Ape Project). Such thinking might startle you. Of course when it gets this close to home, it's often difficult to remain objective!

What Are Fossils and How Do They Form?

Much of what we know about the history of life comes from studying **fossils**, which are traces of ancient organisms that can be formed in many ways. The oldest fossils found thus far date back more than 3 billion years; because they are the remains of microorganisms, they are extremely small and are called *microfossils*.

These very early traces of life are fragile and very rare. Most of our evidence comes from a later time and usually in the form of pieces of shells, bones, or teeth, all of which, even in a living animal, were already partly made of mineral, giving them a head start in the fossilization process. After the organism died, these "hard" tissues were further impregnated with other minerals, being eventually transformed into a stone-like composition through a process called **mineralization** (Fig. 5-7). The chemical exchange of minerals between the dead organism and the surrounding burial environment (known as *diagenesis*) is what turns bones and teeth into fossils.

There are, however, many other ways in which life-forms have left traces of their existence. Sometimes insects were trapped in tree resin, which later became hardened and chemically altered. Because there was little or no oxygen inside the hardened amber, the insects have remained remarkably well preserved for millions of years, even with soft tissue and DNA still present (Fig. 5-8). This fascinating circumstance led author Michael Crichton to conjure the events depicted in the novel (and motion picture) *Jurassic Park*.

Dinosaur footprints as well as much more recent hominin tracks, leaf imprints in hardened mud or similar impressions of small organisms, and even the traces of dinosaur feathers—all are considered fossils. Recently, beautifully preserved theropod dinosaur feathers have been discovered in northeastern China (dated to approximately 125 mya). These remains are so superbly preserved that even microscopic

adaptive zone A general ecological lifestyle more basic than the narrower ecological niche characteristic of an individual species.

fossils Traces or remnants of organisms found in geological beds on the earth's surface.

mineralization The process in which parts of animals (or some plants) become transformed into stone-like structures. Mineralization usually occurs very slowly, as water carrying minerals—such as silica or iron—seeps into the tiny spaces within a bone. In some cases, the original minerals within the bone or tooth can be completely replaced, molecule by molecule, with other minerals.

John Cancalosi/Alamy

Phil Degginger/Alamy

Elwyn Simons

Shoshannah White/Aurora Photos

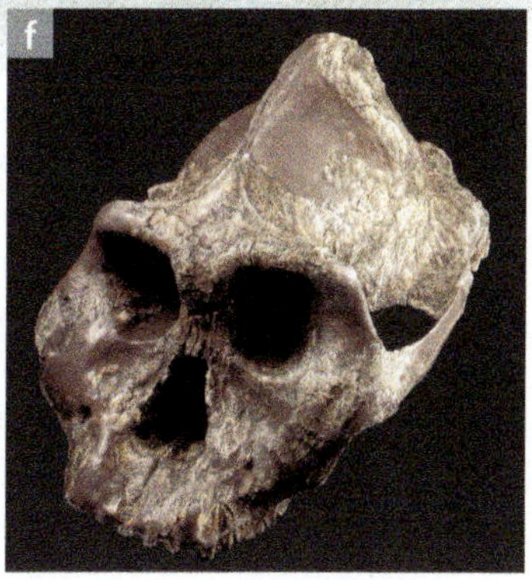

Russell L. Ciochon

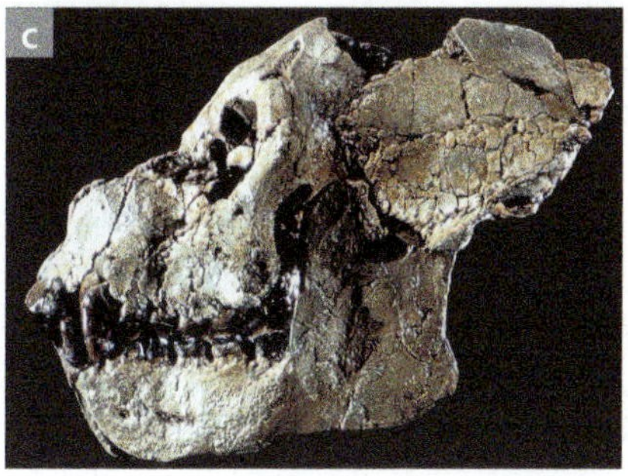

Marvin Dembinsky Photo Associates/Alamy

▲ **Figure 5-7**

Examples of mineralized fossils. (**a**) A mineralized snake cast from geological deposits in Wyoming (dated to about 50 mya). (**b**) A fossil dragonfly from Brazil, dated to more than 100 mya. (**c**) An early primate skull from Egypt, dated to about 30 mya. (**d**) A fossil fish (a relative of the piranha) from the same deposits as the snake in part (**a**), also dated to approximately 50 mya. (**e**) An ammonite fossil, an extinct Cretaceous period marine mollusk related to the living octopus and squid. (**f**) A fossilized skull of a hominin from East Africa, dated to 2.5 mya.

Kazuo Unno/Minden Pictures

◀ **Figure 5-8**

A spider fossilized in amber.

cell structures have been identified. These tiny structures directly influenced feather color in ancient dinosaurs; what's more, these same structures influence feather color in modern birds. Researchers are now able to deduce that some stripes in the feathers of one dinosaur were chestnut/reddish brown in color (Zhang et al., 2010)!

A spectacular discovery of a 47-million-year-old early primate fossil was widely publicized in 2009. This fossil is remarkable, preserving more than 95 percent of the skeleton as well as outlines of soft tissue and even fossilized remains of digestive tract contents (see Chapter 8) (Franzen et al., 2009). The amazing preservation of this small primate occurred because it died on the edge of a volcanic lake and was quickly covered with sediment. It reminds us that whether a dead animal will become fossilized and how much of it will be preserved depends partly on *how* it dies, but even more on *where* it dies. In fact, the likelihood that a dead organism will survive to become a fossil is quite low.

Some ancient organisms have left vast amounts of fossil remains. Indeed, limestone deposits can be hundreds of feet thick and are largely made up of fossilized remains of marine shellfish (see Chapter 2). However, fossils of land animals are not nearly so common. After an animal dies—let's say it's an early hominin from 2 mya—it will most likely be scavenged by carnivores, and then its bones will be scattered and broken and eventually decompose. After just a few weeks, there will be hardly anything left to fossilize. But suppose, by chance, this recently deceased hominin was quickly covered by sediment, perhaps by sand and mud in a streambed or along a lakeshore or by volcanic ash from a nearby volcano. As a result, the long, slow process of mineralization might eventually turn at least some parts of the hominin into a fossil.

The study of how bones and other materials come to be buried in the earth and preserved as fossils is called **taphonomy** (from the Greek *taphos*, meaning "study of the grave"). Such studies focus on everything that happens to an organism once it has died, making it the life history of the dead, so to speak. Among the topics that taphonomists try to understand are processes of sedimentation and burial, including the action of streams, preservation properties of bone, and the role of carnivores in scavenging animal carcasses.

Humans Are Vertebrates: Distant Connections through Geological Time

Biologists must contend not only with the staggering array of living and extinct lifeforms but also the vast amount of time that life has been evolving on earth. Again, scientists have devised simplified schemes—but in this case to organize *time*, not biological diversity.

Geologists have formulated the **geological time scale** (Fig. 5-9), in which very large time spans are organized into eras that include one or more periods. Periods, in turn, can be broken down into epochs. For the time span encompassing vertebrate evolution, there are three eras: the Paleozoic, Mesozoic, and Cenozoic. The earliest vertebrates are present in the fossil record dating to early in the Paleozoic at 500 mya, and their origins are probably much older. It's the vertebrates' capacity to form bone that accounts for their more complete fossil record *after* 500 mya.

During the Paleozoic, several varieties of fishes (including the ancestors of modern sharks and bony fishes) as well as the first four-limbed organisms (amphibians and reptiles) appeared on earth. At the end of the Paleozoic, close to 250 mya, several varieties of mammal-like reptiles were also diversifying. It's generally thought that some of these forms ultimately gave rise to the mammals.

taphonomy The study of how bones and other materials come to be buried in the earth and preserved as fossils.

geological time scale The organization of earth history into eras, periods, and epochs; commonly used by geologists and paleoanthropologists.

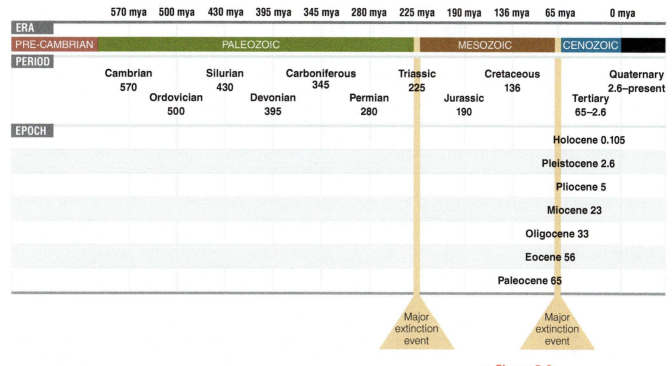

▲ Figure 5-9
Geological time scale.

The evolutionary history of vertebrates and other organisms during the Paleozoic and Mesozoic was profoundly influenced by geographical events. We know that the positions of the earth's continents shifted dramatically during the last several hundred million years. This process, called **continental drift**, is explained by the geological theory of *plate tectonics*, which states that the earth's crust is a series of gigantic moving and colliding plates. Such massive geological movements can induce volcanic activity (as, for example, all around the Pacific Rim), mountain building (for example, the Himalayas), and earthquakes. Living on the juncture of the Pacific and North American plates, residents of the Pacific coast of the United States are acutely aware of some of these consequences, as illustrated by the explosive volcanic eruption of Mt. St. Helens and the frequent earthquakes in Alaska and California.

While reconstructing the earth's physical history, geologists have determined the earlier, much altered positions of major continental landmasses. During the late Paleozoic, the continents came together to form a single colossal landmass called *Pangea*. (In reality, the continents had been drifting on plates, coming together and separating, long before the end of the Paleozoic around 225 mya.) During the early Mesozoic, the southern continents (South America, Africa, Antarctica, Australia, and India) began to split off from Pangea, forming a large southern continent called *Gondwanaland* (Fig. 5-10a). Similarly, the northern continents (North America, Greenland, Europe, and Asia) were consolidated into a northern landmass called *Laurasia*. During the Mesozoic, Gondwanaland and Laurasia continued to drift apart and to break up into smaller segments. By the end of the Mesozoic (about 65 mya), the continents were beginning to assume their approximate current positions (Fig. 5-10b).

The evolutionary ramifications of this long-term continental drift were profound. Groups of animals became effectively isolated from one another by oceans, significantly influencing the distribution of mammals and other land vertebrates. These continental movements continued in the Cenozoic and indeed are still happening, although without such dramatic results.

During most of the Mesozoic, reptiles were the dominant land vertebrates; they exhibited a broad expansion into a variety of *ecological niches*, which included aerial and marine habitats. The most famous of these highly successful Mesozoic reptiles

continental drift The movement of continents on sliding plates of the earth's surface. As a result, the positions of large landmasses have shifted drastically during the earth's history.

A Closer Look Deep Time

The vast expanse of time during which evolution has occurred on earth staggers the imagination. Indeed, this fundamental notion of what John McPhee has termed "deep time" is not really understood or, in fact, widely believed. Of course as we've emphasized beginning in Chapter 1, *belief*, as such, is not part of science. But observation, theory building, and testing are. Still, in a world populated mostly by nonscientists, the concept of deep time, crucial as it is to geology and anthropology, is resisted by many people. This situation really isn't surprising; the very notion of deep time is in many ways counterintuitive. Human beings tend to measure their existence in months, years, and the span of human lifetimes.

But what are these durations as measured against geological or galactic phenomena? In a real sense, these vast time expanses are beyond human comprehension. We can reasonably fathom the reaches of human history stretching to about 5,000 years ago. In a leap of imagination, we can perhaps even begin to grasp the stretch of time back to the cave painters of France and Spain, approximately 17,000 to 25,000 years ago. How do we relate, then, to a temporal span that's 10 times this one, back to 250,000 years ago, about the time of the earliest *Homo sapiens*—or to 10 times this span to 2,500,000 years ago (about the time of the appearance of our genus, *Homo*)? And when we multiply this last duration another 1,000 times (to 2,500,000,000), we're back to a time of fairly early life-forms. We'd have to reach still further into earth's past, another 1.5 billion years, to approach the *earliest* documented life.

The dimensions of these intervals are humbling to say the least. The discovery in the nineteenth century of deep time (see Chapter 2), what the late Stephen Jay Gould called "geology's greatest contribution to human thought," plunged one more dagger into humanity's long-cherished view of itself as something special. Astronomers had previously established how puny our world was in the physical expanse of space, and then geologists showed that even on our own small planet we were but residues dwarfed within a river of time "without a vestige of a beginning or prospect of an end" (from James Hutton, a founder of modern geology and one of the discoverers of deep time). It's no wonder that people resist the concept of deep time; it not only stupefies our reason but also implies a sense of collective meaninglessness and reinforces our individual mortality. Geologists, astronomers, and other scholars have struggled for over a century, with modest success, to translate the tales told in rocks and hurtling stars into terms that everyone could understand. Various analogies have been attempted—metaphors,

Kimberly Deprey/iStockphoto.com

▲ **Figure 1**

Geological exposures at the Grand Canyon. Some of the sediments are almost 2 billion years old and have been cut through by the Colorado River over the last 6 million years.

▶ **Figure 5-10**

Continental drift. (**a**) Positions of the continents during the Mesozoic (ca. 125 mya). Pangea is breaking up into a northern landmass (Laurasia) and a southern landmass (Gondwanaland). (**b**) Positions of the continents at the beginning of the Cenozoic (ca. 65 mya).

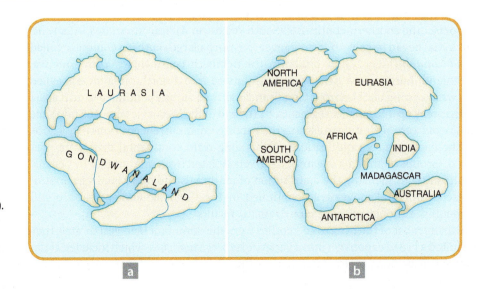

a

b

really—drawn from common experience. Among the most successful of these attempts is a "cosmic calendar" devised by eminent astronomer Carl Sagan in his book *The Dragons of Eden* (1977). In this version of time's immensity, Sagan likens the passage of geological time to that of one calendar year.

The year begins on January 1 with the Big Bang, the cosmic explosion marking the beginning of the universe and the beginning of time. In this version, the Big Bang is set at 15 billion years ago,* with some of the major events in the geological past as follows:

Time Unit Conversion Using the Cosmic Calendar

1 year = 15,000,000,000 years	1 hour = 1,740,000 years
1 month = 1,250,000,000 years	1 minute = 29,000 years
1 day = 41,000,000 years	1 second = 475 years

		Appearance of early hominoids (apes and humans)	*December 31 Events* 12:30 P.M.
Big Bang	January 1	First hominins	9:30 P.M.
Formation of the earth	September 14	Extensive cave painting in Europe	11:59 P.M.
Origin of life on earth (approx.)	September 25	Invention of agriculture	11:59:20 P.M.
Significant oxygen atmosphere begins to develop	December 1	Renaissance in Europe; Ming dynasty in China; emergence of scientific method	11:59:59 P.M.
Precambrian ends; Paleozoic begins; invertebrates flourish	December 17		
Paleozoic ends and Mesozoic begins	December 25	Widespread development of science and technology; emergence of a global culture; first steps in space exploration; mass extinctions caused by humans	NOW: the first second of the New Year
Cretaceous period: first flowers; dinosaurs become extinct	December 28		
Mesozoic ends; Cenozoic begins; adaptive radiation of placental mammals	December 29		

*Recent evidence gathered by the Hubble Space Telescope has questioned the established date for the Big Bang. However, even the most recent data are somewhat contradictory, suggesting a date from as early as 16 billion years ago (indicated by the age of the oldest stars) to as recent as 8 billion years ago (indicated by the rate of expansion of the universe). Here we'll follow the conventional dating of 15 billion years; if you apply the most conservative approximation (8 billion years), the calibrations shift as follows: 1 day = 22,000,000 years; 1 hour = 913,000 years; 1 minute = 15,000 years. Using these calculations, for example, the first hominins appear on December 31 at 7:37 P.M., and modern humans (*Homo sapiens*) are on the scene at 11:42 P.M.

were the dinosaurs, which themselves evolved into a wide array of sizes and species and adapted to a variety of lifestyles. Dinosaur paleontology, never a boring field, has advanced several startling notions in recent years: that many dinosaurs were "warm-blooded"; that some varieties were quite social and probably also engaged in considerable parental care; that many forms became extinct because of major climate changes to the earth's atmosphere from collisions with comets or asteroids; and, finally, that not all dinosaurs became entirely extinct and have many descendants still living today (that is, all modern birds). (See Fig. 5-11 for a summary of major events in early vertebrate evolutionary history.)

The Cenozoic is divided into two periods, the Tertiary (about 63 million years in duration) and the Quaternary, from about 2.6 mya up to and including the present (see Fig. 5-9). Paleontologists often refer to the next, more precise level of subdivision within the Cenozoic as the **epochs**. There are seven epochs within the Cenozoic: the Paleocene, Eocene, Oligocene, Miocene, Pliocene, Pleistocene, and Holocene, the last often referred to as the Recent epoch.

epochs Categories of the geological time scale; subdivisions of periods. In the Cenozoic era, epochs include the Paleocene, Eocene, Oligocene, Miocene, and Pliocene (from the Tertiary Period) and the Pleistocene and Holocene (from the Quaternary Period).

570 mya	500 mya	430 mya	395 mya	345 mya
ERA				
		PALEOZOIC		
PERIOD				
Cambrian	**Ordovician**	**Silurian**	**Devonian**	**Carboniferous**
Trilobites abundant; also brachiopods, jellyfish, worms, and other invertebrates	First fishes; trilobites still abundant; graptolites and corals become plentiful; possible land plants	Jawed fishes appear; first air-breathing animals; definite land plants	Age of Fishes; first amphibians and first forests appear	First reptiles; radiation of amphibians; modern insects diversify

▲ **Figure 5-11**
This time line depicts major events in early vertebrate evolution.

Humans Are Also Mammals: Closer Connections

We can learn about mammalian evolution from fossils as well as from studying the DNA of living species (Bininda-Emonds et al., 2007). Studies using both of these approaches suggest that all the living groups of mammals (that is, all the orders) had diverged by 75 mya. Only later, several million years following the beginning of the Cenozoic, did the various current mammalian subgroups (that is, the particular families) begin to diversify.

Today there are over 5,400 species of mammals, and we could call the Cenozoic the Age of Mammals. It is during this era that, along with birds, mammals replaced earlier reptiles as the dominant land-living vertebrates.

How do we account for the relatively rapid success of the mammals during the late Mesozoic and early Cenozoic? Several characteristics relating to learning and general flexibility of behavior are of prime importance. Mammals were selected for larger brains than those typically found in reptiles, making them better equipped to process information. In particular, the cerebrum became generally enlarged, especially the outer covering, the **neocortex**, which controls higher brain functions (Fig. 5-12). In some mammals, the cerebrum expanded so much that it came to constitute most of the brain volume; the number of surface convolutions also increased, creating more surface area and thus providing space for even more nerve cells (neurons). As we'll see in Chapter 6, this trend is even further emphasized among the primates.

neocortex The more recently evolved portions of the cortex of the brain that are involved with higher mental functions and composed of areas that integrate incoming information from different sensory organs.

▶ **Figure 5-12**
Lateral view of the brain in fishes, reptiles, and primates. You can see the increased size of the cerebral cortex (neocortex) of the primate brain. The cerebral cortex integrates sensory information and selects responses.

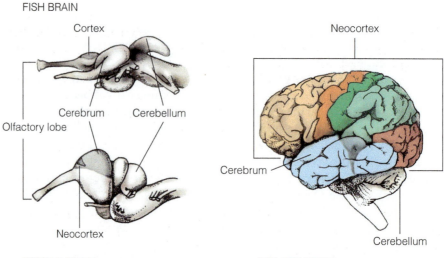

FISH BRAIN

Cortex

Cerebrum   Cerebellum

Olfactory lobe

Neocortex

REPTILE BRAIN

Neocortex

Cerebrum

Cerebellum

PRIMATE BRAIN

280 mya	225 mya	190 mya	136 mya	65 mya

MESOZOIC

Permian

Reptile radiation; mammal-like reptiles appear

Triassic

Reptiles further radiate; first dinosaurs; egg-laying mammals

Jurassic

Great Age of Dinosaurs; flying and swimming dinosaurs appear; first toothed birds

Cretaceous

Placental and marsupial mammals appear; first modern birds

Major extinction event

Major extinction event

For such a large and complex organ as the mammalian brain to develop, a longer, more intense period of growth is required. Slower development can occur internally (*in utero*) as well as after birth. Internal fertilization and internal development aren't unique to mammals, but the latter was a major innovation among terrestrial vertebrates. Other forms (most fishes and reptiles—including birds) lay eggs, and "prenatal" development occurs externally, outside the mother's body. Mammals, with very few exceptions, give birth to live young. Even among mammals, however, there's considerable variation among the major groups in how mature the young are at birth; **placental** mammals, including ourselves, show the longest period of *in utero* development.

Another distinctive feature of mammals is the dentition. While many living reptiles (such as lizards and snakes) consistently have similarly shaped teeth (called a *homodont* dentition), mammals have differently shaped teeth (Fig. 5-13). This varied pattern, termed a **heterodont** dentition, is reflected in the ancestral (primitive) mammalian arrangement of teeth, which includes three incisors, one canine, four premolars, and three molars in each quarter of the mouth. So, with 11 teeth in each quarter of the mouth, the ancestral mammalian dental complement includes a total of 44 teeth. Such a heterodont arrangement allows mammals to process a wide variety of foods. Incisors are used for cutting, canines for grasping and piercing, and premolars and molars for crushing and grinding.

A final point regarding teeth relates to their disproportionate representation in the fossil record. As the hardest, most durable portion of a vertebrate skeleton, teeth have the greatest likelihood of becoming fossilized (that is, mineralized), because teeth are predominantly composed of mineral to begin with. As a result, the vast majority of available fossil data for most vertebrates, including primates, consists of teeth.

Another major adaptive complex that distinguishes contemporary mammals from reptiles (except birds) is the maintenance of a constant internal body temperature. Known colloquially (and incorrectly) as warmbloodedness, this crucial physiological adaptation is also seen in contemporary birds and may have characterized many dinosaurs as well. Except for birds, reptiles maintain a constant internal body

placental A type (subclass) of mammal. During the Cenozoic, placentals became the most widespread and numerous mammals and today are represented by upward of 20 orders, including the primates.

heterodont Having different kinds of teeth; characteristic of mammals, whose teeth consist of incisors, canines, premolars, and molars.

a REPTILIAN (alligator): homodont

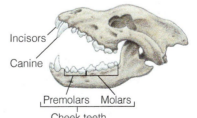

Incisors

Canine

Premolars   Molars

Cheek teeth

b MAMMALIAN: heterodont

◀ **Figure 5-13**
Reptilian and mammalian teeth.

▲ Figure 5-14
A duck-billed platypus (monotreme).

▲ Figure 5-15
A wallaby with an infant in its pouch (marsupials).

endothermic (*endo*, meaning "within" or "internal," and *thermic*, meaning "heat"). Able to maintain internal body temperature by producing energy through metabolic processes within cells; characteristic of mammals, birds, and perhaps some dinosaurs.

adaptive radiation The relatively rapid expansion and diversification of life-forms into new ecological niches.

temperature through exposure to the sun; these reptiles are said to be *ectothermic*. In mammals and birds, however, energy is generated *internally* through metabolic activity (by processing food or by muscle action); for this reason, mammals and birds are said to be **endothermic**.

There are three major subgroups of living mammals: the egglaying mammals, or monotremes; the pouched mammals, or marsupials; and the placental mammals. The monotremes, of which the platypus is one example (Fig. 5-14), are extremely primitive and are considered more distinct from marsupials or placentals than these two subgroups are from each other. The sequencing of the full genome of the platypus (Warren et al., 2008) has confirmed the very ancient origins of the monotremes and their distinctiveness from other mammals.

The most notable difference between marsupials and placentals concerns fetal development. In marsupials, the young are born extremely immature and must complete development in an external pouch (Fig. 5-15). But placental mammals develop over a longer period of time *in utero*, made possible by the evolutionary development of a specialized tissue (the placenta) that provides for fetal nourishment.

With a longer gestation period, the central nervous system develops more completely in the placental fetus. What's more, after birth, the "bond of milk" between mother and young allows more time for complex neural structures to form. We should also emphasize that from a *biosocial* perspective, this dependency period not only allows for adequate physiological development but also provides for a wider range of learning stimuli. That is, a vast amount of information is channeled to the young mammalian brain through observation of the mother's behavior and play with age-mates. It's not enough to have evolved a brain capable of learning. Collateral evolution of mammalian social systems has ensured that young mammalian brains are provided with ample learning opportunities and are thus put to good use.

Processes of Macroevolution

As we noted earlier, evolution operates at both micro- and macroevolutionary levels. We discussed evolution primarily from a microevolutionary perspective in Chapter 4; in this chapter, our focus is on macroevolution. Macroevolutionary mechanisms operate more on the whole species than on individuals or populations, and they take much longer than microevolutionary processes to have a noticeable impact.

Adaptive Radiation

As we mentioned in Chapter 2, the potential capacity of a group of organisms to multiply is practically unlimited, but its ability to increase its numbers is regulated largely by the availability of resources (food, water, shelter, mates, and space). As population size increases, access to resources decreases, and the environment will ultimately prove inadequate. Depleted resources induce some members of a population to seek an environment in which competition is reduced and the opportunities for survival and reproductive success are increased. This evolutionary tendency to exploit unoccupied habitats can eventually produce an abundance of diverse species.

This story has been played out countless times during the history of life, and some groups have expanded extremely rapidly. Known as **adaptive radiation**, this evolutionary process can be seen in the divergence of the stem reptiles into the profusion of different forms of the late Paleozoic and especially those of the

Mesozoic. It's a process that takes place when a life-form rapidly takes advantage, so to speak, of the many newly available ecological niches.

The principle of evolution illustrated by adaptive radiation is fairly simple, but important. It may be stated this way: A species or group of species will diverge into as many variations as two factors allow. These factors are (1) its adaptive potential and (2) the adaptive opportunities of the available niches.

In the case of reptiles, there was little divergence in the very early stages of evolution, when the ancestral form was little more than one among a variety of amphibian water dwellers. Later, a more efficient egg (one that could incubate out of water) developed in reptiles; this new egg, with a hard, watertight shell, had great adaptive potential, but initially there were few zones to invade. When reptiles became fully terrestrial, however, a wide array of ecological niches became accessible to them. Once freed from their attachment to water, reptiles were able to exploit landmasses with no serious competition from any other animal. They moved into the many different ecological niches on land (and to some extent in the air and sea), and as they adapted to these areas, they diversified into a large number of species. This spectacular radiation burst forth with such evolutionary speed that it may well be termed an adaptive explosion.

Of course, the rapid expansion of placental mammals during the late Mesozoic and throughout the Cenozoic is another excellent example of adaptive radiation. The worldwide major extinction event at the end of the Mesozoic, as the dinosaurs disappeared, left thousands of econiches vacant. Small-bodied, mostly nocturnal mammals had been around for at least 70 million years, and once they were no longer in competition with the dinosaurs, they were free to move into previously occupied habitats. Thus, over the course of several million years, there was a major adaptive radiation of mammals as they diversified to exploit previously unavailable habitats.

Generalized and Specialized Characteristics

Another aspect of evolution closely related to adaptive radiation involves the transition from *generalized* characteristics to *specialized* characteristics. These two terms refer to the adaptive potential of a particular trait. A trait that's adapted for many functions is said to be generalized, whereas one that's limited to a narrow set of functions is said to be specialized.

For example, a generalized mammalian limb has five fairly flexible digits adapted for many possible functions (grasping, weight support, and digging). In this respect, human hands are still quite generalized. On the other hand (or foot), there have been many structural modifications in our feet to make them suited for the specialized function of stable weight support in an upright posture.

The terms *generalized* and *specialized* are also sometimes used when speaking of the adaptive potential of whole organisms. Consider, for example, the aye-aye of Madagascar, an unusual primate species. The aye-aye is a highly specialized animal, structurally adapted to a narrow, rodent/woodpecker-like econiche—digging holes with prominent incisors and removing insect larvae with an elongated bony middle finger (Fig. 5-16).

It's important to note that only a generalized ancestor can provide the flexible evolutionary basis for rapid

▼ **Figure 5-16**

An aye-aye, a specialized primate native to Madagascar. Note the elongated middle finger, which is used to probe under bark for insects.

Nigel J. Dennis/Gallo Images/Encyclopedia/Corbis

diversification. Only a generalized species with potential for adaptation to varied ecological niches can lead to all the later diversification and specialization of forms into particular ecological niches.

An issue that we've already raised also bears on this discussion: the relationship of ancestral and derived characters. It's not always the case, but ancestral characters *usually* tend to be more generalized. And specialized characteristics are nearly always derived as well.

Working Together: Microevolution and Macroevolution

For many years, evolutionary biologists generally agreed that microevolutionary mechanisms could be translated directly into the larger-scale macroevolutionary changes, especially the most central of all macroevolutionary processes, speciation. However, four decades ago, some leading evolutionary biologists challenged this traditional view.

Over the last 40 years evolutionary biologists have debated whether there are fundamental differences between the processes of microevolution and macroevolution. This discussion continues, and divergent views, framed as specific hypotheses, are further tested against new evidence. At present, the major difference seems to be one of *scale*. That is, both processes are driven by similar factors; however, macroevolution takes much longer than microevolution to occur.

For example, several species of very early hominins evolved over more than 5 million years, initially separating from their common ancestor with chimpanzees, and some of these species eventually adapted to more ground-living niches. These changes clearly reflect macroevolutionary processes. Much more recently, some modern human populations adapted in just a couple of thousand years to living at high altitudes, which was made possible by changes in particular genes. This is a good example of microevolution.

We should note that rates of evolutionary change can speed up at certain times and slow down during others. Most crucially, natural selection is influenced by how fast the environment is changing (and how fast genetic changes appear and spread within a species). Both fossil and molecular evidence (Pagel et al., 2006) indicate that both gradual (slow) and rapid (also called "punctuated") changes have occurred in the evolution of both plant and animal species.

In all lineages, the pace assuredly speeds up and slows down due to factors that influence the size and relative isolation of populations. As we've said, environmental changes that influence the pace and direction of natural selection must also be considered. So, in general accordance with the Modern Synthesis and as indicated by molecular evidence, microevolution and macroevolution needn't be considered separately, as some evolutionary biologists have suggested. Some groups of primates, for instance, simply have slower or faster rates of speciation, which is why Old World monkeys typically speciate more slowly than the great apes.

How Do We Know?

We know about earlier life-forms directly from fossils, of which tens of trillions have formed over the vast time that life has existed on earth. We also know about "deep time" in earth's geological history, and the age when fossils formed over the last 3 billion years, from studies made by geologists who use precise dating techniques (the latter to be discussed in Chapter 9). But have you ever wondered why hominin fossil discoveries are so rare? Paleoanthropologists rightly acknowledge that the fossil record is incomplete, limiting their ability to interpret relationships between extinct hominin species. Indeed, we have only a small sample of the diversity of our ancestors, the ancient hominins, who once lived on the landscape.

Throughout time, the forces of nature have removed the evidence of nearly all hominin existence. What are these forces of nature? Earlier in this chapter, we discussed the role of taphonomic processes (that is, the postmortem events that occur to organisms from the time of death to the time of their discovery by researchers) in regard to the formation of the fossil record. Modern taphonomic studies have identified a number of factors that result in the destruction and removal of animal carcasses from the landscape, including carnivore and rodent scavenging, freeze-thaw and wet-dry cycles, transport of remains by water, sun exposure, invasion by microbes and plants, and trampling by large animals (Denys, 2002; Pokines and Symes, 2013). In fact, the most important factor contributing to the preservation of vertebrate skeletons is rapid burial. By being buried, an animal carcass avoids many of the taphonomic processes that occur on the earth's surface. Once buried, skeletal preservation is largely determined by the burial environment, especially the pH of the surrounding soil and groundwater that chemically exchange with the remains. High-pH soils are acidic and often result in poor skeletal preservation, even at short time intervals; lower-pH soils are more alkaline and therefore more conducive to skeletal preservation (Denys, 2002). The size, shape, and density of a particular skeletal or dental element are also important factors influencing skeletal preservation. When we consider all the factors that could potentially affect the preservation of hominin remains, it is surprising that we have the fossil record that we do. One explanation is that hominin species often spent time near lakes (generally an alkaline environment), which could account for their preservation, especially in East African sites. In other areas (for example, South Africa), skeletal preservation was facilitated through their deposition and rapid burial within limestone caves.

What Do You Think?

Can you identify some of the taphonomic processes that would affect the preservation of animal carcasses in your local area? Are there any known fossil deposits nearby? Would you expect remains to fossilize there? Why or why not? ■

Summary of Main Topics

- All life-forms are classified according to the Linnaean taxonomic system, which classifies organisms based on their homologous traits (shared) rather than their analogous traits (homoplasies).
- Evolutionary systematics and cladistics are the two major types of classification. Evolutionary systematics uses homologous characteristics to make hypotheses regarding evolutionary relationships as well as ancestor-descendant relationships and shows the latter through time as a phylogenetic tree. Cladistics more rigorously uses only specific sorts of homologous characteristics (derived ones) and doesn't attempt to draw ancestor-descendant conclusions or show evolutionary relationships through time; conclusions are shown in a cladogram.

- According to the biological species concept, species are groups of individuals capable of fertile interbreeding but are reproductively isolated from other such groups. There are also other definitions of species suggested by biologists, but this one is the most widely used.
- Fossils are traces of ancient organisms that can form through a number of methods, and include fragments of shell, bones, and teeth as well as impressions left from ancient animals (for example, footprints and cast impressions). The fossilization process often involves the conversion of hard tissues to a stone-like material due to a process known as mineralization.
- Vertebrates are animals with a segmented backbone (vertebral column), a developed brain, and paired sensory structures. Vertebrates

include fishes, amphibians, reptiles (including birds), and mammals.
- Humans are placental mammals that (along with some other mammals) are characterized by development *in utero* (that is, live birth), differently shaped (heterodont) teeth, more complex brains, and maintenance of a constant internal body temperature (endothermic). Placental mammals in particular have even more complex brains (with a large neocortex), longer periods of development, and more complex social behavior.
- Macroevolution takes many hundreds or thousands of generations and can result in the appearance of new species (a process called *speciation*). Microevolution can occur within just a few generations and results in small genetic differences between populations of a species.

Critical Thinking Questions

1. Remains of a fossil mammal have been found on your campus. If you adopt a cladistic approach, how would you determine (a) that it's a mammal rather than some other kind of vertebrate (discuss specific characters it possesses), (b) what kind of mammal it is, and (c) how it *might* be related to one or more living mammals?

2. Why is taxonomy important to interpreting the fossil record? What are some of the areas of confusion in applying the biological species concept to fossils? Explain how the paleospecies concept is used.

3. For the same fossil find (and your interpretation) in question 2, draw an interpretive figure using cladistic analysis (that is, draw a cladogram). Next, using more traditional evolutionary systematics, construct a phylogenetic tree. Last, explain the differences between the cladogram and the phylogenetic tree (be sure to emphasize the fundamental ways in which the two schemes differ).

4. a. Humans are fairly generalized mammals. What do we mean by this, and what specific features (characters) would you select to illustrate this statement?
   b. More precisely, humans are *placental* mammals. How do humans and all other placental mammals differ from the other two major groups of mammals?

CONNECTIONS

Humans are both vertebrates and mammals, and their evolutionary history over many millions of years explains our early roots.

Because humans are primates, we share many biological characteristics with other primate species.

Partly because of common evolutionary history, many human behaviors are also seen in other primates.

Survey of the Living Primates

6

Primate Characteristics

Limbs and Locomotion

Dentition and Diet

The Senses and the Brain

Maturation, Learning, and Behavior

Primate Adaptations

Evolutionary Factors

Geographical Distribution and Habitats

Diet and Teeth

Locomotion

Primate Classification

A Survey of the Living Nonhuman Primates

Lemurs and Lorises

Tarsiers

Anthropoids: Monkeys, Apes, and Humans

Hominoids: Apes and Humans

Endangered Primates

The Bushmeat Trade

Student Learning Objectives After studying the material in this chapter, you should be able to:

▶ Describe the major characteristics of primates.

▶ Summarize the anatomical adaptations of primates.

▶ Outline the primate taxonomy.

▶ Discuss the major categories of nonhuman primates, their geographic distribution, and how they differ from one another.

▶ List some of the many reasons why over half of all nonhuman primate species are threatened or highly endangered today.

Chimpanzees aren't monkeys, and neither are gorillas or orangutans. They're apes. And even though most people think that monkeys and apes are basically the same, they aren't. Yet how many times have you seen a greeting card or magazine ad with a picture of a chimpanzee and a phrase that says something like, "Don't monkey around" or "No more monkey business"? Or maybe you've seen people at zoos making fun of primates. While these things may seem trivial, they really aren't, because they demonstrate just how little most people know about our closest relatives. This is extremely unfortunate, because by better understanding these relatives, we can better understand ourselves. And just as important, we can also

A baboon drinking water.

Melanie Beasley; Top Images: © Cengage Learning; Lynn Kilgore; David Haring try to preserve the many nonhuman primate species that are critically endangered today. Indeed, many will go extinct in the next 30 years or so if steps aren't taken now to save them.

One way to understand any organism is to compare its anatomy and behavior with that of other closely related species. This comparative approach helps explain how and why physiological and behavioral systems evolved as adaptive responses to various selective pressures throughout the course of evolution. This statement applies to humans just as it does to any other species. If we want to identify the components that have shaped the evolution of our species, a good starting point is to compare ourselves with our closest living relatives, the nonhuman primates (lemurs, lorises, tarsiers, monkeys, and apes).

Exactly how many nonhuman primate species there are is not entirely clear because the taxonomic status of many groups has not been clarified. Furthermore, new species are still being discovered. Between 1990 and 2009, a total of 86 new primate species and subspecies were described (Mittermeier et al., 2009). While some authors believe that there may be more than 485 nonhuman primate species (Rylands and Mittermeier, 2014), most feel more comfortable with an estimate of 230 to 270.

This chapter describes the physical characteristics that define the order **Primates**, gives a brief overview of the major groups of living primates, and introduces some methods currently used to compare living primates genetically. (For a comparison of human and nonhuman skeletons, see Appendix A.) But before going any further, we again want to call attention to a few common misunderstandings about evolutionary processes.

Evolution is not a goal-directed process. Therefore the fact that lemurs appeared earlier than **anthropoids** doesn't mean that lemurs "progressed" or "advanced" to become anthropoids. Living primates aren't in any way "superior" to their evolutionary predecessors or to one another. Consequently, in discussions of major groupings of contemporary nonhuman primates, there is no implied superiority or inferiority of any of these groups. Each lineage or species has come to possess unique qualities that make it better suited to a particular habitat and lifestyle than others. Given that all contemporary organisms are "successful" results of the evolutionary process, it's best to completely avoid such loaded terms as *superior* and *inferior*. Finally, you shouldn't make the mistake of thinking that contemporary primates (including humans) necessarily represent the final stage or apex of a lineage, because we all continue to evolve as lineages. Actually, the only species that represent final evolutionary stages of particular lineages are those that become extinct.

Primate Characteristics

As you learned in Chapter 5, all primates share many characteristics with other placental mammals. Some of these basic mammalian traits are body hair; a relatively long gestation period followed by live birth; mammary glands (thus the term *mammal*); *heterodonty* (that is, different types of teeth, including incisors, canines, premolars, and molars; the ability to maintain a constant internal body temperature through physiological means (called *endothermy*; see Chapter 5); increased brain size; and a considerable capacity for learning and behavioral flexibility. So, to differentiate primates as a distinct group from other mammals, we must describe those characteristics that, taken together, set primates apart.

It isn't easy to identify single traits that define the primate order because, compared with most mammals, primates have remained quite *generalized*. This

primates Members of the mammalian order Primates (pronounced "pry-may´-tees"), which includes lemurs, lorises, tarsiers, monkeys, apes, and humans.

anthropoids Members of the primate infraorder Anthropoidea (pronounced "an-throw-poid´-ee-uh"), which includes monkeys, apes, and humans.

means that primates have retained several ancestral (that is, primitive) mammalian traits that many other mammals have lost over time. In response to particular selective pressures, some mammalian groups have become increasingly specialized, or derived. For example, through the course of evolution, horses and cattle have undergone a reduction in the number of digits (fingers and toes) from the ancestral pattern of five to one and two, respectively. These species have also developed hard, protective coverings over their feet in the form of keratinized hooves (Fig. 6-1a). This foot structure is beneficial in prey species, because their survival depends on speed and stability, but it restricts them to only one type of locomotion. Moreover, limb function is limited to support and movement, and the ability to manipulate objects is lost completely.

Primates can't be defined by one or even a few traits they share in common because they *aren't* as specialized as many mammals. Therefore primatologists have drawn attention to a group of characteristics that more or less characterize the entire primate order. Still, these are a set of general tendencies that are not equally expressed in all primates. In addition, while some of these traits are unique to primates, many others are retained ancestral mammalian characteristics shared with other mammals. The following sections are designed to give you a general anatomical and behavioral picture of the primates. Concentrating on certain ancestral mammalian traits along with more specific, derived ones has been the traditional approach of primatologists, and it's still used today. In their limbs and locomotion, teeth, diet, senses, brain, and behavior, primates reflect a common evolutionary history with adaptations to similar environmental challenges, primarily as highly social, arboreal animals.

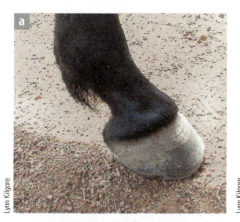

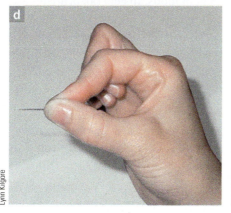

▲ **Figure 6-1**

(**a**) A horse's front foot, homologous with a human hand, has undergone reduction from five digits to one. (**b**) Although raccoons are capable of considerable manual dexterity and can easily pick up small objects with one hand, they have no opposable thumb. (**c**) Many monkeys are able to grasp objects with an opposable thumb, whereas others have very reduced thumbs. (**d**) Humans are capable of a "precision grip." (**e**) Chimpanzees, with their reduced thumbs, are capable of a precision grip but frequently use a modified form.

Limbs and Locomotion

The study of primate limb structures provides important information regarding locomotion and behavior. For example, we can see evidence of a primate's locomotive patterns in several different anatomical regions of the body.

1. *A tendency toward an erect posture (especially in the upper body)* (derived trait). All primates show this tendency to some degree; it's variously associated with sitting, leaping, standing, and occasionally bipedal locomotion.
2. *A flexible, generalized limb structure, which allows most primates to practice numerous forms of locomotion* (ancestral trait). Primates have retained some bones (such as the clavicle, or collarbone) and certain abilities (like rotation of the forearm) that have been lost in more specialized mammals such as horses (Fig. 6-1a). Various aspects of hip and shoulder **morphology** provide primates with a wide range of limb movement and function. Thus, by maintaining a generalized locomotor anatomy, primates aren't restricted to one form of movement, as are many other mammals. Primates also use their limbs for many activities besides locomotion.
3. *Prehensile hands (and sometimes feet)* (derived trait). Many animals can manipulate objects, but not as skillfully as primates (Fig. 6-1b). All primates use their hands and frequently their feet to grasp and manipulate objects. This ability is variably expressed and is enhanced by several characteristics, including:

    a. *Retention of five digits on the hands and feet* (ancestral trait). This trait varies somewhat throughout the order, with some species having reduced thumbs or second digits.
    b. *An opposable thumb and, in most species, a divergent and partially opposable big toe* (derived trait). Most primates are capable of moving the thumb so that it comes in contact with the second digit or with the palm of the hand (Fig. 6-1c–e).
    c. *Nails instead of claws* (derived trait). This characteristic is seen in all primates except two groups of New World monkeys. All lemurs and lorises also have a claw on one digit, known as a grooming claw.
    d. *Tactile pads enriched with sensory nerve fibers at the ends of digits* (derived trait). This characteristic enhances the sense of touch.

Dentition and Diet

The study of the dentition provides clues regarding the dietary patterns of primates. While tooth morphology reflects adaptations to different diets, primates as a group consume a wide range of resources.

1. *Lack of dietary specialization* (ancestral trait). This trait is typical of most primates, who tend to eat a wide assortment of foods. In general, primates are **omnivorous**.
2. *A generalized dentition* (ancestral trait). Primate teeth aren't specialized for processing only one type of food, a characteristic related to a general lack of dietary specialization.

The Senses and the Brain

Primates (**diurnal** ones in particular) rely heavily on vision and less on **olfaction**, especially when compared with other mammals. This emphasis is reflected in evolutionary changes in the skull, eyes, and brain (derived trait).

1. *Color vision* (derived trait). This is a characteristic of all Old World diurnal primates. Some New World species don't have the full range of color vision, and **nocturnal** primates lack color vision.

morphology The form (shape, size) of anatomical structures; can also refer to the entire organism.

omnivorous Having a diet consisting of many food types, such as plant materials, meat, and insects.

diurnal Active during the day.

olfaction The sense of smell.

nocturnal Active during the night.

stereoscopic vision The condition whereby visual images are, to varying degrees, superimposed. This provides for depth perception, or viewing the external environment in three dimensions. Stereoscopic vision is partly a function of structures in the brain.

binocular vision Vision characterized by overlapping visual fields provided by forward-facing eyes. Binocular vision is essential to depth perception.

hemisphere One of the two halves of the cerebrum, which are connected by a dense mass of fibers. (The cerebrum is the large rounded outer portion of the brain.)

neocortex The more recently evolved portions of the cortex (outer layer) of the brain that are involved with higher mental functions and composed of areas that integrate incoming information from different sensory organs.

sensory modalities Different forms of sensation (e.g., touch, pain, pressure, heat, cold, vision, taste, hearing, and smell).

2. *Depth perception* (derived trait). Primates have **stereoscopic vision**, or the ability to perceive objects in three dimensions. This is made possible through a variety of mechanisms, including:

a. *Eyes placed toward the front of the face (not to the sides).* This position provides for overlapping visual fields, or **binocular vision** (Fig. 6-2).

b. *Visual information from each eye transmitted to visual centers in both hemispheres of the brain.* In nonprimate mammals, most optic nerve fibers cross to the opposite **hemisphere** at the base of the brain. In primates, about 40 percent of the fibers remain on the same side, so that both hemispheres receive much of the same information.

c. *Visual information organized into three-dimensional images by specialized structures in the brain itself.* The capacity for stereoscopic vision depends on each hemisphere of the brain receiving visual information from both eyes and from overlapping visual fields.

3. *Decreased reliance on the sense of smell (olfaction)* (derived trait). This trend is expressed as an overall reduction in the size of olfactory structures in the brain. A corresponding reduction of the entire olfactory apparatus has also resulted in decreased size of the snout in most species. This is related to an increased dependence on vision. Some species, such as baboons, have large muzzles; however, this isn't related to olfaction but rather to the necessity of accommodating large canine teeth (see "A Closer Look: Primate Cranial Anatomy").

4. *Expansion and increased complexity of the brain* (derived trait). This is a general trend among placental mammals, but it's especially characteristic of primates. In primates, this expansion is most evident in the visual and association areas of the **neocortex** (portions of the brain where information from different **sensory modalities** is combined). Expansion in regions involved with sensory and motor functions of the hand is seen in many primate species, particularly humans.

Maturation, Learning, and Behavior

Primates have unusually long gestation periods, slow growth and development, and greater longevity when compared with other mammals. These characteristics are associated with several behavioral and social patterns.

1. *A more efficient means of fetal nourishment, longer periods of gestation, reduced numbers of offspring (with single births the norm), delayed maturation, and extension of the entire life span* (derived trait).

2. *A greater dependence on flexible, learned behavior* (derived trait). This trend is correlated with delayed maturation and subsequently longer periods of infant and subadult dependency on at least one parent. Because of these trends,

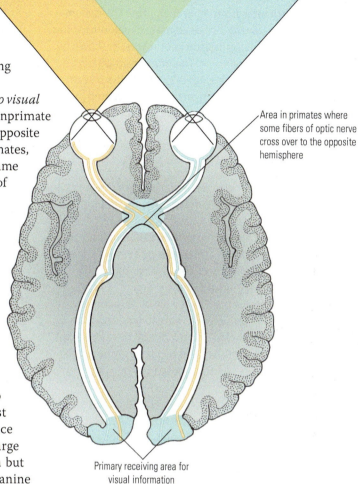

Area in primates where some fibers of optic nerve cross over to the opposite hemisphere

Primary receiving area for visual information

▲ **Figure 6-2**

This simplified diagram shows the overlapping visual fields that permit binocular vision in primates with eyes positioned at the front of the face. (The green-shaded area in front of the eyes represents the area of overlap.) Stereoscopic vision (three-dimensional vision) is provided in part by binocular vision and in part by the transmission of visual stimuli from each eye to both hemispheres of the brain. This is illustrated by the blue and gold lines, representing nerve fibers that transmit information from each eye to visual receiving areas at the rear of *both* sides of the brain. (In nonprimate mammals, most or all visual information crosses over to the hemisphere opposite the eye in which it was initially received.)

A Closer Look Primate Cranial Anatomy

Several anatomical features of the cranium distinguish primates from other mammals. The mammalian trend toward increased brain development has been further emphasized in primates, as shown by a relatively enlarged braincase. The primate emphasis on vision is further reflected in generally large eye sockets; the decreased dependence on olfaction is indicated by reduction of the snout and corresponding flattening of the face (Fig. 1).

Here are some of the specific anatomical details seen in modern and most fossil primate crania:

1. The primate face is shortened and the size of the braincase relative to that of the face is enlarged compared with other mammals (see Fig. 1).

2. Unlike the eye sockets seen in other mammals, primate eye sockets are enclosed at the sides by a ring of bone called the *postorbital bar* (see Fig. 1). Also, in tarsiers, monkeys, apes, and humans, there is a plate of bone at the back of the eye orbit called the *postorbital plate*, a feature that isn't present in lemurs, lorises, and other mammals. The functional significance of these structures hasn't been thoroughly explained, but it may be related to stresses on the eye orbits imposed by chewing (Fleagle, 1999).

3. The region of the skull that contains the structures of the middle ear is completely encircled by a bony structure called the *auditory bulla*. In primates, the floor of the auditory bulla is derived from a segment of the temporal bone (Fig. 2). Of all the skeletal structures, most primate paleontologists consider the postorbital bar and the

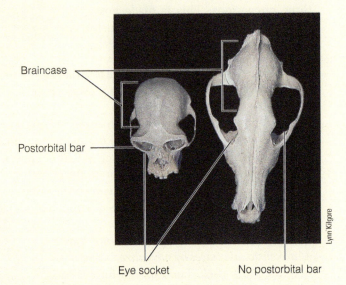

Braincase

Postorbital bar

Eye socket

No postorbital bar

Lynn Kilgore

▲ **Figure 1**

The skull of a gibbon (left) compared with that of a red wolf (right). Note that the absolute size of the braincase in the gibbon is slightly larger than that of the wolf, even though the wolf (at about 80 to 100 pounds) is six times the size of the gibbon (about 15 pounds).

derivation of the auditory bulla to be the two best diagnostic traits of the primate order.

4. The base of the skull in primates is somewhat flexed, so that the muzzle (mouth and nose) is positioned lower relative to the braincase (Fig. 3). This arrangement provides for the exertion of greater force during chewing, which is particularly needed for crushing and grinding tough vegetable fibers, seeds, and hard-shelled fruits.

---

parental investment in each offspring is increased. Although fewer offspring are born, they receive more parental care.

3. *The tendency to live in social groups and the permanent association of adult males with the group* (derived trait). Except for some nocturnal species, primates tend to associate with other individuals. Also, the permanent association of adult males with the group is uncommon in most mammals but widespread in primates.

4. *The tendency toward diurnal activity patterns* (derived trait). This is seen in most primates: Lorises, tarsiers, one monkey species, and some lemurs are nocturnal; all the rest (the other monkeys, apes, and humans) are diurnal.

Primate Adaptations

In this section, we consider how primate anatomical traits evolved as adaptations to environmental circumstances. It's important to remember that when you see the phrase *environmental circumstances*, it refers to several interrelated variables,

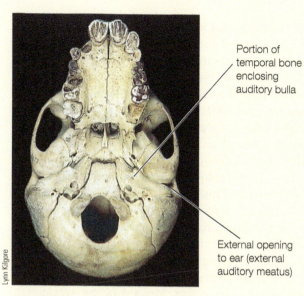

Portion of temporal bone enclosing auditory bulla

External opening to ear (external auditory meatus)

Lynn Kilgore

▲ **Figure 2**
The base of an adolescent chimpanzee skull. (In an adult animal, the bones of the skull would be fused together and would not appear as separate elements, as shown here.)

▶ **Figure 3**
The skull of a male baboon (**a**) compared with that of a red wolf (**b**). The angle at the base of the baboon skull is due to flexion. The corresponding area of the wolf skull is relatively flat. Note the forward-facing position of the eye orbits above the snout in the baboon. Also note that in the baboon, the enlarged muzzle does *not* reflect a heavy reliance on the sense of smell. Rather, it serves to support very large canine teeth, the roots of which curve back through the bone for as much as 1½ inches. Photos not to scale.

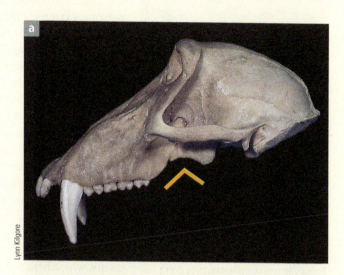

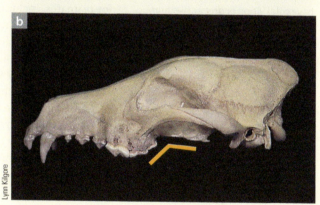

Lynn Kilgore

including climate, diet, habitat (woodland, grassland, forest, and so on), and predation pressure.

Evolutionary Factors

Traditionally, the group of characteristics shared by primates has been explained as the result of an adaptation to **arboreal** living. While other mammals were adapting to various ground-dwelling lifestyles and even marine environments, the primates found their **adaptive niche** in the trees. A number of other mammals were also adapting to arboreal living; but though many of them nested in the trees, they continued to forage for food on the ground (Fig. 6-3). However, throughout the course of evolution, primates increasingly found food (leaves, seeds, fruits, nuts, insects, and small mammals) in the trees themselves. Over time, this dietary shift enhanced a general trend toward *omnivory*, and this trend in turn led to the retention of the generalized dentition that's characteristic of most primates.

arboreal Tree living; adapted to life in the trees.

adaptive niche An organism's entire way of life: where it lives, what it eats, how it gets food, how it avoids predators, and so on.

▲ **Figure 6-3**
Gray squirrels are extremely well adapted to life in the trees, where they nest, sleep, play, and frequently eat. However, unlike primates, they don't have color vision or prehensile thumbs and big toes. They also have claws instead of nails.

Increased reliance on vision coupled with grasping hands and feet are also adaptations to an arboreal lifestyle. In a complex, three-dimensional environment with uncertain footholds, acute color vision with depth perception is, for obvious reasons, extremely beneficial.

An alternative to this traditional *arboreal hypothesis* is based on the fact that animals such as squirrels are also arboreal, yet they haven't evolved primate-like adaptations such as prehensile hands or forward-facing eyes. But visual predators, such as cats and owls, do have forward-facing eyes, and this fact may provide insight into an additional factor that could have shaped primate evolution.

Actually, forward-facing eyes (which facilitate binocular vision), grasping hands and feet, and the presence of nails instead of claws may not have come about solely as adaptive advantages in a purely arboreal setting. They may also have been the hallmarks of an arboreal visual predator. The *visual predation hypothesis* argues that early primates may first have adapted to shrubby forest undergrowth and the lowest tiers of the forest canopy, where they hunted insects and other small prey (Cartmill, 1972, 1992). In fact, many smaller primates occupy just such an econiche today.

Sussman (1991) suggested that the basic primate traits were developed in conjunction with another major evolutionary occurrence: the appearance of flowering plants, which began around 140 mya. Flowering plants provide numerous resources for primates, including nectar, seeds, and fruits. Sussman argued that since visual predation isn't common among modern primates, forward-facing eyes, grasping hands and feet, omnivory, and *color vision* may have arisen in response to the demand for fine visual and tactile discrimination. Certainly this type of discrimination is necessary when feeding on small food items such as fruits, berries, and seeds among branches and stems (Dominy and Lucas, 2001).

These hypotheses aren't mutually exclusive. The complex of primate characteristics might well have originated in nonarboreal settings and certainly could have been stimulated by the new econiches provided by evolving flowering plants. But at some point primates did take to the trees, and that's where most of them still live today.

Geographical Distribution and Habitats

With just a couple of exceptions, nonhuman primates are found in tropical or semitropical areas of the New and Old Worlds. In the New World, these areas include southern Mexico, Central America, and parts of South America. Old World primates are found in Africa, India, Southeast Asia (including numerous islands), and Japan (Fig. 6-4 on pp. 152–153).

Even though most nonhuman primates are arboreal and live in forest or woodland habitats, some Old World monkeys (for example, baboons) spend much of the day on the ground. The same is true for the African apes (gorillas, chimpanzees, and bonobos). Nevertheless, all nonhuman primates spend some time in the trees, especially when sleeping.

Diet and Teeth

Omnivory is one example of the overall lack of specialization in primates. Although all primates tend to emphasize some food items over others, most eat a combination of fruits, nuts, seeds, leaves, other plants, and insects. Many also get animal protein from birds and amphibians. Some (capuchins, baboons, bonobos, and especially chimpanzees) occasionally kill and eat small mammals, including other primates. Others, such as African colobus monkeys and the leaf-eating monkeys (langurs) of India and Southeast Asia, have become more specialized and mostly eat leaves.

This wide and varied menu is a good example of the advantages of having a generalized diet, especially in less predictable environments; if one food source fails (for example, during drought or because of human activities), other options may still be available. The downside of being generalized is that there may be competition for resources with other species that eat the same things. Specialization, where a species has a narrow ecological niche and eats only one or two things, can be advantageous in this regard because these species don't have much competition from others; but it can be catastrophic if the food supply disappears.

Like nearly all other mammals, primates have four kinds of teeth: incisors and canines for biting and cutting, and premolars and molars for chewing and grinding. Biologists use what's called a **dental formula** to describe the number of each type of tooth that typifies a species. A dental formula indicates the number of each tooth type in each quadrant of the mouth (Fig. 6-5 on p. 154). For example, all Old World *anthropoids* (monkeys, apes, and humans) have two incisors, one canine, two premolars, and three molars on each side of the midline in both the upper and lower jaws, for a total of 32 teeth. This is represented by the following dental formula:

$$\frac{2.1.2.3 \text{ (upper)}}{2.1.2.3 \text{ (lower)}}$$

The dental formula for a generalized placental mammal is 3.1.4.3 (three incisors, one canine, four premolars, and three molars). Primates have fewer teeth than this ancestral pattern because of a general evolutionary trend toward fewer teeth in many mammal groups. Consequently the number of each type of tooth varies between lineages. For example, in most New World monkeys, the dental formula is 2.1.3.3 (two incisors, one canine, three premolars, and three molars). (See Fig. 6-5 for a comparison of the dental formulae for modern humans and New World Monkeys). Some New World Monkeys (marmosets and tamarins) have lost their third molars, but still have three premolars in each quadrant of the dentition. Dental formulae can be abbreviated (for example, 2.1.2.3) when the upper and lower jaws have the same numbers for each tooth type; however, both the upper and lower should be indicated for species that have different numbers for each tooth type.

The overall lack of dietary specialization in primates is reflected in the lack of specialization in the size and shape of the teeth because tooth shape and size are directly related to diet. Carnivores typically have premolars and molars with high, pointed **cusps** adapted for tearing meat (*carnassial teeth*); but herbivores, such as cattle and horses, have premolars with broad, flat surfaces (*lophodont teeth*) suited to chewing tough grasses and other plant materials. Most primates have premolars and molars with low, rounded cusps—a molar morphology that enables them to process most types of foods. For apes and humans in particular, molar cusps are low and rounded to facilitate grinding of foods (*bunodont teeth*). So throughout their evolutionary history, the primates have developed a dentition adapted to a varied diet, and the capacity to exploit many foods has contributed to their overall success during the last 50 million years.

Locomotion

Almost all primates are, at least to some degree, **quadrupedal**, meaning that they use all four limbs to support the body during locomotion. However, most primates use more than one form of locomotion, and they're able to do this because of their generalized anatomy.

Vertical clinging and leaping, another form of locomotion, is characteristic of some lemurs and tarsiers. As the term implies, vertical clingers and leapers support themselves vertically by grasping onto trunks of trees or other large plants

dental formula Numerical device that indicates the number of each type of tooth in each quadrant of the upper and lower jaws.

cusps The bumps on the chewing surface of premolars and molars.

quadrupedal Using all four limbs to support the body during locomotion; the basic mammalian (and primate) form of locomotion.

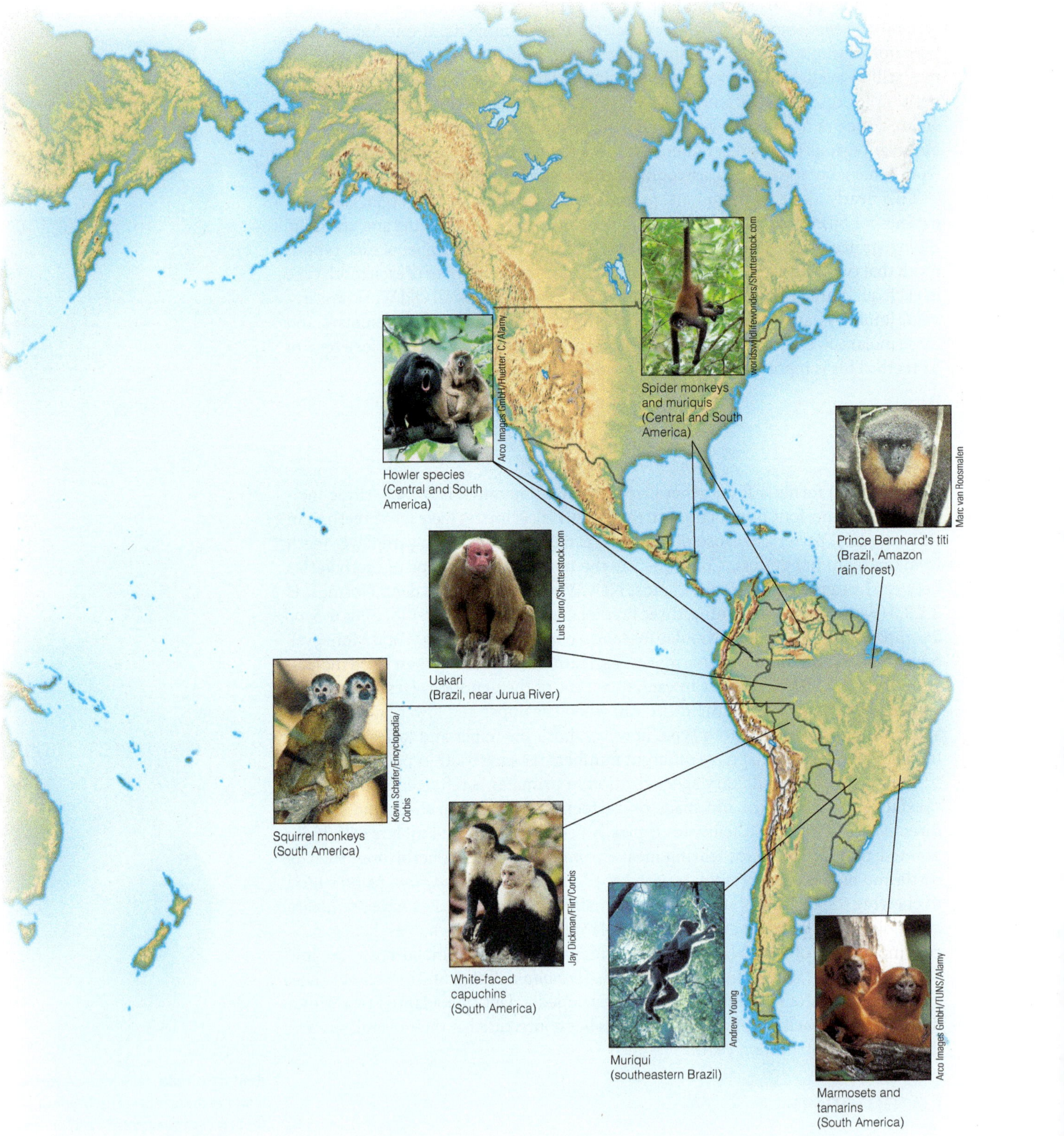
Spider monkeys and muriquis (Central and South America)
worldswildlifewonders/Shutterstock.com
Howler species (Central and South America)
Arco Images GmbH/Huetter, C./Alamy
Prince Bernhard's titi (Brazil, Amazon rain forest)
Marc van Roosmalen
Uakari (Brazil, near Jurua River)
Luis Louro/Shutterstock.com
Squirrel monkeys (South America)
Kevin Schafer/Encyclopedia/Corbis
White-faced capuchins (South America)
Jay Dickman/Flirt/Corbis
Muriqui (southeastern Brazil)
Andrew Young
Marmosets and tamarins (South America)
Arco Images GmbH/TUNS/Alamy

▲ **Figure 6-4**
Geographical distribution of living nonhuman primates. Much original habitat is now very fragmented.

Macaque species (North Africa, India, Southeast Asia, China, and Japan)
Jean De Rousseau

Gibbons and siamangs (Southeast Asia, islands, and China)
Lynn Kilgore

Baboon species (throughout sub-Saharan Africa)
Melanie Beasley

Cercopithecus species (throughout sub-Saharan Africa)
Melanie Beasley

Tarsier species (southeast Asian islands)
Nick Garbutt/Steve Bloom Images/Alamy

Loris species (Africa, India, and Southeast Asia)
Ian Butler Borneo/Alamy

Mountain and lowland gorillas (western and central Africa)
Lynn Kilgore

Langur species (colobines) (India, southern Asia, and south China)
Cyril Ruoso/Minden Pictures/Getty Images

Lemurs (Madagascar)
Fred Jacobs

Orangutans (Borneo and Sumatra)
Thomas Marent/Rolfnp/Rolf Nussbaumer Photography/Alamy

Chimpanzees and bonobos (across central Africa)
Melanie Beasley

Galago species (throughout sub-Saharan Africa)
Federico Veronesi/Getty Images

Colobus species (throughout sub-Saharan Africa)
Robert Jurmain

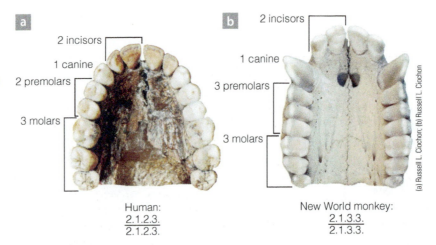

▶ **Figure 6-5**

(**a**) The human maxilla illustrates a dental formula characteristic of all Old World monkeys, apes, and humans. (**b**) The New World monkey (*Cebus*) maxilla shows the dental formula typical of most New World monkeys. (Not to scale; the monkey maxilla is actually much smaller than the human maxilla.)

a
2 incisors
1 canine
2 premolars
3 molars

Human:
2.1.2.3.
2.1.2.3.

b
2 incisors
1 canine
3 premolars
3 molars

New World monkey:
2.1.3.3.
2.1.3.3.

(a) Russell L. Ciochon; (b) Russell L. Ciochon

while their knees and ankles are tightly flexed (Fig. 6-6). By forcefully extending their long hind limbs, they can spring powerfully away either forward or backward.

Brachiation, or arm swinging, is a suspensory form of locomotion in which the body moves by being alternatively supported by one forelimb and then the other. (You may have brachiated as a child on "monkey bars" in playgrounds, although these would more appropriately be called "ape bars".) Because of anatomical modifications at the shoulder joint, apes and humans are capable of true brachiation. However, only the small gibbons and siamangs of Southeast Asia use this form of locomotion almost exclusively (Fig. 6-7).

Brachiation is seen in species characterized by arms longer than legs; a short, stable lower back; long curved fingers; and shortened thumbs. Because these are traits seen in all the apes, it's believed that although none of the great apes (orangutans, gorillas, bonobos, and chimpanzees) habitually brachiates today, they probably inherited these characteristics from brachiating or climbing ancestors.

Some New World monkeys, such as spider monkeys and muriquis, are called semibrachiators because they practice a combination of leaping with some arm swinging. Also, some New World monkeys enhance arm swinging and other suspensory behaviors by using a *prehensile tail*, which serves as an effective grasping fifth hand. It's important to mention here that prehensile tails are exclusively a New World phenomenon; they aren't seen in any Old World primates.

Lastly, all the apes to varying degrees have arms that are longer than legs, and some (gorillas, bonobos, and chimpanzees) practice a special form of quadrupedalism called *knuckle walking*. Because their arms are so long relative to their legs, instead of walking with the palms of their hands flat on the ground as some monkeys do, they support the weight of their upper body on the back surfaces of their bent fingers (Fig. 6-8).

Cyril Ruoso/Feature Stories/Ring-tailed Lemurs/Minden picture

▲ **Figure 6-6**

Ring-tailed lemurs in a typical vertical clinging posture. They also spend some time on the ground, where they walk quadrupedally.

Terry Whittaker/Science Source

▶ **Figure 6-7**

White-handed gibbon brachiating. Note the very long arms and long, curved fingers.

Primate Classification

The living primates are commonly categorized into their respective subgroups, as shown in Figure 6-9. This taxonomy is based on the system originally established by Linnaeus (see Chapter 2). The primate order, which comprises approximately 230 species, belongs to a larger group, the class Mammalia (see Chapter 5).

In any taxonomic system, as you learned in Chapter 5, animals are organized into increasingly specific categories. For example, the order Primates includes *all* primates. But at the next level down, the *suborder*, primates are divided into two smaller categories: **Strepsirrhini** (lemurs and lorises) and **Haplorhini** (tarsiers, monkeys, apes, and humans). Therefore the suborder distinction is narrower, or more specific. At the suborder level, the lemurs and lorises are distinct as a group from all the other primates. This classification makes the biological and evolutionary statement that all the lemurs and lorises are more closely related to one another than they are to any of the other primates. Likewise, humans, apes, monkeys, and tarsiers are more closely related to one another than they are to the lorises and lemurs.

The taxonomy shown in Figure 6-9 is a modified version of a similar system that biologists and primatologists have used for decades. The traditional system is based on physical similarities between species and lineages; however, sometimes this approach leads to erroneous conclusions. For instance, some New and Old World monkeys resemble each other anatomically; evolutionarily, however, they're quite distinct, having diverged from a common ancestor perhaps as long as 40 mya. By considering only physical characteristics, it's possible to overlook the unknown effects of separate evolutionary history (see the discussion of homoplasy in Chapter 5). But thanks to the rapidly growing number of species whose genomes have been sequenced, geneticists can now make direct comparisons between the genes and indeed the entire genetic makeup of different species. This kind of analysis, called *comparative genomics*, gives us a much more accurate picture of evolutionary and biological relationships between species than was possible even as recently as the late 1990s. So once again, we see how changing technologies influence the refining of older hypotheses and the development of new ones.

A complete draft sequence of the chimpanzee genome was completed in 2005 (Chimpanzee Sequencing and Analysis Consortium, 2005)—a major milestone in human comparative genomics. Comparisons of the genomes of different species are extremely important because they reveal such differences in DNA as the number of nucleotide substitutions and/or deletions that have occurred since related species last shared a common ancestor. Geneticists estimate the rate at which genes change and then use this information, combined with the amount of change they observe, to estimate when related species diverged from their last common ancestor.

Wildman and colleagues (2003) compared nearly 100 human genes with their chimpanzee, gorilla, and orangutan counterparts. Their results supported some earlier studies, which had concluded that humans are most closely related to chimpanzees and that the protein-coding DNA sequences of the two species are 98.4 to 99.4 percent identical. The results of the study also estimated that the chimpanzee and human lineages diverged between 6 and 7 mya. These results are consistent with the molecular findings of several other studies (Chen and Li, 2001; Clark et al., 2003; Steiper and Young, 2006). Other research has substantiated these figures, but it has also revealed more variation in noncoding DNA segments and portions that have been inserted, deleted, or duplicated. So when the *entire* genome is considered, reported DNA differences between chimpanzees and humans range from 2.7 percent (Cheng et al., 2005) to 6.4 percent (Demuth et al., 2006). These aren't substantial differences, but perhaps the most important discovery of all is

Lynn Kilgore

▲ **Figure 6-8**
Chimpanzee knuckle walking. Note how the weight of the upper body is supported on the knuckles and not the palm of the hand.

brachiation Arm swinging, a form of locomotion used by some primates. Brachiation involves hanging from a branch and moving by alternately swinging from one arm to the other.

Strepsirrhini (strep´-sir-in-ee) The primate suborder that includes lemurs and lorises. (Colloquial form: strepsirrhine.)

Haplorhini (hap´-lo-rin-ee) The primate suborder that includes tarsiers, monkeys, apes, and humans. (Colloquial form: haplorhine.)

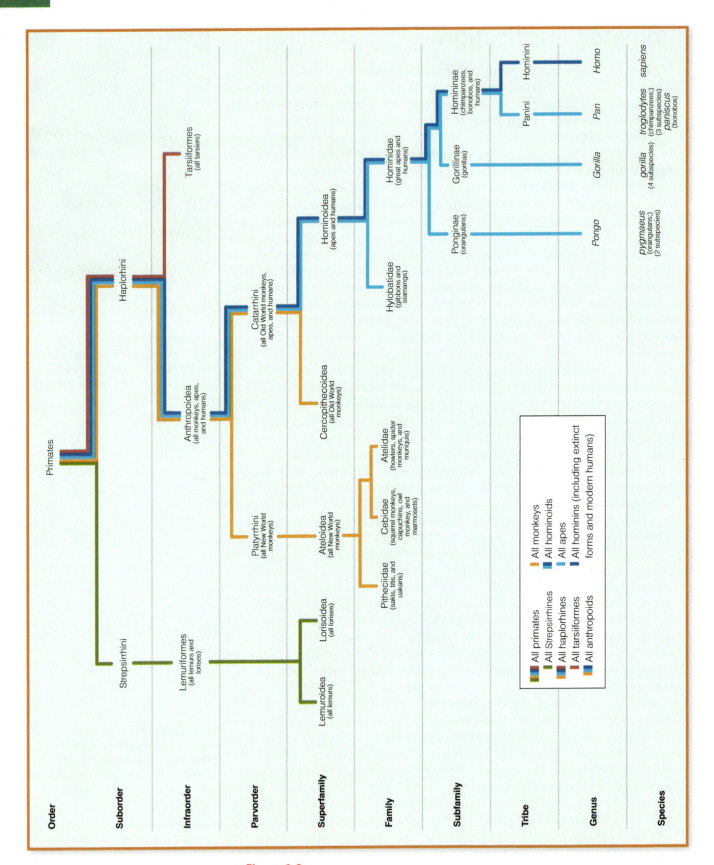

▲ **Figure 6-9**
Primate taxonomic classification. This abbreviated taxonomy illustrates how primates are grouped from broader categories (e.g., the order Primates) into increasingly specific ones (species). Except for the great apes and humans, only the more general categories are shown.

that humans have much more non-protein-coding DNA than do the other primates that have thus far been studied. Now that geneticists are beginning to understand some of the functions of non-protein-coding DNA, they hope to explain why humans have so much of it and how it makes us different from our closest relatives.

A Survey of the Living Nonhuman Primates

In this section, we discuss the major primate subgroups. Since it's beyond the scope of this book to cover any species in great detail, we present a brief description of each major grouping, taking a closer look at the apes.

▲ Figure 6-10
The moist surface of this cow's nose enhances her sense of smell. Many mammals have rhinaria.

Lemurs and Lorises

The suborder Strepsirrhini includes the lemurs and lorises, the most nonderived or primitive living primates. Remember that by *primitive* we mean that lemurs and lorises are more similar anatomically to their earlier mammalian ancestors than are the other primates (tarsiers, monkeys, apes, and humans). For example, they retain certain ancestral characteristics, such as a more pronounced reliance on *olfaction*. Their greater olfactory capabilities (compared with other primates) are reflected in the presence of a moist, fleshy pad, or **rhinarium**, at the end of the nose and a relatively long snout (Fig. 6-10).

Many other characteristics distinguish lemurs and lorises from the other primates, including eyes placed more to the side of the face, differences in reproductive physiology, and shorter gestation and maturation periods. Lemurs and lorises also have a unique derived trait called a "dental comb" (Fig. 6-11), formed by forward-projecting lower incisors and canines. These modified teeth are used in both grooming and feeding. One other characteristic that sets lemurs and lorises apart is the retention of a claw (called a "grooming claw") on the second toe.

▲ Figure 6-11
Lemur dental comb, formed by forward-projecting incisors and canines.

rhinarium (rine-air′-ee-um) The moist, hairless pad at the end of the nose seen in most mammalian species. The rhinarium enhances an animal's ability to smell.

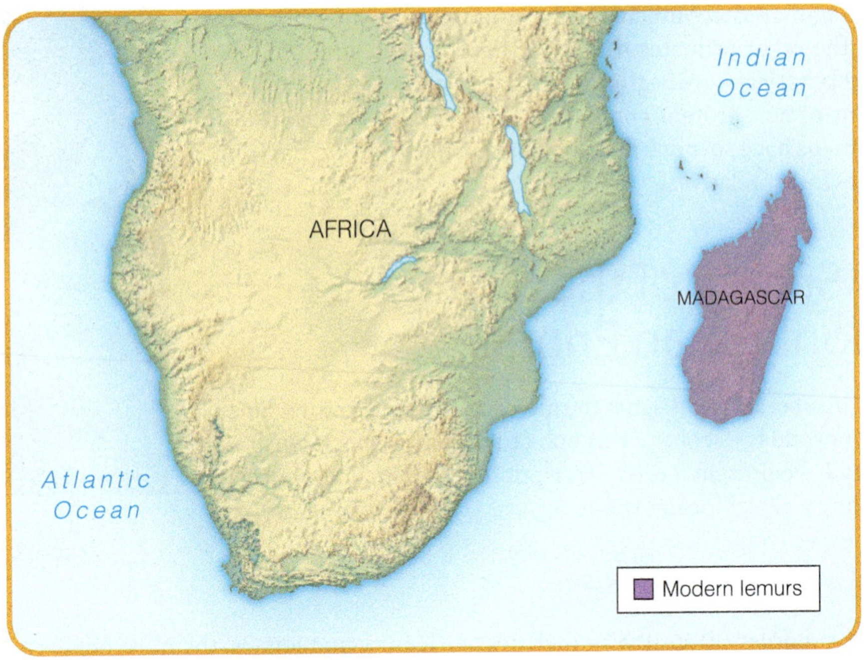

▶ **Figure 6-12**
Geographical distribution of modern lemurs.

Lemurs Lemurs are found only on the island of Madagascar and adjacent islands off the east coast of Africa (Fig. 6-12). As the only nonhuman primates on Madagascar, lemurs diversified into many and varied ecological niches without competition from monkeys and apes. Thus the 103 known lemur species on Madagascar today represent a kind of lost world, an evolutionary pattern that vanished elsewhere. It is a tragedy that, with 91 percent of lemur species now threatened with extinction, lemurs are possibly the most endangered group of vertebrates in the world (Mittermeier et al., 2014).

Lemurs range in size from the tiny Madame Berthe's mouse lemur, with a body length (head and trunk) of only 3 inches, to the indri, with a body length of 2 to 3 feet (Nowak, 1999). Typically the larger lemurs are diurnal and eat a wide variety of foods, such as leaves, fruits, buds, bark, and shoots, but the tiny mouse and dwarf lemurs are nocturnal insectivores.

There is a great deal of behavioral variation among lemur species. Some are mostly arboreal, but others, such as ring-tailed lemurs (see Fig. 6-6), are more terrestrial. Some arboreal species are quadrupeds, and others (sifakas, ring-tails, and indris) are vertical clingers and leapers (Fig. 6-13). Several species (for example, ring-tailed lemurs and sifakas) live in groups of 10 to 25 animals comprising males and females of all ages. However, indris are among the few primates that live in social units composed of mated pairs and dependent offspring. Additionally, several nocturnal forms are mostly solitary.

Lorises Lorises (Fig. 6-14), which somewhat resemble lemurs, were able to survive in Africa and Asia by being nocturnal. In this way, they were (and are) able to avoid competition with more recently evolved primates, the diurnal monkeys.

There are at least eight loris species, all of which are found in tropical forest and woodland habitats of India, Sri Lanka, Southeast Asia, and Africa. Also included in the same general category are six to nine galago species, sometimes called bush babies (Bearder, 1987; Nowak, 1999), which are widely distributed throughout most of the forested and woodland savanna areas of sub-Saharan Africa (Fig. 6-15).

Locomotion in some lorises is a slow, cautious, climbing form of quadrupedalism. All galagos, however, are highly agile vertical clingers and leapers. Some lorises and galagos are almost entirely insectivorous, while others also eat combinations

Fred Jacobs

◀ **Figure 6-13**
Verreaux's sifakas are another lemur species.

of fruits, leaves, and other plant products. Lorises and galagos frequently forage alone, but feeding ranges can overlap, and two or more females may feed and even nest together. Females also leave young infants behind in nests while they search for food (referred to as *parking*). Leaving infants alone is extremely uncommon among primates. With these exceptions, all primate infants are always carried by a parent, usually the mother, from the time they're born.

Lemurs and lorises represent the same general adaptive level. Both groups exhibit good grasping and climbing abilities and a well-developed visual apparatus; however, vision is not completely stereoscopic, and in diurnal species, color vision may not be as well developed as in anthropoids.

Tarsiers

There are five recognized tarsier species (Nowak, 1999), all of which are restricted to islands of Southeast Asia (Malaysia, Borneo, Sumatra, and the Philippines), where they inhabit a wide range of habitats, from tropical forest to backyard gardens (Figs. 6-16 and 6-17). Tarsiers are nocturnal insectivores that use vertical clinging and leaping to surprise prey (which may also include small vertebrates) on lower branches and shrubs. They appear to form stable pair bonds, and the

Ian Butler Borneo/Alamy

▲ **Figure 6-14**
A slow loris in Malaysia. Note the large forward-facing eyes and rhinarium.

Federico Veronesi/Getty Images

◀ **Figure 6-15**
Galago, or "bush baby."

Nick Garbutt/Steve Bloom Images/Alamy

▲ **Figure 6-16**
Bornean tarsier.

▲ **Figure 6-17**
Geographical distribution of the various tarsier species.

basic tarsier social unit is a mated pair and their young offspring (MacKinnon and MacKinnon, 1980).

Tarsiers are highly specialized (derived) animals that have several unique characteristics. In the past, primatologists believed that tarsiers were more closely related to lemurs and lorises than to other primates because they share several traits with them. Consequently they were classified in the same suborder as lemurs and lorises. However, tarsiers actually present a complex blend of characteristics not seen in any other primate. One of the most obvious is their enormous eyes, which dominate much of the face and are immobile within their sockets. To compensate for the inability to move their eyes, tarsiers, like owls, can rotate their heads 180 degrees. A tarsier's eye is about the same size as its brain!

In addition, tarsiers possess certain anthropoid characteristics (for example, they have a fused frontal bone and lack a rhinarium like monkeys, apes, and humans), and DNA studies have indicated that they are more closely related to monkeys, apes, and humans than to lemurs and lorises. Therefore, although there is still some debate as to the taxonomic status of tarsiers, they are now classified in the suborder Haplorhini, along with the anthropoids (see Fig. 6-9 and Appendix A).

Anthropoids: Monkeys, Apes, and Humans

Although there is much variation among anthropoids, they share certain features that, taken together, distinguish them as a group from lemurs and lorises. Here's a partial list of these anthropoid traits:

1. A larger average body size
2. A larger brain in absolute terms and relative to body weight
3. Reduced reliance on olfaction, indicated by absence of a rhinarium and a reduction in the relative size of olfactory-related structures in the brain

4. Increased reliance on vision, with forward-facing eyes placed more to the front of the face
5. A greater degree of color vision
6. Back of eye socket protected by a bony plate (*post-orbital closure*)
7. Blood supply to the brain different from that of lemurs and lorises
8. Fusion of the two sides of the mandible at the midline to form one bone (in lemurs and lorises, they're two distinct bones joined by cartilage at the middle of the chin)
9. More generalized dentition, as seen in the absence of a dental comb and some other features
10. Differences in female internal reproductive anatomy
11. Longer gestation and maturation periods
12. Increased parental care
13. More mutual grooming

Approximately 85 percent of all primates are monkeys and newly discovered species are still being described. Monkeys are divided into two groups separated by geographical area (New World and Old World), as well as at least 40 million years of separate evolutionary history.

New World Monkeys   The approximately 70 New World monkey species can be found in a wide range of arboreal environments throughout most forested areas in southern Mexico and Central and South America (Fig. 6-18). They exhibit a wide range of variation in size, diet, and ecological adaptation (Fig. 6-19). In size, they vary from the tiny marmosets and tamarins (about 12 ounces) to the 20-pound howler

◀ **Figure 6-18**
Geographical distribution of New World monkeys.

Male uakari

Squirrel monkeys

Prince Bernhard's titi monkey (discovered in 2002)

White-faced capuchins

Female muriqui with infant

▲ **Figure 6-19**

Some New World monkeys.

◀ **Figure 6-20**
Golden lion tamarins.

▶ **Figure 6-21**
Male, female, and infant howler monkeys. Illustrating why they're called "howlers." The roaring sound they make is among the loudest of mammalian vocalizations.

Arco Images GmbH/TUNS/Alamy

Arco Images GmbH/Huetter, C./Alamy

monkeys (Figs. 6-20 and 6-21). New World monkeys are almost exclusively arboreal, and some never come to the ground. Like the Old World monkeys, all except one species (the owl monkey) are diurnal.

One characteristic that distinguishes New and Old World monkeys is the shape of the nose. New World monkeys have broad noses with outward-facing nostrils; Old World monkeys have narrower noses with downward-facing nostrils. To verify this, compare the white-faced capuchins in Figure 6-19 with the Sykes monkey in Figure 6-24 or with your own downward-facing nostrils. This difference in nose form has given rise to the terms *platyrrhine* (flat-nosed) and *catarrhine* (downward-facing nose) to refer to New and Old World anthropoids, respectively. The more formal terminology used in primate classification is shown in Fig. 6-9 and will be discussed in more detail in Chapter 8.

In addition to being the smallest of all monkeys, marmosets and tamarins have several other distinguishing features. They have claws instead of nails and a 2.1.3.2 dental formula, and unlike other primates, they usually give birth to twins instead of a single infant. They're mostly insectivorous, although marmosets eat gum from trees and tamarins also eat fruit. Marmosets and tamarins are quadrupedal, and they use their claws for climbing. These tiny monkeys live in social groups usually composed of a mated pair or a female and two adult males and their offspring. This type of mating pattern is rare among mammals. Indeed, marmosets and tamarins are among the few primate species in which males are extensively involved in infant care (a truly progressive society!).

▲ **Figure 6-22**
Spider monkey. Note use of prehensile tail for suspension.

Cercopithecidae (serk-oh-pith´-eh-see-dee) The taxonomic family that includes all Old World monkeys.

Cercopithicinae (serk-oh-pith´-eh-see-nee) Taxonomic subfamily of Old World monkeys that have cheek pouches for storing food. Includes macaques, baboons, and several other species of monkey that use both arboreal and terrestrial habitats.

cercopithecines (serk-oh-pith´-eh-seens) Common name for members of the subfamily of Old World monkeys that includes baboons, macaques, and guenons.

Colobinae (kole´-uh-bi-nay) Taxonomic subfamily of Old World leaf-eating monkeys that have reduced thumbs and multi-chambered stomachs. Includes colobus monkeys, proboscis monkeys, and langurs.

colobines (kole´-uh-bines) Common name for members of the subfamily of Old World monkeys that includes the African colobus monkeys and Asian langurs.

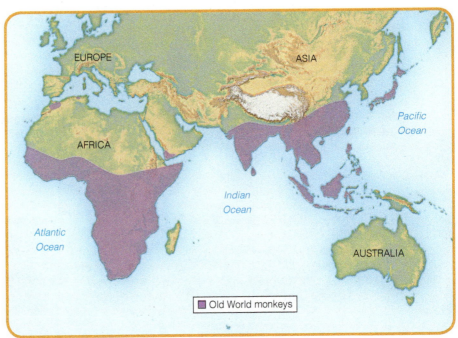

▲ **Figure 6-23**
Geographical distribution of living Old World monkeys.

Other New World species range in size from squirrel monkeys (weighing only 1.5 to 2.5 pounds and having a body length of 12 inches) to the larger howlers (as much as 22 pounds in males and around 24 inches long).

New World monkeys rely on a combination of fruits and leaves supplemented to varying degrees with insects. Most are quadrupedal; but some, such as spider monkeys (Fig. 6-22), are semibrachiators. Howlers, muriquis, and spider monkeys also have prehensile tails that are used not only in locomotion but also for hanging from branches. Socially, most New World monkeys live in mixed-sex groups of all age categories. Some (such as titis) form monogamous pairs and live with their subadult offspring.

Old World Monkeys Except for humans, Old World monkeys are the most widely distributed of all living primates. They're found throughout sub-Saharan Africa and southern Asia, ranging from tropical jungle habitats to semiarid desert and even to seasonally snowcovered areas in northern Japan (Fig. 6-23).

All Old World monkeys are placed in one taxonomic family, **Cercopithecidae** (serk-oh-pith´-eh-see-dee). In turn, this family is divided into two subfamilies: the **Cercopithecinae** (serk-oh-pith´-eh-see-nee), which are the **cercopithecines** (serk-oh-pith´-eh-seens) and the **Colobinae**, which are the **colobines** (kole´-uh-bines). Most Old World monkeys are quadrupedal and primarily arboreal, but some (such as baboons) spend a great deal of time on the ground and return to the trees at night.

The cercopithecines are more generalized than colobines. They're more omnivorous and, as a group, will eat almost anything: fruits, seeds, leaves, grasses, tubers, roots, nuts, insects, birds' eggs, amphibians, small reptiles, and small mammals (the last seen in baboons).

The majority of cercopithecine species, such as the mostly arboreal guenons (Dutch for *clown*; Fig. 6-24) and the more terrestrial baboons (Fig. 6-25), are found in Africa. The many macaque species (including the well-known rhesus monkeys), however, are widely distributed in southern Asia and India.

▲ **Figure 6-24**
Adult male Sykes monkey, one of several guenon species.

▲ **Figure 6-25**
Hamadryas baboons are found in Ethiopia. Note how much larger the male (at right) is than the female. The male also has much longer hair around the head and shoulders, which produces a distinctive mane.

Colobine species have a narrower range of food preferences and mainly eat mature leaves, which is why they're also called leaf-eating monkeys. The colobines are found mainly in Asia, but both the red colobus and black-and-white colobus are exclusively African (Fig. 6-26). Other colobines include several Asian langur species and the proboscis monkey of Borneo (Fig. 6-27).

Locomotion in Old World monkeys includes arboreal quadrupedalism in guenons, macaques, and langurs; terrestrial quadrupedalism in baboons and macaques; and semibrachiation and acrobatic leaping in colobus monkeys.

▲ **Figure 6-26**
Black-and-white colobus monkeys.

▲ **Figure 6-27**
Male proboscis monkey. The nose (which gives the species its common name) is much larger in males than in females.

Marked differences in body size or shape between the sexes, referred to as **sexual dimorphism**, are typical of some terrestrial species and are especially pronounced in baboons. In these species, male body weight (up to 80 pounds in baboons) may be twice that of females.

Females of several species (especially baboons and some macaques) have pronounced cyclical changes of the external genitalia. These changes, which include swelling and redness, are associated with estrus, a hormonally initiated period of sexual receptivity in female nonhuman mammals correlated with ovulation. They serve as visual cues to males that females are sexually receptive.

Old World monkeys live in a few different kinds of social groups. Colobines tend to live in small groups, with only one or two adult males. Savanna baboons and most macaque species are found in large social units comprising several adults of both sexes and offspring of all ages. Monogamous pairing isn't common in Old World monkeys, but it's seen in a few langur species and possibly one or two guenon species.

Old and New World Monkeys: A Case of Homoplasy We've mentioned several differences between New and Old World monkeys, but the fact remains that they're all monkeys. That is, they're all adapted to a similar (primarily arboreal) way of life. Except for South American owl monkeys, they're all diurnal. All live in social groupings; all are omnivorous to varying degrees; and all are quadrupedal (though there are variations of this general locomotor pattern).

These similarities are even more striking when you consider that New and Old World monkeys have followed separate evolutionary paths for at least 40 million years. It was once believed that both lineages evolved independently from separate early primate ancestors; but today the consensus is that both New and Old World monkeys arose in Africa from a common monkey ancestor. The animals that gave rise to today's New World species reached South America by "rafting" over on chunks of land that had broken away from mainland areas (Hoffstetter, 1972; Ciochon and Chiarelli, 1980b). It is remarkable that the two forms haven't become more different from one another. The arboreal adaptations we see in both New and Old World monkeys are examples of homoplasy resulting from adaptations in geographically distinct populations that have responded to similar selective pressures. This phenomenon, which we'll explain more fully in Chapter 8, probably happened many times over the course of several million years.

Hominoids: Apes and Humans

Apes and humans are classified together in the same superfamily, **Hominoidea** (Hom·i·noi·dea), which are the **hominoids**. Apes are found in Asia and Africa. The small-bodied gibbons and siamangs live in Southeast Asia, and the two orangutan subspecies live on the islands of Borneo and Sumatra (Fig. 6-28). In Africa, until the mid- to late twentieth century, gorillas, chimpanzees, and bonobos occupied the forested areas of western, central, and eastern Africa, but their habitat is now extremely fragmented, and all are now threatened or highly endangered. Apes and humans differ from monkeys in numerous ways:

1. Generally larger body size (except for gibbons and siamangs)
2. No tail
3. Shorter and more stable lower back
4. Arms longer than legs (only in apes)
5. Anatomical differences in the shoulder joint, which facilitate suspensory feeding and locomotion
6. Generally more complex behavior

sexual dimorphism Differences in physical characteristics between males and females of the same species. For example, humans are slightly sexually dimorphic for body size, with males being taller, on average, than females of the same population. Sexual dimorphism is very pronounced in many species, such as gorillas.

Hominoidea Taxonomic superfamily that includes all apes and humans (tailless primates).

hominoids Members of the primate superfamily (Hominoidea), which includes apes and humans.

territorial Pertaining to the protection of all or a part of the area occupied by an animal or group of animals. Territorial behaviors range from scent marking to outright attacks on intruders.

◀ **Figure 6-28**
Geographical distribution of living Asian apes.

7. More complex brain and enhanced cognitive abilities
8. Increased period of infant development and dependency

Gibbons and Siamangs   The eight gibbon species and the closely related sia-mangs are the smallest of the apes, with long, slender bodies that weigh approxi-mately 13 pounds in gibbons (Fig. 6-29) and around 25 pounds in siamangs. Their most distinctive anatomical features are adaptations to feeding while hanging from tree branches, or brachiation, at which gibbons and siamangs excel. In fact, gib-bons and siamangs are more dedicated to brachiation than any other primate, a fact reflected in their extremely long arms, long, permanently curved fingers, short thumbs, and powerful shoulder muscles. (Their arms are so long that when they're on the ground, they have to walk bipedally with their arms raised to the side.) Gibbons and siamangs mostly eat fruits, although they also consume a variety of leaves, flowers, and insects.

The basic social unit of gibbons and siamangs comprises an adult male and female with dependent offspring. Although they've been described as monoga-mous, in reality members of a pair do sometimes mate with other individuals. Like marmosets and tamarins, male gibbons and siamangs are very much involved in rearing their young. Both males and females are highly **territorial** and protect their territories with elaborate whoops and siren-like "songs," lending them the name "the singing apes of Asia."

Many gibbon species are critically endangered today. The eastern blackcrested gibbon for example, is now represented by 18 known groups living in small areas along the border between Vietnam and China. The total number of animals living in these groups was estimated at approximately 110 individuals in 2007 (Dat et al., 2008). Much of the remaining habitat is threatened by forest clearing

Gerry Ellis/Minden Pictures

▲ **Figure 6-29**
White-handed cream-colored gibbon. The combination of a much reduced thumb and extremely elongated fingers and shortened thumb enhances the ability to brachiate.

for cultivation and livestock. Moreover, hunting is always a problem. With so few animals living in dispersed groups, the survival of this species is in doubt, but conservation efforts are under way.

Orangutans   Orangutans (*Pongo pygmaeus*) (Fig. 6-30) are represented by two subspecies found today only in heavily forested areas on the Indonesian islands of Borneo and Sumatra. The name *orangutan* (which has no final g and should never be pronounced "o-rang-utang") means "wise man of the forest" in the language of the local people. But despite this somewhat affectionate-sounding label, orangutans are severely threatened with extinction in the wild because of poaching by humans and continuing habitat loss on both islands. Habitat loss is especially severe on Sumatra, where land is continuously being cleared for coffee cultivation, wood pulp for paper products, and—most important of all—palm oil production. Additionally, orangutans are shot as pests and infants find their way into the pet trade. Today an estimated 6,600 Sumatran orangutans live in fragmented habitats in northern Sumatra (Singleton et al., 2009). That may seem like a relatively high number, but Sumatra's forests are currently being cleared at a rate of 300 football fields every hour, 24 hours a day. Indeed, half of the forest that existed in 1985 was destroyed by 2012.

Orangutans are slow, cautious climbers whose form of locomotion can best be described as four-handed, referring to their use of all four limbs for grasping and support. Although they're almost completely arboreal, orangutans sometimes travel on the ground, walking on their fists. They exhibit pronounced sexual dimorphism; males may weigh more than 200 pounds whereas females typically weigh less than 100 pounds. In the wild, orangutans lead largely solitary lives, although adult females are usually accompanied by one or two dependent offspring. They're primarily **frugivorous** but may also eat bark, leaves, insects, and (rarely) meat.

frugivorous Having a diet composed primarily of fruits.

▲ **Figure 6-30**
Bornean orangutans. (**a**) Female with infant. (**b**) Male.

(a) Thomas Marent/Rolfnp/Rolf Nussbaumer Photography/Alamy, (b) Thomas Marent/Minden pictures

Gorillas The largest of all living primates, gorillas (*Gorilla gorilla*) are found in forested areas of western and eastern equatorial Africa (Fig. 6-31). There are four generally recognized gorilla subspecies. Of these, Western lowland gorillas (Fig. 6-32) are the most numerous and are found in several countries of west-central Africa. In 1998, Doran and McNeilage estimated their population size at perhaps 110,000, but Walsh and colleagues (2003) suggested that their numbers were far lower. Staggeringly, in August 2008, the Wildlife Conservation Society reported the discovery of an estimated 125,000 western lowland gorillas in the northern region of the Democratic Republic of the Congo (DRC, formerly Zaire)! This is extremely encouraging news, but it doesn't mean that gorillas are out of danger. To put this figure into perspective, consider that a large football stadium can hold around 70,000 people. So next time you see a stadium packed with fans, think about the fact that you're perhaps looking at a crowd that numbers around half of all the western lowland gorillas on earth. Unless the DRC government, acting with wildlife conservation groups, can set aside more land as national parks and protect the gorillas from hunting and disease, it's probable that western lowland gorillas face extinction in the wild.

Cross River gorillas, a West African subspecies, were identified in the early 1900s but thought to be extinct until the 1980s, when primatologists became aware of a few small populations in areas along the border between Nigeria and Cameroon (Sarmiento and Oates, 2000). Primatologists believe that there may be only 250 to 300 of these animals; thus Cross River gorillas are among the most endangered of all primates. Currently the International Union for the Conservation of Nature and Natural Resources (IUCN) is developing plans to protect this vulnerable and little-known subspecies (Oates et al., 2007).

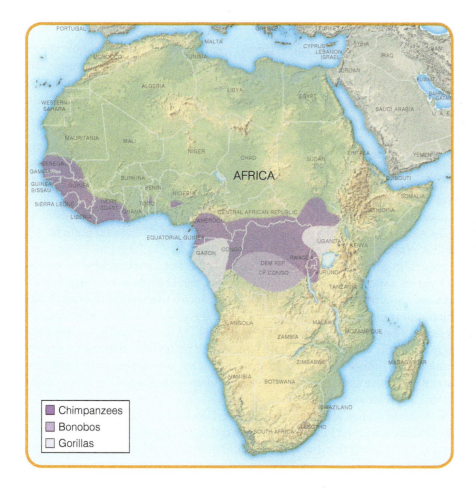

◀ **Figure 6-31**
Geographical distribution of living African apes.

■ Chimpanzees
■ Bonobos
□ Gorillas

Michael Krabs/ImageBroker/Alamy

Duncan Usher/Alamy

▲ **Figure 6-32**
Lowland gorillas. (**a**) Male. (**b**) Female with infant.

Eastern lowland gorillas, which haven't been studied in detail, live near the eastern border of the DRC. At present, their numbers are unknown but suspected to be around 17,000. (You wouldn't need a very large football stadium to hold this many people.) Owing to warfare in the region, researchers fear that many of these gorillas have been killed, but it's impossible to know how many.

Mountain gorillas (Fig. 6-33), the most extensively studied of the four subspecies, are restricted to the mountainous areas of central Africa in Rwanda, the DRC, and Uganda. There have probably never been many mountain gorillas, and as of 2012, they number only about 880 animals, making them one of the more endangered primate species.

Like all gorillas, mountain gorillas exhibit marked sexual dimorphism, with males weighing up to 400 pounds and females around 150 to 200 pounds. Adult gorillas, especially males, are primarily terrestrial.

Mountain gorillas live in groups composed of one or sometimes two large silverback males, a variable number of adult females, and their subadult offspring. (The term *silverback* refers to the saddle of white hair across the backs of fully adult males, which appears around the age of 12 or 13 years.) A silverback male may tolerate the presence of one or more young adult "blackback" males (probably his sons) in his group. Typically but not always, both females and males leave their **natal group** as young adults. Females join other groups, and males, who appear to be less likely to emigrate, may live alone for a while or may join up with other males before eventually forming their own groups.

Systematic studies of free-ranging western lowland gorillas weren't begun until the mid-1980s, so even though they're the only gorillas you'll see in zoos, we don't know as much about them as we do about mountain gorillas. The social structure

natal group The group in which animals are born and raised. (*Natal* pertains to birth.)

(a) Thomas Marent/Minden pictures; (b) Lynn Kilgore

▲ **Figure 6-33**
Mountain gorillas. (**a**) A male silverback mountain gorilla with his group in the background. (**b**) Female.

of western lowland gorillas is similar to that of mountain gorillas, but groups are smaller and somewhat less cohesive.

All gorillas are almost exclusively vegetarian. Mountain and western lowland gorillas concentrate primarily on leaves, pith, and stalks, but western lowland gorillas eat more fruit. Western lowland gorillas, unlike mountain gorillas (which avoid water), also frequently wade through swamps while foraging on aquatic plants (Doran and McNeilage, 1998).

Perhaps because of their large body size and enormous strength, gorillas have long been considered vicious; but in reality, they're usually shy and gentle. However, this doesn't mean they're never aggressive. In fact, among males, competition for females can be extremely violent. As might be expected, males will attack to defend their group from any perceived danger, whether it's another male gorilla or a human hunter. Still, the reputation of gorillas as murderous beasts is the result of uninformed myth making and little else.

Chimpanzees   The three subspecies of common chimpanzee (*Pan troglodytes*) are probably the best known of all nonhuman primates, even though many people mistake them for monkeys (Fig. 6-34). Chimpanzees are often misunderstood because of zoo exhibits, circus acts, television shows, and movies; thus their true nature was unknown until years of fieldwork with wild chimpanzee groups provided a

▼ **Figure 6-34**
Female chimpanzee with adolescent.

Melanie Beasley

more accurate picture. Today chimpanzees are found in equatorial Africa, in a broad belt from the Atlantic Ocean in the west to Lake Tanganyika in the east (refer back to Fig. 6-31). However, within this large geographical area, their range is very patchy, and it's becoming even more so with continuous habitat destruction.

In many ways, chimpanzees are anatomically similar to gorillas, with corresponding limb proportions and upper-body shape. However, the ecological adaptations and behaviors of chimpanzees and gorillas differ, with chimpanzees spending more time in the trees. Chimpanzees are also frequently excitable, active, and noisy, whereas gorillas tend to be placid and quiet.

Chimpanzees are smaller than orangutans and gorillas, and although they're sexually dimorphic, sex differences aren't as pronounced as in gorillas and orangutans. A male chimpanzee may weigh 150 pounds, but females can weigh at least 100 pounds. In addition to quadrupedal knuckle walking, chimpanzees (particularly youngsters) may brachiate. When on the ground, they frequently walk bipedally for short distances when they are carrying food or other objects.

Chimpanzees consume a wide variety of foods, including fruits, leaves, insects (for example, ants, termites, and caterpillars), nuts, birds' eggs, berries, and small mammals. Moreover, both males and females occasionally take part in group hunting efforts to kill small mammals such as young bushpigs and antelope. Their prey also includes monkeys, especially red colobus. When hunts are successful, the members of the hunting party share the prey.

Chimpanzees live in large fluid communities ranging in size from 10 to as many as 100 individuals. A group of closely bonded males forms the core of chimpanzee communities in many locations, especially in East Africa (Goodall, 1986; Wrangham et al., 1992). However, for some West African groups, females appear to be more central to the community (Boesch, 1996; Boesch and Boesch-Achermann, 2000; Vigilant et al., 2001). Relationships among closely bonded males aren't always peaceful or stable, yet these males cooperatively defend their territory and are highly intolerant of unfamiliar chimpanzees, especially males.

Even though chimpanzees live in communities, it's rare for all members to be together at the same time. Rather, they tend to come and go, thus they don't encounter the same individuals on a daily basis. Adult females usually forage either alone or in the company of their offspring, a grouping that might include several animals, since females with infants sometimes accompany their own mothers and siblings. These associations have been reported for the chimpanzees at Gombe National Park, where about 40 percent of females remain in the group in which they were born (Williams, 1999). But in most other areas, females leave their natal group to join another community. This behavioral pattern reduces the risk of mating with close male relatives, because males apparently never leave the group in which they were born.

Chimpanzee social behavior is extremely complex, and individuals form lifelong attachments with friends and relatives. If they continue to live in their natal group, the bond between mothers and infants can remain strong until one of them dies. This may be a considerable period of time, because many wild chimpanzees live well into their 40s and even longer.

Bonobos   Bonobos (*Pan paniscus*) are found only in an area south of the Zaire River in the DRC (Fig. 6-35). Not officially recognized by European scientists until the 1920s, they remain among the least studied of the great apes. Although ongoing field studies have produced much information (Susman, 1984; Kano, 1992), research has been hampered by civil war. There are currently no accurate counts of bonobos, but their numbers are believed to be between 29,000 and 50,000 (Fruth et al., 2008). The 50,000 estimate is probably optimistic at this point and bonobos are

Ellen Ingmanson

◀ **Figure 6-35**
Female bonobos with young.

highly threatened by human hunting, habitat loss, and disturbance due to political strife and warfare in the region.

Because bonobos bear a strong resemblance to common chimpanzees but are slightly smaller, they've been called "pygmy chimpanzees." Actually, the differences in body size aren't great, but bonobos are less stocky. They also have longer legs relative to arms, a relatively smaller head, and a dark face from birth.

Bonobos are more arboreal than chimpanzees, and they're less excitable and aggressive. Although aggression isn't unknown, it appears that physical violence both within and between groups is uncommon. Like chimpanzees, bonobos live in geographically based fluid communities, and they eat many of the same foods, including occasional meat derived from small mammals (Badrian and Malenky, 1984). But bonobo communities aren't centered around a group of males. Instead, male-female bonding is more important than in chimpanzees and most other nonhuman primates (Badrian and Badrian, 1984). This may be related to bonobo sexuality, which differs from that of other nonhuman primates in that copulation is frequent and occurs throughout a female's estrous cycle. That is, among bonobos sex is not linked solely to reproduction. In fact, bonobos are famous for their sexual behavior, since they copulate frequently and use sex to defuse potentially tense situations. Sexual activity between members of the same sex is also common (Kano, 1992; de Waal and Lanting, 1997). Given this aspect of bonobo behavior, it's perhaps not surprising that they've been called the "make love, not war" primate society.

Humans Humans (*Homo sapiens*) are the only living representatives of the habitually bipedal primates (hominin tribe). Our primate heritage is evident in our overall anatomy and genetic makeup and in many behavioral aspects. Except for reduced canine size, human teeth are typical primate (especially ape) teeth. The human dependence on vision and decreased reliance on olfaction as well as flexible limbs and grasping hands are rooted in our primate, arboreal past (Fig. 6-36).

Humans in general are omnivorous, although all societies observe certain culturally based dietary restrictions. Even so, as a species with a rather generalized digestive system, we're physiologically adapted to benefit from an extremely wide assortment of foods. Perhaps to our detriment, we also share with our relatives a

▲ **Figure 6-36**
Playground equipment frequently allows children to play in ways that reflect their arboreal heritage.

fondness for sweets that originates from the importance of high-energy fruits eaten by many nonhuman primates.

But humans are obviously unique among primates and indeed among all animals. For example, no member of any other species has the ability to write or think about how it differs from other life-forms. This ability is rooted in the fact that during the last 800,000 years of human evolution, brain size has increased dramatically, and there have also been many other neurological changes.

Humans are also completely dependent on culture. Without cultural innovation, it would never have been possible for us to leave the tropics. As it is, humans inhabit every corner of the planet except for Antarctica, and we've even established outposts there. And lest we forget, a fortunate few have even walked on the moon! None of the technologies (indeed, none of the other aspects of culture) that humans have developed over the last several thousand years would have been possible without the highly developed cognitive abilities that we alone possess. Nevertheless, the neurological basis for **intelligence** is rooted in our evolutionary past, and it's something that connects us to other primates. Indeed, research has demonstrated that several nonhuman primate species—most notably chimpanzees, bonobos, and gorillas—display a level of problem solving and insight that most people would have considered impossible 30 years ago (see Chapter 7).

Humans are uniquely predisposed to use spoken language, and some 5,000 years ago, we also developed writing. Our advanced capacity for language exists because during the course of human evolution, certain neurological and anatomical structures were modified in ways not seen in any other species. But even though nonhuman primates aren't anatomically capable of producing speech, research has shown that, to varying degrees, the great apes are able to communicate by using symbols, which is a foundation for language that humans and the great apes (to a limited degree) have in common.

Aside from cognitive abilities, the one other trait that sets humans apart from other primates (and indeed other mammals) is our unique form of striding, *habitual* bipedal locomotion. This particular trait appeared early in the evolution of our lineage and, over time, we've become more efficient at it because of related changes in the musculoskeletal anatomy of the pelvis, leg, and foot. Early hominins increasingly adopted bipedalism because it was advantageous to them. As primates and especially as apelike primates, they were already behaviorally predisposed to, and anatomically capable of, at least short-term bipedal walking before they adopted it wholeheartedly. So although it's certainly true that human beings are unique intellectually, and in some ways anatomically, we're still primates. As a matter of fact, humans are basically exaggerated African apes.

intelligence Mental capacity; ability to learn, reason, or comprehend and interpret information, facts, relationships, and meanings; the capacity to solve problems, whether through the application of previously acquired knowledge or through insight.

Endangered Primates

In September 2000, scientists announced that a subspecies of red colobus, named Miss Waldron's red colobus, indigenous to the West African countries of Ghana and the Ivory Coast, had officially been declared extinct. This announcement came after a 6-year search for this 20-pound monkey, which hadn't been seen for 20 years (Oates et al., 2000). Since this announcement was published, there has been compelling evidence that at least a few of these monkeys may still survive, although there have been no confirmed sightings of live animals.

Closely following in the footsteps of Miss Waldron's red colobus to extinction was the Yunnan white-handed gibbon of China, last observed in 1988 and last heard in 1992. Grueter and colleagues (2009) suggest that the last surviving groups of this species probably disappeared in the late 1990s, again due to human hunting and habitat loss. Tragically, because several of the gibbon species indigenous to China number less than 100 individuals, the extinction of these species is likely to occur in the near future. We can hope that the pronouncements of the extinction of Miss Waldron's red colobus and the Yunnan white-handed gibbon were premature. But even if they were, the twenty-first century will see the extinction of many nonhuman primates. In fact, as of this writing, approximately 70 percent of all nonhuman primate species are in jeopardy (Table 6-1).

A Closer Look

Aye-Ayes: Victims of Derived Traits and Superstition

The primate order is filled with a variety of fascinating animals, although few seem as unusual as the aye-aye (*Daubentonia madagascariensis*), a type of lemur. This is because most primates aren't as derived as the aye-aye. Today, aye-ayes are the only members of their genus. A second species (a subfossil lemur) was exterminated by humans during the last few centuries, and the aye-aye was unknown (at least to Western science) until 1961. Like all lemurs, aye-ayes are found only on the island of Madagascar, where they occupy a niche similar to that of woodpeckers. Like woodpeckers, which aren't found on Madagascar, aye-ayes feed on insects and grubs that live in tree bark. On the ground they also find these same foods in logs. But instead of using a long beak to drill for hidden prey, this nocturnal primate uses an extremely specialized, elongated bony middle finger to tap, tap, tap along a tree trunk, listening for hollow spaces (Fig. 1). When an aye-aye finds a hollow space where a grub might be hiding, it tears through the bark with its continuously growing incisor teeth (a rodent-like trait) and scoops out the unlucky larva with the long nail at the end of its peculiar middle finger.

Aye-aye dentition is also quite derived and specialized for this particular dietary niche. The aye-aye dental formula of

$$\frac{1.0.1.3}{1.0.0.3}$$

isn't unique only among primates; it's unique among all mammals. As you can see, aye-ayes have no canine teeth and no lower premolars, although there's one upper premolar (Hershkovitz, 1977).

This perhaps strange-looking primate, which seems to have a permanent "bad hair day," is about the size of a small house cat and has little of the appeal of, say, a galago. Unfortunately, many Malagasy (the human inhabitants of Madagascar) find the aye-aye's appearance less than endearing. In fact, many think aye-ayes are bad luck and don't realize that they're simply harmless primates making a living as best they can.

Sadly, human imagination may prove this primate's undoing. Aye-ayes are variously thought to be heralds of evil or killers who creep into thatched huts and puncture their victim's aorta with their frightening middle finger (Goodman and Schütz, 2000). And some Malagasy superstitiously believe that should an aye-aye point its long middle finger at you, you will die. So it seems that cruel fate and humans have pointed their own finger of condemnation at the aye-aye, for only about 2,500 live in the wild and only a dozen or so in captivity.

◀ **Figure 1**

This nineteenth-century drawing of an aye-aye perfectly illustrates the elongated middle finger used for digging insects and grubs from logs and tree bark.

Lynn Kilgore

Table 6-1 | List of 16 of the Most Highly Endangered Nonhuman Primate Species

Species	Region/Country	Estimated Population Size	Threats
AFRICA			
Cross River gorilla	Cameroon, Nigeria	300	Restricted range: habitat loss due to agriculture and development; hunting for bushmeat and the pet trade; snares for trapping other animals
Rondo dwarf galago	Tanzania	No reliable estimates	Habitat loss (agriculture, logging, and charcoal production); fragmented range contributing to nonviable population size; locally extinct in many former ranges; may be extinct in Ghana
Roloway guenon	West Africa (Côte d'Ivoire and Ghana)	No reliable estimates	Extensively hunted for bushmeat trade; habitat loss (cultivation, including palm oil) and habitat fragmentation with resulting nonviable population size
Kipunji	Montane forests in southern Tanzania	1,117	Hunting and habitat loss; groups mostly isolated from each other because of extreme fragmentation of forest; this species already highly endangered when scientists discovered it in late 2003
Niger Delta Red Colobus	Niger River Delta, Nigeria	No reliable estimates	Commercial bushmeat hunting; habitat destruction due to logging, canal construction, and oil extraction activities
MADAGASCAR			
Northern sportive lemur	Northern Madagascar	18	Deforestation for charcoal and hunting; extreme habitat fragmentation with resulting nonviable population size
Greater bamboo lemur	Rain forests of southeastern Madagascar	100–160	Habitat loss due to mining, illegal logging, slash-and-burn agriculture; hunting; reduced drinking water due to climate change; bamboo cutting (this species relies heavily on bamboo)
Silky sifaka	Northeastern Madagascar	100–1,000	Hunting; habitat loss due to slash-and-burn agriculture and logging for fuel and precious woods for export (e.g., rosewood)
ASIA			
Sumatran orangutan	Indonesia (Sumatra)	6,600	Habitat loss due to logging, forest clearing for agriculture, especially oil palm plantations and road construction; killing for food, pet trade (infants), and as means of "pest" control
Eastern black-crested gibbon	Vietnamese-Chinese border	110	Habitat loss (cultivation, firewood, charcoal); small, isolated populations
Tonkin snub-nosed monkey	Northeastern Vietnam	200	Hunting; habitat loss (charcoal production, cultivation); and small, isolated populations
Cat Ba (golden-headed) langur	Cat Ba Island, Vietnam	60–70	Hunting for body parts used in traditional medicines
Javan slow loris	Java, Indonesia	No reliable estimates	Habitat loss due to forest clearing; capture for uncontrolled, extensive wildlife trade (traditional medicines and pets)
NEW WORLD			
Cottontop tamarin	Northwestern Colombia	Fewer than 6,000	Habit loss and fragmentation (logging, oil palm plantations, agriculture, logging); pet trade
Brown (variegated) spider monkey (2 subspecies)	Colombia and Venezuela	No reliable estimates	Habitat loss (agriculture, cattle ranching); hunting for food and pet trade
Peruvian yellow-tailed woolly monkey	Tropical Andean forests, Peru	No reliable estimates	Habitat loss and fragmentation (agriculture, roads, logging, influx of large numbers of humans); hunting (food, skins, and pet trade)

Source: R. A. Mittermeier, C. Schwitzer, A. B. Rylands, et al., "Primates in Peril: The World's Top 25 Most Endangered Primates, 2012–2014." Washington: IUCN/SCC Primate Specialist Group, Conservation International, and International Primatological Society, 2014.

There are three basic reasons for the worldwide depletion of nonhuman primates: habitat destruction, human hunting, and live capture for export or local trade. Underlying these three causes is one major factor: unprecedented human population growth, particularly in developing countries, where most nonhuman primates live.

The developing nations of Africa, Asia, and Central and South America are home to over 90 percent of all nonhuman primate species. During the 1990s, these countries—aided by Europe, China, and the United States—destroyed an average of 39 million acres of forest per year. The destruction declined between 2000 and 2010 to about 32 million acres a year, largely because of restrictions in Brazil (Tollefson, 2008, 2012). Whether these restrictions will hold remains to be seen.

The motivation behind deforestation is, of course, economic: the short-term gains from clearing forests to create immediately available (but frequently poor) farmland or ranchland; the use of trees for lumber, charcoal, and paper products; large-scale mining operations (with their necessary roads); and more recently, oil and gas exploration. People in many developing countries are also critically short of fuel, and lacking electricity, they use whatever firewood they can get. In addition, the demand for tropical hardwoods (such as mahogany, teak, and rosewood) in the United States, Europe, and Japan continues unabated, creating an enormously profitable market for rain forest products.

The demand for wood has resulted in conflict with conservationists, especially in parts of South America and central Africa. For example, mountain gorillas are among the most endangered nonhuman primate species on earth, and tourism is the only real hope of salvation for these magnificent animals. For this reason, several gorilla groups in Rwanda, Uganda, and the DRC have been habituated to humans and are protected by park rangers. Nevertheless, poaching, civil war, and land clearing have continued to take a toll on these small populations. For example, in 2007, 10 mountain gorillas were shot in the Virunga Volcanoes Conservation Area shared by Uganda, Rwanda, and the DRC (Fig. 6-37). The gorillas weren't killed for meat or because they were raiding crops. They were killed because the presence and protection of mountain gorillas are obstacles to people and corporations who profit from the destruction of the forests. But gorillas are not the only primates to have been shot in the Virungas. In the past few years, more than 140 park rangers have been killed while protecting wildlife.

Brent Stirton Images/Getty Images

◀ **Figure 6-37**
Congolese villagers carrying the body of a silverback gorilla shot and killed in the July 2007 attack. His body was buried with the other members of his group who were also killed.

The situation in Virunga National Park in the DRC is typical of problems facing wildlife and forests everywhere. Founded in 1925, Virunga National Park, a UNESCO World Heritage Site, is the oldest national park in Africa. It encompasses some 3,000 square miles and is one of the most ecologically diverse areas in the world. It is home to three great ape species, including around 300 mountain gorillas (roughly a third of the entire species), the extremely endangered Grauer's (eastern lowland) gorillas, and chimpanzees. Sadly, it is an area that has been plagued by more or less continuous warfare since the 1970s, and now, conflict has emerged over its most valuable asset: oil.

In 2010, SOCO, a British oil company, obtained permits for oil exploration within the park boundaries. Oil exploration is not permitted in any World Heritage Site, but limited testing was done and operations were completed in 2014. However, SOCO has not relinquished its exploration rights, which it could still sell to another party. (It is worth noting that other major petroleum companies, such as Shell and Total, canceled plans for similar operations in response to international opposition.) Moreover, in 2015, the government of the DRC entered into negotiations with UNESCO to redraw some of the park boundaries to allow possible oil exploration and extraction. This is not something to which UNESCO is likely to agree.

In 2014, Dr. Emmanuel de Merode, a Belgian by birth and director of Virunga National Park, was ambushed and shot while driving in the park. Fortunately, he was rescued. Interestingly, this attack occurred as he was returning from the capital city of the DRC, where he had just delivered documents pertaining to the activities of SOCO, who subsequently denied any involvement in the attack. However, it is abundantly clear that protecting highly endangered species, including our closest relatives, is a very dangerous business indeed.

The attack on Dr. de Merode coincided with the release of *Virunga*, a highly acclaimed documentary film about the Virunga National Park and the threats to its existence. One of its executive producers is the actor Leonardo di Caprio, who has won many awards for this film.

Africa is not the only place where nonhuman primates face increasing challenges from international business. In Indonesia (which includes Sumatra and part of Borneo) and Malaysia (which also includes part of Borneo), the palm oil industry is responsible for the clearing of vast stretches of rain forest, home to primates, elephants, tigers, and many other highly endangered species.

Palm oil is a vegetable oil that is found in almost any household product you care to name: from cosmetics, to soaps and lotions, to countless food items. In fact, it is estimated that about half of all packaged products now contain palm oil. An estimated 85 percent of the world's palm oil is derived from plantations in Malaysia and Indonesia in areas that, until recently, were the tropical forest homes of tigers, elephants, and several primate species, including orangutans (on the islands of Borneo and Sumatra). Between 1990 and 2010, it is estimated that Indonesia, Malaysia, and Papua New Guinea cleared around 9 million acres of forest for the development of palm oil plantations (Neme, 2014). This extremely rapid deforestation has had devastating consequences for the nonhuman animals that live in these forests. Although it is illegal in Malaysia and Indonesia to kill orangutans, it is an extremely common occurrence. Because forests are frequently burned, orangutans and other animals die in fires. Those that survive forest clearing often starve to death, and survivors that turn to oil palm trees for food are killed by farmers. Unfortunately, orphaned infants are often captured and sold into the illegal wildlife trade.

One hundred years ago, an estimated 300,000 orangutans are thought to have lived in the wild. Today these numbers are dramatically reduced, with approximately 50,000 orangutans on Borneo and fewer than 6,000 surviving on the island of Sumatra. Given the pace of deforestation, combined with hunting for meat and the pet trade, both orangutan subspecies are endangered. But the Sumatran orangutan is now in grave danger of extinction in the wild.

Fortunately, there may be cause for hope, at least regarding the expansion of palm oil plantations. For more than a decade, environmental groups and manufacturers have been working toward the development of sustainable palm oil production. This would provide for the production of palm oil with little or no continued deforestation. Although this seems like an unattainable goal, in 2013, the world's largest palm oil company, along with another major producer, committed to a zero deforestation policy. Customers of these two producers include the names of some of the most recognizable products in the world, including Kellogg's, Procter & Gamble, Nestlé, and ConAgra. This is an enormous step forward, and although there are a myriad of details to be dealt with, the initiative taken by large multinational corporations means that there may be real progress in slowing the rate of habitat destruction, not only for orangutans, but also for the thousands of other species that depend on the forests of Indonesia and Malaysia for survival.

The Bushmeat Trade

Until the late 1990s, habitat loss was the single greatest threat to nonhuman primates. But in the past few years, human hunting has become an equally important factor in some parts of the world (Fig. 6-38). During the 1990s, primatologists and conservationists became aware of a rapidly developing trade in *bushmeat*, meat from wild animals, especially in Africa. The current slaughter, which now accounts for an annual loss of tens of thousands of nonhuman primates and other animals, has been compared to the near extinction of the American bison in the nineteenth century.

Wherever nonhuman primates live, people have always hunted them for food. But in the past subsistence hunting wasn't a serious threat to entire primate populations and certainly not to entire species. But now, hunters armed with automatic rifles can and do wipe out an entire group of monkeys or gorillas in minutes. In fact, it's possible to buy bushmeat outside the country of origin. In major cities throughout Europe and the United States, illegal bushmeat is readily available to immigrants

(a) John Oates; (b) Jenny Pate/Robert Harding World Imagery/Getty Images

▲ **Figure 6-38**

(a) Red-eared guenons (with red tails) and Preuss's guenons for sale in a bushmeat market, Malabo, Equatorial Guinea. (b) Body parts, mostly from various monkey species, for sale in a West African market.

who want traditional foods or to nonimmigrants who think it's trendy to eat meat from exotic and frequently endangered animals.

It's impossible to know how many animals are killed each year, but the estimates are staggering. The Society for Conservation Biology estimates that about 6,000 kg (13,228 pounds) of bushmeat is taken through just seven western cities (New York, London, Toronto, Paris, Montreal, Chicago, and Brussels) every month. No one knows how much of this meat is from primates, but this figure represents only a tiny fraction of all the animals being slaughtered, because much smuggled meat isn't detected at ports of entry. Also, the international trade is thought to account for only about 1 percent of the total (Marris, 2006).

Quite clearly, slowly reproducing species such as primates, which number only a few hundred or a few thousand animals, cannot and will not survive this onslaught for more than a few years. In addition, hundreds of infants, orphaned by the bushmeat trade, are sold in markets as pets. Although a few of these traumatized orphans make it to sanctuaries, most die within days or weeks of capture (Fig. 6-39).

Logging has been a major factor in the development of the bushmeat trade. The construction of logging roads, mainly by French, German, and Belgian lumber companies, has opened up vast tracts of previously inaccessible forest to hunters. What has emerged is a multimillion-dollar trade in bushmeat, a trade in which logging company employees and local government officials participate with hunters, villagers, market vendors, and smugglers to cater to local and overseas markets. In other words, the hunting of wild animals for food, particularly in Africa, has quickly shifted from a subsistence activity to a commercial enterprise of international scope.

Although the slaughter may be best known in Africa, it's by no means limited to that continent. In South America, for example, the hunting of nonhuman primates for food is common, although it has not become a commercial enterprise on the scale seen in Africa and parts of Asia. Nevertheless, one report documented that in less than 2 years, one family of Brazilian rubber tappers killed almost 500 members of various large-bodied species, including spider monkeys, woolly monkeys, and howlers (Peres, 1990). Moreover, live capture and illegal trade in endangered primate species continue unabated in China and Southeast Asia, where nonhuman primates are not only eaten but also funneled into the exotic pet trade. Just as importantly, primate body parts also figure prominently in traditional medicines.

▶ **Figure 6-39**
Orphaned bonobo infants being cared for at a bonobo sanctuary in the Democratic Republic of the Congo.

Cyril Ruoso/Minden picture

With increasing human population size, the enormous demand for these products (and products from other, nonprimate species, such as tigers) has placed many species in extreme jeopardy (Table 6-1).

As a note of optimism, in November 2007, the DRC government and the Bonobo Conservation Initiative (in Washington, D.C.) created a bonobo reserve consisting of 30,500 km². This amounts to about 10 percent of the land in the DRC, and the government has stated that its goal is to set aside an additional 5 percent for wildlife protection (News in Brief, 2007). This was a huge step forward. But as of this writing, warfare has once again begun in the DRC and, tragically, some of the fighting is happening in the gorilla sector.

Many conservation groups are working to protect nonhuman primates. These include, among many others, Conservation International, the World Wildlife Fund, Wildlife Direct, the International Primate Protection League, the Great Ape Trust, the Jane Goodall Institute, and the Orangutan Conservancy. In 2000, the United Nations Environmental Program established the Great Ape Survival Project (GRASP). GRASP is an alliance of many of the world's major great ape conservation and research organizations. It goes without saying that GRASP and other organizations must succeed if the great apes are to survive in the wild for even a few more decades.

If you are in your 20s or 30s, you will certainly live to hear of the extinction of some of our marvelous cousins. Many more will undoubtedly slip away unnoticed. Tragically, in most cases this will occur before we've even gotten to know them. Each species on earth is the current result of a unique set of evolutionary events that, over millions of years, has produced a finely adapted component of a diverse ecosystem. When it becomes extinct, that adaptation and that part of biodiversity is lost forever. What a tragedy it will be if, through our own mismanagement and greed, we awaken to a world without chimpanzees, mountain gorillas, lemurs, or the tiny, exquisite cotton-topped tamarin. When this day comes, we truly will have lost a part of ourselves, and we will certainly be the poorer for it.

How Do We Know?

Most people don't know much about nonhuman primates, and of those who do, a majority don't realize how seriously endangered they are. What's worse, many who do know don't really care because their lives won't substantially change if, say, chimpanzees become extinct in the wild. (Although there could still be captive chimpanzees for a few more decades, this isn't seen as a viable long-term solution.)

The fact is, it *is* important that we know about nonhuman primates, not only for the anthropocentric reason that we can better understand ourselves (although this is true), but also because the living nonhuman primates are the current representatives of a lineage that goes back approximately 60 million years. They can provide a great deal of information as to how evolutionary processes have produced the diversity we see in our own lineage today. From comparative studies, we can identify the genetic causes for certain conditions (such as AIDS) that humans are susceptible to but chimpanzees are able to resist. Although this information may not help us decide what kind of car to buy or what to have for dinner, it is permitting us to unravel the genetic and behavioral links that connect all primates, including ourselves, in a network of adaptation and evolution. Lastly, the nonhuman primates (and other species, too) are important in their own right, and it's up to us to make sure they survive into the next century. Indeed, this is going to be a truly formidable task.

What Do You Think?

In this section, you learned about some of the reasons primates are important to us today, including our understanding of biodiversity, evolution, and medicine. Can you think of some other ways in which the study of primates enriches our lives today? What would be the loss to science and humanity if, for example, the chimpanzee were to become extinct? ∎

Summary of Main Topics

- As a group, primates are very generalized, meaning they've retained many anatomical characteristics that were present in early ancestral mammalian species. These traits include five digits on the hands and feet, different kinds of teeth (*heterodonty*), and a skeletal anatomy and limb structure that allow for different forms of locomotion (climbing, brachiation, quadrupedalism, and bipedalism). Primates have grasping hands, and most have an opposable thumb, which facilitates this ability. (Some species are more specialized in that their thumbs are reduced or even absent.) Many primates, such as chimpanzees and bonobos, also have opposable big toes.

- Most primates are omnivorous, although certain species focus on only certain foods. For example, the colobines (colobus monkeys and langurs) primarily eat leaves. In general, primates have relatively larger, more complex brains than other mammals. Consequently they are comparatively more intelligent and exhibit more complex behaviors. This is especially true of monkeys, apes, and humans. Primates rely more on vision than olfaction, and diurnal primates (with some New World exceptions) have full color vision. Correspondingly, the areas of the brain related to vision are larger and more complex than the areas related to olfaction. Almost all nonhuman primates are arboreal and spend at least part of their time in trees.

- The order Primates is divided into two suborders: Strepsirrhini (lemurs and lorises) and Haplorhini (tarsiers, monkeys, apes, and humans).

- The mammalian order Primates includes humans and approximately 230–270 nonhuman species: apes, monkeys, tarsiers, and lemurs. Most nonhuman primates live in tropical and subtropical regions of Africa, India, Asia, Mexico, and South America.

- Because of human hunting and habitat loss, the majority of nonhuman primates are endangered today, and many are on the verge of extinction. Without concerted efforts to preserve primate habitat and control hunting, many species will probably be extinct by as soon as 2050.

Critical Thinking Questions

1. What are some human characteristics that reflect a common ancestry between nonhuman primates and ourselves? Although we didn't really discuss this topic in the chapter, can you think of some ways in which humans are more similar to chimpanzees than to monkeys?

2. How do you think continued advances in genetic research will influence how we look at our relationship with nonhuman primates?

3. How does a classification scheme reflect biological and evolutionary changes in a lineage? Can you give an example of suggested changes to how primates are classified? What do you think most people's reaction would be to hearing that scientists are placing the great apes into the same taxonomic family as humans?

4. Pretend you are at the zoo and are observing a primate exhibit featuring monkeys. What traits could be used to determine whether the exhibit features a New World or Old World monkey species?

5. What factors threaten the existence of nonhuman primates in the wild? What can you do to help save nonhuman primates from extinction? Why is this important for society?

CONNECTIONS

Humans are primates and share many biological characteristics with other primates.

Partly because of common evolutionary history, many human behaviors are also seen in other primates.

Fossil evidence indicates our primate origins date to at least 65 million years ago.

Primate Behavior

The Evolution of Behavior

Some Factors That Influence Social Structure

Why Be Social?

Primate Social Behavior

Dominance

Communication

Aggressive and Affiliative Behaviors within Groups

Reproduction and Reproductive Behaviors

Reproductive Strategies

Sexual Selection

Is Infanticide a Reproductive Strategy?

Mothers, Fathers, and Infants

Nonhuman Primate Models for the Evolution of Human Behavior

Brain and Body Size

Language

The Evolution of Language

Primate Cultural Behavior

Conflict between Groups

Prosocial Behaviors: Affiliation, Altruism, and Cooperation

Altruism

The Primate Continuum

Student Learning Objectives   After studying the material in this chapter, you should be able to:

▶ Explain why behavioral ecology is an important framework for understanding the evolution of behavior among primates, including humans.

▶ Describe some of the factors used to explain why primates are social.

▶ Discuss how dominance hierarchies and forms of communication function within primate societies.

▶ Discuss the differences between male and female reproductive strategies.

▶ Describe how primates have been used as models for the evolution of human behavior.

▶ Define language and discuss how research has shown that many nonhuman primates have a capacity to communicate symbolically. You should also be able to provide examples of how wild nonhuman primates have been observed to communicate symbolically.

▶ Explain the evidence for culture in many nonhuman species, including some that aren't primates.

▶ Discuss evidence for affiliation, altruism, and cooperation in nonhuman primates. Discuss altruism and empathy and explain how these examples can help us understand the evolution of these capacities in our own species.

▶ Discuss the importance of studying humans and other nonhuman primates as part of a biological and behavioral continuum.

D o you think cats are cruel when they play with mice? Or if you've ever fallen off a horse when it suddenly jumped sideways for no apparent reason, did you think it threw you deliberately? If you answered yes to either of these questions, you wouldn't be alone. To most people, it does seem cruel for a cat to torment a mouse for no

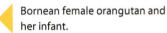
Bornean female orangutan and her infant.

obvious reason; and more than one rider has blamed their horse for intentionally throwing them (it has been known to happen). But these commonly held views indicate how little most people really know about nonhuman animal **behavior**.

Behavior is extremely complex, especially in mammals and birds, because it's been shaped over evolutionary time by interactions between genetic and environmental factors. Most people don't give this much thought, and even those who do don't necessarily accept this basic premise. For example, many social scientists object to the notion of genetic influences on human behavior because of concerns that it implies that behaviors are fixed and can't be modified by experience (learning). This view could, in turn, be used to support racist and sexist ideologies. Nevertheless, there is a substantial body of scientific evidence that genes indeed have a considerable influence on individual behavior, human and otherwise.

Also, there's the prevailing notion of a fundamental divide between humans and all other animals. Most people see themselves as uniquely set apart from all other species. At the same time, and in obvious contradiction, people sometimes assign certain human attributes to other species in order to explain behaviors (for example, cats are cruel to play with mice). Of course this isn't a valid thing to do for the simple reason that other animals aren't human. Cats sometimes play with mice because that's how, as kittens, they learn to hunt. Cruelty doesn't enter into it because the cat has no concept of cruelty and no idea of what it's like to be the mouse.

Likewise, a horse usually doesn't deliberately throw you off when it hears leaves rattling in a shrub. It jumps because its behavior has been shaped by thousands of generations of equine ancestors who leaped first and asked questions later. It's important to understand that just as cats evolved as predators, horses evolved as prey animals, and their evolutionary history is littered with unfortunate animals that didn't jump at a sound in a shrub. In many cases, those ancestral horses learned, too late, that the sound wasn't caused by a breeze. This is a mistake that prey animals often fail to survive, and those that don't leap first tend to leave fewer descendants than those who don't wait to see why the leaves are shaking.

Obviously, this chapter isn't about cats and horses. It's about what we know and hypothesize about the individual and social behaviors of nonhuman primates. We begin here with the familiar examples of cats and horses because we want to point out that many basic behaviors have been shaped by the evolutionary history of particular species. So, if we want to discover the underlying principles of behavioral evolution, we must first identify the interactions between a number of environmental and physiological variables.

The Evolution of Behavior

Scientists study primates from an **ecological** and evolutionary perspective, focusing on the relationship between behaviors (both individual and social), the natural environment, and various physiological traits. This approach, called **behavioral ecology**, is based on the assumption that all of the biological components of ecological systems (animals, plants, and even microorganisms) evolved together. Behaviors are thus adaptations to environmental circumstances that existed in the past and remain in the present.

Briefly, the cornerstone of this perspective is that *behaviors have evolved through the operation of natural selection;* that is, behaviors are subject to natural selection in the same way that physical characteristics are. The underlying assumption is that certain behaviors are influenced by genes and are therefore subject to natural selection in the same way that physical characteristics are. Therefore behavior constitutes a phenotype, and individuals whose behavioral phenotypes increase reproductive fitness will pass on their genes at a faster rate than others. However, this

behavior Anything organisms do that involves action in response to internal or external stimuli; the response of an individual, group, or species to its environment. Such responses may or may not be deliberate and they aren't necessarily the results of conscious decision making.

ecological Pertaining to the relationships between organisms and all aspects of their environment (temperature, predators, nonpredators, vegetation, availability of food and water, types of food, disease organisms, parasites, etc.).

behavioral ecology The study of the evolution of behavior, emphasizing the role of ecological factors as agents of natural selection. Behaviors and behavioral patterns have been favored because they increase the reproductive fitness of individuals (i.e., they are adaptive) in specific environmental contexts.

doesn't mean that primatologists think that genes code for specific behaviors, such as a gene for aggression, another for cooperation, and so on. The study of complex behaviors from an evolutionary viewpoint does not imply a one gene–one behavior relationship, nor does it suggest that behaviors that are influenced by genes can't be modified through learning.

In insects and other invertebrates, behavior is mostly under genetic control. In other words, most behavioral patterns in these species aren't learned; they're innate. But in many vertebrates, especially birds and mammals, the proportion of behavior that's due to learning is substantially increased and the proportion under genetic control is reduced. This is especially true of primates; and in humans, who are so much a product of culture, most behavior is learned.

Behavioral genetics, the study of how genes affect behavior, is a relatively new field, and we don't yet know the extent to which genes actually influence behavior in humans or other species. What we do know is that behavior must be viewed as the product of *complex interactions between genetic and environmental factors.* The limits and potentials for learning, and for behavioral flexibility, vary considerably among species. In some groups, such as primates, the potentials are extremely broad; in others, such as insects, they aren't. Ultimately, those limits and potentials are set by genetic factors that have been subjected to natural selection throughout the evolutionary history of every species. That history, in turn, has been shaped by the ecological setting not only of living species *but also of their ancestors.*

One of the major goals of primatology is to discover how certain behaviors influence reproductive fitness and how ecological factors have shaped the evolution of those behaviors. Although the actual mechanics of behavioral evolution aren't yet fully understood, new methods and technologies are helping scientists answer many questions. For example, genetic analysis has recently been used to establish paternity in a few primate groups, and this has helped support hypotheses about some behaviors in males. But in general, an evolutionary approach to the study of behavior doesn't provide definitive answers to many research questions. Rather, it offers primatologists a valuable framework through which to analyze data and generate and test hypotheses concerning behavioral patterns. (Remember, the development and testing of new hypotheses is how scientific research is done.)

Because primates are among the most social of animals, social behavior is one of the major topics in primate research (Fig. 7-1). This is a broad subject that includes all aspects of behaviors that occur in social groupings, even some you may not think of as social behaviors, such as feeding or mating. To understand the function of one behavioral element, it's necessary to determine how it's influenced by numerous interrelated factors. As an example, we'll consider some of the more important variables that influence **social structure**. Bear in mind that social structure itself influences individual behavior, thus in many cases the distinctions between social and individual behaviors are blurred.

social structure The composition, size, and sex ratio of a group of animals. The social structure of a species is, in part, the result of natural selection in a specific habitat, and it guides individual interactions and social relationships.

▼ **Figure 7-1**
These proboscis monkeys in Malaysia provide a good example of a small nonhuman primate group.

Barbara Walton/epa/Corbis Wire/Corbis

Some Factors That Influence Social Structure

Body Size As a rule, larger animals require fewer calories per unit of weight than smaller animals because larger animals have less surface area relative to body mass than smaller animals. Since body heat is lost at the surface, larger animals can retain heat more efficiently, so they need less energy overall. It may seem strange, but two 10-pound monkeys require more food than one 22-pound monkey (Fleagle, 1999).

▲ **Figure 7-2**
Dwarf mouse lemur.

Basal Metabolic Rate (BMR) The BMR concerns **metabolism**, the rate at which the body uses energy to maintain all bodily functions while in a resting state. It's closely correlated with body size. In general, therefore, smaller animals have a higher BMR than larger ones (Fig. 7-2). Consequently, smaller primates, such as galagos and marmosets, require an energy-rich diet high in protein (insects), fats (nuts and seeds), and carbohydrates (fruits and seeds). Some larger primates, which tend to have a lower BMR and reduced energy requirements relative to body size, can do well with less energy-rich foods, such as leaves.

Diet Because the nutritional requirements of animals are related to body size and BMR, all three have evolved together. Therefore when primatologists study the relationships between diet and behavior, they consider the benefits in terms of energy (calories) derived from various food items against the costs (energy expended) of obtaining and digesting them. While small-bodied primates focus on high-energy foods, such as sugar-containing fruits or protein sources, larger ones don't necessarily need to, at least not to the same degree. For instance, gorillas eat leaves, pith from bamboo stems, and other types of vegetation. These foods have less caloric value than fruits, nuts, and seeds, but they still serve these animals well because gorillas tend to spend much of the day eating and they don't expend a great deal of energy getting food (Fig. 7-3).

Some monkeys, especially colobines (colobus and langur species), are primarily leaf eaters. Compared with many other monkeys, they're fairly large-bodied. They've also evolved elongated intestines and pouched stomachs that enable them, with the assistance of intestinal bacteria, to digest the tough fibers and cellulose in leaves. Moreover, in at least two langur species, there's a duplicated gene that produces an enzyme that further helps with digestion. This gene duplication isn't found in other primates that have been studied, so the duplication event probably occurred after colobines and cercopithecines last shared a common ancestor (Zhang et al., 2002).

metabolism The chemical processes within cells that break down nutrients and release energy for the body to use. (When nutrients are broken down into their component parts, such as amino acids, energy is released and made available for the cells to use.)

▲ **Figure 7-3**
This male mountain gorilla has only to reach out to find something to eat.

◀ **Figure 7-4**
Gelada baboons live in one-male–multifemale groups that combine to form troops that can number more than 300 animals.

Having a second copy of the gene would have been advantageous to colobine ancestors, who were probably already eating some leaves, so natural selection favored it to the point that it was established in the lineage. (The discovery of this gene duplication is another example of how new technologies help explain behavior—in this case, dietary differences.)

Distribution of Resources Various kinds of foods are distributed in different ways. Leaves can be abundant and dense and therefore support large groups of animals. Insects, on the other hand, may be widely scattered; therefore the animals that rely on them usually feed alone or with only one or two others.

Fruits, nuts, and berries occur in dispersed trees and shrubs. These are most efficiently exploited by smaller groups of animals, so large groups frequently break up into smaller subunits while feeding. Such subunits may consist of one-male–multifemale groups (for example, some baboons) or **matrilines** (for example, macaques). Species that subsist on abundantly distributed resources may also live in one-male groups, and because food is plentiful, these one-male units are able to join with others to form large, stable communities (for example, howlers and some baboons) (Fig. 7-4). To the casual observer, these communities can appear to be multimale-multifemale groups. (See "A Closer Look: Types of Nonhuman Primate Social Groups" on page 190)

Some species that depend on foods distributed in small clumps are protective of resources, especially if their feeding area is small enough to be defended. Some live in small groups composed of a mated pair (siamangs) or a female with one or two males (for example, marmosets and tamarins) and their offspring. Last, foods such as fruits, nuts, and berries are only seasonally available; therefore primates that rely on them must eat a wide variety of foods. This is another factor that tends to favor smaller feeding groups.

Predation Depending on their size, primates are vulnerable to many types of predators, including snakes, birds of prey, leopards, wild dogs, and even other primates. Their responses to predation depend on their body size, social structure, and the type of predator. Typically, where predation pressure is high and body size is small, large communities are advantageous. These may be multimale-multifemale groups or congregations of one-male–multifemale groups.

matrilines Groups that consist of a female, her daughters, and their offspring. Matrilines are common among macaques.

A Closer Look Types of Nonhuman Primate Social Groups

1. *One-male–multifemale:* a single adult male, several adult females, and their offspring. This is the most common primate mating structure, in which only one male actively breeds, and it's typically formed by a male joining a kin group of females. Females usually form the permanent nucleus of the group. Examples: guenons, gorillas, some spider monkeys, patas, some langurs, and some colobus monkeys. In many species, several one-male groups may form large congregations.

2. *Multimale-multifemale:* several adult males, several adult females, and their young. Many of the males reproduce. The presence of several males in the group may lead to tension and to the formation of a dominance hierarchy. Examples: some lemurs, macaques, mangabeys, savanna baboons, vervets, squirrel monkeys, some spider monkeys, and chimpanzees. In some species (vervets, baboons, and macaques), females are members of matrilines, or groups composed of a female, her female offspring, and their offspring. These kin groups are ranked relative to one another in a hierarchy.

3. *Monogamous pair:* a mated pair and their young. The term *monogamous* is somewhat misleading because matings with individuals other than partners aren't uncommon. Species that form pairs are usually arboreal, show minimal sexual dimorphism, and are frequently territorial. Adults don't normally tolerate other adults of the same sex. This grouping isn't found among the great apes, and it's the least common breeding structure among nonhuman primates. Examples: siamangs, gibbons, indris, titis, sakis, owl monkeys, and pottos. Males may directly participate in infant care.

4. *Polyandrous:* one female and two males. This social group is seen only in some New World monkeys (marmosets and tamarins). Males participate in infant care.

5. *Solitary:* individual who forages for food alone. This is seen in nocturnal primates such as aye-ayes, lorises, and galagos. In some species, adult females may forage in pairs or may be accompanied by offspring. Also seen in orangutans.

There are also other groupings, such as foraging groups, hunting groups, all-female or all-male groups, and so on. Like humans, nonhuman primates don't always maintain one kind of group; one-male–multifemale groups may sometimes form multimale-multifemale groups, and vice versa. Hamadryas and Gelada baboons, for example, are described as living in one-male groups, but they form large herds at night as they move to the safety of sleeping cliffs.

Dispersal Dispersal is another factor that influences social structure and relationships within groups. As is true of most mammals (and indeed most vertebrates), members of one sex leave the group in which they were born (their *natal* group) about the time they become sexually mature. Male dispersal is the more common pattern (for example, ring-tailed lemurs, vervets, and macaques, to name a few). However, female dispersal occurs in some colobus species, hamadryas baboons, chimpanzees, and mountain gorillas. In species where the basic social structure is a mated pair, offspring of both sexes either leave or are driven away by their parents (for example, gibbons and siamangs).

Dispersal may have more than one outcome. When females leave, they join another group. Males may do likewise, but in some species (for example, gorillas), they may live alone for a time, or they may temporarily join an all-male "bachelor" group until they're able to establish a group of their own. But the common theme is that individuals who disperse usually find mates outside their natal group. This has led primatologists to conclude that the most valid explanations for dispersal are related to two major factors: reduced competition between males for mates and, more importantly, the decreased likelihood of close inbreeding.

Life Histories **Life history traits** are characteristics or developmental stages that typify members of a given species and influence potential reproductive rates. Examples of life history traits include length of gestation, length of time between pregnancies (interbirth interval), period of infant dependency and age at weaning, age at sexual maturity, and life expectancy.

life history traits Characteristics and developmental stages that influence reproductive rates. Examples include longevity, age at sexual maturity, and length of time between births.

Life history traits have important consequences for many aspects of social life, and they can also be critical to species survival. In species that live in marginal or unpredictable habitats, shorter life spans can be advantageous. Members of these species mature early and have short interbirth intervals, so reproduction can occur at a relatively fast rate in a habitat that doesn't favor longevity (Strier, 2003). Conversely, longer-lived species, such as gorillas, are better suited to stable environmental conditions. The extended life spans of the great apes in particular, characterized by later sexual maturation and long interbirth intervals of three to five years, means that most females will raise only three or four offspring to maturity. Today, this slow rate of reproduction increases the threat of extinction for all the great apes, which are being hunted at a rate that far outpaces their replacement capacities.

Strategies Strategies are behaviors that increase individual reproductive success. They also influence the structure and dynamics of primate social groups. We're accustomed to using the word *strategies* to mean deliberate schemes or plans purposefully designed to achieve goals. But in the context of nonhuman behavioral ecology, strategies are seen as products of natural selection, and no conscious planning or motivation is implied (Strier, 2003). Several kinds of strategies are discussed in behavioral studies, including *life history strategies, feeding strategies, social strategies, reproductive strategies*, and *predator avoidance strategies*.

Distribution and Types of Sleeping Sites Gorillas are the only nonhuman primates that sleep on the ground. Primate sleeping sites can be in trees or on cliff faces, and their spacing can be related to social structure and predator avoidance (Fig. 7-5).

Activity Patterns Most primates are diurnal, but galagos, lorises, aye-ayes, tarsiers, and New World owl monkeys are nocturnal. Nocturnal primates tend to forage for food alone or in groups of two or three, and many avoid predators by hiding (note that these groups have very large eyes relative to their body size).

Human Activities As you saw in Chapter 6, virtually all nonhuman primate populations are now impacted by human hunting and forest clearing. These activities severely disrupt and isolate groups, reduce numbers, reduce resource availability, and eventually lead to extinction.

Why Be Social?

Group living exposes animals to competition with other group members for resources; so why don't primates live alone? After all, competition can lead to injury or even death, and it's costly in terms of energy expenditure. One widely accepted answer to this question is that the costs of competition are offset by the benefits of predator defense. Multimale–multifemale groups are advantageous in areas where predation pressure is high, particularly in mixed woodlands and on open savannas. Leopards are the most significant predator of terrestrial primates (Fig. 7-6), and the chances of escaping a leopard attack are far greater for an animal that lives in a group than for a single individual.

Savanna baboons have long been used as an example of these principles. They live in semiarid grassland and broken woodland habitats throughout sub-Saharan Africa. To avoid nocturnal predators, savanna baboons sleep in trees, but they spend much of the day on the ground foraging for food. If a predator appears, baboons flee back into the trees; but if they're some distance from safety, adult males (and sometimes females) may join forces to chase the intruder.

Hoberman Collection/Alamy

▲ **Figure 7-5**
Chacma baboon having an afternoon nap. Almost all primates sleep in the safety of trees or on cliffs if there are no trees around. They also often take naps during the day. The fact that many humans have a midafternoon "lull" may reflect a primate tendency for afternoon drowsiness.

John Dominis/The LIFE Picture Collection/Getty Images

▶ **Figure 7-6**

When a baboon strays too far from its troop, as this one has done, it's more likely to fall prey to predators. Leopards are the most serious nonhuman threat to terrestrial primates.

As effective as increased numbers can be in preventing predation, there are other explanations for primate sociality. One is that larger social groups can outcompete smaller groups of conspecifics foraging in the same area (Wrangham, 1980). Wrangham also suggests that large multimale–multifemale groups evolved because males were attracted to related females living together. And last, females may tolerate familiar males, since they can provide protection against other, potentially infanticidal males.

There is probably no single answer to the question of why primates live in groups. More than likely, predator avoidance is a major factor but not the only one. Group living evolved as an adaptive response to a number of ecological variables, and it has served primates well for a very long time.

Primate Social Behavior

Because primates solve their major adaptive problems in a social context, we should expect them to behave in ways that reinforce the integrity of the group. The better known of these are described here. Remember, all these behaviors have evolved as adaptive responses during more than 50 million years of primate evolution. The "At a Glance" on page 193 outlines several key factors that influence primate social strategies.

Dominance

Many primate societies are organized into **dominance hierarchies**, which impose a certain degree of order by establishing parameters of individual behavior. Although aggression is frequently used to increase an animal's status within the group, dominance hierarchies usually reduce the amount of actual physical violence. Not only are lower-ranking animals unlikely to attack or even threaten a higher-ranking one; what's more, dominant animals are also able to exert control simply by making a threatening gesture. Individual rank or status can be measured by access to resources, including food items and mating partners. Dominant animals (alpha males and females) are given priority by others, and they rarely give way in confrontations.

Many primatologists think that the primary benefit of dominance is the increased reproductive success of high-ranking animals. This is true in many cases, but there's good evidence that lower-ranking males also mate successfully. High-ranking females

dominance hierarchies Systems of social organization wherein individuals within a group are ranked relative to one another. Higher-ranking animals have greater access to preferred food items and mating partners than lower-ranking individuals. Dominance hierarchies are sometimes called "pecking orders."

At a Glance   Primate Social Strategies

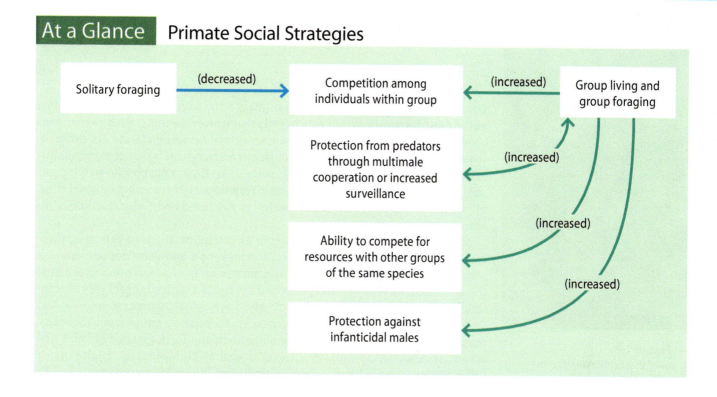

also have higher reproductive success because they have greater access to food than subordinate females. Therefore they obtain more energy for the production and care of offspring (Fedigan, 1983).

Pusey and colleagues (1997) demonstrated that the offspring of high-ranking female chimpanzees at Gombe Stream National Park in Tanzania had significantly higher rates of infant survival than those of lower-ranking females. Moreover, daughters of these high-ranking females matured faster, which meant they had shorter interbirth intervals and consequently produced more offspring.

An individual's position in the hierarchy isn't permanent; rather, it changes throughout life and is influenced by many factors, including sex, age, level of aggression, amount of time spent in the group, intelligence, motivation, and sometimes the mother's social position (particularly true of macaques).

In species organized into groups containing a number of females associated with one or several adult males, males are generally dominant to females. Within such groups, males and females have separate hierarchies, although very high-ranking females can dominate the lowest-ranking males, particularly young ones. But there are exceptions to this pattern of male dominance. In many lemur species, females are the dominant sex. Moreover, in species that form bonded pairs (for example, indris and gibbons), males and females are codominant.

All primates learn their position in the hierarchy. From birth, an infant is carried by its mother, and it observes how she responds to every member of the group. Just as importantly, it sees how others react to her. Dominance and subordination are indicated by gestures and behaviors, some of which are universal throughout the primate order (including humans), and this gestural repertoire is part of every youngster's learning experience.

Young primates also acquire social rank through play with age peers, and as they spend more time with playgroups, their social network widens. Competition and rough-and-tumble play allow them to learn the strengths and weaknesses of peers, and they carry this knowledge with them throughout their lives. Thus, through early contact with their mothers and subsequent exposure to peers, young primates learn

▲ **Figure 7-7**
A "yawn" that exposes long canine teeth is a common threat gesture in many primate species. Here an adult male baboon combines it with an "eyelid flash," closing the eyes to expose light-colored eyelids that enhance the visual effect of the threat.

to negotiate their way through the complex web of social interactions that makes up their daily lives.

Communication

Communication is universal among animals; it includes scents and unintentional **autonomic** responses as well as behaviors that convey meaning. Such attributes as body posture provide information about an animal's emotional state. For example, crouching indicates submission, insecurity, or fear, and this is true of many nonprimate animals too (for example, dogs). At the same time, a purposeful striding gait implies confidence. Moreover, autonomic responses to threatening or novel stimuli, such as raised body hair (most species) or enhanced body odor (gorillas), indicate excitement or fear.

Many intentional behaviors also serve as communication. In primates, these include a wide variety of gestures, facial expressions, and vocalizations, some of which we humans share. Among many primates, an intense stare indicates a mild threat; indeed, we humans find prolonged eye contact with strangers very uncomfortable. (For this reason people should avoid eye contact with captive primates.) Other threat gestures include a quick yawn to expose canine teeth (baboons, macaques; Fig. 7-7), crouching and bobbing back and forth (patas monkeys), and branch shaking (many monkey species as well as chimpanzees). High-ranking baboons mount the hindquarters of subordinates to express dominance (Fig. 7-8). Mounting may also serve to defuse potentially tense situations by indicating something like, "It's okay, apology accepted."

Primates also use a variety of behaviors to indicate submission, reassurance, or amicable intentions. Most primates crouch to show submission, and baboons also present or turn their hindquarters toward an animal they want to appease. Reassurance takes the form of touching, patting, hugging, and holding hands (Fig. 7-9). **Grooming** also serves in a number of situations to indicate submission or reassurance.

communication Any act that conveys information to another individual. Frequently, the result of communication is a change in the behavior of the recipient. Communication may not be deliberate but may instead be the result of involuntary processes or a secondary consequence of an intentional action.

autonomic Pertaining to physiological responses not under voluntary control. An example in chimpanzees would be the erection of body hair during excitement. Blushing is a human example. Both convey information regarding emotional states, but neither is deliberate, and communication isn't intended.

grooming Picking through fur to remove dirt, parasites, and other materials that may be present. Social grooming is common among primates and reinforces social relationships.

▲ **Figure 7-8**
One young male savanna baboon mounts another as an expression of dominance.

A wide variety of facial expressions indicating emotional state is seen in chimpanzees and especially in bonobos (Fig. 7-10). These include the well-known play face (also seen in several other primate and nonprimate species) associated with play behavior and the fear grin indicating fear and submission.

Not surprisingly, vocalizations play a major role in primate communication. Some, such as the bark of a baboon that has just spotted a leopard, are unintentional startled reactions. Others, such as the chimpanzee food grunt, are heard only in specific contexts; in this case in the presence of food. These vocalizations, whether deliberate or not, inform others of the possible presence of predators or food.

Primates (and other animals) also communicate through **displays**, which are more complicated, frequently elaborate combinations of behaviors. For example, the exaggerated courtship dances of many male birds, often enhanced by colorful plumage, are displays. Chest slapping and tearing vegetation are common gorilla threat displays. Likewise an angry chimpanzee, with hair on end, may charge an opponent while screaming, waving its arms, and tearing vegetation (Fig. 7-11).

All nonhuman animals use various body postures, vocalizations, and facial expressions to transmit information. But the array of communicative devices is much richer among nonhuman primates, even though they don't use **language** the way humans do. Communication is important because it's what makes social

▲ **Figure 7-9**
Adolescent savanna baboons holding hands.

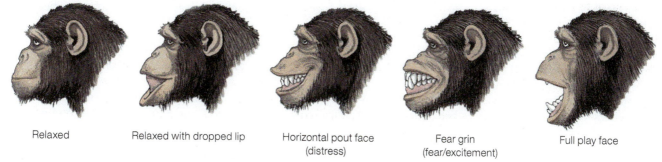

Relaxed   Relaxed with dropped lip   Horizontal pout face (distress)   Fear grin (fear/excitement)   Full play face

▲ **Figure 7-10**
Chimpanzee facial expressions.

◀ **Figure 7-11**
Male chimpanzee display. Note how the hair on his arms and shoulders is raised to make him look larger.

displays Sequences of repetitious behaviors that serve to communicate emotional states. Nonhuman primate displays are most frequently associated with reproductive or agonistic behavior. Examples include chest slapping in gorillas and, in male chimpanzees, dragging and waving branches while charging and threatening other animals.

language A standardized system of arbitrary vocal sounds, written symbols, and gestures used in communication.

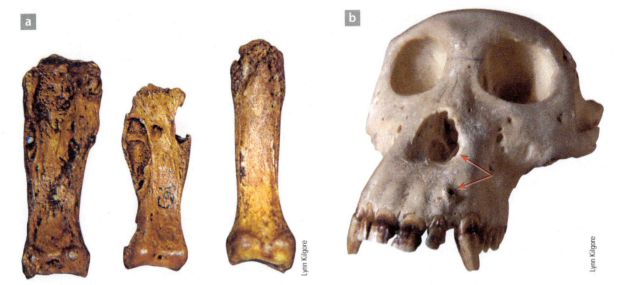

Lynn Kilgore

Lynn Kilgore

▲ **Figure 7-12**

(**a**) These finger bones are from a female chimpanzee named Gilka, a member of Jane Goodall's study group in Tanzania. On more than one occasion, observers saw another female attack Gilka, and during one attack, Gilka was badly bitten on the hand. Afterward she suffered periodically from running sores on her hand. The cavities and deformation in these bones indicate severe infection of the marrow cavity, probably resulting from the bite wound. (**b**) This male chimpanzee cranium from West Africa exhibits a healed bite wound beneath the nose (arrow) most likely inflicted by another chimpanzee. Also, the left margin of the nasal opening shows irregularities that may have been caused by an infection, perhaps related to the injury.

living possible. Through submissive gestures, aggression is reduced and physical violence is less likely. Likewise, friendly intentions and relationships are reinforced through physical contact and grooming. Indeed, we humans can see ourselves in other primates most clearly in their use of nonverbal communication, particularly because some of their gestures and facial expressions carry the same meaning as ours do.

Aggressive and Affiliative Behaviors within Groups

Aggression Within primate societies, there is an interplay between aggressive behaviors, which can lead to group disruption, and **affiliative behaviors**, which promote group cohesion. Conflict within a group frequently develops out of competition for resources, including mating partners or food. Instead of actual attacks or fighting, most aggression within a group occurs in the form of various signals and displays, frequently within the context of a dominance hierarchy. Most tense situations are resolved through various submissive and appeasement behaviors.

But conflicts aren't always resolved peacefully; in fact, they can have serious and even fatal consequences. For example, high-ranking female macaques frequently intimidate, harass, and even attack lower-ranking females to keep them away from food. Dominant females consistently chase subordinates away from food and have even been observed taking food from their mouths. In some cases, low-ranking females suffer weight loss and poor nutrition, which in turn may also result in lower reproductive success because they're less able to rear offspring to maturity simply because they don't get enough to eat (Silk et al., 2003).

Competition between males for mates frequently results in injury and even death (Fig. 7-12). In species that have a distinct breeding season, such as New World squirrel monkeys, conflict between males is most common during that time. In species not restricted to a mating season, such as baboons and chimpanzees, competition between males can be ongoing.

Affiliative Behaviors Even though conflict can be destructive, a certain amount of aggression helps maintain order within groups and protects either individual or group resources. Fortunately, there are many affiliative behaviors that reinforce bonds between individuals, promote group cohesion, minimize actual violence, and defuse potentially dangerous situations. Common affiliative behaviors include reconciliation, consolation, and simple amicable interactions between friends

affiliative behaviors Amicable associations between individuals. Affiliative behaviors, such as grooming, reinforce social bonds and promote group cohesion.

and relatives. Most such behaviors involve various forms of physical contact such as touching, hand holding, hugging, and grooming (Fig. 7-13). In fact, physical contact is one of the most important factors in primate development, and is crucial in promoting peaceful relationships and reinforcing bonds in many primate social groups.

Grooming is one of the most important affiliative behaviors in many primate species. Although it occurs in other animal species, social grooming is mostly a primate activity and plays an important role in day-to-day life. Because grooming involves using the fingers to pick through the fur of another individual (or one's own) to remove insects, dirt, and other materials, it serves hygienic functions. But it's also an immensely pleasurable activity that members of some species, especially chimpanzees, engage in for long periods of time.

Grooming occurs in a variety of contexts. Mothers groom infants; males groom sexually receptive females; subordinate animals groom dominant ones, sometimes to gain favor; and friends groom friends. In general, grooming is comforting. It restores peaceful relationships after conflict, and provides reassurance during tense situations. In short, grooming reinforces social bonds and consequently helps strengthen and maintain a group's structure.

Social relationships are crucial to nonhuman primates, and bonds between individuals can last a lifetime. These relationships serve many functions. Individuals of many species form alliances in which members support each other against outsiders. Alliances, or coalitions, as they're also called, can be used to enhance the status of members. In fact, chimpanzees rely so heavily on coalitions and are so skillful politically that an entire book, appropriately titled *Chimpanzee Politics* (de Waal, 2007), is devoted to the topic.

▼ **Figure 7-13**

Grooming primates. (**a**) Mandrills. (**b**) Savanna baboons. (**c**) Japanese macaques. (**d**) Chimpanzees.

Reproduction and Reproductive Behaviors

In most primate species as in most mammals, sexual behavior is tied to the female's reproductive cycle, with females being receptive to males only when they're in estrus. Estrus is characterized by behavioral changes and, in Old World monkeys and apes that live in multimale groups, it is also accompanied by swelling and changes in color of the skin around the genital area. These changes serve as visual cues of a female's readiness to mate (Fig. 7-14).

Permanent bonding between males and females isn't common among nonhuman primates. However, male and female savanna baboons sometimes form mating consortships. These temporary relationships last while the female is in estrus, and the two spend most of their time together, mating frequently. Mating consortships are common among bonobos. In fact, male and female bonobos may spend several weeks primarily in each other's company. During this time they mate often, even when the female is not in estrus.

Such a male-female bond may result in increased reproductive success for both sexes. For the male, there is the increased likelihood that he will be the father of any infant the female conceives. At the same time, the female potentially gains protection from predators or other members of her group, and perhaps assistance in caring for offspring she may already have.

Reproductive Strategies

Reproductive strategies, and especially how they differ between the sexes, have been a primary focus of primate research. The goal of these strategies is to produce and successfully rear to adulthood as many offspring as possible.

Primates are among the most **K-selected** of mammals. By this we mean that individuals produce only a few young, in whom they invest a tremendous amount of parental care. Contrast this pattern with **r-selected** species, where individuals

reproductive strategies Behaviors or behavioral complexes that have been favored by natural selection to increase individual reproductive success. The behaviors need not be deliberate, and they often vary considerably between males and females.

K-selected Pertaining to K-selection, an adaptive strategy whereby individuals produce relatively few offspring, in whom they invest increased parental care. Although only a few infants are born, chances of survival are increased for each one because of parental investments of time and energy (compared with r-selected species). Birds, elephants, and canids (wolves, coyotes, and dogs) are examples of K-selected nonprimate species.

r-selected Pertaining to r-selection, a reproductive strategy that emphasizes relatively large numbers of offspring and reduced parental care (compared with K-selected species). *K-selection* and *r-selection* are relative terms; for example, mice are r-selected compared with primates but K-selected compared with insects.

▲ **Figure 7-14**
Estrous swelling in a female Celebes crested macaque.

produce large numbers of offspring but invest little or no energy in parental care. Good examples of r-selected species include insects, most fishes, and, among mammals, mice and rabbits.

Considering the degree of care required by young dependent primate offspring, it's clear that an enormous investment by at least one parent is necessary, and in most species the mother carries most of the burden certainly before, and also after the birth. Primates are completely helpless at birth. They develop slowly, and consequently, are exposed to expanded learning opportunities within a social environment. Therefore what we see in ourselves and our close primate relatives (and presumably in our more recent ancestors as well) is a strategy in which at least one parent, usually the mother, makes an extraordinary investment to produce a few "high-quality," slowly maturing offspring.

Finding food and mates, avoiding predators, and caring for and protecting dependent young are difficult challenges for nonhuman primates. In most species, males and females use different strategies to meet these challenges.

Female primates spend almost all their adult lives either pregnant, lactating, and/or caring for offspring, and the resulting metabolic demands are enormous. A pregnant or lactating female, although perhaps only half the size of her male counterpart, may require about the same number of calories per day. Even if these demands are met, her physical resources may be drained. For example, analysis of chimpanzee skeletons from Gombe showed significant loss of bone and bone mineral in older females (Sumner et al., 1989).

Given these physiological costs, and the fact that her reproductive potential is limited by lengthy interbirth intervals, a female's best strategy is to maximize the amount of resources available to her and her offspring. Indeed, as we discussed earlier, females of many primate species (marmosets, gibbons, and macaques, to name a few) are highly competitive with other females and aggressively protect resources. In other species (chimpanzees, for example), females distance themselves from others to avoid competition. Males, however, face a different set of challenges. Having little investment in the rearing of offspring and the continuous production of sperm, it's to the male's advantage to secure as many mates and produce as many offspring as possible.

Sexual Selection

Sexual selection is one outcome of different mating strategies. First described by Charles Darwin, it is a type of natural selection that operates on only one sex, usually males. The selective agent is male competition for mates and, in some species, mate choice by females. The long-term effect of sexual selection is to increase the frequency of those traits in males that lead to greater success in acquiring mates.

In the animal kingdom, numerous male attributes are the result of sexual selection. For example, female birds of many species are attracted to males with more vividly colored plumage. Selection has thus increased the frequency of alleles that influence brighter coloration in males, and in these species (peacocks are a good example), males are more colorful than females.

Sexual selection in primates is most common in species in which mating is **polygynous** and there is considerable male competition for females. In these species, sexual selection produces dimorphism with regard to a number of traits, most noticeably body size (Fig. 7-15). As you have seen, the males of many primate species are considerably larger than females, and they also have larger canine teeth. Conversely, in species that live in pairs (such as gibbons) or where male competition is reduced, sexual dimorphism in body size and canine teeth is either reduced or nonexistent. For this reason, the presence or absence of sexual dimorphism in a species can be a reasonably good indicator of mating structure.

sexual selection A type of natural selection that operates on only one sex within a species. It's the result of competition for mates, and it can lead to sexual dimorphism with regard to one or more traits.

polygynous Pertaining to polygyny; a mating system in which a male mates with more than one female. This is the most common mating pattern found in mammals, including most primates.

▲ **Figure 7-15**
Female and male mandrills are among the many good examples of sexual dimorphism and sexual selection among primates. Adult male mandrills are about twice the size of females and are much more colorful.

Is Infanticide a Reproductive Strategy?

One way males may increase their chances of reproducing is to kill infants fathered by other males. This explanation was first offered in an early study of Hanuman langurs in India (Hrdy, 1977). Hanuman langurs (Fig. 7-16) typically live in groups composed of one adult male, several females, and their offspring. Males without mates form "bachelor" groups that frequently forage within sight of one-male–multifemale units. These peripheral males occasionally attack and defeat a reproductive male and drive him from his group. Sometimes, following such a takeover, the new male kills some or all of the group's infants that were fathered by the previous male.

At first glance, infanticide would appear to be counterproductive, especially for a species as a whole. However, individuals act to maximize their own reproductive success, no matter what effect their actions may have on the group or species. Even though they aren't really aware of it, by killing infants fathered by other animals, male langurs may in fact increase their own chances of fathering offspring. This is because a female doesn't come into estrus while she is producing milk and nursing an infant; therefore she isn't sexually available. But when a female loses an infant, she resumes cycling and becomes sexually receptive. Thus, by killing a nursing infant, a new male avoids having to wait two to three years for it to be weaned before he can mate with its mother. This could be advantageous for him because chances are good that he won't even be in the group for two or three years. Moreover, he also doesn't expend energy and put himself at risk defending infants who don't carry his genes.

Hanuman langurs aren't the only primates that practice infanticide. It has been observed or surmised among many primates, including red colobus, savanna baboons, orangutans, gorillas, chimpanzees (Struhsaker and Leyland, 1987), and humans. (We should also mention that infanticide occurs in numerous nonprimate species, including rodents, cats, and horses.)

In the majority of reported nonhuman primate examples, infanticide coincides with the transfer of a new male into a group or, as among chimpanzees, an encounter with an unfamiliar female and infant. Numerous objections to this explanation of infanticide have been raised. Alternative explanations have included competition for resources (Rudran, 1973), aberrant behaviors related to human-induced overcrowding (Curtin and Dohlinow, 1978), and inadvertent killing during conflict between animals (Bartlett et al., 1993). But others (Struhsaker and Leyland, 1987; Hrdy et al., 1995) maintain that the incidence and patterning of infanticide by males are not only significant but also consistent with the assumptions established by theories of behavioral evolution.

In a study published in 2003, Henzi and Barrett reported that when chacma baboon males migrate into a new group, they "deliberately single out females with young infants and hunt them down"

▼ **Figure 7-16**
Hanuman langurs.

Peter Henzi

▲ **Figure 7-17**

An immigrant male chacma baboon chases a terrified female and her infant (clinging to her back). Resident males interceded to stop the chase.

(Fig. 7-17). The importance of these findings is the conclusion that, at least in chacma baboons, newly arrived males consistently try to kill infants, and their attacks are highly aggressive and purposeful. However, reports such as these don't prove that infanticide increases a male's reproductive fitness. In order to do this, primatologists must demonstrate two crucial facts:

1. Infanticidal males *do not* kill their own offspring.
2. Once a male has killed an infant, he subsequently fathers another infant with the victim's mother.

These statements are hypotheses that can be tested; and to do this, Borries and colleagues (1999) collected DNA samples from the feces of infanticidal males and their victims' remains in several groups of free-ranging Hanuman langurs. This was done to determine if these males killed their own offspring. Their results showed that in all 16 cases where infant and male DNA was available, the males were not related to the infants they either attacked or killed. Moreover, DNA analysis also showed that in 4 out of 5 cases in which a victim's mother subsequently gave birth, the new infant was fathered by the infanticidal male. The application of DNA technology to a long-unanswered question has provided strong evidence suggesting that infanticide may indeed give males an increased chance of fathering offspring. Moreover, this study provides another example of how science works: hypotheses are refined and further tested as new discoveries are made or, as in this case, new technologies are developed.

Mothers, Fathers, and Infants

The basic social unit among all primates is a female and her infants (Fig. 7-18). Except in those species in which monogamy or **polyandry** occurs, or in which the social group is a bonded pair, males usually don't directly participate in the rearing of offspring.

The mother–infant bond begins at birth. Although the exact nature of the bonding process isn't fully understood, there appear to be predisposing innate factors that strongly attract the female to her infant, so long as she herself has had a sufficiently normal experience with her own mother. This doesn't mean that primate mothers have innate knowledge of how to care for an infant. They don't. Monkeys and apes raised in captivity without contact with their own mothers not only don't know how to care for a newborn infant but also may be afraid of it and attack or even kill it. Thus learning is essential to establishing a mother's attraction to her infant.

polyandry A mating system wherein a female continuously associates with more than one male (usually two or three) with whom she mates. Among nonhuman primates, polyandry is seen only in marmosets and tamarins. It also occurs in a few human societies.

David Haring

Melanie Beasley

Robert Jurmain

Eric Gevaert/Alamy

Melanie Beasley

◀ **Figure 7-18**
Primate mothers with young.
(**a**) Mongoose lemurs.
(**b**) Chimpanzees.
(**c**) Sykes monkeys.
(**d**) Squirrel monkeys.
(**e**) Savanna baboons.

The importance of a normal relationship with the mother has been demonstrated by field and laboratory studies. From birth, infant primates are able to cling to their mother's fur, and they're in more or less constant physical contact with her for several months. During this critical period, infants develop a closeness with their mothers that doesn't always end with weaning. In some species it may be maintained until one or the other dies.

Gerry Ellis/Minden Pictures

◀ **Figure 7-19**

(**a**) This male savanna baboon is holding a very young infant as its mother looks on. (**b**) Infant mountain gorilla with silverback male. It's not certain that these males are actually the fathers of the infants, but they are exhibiting parental behavior.

In some species, presumed fathers also participate in infant care (Fig. 7-19). Male siamangs actively care for their offspring, and marmoset and tamarin males provide most of the direct infant care. In fact, marmoset and tamarin offspring (frequently twins) are usually carried on the male's back and transferred to their mother only for nursing.

Even in species where males aren't directly involved in infant care, they may take more than a casual interest in infants, and this is especially true of hamadryas and savanna baboons. But to establish that baboons exhibit paternal care, it's necessary to establish paternity. Buchan and colleagues (2003) did just that by analyzing the DNA of sub-adults and males. They showed that during disputes, males intervened on behalf of their offspring significantly more often than they did for unrelated juveniles. Because disputes can lead to severe injury, Buchan and colleagues considered the male intervention an example of true paternal care.

Paul Souders/Getty Images

Nonhuman Primate Models for the Evolution of Human Behavior

In Chapter 1 we said that primates, chimpanzees in particular, are often used as models for early hominin behavior. But once the human and chimpanzee lineages diverged from a common ancestor, they traveled down different evolutionary paths and continued to evolve in response to different environmental pressures. Consequently no living species, not even chimpanzees, can perfectly serve as representatives of early hominin adaptations.

Primatologists examine behavioral patterns that have evolved as adaptive responses in nonhuman primates, always keeping in mind the enormous degree of flexibility in primate behavior. Then they identify similar patterns in humans and try to draw conclusions about the ecological and genetic factors that may have produced similarities (and differences) between our closest relatives and ourselves. This approach places the study of human behavior firmly within an evolutionary context.

As a separate lineage, our own evolutionary story probably began with a behavioral shift to exploiting a mixed woodland habitat, an econiche different from that of the great apes, and this new adaptation required spending more time on the ground and exploiting different types of resources. These factors, in turn, selected for additional behavioral and anatomical adaptations, at the same time that other hominoids were responding to different environmental pressures.

Brain and Body Size

One predominant characteristic that clearly differentiates humans from other primates is relative brain size, by which we mean the proportion of some measure of body size, such as weight, that's accounted for by the brain. Brain size and body size are closely correlated. Clearly an animal the size of a chimpanzee (about 100 to 150 pounds) has a larger brain than a 2 pound squirrel monkey. But, the ratio between brain size and body weight is not the same in all species.

The predictable relationship between body and brain size has been called the "index of **encephalization**" (Jerison, 1973). The degree of encephalization is used to estimate the expected brain size for any given body size. Most primates are close to predicted ratios for brain–body size, but there's one notable exception: ourselves. (New World capuchins and squirrel monkeys also show a degree of encephalization that considerably exceeds predictions.) Brain size in modern humans is well beyond what would be expected for a primate of similar body weight (approximately three times larger than expected!). It's this degree of encephalization that must be explained as a unique and central component of relatively recent human evolution. Indeed, studies of fossil hominins have clearly demonstrated that early members of the genus *Homo* as well as even older less derived hominins (*Australopithecus*) weren't nearly as encephalized as modern humans are.

Beyond simple comparisons of brain size between different species, it's more appropriate to emphasize the relative size of certain structures in the brain. Primitive (ancestral) brains, such as those of reptiles, are mostly composed of structures related to basic physiological functions, and there's a small cortex that receives sensory (especially olfactory) information. As discussed in Chapter 5, in mammals, the relative size of the most recently evolved layer of the cortex, called the neocortex, has increased. This increase permits a more detailed analysis and interpretation of incoming sensory information and therefore more complex behavior. In primates, expansion of the neocortex has accounted for much of the increase in brain size (Fig. 7-20). The primate neocortex is partly composed of many complex association areas. It's the part of the brain that, in humans, is associated with cognitive functions related to reasoning, complex problem solving, forethought, and language. The neocortex accounts for about 80 percent of the total volume of the human brain (Dunbar, 1998).

Timing of brain growth is also important. In nonhuman primates, the most rapid period of brain growth occurs shortly before birth; but in humans, it occurs after birth. Human prenatal brain growth is restricted so that the infant can pass through the birth canal. As it is, the size of the head in human newborns makes childbirth more difficult in humans than in any other primate. Thus, in humans, the brain grows rapidly for at least the first five years after birth. Because brain tissue is the most costly of all body tissues in terms of energy consumed, the metabolic costs of

encephalization The proportional size of the brain relative to some estimate of overall body size, such as weight. More precisely, the term refers to increases in brain size beyond what would be expected given the body size of a particular species.

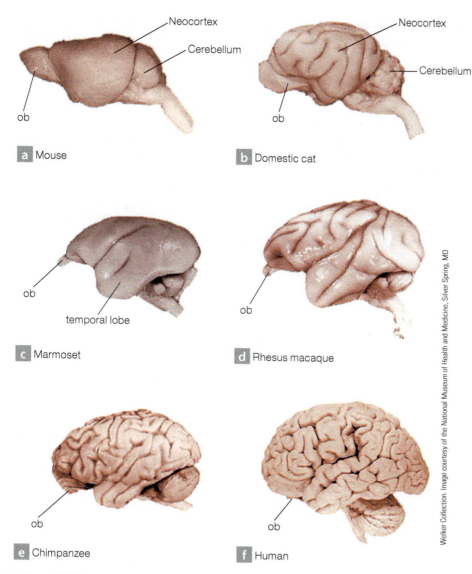

Welker Collection. Image courtesy of the National Museum of Health and Medicine, Silver Spring, MD

▲ **Figure 7-20**

Comparisons of mammalian brains as seen in these left lateral views (front is to left). Expansion of the neocortex, the outer layers of the cerebral hemispheres, has been the most significant trend during the evolution of the mammalian brain. This is especially evident in the size of the neocortex relative to that of the olfactory bulb (ob) at the front of the brain. The olfactory bulb is the termination point of sensory fibers that send olfactory information from the nose to the brain. A relatively large olfactory bulb indicates a greater dependence on the sense of smell. Compare the size of this organ, relative to the neocortex, in these brains. In the mouse and cat, it's particularly large, but it becomes smaller in primates. In humans, it's barely visible. In fact, in chimpanzees and humans, the neocortex is all that's visible from the top and sides except for the cerebellum. Also note the increasingly convoluted surface of the neocortex. This is due to cortical folding, which allows more neurons to be packed into a limited space. Increasing the number of neurons provides more interconnections between areas of the brain, allowing more information to be processed. The marmoset exhibits less cortical folding than the cat, but its temporal lobe (part of the neocortex) is better defined, and brain size relative to body size is greater. As you can see, cortical folding is most pronounced in humans. (Illustrations are shown approximately the same size and not to scale.) (Photos provided by the University of Wisconsin–Madison Comparative Mammalian Brain Collection: http://brainmuseum.org. Preparation of these images and specimens was funded by the National Science Foundation and the National Institutes of Health.)

▶ **Figure 7-21**

These young raccoons are extremely intelligent and forage for a wide assortment of foods in a complex environment. However, they don't spend their entire lives in social groups and their relative (and absolute) brain size is smaller than that of similarly sized primates.

such rapid and sustained neurological growth are enormous, requiring more than 50 percent of an infant's metabolic output (Aiello, 1992).

In evolutionary terms, the metabolic costs of a large brain must be compensated for by benefits. That is, large brains would not have evolved if they didn't offer some advantage (Dunbar, 1998). Various hypotheses have been proposed for the evolution of large brains in primates, and many scientists in the past focused on problems related to getting food and the kinds of foods a species eats. For example, some monkeys (with a smaller relative brain size) primarily eat leaves, which, although plentiful, aren't an energy-rich food source. Primates need a complex brain in order to be familiar with their home range; to be aware of when seasonal foods are available; and to solve the problem of extracting foods from shells, hard peels, and even underground roots. But these are problems for all foraging species (squirrels and raccoons, for example), yet these animals haven't evolved such relatively large brains (Fig. 7-21).

Another explanation, the social brain hypothesis, proposes that primate brains increased in relative size and complexity because primates live in social groups. The demands of social living are numerous, and primates must be able to negotiate a complex web of interactions, including competition, alliance formation, forming and maintaining friendships, and avoiding certain individuals. Therefore Barton and Dunbar (1997) suggested that intelligence evolved not only to solve physical problems (such as finding food and avoiding predators) but also to analyze and use social information, such as which animals are dominant, who forms alliances with whom, and whom to avoid.

Language

The development of language was one of the most significant events in human evolution. We have already described several behaviors and autonomic responses that convey information in nonhuman primates. But although we emphasized the importance of communication to primate social life, we also said that nonhuman primates don't use language the way humans do.

The view traditionally held by most linguists and behavioral psychologists has been that nonhuman communication consists of mostly involuntary vocalizations and actions that convey information solely about an animal's emotional state (anger, fear, and so on). Nonhuman animals haven't been considered capable of communicating about external events, objects, or other animals, either in close proximity or removed in space or time. For example, when a startled baboon barks, other group members know only that it may have been surprised or frightened. But they don't necessarily know why it barked until they look around to see what provoked it. In general, then, it's been assumed that in nonhuman animals, including primates, vocalizations, facial expressions, body postures, and so on don't refer to specific external phenomena.

But these views have been challenged for years (Steklis, 1985; King, 1994, 2004). For example, vervet monkeys (Fig. 7-22) use specific vocalizations to refer to particular categories of predators, such as snakes, birds of prey, and leopards (Struhsaker, 1967; Seyfarth et al., 1980a,b). The fact that vervets use distinct vocalizations to refer to specific components of the external environment demonstrates that their calls aren't involuntary and they don't refer solely to the individual's emotional state (alarm), although this information is certainly conveyed. While these findings dispel certain long-held misconceptions about nonhuman communication (at least for some species), they also indicate certain limitations. Vervet communication is restricted to the present; as far as we know, no vervet can refer to a predator it saw yesterday or one it might see in the future. When researchers made tape recordings of various vervet alarm calls and played them back within hearing distance of wild vervets, they saw different responses to various calls. When the monkeys heard leopard-alarm calls, they climbed trees; they looked up when they heard eagle-alarm calls; and they responded to snake-alarm calls by looking at the ground around them. A tarsier predation study in Indonesia found similar results and showed that tarsiers use different vocalizations based on the type of predator (snakes versus birds of prey) present in the environment (Gursky, 2003).

Humans use *language*, a set of written and/or spoken symbols that refer to concepts, other people, objects, and so on. This set of symbols is said to be arbitrary because the symbol itself has no inherent relationship with whatever it stands for. For example, the English word *flower*, when written or spoken, neither looks, smells, nor feels like the thing it represents. Humans can also recombine their linguistic symbols in an infinite number of ways to create new meanings, and we can use language to refer to events, places, objects, and people far removed in both space and time. For these reasons, language is described as an open system of communication, based on the human ability to think symbolically.

◀ **Figure 7-22**
A group of vervets.

Lynn Kilgore

Language, as distinct from other forms of communication, has always been considered a uniquely human achievement, setting humans apart from the rest of the animal kingdom. But reports from psychologists, especially those who work with chimpanzees, leave little doubt that apes can learn to interpret visual signs and use them in communication. Other than humans, no mammal can speak. However, the fact that apes can't speak has less to do with lack of intelligence than with differences in the anatomy of the vocal tract and language-related structures in the brain.

Beginning in the 1960s, after unsuccessful attempts by others to teach young chimpanzees to speak, psychologists Beatrice and Allen Gardner designed a study to test language capabilities in chimpanzees by teaching ASL (American Sign Language for the deaf) to an infant female named Washoe. The project began in 1966, and in three years, Washoe had acquired at least 132 signs. "She asked for goods and services, and she also asked questions about the world of objects and events around her" (Gardner et al., 1989, p. 6).

Years later, an infant chimpanzee named Loulis was placed in Washoe's care, and she adopted him. Psychologist Roger Fouts and colleagues wanted to know if Loulis would spontaneously acquire signing skills through contact with Washoe and other chimpanzees in the study group. Within just eight days, Loulis began to imitate signs the other chimpanzees were making. Also, Washoe deliberately taught Loulis how to make some signs. For example, when she wanted him to sit down, "Washoe placed a small plastic chair in front of Loulis, and then signed CHAIR/SIT to him several times in succession, watching him closely throughout" (Fouts et al., 1989, p. 290).

There have been other chimpanzee language experiments. A female named Sara was taught to recognize plastic chips as symbols for various objects. Importantly, the chips did not resemble the objects they represented. For example, the chip that represented an apple was neither round nor red. The fact that Sara was able to use the chips to communicate is significant because her ability to associate chips with concepts and objects to which they bore no similarity implies some degree of symbolic thought. And at the Yerkes Regional Primate Research Center in Atlanta, Georgia, two male chimpanzees, Sherman and Austin, learned to communicate using a series of lexigrams, or geometric symbols, imprinted on a computer keyboard (Savage-Rumbaugh, 1986).

Other apes have also shown language abilities. The most famous of these is Koko, a female lowland gorilla who was taught to use ASL by Dr. Francine Patterson in the 1970s. Furthermore, Michael, an adult male gorilla who was also involved in the same study until his death in 2000, had a considerable vocabulary, and the two gorillas regularly communicated with each other using sign language.

In the late 1970s, a 2-year-old male orangutan named Chantek (also at Yerkes) acquired approximately 140 signs, which he sometimes used to refer to objects and people not present. Chantek also invented signs and recombined them in novel ways, and he appeared to understand that his signs were representations of items, actions, and people (Miles, 1990).

Several people have questioned this type of experimental work. Do the apes really understand the signs they learn or are they merely imitating their trainers? Do they learn that a symbol refers to or represents an object, or do they only understand that making a symbol will produce that object?

Partly in an effort to address some of these questions, psychologist Sue Savage-Rumbaugh taught the two chimpanzees Sherman and Austin to use symbols for *categories* of objects, such as "food" or "tool." This was done in recognition of the fact that in previous studies, apes had been taught symbols for specific items, not categories. Using a symbol as a label isn't the same thing as understanding the *representational value* of the symbol. But if chimpanzees could classify things into groups, it would indicate that they can use symbols referentially.

Sherman and Austin were taught to recognize familiar food items, for which they routinely used symbols, as belonging to a broader category referred to by yet another symbol, "food." They were then introduced to unfamiliar food items, for which they had no symbols, to see if they would place them in the food category. The fact that they scored high in this experiment showed that they could categorize unfamiliar objects. More importantly, it was clear that they could assign symbols to indicate an object's membership in a broad grouping. This ability strongly indicated that the chimpanzees understood that the symbols represented not only objects but also groups of objects (Savage-Rumbaugh and Lewin, 1994).

One criticism of the conclusions drawn from the ape language studies has been that young chimpanzees must be *taught* to use symbols, while human children spontaneously acquire language through exposure without being deliberately taught. Therefore it was significant when Savage-Rumbaugh and her colleagues reported that Kanzi, an infant male bonobo, was spontaneously acquiring and using symbols at the age of 2½ years (Savage-Rumbaugh et al., 1986) (Fig. 7-23).

While Kanzi showed a remarkable degree of cognitive complexity, it remains clear that apes don't acquire and use language in the same way humans do. Nonetheless, we now have abundant evidence that humans aren't the only species capable of some degree of symbolic thought and complex communication.

The Evolution of Language

From an evolutionary perspective, the ape language experiments may suggest clues to the origins of human language. It's also highly significant that free-ranging great apes use some gestures for communication (King, 2004). In fact, it's possible that the last common ancestor we share with the living great apes had communication capabilities similar to those we see in these species. Thus we need to identify the factors that enhanced the adaptive value of these abilities in our own lineage.

While increased brain size played a crucial role in human evolution, it was changes in preexisting neurological structures that permitted the development of language. Current evidence suggests that new structures and novel connections haven't generally been the basis for most of the neurological differences we see among species. Rather, reorganization, elaboration, and/or reduction of existing

◀ Figure 7-23

The bonobo Kanzi, as a youngster, using lexigrams to communicate with human observers.

structures, as well as shifts in the proportions of existing connections, have been far more important (Deacon, 1992). It's also important to understand that the neurological changes that enhanced language development in humans wouldn't have occurred if early hominins hadn't already acquired the behavioral and neurological foundations that made them possible. For reasons we don't yet fully understand, communication became increasingly important during the course of human evolution, and natural selection favored anatomical and neurological changes that enhanced our ancestors' ability to use spoken language.

In most people, language function is located in the left hemisphere, meaning it's lateralized. (The left hemisphere is the dominant hemisphere in most people, and since it controls motion on the right side of the body, most people are right-handed.) Two regions in particular, Broca's area in the left frontal lobe and Wernicke's area in the left temporal lobe, are directly involved in the production and perception, respectively, of spoken language (Fig. 7-24).

Broca's area is located in the motor cortex immediately adjacent to a region that controls the movement of muscles in the face, lips, larynx, and tongue. When a person is speaking, information is sent to Broca's area, where it's organized *specifically for communication*. Then it's sent to the adjacent motor areas, which in turn activate the muscles involved in speech. We know that Broca's area operates this way because when it's damaged, speech production is impaired, even though there's no muscle paralysis. Paralysis occurs only when nearby areas that control facial muscles are damaged, not when the damage is confined to Broca's area.

Wernicke's area is an association area that lies near structures involved in the reception of sound. A lesion in Wernicke's area doesn't impair hearing, but it severely affects language comprehension. This, in turn, interferes with speech production because auditory information that is related *specifically to language* is sent from Wernicke's area to Broca's area by way of a bundle of nerve fibers connecting the two regions.

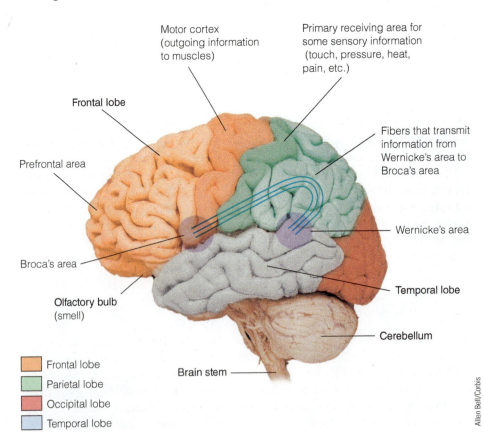

▶ **Figure 7-24**
Left lateral view of the human brain, showing major regions and areas involved in language. Information that is to be used in speech is sent from Wernicke's area via a bundle of nerve fibers to Broca's area.

Motor cortex
(outgoing information
to muscles)

Primary receiving area for
some sensory information
(touch, pressure, heat,
pain, etc.)

Frontal lobe

Prefrontal area

Fibers that transmit
information from
Wernicke's area to
Broca's area

Broca's area

Wernicke's area

Olfactory bulb
(smell)

Temporal lobe

Cerebellum

Brain stem

Frontal lobe
Parietal lobe
Occipital lobe
Temporal lobe

Allen Bell/Corbis

But the perception and production of speech involve much more than these two areas, and the use of written language requires still other neurological structures. Eventually, information relating to all the senses (visual, olfactory, tactile, and auditory) is combined and relayed to Broca's area, where it's translated for speech production. This uniquely human ability depends on the interconnections between receiving areas for all sensory stimuli. While the brains of other species have such areas, they don't have the ability to transform sensory information for the purpose of using language—or maybe they do at least to some degree.

Cantalupo and Hopkins (2001) report that magnetic resonance imaging of chimpanzee, bonobo, and gorilla brains demonstrates that in these species a region analogous to part of Broca's area is larger on the left side than on the right. These authors further report that in captive great ape studies, gestures are preferentially made by the right hand (controlled by the left hemisphere), especially when gestures are combined with vocalizations. This study suggests, therefore, that perhaps the anatomical basis for the development of left-hemisphere dominance in speech production in humans was present, at least to an incipient degree, in the last common ancestor of humans and the African great apes.

Specialization of auditory centers of the left hemisphere for language may have preceded the evolutionary divergence of humans and apes. A team of neuroscientists has shown that, to a degree, rhesus macaques also have this type of lateralization (Poremba et al., 2004). In these monkeys, evidence suggests that the left temporal lobe is specialized for processing the vocalizations of other rhesus macaques in particular.

The identification of a regulatory gene involved in speech may provide another piece to the puzzle of the evolution of human language. This gene, called *FOXP2*, produces a protein that influences the expression of other genes. In turn, those genes control the embryological development of brain circuits that relate to language in humans. People who inherit a particular *FOXP2* mutation have developmental disorders in the brain that cause severe speech and language impairment (Lai et al., 2001).

The *FOXP2* gene isn't unique to humans. In fact, it's present in mice, indicating that all mammals probably have it. But while *FOXP2* is important to neurological development in nonhuman mammals, it has nothing to do with language in these species. When researchers compared the human form of the *FOXP2* protein with that of chimpanzees and gorillas, they found that the human protein differed from the two ape versions by two amino acid substitutions. This means that since humans last shared a common ancestor with chimpanzees and gorillas, the gene has undergone two point mutations during the course of human evolution. But in chimpanzees and gorillas, it hasn't changed.

The *FOXP2* gene is the first gene demonstrated to influence language development. It varies between ourselves and closely related species, indicating not only that natural selection has acted on it in our lineage but also that the *FOXP2* protein may have played a role in the development of language capacities in humans. The "At a Glance" on page 212 outlines several key factors that likely influenced the evolution of human language.

Primate Cultural Behavior

One important trait that makes primates, and especially chimpanzees, attractive as models for early hominin behavior may be called cultural behavior. Although many cultural anthropologists and others prefer to use the term *culture* specifically to refer to human activities, most biological anthropologists consider it appropriate to apply the term to many nonhuman primate behaviors too (McGrew, 1992, 1998; de Waal, 1999; Whiten et al., 1999).

At a Glance   Evolution of Human Language

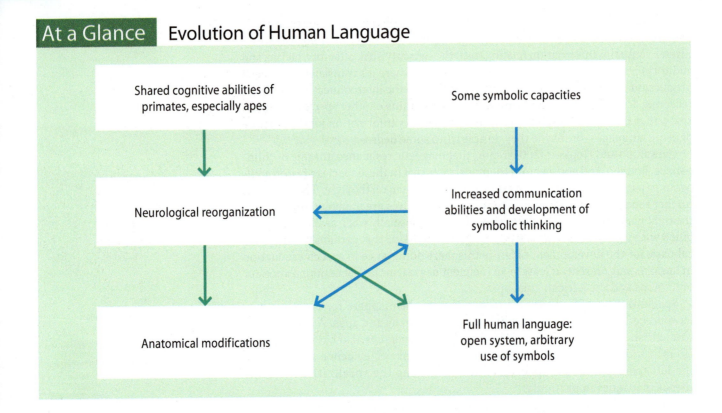

Cultural behavior is *learned*, not genetically determined, although the capacity to learn is greatly influenced by genes. Whereas humans deliberately teach their young, free-ranging nonhuman primates (with the exception of a few reports) don't appear to do so. But at the same time, like young nonhuman primates, human children also acquire a tremendous amount of knowledge through observation rather than instruction (Fig. 7-25). By watching their mothers and other members of their group, nonhuman primate infants learn about food items, appropriate behaviors, and how to use and modify objects to achieve certain ends. In turn, their own offspring will observe their activities. What emerges is a *cultural tradition* that may eventually come to typify an entire group or even a species.

The earliest reported example of cultural behavior concerned a study group of Japanese macaques on Koshima Island, Japan. In 1952, Japanese researchers began feeding the macaques unwashed sweet potatoes. The following year, a young female (named Imo) started washing her potatoes before eating them. Within three years, several other monkeys were also washing their potatoes. The researchers pointed out that dietary habits and food preferences are learned and that potato washing is an example of nonhuman culture (Boesch and Tomasello, 1998). Because the practice arose as an innovative solution to a problem (removing dirt) and gradually spread through the troop until it became a tradition, it was seen as containing elements of human culture.

A study of orangutans listed 19 behaviors that showed sufficient regional variation to be classed as "very likely cultural variants" (van Schaik et al., 2003). Four of these were differences in how nests were used or built. Other behaviors that varied included the use of branches to swat insects and pressing leaves or hands to the mouth to amplify sounds.

The use of tools or objects to accomplish tasks has always been considered one of the hallmarks of being human. In fact, tool use and language have traditionally been said to set humans apart from other animals. However, we now know

▲ **Figure 7-25**
(**a**) This little girl is learning basic computer skills by watching her older sister. (**b**) A chimpanzee learns the art of termiting through intense observation.

that humans are not the only animals that use tools. A few nonhuman primates also use tools, with chimpanzees being the most notable example. What's more, tool use isn't even restricted to primates. New Caledonian crows modify and use leaf stems to probe for insect larvae, and in captivity, they've bent wire to make "hooks" to obtain food (Hunt, 1996; Weir et al., 2008); and sea otters use rocks to crack open abalone shells (Fig. 7-26). Nevertheless, tool use is most elaborate among primates and, needless to say, no other species even comes close to developing tools to the degree that humans have. But human technology had to begin somewhere, so we briefly discuss some of the many examples of tool use in nonhuman primates.

Reports of tool use by gorillas aren't common, but Breuer and colleagues (2005) reported seeing two female lowland gorillas in the DRC using branches as tools. In one case, a gorilla used a branch to test the depth of a pool of water. Then, as she waded bipedally through the pool, she used the branch again, this time as a walking stick (Fig. 7-27).

◀ **Figure 7-26**
This California sea otter is eating a clam it has opened with a rock. It's common for sea otters to put their shell-cracking rocks on their stomachs as they eat, just in case they should need them again.

Thomas Breuer/WCS

▲ **Figure 7-27**
A female lowland gorilla uses a "wading stick" (in her right hand) for support.

Chimpanzees exhibit more complex forms of tool use than any other nonhuman primate. This point is very important, because traditionally, tool use (along with language) was said to set humans apart from other animals. Chimpanzees crumple and chew handfuls of leaves, which they dip into tree hollows where water accumulates.

Then they suck the water from the newly made "leaf sponges." Leaves are also used to wipe substances from fur. Twigs are used as toothpicks, stones as weapons, and objects such as branches and stones may be dragged or rolled to enhance displays.

They routinely insert twigs and grass blades into termite mounds in a practice primatologists call "termite fishing" (refer back to Fig. 7-25). The termites seize the twig in an attempt to protect their nest, and, unfortunately for them, they become a light snack once the chimpanzee pulls the twig out of the mound. Importantly, chimpanzees frequently modify some of their stems and twigs by stripping the leaves—in effect, making a tool. For example, chimpanzees often choose a particular piece of vine, twig, or palm frond, remove leaves or other extraneous material, and then break off portions until it's the proper length. Chimpanzees have also been seen making these tools even before the termite mound is in sight.

The modification of natural objects for use as tools has several implications for nonhuman primate intelligence. First, the chimpanzees are involved in an activity that prepares them for a future task at a somewhat distant location, and this implies planning and forethought. Second, attention to the shape and size of the raw material indicates that chimpanzees have a preconceived idea of what the finished product needs to be in order to be useful. To produce a tool, even a simple one, based on a concept is an extremely complex behavior that, as we now know, is not the exclusive domain of humans.

Primatologists have been aware of termite fishing and similar behaviors since the 1960s, but they were surprised by the discovery that chimpanzees also use tools to catch small prey. Pruetz and Bertolani (2007) reported that savanna chimpanzees in Senegal, West Africa, sharpen small branches to use as thrusting spears for capturing galagos. This is the first report of a nonhuman primate hunting with what is basically a manufactured weapon.

On 22 occasions, 10 different animals jabbed sharpened sticks into cavities in branches and trunks to extract galagos from their sleeping nests. In much the same way they modify termiting sticks, these chimpanzees had stripped off side twigs and leaves. But they'd also chewed the ends to sharpen them, in effect producing small thrusting "spears."

After several thrusts, the chimpanzee would reach into the opening to see if there was anything to be had. Observers saw only one galago being retrieved and eaten, and although it wasn't moving or vocalizing, it was unclear if it had actually been killed by the "spear" (Pruetz and Bertolani, 2007).

In several West African study groups, chimpanzees use unmodified stones as hammers and anvils (Fig. 7-28) to crack nuts and hard-shelled fruits (Boesch et al., 1994; Matsuzawa et al., 2011). Interestingly, stone hammers and platforms are used only in West African groups and not in East Africa. Likewise, termite fishing is seen in Central and East Africa, but apparently it's not done in West African groups (McGrew, 1992).

The fact that chimpanzees show regional variation in the types of tools they use is significant because these variations are cultural differences. Chimpanzees also exhibit regional dietary preferences (Nishida et al., 1983; McGrew, 1992, 1998). For example, oil palm fruits and nuts are eaten at many locations, including Gombe. But even though oil palms also grow in the Mahale Mountains (only about 90 miles from Gombe), the chimpanzees there seem to ignore them. Such regional patterns in tool use and food preferences are very similar to the cultural differences typical of humans. Therefore it's possible that this kind of variation existed in early hominins too.

So far we've focused on tool use and culture in great apes, but they aren't the only nonhuman primates that consistently use tools and exhibit elements of cultural behavior. Primatologists have been studying tool use in capuchin (*Cebus*) monkeys for over 30 years. Capuchins are found in South America in Colombia, Venezuela, Brazil, and northern Argentina. They are the most encephalized of all monkeys and, while forest-dwelling capuchin species are arboreal, other species live in a more savanna-like habitat, and these spend a fair amount of time on the ground. It's these more terrestrial monkeys that have been studied because of their tool use.

Many of the capuchin tool-using behaviors parallel those we've discussed for chimpanzees. Capuchins use leaves to extract water from cavities in trees (Phillips, 1998), and they use small, modified branches to probe holes in logs for invertebrates (Westergaard and Fragaszy, 1987). But what they've really become known for is using stones to obtain food. They use stones to smash foods into smaller pieces, crack palm nuts, break open hollow tree branches and logs, and dig for tubers and insects. Capuchins are the only monkeys known to use stones as tools and the only nonhuman primates to dig with stones (Visalberghi, 1990; Moura and Lee, 2004; Ottoni and Izar, 2008).

The importance of palm nuts as a food source is revealed by the enormous effort required to obtain them. Adult female and male capuchins weigh around 6 to 8 pounds, respectively, yet they walk bipedally carrying stones that weigh as much as 2 pounds (25 to 40 percent of their own body weight) (Fragaszy et al., 2004; Visalberghi et al., 2007). Because the stones are heavy, it's difficult for capuchins to sit while cracking nuts, so they frequently stand bipedally, raise the hammer stone with both hands, and then pound the nut using their entire body (Fig. 7-29).

Capuchins who use stones to crack nuts and dig for roots have one extremely important thing in common with chimpanzees who dig with sticks and hunt galagos with sharpened branches: They all live in seasonally dry, open woodland environments and not in forests. In general, this is similar to the habitat occupied by early hominins. Of course capuchins and chimpanzees aren't hominins, but those populations that live in more marginal environmental settings face many of the same challenges encountered by early hominins. Moreover, chimpanzees and capuchins are among the most encephalized nonhuman primates and have manipulative abilities similar to those of early hominins. By further studying these behaviors, researchers hope to better understand how dry, relatively open habitats, where resources are more scarce and unpredictable (compared with forest environments), may have been the context that stimulated the use of tools as a means of obtaining otherwise inaccessible foods. Culture has become the environment in which modern humans live. Quite clearly, the use of sticks in termite fishing and hammer stones to crack nuts is

Nimba/Tetsuro Matsuzawa

▲ **Figure 7-28**

Chimpanzees in Bossou, Guinea, West Africa, use a pair of stones as a hammer and anvil to crack oil palm nuts. Although the youngster isn't being deliberately taught to use stone tools, it's learning about them through observation.

Noemi Spagnoletti

▲ **Figure 7-29**
This female capuchin must use most of her strength to smash a palm nut with a heavy stone, especially when carrying her infant on her back. Meanwhile, just by observing, her infant is learning the nut-smashing technique.

anthropocentric Viewing nonhuman organisms in terms of human experience and capabilities; emphasizing the importance of humans over everything else.

core area The portion of a home range containing the highest concentration and most reliable supplies of food and water. The core area is defended.

territories Portions of an individual's or group's home range that are actively defended against intrusion, especially by members of the same species.

hardly comparable to modern human technology. However, modern human technology is rooted in behaviors such as these. This doesn't mean that nonhuman primates are "on their way" to becoming human. Remember, evolution isn't goal directed, and, even if it were, there's nothing to dictate that modern humans necessarily constitute an evolutionary goal. Such a conclusion is a purely **anthropocentric** view and has no validity in discussions of evolutionary processes.

Conflict between Groups

For many primate species, especially those whose ranges are small, contact with one or more other groups of conspecifics is a daily occurrence, and the nature of these encounters can vary from one species to another. Primate groups are associated with a *home range*, where they remain permanently. (Although individuals may leave their home range and join another community, the group itself remains in a particular area.) Within the home range is a portion called the **core area**. This area contains the highest concentration of predictable resources, and it's where the group is most likely to be found. Although portions of the home range may overlap with that of one or more other groups, core areas of adjacent groups don't overlap. The core area can also be said to be a group's territory; it's the portion of the home range defended against intrusion. In some species, however, other areas of the home range may also be defended.

Not all primates are territorial. In general, territoriality is associated with species whose ranges are sufficiently small to permit patrolling and protecting (such as gibbons and vervets). But male chimpanzees are highly intolerant of unfamiliar chimpanzees, especially other males, and fiercely defend their **territories** and resources. Therefore interactions between groups of chimpanzees almost always include aggressive displays, chasing, and sometimes fighting.

In recent years, a good deal of attention has been focused on lethal attacks by male coalitions on other chimpanzees. Such attacks occur when a number of chimpanzees attack and sometimes kill one or two others, who may or may not be members of the same group. Lethal aggression is relatively common between groups of chimpanzees. It has also been reported for a few monkey species, including capuchins (Gros-Louis et al., 2003).

Groups of male chimpanzees, sometimes accompanied by one or two females, patrol the boundaries of their home range and sometimes enter another group's territory (Wrangham, 1999; Wilson et al., 2004). While they're patrolling, chimpanzees travel silently in compact groupings (Fig. 7-30). They stop frequently to sniff, look around, or climb tall trees, where they may sit for an hour or more surveying the region. During such times, they appear to be tense, and a sudden sound, such as a snapping twig, causes them to touch or embrace each other for reassurance (Goodall, 1986). It's apparent from their nervous behavior and uncharacteristic silence that they know they're venturing into a potentially dangerous situation.

Before they enter peripheral areas, chimpanzees usually hoot and display to determine if other animals are present. If members of another community appear, some form of aggression occurs until one group retreats. But if the intruders encounter a female with an infant or a lone male, they will almost certainly attack, and chances are good that an infant or a single male will be killed. (Mothers of killed infants are frequently allowed to escape.)

for themselves and another animal, both capuchins and bonobos most frequently chose the latter option (Lakshminarayan and Santos, 2008; Hare and Kwetuenda, 2010). Indeed, bonobos showed a clear preference for eating with another unrelated individual even when it meant sharing highly desirable food items.

▲ **Figure 7-32**
(**a**) Children often try to help others. (**b**) This man is carrying an elderly neighbor to safety during a flood in Utah.

Altruism

Altruism is behavior that benefits another individual while involving some risk or sacrifice to the performer. Cooperation, assistance, and altruism are fairly common in many primate species, and altruistic acts sometimes contain elements of compassion. It's somewhat risky to use the term compassion because in humans, compassion is motivated by **empathy** for another individual. We don't know for sure whether nonhuman primates can empathize with another's suffering or misfortune, but laboratory research has indicated that some of them probably do. The degree to which chimpanzees and other primates are capable of empathy is debated by primatologists. Some believe there is substantial evidence for it (de Waal, 1996, 2007), but others remain unconvinced (Silk et al., 2005). Certainly, there are many examples, mostly from chimpanzee studies, of actions that resemble compassionate behavior in humans. Examples include protecting victims during attacks, helping younger siblings, and remaining near ill or dying relatives or friends.

Some other examples involve chimpanzees attempting to rescue others who have fallen into water. Because chimpanzees can't swim, jumping into water is a life-threatening action. Nevertheless, there are several reports of chimpanzees doing just that, especially in zoos where water-filled moats sometimes surround portions of chimpanzee exhibits. In one case, an adult male actually drowned while trying to save an infant that had fallen into the water (de Waal, 2007).

The most fundamental of altruistic behaviors, protecting dependent offspring, is ubiquitous among mammals and birds; in most species, altruistic acts are confined to this context. Among primates, however, recipients of altruistic acts may include individuals who aren't offspring and who may not even be closely related to the performer.

Chimpanzees routinely come to the aid of relatives and friends, female Hanuman langurs join forces to protect infants from infanticidal males, and male baboons protect infants and cooperate to chase predators. In fact, the primate literature abounds with examples of altruistic acts—individuals placing themselves at risk to protect others from attack.

altruism Actions that benefit another individual but at some potential risk or cost to oneself.

empathy The ability to identify with the feelings and thoughts of another individual.

One very intriguing report concerns the attempted rescue of a young adult male baboon who, at some distance from his group, was being chased by a hyena. Suddenly, observers saw an adult female racing toward the hyena in what turned out to be a vain attempt to rescue the male (Stelzner and Strier, 1981; Strier, 2003). The female wasn't the victim's mother, and a female baboon is no match for a hyena. So why would she place herself in serious danger to help an animal to whom, as far as was known, she wasn't closely related? We don't know, but this was clearly an altruistic albeit unsuccessful act.

Adopting orphans is a form of altruism that has been reported for capuchins, macaques, baboons, and especially chimpanzees. When chimpanzee youngsters are orphaned, they're routinely adopted, usually by older siblings, who are solicitous and highly protective. Adoption is crucial to the survival of orphans, who certainly wouldn't survive on their own.

Evolutionary explanations of altruism are based on the premise that individuals are more likely to perform risky or self-sacrificing behaviors for the benefit of a relative who shares genes with the performer. According to this hypothesis, known as *kin selection*, an individual may enhance his or her reproductive success by saving the life of a relative. Even if the performer's life is lost because of the act, the relative may survive to reproduce and pass on genes that both individuals shared.

There's also the hypothesis of reciprocal altruism, where the recipient of an altruistic act (that is, the one who benefits) may later return the favor. Coalitions, or alliances between two or more individuals, are an often cited example of reciprocal altruism, and they're common among baboons and chimpanzees. As we mentioned earlier, members of alliances support and defend one another in conflicts with others and may use the alliance to increase their status within the group hierarchy. Even though reciprocal altruism may occur, it's a hypothesis that needs further testing.

Group selection is a third hypothesis that some primatologists have supported. According to this model, an individual may act altruistically to benefit other group members because ultimately it's to the performer's benefit that the group be maintained. If the altruist dies, genes he or she shares with other group members may still be passed on (as in kin selection). But there's a problem with group selection theory: According to natural selection theory, individual reproductive success is enhanced by acting selfishly, and the individual is the object of natural selection.

Although the group selection issue hasn't been resolved, we do know that for many reasons primates, including humans, have a better chance of surviving and reproducing if they live in groups. Given this important fact, any behavioral mechanism that reinforces the integrity and cohesion of social groupings works to the advantage of individual group members. These mechanisms include altruism, perhaps a form of compassion, and a certain degree of empathy (de Waal, 2007).

Primatologist Frans de Waal has published extensively on empathy and altruism in chimpanzees. He points out that theories of kin selection, reciprocal altruism, and group selection ultimately explain altruism and cooperation in terms of selfishness. But this is the explanation of how the behaviors evolved, not the motivation of the animal performing the altruistic act, and de Waal views the immediate motivation as a function of "sensitivity to the needs of others," or empathy. He states, "In humans, the most commonly assumed motivation behind altruism is empathy. We identify with another in need, pain, or distress, which induces emotional arousal that may translate into sympathy and helping. Inasmuch as there are signs of empathy in other animals, from rodents to primates, the same hypothesis may apply" (de Waal, 2007, p. 1406).

The issue of empathy is much discussed, and not all primatologists agree that nonhuman primates possess a true capacity for it. Nonetheless, many behaviors certainly support the hypothesis that empathy is a behavioral trait that other species have at least to some degree. Further studies no doubt will clarify the issue and provide yet another example of behavioral continuity between other primates and ourselves.

The Primate Continuum

It's an unfortunate fact that humans generally view themselves as separate from the rest of the animal kingdom. This perspective is partly due to a prevailing lack of knowledge of the behavior and abilities of other species. Moreover, these notions are continuously reinforced through exposure to advertising, movies, and television (Fig. 7-33).

For decades, behavioral psychology taught that animal behavior represents nothing more than a series of conditioned responses to specific stimuli. (This perspective is very convenient for those who exploit nonhuman animals, for whatever purposes, and want to remain guilt-free.) Fortunately this attitude has begun to change in recent years to reflect a growing awareness that humans, although in many ways unquestionably unique, are nevertheless part of a **biological continuum** as well as a behavioral continuum. We are connected not only to our closest relatives, the other primates, but also to all life on earth.

Where do humans fit in this continuum? The answer depends on the criteria used. Certainly we're the most intelligent species if we define intelligence in terms of problem-solving abilities and abstract thought. However, if we look more closely, we recognize that the differences between ourselves and our primate relatives, especially chimpanzees and bonobos, are primarily quantitative and not qualitative.

Although the human brain is absolutely and relatively larger, neurological processes are functionally the same. The necessity of close bonding with at least one parent and the need for physical contact are essentially the same. Developmental stages and dependence on learning are similar. Indeed, even in the capacity for cruelty and aggression combined with compassion, tenderness, and altruism, as exhibited by chimpanzees, we see a close parallel to the dichotomy between "evil" and "good" so long recognized in ourselves. The main difference between how chimpanzees and humans express these qualities (and therefore the dichotomy) is one of degree. Humans are much more adept at cruelty and compassion, and we can reflect on our behavior in ways that chimpanzees cannot. Like the cat that plays with a mouse, chimpanzees don't seem to understand the suffering they inflict on others. But humans do. Likewise, while an adult chimpanzee may sit next to a dying relative, it doesn't seem to feel the intense grief a human normally does in the same situation.

biological continuum Refers to the fact that organisms are related through common ancestry and that behaviors and traits seen in one species are also seen in others to varying degrees. (When expressions of a phenomenon continuously grade into one another so that there are no discrete categories, they are said to exist on a continuum. Color is one such phenomenon.)

▼ **Figure 7-33**
Stereotypes and misconceptions many people have of our closest relatives are illustrated by (**a**) this unfortunate advertising display and (**b**) a well-meaning but ill-informed poster.

To arrive at any understanding of what it is to be human, it's important to recognize that many of our behaviors are elaborate extensions of those of our hominin ancestors and close primate relatives. The fact that so many of us prefer to bask in the sun on a beach with hundreds or thousands of others reflects our heritage as social animals adapted to life in the tropics. And the sweet tooth that afflicts so many of us is a result of our earlier primate ancestors' predilection for the high-energy sugar contained in ripe fruit. Thus it's important to recognize our primate heritage as we explore how humans came to be and how we continue to adapt.

How Do We Know?

Researchers have long debated whether culture exists in nonhuman animals, such as the great apes, monkeys, sea otters, various species of birds, and whales. Much of this research has centered on identifying the core components of culture as they pertain to the evolution of the hominin lineage. Among nonhuman primates, chimpanzees have received the most attention, which in part reflects the wide array of potential cultural behaviors documented by researchers as well as their anatomical, genetic, and behavioral similarities to humans. Culture is typically defined as those things that are learned, shared, and socially transmitted within a society and across generations. Cultural transmission is facilitated in *our* species through language, writing, and other forms of symbolic or nonverbal communication. However, among nonhuman animals, novel cultural behaviors introduced by individuals rarely have lasting power. Without a means of recording cultural

information, cultural traditions, once introduced, often disappear without a trace. Boesch and Tomasello (1998) used a ratchet tool as an analogy to describe the propensity for failures in cultural transmission among nonhuman animals. In humans, the ratchet advances as cultural behaviors are socially transmitted, shared, and passed on to future generations. However, among other animals, the ratchet often slips, resulting in the loss of new cultural behaviors in the next generation.

Chimpanzees of the Taï Forest (Côte d'Ivoire) routinely crack *Coula* nuts, which represent both a learned and shared behavior undertaken primarily by females (Boesch and Tomasello, 1998). Primatologists have even observed a few instances of mothers teaching their offspring the art of nut cracking. A comparison between two chimpanzee populations living on opposite sides of the N'Go River found that the eastern Taï chimpanzee population does not crack *Coula* nuts (even though they are available), whereas the western

population is heavily invested in nut cracking. Because these populations live in essentially the same environment, it is likely that these differences reflect cultural behavior (and not instinctual behavior). For many researchers, chimpanzees, as well as many other nonhuman primate and nonprimate species, show clear evidence of cultural behaviors. How this differs from culture in *our* species centers on the human capacity to accumulate and transmit cultural behaviors and knowledge across generations through oral history and systems of writing and symbols.

What Do You Think?

Do you think that by studying evidence of culture in nonhuman primates, we will have a better understanding of the development of culture in hominin evolution? What are some of the challenges and limitations to studying evidence of culture in nonhuman animals? ◼

Summary of Main Topics

- The fundamental principle of behavioral evolution is that aspects of behavior (including social behavior) are influenced by genetic factors. Because some behavioral elements are influenced by genes, natural selection can act on them in the same way it acts on anatomical characteristics. Behavioral ecology is the discipline that examines behavior from the perspective of complex ecological relationships and the role of natural selection as it favors behaviors that increase reproductive fitness. This approach generates many models of behavioral evolution that can be applied to all species, including humans.

- Primatologists have provided various explanations for why primates live in social groups (for example, predator avoidance and competition for resources with other groups).
- Primates are among the most social of animals, but within social groups there is competition for resources, and conflict. Dominance hierarchies help to reduce the amount of physical aggression. Also, there are numerous amicable behaviors, such as grooming, that maintain peaceful relationships between individuals.
- Life history traits or strategies (developmental stages that characterize a species) are important to the reproductive success of individuals. These traits include length of gestation, number of offspring per birth, interbirth interval, age of sexual

maturity, and longevity. Although these characteristics are strongly influenced by the genome of any species, they're also influenced by environmental and social factors, such as nutrition and social status. In turn, nutritional requirements are affected by body size, diet, and basal metabolic rate (BMR).

- Nonhuman primates (especially chimpanzees and other great apes) are often used as models for understanding the evolution of human behavior.
- Communication makes it possible to live in social groups. It occurs in many forms, including vocalizations and gestures. Some primate species are able to communicate about certain aspects of the external environment, indicating some ability to think symbolically. Long-term language studies with the great apes have shown that these species have the ability to communicate

using different kinds of symbols, including sign language.

- Several nonhuman primates exhibit aspects of culture, including tool use and regional variation in dietary preferences. These variations represent cultural traditions that were perhaps present in early hominins. Variation in cultural behavior and the transmission of these behaviors from one individual to another through observation and learning are hallmarks of human culture. Nonhuman primates exhibit certain aspects of culture, although none of these species have adopted culture as an adaptive strategy the way humans have.
- Affiliative behaviors such as grooming, hugging, and helping others (altruism) also promote group cohesion.
- Biological and behavioral continuity within the primate order reveals how humans are connected to our closest relatives and allows us to explain some aspects of human behavior.

Critical Thinking Questions

1. Apply some of the topics presented in this chapter to some nonprimate species with which you are familiar. Can you develop some hypotheses to explain the behavior of some domestic species? You might want to speculate on how behavior in domestic animals may differ from that of their wild ancestors. (Chapter 2 might help you here.)

2. We used birds as an example of sexual dimorphism resulting from sexual selection. But there are some bird species in which males, not females, sit on the nest to warm and protect the eggs.

These males are less colorful than the females. How would you explain this? (Hint: Sexual selection may not be the only factor involved in sexual dimorphism in bird coloration.) Try to come up with two examples on how the behavioral ecology of nonhuman primates may be helpful in explaining specific human behaviors.

3. How might infanticide be seen as a reproductive strategy for males? What would you say if you saw a newspaper article that applied this concept (not the act itself) to human males? Do you think

some people would object? Why or why not?

4. What evidence is there for culture among nonhuman primates? Do you think the evidence is convincing? Why or why not?

5. Do you think that knowing about aggression between groups of chimpanzees is useful in understanding conflicts between human societies? Why or why not?

6. Why are the language capabilities of nonhuman primates important to our understanding of how our own species may have acquired language?

CONNECTIONS

Partly because of common evolutionary history, many human behaviors are also seen in other primates.

Fossil evidence indicates our primate origins date to at least 65 million years ago.

Paleoanthropology, which includes physical anthropology, archaeology, and geology, provides the scientific basis to understand hominin evolution.

Overview of the Fossil Primates

Background to Primate Evolution: Late Mesozoic

Primate Origins

Made to Order: Archaic Primates

Eocene Euprimates

Lemur Connections? The Adapoids

Closer Connections to Living Primates: The Evolution of True Lemurs and Lorises

Tarsier Connections? The Omomyoids

Evolution of True Tarsiers

Eocene and Oligocene Early Anthropoids

Oligocene Primates

True Anthropoids

Early Platyrrhines: New World Anthropoids

Miocene Primates

Monkeying Around

Aping Monkeys

True Apes

Evolution of Extant Hominoids

Hylobatids: The Lesser Apes

The African Great Apes

Asia's Lone Great Ape

Cranial reconstruction and artist rendering of *Pliobates*, a new small-bodied apelike primate from Spain.

Marta Palmero/Institut Català de Paleontologia Miquel Crusafont (ICP); Top Images: David Haring; Russell L. Ciochon; Institute of Human Origins, photo by Nanci Kahn

Student Learning Objectives   After studying the material in this chapter, you should be able to:

▶ Outline the seven geological epochs of the Cenozoic and indicate which primate groups emerged during each epoch.

▶ Describe the earliest evidence for the emergence of the primate order and the characteristics of these early fossils (e.g., the plesiadapiforms).

▶ Describe the earliest evidence for the emergence of the euprimates and the characteristics of these fossil strepsirrhines and early haplorhines.

▶ Discuss the evidence for the earliest true anthropoids from the Oligocene and indicate where these fossils are located.

▶ Describe the evolution and subsequent dispersal of the superfamily Hominoidea (apes and humans) during the Miocene.

▶ Discuss the relationship between fossil apes of the Middle to Late Miocene and with extant apes in Africa and Asia.

When gazing into the eyes of a great ape, we see in them something unique that we feel inside ourselves. Often, however, when looking into the eyes of a galago ("bush baby"), we see nothing but an appealing, small animal that we might like to take home as a pet (see Fig. 6-15 in Chapter 6). When most of us think back to the origins of our own species, we generally stop once we've evoked the idea of an upright-walking ape ancestor. But have you ever considered extending your family tree to the baboons you may see in a wildlife park or to the lemurs or bush babies you see in the zoo? You might think, "How can a creature so small and, well, *animal*-like have anything to do with us or our evolutionary background?" In this chapter, we focus on bridging the gap between these creatures and ourselves—between **strepsirrhines** and **haplorhines**—to help us better understand our own evolutionary history.

As we've seen in Chapters 6 and 7, some of our primate cousins share many of the traits we generally think of as uniquely human. Many of these similarities can be traced to shared origins in highly social groups living in the trees. We see these origins not only in the structure of our body and in the retention of many primitive features, such as pentadactyly (five fingers and toes) and unfused lower arm bones, but also in more **"derived"** skeletal traits that came later. Among the most important of these derived primate traits are evolutionary trends toward a more **orthograde** (upright) body position and more forward-facing eyes. Distinguishing these uniquely primate features in the fossil record as being different from those traits found in more distantly related mammalian cousins is the first step in recognizing our own beginnings. As we move in time through the Cenozoic era (see Chapter 5), we see in rough form the recapitulation of our own (primate) order from "primitive" to highly derived. We'll also trace the development of mammals that resemble us more and more over time until we conclude this chapter in the Miocene, 23 to 5 million years ago (mya), with the emergence of the first hominoids (apes) and then the first possible hominins (humans). As you'll see, our ability to recognize primate families in the fossil record not only uses the same skills that allow us to discover our later human origins but also enables us to organize these creatures into meaningful groups.

This organization means that you'll face a multitude of taxonomic designations. These names aren't meant to scare you, but they should impress upon you how successful past lineages of primates have been—in fact, much more so than they are now. As you'll see, learning about the earliest beginnings and recent past of our primate order can lend powerful perspective and meaning to our own origins, even though most of the fossil groups discussed in this chapter never led to any extant (currently living) forms, and even fewer are related to our own hominin ancestors.

Background to Primate Evolution: Late Mesozoic

The exact origins of the earliest primates aren't well understood; in fact, they're shrouded in some degree of mystery. We *do* know that following the extinction of the dinosaurs at the end of the Mesozoic, the reign of the giant reptiles was over and the Age of Mammals had begun. Primates were just one of the many groups of small mammals that were left to diversify and explore the many niches left vacant with the passing of the dinosaurs.

Primates began to diverge from closely related mammalian lineages during the Cretaceous, right around the mass extinction of dinosaurs. Some scientists place these closely related ("sister") lineages into a **superorder** that includes tree shrews, flying lemurs (also known as the colugos, which don't fly and aren't lemurs), and primates (Fig. 8-1). **Sister groups** are the related new clades that result from the splitting of a single common lineage. It's interesting to note that the closest relatives of this superorder are rabbits, rodents, and their relatives.

This diversification of early mammals took place in a global tropical climate that accompanied the emergence of modern plants—although neither the exact region where primates first evolved nor the precise pressures that molded their adaptations are known. These uncertainties continue to intrigue scientists even today.

strepsirrhines (strep-sir´-rines) Members of the primate suborder Strepsirrhini, which includes lemurs and lorises.

haplorhines (hap-lore´-ines) Members of the primate suborder Haplorhini, which includes tarsiers, monkeys, apes, and humans.

derived Being or having a feature that is not present in the ancestral form.

orthograde Referring to an upright body position. This term relates to the position of the head and torso during sitting, climbing, etc., and doesn't necessarily mean that an animal is bipedal.

superorder A taxonomic group ranking above an order and below a class or subclass.

sister groups The relationship of new clades that result from the splitting of a single common lineage.

Primate Origins

The Cenozoic era is the broad time period during which most of primate evolution has unfolded (and continues to unfold). This time period is divided into seven epochs, the oldest of which is called the Paleocene (beginning 65 mya). For each of these broad epochs, we can roughly attribute a particular phase of primate evolution and development. However, evolution knows no temporal bounds, so the time line for these phases will always be imperfectly defined (more precise dates and particular fossil primate groups are discussed later in this chapter):

- Paleocene (65 to 55.8 mya): first archaic primates, plesiadapiforms
- Eocene (55.8 to 33 mya): first euprimates, early strepsirrhines and haplorhines
- Oligocene (33 to 23 mya): early catarrhines, precursors to monkeys and apes
- Miocene (23 to 5.3 mya): monkeys and apes; first humanlike creatures
- Pliocene (5.3 to 2.6 mya): early hominin diversification
- Pleistocene (2.6 to 0.105 mya): early *Homo* and its descendants
- Holocene (0.105 mya to present): modern humans

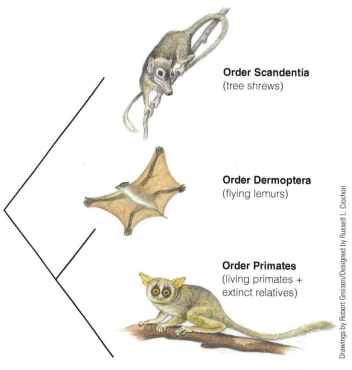

Order Scandentia
(tree shrews)

Order Dermoptera
(flying lemurs)

Order Primates
(living primates + extinct relatives)

Drawings by Robert Greisen/Designed by Russell L. Ciochon

▲ **Figure 8-1**
The superorder which includes the sister orders of tree shrews, flying lemurs, and primates.

Paleontological evidence indicates that the first indisputable primates emerged just before the Eocene epoch (56 mya). Given that this is their first occurrence in the fossil record, it has led many primate biologists to hypothesize that the initial radiation of archaic primates must have occurred long before this, perhaps during the late Cretaceous to early Paleocene time period (68 to 62 mya) (Miller et al., 2005; Bloch et al., 2007; Chester et al., 2015). Still, our search for the key time of evolutionary divergence—that is, the time when the last common ancestor of primates and their closest relatives lived—remains tricky. The **last common ancestor (LCA)** is the hypothetical species that was the last to exist before it speciated into the myriad of sister orders related to primates. This critical species is often difficult to pinpoint morphologically since it doesn't yet have the shared derived traits found in the **crown group** (Fig. 8-2). This means that researchers can't confidently associate it with any given fossil. A crown group is easier to identify because it includes all of the **taxa** that come *after* a major speciation event. All extant (currently living) groups and fossils sharing their specific derived traits are crown. Despite its lack of the clade's derived traits, the LCA also belongs to the crown group. On the other hand, the **stem group** includes all of the taxa in a clade *before* a major speciation event. For this reason, like the LCA, stem group taxa are often difficult to recognize in the fossil record. In spite of this, many scientists feel more comfortable classifying uncertain taxa as stem rather than committing them to the crown group (see Chapter 5 for a more complete discussion of phylogenetic concepts).

Thus the time when we can first *confidently* identify an archaic primate is almost assuredly an underestimate of the actual time of divergence (the assumed date when the last common ancestor lived). Molecular data, on the other hand, have often provided us with *overestimates* of this time (Steiper and Young, 2008; Wilkinson et al., 2011). What is important to realize, however, is that (1) since molecular estimates of divergence dates (see "A Closer Look: Building Family Trees from Genes," p. 228) are

last common ancestor (LCA) The final evolutionary link between two related groups.

crown group All of the taxa that come after a major speciation event. Crown groups are easier to identify than stem groups because the members possess the clade's shared derived traits.

taxa (*sing.* taxon) A taxonomic group of any rank (e.g., species, family, or class).

stem group All of the taxa in a clade before a major speciation event. Stem groups are often difficult to recognize in the fossil record since they don't often have the shared derived traits found in the crown group.

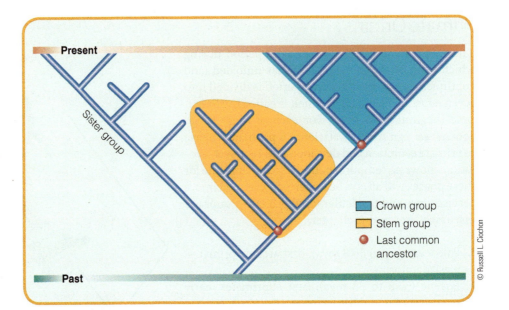

▶ **Figure 8-2**
Visual representation of crown group, stem group, and last common ancestor concepts. In this example both the stem group and crown group have last common ancestors.

© Russell L. Ciochon

A Closer Look Building Family Trees from Genes

Molecular anthropology uses genetics to investigate the biology and evolution of humans and our closest relatives, the nonhuman primates. Before we can test specific hypotheses about primate evolution and adaptation, we must understand how primate species are related to each other. Molecular anthropologists use proteins, genes, and even genomes to test hypotheses regarding the relationships within the primate order. The use of molecular methods in this manner has revolutionized our knowledge of primate systematics and revealed evolutionary relationships that have otherwise been difficult to resolve. This primate tree (Fig. 1) is compiled from recent research performed by three teams of molecular anthropologists (Jameson et al., 2011; Perelman et al., 2011; Steiper and Seiffert, 2012).

Molecular anthropologists can use DNA sequences to make inferences as to how long ago primate species last shared a common ancestor. Since mutations in DNA occur at a relatively constant rate, the differences between two samples are proportional to the time since they last shared a common ancestor. This is often referred to as the "molecular clock." In primates, there is variation between species in the speed of their "molecular clocks" based on life histories including brain and body size and generation time, the time between generations. Large-bodied apes take longer to mature and produce offspring, which slows down the "clock" for these species. The fossil record can calibrate these "clocks" with information about when species on a tree diverged from one another as well as giving size estimates for fossil species to infer the rate of their "clocks." As with the construction of gene trees, molecular divergence dates are best inferred from multiple parts of the genome in order to ensure that divergences calculated from different regions are generally consistent. Because early primates were much smaller than modern primates, they would have had faster "molecular clocks." This results in many primate divergence times inferred from molecular data to be much older than expected if left uncorrected (Steiper and Seiffert, 2012).

Advances in genome sequencing technology now allow for the collection of unprecedented amounts of molecular data. In this new age of genomics, molecular anthropologists are now using genome-scale data to further examine the evolutionary relationships of extant primate species as well as to identify the genotypes that underlie distinctly modern human characteristics.

calibrated using known fossil dates, the two approaches are inextricably linked, and (2) determining the appropriate rate of mutation, which joins these two together, can be tricky. Together, these two approaches (morphological and molecular) now place the origins of indisputable primates at some time during the Paleocene-Cretaceous transition, about 66 mya (Steiper and Seiffert, 2012).

Made to Order: Archaic Primates

Fossil evidence indicates that during the earliest Paleocene to early Eocene, between 65 and 52 mya, a major radiation of archaic primates known as the plesiadapiforms occurred. Plesiadapiforms are members of an extinct group that occupies a controversial position in primate phylogeny. When first discovered, these creatures were considered early members of the primate order, but in the 1960s this conclusion was reversed and they were treated as their own order, Plesiadapiformes. In recent years, however, the careful analysis of an amazing array of more newly discovered fossils has once again placed plesiadapiforms back within Primates (Bloch and Silcox, 2001; Silcox, 2001; Bloch and Boyer, 2002; Bloch

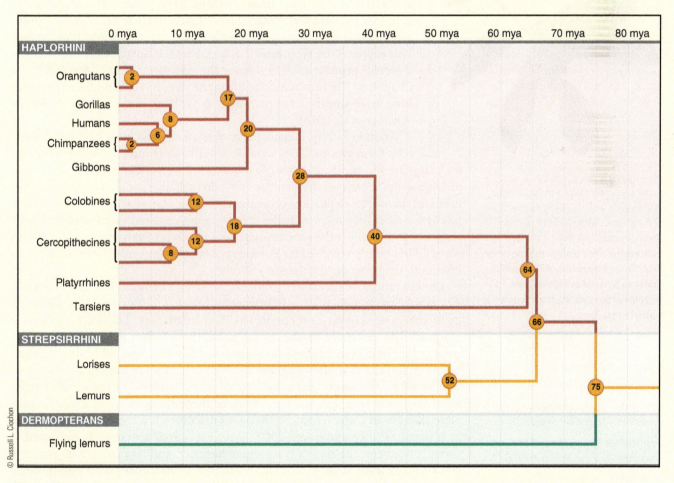

Figure 1 ▲
Molecular primate family tree based on the works of three research teams (see text). Dates of divergence are noted in the gold-colored nodes.

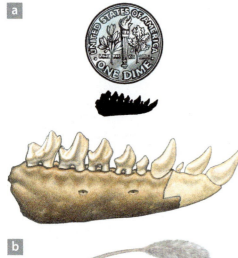

Drawings by Robert Greisen (a) and Doug Boyer (b)/Layout by Russell L. Ciochon

▲ **Figure 8-3**

Artist's representations of *Purgatorius*. (**a**) Rendering of the best-preserved jaw of *Purgatorius* with the front portion reconstructed. The dime is present to indicate the small scale of the specimen. (**b**) An artist's depiction of *Purgatorius*. The tarsals (feet) have specialized features which indicate that *Purgatorius* was arboreal.

semiorder The taxonomic category above suborder and below order.

euprimates "True primates." This term was coined by Elwyn Simons in 1972.

postcranial Referring to all or part of the skeleton not including the skull. The term originates from the fact that in quadrupeds the body is posterior to the head; the term literally means "behind the head."

et al., 2007; Chester et al., 2015). They are now gaining acceptance as a **semiorder** within Primates that is separate from the later **euprimates** (Silcox, 2007).

Plesiadapiforms are best known from a large number of fossil finds from the American West (especially Montana and Wyoming). Some of the more recent finds of these Paleocene mammals, particularly those from Clarks Fork Basin, Wyoming, have yielded a variety of nearly complete skeletons. Some members of this group exhibit a striking continuity of traits with some of the earliest strepsirrhines from the later Eocene epoch. Although as many as six families are commonly recognized within this group, we'll concentrate on the three families that are most pertinent for this discussion.

The first family, Purgatoriidae, counts among their numbers the oldest recognized archaic primate, *Purgatorius* (Clemens, 1974) (Fig. 8-3). Members of this extinct genus are believed to have been about the size of modern rats, and at least two (and perhaps as many as four) species lived in the American Northwest during the earliest Paleocene about 65 mya (Lofgren, 1995; Clemens, 2004; Bloch et al., 2007). Evidence of a radiation of this kind, however, most likely indicates an origin in the late Cretaceous or early Paleocene, 68 to 65 mya (see "A Closer Look: Building Family Trees from Genes" on p. 228). Based on *Purgatorius'* placement at the base of their sister lineages (think "stem group"), it is important to note that **postcranial** material from Garbani Channel in northeastern Montana (dated to ~ 65 mya) reveals arboreal adaptation within the feet. This supports the hypothesis that an arboreal adaptation has been a prime mover in primate evolution since the very beginning of the order (see Chapter 6). This adaptation to life in the trees has differentiated primates from other similar-sized mammals as far back as the earliest Paleocene (Chester et al., 2015).

Another family, Plesiadapidae, was among the more successful plesiadapiform groups. They were chipmunk- to groundhog-sized mammals with large incisors similar to those of a rodent. However, unlike rodents, plesiadapid incisors weren't continuously growing and didn't self-sharpen, suggesting that they used their incisors for a purpose other than gnawing. Some have suggested that this family subsisted on a vegetative diet of leaves supplemented with fruits. The best-known of this family is the genus *Plesiadapis*, which probably originated in North America but went on to colonize Europe via a land bridge across Greenland before eventually dying out during the early Eocene.

The last family we'll look at, Carpolestidae (whose name means "fruit stealer"), was quite common during the Paleocene in North America and Asia, although its members were never as successful as the plesiadapids. These creatures were much smaller, generally mouse- to rat-sized, though they exhibit the typically enlarged incisors seen in these early groups. They also have additional specialized dental traits that allowed them to efficiently process fibrous vegetation as well as nuts and insects. For a long time, carpolestids were known only from fossil teeth and jaws, but our knowledge of them changed when a nearly complete skeleton of *Carpolestes* (Fig. 8-4) was discovered in the Clarks Fork Basin, in Wyoming (Bloch and Boyer, 2002). The Clarks Fork specimen is estimated at about 3.5 ounces, the size of the average hamster, and its postcranial anatomy reveals many traits adapted to a highly arboreal environment (particularly since it had opposable grasping big toes with nails instead of claws). But unlike later euprimates that were fully adapted to living in the trees, *Carpolestes* displays no adaptations for leaping, though it was almost certainly a terminal branch feeder (Sargis et al., 2007).

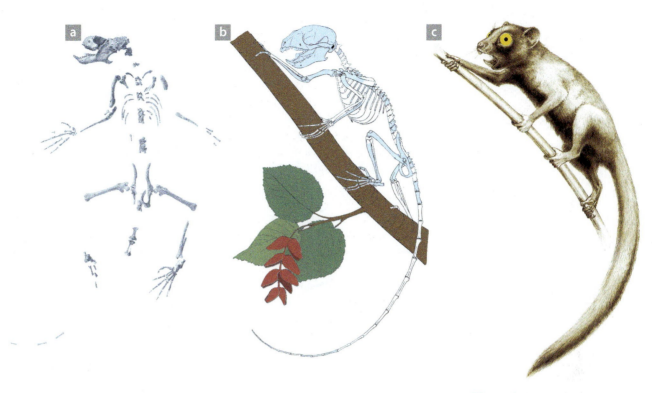

▲ **Figure 8-4**

Nearly complete skeleton of *Carpolestes* discovered in the Clarks Fork Basin of Wyoming. (**a**) *Carpolestes* as it was discovered. (**b**) Reconstructed skeleton of *Carpolestes*. (**c**) Artist's rendering of *Carpolestes* as it might have looked in life.

(From "Grasping Primate Origins", by Jonathan I. Bloch and Doug M. Boyer. *Science Magazine*, Vol. 298, pp.1606–1610, Fig. 2, November 22, 2002. Reprinted with permission from AAAS.)

Eocene Euprimates

During the Eocene epoch (55.8 to 33 mya) we see the gradual extinction of the plesiadapiforms and their replacement by the euprimates (Fig. 8-5). These mammals, unlike the plesiadapiforms, have definite recognizable and modern derived primate traits, such as forward-facing eyes, greater encephalization, a postorbital bar, nails instead of claws at the ends of their fingers and toes, and an opposable big toe (see Chapter 6). These and other basic primate features suggest an adaptation to environmental conditions that were fundamentally different from those experienced by the plesiadapiforms, as this was a warmer climate with year-round rainfall and lush, broad-leaved evergreen forests.

At the beginning of the Eocene epoch, North America and Europe were connected; they didn't split apart until the middle Eocene. Meanwhile, during the middle to late Eocene, North America was sporadically connected to Asia via the Bering land bridge. These early connections between these three continents meant that they shared many common species. In contrast, the continents of Africa, Antarctica, Australia, and South America remained isolated by large bodies of water. Following the end of the reign of dinosaurs, the Eocene was a time of rapid diversification for *all* mammals, not just the primates. As a result, the variety of animals known from this time period is much greater than that known from the earlier Paleocene Epoch.

Euprimates were part of this wave of diversification and adaptive radiation (see Chapter 5). They came on the scene around 56 mya—nearly simultaneously, it seems—in North America, Europe, and Asia. There are two main branches of euprimates grouped into different superfamilies (Adapoidea and Omomyoidea). These two superfamilies include primitive primates described as being either more lemurlike (adapoid) or tarsier- or galagolike (omomyoid). Both groups have been well known from cranial, dental, and postcranial remains from North America and Europe, as well as now from more fossil finds in Asia and Africa.

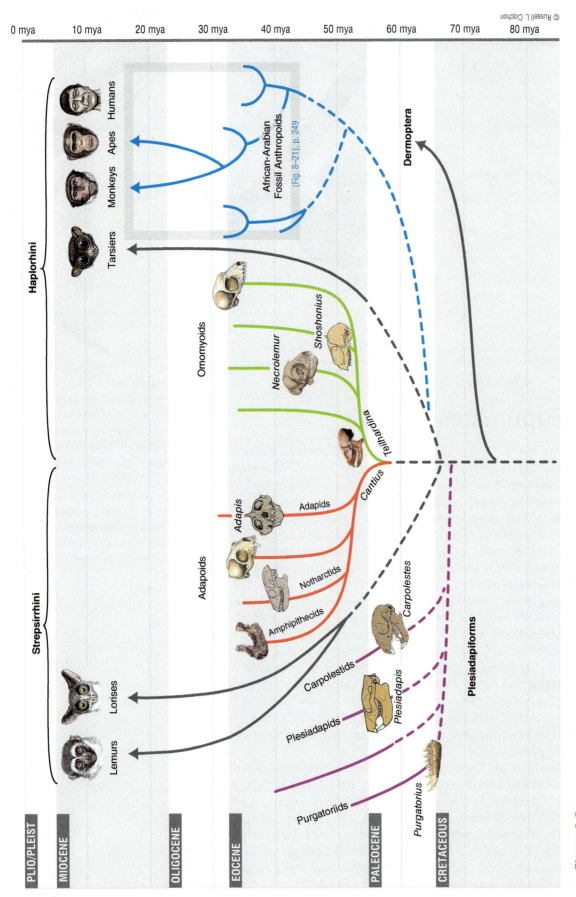

▲ **Figure 8-5**

Family tree of euprimates and their relationships to modern strepsirrhine and haplorhine groups. Colors represent major groupings within the primates. Red is for the lemurlike adapoids, green is for the tarsierlike omomyoids, purple is for the plesiadapiforms, and blue represents the Fayum early anthropoid radiation.

Lemur Connections? The Adapoids

The adapoids are the best known of the Eocene stem strepsirrhines and include more than 35 genera that we know of; their actual biodioversity during the Eocene was surely far greater. These are the most primitive of the euprimates, as recognized by their dental anatomy. Their primitive dental formula (2.1.4.3; see Chapter 6) provided a generalized ancestral baseline from which many later, more derived varieties of dental specializations could evolve. The adapoids are divided into five families, based mostly on biogeographical distinctions. The most prominent are the notharctids of North America (predominantly) and the adapids of Europe.

The first of the two major adapoid families, the notharctids, includes the genus *Cantius*. This was the earliest notharctid and one of the earliest of any of the adapoids. This small- to medium-sized animal is known primarily from North America, with just two species reported from Europe. Cranial and skeletal remains indicate that it was a diurnal creature, foraging during the day. It also probably traveled very rapidly through the trees, leaping quadrupedally. Traits of its mandible and its primitive dental formula of 2.1.4.3 indicate that it was probably a fruit eater. Another prominent notharctid was unveiled in 2009 to great fanfare. This 47-million-year-old creature, *Darwinius* (nicknamed "Ida"), does not appear to have had a dental comb or a grooming claw, which its scientific proponents argued was evidence that the adapoids are much more than mere lemur relatives (Fig. 8-6). In fact, these researchers went on to sensationally assert that Ida and other adapoids were basal haplorhines, a position not supported by the preponderance of scientific evidence (Franzen et al., 2009). Ironically, just months later, a new adapid from Egypt solidified the adapoid position as a stem strepsirrhine group and helped bolster the hypothesis that apparent similarities to higher primates are indicative of convergent evolution (Seiffert et al., 2009).

This informative fossil, dating to about 37 mya, represents *Afradapis*, a previously unknown large-bodied adapiform genus. *Afradapis* belongs to the second major family of adapoids, appropriately called the adapids, which abruptly appeared in Europe near the end of the Eocene and just as quickly became extinct. For this reason, phylogenetic relations for this group are not well understood, although the adapids probably emigrated from another continent, most likely Asia. This conclusion is supported by new discoveries in southern China where six new genera of strepsirrhines have been described from the early Oligocene (Ni et al., 2016).

Remember that in Chapter 5 we introduced the terms *homology* (similar traits based on descent) and *homoplasy* (similar traits that evolve independently in different groups) and talked about the example of theropod dinosaurs and birds sharing derived traits. The teeth of *Afradapis* indicate that it may have exploited anthropoid-like feeding niches in Africa, eating leaves like a monkey (Seiffert et al., 2010). This example of convergent evolution due to shared dietary patterns (very common in early primate evolution) means that adapoids might have been the first primates to exploit anthropoid-like feeding niches in Africa. If true, this could have some important implications with regard to the role that potential ecological competition might have played in the early evolution of stem strepsirrhine and haplorhine groups, explaining some of these early apparent convergences (Seiffert et al., 2009).

Perhaps the best-known fossil of this group is called *Adapis*. It was not only the first nonhuman fossil primate named but was also first described by the well-known nineteenth-century naturalist Georges Cuvier. As you may remember from Chapter 2, Cuvier didn't believe in evolving lineages, even going so far as to state, in 1812, *"l'homme fossile n'existe pas"* ("fossil man does not exist"). By this he also

▲ **Figure 8-6**
Skeleton of *Darwinius*, nicknamed "Ida."

Martin Shields/Alamy

meant fossil primates. So it's ironic that in 1822, it was Cuvier who described and named the first fossil primate. Unfortunately for him, he confused the remains for that of an ungulate (a hoofed mammal); however, shortly after his death in 1837, the fossil was correctly identified as a primate. *Adapis'* dental formula remains primitive (2.1.4.3), and some have argued that an incipient dental comb (a lemur feature) could be recognized in this fossil genus. (You may recall from Chapter 6 that a dental comb is a specialization of the front teeth in the lower jaw; the teeth are elongated and project forward like a small comb.) A slow arboreal quadruped, *Adapis* most likely spent its time foraging for leaves during the daytime hours. The "At a Glance" below lists key early primate names.

Closer Connections to Living Primates: The Evolution of True Lemurs and Lorises

As we've mentioned, the adapoids were fairly lemurlike in their overall pattern, and they show distinctive primate tendencies. Although the ancient adapoids do resemble lemurs in overall anatomical body plan, this is mostly because modern lemurs retain some ancestral traits. The adapoid fossils don't show the same specializations seen in crown members of lemurs, galagos, and lorises, such as development of the dental comb. For this reason we may say that modern-day lemurs, galagos, and lorises have retained many "primitive" aspects of anatomy, though there's no clear evolutionary relationship between the Eocene adapoids and these latter-day creatures (but see Kay et al., 2004; Ross et al., 2004).

It's important to note that the evolution of lemurs and other strepsirrhines is of great interest to researchers because of their basal position as the sister group to all other primate lineages (Horvath and Willard, 2007; Horvath et al., 2008). Accordingly, information related to their initial emergence and dispersal can be used to better calibrate subsequent primate divergence dates.

Lorisoids (lorises and galagos) are the earliest examples of strepsirrhine primates in the fossil record. These small primitive creatures have been found in late Eocene

At a Glance   Key Early Primate Names

Genus Name	Epoch	Sites/Regions	The Big Picture
Purgatorius	Paleocene	American Southwest, Montana	Plesiadapiform; first known archaic primate.
Carpolestes	Paleocene	North America and Asia	Highly arboreal, terminal branch feeder that possessed opposable grasping big toes with nails instead of claws.
Darwinius	Early Eocene	Messel, Germany	Adapoid genus named to commemorate the bicentenary of the birth of Charles Darwin; known from one astonishingly complete and well-preserved fossil.
Teilhardina	Early Eocene	North America, Europe, Asia	Omomyoid genus whose lineage demonstrates that all euprimates likely engaged in a rapid westward dispersal from Asia to Europe and finally, North America.
Archaeolemur	Holocene (modern epoch)	Madagascar	Subfossil lemur with fused mandible and bilophodont molars; converged upon monkey anatomy in a monkey-less environment.

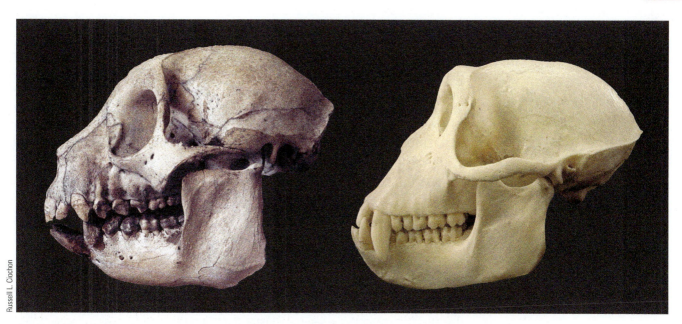

Russell L. Ciochon

▲ **Figure 8-7**

Comparison of the skull of *Archaeolemur* (left) and a macaque monkey. Note how the lemur resembles the monkey in the shape of the jaw, teeth, and overall cranial form. This is an excellent example of convergent evolution.

deposits of the Fayum Depression in Egypt, an area that we'll discuss in more detail shortly. A late Eocene (circa 34 mya) fossil find from Egypt appears to have had a dental comb (Stevens and Heesy, 2006). This and other features have led to the conclusion that it's a stem galagid. Together with molecular evidence (Seiffert et al., 2003), it can be inferred that lorises and galagos (also known as "bush babies") likely diverged by the close of the middle Eocene.

The existence of an early African bush baby in Egypt during this time indicates that stem strepsirrhines initially evolved on the African mainland. These primates likely colonized Madagascar to give rise to crown lemuriforms, which would mean that lemurs have *never* existed outside of this tiny island (Seiffert et al., 2005a). The colonization itself most likely occurred when these animals crossed the Mozambique Channel, perhaps by unintentionally rafting over on drifting debris (Yoder et al., 1996, 2003; Kappeler, 2000; Ali and Huber, 2010), a phenomenon that most likely had its heyday during the early Cenozoic, before a change to modern ocean currents between Madagascar and the mainland (Samonds et al., 2012). Additionally, other biogeographical mechanisms, such as "**island hopping**," have been suggested (McCall, 1997; Arnason et al., 2000), though, as you will see, these may have had a bigger hand in the original monkey colonization of South America (see "A Closer Look: Island Hopping and Primate Evolution," on page 244).

There are few if any truly fossilized lemur remains in Madagascar; but there are numerous **subfossil** lemurs. These unfossilized skeletal remains are too recent to have become completely mineralized into fossils. Many of these extinct subfossil lemurs were colossal compared with the lemurs of today—indeed, some of them were up to five times as big! Despite their large size, they were mostly tree-dwelling and likely diurnal. Most interesting of all, many filled unusual ecological niches not shared by any living lemurs. Many of these peculiar adaptations provide examples of convergence with higher primate niches found elsewhere in the Old World. For instance, the extinct *Archaeolemur* (Fig. 8-7), with its fused mandible and **bilophodont** molars, in many ways more closely resembled a monkey than the 37-pound lemur that it was (Fleagle, 2013). What's more, the sulcal (grooved) pattern of *Archaeolemur*'s brain was similar to that seen in higher primates (Martin, 1990). Based on this evidence, we can see this group as converging on a monkey-like role on a monkeyless island.

The best known of the giant lemurs, however, is the 170-pound *Megaladapis*; it was built like a koala on steroids. Its koala-like similarities are due to a convergence of dietary patterns, since these slow-climbing oversized lemurs cropped leaves with their

island hopping Traveling from one island to the next.

subfossil Bone not old enough to have become completely mineralized as a fossil.

bilophodont Referring to molars that have four cusps oriented in two parallel rows, resembling ridges, or "lophs." This trait is characteristic of Old World monkeys.

front incisors much like modern koalas (Tattersall, 1982). Unfortunately this specialized forest dweller became extinct with the appearance of humans on the island, when the trees were cleared for farmland. Sadly, the *Megaladapis* story isn't unusual; most of the 16 subfossil species discovered went extinct within the last 2,000 years—at the same time that humans began colonizing the island. Because these large-bodied lemurs (over 22 pounds) had low reproductive rates, the predation and deforestation carried out by these early peoples rapidly caused the extinction of these massive animals (Catlett et al., 2010). Unfortunately the remaining lemurs of Madagascar will meet the same fate unless the continued destruction of their habitat by humans ceases.

Tarsier Connections? The Omomyoids

The tarsier-like omomyoids, the earliest haplorhine group, are more taxonomically diverse than the adapoids. They're often called tarsier-like because the European specimens of this group more closely resemble the tarsier, though no specific phylogenetic connection has been made. They have a similar dental formula to living tarsiers (1.1.3.3) as well as large orbits and small snouts. Earlier members of this group are somewhat more generalized than later ones, and some researchers hypothesize that they represent the stock for all later haplorhines—that is, tarsiers, New World monkeys, Old World monkeys, apes, and humans (Ross, 2000). **Paleoprimatologists** have traced this successful radiation from primarily the Eocene and early Oligocene of North America and Europe, with a small number also known from Asia.

Members of the genus *Teilhardina* (Fig. 8-8) are found on three continents (although a recent analysis disputes whether all the attributed material belongs in the same genus; see Tornow, 2008). The fossil record appears to show that the earliest euprimates (including all adapoids and omomyoids) engaged in a rapid westward dispersal, with evidence pointing to Asia as the euprimates' starting point. In fact, analysis of related species of *Teilhardina* has shown that the oldest and most primitive members were from Asia while the youngest were from North America. A comprehensive comparison of more than 25 specimens from Bighorn Basin, Wyoming, clearly demonstrates that the North American specimens are more derived than those found in Europe or Asia (Rose et al., 2011). This evidence would tend to support a westward migration of euprimates from Asia, through Europe, and eventually to North America (Smith et al., 2006) (Fig. 8-9). There was significant global warming at the very beginning of the Eocene which opened high-latitude land bridges between these continents which allowed *Teilhardina* to migrate.

Other Eocene fossils of the family Omomyidae from North America (*Shoshonius*) and Europe (*Necrolemur*) are also thought to be closely related to the tarsier. Like

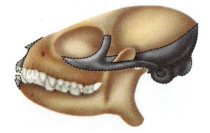

▲ **Figure 8-8**
An artist's reconstruction of *Teilhardina*, with areas in gray representing missing fragments. (Based on drawing from Xijum Ni, IVPP, Chinese Academy of Sciences.)

paleoprimatologists Anthropologists specializing in the study of the nonhuman primate fossil record.

▶ **Figure 8-9**
The rapid westward dispersal of euprimates of the genus *Teilhardina*. Analysis of related species of *Teilhardina* shows that the oldest and most primitive members were from Asia, while the youngest were from North America.

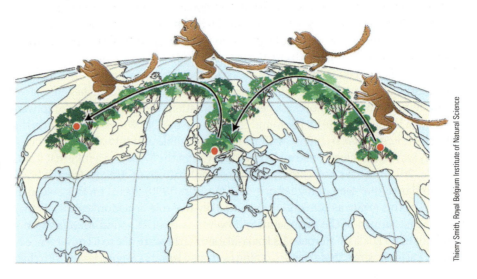

Thierry Smith, Royal Belgium Institute of Natural Science

modern tarsiers, these animals apparently possessed large convergent eye orbits as well as details of the ear region that unite them to the tarsier group. In addition, there is some evidence that *Necrolemur* may have had a fused tibia and fibula as well as an elongated calcaneus, a leverlike construction (much like that seen in a jackrabbit) that gives modern tarsiers their fantastic leaping abilities. However, many researchers conclude that these similarities are superficial ones, not necessarily indicating any unique (that is, shared derived) relationship. Even so, at least one feature, the position of the olfactory portion of the brain that processes scent, links these Eocene forms with later tarsiers though not with anthropoids (Fleagle, 2013).

Evolution of True Tarsiers

The fossil record for the tarsier family tree was missing most of its branches until recently. Several new finds have added valuable information to our understanding of tarsier evolution. In 2013, the discovery of a nearly complete and partly articulated skeleton of a tarsiiform primate was recovered in a limestone slab from the early Eocene of China, some 55 mya (Ni et al., 2013). This partial skeleton, named *Archicebus,* is the sister group to all later tarsiiform primates including the living Tarsiidae. This small primate, the size of modern pygmy mouse lemur, had a long tail and hind limbs that suggest that it was arboreal, but it lacked the specialized feet that modern tarsiers use for vertical clinging and leaping. The relatively large orbits indicate a high reliance on vision for locomotion and catching its insect prey, but are smaller than those of nocturnal primates, suggesting that *Archicebus* was diurnal. Cranial remains from the Middle Eocene of China indicate that by 45 mya tarsiiform orbital anatomy was virtually identical to living tarsiers and most likely indicates that they were nocturnal (Rossie et al., 2006). A tarsiiform from the middle Miocene of Thailand is so extremely bug-eyed in its orbital size that it falls outside the range of variation for extant members of the genus (Chaimanee et al., 2011). From these fossils it has been generally concluded that modern tarsiers have retained essentially the same body plan that they had in the Eocene, though their current restriction to the islands of Southeast Asia is a relatively new condition. Molecular evidence has shown that the five extant (currently existing) species of tarsiers diverged in the Miocene (Wright et al., 2003); and as you learned in Chapter 6, all living tarsiers are now limited to a few islands in Southeast Asia.

Toward the end of the Eocene, there was a shift from tropical to drier and more seasonal climates. This change led to more diverse landscapes, opening many niches for the highly adaptable primates to exploit. This backdrop sets the stage for our next saga in primate origins—that of our own infraorder, Anthropoidea. Of course tarsiers and strepsirrhine primates have continued to evolve since the Eocene, but we'll now focus on those primates most directly related to our own evolution as humans. For a comparison of strepsirrhines and anthropoids, see Figure 8-10.

Eocene and Oligocene Early Anthropoids

It's important to realize that when we're trying to interpret the past, things aren't as straightforward as they may at first seem. In addition to the debate about the earliest emergence of strepsirrhines and tarsiers (and therefore the most "primitive" members of Primates), we're equally unsure about the origins of anthropoid primates—the ones that eventually led to apes and monkeys as well as to our own lineage.

In recent years, new discoveries have led scientists to dispute an adapoid or even omomyoid origin of anthropoids, with some advocating that crown haplorhines (tarsiers and anthropoids) are a sister group to omomyoids as a whole (Bajpai et al., 2008; Williams et al., 2010).

Lemuriforms

Anthropoids

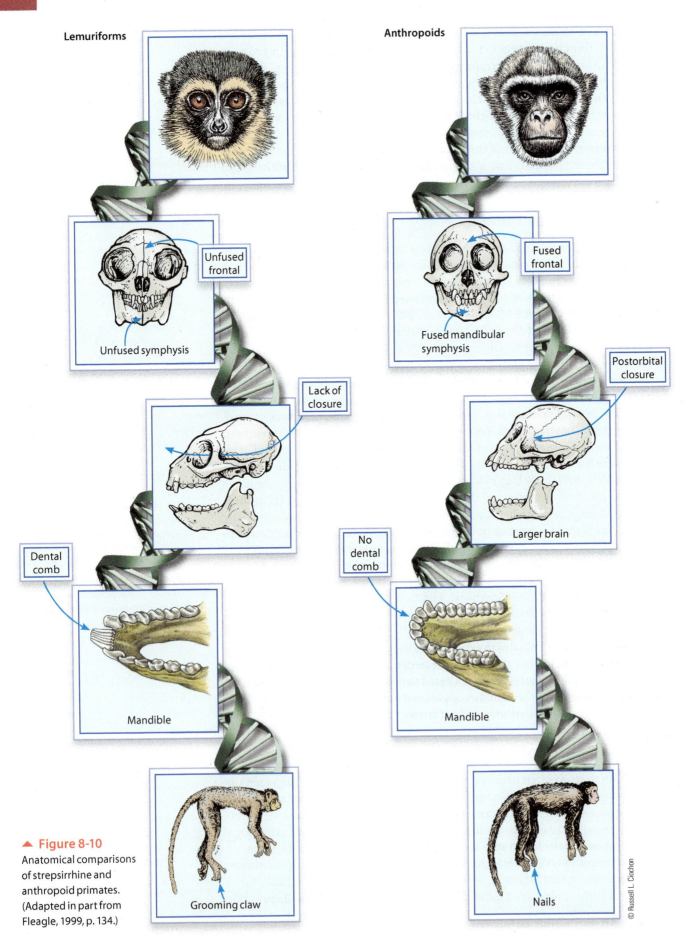

Unfused frontal

Unfused symphysis

Fused frontal

Fused mandibular symphysis

Lack of closure

Postorbital closure

Dental comb

No dental comb

Larger brain

Mandible

Mandible

Grooming claw

Nails

▲ **Figure 8-10**

Anatomical comparisons of strepsirrhine and anthropoid primates. (Adapted in part from Fleagle, 1999, p. 134.)

© Russell L. Ciochon

The Fayum Depression in Egypt (see "A Closer Look: Primate Diversity in the Fayum," below), an arid region today, provides most of our early anthropoid record for the Eocene and Oligocene. Over the last five decades, paleoprimatologist Elwyn Simons and colleagues have excavated this rich area and found a remarkable array of fossil primates. One of these discoveries, *Biretia*, is precisely dated to 37 mya and represents the most complete remains of an early African anthropoid. This small primate, weighing just under a pound, exhibits dental morphology typical of that expected for a basal (most primitive) anthropoid. Surprisingly though, the structure of the upper molar tooth roots points to large orbits, implying that *Biretia* was nocturnal (Seiffert et al., 2005b). This is interesting because, as

A Closer Look Primate Diversity in the Fayum

Today El-Fayuom, or the Fayum, is an Egyptian province about 40 miles southwest of Cairo. In the Eocene and Oligocene epochs, it was a swampy forest playground for primates. Now all that's left of that primate Eden is chunks of petrified wood, flotsam adrift in the vast desert of the Sahara. The name Fayum probably comes from the ancient Egyptian word *Baym*, meaning "lake or sea" and referring to the area's proximity to a large lake near the Nile. Nowadays, though, the last thing anyone would associate with this arid region is a body of water.

In 1906, the first primate ever discovered in Egypt was unearthed and later identified as *Apidium*. Many considered this discovery, hailed as a "dawn ape," to be the earliest relative of apes and monkeys. Though several primate fossils were discovered in the early 1900s, it wasn't until 1961 that the dogged persistence of Elwyn Simons led to the unearthing of the Fayum's true fossil primate abundance. Simons conducted fieldwork in the Fayum from 1961 to 2012 before passing away in March of 2016. Through the efforts of Simons and colleagues (Fig. 1), the Fayum primates are the best-studied fossils in the region and far and away the most abundant late Eocene and Oligocene finds from anywhere in the world, and they shape many of our views regarding the diversification of strepsirrhines, tarsiers, monkeys, and apes. These fossils are often referred to as the "lower-sequence primates" and "upper-sequence primates," according to their placement in the stratigraphic section. From these Eocene (lower) and Oligocene (upper) sediments, over 20 genera are known, presenting us with a wide variety of dietary niches. What's most surprising, however, is that both the strepsirrhines and some anthropoids exploited a frugivorous (fruit-eating) lifestyle, challenging the idea that ecological changes might account for the emergence of the latter group (Kirk and Simons, 2001). So for the time being, anthropoid origins remain as enigmatic as the Sphinx.

◀ **Figure 1**
Elwyn Simons and colleagues toil in the harsh heat of the Fayum in Egypt while collecting fossils of the earliest anthropoids. These fossils are so small that workers must excavate with their faces close to the ground.

Russell L. Ciochon

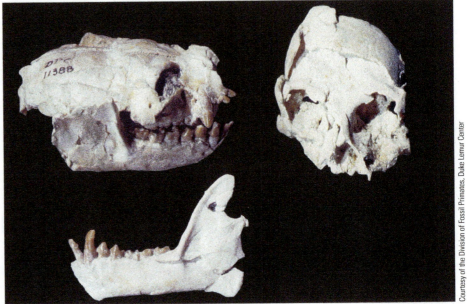

▶ **Figure 8-11**

Three views of *Catopithecus*, the earliest anthropoid genus to preserve a skull. These elements give us our first view of early catarrhine cranial anatomy, including fully enclosed orbits.

discussed in Chapter 6, the general trend for Anthropoidea is toward a diurnal activity pattern. Simons has placed these fossils, based on their dental characters, into the extinct superfamily Parapithecoidea. This superfamily is significant as the most primitive anthropoid group and therefore the possible root stock from which the entire New World anthropoid evolutionary group (that is, clade) evolved.

The later Oligocene evolution of these very early anthropoids (Seiffert et al., 2005b) is discussed in the next section. Somewhat more recent (dating to around 35 mya) are the Fayum primate genera from the family Oligopithecidae, including *Catopithecus* (Fig. 8-11), which clearly possessed anthropoid features (such as complete postorbital closure) and some derived **catarrhine** features (such as a 2.1.2.3 dental formula). These Fayum discoveries help fill the gap between later (more derived) anthropoids and the middle Eocene primates of Libya (Jaeger et al., 2010). Most scientists, though there are exceptions (notably, Chaimanee et al., 2012), agree that the earliest fossil anthropoids appear to have been from Africa. Current molecular and biogeographical data apparently confirm that anthropoids had an African origin, much like the African origin of our own genus, *Homo* (Miller et al., 2005).

Oligocene Primates

The vast majority of Old World primate fossils of the Oligocene epoch (33 to 23 mya) come from just one region, the Fayum Depression in Egypt—the same area that has yielded abundant late Eocene remains. Altogether, well over 1,000 primate specimens have been retrieved from the Fayum, representing a remarkable paleontological record of what was once an extremely rich primate ecosystem.

True Anthropoids

The early primates of the Oligocene are generally placed into three families: the oligopithecids, parapithecids, and propliopithecids. Members of the oligopithecid family are among the earliest catarrhine (Old World) anthropoid primates, with some also known from the late Eocene of the Fayum in Egypt. One of these early taxa, *Catopithecus* (mentioned earlier), is represented by several crushed crania. Analyses of these fragmentary remains, with their complete postorbital closure

catarrhine Member of Catarrhini, a parvorder of Primates, one of the three major divisions of the suborder Haplorhini. It contains the Old World monkeys, apes, and humans.

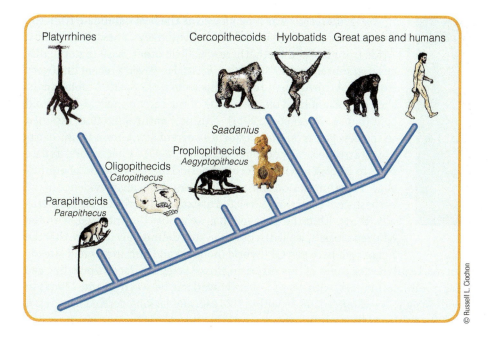

◀ **Figure 8-12**

Diagram of the phyletic relationships (cladogram) of Fayum early anthropoids and living catarrhines (monkeys, apes, and humans). (Adapted from Fig. 13-18 in Fleagle, 1999, p. 418.)

and derived 2.1.2.3 dental formula, have led paleoprimatologists to conclude that *Catopithecus* is the earliest catarrhine.

The most abundant of the Oligocene fossils from the Fayum are from the parapithecid family, and they belong to the genus *Apidium*. About the size of a squirrel, *Apidium* had several anthropoid-like features, but it also possessed some unusual dental features. *Apidium* fossils exhibit a dental formula of 2.1.3.3, indicating that *Apidium* probably appeared near when Old and New World anthropoids diverged. As noted, this makes the earlier relatives of *Apidium* possible candidates as ancestors of New World anthropoids (that is, **platyrrhines**, see discussion in next section on "Early Platyrrhines: New World Anthropoids"; Fig. 8-12). The teeth also suggest a diet composed of fruits and probably some seeds. Another interesting feature suggests something about this animal's social behavior: an unusually large degree of sexual dimorphism in canine size may indicate that *Apidium* lived in polygynous social groups of a single male and multiple females and offspring. Limb remains show that this creature was a small arboreal quadruped, adept at leaping and springing. We now know much more about the cranial anatomy of the parapithecids thanks to the discovery of a complete skull of the genus *Parapithecus* (Fig. 8-13), a close relative of *Apidium*.

Members of the third major family are called the propliopithecids. They include possibly the most significant fossil genus from the Fayum, *Aegyptopithecus* (Fig. 8-14). This genus has been proposed as the ancestor of both later Old World monkeys and hominoids. *Aegyptopithecus* is known from several well-preserved crania, numerous jaw fragments, and a fair number of limb bones. The largest of the Fayum anthropoids, *Aegyptopithecus* was roughly the size of a modern howler monkey at 13 to 18 pounds, with considerable sexual dimorphism. With a dental formula of 2.1.2.3, *Aegyptopithecus* shares the derived catarrhine dental formula. The skull is small and resembles a modern monkey skull in certain details, while the brain size appears to have been at best strepsirrhine-like; some even consider it so primitive as to be non-primate-like. In fact, a reappraisal of intracranial size has determined that given the small brain size of this genus, greater encephalization must have evolved independently within the two anthropoid **parvorders**, Platyrrhini and Catarrhini (Simons et al., 2007). Postcranial evidence reveals that *Aegyptopithecus* was likely a short-limbed, heavily muscled, slow-moving arboreal quadruped.

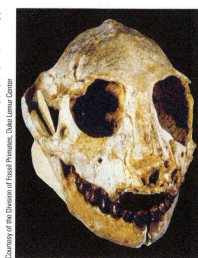

▲ **Figure 8-13**

Parapithecus belongs to the group of Fayum anthropoids most closely related to the ancestry of New World monkeys.

platyrrhines Members of Platyrrhini, a parvorder of Primates, one of the three major divisions of the suborder Haplorhini. These include only the New World monkeys.

parvorder A taxonomic group below infraorder.

Courtesy of the Division of Fossil Primates, Duke Lemur Center

▲ Figure 8-14

Skull of *Aegyptopithecus*. This genus has historically been proposed as the ancestor of both Old World monkeys and hominoids.

▼ Figure 8-15

Skull of *Saadanius*. This genus has recently been proposed as the ancestor of *both* Old World monkeys and hominoids.

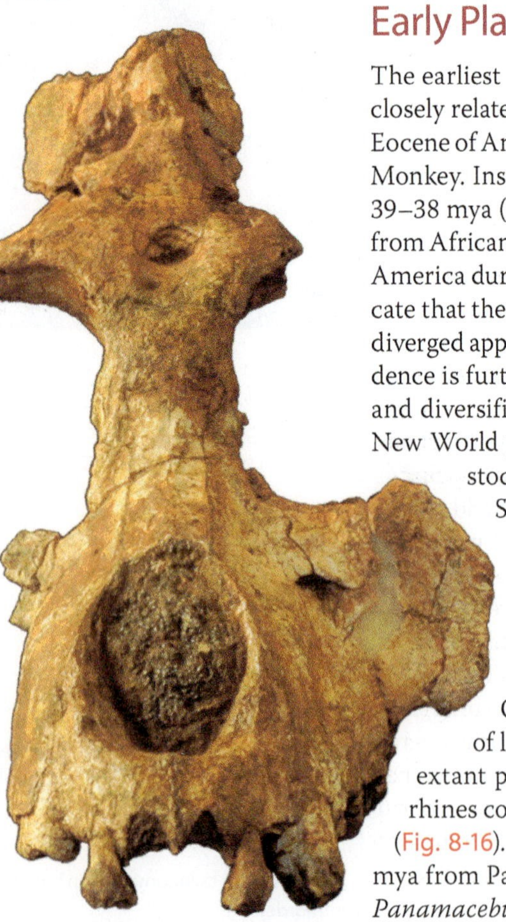

University of Michigan Museum of Paleontology

Aegyptopithecus was long viewed as the best candidate from the Fayum to have given rise to Old World monkeys, apes, and humans. Aside from isolated teeth, there was little other fossil material discovered subsequent to *Aegyptopithecus*. However, a recent discovery from the Afro-Arabian region, this time from Saudi Arabia, might shed important light on the timing of the cercopithecoid-hominoid split (but see Pozzi et al., 2011). This new anthropoid find, assigned to the new genus *Saadanius*, defies current attribution to any existing catarrhine family or superfamily (Fig. 8-15). What's more, its date of 29 to 28 mya is within a critical period in the evolution of our lineage. This time period is so crucial because it bridges evidence of the earliest stem catarrhines (related to extant catarrhines but not actually from within the lineage), that we've just summarized, with the Miocene fossils, we'll discuss later, that definitively indicate that the major split between Old World monkeys and hominoids had already occurred. Until the discovery of this surprising fossil, scientists faced a puzzling gap of many millions of years, with very few fossils available between 30 and 23 mya to provide insight. *Saadanius* dates to within this gap, and lacking derived features of either cercopithecoids or hominoids, suggests that the split between these lines had not yet occurred. *Saadanius'* most significant features in this respect include a projecting midface, a tubelike middle ear, and large broad molars. The tubelike middle ear is especially important, as it is a characteristic that it shares with crown catarrhines (monkeys, apes, and humans) to the exclusion of the propliopithecids. This would make *Saadanius* an advanced stem catarrhine, though perhaps intermediate between *Aegyptopithecus* and Miocene monkeys and apes (Zalmout et al., 2010).

Early Platyrrhines: New World Anthropoids

The earliest anthropoids found in the New World date to the late Eocene and are closely related to the early African anthropoids. *Perupithecus* comes from the late Eocene of Amazonian Peru—however it does not resemble any modern New World Monkey. Instead it has been linked to *Talahpithecus* from North Africa, dated to 39–38 mya (Jaeger et al., 2010; Bond et al., 2015). Early platyrrhines likely evolved from African anthropoids similar to those found in the Fayum who arrived in South America during the late Eocene (45 to 35 mya). In fact, recent molecular data indicate that the platyrrhine-catarrhine (New World–Old World anthropoid) lineages diverged approximately between 50 and 35 mya (Steiper and Young, 2006). This evidence is further bolstered by fossil and molecular evidence concerning the arrival and diversification of caviomorph rodents (for example, guinea pigs, chinchillas, New World porcupines, and their relatives). "Cavies" also originate from African stock and were the only other group of terrestrial mammals to colonize South America at the same time as platyrrhines (Poux et al., 2006).

After *Perupithecus* arrived in South America, these early platyrrhines most likely would have undergone an adaptive radiation. *Branisella* represents a remnant of the first platyrrhine radiation and is so primitive that it's not placed in any living platyrrhine lineage. *Branisella* is a genus of small monkeys (about 2 pounds) from the late Oligocene of Bolivia. *Branisella* represents a side branch from the clade of living New World monkeys that includes the last common ancestor of extant platyrrhines. Molecular evidence supports this view, as living platyrrhines converge on a shared ancestor that is only 25 mya (Perelman et al., 2011) (Fig. 8-16). The oldest known crown platyrrhine, *Panamacebus*, is dated to 21 mya from Panama and is most closely related to fossil cebines (Bloch et al., 2016). *Panamacebus* was discovered during an expansion of the Panama Canal on the

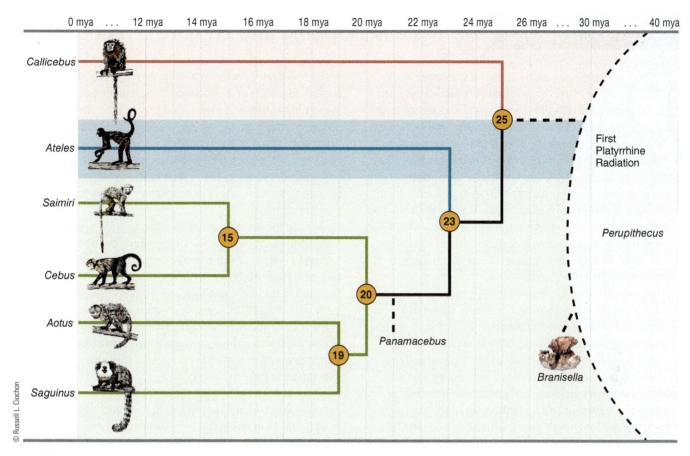

▲ **Figure 8-16**

Cladogram of extant groups of New World monkeys based on molecular evidence, with dates of divergence noted in the gold nodes (Perelman et al., 2011). *Perupithecus* and *Branisella* are representative of the basal adaptive radiation of the stem group of New World monkeys, unrelated to the crown group species living today, and have been positioned accordingly. On the other hand, the newly discovered *Panamacebus* has been positioned within the crown group.

most southern end of the North American landmass. This is the first evidence of an overwater crossing, by way of "island hopping," of platyrrhines between North and South America (Fig. 8-17).

Since South America was an island continent until 5 to 3 mya, all of the theories for the origin of platyrrhines involve overwater crossing. Multiple theories have been proposed in an attempt to explain the mysterious arrival of platyrrhines in South America including Antarctic migration and South Atlantic "island hopping." The first scenario contends that migration could have been accomplished by passing through the Antarctic—first crossing by water from Africa south to Antarctica and then crossing a land bridge that linked Antarctica to South America. The more likely scenario for the arrival of platyrrhines in South America involves their floating between closely spaced islands across the Atlantic Ocean from Africa to South America on rafts made of naturally formed mats of vegetation (see "A Closer Look: Island Hopping and Primate Evolution," on page 244). The rafting scenario is supported by the fact that during the Eocene, South America and Africa were closer to each other than they are today. An additional drop in sea level would have further decreased the distance between Africa and South America and may have exposed mid-Atlantic islands, allowing early platyrrhines to "raft" their way to South America (Ciochon and Chiarelli, 1980b; Houle, 1999; Poux and Douzery, 2004). Paleo-oceanographic modeling has indicated that paleocurrent directions at this

A Closer Look Island Hopping and Primate Evolution

Despite the peculiar images this statement might conjure, island hopping and the associated phenomenon of rafting are actually well-recognized methods of animal migration for some vertebrates. In fact, there's documented evidence of a natural raft carrying a crocodile 685 miles from Java to the Cocos Islands in 1930 (Ciochon and Chiarelli, 1980a). Admittedly such instances of natural rafting are rare; but given the geological span of time, even unlikely events (such as you winning the lottery or monkeys floating to South America) become likely. This idea is known as the sweepstakes model, and it was popularized by evolutionist G. G. Simpson (contributor to the Modern Synthesis, discussed in Chapter 4).

As better information regarding the rare availability of land bridges has been absorbed, scientists are relying more and more on sweepstakes models such as rafting to explain events that are otherwise impossible to explain. Such is the case for the lemur population of Madagascar and the New World monkeys. In both circumstances, we have the relatively sudden appearance of primates in areas where no ancestor is present and for which migration could only have been predominantly over a large body of water. The existence of islands that are now submerged as intermediates accompanied by short instances of natural rafting could have accommodated such an otherwise unlikely route of travel. Coincidentally, Africa is the apparent source of both the lemur and platyrrhine root stock.

The scenario goes like this: A female primate and her mate live on the edge of a river. During one particularly nasty storm, their home is disconnected from the mainland, becoming a natural houseboat of sorts. The storm rages, and the entire raft is carried out to sea. Days later, the bedraggled primates wash ashore at their new home (Fig. 1). The rest is history. Or is it?

Recently scientists reevaluated this sweepstakes model, exposing some serious flaws. To be a lucky ticket holder, the primates would have to actually survive the voyage or the whole model is useless. In 1976, Simons calculated that it would take only 4 to 6 days for most small primates to succumb to the combined effects of lacking food and water and experiencing salt imbalance and exposure (Simons, 1976). The shortest distance today from the African mainland to Madagascar is 249 miles. Even with a stiff continuous wind, it would take 10 days to make the journey, so the migrant lemurs would be comatose days before. The first platyrrhines would have had to cross 800 miles—that's an intolerably lengthy journey for a thirsty primate.

Despite these shortcomings, rafting is still viewed by many as the best explanation that we have for these dispersals—short of some even more obscure method of transportation. Additionally, rafting is presumed to have been the method of the primate colonization of Madagascar (Samonds et al., 2012). Combined with the probable existence of islands intermediate to Madagascar and the New World during the times of these voyages, it's quite possible that the primates were first washed up on one of these isles and only later rafted to their current residences. This would mean that they would not have to cross the entire span in one daunting voyage but would instead engage in island hopping. In addition, Alain Houle (1998) has researched the idea of "floating islands" as a mode of distant dispersal of small- to medium-sized vertebrates. These vegetation rafts could have supported microhabitats that would have permitted small vertebrates, such as primates, to cross ocean barriers and reach far distant islands. Additional random dispersals on vegetation rafts from these distant islands would ultimately have allowed primates to colonize the New World.

▶ **Figure 1**

An artist's rendering of the South Atlantic populating scenario called island hopping, which would allow primates to take their time in moving from one island to another before finally reaching South America.

Drawing by Robert Greisen/Design by Russell L. Ciochon

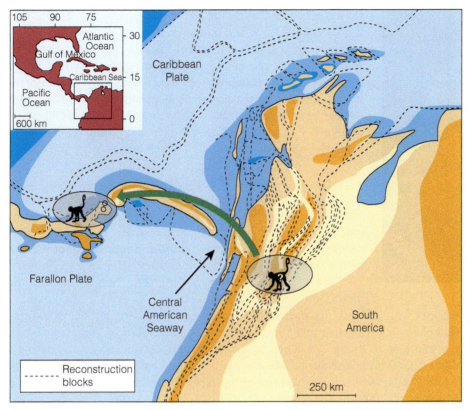

◀ **Figure 8-17**
Palaeogeographic reconstruction showing hypothetical dispersal route of *Panamacebus* across the Central American Seaway in the early Miocene. Crossing this seaway would have required "island hopping." (Based on drawing from Bloch et al., 2016.)

time may have favored this method of dispersal (Ali and Huber, 2010). Though it sounds fanciful, this method of accidental colonization has actually been used very recently to explain early hominin colonization of islands in Southeast Asia without the use of swimming or seafaring technology (Ruxton and Wilkinson, 2012).

Miocene Primates

Throughout the Miocene we see diversification of the anthropoids into the groups we're familiar with today. The cercopithecoid monkeys and the hominoids competed for the dominant position on the primate landscape in the Old World, with the former finally emerging victorious. Today the number of ape groups is very limited compared with the diversity they enjoyed in the Miocene, while cercopithecoids remain relatively varied and abundant.

Monkeying Around

Following the emergence of Afro-Arabian stem catarrhines like *Aegyptopithecus* and *Saadanius*, we have evidence of further diversification of later catarrhines—namely, the Old World monkeys and the hominoids. A new Oligocene discovery, *Nsungwepithecus*, dated to 25 mya from Tanzania bridges the gap between earlier forms like *Saadanius* and Miocene Old World monkeys (Stevens et al., 2013). This transitional specimen exhibits incomplete bilophodonty and supports the 28-mya molecular divergence date of Old World Monkeys and apes. The cercopithecoids, as the Old World monkeys are known, fall into two families—one extinct (called the victoriapithecids) and the other the living cercopithecids. The late Miocene was a highly successful time for the radiation of monkeys in the Old World. Their more immediate descendants, which evolved during the Plio-cene and the Pleistocene, were much more varied in size, locomotion, and diet

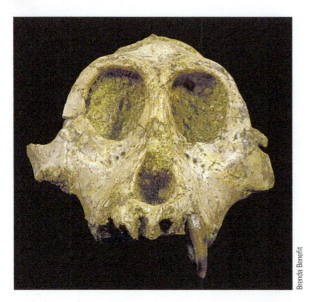

Brenda Benefit

▲ **Figure 8-18**

Skull of *Victoriapithecus*, the common ancestor of all living Old World monkey.

than their counterparts today. For a comparison of New World monkeys and Old World monkeys, see Figure 8-19.

The extinct family Victoriapithecidae represents the earliest members of the lineage leading to present-day Old World monkeys. The victoriapithecids were found throughout northern and eastern Africa as early as 24 mya (Gutiérrez, 2011), predating the split between the two extant subfamilies of Old World monkeys—the colobines (leaf-eating monkeys) and the cercopithecines (cheek-pouch monkeys)—which occurred around 18 mya (Perelman et al., 2011). If accurate, this would conform well to a molecular clock date of about 28 mya for the cercopithecoid-hominoid split. Since they're more "primitive" in many features than either colobines or cercopithecines, the victoriapithecids may represent the basal cercopithecoid and therefore the last common ancestors of crown Old World monkeys, but it's also possible that they represent an extinct sister group (Jablonksi and Frost, 2010; Gutiérrez, 2011). The best known of the victoriapithecids is *Victoriapithecus* (Fig. 8-18), a small monkey whose cranium exhibits a mosaic of later colobine and cercopithecine features that place it close to the root of both subfamilies. The molars of *Victoriapithecus*, like those of all living Old World monkeys, exhibit bilophodonty, indicating a diet of hard fruits and seeds. Meanwhile postcranial skeletal features demonstrate similarities to living terrestrial monkeys (Benefit and McCrossin, 1997; Miller et al., 2009).

By 12 mya, the victoriapithecids had been replaced by monkeys whose direct descendants are still alive today—that is, cercopithecines and colobines (see Chapter 6). Fossils of the first true colobine are found in African deposits dating to approximately 9 mya. These monkeys were smaller than most living forms, though—at 8 to 9 pounds—they weren't lightweights. Following their first appearance in Africa, the colobines quickly radiated into Europe and Asia. As you'll see, this was when Eurasian ape groups also began reentering Africa.

You may not know it, but you're probably already familiar with members of Cercopithecinae, a subfamily of the family Cercopithecidae. This subfamily includes monkeys such as today's macaques (for example, the rhesus monkeys used in labs) and baboons. Most fossil macaques appear remarkably similar to each other and to living forms, indicating that ancestral macaque morphology has been retained for more than 5 million years. This is bolstered by molecular evidence indicating that *Macaca* diverged from *Papio* (the modern baboon) about 8 mya (Perelman et al., 2011).

In East Africa, the baboon-like *Theropithecus* was the dominant cercopithecine genus of the Plio-Pleistocene (Fig. 8-20). Adaptations of the hands and teeth indicate that all species of *Theropithecus* exploited a dietary niche consisting almost exclusively of grasses—a unique diet among primates that feed on small objects. This group contains some notable fossil specimens, among them the largest monkey, weighing 225 pounds, that ever lived. *Theropithecus* was an incredibly successful genus throughout much of the Pliocene and Early Pleistocene; but at some time during the Middle Pleistocene, most of its members went extinct, leaving a single remaining species—the gelada (*Theropithecus gelada*). While we don't completely understand exactly what caused these extinctions, many researchers hypothesize that competition with the closely related *Papio* baboons of today was a major factor. Today, the living gelada is confined to the high wet grasslands of the Amhara Plateau, in Ethiopia, an ecological zone where no *Papio* baboons are found. The "At a Glance" on page 250 lists key early anthropoid names.

New World Monkeys

Old World Monkeys

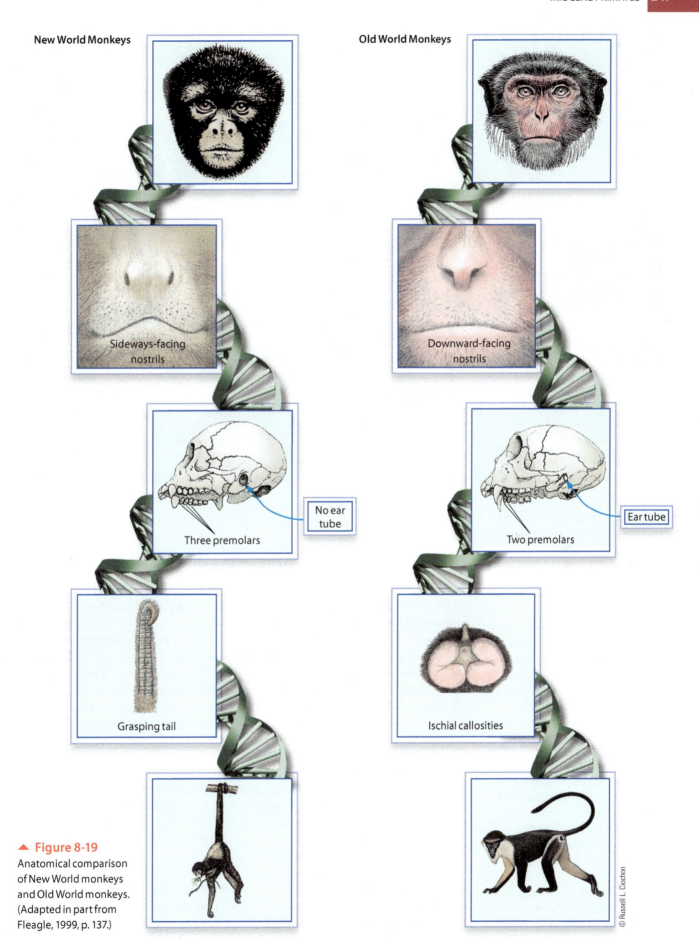

Sideways-facing nostrils

Downward-facing nostrils

Three premolars

No ear tube

Two premolars

Ear tube

Grasping tail

Ischial callosities

▲ **Figure 8-19**

Anatomical comparison of New World monkeys and Old World monkeys. (Adapted in part from Fleagle, 1999, p. 137.)

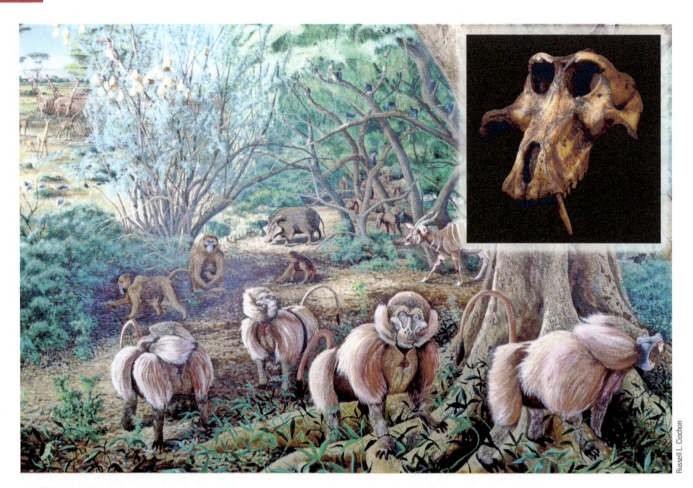

Russell L. Ciochon

▲ **Figure 8-20**
Skull of *Theropithecus brumpti*, the most bizarre fossil monkey (inset). An artist's rendering of *Theropithecus* on the landscape in the Omo Basin of Ethiopia about 3 mya.

▶ **Figure 8-21 (opposite page)**
Family tree of early catarrhines and their relationships to modern Old World monkeys and apes. Red is for living apes and their immediate ancestors (Hominoidea), green is for the Old World monkeys and their immediate ancestors (Cercopithecoidea), orange is for precursors to apes (Proconsuloidea), purple is for the primitive catarrhines (Pliopithecoidea), and blue represents the Fayum early anthropoid radiation. Note that the genus *Pliobates* appears in two possible locations due to uncertainties in its phylogenetic placement.

Y-5 molar Molar that has five cusps with grooves running between them, forming a Y shape. This is characteristic of hominoids.

Aping Monkeys

By the end of the Oligocene, the world's major continents were located about where they are today. During the Miocene (23 to 5.3 mya), however, the drifting of South America and Australia away from Antarctica significantly altered ocean currents. At the same time, the South Asian Plate continued to ram into Asia, producing the Himalayan Plateau. Together, these major paleogeographical modifications significantly affected the climate, causing the early Miocene to be considerably warmer and wetter than the Oligocene. As a result, subtropical dense woodlands became the dominant environments of Africa during the early Miocene. It was in this forested environment of Africa that the first apelike primates evolved.

The Apelike Proconsuloids Molecular evidence suggests that the evolutionary lineages leading to monkeys and apes diverged approximately 28 mya (Steiper and Seiffert, 2012) (Fig. 8-21), which is consistent with the fossil evidence following the recent discovery of *Saadanius*, the Oligocene advanced stem catarrhine (Zalmout et al., 2010). Not surprisingly, the first apelike fossils share many postcranial characteristics with monkeys. In fact, in many of these early forms of the superfamily Proconsuloidea, the only apelike feature is the presence of the **Y-5 molar** pattern. As shown in Figure 8-22, the ape molars have five cusps separated by a "Y" groove, as opposed to the monkey's typical four bilophodont cusps. Consequently proconsuloids were once commonly called dental apes, reflecting their apelike teeth but monkey-like postcranial skeleton. Today, proconsuloids are widely viewed as general precursors to all later hominoids (Harrison, 2010a; Harrison, 2010b; but see Zalmout et al., 2010).

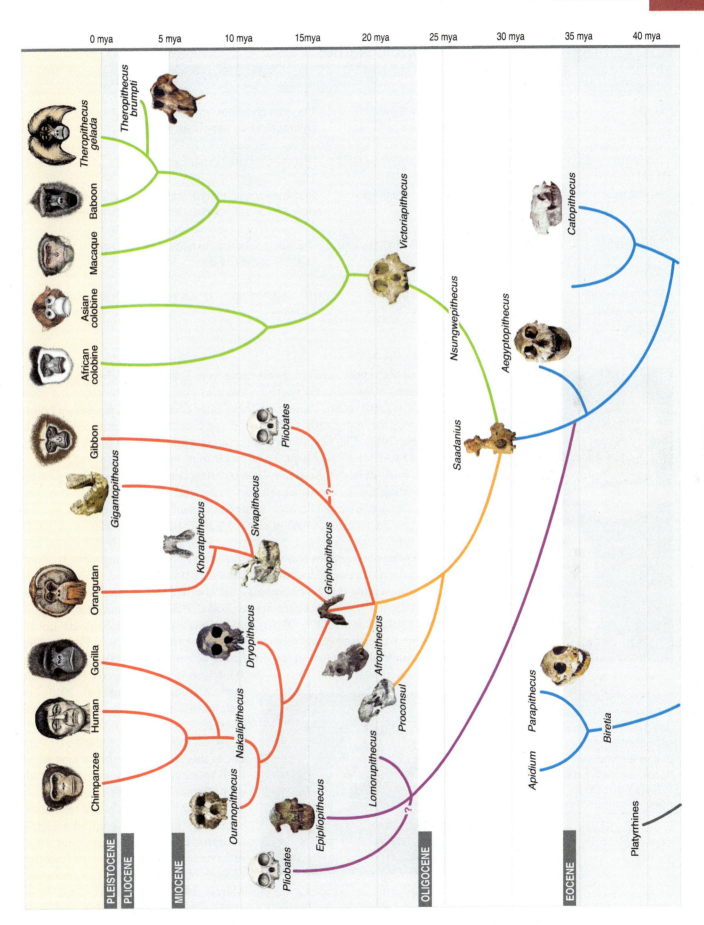

0 mya   5 mya   10 mya   15mya   20 mya   25 mya   30 mya   35 mya   40 mya

Theropithecus brumpti

Theropithecus gelada

Baboon

Macaque

Asian colobine

African colobine

Gibbon

Gigantopithecus

Orangutan

Gorilla

Human

Chimpanzee

Victoriapithecus

Nsungwepithecus

Catopithecus

Aegyptopithecus

Saadanius

Pliobates

Khoratpithecus

Sivapithecus

Griphopithecus

Dryopithecus

Afropithecus

Nakalipithecus

Proconsul

Ouranopithecus

Lomorupithecus

Epipliopithecus

Parapithecus

Biretia

Apidium

Pliobates

Platyrrhines

PLEISTOCENE

PLIOCENE

MIOCENE

OLIGOCENE

EOCENE

At a Glance   Key Early Anthropoid Names

Genus Name	Epoch	Sites/Regions	The Big Picture
Biretia	Late Eocene	The Fayum (Egypt); North Africa	The most complete remains of an early African anthropoid; may have been nocturnal.
Saadanius	Oligocene	Saudi Arabia; Afro-Arabia	First stem catarrhine; has ear tube.
Perupithecus	Late Eocene	Peru; South America	First known fossil platyrrhine; more closely resembles early African anthropoids than crown platyrrhines.
Panamacebus	Early Miocene	Panama; North American landmass	The oldest know crown platyrrhine; the earliest known member of the Cebidae.
Victoriapithecus	Middle Miocene	Kenya and Uganda; East Africa	Has bilophodont molar pattern; ancestor of all Old World monkeys.

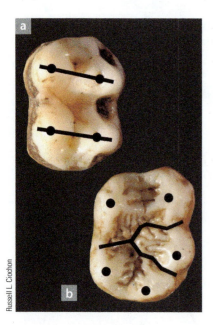

Russell L. Ciochon

▲ **Figure 8-22**

Comparison of (**a**) bilophodont molars, as found in cercopithecoids, and (**b**) Y-5 molars, as seen in hominoids. (**a**) Notice that the four cusps are positioned in two parallel rows or lobes. (**b**) See how the five cusps are arranged so that a Y-shaped valley runs between them.

Nearly all of the proconsuloid fossils come from East Africa, although some fossils have been recovered as far south and west as Namibia, on the southern coast of Africa. The fossil record shows that these early apelike creatures were a highly diverse group, varying greatly in both size and locomotor patterns (Gebo et al., 1997; Fleagle, 2013). The best known of the proconsuloids is the genus *Proconsul*, which lived in Africa 20 to 17 mya. The first example of *Proconsul*, a skull, was discovered on Rusinga Island, Kenya, in 1948 by esteemed fossil hunter Mary Leakey. This fruit-eating apelike creature roamed a wide range of environments from rainforest to open woodlands. Though generally considered small-bodied, various *Proconsul* species actually ranged in size from 10 to 150 pounds (Harrison, 2002). *Proconsul* exhibits a generalized cranium (Fig. 8-23) and an apelike Y-5 dental pattern, but postcranial remains show that *Proconsul's* limbs and long torso retained adaptations for quadrupedal locomotion similar to that of monkeys. Scientists are increasingly accepting that *Proconsul* may not have had a tail, which could indicate that this particular hominoid characteristic had a relatively ancient origin (Begun, 2003; Nakatsukasa et al., 2004; Ward, 2005). However, the proconsuloids' uncertain position has caused many researchers to place them outside of Hominoidea (in Proconsuloidea), just prior to the divergence of hominoids and cercopithecoids (Harrison, 2010b; but see McCollum et al., 2010, and Zalmout et al., 2010). For a comparison of Old World monkeys and apes, see Figure 8-25 on page 252.

Afropithecus, a more derived member of this superfamily, had a long snout with procumbent incisors that protruded horizontally from its face (Fig. 8-24). Its relatively thickly enameled teeth indicate that *Afropithecus* enjoyed a diet of hard fruits, while the sexual dimorphism of its molars and premolars exceeds that of even of living gorillas (Andrews and Martin, 1987; Leakey et al., 1988; Rose, 1993). The few known limb and hand bones point toward a quadrupedal

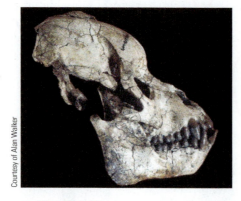

Courtesy of Alan Walker

▲ **Figure 8-23**

Skull of *Proconsul*, the best known of the early Miocene precursors to apes.

arboreal lifestyle. Known from both Kenya *and* Saudi Arabia between 16 and 18 mya, *Afropithecus* provides compelling evidence of transcontinental migration into Europe and likely provided the basal stock from which the later true ape radiations emerged. Researchers now conclude that *Afropithecus* was likely the first apelike primate to leave Africa about 17.5 mya (Begun et al., 2012).

Members of the superfamily Pliopithecoidea, like the proconsuloids, are also generally known from the early Miocene, though they're more primitive in their features than all other catarrhines. Most evidence indicates that the pliopithecoids were an early small-bodied (6 to 44 pounds) group of stem catarrhines that branched off before the cercopithecoid-hominoid split. A highly successful group once thought to be related to extant hylobatids, they underwent a rapid adaptive radiation in the Miocene (Begun, 2002; Alba et al., 2010).

Toward the end of the early Miocene, around 19 mya, the Arabian Plate moved to its current location, forming a land bridge between Africa and Eurasia. Major animal migrations could then take place between the two previously separated land masses. It's thought that African pliopithecoids were among the first transcontinental primate migrants and, importantly, represent the first anthropoids to colonize both Asia and Europe. Researchers thus commonly agree that the pliopithecoids were the first stem catarrhines to leave Africa. For many years, however, this migration was only assumed, since pliopithecoid fossil remains were known only from Eurasia. But in 2006, a new genus of pliopithecoid, *Lomorupithecus*, was described from Uganda. Dating to the early Miocene (nearly 20 mya), *Lomorupithecus* could be the earliest member of this group, and—as predicted—it's from Africa (Rossie and MacLatchy, 2006)! Though still more recent in age than *Saadanius*, the pliopithecoids' more primitive features indicate that they actually diverged earlier, possibly giving rise to the early primitive catarrhine group to which *Saadanius* belongs, among others (Begun, 2002; Alba et al., 2010). This find could provide the proof that pliopithecoids had their roots in Africa, bringing this idea from the realm of conjecture into reality. The pliopithecoids enjoyed an intense and prolific radiation early on, but it appears that later, during the Pliocene, their success ended. All forms went extinct, with no known living descendants.

Russell L. Ciochon

▲ **Figure 8-24**
Skull of *Afropithecus*, the first apelike primate to leave Africa.

A New Small-Bodied Ape?

In 2015, researchers announced the discovery of a skull and partial skeleton of a new small-bodied ape, *Pliobates,* found in Catalonia, Spain (Alba et al., 2015) (Figure 8-26). Dated at 11.6 mya, this small apelike creature does not fit any existing model of ape evolution. According to Spanish researchers, *Pliobates* "exhibits a mosaic of primitive (stem catarrhine-like) and derived (extant hominoid-like) features that forces us to reevaluate the role of small-bodied catarrhines in ape evolution" (Alba et al., 2015, p. 528). Its relatively large brain volume, goggle-like orbital rims, hominoid-like wrist, and humerus morphology hint at a potential ancestry to gibbons. Yet, its lack of a tubelike middle ear that all living catarrhines possess makes it more primitive than the 28-mya *Saadanius* (Benefit and McCrossin, 2015). This combination of primitive and derived features is an excellent example of the complexities of mosaic evolution and homoplasy. *Pliobates* can be placed in multiple lineages depending on which features are given the most importance. If *Pliobates* is an early ape related to gibbons, then the boney ear tube found in all living Old World monkeys and apes would have to independently evolve multiple times in the cercopithecoid and hominoid lineages. Alternately, *Pliobates* could be a member of the Pliopithecoidea that branched off prior to the split between cercopithecoids and hominoids. Pliopithecoids lack a boney ear tube and possess a primitive elbow joint morphology like that seen in *Pliobates*. In this scenario *Pliobates* would have convergently evolved a hominoid-like wrist possibly as an adaptation for a more arboreal habitat. As the phylogenetic position is difficult to determine, we have placed *Pliobates* in two locations on the early catarrhine family tree (see Fig. 8-21).

Old World Monkeys

Apes

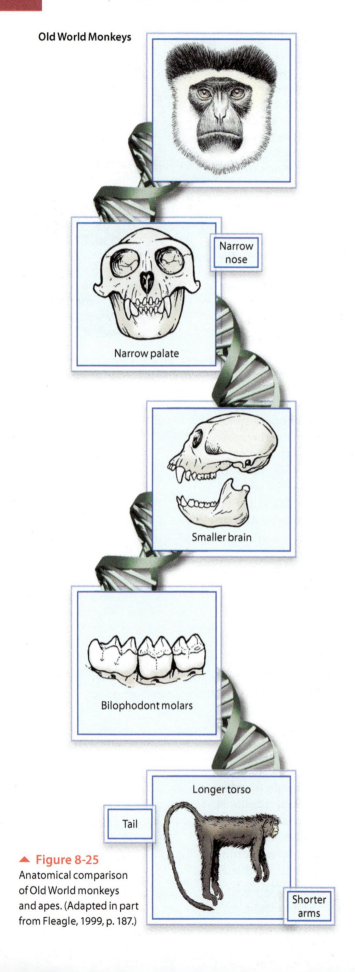

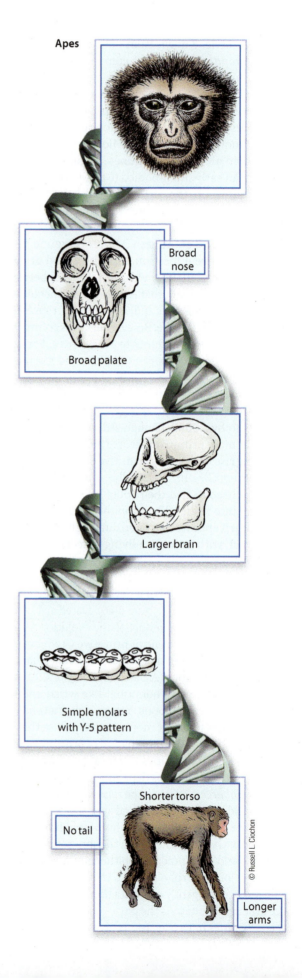

Narrow nose

Broad nose

Narrow palate

Broad palate

Smaller brain

Larger brain

Bilophodont molars

Simple molars with Y-5 pattern

Longer torso

Shorter torso

Tail

No tail

Shorter arms

Longer arms

© Russell L. Ciochon

▲ **Figure 8-25**
Anatomical comparison of Old World monkeys and apes. (Adapted in part from Fleagle, 1999, p. 187.)

True Apes

The first true apes, those belonging to the superfamily Hominoidea, appear during the early to middle Miocene, 17 mya, first in Europe, presumably coming from an African proconsuloid ancestor (Begun et al., 2012) (Fig. 8-27). These earliest hominoids are united by thick enamel on their molars, which appears to have been a trait that was important in their ability to adapt to a variety of new non-African paleoenvironments (Böhme et al., 2011). What this tells us is that hard-object feeding (such as tough, fibrous fruits and nuts) was a key feature of these new environments (Alba et al., 2010). The "At a Glance" below lists key fossil ape names.

West Side Story: True Apes in Europe Miocene Europe was a much different continent from that which we know today. The climate was warm and humid, with a landscape dominated by lush subtropical forests. It was these swampy forests that attracted a diverse group of animals, of which stem hominoids were a part. Sometime during the early-middle Miocene *Afropithecus* ventured out of Africa via land bridges, crossing parts of the modern Middle East to give rise to the first true apes in Europe. Although the initial hominoid (true ape) radiation was widespread geographically, so far we've found only scant evidence of it from scattered localities in France, Spain, Italy, Greece, Austria, Germany, Slovakia, and Hungary.

Dated to roughly 17 mya, the earliest of these true apes, *Griphopithecus*, is known first from southern Germany and later from Slovakia and Turkey. Similar to what we saw with the earlier proconsuloids, the earliest apelike features are in the dentition, with the retention of more monkey-like postcrania. However, unlike many proconsuloids, *Griphopithecus* and later true apes all lack a tail, one of the distinguishing traits of hominoids (see Chapter 6; see Fig. 8-25). Their limb proportions were roughly similar and there is no evidence of the more suspensory adaptations we see in later apes, but their hands do indicate a greater grip than that of your average monkey. Additionally, *Griphopithecus'* thickly enameled and more generalized teeth made it possible for this ape to exploit a variety of different environments, which was perhaps key in allowing it to migrate from Turkey and into the Asian continent at about 15 mya. In fact, David Begun has gone so far as to propose that *Griphopithecus*

Marta Palmero/Institut Català de Paleontologia Miquel Crusafont (ICP)

▲ **Figure 8-26**
Cranial reconstruction and artist rendering as it might have looked in life of *Pliobates*, a new small-bodied apelike primate from Spain.

At a Glance   Key Fossil Ape Names

Genus Name	Epoch	Sites/Regions	The Big Picture
Afropithecus	Miocene	Kenya; Africa	The first apelike primate to leave Africa; may have given rise to the European apes; thick-enameled teeth and Y-5 pattern molars.
Griphopithecus	Miocene	Germany, Slovakia, Turkey; Eastern Europe/Western Asia	The first true ape; may have given rise to both the later radiations of European and Asian apes; no tail.
Ouranopithecus	Late Miocene	Greece; Europe	Fossil great ape; believed by many to have returned to Africa to give rise to the living great apes and humans.
Khoratpithecus	Late Miocene	Thailand, Myanmar; Asia	Part of the Asian fossil great ape radiation; stem orangutan.
Gigantopithecus	Miocene-Pleistocene	China, Vietnam, India, Myanmar; Asia	The largest ape that ever lived; only great ape to go extinct in the Pleistocene.

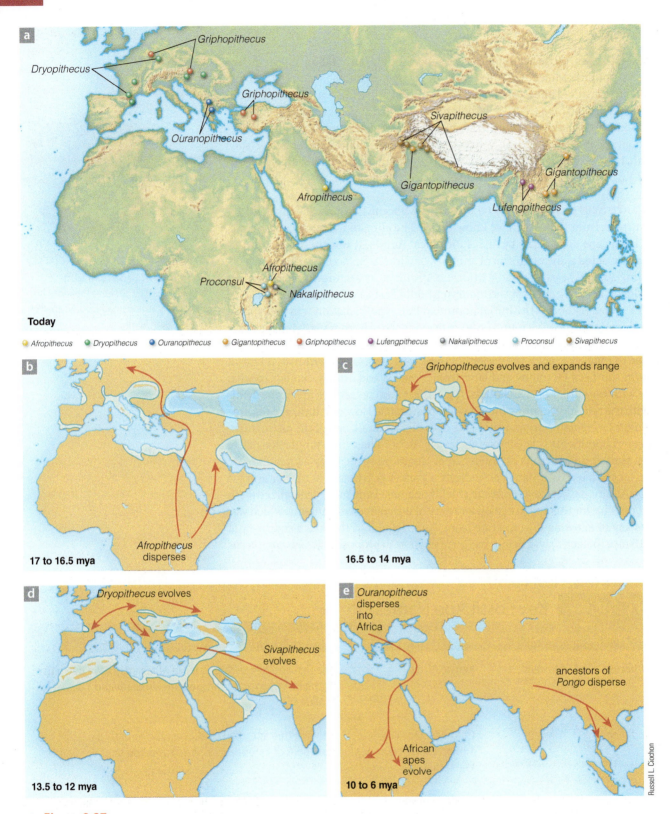

▲ **Figure 8-27**

Model providing geographical context for the evolution and dispersal of the Miocene apes. (**a**) Map of present-day Africa, Europe, and Asia showing ape and proto-ape fossil localities. Maps (**b–e**) are paleogeographic maps showing the locations of inland seas at various time intervals in the Miocene: (**b**) 17 to 16.5 mya, first dispersal of apelike *Afropithecus* out of Africa into Europe; (**c**) 16.5 to 14 mya, *Griphopithecus* evolves and expands its range throughout Europe and into western Asia; (**d**) 13.5 to 12 mya, *Dryopithecus* evolves and disperses in Europe and *Sivapithecus* evolves and disperses in southern Asia; (**e**) 10 to 6 mya, *Ouranopithecus* disperses from southern Europe back into Africa to give rise to the African great apes and humans, in Asia the ancestors of *Pongo* disperse into southern China and Southeast Asia. (Maps modified after Begun, 2003 and Begun et al., 2012.)

represents a Eurasian linchpin in hominoid evolution, providing the stock from which both European and Asian apes later derived (Begun, 2010; Begun et al., 2012).

The best-known European hominoid of the middle Miocene (circa 12 to 10 mya) is *Dryopithecus*, from southern France and northern Spain (Fig. 8-28). Unlike *Griphopithecus*, *Dryopithecus* resembles modern hominoids in many cranial and postcranial features, including long arms, large hands, and long fingers—all signifying an ability to brachiate. The relatively thinly enameled teeth of *Dryopithecus* imply an unusual diet of both fruits and leaves (Begun, 1994). Also, these skeletal and dental remains suggest that unlike most other great apes, *Dryopithecus* was a highly arboreal species, rarely descending from its high-canopy forested habitat.

As the Miocene progressed, the formerly subtropical environment of Europe began to cool and the swampy parts began to dry. These changes led to the extinction of many forest-adapted animals, though others met this more open, grassy environment with increased body size and/or more complex dentition (Begun et al., 2012). One of these "new apes" was the late Miocene (9.6 to 8.7 mya) European fossil hominoid *Ouranopithecus*, whose face shares many features with the living African great apes, including large browridges and a wide distance between the eye orbits (Fig. 8-29). *Ouranopithecus'* powerful jaws, with small canines and extremely thick molar enamel, led some researchers to postulate that these hominoids subsisted on a diet consisting of relatively hard foods, such as nuts (Ungar and Kay, 1995). The variation in both body and canine size indicates a range of sexual dimorphism comparable to that of the modern gorilla, which these animals resemble in size. *Ouranopithecus* is a taxon to watch, as it will come up later in our discussion of the emergence of the African apes. For the time being, the most likely position of *Ouranopithecus* appears to be as a separate sister clade to the extant African apes and to humans (Begun et al., 2012).

East Side Story: Asian Radiation

Hominoids do not appear to have colonized Asia until about 15 mya (Heizmann and Begun, 2001). This initial incursion is first recorded at the site of Paşalar in southwestern Turkey and is marked by the expansion of *Griphopithecus*, a European genus, into western Asia (Begun et al., 2012). The hominoids of the middle and late Miocene of Asia represent one of the most varied Miocene fossil ape assemblages. These Asian fossil apes are geographically dispersed from Turkey in the west to China in the east.

Sivapithecus dates to the middle and late Miocene and has been recovered from southern Asia, in the Siwalik Hills of India and Pakistan. Included in this large collection are a multitude of mandibles, many postcranial remains, and a partial cranium, including most of the face. *Sivapithecus* was a large hominoid, ranging from 70 to 150 pounds; it probably inhabited a mostly arboreal niche. The most characteristic anatomical aspects of *Sivapithecus* are seen in the face, which exhibits a concave profile (dished face), broad **zygomatics** (cheekbones), and a procumbent (projecting) maxilla and incisors remarkably resembling the face of the modern orangutan (Pilbeam, 1982) (Fig. 8-30). It's important to note that the body of *Sivapithecus* is distinctly unlike that of living orangutans or any other known hominoid for that matter. For example, the forelimb exhibits a unique mixture of traits, probably indicating some mode of arboreal quadrupedalism with no ability for brachiation (Pilbeam et al., 1990).

One of *Sivapithecus'* descendants from the late Miocene through the Pleistocene, *Gigantopithecus* ("Giganto"), was discovered in a rather unconventional way. For thousands of years, Chinese pharmacists have used fossils as ingredients in potions intended to cure ailments ranging from backache to sexual impotence. In 1935, Dutch paleoanthropologist Ralph von Koenigswald came across several large fossil primate molars in a Hong Kong apothecary shop. He named

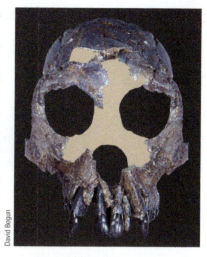

David Begun

▲ **Figure 8-28**
Skull of *Dryopithecus*, one of the earliest European apes. The left side is reconstructed as a mirror image of the complete right side.

▼ **Figure 8-29**
Ouranopithecus, possible extinct relative of the African apes. Notice that the face shares many features with living African great apes, including large browridges and a wide distance between the eye orbits. The upper left side is reconstructed as a mirror image of the complete right side.

Laboratory of Geology and Palaeontology, Aristotle University of Thessaloniki

zygomatics Cheekbones.

David Pilbeam

▲ **Figure 8-30**

Comparison of a modern chimpanzee (left), *Sivapithecus* (middle), and a modern orangutan (right). Notice that both *Sivapithecus* and the orangutan exhibit a dished face, broad cheekbones, and projecting maxilla and incisors.

these fossil teeth *Gigantopithecus*, meaning "gigantic ape," and the species *blacki*, in honor of his late friend and colleague Davidson Black (the discoverer of "Peking Man"). Subsequent researchers were able to source the teeth to China's southernmost Guangxi Province, a karstic (eroded limestone) region of great rock towers riddled with caves. A Giganto tooth found recently in Thailand suggests that the giant apes' habitat extended farther than originally described (Bocherans et al., 2015).

While four lower jaws and almost 2,000 isolated teeth of the extinct ape have been found, no other bones have turned up (Fig. 8-31). Based only on the jaws and teeth, however, researchers can attempt to reconstruct both the animal and its way of life. Estimates based on the massive mandibles indicate that the Chinese species of Giganto likely weighed more than 500 pounds and was possibly 8 feet tall standing erect on its hind legs (though it was most likely a terrestrial fist walker). This makes *Gigantopithecus* the largest primate that ever lived. But Giganto wasn't always the king of apes that it became in later years. Evidence shows that this great ape increased in size as the genus evolved, which follows a trend seen in other large Pleistocene mammals, such as the mammoth. The earlier Indian and Pakistani *Gigantopithecus giganteus* (8.6 mya), despite its specific name, was about half the size of the later Chinese and Southeast Asian *Gigantopithecus blacki* (around 2.0 mya).

The comparatively small incisors and canines, very thick enamel on the cheek teeth, and massive, robust jaws led to the inevitable conclusion that the animal was adapted to the consumption of tough, fibrous foods by cutting, crushing, and grinding them. Some researchers have argued that Giganto's huge mandible and dentition were an adaptation for a diet consisting primarily of bamboo, much like that of the giant panda. More detailed studies of the teeth concluded that while Giganto ate some bamboo, its diet contained a much wider range of plants and fruits including durian, a tropical fruit with a tough outer skin (Ciochon et al., 1990; Zhao and Zhang, 2013) (Fig. 8-32).

▶ **Figure 8-31**

Comparison of the mandibles and teeth of *Gigantopithecus* and *Homo sapiens*. Notice that Giganto's jaw is almost three times the size of the human's, as are the teeth.

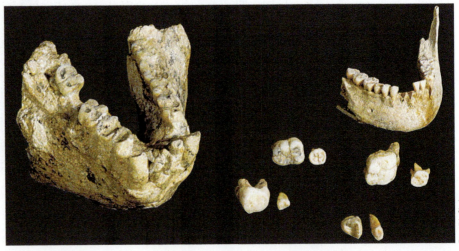

Russell L. Ciochon

Sadly, at some time near the end of the Middle Pleistocene, around 300,000 years ago (ya), Giganto went extinct. The animal had flourished for more than 8.5 million years, but climatic and environmental change proved too much for the vegetarian giant as China's bamboo forests gave way to spreading grasslands (Bocherens et al., 2015).

Another ape from Asia, *Lufengpithecus*, has been recovered from localities in southern China and dated to the late Miocene (10 to 6 mya) (Ji et al., 2013). This medium-sized ape, with an estimated adult body weight of about 110 pounds, is known from one of the most complete fossil ape assemblages: 7 crania, 41 mandibles, over 650 isolated teeth, and, most recently, postcrania including finger bones and a femur (Xu and Lu, 2007). With its narrow interorbital distance, ovoid orbits, and curved phalanges (Fig. 8-33), some Chinese researchers have argued that *Lufengpithecus* is related to the modern orangutan. Additional information from the recovery of two new crania has lead other researchers to conclude that it is a stem member of the hominid (great ape and human) clade, perhaps related to the European *Dryopithecus* (Kelley and Gao, 2012; Ji et al., 2013). *Lufengpithecus* is also noted for its existence within a protected area created by the uplift of the Tibetan Plateau—the result of Himalayan mountain building (Harrison et al., 2002). Within this refuge, a sort of "lost world," *Lufengpithecus* survived until at least 6 mya.

Recent discoveries from Pleistocene cave sites in southern China have revealed the presence of an additional unnamed "mystery ape" (Ciochon, 2009). These caves have long yielded teeth belonging to *Gigantopithecus* and have recently produced more diminutive teeth and jaws initially identified as belonging to an early human. Following more rigorous analysis, these teeth can no longer be considered human and are too small to be those of either Giganto or the orangutan *Pongo;* therefore they are now thought to belong to a previously unknown, medium-sized Pleistocene ape. Six cave sites have yielded an upper jaw, lower jaw, and numerous isolated teeth of this new ape. Current evidence points to the existence of three distinct great ape lineages in Pleistocene Asia: the massive *Gigantopithecus*, the large-bodied *Pongo*, and the medium-sized "mystery ape." As you've seen in Chapter 6, this Asian hominoid diversity has dwindled in modern times, just as it has in Africa and elsewhere in the world.

▲ **Figure 8-32**

An artist's rendering of *Gigantopithecus* enjoying a meal of the tasty but tough tropical fruit known as durian.

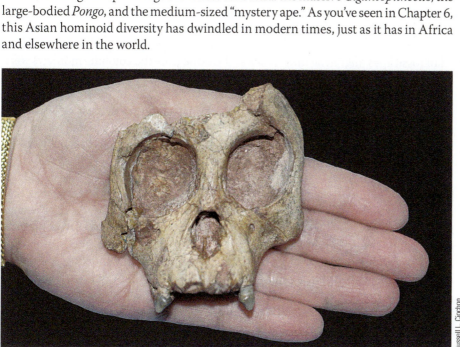

◀ **Figure 8-33**

Skull of a *Lufengpithecus* juvenile from the late Miocene of Yunnan Province, China. Current research shows this Asian ape likely had affinities to European *Dryopithecus*.

Evolution of Extant Hominoids

Hylobatids: The Lesser Apes

Molecular evidence indicates that the gibbon–great ape split occurred 20 mya (Perelman et al., 2011). This would place their divergence around the time that migration into Eurasia from Africa would have first become geographically possible (Pilbeam, 1996; Thinh et al., 2010). The molecular evidence also shows that extant hylobatids (lesser apes, such as gibbons) only diverged from one another between 9 to 6 mya (Perelman et al., 2011), with 9-million-year-old *Yuanmoupithecus* supporting that date (Harrison et al., 2008). For many years, researchers had considered pliopithecoids as possible gibbon ancestors owing to similarities in the shape of the face. But pliopithecoids and Oligocene catarrhines actually share numerous primitive features, including the lack of a tubelike middle ear, the presence of a small tail, and an elbow joint that's strikingly similar to those of various Fayum primates. These features, as well as their monkey-like limb proportions, clearly remove pliopithecoids from consideration as the ancestors of modern gibbons. From molecular evidence and from fossil remains of the small-bodied Chinese stem hylobatid *Yuanmoupithecus* (Harrison et al., 2008), however, we can determine that the gibbon radiation most likely began in mainland Asia, perhaps in China, before dispersing southward to Malaysia and Sumatra via tropical forests connected by the land bridges of the Miocene. Once in Sumatra, gibbons differentiated into two taxa, including the modern *Hylobates*, which eventually made their way into Borneo and Java via the same route, though multiple migrations via these land bridges is possible (Chatterjee, 2006; Harrison et al., 2008; Thinh et al., 2010).

The African Great Apes

Recent molecular studies suggest that gorillas diverged from humans and chimpanzees about 8 mya, with the divergence between humans and chimpanzees occurring at 6.6 mya (Perelman et al., 2011). If these estimates are right, then the late Miocene (11 to 5 mya) becomes a crucial period for understanding African great apes and human origins. Strangely, hominoids disappear from the African fossil record about 13 mya, not to appear again until the late Miocene about 10 mya. This African "ape gap" (Hill, 2007) has led researchers to hypothesize that the appearance of hominoids in Africa during the late Miocene was the result of Eurasian fossil apes migrating into Africa at the same time the colobine monkeys were dispersing from Africa.

European *Ouranopithecus* (9.6 to 8.7 mya), a large-bodied hominoid from Greece, is considered the best candidate for a stem African ape/human ancestor. This argument is based primarily on the facial similarities discussed earlier. This out-of-Europe ape lineage later migrated into Africa at some time during the late Miocene, producing the African ape–human line (see Chapter 10).

The 9.9- to 9.8-million-year-old *Nakalipithecus* from Kenya may be close to the last common ancestor of the African great apes and humans. *Nakalipithecus* is reconstructed as having been comparable in size to a female gorilla, with dental features that indicate a hard-object diet, both suggestive of a **terrestrial** lifestyle (substantial ground living) (Kunimatsu et al., 2007; Nakatsukasa and Kunimatsu, 2009). Size and dental similarities between *Nakalipithecus* and the slightly younger *Ouranopithecus* (the two are separated by only 200 to 300 thousand years) may be due to the two having lived in similar environments, or an ancestor-descendent relationship, or as some scientists argue, they are actually members of the same taxon. Despite its still ambiguous phylogenetic affiliation, it is clear that the Samburu Hills of northern Kenya, where *Nakalipithecus* was found, were a hotbed of hominoid

terrestrial Living and locomoting primarily on the ground.

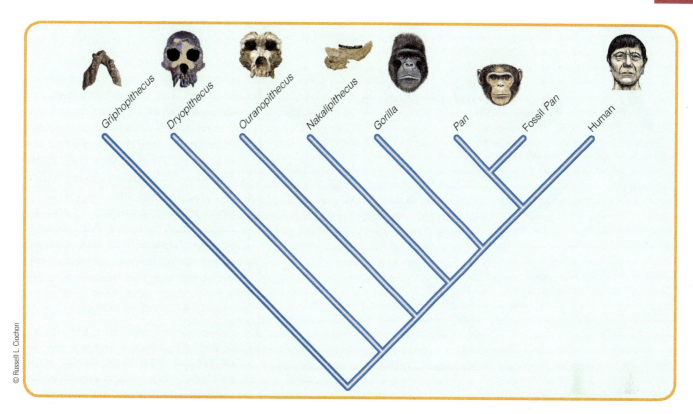

▲ **Figure 8-34**

Cladogram of Homininae showing the relationships of gorillas, chimpanzees, and humans with their fossil ape relatives. *Griphopithecus* is the sister group of the Homininae.

diversity, with at least two other genera known from this region during the Miocene (Nakatsukasa and Kunimatsu, 2009) (Fig. 8-34).

In 2005, researchers discovered several teeth of a fossil chimpanzee at a site near Lake Baringo, in Kenya. This discovery adds some fossil time depth to at least the *Pan* lineage. These fossil chimpanzee teeth date to approximately 500,000 ya and represent the first and only fossils belonging to the genus *Pan* (such fossils are rare because tropical forest environments aren't conducive to preserving organic remains). Also note that these fossils are quite late, several million years after the chimpanzee lineage diverged from hominins. Although currently not assigned to a particular chimpanzee species, the fossil teeth exhibit greater similarities to the common chimpanzee (*Pan troglodytes*) than to bonobos (*Pan paniscus*) (McBrearty and Jablonski, 2005).

Another reason why African ape and chimpanzee fossils in particular may seem so rare is the difficulty in identifying them as such and not as early hominins. As we will see in Chapter 10, the controversial and now iconic rebranding of *Ardipithecus*, a previously described genus, reveals a complex and unexpected mix of primitive and derived traits, meaning that the last common ancestor of the African apes and humans may not have looked like either group as we know them now (Lovejoy, 2009; Shreeve, 2009). In fact, a number of researchers believe, that under further examination, this genus will be revealed not as a hominin but rather as a descendant of a late Miocene African ape. However, given the shortage of African hominoid fossils, why can't that be good enough? Still, if these aren't our distant relatives, where *do* we come from? In Chapter 10, we'll seek answers to this question.

Asia's Lone Great Ape

Of all the living apes, the orangutan's ancestry is probably the best documented. Recall that the European *Griphopithecus* expanded its range into western Asia

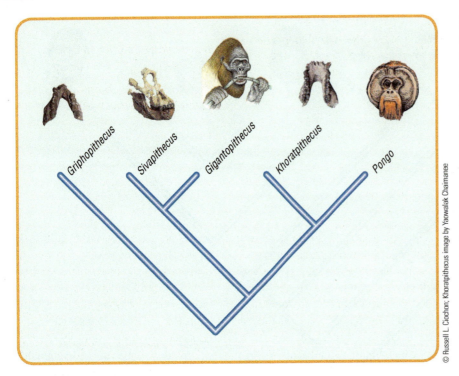

▲ **Figure 8-35**

Cladogram of Ponginae showing the relationship of the orangutan with its fossil ape relatives. *Griphopithecus* is the sister-group of the Ponginae.

(Paşalar, Turkey) beginning approximately 15 mya, so it may be viewed as the progenitor of later Asian apes (Begun et al., 2012). Current evidence indicates that *Sivapithecus* gave rise to *Gigantopithecus* (some time before 9 mya) as well as to another ape *Khoratpithecus,* and then finally to the orangutan (*Pongo*). Since the earliest *Sivapithecus* fossils date to more than 12 mya, it's clear that the branching event separating orangutans and the lineage leading to the African great apes and humans must have occurred before then. In fact, molecular evidence indicates that this divergence of African and Asian apes took place approximately 17 mya (Perelman et al., 2011). The relationship between *Sivapithecus* and *Pongo* is based primarily on cranial similarities, though their vastly differing postcranial anatomies raise questions regarding their evolutionary proximity to each another.

Another fossil ape, *Khoratpithecus,* shows a closer evolutionary relationship to the orangutan. *Khoratpithecus* is a late Miocene ape known from three localities, two in Thailand and one in Myanmar, dated from 9 to 7 mya (Chaimanee et al., 2004; Jaeger et al., 2011). It shares some dental similarities with living orangutans. More importantly, it is the only known fossil ape with the unique dental arcade shape and mandibular symphysis morphology that is found only in living orangutans. These shared derived features include large anterior dentition, absence of an attachment for the anterior digastric muscle, and very large third molar (Chaimanee et al., 2006). This is strong evidence that *Khoratpithecus* is the most likely ancestor of the orangutan (Fig. 8-35).

How Do We Know?

We know a great deal about the earliest primates and their ancestors based mostly on fossil finds. However, the number of fossils (especially complete ones) that have been discovered from the Paleocene through the Miocene is still relatively small compared with later taxa, but the teeth in particular are very informative regarding dietary habits and paleoenvironments. For example, molar tooth crown morphology often reveals clues regarding a primate's diet; more rounded molar cusps serve as ideal grinding surfaces for a wide variety of food resources (most commonly fruit), whereas molars with two ridges of enamel (bilophodont molars) reflect a partial specialization for leaf-eating. By comparing the shape, size, and morphology of teeth and jaws of modern primates with those of fossil primates, researchers can make inferences about ancient primate diet (Ungar, 2002). In addition, dental wear patterns on the occlusal (chewing) surfaces of teeth can provide significant insight on diet. Analysis of both macrowear (tooth wear observable to the naked eye) and microwear (microscopic scratches and pits observed on the occlusal surface of teeth) patterns on modern primates with known diets can be used to create a baseline for comparison with fossil primate dentitions (Ungar, 2002). For example, primates that consume large quantities of fruit tend to show higher ratios of microscopic pits to scratches compared to leaf-eating primates. Although complex to interpret, similarities in tooth wear patterns between modern and fossil primate groups could reflect similar dietary

© Russell L. Ciochon; Khoratpithecus image by Yaowalak Chaimanee

adaptions. Finally, chemical analysis, such as stable isotope analysis and trace elemental analysis, of teeth can be used to reconstruct fossil primate diet. Because teeth are more resistant to diagenesis than bone, they are more likely to preserve dietary signatures.

Isotopic analysis and trace element analysis can provide information regarding the specific dietary niches used by a fossil primate group, as well as the types of plant and animals that were exploited.

What Do You Think?

What are some of the challenges with reconstructing the diet of fossil primates? What lines of evidence do you think are the most reliable? ■

Summary of Main Topics

- Primates began diverging from closely related mammalian lineages at the end of the Cretaceous right around the mass extinction of the dinosaurs. The Cenozoic comprises seven geological epochs (Paleocene, Eocene, Oligocene, Miocene, Pliocene, Pleistocene, and the Holocene).
- Beginning in the Paleocene, the earliest primate ancestors were probably little more than arboreally adapted insectivores, much like modern tree shrews.
- In the Eocene, we see an abundant diversification of readily identifiable euprimates, with the lemurlike adapoids and the tarsierlike omomyoids (fossil strepsirrhines) beginning their evolutionary radiations. As demonstrated by recent evidence from the Fayum and other locations in Africa, early haplorhine origins also date to a time in the middle Eocene.

- Old and New World anthropoids apparently shared their last common ancestry in the Eocene or early Oligocene and have gone their separate evolutionary ways ever since. In the Old World, the Oligocene reveals numerous possible early anthropoid ancestors, again mostly at the Fayum, but none of the modern lineages (Old World monkeys, gibbons, large-bodied apes) can definitely be traced to this time.
- The Miocene reveals the first Old World monkeys and a highly complex array of ape forms; many large-bodied varieties are represented from remains discovered in Africa, Asia, and Europe. Some early forms from Kenya and Uganda (the proconsuloids) are more primitive than all of the hominoids from Eurasia. It is likely that one of these (*Afropithecus*) migrated into Europe to give rise to the later true apes. The first

true ape, *Griphopithecus*, is known from the early-middle Miocene of Europe, which is where apes had their initial origin and adaptive radiation. Later they made their way into Asia and finally back into Africa.
- Connecting fossil ape species of the Middle and Late Miocene with modern-day apes has been problematic. Though there's little firm evidence tying Miocene fossil forms to living apes or humans, morphological evidence suggests that *Yuanmoupithecus* may be related to the gibbon, and *Khoratpithecus* is probably closely related to the orangutan. *Ouranopithecus* or a related form may have migrated back into Africa, where the more recently discovered *Nakalipithecus* might be an ancestor of the African apes.

Critical Thinking Questions

1. How do molecular and fossil age estimates differ? How can they be used to give us a more complete view of the past?

2. Why is it difficult to distinguish the earliest members of the primate order from other placental mammals? If you found a nearly complete skeleton of an early Paleocene mammal, what structural traits

might lead you to determine that it was a euprimate?

3. Compare and contrast the adapoids and omomyoids with living members of the primate order. Why do we call them lemur- or tarsierlike and not lemurs and tarsiers?

4. Where is the Fayum, and why is it significant in primate evolution? Are there any other sites where so

many fossil primates have been found? Why or why not?

5. Where do the first true apes arise and from where do they migrate? How are the earliest forms different from extant groups and to whom are they most closely related?

CONNECTIONS

Fossil evidence indicates our primate origins date to at least 65 million years ago.

Paleoanthropology, which includes physical anthropology, archaeology, and geology, provides the scientific basis to understand hominin evolution.

The first more human-like animals (hominins) appeared in Africa around 6 mya ago and evolved into a variety of different species.

Paleoanthropology: Reconstructing Early Hominin Behavior and Ecology

9

Understanding Our Direct Evolutionary Connections: What's a Hominin?

What's in a Name?

Biocultural Evolution: The Human Capacity for Culture

Discovering Human Evolution: The Science of Paleoanthropology

Connecting the Dots through Time: Paleoanthropological Dating Methods

Experimental Archaeology

Stone Tool (Lithic) Technology

Analysis of Bone

Reconstruction of Early Hominin Environments and Behavior

Why Did Hominins Become Bipedal?

Student Learning Objectives   After studying the material in this chapter, you should be able to:

▸ Explain what is meant by *mosaic evolution* and why it is an important concept in understanding hominin evolution.

▸ Explain what is meant by *biocultural evolution* and provide examples of how it might have influenced the development of the earliest cultural behavior in hominins and also simultaneously influenced biological/anatomical changes in them.

▸ Describe why paleoanthropology is necessarily a multidisciplinary science and discuss the major subdisciplines that contribute to it.

▸ Compare and contrast relative versus chronometric dating methods and describe some of the major techniques used.

▸ Discuss what the earliest tools thus far discovered looked like and explain how they may have been made.

▸ Describe the different hypotheses that try to account for the evolution of bipedal locomotion and discuss the strengths and weaknesses of each.

A portion of a pig's tusk, a small sample of volcanic sediment, a battered rock, a primate's molar: What do these seemingly unremarkable remains have in common, and more to the point, why are they of interest to paleoanthropologists? First of all, if they're all discovered at sites in Africa or Eurasia, they *may* be quite ancient—indeed, perhaps millions of years old. Further, some of these materials actually inform scientists directly of

NASA satellite image showing East Africa.

NASA/Science Photo Library/Photo Researchers;
Top Images: Russell L. Ciochon; Institute of Human Origins, photo by Nanci Kahn

quite precise dating of the finds. Last and most exciting, some of these finds may have been modified, used, and discarded by bipedal creatures who looked and behaved in some ways like ourselves but were in other respects very different. And what of that molar? Is it a fossilized remnant of an ancient hominin? These are the kinds of questions asked by paleoanthropologists, and to answer them, these researchers travel to remote locales across the Old World.

How do we distinguish possible hominins from other types of animals (most notably from other primates), especially when all we have are fragmentary fossil remains from just a small portion of a skeleton? How do humans and our most distant ancestors compare with other animals? In the last three chapters, we've seen how humans are classified as primates, structurally, genetically, and behaviorally, and how our evolutionary history coincides with that of other mammals and specifically other primates. Even so, we're a unique kind of primate, and our ancestors have been adapted to a particular lifestyle for several million years. Some late Miocene apes probably began this process close to 7 mya, though better-preserved fossil discoveries reveal more definitive evidence of hominins shortly after 4 mya.

We're able to determine the hominin nature of these remains by more than the structure of teeth and bones; we know that these animals were hominins also because of the way they behaved—emphasizing once again the *biocultural* nature of human evolution. In this chapter, we'll discuss the methods scientists use to explore early hominin behavior and ecology.

Understanding Our Direct Evolutionary Connections: What's a Hominin?

The earliest evidence of hominins that has been found dates to the end of the Miocene and mainly includes dental and cranial remains. However, dental features alone do not fully describe the unique features of hominins, and they certainly are not distinctive of the later stages of human evolution. Modern humans, as well as our most immediate hominin ancestors, are distinguished from the great apes by more obvious features than tooth and jaw dimensions. For example, various scientists have pointed to such distinctive hominin characteristics as bipedal locomotion, large brain size, and toolmaking behavior as being significant (at some stage) in defining what makes a hominin.

It's important to recognize that all these characteristics did not develop simultaneously or at the same pace. In fact, over the last several million years of hominin evolution, a very different pattern has been evident, in which the various components (dentition, locomotion, brain size, and toolmaking) have developed at quite different rates. This pattern, in which anatomical traits and behavioral systems evolve at different rates, is called **mosaic evolution**. As we first pointed out in Chapter 1 and will emphasize in this and the next chapter, the single most important defining characteristic of the full course of hominin evolution is bipedal locomotion. In the earliest stages of hominin emergence, skeletal evidence indicating bipedal locomotion is the only truly reliable indicator that these fossils were indeed hominins. But in later stages of hominin evolution, other features, especially those relating to brain development and behavior, become highly significant (Fig. 9-1).

These behavioral aspects of hominin emergence—particularly toolmaking—are what we'd like to emphasize in this chapter. Important structural attributes of the hominin brain, teeth, and especially locomotor apparatus are discussed in the next chapter, where we investigate early hominin anatomical adaptations in greater detail.

mosaic evolution A pattern of evolution in which the rate of evolution in one functional system varies from that in other systems. For example, in hominin evolution, the dental system, locomotor system, and neurological system (especially the brain) all evolved at markedly different rates.

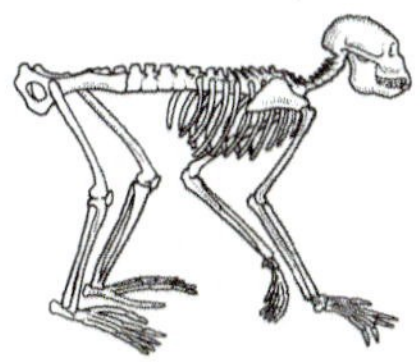

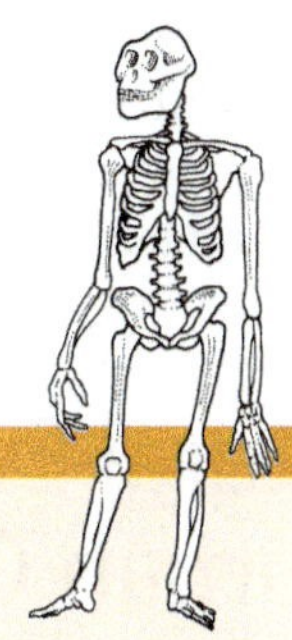

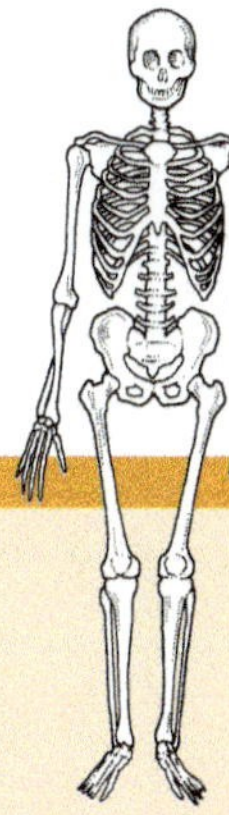

(Miocene, generalized hominoid)	(Early hominin)	(Modern *Homo sapiens*)				
20 mya		4 mya	3 mya	2 mya	1 mya	0.5 mya

LOCOMOTION

Quadrupedal: long pelvis; some forms capable of considerable arm swinging, suspensory locomotion	Bipedal: shortened pelvis; some differences from later hominins, showing smaller body size and long arms relative to legs; long fingers and toes; probably capable of considerable climbing	Bipedal: shortened pelvis; body size larger; legs longer; fingers and toes not as long

BRAIN

Small compared to hominins, but large compared to other primates; a fair degree of encephalization	Larger than Miocene forms, but still only moderately encephalized; prior to 6 mya, no more encephalized than chimpanzees	Greatly increased brain size—highly encephalized

DENTITION

Large front teeth (including canines); molar teeth variable, depending on species; some have thin enamel caps, others thick enamel caps	Moderately large front teeth (incisors); canines somewhat reduced; upper canine/lower first premolar lack honing complex; molar tooth enamel caps very thick	Small incisors; canines further reduced; canine/premolar honing complex absent; molar tooth enamel caps thick

TOOLMAKING BEHAVIOR

Unknown—no stone tools; probably had capabilities similar to chimpanzees	In earliest stages unknown; no stone tool use prior to 2.6 mya; probably somewhat more oriented toward tool manufacture and use than chimpanzees	Stone tools found after 2.6 mya; increasing trend of cultural dependency apparent in later hominins

▲ **Figure 9-1**
Mosaic evolution of hominin characteristics: a postulated time line.

What's in a Name?

Throughout this book, we refer to members of the human family as hominins (the technical name for members of the tribe Hominini). Most professional paleoanthropologists now prefer this terminology, since it more accurately reflects evolutionary relationships. As we mentioned briefly in Chapter 6, the more traditional classification of hominoids is not as accurate and actually misrepresents key evolutionary relationships.

Over the last several years detailed molecular evidence has clearly shown that the great apes (traditionally classified as pongids and including orangutans, gorillas, chimpanzees, and bonobos) do not make up a coherent evolutionary group sharing a single common ancestor and thus are not a *monophyletic* group. Indeed, the molecular data indicate that the African great apes (gorillas, chimpanzees, and bonobos) are significantly more closely related to humans than is the orangutan. What's more, at an even closer evolutionary level, we now know that chimpanzees and bonobos are yet more closely linked to humans than is the gorilla. Hominoid classification has been significantly revised to show these more complete relationships, and two further taxonomic levels (subfamily and tribe) have been added.

We should mention a couple of important ramifications of this new classification. First, it further emphasizes the *very* close evolutionary relationship of humans with African apes and most especially with chimpanzees and bonobos. Second, the term *hominid*, which has been used for decades to refer to our specific evolutionary lineage, has a quite different meaning in the revised classification; now it refers to *all* great apes and humans together.

Biocultural Evolution: The Human Capacity for Culture

One of the most distinctive behavioral features of humans is our extraordinary elaboration of and dependence on **culture**. Certainly other primates, and many other animals for that matter, modify their environments. As we saw in Chapter 7, chimpanzees especially are known for such behaviors as using termite sticks, and some chimpanzees as well as capuchin monkeys even carry rocks to use for crushing nuts. Because of such observations, we're on shaky ground when it comes to drawing sharp lines between early hominin toolmaking behavior and that exhibited by other animals.

Another point to remember is that human culture, at least as it's defined in contemporary contexts, involves much more than toolmaking capacity. For humans, culture integrates an entire adaptive strategy involving cognitive, political, social, and economic components. *Material culture*—or the tools humans use—is but a small portion of this cultural complex.

Still, when we examine the archaeological record of earlier hominins, what's available for study is almost exclusively limited to material culture, especially the bits and pieces of broken stone left over from tool manufacture. This is why it's extremely difficult to learn anything about the earliest stages of hominin cultural development before the regular manufacture of stone tools. As you'll see, this most crucial cultural development has been traced to approximately 2.6 mya (Semaw et al., 2003). Yet because of our contemporary primate models, we can assume that hominins were undoubtedly using other kinds of tools (made of perishable materials) and displaying a whole array of other cultural behaviors long before then. But with no "hard" evidence preserved in the archaeological record, our understanding of the early development of these nonmaterial cultural components remains elusive.

The fundamental basis for human cultural success relates directly to our cognitive abilities. Again, we're not dealing with an absolute distinction but a relative one. As you've already learned, other primates, as documented in the great apes, have some of the language capabilities exhibited by humans. Even so, modern humans display these abilities in a complexity several orders of magnitude beyond that of any other animal. And only humans are so completely dependent on symbolic communication and its cultural by-products that contemporary *Homo sapiens* could not survive without them.

At this point you may be wondering when the unique combination of cognitive, social, and material cultural adaptations became prominent in human evolution. In answering that question we must be careful to recognize the complex nature of culture; we can't expect it to always contain the same elements across species (as when comparing ourselves with nonhuman primates) or through time (when trying to reconstruct ancient hominin behavior). Richard Potts (1993) has critiqued such overly simplistic perspectives and suggests instead a more dynamic approach,

culture Behavioral aspects of human adaptation, including technology, traditions, language, religion, marriage patterns, and social roles. Culture is a set of learned behaviors transmitted from one generation to the next by nonbiological (i.e., nongenetic) means.

one that incorporates many subcomponents (including aspects of behavior, cognition, and social interaction).

We know that the earliest hominins almost certainly didn't regularly manufacture stone tools (at least none that have been found and identified as such). These earliest members of the hominin lineage, dating back to approximately 6 to 5 mya, may have carried objects such as naturally sharp stones or stone flakes, parts of carcasses, and pieces of wood around their home ranges. At the very least, we would expect them to have displayed these behaviors to at least the same degree as exhibited by living chimpanzees.

Also, as you'll see in the next chapter, by around 6 mya, hominins had developed one crucial advantage: They were bipedal and so could more easily carry all kinds of objects from place to place. Ultimately, the efficient exploitation of resources widely distributed in time and space would most likely have led to using "central" spots where key components—especially stone objects—were cached, or collected (Potts, 1991; see "A Closer Look: What Were Early Hominins Doing, and How Do We Know?" on pages 268–269).

What we know for sure is that over a period of several million years, during the formative stages of hominin emergence, many components interacted, but not all of them developed simultaneously. As cognitive abilities developed, more efficient means of communication and learning resulted. Largely because of consequent neurological reorganization, more elaborate tools and social relationships also emerged. These, in turn, selected for greater intelligence, which in turn selected for further neural elaboration. Quite clearly these mutual dynamic interactions are at the very heart of what we call hominin *biocultural* evolution.

Discovering Human Evolution: The Science of Paleoanthropology

To adequately understand human evolution, we obviously need a broad base of information. It's the paleoanthropologist's task to recover and interpret all the clues left by early hominins. *Paleoanthropology* is defined as "the study of ancient humans." As such, it's a diverse **multidisciplinary** pursuit seeking to reconstruct every possible bit of information concerning the dating, anatomy, behavior, and ecology of our hominin ancestors. Over the past few decades, the study of early humans has marshaled the specialized skills of many different kinds of scientists. This growing and exciting adventure includes but is not limited to geologists, vertebrate paleontologists, archaeologists, physical anthropologists, and paleoecologists (Table 9-1).

Geologists, usually working with other paleoanthropologists, do the initial surveys to locate potential early hominin sites. Many sophisticated techniques aid in

Table 9-1	Subdisciplines of Paleoanthropology	
Physical Sciences	**Biological Sciences**	**Social Sciences**
Geology	Physical anthropology	Archaeology
Stratigraphy	Paleoecology	Ethnoarchaeology
Petrology	Paleontology	Cultural anthropology
(rocks, minerals)	(fossil animals)	Ethnography
Pedology (soils)	Palynology	Psychology
Geomorphology	(fossil pollen)	
Geophysics	Primatology	
Chemistry		
Taphonomy		

multidisciplinary Pertaining to research involving mutual contributions and the cooperation of experts from various scientific fields, or disciplines.

A Closer Look What Were Early Hominins Doing, and How Do We Know?

Many years ago, the popular interpretation of the bone refuse and stone tools discovered at Olduvai Gorge and other sites suggested that most or all of these materials resulted from hominin activities. However, a later and more comprehensive reanalysis of the bone remains from Olduvai localities has challenged this view (Binford, 1981, 1983). Olduvai is so important because it has the most complete and best studied paleoanthropological record of any early hominin site in the world. Archaeologist Lewis Binford has criticized those who are drawn too quickly to concluding that these bone scatters are the remnants of hominin behavior patterns while simultaneously ignoring the possibility of other explanations.

From information concerning the kinds of animals present, which body parts were found, and the differences in preservation among these skeletal elements, Binford has concluded that much of what's preserved can be explained by carnivore activity. This conclusion has been reinforced by certain details observed by Binford himself in Alaska—details on animal kills, scavenging, the transportation of elements, and preservation that are the result of wolf and dog behaviors. Binford describes his approach:

> I took as "known," then, the structure of bone assemblages produced in various settings by animal predators and scavengers; and as "unknown" the bone deposits excavated by the Leakeys at Olduvai Gorge. Using mathematical and statistical techniques I considered to what degree the finds from Olduvai Gorge could be accounted for in terms of the results of predator behavior and how much was "left over." (Binford, 1983, pp. 56–57)

Binford isn't arguing that all of the remains found at Olduvai resulted from nonhominin activity. In fact, he recognizes that "residual material" was consistently found on surfaces with high tool concentration "which could not be explained by what we know about African animals" (Binford, 1983).

Support for the idea that early hominins utilized at least some of the bone refuse has come from a totally different perspective. Researchers have analyzed (both macroscopically and microscopically) the cut marks left on fossilized bones. By experimenting with modern materials, they've been able to delineate more clearly the differences between marks left by stone tools and those left by animal teeth or other factors (Bunn, 1981; Potts and Shipman, 1981). Analyses of bones from several early localities at Olduvai have shown unambiguously that hominins used these specimens and left telltale cut marks from their stone tools. The sites investigated so far reveal a somewhat haphazard cutting and chopping, apparently unrelated to deliberate disarticulation. So the conclusion is that hominins scavenged carcasses, probably of carnivore kills, and did *not* hunt large animals themselves (Shipman, 1983). As we'll see in a moment, new evidence of possible cut marks as well as indications of pounding to get at the marrow has been found at a site in Ethiopia dating as far back as 3.4 mya.

Following and expanding on the experimental approaches pioneered by Binford, Bunn, and others, Robert Blumenschine, of Rutgers University, has more recently conducted a more detailed analysis of the Olduvai material. Like his predecessors, Blumenschine has also concluded that the cut marks on animal bones are the result of hominin processing (Blumenschine, 1995). Blumenschine and colleagues further surmise that most meat acquisition (virtually all from large animals) was the result of scavenging (from remains of carnivore kills or from animals that died from natural causes). In fact, these researchers suggest that scavenging was a crucial adaptive strategy for early hominins and considerably influenced their habitat usage, diet, and utilization of stone tools (Blumenschine and Cavallo, 1992; Blumenschine and Peters, 1998). What's more, Blumenschine and colleagues have developed a model detailing how scavenging and other early hominin adaptive strategies integrate into patterns of land use (that is, differential utilization of various niches in and around Olduvai). From this model, they formulated specific hypotheses concerning the predicted distribution of artifacts and animal remains in different areas at Olduvai. Subsequent excavations at Olduvai were aimed specifically at testing these hypotheses.

this search, including aerial and satellite imagery (Fig. 9-2), though the most common way to find these sites is simply to trip over fossil remains. Vertebrate paleontologists are usually involved in this early survey work, helping to find fossil beds containing faunal (animal) remains, because where conditions are favorable for the preservation of bone from such species as pigs and elephants, hominin remains may also be preserved. Paleontologists also can (through comparison with known faunal sequences) give quick and dirty approximate age estimates of fossil sites in the

If early hominins (close to 2 mya) weren't hunting consistently, what did they obtain from scavenging the kills of other animals? One obvious answer is whatever meat was left behind. However, the position of the cut marks suggests that early hominins were often hacking at non-meat-bearing portions of the skeletons. Perhaps they were after bone marrow and brain, resources not fully exploited by other predators and scavengers (Binford, 1981; Blumenschine and Cavallo, 1992).

Exciting discoveries from the Bouri Peninsula of the Middle Awash of Ethiopia provide the best evidence yet for meat and marrow exploitation by early hominins. Dated to 2.5 mya (that is, as old as the oldest known firmly dated artifacts), antelope and horse fossils from Bouri show telltale incisions and breaks, indicating that bones were not only smashed to extract marrow but also cut, ostensibly to retrieve meat (de Heinzelin et al., 1999). The researchers who analyzed these materials have suggested that the greater dietary reliance on animal products may have been important in stimulating brain enlargement in the lineage leading to genus *Homo*.

Another recent research twist relating to the reconstruction of early hominin diets has come from the biochemical analysis of some hominin teeth from South Africa (dating to about the same time range as hominins from Olduvai—or perhaps slightly earlier). In an innovative application of **stable carbon isotope** analysis, Matt Sponheimer and Julia Lee-Thorp found that these early hominin teeth revealed telltale chemical signatures relating to diet (Sponheimer and Lee-Thorp, 1999). In particular, the proportions of stable carbon isotopes indicated that these early hominins ate either grass products (such as seeds) or meat/marrow from animals that in turn had eaten grass products (that is, the hominins might well have derived a significant portion of their diet from meat or other animal products). What's more, newly collected stable carbon isotope data from another South African early hominin show a quite different diet from that of other South African finds and, indeed almost all other early hominins (Henry et al., 2012) (see Chapter 10). This evidence comes from an exciting new

▲ **Figure 1**

Hyenas scavenging a buffalo carcass in East Africa. Early hominins also scavenged animals that had been killed by predators. In so doing, they almost certainly competed with hyenas and other scavengers.

perspective that provides a more direct indicator of early hominin diets. While it's not clear how much meat these early hominins consumed, these new data do suggest that they were consistently exploiting more open regions of their environment. Moreover, a new laser technology makes it possible to detect, from a single tooth, what sorts of foods were eaten from year to year and even seasonally within the same year. Sponheimer, Thorp, and colleagues have used this new approach to show that some early hominins were able to flexibly move between different environments and exploit seasonally available foods (Sponheimer et al., 2006). To demonstrate that stable isotope data are accurate, researchers need to evaluate the influence of chemical changes (*diagenesis*) to bones and teeth that occurred during fossilization. Stable isotope methods will continue to play a prominent role in the reconstruction of hominin diets and paleoenvironments.

field without having to wait for the results of more time-consuming (though more accurate) analyses that will later be performed in a lab (Fig. 9-3).

Once identified, fossil beds likely to contain hominin finds are subjected to extensive field surveying. For some sites, generally those postdating 2.6 mya (roughly the age of the oldest firmly identified human artifacts), archaeologists take over in the search for hominin material traces. We don't necessarily have to find remains of early hominins themselves to know that they consistently occupied a

stable carbon isotopes Isotopes of carbon that are produced in plants in differing proportions, depending on environmental conditions. By analyzing the proportions of the isotopes contained in fossil remains of animals (who ate the plants), it's possible to reconstruct aspects of ancient diet and environments (particularly temperature and aridity).

Goddard Space Flight Center, NASA

▲ **Figure 9-2**
Satellite photo of geological exposures in northern Tanzania, near Olduvai Gorge. The mountainous regions are part of the Rift Valley. The lake has formed inside a volcanic crater.

artifacts   Objects or materials made or modified for use by hominins. The earliest artifacts are usually tools made of stone or occasionally bone.

particular area. Such material clues as **artifacts** inform us directly about early hominin activities. Modifying rocks according to a consistent plan or simply carrying them around from one place to another over fairly long distances and distributing them in a manner not explained by natural means—like movement due to streams or glaciers—is characteristic of no other animal but a hominin. So when we see such material evidence at a site, we know without a doubt that hominins were once present there.

We've suspected for a while that hominins likely used stone and other materials for a long time before they began modifying rock to a consistent (and recognizable) pattern. After all, chimpanzees carry rocks short distances and bash nuts with them (see Chapter 8). New evidence from the Dikika site in Ethiopia might indicate that hominins were using stone in an even more sophisticated way as far back as 3.4 mya (McPherron et al., 2010). No stone tools were found, but two animal bones show possible cut marks (see "A Closer Look," on page 268) as well as other marks suggesting that the bones were pounded with unmodified rocks (ostensibly to slice away meat and retrieve marrow). While it's true that this evidence doesn't mean that hominins were yet modifying rocks consistently to make tools, it potentially shows advanced behavior, including scavenging, meat eating, and marrow extraction that have not previously been considered possible for very early hominins. These finds are extremely important and have been very carefully investigated. However, just the two bones by themselves (and no stone tools) are not enough evidence for many paleoanthropologists to be entirely convinced that the eating of meat and marrow were yet typical behaviors of such ancient hominins (Domínguez-Rodrigo et al., 2010). Indeed, some researchers have argued that most of these modifications were caused by animal trampling, and that the purported cut marks are ambiguous at best (Domínguez-Rodrigo et al., 2010; Domínguez-Rodrigo and Alcala, 2016).

In 2011, crude stone tools were discovered by Sonia Harmand at the site of Lomekwi 3, located along the western shore of Lake Turkana, Kenya. Analyses by Harmand and colleagues (2015) of the tools and the geological deposits they are found in suggest that the tools date to 3.3 mya. If the geological context is correct, these finds would push back the date of the earliest stone tools approximately

▶ **Figure 9-3**
A geologist is shown making entries on a detailed map as he surveys a large area of exposures in the Hadar region of northeastern Ethiopia.

Institute of Human Origins, photo by Nanci Kahn

▲ **Figure 9-4**

Location of sites where early evidence of stone tools has been discovered. The dates shown for each site represent the earliest dated tools found at that location.

*Interpretation of the Dikika evidence is controversial. It includes bones with presumed cut marks. However, no stone tools have been found. Some researchers have argued that these modifications are in fact crocodile tooth marks or trampling damage instead of cut marks.

700,000 years earlier than the Oldowan tools from Gona, Ethiopia. However, controversy remains over the association of the stone tools and the deposits at Lomekwi 3. Domínguez-Rodrigo and Alcala (2016) have recently argued that the tools may not have originated from the geological context that was dated to 3.3 mya. This could suggest that the tools are not as old as originally claimed. Clearly more research is needed to substantiate the dates of these early tools.

Once an area has clearly been demonstrated to be a hominin site, much more concentrated research begins (Fig. 9-4). We should point out that a more mundane but significant aspect of paleoanthropology not reflected in Table 9-1 is the financial one. Just the initial survey work in usually remote areas costs many thousands of dollars, and mounting a concentrated research project costs several hundred thousand dollars more. This is why many projects are undertaken in areas where promising surface finds have already been made. Massive financial support is required from government agencies and private donations; therefore, it's unrealistic just to dig at random places. A great deal of a paleoanthropologist's effort and time is necessarily devoted to writing grant proposals or speaking on the lecture circuit to raise the required funds for this work.

Once the financial hurdle has been cleared, a coordinated research project can begin. Usually headed by an archaeologist or physical anthropologist, the field crew continues to survey and map the target area in great detail. In addition, field crew members begin searching carefully for bones and artifacts eroding out of the soil, taking pollen and soil samples for ecological analysis, and carefully collecting rock and other samples for use in various dating techniques. If, at this early stage of exploration, members of the field crew find fossil hominin remains, they will feel very lucky indeed. The international press usually considers human fossils the most exciting kind of discovery—a fortunate circumstance that produces wide publicity and often ensures future financial support. More likely, the crew will accumulate much information on the geological setting, ecological data (particularly faunal remains), and, with some luck, artifacts and other archaeological traces.

Although paleoanthropological fieldwork is typically a long and arduous process, the detailed analyses of collected samples and other data back in the laboratory are even more time-consuming. Archaeologists must clean, sort, label, and identify all artifacts, and vertebrate paleontologists must do the same for all faunal remains. Knowing the kinds of animals represented—whether forest browsers, woodland species, or open-country forms—greatly helps in reconstructing the local *paleoecological* settings in which early hominins lived. Analysis of the fossil pollen collected from hominin sites by a scientist called a palynologist further aids in developing a detailed environmental reconstruction. All these paleoecological analyses can assist in reconstructing the diet of early humans. Also, the **taphonomy** of the site must be worked out to understand its depositional history—that is, how the site formed over time and if its present state is in a *primary* or *secondary* **context**.

In the concluding stages of interpretation, the paleoanthropologist draws together these essentials:

1. *Dating*: geological, paleontological, geophysical
2. *Paleoecology*: paleontology, palynology, geomorphology, taphonomy
3. *Archaeological traces of behavior*
4. *Anatomical evidence from hominin remains*

By analyzing all this information, scientists try to "flesh out" the kind of creature that may have been our direct ancestor (or at least a very close relative). Primatologists may assist here by showing the detailed relationships between the anatomical structure and behavior of humans and that of contemporary non-human primates. Cultural anthropologists and ethnoarchaeologists (who study the "archaeology" of living groups by examining their material remains) may contribute ethnographic information concerning the varied nature of modern human behavior, particularly ecological adaptations of those contemporary hunter-gatherer groups exploiting roughly similar environmental settings as those reconstructed for a hominin site.

The end result of years of research by dozens of scientists will (we hope) produce a more complete and accurate understanding of human evolution—how we came to be the way we are. Both biological and cultural aspects of our ancestors contribute to this investigation, each process developing in relation to the other.

taphonomy (*taphos*, meaning "tomb") The study of how bones and other materials came to be buried in the earth and preserved as fossils. Taphonomists study the processes of sedimentation, the action of streams, preservation properties of bone, and carnivore disturbance factors.

context The environmental setting where an archaeological trace is found. Primary context is the setting in which the archaeological trace was originally deposited. A secondary context is one to which it has been moved (such as by the action of a stream).

Connecting the Dots through Time: Paleoanthropological Dating Methods

An essential objective of paleoanthropology is to place sites and fossils into a time frame. In other words, we want to know how old they are. How, then, do we date sites—or more precisely, the geological strata, or layers, in which sites are found? The question is both reasonable and important, so let's examine the dating techniques

Robert Jurmain

◀ **Figure 9-5**

View of the main gorge at Olduvai Gorge in Tanzania. Note the clear sequence of geological beds. The discontinuity in the stratigraphic layers (to the right of the red arrow) is a major fault line. The stratigraphy at Olduvai is exceptionally well preserved, although even here you can see that it can be complicated.

used by paleontologists, archaeologists, and other scientists involved in paleoanthropological research.

Scientists use two kinds of dating for this purpose: relative dating and **chronometric dating** (also known as *absolute dating*). Relative dating methods tell us that something is older or younger than something else but not by how much. If, for example, a cranium is found at a depth of 50 feet and another cranium at 70 feet at the same site, we usually assume that the specimen discovered at 70 feet is older. We may not know the date (in years) of either one, but we'd know that one is older (or younger) than the other. Although this may not satisfy our curiosity about the actual number of years involved, it would give us some idea of the evolutionary changes in cranial morphology (structure), especially if we found several crania at different levels and compared them.

This method of relative dating is based on **stratigraphy** and was one of the first techniques to be used by scientists working with the vast period of geological time. Stratigraphy, in turn, is based on the **principle of superposition**, which states that a lower stratum (layer) is older than a higher stratum. Because much of the earth's crust has been laid down by layer after layer of sedimentary rock, much like the layers of a cake, stratigraphy has been a valuable aid in reconstructing the history of the earth and the life upon it.

Stratigraphic dating does, however, have some problems. Earth disturbances, such as volcanic activity, river activity, and mountain building, may shift strata and the objects within them; in such cases the chronology of the material may be difficult or even impossible to reconstruct. What's more, it's impossible to accurately determine the time period of a particular stratum—that is, how long it took to accumulate (Fig. 9-5).

Another method of relative dating is *fluorine analysis*, which applies only to bones (Oakley, 1963). Bones in the earth are exposed to the seepage of groundwater, which usually contains fluorine. The longer a bone lies in the earth, the more fluorine it will incorporate during the fossilization process. Bones deposited at the same time in the same location thus should contain the same amount of fluorine. Professor Kenneth Oakley, of the British Museum, used this technique in the early 1950s to expose the Piltdown (England) hoax by demonstrating that a human skull was considerably older than the jaw (ostensibly also human) found with it (Weiner, 1955).

chronometric dating (*chrono*, meaning "time," and *metric*, meaning "measure") A dating technique that gives an estimate in actual numbers of years; also known as absolute dating.

stratigraphy Study of the sequential layering of deposits.

principle of superposition In a stratigraphic sequence, the lower layers were deposited before the upper layers. Or, simply put, the stuff on top of a heap was put there last.

When a discrepancy in the fluorine content led Oakley and others to examine the bones more closely, they found that the jaw was not that of a hominin at all but of a young adult orangutan!

Unfortunately, fluorine analysis is useful only with bones found at the same location. Because the amount of fluorine in groundwater is based on local conditions, it varies from place to place. Also, some groundwater may not contain any fluorine. For these reasons it's impossible to use fluorine analysis when comparing bones from different localities.

In both stratigraphy and fluorine analysis, it's impossible to calculate the actual age of a geological stratum and the objects within it. To determine the age in years, scientists have developed various chronometric techniques based on the phenomenon of radioactive decay. Actually, the theory is pretty simple: Certain radioactive isotopes of elements are unstable, causing them to decay and form an isotopic variation of another element. Since the rate of decay follows a definite mathematical pattern, the radioactive material forms an accurate geological time clock. By measuring the amount of decay in a particular sample, scientists can calculate the number of years it took for that amount of decay to accumulate. Chronometric techniques have been used for dating the immense age of the earth as well as artifacts less than 1,000 years old. Several techniques have been employed for a number of years and are now quite well known.

The most important chronometric technique used to date early hominins involves potassium-40 (^{40}K), which has a **half-life** of 1.25 billion years and produces argon-40 (^{40}Ar). Known as the K/Ar or potassium-argon method, this procedure has been extensively used by paleoanthropologists in dating materials in the 1- to 5-million-year range, especially in East Africa, where past volcanic activity makes this dating technique possible. A variant of this technique, the ^{40}Ar/^{39}Ar method, has also been used to date several hominin localities. The ^{40}Ar/^{39}Ar method permits the analysis of smaller samples (even single crystals), reduces experimental error, and is more precise than standard K/Ar dating. Consequently, it can be used to date a wide chronological range—indeed, the entire hominin record, even up to modern times. Recent applications have provided excellent dates for several early hominin sites in East Africa (discussed in Chapter 10) as well as somewhat later sites in Java (discussed in Chapter 11). In fact, the technique was used to date the famous Mt. Vesuvius eruption of A.D. 79, which destroyed the city of Pompeii, as documented by ancient historians. Remarkably, the midrange date obtained by the ^{40}Ar/^{39}Ar technique was A.D. 73, just six years from the known date (Renne et al., 1997)! And still another radiometric dating method, this one measuring the decay of uranium into lead (the U/Pb method, with a half-life of 4.47 million years), has been used recently in South Africa to date hominin sites (De Ruiter et al., 2009; Dirks et al., 2010). Organic material, such as bone, can't be directly dated by these techniques; but the rock matrix in which the bone is found can be. Scientists used K/Ar dating to obtain a minimum date for the deposit containing the *Zinjanthropus* cranium discovered at Olduvai by dating a volcanic layer above the fossil (Fig. 9-6).

Rocks that provide the best samples for K/Ar and ^{40}Ar/^{39}Ar dating are those that have been heated to an extremely high temperature, such as that generated by volcanic activity. When the rock is in a molten state, argon, a gas, is driven off. As the rock cools and solidifies, ^{40}K continues to break down to argon; but now the gas is physically trapped in the cooled rock. To obtain the date of the rock, scientists reheat it and measure the escaping gas. Because the rock must in the past have been exposed to extreme heat, this limits these techniques to areas where sediments have been superheated, such as regions of past volcanic activity or meteorite falls.

Another well-known radiometric method popular with archaeologists makes use of carbon-14 (^{14}C), with a half-life of 5,730 years. It has been used to measure the age of organic materials (such as wood, bone, cloth, and plant remains) dating from less

half-life The time period in which one-half the amount of a radioactive isotope is converted chemically to a daughter product. For example, after 1.25 billion years, half the potassium-40 (^{40}K) remains; after 2.5 billion years, one-fourth remains.

than 1,000 years to more than 75,000 years ago, although accuracy is reduced for materials more than 40,000 years old. Since this technique is used to study the latter stages of hominin evolution, its applications relate to material discussed in Chapters 12 and 13.

Some inorganic artifacts can be directly dated through the use of **thermoluminescence (TL)**. This method, too, relies on the principle of radiometric decay. Stone material used in manufacturing tools invariably contains trace amounts of radioactive elements, such as uranium or thorium. As the rock gets heated (perhaps by accidentally falling into a campfire or deliberately being heated to help in its production), the rapid heating releases displaced beta particles trapped within the rock. As the particles escape, they emit a dull glow known as thermoluminescence. After that, radioactive decay resumes within the fired stone, again building up electrons at a steady rate. To determine the age of an archaeological sample, the researcher must heat the sample to 500°C and measure its thermoluminescence, from which the date can be calculated. Used especially by archaeologists to date ceramic pots from recent sites, TL can also be used to date burned flint tools from earlier hominin sites.

Like TL, two other techniques used to date sites from the latter phases of hominin evolution (where neither K/Ar nor radiocarbon dating is possible) are uranium series dating and electron spin resonance (ESR) dating. Uranium series dating relies on the radioactive decay of short-lived uranium isotopes, and ESR is similar to TL because it's based on measuring trapped electrons. However, while TL is used on heated materials such as clay or stone tools, ESR is used on the dental enamel of animals. All three of these dating methods have been used to provide key dating controls for hominin sites discussed in Chapters 11 through 13.

You should realize that none of these methods is precise. Each one has problems that must be carefully considered during laboratory measurement and in collecting material to be analyzed. Because the methods aren't perfectly accurate, approximate dates are given as probability statements with an error range. For example, a date given as 1.75 ± 0.2 mya should be read as having a 67 percent chance that the actual date lies somewhere between 1.55 and 1.95 mya (see "A Closer Look: Chronometric Dating Estimates").

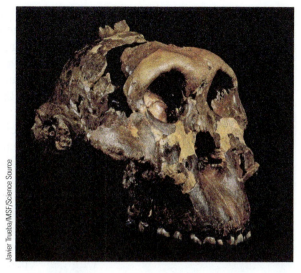

Javier Trueba/MSF/Science Source

▲ **Figure 9-6**
Zinjanthropus cranium, discovered at Olduvai Gorge and dated to 1.75 mya. This dating (using the potassium/argon method) was extraordinarily important, because previously most paleoanthropologists didn't think hominins appeared until around a million years ago.

thermoluminescence (TL) (ther-mo-loo-min-ess´-ence) A technique for dating certain archaeological materials (such as stone tools) that were heated in the past and that, upon reheating, release the stored energy of radioactive decay as light.

A Closer Look Chronometric Dating Estimates

Chronometric dates are usually determined after testing several geological samples. The dates that result from such testing are combined and expressed statistically. For example, say that five different samples are used to give the K/Ar date 1.75 ± 0.2 mya for a particular geological bed. The individual results from all five samples are totaled together to give an average date (here, 1.75 mya), and the standard deviation is calculated (here, 0.2 million years; that is, 200,000 years). The dating estimate is then reported as the mean plus or minus (±) 1 standard deviation. Those of you who have taken statistics will realize that (assuming a normal distribution) 67 percent of a distribution of dates is included within 1 standard deviation (±) of the mean. Thus, the chronometric result, as shown in the reported range, is simply a probability statement that 67 percent of the dates from all the samples tested fell within the range of dates from 1.55 to 1.95 mya. You should carefully read chronometric dates and study the reported ranges. It's likely that the smaller the range, the more samples were analyzed. Smaller ranges mean more precise estimates; better laboratory controls will also increase precision.

Institute of Human Origins, Don Johanson

▲ **Figure 9-7**

A geologist carefully takes a sample of sediment containing magnetically charged particles for paleomagnetic dating. He must very precisely record the exact compass orientation so that it can be correlated with the sequence of magnetic orientations.

An important means of cross-checking dates is called **paleomagnetism**. This technique is based on the constantly shifting nature of the earth's magnetic pole. Of course, the earth's magnetic pole is now oriented in a northerly direction, but this hasn't always been so. In fact, the orientation and intensity of the geomagnetic field have undergone numerous documented changes in the last few million years. From our current viewpoint, we call a northern orientation "normal" and a southern one "reversed." Paleomagnetic dating is accomplished by carefully taking samples of sediments that contain magnetically charged particles. Since these particles maintain the magnetic orientation they had when they were consolidated into rock (millions of years ago), we have a kind of "fossil compass" (Fig. 9-7). Then the paleomagnetic sequence is compared against the K/Ar dates to see if they agree. Some complications may arise, but once these oscillations in the geomagnetic pole are worked out, the sequence of paleomagnetic orientations can provide a valuable cross-check for K/Ar age determinations. Paleomagnetic dating has also been used recently in South Africa to confirm the U/Pb dates from a newly discovered hominin site (Dirks et al., 2010).

A final dating technique used at several African sites is based on the regular evolutionary changes in well-known groups of mammals. This technique, called *faunal correlation,* or **biostratigraphy**, provides yet another means of cross-checking the other methods. This technique employs some of the same methods used in relative stratigraphic dating, but it incorporates information on sequences of faunal remains from different sites. For instance, the presence of particular fossil pigs, elephants, antelopes, rodents, and carnivores in areas where dates are known (by K/Ar, for example) can be used to extrapolate an approximate age for other, more hard-to-date sites by noting which genera and species are present at those sites.

All these methods—K/Ar dating, paleomagnetism, and biostratigraphy—have been used in dating early hominin sites. So many different dating techniques are necessary because no single method is perfectly reliable by itself. Sampling error, contamination, and experimental error can all introduce ambiguities into our so-called absolute dates. Because the sources of error are different for each technique, however, cross-checking among several independent methods is the most reliable way of authenticating the chronology for early hominin sites.

Experimental Archaeology

Simply classifying artifacts into categories and types is not enough. We can learn considerably more about our ancestors by understanding how they made and used their tools. It is, after all, the artifactual traces of prehistoric tools of stone (and, to a lesser degree, bone) that provide much of our information concerning early human behavior. Tons of stone debris litter archaeological sites worldwide. A casual walk along the bottom of Olduvai Gorge could well be interrupted every few seconds by tripping over prehistoric tools!

Clearly, archaeologists are presented with a wealth of information revealing at least one part of human material culture. What do these artifacts tell us about our ancestors? How were these tools made, and how were they used? To answer these questions, contemporary archaeologists have tried to reconstruct prehistoric techniques of stone toolmaking, butchering, and so forth. In this way, experimental archaeologists are, in a sense, trying to re-create the past.

paleomagnetism   Dating method based on the earth's shifting magnetic pole.

biostratigraphy   A relative dating technique based on the regular changes seen in evolving groups of animals as well as the presence or absence of particular species.

Stone Tool (Lithic) Technology

Stone is by far the most common residue of prehistoric cultural behavior. For this reason, archaeologists have long been keenly interested in this material.

When struck properly, certain types of stone will fracture in a controlled way; these nodules are called **blanks**. The smaller piece that comes off is called a **flake**, while the larger remaining chunk is called a **core** (Fig. 9-8). Both core and flake have sharp edges that are useful for cutting, sawing, or scraping. The earliest hominin cultural inventions probably used nondurable materials that didn't survive archaeologically (such as digging sticks or ostrich eggshells used as watertight containers). Still, a basic human invention was the recognition that stone can be fractured to produce sharp edges.

For many years, it's been assumed that in the earliest known stone tool industry (that is, the Oldowan), both core and flake tools were deliberately manufactured as final, desired products. Such core implements as "choppers" were thought to be central artifactual components of these early **lithic** assemblages (in fact, the Oldowan is often depicted as a "chopping tool industry"). However, detailed reevaluation of these artifacts has thrown these traditional assumptions into doubt. By carefully analyzing the attributes of Oldowan artifacts from Olduvai, Potts (1991, 1993) concluded that the so-called core tools really weren't tools after all. He suggests instead that early hominins were deliberately producing flake tools, and the various stone choppers were simply "incidental stopping points in the process of removing flakes from cores" (Potts, 1993, p. 60). As Potts concludes, "The flaked stones of the Oldowan thus cannot be demonstrated to constitute discrete target designs, but can be shown to represent simple by-products of the repetitive act of producing sharp flakes" (Potts, 1993, pp. 60–61).

Breaking rocks by bashing them together is one thing. Producing consistent results, even apparently simple flakes, is quite another. You might want to give it a try, just to appreciate how difficult making a stone tool can be. It takes years of practice before modern stone **knappers** learn the intricacies—the type of rock to choose, the kind of hammer to employ, the angle and velocity with which to strike, and so on. Such experience allows us to appreciate how skilled in stoneworking our ancestors truly were.

Flakes can be removed from cores in various ways. The object in making a tool, however, is to produce a usable cutting surface. By reproducing results similar to those of earlier stoneworkers, experimental archaeologists can infer which kinds of techniques *might* have been employed.

For example, the nodules (now thought to be blanks) found in sites in Bed I at Olduvai (circa 1.85 to 1.2 mya) are flaked on one side only (that is, *unifacially*). It's possible, but by no means easy, to produce such implements by hitting one stone—the hammerstone—against another—the core—in a method called **direct percussion** (Fig. 9-9).

However, in later sites, particularly well studied at Olduvai (circa 400,000 ya*), most of the tools are flaked on both sides (that is, *bifacially*) and have long rippled edges. Such a result can't be reproduced by direct percussion with just a hammerstone. The edges must have been straightened ("retouched") with a "soft" hammer, such as bone or antler.

Reproducing implements similar to those found in later stages of human cultural development calls for even more sophisticated techniques. Tools such as the delicate **microliths** found in the uppermost beds at Olduvai (circa 17,000 ya), the

▲ **Figure 9-8**
Flake and core.

▲ **Figure 9-9**
Direct percussion.

blanks In archaeology, stones suitably sized and shaped to be further worked into tools.

flake A thin-edged fragment removed from a core.

core A stone reduced by flake removal. A core may or may not itself be used as a tool.

lithic (*lith*, meaning "stone") Referring to stone tools.

knappers People (frequently archaeologists) who make stone tools.

direct percussion Striking a core or flake with a hammerstone.

microliths (*micro*, meaning "small," and *lith*, meaning "stone") Small stone tools usually produced from narrow blades punched from a core; found especially in Africa during the latter part of the Pleistocene.

*y.a. = years ago

▲ **Figure 9-10**
Pressure flaking.

superb Solutrean blades from Europe (circa 20,000 ya), and the expertly crafted Folsom projectile points from the New World (circa 10,000 ya) all require a mastery of stone matched by few knappers today.

To reproduce implements like those just mentioned, the knapper must remove extremely thin flakes. This can be done only through **pressure flaking**—for example, using a pointed piece of bone, antler, or hard wood and pressing firmly against the stone (Fig. 9-10).

Once the tools were manufactured, our ancestors used them in ways that we can infer through further experimentation. For example, archaeologists from the Smithsonian Institution successfully butchered an entire elephant (which had died in a zoo) using stone tools they had made for that purpose (Park, 1978). Other archaeologists have cut down (small) trees using stone axes they had made.

Ancient tools themselves may carry telltale signs of how they were used. Lawrence Keeley performed a series of experiments in which he manufactured flint tools and then used them in diverse ways—whittling wood, cutting bone, cutting meat, and scraping skins. Viewing these implements under a microscope at fairly high magnification revealed patterns of polishes, striations, and other kinds of **microwear**. What's most intriguing is that these patterns varied depending on how the tool was used and which material was worked. For example, Keeley was able to distinguish among tools used on bone, antler, meat, plant materials, and hides. In the last case, he was even able to determine if the hides were fresh or dried! Orientations of microwear markings also give some indication of how the tool was used (such as for cutting or scraping). Because these experiments into stone tool manufacture and use reveal valuable information about variations in microwear morphology, researchers are able to use the experimentally produced data to make inferences about specific stone tool usage in the past. For example, the 9,000-year-old Paleoindian flake from Nebraska shown in Figure 9-11 shows microwear polish from cutting antler or bone. Evidence of microwear polish has been examined on even the extremely early hominin stone tools from Koobi Fora (East Lake Turkana), in Kenya (Keeley and Toth, 1981).

Advances in tool use studies include the application of scanning electron microscopy (SEM). Working at 10,000× magnification, researchers have found that the edges of stone implements sometimes retain plant fibers and amino acids as well as nonorganic residues, including **phytoliths**. Because phytoliths produced by different plant species are distinctive, there is good potential for identifying the botanical materials that came in contact with the tool during its use (Rovner, 1983). Such work is most exciting; for the first time, we may be able to make definite statements concerning the uses of ancient tools. In addition, phytoliths have also been found in the dental calculus (that is, plaque) on some Neandertal teeth as well as recently on 2-million-year-old hominins from South Africa (Henry et al., 2012). The findings for the early African hominins provided quite a surprise.

pressure flaking A method of removing flakes from a core by pressing a pointed implement (e.g., bone or antler) against the stone.

microwear Polishes, striations, and other diagnostic microscopic changes on the edges of stone tools.

phytoliths (*phyto*, meaning "hidden," and *lith*, meaning "stone") Microscopic silica structures formed in the cells of many plants, particularly grasses.

Analysis of Bone

Experimental archaeologists are also interested in the ways in which bone is altered by human and natural forces. Other scientists are vitally concerned with this process as well; in fact, it has produced an entire new branch of paleoecology—taphonomy. Taphonomists have carried out comprehensive research on how natural factors influence bone deposition and preservation. In South Africa, C. K. Brain collected data on contemporary African butchering practices, carnivore (for example, canids) disturbances of carcasses, and so forth and then correlated these factors with the kinds and numbers of elements usually found in bone accumulations (Brain, 1981). In this way, he was able to account for the accumulation of most of the bones in South African cave sites. Likewise, in East African game parks, observations have been made on decaying animals to measure the effects of weathering, carnivore chewing, and trampling (Behrensmeyer et al., 1979; Perkins, 2003).

Further insight into the many ways bone is altered by natural factors has come from experimental work in the laboratory (Boaz and Behrensmeyer, 1976). In an experiment conducted at the University of California, Berkeley, human bones were put into a running-water trough. Researchers observed how far the water carried different pieces and recorded how much and what kind of damage was done. Such information is extremely useful in interpreting early hominin sites. For example, the distribution of hominin fossils at Olduvai suggests that active water transport was less prevalent there than in the Omo River Valley in southern Ethiopia.

Detailed examination of bones may also provide evidence of butchering and bone breakage by hominins, including cut and percussion marks left by stone tools. Great care must be taken to distinguish marks left on bone by carnivore or rodent gnawing, weathering processes, hoof marks, or even normal growth. High magnification of a cut made by a stone tool may reveal a minutely striated and roughened groove scored into the bone's surface. Many such finds have been recognized at early hominin sites, including Olduvai Gorge (Bunn, 1981; Potts and Shipman, 1981). (See "A Closer Look," pp. 268–269.)

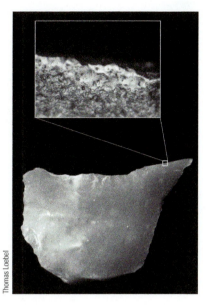

▲ **Figure 9-11**

Photomicrograph (200×) showing polish resulting from bone modification on a 9,000-year-old stone tool excavated from the O. V. Clary site in Nebraska by Dr. M.G. Hill, of Iowa State University.

Reconstruction of Early Hominin Environments and Behavior

Now that we've reviewed the many methods used by paleoanthropologists to collect their varied data, we can look at the intriguing ways in which this information is *interpreted*. Be aware that much of this interpretation is quite speculative and less amenable to scientific verification than more concrete sources of data (for example, that relating to dating, geology, or hominin anatomy). (In Chapter 1, we discussed how hypotheses are developed and tested by scientists, noting the requirement that *scientific* explanations be falsifiable.)

Paleoanthropologists are keenly interested not just in *how* early hominins evolved but also in *why* the process occurred the way it did. Accordingly, they frequently use the data available as a basis for broad, speculative scenarios that try to explain both early hominin adaptations to a changing environment and the new behaviors that these hominins adopted. Such scenarios are fascinating, and paleoanthropologists enjoy constructing them (and certainly many in the general public enjoy reading them). Without doubt, for scientists and laypersons alike, our curiosity inevitably leads to intriguing and sweeping generalizations. Still, in the following discussion, we'll focus on what is *known* from the paleoanthropological record itself and separate that from the more speculative conclusions. You, too, should evaluate these explanations with a critical eye and try to identify the empirical basis for each type of reconstruction. It's important not to accept a scenario merely because it's appealing (often because it's simple) or just because it seems plausible. We must always ask ourselves what kinds of evidence support a particular contention, how generally the explanation fits the evidence (that is, how consistent it is with different types of data from varied sources), and what types of new evidence might either help to verify or potentially falsify the interpretation.

Why Did Hominins Become Bipedal?

As we've noted several times, the adaptation of hominins to bipedal locomotion was *the* most fundamental adaptive shift among the early members of our lineage. But what were the factors that initiated this crucial change? Ecological theories have long been thought to be central to the development of bipedalism. Clearly, however, environmental influences would have to have occurred *before* evidence of well-adapted bipedal behavior could appear. In other words, the major shift would have been at the end of the Miocene. Although the evidence indicates that no *sudden* wide ecological change took place at that time, locally forests probably did become patchier as rainfall became more seasonal. Given the changing environmental conditions, did hominins come to the ground to seize the opportunities offered in these more open habitats? Did bipedalism quickly ensue, stimulated somehow by this new way of life? At a very general level, the answer to these questions is yes. Obviously, hominins did at some point become bipedal, and this adaptation took place on the ground. Likewise, hominins are more adapted to mixed and open-country habitats than are our closest modern ape cousins. Successful terrestrial bipedalism probably made possible the further adaptation to more arid, open-country terrain. Still, this rendition simply tells us *where* hominins found their niche, not *why*.

As always, it's wise to be cautious in speculating about causation in evolution. It is all too easy to draw superficial conclusions. For example, scientists often surmise that the mere availability of ground niches (and perhaps that there were no direct competitors for them) inevitably led the earliest hominins to terrestrial bipedalism. But consider this: Plenty of mammalian species, including some nonhuman primates, also live mostly on the ground in open country—and they aren't bipedal. Clearly, beyond such simplistic environmental generalizations, some more complex explanation for hominin bipedalism is required. There must have been something more than just an environmental opportunity to explain this adaptation to such a unique lifestyle.

Another issue sometimes overlooked in the discussion of early hominin bipedal adaptation is that these creatures did not suddenly become completely terrestrial; but they also didn't slouch about, as cartoon illustrations of a linear progression of human evolution would suggest. We know, for example, that all terrestrial species of nonhuman primates (including savanna baboons, hamadryas baboons, and patas monkeys; see Chapter 7) regularly seek out safe sleeping sites off the ground. These safe havens help protect against predation and are usually found in trees or on cliff faces. Likewise, early hominins almost certainly sought safety at night in the trees, even after they became well adapted to terrestrial bipedalism during daytime foraging. What's more, the continued opportunities for feeding in the trees would most likely have remained significant to early hominins well after they were also utilizing ground-based resources.

Various hypotheses explaining why hominins initially became bipedal have been suggested and are summarized in Table 9-2. The primary influences claimed to have stimulated the shift to bipedalism include acquiring the ability to carry objects (and offspring), hunting on the ground, gathering of seeds and nuts, feeding from bushes, improved thermoregulation (that is, keeping cooler on the open savanna), having a better view of open country (to spot predators), walking long distances, and provisioning by males of females with dependent offspring.

These are all creative scenarios, but once again they're not very conducive to rigorous testing and verification. Still, two of the more ambitious scenarios proposed by Clifford Jolly (1970) and Owen Lovejoy (1981) deserve further mention. Both of these views sought to link several aspects of early hominin ecology, feeding, and social behavior and both utilized models derived from studies of contemporary nonhuman primates.

Jolly's seed-eating hypothesis used the feeding behavior and ecology of gelada baboons as an analogy for very early hominins. Seed eating is an activity that requires keen hand-eye coordination, with presumed bipedal shuffling potentially improving the efficiency of foraging. In this view, early hominins are hypothesized

Table 9-2 | Possible Factors Influencing the Initial Evolution of Bipedal Locomotion in Hominins

Factor	Speculated Influence	Comments
Carrying (objects, tools, weapons, infants)	Upright posture freed the arms to carry various objects (including offspring).	Charles Darwin emphasized this view, particularly relating to tools and weapons; however, evidence of stone tools is found much later in the record than first evidence of bipedalism.
Hunting	Bipedalism allowed carrying of weapons, more accurate throwing of certain weapons, and improved long-distance walking.	Systematic hunting is now thought not to have been practiced until after the origin of bipedal hominins.
Seed and nut gathering	Feeding on seeds and nuts occurred while standing upright.	Model initially drawn from analogy with gelada baboons (see text).
Feeding from bushes	Upright posture provided access to seeds, berries, etc., in lower branches; analogous to adaptation seen in some specialized antelope.	Climbing adaptation already existed as prior ancestral trait in earliest hominins (i.e., bush and tree feeding already was established prior to bipedal adaptation).
Thermoregulation (cooling)	Vertical posture exposes less of the body to direct sun; increased distance from ground facilitates cooling by increased exposure to breezes.	Works best for animals active midday on savanna; moreover, adaptation to bipedalism may have initially occurred in woodlands, not on savanna.
Visual surveillance	Standing up provided better view of surrounding countryside (view of potential predators as well as other group members).	Behavior seen occasionally in terrestrial primates (e.g., baboons); probably a contributing factor, but unlikely as "prime mover."
Long-distance walking	Covering long distances was more efficient for a biped than for a quadruped (during hunting or foraging); mechanical reconstructions show that bipedal walking is less energetically costly than quadrupedalism (this is not the case for bipedal running).	Same difficulties as with hunting explanation; long-distance foraging on ground also appears unlikely adaptation in earliest hominins.
Male provisioning	Males carried back resources to dependent females and young.	Monogamous bond suggested; however, most skeletal data appear to falsify this part of the hypothesis (see text).

to have adapted to open country and bipedalism as a result of their primary adaptation to eating seeds and nuts (found on the ground). The key assumption is that early hominins were eating seeds acquired in similar ecological conditions to those of contemporary gelada baboons.

Lovejoy, meanwhile, has combined presumed aspects of early hominin ecology, feeding, pair bonding, infant care, and food sharing to devise his creative scenario. This view hinges on these assumptions: (1) that the earliest hominins had offspring at least as K-selected (see Chapter 7) as other large-bodied hominoids; (2) that hominin males ranged widely and provisioned females and their young, who remained more tied to a "home base"; and (3) that males were paired monogamously with females.

As we've noted, while not strictly testable, such scenarios do make certain predictions that can be potentially falsified or upheld. Accordingly, aspects of each scenario can be evaluated in light of more specific data (obtained from the paleoanthropological record). Regarding the seed-eating hypothesis, predictions relating to the size of the back teeth in most early hominins are met, but the proportions of the front teeth in many forms aren't what we'd expect to see in a committed seed eater. Besides, the analogy with gelada baboons is not as informative as once thought; these animals actually don't eat that many seeds and certainly aren't habitual bipeds. Finally, many of the characteristics that Jolly suggested were restricted to hominins (and geladas) and are also found in several late Miocene hominoids (who weren't hominins—nor obviously bipeds). Thus, regarding the seed-eating hypothesis, the proposed dental and dietary adaptations don't appear to be linked specifically to hominin origins or bipedalism.

Further detailed analyses of data have also questioned crucial elements of Lovejoy's male-provisioning scenario. The evidence that appears to most contradict this view is that all early hominins were quite sexually dimorphic (McHenry, 1992). According to Lovejoy's model (and analogies with contemporary monogamous nonhuman primates such as gibbons), there shouldn't be such dramatic differences in body size between males and females. Recent studies (Reno et al., 2003, 2005) have questioned this conclusion, suggesting that sexual dimorphism was only moderate at least for one species (*Australopithecus afarensis*). Further evaluation of another, even earlier hominin (*Ardipithecus*) has led Lovejoy to continue to forcefully argue for his male-provisioning model (Lovejoy, 2009). From a wider perspective, these conclusions appear at odds with most of the evidence regarding early hominins. What's more, the notions of food sharing (presumably including considerable meat), home bases, and long-distance provisioning are questioned by more controlled interpretations of the archaeological record.

Another imaginative view is also relevant to this discussion of early hominin evolution, since it relates the adaptation to bipedalism (which was first) to increased brain expansion (which came later). This interpretation, proposed by Dean Falk, suggests that an upright posture put severe constraints on brain size (since blood circulation and drainage would have been altered and cooling would consequently have been more limited than in quadrupeds). Falk thus hypothesizes that new brain-cooling mechanisms must have coevolved with bipedalism; this view is articulated in what she calls the "radiator theory" (Falk, 1990). Falk further surmises that the requirement for better brain cooling would have been particularly marked as hominins adapted to open-country ground living on the hot African savanna. Another interesting pattern observed by Falk concerns two varying cooling adaptations found in different early hominin species. She thus suggests that the type of "radiator" adapted in the genus *Homo* was particularly significant in reducing constraints on brain size—which presumably limited some other early hominins. The radiator theory works well, since it helps to explain not only the relationship of bipedalism to later brain expansion but also why only some hominins became dramatically encephalized.

The radiator theory, too, has been criticized by some paleoanthropologists. Most notably, the presumed species distinction concerning varying cooling mechanisms is not as obvious as suggested by the hypothesis. Both types of venous drainage systems can be found in contemporary *Homo sapiens* as well as within various early hominin species (that is, the variation is intraspecific, not just interspecific). Indeed, in some early hominin specimens, both systems can be found in the same individual (expressed on either side of the skull). Besides, as Falk herself has noted, the radiator itself didn't lead to larger brains; it simply helped reduce constraints on increased encephalization among hominins. It thus requires some further mechanism (prime mover) to explain why, in some hominin species, brain size increased the way it did.

As with any such ambitious effort, it's all too easy to find holes. Falk aptly reminds us that "the search for such 'prime movers' is highly speculative, and these theories do not lend themselves to hypothesis testing" (Falk, 1990, p. 334). Even so, the attempt to interrelate various lines of evidence, the use of contemporary primate models, and predictions concerning further evidence obtained from paleoanthropological contexts all conform to sound scientific methodology. All the views discussed here have contributed to this venture—one not just aimed at understanding our early ancestors but also seeking to refine its methodologies and scientific foundation.

How Do We Know?

This entire chapter is all about how we can learn about the age, behavior, and environments of our early hominin relatives. Most importantly is the key hominin adaptation to bipedal locomotion. The evolution of bipedalism contributed to the success of our ancestors and likely to our own success as well. There are many theories regarding the origin of bipedalism, and it's unclear which explanation is the most likely to be correct. It's also important to remember that evolutionary processes represent a series of trade-offs rather than a path toward perfection, so it's not surprising that some of the anatomical changes allowing bipedalism are less than optimal. In fact, the "imperfections" are pretty good evidence against intelligent design. What sort of designer would have a birth canal so narrow and twisted that the baby has to undergo a series of rotations in order to pass its head and shoulders through

the canal? In fact, complications of birth are a major cause of death in women throughout the world today, especially in the less industrialized nations.

W. M. Krogman wrote a thought-provoking article in 1951 entitled "The Scars of Human Evolution," in which he discussed the ubiquitous back problems that most of us have as a result of being bipedal. After all, the limb structure we have inherited initially evolved over millions of years in quadrupeds and has since been stitched together to function in an animal walking around on just two legs. The difficulties have probably gotten worse since Krogman wrote the article, given that one of the reasons we have back problems is all the sitting (often with bad posture) that we do—like sitting in front of the computer or being hunched over a textbook. Anthropologist Robert Anderson, who also happens to be a chiropractor, argues that if we are taught proper walking techniques as children and are

more careful of the way we sit, walk, lift, and carry, then we can prevent many of the back problems (especially lower back pain) so often encountered as people enter midlife. In this way, by considering how bipedalism evolved, we may be able to adopt walking and sitting habits that keep our spines more healthy throughout our lives.

What Do You Think?

In many ways, modern human lifestyles are at odds with our bipedal locomotion. At no point in history have humans been as inactive as today (especially in developed nations), which has led to a number of physical ailments such as obesity, loss of mobility, and lower back pain. What are some other "scars of evolution"? What are some ways we can alleviate these issues? ■

Summary of Main Topics

- Early hominins evolved at the end of the Miocene. Hominins show a pattern of mosaic evolution over the past six million years. More recent genetic data demonstrate that humans and chimpanzees are more closely related to one another than either is to other great apes.
- Paleoanthropologists use a biocultural approach to understand the evolution of the hominin lineage.
- The most important subfields of paleoanthropology are geology, paleontology, archaeology, and physical anthropology.
- The two types of dating techniques are relative dating and chronometric dating. Stratigraphy and paleomagnetism are the two most important examples of relative dating; potassium-argon dating and radiocarbon (^{14}C) dating are the most important examples of chronometric dating.
- Experimental archaeology provides a means from which to test hypotheses about past human behavior, including the function of stone tools. The first confidently dated stone tools thus far discovered date to about 2.6 mya. These tools include mostly simple flake implements and the discarded cores from which they were struck.
- Bipedal locomotion is thought to have been significantly influenced by one or more of the following: carrying objects, seed gathering or feeding from bushes, visual spotting of predators, and longdistance walking (the latter coming more recently in human evolution).

Critical Thinking Questions

1. You are leading a paleoanthropological expedition aimed at discovering an early hominin site dating to the Pliocene. In what part of the world will you pick your site, and why? After selecting a particular region, how will you identify which area(s) to survey on foot?
2. Why is it important to have accurate dates for paleoanthropological localities? Why is it necessary to use more than one kind of dating technique?
3. What do we mean when we say that early hominins displayed cultural behavior? What types of behavior do you think this would have included? (Imagine that you've been transported back in time by a time machine, and you're sitting in a tree watching a group of hominins at Olduvai Gorge 1.5 mya.)
4. Why is the reconstruction of hominin environments and behavior important to understanding the evolution of hominins?
5. What do we mean when we say that human evolution is biocultural? How do paleoanthropologists investigate early hominins using such a biocultural perspective?

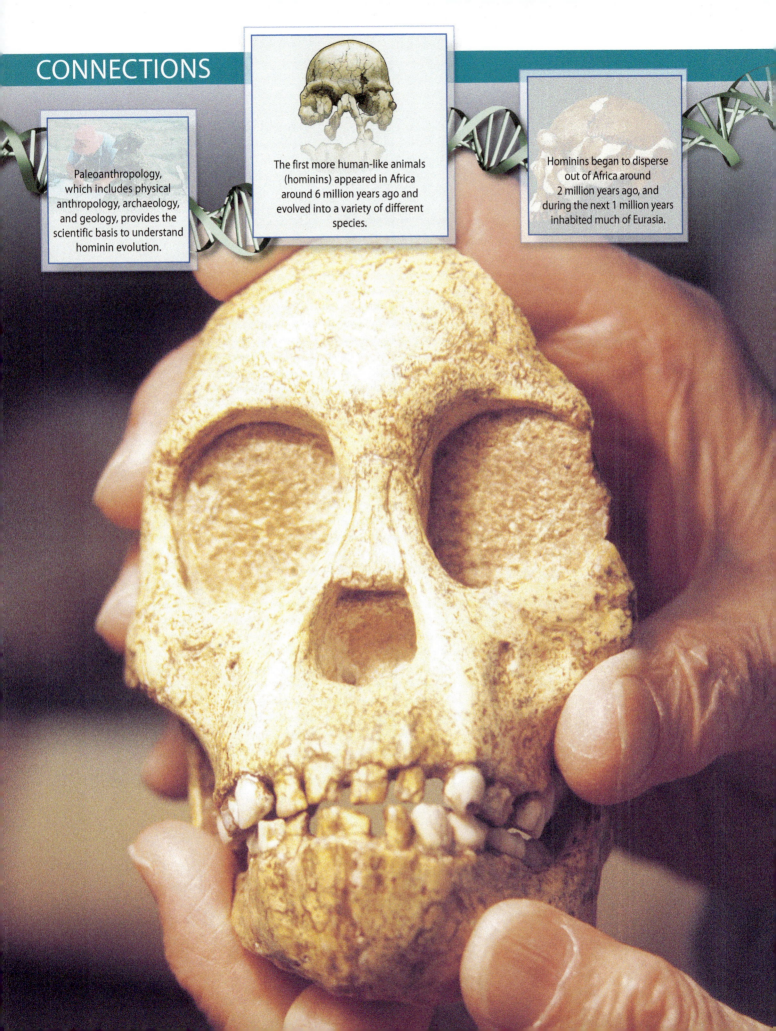

CONNECTIONS

Paleoanthropology, which includes physical anthropology, archaeology, and geology, provides the scientific basis to understand hominin evolution.

The first more human-like animals (hominins) appeared in Africa around 6 million years ago and evolved into a variety of different species.

Hominins began to disperse out of Africa around 2 million years ago, and during the next 1 million years inhabited much of Eurasia.

Hominin Origins in Africa

10

Walking the Walk: The Bipedal Adaptation

The Mechanics of Walking on Two Legs

Digging for Connections: Early Hominins from Africa

Pre-Australopiths (6.0+ to 4.4 mya)

Australopiths (4.2 to 1.2 mya)

A Contemporaneous and Very Different Kind of Hominin

Later More Derived Australopiths (3.0 to 1.2 mya)

New Connections: A Transitional Australopith?

Closer Connections: Early *Homo* (2.0 to 1.4 mya)

Interpretations: What Does It All Mean?

Seeing the Big Picture: Adaptive Patterns of Early African Hominins

Student Learning Objectives   After studying the material in this chapter, you should be able to:

▶ Describe the basic mechanics of bipedal locomotion and explain why evidence of bipedal locomotion is so important in the study of hominin evolution.

▶ Outline the three major early hominin groups from Africa, including species, important site locations, anatomical features, and dates.

▶ Describe what is considered the earliest evidence of the genus *Homo*, where and when these hominins lived, and what all this tells us about human evolution.

▶ Discuss the basic steps of a paleoanthropological investigation, beginning with locating sites and ending with publication of final research results.

▶ Outline the major adaptive patterns of early hominins.

Our species today dominates earth because we use our brains and cultural inventions to invade every corner of the planet. Yet, around 5 million years ago, our ancestors were little more than bipedal apes, confined to a few regions in Africa. What were these creatures like? When and how did they begin their evolutionary journey?

In Chapter 9, we discussed the techniques paleoanthropologists use to locate and excavate sites, as well as the multidisciplinary approaches used to interpret discoveries. In this chapter, we turn to the physical evidence of the hominin fossils themselves. The earliest fossils identifiable as hominins are all from Africa. They date from as early as 6+ mya; after 4 mya,

The Taung child (*Australopithecus africanus*) skull.

Robert Jurmain; Top Images: Institute of Human Origins photo by Nanci Kahn; © Cengage Learning; Russell L. Ciochon

species of these early hominins become more plentiful and widely distributed in Africa. It's fascinating to think about all these quite primitive early members of our family tree living side by side for millions of years, especially when we also try to figure out how they managed to coexist with their different adaptations. Most of these species became extinct. Why? And were some of these apelike animals possibly our direct ancestors?

Hominins, of course, evolved from earlier apes (dating to the later Miocene), and in Chapter 8 we discussed the fossil evidence of prehominin primates. These fossils provide us with a context within which to understand the subsequent evolution of the human lineage. In recent years, paleoanthropologists from several countries have been excavating sites in Africa, and many exciting new finds have been uncovered. However, because many such discoveries are so recent, detailed evaluations are still in progress, and conclusions must remain tentative.

One thing is certain, however. The earliest members of the human lineage were confined to Africa. Only much later did their descendants disperse from the African continent to other areas of the Old World. (This "out of Africa" saga will be the topic of the next chapter.)

Walking the Walk: The Bipedal Adaptation

In our overview in Chapter 9 of behavioral reconstructions of early hominins, we highlighted several hypotheses that attempt to explain *why* bipedal locomotion first evolved in the hominins. Here we turn to the specific anatomical (that is, **morphological**) evidence showing us when, where, and how hominin bipedal locomotion evolved. From a broader perspective, we've noted a tendency in all primates for erect body posture and some bipedalism. Of all living primates, however, efficient bipedalism as the primary (habitual) form of locomotion is seen *only* in hominins. Functionally, the human mode of locomotion is most clearly shown in our striding gait, where weight is alternately placed on a single fully extended hind limb. This specialized form of locomotion has developed to a point where energy levels are used at near peak efficiency among modern humans. Our manner of bipedal locomotion is a far cry from what we see in nonhuman primates, who move bipedally with hips and knees bent and maintain balance clumsily and inefficiently, tottering along rather than striding.

From a survey of our close primate relatives, it's apparent that while still in the trees, our ancestors were adapted to a fair amount of upper-body erectness. Strepsirrhines, monkeys, and apes all spend considerable time sitting erect while feeding, grooming, or sleeping. Presumably, our early ancestors displayed similar behavior. What caused these forms to come to the ground and embark on the unique way of life that would eventually lead to humans is still the subject of much speculation. Perhaps natural selection favored some Miocene hominoids coming occasionally to the ground to forage for food on the forest floor and forest fringe. In any case, once they were on the ground and away from the immediate safety offered by trees, bipedal locomotion could become a tremendous advantage. (For a discussion of some specific hypotheses that have tried to explain the early evolution of bipedal locomotion, see Chapter 9.)

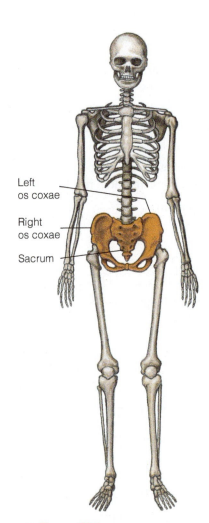

Left
os coxae

Right
os coxae

Sacrum

▲ **Figure 10-1**
The human pelvis: various elements shown on a modern skeleton.

The Mechanics of Walking on Two Legs

Our mode of locomotion is indeed extraordinary, involving, as it does, a unique kind of activity in which "the body, step by step, teeters on the edge of catastrophe" (Napier, 1967, p. 56). In this way, the act of human walking is the act of *almost*

morphological Pertaining to the form and structure of organisms.

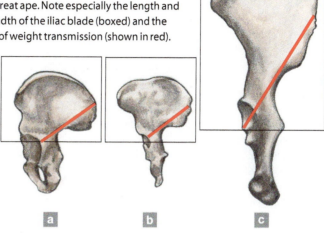

▼ **Figure 10-3**

Ossa coxae. (**a**) *Homo sapiens*. (**b**) Early hominin (australopith) from South Africa. (**c**) Great ape. Note especially the length and breadth of the iliac blade (boxed) and the line of weight transmission (shown in red).

a   b   c

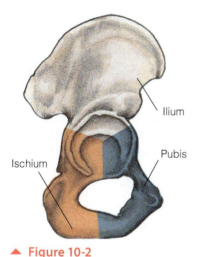

▲ **Figure 10-2**

The human os coxae, composed of three bones (right side shown).

Ilium

Ischium

Pubis

falling repeatedly! The problem is to maintain balance on the "stance" leg while the "swing" leg is off the ground. In fact, during normal walking, both feet are simultaneously on the ground only about 25 percent of the time, and this figure becomes even less as we walk (or run) faster.

Maintaining a stable center of balance in this complex form of locomotion calls for many drastic structural/anatomical alterations in the basic primate quadrupedal pattern. The most dramatic changes are seen in the pelvis. The pelvic girdle is composed of three elements: two hip bones, or ossa coxae (*sing.*, os coxae), joined at the back to the sacrum (Fig. 10-1). In a quadruped, the ossa coxae are vertically elongated bones positioned along each side of the lower portion of the spine and oriented more or less parallel to it. In hominins, the pelvis is comparatively much shorter and broader and extends around to the side (Fig. 10-2). This configuration helps to stabilize the line of weight transmission in a bipedal posture from the lower back to the hip joint (Fig. 10-3).

Several consequences resulted from the remodeling of the pelvis during early hominin evolution. Broadening the two sides and extending them around to the side and front of the body produced a basin-shaped structure that helps support the abdominal organs (*pelvis* means "basin" in Latin). These alterations also repositioned the attachments of several key muscles that act on the hip and leg, changing their mechanical function. Probably the most important of these altered relationships is that involving the gluteus maximus, the largest muscle in the body, which in humans forms the bulk of the buttocks. In quadrupeds, the gluteus maximus is positioned to the side of the hip and functions to pull the thigh to the side and away from the body. In humans, this muscle is positioned behind the hip; this arrangement allows it, along with the hamstrings, to extend the thigh, pulling it to the rear during walking and running (Fig. 10-4). The gluteus maximus is a truly powerful extensor of the thigh and provides additional force, particularly during running and climbing.

Modifications also occurred in other parts of the skeleton because of the shift to bipedalism. The most

▼ **Figure 10-4**

Comparisons of important muscles that act to extend the hip. Note that the attachment surface (origin, shown in black) of the gluteus maximus in humans (**a**) is farther in back of the hip joint than in a chimpanzee standing bipedally (**b**). Conversely, in chimpanzees, the hamstrings are farther in back of the knee.

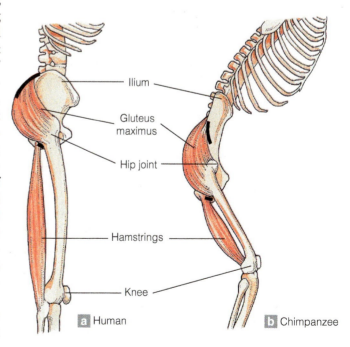

Ilium

Gluteus maximus

Hip joint

Hamstrings

Knee

a Human   b Chimpanzee

significant of these, summarized in "A Closer Look: Major Features of Bipedal Locomotion," include (1) repositioning of the foramen magnum, the opening at the base of the skull through which the spinal cord emerges; (2) the addition of spinal curves that help to transmit the weight of the upper body to the hips in an upright posture; (3) shortening and broadening of the pelvis and the stabilization of weight transmission (discussed earlier); (4) lengthening of the hind limb, thus increasing stride length (distance between two successive placements of the same foot); (5) angling of the femur (thighbone) inward to bring the knees and feet closer together under the body; and (6) several structural changes in the foot,

A Closer Look   Major Features of Bipedal Locomotion

During hominin evolution, several major structural features throughout the body have been reorganized (from those seen in other primates), facilitating efficient bipedal locomotion. These are illustrated here, beginning with the head and progressing to the foot: (**a**) The foramen magnum (shown in blue) is repositioned farther underneath the skull, so that the head is more or less balanced on the spine (and thus requiring less robust neck muscles to hold the head upright). (**b**) The spine has two distinctive curves—a backward (thoracic) one and a forward (lumbar) one—that keep the trunk (and weight) centered above the pelvis. (**c**) The pelvis is shaped more in

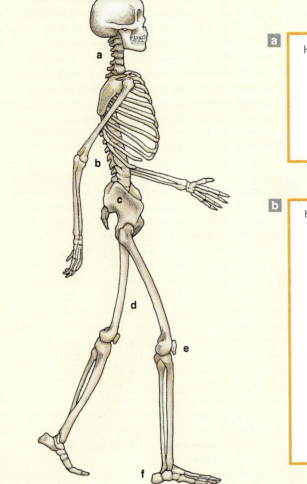

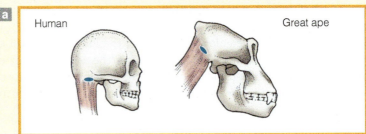

a

Human   Great ape

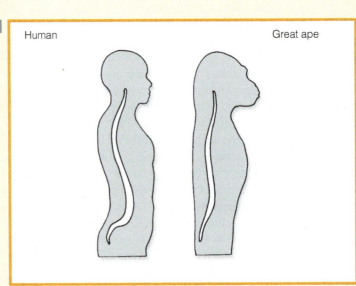

b

Human   Great ape

including the development of a longitudinal arch and realignment of the big toe in parallel with the other toes (that is, making it no longer divergent).

As you can appreciate, the evolution of hominin bipedalism required complex anatomical reorganization. For natural selection to produce anatomical change of the magnitude seen in hominins, the benefits of bipedal locomotion must have been significant indeed! We mentioned in Chapter 9 several possible adaptive advantages that bipedal locomotion may have conferred upon early hominins. But these all remain hypotheses (since they can't be tested, they could more accurately be called scenarios), and we have inadequate data for testing the various proposed models.

the form of a basin to support internal organs; the ossa coxae (specifically, the iliac blades) are also shorter and broader, thus stabilizing weight transmission. (**d**) The lower limbs are elongated, as shown by the proportional lengths of various body segments (for example, in humans the thigh comprises 20 percent of body height, while in gorillas it comprises only 11 percent). (**e**) The femur is angled inward, keeping the legs more directly under the body; modified knee anatomy also permits full extension of this joint. (**f**) The big toe is enlarged and brought in line with the other toes; a distinctive longitudinal arch also forms, helping to absorb shock and adding propulsive spring.

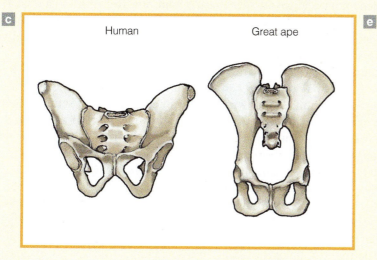

c

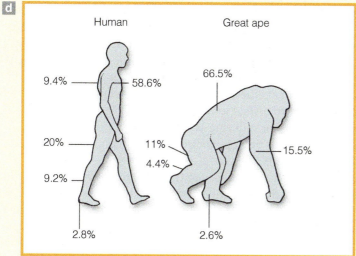

d

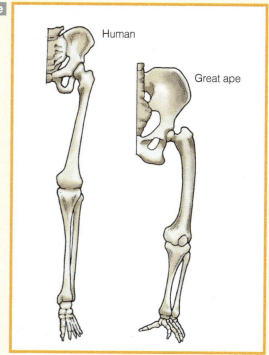

e

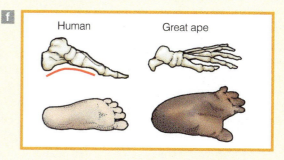

f

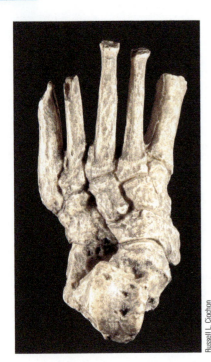

▲ **Figure 10-5**
A nearly complete hominin foot
(OH 8) from Olduvai Gorge, Tanzania.

Still, given the anatomical alterations required for efficient bipedalism, some major behavioral stimuli must have influenced its development. When they interpret evolutionary history, biologists are fond of saying that form follows function. In other words, during evolution, organisms don't undergo significant reorganization in structure *unless* these changes—over many generations—assist individuals in some functional capacity (and in so doing increase their reproductive success). Such changes didn't necessarily occur all at once, but probably evolved over a fairly long period of time. Even so, once behavioral influences initiated certain structural modifications, the process gained momentum and proceeded irreversibly.

We say that hominin bipedalism is both habitual and obligate. By **habitual bipedalism,** we mean that hominins, unlike any other primate, move bipedally as their primary and most efficient mode of locomotion. By **obligate bipedalism**, we mean that hominins are committed to bipedalism and cannot locomote efficiently in any other way. For example, the loss of grasping ability in the foot makes climbing much more difficult for humans (although by no means impossible). The central task, then, in trying to understand the earliest members of the hominin lineage is to identify anatomical features that indicate bipedalism and to interpret to what degree these individuals were committed to this form of locomotion (that is, was it a habitual or obligate biped?).

What structural patterns are observable in early hominins, and what do they imply regarding locomotor function? By at least 4 mya, all the major structural changes required for bipedalism are seen in early hominins from Africa (at least as far as the evidence permits conclusions to be drawn). In particular, the pelvis, as clearly documented by several excellently preserved specimens, was dramatically modified to support weight in a bipedal stance (see Fig. 10-3b).

Other structural changes shown after 4 mya in the earliest relatively complete hominin postcranial remains further confirm the pattern seen in the pelvis. For example, the vertebral column (as known from specimens in East and South Africa) shows the same curves as in modern hominins. The lower limbs are also elongated, and they seem to be proportionately about as long as in modern humans (although the arms are longer in these early hominins). Further, the angle of weight support from the hip to the knee is very similar to that seen in *Homo sapiens*.

Fossil evidence of early hominin foot structure has come from two sites in South Africa; especially important are some fossils from **Sterkfontein** (Clarke and Tobias, 1995). These specimens, including four articulating elements from the ankle and big toe, indicate that the heel and longitudinal arch were both well adapted for a bipedal gait. But the paleoanthropologists (Ron Clarke and Phillip Tobias) who analyzed these remains also suggest that the large toe was *divergent*, unlike the hominin pattern shown in "A Closer Look: Major Features of Bipedal Locomotion." If the large toe really did possess this anatomical position (and this is disputed), it most likely would have aided the foot in grasping. In turn, this grasping ability (as in other primates) would have enabled early hominins to more effectively exploit arboreal habitats. Finally, because changes in anatomical structures are always constrained by a set of complex functional compromises, a foot highly capable of grasping and climbing is less useful as a stable platform during bipedal locomotion. Some researchers therefore see early hominins as perhaps not quite as fully committed to bipedal locomotion as were later hominins.

Further evidence for evolutionary changes in the foot comes from two sites in East Africa where numerous fossilized elements have been recovered (Fig. 10-5). As in the remains from South Africa, the East African fossils suggest a well-adapted bipedal gait. The arches are developed, but some differences in the ankle also imply that considerable flexibility was possible (again, probably indicating some continued adaptation to climbing). From this evidence some researchers have concluded that many forms of early hominins probably spent considerable time in the trees.

habitual bipedalism Bipedal locomotion as the form of locomotion shown by hominins most of the time.

obligate bipedalism Bipedalism as the *only* form of hominin terrestrial locomotion. Since major anatomical changes in the spine, pelvis, and lower limbs are required for bipedal locomotion, once hominins adopted this mode of locomotion, other forms of locomotion on the ground became impossible.

Sterkfontein (sterk´-fawn-tane)

What's more, they may not have been quite as efficient bipedally as has previously been suggested. Nevertheless, most researchers maintain that early hominins from Africa displayed both habitual and obligate bipedalism (despite the new evidence from South Africa and the earliest traces from central and East Africa, all of which will require further study).

Digging for Connections: Early Hominins from Africa

As you are now well aware, a variety of early hominins lived in Africa, and we'll cover their comings and goings over a 5-million-year period, from at least 6 to 1 mya. It's also important to keep in mind that these hominins were geographically widely distributed, with fossil discoveries coming from Central, East, and South Africa. Paleoanthropologists generally agree that among these early African fossils, there were at least six different genera, which in turn may comprise at least 14 different species. (Note: Some poorly represented or controversial genera and species are omitted from this chapter in the interest of clarity.) At no time and in no other place were hominins ever as diverse as these very ancient members of our family tree. As you'll see in a minute, some of the earliest fossils thought by many researchers to be hominins are primitive in some ways and unusually derived in others. In fact, some paleoanthropologists remain unconvinced that they are really hominins.

As you've already guessed, there are quite a few different fossils from many sites; their formal naming can be difficult to pronounce and not easy to remember. So we'll try to discuss these fossil groups in a way that's easy to understand. Our primary focus will be to organize them by time and by major evolutionary trends. In so doing, we recognize three major groups:

1. Pre-australopiths—the earliest and most primitive (possible) hominins (6.0+ to 4.4 mya)
2. Australopiths—diverse forms, some more primitive, others highly derived (4.2 to 1.2 mya)
3. Early *Homo*—the first members of our genus (2.8+ to 1.4 mya)

Pre-Australopiths (6.0+ to 4.4 mya)

The oldest and most surprising of these earliest hominins is represented by a cranium discovered at a central African site called Toros-Menalla in the modern nation of Chad (Brunet et al., 2002) (Fig. 10-6). Provisional dating using faunal correlation (biostratigraphy) suggests a date of between 7 and 6 mya (Vignaud et al., 2002). Closer examination of the evidence used in obtaining this biostratigraphic date now has led many paleoanthropologists to suggest that 6 mya is more likely.

The morphology of the fossil is unusual, with a combination of characteristics unlike that found in other early hominins. The braincase is small, estimated at no larger than a modern chimpanzee's (preliminary estimate in the range of 320 to 380 cm^3), but it is massively built, with pronounced brow ridges in front, a crest on top, and large muscle attachments in the rear. Yet, combined with these apelike features is a smallish vertical face containing front teeth very unlike an ape's. In fact, the lower face, being more tucked in under the brain case

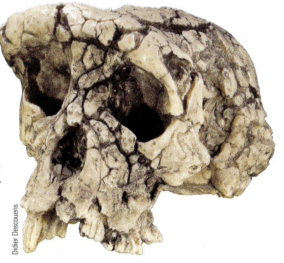

▼ **Figure 10-6**
A nearly complete cranium of *Sahelanthropus* from Chad, dating to approximately 6 mya or somewhat older.

Didier Descouens

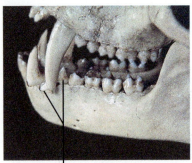

Sectorial lower first premolar

▲ **Figure 10-7**

Canine/lower first premolar honing complex, typical of most Old World anthropoids, but lacking in most hominins (shown here in a male patas monkey). Note how the large upper canine shears against the elongated surface of the lower first premolar.

honing complex The shearing of a large upper canine with the first lower premolar, with the wear leading to honing of the surfaces of both teeth. This anatomical pattern is typical of most Old World anthropoids but is mostly absent in hominins.

(and not protruding, as in most other early hominins), is more of a *derived* feature more commonly expressed in much later hominins (especially members of genus *Homo*). What's more, unlike the dentition seen in apes (and some early hominins), the upper canine is reduced and is worn down from the tip (rather than shearing along its side against the first lower premolar). The lack of such a shearing canine/premolar arrangement (called a **honing complex**) (Fig. 10-7) is viewed by many researchers as an important derived characteristic of early hominins (White et al., 2010). Other experts are not entirely convinced and suggest that it could just as easily have evolved in both hominins and other hominoids because of homoplasy (Wood and Harrison, 2011).

In recognition of this unique combination of characteristics, paleoanthropologists have placed the Toros-Menalla remains into a new genus and species of hominin, *Sahelanthropus tchadensis* (Sahel being the region of the southern Sahara Desert in North Africa) (Fig. 10-8). These new finds from Chad have forced an immediate and significant reassessment of early hominin evolution. Two cautionary comments, however, are in order. First, as we noted, the dating is only approximate, since it is based on biostratigraphic correlation with sites in Kenya (1,500 miles to the east). Second, and perhaps more serious, is the hominin status of the Chad fossil. Given the facial structure and dentition, it's difficult to see how *Sahelanthropus* could be anything but a hominin. However, the position of its foramen magnum is intermediate between that of a quadrupedal ape and that of a bipedal hominin, making it unclear if its skull would have been balanced over a bipedal spinal column (Fig. 10-9); for this and other reasons, some researchers (Wolpoff et al., 2002) suggest that at this time, "ape" may be a better classification for *Sahelanthropus*. As we have previously said, the best-defining anatomical characteristics of hominins relate to bipedal locomotion. Unfortunately, no postcranial elements have been recovered from Chad—at least not yet. Consequently, we do not yet know the locomotor behavior of *Sahelanthropus for certain*, and this raises even more fundamental questions: What if further finds show this form not to be bipedal? Should we still consider it a hominin? What, then, are the defining characteristics of our lineage? For all these reasons, several paleoanthropologists have recently grown more skeptical regarding the hominin status of all the pre-australopith finds, and Bernard Wood (2010) prefers to call them "possible hominins."

Probably living at about the same time as *Sahelanthropus*, two other very early (possible) hominin genera have been found at sites in central Kenya in the Tugen Hills and from the Middle Awash area of northeastern Ethiopia. The earlier of these finds (dated by radiometric methods to around 6 mya) comes from the Tugen Hills and includes mostly dental remains, and also some quite complete lower limb bones. These fossils have been placed in a separate early hominin genus called *Orrorin*. The postcranial remains are especially important, since they seem to indicate bipedal locomotion (Pickford and Senut, 2001; Senut et al., 2001; Galik et al., 2004; Richmond and Jungers, 2008). As a result of these further analyses, *Orrorin* is the pre-australopith generally recognized as having the best evidence to establish it as a hominin among all late Miocene-age fossils.

The last group of possible hominins dating to the late Miocene (that is, earlier than 5 mya) comes from the Middle Awash in the Afar Triangle of Ethiopia. Radiometric dating places the age of these fossils in the very late Miocene, 5.8 to 5.2 mya. The fossil remains themselves are very fragmentary. Some of the dental remains resemble some later fossils from the Middle Awash (discussed shortly), and Yohannes Haile-Selassie, the researcher who first found and described these earlier materials, has provisionally assigned them to the genus *Ardipithecus* (Haile-Selassie et al., 2004). In addition, some postcranial elements have been preserved—most informatively a toe bone, a phalanx from the middle of the foot (see Appendix A,

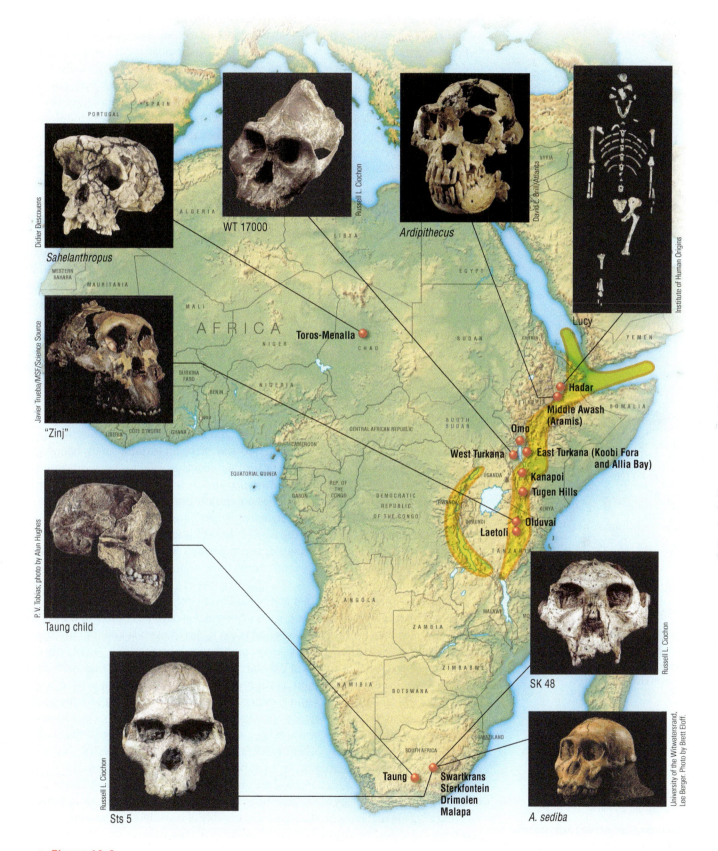

Didier Descouens

Sahelanthropus

Russell L. Ciochon

WT 17000

Ardipithecus

David L. Brill/Atlanta

Institute of Human Origins

Lucy

Javier Trueba/MSF/Science Source

"Zinj"

P. V. Tobias; photo by Alun Hughes

Taung child

Toros-Menalla

Hadar

Middle Awash
(Aramis)

Omo

West Turkana

East Turkana (Koobi Fora
and Allia Bay)

Kanapoi
Tugen Hills

Olduvai

Laetoli

Russell L. Ciochon

Sts 5

Russell L. Ciochon

SK 48

University of the Witwatersrand,
Lee Berger. Photo by Brett Eloff.

A. sediba

Taung

Swartkrans
Sterkfontein
Drimolen
Malapa

▲ Figure 10-8

Early hominin fossil finds (pre-australopith and australopith localities). The Rift Valley in East Africa is shown in gold.

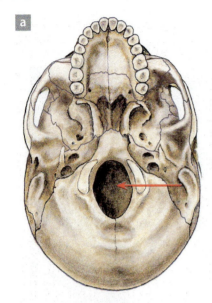

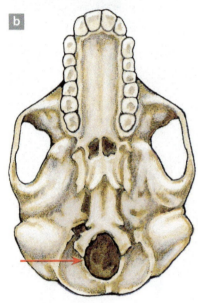

Fig. A-8). From clues in this bone, Haile-Selassie concludes that this primate was a well-adapted biped (once again, the best-supporting evidence of hominin status).

From another million years or so later in the geological record in Ethiopia's Middle Awash region, a very large and significant assemblage of fossil hominins has been discovered at a site called **Aramis** (White et al., 2009). Radiometric dating firmly places these remains at about 4.4 mya. The site, represented by a 6-foot-thick bed of bones, has yielded more than 6,000 fossils. These abundant finds include both large and small vertebrates—birds and other reptiles and even very small mammals. Additionally, fossil wood and pollen samples have been recovered. All this information is important for understanding the environments in which these ancient hominins lived.

Hominin fossil remains from Aramis include several individuals, the most noteworthy being a partial skeleton. From this important site a total of at least 36 other hominins are represented by isolated teeth, cranial bones, and a few limb bones. All the bones were extremely fragile and fragmentary and required many years of incredibly painstaking effort to clean and reconstruct. Indeed, it took 15 years before the partial skeleton was in good enough condition to be intensively studied. But the wait was well worth it, and in 2009, Tim White and colleagues published their truly remarkable finds. By far the most informative fossil is the partial skeleton. Even though it was found crushed and fragmented, the years of work and computer imaging have now allowed researchers to interpret this 4.4-million-year-old individual. Nicknamed "Ardi," this individual has more than 50 percent of its skeleton represented; however, since it was found in such poor condition, any reconstruction must be seen as provisional and open to varying interpretations. Ardi has been sexed as female and contains several key portions, including a skull, a pelvis, and almost complete hands and feet (White et al., 2009; Fig. 10-10).

Ardi's brain size, estimated between 300 and 350 cm³, is quite small, being no larger than a chimpanzee's. However, it is much like that seen in *Sahelanthropus*, and overall the skulls of the two hominins also appear to be similar. The preservation of much of the postcranial skeleton is potentially crucial, because key body elements, such as the pelvis and the foot, are only very rarely discovered, in part due to their low bone density. This is the *earliest* hominin for which we have so many different parts of the body represented, and it permits researchers to hypothesize more confidently about body size and proportions and, perhaps most crucially of all, the mode of locomotion.

Height is estimated at close to 4 feet, with a body weight of around 110 pounds. Compared to other early hominins, such a body size would be similar to that of a male and well above average for a female (Table 10-1). The pelvis and foot are preserved well enough to allow good-quality computer reconstructions. According to White and colleagues, both areas of the body show key anatomical changes indicating that *Ardipithecus* was a competent biped. For example, the ilium is short and broad (see Figs. 10-2 and 10-3), and the foot has been modified to act as a prop for propulsion during walking.

However, Ardi also presents some big surprises. While the shape of the ilium seems to show bipedal ability, other parts of the pelvis show more ancestral ("primitive") hominoid characteristics. In fact, the paleoanthropologists who analyzed the skeleton concluded that Ardi likely walked quite adequately but might well have had difficulty running (Lovejoy et al., 2009a, b). The foot is also an odd mix of features, showing a big toe that is highly divergent and capable of considerable grasping. Some researchers are not convinced that Ardi was bipedal, and considering all her other primitive characteristics, some have questioned whether *Ardipithecus* was really a hominin at all (Sarmiento, 2010). The extent of reconstruction that was required (for the skull and pelvis especially) adds further uncertainty to understanding this crucial discovery. One thing that everyone agrees on is that Ardi was an able

▲ **Figure 10-9**
Position of the foramen magnum in **(a)** a human and **(b)** a chimpanzee. Note the more forward position in the human cranium.

Aramis (air-ah-miss)

australopiths A colloquial name referring to a diverse group of Plio-Pleistocene African hominins. Australopiths are the most abundant and widely distributed of all early hominins and are also the most completely studied.

climber who likely was well adapted to walking on all fours along the tops of branches. It seems clear that she spent a lot of time in the trees.

Accepting for the moment that *Ardipithecus* was a hominin, it was a very primitive one, displaying an array of characteristics quite distinct from all later members of our lineage. In fact, its combination of characteristics is very odd and unique among our lineage. The new evidence that Ardi provides has not convinced all paleoanthropologists that *Ardipithecus* or any of the other very early pre-australopiths are hominins (Wood and Harrison, 2011); indeed, Ardi's very odd anatomy has caused doubts to increase. One thing is for sure: It would take a considerable adaptive shift in the next 200,000 years to produce the more derived hominins we'll discuss in a moment. All of these considerations have not only intrigued professional anthropologists but also captured the imagination of the general public. When did the earliest member of our lineage first appear? The search goes on, and professional reputations are made and lost in this quest.

Another intriguing aspect of all these late Miocene/early Pliocene locales (that is, Toros-Menalla, Tugen Hills, early Middle Awash sites, and Aramis) relates to the ancient environments associated with these earliest hominins. Rather than the more open grassland savanna habitats so characteristic of most of the later hominin sites, the environment at all these early locales is more heavily forested. Perhaps at Aramis and these other ancient sites we are seeing the very beginnings of hominin divergence, not long after the division from the African apes. The "At a Glance" outlines key features of early hominin fossil discoveries and site locations.

Australopiths (4.2 to 1.2 mya)

The best-known, most widely distributed, and most diverse of the early African hominins are colloquially called **australopiths**. In fact, this varied and highly successful group of hominins is made up of two closely related genera, *Australopithecus* and *Paranthropus*. These hominins have an established time range of over 3 million years, stretching back as early as 4.2 mya and not becoming extinct until apparently close to 1 mya—making them the longest-enduring hominins yet documented. In addition, these hominins have been found in all the major geographical areas of Africa that have, to date, produced early hominin finds, namely, South Africa, Central Africa (Chad), and East Africa. From all these areas combined, there appears to have been considerable complexity in terms of evolutionary diversity, with numerous species now recognized by most paleoanthropologists.

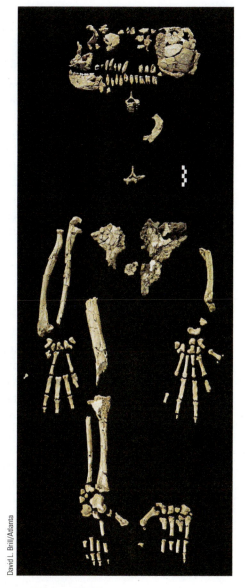

David L. Brill/Atlanta

▲ Figure 10-10

A mostly complete (but fragmented) skeleton of *Ardipithecus*. Dating to about 4.4 mya, this is the earliest hominin skeleton yet found containing so many different portions of the body.

Table 10-1	Estimated Body Weights and Stature in Plio-Pleistocene Hominins			
	Body Weight		**Stature**	
	Male	Female	Male	Female
A. afarensis	45 kg (99 lb)	29 kg (64 lb)	151 cm (59 in.)	105 cm (41 in.)
A. africanus	41 kg (90 lb)	30 kg (65 lb)	138 cm (54 in.)	115 cm (45 in.)
A. robustus	40 kg (88 lb)	32 kg (70 lb)	132 cm (52 in.)	110 cm (43 in.)
A. boisei	49 kg (108 lb)	34 kg (75 lb)	137 cm (54 in.)	124 cm (49 in.)
H. habilis	52 kg (114 lb)	32 kg (70 lb)	157 cm (62 in.)	125 cm (49 in.)

Source: After McHenry, 1992. Note: Reno et al. (2003) conclude that sexual dimorphism in *A. afarensis* was considerably less than shown here.

At a Glance Key Pre-Australopith Discoveries

Date	Region	Hominin	Site	Evolutionary Significance
4.4 mya	East Africa	*Ardipithecus ramidus*	Aramis	Large collection of fossils, including partial skeletons; bipedal, but derived.
5.8–5.2 mya		*Ardipithecus*	Middle Awash	Fragmentary, but possibly bipedal.
~6.0 mya		*Orrorin tugenensis*	Tugen Hills	First hominin with post-cranial remains; possibly bipedal.
~7.0– 6.0 mya	Central Africa	*Sahelanthropus tchadensis*	Toros-Menalla	Oldest potential hominin; well-preserved cranium; very small-brained; possibly bipedal.

There are two major subgroups of australopiths: an earlier one that is more anatomically primitive and a later one that is much more derived. These earlier australopiths, dated 4.2 to 3.0 mya, show several more primitive (ancestral) hominin characteristics than the later australopith group, whose members are more derived, some extremely so. These more derived hominins lived after 2.5 mya and are composed of two different genera, together represented by at least five different species. (See Appendix C for a complete listing and more information about early hominin fossil finds.)

Given the 3-million-year time range as well as quite varied ecological niches, there are numerous intriguing adaptive differences among these varied australopith species. We'll discuss the major adaptations of the different species in a moment. But first let's emphasize the major features that all australopiths share:

1. They are all clearly bipedal (although not necessarily identical to *Homo* in this regard).
2. They all have relatively small brains (at least compared to *Homo*).
3. They all have large teeth, particularly the back teeth, with thick to very thick enamel on the molars.

In short, then, all these australopith species are relatively small-brained, large-toothed bipeds.

The earliest australopiths, dating to 4.2 to 3.0 mya, come from East Africa from a couple of sites in northern Kenya as well as two other sites in the Middle Awash region of Ethiopia (in the same area where *Ardipithecus* was discovered). Among the fossil finds of those earliest australopiths so far discovered, a few postcranial pieces clearly indicate that locomotion was bipedal. There are, however, a few primitive features in the dentition, including a large canine and a **sectorial** lower first premolar (see Fig. 10-7).

Since these particular fossils have initially been interpreted as more primitive than all the later members of the genus *Australopithecus*, paleoanthropologists have provisionally assigned them to a separate species. This important fossil species is now called *Australopithecus anamensis*, and some researchers suggest that it is a potential ancestor for many later australopiths as well as perhaps early members of the genus *Homo* (White et al., 2006) (see Fig. 10-11).

Slightly later and much more complete remains of *Australopithecus* have come primarily from the sites of Hadar (in Ethiopia) and Laetoli (in Tanzania). Much of this material has been known for over four decades, and the fossils have been

sectorial Adapted for cutting or shearing; among primates, this term refers to the compressed (side-to-side) first lower premolar, which functions as a shearing surface with the upper canine.

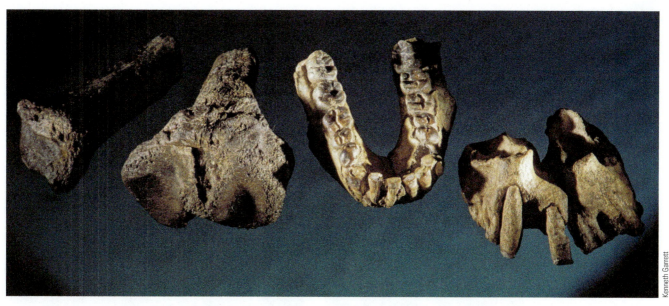

▲ **Figure 10-11**
Fossil remains of *Australopithecus anamensis* from the Middle Awash region of Ethiopia. In addition to teeth and jaw fragments, several postcranial pieces were also found (hand and foot bones, pieces of vertebrae, and part of a femur and tibia).

very well studied; indeed, in certain instances, they are quite famous. For example, the Lucy skeleton was discovered at Hadar in 1974, and the Laetoli footprints were first found in 1978. These hominins are classified as members of the species *Australopithecus afarensis*.

Literally thousands of footprints have been found at Laetoli, representing more than 20 different kinds of animals (Pliocene elephants, horses, pigs, giraffes, antelopes, hyenas, and an abundance of hares). Several hominin footprints have also been found, including a trail more than 75 feet long made by at least two—and perhaps three—individuals (Leakey and Hay, 1979) (Fig. 10-12; also refer to Fig. 1-1 from Chapter 1). Such discoveries of well-preserved hominin footprints are extremely important in furthering our understanding of human evolution. For the first time, we can make *definitive* statements regarding the locomotor pattern and stature of early hominins.

◄ **Figure 10-12**
Hominin footprint from Laetoli, Tanzania. Note the deep impression of the heel and the large toe (arrow) in line (adducted) with the other toes.

▶ **Figure 10-13**
(a) "Lucy," a partial hominin skeleton, discovered at Hadar in 1974. This individual is assigned to *Australopithecus afarensis*. **(b)** Artist's reconstruction of a female *A. afarensis* derived from study of the Lucy skeleton.

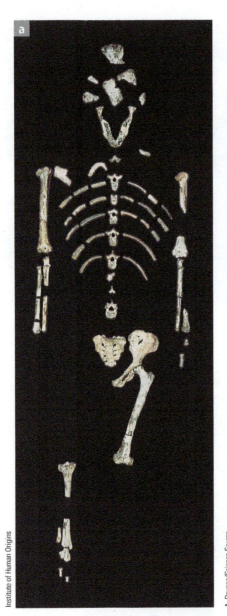

Institute of Human Origins

A. Daynes/Science Source

Studies of these impression patterns clearly show that the mode of locomotion of these hominins was bipedal (Day and Wickens, 1980). Some researchers, however, have concluded that *A. afarensis* was not bipedal in quite the same way that modern humans are. From detailed comparisons with modern humans, estimates of stride length, cadence, and speed of walking have been ascertained, indicating that the Laetoli hominins moved in a slower ("strolling") fashion with a rather short stride.

One extraordinary discovery at Hadar is the Lucy skeleton (Fig. 10-13), found eroding out of a hillside by Don Johanson. This fossil is scientifically designated as Afar Locality (AL) 288-1 but is usually just called Lucy (after the popular Beatles song "Lucy in the Sky with Diamonds"). Representing almost 40 percent of a skeleton, this is one of the most complete individuals from anywhere in the world for the entire period before about 100,000 years ago.

Because the Laetoli area was covered periodically by ashfalls from nearby volcanic eruptions, accurate dating is possible and has provided dates of 3.7 to 3.5 mya. Dating from the Hadar region hasn't proved as straightforward; however, more complete dating calibration using a variety of techniques has determined a range of 3.9 to 3.0 mya for the hominin discoveries from this area.

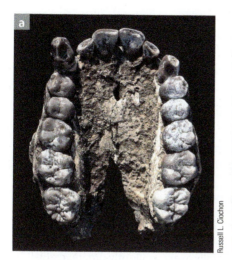

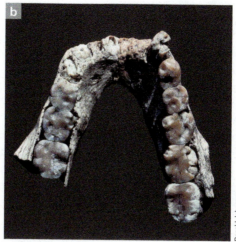

Russell L. Ciochon

Donald Johanson

◀ **Figure 10-14**

Jaws of *Australopithecus afarensis*. **(a)** Maxilla, AL 200-1a, from Hadar, Ethiopia. (Note the parallel tooth rows and large canines.) **(b)** Mandible, LH 4, from Laetoli, Tanzania. This fossil is the type specimen for the species *Australopithecus afarensis*.

Several hundred *A. afarensis* specimens, representing a minimum of 60 individuals (and perhaps as many as 100), have been excavated from Laetoli and Hadar. At present, these materials represent the largest *well-studied* collection of early hominins and as such are among the most significant of the hominins discussed in this chapter.

Without question, *A. afarensis* is more primitive than any of the other later australopith fossils from South or East Africa (discussed shortly). By *primitive* we mean that *A. afarensis* retains more ancestral features than later-occurring hominin species. That is, *A. afarensis* shares more primitive features with some late Miocene apes and with living great apes than do later hominins, who display more derived characteristics.

For example, the teeth of *A. afarensis* are quite primitive. The canine teeth are often large and pointed, which are apelike traits. Moreover, the lower first premolar is semisectorial (that is, it provides a shearing surface for the upper canine), and the tooth rows are parallel, even converging somewhat toward the back of the mouth, similar to apes (Fig. 10-14).

The cranial portions that are preserved also display several primitive hominoid characteristics, including a crest in the back as well as several primitive features of the cranial base. Cranial capacity estimates for *A. afarensis* show a mixed pattern compared to later hominins. A provisional estimate for the one partially complete cranium—apparently a large individual—gives a figure of 500 cm³, but another even more fragmentary cranium is apparently quite a bit smaller and has been estimated at about 375 cm³ (Holloway, 1983). Thus for some individuals (probable males), *A. afarensis* is well within the range of other australopith species (see "A Closer Look: Cranial Capacity"); but others (probable females) may have a significantly smaller cranial capacity. However, a detailed depiction of cranial size for *A. afarensis* is not possible at this time; this part of the skeleton is unfortunately too poorly represented. One thing is clear: *A. afarensis* had a small brain, probably averaging for the whole species not much over 420 cm³.

On the other hand, a large assortment of postcranial pieces representing almost all portions of the body of *A. afarensis* has been found. Initial impressions suggest that relative to lower limbs, the upper limbs are longer than in modern humans (also a primitive Miocene ape condition). (This statement, however, does not mean that the arms of *A. afarensis* were longer than the legs.) In addition, the wrist, hand, and foot bones show several differences from modern humans (Sussman et al., 1985). From such excellent postcranial evidence, stature can be confidently estimated:

A Closer Look Cranial Capacity

Cranial capacity, usually reported in cubic centimeters, is a measure of brain size, or volume. The brain itself, of course, doesn't fossilize. However, the space once occupied by brain tissue (the inside of the cranial vault) is sometimes preserved, at least in those cases where fairly complete crania are recovered.

For purposes of comparison, it's easy to obtain cranial capacity estimates for contemporary species (including humans) from analyses of skeletonized specimens in museum collections. From studies of this nature, estimated cranial capacities for modern hominoids have been determined as follows (Tobias, 1971, 1983):

	Range (cm³)	Average (cm³)
Human	1,150–1,750*	1,325
Chimpanzee	285–500	395
Gorilla	340–752	506
Orangutan	276–540	411
Bonobo	—	350

*The range of cranial capacity for modern humans is very large—in fact, even greater than that shown (which approximates cranial capacity for the majority of contemporary *H. sapiens* populations).

These data for living hominoids can then be compared with those obtained for early hominins:

	Average (cm³)
Sahelanthropus	~350
Orrorin	Not currently known
Ardipithecus	~420
Australopithecus anamensis	Not currently known
Australopithecus afarensis	438
Later australopiths	410–530
Early members of genus *Homo*	631

As the tabulations indicate, cranial capacity estimates for australopiths fall within the range of most modern great apes, and gorillas actually average slightly greater cranial capacity than that seen in most early hominins. It's important to remember, however, that gorillas are very large animals, whereas most early hominins probably weighed on the order of 100 pounds (see Table 10-1). Since brain size is partially correlated with body size, comparing such different-sized animals can't be justified. Compared to living chimpanzees (most of which are slightly larger than early hominins) and bonobos (which are somewhat smaller), australopiths had *proportionately* about 10 percent bigger brains; so we would say that these early hominins were more *encephalized*.

A. afarensis was a short hominin. From her partial skeleton, Lucy is estimated to have been only 3 to 4 feet tall. However, Lucy—as demonstrated by her pelvis—was probably a female, and there is evidence of larger individuals as well. The most economical hypothesis explaining this variation is that *A. afarensis* was quite sexually dimorphic: The larger individuals are male, and the smaller ones, such as Lucy, are female. Estimates of male stature can be approximated from the larger footprints at Laetoli, inferring a height of just under 5 feet. If we accept this interpretation, *A. afarensis* was a very sexually dimorphic hominin indeed. In fact, for overall body size, this species may have been as dimorphic as *any* living primate (that is, as much as gorillas, orangutans, or baboons). However, the degree of sexual dimorphism has been re-examined by Reno and Lovejoy (2015), who conclude that sex differences in body size are less pronounced than what was previously thought.

Significant further discoveries of *A. afarensis* have come from Ethiopia in the last few years, including two further partial skeletons. The first of these is a mostly complete skeleton of an *A. afarensis* juvenile discovered at the Dikika locale in northeastern Ethiopia, very near the Hadar sites mentioned earlier (Fig. 10-15). What's more, the juvenile skeleton comes from the same geological horizon as Hadar, with very similar dates of 3.3 to 3.2 mya (Alemseged et al., 2006).

This find of a 3-year-old hominin is remarkable because it's the first example of a very well-preserved immature hominin prior to about 100,000 years ago. From the individual's extremely well-preserved teeth, scientists hypothesize that she was female. A comprehensive study of her developmental biology has already begun, and many more revelations are surely in store as the Dikika fossil is more completely

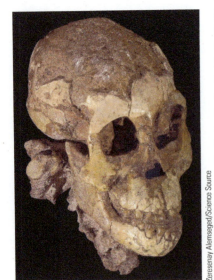

▲ **Figure 10-15**
Complete skull with attached vertebral column of the juvenile skeleton from Dikika, Ethiopia (dated to about 3.3 mya).

Zeresenay Alemseged/Science Source

cleaned and studied. Initial results, accounting for her immature age, show a skeletal pattern quite similar to what we'd expect in an *A. afarensis* adult. What's more, the limb proportions, anatomy of the hands and feet, and shape of the scapula (shoulder blade) reveal a similar "mixed" pattern of locomotion. The foot and lower limb indicate that this young hominin would have been a terrestrial biped. Further analysis of her shoulder confirms that she was also capable of climbing about quite ably in the trees (Green and Alemseged, 2012).

The second recently discovered *A. afarensis* partial skeleton comes from the Woranso-Mille research area in the central Afar, only about 30 miles north of Hadar (Haile-Selassie et al., 2010). The dating places the find at close to 3.6 mya (almost 400,000 years earlier than Lucy). Moreover, this individual was considerably larger than Lucy and likely was male. Analysis of bones preserved in this new find reinforces what was previously known about *A. afarensis* as well as adding some further insights. The large degree of sexual dimorphism and well-adapted bipedal locomotion agree with prior evidence. Mbua and colleagues (2016) recently reported on specimens identified as *A. afarensis* excavated from the site of Kantis, located in the highlands of Kenya along the Gregory Rift Valley. This new discovery has significantly expanded the known range of *A. afarensis*, and faunal and isotope studies indicate a different dietary specialization among these individuals compared to their contemporaries from Ethiopia.

What makes *A. afarensis* a hominin? The answer is revealed by its manner of locomotion. From the abundant limb bones recovered from Hadar and other locales, as well as those beautiful footprints from Laetoli, we know unequivocally that *A. afarensis* walked bipedally when on the ground. (At present, we do not have nearly such good evidence concerning locomotion for *any* of the earlier hominin finds.) Whether Lucy and her contemporaries still spent considerable time in the trees and just how efficiently they walked have become topics of some debate. Most researchers, however, agree that *A. afarensis* was an efficient habitual biped while on the ground. These hominins were also clearly *obligate* bipeds, which would have hampered their climbing abilities but would not necessarily have precluded arboreal behavior altogether.

Australopithecus afarensis is a crucial hominin group. Since it comes after the earliest, poorly known group of pre-australopith hominins, but prior to all later australopiths as well as *Homo*, it is an evolutionary bridge, linking together much of what we assume are the major patterns of early hominin evolution. The fact that there are many well-preserved fossils and that they have been so well studied also adds to the paleoanthropological significance of *A. afarensis*. The consensus among most experts over the last several years has been that *A. afarensis* is a potentially strong candidate as the ancestor of *all* later hominins. Some ongoing analysis has recently challenged this hypothesis (Rak et al., 2007), but at least for the moment, this new interpretation has not been widely accepted. Still, it reminds us that science is an intellectual pursuit that constantly reevaluates older views and seeks to provide more systematic explanations about the world around us. When it comes to understanding human evolution, we should always be aware that things might change. So stay tuned.

A Contemporaneous and *Very* Different Kind of Hominin

From Woranso-Mille, the same site in the central Afar where researchers recently discovered a partial *A. afarensis* skeleton, they have also uncovered a partial foot dated to about 3.4 mya (Haile-Selassie et al, 2012). However, the partial foot remains, which include several nicely preserved toe bones, are very different from those of

A. afarensis and other obligate bipeds. The new find shows a divergent opposable big toe and other apelike features that strongly suggest that this animal was a good climber. At the same time there are some other characteristics suggesting that it probably could walk bipedally on the ground, although not in a manner like *A. afarensis* or any later hominin. This odd mix of characteristics looks most like that of *Ardipithecus*, which lived a full million years earlier. Without more complete fossil remains, it's impossible, for now, to assign this new find to a particular species. One thing is for sure: It isn't *A. afarensis*! So, there were two different lineages living side by side, each with very different foot anatomy and varied forms of locomotion. The researchers who have studied these new foot fossils as well as some other experts (Lieberman, 2012) think it was a hominin that was at least partially bipedal. On both counts, we'll have to wait and see.

At the same site, Haile-Selassie and colleagues (2015) also found hominin dental remains dating from 3.3–3.5 mya. Although not associated with the partial foot remains discussed above, these dental remains may belong to the same species. These dental remains match most closely with *Australopithecus*, although the authors argue that they belong to a new species (*A. deyiremeda*); however, additional fossil evidence and continued study of this material are needed to better understand its phylogenetic placement on the hominin tree.

Later More Derived Australopiths (3.0 to 1.2 mya)

Following 3.0 mya, hominins became more diverse in Africa. As they adapted to varied niches, australopiths became considerably more derived. In other words, they show physical changes making them quite distinct from their immediate ancestors.

In fact, there were at least three separate lineages of hominins living (in some cases side by side) between 2.0 and 1.2 mya. One of these is a later form of *Australopithecus*; another is represented by the highly derived three species that are often assigned to the genus *Paranthropus*; and the last consists of early members of the genus *Homo*. Here we'll discuss *Paranthropus* and *Australopithecus*. *Homo* will be discussed in the next section.

The most derived australopiths are the various members of *Paranthropus*. While all australopiths have large teeth, *Paranthropus* has the largest teeth of all, especially as seen in its huge premolars and molars. Along with these massive back teeth, these hominins show a variety of other specializations related to powerful chewing (Fig. 10-16). For example, they all have large, deep lower jaws and large attachments for muscles associated with chewing. In fact, these chewing muscles are so prominent that major anatomical alterations evolved in the architecture of their face and skull vault. In particular, the *Paranthropus* face is flatter than that of any other australopith; the broad cheekbones (to which the masseter muscle attaches) flare out; and a ridge develops on top of the skull (this is called a **sagittal crest**, and it's where the temporal muscle attaches).

All these morphological features indicating strong chewing suggest that *Paranthropus* likely was adapted for a diet emphasizing rough vegetable foods. However, this does not mean that these very large-toothed hominins did not also eat a variety of other foods, perhaps including some meat. In fact, sophisticated chemical analyses of *Paranthropus* teeth suggest that their diet may have been quite varied (Sponheimer et al., 2006).

The first member of the *Paranthropus* evolutionary group (clade) comes from a site in northern Kenya on the west side of Lake Turkana. This key find is that of a nearly complete skull, called the "Black Skull" (owing to the chemical staining from manganese-rich soil during fossilization), dating to approximately 2.5 mya

sagittal crest A ridge of bone that runs down the middle of the cranium like a short Mohawk. This serves as the attachment for the large temporal muscles, indicating strong chewing.

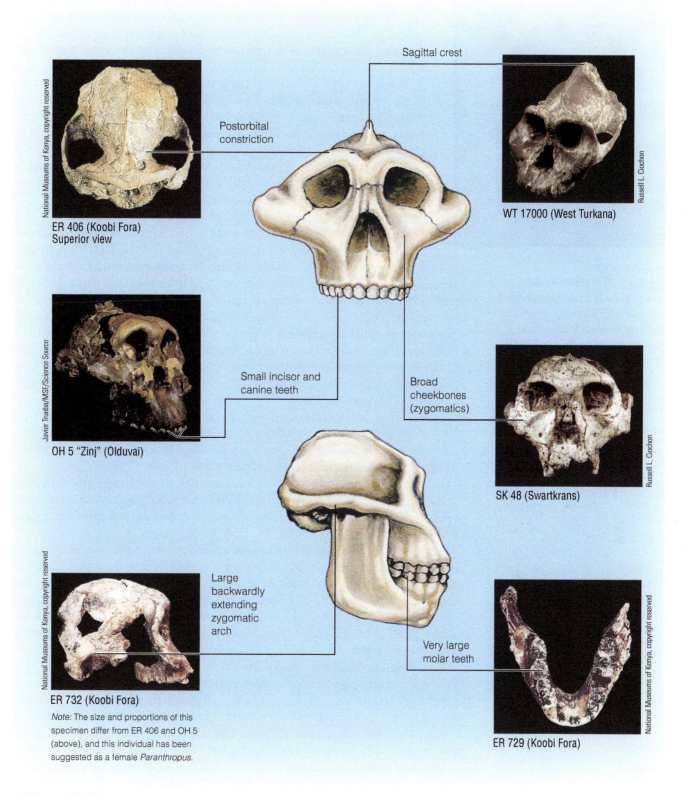

Sagittal crest

Postorbital constriction

National Museums of Kenya, copyright reserved

ER 406 (Koobi Fora)
Superior view

Javier Trueba/MSF/Science Source

OH 5 "Zinj" (Olduvai)

Small incisor and canine teeth

Russell L. Ciochon

WT 17000 (West Turkana)

Broad cheekbones (zygomatics)

Russell L. Ciochon

SK 48 (Swartkrans)

National Museums of Kenya, copyright reserved

ER 732 (Koobi Fora)

Large backwardly extending zygomatic arch

Very large molar teeth

National Museums of Kenya, copyright reserved

ER 729 (Koobi Fora)

Note: The size and proportions of this specimen differ from ER 406 and OH 5 (above), and this individual has been suggested as a female *Paranthropus.*

▲ **Figure 10-16**

Morphology and variation in *Paranthropus.* (Note both typical features and range of variation as shown in different specimens.)

▲ **Figure 10-17**

The "Black Skull," discovered at West Lake Turkana. This specimen is usually assigned to *Paranthropus aethiopicus*. It's called the Black Skull because of its dark color due to the fossilization (mineralization) process.

(Fig. 10-17). This skull, with a cranial capacity of only 410 cm³, is among the smallest for any hominin known, and it has other primitive traits reminiscent of *A. afarensis*. For example, there's a compound crest in the back of the skull, the upper face projects considerably, and the upper dental row converges in back (Kimbel et al., 1988).

However, here's what makes the Black Skull so fascinating: Mixed into this array of distinctively primitive traits are a host of derived ones that link it to other, later *Paranthropus* species (including a broad face, a very large palate, and a large area for the back teeth). This mosaic of features seems to place this individual between earlier *A. afarensis* on the one hand and the later *Paranthropus* species on the other. Because of its unique position in hominin evolution, the Black Skull (and the population it represents) has been placed in a new species, *Paranthropus aethiopicus*.

Around 2 mya, different varieties of even more derived members of the *Paranthropus* lineage were on the scene in East Africa. As well documented by finds dated after 2 mya from Olduvai and East Turkana, *Paranthropus* continued to have a relatively small cranial capacity (ranging from 510 to 530 cm³) and a very large, broad face with massive back teeth and lower jaws. The larger (probably male) individuals also show the characteristic raised ridge (sagittal crest) along the midline of the cranium. Females are not as large or as robust as the males, indicating a fair degree of sexual dimorphism. In any case, the East African *Paranthropus* individuals are all extremely robust in terms of their teeth and jaws—although in overall body size they are much like other australopiths. Since these somewhat later East African *Paranthropus**fossils are so robust, they are usually placed in their own separate species, *Paranthropus boisei*.

Paranthropus fossils have also been found at several sites in South Africa. The geological context in South Africa usually does not allow as precise chronometric dating as is possible in East Africa. Based on less precise dating methods, *Paranthropus* in South Africa existed about 2.0 to 1.2 mya.

Paranthropus in South Africa is very similar to its close cousin in East Africa, but it's not quite as dentally robust. As a result, paleoanthropologists prefer to regard South African *Paranthropus* as a distinct species—one called *Paranthropus robustus*.

Despite the suite of shared traits found among the three recognized species of *Paranthropus*, there remains some controversy over their taxonomic status. For example, some researchers prefer to group all of these derived species with the genus *Australopithecus*, in part because it is possible that the East African and South African forms evolved their features through homoplasy. The debate is far from resolved and, at this point, it makes more sense to classify them as a separate genus, *Paranthropus*.

What became of *Paranthropus*? After 1 mya, these hominins seem to have vanished without leaving any descendants. Nevertheless, we should be careful not to think of them as evolutionary "failures." After all, they lasted for 1.5 million years, during which time they expanded over a considerable area of sub-Saharan Africa. Moreover, while their extreme dental/chewing adaptations may seem peculiar to us, they represent a fascinating "evolutionary experiment" in hominin evolution, as well as an innovation that worked for a long time. Still, these large-toothed cousins of ours did eventually die out. It remains to us, the descendants of another hominin lineage, to find their fossils, study them, and ponder what these creatures were like.

---

*Note that these later East African *Paranthropus* finds are at least 500,000 years later than the earlier species (*P. aethiopicus*, exemplified by the Black Skull).

No fossil finds of the genus *Australopithecus* more recent than 3 mya have yet been found in East Africa. As you know, their close *Paranthropus* kin were doing quite well during this time. Whether *Australopithecus* actually did become extinct in East Africa around 3 mya or whether we just haven't yet found their fossils is impossible to say at this point.

South Africa, however, is another story. A very well-known *Australopithecus* species has been found at four sites in southernmost Africa, in a couple of cases in limestone caves very close to where *Paranthropus* fossils have also been found.

In fact, the very first early hominin discovery from Africa (indeed, from *anywhere*) came from the Taung site and was discovered back in 1924. The story of the discovery of the beautifully preserved child's skull from Taung is a fascinating tale (Fig. 10-18). When first published in 1925 by a young anatomist named Raymond Dart (Fig. 10-19), most experts were unimpressed by the small-brained specimen of a 3- to 4-year-old child. They believed that our earliest ancestors would be easily identifiable by their larger brains and thought of Africa as an unlikely place for the origins of hominins. These skeptics, who for a long time had been focused on European and Asian hominin finds, were initially unprepared to acknowledge Africa's central place in human evolution. Only years later, following many more African discoveries from other sites, did professional opinion shift. With this admittedly slow scientific awareness came the eventual consensus that the Taung specimen (which Dart classified as *Australopithecus africanus*, which means southern ape of Africa) was indeed an ancient member of the hominin family tree.

Like other australopiths, the "Taung child" (the type specimen) and other *A. africanus* individuals (Fig. 10-20) were small-brained, with an adult cranial capacity of about 440 cm³. In fact, the Taung child is quite remarkable for its preservation of a natural **endocast**. It was this fossilized cast of the external morphology of the right side of the child's brain that led Dart to recognize it as hominin and not an ape. As a recent reassessment of this brain cast has shown, *A. africanus* already had a pattern of brain development more in line with that of later hominins (Falk et al., 2012). *A. africanus* was also large-toothed relative to later hominins, although not as extremely so as *Paranthropus*. Moreover, from very well-preserved postcranial remains from Sterkfontein, we know that these individuals were also were well-adapted bipeds. The ongoing excavation of the remarkably complete skeleton at Sterkfontein should tell us a lot about *A. africanus*' locomotion, body size and proportions, and much more (Fig. 10-21). This skeleton has been recently re-dated to 3.67 mya using radioisotope methods of the limestone deposits that encased the fossil (Granger et al., 2015), although this will likely remain controversial. The skull and left arm have been removed, but much of the skeleton is still being carefully excavated within the cave.

The precise dating of *A. africanus*, as with most other South African hominins, has been disputed. Over the last several years, it's been assumed that this species existed as far back as 3.3 mya. However, the most recent analyses suggest that *A. africanus* lived approximately between 3 and 2 mya (Walker et al., 2006; Wood, 2010) (Fig. 10-22 on p. 309). The more recent dating evidence from Sterkfontein, however, may extent this back further in time.

New Connections: A Transitional Australopith?

As we'll see in the next section, almost all the evidence for the earliest appearance of our genus, *Homo*, has come from East Africa. So it's no surprise that most researchers have assumed that *Homo* probably first evolved in this region of Africa.

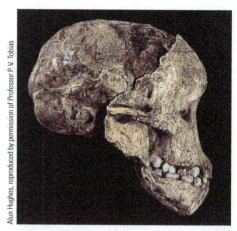

▲ **Figure 10-18**
The Taung child's skull, discovered in 1924. There is a fossilized endocast of the brain in back, with the face and lower jaw in front.

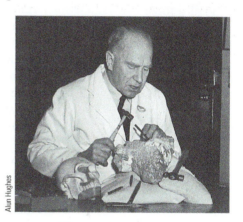

▲ **Figure 10-19**
Raymond Dart, shown working in his laboratory.

endocast A solid impression of the inside of the skull vault, often preserving details relating to the size and surface features of the brain.

▲ **Figure 10-20**

Adult cranium of *Australopithecus africanus* from Sterkfontein.

However, new and remarkably well-preserved fossil discoveries from South Africa may challenge this view. In 2008, paleoanthropologists discovered two partial skeletons at the Malapa Cave, located just a few miles from Sterkfontein and Swartkrans (see Fig. 10-8). Actually, the first find was made by the lead researcher's 9-year-old son, Matthew, while out walking the family dog. His father (Lee Berger, from the University of Witwatersrand) and colleagues have been further investigating inside the cave, where several skeletons may be buried; they announced and described these finds in 2010 (Berger et al., 2010). Recently, much more detailed analyses have been published in a series of papers in 2013 (Churchill et al., 2013; de Ruiter et al., 2013; DeSilva et al., 2013; Irish et al., 2013; Schmid et al., 2013; Williams et al., 2013). Current interpretations of the site context suggest that the two individuals likely fell through a fissure into a deep cave shaft (Dirks et al., 2010). In fact, both individuals demonstrate clear evidence of bone fractures that occurred at or around the time of death (that is, perimortem), consistent with a fall into the cave shaft (L'Abbé et al., 2015).

Using paleomagnetic dating as well as more precise radiometric techniques than have been used before in South Africa (Dirks et al., 2010; Pickering et al., 2011) (see Chapter 9), the fossils are dated to just a little less than 2 mya and show a fascinating mosaic of primitive australopith characteristics along with a few derived features more suggestive of *Homo*. In addition, the dentition and jaws of these individuals show shape and size differences with other hominins, including South African specimens (de Ruiter et al., 2013; Irish et al., 2013). Because of this unique anatomical combination, these fossils have been assigned to a new species, *Australopithecus sediba* (*sediba* means "wellspring" or "fountain" in the local language). Australopith-like characteristics seen in *A. sediba* include a small brain (estimated at 420 cm³), the australopith shoulder joint, long arms with curved fingers, and several primitive traits in the feet. In these respects *A. sediba* most resembles *A. africanus*, its potential immediate South African predecessor. The analysis of the lower limb anatomy suggests that *A. sediba* would have swayed side-to-side while walking, an unusual form of bipedal locomotion (DeSilva et al., 2013). However, evidence of powerful upper

▶ **Figure 10-21**

The approximately 3.67-million-year-old skeleton from the limestone matrix at Sterkfontein Cave, South Africa. Clearly seen are the cranium (with articulated mandible) and the upper arm bone.

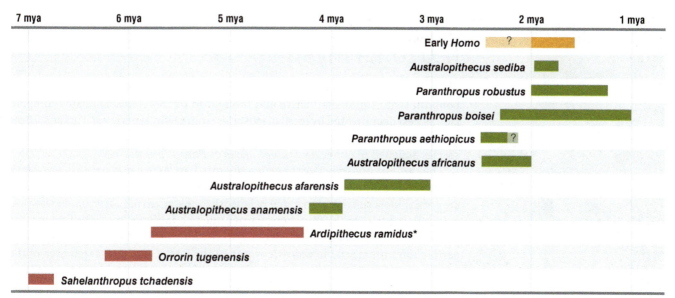

7 mya	6 mya	5 mya	4 mya	3 mya	2 mya	1 mya

Early *Homo* ?

Australopithecus sediba

Paranthropus robustus

Paranthropus boisei

Paranthropus aethiopicus ?

Australopithecus africanus

Australopithecus afarensis

Australopithecus anamensis

*Ardipithecus ramidus**

Orrorin tugenensis

Sahelanthropus tchadensis

*The earlier *Ardipithecus* specimens (5.8–5.2 mya) are placed in a separate species.

▲ **Figure 10-22**
Time line of early African hominins. Note that most dates are approximations. Question marks indicate those estimates that are most tentative.

limbs, the orientation of the shoulder, and other anatomical features suggest it likely retained adaptations to arboreal habitats, a common finding in earlier australopiths (Churchill et al., 2013).

On the other hand, some other aspects of *A. sediba* more closely resemble *Homo*. Among these characteristics are short fingers, a more flexible lower spine (as well as five lumbar vertebrae like modern humans), and possible indications of brain reorganization (see Fig. 10-23). All this is very new and quite complex. Indeed, initial paleoanthropological interpretations are highly varied (Balter, 2010; Gibbons, 2011a; Pickering et al., 2011; Kimbel, 2013). It will take some time for experts to figure it out.

What's more, new dental evidence shows that *A. sediba* had a surprising diet, at least one that is unusual for a hominin. Using an array of methods—including stable carbon isotopes, phytolith residues in dental calculus, and dental microwear (see Chapter 9 for discussion of all three methods)—Amanda Henry and colleagues have analyzed teeth from both skeletons thus far excavated at Malapa (Henry et al., 2012). Their results indicate that *A. sediba* primarily ate leaves, fruit, wood, and bark, along with a few grasses. Unlike that seen in most other early hominins, there is no evidence of a dietary focus on grass resources or meat, which are more typically found in more open savanna habitats. Indeed, *A. sediba*'s diet appears to more closely resemble that of chimpanzees rather than that of most other hominins. The closest early hominin similarity is with *Ardipithecus*. These findings indicate that in anatomy as well as behavior, early hominins were an extremely varied group.

Remember, too, that there are more fossils still to be unearthed at Malapa. The initial consensus among paleoanthropologists is that *A. sediba* is quite different from other australopiths and shows a surprising and unique mix of primitive and derived characteristics. How it fits in with the origins of *Homo* remains to be determined. Certainly, more detailed studies of the *A. sediba* fossils, including further comparisons with other early hominins will help to further our understanding where *A. sediba* fits in (Fig. 10-24). For the moment, most paleoanthropologists still think that the best evidence for the origins of our genus comes from East Africa.

University of the Witwatersrand, Lee Berger. Photo by Brett Eloff.

▲ **Figure 10-23**
A. sediba skull, found at Malapa Cave, South Africa.

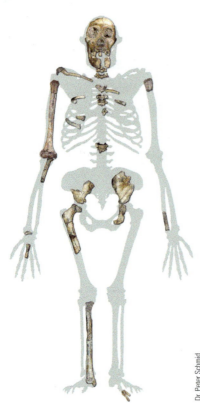

Dr. Peter Schmid

▲ **Figure 10-24**

One of the two partial *A. sediba* skeletons so far discovered at Malapa Cave, showing those elements that were preserved.

Plio-Pleistocene Pertaining to the Pliocene and first half of the Pleistocene, a time range of 5 to 1 mya. For this time period, numerous fossil hominins have been found in Africa.

Closer Connections: Early *Homo* (2.0 to 1.4 mya)

In addition to the australopith remains, there's another largely contemporaneous hominin that is quite distinctive and thought to be more closely related to us. In fact, as best documented by fossil discoveries from Olduvai and East Turkana, these materials have been assigned to the genus *Homo*—and thus are different from all species assigned to either *Australopithecus* or *Paranthropus*.

The earliest appearance of the genus *Homo* in East Africa may date prior to 2 mya (and thus considerably before *A. sediba*). A discovery in the 1990s from the Hadar area of Ethiopia suggested to many paleoanthropologists that early *Homo* was present in East Africa by 2.3 mya; however, we must be cautious, since the find is quite incomplete (including only one upper jaw) (Kimbel et al., 1996). More recently, a partial hominin mandible was discovered in the Ledi-Geraru research area of the Afar region of Ethiopia (Villmoare et al., 2015). This lower jawbone, dated to about 2.8 mya, has provided the earliest possible evidence of the genus *Homo* (DiMaggio et al., 2015). Although the researchers did not classify the jaw into a particular species, they argue that it shows morphology more consistent with early *Homo* than with earlier hominins, such as the australopithecines (Villmoare et al., 2015). Hawks and colleagues (2015) caution against classifying the fossil into the genus *Homo*, and have argued that the taxonomic status of the mandible is uncertain. More complete remains will be needed to better understand where these Late Pliocene specimens fit into the hominin lineage.

Better-preserved evidence of a **Plio-Pleistocene** hominin with a significantly larger brain than seen in australopiths was first suggested by Louis Leakey in the early 1960s on the basis of fragmentary remains found at Olduvai Gorge in Tanzania. Leakey and his colleagues gave a new species designation to these fossil remains, naming them *Homo habilis*. There may, in fact, have been more than one species of *Homo* living in Africa during the Plio-Pleistocene. Therefore, more generally, we'll refer to them all as "early *Homo*." The species *Homo habilis* comprises particularly those early *Homo* fossils from Olduvai and the Turkana Basin.

The *Homo habilis* material at Olduvai dates to about 1.8 mya, but owing to the fragmentary nature of the fossil remains, evolutionary interpretations have been difficult. The most immediately obvious feature distinguishing the *H. habilis* material from the australopiths is cranial size. For all the measurable early *Homo* skulls, the estimated average cranial capacity is 631 cm³, compared to 520 cm³ for all measurable *Paranthropus* specimens and 442 cm³ for *Australopithecus* crania (McHenry, 1988), including *A. sediba* (see "A Closer Look: Cranial Capacity," p. 302). Early *Homo*, therefore, shows an increase in cranial size of about 20 percent over the larger of the australopiths and an even greater increase over some of the smaller-brained forms. In their initial description of *H. habilis*, Leakey and his associates also pointed to differences from australopiths in cranial shape and in tooth proportions.

The naming of this fossil material as *Homo habilis* ("handy man") was meaningful from two perspectives. First of all, Leakey argued that members of this group were the early Olduvai toolmakers. Second, and most significantly, by calling this group *Homo*, Leakey was arguing for at least *two separate branches* of hominin evolution in the Plio-Pleistocene. Clearly, only one could be on the main branch eventually leading to *Homo sapiens*. By labeling this new group *Homo* rather than *Australopithecus*, Leakey was guessing that he had found our ancestors.

Because the initial evidence was so fragmentary, most paleoanthropologists were reluctant to accept *H. habilis* as a valid species distinct from all australopiths. Later discoveries, especially from Lake Turkana, of better-preserved fossils have shed further light on early *Homo* in the Plio-Pleistocene. The most important of this

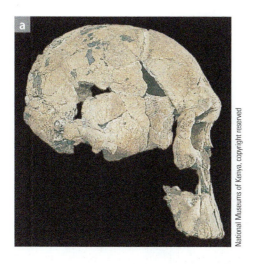

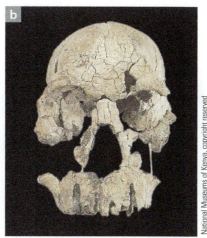

◀ **Figure 10-25**

A nearly complete early *Homo* cranium from East Lake Turkana (ER 1470), one of the most important single fossil hominin discoveries from East Africa. **(a)** Lateral view. **(b)** Frontal view.

additional material is a nearly complete cranium (Fig. 10-25). With a cranial capacity of 775 cm³, this individual is well outside the known range for australopiths and actually overlaps the lower boundary for later species of *Homo* (that is, *Homo erectus*, discussed in the next chapter). In addition, the shape of the skull vault is in many respects unlike that of australopiths. However, the face is still quite robust (Walker, 1976), and the fragments of tooth crowns that are preserved indicate that the back teeth in this individual were quite large.* The East Turkana early *Homo* material is generally contemporaneous with the Olduvai remains. The oldest fossils date to about 1.8 mya, but another specimen found a few years ago dates to as recently as 1.44 mya, making it by far the latest surviving early *Homo* fossil yet found (Spoor et al., 2007). In fact, this discovery indicates that a species of early *Homo* coexisted in East Africa for several hundred thousand years with *H. erectus*, with both species living in the exact same area on the eastern side of Lake Turkana. Recent reassessments of early *Homo* fossils further identified a high level of variation (especially in jaw morphology), which suggests the presence of at least two early *Homo* species (Spoor at al., 2015). This new evidence raises numerous fascinating questions regarding how two or more closely related species of early *Homo* existed for so long in the same region.

As in East Africa, early members of the genus *Homo* have also been found in South Africa, and these fossils are considered more distinctive of *Homo* than is the *transitional* australopith, *A. sediba*. At both Sterkfontein and Swartkrans, fragmentary remains have been recognized as most likely belonging to *Homo* (Fig. 10-26).

On the basis of evidence from Olduvai, East Turkana, and Hadar, we can reasonably postulate that at least one species (and possibly two) of early *Homo* was present in East Africa perhaps before 2 mya, developing in parallel with an australopith species. These hominin lines lived contemporaneously for at least 1 million years, after which the australopiths apparently disappeared forever. One lineage of early *Homo* likely evolved into *H. erectus* about 1.8 mya. Any other species of early *Homo* became extinct sometime after 1.4 mya.

Interpretations: What Does It All Mean?

By this time, you may think that anthropologists are obsessed with finding small fragments of bones and teeth buried in the ground and then giving them confusing

*In fact, some researchers have suggested that all these "early *Homo*" fossils are better classified as *Australopithecus* (Wood and Collard, 1999a).

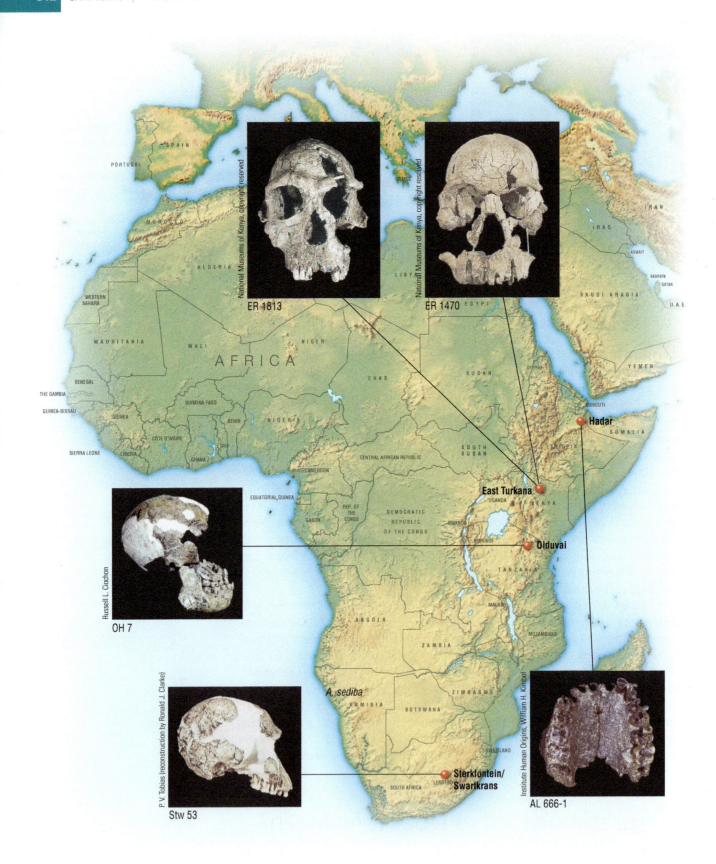

ER 1813

ER 1470

OH 7

Stw 53

AL 666-1

Hadar

East Turkana

Olduvai

A. sediba

Sterkfontein/
Swartkrans

▲ **Figure 10-26**
Early *Homo* fossil finds.

numbers and taxonomic labels that are impossible to remember. However, it's important to realize that the collection of all the basic fossil data is the foundation of human evolutionary research. Without fossils, our speculations would be largely hollow—and most certainly not scientifically testable. Several large, ongoing paleoanthropological projects are now collecting additional data in an attempt to answer some of the more perplexing questions about our evolutionary history.

The numbering of specimens, which may at times seem somewhat confusing, is an effort to keep the designations neutral and to make reference to each individual fossil as clear as possible. The formal naming of finds as *Australopithecus*, *Paranthropus*, or *Homo habilis* should come much later, since it involves a lengthy series of complex analyses and interpretations. Assigning generic and specific names to fossil finds is more than just a convenience; when we attach a particular label, such as *A. afarensis*, to a particular fossil, we should be fully aware of the biological implications of such an interpretation.

From the time that fossil sites are first located until the eventual interpretation of hominin evolutionary patterns, several steps take place. Ideally, they should follow a logical order, for if interpretations are made too hastily, they confuse important issues for many years. Here's a reasonable sequence:

1. Selecting and surveying sites
2. Excavating sites and recovering fossil hominins
3. Designating individual finds with specimen numbers for clear reference
4. Cleaning, preparing, studying, and describing fossils
5. Comparing with other fossil material—in a chronological framework if possible
6. Comparing fossil variation with known ranges of variation in closely related groups of living primates and analyzing ancestral and derived characteristics
7. Assigning taxonomic names to fossil material
8. Publishing results and interpretations in peer-reviewed sources

But the task of interpretation still isn't complete, for what we really want to know in the long run is what happened to the populations represented by the fossil remains. In looking at the fossil hominin record, we're actually looking for our ancestors. In the process of eventually determining those populations that are our most likely antecedents, we may conclude that some hominins are on evolutionary side branches. If this conclusion is accurate, those hominins necessarily must have become extinct. It's both interesting and relevant to us as hominins to try to find out what influenced some earlier members of our family tree to continue evolving while others died out.

Although a clear evolutionary picture is not yet possible for organizing all the early hominins discussed in this chapter, there are some general patterns that for now make good sense (Fig. 10-27). New finds may of course require serious alterations to this scheme. Science can be exciting, but it can also be frustrating to many in the general public looking for simple answers to complex questions. For well-informed students of human evolution, it's most important to grasp the basic principles of paleoanthropology, *how* interpretations are made, and *why* they must sometimes be revised. This way you'll be prepared for whatever shows up tomorrow.

Seeing the Big Picture: Adaptive Patterns of Early African Hominins

As you are aware by now, there are several different African hominin genera and certainly lots of species. This in itself is interesting. Speciation was occurring quite

▶ **Figure 10-27**
A tentative early hominin phylogeny. Note the numerous question marks, indicating continuing uncertainty regarding evolutionary relationships.

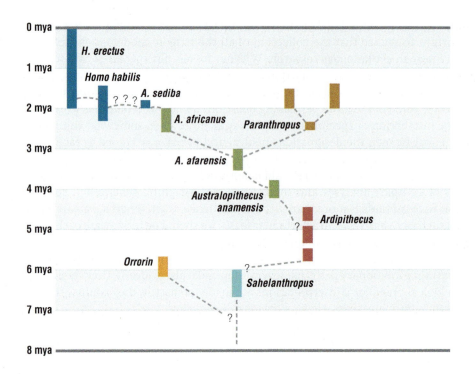

frequently among the various lineages of early hominins—more frequently, in fact, than among later hominins. What explains this pattern?

Evidence has been accumulating at a furious pace in the last decade, but it's still far from complete. What's clear is that we'll never have anything approaching a complete record of early hominin evolution, so some significant gaps will remain. After all, we're able to discover hominins only in those special environmental contexts where fossilization was likely. All the other potential habitats they might have exploited are now invisible to us.

Still, patterns are emerging from the fascinating data we do have. First, it appears that early hominin species (pre-australopiths, *Australopithecus*, *Paranthropus*, and early *Homo*) all had restricted ranges. It's therefore likely that each hominin species exploited a relatively small area with specific niches and could easily have become separated from other populations of its own species. So genetic drift (and to some extent natural selection) could have led to rapid genetic divergence and eventual speciation.

Second, most of these species appear to have been at least partially tied to arboreal habitats, although there's disagreement on this point regarding early *Homo* (see Wood and Collard, 1999b; Foley, 2002). Also, *Paranthropus* was probably somewhat less arboreal than *Ardipithecus* or *Australopithecus*. These very large-toothed hominins apparently concentrated on a diet of coarse, fibrous plant foods, such as roots. Exploiting such resources may have routinely taken these hominins farther away from the trees than their dentally more gracile—and perhaps more omnivorous—cousins.

Third, except for some early members of the genus *Homo*, there's very little in the way of an evolutionary trend of increased body size or of markedly greater encephalization. Beginning with *Sahelanthropus*, brain size was no more than that in chimpanzees—although when accounting for body size, this earliest of all known hominins may have had a proportionately larger brain than any living ape. Close to 5 million years later (that is, the time of the last surviving australopith species), relative brain size increased by no more than 10 to 15 percent. Perhaps tied to this relative stasis in brain capacity, there's no absolute association of any of these hominins with patterned stone tool manufacture (see Chapter 9).

Although conclusions are becoming increasingly controversial, for the moment early *Homo* appears to be a partial exception. This group shows both increased encephalization and numerous occurrences of likely association with stone tools (though at many of the sites, australopith fossils were *also* found).

Last, all of these early African hominins show an accelerated growth and development pattern (similar to that seen in African apes)—one quite different from the *delayed* growth and development pattern characteristic of *Homo sapiens* (and our immediate precursors). This apelike development is also seen in some early *Homo* individuals (Wood and Collard, 1999a). Rates of development can be accurately reconstructed by examining dental growth markers (Bromage and Dean, 1985; Smith, 2008; Smith et al., 2015), and these data may provide a crucial window into understanding this early stage of hominin evolution.

These African hominin predecessors were rather small, able bipeds, but still closely tied to arboreal and/or climbing niches. They had fairly small brains and, compared to later *Homo*, matured rapidly. It would take a major evolutionary jump to push one of their descendants in a more human direction. For the next chapter in this more human saga, read on.

How Do We Know?

We know a great deal about early hominin evolution, especially from a large number of fossils, which now include thousands of individual elements—representing more than 500 individuals. What's more, some of these finds are quite complete, including some remarkable skeletons discovered recently in South and East Africa. By comparing these finds with modern humans and apes, we can interpret the anatomy and likely function of these early hominins. For paleoanthropologists, the advent of bipedalism is often considered the key transition marking the beginning of the hominin lineage. In fact, researchers often identify fossils as *hominin* when evidence suggests bipedal anatomy. But how do we recognize this evidence? Fortunately, both direct and indirect evidence for bipedalism can be found throughout almost the entire skeleton, as well as in fossilized footprints such as the ones discovered at Laetoli in Tanzania. Bipedal locomotion required major changes in skeletal anatomy as well as the orientation of muscles and ligaments. For cranial remains, evidence for bipedalism includes more anterior placement of the foramen magnum, smaller muscle attachments in the nuchal area at the back of the skull, and a high degree of flexion of the cranial base. Evidence from the vertebral column includes an increase in vertebral size from the neck down to the lower back, indicating a weight-bearing spine. Further, the concave curve in the neck area, convex curve in the mid-back, and concave curve in the lower back area all help to balance the weight of different body regions over their respective centers of gravity. Evidence for bipedalism is more difficult to infer from the arm and hand, although robust arm bones and curved finger bones in fossils suggest some emphasis on arboreal locomotion (a finding in most early hominin species). Clear evidence of bipedalism can also be found in the pelvis, lower limb, and foot. For pelvic remains, the wide, flared ilium is a key indicator of bipedalism (designed to stabilize weight transmission), whereas quadrupedal primates have a narrow, elongated ilium. In the lower limb, the femur slants inward to position the knees under the center of gravity. Thus, a fossilized femur can provide definitive evidence for bipedalism. Lastly, fossilized foot remains can provide telltale signs of bipedalism, such as a large heel bone and a robust first metatarsal (reflecting the heel-to-toe strike in bipedal locomotion), by the presence of a longitudinal arch in the foot that aids in propulsion and acts as a shock absorber, and by a big toe that is in line with the rest of the foot.

What Do You Think?

Definitive evidence for bipedalism can be tracked to at least 4 mya, although it is likely that the very earliest hominin groups were also bipedal. What are some of the limitations of attempting to interpret anatomical evidence for bipedal locomotion in highly fragmented and incomplete fossil specimens?

Summary of Main Topics

- Bipedalism evolved as a new loco-motor strategy during the Late Miocene among the earliest homi-nin lineage. This new form of loco-motion evolved in a mosaic pattern from habitual bipedalism toward obligate bipedalism.

- The earliest possible members of our lineage date back to about 6 mya, and for the next 4 million years, they stayed geographically restricted to Africa, where they diversified into many different forms. During this several-million-year span, at least six different hominin genera and at least 14 species have been identi-fied from the available fossil record. These earliest African hominins fit into two major groupings:
  - Pre-australopiths (6.0+ to 4.4 mya), including three genera of very early, and still primitive, possible hominins (*Sahelanthro-pus*, *Orrorin*, and *Ardipithecus*).

- Australopiths (4.2 to 1.2 mya): Early, more primitive australo-pith species (4.2 to 3.0 mya), including *Australopithecus ana-mensis* and *Australopithecus afarensis*. These are the earliest definite hominins. Later, more derived australopith species (2.5 to 1.2 mya) include two genera (*Paranthropus* and later species of *Australopithecus*). A recently discovered species (*A. sediba*), shows a combination of features that some researchers hypoth-esize as transitional between *Australopithecus* and early *Homo* (but this view remains controversial).

- Early *Homo* (2.0+? to 1.4 mya), including the first members of our genus (e.g., *Homo habilis*), who around 2 mya likely diverged into more than one species. New dates tentatively suggest the roots of early *Homo* may trace back to 2.8–2.4 mya.

- Formal naming of fossil hominin remains into species is a complex process, and involves assessment of site context, dates, fossil morphol-ogy, comparison with other fos-sil specimens, and publication of results in peer-reviewed sources.

- Restricted home ranges may have facilitated rapid speciation within hominin lineages. Genetic drift and natural selection likely accounted for divergences with-in lineages during the Late Mio-cene and Pliocene. Early hominins show evidence of a slight degree of encephalization over great apes, although growth and development follows an apelike pattern. Early hominins continued to use both arboreal habitats, although terres-trial habitats likely became more important over time.

Critical Thinking Questions

1. In what ways are the remains of *Sahelanthropus*, *Orrorin*, and *Ardipithecus* considered primi-tive? How do we know that these forms are hominins? How sure are we?

2. Assume that you are in the lab-oratory analyzing the "Lucy" *A. afarensis* skeleton. You also have complete skeletons from a chim-panzee and a modern human. (a) Which parts of the Lucy skeleton are more similar to the chimpan-zee? Which are more similar to the human? (b) Which parts of the Lucy skeleton are *most informa-tive* regarding hominin status?

3. Discuss two current disputes regarding taxonomic issues con-cerning early hominins. Try to give support for alternative positions.

4. What is a phylogeny? Construct one for early hominins (6.0 to 1.0 mya). Make sure you can describe the conclusions to which your scheme leads. Also, try to defend it.

5. Write down a list of the areas of expertise needed to conduct a paleoanthropological inves-tigation from start to finish. Then list what each specialty contributes to the overall pro-ject. Why are multidisciplinary efforts so important for ensur-ing success?

The first more human-like animals (hominins) appeared in Africa around 6 million years ago and evolved into a variety of different species.

Hominins began to disperse out of Africa around 2 million years ago, and during the next 1 million years inhabited much of Eurasia.

The immediate predecessors of modern humans, including the Neandertals, were much like us, but had some anatomical and behavioral differences.

The First Dispersal of the Genus *Homo:* *Homo erectus* and Contemporaries

11

A New Kind of Hominin

The Morphology of *Homo erectus*

Body Size

Brain Size

Cranial Shape

The Geographic Range of *Homo erectus*

The First Homo erectus: Homo erectus from Africa

A New Hominin Discovery in South Africa

Who Were the Earliest African Emigrants?

Homo erectus from Indonesia

Homo erectus from China

Asian and African Homo erectus: A Comparison

Later Homo erectus from Europe

Technological Trends During the Time of *Homo erectus*

Seeing the Connections: Interpretations of *Homo erectus*

Something New and Different: The "Little People"

Student Learning Objectives After studying the material in this chapter, you should be able to:

▶ Discuss why *Homo erectus* marks an adaptive shift in hominin evolution.

▶ Describe the key morphological characteristics of *H. erectus*.

▶ Discuss the geographic range of *H. erectus* and compare it to that of earlier hominins.

▶ Discuss what sorts of tools are associated with *H. erectus* and what they tell us about their cultural adaptations.

▶ Compare the Dmanisi discoveries with *H. erectus* from Africa and Europe and discuss how the Dmanisi hominins complicate earlier hypotheses regarding hominin dispersal.

▶ Describe the major physical features of *Homo floresiensis* and explain why the discovery of this hominin was such a surprise.

I t's estimated that more than 2 million people now cross national borders every day. Some travel for business, some for pleasure, and others may be seeking refuge from persecution in their own countries. Regardless, it seems that modern humans have wanderlust—a desire to see distant places. Our most distant hominin ancestors were essentially homebodies, staying in fairly restricted areas, exploiting the local resources, and trying to stay out of harm's way. In this respect, they were much like other primate species.

 Skull from Dmanisi, Republic of Georgia.

David Lordkipanidze; Top Images: © Cengage Learning; Russell L. Ciochon; Harry Nelson

One thing is certain: All of these early hominins were restricted to Africa. When did hominins first leave Africa? What were they like, and why did they leave their ancient homeland? In what ways did they differ physically from their australopith and early *Homo* forebears, and did they have new behavioral and cultural capabilities that helped them successfully exploit new environments?

It would be a romantic misconception to think of these first hominin transcontinental emigrants as "brave pioneers, boldly going where no one had gone before." They weren't deliberately striking out to go someplace in particular. It's not as though they had a map! Still, for what they did, deliberate or not, we owe them a lot.

Sometime close to 2 mya, something decisive occurred in human evolution. As the title of this chapter suggests, for the first time, hominins expanded widely out of Africa into other areas of the Old World. Because all the early fossils have been found *only* in Africa, it seems that hominins were restricted to that continent for perhaps as long as 5 million years. The later, more widely dispersed hominins were quite different both anatomically and behaviorally from their African ancestors. They were much larger in body size, were more committed to a completely terrestrial habitat, used more elaborate stone tools, and probably supplemented their diets with meat.

There is some variation among the different geographical groups of these highly successful hominins, and anthropologists still debate how to classify them. In particular, more recent discoveries from the Republic of Georgia over the last couple of decades have forced a major reevaluation of exactly which hominin species were the first to leave Africa (Fig. 11-1 on pp. 322–323).

Nevertheless, after 2 mya, there's less diversity among African hominins than is apparent in their pre-australopith and australopith predecessors. Consequently there is nearly universal agreement that the hominins found outside of Africa are all members of genus *Homo*. Thus taxonomic debates focus solely on how many species are represented. The early *Homo* species for which we have the most evidence, both physically and culturally, is called *Homo erectus*. Furthermore, this is the one group of early humans that most paleoanthropologists have recognized for decades and still agree on. Thus, in this chapter we'll focus our discussion on *Homo erectus*. We will, however, also discuss alternative interpretations that "split" the fossil sample into more species.

A New Kind of Hominin

The discovery of fossils now referred to as *Homo erectus* began in the late nineteenth century. Later in this chapter, we'll discuss the historical background of these earliest discoveries in Java and the somewhat later discoveries in China. For these fossils, as well as several from Europe and North Africa, a variety of taxonomic names have been suggested.

It's important to realize that such taxonomic *splitting* was quite common during the late nineteenth century, in the early years of paleoanthropology. More systematic biological thinking came to the fore only after World War II, with the incorporation of the Modern Synthesis (that is, the integration of natural selection theory and genetics) into paleontology. Most of the fossils that were given these varied names are now placed in the species *Homo erectus*—or at the very least have been lumped into one genus (*Homo*).

In the last few decades, discoveries from East Africa of firmly dated fossils have established the clear presence of *Homo erectus* by 1.7 mya and even a little earlier in western Asia, in the Republic of Georgia (Ferring et al., 2011). Some researchers see several anatomical differences between these African representatives of a *Homo erectus*-like hominin and their Asian cousins (hominins that almost everybody refers to as *Homo erectus*). Thus they place the African fossils into a separate species, one they call *Homo ergaster* (Andrews, 1984; Wood, 1991).

As we will discuss, there are some anatomical differences between the African specimens and those from Asia; however, they are all clearly *closely* related and likely represent geographical varieties of a single species. We'll thus recognize them as a single species and refer to them collectively as *Homo erectus*.

Most analyses show that *H. erectus* is quite different from their more ancient African predecessors. An increase in body size and robusticity, changes in limb proportions (especially longer lower limbs), and an increase in brain size (that is, more encephalized) all indicate that these hominins were more like modern humans in their adaptive pattern than their African ancestors were. It's clear from most of the fossils usually classified as *Homo erectus* that a major adaptive shift had taken place—one setting hominin evolution in a distinctly more human direction.

We mentioned that there is considerable variation among different regional populations defined as *Homo erectus*. More recent discoveries in western Asia show even more dramatic variation, suggesting that some of these hominins may not fit closely with this general adaptive pattern (discussed later in this chapter). For the moment, however, let's review the common features found in most of these fossils.

The Morphology of *Homo erectus*

Homo erectus populations lived in very different environments over much of the Old World. They all, however, shared several common physical traits.

Body Size

Anthropologists estimate that some *H. erectus* adults weighed well over 100 pounds, with an average adult height of about 5 feet 6 inches (McHenry, 1992; Ruff and Walker, 1993; Walker and Leakey, 1993). Another point to keep in mind is that *H. erectus* was quite sexually dimorphic—at least as indicated by the East African specimens.

Increased height, especially leg length, and weight in *H. erectus* are also associated with a dramatic increase in robusticity. In fact, a heavily built body was to dominate hominin evolution not just during *H. erectus* times but through the long transitional era of premodern forms as well. Only with the appearance of anatomically modern *H. sapiens* did a more gracile skeletal structure emerge, one that still characterizes most modern populations.

Brain Size

Although *Homo erectus* differs in several respects from both early *Homo* (for example, *Homo habilis*) and *Homo sapiens*, the most obvious feature is internal cranial size—which is closely related to brain size. Early *Homo* had cranial capacities ranging from as small as 500 cm³ to as large as 800 cm³. *H. erectus*, on the other hand, shows considerable brain enlargement, with a cranial capacity of about 700* to 1,250 cm³ (and a mean of approximately 900 cm³).

As we've discussed, brain size is closely linked to overall body size. So it's important to note that along with an increase in brain size, *H. erectus* was also considerably larger than earlier members of the genus *Homo*. In fact, when we compare *H. erectus* with the larger-bodied early *Homo* individuals, *relative* brain size is about the same (Walker, 1991). What's more, when we compare the relative brain size of *H. erectus* with that of *H. sapiens*, we see that *H. erectus* was considerably less encephalized than later members of the genus *Homo*.

---

*Even smaller cranial capacities are seen in recently discovered fossils from the Caucasus region of the Republic of Georgia at a site called Dmanisi. We'll discuss these fossils in a moment.

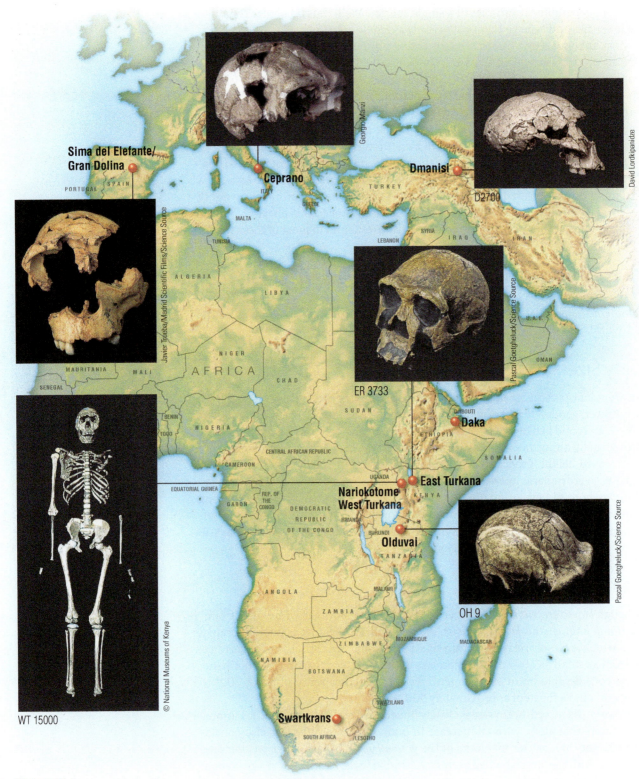

▲ **Figure 11-1**

Major *Homo erectus* sites and localities
of other contemporaneous hominins.

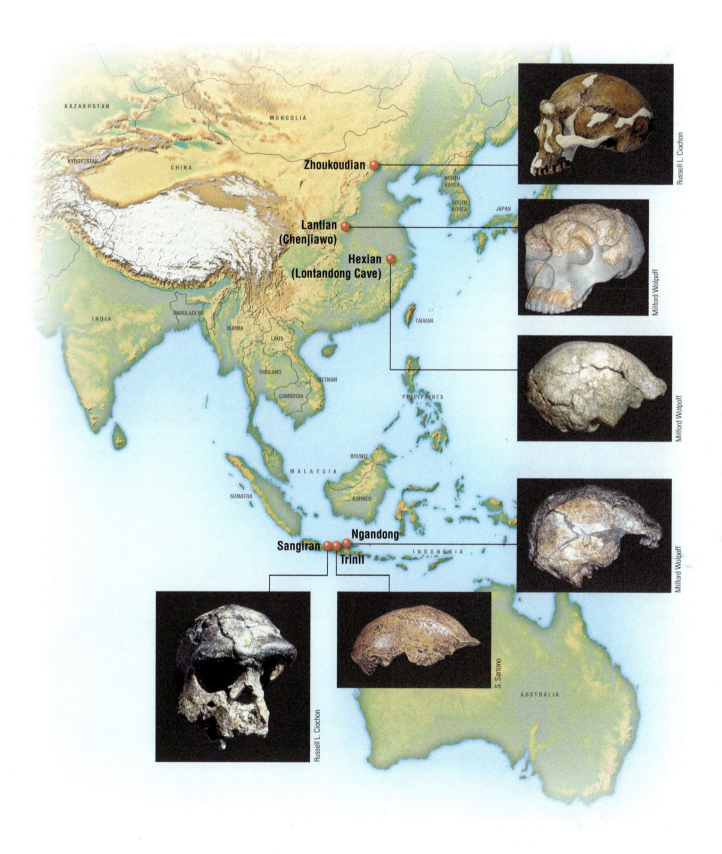

Zhoukoudian

Lantian
(Chenjiawo)

Hexian
(Lontandong Cave)

Ngandong

Sangiran

Trinil

Russell L. Ciochon

Milford Wolpoff

Milford Wolpoff

Milford Wolpoff

Russell L. Ciochon

S. Sartono

Cranial Shape

nuchal torus (nuke´-ul) (*nucha*, meaning "neck") A projection of bone in the back of the cranium where neck muscles attach. These muscles hold up the head.

Homo erectus crania display a highly distinctive shape, partly because of increased brain size but probably more correlated with increased body size. The ramifications of this heavily built cranium are reflected in thick cranial bone (in most specimens), large browridges (supraorbital tori) above the eyes, and a projecting **nuchal torus** at the back of the skull (Fig.11-2).

▼ **Figure 11-2**
Morphology and variation in *Homo erectus*.

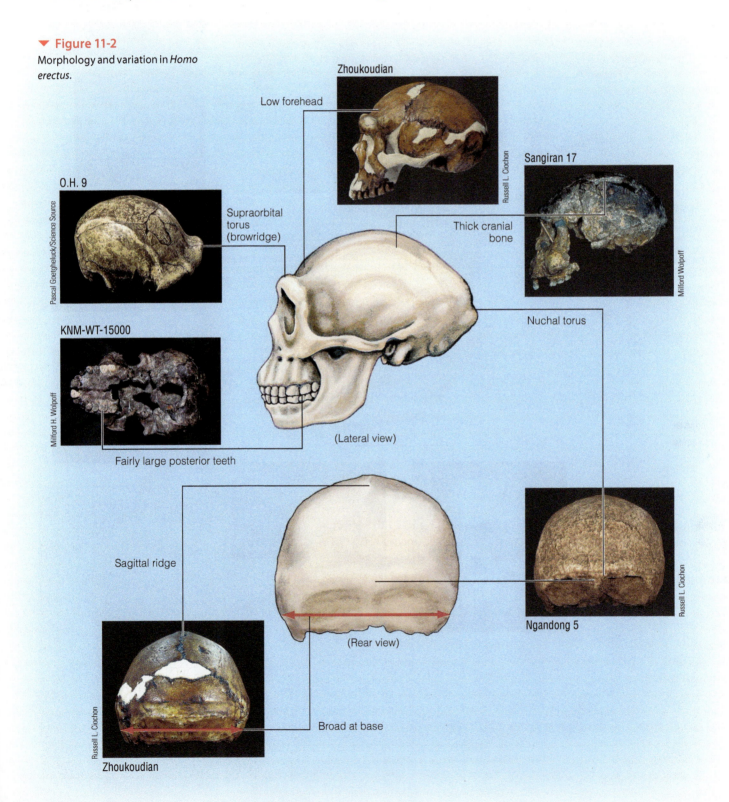

Zhoukoudian

Low forehead

Sangiran 17

O.H. 9

Supraorbital torus (browridge)

Thick cranial bone

Nuchal torus

KNM-WT-15000

(Lateral view)

Fairly large posterior teeth

Ngandong 5

Sagittal ridge

(Rear view)

Broad at base

Zhoukoudian

The braincase is long and low, receding from the large browridges with little forehead development. Also, the cranium is wider at the base compared with earlier *and* later species of genus *Homo*. The maximum breadth of the cranium is located below the ear canal, giving the cranium a pentagonal shape (when viewed from behind). In contrast, the skulls of early *Homo* and *H. sapiens* have more vertical sides, and the maximum width is above the ear canals.

Most specimens also have a sagittal keel running along the midline of the skull. Very different from a sagittal crest, the keel is a small ridge that runs front to back along the sagittal suture (shaped like a keel on the bottom of a boat). The sagittal keel, browridges, and nuchal torus don't seem to have served an obvious adaptive function, but most likely reflect bone buttressing in a very robust skull.

The Geographic Range of *Homo erectus*

The First *Homo erectus: Homo erectus* from Africa

Where did *Homo erectus* first appear? The answer seems fairly simple: Most likely, this species initially evolved in Africa. Two important pieces of evidence help to support this hypothesis. First, *all* of the earlier hominins prior to the appearance of *H. erectus* come from Africa. What's more, by 1.7 mya, there are well-dated fossils of this species at East Turkana, Kenya, and not long after that at other sites in East Africa.

But there's a small wrinkle in this tidy view of human evolution. We now know that at about 1.8 mya, similar populations were already living far away in western Asia, and by 1.6 mya, in Indonesia. So, adding these pieces to our puzzle, it seems likely that *H. erectus* first arose in East Africa and then very quickly migrated to other continents; nevertheless, as we'll see shortly, the dating of sites from Africa and elsewhere does not yet clearly confirm this hypothesis. Let's first review the African *H. erectus* specimens dated at 1.7 to 1 mya, and then we'll discuss those populations that emigrated to Europe, and western and eastern Asia.

The earliest of the East African *H. erectus* fossils come from East Turkana, from the same area where earlier australopith and early *Homo* fossils have been found (see Chapter 10). Indeed, it seems likely that in East Africa around 2.0 to 1.8 mya, some form of early *Homo* evolved into *H. erectus*.

The most significant *H. erectus* fossil from East Turkana is a nearly complete skull (ER 3733; Fig. 11-3). Recently redated at 1.7 mya, this fossil is about the same age (or even just a little younger) than some other fossils outside of Africa; nevertheless, for now, it certainly is the oldest known member of this species from Africa (Lepre and Kent, 2010). The cranial capacity is estimated at 848 cm³, in the lower range for *H. erectus* (700 to 1,250 cm³), which isn't surprising considering its early date. A second very significant find from East Turkana is notable because it has the smallest cranium of any *H. erectus* specimen from anywhere in Africa. Dated to around 1.5 mya, the skull has a cranial capacity of only 691 cm³. As we'll see shortly, there are a couple of crania from western Asia that are even smaller. The small skull from East Turkana also shows more gracile features (such as smaller browridges) than do other East African *H. erectus* individuals, but it preserves the overall *H. erectus* vault shape. It's been proposed that perhaps this individual is a female and that the variation indicates a very high degree of sexual dimorphism in this species (Spoor et al., 2007).

Another remarkable discovery was made in 1984 by Kamoya Kimeu, a member of Richard Leakey's team known widely as an outstanding fossil hunter. Kimeu discovered a small piece of skull

▼ **Figure 11-3**

Nearly complete skull of *Homo erectus* from East Lake Turkana, Kenya, dated to approximately 1.7 mya.

Pascal Goetgheluck/Science Source

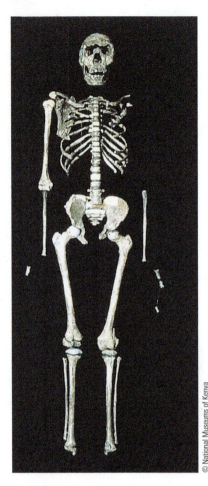

© National Museums of Kenya

▲ **Figure 11-4**

WT 15000 from Nariokotome, Kenya: The "Nariokotome boy" is the most complete *H. erectus* specimen yet found.

on the west side of Lake Turkana at a site known as **Nariokotome**. Excavations produced the most complete *H. erectus* skeleton ever found (Fig. 11-4). Known formally as WT 15000, the almost complete skeleton includes facial bones, a pelvis, and most of the limb bones, ribs, and vertebrae; it is chronometrically dated to about 1.6 mya (Walker and Leakey, 1993).

Such well-preserved postcranial elements make for a very unusual and highly useful discovery, because these elements are scarce at other *H. erectus* sites. The skeleton is that of a juvenile about 8 years of age with an estimated height of about 5 feet 3 inches (Walker and Leakey, 1993; Dean and Smith, 2009).

Some estimates have hypothesized that the adult height of this individual could have been about 6 feet. However, this conclusion is contentious, since it assumed that the growth pattern of this species was similar to that of modern humans. In fact, more recent and more detailed analyses find the developmental pattern in this and other *H. erectus* individuals to actually be more like that of an ape (Dean and Smith, 2009). What's more, it now seems unlikely that this individual would have experienced the typical adolescent growth spurt seen in modern humans (see Chapter 16). A recent reexamination of the Nariokotome skeleton's growth and development pattern generated hypothetical growth curves based on modified growth curves for both humans and chimpanzees (Graves et al., 2010). By estimating how much growth remained at the time of death, the researchers suggested that maximum height would have been completed by around 12 years of age; thus, their revised stature estimate suggests an adult height of between 5 feet and 5 feet 7 inches (mean of 5 feet 4 inches). They further suggest that some of the confusion regarding the Nariokotome skeleton's estimated age may be related to a pathological condition that affected the fusion of the growth plates in the long bones.

Nevertheless, the postcranial bones look very similar, though not quite identical, to those of modern humans. And the recent publication describing additional vertebral and rib fragments indicates that the modern human spine and rib cage shape were already present (Haeusler et al., 2011). The cranial capacity of WT 15000 is estimated at 880 cm³. Brain growth was nearly complete, and the adult cranial capacity would have been approximately 909 cm³, or twice that of the australopith mean (Begun and Walker, 1993; Falk, 2012). Based on size and the degree of robusticity, many researchers argue that the skeleton is male.

Other important *H. erectus* finds have come from Olduvai Gorge, in Tanzania. These fossils include a very robust skull discovered by Louis Leakey in 1960. The skull, dated to 1.4 mya, has a well-preserved cranial vault with just a small part of the upper face. Estimated at 1,067 cm³, its cranial capacity is the largest of all the African *H. erectus* specimens. The browridge is massive, the largest known for any hominin, but the walls of the cranial vault are relatively thin. This last characteristic is seen in most East African *H. erectus* specimens; in this respect, they differ from Asian *H. erectus*, in which cranial vault bones are thick.

Three other sites from Ethiopia have yielded *H. erectus* fossils, the most noteworthy coming from the Gona area and the Daka locale, both in the Awash River region of eastern Africa (Gilbert and Asfaw, 2008). As you've seen, numerous remains of earlier hominins have come from this area (see Chapter 10 and Appendix C).

A recently discovered nearly complete female *H. erectus* pelvis comes from the Gona area in Ethiopia and is dated to approximately 1.3 mya (Simpson et al., 2008). It is a particularly interesting find because *H. erectus* postcranial remains are so rare, and this is the first *H. erectus* female pelvis yet found. The Gona pelvis is very different from the Nariokotome pelvis and is unusual for its considerable width, along with a short stature. It's possible that this may reflect considerable sexual dimorphism. This fossil also reveals some tantalizing glimpses of likely *H. erectus* growth and development. The pelvis has a very wide birth canal, indicating that quite large-brained infants could have developed *in utero* (before birth); in fact, it's

Nariokotome (nar´-ee-oh-koh´-tow-may)

At a Glance — Key *Homo erectus* Discoveries from Africa

Date	Site	Evolutionary Significance
1.4 mya	Olduvai	Large individual, very robust (male?) *H. erectus*
1.6 mya	Nariokotome, W. Turkana	Nearly complete skeleton; young male
1.7 mya	E. Turkana	Oldest well-dated *H. erectus* in Africa; great amount of variation seen among individuals, possibly due to sexual dimorphism

possible that a *H. erectus* newborn could have had a brain that was as large as what's typical for modern human babies (DeSilva, 2011). These factors indicate a modern compromise between the demands of obligate bipedalism and that of birthing large-brained infants.

This evidence has led researchers to suggest that *H. erectus* prenatal brain growth was more like that of later humans and quite different from that found in apes or in australopiths such as Lucy. However, it's also evident that *H. erectus* brain growth after birth was more rapid than it is in modern humans. The Gona female was in some ways quite primitive, especially her unusually small body size (approximately 81 pounds, as estimated by the size of her hip joint). Some anthropologists conclude from this evidence that the Gona pelvis may actually have come from an australopith rather than from *H. erectus* (or any other species of *Homo*) (Ruff, 2010).

Another recent discovery from the Middle Awash of Ethiopia of a mostly complete cranium from Daka is also important because this individual (dated at approximately 1 mya) is more like Asian *H. erectus* than are most of the earlier East African remains we've discussed (Asfaw et al., 2002; Gilbert and Asfaw, 2008). Consequently, the suggestion by several researchers that East African fossils are a different species from (Asian) *H. erectus* isn't supported by the morphology of the Daka cranium (Fig. 11-5).

In fact, a cladistics analysis of traits found in *H. erectus* crania was unable to identify meaningful regional variation, supporting a single species argument (Asfaw et al., 2002; Gilbert et al., 2003; Gilbert 2008). The "At a Glance" summarizes information on some of the key African *H. erectus* discoveries.

A New Hominin Discovery in South Africa

In 2013, a massive trove of fossil hominins was discovered in the Dinaledi Chamber of the Rising Star cave system in South Africa. The initial discovery was made by expert cavers who navigated their way through the treacherous cave system into the chamber. They notified Dr. Lee Berger, of the University of Witwatersrand, of the discovery, who in turn recruited a team of six researchers who were petite enough to navigate the cave system to reach the fossils (Berger et al., 2015). In an unprecedented move, Berger assembled a team of over 60 scientists to study the fossils in detail and to quickly publish results on the discovery (Berger et al., 2015; Dirks et al., 2015). The analysis revealed a new species, *Homo naledi*, represented by 1,550 well-preserved fossil specimens which collectively comprise at least 15 individuals—the largest fossil hominin discovery in all of Africa!

▼ **Figure 11-5**

Daka cranium from the Middle Awash region of Ethiopia, dated to 1.0 mya. This specimen shows many similarities with *Homo erectus* finds from Indonesia and China as well as Europe.

David L. Brill/Atlanta

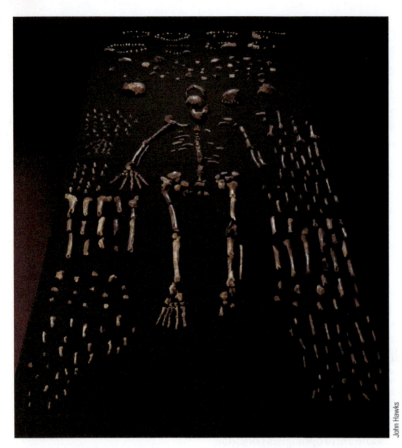

John Hawks

▲ **Figure 11-6**

A reconstructed skeleton of *Homo naledi*, surrounded by the partial skeletal remains of at least 14 additional individuals. Reliable dating of this tremendous fossil discovery is underway, and additional discoveries within the Rising Star cave system are anticipated.

At least one composite individual was able to be reconstructed, demonstrating the overall anatomy of a single individual (Fig. 11-6). How these fossils ended up in the cave's chamber is a matter of debate. They do not appear to have been washed into the cave by water or to have been dragged into the chamber as carnivore meals (no evidence of micro-abrasion or tooth marks were found on the hominin bones). Further, there is no evidence of hominins utilizing the cave as a living area (Berger et al., 2015; Dirks et al., 2015). The researchers hypothesize that the context suggests deliberate disposal of the dead, although they do not rule out the possibility of a mass mortality event or natural death trap scenario (Dirks et al., 2015). All anatomical regions of the skeleton are represented, as are both males and females, and the very young (for example, neonates) to the very old (Dirks et al., 2015).

Anatomically, *Homo naledi* shows a mosaic of both primitive and derived features. For example, the upper half of the body is more australopith-like, including the small cranial capacity (approximately 465 cm^3), curved fingers, and morphology of the upper limb. The lower half of the body more closely resembles the genus *Homo*, especially the anatomy of the legs and feet. In addition, *Homo naledi* shows a number of features consistent with *Homo erectus*, including reduced jaws and teeth, a more derived wrist and hand, a pentagonal skull shape (when viewed from the back), and a well-developed supraorbital and nuchal torus (Berger et al., 2015).

One major question that has yet to be answered regarding *Homo naledi* is its geological age. Dating of South African cave sites is notoriously difficult, and the Rising Star system is no exception. Dembo and colleagues (2016) hypothesize that *Homo naledi* may date as recent as 912,000 ya, although this is a phylogenetic estimate (not based on chronometric dating). Morphologically, *Homo naledi* could be ancestral to *Homo erectus*. Hawks and Berger (2016) have recently addressed the implications of various hypothetical dates of the fossils; however, until chronometric dates are produced from the site, the taxonomic status of *Homo naledi* will remain an open question to many researchers. Regardless, it is likely that these fossils have a close affinity to *Homo erectus*. Ongoing work in the Dinaledi Chamber is likely to yield many more *Homo naledi* fossils.

Who Were the Earliest African Emigrants?

The fossils from East Africa imply that a new adaptive pattern in human evolution appeared in Africa not long after 2 mya. Until recently, *Homo erectus* sites outside Africa all have reported dates that are later than the earliest finds of this species in Africa, leading paleoanthropologists to assume that the hominins who migrated to Asia and Europe descended from earlier African ancestors. Also, these travelers look like *Homo*, with longer limbs and bigger brains. Because *H. erectus* originated in East Africa, they were geographically closest to areas connected to Eurasia (through the Middle East) and thus were probably the first to leave the continent. We can't be sure why these hominins left—were they following animal migrations, or was it simply population growth and expansion?

a

b

David Lordkipanidze

David Lordkipanidze

c

d

David Lordkipanidze

David Lordkipanidze

◀ **Figure 11-7**
Dmanisi crania discovered in 1999 and 2001 and dated to 1.8 to 1.7 mya. **(a)** Specimen 2282. **(b)** Specimen 2280. **(c)** Specimen 2700. **(d)** Specimen 4500 (cranium) with articulated specimen 2600 (mandible).

What we do know is that we're seeing a greater range of physical variation in the specimens outside of Africa and that the emigration out of Africa happened earlier than we had previously thought. Current evidence shows *H. erectus* in East Africa about 1.7 mya, while similar hominins were living in the Caucasus region of western Asia *even a little earlier*, about 1.8 mya.* Eventually hominins made it all the way to the island of Java, Indonesia, by 1.6 mya! It took *H. erectus* less than 200,000 years to travel from East Africa to Southeast Asia. Let's look at this fascinating evidence.

The site of **Dmanisi**, in the Republic of Georgia, has produced several individuals, giving us a unique look at these first possible travelers (see Fig. 11-7a–d). The age of this crucial site has recently been radiometrically dated to 1.81 mya (Garcia et al., 2010). The Dmanisi crania are similar to those of *H. erectus* (for example, the long, low braincase, wide base, and sagittal keeling; see especially Fig. 11-7b, and compare with Fig. 11-2). However, other characteristics of the Dmanisi individuals are different from other hominins outside Africa. In particular, one of the most complete fossils (specimen 2700; see Fig. 11-7c) has a less robust and thinner browridge, a projecting lower face, and a relatively large upper canine. At least when viewed from the front, this skull is more reminiscent of the smaller early *Homo* specimens from East Africa (such as *Homo habilis*) than it is of *H. erectus*. Also, specimen 2700's cranial capacity is very small—estimated at only 600 cm³, well within the range of early *Homo*. In fact, all four Dmanisi crania so far described have relatively small cranial capacities—estimated at 550 cm³, 630 cm³, 650 cm³, and 780 cm³.

The most recently reported specimen, discovered in 2005, is a complete skull, indeed the most complete skull of early *Homo* (Lordkipanidze et al., 2013). The cranium, known as D4500 (Fig. 11-7d), fits perfectly with a mandible discovered a decade earlier (D2600). This skull shows several primitive traits, including a small cranial vault and a massive, prognathic face. In fact, this skull has the smallest cranial capacity of all Dmanisi finds (~550 cm³). This specimen is especially important because of its completeness and lack

*Note that these dates are based solely on what has been discovered so far.

| **Dmanisi** (dim´-an-eese´-ee)

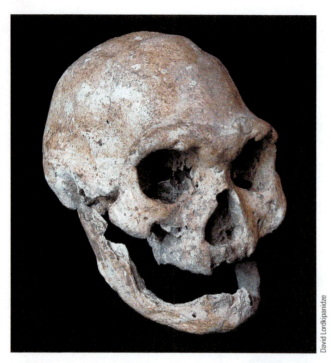

David Lordkipanidze

▲ **Figure 11-8**

A recently discovered cranium from Dmanisi, almost totally lacking in teeth (with both upper and lower jaws showing advanced bone resorption).

of distortion, providing a clear idea of what it looked like, and exactly how the face and vault fit together. Lordkipanidze and colleagues (2013) hypothesize that the skull may be associated with postcranial materials found at the site, which suggests similar body proportions as found in modern humans.

Another remarkable find from Dmanisi is the nearly complete cranium of an older adult male; and surprisingly for such an ancient find, he died with only one tooth remaining in his jaws (Lordkipanidze et al., 2006). Because his jawbones show advanced bone loss (which occurs following tooth loss), it seems that he lived for several years without being able to chew his food efficiently (Fig. 11-8). As a result, it probably would have been difficult for him to maintain an adequate diet.

Researchers have also recovered some stone tools at Dmanisi. The tools are similar to the Oldowan industry from Africa, as would be expected for a site dated earlier than the beginning of the **Acheulian** industry; this later and very important tool industry is first found associated with African *H. erectus* about 1.6 mya.

Some of the most recent evidence from Dmanisi includes several postcranial bones coming from at least four individuals (Lordkipanidze et al., 2007). This evidence is especially important because it allows us to make comparisons with what is known of *H. erectus* from other areas. The Dmanisi fossils have an unusual combination of traits. They weren't especially tall, having an estimated height ranging from about 4 feet 9 inches to 5 feet 5 inches. Certainly, based on this evidence, they seem smaller than the full *H. erectus* specimens from East Africa or Asia. Yet, although very short in stature, they still show body proportions (such as leg length) like that of *H. erectus* (and *H. sapiens*) and quite different from that seen in earlier hominins.

Based on the evidence from Dmanisi, we can assume that *Homo erectus* was the first hominin to leave Africa. Although the Dmanisi specimens are small in both stature and cranial capacity, they have specific characteristics that identify them as *H. erectus* (for example, a sagittal keel and low braincase). So for now, the Dmanisi hominins are thought to be *H. erectus*, although an early and quite different variety from that found almost anywhere else.

The recent evidence raises important and exciting possibilities. The Dmanisi findings suggest that the first hominins to leave Africa were quite possibly a small-bodied very early form of *H. erectus*, possessing smaller brains than later *H. erectus* and carrying with them a typical African Oldowan stone tool culture.

Also, the Dmanisi hominins had none of the adaptations hypothesized to be essential to hominin migration—that is, being tall and having relatively large brains. Recent analyses do not support two separate migrations out of Africa during the Early Pleistocene (Lordkipanidze et al., 2013), suggesting the Dmanisi hominins could be closely related to the well-recognized *H. erectus* populations of Java and China. The scientific community has only just recently reached a point where it is able to absorb these data, though it's still too soon to predict what further revisions may be required.

Homo erectus from Indonesia

After the publication of *On the Origin of Species*, debates about evolution were prevalent throughout Europe. While many theorists simply stayed home and debated the merits of natural selection and the likely course of human evolution, one young Dutch anatomist decided to go find evidence of it. Eugene Dubois (1858–1940) enlisted in the Dutch East Indian Army and was shipped to the island of Sumatra, Indonesia, to look for what he called "the missing link."

Acheulian (ash´-oo-lay-en) Pertaining to a stone tool industry from the Early and Middle Pleistocene; characterized by a large proportion of bifacial tools (flaked on both sides). Acheulian tool kits are common in Africa, Southwest Asia, and western Europe, but they're thought to be less common elsewhere. Also spelled Acheulean.

In October 1891, after moving his search to the neighboring island of Java, Dubois' field crew unearthed a skullcap along the Solo River near the town of Trinil—a fossil that was to become internationally famous as the first recognized human ancestor (Fig. 11-9). The following year, a human femur was recovered about 15 yards upstream in what Dubois claimed was the same level as the skullcap, and he assumed that the skullcap (with a cranial capacity of slightly over 900 cm³) and the femur belonged to the same individual.

Counting the initial find plus later discoveries, so far, all the Javanese *H. erectus* fossil remains have come from six sites located in the eastern part of the island. The dating of these fossils has been hampered by the complex nature of Javanese geology, but it's generally accepted that most of the fossils belong to the Early to Middle **Pleistocene** and are between 1.6 and 1 million years old. The island of Java continues to yield new hominin fossils, with the discovery in 2001 of a *H. erectus* upper jaw at the fossil-rich Sangiran Dome (see "A Closer Look," pp. 332–333). Very well-controlled ⁴⁰Ar/³⁹Ar dating places this fossil very close to an age of 1.5 mya. Comparisons of this newly described jaw with Chinese and Western *Homo erectus* (from Georgia and Africa), as well as with *Homo habilis* reveal some interesting differences. These differences seem to indicate that there were two separate population sources for the earlier Sangiran *H. erectus* and later Zhoukoudian *H. erectus*, which you will be introduced to in a moment (Zaim et al., 2011).

What's more, there was also a very late-surviving *H. erectus* group in Java that apparently managed to survive there until less than 100,000 years ago, and possibly as recent as 27,000 years ago. These fossils from the Ngandong site are by far the most recent group of *H. erectus* fossils from Java or anywhere else. At Ngandong, an excavation along an ancient river terrace produced 11 mostly complete hominin skulls. Some estimates of the age of the Ngandong *H. erectus* fossils initially suggested an age of only 52,000 to 27,000 years ago (ya). These dates are quite controversial, but further evidence has established a *very late survival* of *H. erectus* in Java (approximately 70,000 to 40,000 ya) (Yokoyama et al., 2008). So these individuals would be contemporary with *H. sapiens*—which, by this time, had expanded widely throughout the Old World and into Australia around 60,000 to 40,000 ya. Recent work on the old excavation site of Ngandong (first excavated in the early 1930s) has led to a rediscovery of the fossil bed where all the *H. erectus* individuals had been found (Ciochon et al., 2009). New dating techniques and fossil identification will be undertaken to better understand site formation processes and taphonomy.

Homo erectus from China

The story of the first discoveries of Chinese *Homo erectus* is another saga filled with excitement, hard work, luck, and misfortune. Europeans had known for a long time that "dragon bones," used by the Chinese as medicine and aphrodisiacs, were actually ancient mammal bones. Scientists eventually located one of the sources of these bones near Beijing at a site called **Zhoukoudian**. Major excavations were undertaken in the 1920s, and in 1929, a fossil skull was discovered. The skull turned out to be a juvenile's, and although it was thick, low, and relatively small, there was no doubt that it belonged to an early hominin.

Zhoukoudian *Homo erectus*

The fossil remains of *H. erectus* discovered in the 1920s and 1930s, as well as some more recent excavations at Zhoukoudian (Fig. 11-10), are by far the largest collection of *H. erectus* material found anywhere. This excellent sample includes 14 skullcaps

S. Sartono

▲ **Figure 11-9**

The famous Trinil skullcap discovered by Eugene Dubois near the Solo River in Java. Discovered in 1891, this was the first fossil human found outside of Europe or Africa.

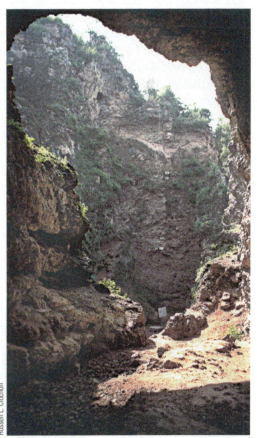

Russell L. Ciochon

▲ **Figure 11-10**

Zhoukoudian cave.

Pleistocene The epoch of the Cenozoic from 2.6 mya until 10,500 ya. Frequently referred to as the Ice Age, this epoch is associated with continental glaciations in northern latitudes.

Zhoukoudian (Zhoh´-koh-dee´-en)

A Closer Look In Search of Ancient Human Ancestors— and a Little Shade

"Whoops!" Upon hearing this exclamation, my colleagues halt their progress along the narrow earthen walkways that outline the flooded rice paddies and make an emerald patchwork quilt on the Java landscape. They turn around and see that I've slipped. Again. Each misstep comes with some good-hearted ribbing as my comrades heave me back onto dry land. Each day we traverse the paddies by way of the thin dikes en route to our research site in central Java. Around us rise great cliffs of ancient soil, striated like an intricately layered cake. Rich green jewel tones dazzle the eye as we pass by peasants laboring in the fields under the hot sun. We, too, are in Java to work, but we toil for a different kind of produce—we seek answers about our early ancestor, *Homo erectus*. As we tread across the paddies to a dusty oxcart path, our eyes comb the adjacent outcrops for darkened silhouettes of fossils—carefully, we note their locations. By the time we reach our destination, our backpacks are filled with curious remains—this one a tooth of a fossil deer, that one a piece of ancient crocodile bone—but no humans. All the fossils are stained crimson or black by the very soils in which they have lain for nearly a million years. As we begin to examine the exposed sediments, we resume our search for more fossils, our sweat-soaked shirts sticking to our skin. It's 9 A.M. and we're already tired and hot, but we quickly brush these distractions away. Our search has just begun.

For the past 15 years, my colleagues and I have been conducting fieldwork in the rice paddies of central Java. You might think it unusual to conduct scientific research in a rice paddy, but you have to "follow the fossils." Ancient sediments in our field area, the Sangiran Dome, were forced to the surface by the pressure of subterranean mud volcanoes about 120,000 years ago. What attracts us to the Sangiran Dome? It's the 1- to 2-million-year-old fossils and sediments that have been unearthed by erosion and other natural processes. This special series of events means that the Sangiran Dome is prime for both discovering the fossils of early humans in their original environmental context and for radiometrically dating them using volcanic sediments—a common occurrence in Java, an island formed by volcanoes.

If the cradle of human origins is Africa, then Asia was one of the playgrounds where our species grew and matured. Around 2 mya, *Homo erectus*, our first widely traveled ancestor, left the African savanna homeland to expand its horizons in the larger world. The first stop on this species' journey was in what is now the Republic of Georgia in western Asia, where four skulls and a partial skeleton have been found. From here, we know that *Homo erectus* ventured onward to East Asia and eventually Java. We know little about the features that attracted these hominins to the Javanese landscape or when the first migration to this island occurred. We do know that over time, the descendants of original *Homo erectus* immigrants evolved, giving us both full-sized primitive peoples with thick skulls and projecting browridges and later the diminutive "Hobbits" on the island of Flores.

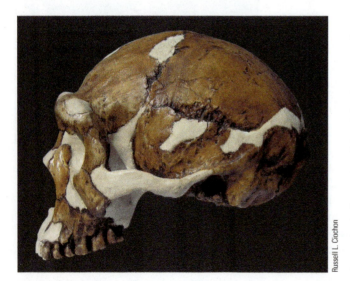

▲ Figure 11-11
Composite cranium of Zhoukoudian *Homo erectus*, reconstructed by Ian Tattersall and Gary Sawyer of the American Museum of Natural History in New York.

(Fig. 11-11), other cranial pieces, and more than 100 isolated teeth, but only a scattering of postcranial elements (Jia and Huang, 1990). Various interpretations to account for this unusual pattern of preservation have been offered, ranging from ritualistic treatment or cannibalism to the more mundane suggestion that the *H. erectus* remains are simply the leftovers of the meals of giant hyenas. The hominin remains were studied and casts were made immediately, which proved invaluable, because the original specimens went missing during the evacuation of Americans from China at the start of World War II.

The hominin remains from China belong to upward of 40 adults and children and together provide a good overall picture of Chinese *H. erectus*. Like the materials from Java, they have typical *H. erectus* features, including a large browridge and nuchal torus. Also, the skull has thick bones, a sagittal keel, and a protruding face and is broadest near the bottom. This site, along with others in China, has been difficult to date accurately. Although Zhoukoudian was previously dated to about 500,000 ya, a relatively new radiometric dating technique that measures isotopes of aluminum and beryllium shows that Zhoukoudian is actually considerably older, with a dating estimate of approximately 780,000 ya (Ciochon and Bettis, 2009; Shen et al., 2009).

Every good realtor will tell you that it's "location, location, location!" What was it about this Asian setting—particularly the island of Java—that drew these ancient immigrants to colonize, as evidenced by the nearly 100 fossils of *Homo erectus* that have been unearthed there over the past century? Was it, perhaps, the rich volcanic soils and the vegetation they fostered that attracted our distant relatives to the Sangiran Dome, or did *Homo erectus* simply follow land-loving animals to the newly emergent environment of central Java? Our research centers on this very issue, using visual and geochemical clues from soils and plant and animal fossils to reconstruct the landscape of Java when *Homo erectus* first arrived millions of years ago.

◀ **Figure 1**

The Sangiran Dome team, composed of researchers from the University of Iowa and the Bandung Institute of Technology, shown here doing a paleoecological analysis of the ancient strata of the dome.

As the sun dips low on the horizon, the valley of the Sangiran Dome dims. At the end of the day, our team reassembles for the trek back to our van, joking and chatting about the day's finds. Our packs are heavy with samples of ancient soils, fossil shells and teeth, and rocks from ancient volcanic eruptions, all being hauled back for analysis. We watch our shadowy likenesses in the murky water of the paddies as we trudge out of the mists of time. In an hour we'll return to the hustle and bustle of Solo and wash away the dirt of ages. But before reentering civilization, we cast one last look into the past and wonder—"What was this place like during the time of our very ancient ancestors?" Was the landscape dominated by palms, mahogany, and cashew-bearing trees, as it is today, or was the countryside completely foreign? The full answers are just beyond our grasp. Perhaps today we carry in our backpacks the answers to these questions. Someday soon we'll be able to look at this landscape as our ancestors did, linking our common histories with modern technology.

—Russell L. Ciochon

Cultural Remains from Zhoukoudian

More than 100,000 artifacts have been recovered from this vast site, which was occupied intermittently for many thousands of years. The earliest tools are generally crude and shapeless, but they become more refined over time. Common artifacts at the site are referred to as cores, perhaps used as "choppers," but, more importantly, retouched flakes were fashioned into scrapers, points, burins, and awls (Fig. 11-12).

◀ **Figure 11-12**
Chinese tools from Middle Pleistocene sites. (Adapted from Wu and Olson, 1985.)

Graver, or burin   Flint awl   Flint point   Quartzite chopper

The way of life at Zhoukoudian has traditionally been described as that of hunter-gatherers who killed deer, horses, and other animals. Fragments of charred ostrich eggshells and abundant deposits of hackberry seeds unearthed in the cave seemed to suggest that these hominins supplemented their diet of meat by gathering herbs, wild fruits, tubers, and eggs. Layers of what appeared to be ash in the cave (over 18 feet deep at one point) were interpreted as indicating the use of fire by *H. erectus*.

However, with the rise of more modern techniques and the infusion of Western scientists, this idyllic picture of Zhoukoudian life was shattered. Lewis Binford and colleagues (Binford and Ho, 1985; Binford and Stone, 1986a,b) reject the description of *H. erectus* as hunters and instead argue that the evidence clearly points more accurately to scavenging. Using advanced archaeological methods, Noel Boaz and colleagues have even questioned whether the *H. erectus* remains at Zhoukoudian represent evidence of hominin habitation of the cave. By comparing the types of bones, as well as the damage to the bones, with that seen in contemporary carnivore dens, Boaz and Ciochon (2001) have suggested that much of the material in the cave likely accumulated through the activities of extinct giant hyenas. In fact, they hypothesize that most of the *H. erectus* remains, too, are the leftovers of hyena meals. Boaz and his colleagues do recognize that the tools in the cave, and possibly the cut marks on some of the animal bones, provide some insight on hominin activities at Zhoukoudian.

Probably the most intriguing archaeological aspect of the presumed hominin behavior at Zhoukoudian has been the long-held assumption that *H. erectus* deliberately used fire inside the cave. Controlling fire was one of the major cultural breakthroughs in prehistory. By providing warmth, a means of cooking, light to further modify tools, and protection, controlled fire would have been a giant technological innovation. However, in the course of further excavations at Zhoukoudian during the 1990s, researchers carefully collected and analyzed soil samples for distinctive chemical signatures that would show whether fire had been present in the cave (Weiner et al., 1998). They determined that burned bone was only rarely found in association with tools. In most cases, the burning appeared to have taken place after fossilization—that is, the bones weren't cooked while fresh. In fact, it turns out that the "ash" layers aren't actually ash but naturally accumulated organic sediment. This last conclusion was derived from chemical testing that showed absolutely no sign of wood having been burned inside the cave. Finally, the "hearths" that have figured so prominently in archaeological reconstructions of presumed fire control at this site apparently aren't hearths at all. They are simply round depressions formed in the past by water.

Despite this debunking of some long-held beliefs, some potential early African sites have yielded evidence suggesting hominin control of fire, though many of these finds are controversial. However, more recent (and convincing) evidence of the use of fire by hominins during the Pleistocene comes from Wonderwerk Cave, in South Africa, dated to 1 mya. Evidence of cooking includes ash deposits and burned bones found in association with Acheulian tools (Berna et al., 2012). What's more, these deposits were located 30 meters within the cave, ruling out lightning as the source of the fire. These findings suggest hominins were adept at cooking and using fire much earlier than previously thought. Debates on the earliest evidence for the use of fire will likely continue. As analytical methods progress, we will have a better understanding of the timing and geographic distribution of this cultural behavior and its implications for the human diet.

Another provisional interpretation of Zhoukoudian's cave geology suggests that the cave wasn't open to the outside, as a habitation site would be, but was accessed only through a vertical shaft. This theory has led archaeologist Alison Brooks to remark, "It wouldn't have been a shelter, it would have been a trap" (quoted in

Wuethrich, 1998). These serious doubts about control of fire, coupled with the suggestive evidence of bone accumulation by carnivores, have led anthropologists Boaz and Ciochon to conclude that the "Zhoukoudian cave was neither hearth nor home" (Boaz and Ciochon, 2001). (See "A Closer Look" on pp. 336–337.)

Other Chinese Sites

More work has been done at Zhoukoudian than at any other Chinese site. Even so, there are other paleoanthropological sites worth mentioning. Three of the more important regions outside of Zhoukoudian are Lantian County (including two sites, often simply referred to as Lantian), Yunxian County, and several discoveries in Hexian County (usually referred to as the Hexian finds).

Originally dated to 1.15 mya, Lantian is older than the fossils at Zhoukoudian (Zhu et al., 2003). In fact, the site was recently redated to between 1.65 and 1.54 mya (Zhu et al., 2015), indicating it could be substantially older than originally thought. However, these dates should be considered tentative due to limitations of paleomagnetic dating.

The cranial remains of two adult *H. erectus* females have been found at the Lantian sites (Woo, 1966; Fig. 11-13a). One of the specimens, an almost complete mandible containing several teeth, is quite similar to those from Zhoukoudian. Two badly distorted crania were discovered in Yunxian County, Hubei Province, in 1989 and 1990 (Li and Etler, 1992). A combination of ESR and paleomagnetism dating methods (see Chapter 9) gives us an average dating estimate of 800,000 to 580,000 ya. If the dates are correct, this would place Yunxian at a similar age to Zhoukoudian in the Chinese sequence. Due to extensive distortion of the crania from ground pressure, it was very difficult to compare these crania with other *H. erectus* fossils; more recently, however, French paleoanthropologist Amélie Vialet was able to restore the crania using sophisticated imaging techniques (Vialet et al., 2005). And from an analysis of the fauna and paleoenvironment at Yunxian, the *H. erectus* inhabitants are thought to have had limited hunting capabilities, since they appear to have been restricted to the most vulnerable prey, namely the young and old animals.

In 1980 and 1981, the remains of several individuals, all bearing some resemblance to similar fossils from Zhoukoudian, were recovered from Hexian County, in southern China (Wu and Poirier, 1995; see Fig. 11-13b). A close relationship has been postulated between the *H. erectus* specimens from the Hexian finds and from Zhoukoudian (Wu and Dong, 1985). Dating of the Hexian remains is unclear, but they appear to be later than Zhoukoudian, perhaps by several hundred thousand years. The "At a Glance" on page 338 summarizes information on some of the key Asian *H. erectus* discoveries.

The Asian crania from Java and China share many similar features, which could be explained by *H. erectus* migration from Java to China possibly as early as 1.6 mya (based on the tentative new dates from Lantian). Asia has a much longer *H. erectus* habitation than Africa (1.8 mya to 40,000 or 70,000 ya versus 1.7 to 1 mya), and it's important to understand the variation seen in this geographically dispersed species.

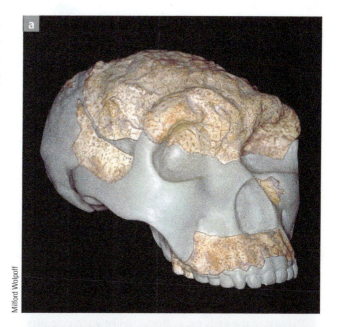

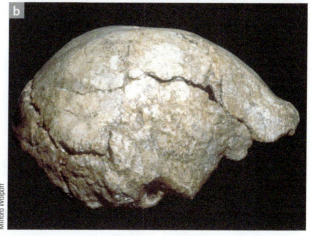

▲ **Figure 11-13**

(a) Reconstructed cranium of *Homo erectus* from Lantian, China, dated to approximately 1.15 mya, and possibly as early as 1.65–1.54 mya. **(b)** Hexian cranium.

A Closer Look

Dragon Bone Hill: Cave Home or Hyena Den?

About 30 miles southwest of Beijing, near Zhoukoudian, is the locality known as Dragon Bone Hill. In the 1920s and 1930s, this cave site yielded the first (and still the largest) cache of fossils of *Homo erectus*, historically known as Peking Man. The remains of about 45 individuals, along with thousands of stone tools, debris from tool manufacture, and thousands of animal bones, were contained within the 100-foot-thick deposits that once completely filled the original cave. Some evidence unearthed at the site suggests to many researchers that these creatures, who lived from about 800,000 to 400,000 ya, had mastered the use of fire and practiced cannibalism. Still, despite years of excavation and analysis, little is certain about what occurred here long ago.

To most of the early excavators, the likely scenario was that these particular early humans lived in the cave where their bones and stone tools were found. The animal bones were likely the remains of meals—proof of their hunting expertise. A more sensational view, first advanced in 1929, was that the cave contained evidence of cannibalism. Skulls were conspicuous among the remains, suggesting to Chinese paleoanthropologist Jia Lanpo that these might be the trophies of headhunters.

But another Chinese paleoanthropologist—Pei Wenzhong, who codirected the early Zhoukoudian excavations—believed that hyenas, not human killers, were responsible for the presence and condition of the skulls and other accompanying damage. In 1939, his views were bolstered by the emerging science of taphonomy, which is the study of how, after death, animal and plant remains become modified, moved, buried, and fossilized (see Chapter 9). Published observations on the way hyenas at the Vienna zoo fed on cow bones led later scientists to reject

▲ **Figure 1**

These illustrations demonstrate the two interpretations of the remains from Dragon Bone Hill: **(a)** the more traditional cave home model and **(b)** the newer, and probably more accurate, hyena den model.

Asian and African *Homo erectus*: A Comparison

The *Homo erectus* remains from East Africa show several differences from the Javanese and Chinese fossils. Some African cranial specimens—particularly ER 3733, presumably a female, and WT 15000, presumably a male—aren't as strongly buttressed at the browridge and nuchal torus, and their cranial bones aren't as thick. Indeed, some researchers are so impressed by these differences, as well as others in the postcranial skeleton, that they're arguing for a separate species status for the African material, to distinguish it from the Asian samples. Bernard Wood, a leading proponent of this view, has suggested that the name *Homo ergaster* be used for the African remains and that *H. erectus* be reserved solely for the Asian material (Wood, 1991). In addition, the very early dates now postulated for the dispersal of *H. erectus* into Asia (Java) would argue that the Asian and African populations were separate (distinct) for more than 1 million years.

the idea of cannibalism, although they continued to look upon the cave as a shelter used by early humans equipped with stone tools and fire (as reflected in the title of *The Cave Home of Peking Man*, published in 1975).

In the mid- to late 1970s, however, Western scientists began to better appreciate and develop the field of taphonomy. One assumption of taphonomy is that the most common species at a fossil site and/or the best-preserved animal remains at the site are most likely the ones to have inhabited the area in life. Of all the mammal fossils from the cave, very few belonged to *H. erectus*—perhaps only 0.5 percent, suggesting that most of the time, this species did not live in the cave. What's more, none of the *H. erectus* skeletons are complete. There's a lack of limb bones—especially of forearms, hands, lower leg bones, and feet—indicating that these individuals died somewhere else and that their partial remains were later carried to the cave. But how?

The answer is suggested by the remains of the most common and complete animal skeletons in the cave deposit—those of the giant hyena, *Pachycrocuta brevirostris*. Had *H. erectus*, instead of being the mighty hunter of anthropological lore, simply met the same unhappy fate as the deer and other prey species in the cave? To test the giant hyena hypothesis, scientists reexamined the fossil casts and a few actual fossils of *H. erectus* from Zhoukoudian for evidence of carnivore damage. Surprisingly, two thirds of the *H. erectus* fossils displayed puncture marks from a carnivore's large, pointed front teeth, most likely the canines of a hyena. What's more, there were long, scraping bite marks, typified

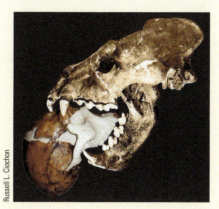

Russell L. Ciochon

◀ Figure 2

A composite image of the skulls of *Pachycrocuta* and *Homo erectus* that shows how the giant hyena may have attacked the face. Recent studies have shown that many of the *Homo erectus* remains from Zhoukoudian show hyena damage.

by U-shaped grooves along the bone, and fracture patterns comparable to those modern hyenas make when they chew bone. One of the *H. erectus* bones, part of a femur, even reveals telltale surface etchings from stomach acid, suggesting it was swallowed and then regurgitated.

Cut marks (made by stone tools) observed on several mammal bones from the cave suggest that early humans did sometimes make use of Zhoukoudian, even if they weren't responsible for accumulating most of the bones. Stone tools left near the cave entrance also attest to their presence. Given its long history, the cave may have served a variety of occupants or at times have been configured as several separate, smaller shelters. Another possibility is that, in a form of time sharing, early humans ventured part way into the cave during the day to scavenge on what the hyenas had not eaten and to find temporary shelter. They might not have realized that the animals, which roamed at twilight and at night, were sleeping in the dark recesses a couple of hundred feet away.

As a result of the discovery of the Daka cranium in Ethiopia and continued comparison of these specimens, this species division has not been fully accepted; the current consensus (and the one we prefer) is to continue referring to all these hominins as *Homo erectus* (Kramer, 1993; Conroy, 1997; Rightmire, 1998; Asfaw et al., 2002). Therefore, as with some earlier hominins, our interpretation of *H. erectus* requires us to recognize a considerable degree of variation within this species. This high degree of variability is likely related to the vast differences in climatic and environmental conditions encountered by ancient humans in the West and in the East. Additionally, the vast distances and island dynamics encountered by *Homo erectus* in the East increased genetic drift, perhaps in some cases producing large enough biological differences to cause speciation (Larick and Ciochon, 2015). We will explore this topic further in later chapters.

At a Glance	Key *Homo erectus* Discoveries from Asia	
Date	**Site**	**Evolutionary Significance**
70,000– 40,000 ya	Ngandong (Java)	Very late survival of *H. erectus* in Java
780,000 ya	Zhoukoudian (China)	Large sample; most famous *H. erectus* site; shows some *H. erectus* populations well adapted to temperate (cold) environments
1.6 mya	Sangiran (Java)	First discovery of *H. erectus* from anywhere; shows dispersal out of Africa into southeast Asia by 1.6 mya

Later *Homo erectus* from Europe

We've talked about *Homo erectus* in Africa, the Caucasus region, and Asia, but there are European specimens as well, found in Spain and Italy. Though not as old as the Dmanisi material, fossils from the Atapuerca region in northern Spain are significantly extending the antiquity of hominins in western Europe. There are several caves in the Atapuerca region, two of which (Sima del Elefante and Gran Dolina) have yielded hominin fossils contemporaneous with *H. erectus*. At this point, however, there is little agreement on the taxonomic status of these fossils from western Europe (Antón, 2013).

The earliest find from Atapuerca (from Sima del Elefante) was discovered recently and dates to 1.2 mya, making it clearly the oldest hominin specimen yet found in western Europe (Carbonell et al., 2008). So far, just one specimen has been found here, a partial jaw with a few teeth. Very provisional analysis suggests that it most closely resembles the Dmanisi fossils. There are also tools and animal bones from the site. As at the Dmanisi site, the implements are simple flake tools similar to those of the Oldowan. Some of the animal bones found at the site also bear the scars of hominin activity, with cut marks indicating the butchering of animal carcasses.

Gran Dolina is a later site, and based on specialized techniques discussed in Chapter 9, it's dated to approximately 850,000 to 780,000 ya (Parés and Pérez-González, 1995; Falguères et al., 1999). Because all the remains so far identified from both these caves at Atapuerca are fragmentary, assigning these fossils to particular species poses something of a problem. Spanish paleoanthropologists who study the Atapuerca hominins have placed them into another (separate) species, which may represent a link between early *Homo* and the later hominins (Bermúdez de Castro et al., 1997; Arsuaga et al., 1999; Bermúdez de Castro et al., 2011). And though they may exhibit some modern features, there is speculation that the hominins of Gran Dolina engaged in a most startling behavior: cannibalism. What's most unsettling about this practice is that the evidence suggests that this was not for ritual purposes or as a last resort. Cut and percussion marks on the hominin bones in question indicate that the bodies were processed much in the same way as any other animal, and all 11 cannibalized individuals represented infant and child remains (Carbonell et al., 2010).

Finally, the southern European discovery of a well-preserved cranium from the Ceprano site in central Italy may be the best evidence yet of *H. erectus* in Europe (Ascenzi et al., 1996). Provisional dating suggested a date between 900,000 and

800,000 ya (Fig. 11-14), but a recent ^{40}Ar/^{39}Ar study has indicated that it more likely dates only as far back as 353,000 ya (Nomade et al., 2011). Philip Rightmire (1998) has concluded that cranial morphology places this specimen quite close to *H. erectus*. Italian researchers have proposed a different interpretation, which classifies the Ceprano hominin as a species separate from *H. erectus*. However, most researchers classify this hominin cranium as *Homo erectus*.

After about 400,000 ya, the European fossil hominin record becomes increasingly abundant. More fossils mean more variation, so it's not surprising that interpretations regarding the proper taxonomic assessment of many of these remains have been debated, in some cases for decades. In recent years, several of these somewhat later "premodern" specimens have been regarded either as early representatives of *H. sapiens* or as a separate species, one immediately preceding *H. sapiens*. These enigmatic premodern humans are discussed in Chapter 12. A time line for the *H. erectus* discoveries discussed in this chapter as well as other finds of more uncertain status is shown in Figure 11-15. The "At a Glance" on page 340 summarizes information on some of the key European *H. erectus* discoveries.

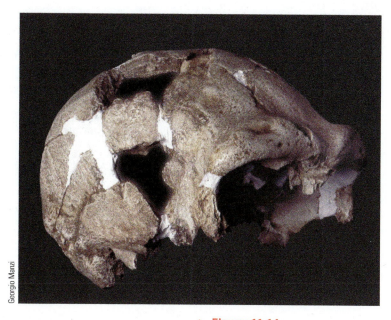

Georgio Manzi

▲ **Figure 11-14**

The Ceprano *Homo erectus* cranium from central Italy, recently dated to 353,000 ya. This is the best evidence for *Homo erectus* in Europe.

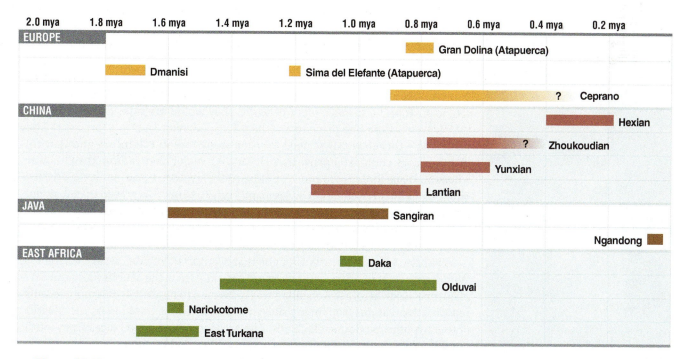

▲ **Figure 11-15**

Time line for *Homo erectus* discoveries and other contemporary hominins. (*Note:* Most dates are only imprecise estimates. However, the dates from East African sites are chronometrically determined and are thus much more secure. The early dates from Java are also radiometric and are gaining wide acceptance.)

At a Glance — Key *Homo erectus* and Contemporaneous Discoveries from Europe and Western Asia

Date	Site	Evolutionary Significance
900,000–350,000 ya	Ceprano (Italy)	Well-preserved cranium; best evidence of full *H. erectus* morphology from any site in Europe
1.2 mya	Sima del Elefante (Atapuerca, Spain)	Oldest evidence of hominins in western Europe, possibly not *H. erectus*
1.80 mya	Dmanisi (Republic of Georgia)	Oldest well-dated hominins outside of Africa; not like full *H. erectus* morphology, but are small-bodied and small-brained

Technological Trends During the Time of *Homo erectus*

The temporal span of *H. erectus* includes two different stone tool industries, one of which was probably first developed by *H. erectus*. Earlier finds indicate that *H. erectus* started out using Oldowan tool technology, which the *H. erectus* emigrants took with them to Dmanisi, Java, and Spain. The newer industry was invented (about 1.6 mya) after these early African emigrants left their original homeland for other parts of the Old World. This new tool kit is called the Acheulian. The important change in this kit was a core worked on both sides, called a biface (known commonly as a hand axe or cleaver; Fig. 11-16). The biface had a flatter shape than seen in the rounder-shaped, earlier Oldowan cores (which were worked to make quick and easy flakes and were soon discarded). Beginning with the Acheulian culture, we find the first evidence that raw materials were being transported more consistently and for longer distances. When Acheulian tool users found a suitable piece of stone, they would often take it with them as they traveled from one place to another. This behavior suggests foresight: They likely knew that they might need to use a stone tool in the future and that this chunk of rock could later prove useful. This is a major change from the Oldowan, where all stone tools are found very close to their raw-material sources. With the biface as a kind of "Acheulian Swiss army knife," these tools served to cut, scrape, pound, and dig. This most useful tool has been found in Africa, parts of Asia, and later in Europe. Take note as well that Acheulian tool kits also include several types of small tools (Fig. 11-17).

For many years, scientists thought that a cultural "divide" separated the Old World, with Acheulian technology found only in Africa, the Middle East, and parts of Europe (elsewhere, the Acheulian was presumed to be absent). But more recently reported excavations from many sites in southern China have forced reevaluation of this hypothesis (Hou et al., 2000). The archaeological assemblages from southern China are securely dated at about 800,000 ya and contain numerous bifaces, very similar to contemporaneous Acheulian bifaces from Africa (see Fig. 11-16). New evidence from India dates the Acheulian in southern Asia to at least 1 mya (Pappu et al., 2011). It now appears likely that cultural traditions relating to stone tool technology were largely equivalent over the *full* geographical range of *H. erectus* and its contemporaries.

William Turnbaugh

▲ **Figure 11-16**
Acheulian biface ("hand axe"), a basic tool of the Acheulian tradition.

Evidence of butchering is widespread at *H. erectus* sites; in the past, such evidence has been cited in arguments for consistent hunting (researchers formerly interpreted any association of bones and tools as evidence of hunting). But some studies now suggest that cut marks on bones from the *H. erectus* time period often overlie carnivore tooth marks. This would mean that hominins weren't necessarily hunting large animals but were scavenging meat and bone marrow from animals killed by carnivores. It's also crucial to mention that they obtained a large amount of their daily calories from gathering wild plants, tubers, and fruits. Like hunter-gatherers of modern times, *H. erectus* individuals most likely consumed most of their daily calories from plant materials.

Seeing the Connections: Interpretations of *Homo erectus*

Several aspects of the geographical, physical, and behavioral patterns shown by *Homo erectus* seem clear. But new discoveries and more in-depth analyses are helping us to reevaluate our prior ideas. The fascinating Dmanisi hominins are perhaps the most challenging piece of this puzzle.

Past theories suggested that *H. erectus* was able to emigrate from Africa owing to more advanced tools and a more modern anatomy (longer legs, larger brains) compared with earlier African hominins. Yet, now we see that what really happened was not this straightforward. Much like the Taung child changed our perspectives on early hominin evolution, the Dmanisi hominins surprisingly reveal that these very early Eurasians still had small brains; moreover, in Dmanisi, Java, and Spain, these hominins were also still using Oldowan-style tools.

What becomes clear is that at least some of the earliest emigrants from Africa didn't yet show the entire suite of *H. erectus* physical and behavioral traits. Additionally, the Dmanisi hominins exhibit a very wide range of variability, making it tempting to conclude that more than one type of hominin is represented; but this is not likely, because all the fossils were found in the same geological context. This degree of apparent intraspecific variation is biologically noteworthy, and it's influencing how paleoanthropologists interpret all of these fossil samples.

This growing awareness of the broad intraspecific variation among some hominins brings us to our second consideration: Is *Homo ergaster* in Africa a separate species from *Homo erectus*, as strictly defined in Asia? Although this interpretation was popular in the last decade, it's now losing support. The finds from Dmanisi raise fundamental issues of interpretation. For example, among four crania from one locality (see Fig. 11-7), we see more variation than between the African and Asian forms, which many researchers have interpreted as different species. Also, the discovery from Daka (Ethiopia) of a young African specimen with Asian traits further weakens the separate-species interpretation of *H. ergaster*.

The separate-species status of the early European fossils from Spain (Sima del Elefante and Gran Dolina) is also not yet clearly established. Recall also that no other western European hominin fossils are known until at least 500,000 years later. Nevertheless, it's quite apparent that later in the Pleistocene, well-established hominin populations were widely dispersed in both Africa and Europe. These later premodern humans are the topic of the next chapter.

In looking back at the evolution of *H. erectus*, we realize how significant this early human was. *H. erectus* had longer lower limbs and thus more efficient bipedalism; was the first species with a cranial capacity approaching the range of *H. sapiens*; became a more efficient scavenger and exploited a wider range of

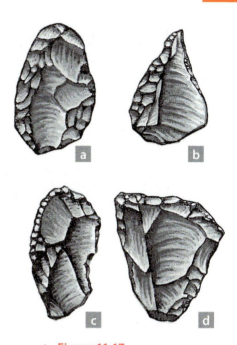

▲ **Figure 11-17**
Small tools of the Acheulian industry.
(a) Side scraper. **(b)** Point. **(c)** End scraper.
(d) Burin.

nutrients, including meat; and ranged across the Old World, from Spain to Indonesia. In short, it was *H. erectus* that transformed hominin evolution to human evolution. As Richard Foley states, "The appearance and expansion of *H. erectus* represented a major change in adaptive strategy that influenced the subsequent process and pattern of human evolution" (1991, p. 425).

Something New and Different: The "Little People"

We mentioned that populations of *Homo erectus* in Java managed to survive on this island long after their cousins had disappeared from other areas (for example, China and East Africa). What's more, even though they persisted well into the Late Pleistocene, physically these Javanese hominins were still similar to other *H. erectus* individuals.

Even more surprising, it seems that other populations possibly branched off from some of these early inhabitants of Indonesia and either intentionally or accidentally found their way to other, smaller islands to the east. There, under even more extreme isolation pressures, they evolved in an astonishing direction. In late 2004, the world awoke to the startling announcement that an extremely small-bodied, small-brained hominin had been discovered in Liang Bua Cave, on the island of Flores, east of Java (Fig. 11-18). Dubbed the "Little Lady of Flores" or simply "Flo," the remains consist of an incomplete skeleton of an adult female (LB1) as well as additional pieces from approximately 13 other individuals, which the press has collectively nicknamed "hobbits." The female skeleton is remarkable in several ways (Fig. 11-19), though in some ways similar to the Dmanisi hominins. First, she was barely 3 feet tall—as short as the smallest australopith—and her brain, estimated at a mere 417 cm³ (Falk et al., 2005), was no larger than that of a chimpanzee (Brown et al., 2004).

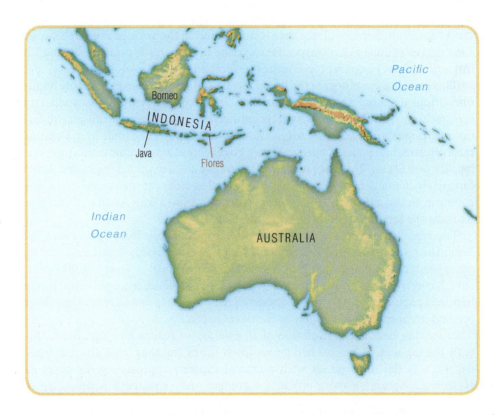

▶ **Figure 11-18**
Location of the Flores site in Indonesia.

Where did they come from? As we said, their predecessors were perhaps *H. erectus* populations like those found on Java. How they got to Flores—some 400 miles away, partly over open ocean—is a mystery. There are several connecting islands, and to get from one to another these hominins may have drifted across on rafts; but there's no way to be sure of this. What's more, these little hominins were apparently living on Flores for a very long time; recently discovered stone tools have been radiometrically dated to at least 1 mya (Brumm et al., 2010). Such an ancient date, as well as the overall similarities to the Dmanisi hominins, suggested to some researchers that *Homo floresiensis* may derive from an early migration of early *Homo* to Southeast Asia (Jungers et al., 2009; Wong, 2009).

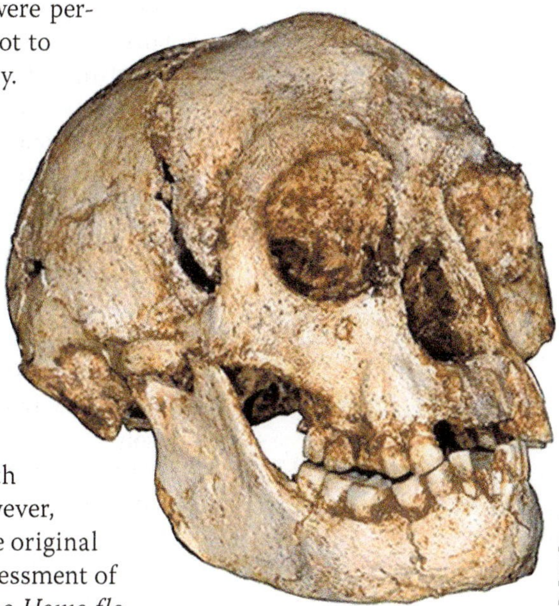

Initial dates suggested that these extraordinary hominins were still living on Flores just 18,000 ya, contemporaneous with *Homo sapiens* (Morwood et al., 2004, 2005; Wong, 2009). However, two recent findings now require a major reinterpretation of these original fossil discoveries. New chronometric dates and a complete reassessment of the stratigraphic context at Liang Bua Cave now indicate that the *Homo floresiensis* fossils actually date between 100,000 and 60,000 ya, significantly older than originally thought (Sutikna et al., 2016). Stone tools associated with *Homo floresiensis* from the site also date from 190,000 to 50,000 ya (Sutikna et al., 2016). Second, recent excavations at the site of Mata Menge, located in the So'a Basin of central Flores, have revealed evidence of a hominin mandible and teeth that closely resemble *Homo floresiensis* (van den Bergh et al., 2016). Of particular importance is that these fossils are chronometrically dated to about 700,000 ya, providing clear evidence for an early Middle Pleistocene origin of *Homo floresiensis* (Brumm et al., 2016). The dates from Mata Menge are consistent with dates derived from the 1 mya radiometrically dated stone tools (mentioned above) found at the nearby site of Wolo Sege, which may reflect the earliest presence of *Homo erectus* on Flores Island (Brumm et al., 2010).

How did they get to be so physically different from all other known hominins? Here we're a little more certain of the answer. Isolated island populations can quite rapidly diverge from their relatives elsewhere. Among such isolated animals, natural selection frequently favors reduced body size. For example, remains of dwarfed elephants have been found on islands in the Mediterranean as well as on some Channel Islands off the coast of southern California. Perhaps most interesting of all, dwarf elephants *also* evolved on Flores; they were found in the same geological beds with the little hominins. The evolutionary mechanism (called "insular dwarfing") thought to explain such extreme body size reduction in both the elephants and the hominins is an adaptation to reduced resources, with natural selection favoring smaller body size (Schauber and Falk, 2008).

Other than short stature, what did the Flores hominins look like? In their cranial shape, thickness of cranial bone, and dentition, they most resemble *H. erectus*, and specifically those from Dmanisi. Still, they have some derived features that also set them apart from all other hominins. For that reason, many researchers have placed them in a separate species, *Homo floresiensis*.

Immediately following the first publication of the Flores remains, intense controversy arose regarding their interpretation (Jacob et al., 2006; Martin et al., 2006). Some researchers have argued that the small-brained hominin (LB1) is actually a pathological modern *H. sapiens* individual afflicted with a severe disorder (microcephaly has been proposed). The researchers who did most of the initial work reject this conclusion and provide some further details to support their original interpretation (for example, Dean Falk and colleagues' further analysis

▲ **Figure 11-19**

Cranium of a *Homo floresiensis* adult female from Flores, Indonesia, now dated between 100,000 and 60,000 ya.

Dr. Peter Brown

of microcephalic endocasts; Falk et al., 2009). Recent analyses of the cranial and postcranial morphology (including bones from the wrist) further support the hypothesis that LB1 represents a separate species (*H. floresiensis*) rather than a pathological individual (Baab et al., 2013; Orr et al., 2013; Westaway et al., 2015).

The conclusion that among this already small-bodied island population the one individual found with a preserved cranium happened to be afflicted with a severe (and rare) growth defect is highly unlikely. Yet, it must also be recognized that long-term, extreme isolation of hominins on Flores leading to a new species showing dramatic dwarfing and even more dramatic brain size reduction is quite unusual.

So where does this leave us? Because a particular interpretation is unlikely, it's not necessarily incorrect. We do know, for example, that such "insular dwarfing" has occurred in other mammals. For the moment, the most comprehensive analyses indicate that a recently discovered hominin species (*H. floresiensis*) did, in fact, evolve on Flores (Nevell et al., 2007; Tocheri et al., 2007; Falk et al., 2008; Schauber and Falk, 2008; Jungers et al., 2009). The more detailed studies of hand and foot anatomy suggest that in several respects, the morphology is like that of *H. erectus* (Nevell et al., 2007; Tocheri et al., 2007) or even early *Homo* (Jungers et al., 2009; Jungers, 2013). The most comprehensive recent analysis reviews all the available data relating to the well-preserved cranium of LB1 (Kaifu et al., 2011). In most respects, the cranium most resembles early *Homo erectus* from Java—which, after all, is very close to Flores. In any case, the morphology of the Flores hominins is different in several key respects from that of *H. sapiens*, including even those rare individuals who show pathological conditions. There is some possibility that DNA can be retrieved from the Flores bones and sequenced, although this has not yet been successful (Jungers, 2013). Although considered a long shot due to poor bone preservation, analysis of this DNA would certainly help solve the mystery. The recent discovery of early Middle Pleistocene *Homo floresiensis* fossils (mentioned above) strongly suggests that insular dwarfing occurred early on after initial settlement on Flores Island (Brumm et al., 2016; van den Bergh et al., 2016).

How Do We Know?

There has been considerable debate regarding the importance of meat consumption in hominin evolution. Large brains are especially metabolically costly, and increases in brain size seem to be correlated with a reduction in the size of the gut—another metabolically costly organ. Known as the *expensive-tissue hypothesis*, Aiello and Wheeler (1995) proposed that increases in brain size during the Pleistocene would have required a shift toward a more nutrient-dense, higher-quality diet, especially one high in protein (that is, one that is more meat-based). Thus, our over-sized brain and smaller than predicted digestive system appear to be linked to a major change in dietary quality, which was likely underway with the evolution of the genus *Homo*.

We can consider both direct and indirect lines of evidence for a shift toward greater meat consumption during the Pleistocene. First, evidence from both stone tools and butchering marks on animal bone suggests a greater emphasis on the processing of animal carcasses, beginning by at least 2.6 mya. In some cases, the bones show evidence of scavenging damage from carnivores that occurred prior to the butchery marks, indicating that the hominins were sometimes getting the leftovers (most likely the fatty-rich marrow from within long bones). Further, stone tools were likely used to cut meat portions into smaller bite-sized pieces, helping to ease the digestion of raw meat. In addition, there is convincing evidence from South Africa for the use of fire to cook animal remains by at least 1 mya. If increased meat consumption helped fuel *Homo erectus'* metabolically costly brain, then selective pressures may have resulted in a decrease in the overall size of the digestive system, and may also account for the reduction in the size of the jaws and teeth relative to earlier hominins. The *expensive-tissue hypothesis* has gained support from many researchers, and actually provides a powerful explanation for many of the anatomical and behavioral patterns observed in hominin evolution. Further, this framework provides a good example of biocultural evolution.

What Do You Think?

We have discussed the role of meat consumption in hominin evolution as an important source of fuel for our oversized and metabolically costly brain. Do you think the *expensive tissue hypothesis* has merit? Why or why not? Can you think of any alternative hypotheses to explain the trend toward larger brain size over the past 2.5 million years? ∎

Summary of Main Topics

- *Homo erectus* is the first hominin found outside of the African continent, and dates to the early Pleistocene (1.8 mya). Although there is regional variation in morphology, many researchers classify all fossils as *Homo erectus.*

- *Homo erectus* differs from early *Homo*, with its larger brain, taller stature, robust build, and changes in facial structure and cranial buttressing.

- *Homo erectus* remains have been found in Africa, Europe, and Asia dating from about 1.8 mya to at least 100,000 ya—and probably even later into the Late Pleistocene; thus this species spanned a period of more than 1.5 million years. *Homo erectus* likely first appeared in East Africa and later migrated to other areas. This widespread and highly successful hominin displays a new and more modern pattern of human evolution.

- Around 1.6 mya, a new stone tool kit, known as the Acheulian, is developed within Africa. These tools largely consist of bifacial hand axes and cleavers and were more specialized and transported over longer distances than Oldowan tools. The Acheulian stone tool technology dispersed outside of Africa but continued to show regional variation. *Homo erectus* probably ate novel foods processed in new ways, including meat as a major source of protein. By using these new tools—and at later sites possibly fire as well—they were also able to move into different environments and successfully adapt to new conditions.

- Early interpretations of *Homo erectus* argued that increases in body size (especially longer legs), brain size, and the use of a more sophisticated stone tool kit was required for expansion outside of Africa. Recent discoveries at the site of Dmanisi in the Republic of Georgia indicate a much earlier dispersal out of Africa (by approximately 1.8 mya). The Dmanisi hominins are shorter-statured, less encephalized, and used a less sophisticated stone tool technology than later *Homo erectus*, suggesting that body size, brain size, and technology were not factors limiting the dispersal of this species.

- *Homo floresiensis* represents an unusual new species discovered on Flores Island in Indonesia. This hominin shows probable evidence of insular dwarfism associated with very short stature, a small brain, and unusual limb proportions. Recent dates and new fossil evidence suggest that *Homo floresiensis* traces its roots in Flores to the early Middle Pleistocene (roughly 700,000 ya).

Critical Thinking Questions

1. Discuss the major differences between the australopiths (see Chapter 10) and *Homo erectus*. What are the major differences in cranial morphology, brain size, body size, and limb proportions?

2. Why is the nearly complete skeleton from Nariokotome so important? What kinds of evidence does it provide?

3. What fundamental questions of interpretation do the fossil hominins from Dmanisi raise? Does this evidence completely overturn the earlier views (hypotheses) concerning *H. erectus* dispersal from Africa? Explain why or why not.

4. How has the interpretation of *H. erectus* behavior at Zhoukoudian been revised in recent years? What kinds of new evidence from this site have been used in this reevaluation, and what does that tell you about modern archaeological techniques and approaches?

5. What are the implications of the most recent discoveries on Flores Island in regard to interpretations of *Homo floresiensis*? How does this help solve the debate regarding the taxonomic status of *Homo floresiensis*?

CONNECTIONS

Hominins began to disperse out of Africa around 2 million years ago, and during the next 1 million years inhabited much of Eurasia.

The immediate predecessors of modern humans, including the Neandertals, were much like us, but had some anatomical and behavioral differences.

Modern humans first evolved in Africa and later spread to other areas of the world, where they occasionally inter-bred with Neandertals and other premodern humans.

Premodern Humans

12

When, Where, and What

The Pleistocene

Dispersal of Middle Pleistocene Hominins

Middle Pleistocene Hominins: Terminology

Premodern Humans of the Middle Pleistocene

Africa

Europe

Asia

A Review of Middle Pleistocene Evolution

Middle Pleistocene Culture

Neandertals: Premodern Humans of the Late Pleistocene

Western Europe

Central Europe

Western Asia

Central Asia

Surprising Connections: Another Contemporary Hominin?

Culture of Neandertals

Technology

Subsistence

Speech and Symbolic Behavior

Burials

Molecular Connections: The Genetic Evidence

Neandertal DNA

Seeing Close Human Connections: Understanding Diversity among Premodern Humans

Excavations at Sima de Los Huesos in Spain.

Javier Trueba/Madrid Scientific Films/Science Source;
Top Images: Russell L. Ciochon; Harry Nelson;
© Cengage Learning

Student Learning Objectives After studying the material in this chapter, you should be able to:

▶ Describe the general time frame and climatic conditions during which early premodern humans lived (generally classified as *Homo heidelbergensis*).

▶ Describe the general areas of the world where these early premodern humans have been found and compare and contrast the physical characteristics of *H. heidelbergensis* with those of *H. erectus*.

▶ Discuss the behavioral patterns of *H. heidelbergensis*.

▶ Describe the time frame during which Neandertals lived, where their remains have been found, and their physical characteristics.

▶ Discuss some of the major cultural innovations displayed by Neandertals and how these compare with those of earlier hominins.

▶ Explain what the information from the whole genome sequencing of Neandertals and Denisovans tells us and why this is important.

▶ Discuss some of the issues with differentiating fossil species that date to the Middle and Late Pleistocene.

What do you think of when you hear the term *Neandertal*? Most people think of imbecilic hunched-over brutes. Yet Neandertals had brains at least as large as ours, and they showed many sophisticated cultural capabilities. What's more, they definitely weren't hunched over but stood fully erect (as hominins had for millions of years). In fact, Neandertals and their immediate predecessors could easily be called human.

That brings us to possibly the most basic of all questions: What does it mean to be human? The meaning of this term is highly varied, encompassing religious, philosophical, and biological considerations. As you know, physical anthropologists primarily concentrate on the biological aspects of the human organism. All living people today are members of one species, sharing a common anatomical pattern and similar behavioral potentials. We call hominins like us "modern" *Homo sapiens*, and in the next chapter, we'll discuss the origin of forms that were essentially identical to people living today.

When in our evolutionary past can we say that our predecessors were obviously human? Certainly, the further back we go in time, the less hominins look like modern *Homo sapiens*. This is, of course, exactly what we'd expect in an evolutionary sequence.

We saw in Chapter 11 that *Homo erectus* took crucial steps in the human direction and defined a new adaptive level in human evolution. In this chapter, we'll discuss the hominins who continued this journey. Both physically and behaviorally, they're much like modern *Homo sapiens*, though they still show several significant differences. So while most paleoanthropologists are comfortable referring to these hominins as "human," we must qualify this recognition a bit to set them apart from fully modern people. Thus, in this text, we'll refer to these fascinating immediate predecessors as "premodern humans."

When, Where, and What

Most of the hominins discussed in this chapter lived during the **Middle Pleistocene**, a period beginning 780,000 ya and ending 125,000 ya. In addition, some of the later premodern humans, including the Neandertals and the Denisovans, lived well into the **Late Pleistocene** (125,000 to 10,500 ya).

The Pleistocene

The Pleistocene has been called the Ice Age because, as had occurred before in geological history, it was marked by periodic advances and retreats of massive continental **glaciations**. During glacial periods, when temperatures dropped dramatically, ice accumulated because more snow fell each year than melted, causing the advance of massive glaciers. As the climate fluctuated, it sometimes became much warmer. During these **interglacials**, the ice that had built up during the glacial periods melted and the glaciers retreated back toward the earth's polar regions. The Pleistocene was characterized by numerous advances and retreats of ice, with at least 15 major and 50 minor glacial advances documented in Europe alone (Delson et al., 2000).

These glaciations, which enveloped huge swaths of Europe, Asia, and North America as well as Antarctica, were mostly confined to northern latitudes. Hominins living at this time—all still restricted to the Old World—were severely affected as the climate, flora, and animal life shifted during these Pleistocene oscillations. The most dramatic of these effects were felt in Europe and northern Asia—less so in southern Asia and Africa.

Still, the climate also fluctuated in the south. In Africa, the main effects were changing rainfall patterns. During glacial periods, the climate in Africa became more arid, while during interglacials, rainfall increased. The changing availability of food resources affected not only the hominins permanently residing in Africa; more importantly, however, migration routes were likely affected by changing climate. For example, during glacial periods (Fig. 12-1), the Sahara Desert expanded, blocking migration in and out of sub-Saharan Africa (Lahr and Foley, 1998).

In Eurasia, glacial advances also greatly affected migration routes. As the ice sheets expanded, sea levels dropped, making more northern regions uninhabitable,

Middle Pleistocene The portion of the Pleistocene epoch beginning 780,000 ya and ending 125,000 ya.

Late Pleistocene The portion of the Pleistocene epoch beginning 125,000 ya and ending approximately 10,500 ya.

glaciations Climatic intervals when continental ice sheets cover much of the northern continents. Glaciations are associated with colder temperatures in northern latitudes and more arid conditions in southern latitudes, most notably in Africa.

interglacials Climatic intervals when continental ice sheets are retreating, eventually becoming much reduced in size. Interglacials in northern latitudes are associated with warmer temperatures, while in southern latitudes the climate becomes wetter.

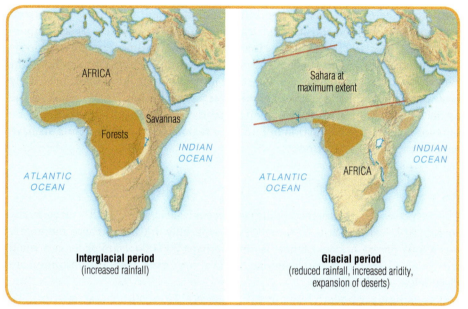

◀ **Figure 12-1**
Changing Pleistocene environments in Africa.

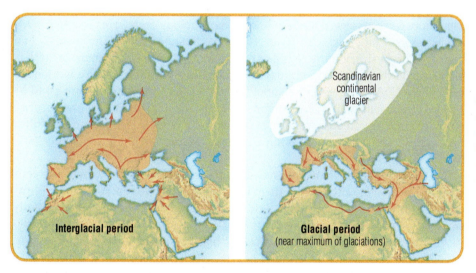

◀ **Figure 12-2**
Changing Pleistocene environments in Eurasia. Orange areas show regions of likely hominin occupation. White areas are major glaciers. Arrows indicate likely migration routes.

and some key passages between areas became blocked by glaciers. For example, during glacial peaks, much of western Europe would have been cut off from the rest of Eurasia (Fig. 12-2).

During the warmer—and in the south wetter—interglacials, the ice sheets shrank, sea levels rose, and certain migration routes reopened (for example, from central Europe into western Europe). Clearly, to understand Middle Pleistocene hominins, it's crucial to view them within their shifting Pleistocene world. As we will see, this had important implications for gene flow, causing some populations to become isolated, leading to genetic drift.

Dispersal of Middle Pleistocene Hominins

Like their *Homo erectus* predecessors, later hominins were widely distributed in the Old World. Discoveries of their presence have come from three continents—Africa, Asia, and Europe. For the first time, Europe became more permanently and densely occupied, with evidence of Middle Pleistocene hominins from England, France, Spain, Germany, Italy, Hungary, and Greece. Africa, as well, continued as a central area of hominin occupation, and finds have come from northern, eastern, and southern Africa. Finally, Asia has yielded several important finds, especially from China. However, these hominins never reached locations occupied by *Homo erectus* within island Southeast Asia. We should point out, though, that these Middle Pleistocene premodern humans didn't vastly extend the geographical range of *Homo erectus*, but rather largely replaced the earlier hominins in previously exploited habitats. One exception appears to be the more successful occupation of Europe, a region where earlier hominins have only sporadically been found.

Middle Pleistocene Hominins: Terminology

The premodern humans of the Middle Pleistocene (that is, after 780,000 ya) generally succeeded *H. erectus.* Still, in some areas—especially in China—there apparently was a long period of coexistence, lasting perhaps 200,000 years or longer; you'll recall that *H. erectus* from Ngandong, in Java, may have lived well into the Late Pleistocene (see Chapter 11).

The earliest premodern humans exhibit several *H. erectus* characteristics: The face is large, the brows are projected, the forehead is low, and in some cases the cranial vault is still thick. Even so, some of their other features show that they were more derived toward modern human morphology than were their *H. erectus* predecessors. Compared with *H. erectus*, these premodern humans possessed an increased brain size, a more rounded braincase (that is, the maximum breadth is higher up on the sides of the cranial vault), a more vertical nose, and a less angled back of the skull (occipital). We should note that the time span encompassed by Middle Pleistocene premodern humans is at least 500,000 years, so it's no surprise that over time we can observe certain trends. Later Middle Pleistocene hominins, for example, show even more brain expansion and an even less angled occipital than do earlier forms.

We know that premodern humans were a diverse group dispersed over three continents. Deciding how to classify them has been disputed for decades, and anthropologists still have disagreements. However, a growing consensus has recently emerged. Beginning perhaps as early as 850,000 ya and extending to about 200,000 ya, the fossils from Africa and Europe are placed within *Homo heidelbergensis*, named after a fossil mandible found near Heidelberg, Germany, in 1907. What's more, some Asian specimens, dating to around 450,000 ya, possibly represent a regional variant of *H. heidelbergensis*.

Until recently, many researchers regarded these fossils as early but more primitive members of *Homo sapiens*. In recognition of this somewhat transitional status, the fossils were called "archaic *Homo sapiens*," with all later humans also belonging to the species *Homo sapiens*. However, most paleoanthropologists now find this terminology unsatisfactory. For example, Phillip Rightmire concludes that "simply lumping diverse ancient groups with living populations obscures their differences" (1998, p. 226). In our own discussion, we recognize *H. heidelbergensis* as a transitional species between *H. erectus* and later hominins (that is, primarily modern *H. sapiens*). Keep in mind, however, that this species was probably an ancestor of both modern humans and Neandertals. It's debatable whether *H. heidelbergensis* actually represents a fully separate species in the biological sense, that is, following the biological species concept (see Chapter 5). Still, it's useful to give this group of premodern humans a separate name to make this important stage of human evolution more easily identifiable. (We'll return to this issue later in the chapter when we discuss the theoretical implications in more detail.)

Premodern Humans of the Middle Pleistocene

Africa

In Africa, premodern fossils have been found at several sites. One of the best known is Kabwe (Broken Hill). At this site in Zambia, fieldworkers discovered a complete cranium (Fig. 12-3) together with other cranial and postcranial elements belonging to several individuals. In this and other African premodern specimens, we can see a mixture of primitive and more derived traits. The skull's massive browridge (one of the largest of any hominin), low vault, and prominent occipital torus recall those of *H. erectus*. On the other hand, the occipital region is less angulated, the cranial vault bones are thinner, and the cranial base is essentially modern. Dating estimates of Kabwe and most of the other premodern fossils from Africa spanned throughout the Middle and Late Pleistocene, but recent estimates have given dates for most of the sites in the range of 600,000–125,000 ya (Klein, 2009; Stringer, 2012).

Bodo is another significant African premodern fossil (Fig. 12-4). A nearly complete cranium, Bodo has been dated to relatively early in the Middle Pleistocene (estimated at 600,000 ya), making it one of the oldest specimens of *H. heidelbergensis* from the African continent (Clark et al., 1994). The Bodo cranium is particularly interesting because it shows a distinctive pattern of cut marks, similar to modifications seen on butchered animal bones. Researchers have thus hypothesized that the Bodo individual was defleshed by other hominins, but for what purpose is not clear. The defleshing may have been related to cannibalism, though it also may have been for some other purpose, such as ritual. In any case, this is the earliest evidence of deliberate bone processing of hominins *by* hominins (White, 1986).

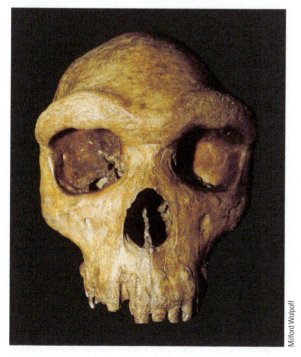

▲ **Figure 12-3**
The Kabwe (Broken Hill) *Homo heidelbergensis* skull from Zambia. Note the very robust browridges.

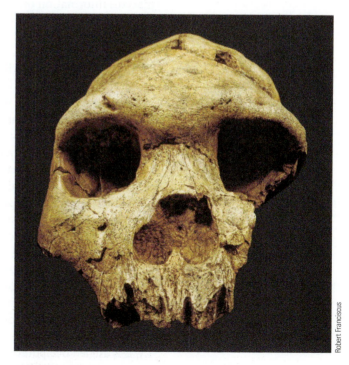

▲ **Figure 12-4**
Bodo cranium, the earliest definitive evidence of *Homo heidelbergensis* in Africa.

At a Glance	Key Premodern Human (*H. heidelbergensis*) Fossils from Africa	
Date	**Site**	**Evolutionary Significance**
130,000 ya	Kabwe (Broken Hill, Zambia)	Nearly complete skull; mosaic of features (browridge very robust, but braincase expanded)
600,000 ya	Bodo (Ethiopia)	Earliest example of African *H. heidelbergensis*; likely evidence of postmortem butchering (e.g., evidence of ritual defleshing or cannibalism)

A number of other crania from South and East Africa also show a combination of retained ancestral with more derived (modern) characteristics, and they're all mentioned in the literature as being similar to Kabwe. The most important of these African finds come from the sites of Florisbad and Elandsfontein (in South Africa) and Laetoli (in Tanzania). A recent reanalysis of hominin cranial remains originally discovered in the early 1970s from Gombore II, located in the Upper Awash region of Ethiopia, suggests the presence of *Homo heidelbergensis* in Africa around 850,000 ya (Profico et al. 2016). Although these fragments represent a very incomplete cranial vault, they provide the earliest potential evidence of *Homo heidelbergensis* in Africa.

The general similarities among all these African premodern fossils indicate a close relationship between them, almost certainly representing a single species (most commonly referred to as *H. heidelbergensis*). These African premodern humans are also quite similar to those found in Europe. The "At a Glance" summarizes information on some of the key African *H. heidelbergensis* discoveries.

Europe

More fossil hominins of Middle Pleistocene age have been found in Europe than in any other region—maybe because more archaeologists have been searching longer in Europe than anywhere else. In any case, during the Middle Pleistocene, Europe was more widely and consistently occupied than it was earlier in human evolution.

The time range of European premodern humans extends the full length of the Middle Pleistocene and beyond. At the earlier end, the Gran Dolina finds from northern Spain (discussed in Chapter 11) are definitely not *Homo erectus*. The Gran Dolina remains may, as proposed by Spanish researchers, be members of a new hominin species (whereas some others prefer to classify them as Neandertals). However, Rightmire (1998) has suggested that the Gran Dolina hominins may simply represent the earliest well-dated occurrence of *H. heidelbergensis*, possibly dating as early as 850,000 ya.

More recent and more completely studied *H. heidelbergensis* fossils have been found throughout much of Europe. Examples of these finds come from Steinheim (Germany), Petralona (Greece), Swanscombe (England), Arago (France), and another cave site at Atapuerca (Spain), known as Sima de los Huesos. Like their African counterparts, these European premoderns have retained certain *H. erectus* traits, but they're mixed with more derived ones—for example, increased cranial capacity, less angled occiput, parietal expansion, and reduced tooth size (Figs. 12-5 and 12-6 on pp. 354–355).

The hominins from the Atapuerca site of Sima de los Huesos are especially interesting. These finds come from another cave in the same area as the Gran Dolina discoveries, but are slightly younger, likely dating to between 500,000 and 400,000 ya (Arnold et al., 2014; Arsuaga et al., 2014). Using a different dating method, a date as early as 600,000 ya has been proposed (Bischoff et al., 2007), but most researchers prefer the more conservative later dates (Green et al., 2010; Wood, 2010; Arnold et al., 2014). A total of at least 28 individuals (including 17 crania) have been recovered from Sima de los Huesos, which literally means "pit of bones." In fact, with more than 4,000 fossil fragments recovered, Sima de los Huesos contains more than 80 percent of all Middle Pleistocene hominin remains in the world (Bermúdez de Castro et al., 2004). Excavations continue at this remarkable site, where bones have somehow accumulated within a deep chamber inside a cave. Paleoanthropologists interpret the hominin morphology as showing several indications of an early Neandertal-like pattern, with arching browridges, a projecting midface, and other Neandertal features (Rightmire, 1998; Stringer, 2012; Arsuaga et al., 2014). Recent mtDNA research on a 400,000-year-old hominin femur from the site indicates a closer relationship with Denisovans (a group discussed later in the chapter) than with Neandertals, ancient humans, or modern humans (Meyer et al., 2014). However, a more recent analysis of nuclear DNA from two hominins from the site found the opposite pattern, suggesting that the hominins of Sima de los Huesos are actually more closely related to Neandertals than Denisovans (Meyer et al., 2015). In this case, the nuclear DNA provides a much more complete picture of the genetic relationships between these hominin groups. The "At a Glance" summarizes information on some of the key European *H. heidelbergensis* discoveries.

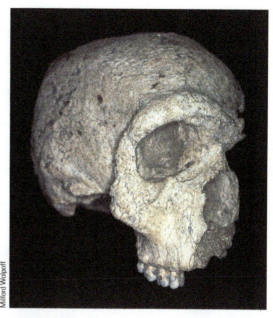

Milford Wolpoff

▲ **Figure 12-5**

Steinheim cranium, a representative of *Homo heidelbergensis* from Germany.

Asia

Like their contemporaries in Europe and Africa, some Asian premodern specimens discovered in China also display both earlier and later characteristics. Previously, Chinese paleoanthropologists suggested that the more ancestral traits, such as a sagittal ridge and flattened nasal bones, are shared with *H. erectus* fossils from Zhoukoudian. They also argued that some of these features can be found in modern *H. sapiens* in China today, suggesting substantial genetic continuity. Despite these superficial similarities, most Chinese researchers today no longer argue that modern Chinese evolved locally in China from a separate *H. erectus* lineage. Whether such regional evolution occurred or whether anatomically modern migrants from Africa displaced local populations is the subject of a major ongoing debate in paleoanthropology. This important controversy will be a central focus of the next chapter.

Dali, the most complete skull of the later Middle or early Late Pleistocene fossils in China, displays *H. erectus* and *H. sapiens* traits, with a cranial capacity

At a Glance	Key Premodern Human (*H. heidelbergensis*) Fossils from Europe	
Date	**Site**	**Evolutionary Significance**
300,000?– 259,000? ya	Swanscombe (England)	Partial skull, but shows considerable brain expansion
600,000?– 400,000 ya	Sima de los Huesos (Atapuerca, northern Spain)	Large sample; very early evidence of Neandertal ancestry (>500,000 ya); earliest evidence of deliberate body disposal of the dead anywhere

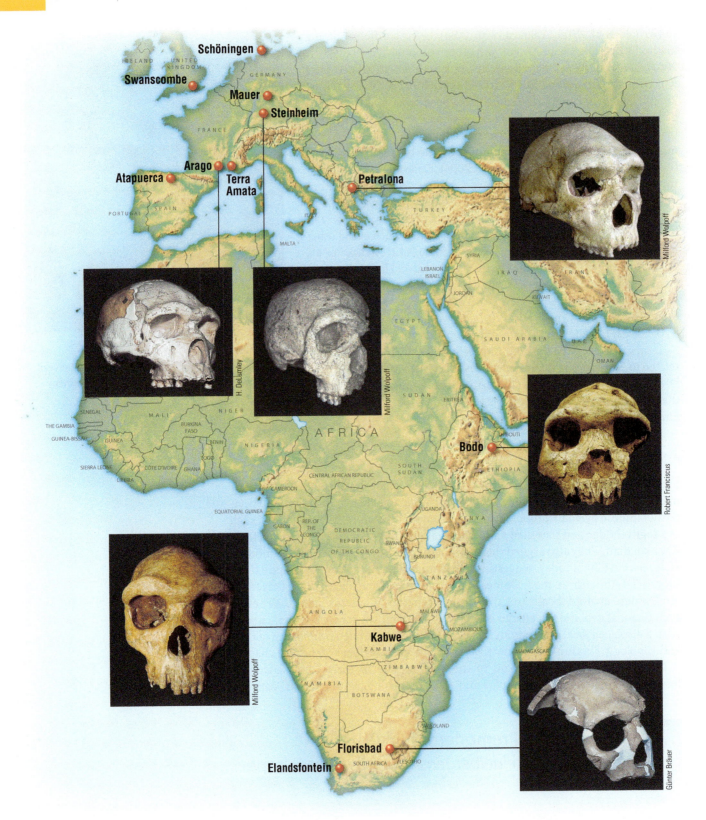

▲ **Figure 12-6**
Fossil discoveries and archaeological localities
of Middle Pleistocene premodern hominins.

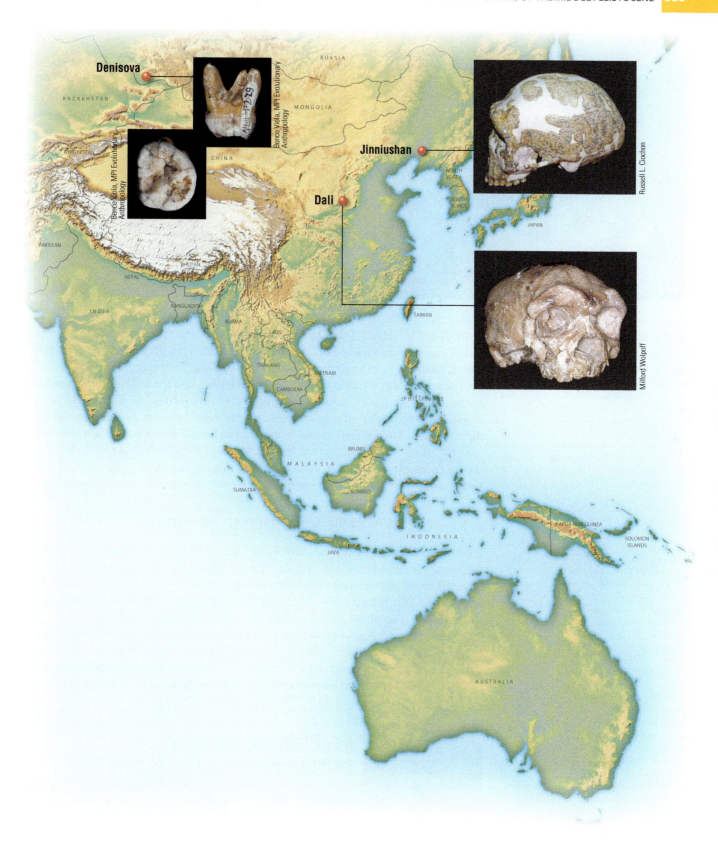

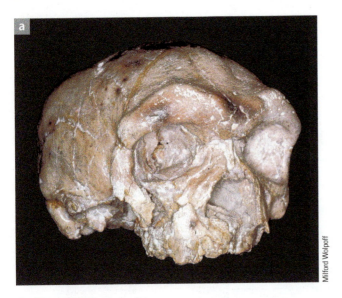

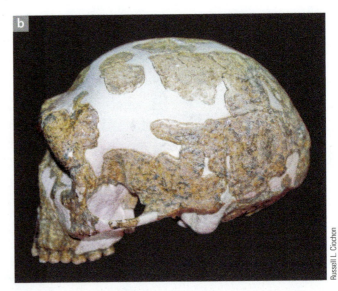

▲ **Figure 12-7**

(**a**) Dali skull and (**b**) Jinniushan skull, both from China. These two crania are considered by some to be Asian representatives of *Homo heidelbergensis*.

of 1,120 cm³ (Fig. 12-7). Like Dali, several other Chinese specimens combine both earlier and later traits. In addition, a partial skeleton from Jinniushan, in northeast China, has been given a provisional date of 200,000 ya (Tiemel et al., 1994). The cranial capacity is fairly large (approximately 1,260 cm³), and the walls of the braincase are thin. These are both modern features, and they're somewhat unexpected in an individual this ancient—if the dating estimate is indeed correct. Just how to classify these Chinese Middle Pleistocene hominins has been a subject of debate and controversy. More recently, though, a leading paleoanthropologist has concluded that they're regional variants of *H. heidelbergensis* (Rightmire, 2004). The "At a Glance" summarizes information on some of the key Asian *H. heidelbergensis* discoveries.

A Review of Middle Pleistocene Evolution

Premodern human fossils from Africa and Europe resemble each other more than they do the hominin fossils from Asia. The mix of some ancestral characteristics—retained from *Homo erectus* ancestors—with more derived features gives the African and European fossils a distinctive look; thus Middle Pleistocene hominins from these two continents are usually referred to as *H. heidelbergensis*.

The situation in Asia isn't so tidy. To some researchers, the remains, especially those from Jinniushan, seem more modern than do contemporary fossils from either Europe or Africa. This observation explains why Chinese paleoanthropologists and some North American colleagues conclude that the Jinniushan remains are early

At a Glance	Key Premodern Human (*H. heidelbergensis*) Fossils from Asia	
Date	**Site**	**Evolutionary Significance**
230,000–180,000 ya	Dali (China)	Nearly complete skull; best evidence of *H. heidelbergensis* in Asia
200,000 ya	Jinniushan (China)	Partial skeleton with cranium showing relatively large brain size; some Chinese scholars suggest it as possible ancestor of early Chinese *H. sapiens*

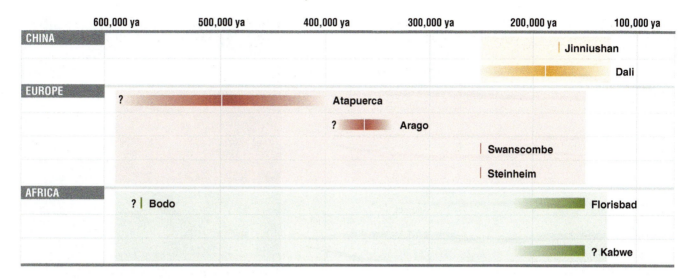

	600,000 ya	500,000 ya	400,000 ya	300,000 ya	200,000 ya	100,000 ya
CHINA						Jinniushan
						Dali
EUROPE	?		Atapuerca			
			?	Arago		
					Swanscombe	
					Steinheim	
AFRICA	?	Bodo				Florisbad
						? Kabwe

▲ **Figure 12-8**
Time line of Middle Pleistocene hominins. Note that most dates are approximations. Question marks indicate those estimates that are most tentative.

members of *H. sapiens*. Other researchers (e.g., Rightmire, 1998, 2004) suggest that they represent a regional branch of *H. heidelbergensis*.

The Pleistocene world forced many small populations into geographical isolation; most of these regional populations no doubt died out. Some, however, did evolve, and their descendants are likely a major part of the later hominin fossil record. In Africa, *H. heidelbergensis* is hypothesized to have evolved into modern *H. sapiens*. In Europe, *H. heidelbergensis* evolved into Neandertals and likely Denisovans as well. Meanwhile, the Chinese premodern populations may all have met with extinction. Right now, though, there's no consensus on the status or the likely fate of these enigmatic Asian Middle Pleistocene hominins (Fig. 12-8).

Middle Pleistocene Culture

The Acheulian technology of *H. erectus* carried over into the Middle Pleistocene with relatively little change until near the end of the period, when it became slightly more sophisticated. Bone, a high-quality tool material, remained practically unused during this time. Stone flake tools similar to those of the earlier era persisted, possibly in greater variety. Some of the later premodern humans in Africa and Europe invented a method—the Levallois technique (Fig. 12-9)—for controlling flake size and shape, resulting in a "turtle back" profile. The Levallois technique required several complex and coordinated steps, suggesting increased cognitive abilities in later premodern populations.

Premodern human populations continued to live in both caves and open-air sites, but they may have increased their use of caves. Did these hominins control fire? Klein (2009), in interpreting archaeological evidence from France, Germany, and Hungary, suggests that they did. What's more, Chinese archaeologists insist that

▼ **Figure 12-9**
The Levallois technique.

Nodule

The nodule is chipped on the perimeter.

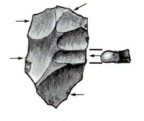

Flakes are radially removed from top surface.

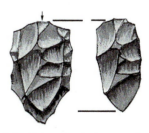

A final blow struck at one end removes a large flake. The flake on the right is the goal of the whole process and is the completed tool.

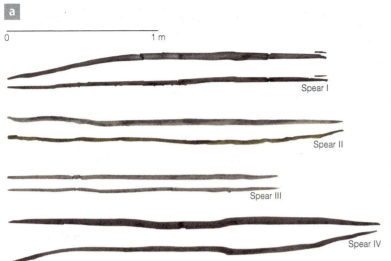

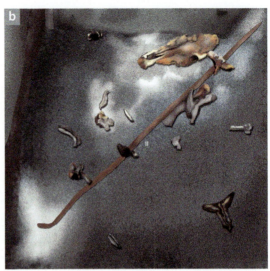

▲ **Figure 12-10**

(a) Fossilized wooden spears from the Schöningen site, Germany (300,000 ya). These large spears were most likely used as throwing weapons for hunting large animals. **(b)** Reconstruction of the association of spear number II and horse remains at the Schöningen site. (Based on Schoch et al., 2008)

many Middle Pleistocene sites in China contain evidence of human-controlled fire. However, the best (and earliest) documented evidence has recently been found in South Africa (Berna et al., 2012). (This new discovery was discussed in Chapter 11.)

We know that Middle Pleistocene hominins built temporary structures, because researchers have found concentrations of bones, stones, and artifacts at several sites. We also have evidence that they exploited many different food sources—fruits, vegetables, seeds, nuts, and bird eggs, each in its own season (Marean et al., 2007). Importantly, they also exploited marine life (including shellfish), a new innovation in human biocultural evolution.

The hunting capabilities of premodern humans, as for earlier hominins, are still greatly disputed. Most researchers have found little evidence supporting widely practiced advanced hunting. Some finds, however, may have caused a shift in this view—especially the discovery in 1995 of remarkable wood spears from the Schöningen site in Germany (Thieme, 1997). These large, extremely well-preserved weapons (now dated to about 300,000 ya) were most likely used as throwing spears, presumably to hunt large animals (Richter and Krbetschek, 2015). Also interesting in this context, the bones of more than 50 horses were recovered at Schöningen. Recent research at the site indicates that these wooden spears and the horse remains are so well preserved because they were submerged within the sediments of an ancient lake that existed at the time. Ongoing studies of these wooden artifacts indicate that at least nine are probable throwing spears, one is a lance, and another is a double pointed stick (Schoch et al., 2015). These artifacts were made out of either spruce or pine, and in at least one case, showed evidence of resharpening of the spear tip (Fig. 12-10).

As documented by the fossil remains as well as artifactual evidence from archaeological sites, the long period of transitional hominins in Europe continued well into the Late Pleistocene (after 125,000 ya). But with the appearance and expansion of the Neandertals and Denisovans, the evolution of premodern humans took a unique turn. We will discuss these important hominin groups next.

Neandertals: Premodern Humans of the Late Pleistocene

Since their discovery more than 150 years ago, the Neandertals have haunted the minds and foiled the best-laid theories of paleoanthropologists. They fit into the general scheme of human evolution, and yet they're misfits. Classified variously either as *H. sapiens* or as belonging to a separate species, they are like us and yet different.

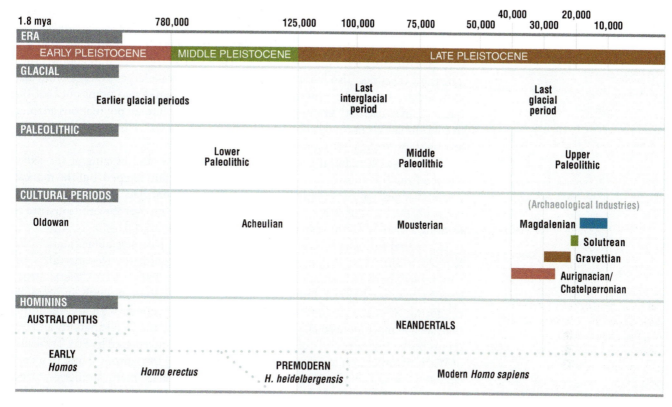

	1.8 mya	780,000	125,000	100,000	75,000	50,000	40,000	20,000	
							30,000	10,000	

ERA — EARLY PLEISTOCENE | MIDDLE PLEISTOCENE | LATE PLEISTOCENE

GLACIAL — Earlier glacial periods | Last interglacial period | Last glacial period

PALEOLITHIC — Lower Paleolithic | Middle Paleolithic | Upper Paleolithic

CULTURAL PERIODS (Archaeological Industries) — Oldowan | Acheulian | Mousterian | Magdalenian | Solutrean | Gravettian | Aurignacian/Chatelperronian

HOMININS — AUSTRALOPITHS | NEANDERTALS | EARLY *Homos* | *Homo erectus* | PREMODERN *H. heidelbergensis* | Modern *Homo sapiens*

▲ **Figure 12-11**
Correlation of Pleistocene subdivisions with archaeological industries and hominins. Note that the geological divisions are separate and different from the archaeological stages (e.g., Late Pleistocene is not synonymous with Upper Paleolithic).

It's not easy to put them in their place. Many anthropologists classify Neandertals within *H. sapiens*, but as a distinctive subspecies, *Homo sapiens neanderthalensis*,* with modern *H. sapiens* designated as *Homo sapiens sapiens*. However, not all experts agree with this interpretation. Recent genetic evidence of interbreeding between Neandertals and early modern humans (Green et al., 2010; Fu et al., 2015) suggests that complete speciation was never attained. This argues against a clear designation of Neandertals as a species separate from *H. sapiens*. However, there are still good reasons to classify them as a different paleospecies from modern humans. We'll discuss this important evidence in more detail in a moment.

Neandertal fossil remains have been found at dates approaching 130,000 ya; but in the following discussion of Neandertals, we'll focus on those populations that lived especially during the last major glaciation, which began about 75,000 ya and ended about 12,000 ya (Fig. 12-11). We should also note that the evolutionary roots of Neandertals apparently reach quite far back in western Europe, as evidenced by the 400,000+-year-old remains from Sima de los Huesos. Some researchers conclude that these hominins are derived enough to be considered members of the Neandertal clade (Stringer, 2012).

The majority of fossils have been found in Europe, where they've been most studied. Our description of Neandertals is based primarily on those specimens, usually called classic Neandertals, from western Europe. Not all Neandertals—including others from eastern Europe and western Asia and those from the interglacial period just before the last glacial one—exactly fit our description of the classic morphology. They tend to be less robust, possibly because the climate in which they lived was not as cold as in western Europe during the last glaciation.

Thal, meaning "valley," is the old spelling; due to rules of taxonomic naming, this spelling is retained in the formal species designation *Homo neanderthalensis* (although the *h* was never pronounced). The modern spelling, *tal*, is used today in Germany; we follow contemporary usage in the text with the spelling of the colloquial *Neandertal*.

One striking feature of Neandertals is brain size, which on average was actually larger than that of *H. sapiens* today. The average for contemporary *H. sapiens* falls between 1,300 and 1,400 cm³, while for Neandertals it was 1,520 cm³. The larger size may be associated with the metabolic efficiency of a larger brain in cold weather. The Inuit (Eskimo), also living in very cold areas, have a larger average brain size than most other modern human populations. We should also point out that the larger brain size in both premodern and contemporary human populations adapted to cold climates is partially correlated with larger body size, which has also evolved among these groups (see Chapter 15).

The classic Neandertal cranium is large, long, low, and bulging at the sides. Viewed from the side, the occipital bone is somewhat bun-shaped, but the marked occipital angle typical of many *H. erectus* crania is absent. The forehead rises more vertically than that of *H. erectus*, and the browridges arch over the orbits instead of forming a straight bar as seen in *H. heidelbergensis* (Fig. 12-12).

Compared with anatomically modern humans, the Neandertal face stands out. It projects almost as if it were pulled forward. Postcranially, Neandertals were very robust, barrel-chested, and powerfully muscled. This robust skeletal structure, in fact, dominates hominin evolution from *H. erectus* through all premodern forms. Still, the Neandertals appear particularly robust, with shorter limbs than seen in most modern *H. sapiens* populations. Both the facial anatomy and the robust postcranial structure of Neandertals have been interpreted by Erik Trinkaus, of Washington University in St. Louis, as adaptations to rigorous living in a cold climate (Trinkaus et al., 1998). Indeed, Neandertals share many similar features, especially in their limb proportions, to modern cold-adapted human populations (Churchill, 2014).

For about 100,000 years, Neandertals lived in Europe and western Asia (Fig. 12-13), and their coming and going have raised more questions and controversies than for any other hominin group. As we've noted, Neandertal forebears were transitional forms dating to the later Middle Pleistocene. However, it's not until the Late Pleistocene that Neandertals become fully recognizable.

Western Europe

One of the most important Neandertal discoveries was made in 1908 at La Chapelle-aux-Saints, a cave in southwestern France. A nearly complete male Neandertal was found buried in a shallow grave in a **flexed** position (Figs. 12-14 and 12-15). Several fragments of nonhuman long bones had been placed over the head, and over them, a bison leg. Around the body were flint tools and broken animal bones (Rendu et al., 2014). Ongoing research at the original site confirms he was deliberately buried; these excavations have mapped out the original grave feature and have even recovered additional skeletal elements associated with this individual (Rendu et al., 2014).

The skeleton was turned over for study to Marcellin Boule, a well-known French paleontologist, who subsequently depicted the La Chapelle Neandertal as a brutish, bent-kneed, not fully erect biped. Because of this exaggerated interpretation, some scholars, and certainly the general public, concluded that all Neandertals were highly primitive creatures.

Why did Boule draw these conclusions from the La Chapelle skeleton? Today, we think he misjudged the Neandertal posture because this adult male skeleton had osteoarthritis of the spine. Also, and probably more importantly, Boule and his contemporaries found it difficult to accept an individual who appeared in any way to depart from the modern pattern as a human ancestor.

flexed The position of the body in a bent orientation, with arms and legs drawn up to the chest.

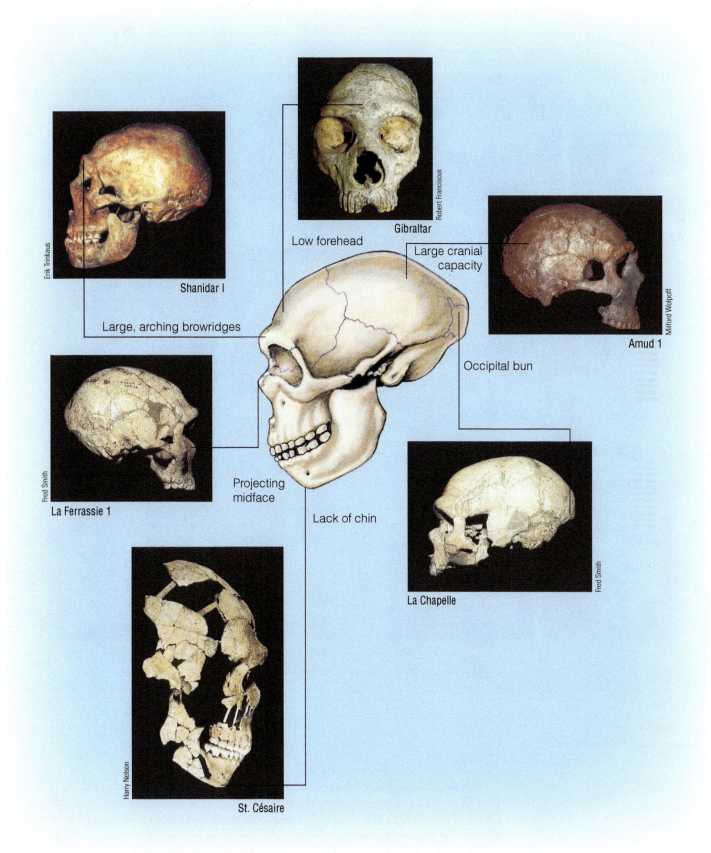

Gibraltar

Low forehead

Large cranial capacity

Shanidar I

Large, arching browridges

Amud 1

Occipital bun

La Ferrassie 1

Projecting midface

Lack of chin

La Chapelle

St. Césaire

▲ Figure 12-12
Morphology and variation in Neandertal crania.

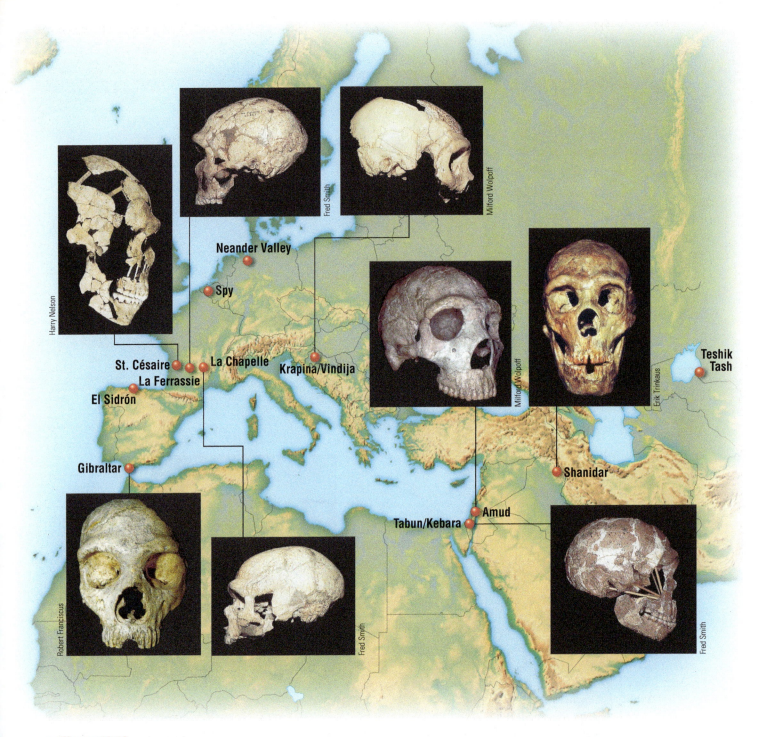

Harry Nelson

Fred Smith

Milford Wolpoff

Neander Valley

Spy

St. Césaire   La Chapelle

La Ferrassie

El Sidrón

Krapina/Vindija

Milford Wolpoff

Erik Trinkaus

Teshik Tash

Gibraltar

Shanidar

Amud

Tabun/Kebara

Robert Franciscus

Fred Smith

Fred Smith

▲ **Figure 12-13**
Fossil discoveries of Neandertals.

The skull of this male, who was possibly at least 40 years of age when he died, is very large, with a cranial capacity of 1,620 cm³. Typical of western European classic forms of Neandertal, the vault is low and long; the browridges are immense, with the typical Neandertal arched shape; the forehead is low and retreating; and the face is long and projecting. The back of the skull is protuberant and bun-shaped (Figs. 12-12 and 12-15).

The La Chapelle skeleton actually isn't a typical Neandertal but an unusually robust male who "evidently represents an extreme in the Neandertal range of variation" (Brace et al., 1979, p. 117). Unfortunately, this skeleton, which Boule claimed didn't even walk completely erect, was widely accepted as "Mr. Neandertal." However, few other Neandertal individuals possess such an exaggerated expression of Neandertal traits as the "Old Man of La Chapelle-aux-Saints."

Dramatic new evidence of Neandertal behavior comes from the El Sidrón site in northern Spain. Dated to about 49,000 ya, fragmented remains of 12 individuals show skeletal evidence indicating that they were smashed, butchered, and likely cannibalized—presumably by other Neandertals (Lalueza-Fox et al., 2011).

Because the remains of all 12 individuals were found together in a cave where their remains had accidentally fallen, they all likely died (were killed) at about the same time. Lying there undisturbed for almost 50,000 years, these individuals reveal several secrets about Neandertal behavior. First, they are hypothesized to all have belonged to the same social group, representing a band of hunter-gatherers. Their ages and sex support this interpretation: three adult males, three adult females, five children/adolescents, and one infant (Lalueza-Fox et al., 2011).

What's more, genetic evidence shows that the adult males were all closely related, but the females weren't. It seems that Neandertals may have practiced a patrilocal form of mating, in which related males stay together and mate with females from other groups (Fig. 12-16 on p. 364).

Some of the most recent of the western European Neandertals come from St. Césaire, in southwestern France, and are dated at about 35,000 ya (Fig. 12-17 on p. 364). At St. Césaire, Neandertal remains were recovered from an archaeological level that also included discarded chipped blades, hand axes, and other stone tools of an **Upper Paleolithic** tool industry associated with Neandertals.

▲ **Figure 12-14**
Artist's reconstruction of a Neandertal adult male based on skeletal remains from La Chapelle, France.

Central Europe

There are quite a few other European classic Neandertals, including significant finds from central Europe (see Fig. 12-13). At Krapina, Croatia, researchers have recovered an abundance of bones—1,000 fragments representing up to 70 individuals—and 1,000 stone tools or flakes (Trinkaus and Shipman, 1992). Krapina is an old site, possibly the earliest showing the full suite of classic Neandertal morphology (Fig. 12-18 on p. 364) dating back to the beginning of the Late Pleistocene (estimated at 130,000 to 110,000 ya). Krapina is also important as an intentional burial site— one of the oldest on record.

About 30 miles from Krapina, Neandertal fossils have also been discovered at Vindija. This site is an excellent source of faunal, cultural, and hominin materials stratified in *sequence* throughout much of the Late Pleistocene. Neandertal fossils from Vindija consist of some 35 specimens dated to between 42,000 and 32,000 ya, making them some of the most recent Neandertals ever discovered (Higham et al., 2006).

As we've seen, the Neandertals from St. Césaire are only slightly older than those from Vindija, making these two sites important for several reasons. Anatomically modern humans were living in both western and central Europe by about 35,000 ya or a bit earlier. So it's possible that Neandertals and modern *H. sapiens* were living quite

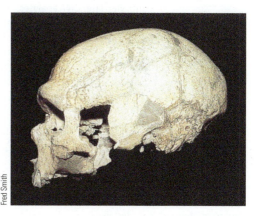

▲ **Figure 12-15**
Specimen from La Chapelle-aux-Saints. Note the occipital bun, projecting face, and low vault.

Upper Paleolithic A cultural period usually not only associated with modern humans but also found with some Neandertals and distinguished by technological innovation in various stone tool industries. Best known from western Europe, similar industries are also known from central and eastern Europe and Africa.

El Sidrón Research Team

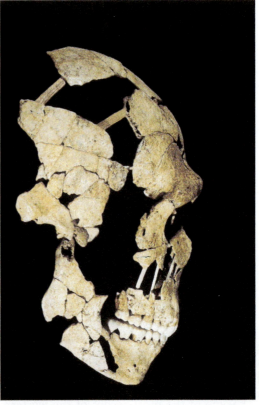

Harry Nelson

▲ **Figure 12-16**
"Clean" excavations at the El Sidrón cave in Spain, where special precautions are used to prevent contamination and allow more controlled later DNA analyses. From this site recent evidence from mtDNA analyses suggests that males likely practiced a patrilocal mating pattern.

▲ **Figure 12-17**
Specimen from St. Césaire, among the "last" Neandertals.

Chatelperronian Pertaining to an Upper Paleolithic industry found in France and Spain, containing blade tools and associated with Neandertals.

close to each other for several thousand years (Fig. 12-19). How did these two groups interact? Evidence from sites in central and southwestern France and northern Spain indicates that Neandertals may have borrowed technological methods and tools (such as blades) from the anatomically modern populations and thereby modified their own tools, creating a new industry, the **Chatelperronian** (Hublin et al., 2012). It's also possible, of course, that early modern *H. sapiens* borrowed cultural innovations from the Neandertals (who, as we'll soon see, were in many ways also quite sophisticated). What's more, we now know that they were *interbreeding* with each other!

▶ **Figure 12-18**
Krapina cranium. (**a**) Lateral view showing characteristic Neandertal traits. (**b**) Three-quarters view.

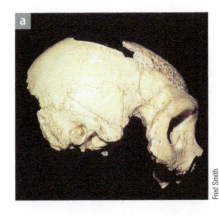

Fred Smith

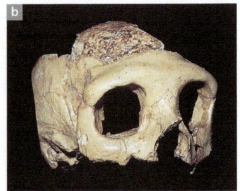

Fred Smith

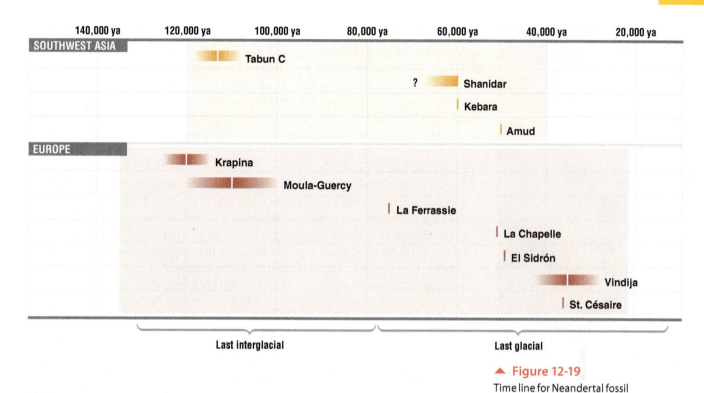

▲ **Figure 12-19**
Time line for Neandertal fossil discoveries.

Western Asia

Israel Many important Neandertal discoveries have also been made in southwest Asia. Neandertal specimens from Israel are more gracile than the classic Neandertals of Europe, though again the overall pattern is clearly Neandertal. One of the best known of these discoveries is from Tabun (Fig. 12-20). Tabun, excavated in the early 1930s, yielded a female skeleton dated by thermoluminescence (TL) at about 120,000 to 110,000 ya. (TL dating is discussed in Chapter 9.) If this dating is accurate, Neandertals at Tabun were generally contemporary with early modern *H. sapiens* found in nearby caves.

A more recent Neandertal burial of a large male comes from Kebara, a neighboring cave at Mt. Carmel. A partial skeleton, dated to 60,000 ya, it contains the most complete Neandertal thorax and pelvis yet found. Also recovered at Kebara is a hyoid—a small bone located in the throat, and the first ever found from a Neandertal; this bone is especially important because it provides information helpful for reconstructing language capabilities.*

▲ **Figure 12-20**
Excavation of the Tabun Cave, Mt. Carmel, Israel.

---

*The Kebara hyoid is identical to that of modern humans, suggesting that Neandertals did not differ from modern *H. sapiens* in this key element.

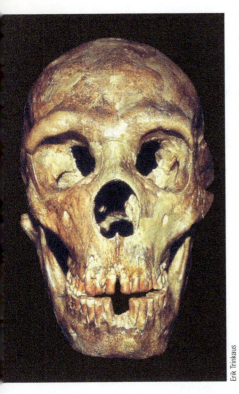

▲ **Figure 12-21**
Shanidar 1. Does he represent Neandertal compassion for the disabled?

Erik Trinkaus

Iraq A most remarkable site is Shanidar Cave, in the Zagros Mountains of northeastern Iraq, where fieldworkers found partial skeletons of nine individuals, four of them deliberately buried. One of the more interesting skeletons recovered from Shanidar is that of a male (Shanidar 1) who lived to be approximately 30 to 45 years old, a considerable age for a prehistoric human (Fig. 12-21). He is estimated to have stood 5 feet 7 inches tall, with a cranial capacity of 1,600 cm³. The skeletal remains of Shanidar 1 also exhibit several other fascinating features:

> There had been a crushing blow to the left side of the head, fracturing the eye socket, displacing the left eye, and probably causing blindness on that side. He also sustained a massive blow to the right side of the body that so badly damaged the right arm that it became withered and useless; the bones of the shoulder blade, collar bone, and upper arm are much smaller and thinner than those on the left. The right lower arm and hand are missing, probably not because of poor preservation . . . but because they either atrophied and dropped off or because they were amputated. (Trinkaus and Shipman, 1992, p. 340)

Besides these injuries, the man had further trauma to both legs, and he probably limped. It's hard to imagine how he could have performed day-to-day activities without assistance. This is why Erik Trinkaus, who has studied the Shanidar remains, suggests that to survive, Shanidar 1 must have been helped by others: "A one-armed, partially blind, crippled man could have made no pretense of hunting or gathering his own food. That he survived for years after his trauma was a testament to Neandertal compassion and humanity" (Trinkaus and Shipman, 1992, p. 341).

Central Asia

Neandertals extended their range even farther to the east, far into central Asia. A discovery made in the 1930s at the site of Teshik-Tash, in Uzbekistan, of a Neandertal child associated with tools of the Mousterian industry suggested that Neandertals had dispersed a long way into Asia. However, owing to poor archaeological control during excavation and the young age of the individual, the find was not considered by all paleoanthropologists as clearly that of a Neandertal. New finds and molecular evaluation have provided crucial evidence that Neandertals did in fact extend their geographical range far into central Asia and perhaps even farther east.

DNA analysis of the Teshik-Tash remains shows that they are clearly Neandertal. What's more, other fragmentary specimens from southern Siberia also show a distinctively Neandertal genetic pattern (Krause et al., 2007b). As we'll see shortly, researchers have recently been able to identify and analyze DNA from several Neandertal specimens. It's been shown that Neandertals and modern humans differ in both their mitochondrial DNA (mtDNA) and nuclear DNA; these results are extremely significant in determining the evolutionary status of the Neandertal lineage. Moreover, in the case of the fragmentary specimens from southern Siberia (dating to 50,000 to 37,000 ya), it was the DNA findings that provided the key evidence in determining whether the hominin is even a Neandertal. In a sense, this is analogous to doing forensic analysis on our ancient hominin predecessors. The "At a Glance" on p. 367 summarizes information on some of the key Neandertal discoveries.

Surprising Connections: Another Contemporary Hominin?

In 2000, 2008, and 2010, researchers found more fragmentary hominin remains in Denisova Cave in the Altai Mountains of southern Siberia. A finger bone and two

At a Glance   Key Neandertal Fossil Discoveries

Date	Site	Evolutionary Significance
42,000– 28,000 ya	Vindija (Croatia)	Large sample (best evidence of Neandertals in eastern Europe); latest well-dated Neandertal site
50,000 ya	La Chapelle (France)	Most famous Neandertal site; historically provided early, but distorted, interpretation of Neandertals
70,000–60,000 ya	Shanidar (Iraq)	Several well-preserved skeletons; good example of Neandertals from southwestern Asia; one individual with multiple injuries
110,000 ya; date uncertain	Tabun (Israel)	Well-preserved and very well-studied fossils showing early evidence of Neandertals in southwestern Asia

teeth were found initially, and these are dated to as old as 80,000–60,000 ya (Meyer et al., 2012). From such incomplete skeletal remains, accurate anatomical species identification is impossible. In prior years, this seemingly meager find would have been stashed away in a cabinet in a museum or university laboratory and mostly forgotten. But in the twenty-first century, we have new ways to study bits and pieces of ancient hominins. So the finger bone was sent to the Max-Planck Institute for Evolutionary Anthropology in Germany to see if DNA analysis could determine to which species it belongs.

Initially, mitochondrial DNA analysis was performed and provided a big surprise: The mtDNA from the hominin at Denisova Cave did not match that of either modern *H. sapiens* or a Neandertal! What's more, the degree of genetic distance suggested to the researchers that this "new" hominin lineage diverged from the modern *H. sapiens*/Neandertal line almost 1 mya (Krause et al., 2010).

Lying in a cool, dry, stable environment inside the cave, the Denisova remains stood a good chance of preserving even more complete ancient DNA. So, the Max Planck team, along with many colleagues from around the world, decided to attempt to sequence the nuclear genome derived from DNA in the finger bone (in which DNA preservation was exceptionally good).

In less than 2 years, they successfully sequenced the *entire* genome from this one small bone—more than 3 billion base pairs—a truly amazing accomplishment (Reich et al., 2010). In 2012 they went even further doing a far more precise sequencing (up to 30× more accurate than the sequence performed previously) of the entire genome from the same finger bone (Meyer et al., 2012). These far more complete data confirmed the earlier findings, most notably that the "Denisovans" were a separate branch of hominins living side by side in central Asia with at least two other lineages of hominins, Neandertals and modern humans (for more details, see "Molecular Connections").

Culture of Neandertals

Anthropologists almost always associate Neandertals, who lived in the cultural period known as the Middle Paleolithic, with the Mousterian industry—although they don't always associate the **Mousterian** industry with just Neandertals (since it is sometimes also found with modern humans). Early in the last glacial period, Mousterian culture extended across Europe and North Africa into the former Soviet

Mousterian Pertaining to the stone tool industry associated with Neandertals and some modern *H. sapiens* groups; also called Middle Paleolithic. This industry is characterized by a larger proportion of flake tools than is found in Acheulian tool kits.

Union, Israel, Iran, and as far east as central Asia and possibly even China. Also, in sub-Saharan Africa, the contemporaneous Middle Stone Age industry is broadly similar to the Mousterian.

Technology

Neandertals extended and diversified traditional methods of making tools, and there's some indication that they developed specialized tools for skinning and preparing meat, hunting, woodworking, and hafting (Fig. 12-22).

Even so, in strong contrast to the following cultural period, the Upper Paleolithic, there's almost no evidence that they used bone tools. Still, Neandertals advanced their technology well beyond that of earlier hominins. It's possible that their technological advances helped provide part of the basis for the remarkable changes of the Upper Paleolithic, which we'll discuss in the next chapter. What's more, Neandertals also were quite advanced in exploiting new food resources as well as fashioning personal adornments.

Subsistence

We know, from the abundant remains of animal bones at their sites, that Neandertals were successful hunters. But though it's clear that Neandertals could hunt large mammals, they may not have been as efficient at this task as Upper Paleolithic modern humans. For example, it wasn't until the beginning of the Upper Paleolithic that the spear-thrower, or atlatl, came into use (see Chapter 13). Soon after that, in Upper Paleolithic groups, the bow and arrow greatly increased efficiency (and safety) in hunting large mammals by putting distance between the hunters and the hunted. Because Neandertals had no long-distance weaponry and were mostly limited to thrusting spears, they may have been more prone to serious injury—a hypothesis supported by paleoanthropologists Thomas Berger and Erik Trinkaus. Berger and Trinkaus (1995) analyzed the pattern of trauma, particularly fractures, in Neandertals and compared it with that seen in contemporary human samples. Interestingly, the pattern in Neandertals, especially the relatively high proportion of head and neck injuries, was most similar to that seen in contemporary rodeo performers. They concluded that "the similarity to the rodeo distribution suggests frequent close encounters with large ungulates unkindly disposed to the humans involved" (Berger and Trinkaus, 1995, p. 841).

Recent archaeological discoveries have shown that Neandertals also expanded their range of available foods to include marine resources—a subsistence strategy

▶ **Figure 12-22**
Examples of the Mousterian tool kit, including (from left to right) a Levallois point, a perforator, and a side scraper.

Randall White

previously thought to have been developed later by modern humans during the Upper Paleolithic. From Gibraltar, evidence has shown that some Neandertals gathered shellfish and hunted seals and dolphins, displaying no difference in their hunting behavior from modern humans of the same region (Stringer et al., 2008).

Speech and Symbolic Behavior

There are a variety of hypotheses concerning the speech capacities of Neandertals, and many of these views are contradictory. Although some researchers argue that Neandertals were incapable of human speech, the prevailing consensus has been that they *were* capable of articulate speech and possibly capable of producing the same range of sounds as modern humans.

Recent genetic evidence likely will help us to determine when fully human language first emerged (Enard et al., 2002; Fisher and Scharff, 2009). In humans today, mutations in a particular gene (named the *FOXP2* gene) are known to produce serious language impairments. From an evolutionary perspective, what is perhaps most significant is the greater variability seen in the alleles at this locus in modern humans as compared with other primates. One explanation for this increased variation is intensified selection acting on human populations. And, as we'll see shortly, DNA evidence from Neandertal fossils shows that these hominins had already made this transformation.

Many researchers are convinced that Upper Paleolithic *H. sapiens* had some significant behavioral advantages over Neandertals and other premodern humans. Was it some kind of new and expanded ability to symbolize, communicate, organize social activities, elaborate technology, obtain a wider range of food resources, or care for the sick or injured? Or was it some other factor? Compared with modern *H. sapiens*, were the Neandertals limited by neurological differences that may have contributed to their demise?

The direct anatomical evidence derived from Neandertal fossils isn't much help in answering these questions. Ralph Holloway (1985) has maintained that Neandertal brains—at least as far as the fossil evidence suggests (from endocasts—both natural and artificial)—aren't significantly different from those of modern *H. sapiens*. What's more, the positioning of the Neandertal vocal tract (determined by the shape of the hyoid bone as well as the shape of the cranial base), along with other morphological features, doesn't appear to have seriously limited their capacity for speech (D'Anastasio et al., 2013).

Most of the reservations about advanced cognitive abilities in Neandertals have been based on archaeological data. However, as more archaeological data have been collected and better dating controls applied to a large number of sites bridging the Mousterian–Upper Paleolithic transition, many of the proposed behavioral differences between Neandertals and early modern humans have blurred. For example, it is now known that, like early *H. sapiens*, Neandertals sometimes used pigment (probably as body ornamentation) and wore jewelry. The most significant recent finds come from two sites in Spain dating to 50,000 to 37,000 ya, and both have a Mousterian stone tool industry. Since these sites were occupied *before* modern *H. sapiens* reached this part of Europe, the most likely conclusion is that the objects found were made by Neandertals (Zilhão et al., 2010). The finds include perforated shells, ostensibly drilled to be used as jewelry, as well as natural pigments that were deliberately brought to the site and applied to the shells and some animal bones (Fig. 12-23 on p. 372).

Neandertals and modern humans coexisted in some parts of Europe for up to 15,000 years, so Neandertals didn't vanish suddenly. Nevertheless, by approximately 41,000–39,000 ya (and possibly as recent as 27,000 kya), they disappear from the

A Closer Look The Evolution of Language

One of the most distinctive behavioral attributes of all modern humans is our advanced ability to use highly sophisticated symbolic language. Indeed, it would be impossible to imagine human social relationships or human culture without language.

When did language evolve? First, we should define what we mean by full human language. As we discussed in Chapter 7, nonhuman primates have shown some elements of language. For example, some chimpanzees, gorillas, and bonobos display the ability to manipulate symbols and a rudimentary understanding of grammar. Still, the full complement of skills displayed by humans includes the extensive use of arbitrary symbols; sophisticated grammar; and a complex, open system of communication.

Most scholars are comfortable attributing such equivalent skills to early members of *H. sapiens*, as early as 200,000 to 100,000 ya. In fact, some researchers have hypothesized that the elaborate technology and artistic achievements, as well as the rapid dispersal, of modern humans were a direct result of behavioral advantages—particularly full language capabilities. More recently, we have come to appreciate that Neandertal cultural abilities were also quite advanced and that the transition to the more elaborate Upper Paleolithic associated with modern humans was not instantaneous.

Clearly, earlier hominins had some form of complex communication; almost everyone agrees that even the earliest hominins did communicate (and the form was at least as complex as that seen in living apes). What's not generally agreed upon is just when the full complement of human language capacity first emerged. Indeed, the controversy relating to this process will continue to ferment, since there's no clear answer to the question. At present, there's not enough evidence available to fully establish the language capabilities of any fossil hominin. We said in Chapter 7 that there are neurological foundations for language and that these features relate more to brain reorganization than to simple increase in brain size. Also, as far as spoken language is concerned, alterations within several anatomical structures—including the brain, tongue and vocal tract—must have occurred at some time during hominin evolution.

Yet, because it's soft tissue, we have no complete record of fossil hominin brains or their vocal tracts. We do have endocasts, which preserve a few external features of the brain. For example, there are several preserved endocasts of australopiths from South Africa. However, the information is incomplete and thus subject to varying interpretations. (For example, did these hominins possess language? If not, what form of communication did they display?) Evidence from the vocal tract has been even more elusive, although recent finds are helping to fill in at least some of the gaps.

In such an atmosphere of fragmentary data, a variety of conflicting hypotheses have been proposed. Some paleoanthropologists argue that early australopiths (3 mya) had language. Others think that such capabilities were first displayed by early *Homo* (perhaps 2 mya). Still others suggest that language didn't emerge fully until the time of *Homo erectus* (2 to 1 mya), or perhaps it was premodern humans (such as the Neandertals) who first displayed such skills. And finally, some researchers assert that language first developed only with the appearance of fully modern *H. sapiens*.

Because the question of language evolution is so fundamental to understanding human evolution (indeed, what it means *to be* human), a variety of creative techniques have

---

fossil and archaeological record (Roebroeks and Soressi, 2016). At some point, as a recognizable human group, Neandertals became an evolutionary dead end. Right now, we can't say exactly what caused their disappearance and ultimate replacement by anatomically modern Upper Paleolithic peoples. Indeed, Neandertals haven't really disappeared altogether, since a few of their genes still can be found today in many human groups (Vernot and Akey, 2014).

Burials

Anthropologists have known for some time that Neandertals deliberately buried their dead. Undeniably, the spectacular discoveries at La Chapelle (Rendu et al., 2014), Shanidar (Trinkaus, 1983), and elsewhere were the direct results of ancient burial, which permits preservation that's much more complete. Such deliberate burial treatment goes back at least 90,000 years at Tabun. From a much older site,

been applied to assess the (limited) evidence that's available. We've already mentioned the analysis of endocasts.

To reconstruct speech capabilities in fossil hominins, the physiology of the vocal tract can also provide some crucial hints, especially the position of the voice box (larynx) within the throat. In adult modern humans, the larynx is placed low in the throat, where it can better act as a resonating chamber. Unfortunately, since all the crucial structures within the vocal tract are soft tissue, they decompose after death, leaving paleoanthropologists to their own imaginations to speculate about the relative positions of the larynx in life. One way to determine the position of the larynx in long-dead hominins is to look at the degree of flexion at the base of the cranium. This flexion can be directly linked to the placement of the larynx in life, since "it shapes the roof of the voice box" (Klein, 1999). In comparisons of fossil hominin crania, it's been determined that full cranial base flexion similar to that found in modern *sapiens* is not found before *Homo heidelbergensis.*

The tongue is, of course, another crucial structure influencing speech. Because it's a site of attachment for one of the muscles of the tongue, the shape and position of the hyoid bone (Fig. 1) can tell us a lot about speech capabilities in earlier hominins. A hyoid located higher up and farther back in the throat allows modern humans to control their tongues much more efficiently and precisely. In the *Australo-pithecus afarensis* child's skeleton (from Dikika,

Ethiopia; see Chapter 10), the hyoid is shaped more like that in a chimpanzee than in a modern human. So it seems most likely that these early hominins weren't able to fully articulate human speech. The only other hyoid found in a fossil hominin comes from the Neandertal skeleton found at Kebara (Israel); quite unlike the australopith condition, it resembles modern hyoids in all respects. We thus have some basis for concluding that the tongue musculature of Neandertals may have been much like our own.

Also potentially informative are possible genetic differences between humans and apes in regard to language. As the human genome is fully mapped (especially identifying functional regions and their specific actions) and compared with ape DNA (the chimpanzee genome is now also completely sequenced at a structural level), we might at long last begin to find a key to solving this great mystery.

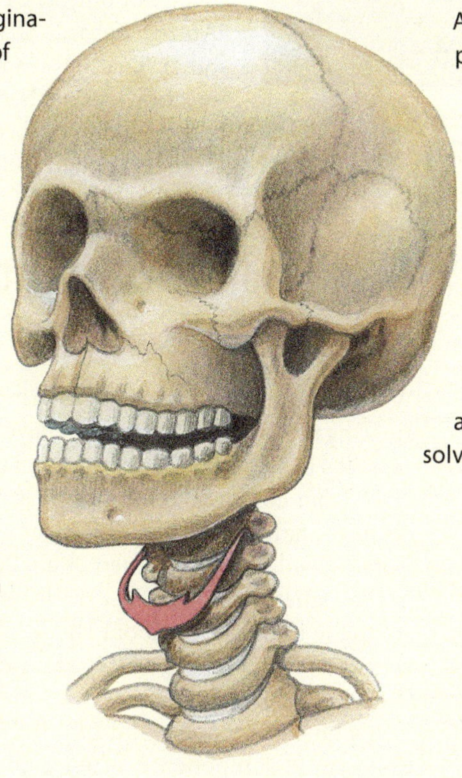

◀ **Figure 1**
The position of the hyoid bone in the throat, shown in a modern human skeleton.

some form of consistent "disposal" of the dead—not necessarily below-ground burial—is evident. As previously discussed, at the site of Sima de los Huesos in Spain, archaeologists found thousands of fossilized bone fragments in a cave at the end of a deep vertical shaft. From the nature of the site and the accumulation of hominin remains, Spanish researchers are convinced that the site demonstrates some form of human activity involving deliberate disposal of the dead (Arsuaga et al., 1997).

The recent dating of Sima de los Huesos to 400,000 ya suggests that Neandertal precursors were already handling their dead in special ways during the Middle Pleistocene. Such behavior was previously thought to have emerged only much later, in the Late Pleistocene. As far as current data indicate, this practice is seen in western European contexts well before it appears in Africa or eastern Asia. For example, in the premodern sites at Kabwe and Florisbad (discussed earlier), deliberate disposal of the dead is not documented, nor is it seen in African early modern sites—for

▲ Figure 12-23
Upper portion of a bivalve shell that has been perforated and stained with pigment, from the Antón rock-shelter site in Spain (dated around 44,000 to 37,000 ya). The reddish inner surface (left) is natural, but the yellow colorant on the outer whitish surface (right) is the result of an added pigment.

example, the Klasies River Mouth, dated at 120,000 to 100,000 ya (see Chapter 13).

Yet, in later contexts (after 35,000 ya), where modern *H. sapiens* remains are found in clear burial contexts, their treatment is considerably more complex than in Neandertal burials. In these later (Upper Paleolithic) sites, grave goods, including bone and stone tools as well as animal bones, are found more consistently and in greater concentrations. Because many Neandertal sites were excavated in the nineteenth or early twentieth century, before more rigorous archaeological methods were developed, many of these supposed burials are now in question. Still, the evidence seems quite clear that deliberate burial was practiced not only at La Chapelle, La Ferrassie (eight graves), Tabun, Amud, Kebara, Shanidar, and Teshik-Tash, but also at several other localities, especially in France. In many cases, the body's position was deliberately modified, placed in the grave in a flexed posture. This flexed position has been found in 16 of the 20 best-documented Neandertal burial contexts (Klein, 2009).

Molecular Connections: The Genetic Evidence

With the revolutionary advances in molecular biology (discussed in Chapter 3), fascinating new avenues of research have become possible in the study of earlier hominins. It's becoming fairly commonplace to extract, amplify, and sequence ancient DNA from contexts spanning the last 10,000 years or so. For example, researchers have analyzed the entire nuclear genome from a 4,000-year-old Inuit (Eskimo) from Greenland (Rasmussen et al., 2010) and the 5,000-year-old "Iceman" found in the Italian Alps. The last of these analyses has provided us with surprisingly complete information about the Iceman. For example, he most likely had brown eyes and was blood-type O; it was even determined that he couldn't digest lactose (Keller et al., 2012).

It's much harder to find usable DNA in even more ancient remains because the organic components, often including the DNA, have been degraded during the fossilization process. Nevertheless, in the past few years exciting results have been announced about DNA found in more than a dozen different Neandertal fossils dated between 50,000 and 32,000 ya. These fossils come from sites in France (including La Chapelle), Germany (from the original Neander Valley locality), Belgium, Italy, Spain, Croatia, Russia (Krings et al., 1997, 2000; Ovchinnikov et al., 2000; Schmitz et al., 2002; Serre et al., 2004; Green et al., 2006), and Siberia (Prüfer et al., 2014). As we previously mentioned, recent ancient DNA evidence strongly suggests that other fossils from central Asia, (most notably, Denisova Cave) dated at 50,000 to 30,000 ya are closely related to Neandertals (Krause et al., 2007a; Prüfer et al., 2014). However, some of the skeletal remains may represent an entirely separate hominin lineage (Krause et al., 2010; Prüfer et al., 2014; Reich et al., 2010).

A recent whole-genome analysis from the finger bone discovered in Denisova Cave (mentioned previously) has also been able to identify the sex of the individual as female and reveal that she had dark skin, brown hair, and brown eyes. Furthermore, it was possible to sequence separately the two DNA strands and thus to tell which genes were inherited from the girl's mother and which ones from her father. Lastly, up to 34 genes that are known to cause disease were found to be different in the Denisovans as compared with modern humans (Meyer et al., 2012). The complete genome also provided another big surprise regarding how these ancient Denisovans are genetically connected to some living human populations. What's more, a toe bone discovered in 2008 from another section of the cave appears to be from a Neandertal and female who lived approximately 50,000 ya (Prüfer et al., 2014). The researchers identified evidence of mixed DNA contributions in this specimen, mostly from Neandertals, and also deriving from Denisovans, early modern humans, and even a fourth (yet to be named) lineage of hominin. Although overall genetic admixture was low, between 3 and 6 percent of this unknown lineage's DNA was found in Denisovan populations. Prüfer and colleagues suggest *H. erectus* as the possible unknown lineage that contributed DNA to the Neandertal genome. Ongoing research will certainly shed new light on the genetic relationships between these Late Pleistocene hominin groups.

Neandertal DNA

Analysis of ancient Neandertal DNA has successfully been accomplished on skeletons dating between 50,000 and 32,000 ya. These fossils come from sites in France (including La Chapelle), Germany (from the original Neander Valley locality), Belgium, Italy, Spain, Croatia, and Russia (Krings et al., 1997, 2000; Ovchinnikov et al., 2000; Schmitz et al., 2002; Serre et al., 2004; Green et al., 2006).

The technique that has been most often used in studying most Neandertal fossils involves extracting mitochondrial DNA (mtDNA), amplifying it through polymerase chain reaction (PCR; see Chapter 3), and sequencing nucleotides in parts of the molecule. Initial results from the Neandertal specimens show that these individuals are genetically more different from contemporary *Homo sapiens* populations than modern human populations are from each other—in fact, about three times as much.

More recently, major advances in molecular biology have allowed much more of the Neandertal genetic pattern to be determined, with the ability to now sequence the entire mtDNA sequence in several individuals (Briggs et al., 2009) as well as big chunks of the *nuclear* DNA (which, as you may recall, contains more than 99 percent of the human genome). In fact, the most exciting breakthrough yet in ancient DNA studies was achieved in 2010 with the completion of the *entire* nuclear genome of European Neandertals (Green et al., 2010). Just a handful of years ago, this sort of achievement would have seemed like science fiction.

This new information has already allowed for crucial (as well as quite surprising) revisions in our understanding of Neandertal and early modern human evolution. First of all, Neandertal DNA is remarkably similar to modern human DNA, with 99.84 percent of it being identical. However, to detect those few (but possibly informative) genes that do differ, the team sequenced the entire genome of five modern individuals (two from Africa and one each from China, France, and New Guinea). To the surprise of almost everyone, the researchers found that many people today still have Neandertal genes! What's more, these Neandertal genes are found only in non-Africans, strongly suggesting that interbreeding occurred between Neandertals and modern *H. sapiens* after the latter had emigrated out of Africa. In fact, the three modern non-African individuals used for comparison in this study all had the same amount of Neandertal DNA. What makes this finding even more startling is that the modern non-African humans evaluated come from widely scattered regions (western Europe, China, and the far South Pacific). Further evidence, including complete genomes from another seven modern people from even more dispersed populations, has further confirmed these findings (Reich et al., 2010).

A Closer Look  Are They Human?

At the beginning of this chapter, we posed the question "What does it mean to be human?" Applying the term *human* to our extinct hominin predecessors is somewhat tricky. Various prior hominin species share with contemporary *Homo sapiens* a mosaic of physical features. For example, they're all bipedal, most (but not all) have fairly small canine teeth, some are completely terrestrial, and some are moderately encephalized (while others are much more so). Thus, the *physical* characteristics that define humanity appear at different times during hominin evolution.

Even more tenuous are the *behavioral* characteristics frequently identified as signifying human status. The most significant of these proposed behavioral traits include major dependence on culture, innovation, cooperation in acquiring food, full language, and elaboration of symbolic representations in art and body adornment. Once again, these characteristics become apparent at different stages of hominin evolution. But distinguishing when and how these behavioral characteristics became established in our ancestors is even more problematic than analyzing anatomical traits. While the archaeological record provides considerable information regarding stone tool technology, it's mostly silent on other aspects of material culture. The social organization and language capabilities of earlier hominins are as yet almost completely invisible.

From the available evidence, we can conclude that *H. erectus* took significant steps in the human direction—well beyond that of earlier hominins. *H. erectus* vastly expanded hominin geographical ranges, achieved the full body size and limb proportions of later hominins, had increased encephalization, and became considerably more dependent on culture for their survival, unlike previous forms, which relied more upon physical adaptations.

H. heidelbergensis (in the Middle Pleistocene) and, to an even greater degree, Neandertals (in the Late Pleistocene) maintained several of these characteristics—such as body size and proportions—while also showing further evolution in the human direction. Most particularly, relative brain size increased further, expanding on average about 22 percent beyond that of *H. erectus* (Fig. 1). Notice, however, that the largest jump in proportional brain size occurs very late in hominin evolution—only with the appearance of fully modern humans.

In addition to brain enlargement, cranial shape also was remodeled in *H. heidelbergensis* and Neandertals, producing a more globular shape of the vault as well as suggesting further neurological reorganization. Stone tool technology also became more sophisticated during the Middle Pleistocene, with the manufacture of tools requiring a more complicated series of steps. Also, for the first time, fire was definitely controlled and widely used; caves were routinely occupied; hominin ranges were successfully expanded throughout much of Europe as well as into northern Asia (that is, colder habitats were more fully exploited); structures were built; the dead were deliberately buried; and more systematic hunting took place.

Some premoderns also were like modern humans in another significant way. Analysis of teeth from a Neandertal shows that these hominins had the same *delayed maturation* found in modern *H. sapiens* (Dean et al., 2001). We don't yet

The best (and simplest) hypothesis for this genetic pattern is that shortly after modern *H. sapiens* migrants left Africa, a small number of them interbred with Neandertals *before* these people and their descendants dispersed to other areas of the world. Researchers were able to sequence the full genome of a ~45,000-ya male from western Siberia. He had the same percent of Neandertal DNA as modern Europeans, indicating that the admixture occurred 60,000 to 50,000 ya (Fu et al., 2014). DNA data from more individuals, both within and outside of Africa, will help clarify this issue. At present, the degree of interbreeding appears to be small but still significant—about 1.5 to 2.1 percent of the total genome for living non-Africans (Prüfer et al., 2014). These low percentages may reflect long-term selection against Neandertal genes in modern humans, especially those located on the X chromosome, which are linked to reduced fertility in males (Sankararaman et al., 2014).

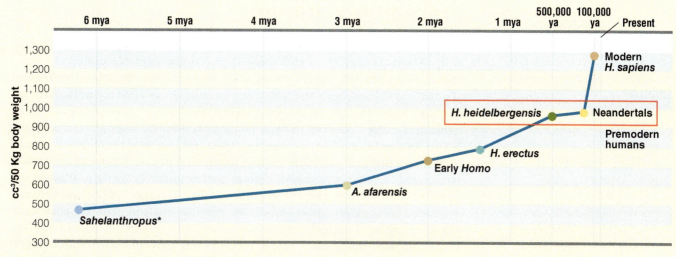

*There are no direct current data for body size in *Sahelanthropus*. Body size is estimated from tooth size in comparison with *A. afarensis*. Data abstracted from McHenry (1992), Wood and Collard (1999a), Brunet (2002), and Carroll (2003).

▲ **Figure 1**

Relative brain size in hominins. The scale shows brain size as cm³ per 50 kg of body weight. Premodern humans have a more than 20 percent increase in relative brain size compared to *H. erectus*, but modern humans show another 30 percent expansion beyond that seen in premodern humans.

have similar data for earlier *H. heidelbergensis* individuals, but it's possible that they, too, showed this distinctively human pattern of development.

Did these Middle and Late Pleistocene hominins have the full language capabilities and other symbolic and social skills of living peoples? It's impossible to answer this question completely, given the types of fossil and archaeological evidence available. Yet, it does seem quite possible that neither *H. heidelbergensis* nor the Neandertals had the entire array of *fully* human attributes. That's why we call them premodern humans.

So, to rephrase our initial question: "Were these hominins human?" We can answer conditionally: They were human—at least mostly so.

We will focus much more on the ancestral connections of modern humans in the next chapter. As you'll see, all of us derive mostly from fairly recent African ancestors. However, when these African migrants came into contact with premodern humans living in Eurasia, some interbreeding occurred with at least two of these premodern groups. We can tell this by distinctive genetic "signatures" that can still be found in living people.

What's more, we've already had tantalizing clues of how we differ from Neandertals as well as from Denisovans in terms of specific genes. For example, genetic studies have found evidence for a mutation in Neandertals that results in pale skin and red hair (Lalueza-Fox et al., 2007; Ding et al., 2014). As these data are further analyzed and expanded, we will surely learn more about the evolutionary development of human anatomy *and* human behavior. In so doing, we'll be able to answer far more precisely the age-old question of "What does it mean to be human?"

Seeing Close Human Connections: Understanding Diversity among Premodern Humans

As you can see, the Middle Pleistocene hominins are a very diverse group, broadly dispersed through time and space. There is considerable variation among them, and it's not easy to get a clear evolutionary picture. We know that regional populations were small and frequently isolated. As environmental conditions changed, hominin populations were likely pushed into smaller and smaller habitable areas, often referred to by biologists as "refugia" (Stewart and Stringer, 2012). As conditions became harsher, these refugia supported fewer people, leading to a dramatic decrease in population size. In turn, such circumstances accelerated the effects of genetic drift as well as intensifying natural selection. Biologist John Stewart and anthropologist Chris Stringer (2012) have recently developed a comprehensive model employing environmental (specifically glacial/interglacial cycles), genetic, and fossil data to explain how in Ice Age Eurasia the development and fate of refuge populations of both premodern and modern humans help explain species distributions, extinctions, and potential opportunities for interbreeding (for example, Neandertals or Denisovans with modern humans).

We must remember, though, that it's virtually certain that many premodern human populations died out, leaving no descendants. So it's a mistake to see an "ancestor" in every fossil find. Still, as a group, these Middle Pleistocene premoderns do reveal some general trends. In many ways, for example, it seems that they were *transitional* between the hominins that came before them (*H. erectus*) and the ones that followed them (modern *H. sapiens*). It's not a stretch to say that all the Middle Pleistocene premoderns derived from *H. erectus* forebears and that some of them, in turn, were probably ancestors of the earliest fully modern humans.

Paleoanthropologists are certainly concerned with such broad generalities as these, but they also want to focus on meaningful anatomical, environmental, and behavioral details as well as the underlying processes. So they consider the regional variability displayed by particular fossil samples as significant—but just how significant is debatable. In addition, increasingly sophisticated theoretical and technological approaches are being used to better understand the processes that shaped the evolution of later *Homo* at both macroevolutionary and microevolutionary levels.

Scientists, like all humans, assign names or labels to phenomena—a point we addressed in discussing classification in Chapter 5. Paleoanthropologists are certainly no exception. Yet, working from a common evolutionary foundation, paleoanthropologists still come to different conclusions about the most appropriate way to interpret the Middle/Late Pleistocene hominins. Consequently, a variety of species names have been proposed in recent years.

Paleoanthropologists who advocate an extreme lumping approach recognize only one species for all the premodern humans discussed in this chapter. These premoderns are classified as *Homo sapiens* and are thus lumped together with modern humans, although they're partly distinguished by such terminology as "archaic *H. sapiens*." As we've noted, this degree of lumping is no longer supported by most researchers. Alternatively, a second, less extreme view postulates modest species diversity and labels the earlier premoderns as *H. heidelbergensis* (Fig. 12-24a).

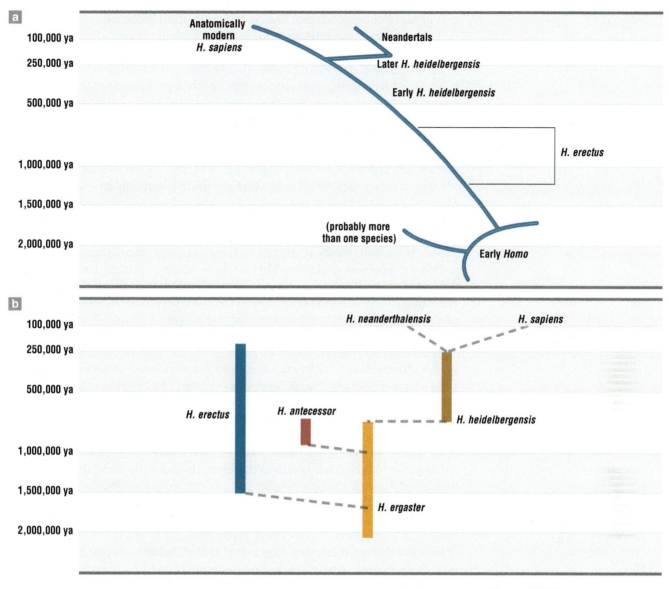

▲ Figure 12-24
(a) Phylogeny of the genus *Homo*. Only very modest species diversity is implied. (b) Phylogeny of genus *Homo* showing considerable species diversity (after Foley, 2002).

At the other end of the spectrum, more enthusiastic paleoanthropological splitters have identified at least two (or more) species distinct from *H. sapiens*. The most important of these, *H. heidelbergensis* and *H. neanderthalensis*, were discussed earlier. This more complex evolutionary interpretation is shown in Figure 12-24b.

We addressed similar differences of interpretation in Chapters 10 and 11, and we know that disparities such as these can be frustrating to students who are new to paleoanthropology. The proliferation of new names is confusing, and it might seem that experts in the field are endlessly arguing about what to call the fossils.

Fortunately, it's not quite that bad. There's actually more agreement than you might think. No one doubts that all these hominins are closely related to each other as well as to modern humans, and everyone agrees that only some of the fossil samples represent populations that left descendants. Where paleoanthropologists disagree is when they start discussing which hominins are the most likely to be closely related to later hominins. The grouping of hominins into evolutionary clusters (clades) and assignment of different names to them is a reflection of differing interpretations—and, more fundamentally, of somewhat differing philosophies.

However, we shouldn't emphasize these naming and classification debates too much. Most paleoanthropologists recognize that a great many of these disagreements result from simple, practical considerations. Even the most enthusiastic splitters acknowledge that the fossil "species" are not true species as defined by the biological species concept (see Chapter 5) (Holliday, 2003). As prominent paleoanthropologist Robert Foley puts it, "It is unlikely they are all biological species. . . . These are probably a mixture of real biological species and evolving lineages of subspecies. In other words, they could potentially have interbred, but owing to allopatry [that is, geographical separation] were unlikely to have had the opportunity" (Foley, 2002, p. 33).

Even so, Foley, along with an increasing number of other professionals, distinguishes these different fossil samples with species names to highlight their distinct position in hominin evolution. That is, these hominin groups are more loosely defined as a type of paleospecies (see Chapter 5) rather than as fully biological species. Giving distinct hominin samples a separate (species) name makes them more easily identifiable to other researchers and makes various cladistic hypotheses more explicit and, equally important, more directly testable.

The hominins that best illustrate these issues are the Neandertals. Fortunately they're also the best known, represented by dozens of well-preserved individuals and also a complete genome. With all this evidence, researchers can systematically test and evaluate many of the differing hypotheses.

Are Neandertals very closely related to modern *H. sapiens*? Certainly. Are they physically and behaviorally somewhat distinct from both ancient and fully modern humans? Yes. Does this mean that Neandertals are a fully separate biological species from modern humans and therefore theoretically incapable of fertilely interbreeding with modern people? Almost certainly not. Finally, then, should Neandertals really be placed in a separate species from *H. sapiens*? For most purposes, it doesn't matter, since the distinction at some point is arbitrary, like looking at a spectrum of colors that grade from red to orange to yellow. Where does one color definitely begin and end? Is that reddish-orange or is it orangey-red? Speciation is, after all, a *dynamic* process and fossil groups such as the Neandertals represent just one point in this process (see Chapter 5), which continues even today.

We can view Neandertals as a distinctive side branch of later hominin evolution. It is not unreasonable to say that Neandertals were likely an incipient species. The much less well-known "Denisovans" from Siberia also likely represent another partially distinct incipient species, separate from both Neandertals and early modern humans. Given enough time and enough isolation, Neandertals and Denisovans likely would have separated completely from their modern human contemporaries. The new DNA evidence suggests that they were partly on their way but had not yet reached full speciation from *Homo sapiens*. Their fate, in a sense, was decided for them as more successful competitors expanded into their habitats. These highly successful hominins were fully modern humans, and in the next chapter we'll focus on their story.

How Do We Know?

A major goal of paleoanthropology is to reconstruct ancient hominin diets. The study of Neandertal diets has been especially contentious, in part, because of the difficulty in reconciling various (and sometimes conflicting) lines of evidence. Researchers have long focused on Neandertal hunting behavior, relying especially on stone tool technology and the remains of the animals the Neandertals consumed. Archaeological evidence does indeed support their role in big game hunting, with ample evidence that they hunted and butchered red deer, horse, and bison. However, more recent evidence has broadened our understanding of Neandertal diets and indicates a more complex subsistence pattern. For example, recent evidence from the southern coast of Spain indicates that Neandertals also intensively exploited marine resources, such as shellfish (Cortés-Sánchez et al., 2011). This contrasts with earlier arguments that only *Homo sapiens* exploited marine resources.

More recent analytical methods are also providing new avenues for understanding Neandertal subsistence practices. For example, stable isotope analysis, a chemical technique, has been used to reconstruct Neandertal diets (Bocherens, 2009; Richards and Trinkaus, 2009; Ecker et al., 2013; Salazar-García et al., 2013). Evidence from stable carbon and nitrogen isotopes of Neandertal bones indicates that they were top level carnivores (that is, were high on the food chain), with most of their dietary protein coming from herbivore meat. This evidence is particularly exciting since the dietary pattern is found across various regions of Europe, and confirms earlier studies based on the analysis of stone tools and animal remains. However, that is not the whole dietary picture. Henry and colleagues (2011) extracted plant microfossils from the calculus (plaque) adhering to the teeth of Neandertals from Belgium and Iraq. They found that these Neandertals also consumed plant foods, such as date palms, legumes, and grass seeds (a close relative of barley). These findings indicate that, like modern humans, Neandertals balanced their diet using protein and fat from animal meat as well as carbohydrates from wild plants. What's more, damage to the structure of many of the recovered grains found in the dental plaque indicates that they derived from plants that had been cooked.

What Do You Think?

We have just discussed some of the different methods researchers use to reconstruct the diets of Neandertals. What are some of the limitations of these methods? How does our modern diet compare with the Neandertal diet? ■

Summary of Main Topics

- Premodern humans (generally classified as *Homo heidelbergensis*) lived during the Middle Pleistocene, a time period spanning 780,000–125,000 ya. These hominins lived during the Ice Age, which consisted of periods of glaciations and interglacial periods.
- Premodern humans from the Middle Pleistocene show similarities both with their predecessors (*H. erectus*) and with their successors (modern *H. sapiens*). They've also been found in many areas of the Old World—in Africa, Asia, and Europe. Most paleoanthropologists call the majority of Middle Pleistocene fossils *H. heidelbergensis*. Similarities between the African and European Middle Pleistocene hominin samples suggest that they can all reasonably be seen as part of this same species, but contemporaneous Asian fossils don't fit as neatly into this model.

- Middle Pleistocene hominins (for example, *Homo heidelbergensis*) continued to use the Acheulian stone tool technology of *Homo erectus*, although this technology becomes more developed over time (for example, the Levallois flaking method). These hominins also likely utilized caves to a greater degree, had mastered the use of fire, and exploited a wider range of food resources than *Homo erectus*.

- Some of the later *H. heidelbergensis* populations in Europe likely evolved into Neandertals, and abundant Neandertal fossil and archaeological evidence has been collected from the Late Pleistocene time span of Neandertal existence, about 130,000 to 35,000 ya (but possibly as recent as 27,000 ya). Neandertals are more geographically restricted than earlier premodern humans and are found in Europe, southwest Asia, and central Asia. Their crania were robust, elongated, and low, with massive projecting browridges. Neandertal cranial capacities exceeded that of modern humans (average of 1,520 cm³). Postcranially, their long bones are short and thick, likely adaptations to the cold climatic conditions of the Late Pleistocene.

- Neandertals are often associated with the Mousterian stone tool industry, although they are not the only hominin group associated with these tools. This stone tool industry is found across Europe, North Africa, Central Asia, and possibly China. Neandertals exploited an even wider range of resources than Middle Pleistocene hominins, and appear to have been specialized

hunters. Current anatomical and genetic evidence suggests they had similar vocal abilities as modern humans. Neandertal sites further show evidence of symbolic behavior, including deliberate disposal of the dead.

- Neandertals have been considered quite distinct from modern *H. sapiens*, but recent genetic evidence confirms that some interbreeding took place between these hominins (likely 80,000 to 50,000 ya). In addition, recent ancient DNA studies on human remains from Denisova Cave in Siberia demonstrate admixture between

Denisovans, Neandertals, modern humans, and even a fourth unknown species of hominin (possibly *Homo erectus*).

- Classifying premodern humans of the Middle and Late Pleistocene is difficult due to the extent of regional variation in morphology and problematic dating of a number of site locales. Recent ancient DNA evidence has provided significant insight on the relationships between different hominin groups, including evidence of genetic admixture between the Neandertals and modern humans.

Critical Thinking Questions

1. How do premodern humans compare anatomically with earlier species, such as *Homo erectus*? How do they compare with modern *Homo sapiens*?

2. Why are Middle Pleistocene hominins so difficult to classify? Further, why is there so much disagreement about naming species during this time period?

3. What is the overall popular conception of Neandertals? Based on

what you have just learned, would you agree with this view? (Cite both anatomical and archaeological evidence to support your conclusion.)

4. What evidence suggests that Neandertals deliberately buried their dead? Do you think the fact that they buried their dead is important? What other novel cultural behaviors do Neandertals demonstrate?

5. How are species defined, both for living animals and for extinct ones? Use the Neandertals to illustrate the problems encountered in distinguishing species among extinct hominins. Contrast specifically the interpretation of Neandertals as a distinct species with the interpretation of Neandertals as a subspecies of *H. sapiens*.

The immediate predecessors of modern humans, including the Neandertals, were much like us, but had some anatomical and behavioral differences.

Modern humans first evolved in Africa and later spread to other areas of the world, where they occasionally interbred with Neandertals and other premodern humans.

Modern human variation is best understood by examining similarities and differences in DNA among populations.

The Origin and Dispersal of Modern Humans

13

Approaches to Understanding Modern Human Origins

The Regional Continuity Model: Multiregional Evolution

Replacement Models

The Earliest Discoveries of Modern Humans

Africa

The Near East

Asia

Australia

Central Europe

Western Europe

Technology and Art in the Upper Paleolithic

Europe

Africa

Summary of Upper Paleolithic Culture

Student Learning Objectives After studying the material in this chapter, you should be able to:

▶ Compare and contrast the two major models that seek to explain modern human origins, giving supporting evidence for each model and explaining why recent molecular evidence has largely resolved this issue.

▶ Describe the major geographical areas and general dating of the key early fossil evidence of modern humans.

▶ Discuss the cultural developments that characterize the Upper Paleolithic as well as contemporaneous cultures in other parts of the world (e.g., Africa) and contrast these with cultural/technological practices of earlier periods.

Today, our species numbers more than 7 billion individuals spread all over the globe, and there are no other living hominins but us. Our last hominin cousin disappeared almost 30,000 ya. Perhaps about 80,000 ya, modern peoples in the Middle East encountered beings that walked on two legs, hunted large animals, made fire, lived in caves, and fashioned complex tools. These beings were the Neandertals, and imagine what it would have been like to be among a band of modern people following game into what is now Israel and coming across these other *humans*, so like yourself in some ways, yet so different in others. It's almost certain that such encounters took place, perhaps many times. How strange would it have been to look into the face of a being sharing so much with you, yet being a total stranger both culturally and,

Cave art of El Castillo, Cantabria, Spain.

Angelo Gandolfi/Nature Picture Library; Top Images: Harry Nelson; © Cengage Learning; Guido Cozzi/Terra /Atlantide Phototravel/Corbis

383

to some degree, biologically? What would you think seeing a Neandertal for the first time? What do you imagine a Neandertal would think seeing you? If a similar encounter had occurred in southern Siberia, modern people would quite likely have been staring into the eyes of a Denisovan. What would that have been like?

At some time, probably close to 200,000 ya, the first modern *Homo sapiens* populations appeared in Africa. Within 150,000 years or so, their descendants had spread across most of the Old World, even expanding as far as Australia (and somewhat later to the Americas).

Who were they, and why were these early modern people so successful? What was the fate of the other hominins, such as the Neandertals, who were already long established in areas outside Africa? Did they continue to evolve as well, leaving descendants among some living human populations? Or did they go extinct, completely swept aside and replaced by African emigrants?

In this chapter, we'll discuss the origin and dispersal of modern *H. sapiens sapiens*. All contemporary populations are placed within this species and subspecies. Most paleoanthropologists agree that several fossil forms of *Homo sapiens*, dating back as far as 100,000 ya, should also be included in the same *fully* modern group as ourselves. In addition, some recently discovered fossils from Africa are also clearly *H. sapiens*, though they show some (minor) differences from living people and could thus be more accurately described as *near*-modern. Still, we can think of these early African humans as well as their somewhat later relatives as "us."

These first modern humans, who had evolved by 195,000 ya, were probably descendants of some of the premodern humans we discussed in Chapter 12. In particular, African populations of *H. heidelbergensis* are the most likely ancestors of the earliest modern *H. sapiens*. The evolutionary events that took place as modern humans made the transition from more ancient premodern forms and then dispersed throughout most of the Old World were relatively rapid, and they raise several basic questions:

1. When (approximately) did modern humans first appear?
2. Where did the transition take place? Did it occur in just one region or in several?
3. What was the pace of evolutionary change? How quickly did the transition occur, and was it uniform across regions?
4. How did the dispersal of modern humans to other areas of the Old World (outside their area of origin) take place?

These questions concerning the origins and early dispersal of modern *Homo sapiens* continue to fuel much controversy among paleoanthropologists. And it's no wonder, for at least some early *H. sapiens* populations are the direct ancestors of all contemporary humans. They were much like us skeletally, genetically, and (most likely) behaviorally. In fact, it's the various hypotheses regarding the behaviors and abilities of our most immediate predecessors that have most fired the imaginations of scientists and laypeople alike. In every major respect, these are the first hominins that we can confidently refer to as *fully* modern human.

In this chapter, we'll also discuss archaeological evidence coming from the Upper Paleolithic cultures. This evidence will give us a better understanding of the technological and social developments during the period when modern humans arose and quickly came to dominate the planet.

The evolutionary story of *Homo sapiens* is really the biological autobiography of all of us. It's a story that still has many unanswered questions, but some general theories can help us organize the many lines of evidence that are now available.

Approaches to Understanding Modern Human Origins

In attempting to organize and explain modern human origins, paleoanthropologists have proposed a few major theories (that is, models) that can be summarized into two contrasting views: the *regional continuity* model and various versions of *replacement* models. These two views are quite distinct, and in some ways they're completely opposed to each other. Since so much of our contemporary view of modern human origins is influenced by the debates linked to these differing models, let's start by briefly reviewing them. Then we'll turn to the fossil evidence and emerging genetic analyses to see what morphology and molecules can contribute to answering the four questions we've posed.

The Regional Continuity Model: Multiregional Evolution

The multiregional continuity model is most closely associated with paleoanthropologist Milford Wolpoff of the University of Michigan and his associates (Wolpoff et al., 1994, 2001). They suggest that local populations—not all, of course—in Europe, Asia, and Africa continued their indigenous evolutionary development from premodern Middle Pleistocene forms to anatomically modern humans. However, if that's true, we have to ask how so many different local populations around the globe happened to evolve with such similar morphology. In other words, how could anatomically modern humans arise separately in different continents and end up so much alike, both anatomically and genetically? The multiregional model answers this question by (1) denying that the earliest modern *H. sapiens* populations originated *exclusively* in Africa and (2) asserting that significant levels of gene flow (migration and interbreeding) between various geographically dispersed premodern populations were extremely likely throughout the Pleistocene.

Through gene flow and natural selection, according to the multiregional hypothesis, local populations would *not* have evolved totally independently from one another, and such mixing would have "prevented speciation between the regional lineages and thus maintained human beings as a single, although obviously *polytypic* [see Chapter 14], species throughout the Pleistocene" (Smith et al., 1989, p. 39). Thus, under a multiregional model, there are no true taxonomic distinctions between modern and premodern hominins. That is, all hominins following *Homo erectus* are classified as a single species: *Homo sapiens*.

In light of emerging evidence over the last few years, advocates of the multiregional model tend not to be dogmatic about the degree of regional continuity. They recognize that a strong influence from modern humans evolving *first* in Africa has left an imprint on populations throughout the world that is still genetically detectable today. Nevertheless, the most recent data suggest that multiregional models, as originally conceived, cannot account for the origins of modern humans (Stringer 2014, 2016). Further, these models provide little insight on the dispersal of modern *H. sapiens*.

Replacement Models

Replacement models all emphasize that modern humans first evolved in Africa and only later dispersed to other parts of the world, where they replaced those hominins already living in these other regions (Stringer and Andrews, 1988; Stringer, 2014, 2016). In recent years, two versions of such replacement models have been proposed, the first emphasizing *complete* replacement.

Complete Replacement Model The complete replacement model proposes that anatomically modern populations arose in Africa within the last 200,000 years and then migrated from Africa, completely replacing populations in Europe and Asia (Stringer and Andrews, 1988). It's important to note that this model doesn't account for a transition from premodern forms to modern *H. sapiens* anywhere in the world except Africa. Stringer and Andrews' original hypothesis argued that anatomically modern humans appeared as the result of a biological speciation event. So in this view, migrating African modern *H. sapiens* could not have successfully interbred with local non-African populations producing fertile offspring because the African modern humans were a *biologically* different species. Under this model, all of the premodern populations outside Africa would be taxonomically classified as belonging to different species of *Homo*. For example, the Neandertals would be classified as *H. neanderthalensis*. This explanation of nonhybridizing speciation would fit nicely with, and, in fact, help explain *complete* replacement; but Stringer has more recently stated that he isn't insistent on this issue (Stewart and Stringer, 2012; Stringer, 2014, 2016). He does suggest that even though there may have been potential for interbreeding, apparently very little actually took place (Stewart and Stringer, 2012; Stringer, 2014, 2016).

Interpretations of the latter phases of human evolution have recently been greatly extended and aided by newly available genetic techniques that have been applied to the question of modern human origins. Drawing genetic data from numerous geographically diverse contemporary human populations, geneticists have precisely determined and compared a wide variety of DNA sequences in order to gain a better understanding of current human variation. The theoretical basis of this approach assumes that at least some of the genetic patterning seen today can act as a kind of window into the past. In particular, the similar genetic patterns observed today between geographically widely dispersed humans are thought to partly reflect migrations occurring in the Late Pleistocene. This hypothesis can be further tested as contemporary and archaic population genetic patterning becomes better documented.

As these new data have accumulated and are being assimilated, reliable relationships are emerging, especially those showing that indigenous African populations have far greater diversity than do populations from elsewhere in the world. The consistency of the results is highly significant because it strongly supports an African origin for modern humans and some subsequent mode of replacement across other regions. What's more, as we will discuss in Chapter 14, new, even more complete nuclear genomic data on contemporary population patterning further confirm these observations.

Certainly, most molecular data come from contemporary individuals, since ancient DNA is not *usually* preserved. Even so, exceptions do occur; for example, the Ice Man and two very recently sequenced 7,000-year-old Iberian hunter-gatherers (Sánchez-Quinto et al., 2012). These cases open another genetic window—one that can directly illuminate the past. As discussed in Chapter 12, mtDNA has been recovered from more than a dozen Neandertal fossils, and most recently, a 400,000-year-old hominin (possibly *H. heidelbergensis*) from the Sima de los Huesos site in Spain (Meyer et al., 2014).

In addition, researchers have sequenced the mtDNA of nine ancient fully modern *H. sapiens* skeletons from sites in Italy, France, the Czech Republic, and Russia (Caramelli et al., 2003; Kulikov et al., 2004; Serre et al., 2004). MtDNA data, however, are somewhat limited because mtDNA is a fairly small segment of DNA; and because it is transmitted between generations without recombination with male DNA, it provides information only regarding the maternal lineage. Indeed, in just the last few years, comparisons of Neandertal and early modern mtDNA have led to some significant misinterpretations. It should be no surprise, though, that data from the vastly larger nuclear genome are far more informative. The "At a Glance" contrasts the multiregional continuity model with the out of Africa model.

At a Glance Scenarios of Modern Human Origins

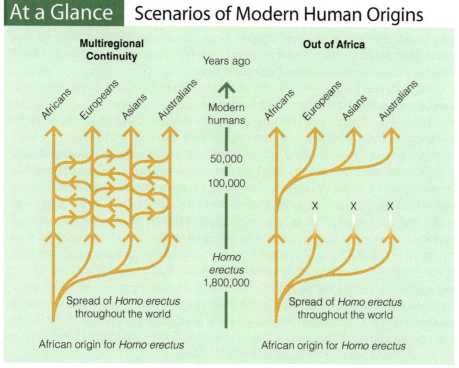

Source: Gibbons (2011b).

As we discussed in Chapter 12, a giant leap forward occurred in 2010 when sequencing of the entire Neandertal nuclear genome was completed. Researchers immediately compared the Neandertal genome with that of people living today and discovered that some populations still retain some Neandertal genes (Green et al., 2010; Reich et al., 2011; Prüfer et al., 2014). Without doubt, we can now conclude that some interbreeding took place between Neandertals and modern humans, arguing against *complete* replacement and supporting some form of *partial* replacement.

Partial Replacement Models For a number of years, several paleoanthropologists, such as Günter Bräuer, of the University of Hamburg, suggested that very little interbreeding occurred—a view supported more recently by John Relethford (2001) in what he described as "mostly out of Africa." The DNA analysis done in 2010 by Green and colleagues confirms that the degree of interbreeding was modest, ranging from 1 to 4 percent in modern populations outside Africa (and perhaps closer to 1.5 to 2.1 percent), while also revealing that contemporary Africans have no trace of Neandertal genes, suggesting that the interbreeding occurred *after* modern humans migrated out of Africa. Another fascinating discovery is that among the modern people so far sampled for these comparisons (five individuals: two African, one European, one Asian, and one Pacific Islander), the three non-Africans all have some Neandertal DNA. The tentative conclusion from these preliminary findings suggests that interbreeding occurred soon after modern humans emigrated out of Africa. The most likely scenario suggests that the intermixing occurred around 80,000 to 50,000 ya, likely in the Middle East and only later in Europe and then Asia. Recent whole-genome sequence data on modern Egyptian and Ethiopian populations further suggest that primary migration routes went through North Africa and into the Middle East during this time frame (Pagani et al., 2015).

These results are very new and are partly based on very limited samples of living people. Technological innovations in DNA sequencing are occurring at an amazing pace, making it faster and cheaper. But it is still a challenge to sequence the more than 3 billion nucleotides each of us has in our nuclear genome. When we have full genomes from more individuals living in many more geographical areas, the patterns of modern human dispersal should become clearer. DNA evidence is beginning to address where modern human–Neandertal interbreeding occurred and where it did not, and also whether some modern human populations interbred with their Neandertal cousins more than others did.

This evidence leads us to ask the question: Were there still other premodern human groups around when modern humans emigrated from Africa—and did they interbreed with modern humans too? As we discussed in Chapter 12, the answer is yes! Detailed DNA evidence from the fragmentary remains from Denisova Cave in southern Siberia show that these hominins had also interbred with modern humans. What's more, these Denisovans may have been quite widespread, since a few of their genes can still be found in Tibetan, New Guinean, some Pacific Islander, and aboriginal Australian populations today (Rasmussen et al., 2011; Reich et al., 2011). This recent research has helped to support what appears to have been (at least) a two-stage migration of modern humans into Asia (after an earlier initial migration of modern humans out of Africa). The earlier of these migrations took place through parts of Southeast Asia and eventually reached the South Pacific (including New Guinea and Australia). In fact, the recent whole genome sequencing using the hair from an Australian Aboriginal man who lived 100 years ago shows that he had Denisovan genes and that Aboriginal populations diverged from other groups 75,000–62,000 ya. The second migration occurred considerably later (38,000–25,000 ya), and it led to the peopling of eastern Asia (Rasmussen et al., 2011).

From his study of fossil remains, Fred Smith of Illinois State University has proposed an "assimilation" model hypothesizing that more interbreeding did take place, at least in some regions (Smith, 2002). To test these hypotheses and answer all the fascinating questions associated with them, we will also need more whole-genome DNA from ancient remains, particularly from early modern human skeletons. This won't be an easy task. Remember, it took 4 years of intensive effort to decode and reassemble the Neandertal genome; however there have been some recent successes (Fu et al., 2014, 2015). We also need to be aware that DNA thousands of years old can be obtained from hominin remains found in environments that have been

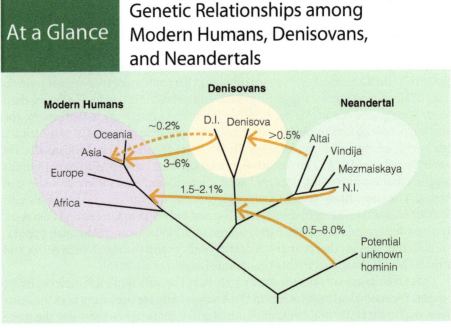

At a Glance

Genetic Relationships among Modern Humans, Denisovans, and Neandertals

Source: Prüfer et al. (2014).

persistently cold (or at least cool). In tropical areas, DNA degrades rapidly, so it seems a long shot that any usable DNA can be obtained from hominins that lived in many extremely large and significant regions (for example, Africa and Southeast Asia). Nevertheless, a very useful approach to partly answer our questions uses the genetic patterning still visible in contemporary humans. From such studies we know that there was more interbreeding and eventual gene flow of Denisovan genes in Asia (and the Pacific) than there was in Europe. The "At a Glance" on page 388 highlights the genetic connections between modern humans, Denisovans, and Neandertals.

The Earliest Discoveries of Modern Humans

Africa

In Africa, several early (around 200,000 to 100,000 ya) fossils have been interpreted as fully anatomically modern forms (Fig. 13-2 on p. 390). The earliest of these specimens comes from Omo Kibish, in southernmost Ethiopia. Using radiometric techniques, the redating of a fragmentary skull (Omo 1) demonstrated that this is the earliest modern human—originating 195,000 ya—yet found in Africa or, for that matter, anywhere (McDougall et al., 2005; Brown et al., 2012). An interesting aspect of fossils from this site concerns the variation shown between two individuals. Omo 1 (Fig. 13-1) is essentially modern in most respects (note the presence of a chin; see Fig. 13-3 on p. 391, where a variety of modern human cranial characteristics are shown). But another ostensibly contemporary cranium (Omo 2) is much more robust and less modern in morphology.

Somewhat later modern human fossils come from the Klasies River Mouth site on the south coast of Africa and from Border Cave, just slightly to the north. Using a variety of dating techniques, paleoanthropologists have dated both sites to about 120,000 to 80,000 ya. The original geological context at Border Cave is uncertain, and the fossils may be younger than those at Klasies River Mouth (Bird et al., 2003). Although a recent reevaluation of the Omo site has provided much more dependable dating, there are still questions about some of the other early African modern fossils. Nevertheless, it now seems very likely that early modern humans appeared in East Africa by shortly after 200,000 ya and had migrated to southern Africa by approximately 100,000 ya. More recently discovered fossils are helping to confirm this view.

Herto The announcement in 2003 of well-preserved *and* well-dated *H. sapiens* fossils from Ethiopia has gone a long way toward filling gaps in the African fossil record. As a result, these fossils are helping to resolve key issues regarding modern human origins. Tim White of the University of California, Berkeley, and his colleagues have been working for three decades in the Middle Awash area of Ethiopia. They've discovered a remarkable array of early fossil hominins (*Ardipithecus* and *Australopithecus*) as well as somewhat later forms (*H. erectus*). From this same area in the Middle Awash, further highly significant discoveries came to light in 1997. For simplicity, these new hominins are referred to as the Herto remains.

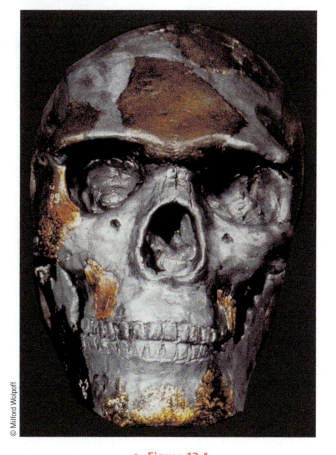

© Milford Wolpoff

▲ **Figure 13-1**
Reconstructed skull of Omo 1, an early modern human from Ethiopia, dated to 195,000 ya. Note the clear presence of a chin.

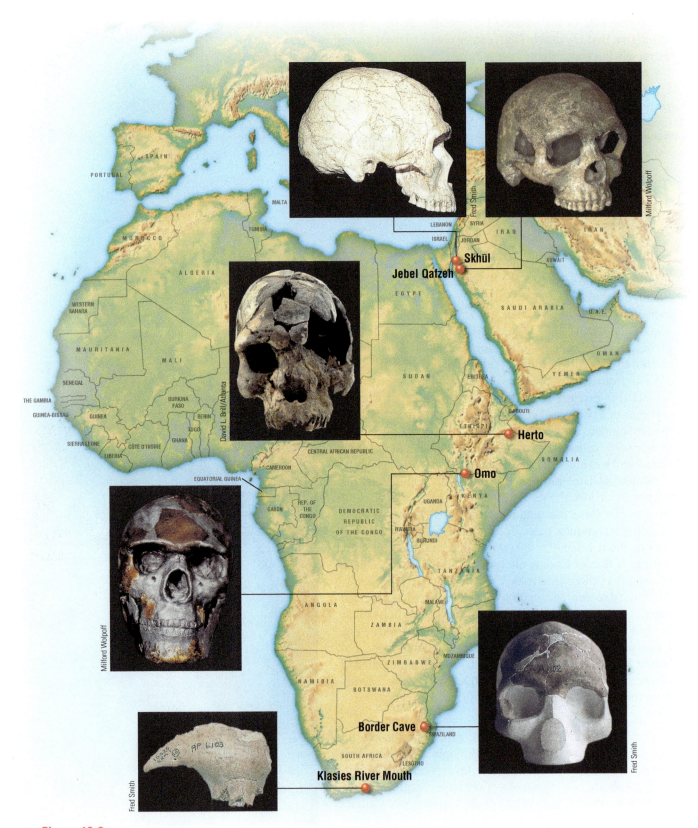

▲ **Figure 13-2**

Modern humans from Africa and the Near East.

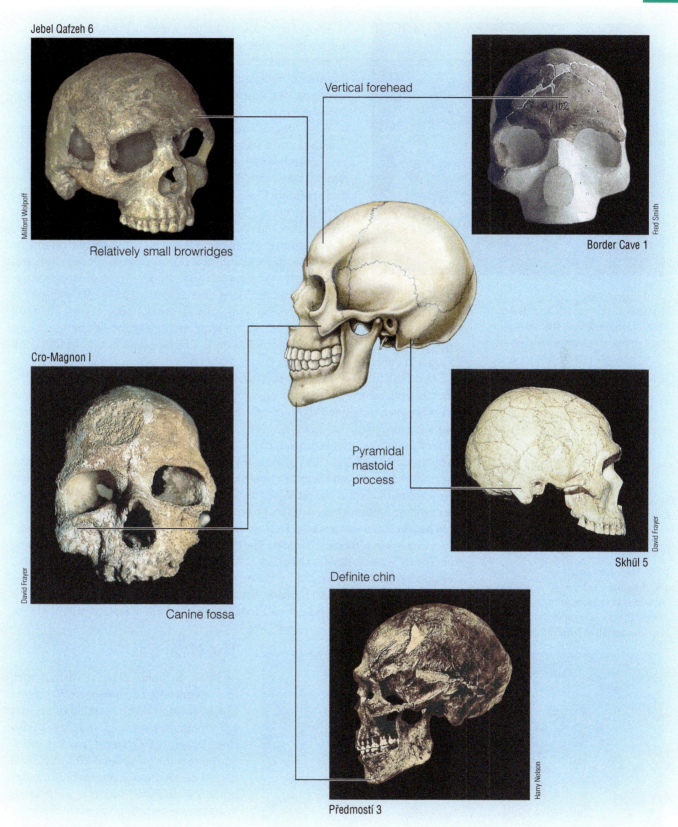

Jebel Qafzeh 6

Milford Wolpoff

Relatively small browridges

Vertical forehead

Border Cave 1

Fred Smith

Cro-Magnon I

David Frayer

Canine fossa

Pyramidal mastoid process

Skhūl 5

David Frayer

Definite chin

Předmostí 3

Harry Nelson

▲ Figure 13-3

Morphology and variation in early specimens of modern *Homo sapiens*.

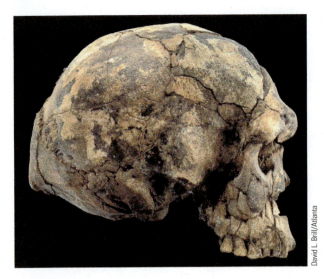

▲ **Figure 13-4**

Herto cranium from Ethiopia, dated 160,000 to 154,000 ya. This is the best-preserved early modern *H. sapiens* cranium yet found.

These Herto fossils include a mostly complete adult cranium, an incomplete adult cranium, a fairly complete (but heavily reconstructed) child's cranium, and a few other cranial fragments. Following lengthy reconstruction and detailed comparative studies, White and colleagues were prepared to announce their findings in 2003.

What they said caused quite a sensation among paleoanthropologists, and it was reported in the popular press as well. First, well-controlled radiometric dating (^{40}Ar/^{39}Ar) securely places the remains between 160,000 and 154,000 ya, making these the best-dated hominin fossils from this time period from anywhere in the world (Hart et al., 2003). Note that this date is clearly *older* than for any other equally modern *H. sapiens* from outside of Africa.

Moreover, the preservation and morphology of the remains leave little doubt about their relationship to modern humans. The mostly complete adult cranium (Fig. 13-4) is very large, with an extremely long cranial vault. The cranial capacity is 1,450 cm³, well within the range of contemporary *H. sapiens* populations. The skull is also in some respects heavily built, with a large, arching browridge in front and a large, projecting occipital protuberance in back. The face does not project, in stark contrast to Eurasian Neandertals.

The overall impression is that this individual is clearly *Homo sapiens*—as are the other fossils from the site. Following comprehensive statistical studies, Tim White and colleagues concluded that, though not identical to modern people, the Herto fossils are near-modern. That is, these fossils "sample a population that is on the verge of anatomical modernity but not yet fully modern" (White et al., 2003, p. 745). To distinguish these individuals from fully modern humans (*H. sapiens sapiens*), the researchers have placed them in a newly defined subspecies: *Homo sapiens idaltu*. The word *idaltu*, from the Afar language, means "elder." More recent analyses of the cranium support these original interpretations (McCarthy and Lucas, 2014).

What, then, can we conclude? First, we can say that these new finds strongly support an African origin of modern humans. The Herto fossils are the right age, and they come from the right place. Besides that, they look much like what we might have predicted. Considering all these facts, they're the most conclusive fossil evidence yet indicating an African origin of modern humans. What's more, this fossil evidence is compatible with a great deal of strong genetic data indicating some form of replacement model for human origins.

The Near East

In Israel, in Skhūl Cave at Mt. Carmel, researchers found early modern *H. sapiens* fossils, including the remains of at least 10 individuals (Figs. 13-5 and 13-6a). Also from Israel, the Qafzeh Cave has yielded the remains of at least 20 individuals (Fig. 13-6b). Although their overall configuration is definitely modern, some specimens show certain premodern features. Skhūl has been dated to between 130,000 and 100,000 ya (Grün et al., 2005), while Qafzeh has been dated to around 120,000 to 92,000 ya (Grün and Stringer, 1991). The time line for these fossil discoveries is shown in Figure 13-7.

▼ **Figure 13-5**

Mt. Carmel, studded with caves, was home to *H. sapiens sapiens* at Skhūl (and to Neandertals at Tabun and Kebara).

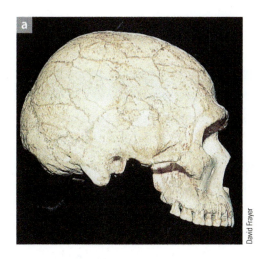

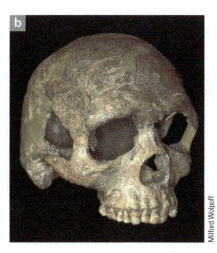

a — David Frayer
b — Milford Wolpoff

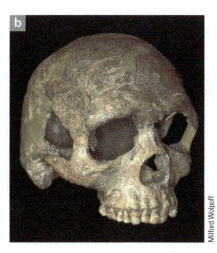

◀ **Figure 13-6**

(**a**) Skhūl 5. (**b**) Qafzeh 6. These specimens from Israel are thought to be representatives of early modern *Homo sapiens*. The vault height, forehead, and lack of prognathism are modern traits.

Such early dates for modern specimens pose some problems for those advocating the influence of local evolution as proposed by the multiregional model. How far back do the premodern populations—that is, Neandertals—appear in the Near East? A chronometric calibration for the Tabun Cave suggests a date as early as 120,000 ya. This dating for these sites, all located *very* close to each other, suggests that there's considerable chronological overlap in the occupation of the Near East by Neandertals and modern humans. This chronological overlap in such a small area (as well as in close proximity to Africa) has led anthropologists to suggest this region as a likely place where Neandertals and modern humans might well have interbred. The "At a Glance" on page 394 summarizes information on some of the key modern *Homo sapiens* discoveries from Africa and the Near East.

▼ **Figure 13-7**

Time line of modern *Homo sapiens* discoveries. Note that most dates are approximations. Question marks indicate those estimates that are most tentative.

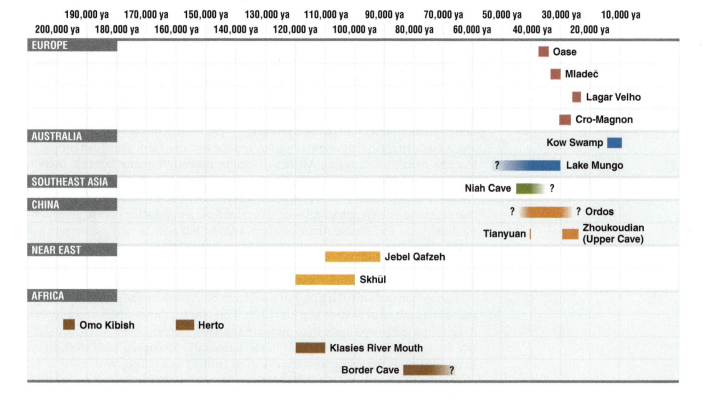

At a Glance	Key Early Modern *Homo sapiens* Discoveries from Africa and the Near East		
Date	**Site**	**Hominin**	**Evolutionary Significance**
110,000 ya	Qafzeh (Israel)	*H. sapiens sapiens*	Large sample (at least 20 individuals); definitely modern, but some individuals fairly robust; early date (>100,000 ya)
115,000 ya	Skhūl (Israel)	*H. sapiens sapiens*	Minimum of 10 individuals; like Qafzeh modern morphology, but slightly earlier date (and earliest modern humans known outside of Africa)
160,000–154,000 ya	Herto (Ethiopia)	*H. sapiens idaltu*	Very well-preserved cranium; date >150,000 ya, the best-preserved early modern human found anywhere
195,000 ya	Omo (Ethiopia)	*H. sapiens*	Dated almost 200,000 ya and the oldest modern human found anywhere; two crania found, one more modern looking than the other

Asia

There are seven early anatomically modern human localities in China, the most significant of which are Upper Cave at Zhoukoudian, Tianyuan Cave (very near Zhoukoudian), and Ordos, in Mongolia (Fig. 13-8). The fossils from these Chinese sites are all fully modern, and all are considered to be from the Late Pleistocene, with dates probably later than 40,000 ya. Many of these dates are controversial and not very precise; for example, Upper Cave at Zhoukoudian has been dated variously to between 10,000 and 29,000 ya (Cunningham and Wescott, 2002).

In addition, some researchers (e.g., Tiemel et al., 1994) have suggested that the Jinniushan skeleton discussed in Chapter 12 hints at modern features in China as early as 200,000 ya. If this date—as early as that proposed for direct antecedents of modern *H. sapiens* in Africa—should prove accurate, it would cast doubt on replacement models. This position, however, is a minority view and is not supported by more recent and more detailed analyses.

Just about 4 miles down the road from the famous Zhoukoudian Cave is another cave called Tianyuan, the source of an important find in 2003. Consisting of a fragmentary skull, a few teeth, and several postcranial bones, this fossil is accurately dated by radiocarbon at close to 40,000 ya (Shang et al., 2007). The skeleton shows mostly modern features but has a few archaic characteristics as well. The Chinese and American team that originally analyzed the remains from Tianyuan proposed that the remains indicate an African origin for modern humans, but that there is also evidence of at least some interbreeding in China with resident archaic (that is, premodern) populations. However, recent nuclear DNA testing on the remains demonstrated that the Tianyuan individual derived from a population ancestral to many modern Asian and Native American populations, but postdated the divergence of Asians from Europeans (Fu et al., 2013). Further, no Denisovan genes were identified in the genetic sequences. Therefore, these remains are those of early modern *H. sapiens* and represent the best-dated context in China.

The second early fossil is a partial skull from Niah Cave on the north coast of the Indonesian island of Borneo (see Fig. 13-8). This is actually not a new find and was, in fact, first excavated more than 50 years ago. However, until recent, more extensive analysis, it had been relegated to the paleoanthropological back shelf owing to uncertainties regarding its archaeological context and dating. Now all this has changed with a better understanding of the geology of the site and new dates strongly

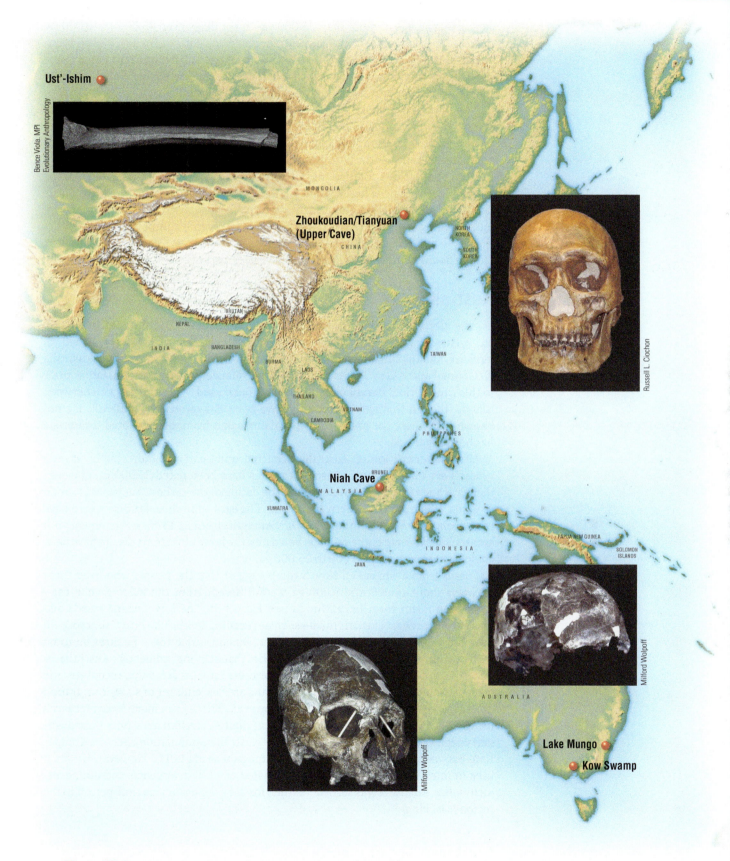

▲ Figure 13-8

Anatomically modern *Homo sapiens* from Asia and Australia.

supporting an age of more than 35,000 ya—most likely even 45,000 to 40,000 ya, making it perhaps older than Tianyuan (Barker et al., 2007). Like its Chinese counterparts, the Niah skull is modern in morphology. It's hypothesized that some population contemporaneous with Niah or somewhat earlier inhabitants of Indonesia was perhaps the first group to colonize Australia.

The third early Asian find was discovered in 2008, and includes a human femur dated to approximately 45,000 ya from the central Asian site of Ust'-Ishim, located in western Siberia. Complete sequencing of the nuclear genome from this individual indicates genetic admixture with Neandertals, at about 2.3 percent, similar to modern non-African populations (Fu et al., 2014). Further, it demonstrated that the individual was male. These findings are important because they provide the earliest genetic information about early modern *Homo sapiens* and show evidence of interbreeding with Neandertal populations. However, it's important to note that the Ust'-Ishim individual does not appear to show a strong affinity to *any* modern human population, suggesting he may have been part of a lineage that went extinct.

Australia

During glacial times, the Indonesian islands were joined to the Asian mainland, but Australia wasn't. Current archaeological evidence suggests that by 47,000 ya, modern humans inhabited Sahul—the area including New Guinea and Australia (O'Connell and Allen, 2015). There is little evidence to suggest colonization prior to this time period. Bamboo rafts may have been used to cross the ocean between islands, though this would certainly have been dangerous and difficult. It's not known just where the ancestral Australians came from, but as noted, Indonesia has been suggested.

Human occupation of Australia occurred quite early, as indicated by several types of evidence. Some archaeological sites have been dated 55,000 ya; however, there has been some controversy about the dating of the earliest Australian human remains, which are all modern *H. sapiens*. The earliest finds so far discovered have come from Lake Mungo, in southeastern Australia (see Fig. 13-8). In agreement with archaeological context and radiocarbon dates, the hominins from this site have been dated at approximately 30,000 to 25,000 ya.

Fossils from a site called Kow Swamp suggest that the people who lived there between about 14,000 and 9,000 ya were different from the more gracile early Australian forms from Lake Mungo (see Fig. 13-8). The Kow Swamp fossils display certain archaic cranial traits—such as receding foreheads, heavy supraorbital tori, and thick bones—that are difficult to explain, since these features contrast with the postcranial anatomy, which matches that of living indigenous Australians. Regardless of the different morphology of these later Australians, recent genetic evidence indicates that all native Australians are descendants of a *single* migration dating back to at least 50,000 ya (Hudjashou et al., 2007). Even more recent research using the whole genome analysis of an Aboriginal Australian male (mentioned earlier) suggests that the divergence of native Australian populations occurred sometime between 75,000 and 62,000 ya (Rasmussen et al., 2011). However, we must keep in mind that these data reflect estimated dates of divergence, and not necessarily when Australia was settled; further, fossil evidence for this time period in the region is lacking.

Central Europe

Central Europe has been a source of many fossil finds, including the earliest anatomically modern *H. sapiens* yet discovered anywhere in Europe. Dated to about 40,000–35,000 ya, these early *H. sapiens* fossils come from discoveries in 2002 at

◀ **Figure 13-9**
Excavators at work within the spectacular cave at Oase, in Romania. The floor is littered with the remains of fossil animals, including the earliest dated cranial remains of *Homo sapiens* in Europe.

Oase Cave in Romania (Fig. 13-9). Here cranial remains of three individuals were recovered, including a complete mandible and a partial skull. While quite robust, they are similar to later modern specimens, as seen in the clear presence of both a chin and a canine fossa (see Fig. 13-3) (Trinkaus et al., 2003; Crevecoeur et al., 2009). DNA was recently analyzed from a modern human male from the site (Fu et al., 2015). Surprisingly, Neandertal DNA comprises approximately 6 to 9 percent of the total genome of this individual. What's more, the researchers estimated that he is only four to six generations (about 200 years) removed from a Neandertal ancestor! Despite these interesting findings, he does not appear to show a close affinity with later modern humans from Europe.

Another early modern human site in central Europe is Mladeč in the Czech Republic (Fig. 13-10 on p. 398). Several individuals have been excavated here and are dated to approximately 31,000 ya. Although there's some variation among the crania, including some with big browridges, Fred Smith (1984) is confident that they're all best classified as modern *H. sapiens* (Fig. 13-11 on p. 399). It's clear that by 28,000 ya, modern humans were widely dispersed in central and western Europe (Trinkaus, 2005).

Western Europe

For several reasons, western Europe (and its fossils) has received more attention than other regions. Over the last 150 years, many of the scholars doing this research happened to live in western Europe, and the southern region of France turned out to be a fossil treasure trove.

As a result of this scholarly interest, a great deal of data accumulated beginning back in the nineteenth century, with little reliable comparative information available from elsewhere in the world. Consequently, theories of human evolution were based almost exclusively on the western European material. It's only been in more recent years, with growing evidence from other areas of the world and the application of new dating techniques, that recent human evolutionary dynamics are being seriously considered from a worldwide perspective.

Western Europe has yielded many anatomically modern human fossils, but by far the best-known sample of western European *H. sapiens* is from the **Cro-Magnon** site, a rock shelter in southern France. At this site, the remains of eight individuals were discovered in 1868.

Cro-Magnon (crow-man´-yon)

▲ **Figure 13-10**

Anatomically modern humans in Europe.

The Cro-Magnon materials are associated with an **Aurignacian** tool assemblage, an Upper Paleolithic industry. Dated at about 28,000 ya, these individuals represent the earliest of France's anatomically modern humans. The so-called Old Man (Cro-Magnon 1) became the original model for what was once termed the Cro-Magnon, or Upper Paleolithic, "race" of Europe (Fig. 13-12). Actually, of course, there's no such valid biological category, and Cro-Magnon 1 is not typical of Upper Paleolithic western Europeans—and not even all that similar to the other two male skulls found at the site.

Most of the genetic evidence, as well as the newest fossil evidence from Africa, argues against continuous local evolution producing modern groups directly from any Eurasian premodern population (in Europe, these would be Neandertals). Still, for some researchers, the issue isn't completely settled. With all the latest evidence, there's no longer much debate that a *large* genetic contribution from migrating early modern Africans influenced other groups throughout the Old World. What's being debated is just how much admixture might have occurred between these migrating Africans and the resident premodern groups. For those paleoanthropologists (e.g., Trinkaus, 2005) who hypothesize that significant admixture (assimilation) occurred in western Europe as well as elsewhere, a child's skeleton from Portugal provides some of the best skeletal evidence of possible interbreeding between Neandertals and anatomically modern *H. sapiens*. This important discovery from the Abrigo do Lagar Velho site was excavated in late 1998 and is dated to 24,500 ya—that's at least 5,000 years more recent than the last clearly identifiable Neandertal fossil. Associated with an Upper Paleolithic industry and buried with red ocher and pierced shell is a fairly complete skeleton of a 4-year-old child (Duarte et al., 1999). In studying the remains, Cidália Duarte, Erik Trinkaus, and their colleagues found a highly mixed set of anatomical features. From this evidence they concluded that the young child was the result of interbreeding between Neandertals and modern humans, and thus supports a partial replacement model of human origins. It's still debatable from this fossil evidence whether interbreeding with Neandertals took place in Portugal this late in time. DNA testing would certainly help to resolve this issue, but has yet to be conducted on the skeleton. Nevertheless, the genetic evidence is unequivocal: Neandertals and modern humans *did* interbreed at some point, though the extent and frequency are presently unknown. The "At a Glance" on page 400 summarizes information on some of the key modern *Homo sapiens* discoveries from Europe and Asia.

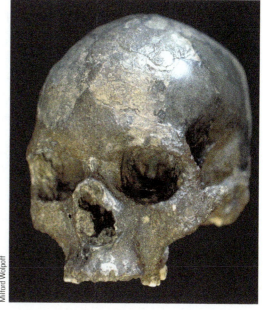

▲ **Figure 13-11**

The Mladeč cranium from the Czech Republic represents a good example of early modern *Homo sapiens* in central Europe. Along with Oase, in Romania, the evidence for early modern *Homo sapiens* appears first in central Europe before the later finds in western Europe.

Aurignacian Pertaining to an Upper Paleolithic stone tool industry in Europe beginning at about 40,000 ya.

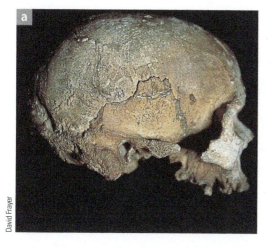

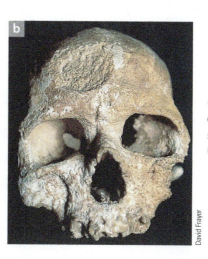

◀ **Figure 13-12**

Cro-Magnon 1 (France). In this specimen, modern traits are quite clear. (**a**) Lateral view. (**b**) Frontal view.

At a Glance	Key Early Modern *Homo sapiens* Discoveries from Europe and Asia		
Date	**Site**	**Hominin**	**Evolutionary Significance**
24,500 ya	Abrigo do Lagar Velho (Portugal)	*H. sapiens sapiens*	Child's skeleton; some suggestion of possible hybrid between Neandertal and modern human—but is controversial
30,000 ya	Cro-Magnon (France)	*H. sapiens sapiens*	Most famous early modern human find in world; earliest evidence of modern humans in France
40,000 ya	Tianyuan Cave (China)	*H. sapiens sapiens*	Partial skull and a few postcranial bones; oldest modern human find from China
45,000–40,000 ya	Niah Cave (Borneo, Indonesia)	*H. sapiens sapiens*	Partial skull recently redated more accurately; oldest modern human find from Asia

Technology and Art in the Upper Paleolithic

Europe

The cultural period known as the Upper Paleolithic began in western Europe approximately 40,000 ya (Fig. 13-13). Upper Paleolithic cultures are usually divided into five different industries based on stone tool technologies: Chatelperronian, Aurignacian, Gravettian, Solutrean, and Magdalenian. Major environmental shifts were also apparent during this period. During the last glacial period, about 30,000 ya, a warming trend lasting several thousand years partially melted the glacial ice. The result was that much of Eurasia was covered by tundra and steppe, a vast area of treeless country dotted with lakes and marshes. In many areas in the north, permafrost prevented the growth of trees but permitted the growth, in the short summers, of flowering plants, mosses, and other kinds of vegetation. This vegetation served as an enormous pasture for herbivorous animals large and small, and carnivorous animals fed off the herbivores. It was a hunter's paradise, with millions of animals dispersed across expanses of tundra and grassland from Spain through Europe and into the Russian steppes.

▶ **Figure 13-13**

Cultural periods of the European Upper Paleolithic and their approximate beginning dates.

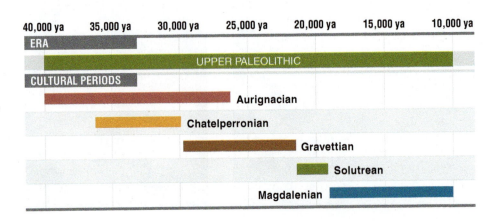

Large herds of reindeer roamed the tundra and steppes, along with mammoths, bison, horses, and a host of smaller animals that served as a bountiful source of food. In addition, humans exploited fish and fowl systematically, apparently for the first time. It was a time of relative abundance, and ultimately Upper Paleolithic people spread out over Eurasia, living in caves and open-air camps and building large shelters. We should recall that many of the cultural innovations seen in the Upper Paleolithic had begun with Neandertals (see Chapter 12). Nevertheless, in looking at the entire Upper Paleolithic, there are notable differences. For example, far more elaborate burials are found, most

Kenneth Garrett

spectacularly at the 24,000-year-old Sungir site near Moscow (Fig. 13-14), where grave goods included a bed of red ocher, thousands of ivory beads, long spears made of straightened mammoth tusks, ivory engravings, and jewelry (Formicola and Buzhilova, 2004). During this period, either western Europe or perhaps portions of Africa achieved the highest population density in human history up to that time.

Humans and other animals in most of Eurasia had to cope with shifts in climate conditions, some of them quite rapid. For example, at 20,000 ya, another climatic "pulse" caused the weather to become noticeably colder in Europe and Asia as the continental glaciations reached their maximum extent for this entire glacial period, which is called the Würm in Eurasia.

As a variety of organisms attempted to adapt to these changing conditions, *Homo sapiens* had a major advantage: the elaboration of increasingly sophisticated technology and probably other components of culture as well. In fact, one of the greatest challenges facing numerous Late Pleistocene mammals was the ever more dangerously equipped humans—a trend that continues today.

The Upper Paleolithic was an age of innovation that can be compared to the past few hundred years in our recent history of amazing technological change. Anatomically modern humans of the Upper Paleolithic not only invented new and specialized tools (Fig. 13-15) but, as we've seen, also experimented with and greatly increased the use of new materials such as bone, ivory, and antler.

Solutrean tools are good examples of Upper Paleolithic skill and likely aesthetic appreciation as well (see Fig. 13-15). In this lithic (stone) tradition, skill in modifying rock (called "knapping") developed to the finest degree ever known. Using specialized flaking techniques, the artisans made beautiful parallel-flaked lance heads, expertly flaked on both surfaces. The lance points are so delicate that they can be considered works of art that quite possibly never served, nor were intended to serve, a utilitarian purpose.

The last stage of the Upper Paleolithic, known as the **Magdalenian**, saw even more advances in technology. The spear-thrower, or atlatl, was a hooked rod made of bone or wood that extended the hunter's arm, enhancing the force and distance of a spear throw (Fig. 13-16). For catching salmon and other fish, the barbed harpoon is a good example of skillful craftsmanship. There's also evidence that bows and arrows may have been used for the first time during this period. The introduction of much more efficient manufacturing methods, such as the punch blade

▲ **Figure 13-14**

Skeletons of two teenagers, a male and a female, from Sungir, Russia. Dated to 24,000 ya, this is the richest find of any Upper Paleolithic grave.

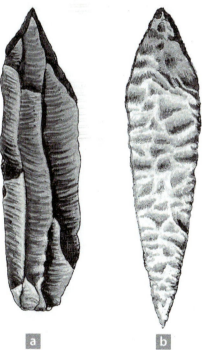

a

b

▲ **Figure 13-15**

(**a**) A burin, a very common Upper Paleolithic tool. (**b**) A Solutrean blade. This is the best-known work of the Solutrean tradition. Solutrean stonework is considered the most highly developed of any Upper Paleolithic industry.

Magdalenian Pertaining to the final phase of the Upper Paleolithic stone tool industry in Europe.

▶ **Figure 13-16**
Spear-thrower (atlatl). Note the carving.

technique (Fig. 13-17), provided an abundance of standardized stone blades. These could be fashioned into **burins** (see Fig. 13-15a) for working wood, bone, and antler; borers for drilling holes in skins, bones, and shells; and knives with serrated or notched edges for scraping wooden shafts into a variety of tools.

By producing many more specialized tools, Upper Paleolithic peoples probably had more resources available to them; moreover, these more effective tools may also have had an impact on the biology of these populations. Emphasizing a biocultural interpretation, C. Loring Brace of the University of Michigan has suggested that with more effective tools as well as the use of fire, allowing for more efficient food processing, modern *H. sapiens* wouldn't have required the large teeth and facial skeletons seen in earlier populations.

In addition to their reputation as hunters, western Europeans of the Upper Paleolithic are even better known for their symbolic representation (what we today recognize as art). There's an extremely wide geographical distribution of symbolic

burins Small, chisel-like tools with a pointed end; thought to have been used to engrave bone, antler, ivory, or wood.

a A large core is selected and the top portion removed by use of a hammerstone.

b The objective is to create a flat surface called a striking platform.

Striking platform

c Next, the core is struck by use of a hammer and punch (made of bone or antler) to remove the long narrow flakes (called blades).

d Or the blades can be removed by pressure flaking.

e The result is the production of highly consistent sharp blades, which can be used, as is, as knives; or they can be further modified (retouched) to make a variety of other tools (such as burins, scrapers, and awls).

▲ **Figure 13-17**
The punch blade technique.

images, best known from many parts of Europe but now also well documented from Siberia, North Africa, South Africa, and Australia. Given a 25,000-year time depth of what we call Paleolithic art, along with its nearly worldwide distribution, we must appreciate that it showed a remarkable range of expression.

Besides cave art, there are many examples of small sculptures excavated from sites in western, central, and eastern Europe. Perhaps the most famous of these are the female figurines, popularly known as "Venuses," found at such sites as Brassempouy in France and Grimaldi in Italy. Some of these figures were realistically carved, and the faces appear to be modeled after actual women. Other figurines may seem grotesque, with sexual characteristics exaggerated, perhaps to promote fertility or serve some other ritual purpose.

Beyond these quite well-known figurines, there are numerous other examples of what's frequently called portable art, including elaborate engravings on tools and tool handles (Fig. 13-18). Such symbolism can be found in many parts of Europe and was already well established early in the Aurignacian, by perhaps as early as 40,000 ya. Recently improved carbon dating used at Geissenklösterle Cave in southwest Germany shows what are thought to be the earliest musical instruments found anywhere (eight flutes made of bone). In addition, sophisticated carved figures were also found, all dating to *at least* 40,000 ya (Higham et al., 2012). Improved dating methods also show early painted representations in several caves in Spain. From the famous cave site at Altamira (dating to 35 kya*) as well as at El Castillo (dating to about 41 kya) come the earliest examples of cave painting from anywhere yet discovered. These new, surprisingly early dates derive from advancements in a radiometric technique called uranium-series dating (see Chapter 9). By using tiny samples of accumulated calcite deposits that form on top of painted or engraved images, archaeologists now have much more accurate ideas of when these images were made (Pike et al., 2012). Remember too that the dates are *minimum* ones: The calcite formed after (perhaps long after) the images were completed.

Innovations in symbolic representations also benefited from and probably further stimulated technological advances. New methods of mixing pigments and applying them were important in rendering painted or drawn images. Engraving and carving on bone and ivory were made easier with the use of special stone tools (see Fig. 13-15). At two sites in the Czech Republic, Dolní Věstonice and Předmostí (both dated at approximately 27,000 to 26,000 ya), small animal figures were fashioned from fired clay. This is the first documented use of ceramic technology anywhere; in fact, it precedes the later invention of pottery by more than 15,000 years.

But it wasn't until the final phases of the Upper Paleolithic, particularly during the Magdalenian, that European prehistoric art reached its climax. Cave art is now known from more than 150 separate sites, the vast majority from southwestern France and northern Spain. Apparently in other areas the rendering of such images did not take place in deep caves. People in central Europe, China, Africa, and elsewhere certainly may have painted or carved representations on rock faces in the open, but these images long since would have disappeared. So we're fortunate that the people of at least one of the many sophisticated cultures of the Upper Paleolithic chose to journey below ground to create their artwork, preserving it not just for their immediate descendants but for us as well. The most spectacular and famous of the cave art sites are Lascaux and Grotte Chauvet in France and Altamira in Spain.

In Lascaux Cave, for example, immense wild bulls dominate what's called the Great Hall of Bulls; also horses, deer, and other animals drawn with remarkable skill

---

*kya = thousand years ago.

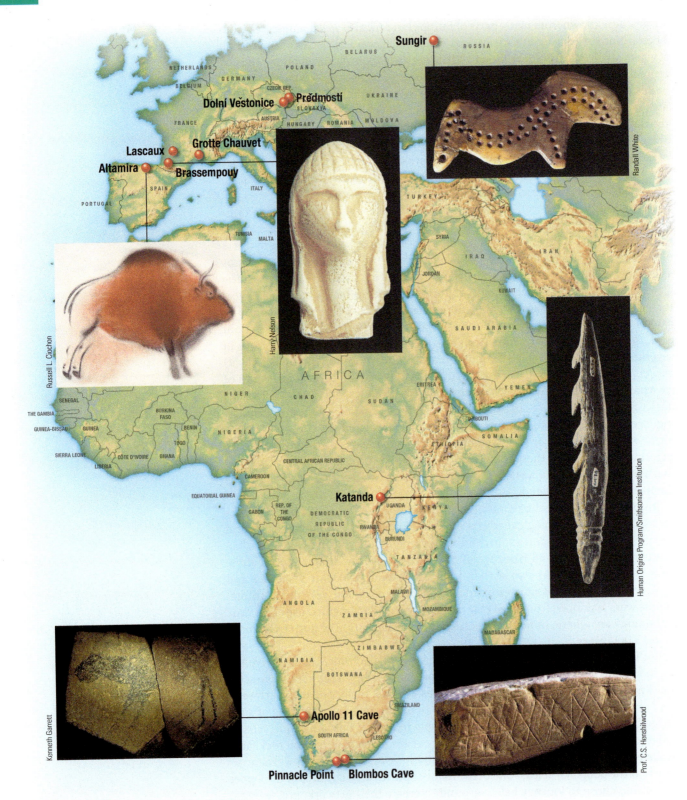

▲ **Figure 13-18**
Symbolic artifacts from the Middle Stone Age of Africa and the Upper Paleolithic in Europe. It is notable that evidence of symbolism is found in Blombos Cave (77,000 ya) and Katanda (80,000 ya), both in Africa, about 45,000 years before any comparable evidence is known from Europe.

adorn the walls in black, red, and yellow. Equally impressive, the walls and ceiling of an immense cave at Altamira are filled with superb portrayals of bison in red and black. The artist even took advantage of bulges in the walls to create a sense of relief (that is, three-dimensionality) in the paintings.

Inside the cave called Grotte Chauvet, preserved unseen for thousands of years, are a multitude of images including dots, stenciled human handprints, and, most dramatically, hundreds of animal representations. Radiocarbon dating has placed the paintings during the Aurignacian, likely more than 35,000 ya, making Grotte Chauvet considerably earlier than the Magdalenian sites of Lascaux and most of the images at Altamira (Balter, 2006). However, as we mentioned above, Altamira and a couple of other Spanish caves contain some images that are now dated even earlier.

Africa

Early accomplishments in rock art, possibly as early as in Europe, are seen in southern Africa (Namibia) at the Apollo 11 rock shelter site, where painted slabs have been identified as dating to between 28,000 and 26,000 ya (Freundlich et al., 1980; Vogelsang, 1998). At Blombos Cave, farther to the south, remarkable bone tools, beads, and decorated ocher fragments are all dated to 73,000 ya (Henshilwood et al., 2004; Jacobs et al., 2006). More recent excavations at the site have revealed the presence of an ocher workshop dating to 100 kya (Henshilwood et al., 2011). Of particular note is the presence of charcoal, bone, hammerstones, and grindstones, all components of the ochre-processing tool kit. Interestingly, evidence of an ochre mixture was found within two abalone shells, and may been used for skin protection or for decoration (Fig. 13-19).

The most recent and highly notable discovery from South Africa comes from another cave located at Pinnacle Point, not far from Blombos (K. Brown et al., 2012). At Pinnacle Point, ocher has been found (perhaps used for personal adornment) as well as clear evidence of systematic exploitation of shellfish and the use of very small stone blades (microliths). What is both important and surprising is that the earliest dates for the site are approximately 165,000 ya, providing the earliest evidence

▼ **Figure 13-19**
Ochre-processing tool kits from Blombos Cave, South Africa, dated to 100 kya.

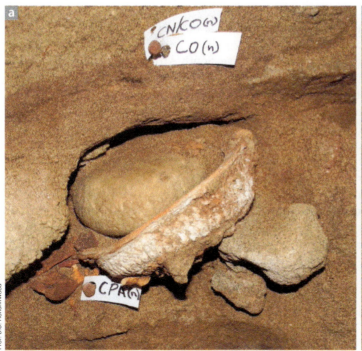

A Closer Look Maybe You *Can* Take It with You

The practice of deliberately burying the dead is an important and distinctive aspect of later human biocultural evolution. We saw in Chapter 12 that Neandertals buried their dead at a number of sites; but we also noted that the assortment of grave goods found in Neandertal burials was pretty sparse.

Something remarkable happened with the appearance and dispersal of modern humans. Suddenly—at least in archaeological terms—graves became much more elaborate. And it wasn't just that many more items were placed with the deceased; it was also the kinds of objects. Neandertal graves sometimes contain a few stone tools and some unmodified animal bones, such as cave bear. But fully modern humans seem to have had more specialized and far more intensive cultural capacities. For example, from 40,000 ya at Twilight Cave, in Kenya, researchers have found 600 fragments of carefully drilled ostrich eggshell beads (Klein and Edgar, 2002). These beads aren't directly associated with a human burial, but they

do show an intensification of craft specialization and possibly a greater interest in personal adornment (although Neandertals in Spain at about the same time were doing similar things, but to a somewhat lesser extent; see Chapter 12).

A locale where such elaborate grave goods (including beads) have been found in association with Upper Paleolithic modern human burials is the famous Cro-Magnon site in southwestern France. Likewise, numerous elaborate grave goods were found with human burials at Grimaldi, in Italy.

No doubt the richest Upper Paleolithic burial sites are those at Sungir, in Russia. Parts of several individuals have been recovered there, dating to about 24,000 ya. Most dramatically, three individuals were found in direct association with thousands of ivory beads and other elaborate grave goods. Two of the individuals, a girl about 9 or 10 years of age and a boy about 12 or 13 years of age, were buried together head to head in a spectacular grave

from anywhere of these behaviors, which are thought by many to be characteristic of modern humans (Marean et al., 2007). The microliths, dated to about 71,000 ya, also show evidence that the stone had been carefully heated, making it easier to modify into such small tools (K. Brown et al., 2009, 2012; Marean, 2010). Other recent finds from Sibudu, another cave site in South Africa dated to around 70,000 ya, show what archaeologist Lyn Wadley and colleagues have identified as traces of compound adhesives made from red ocher and plant gum, which were then used to haft stone tools to handles, as well as indirect evidence of the possible use of snares and traps to catch small animals (Wadley, 2009; Wadley et al., 2009). Wadley and colleagues conclude that such traces of behavior show evidence of what she terms "complex cognition," since they appear to indicate an understanding of basic chemical reactions. Recent work at Border Cave, South Africa, has also found evidence of a suite of complex behaviors, including use of notched bones, wooden digging sticks, bone awls, bone points, and organic residue likely used for hafting, and as well as possible evidence of a wooden poison applicator. These well-preserved organic materials suggest that modern hunter-gatherer adaptations were well developed by 44,000 ya (d'Errico et al., 2012).

In central Africa there was also considerable use of bone and antler, some of it possibly quite early. Excavations in the Katanda area of the eastern portion of the Democratic Republic of the Congo (see Fig. 13-18) have shown remarkable development of bone craftwork. Dating of the site is quite early, with initial ESR and TL dating results indicating an age of 80,000 ya (Feathers and Migliorini, 2001). Preliminary reports have demonstrated that these technological achievements rival those of the more renowned European Upper Paleolithic (Yellen et al., 1995).

Indonesia Recent studies of rock art from Sulawesi, Indonesia have revealed evidence of Late Pleistocene occupation of the Maros region. Uranium-series dating on minerals (*speleothems*) associated with 12 human hand stencils and two animal figurines from seven cave sites produced dates between about 40,000 and

(see Fig. 13-14). The more than 10,000 beads excavated here were probably woven into clothing, a task that would have been extraordinarily time-consuming. The two individuals were placed directly on a bed of red ocher, and with them were two magnificent spears made of straightened mammoth tusks—one of them more than 6 feet (240 cm) long! What's more, there were hundreds of drilled fox canine teeth, pierced antlers, and ivory carvings of animals as well as ivory pins and pendants (Formicola and Buzhilova, 2004).

The production of all of these items, which were so carefully placed with these two young individuals, took thousands of hours of labor. Indeed, one estimate suggests that it took 10,000 hours just to make the beads (Klein and Edgar, 2002). What were the Magdalenian people who went to all this trouble thinking? The double burial is certainly the most extravagant of any from the Upper Paleolithic, but another at Sungir is almost as remarkable. Here, the body of an adult male—perhaps about 40 years old when he died—was also

found with thousands of beads, and he, too, was carefully laid out on a bed of red ocher.

Sungir is likely a somewhat extraordinary exception; still, far more elaborate graves are often found associated with early modern humans than was ever the case in earlier cultures. At Sungir, and to a lesser extent at other sites, it took hundreds or even thousands of hours to produce the varied and intricate objects.

The individuals who were buried with these valuable goods must have been seen as special. Did they have unique talents? Were they leaders or the children of leaders? Or did they have some special religious or ritual standing? To be sure, this evidence is the earliest we have from human history revealing highly defined social status. Thousands of years later, the graves of the Egyptian pharaohs express the same thing—as do the elaborate monuments seen in most contemporary cemeteries. The Magdalenians and other Upper Paleolithic cultures were indeed much like us. They, too, may have tried to defy death and "take it with them"!

35,000 ya, comparable in age with oldest cave art in Europe (Fig. 13-20; Aubert et al., 2014; van den Bergh et al., 2016). These incredible discoveries indicate that human artistic expression was much more widespread during the Upper Paleolithic than previously thought.

Summary of Upper Paleolithic Culture

In looking back at the Upper Paleolithic, we can see it as the culmination of 2 million years of cultural development. Change proceeded incredibly slowly for most of the Pleistocene, but as cultural traditions and materials accumulated, and the brain—as well as, we assume, intelligence—expanded and reorganized, the rate of change quickened.

Cultural evolution continued with the appearance of early premodern humans and moved a bit faster with later premodern humans. Neandertals in Eurasia and their contemporaries elsewhere added deliberate burials, body ornamentation, technological innovations, and much more.

Building on existing cultures, Late Pleistocene populations attained sophisticated cultural and material heights in a seemingly short (by previous standards) burst of exciting activity. In Europe and southern and central Africa, particularly, there seem to have been dramatic cultural innovations, among them big game hunting with new weapons, such as harpoons, spear-throwers, and eventually bows and arrows. Other innovations included needles, "tailored" clothing, hafting of tools, and burials with elaborate grave goods—a practice that may indicate some sort of status hierarchy.

This dynamic age was doomed, or so it seems, by the climate changes of about 10,000 ya. As the temperature slowly rose and the glaciers retreated (beginning with the end of the last glacial maximum, 19,000 ya), animal and plant species were seriously affected, and these changes, in turn, affected humans. As traditional prey

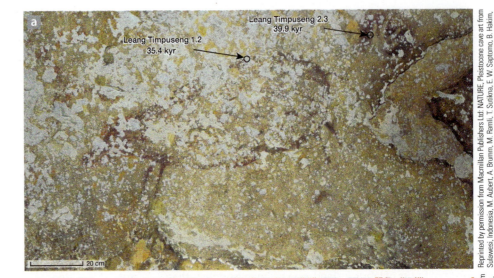

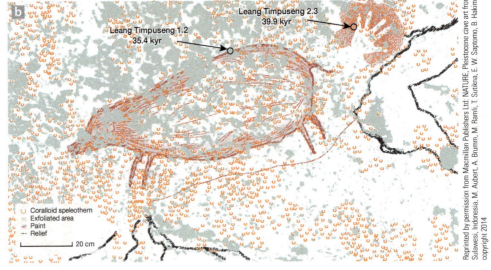

> ▶ **Figure 13-20**
> Rock art from Leang Timpuseng, Sulawesi, Indonesia, showing a hand stencil and an animal depiction. Dating of spelothems provides an age of 40–35 kya.

Corralloid speleothem
Exfoliated area
Paint
Relief

Reprinted by permission from Macmillan Publishers Ltd: NATURE, Pleistocene cave art from Sulawesi, Indonesia, M. Aubert, A. Brumm, M. Ramli, T. Sutikna, E. W. Saptomo, B. Hakim, copyright 2014

animals were depleted or disappeared altogether, humans had to seek other means of obtaining food.

The grinding of hard seeds or roots became important, and as humans grew more familiar with propagating plants, they began to domesticate both plants and animals. Human dependence on domestication became critical, and with it came permanent settlements, new technology, and more complex social organization. This continuing story of human biocultural evolution will be the topic of the remainder of this text.

How Do We Know?

One surprising fact revealed by DNA research on both living and ancient modern humans is the lack of genetic diversity. Studies on modern populations clearly indicate that more variation exists *within* groups than *between* groups. Collectively, these results suggest that *Homo sapiens* experienced a bottleneck effect in the past, which significantly reduced genetic diversity. A key study conducted more than 25 years ago discovered this through analysis of modern mtDNA from 147 individuals representing five different geographical regions of the world (Cann et al., 1987). More importantly, the research team found the highest number of mtDNA mutations among individuals of African ancestry, suggesting that the African lineage represented the oldest population and the ultimate source of all modern humans. Through comparison of genetic mutations between groups, Cann and colleagues (1987) developed a mitochondrial DNA clock, which is based on the assumption that mutations in mtDNA accumulate at a fairly regular rate. Groundbreaking at the time, this research suggested that all modern humans can trace their ancestry to an African population that lived between 200,000 and 100,000 ya.

Although the original study was heavily criticized by both paleoanthropologists (especially those supporting multiregional evolution) and geneticists at the time, more recent work using both mtDNA and nuclear DNA strongly supports the original interpretations (Jobling et al., 2013). What's more, detailed fossil evidence of modern humans during the Late Pleistocene supports this model, with the oldest *H. sapiens* fossils found in East Africa. Thankfully, we are now in an era where geneticists and paleoanthropologists work closely together to resolve questions about human origins.

What Do You Think?

We just discussed some of the genetic techniques used to trace the origins of modern humans. What different kinds of information can be derived from genetic studies versus morphological studies of fossils? Why do you think it's important to integrate different perspectives for understanding human origins? ■

Summary of Main Topics

- The two main hypotheses that have been used to explain the origin and dispersal of modern humans include the regional continuity model and the replacement model. The regional continuity model suggests that different groups of modern people evolved from local populations of premodern humans. Various replacement models, especially those emphasizing partial replacement, suggest that modern humans originated in Africa and migrated to other parts of the world. However, when they came into contact with premodern human groups, they did not completely replace them, but interbred with them to some extent. Recent DNA evidence from ancient Neandertals as well as from modern people demonstrates that some low level of interbreeding did take place, probably between 80,000 and 50,000 ya. These findings support a partial replacement model. Archaeological finds and some fossil evidence (although the latter is not as well established) also support the view that intermixing occurred between modern *H. sapiens* and Neandertals.

- The earliest finds of modern *H. sapiens* come from East Africa (Ethiopia), with the oldest dating to about 195,000 ya. Another find from Herto is very well dated (160,000 ya) and is the best evidence of an early modern human from anywhere at this time. Modern humans are found in South Africa beginning around 100,000 ya, and the first anatomical modern *H. sapiens* individuals are found in the Middle East, dating to perhaps more than 100,000 ya.

- The Upper Paleolithic is a cultural period showing many innovations in technology, development of more sophisticated (cave) art, and very elaborate burials rich in grave goods. Similar cultural developments occurred in Eurasia, Africa, and Indonesia.

Critical Thinking Questions

1. What anatomical characteristics define *modern* as compared with *premodern* humans? Assume that you're analyzing an incomplete skeleton that may be early modern *H. sapiens*. Which portions of the skeleton would be most informative, and why?

2. What recent evidence supports a partial replacement model for an African origin and later dispersal of modern humans? Do you find this evidence convincing? Why or why not? Can you propose an alternative that has better data to support it?

3. Why are the fossils discovered from Herto so important? How does this evidence influence your conclusions in question 2?

4. What archaeological evidence shows that modern human behavior during the Upper Paleolithic was significantly different from that of earlier hominins? Compare and contrast some key differences in burial contexts between modern humans and the Neandertals. What do you think accounts for these differences?

5. Why do you think some Upper Paleolithic people painted in caves? Why don't we find such evidence of cave painting from a wider geographical area?

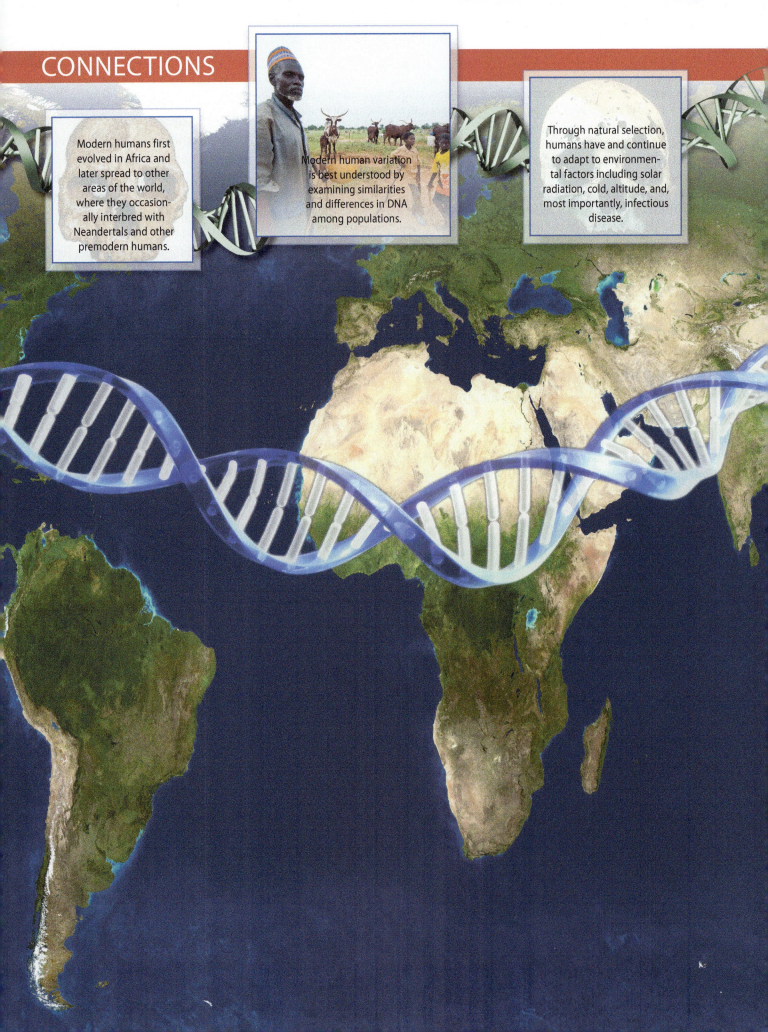

CONNECTIONS

Modern humans first evolved in Africa and later spread to other areas of the world, where they occasionally interbred with Neandertals and other premodern humans.

Modern human variation is best understood by examining similarities and differences in DNA among populations.

Through natural selection, humans have and continue to adapt to environmental factors including solar radiation, cold, altitude, and, most importantly, infectious disease.

Modern Human Biology: Patterns of Variation

14

Historical Views of Human Variation

The Concept of Race

Contemporary Interpretations of Human Variation

Human Polymorphisms

Polymorphisms at the DNA Level

Population Genetics

Calculating Allele Frequencies

Evolution in Action: Modern Human Populations

Human Biocultural Evolution

Student Learning Objectives After studying the material in this chapter, you should be able to:

▸ Outline historical views on human variation.

▸ Explain why the concept of race is invalid from a biological perspective.

▸ Discuss contemporary views on human variation based on studies of human polymorphisms.

▸ Explain how population genetics is used to examine microevolution.

▸ Describe two specific examples of biocultural evolution in regard to modern human populations.

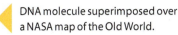

A t some time or other, you've probably been asked to specify your "race" or "ethnicity" on an application or census form. Did that bother you, and if so, why? Usually, you can choose from a few racial/ethnic categories. Was it easy to pick one? Where would your parents and grandparents fit in?

Notions about human diversity have played an extremely important role in human relations for at least a few thousand years, and they still influence political and social perceptions. While we'd like to believe that informed views have become almost universal, the gruesome tally of genocidal/ethnic cleansing atrocities in recent years tells us that tragically, worldwide, we have a long way to go before tolerance becomes the norm.

DNA molecule superimposed over a NASA map of the Old World.

Unfortunately there are probably hundreds (if not thousands) of popular misconceptions regarding human diversity, and to make matters worse, many people seem unwilling to accept what science has to say on the subject. Many misconceptions, especially those regarding how race is defined and categorized, are rooted in cultural history over the last few centuries.

In Chapters 3 and 4, we saw how physical characteristics are influenced by the DNA in our cells. We discussed how people inherit genes from their parents and how variations in those genes (alleles) can produce different expressions of traits. We also focused on how the basic principles of inheritance are related to evolutionary change.

In this chapter, we'll continue to deal with topics that directly relate to genetics—namely, biological diversity in humans and how biocultural evolution influences the ways in which humans adapt to environmental challenges. After discussing historical attempts to explain human phenotypic variation and racial classification, we'll examine contemporary methods of interpreting diversity. In recent years, several new techniques have emerged that permit direct examination of the DNA molecule, revealing differences among people even at the level of single nucleotides. But as discoveries of different levels of diversity emerge, geneticists have also shown that our species is remarkably uniform genetically, particularly when compared with other species.

Historical Views of Human Variation

The first step toward understanding diversity in nature is to organize it into categories that can then be named, discussed, and perhaps studied. Historically, when different groups of people came into contact with each other, they tried to account for the physical differences they saw. Because skin color was so noticeable, it was one of the more frequently explained phenotypic traits, and most systems of racial classification were based on it.

As early as 1350 B.C.E., the ancient Egyptians had classified humans based on their skin color: red for Egyptian, yellow for people to the east, white for those to the north, and black for sub-Saharan Africans (Gossett, 1963). In the sixteenth century, after the European discovery of the New World, several western European countries embarked on a period of intense exploration and colonization in both the New and Old Worlds. One result of this contact was an increased awareness of human diversity.

Throughout the eighteenth and nineteenth centuries, European and American scientists concentrated on describing and classifying biological variation in humans and also in nonhuman species. The first scientific attempt to describe the newly discovered variation among human populations was Linnaeus's taxonomic classification (see Chapter 2), which placed humans into four separate categories. Linnaeus assigned behavioral and intellectual qualities to each group, with the least complimentary descriptions going to sub-Saharan Africans. This ranking system was typical of the period and reflected the almost universal European view that Europeans were superior to everyone else.

Johann Friedrich Blumenbach (1752–1840), a German anatomist, classified humans into five races. Blumenbach's categories came to be described simply as white, yellow, red, black, and brown, but he also used criteria other than skin color. What's more, he emphasized that racial categories based on skin color were arbitrary and that many traits, including skin color, weren't discrete phenomena. Blumenbach pointed out that classifying all humans using such a system would completely omit everyone who didn't fall into a specific category. Blumenbach and others also recognized that traits such as skin color showed overlapping expression between groups.

Most Europeans ignored these complexities, so that by the mid-nineteenth century populations were ranked on a scale based primarily on skin color (along with physical aspects of the head, nose, eyes, and hair), again with sub-Saharan Africans at the bottom. The Europeans themselves were also ranked, with northern, light-skinned populations considered superior to their southern, somewhat darker-skinned neighbors in Italy and Greece.

To many Europeans, the fact that non-Europeans weren't Christian suggested that they were "uncivilized" and implied an even more basic inferiority of character and intellect. This view was rooted in a concept called **biological determinism**, which in part holds that there is an association between physical characteristics and such attributes as intelligence, morals, values, abilities, and even social and economic condition. In other words, cultural variations were thought to be inherited in the same way that biological variations are. It followed, then, that there are inherent behavioral and cognitive differences between groups and that some groups are by nature superior to others. Unfortunately, many people still hold these views, and following this logic, it's a simple matter to justify the persecution and even enslavement of other peoples simply because their outward appearance differs from what is familiar.

After 1850, biological determinism was a constant theme underlying common thinking as well as scientific research in Europe and the United States. Most people—including such notables as Thomas Jefferson, Georges Cuvier, Benjamin Franklin, Charles Lyell, Abraham Lincoln, Charles Darwin, and Supreme Court justice Oliver Wendell Holmes—held deterministic (and what today we'd call racist) views. Commenting on this usually deemphasized characteristic of more respected historical figures, the late evolutionary biologist Stephen J. Gould (1981, p. 32) remarked that "all American culture heroes embraced racial attitudes that would embarrass public-school mythmakers."

Francis Galton (1822–1911), Charles Darwin's cousin, shared a growing fear among nineteenth-century Europeans that "civilized society" was being weakened by the failure of natural selection to completely eliminate unfit and inferior members (Greene, 1981, p. 107). Galton wrote and lectured on the necessity of "race improvement" and suggested government regulation of marriage and family size, an approach he called **eugenics**. Although eugenics had its share of critics, its popularity flourished throughout the 1930s. Nowhere was it more attractive than in Germany, where the viewpoint took a horrifying turn. The false idea of pure races was increasingly extolled as a means of reestablishing a strong and prosperous state. Eugenics was seen as scientific justification for purging Germany of its "unfit," and many of Germany's scientists continued to support the policies of racial purity and eugenics during the Nazi period (Proctor, 1988, p. 143), when these policies served as justification for condemning millions of people to death.

At the same time, many scientists were turning away from racial typologies and classification in favor of a more evolutionary approach. No doubt for some, this shift in direction was motivated by their growing concerns over the goals of the eugenics movement. Probably more important, however, was the synthesis of genetics and Darwin's theories of natural selection during the 1930s. As discussed in Chapter 4, this breakthrough influenced all the biological sciences, and some physical anthropologists soon began applying evolutionary principles to the study of human variation.

The Concept of Race

All contemporary humans are members of the same **polytypic** species, *Homo sapiens*. A polytypic species is composed of local populations that differ in the expression of one or more traits. It's crucial to emphasize that even *within* local populations, there's a great deal of genotypic and phenotypic variation among individuals.

biological determinism The concept that phenomena, including various aspects of behavior (e.g., intelligence, values, morals) are governed by biological (genetic) factors; the inaccurate association of various behavioral attributes with certain biological traits, such as skin color.

eugenics The philosophy of "race improvement" through the forced sterilization of members of some groups and increased reproduction among others; an overly simplified, often racist view that's now discredited.

polytypic Referring to species composed of populations that differ in the expression of one or more traits.

A Closer Look Racial Purity: A False and Dangerous Ideology

During the late nineteenth and early twentieth centuries, a growing sense of nationalism swept Europe and the United States. At the same time, an increased emphasis on racial purity was coupled with the more dangerous aspects of what's known as biological determinism. The concept of pure races is based in part on the notion that in the past, races were composed of people who conformed to idealized types and were similar in appearance and intellect. According to this concept, over time some variation was introduced into these pure races through interbreeding with other groups. Increasingly, this type of "contamination" was seen as a threat to be avoided.

In today's terminology, pure races would be said to be genetically homogenous, or to possess little genetic variation. Therefore everyone would have the same alleles at most of their loci. Actually, we do see this situation in "pure breeds" of domesticated animals and plants, developed deliberately by humans through selective breeding. We also see many of the detrimental consequences of such genetic uniformity in various congenital abnormalities, such as hip dysplasia in some breeds of dogs.

With our current understanding of genetic principles, we're able to appreciate the potentially negative outcomes of matings between genetically similar individuals. For example, we know that inbreeding increases the likelihood of offspring who are homozygous for certain deleterious recessive alleles. We also know that decreased genetic variation in a species diminishes the potential for natural selection to act, thus compromising that species' ability to adapt to certain environmental fluctuations. What's more, in genetically uniform populations, individual fertility can be seriously reduced, potentially with disastrous consequences for the entire species. So, even if pure human races did exist at one time (and they didn't), it would not have been a genetically desirable condition, and these groups most certainly would have been at an evolutionary disadvantage.

In northern Europe, particularly Germany, and in the United States, racial superiority was increasingly embodied in the so-called Aryan race. *Aryan* is a term that's still widely used, albeit erroneously, with biological connotations. Actually, *Aryan* doesn't refer to a biological population, as most people who use the term intend it. Rather, it's a linguistic term that refers to an ancient language group that was ancestral to the Indo-European family of languages, and it's the word from which the name Iran is derived.

By the early twentieth century, the "Aryans" had been transformed into a mythical superrace of people whose noble traits were embodied in an extremely idealized "Nordic type." The true Aryan was held to be tall, blond, blue-eyed, strong, industrious, and "pure in spirit." Nordics were extolled as the developers of all ancient "high" civilizations and as the founders of modern industrialized nations. (It would appear that the ancient cultures of the Indus Valley, China, Arabia, Mexico, Zimbabwe, Greece, and Rome were unknown.) In Europe, there was growing emphasis on the superiority of northwestern Europeans as the modern representatives of "true Nordic stock," while southern and eastern Europeans were viewed as inferior.

In the United States, there prevailed the strongly held opinion that America was "originally" settled by Christian Nordics. One wonders how Native Americans could have been so conveniently forgotten. Before about 1890, most recent newcomers to the United States had come from Germany, Scandinavia, Great Britain, and Ireland. But by the

▲ **Figure 1**

Emaciated survivors of one of the largest Nazi concentration camps, at Ebensee, Austria, liberated by U.S. Army troops in May 1945.

Nevertheless, in discussions of human variation, most people typically have emphasized and grouped together various characteristics, such as skin color, face shape, nose shape, hair color, hair form (curly or straight), and eye color. Those individuals who have particular combinations of these and other traits have been placed together in categories associated with specific geographical localities. Traditionally, such categories have been called *races*.

1890s, the pattern of immigration had changed. The arrival of increasing numbers of Italians, Turks, Greeks, and eastern European Jews among the thousands of newcomers raised fears that society was being contaminated by immigration from southern and eastern Europe.

Also in the United States, there were concerns about the large population of former slaves and their descendants. As African Americans left the South to work in the factories of the North, many unskilled white workers felt economically threatened by this competition. It was no coincidence that the Ku Klux Klan, which had been inactive for some years, was revived in 1915 and by the 1920s was preaching vehement opposition to African Americans, Jews, and Catholics in support of the supremacy of the white, Protestant "Nordic race." These sentiments were widespread in the general population, although they didn't always take the extreme form advocated by the Klan. One result of these views was the Immigration Restriction Act, passed by Congress in 1924, which was aimed at curtailing the immigration of non-Nordics, including Italians, Jews, and eastern Europeans, in order to preserve "America's Nordic heritage."

To avoid the further "decline of the superior race," many states practiced policies of racial segregation until the mid-1950s. Particularly in the South, segregation laws resulted in an almost total separation of whites and blacks except where blacks were employed as servants or laborers. There were also laws against marriage between whites and blacks in over half the states, and unions between whites and Asians were frequently illegal. In several states, marriage between whites and blacks was punishable as either a misdemeanor or a felony, and astonishingly, some of these laws weren't repealed until the late 1950s or early 1960s. Likewise, in Germany, by 1935, the newly instituted Nuremberg Laws forbade marriage or sexual intercourse between so-called Aryan Germans and Jews.

The fact that belief in racial purity and superiority led ultimately to the Nazi death camps in World War II is undisputed (except for continuing efforts by certain white supremacist and neo-Nazi organizations). It's one of the great tragedies of the twentieth century that some of history's most glaring examples of discrimination and brutality were perpetrated by people who believed their actions to be based in

MSGT Rose Reynolds

▲ **Figure 2**

Victims of genocide in Rwanda resulting from tribal warfare in 1994.

scientific principles. In reality, there's absolutely no evidence to suggest that "pure" human races ever existed. Indeed, such an idea flies in the face of everything we know about natural selection, recombination, and gene flow. The degree of genetic uniformity throughout our species (compared with some other species), as evidenced by mounting data from mitochondrial and nuclear DNA analysis, argues strongly that there has always been gene flow between human populations and that genetically homogenous races are nothing more than fabrications.

We all think we know what we mean by the word *race*, but in reality the term has had various meanings since the 1500s, when it first appeared in the English language. Race has been used synonymously with *species*, as in "the human race." Since the 1600s, *race* has also referred to various culturally defined groups, and this meaning is still common. For example, you'll hear people say, "the English race" or "the Japanese race," when they actually mean nationality. Another phrase you've probably heard is "the Jewish race," when the speaker is really talking about a particular ethnic and religious identity. The category "Hispanic" is equally problematic. Technically, it refers largely to the Spanish speaking populations of Latin America; however, it is often used socially as a racial or ethnic term (despite the fact that it is applied to biologically and culturally heterogeneous populations).

So, even though *race* is usually a term with biological connotations, it also has enormous social significance. And there's still a widespread perception that certain physical traits (skin color in particular) are associated with numerous cultural attributes (such as occupational preferences or even morality). As a result, in many cultural contexts, a person's social identity is strongly influenced by the way he or she expresses those physical traits traditionally used to define "racial groups." Characteristics such as skin color are highly visible, and they make it easy to immediately and superficially place people into socially defined categories. However, so-called racial traits aren't the only phenotypic expressions that contribute to social identity. Sex and age are also critically important. But aside from these two variables, an individual's biological and/or ethnic background is still inevitably a factor that influences how he or she is initially perceived and judged by others.

References to national origin (for example, African, Asian) as substitutes for racial labels have become more common in recent years, both within and outside anthropology. Within anthropology, the term *ethnicity* was proposed in the early 1950s to avoid the more emotionally charged term *race*. Strictly speaking, *ethnicity* refers to cultural factors, but the fact that the words *ethnicity* and *race* are often used interchangeably reflects the social importance of phenotypic expression and demonstrates once again how phenotype is mistakenly associated with culturally defined variables.

In its most common biological usage, the term *race* refers to geographically patterned phenotypic variation within a species. By the seventeenth century, naturalists were beginning to describe races in plants and nonhuman animals. They had recognized that when populations of a species occupied different regions, they sometimes differed from one another in the expression of one or more traits. But even today, there are no established criteria for assessing races of plants and animals, including humans. As a result, biologists now almost never refer to "races" of other species but more typically talk about *populations* or, for major subdivisions, *subspecies*.

Before World War II, most studies of human variation focused on visible phenotypic variation between large, geographically defined populations, and these studies were largely descriptive. But in the last 60 years or so, the emphasis has shifted to examining the differences in allele frequencies (and, more basically, DNA differences) within and between populations, as well as considering the adaptive significance of phenotypic and genotypic variation. This shift in focus occurred partly because of the Modern Synthesis in biology. But now, armed with genome data sets for populations, biologists have an unprecedented opportunity to study and explain human variation and the role that evolutionary factors have played in producing it (Pritchard, 2010).

In the twenty-first century, the application of evolutionary principles to the study of modern human variation has replaced the superficial nineteenth-century view of *race based solely on observed phenotype*. Additionally, the genetic emphasis has dispelled previously held misconceptions that races are fixed biological entities that don't change over time and are composed of individuals who all conform to a particular *type*.

Clearly, there are visible phenotypic differences between humans, and some of these roughly correspond to particular geographical locations. But we need to ask if there's any adaptive significance attached to these differences. Is genetic drift a factor? What is the degree of underlying genetic variation that influences phenotypic variation? What influence has culture had in the past? These questions place considerations of human variation within a contemporary evolutionary, biocultural framework.

Although, as a discipline, physical anthropology is rooted in attempts to explain human diversity, no contemporary scholar subscribes to pre–Modern Synthesis concepts of races (human or nonhuman) as fixed biological entities. Also, anthropologists recognize that such outdated concepts of race are no longer valid, because the amount of genetic variation accounted for by differences *between* groups is vastly exceeded by the variation that exists *within* groups. Many physical anthropologists also argue that race is an outdated creation of the human mind that attempts to simplify biological complexity by organizing it into categories. So, human races are a product of the human tendency to impose order on complex natural phenomena. In this view, simplistic classification may have been an acceptable approach 100 years ago, but given the current state of genetic and evolutionary science, it's meaningless.

However, even though racial categories based on outwardly expressed variations are invalid, many biological anthropologists continue to study differences in such traits as skin or eye color because these characteristics, and the genes that influence them, can yield information about population adaptation, genetic drift, mutation, and gene flow. Forensic anthropologists, in particular, find the phenotypic criteria associated with ancestry (especially in the skeleton) to have practical applications. Law enforcement agencies frequently call on these scientists to help identify human skeletal remains. Because unidentified human remains are often those of crime victims, identification must be as accurate as possible. The most important variables in such identification are the individual's sex, age, stature, and ancestry. Using metric and nonmetric criteria, forensic anthropologists employ various techniques for establishing broad population affinity (that is, a likely relationship) for a particular individual, and for most applications their findings are accurate about 80 percent of the time (Ousley et al., 2009).

Another major limitation of traditional classification schemes derives from their inherently *typological* nature, meaning that categories are distinct and based on stereotypes or ideals that comprise a specific set of traits. So in general, typologies are inherently misleading because any grouping always includes many individuals who don't conform to all aspects of a particular type. In any so-called racial group, there are individuals who fall into the normal range of variation for another group based on one or several characteristics. For example, two people of different ancestry might differ in skin color, but they could share any number of other traits, including height, head shape, hair color, eye color, and ABO blood type. In fact, they could easily share more similarities with each other than they do with many members of their own populations (Fig. 14-1).

To blur this picture further, the characteristics that have traditionally been used to define races are *polygenic*; that is, they're influenced by more than one gene and therefore exhibit a continuous range of expression. So it's difficult, if not impossible, to draw distinct boundaries between populations with regard to many traits. This limitation becomes clear if you ask yourself: At what point is hair color no longer dark brown but medium brown, or no longer light brown but dark blond? (Look back at Fig. 4-16 for an illustration of variability in eye color.)

The scientific controversy over race will fade as we enhance our understanding of the genetic diversity (and uniformity) of our species. Given the rapid changes in genome studies, and because very few genes actually contribute to outward expressions of phenotype, dividing the human species into racial categories isn't a biologically meaningful way to look at human variation. Among the general public, variations on the theme of race will undoubtedly continue

▶ **Figure 14-1**

Some examples of phenotypic variation among Africans. **(a)** San (South African). **(b)** West African (Bantu). **(c)** Ethiopian. **(d)** Ituri (central African). **(e)** North African (Tunisian).

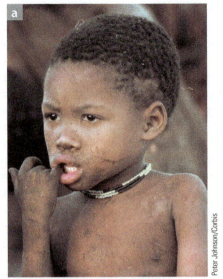

Peter Johnson/Corbis

Charles Lenars/Josette Lenars/Terra/Corbis

Martin Harvey/Documentary Value/Gallo Images/Corbis

Otto Lang/Historical/Corbis

Lynn Kilgore

to be the most common view of human biological and cultural variation. Keeping all this in mind, it's up to anthropologists to continue exploring the issue so that, to the best of our abilities, accurate information about human variation will be available to anyone who seeks informed explanations of complex phenomena.

Contemporary Interpretations of Human Variation

Because the physical characteristics (such as skin color and hair form) that are used to define race are *polygenic*, precisely measuring the genetic influence on them hasn't been possible (although geneticists are getting closer). Physical anthropologists and other biologists who study modern human variation have largely abandoned the traditional perspective of describing superficial phenotypic characteristics in favor of examining differences in the frequencies of genes.

Beginning in the 1950s, studies of modern human variation focused on the various components of blood as well as other aspects of body chemistry. Such traits as the ABO blood types are phenotypes, but they're also direct products of the genotype. (Recall that protein-coding genes direct cells to make proteins, and the antigens on blood cells and many constituents of blood serum are partly composed of proteins; Fig.14-2.) During the twentieth century, this perspective met with a great deal of success, as eventually dozens of loci were identified and the frequencies of many specific alleles were obtained from numerous human populations. Even so, in all these cases, it was the phenotype that was observed, and information about the underlying genotype remained largely unobtainable. But beginning in the 1990s, with the advent of genomic studies, new techniques were developed. Now that we can directly sequence DNA, we can actually identify entire genes and even larger DNA segments and make comparisons between individuals and populations. A decade ago, only a small portion of the human genome was accessible to physical anthropologists, but now we have the capacity to obtain DNA profiles for virtually every human population on earth. And we can expect that in the next decade, our understanding and knowledge of human biological variation and adaptation will dramatically increase.

Human Polymorphisms

Traits (or the DNA sequences that code for them) that differ in expression between populations and individuals are called **polymorphisms**, and they're the main focus of human variation studies. A genetic trait is *polymorphic* if the locus that governs it has two or more alleles. (See Chapter 4 for a discussion of the ABO blood group system, which is governed by three alleles at one locus.) A locus can consist of hundreds of nucleotides or just one nucleotide.

Understanding polymorphisms requires evolutionary explanations, and geneticists use polymorphisms as a principal tool to understand evolutionary processes in modern populations. By using these polymorphisms to compare gene frequencies between different populations, we can begin to reconstruct the evolutionary events that link human populations with one another.

The ABO system is interesting from an anthropological perspective because the frequencies of the *A*, *B*, and *O* alleles vary tremendously among humans. In most groups, *A* and *B* are rarely found in frequencies greater than 50 percent, and usually their frequencies are much lower. Still, most human groups are polymorphic for all three alleles, but there are exceptions. For example, in native South American Indians, frequencies of the *O* allele reach 100 percent. Exceptionally high frequencies of *O* are also found in

polymorphisms Loci with more than one allele. Polymorphisms can be expressed in the phenotype as the result of gene action (as in ABO), or they can exist solely at the DNA level within noncoding regions.

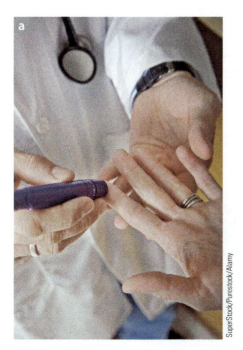

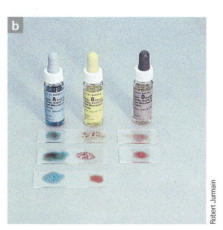

◀ **Figure 14-2**
Blood typing. **(a)** A blood sample is drawn. **(b)** A few drops of blood are treated with commercially available chemicals for detecting the ABO and Rh blood types. The glass slides below the blue- and yellow-labeled bottles show reactions for the ABO system: The blood on the top slide is type AB; the middle is type B; and the bottom is type A. The two samples to the right depict Rh-negative blood (top) and Rh-positive blood (bottom).

SuperStock/Purestock/Alamy

Robert Jurmain

northern Australia, and some islands off the Australian coast show frequencies exceeding 90 percent. In these populations, the high frequencies of the *O* allele are probably due to genetic drift (founder effect), although the influence of natural selection can't be entirely ruled out.

Besides ABO, there are many other red blood cell phenotypes, each under the control of a different genetic locus. These include the well-known Rh blood group as well as the less familiar Duffy and MN blood groups. Some antigens on white blood cells are also polymorphic. Called human leukocyte antigens (HLAs) in humans, these are crucial to the immune response because they allow the body to recognize and resist potentially dangerous infections. But unlike simple polymorphisms, such as ABO (one locus with three alleles) or MN (one locus with only two alleles), the HLA system is governed by perhaps hundreds of alleles at six different loci. Therefore, the HLA system is by far the most polymorphic genetic system known in humans.

Because there are so many HLA alleles, they're useful in showing patterns of human population diversity. For example, Lapps, Sardinians, and Basques differ in HLA allele frequencies from other European populations, and these data coincide with allele frequency distributions for ABO, MN, and Rh (Fig. 14-3). Founder effect is the most likely explanation for the distinctive genetic patterning in these smaller, traditionally more isolated groups. Likewise, some of the atypical frequencies of HLA alleles characteristic of certain populations in Australia and New Guinea probably result from founder effect. Natural selection has also influenced the evolution of HLA alleles in humans, especially as related to infectious disease. For example, certain HLA antigens appear to be associated with resistance to malaria and hepatitis B and perhaps to HIV as well. And finally, one physiological and evolutionary influence of HLA concerns male fertility. Data suggest that some HLA antigens are found in higher frequencies in infertile males, suggesting that there may be some influence of two or more HLA loci on sperm production and function (van der Ven et al., 2000).

Another well-studied polymorphism is the ability to taste an artificial substance called phenylthiocarbamide (PTC). While many people perceive PTC as extremely bitter, others don't taste it at all. The mode of inheritance follows a Mendelian pattern, with two alleles (*T* and *t*). The ability to taste PTC is a

▶ **Figure 14-3**
People in Sardinia, a large island off the west coast of Italy, differ from other European populations in allele frequencies at some loci.

dominant trait, while the inability to taste it is recessive. So, "nontasters" are homozygous (*tt*) for the recessive allele. The frequency of PTC tasting varies considerably in human populations, and the evolutionary explanation for the patterns of variation isn't clear. But it's possible that perceiving substances as bitter could be advantageous, especially in children, because poisonous plants are often bitter. Thus heightened sensitivity to bitter substances increases the likelihood that toxic substances will be avoided.

Polymorphisms at the DNA Level

As a result of the Human Genome Project, we've gained remarkable insights into human variation at the DNA level, and molecular biologists have recently discovered many variations in the human genome. For example, there are thousands of DNA segments called copy number variants (CNVs), where DNA segments are repeated, in some cases just a few times and in other cases hundreds of times. These segments vary tremendously from person to person; in fact, every person has a unique arrangement that defines that individual's distinctive "DNA fingerprint."

Researchers are expanding their approach to map patterns of variation for individual nucleotides. As you know, point mutations have been recognized for some time. But what's only recently been appreciated is that single-nucleotide changes also frequently occur in *non-protein-coding* portions of DNA. These point mutations, together with those in coding regions of DNA, are all referred to as *single-nucleotide polymorphisms (SNPs)*. From years of detailed analyses, about 15 million SNPs have been recognized. These are dispersed throughout the human genome (the majority found in noncoding DNA), and they're extraordinarily variable (Durbin, 2010). SNPs are only one of several recent genetic discoveries and indeed, geneticists have gained access to a vast biological "library" that documents the genetic history of our species. The "At a Glance" outlines an example of a genetic polymorphism used to study human variation.

At a Glance — Genetic Polymorphisms Used to Study Human Variation

Phenotypically ascertained	DNA based
↓	↓
Examples: Red blood cell antigens (ABO, MN, etc.) White blood cell antigens (HLA) PTC	Examples: Microsatellites (multiple repeats along a chromosomal region) *Alus* (single repeats that can jump between chromosomes) Single nucleotide polymorphisms (SNPs) (change in single nucleotide within coding or noncoding DNA)
↓	↓
Note: Most of these traits are subject to natural selection.	Note: Most of these characteristics are neutral and therefore not influenced by natural selection.

The field of **population genetics** is taking advantage of these new discoveries. While traditional polymorphic traits, such as ABO, are still being studied, researchers are directing more and more attention to the remarkably variable DNA polymorphisms. These molecular applications are now being widely used to evaluate human variation at a microevolutionary level, and this information provides far more accurate measures of within- and between-group variation than was previously possible. Besides that, we can now use the vast amount of new data to more fully understand very recent events in human population history, including the many roles of natural selection, genetic drift, gene flow, and mutation. As an example of how far the study of human variation has moved toward a molecular approach, more than 95 percent of papers dealing with population variation presented at a recent anthropology conference made use of DNA polymorphisms obtained from populations from all over the world.

The most recent and most comprehensive population data regarding worldwide patterns of variation come from scans of extremely large portions of DNA, called "whole-genome" analysis. Three recent studies have evaluated molecular information for the entire genome in more than 1,000 individuals. The first two studies each identified and traced the patterning of more than 500,000 SNPs as expressed in a few dozen populations worldwide (Jakobsson et al., 2008; Li et al., 2008). A recent study, called the 1000 Genomes Project, is a massive collaboration of more than 400 scientists worldwide; its preliminary findings reported on close to 15 million SNPs (as well as other DNA variants such as insertions and

population genetics The study of the frequency of alleles, genotypes, and phenotypes in populations from a microevolutionary perspective.

A Closer Look

What DNA Tells Us about Ancient Human Migrations

Recent investigations using whole genome sequencing have greatly expanded our knowledge of the origins and migration patterns of modern populations. Two recent studies have focused on ancestry in African populations. In the first study (Schuster et al., 2010) two South African individuals had their full genomes sequenced and analyzed, one a San, and the other a descendant of Bantu-speaking ancestors. Interestingly, the South African of Bantu descent is quite a well-known individual, Archbishop Desmond Tutu (Fig.1). In addition, another three San individuals were evaluated for partial genomes (focusing on protein-coding regions). A more recent investigation (Lachance et al., 2012) expanded the sample to hunter-gatherers from other regions of Africa (including two populations from Tanzania in eastern Africa and a pygmy group from Cameroon in western Africa). Whole genome sequences were obtained from five individuals from each group, and the results reinforced earlier work as well as providing a few surprises. First, the variation found in all these African

▲ **Figure 1**

Archbishop Desmond Tutu, who recently had his entire genome sequenced. This information was compared with that of other South African individuals of different ancestries.

hunter-gatherer populations far exceeds that in other groups in Africa or anywhere else in the world. Second, initial evidence suggests some interbreeding with archaic hominins occurred perhaps as early as has been more fully documented in Eurasia (that is, interbreeding with Neandertals and Denisovans around 50,000 ya).

The results emphasize how genetically diverse are African hunter-gatherer populations. In fact, two San individuals are as genetically distinct from each other as, for example, is a European from an Asian individual. The degree of uniqueness ("private alleles") found among the San and other hunter-gatherers is much further supported by information from the whole genome sequencing used in this research. Strikingly, the researchers found in their small sample of five South African men 1.3 million novel DNA differences not reported previously in other populations. This is quite astounding as it expands the range of known genetic variants for *Homo sapiens* by more than 10 percent from what has been reported previously for the whole world.

deletions); indeed, with more detailed sequencing methods and more sophisticated analyses, the researchers concluded that they already had discovered the molecular basis for 95 percent of all fairly common patterns of human variation (Durbin, 2010). They have also identified between 50 and 100 gene variants associated with disease. Rather than relying on scans of DNA segments (which locate SNPs), this study also made use of the latest sequencing techniques of human genomes and could thus quite accurately reconstruct the *entire* genome for 179 individuals (with an ultimate goal of completing whole genome sequences for 2,500 people from all around the world). These more complete data, particularly as they are enhanced further, will provide the basis for the next generation of human population genetics studies.

So far, the results of these new studies are highly significant because they confirm earlier findings from more restricted molecular data, and they also provide new insights. The higher degree of genetic variation seen in African populations as compared with any other geographical group was once again clearly seen. All human populations outside Africa have much less genetic variation than is seen in Africa. These findings further verify the earlier genetic studies (as well as fossil discoveries) that suggest a fairly recent African origin of all modern humans (as discussed in Chapter 13). Moreover, these new data shed light on the genetic relationships between populations worldwide and the nature of human migrations out of Africa (see "A Closer Look: What DNA Tells Us about Ancient Human Migrations"). They also provide evidence of the role of genetic drift (founder effect) in recent human evolution as successively smaller populations

Based on the best current evidence, major migration(s) of modern humans out of Africa took place 50,000 to 60,000 ya. One hypothesis proposed two major migration routes. One of these was a "northern" route, up through the Nile Valley in North Africa, directly into the Middle East. A second route suggests a migration from East Africa across the mouth of the Red Sea, into Arabia, then along south Asia (notably southern India), and eventually all the way to Australia, reaching there as early as 50,000 ya (Kayser, 2010).

This dual out-of-Africa migration hypothesis has mostly been based on mtDNA and Y chromosome data. More complete nuclear DNA evidence better supports a single (southern) route deriving from East Africa (Campbell and Tishkoff, 2010), with some descendants traveling north and a larger migration following the southern tier (Majumder, 2010; Stoneking and Deflin, 2010).

Once they had dispersed out of Africa, human populations fairly quickly spread throughout the Old World. As mentioned in Chapter 13, there appear to have been two separate major migrations in Asia. One of these occurred earlier (perhaps as far back as 75,000 ya) and followed along Southeast Asia, through Pacific Island chains, and eventually all the way to Australia. The second Asian dispersal occurred sometime after 40,000 ya and led to the first modern human occupation of East Asia; it included the ancestors of Han Chinese populations (Rasmussen et al., 2011). These ancient travels are revealed to us through the analysis of DNA patterns in contemporary populations as well as some remarkable discoveries from ancient DNA. For example, the population history of Southeast Asia/Pacific Island/Australia populations was influenced by early interbreeding of modern humans with Denisovans. As we mentioned in Chapter 13, we can still see the traces of this ancient gene flow from the whole genome sequencing of hair from an aboriginal Australian who died 100 years ago!

European modern human population history can be traced back to about 45,000 ya, and further genetic data suggest at least four subsequent significant migration episodes, culminating in historical times, about 5,000 ya (Soares et al., 2010). The origins of New World populations posed perhaps the biggest enigma regarding the worldwide history of major population expansions. Unquestionably, all the genetic data confirm that Native Americans have Asian origins. However, the most comprehensive recent data based on comparative analysis of more than 350,000 SNPs from both the Americas and Siberia suggest there were at least three separate migrations from Asia (Reich et al., 2012). The earliest of these, called the "First Americans," left traces throughout the New World, while the latter two migrations included, respectively, ancestors of both Aleut and Inuit populations and members of the Na-Dene–speaking language group found in Canada (and perhaps the United States, although no DNA samples were made available by any Native American groups other than in Alaska).

split off from larger ones. Finally, preliminary results suggest that the patterning of human variation at the global level may help scientists identify genetic risk factors that influence how susceptible different populations are to various diseases. Specifically, the relative genetic uniformity in non-African populations (for example, European Americans) as compared with those of more recent African descent (for example, African Americans) exposes the former to a greater risk of developing disease (Lohmueller et al., 2008). How such information might be put to use, however, is controversial.

All these genetic data, including the more traditional polymorphisms (such as blood groups) and the vast new DNA-based evidence, point in the same direction: Genetically, humans differ individually within populations far more than large geographical groups ("races") differ from each other. Does this mean, as eminent geneticist Richard Lewontin concluded 40 years ago, that there's no biological value in the further study of geographical populations (Lewontin, 1972)? Even with all our new information, the answer isn't entirely clear. Some of the recent genetic evidence from patterns of two different types of CNVs (Rosenberg et al., 2002; Bamshad et al., 2003) has pointed to broad genetic correlations that consistently indicate an individual's geographical ancestry. We must consider some important points here, however. These geographically patterned genetic clusters aren't "races" as traditionally defined, and so they aren't closely linked to simple patterns of phenotypic variation (such as skin color). What's more, the correlations are broad, so not all individuals can be easily classified. In fact, many people would probably be misclassified, even when the best information for dozens of genetic loci is used.

This debate isn't entirely academic, and it really never has been. Just consider the destructive social impact that the misuse of the race concept has caused over the last few centuries. A contemporary continuation of the debate concerns the relationship of ancestry and disease. It's long been recognized that some disease-causing genes are more common in certain populations than in others (such as the allele that causes sickle-cell anemia). The much more complete data on human DNA patterns have further expanded our knowledge, showing, for example, that some people are more resistant than others to HIV infection (see Chapter 15 for further discussion). Does this mean that a person's ancestry provides valuable medical information in screening or even treating certain diseases?

Some experts argue that such information is medically helpful (e.g., Rosenberg et al., 2002; Bamshad and Olson, 2003; Burchard et al., 2003). What's more, official federal guidelines recently issued by the U.S. Food and Drug Administration recommend the collection of ancestry data ("race/ethnic identity") in all clinical trials testing new drugs. Other researchers disagree and argue that such information is at best tenuous (King and Motulsky, 2002) or that it has no obvious medical use (e.g., Cooper et al., 2003). A major difficulty fueling this controversy has been poor communication between biomedical researchers and anthropologists and other evolutionary biologists. To allow for a more balanced and useful approach, anthropologist Clarence Gravlee has argued for adoption of a "more complex biocultural view of human biology" (2009, p. 54).

Even the general public has weighed in on this issue, defeating a 2003 California ballot measure that would have restricted the collection of "racial" (ethnic) information on medical records. There are no easy answers to the questions we've raised, and this is an even stronger argument for an informed public. The subject of race has been contentious, and anthropology and other disciplines have struggled to come to grips with it. Our new genetic tools have allowed us to expand our knowledge at a rate far beyond anything seen previously. But increased information alone doesn't permit us to fully address all human concerns. How we address diversity, both individually and collectively, must balance the potential scientific benefits against a history of social costs.

Population Genetics

As we defined it in Chapter 4, a *population* is a group of interbreeding individuals. More precisely, a population is the group within which an individual is most likely to find a mate. As such, a population is marked by a degree of genetic relatedness and shares a common **gene pool**.

In theory, this is a straightforward concept. In every generation, the genes (alleles) are mixed by recombination and rejoined through mating. What emerges in the next generation is a direct product of the genes going into the pool, which in turn is a product of who is mating with whom.

In practice, however, describing human populations is difficult. The largest human population that can be described is our entire species. All members of a species are *potentially* capable of interbreeding but are incapable of producing fertile offspring with members of other species. Our species, like any other, is thus a *genetically closed system*. The problem arises not in describing who can potentially mate with whom but in determining the exact pattern of those individuals who are doing so.

Factors that determine mate choice are geographical, ecological, and social. If individuals are isolated on a remote island in the middle of the Pacific Ocean, there isn't much chance that they'll find mating partners outside the immediate vicinity. Such **breeding isolates** are fairly easily defined and are ideal for microevolutionary studies. Geography plays a dominant role in producing these isolates by severely limiting the range of available mating partners. But even within these limits, cultural rules can easily play a deciding role by stipulating who is most appropriate among those who are potentially available.

Human population segments are defined as groups with relative degrees of **endogamy** (marrying/mating within the group). But these aren't totally closed systems. Gene flow often occurs between groups, and individuals may choose mating partners from distant locations. With the advent of modern transportation, the rate of **exogamy** (marrying/mating outside the group) has dramatically increased.

Today, most humans aren't clearly defined as members of particular populations because they don't belong to a breeding isolate. Inhabitants of large cities may appear to be members of a single population; but within the city, there's a complex system of social, ethnic, and religious boundaries that are crosscut to form smaller population segments. Besides being members of these highly open local population groupings, we're simultaneously members of overlapping gradations of larger populations—the immediate geographical region (a metropolitan area or perhaps an entire state), a section of the country, the entire nation, and ultimately the whole species.

After identifying specific human populations, the next step is to find out what evolutionary forces, if any, are operating on them. To determine whether evolution is taking place at a given genetic locus, we measure allele frequencies for specific traits. We then compare these observed frequencies with those predicted by a mathematical model called the **Hardy-Weinberg theory of genetic equilibrium**. This model gives us a baseline set of evolutionary expectations under known conditions.

The Hardy-Weinberg theory establishes a set of conditions in a hypothetical population where no evolution occurs. In other words, no evolutionary forces are acting and all genes have an equal chance of recombining in each generation (that

gene pool The total complement of genes shared by the reproductive members of a population.

breeding isolates Populations that are clearly isolated geographically and/or socially from other breeding groups.

endogamy Mating with individuals from the same group.

exogamy Mating pattern whereby individuals obtain mating partners from groups other than their own.

Hardy-Weinberg theory of genetic equilibrium The mathematical relationship expressing—under conditions in which no evolution is occurring—the predicted distribution of alleles in populations; the central theorem of population genetics.

is, there's random mating of individuals). More precisely, the conditions that such a population would be *assumed* to meet are as follows:

1. The population is infinitely large; this eliminates the possibility of random genetic drift—that is, changes in allele frequencies due to chance.
2. There's no mutation; thus, no new alleles are being added by changes in genes.
3. There's no gene flow; thus there's no exchange of genes with other populations that could alter allele frequencies.
4. Natural selection isn't operating; thus specific alleles offer no advantage over others that might influence reproductive success.
5. Mating is random; therefore, there's nothing to influence who becomes mating partners with whom; all females are assumed to have an equal chance of mating with any male, and vice versa.

If all these conditions are met, allele frequencies won't change from one generation to the next (that is, no evolution will take place), and as long as these conditions prevail, the population maintains a permanent equilibrium. This equilibrium model provides population geneticists with a standard against which they can compare actual circumstances. Notice that the conditions defining the Hardy-Weinberg equilibrium constitute an idealized, hypothetical state. In the real world, no actual population would fully meet any of these conditions. But don't be confused by this distinction. By explicitly defining the allele frequencies that would be expected if no evolutionary change were occurring (that is, in equilibrium), we establish a baseline with which to compare the allele frequencies we actually observe in real human populations.

If the observed frequencies differ from those of the expected model, we can then say that evolution is taking place at the locus in question. The alternative, of course, is that the observed and expected frequencies don't differ enough that we can confidently say that evolution is occurring at a particular locus in a population. In fact, this is often what happens; in such cases, population geneticists aren't able to clearly define evolutionary change at the particular locus under study. The "At a Glance" on page 427 outlines the process of conducting population genetics research.

The simplest way to do a microevolutionary study is to observe a genetic trait that follows a simple Mendelian pattern and has only two alleles (*A* and *a*). Remember that there are only three possible genotypes: *AA*, *Aa*, and *aa*. Proportions of these genotypes (*AA:Aa:aa*) are a function of the allele frequencies themselves (percentage of *A* and percentage of *a*). To provide uniformity for all genetic loci, a standard notation is employed to refer to these frequencies:

Frequency of dominant allele (*A*) = p
Frequency of recessive allele (*a*) = q

Since in this case there are only two alleles, their combined total frequency must represent all possibilities. In other words, the sum of their separate frequencies must be 1:

p q
(Frequency of *A* alleles) + (Frequency of *a* alleles) = 1 (100% of alleles at the locus in question)

To determine the expected proportions of genotypes, we compute the chances of the alleles combining with one another in all possible combinations. Remember, they all have an equal chance of combining and no new alleles are being added. These probabilities are a direct function of the frequency of the two alleles. The chances of all possible combinations occurring randomly can be simply shown as

At a Glance · Population Genetics Research

Selection of population (frequently an isolate)

Collection of samples (blood samples or swabs from inside mouth)

Analysis of specific gene patterns; loci and alleles determined from expressed phenotype (as in ABO) or directly at DNA level (as in microsatellites)

Calculation of allele frequencies in population

Determination of evolutionary status using Hardy-Weinberg equilibrium formula

Null hypothesis; population in equilibrium at loci tested; no evolution

or

Population not in equilibrium; population is evolving

Evolutionary process explained by natural selection, genetic, drift, gene flow, and/or mutation

$$
\begin{array}{cccc}
 & p & + & q \\
\times & p & + & q \\
\hline
 & pq & + & q^2 \\
p^2 & + & pq & \\
\hline
p^2 & + & 2pq & + & q^2
\end{array}
$$

Mathematically, this is known as a binomial expansion and can also be shown as:

$$(p + q)(p + q) = p^2 + 2pq + q^2$$

What we have just calculated is simply:

Allele Combination	Genotype Produced	Expected Proportion in Population
Chances of A combining with A	AA	$p \times p = p^2$
Chances of A combining with a;	Aa	$p \times q =$
a combining with A	aA	$p \times q =$ $2pq$
Chances of a combining with a	aa	$q \times q = q^2$

Thus, p^2 is the frequency of the AA genotype, $2pq$ is the frequency of the Aa genotype, and q^2 is the frequency of the aa genotype, where p is the frequency of the dominant allele and q is the frequency of the recessive allele in a population.

Calculating Allele Frequencies

We can best demonstrate how geneticists use the Hardy-Weinberg formula by giving an example. Let's assume that a population contains 200 individuals, and we'll use the MN blood group locus as the gene to be measured. The two alleles of the MN locus produce two antigens (M and N) that are similar to the ABO antigens and are also located on red blood cells. Because the M and N alleles are codominant, we can ascertain everyone's phenotype by taking blood samples and testing them in a process very similar to that for ABO (see Fig. 14-2). From the phenotypes, we can then directly calculate the observed allele frequencies. So let's see what we can determine.

All 200 individuals are tested, and the observed data for the three phenotypes are as follows:

Genotype	Number of Individuals*	Percent	Number of Alleles				
			M	*N*			
MM	80	40	160	0			
MN	80	40	80	80			
NN	40	20	0	80			
Totals	200	100	240 +	160	=	400	
	Proportion		0.6 +	0.4	=	1	

---

*Each individual has two alleles, so a person who's *MM* contributes two *M* alleles to the total gene pool, a person who's *MN* contributes one *M* and one *N*, and a person who's *NN* contributes two *N* alleles. For the *MN* locus, then, 200 individuals contribute 400 alleles.

From these observed results, we can count the number of M and N alleles and thus calculate the observed allele frequencies:

p = frequency of M = 0.6
q = frequency of N = 0.4

The total frequency of the two alleles combined should always equal 1. As you can see, they do.

Next, we need to calculate the expected genotypic proportions. This calculation comes directly from the Hardy-Weinberg equilibrium formula: $p^2 + 2pq + q^2 = 1$.

p^2 = (.6)(.6) = .36

$2pq$ = 2(.6)(.4) = 2(.24) = .48

q^2 = (.4)(.4) = .16

Total 1.00

There are only three possible genotypes: MM, MN, and NN. The total of the relative proportions should equal 1. Again, as you can see, they do.

Finally, we need to compare the two sets of data—that is, the observed frequencies (what we actually found in the population) with the expected frequencies (those predicted by Hardy-Weinberg under conditions of genetic equilibrium). How do these two sets of data compare?

	Expected Frequency	Expected Number of Individuals	Observed Frequency	Actual Number of Individuals with Each Genotype
MM	.36	72	.40	80
MN	.48	96	.40	80
NN	.16	32	.20	40

We can see that although the match between observed and expected frequencies isn't perfect, it's close enough statistically to satisfy equilibrium conditions. Since our population isn't a large one, sampling may easily account for the small degree of observed differences. Our population is therefore probably in equilibrium (that is, it's not evolving at this locus).

Of course, the observed allele frequencies do sometimes vary enough from equilibrium predictions to suggest that the population isn't in equilibrium—that is, it's evolving. For example, consider the locus influencing PTC tasting. What makes PTC tasting such a useful characteristic is how easy it is to identify. Unlike blood antigens such as ABO or MN, PTC tasting can be tested by simply having subjects place a thin paper strip on their tongues. This paper contains concentrated PTC, and people either taste it or they don't. So testing is quick, inexpensive, and doesn't involve a blood test. With such an efficient means of screening subjects, we now consider a sample population of 500 individuals. The results from observing the phenotypes and calculations of expected genotypic proportions are shown in

A Closer Look

Calculating Allele Frequencies: PTC Tasting in a Hypothetical Population

For the PTC tasting trait, it's assumed that there are two alleles, *T* and *t*. Also, while dominance is displayed, it's incomplete. So it's theoretically possible to ascertain the phenotypes of heterozygotes. To simplify calculations for this example, we assume that all heterozygotes can be ascertained.

In our population of 500 individuals, we find the following observed phenotypic frequencies:

Genotype	Number of Individuals	Percent	Number of Alleles *T*	Number of Alleles *t*
TT	125	25	250	0
Tt	325	65	325	325
tt	50	10	0	100
Totals	500	100	575	425

Thus, the observed allele frequencies are

$T(p)$ = .575
$t(q)$ = .425

The expected genotypic proportions are

p^2 = (.575)(.575) = .33
$2pq$ = 2(.575)(.425) = .49
q^2 = (.425)(.425) = .18

Now we compare the observed and expected genotypic frequencies:

	Expected Frequency	Expected Number of Individuals	Observed Frequency	Actual Number of Individuals with Each Genotype
TT	.33	165	.25	125
Tt	.49	245	.65	325
tt	.18	90	.10	50

These results show considerable departures of the observed genotypic proportions from those predicted under equilibrium conditions. Both types of homozygotes (*TT* and *tt*) are less commonly observed than expected, while the heterozygote (*Tt*) is more common than expected. A statistical test (called a chi-square) can be performed to test the statistical significance of this difference. The results of this test are shown in Appendix C.

"A Closer Look: Calculating Allele Frequencies: PTC Tasting in a Hypothetical Population." You'll find additional examples of population genetics calculations in Appendix D.

Evolution in Action: Modern Human Populations

Once a population has been defined, it's possible to determine whether allele frequencies are stable (that is, in genetic equilibrium) or changing. As we've seen, the Hardy-Weinberg formula provides the tool to establish whether allele frequencies are indeed changing. But what factors cause changes in allele frequencies? There are a number of factors, including:

1. Production of new variation (that is, mutation)
2. Redistribution of variation through gene flow or genetic drift
3. Selection of "advantageous" allele combinations that promote reproductive success (that is, natural selection)

Notice that factors 1 and 2 constitute the first stage of the evolutionary process, as first emphasized by the Modern Synthesis, while factor 3 is the second stage (see Chapter 4). There's also another factor, as implied by the condition of genetic equilibrium that under idealized conditions all matings are random. Thus, an evolutionary alteration (that is, deviation from equilibrium) is called **nonrandom mating**.

Nonrandom Mating Although sexual recombination doesn't itself alter allele frequencies, any consistent bias in mating patterns can change the genotypic proportions. By affecting genotype frequencies, nonrandom mating causes deviations from Hardy-Weinberg expectations of the proportions p^2, $2pq$, and q^2. It therefore sets the stage for the action of other evolutionary factors, particularly natural selection.

A form of nonrandom mating, called assortative mating, occurs when individuals of either similar phenotypes (positive assortative mating) or dissimilar phenotypes (negative assortative mating) mate more often than expected by Hardy-Weinberg predictions. However, in the vast majority of human populations, neither factor appears to have much influence.

Inbreeding is a second type of nonrandom mating, and it can have important medical and evolutionary consequences. Inbreeding occurs when relatives mate more often than expected. Such matings will increase homozygosity, since relatives who share close ancestors will probably also share more alleles than two unrelated people would. When relatives mate, their offspring have an increased probability of inheriting two copies of potentially harmful recessive alleles from a relative (perhaps a grandparent) they share in common. Many potentially deleterious genes that are normally "masked" in heterozygous carriers may be expressed in homozygous offspring of inbred matings and therefore "exposed" to the action of natural selection. Among offspring of first-cousin matings in the United States, the risk of congenital disorders is 2.3 times greater than it is for the overall population. Matings between especially close relatives (incest) often lead to multiple genetic defects.

All societies have incest taboos that ban matings between close relatives, such as between parent and child or brother and sister. Thus these matings usually occur less frequently than predicted under random mating conditions. Whether biological factors also interact to inhibit such behavior has long been a topic of debate among anthropologists. For many social, economic, and ecological reasons, exogamy is an advantageous strategy for hunting and gathering societies. Selective pressures may also play a part, since highly inbred offspring have a greater chance of expressing a recessive genetic disorder and thereby lowering their reproductive fitness. What's

nonrandom mating Pattern of mating in which individuals choose mating partners preferentially, with mate choice based on criteria such as social status, ethnicity, or biological relationship. In nonrandom mating, an individual doesn't have an equal chance of mating with all other individuals in the group.

inbreeding A type of nonrandom mating in which relatives mate more often than predicted under random mating conditions.

more, inbreeding reduces genetic variability among offspring, potentially reducing reproductive success (Murray, 1980). In this regard, it's interesting to note that **incest avoidance** is widespread among vertebrates. Detailed studies of free-ranging chimpanzees indicate that they usually avoid incestuous matings within their family groups, although exceptions do occur (Constable et al., 2001). In fact, in most primate species, adults of one sex consistently find mating partners from groups other than the one in which they were reared (see Chapter 7). As we've seen, recognition of close kin apparently is an ability displayed by several (perhaps all) primates. Primatologists are currently investigating this aspect of our primate cousins. Apparently both biological factors (in common with other primates) and uniquely human cultural factors have interacted during hominin evolution to produce this universal behavioral pattern among contemporary societies.

Human Biocultural Evolution

We've defined *culture* as the human strategy of adaptation. Human beings live in cultural environments that are continually modified by human activity; thus evolutionary processes are understandable only within this cultural context. We've discussed at length how natural selection operates within specific environmental settings. For humans and many of our hominin ancestors, this means an environment dominated by culture. For example, the sickle-cell allele hasn't always been an important genetic factor in human populations. Before the development of agriculture, humans rarely, if ever, lived close to mosquito-breeding areas. With the spread in Africa of **slash-and-burn agriculture,** perhaps in just the last 2,000 years, penetration and clearing of tropical rain forests occurred. This deforestation created open, stagnant pools that provided prime mosquito-breeding areas in close proximity to human settlements. DNA analyses have further confirmed such a recent origin and spread of the sickle-cell allele in West Africa. A study of a population from Senegal has estimated the origin of the Hb^s mutation in this group between 2,100 and 1,250 ya (Currat et al., 2002).

So quite recently, and for the first time, malaria struck human populations with its full impact; and it became a powerful selective force. No doubt, humans attempted to adjust culturally to these circumstances, and many biological adaptations also probably came into play. The sickle-cell trait is one of these biological adaptations. But there's a definite cost involved with such an adaptation. Carriers have increased resistance to malaria and presumably higher reproductive success, though some of their offspring may be lost to the genetic disease sickle-cell anemia. Thus, there is a counterbalancing of selective forces, with an advantage for carriers only in malarial environments. (The genetic patterns of recessive traits such as sickle-cell anemia are discussed in Chapter 4.)

Following World War II, extensive DDT (dichlorodiphenyltrichloroethane) spraying by the World Health Organization began systematic control of mosquito-breeding areas in the tropics. Forty years of DDT spraying killed millions of mosquitoes; but at the same time, natural selection acted to produce several strains of DDT-resistant mosquitoes (Fig. 14-4). Accordingly, especially in the tropics, malaria is again on the rise, with up to 500 million new cases reported annually and more than 1 million people dying each year. More than 90 percent of these cases occur in sub-Saharan Africa, and most often affect children under 5 years of age.

A genetic characteristic (such as sickle-cell trait) that provides a reproductive advantage to heterozygotes in certain environments is a clear example of natural selection in action among human populations. The precise evolutionary mechanism in the sickle-cell example is called a **balanced polymorphism**. A polymorphism, as we've defined it, is a trait with more than one allele at a locus in a population. But

incest avoidance In animals, the tendency not to mate with close relatives. This tendency may be due to various social and ecological factors that keep the individuals apart. There may also be innate factors that lead to incest avoidance, but these aren't well understood.

slash-and-burn agriculture A traditional land-clearing practice involving the cutting and burning of trees and vegetation. In many areas, fields are abandoned after a few years and clearing occurs elsewhere.

balanced polymorphism The maintenance of two or more alleles in a population due to the selective advantage of the heterozygote.

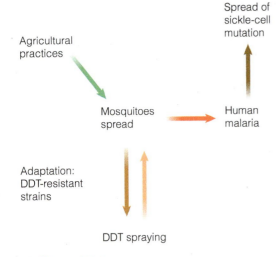

▲ **Figure 14-4**
Evolutionary interactions affecting the frequency of the sickle-cell allele.

when a harmful allele (such as the sickle-cell allele) has a higher frequency than can be accounted for by mutation alone, a more detailed evolutionary explanation is required. In this case, the additional mechanism is natural selection.

This brings us to the second part of the term. By *balanced* we mean the interaction of selective pressures operating on specific alleles in a particular environment (in this case, the sickle-cell alleles in malarial areas). Some individuals (mainly homozygous normals) will die of the infectious disease malaria. Others (homozygous recessives) will die of the inherited disease sickle-cell anemia. Thus, the individuals with the highest reproductive success are the heterozygotes who have sickle-cell trait. These heterozygotes pass both the normal allele (Hb^A) and the sickle-cell allele (Hb^S) to offspring, thus maintaining both alleles at fairly high frequencies. Since one allele in this population won't significantly increase in frequency over the other allele, this situation will become "balanced" and will persist as long as malaria continues to be a selective factor.

Lactose intolerance, which involves an individual's ability to digest milk, is another example of human biocultural evolution. In all human populations, infants and young children are able to digest milk, an obvious necessity for any young mammal. One ingredient of milk is *lactose*, a sugar that's broken down by the enzyme lactase. In most mammals, including many humans, the gene that codes for lactase production "switches off" in adolescence. Once this happens, if a person drinks fresh milk, the lactose ferments in the large intestine, leading to diarrhea and severe gastrointestinal upset. So, as you might expect, adults stop drinking fresh milk. Among many African and Asian populations (a majority of humankind today), most adults are lactose-intolerant (Table 14-1). But in other populations, including some Africans and Europeans, adults continue to produce lactase and are able to digest fresh milk. This continued production of lactase is called **lactase persistence**. Warinner and colleagues (2014) recently identified the milk protein beta-lactoglobulin in the dental calculus (plaque deposits on teeth) of ancient Europeans, providing direct evidence for the early consumption of milk during the Bronze Age (about 5000 ya).

Evidence has suggested a simple dominant mode of inheritance for lactase persistence in adults. The environment also plays a role in expression of the trait—that is, whether a person will be lactose-intolerant—since intestinal bacteria can somewhat buffer the adverse effects of drinking fresh milk. Because these bacteria increase with previous exposure, some tolerance can be acquired, even in individuals who genetically are not lactase-persistent.

Throughout most of hominin evolution, milk was unavailable after weaning; therefore, there *may* be a selective advantage to switching off the gene that codes for lactase production. So why can some adults (the majority in some populations) tolerate milk? The distribution of lactose-tolerant populations may provide an answer to this question, and it suggests a powerful cultural influence on this trait.

Europeans, who are generally lactose-tolerant, are partly descended from Middle Eastern populations. Often economically dependent on pastoralism, these groups raised cows and/or goats and probably drank considerable quantities of milk. In such a cultural environment, strong selection pressures apparently favored lactose tolerance, a trait that has been retained in modern Europeans. Genetic evidence from north-central Europe supports this interpretation. DNA analysis of both cattle and humans suggests that these species have, to some extent, influenced each other genetically. The interaction between humans and cattle resulted in cattle that produce high-quality milk and humans with the ability to digest it (Beja-Pereira

lactase persistence In adults, the continued production of lactase, the enzyme that breaks down lactose (milk sugar). This allows adults in some human populations to digest fresh milk products. The discontinued production of lactase in adults leads to lactose intolerance and the inability to digest fresh milk.

et al., 2003). In other words, more than 5,000 ya, populations of north-central Europe were selectively breeding cattle for higher milk yields. And as these populations were increasing their dependence on fresh milk, they were inadvertently selecting for the gene that produces lactase persistence.

But perhaps even more informative is the distribution of lactose tolerance in Africa, where the majority of people are lactose-intolerant. Groups such as the Fulani and Tutsi have been pastoralists for perhaps thousands of years and have much higher rates of lactase persistence than nonpastoralists (Fig. 14-5). Presumably, like their European counterparts, they've retained the ability to produce lactase because of their continued consumption of fresh milk (Powell and Tishkoff, 2003).

Molecular evidence has supported this hypothesis, showing a similar coevolution of humans and cattle in East Africa (Tishkoff et al., 2007). The pattern of DNA mutations (SNPs) in Africa is different from that seen in Europe, strongly suggesting that lactase persistence has evolved independently in the two regions. In fact, the data show that lactase persistence has evolved several times just in East Africa. The importance of cattle domestication in providing milk for human groups was clearly a cultural and dietary shift of major importance. As humans selectively bred cattle to produce more and higher-quality milk, they promoted fairly rapid evolution in these animals. At the same time, humans in different areas coevolved through natural selection as allele frequencies shifted to produce higher frequencies of lactase persistence.

As we've seen, the geographical distribution of lactase persistence is related to a history of cultural dependence on fresh milk products. There are, however, some populations that rely on dairying but don't have high rates of lactase persistence (Fig. 14-6). It's been suggested that such groups have traditionally consumed their milk in the form of cheese and yogurt, in which the lactose has been broken down by bacterial action.

Table 14-1 | Frequencies of Lactase Persistence

Population Group	Percent
U.S. whites	81–98
Swedes and Danes	>90
Swiss	88
U.S. blacks	23–30
Ibos	1
Bantu	10
Fulani	50
Chinese	1
Thais	1
Asian Americans	<5
Native Americans	85

Source: Lerner and Libby, 1976, Tishkoff et al., 2007.

◀ **Figure 14-5**
Fulani cattle herder with his cattle.

▶ **Figure 14-6**

Natives of Mongolia rely heavily on milk products from goats and sheep but consume these foods mostly in the form of cheese and yogurt.

Michael S Yamashita/Documentary Value/Corbis

The interaction of human cultural environments and changes in lactose tolerance in human populations is another example of biocultural evolution. In the last few thousand years, cultural factors have initiated specific evolutionary changes in human groups. Such cultural factors have probably influenced the course of human evolution for at least 3 million years, and today they are of paramount importance.

How Do We Know?

Forensic anthropologists are routinely asked by law enforcement to assess various biological parameters from unidentified skeletal remains, such as a decedent's sex, age at death, stature, and ancestry. Although each of these areas has a long history of study within physical anthropology, none has been as controversial as ancestry estimation. Craniofacial shape is highly heritable and ultimately reflects geographically patterned genetic variation. Early physical anthropologists focused on identifying "race" from the skull, primarily using craniofacial morphology and nonmetric traits of the skull (for example, nasal bone shape, eye orbit shape, degree of projection of the midfacial region). These determinations were typically

made by comparing an unknown skull with stereotypical skull "types" or by comparing nonmetric traits to very small reference samples of known geographical origin. The 1960s marked the beginning of the shift away from a racial typology approach toward the study of skeletal variation as a continuum. Today, most forensic anthropologists have abandoned typological approaches and accept that race is not a meaningful biological construct. In fact, there is no single skeletal trait or measurement that can accurately separate out individuals into meaningful geographical types. Over the past few decades, forensic anthropologists have increasingly focused on cranial measurements and morphoscopic traits (traits that can be scored based on their expression,

such as the anterior nasal spine at the base of the nasal aperture). These data can be compared against datasets of individuals of known ancestry using computer software programs, such as Fordisc (Jantz and Ousley, 2005). These approaches appropriately place ancestry assessment within a statistical framework and also recognize that estimations reflect an individual's ultimate genetic origin. For example, an unknown skull may be classified as being of African, European, or Asian ancestry or classified as an even smaller subgroup within these broad categories (depending on which reference samples are represented in the database). Often, ancestry assessments translate to social or ethnic categories, which may provide investigative leads to law enforcement agencies charged with identifying victims. When used cautiously (and recognizing when classification statistics are too low to make an estimation), forensic anthropologists have been able to produce moderate to high levels of success in correctly assessing ancestry from the skeleton.

What Do You Think?

Many social scientists have criticized forensic anthropologists for continuing to assess ancestry from the skeleton. Some are also equally critical of genetic approaches used to estimate ancestry. Do you think ancestry estimation can provide meaningful information to law enforcement? In other words, do you think it has validity, or should it be avoided altogether? Can you think of some areas of confusion that forensic anthropologists may encounter when assessing ancestry? ■

Summary of Main Topics

- Physically visible traits, traditionally used in attempts to classify humans into clearly defined groups ("races"), have emphasized such features as skin color, hair color, hair form, head shape, and nose shape. However, all of these physical characteristics are not only influenced by several genetic loci but are also modified by the environment. As a result, these traditional markers of race aren't reliable indicators of genetic relationships, and they're not biologically useful in depicting patterns of human diversity.

- Since the middle of the twentieth century, more precise techniques have allowed a far better understanding of actual patterns of human variation, beginning with information obtained from the phenotypic expression of Mendelian traits such as blood groups. Population genetics analyses of several of these genetic polymorphisms proved useful in showing broad patterns, such as the high degree of within-population variation and the relatively minor amount of between-population variation. Since the 1990s, the development and rapid application of comparative genomics have drastically expanded genetic data. These powerful new tools allow evaluation of human population variation using thousands (or hundreds of thousands) of precisely defined DNA sequences. Such population studies are aimed at reconstructing the microevolutionary population history of our species and understanding the varied roles of natural selection, genetic drift, gene flow, and mutation.

- The field of population genetics has provided a means from which to identify evidence of a change in allele frequency from one generation to the next (that is, evolutionary change). The Hardy-Weinberg formula provides an important tool to establish whether allele frequencies are indeed changing.

- For humans, of course, culture also plays a crucial evolutionary role. Interacting with biological influences, these factors define the distinctive biocultural nature of human evolution. Two excellent examples of recent human biocultural evolution relate to resistance to malaria (involving the sickle-cell allele) and lactase persistence.

Critical Thinking Questions

1. Imagine you're with a group of friends discussing human diversity and the number of races. One friend says there are three clearly defined races, a second says five, while the third isn't sure. Would you agree with any of them? Why or why not?

2. For the same group of friends mentioned in question 1 (none of whom have had a course in biological anthropology), how would you explain how scientific knowledge fits (or doesn't fit) with their preconceived notions about human races?

3. Explain how the concept of race has developed in the Western world. How have current genetic studies changed this view? How is the biological construct of race different from the social construct of race?

4. Explain how modern genetic studies can contribute to our understanding of biological variation in humans. Be as specific as possible.

CONNECTIONS

Modern human variation is best understood by examining similarities and differences in DNA among populations.

Through natural selection, humans have and continue to adapt to environmental factors including solar radiation, cold, altitude, and, most importantly, infectious disease.

Human development and adaptation are best understood from an evolutionary perspective.

Modern Human Biology: Patterns of Adaptation

15

The Adaptive Significance of Human Variation

Solar Radiation and Skin Color

The Thermal Environment

High Altitude

Infectious Disease

The Continuing Impact of Infectious Disease

Human Skeletal Biology: What Bones Can Tell Us about Ancient Diseases, Trauma, and Lifestyles

Evidence of Prehistoric Diseases

Reconstruction of Prehistoric Behavioral Patterns

Student Learning Objectives After studying the material in this chapter, you should be able to:

▶ Discuss the role of natural selection in influencing skin pigmentation, body shape, and limb proportions, as well as human adaptive responses to altitude, heat, and cold.

▶ Explain how infectious disease became a selective force in human evolution. You should be able to give examples.

▶ Discuss why infectious diseases continue to present a major health crisis to modern populations across the world.

▶ Discuss in general what pathological conditions skeletal biologists have studied in archaeological human skeletons.

I n previous chapters, we explored the genetic bases for biological variation within and between human populations. We discussed how, as a species, humans are remarkably genetically uniform compared with our closest primate relatives. We've also placed these discussions within an evolutionary framework, emphasizing the roles of natural selection and genetic drift in human evolution. With this foundation, we can turn our attention to some of the many challenges we have faced through our evolutionary journey and consider some of the ways we've met these challenges as a species, as populations, and as individuals.

Early humans migrated out of Africa some 200,000 to 100,000 ya, and we now permanently inhabit the entire planet except for the oceans, the highest mountain peaks, and Antarctica. But as human populations spread over the earth, they had to cope with variations in ultraviolet (UV) radiation, altitude, temperature, humidity, diet, and infectious diseases. All of these factors, plus the fact that populations were separated from one another by enormous distances, have combined to produce many forms of adaptation in our species.

The Adaptive Significance of Human Variation

As you know, when biological anthropologists study human variation, they consider all evolutionary factors. But natural selection favoring adaptive traits was the most important mechanism that produced the variation we see today. We must also bear in mind that to accommodate differences in climate, terrain, and available resources, humans had to adopt lifestyles that differed with regard to technology and diet. As time passed, and especially after the domestication of plants and animals beginning around 14,000 ya, cultural changes, including dietary practices, exerted an even greater degree of selective pressure. Thus, as populational differences in lactose tolerance demonstrate, the interaction between culture and biology became ever more important to human adaptive responses, and this interaction was responsible for changes in the frequencies of many alleles. Since the sequencing of the human genome in 2003, geneticists, armed with an array of new technologies, have been looking at the genes that govern adaptive traits in many populations. Specifically, they've been focusing on single nucleotide polymorphisms, or SNPs, studying how differences in single DNA bases alter gene action and how their frequencies vary between populations. Within the next few years, our understanding of many aspects of human adaptation will increase dramatically, owing to advances in genetic research that will allow the testing not only of long-held hypotheses but also of new ones.

To survive, all organisms need to maintain the normal functions of internal organs, tissues, and cells. What's more, they must accomplish this task in the context of an ever-changing environment. Even during the course of a single, seemingly uneventful day, there are numerous fluctuations in temperature, wind, solar radiation, humidity, and so on. Physical activity also results in physiological **stress**. The body must accommodate all these changes in order to maintain internal constancy, or **homeostasis**, and all life forms have evolved physiological mechanisms that, within limits, achieve this goal.

Physiological responses to environmental change are influenced by genetic factors. We've already defined adaptation as a response to environmental conditions in populations and individuals. In a broader sense, *adaptation* refers to long-term evolutionary (that is, genetic) changes that characterize all individuals within a population or species.

Examples of long-term adaptations in humans include physiological responses to heat (sweating) or excessive levels of UV light (deeply pigmented skin near the equator). These characteristics are the results of evolutionary change in our species, and they don't vary because of short-term environmental change. For example, the ability to sweat isn't lost in people who spend their lives in predominantly cool areas. Likewise, individuals born with dark skin won't become pale, even if they're never exposed to sunlight.

Acclimatization is another kind of physiological response to changing environmental conditions in individuals. Most forms of acclimatization are temporary and last only until environmental conditions return to their former state. The physiological responses to environmental stressors are at least partially influenced by

stress In a physiological context, any factor that acts to disrupt homeostasis; more precisely, the body's response to any factor that threatens its ability to maintain homeostasis.

homeostasis A condition of balance, or stability, within a biological system, maintained by the interaction of physiological mechanisms that compensate for changes (both external and internal).

acclimatization Physiological responses to changes in the environment that occur during an individual's lifetime. Such responses may be temporary or permanent, depending on the duration of the environmental change and when in the individual's life it occurs. The capacity for acclimatization may typify an entire population or species, and because it's under genetic influence, it's subject to evolutionary factors such as natural selection and genetic drift.

genetic factors, and also are affected by the duration and severity of the exposure, technological buffers (such as shelter or clothing), individual behavior, weight, and overall body size.

The simplest form of acclimatization is a temporary and rapid adjustment to an environmental change (for example, tanning). Another example is one you may not know about although you've probably experienced it. This is the rapid increase in hemoglobin production that occurs in low-altitude residents who travel to higher elevations. (It's happened in your own body if you've spent a few days in the mountains.) In both of these examples, the physiological changes are temporary. Tans fade when exposure to sunlight is reduced, and hemoglobin production drops to original levels after returning to lower elevations.

Another type of acclimatization, called developmental acclimatization, results from exposure to an environmental challenge during growth and development. Because this kind of acclimatization is incorporated into an individual's physiology, it isn't reversible. Certain physiological responses seen in lifelong residents of high altitude are examples of developmental acclimatization.

In this section, we present some of the many examples of how humans respond to environmental challenges. Some of these examples describe adaptations that characterize our entire species; others are shared by most or all members of only certain populations.

Solar Radiation and Skin Color

For many years, skin color has been cited as an example of adaptation through natural selection in humans. In general, pigmentation in indigenous populations prior to European contact (beginning around A.D. 1500) followed a particular geographical distribution, especially in the Old World. This pattern pretty much holds true today. As Figure 15-1 shows, populations with the most pigmentation are found in the tropics, while lighter skin color is associated with more northern latitudes, especially among the long-term inhabitants of northwestern Europe.

▼ **Figure 15-1**

Geographical distribution of skin color in indigenous human populations. (After Biasutti, 1959.)

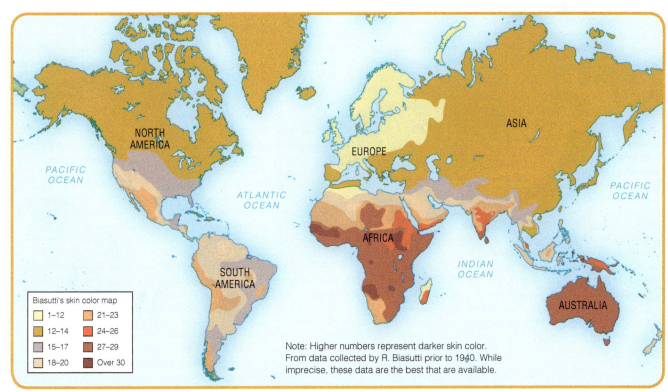

Biasutti's skin color map

1–12	21–23
12–14	24–26
15–17	27–29
18–20	Over 30

Note: Higher numbers represent darker skin color. From data collected by R. Biasutti prior to 1940. While imprecise, these data are the best that are available.

Three substances influence skin color: hemoglobin, the protein carotene, and, most important, the pigment melanin. Melanin is a granular substance produced by cells called melanocytes, located in the outer layer of the skin (Fig. 15-2). Melanin is extremely important because it acts as a built-in sunscreen by absorbing potentially dangerous ultraviolet (UV) rays that are present but not visible in sunlight. So melanin protects us from overexposure to UV radiation, which frequently causes genetic mutations in skin cells. These mutations can lead to skin cancer, which, if left untreated, can eventually spread to other organs and even cause death (see "A Closer Look: Skin Cancer and UV Radiation").

As mentioned earlier, exposure to sunlight triggers a protective mechanism in the form of tanning, the result of a temporary increase in melanin production (acclimatization). This response occurs in all humans except albinos, who carry a genetic mutation that prevents their melanocytes from producing melanin. But even people who do produce melanin differ in their ability to tan. For instance, in all populations, women tend not to tan as deeply as men. More importantly, however, people of northern European descent tend to have very fair skin, blue eyes, and light hair. Their cells produce only small amounts of melanin and, when exposed to sunlight, they have almost no ability to increase production. But in areas closest to the equator (the tropics), where the sun's rays are most direct and where exposure to UV light is most intense and constant, natural selection has favored

▼ **Figure 15-2**
Ultraviolet rays penetrate the skin and can eventually damage DNA within skin cells. The three major types of cells that can be affected are squamous cells, basal cells, and melanocytes.

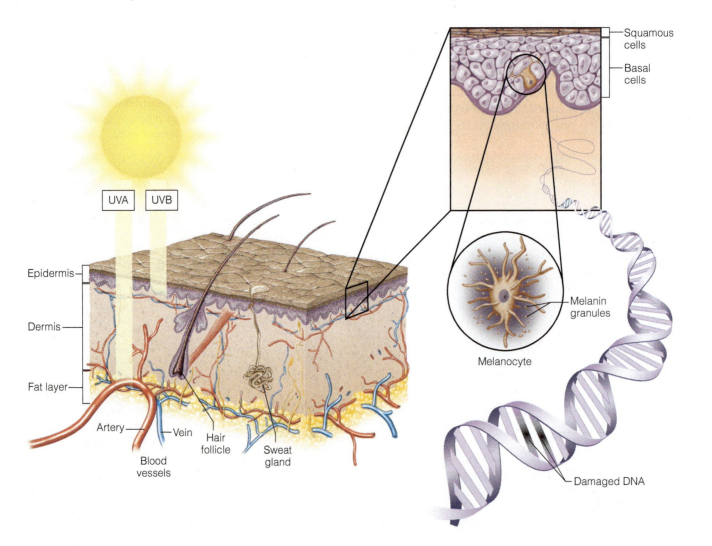

deeply pigmented skin. In considering the cancer-causing effects of UV radiation from an evolutionary perspective, keep in mind these three points:

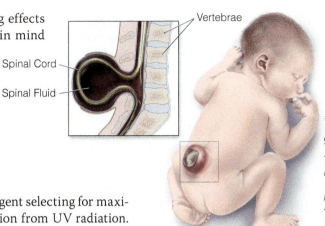

1. Early hominins lived in the tropics, where solar radiation is more intense than in temperate areas to the north and south.
2. Unlike most modern city dwellers, early hominins were constantly exposed to solar radiation.
3. Early hominins likely didn't wear protective clothing.

Under these conditions, UV radiation was a powerful agent selecting for maximum levels of melanin production as a means of protection from UV radiation. Physical anthropologists have long considered this protection to be very important, because UV radiation is the most common cause of skin cancer. There's an important objection to this hypothesis, however. As we mentioned in Chapter 4, natural selection can act only on traits that affect reproduction. Because cancers tend to occur later in life, after people have had their children, it should theoretically be difficult for selection to act effectively against a factor that might facilitate the development of cancer. This is probably true in general, but in one African study it was shown that all albinos in dark-skinned populations of Nigeria and Tanzania had either precancerous lesions or skin cancer by the age of 20 (Robins, 1991). This evidence suggests that in early hominins of reproductive age, less pigmented skin could potentially have reduced individual reproductive fitness in regions of intense sunlight.

However, Jablonski (1992) and Jablonski and Chaplin (2000, 2010) disagree that skin cancer was the most important factor; they have provided convincing evidence for another, probably more important explanation for heavily pigmented skin in the tropics. This explanation concerns the degradation of folate by UV radiation. Folate is a B vitamin that is not stored in the body and must be replenished through dietary sources such as leafy green vegetables and certain fruits. Adequate levels of folate are required for cell division, and this is especially important during embryonic and fetal development, when cell division is rapid and ongoing. In pregnant women, insufficient levels of folate are associated with numerous fetal developmental disorders, including **neural tube** defects such as **spina bifida** (Fig. 15-3). The consequences of severe neural tube defects can include pain, infection, paralysis, and even failure of the brain to develop. Given the importance of folate to many processes related to reproduction, it's clear that maintaining adequate levels of this vitamin contributes to individual reproductive fitness.

Studies have shown that UV radiation rapidly depletes serum folate levels in both laboratory animals and light-skinned people. These findings have implications for pregnant women, children, and the evolution of dark skin in early hominins. Jablonski (1992) has proposed that the earliest hominins may have had light skin covered with dark hair, as seen in chimpanzees and gorillas (who have darker skin on exposed body parts, such as the face and hands). But as loss of body hair occurred in hominins, dark skin evolved rather rapidly as a protective response to the damaging effects of UV radiation on folate.

The maintenance of sufficient levels of folate and, perhaps to a lesser degree, the occurrence of skin cancer have no doubt been selective agents that have favored dark skin in populations living where UV radiation is most intense. Therefore we have good explanations for darker skin in the tropics. But what about less pigmented skin? Why do indigenous populations in higher latitudes, farther from the equator, have lighter skin? There are several closely related hypotheses, and recent studies have added strength to these arguments.

▲ **Figure 15-3**

Spina bifida occurs when the back of the vertebral column (spine) fails to close during embryonic development. It ranges from mild to lethal. In this illustration the last two lumbar vertebrae failed to fuse and the spinal cord has protruded through the opening.

neural tube In early embryonic development, the anatomical structure that develops to form the brain and spinal cord.

spina bifida A condition in which one or more of the vertebral arches fail to fuse and form a protective barrier around the spinal cord.

As hominins migrated out of Africa and into Asia and Europe, they faced new selective pressures. In particular, those populations that eventually occupied northern Europe encountered cold temperatures and cloudy skies, frequently during summer as well as winter. Winter also meant many fewer hours of daylight, and with the sun well to the south, solar radiation was very indirect. What's more, people in these areas wore animal skins and other types of clothing, which blocked the sun's rays. For some time, researchers proposed that because of reduced exposure to sunlight, the advantages of deeply pigmented skin in the tropics no longer applied, and selection for melanin production may have been relaxed.

However, relaxed selection for dark skin doesn't adequately explain the very depigmented skin seen in some northern Europeans. In fact, natural selection appears to have acted very rapidly against darker skin as humans moved to northern latitudes. This is because the need for a physiological UV filter was outweighed by another extremely important biological necessity, the production of vitamin D. The theory concerning the role of vitamin D is called the *vitamin D hypothesis*.

Since the early twentieth century, scientists have known that vitamin D is essential for the mineralization and normal growth of bones during infancy and childhood because it enables the body to absorb calcium (the major source of bone mineral) from dietary sources. Vitamin D is also required for the continued mineralization of bones in adults. Many foods, including fish oils, egg yolk, butter, cream, and liver, are good sources of vitamin D. But the body's primary source of vitamin D is its own ability to synthesize it through the interaction of UV radiation and a form of cholesterol found in skin cells. Therefore adequate exposure to sunlight is essential to normal bone growth.

Insufficient amounts of vitamin D during childhood result in rickets, a condition that leads to skeletal deformities, especially in the weight-bearing bones of the legs and pelvis. Thus, people with rickets frequently have bowed legs and pelvic deformities (Fig. 15-4). Pelvic deformities are of particular concern for pregnant women because they can lead to a narrowing of the birth canal. Without surgical intervention, both the mother and her infant can die during childbirth, thus allowing natural selection to act powerfully in favor of any mechanism that provides proper bone mineralization.

During the latter decades of the nineteenth century in the United States, African American inhabitants of northern cities suffered a higher incidence of rickets than whites. (The solution to this problem was fairly simple: the supplementation of vitamin D–fortified milk.) Another example is seen in Britain, where darker-skinned East Indians and Pakistanis show a higher incidence of rickets than do people with lighter skin (Molnar, 1983; Ashraf and Mughal, 2002).

In addition to its role in bone mineralization, vitamin D has many other critical functions. In the body, vitamin D is converted to a different molecule called 1,25D, which can attach directly to DNA, and act to regulate more than 1,000 different genes (Tavera-Mendoza and White, 2007). Some of these genes are involved in cell replication, and because 1,25D influences this activity, it appears to provide some protection against certain cancers, especially prostate and colon cancer (Lin and White, 2004). (Cancer is caused by uncontrolled cell replication.) Moreover, 1,25D reduces inflammation and may eventually be used as a basis for treating certain diseases, including multiple sclerosis (Tavera-Mendoza and White, 2007).

Other genes influenced by 1,25D produce proteins that act as natural antibiotics to kill certain bacteria and viruses, one of which is *Mycobacterium tuberculosis* (*M. tuberculosis*), the bacterium that causes tuberculosis (TB). Liu et al. (2006) demonstrated how 1,25D is involved in the destruction of *M. tuberculosis* in infected cells. The fact that exposure to UV radiation is necessary for vitamin D synthesis

▼ **Figure 15-4**

An X-ray of a child with rickets. Note that the leg bones have not properly mineralized due to lack of vitamin D. Thus, they are bowed because they are not strong enough to support the child's body weight.

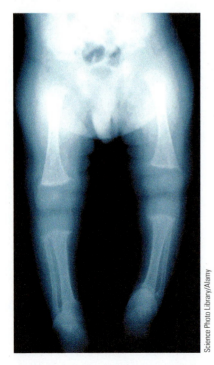

Science Photo Library/Alamy

probably explains why, in the early twentieth century, TB patients often improved after being sent to sanitariums in sunny locations.

The influence of latitude and skin pigmentation on levels of 1,25D in the body has been demonstrated by epidemiological studies of modern populations. For example, one study revealed that 92 percent of more than 400 girls in several northern European countries were severely deficient in 1,25D during the winter months. Also, the fact that African Americans appear to have about half the amount of 1,25D seen in European Americans illustrates the role of increased pigmentation in reducing vitamin D levels in more northern latitudes (Tavera-Mendoza and White, 2007). This fact is significant because African Americans have a higher incidence of TB than European Americans (Liu et al., 2006).

As you can see, vitamin D is an immensely important factor in the body's response to a number of conditions, many of which influence reproductive success. This evidence substantially supports the vitamin D hypothesis and argues for strong and rapid positive selection for lighter skin in northern latitudes. Furthermore, the vitamin D evidence is strongly supported by recent genetic studies.

At least 100 genes are thought to be involved in pigmentation in vertebrates. One of the more important of these genes, referred to as *MC1R*, affects coloration in all mammals. The human version of this gene has at least 30 alleles, some of which are associated with red hair combined with fair skin and a tendency to freckle (Lin and Fisher, 2007). As we mentioned in Chapter 13, research on Neandertal DNA has revealed that some Neandertals probably had red hair and fair skin. Research on Neandertal DNA has shown that some Neandertals carried an *MC1R* allele that reduces the amount of pigment in skin and hair, but it's *not* an allele that occurs in modern humans. Therefore less pigmented skin developed in two hominin species but through different mutations in the same gene. This fact strongly reinforces the hypothesis that there is a significant selective advantage to having lighter skin in northern latitudes.

Lastly, evidence for the importance of vitamin D is provided by the recent discovery of yet another gene, called *SCL24A5*, which we'll refer to simply as *SCL* (Lamason et al., 2005). This gene and its effects on pigmentation were first discovered in zebrafish, and just to emphasize (yet again) the concept of biological continuity or connections between species, we'll point out that approximately 68 percent of the sequences of DNA bases in the human and zebrafish *SCL* genes are the same (Balter, 2007).

Like *MC1R*, the *SCL* gene is involved in melanin production. This gene has two primary alleles that differ by one single base substitution; that is, one allele arose as a point mutation. The original form (allele) of the gene is present in 93 to 100 percent of Africans, Native Americans, and East Asians. However, and most importantly, virtually 100 percent of Europeans and European Americans have the more recent (mutated) allele that inhibits melanin production. These frequencies provide yet more compelling evidence of very strong selection for lighter skin in northern latitudes. In fact, it appears that natural selection favored the mutated allele to the point that it became the only *SCL* allele in northern European populations.

But there's a question that has yet to be answered. (Actually, there are several questions, but we'll mention only one.) In East Asians, the frequency of the original melanin-producing allele is the same as in sub-Saharan Africans, yet on average, skin color in East Asians is fairly light. Lamason and colleagues (2005) argue that this means that in East Asian populations, there are other, as yet unidentified genes that interact with the *SCL* locus to reduce skin pigmentation. Certainly, several other genes that contribute to skin pigmentation have been identified, but none has yet been shown to have the same degree of variation between populations.

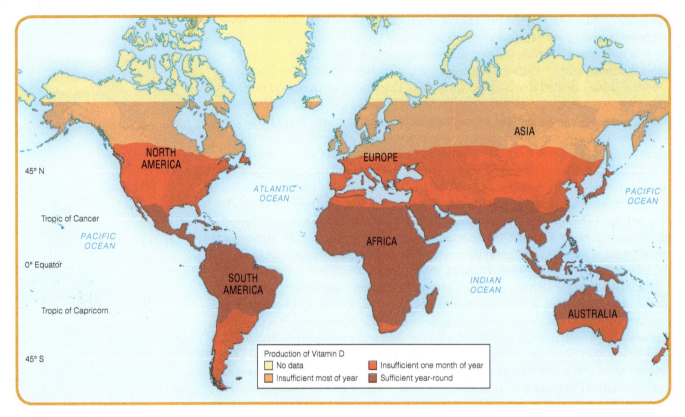

▲ Figure 15-5

Populations indigenous to the tropics (brown band) receive enough UV radiation for vitamin D synthesis year-round. The dark orange band shows areas where people with moderately pigmented skin don't receive enough UV light for vitamin D synthesis for one month of the year. The light orange band shows areas where even light skin doesn't receive enough UV light for vitamin D synthesis during most of the year. (Adapted from Jablonski and Chaplin, 2000, 2002.)

Jablonski and Chaplin (2000) have looked at the potential for vitamin D synthesis in people of different skin color based on the yearly average UV radiation at various latitudes (Fig. 15-5). Their conclusions support the vitamin D hypothesis to the point of stating that the requirement of vitamin D synthesis in northern latitudes was as important to natural selection as the need for protection from UV radiation in tropical regions.

Except for a person's sex, more social importance has been attached to skin color than to any other single human biological trait. But there's absolutely no valid reason for this. Aside from its adaptive significance relative to UV radiation, skin color is no more important physiologically than many other biological characteristics. But from an evolutionary perspective, skin color provides an outstanding example of how the forces of natural selection have produced geographically patterned variation as the result of two conflicting selective forces: the need for protection from overexposure to UV radiation on the one hand and the need for adequate UV exposure for vitamin D synthesis on the other.

The Thermal Environment

Mammals and birds have evolved complex mechanisms to maintain a constant internal body temperature. While reptiles must rely on exposure to external heat sources to raise body temperature and energy levels, mammals and birds have physiological mechanisms that, within certain limits, increase or reduce the loss of body heat. The optimum body temperature for normal cellular functions is species-specific, and for humans, it's approximately 98.6°F.

People are found in a wide variety of habitats, with thermal environments ranging from over 120°F (for example, Danakil Desert, Ethiopia) to lower than −60°F (for example, Oymyakon, Russia). In such extremes, particularly cold, human life would not be possible without cultural innovations. But even accounting for the artificial environments we live in, such external conditions expose the human body to enormous physiological stress.

Response to Heat   All available evidence suggests that the earliest hominins evolved in the warm-to-hot woodlands and savannas of East Africa. The fact that humans cope better with heat, especially dry heat, than they do with cold is testimony to the long-term adaptations to heat that evolved in our ancestors.

In humans as well as some other species such as horses, sweat glands are distributed throughout the skin. This wide distribution of sweat glands makes it possible to lose heat at the body's surface through **evaporative cooling**, a mechanism that has evolved to the greatest degree in humans. In fact, perspiration is the most important factor in heat dissipation in humans.

The capacity to dissipate heat by sweating is seen in all human populations to an almost equal degree, with the average number of sweat glands per individual (approximately 1.6 million) being fairly constant. However, there is some variation, since people who are not generally exposed to hot conditions do experience a period of acclimatization that initially involves significantly increased perspiration rates (Frisancho, 1993). An additional factor that enhances the cooling effects of sweating is increased exposure of the skin through reduced amounts of body hair. We don't know when in our evolutionary history we began to lose body hair, but it represents a species-wide adaptation (although, on average, some populations have more body hair than others).

Heat reduction through evaporation can be expensive, and indeed dangerous, because of the loss of water and electrolytes, such as sodium and chloride. For example, a person engaged in heavy work in high heat can lose up to 3 liters of water per hour. To appreciate the importance of this fact, consider that losing 1 liter of water is approximately equivalent to losing 1.5 percent of total body weight, and losing 10 percent of body weight can be life threatening. Thus water must be continuously replaced when you exercise on a hot day.

Basically, there are two types of heat, arid and humid. Arid environments, such as those of the southwestern United States, the Middle East, and parts of Africa, are characterized by high temperatures, wind, and low precipitation levels. Humid heat occurs in regions with a great deal of vegetation and precipitation, conditions found in the eastern and southern United States, parts of Europe, and much of the tropics. Because the increased water vapor in humid climates inhibits the evaporation of sweat on the skin's surface, humans adjust much more readily to dry heat. In fact, people exercising in dry heat may be unaware that they're sweating because the perspiration evaporates as soon as it reaches the skin's surface. While rapid evaporation increases comfort, it can lead to dehydration. Therefore in dry heat, it's important to keep drinking water, even if you aren't particularly thirsty.

Another mechanism for radiating body heat is vasodilation, which occurs when capillaries near the skin's surface widen to increase blood flow to the skin. The visible effect of **vasodilation** is flushing, or increased redness and warming of the skin, particularly of the face. But the physiological effect is to permit heat, carried by the blood from the interior of the body, to be emitted from the skin's surface to the surrounding air. (Some drugs, including alcohol, also produce vasodilation; this accounts for the increased redness and warmth of the face in some people after a couple of alcoholic drinks.)

Body size and proportions are also important in regulating body temperature. In fact, there seems to be a general relationship between climate and body size and shape in birds and mammals. In general, within a species, body size (weight) increases as distance from the equator increases (higher latitude correlates with lower temperature). In humans, this relationship holds up fairly well, but there are many exceptions.

evaporative cooling   A physiological mechanism that helps prevent the body from overheating. It occurs when perspiration is produced from sweat glands and then evaporates from the surface of the skin.

vasodilation   Expansion of blood vessels, permitting increased blood flow to the skin. Vasodilation permits warming of the skin and facilitates radiation of warmth as a means of cooling. Vasodilation is an involuntary response to warm temperatures, various drugs, and even emotional states (blushing).

A Closer Look Skin Cancer and UV Radiation

Even though we know we can't live without it, most people tend to take their skin for granted. The many functions of this complex organ (and skin is an organ) are vital to life. Yet most of us thoughtlessly expose our skin to any number of environmental assaults and especially abuse it with overexposure to the sun, practically to the point of charbroiling. For these reasons, we think it's appropriate here to examine a little more closely this watertight, evolutionary achievement that permits us to live on land, just as it allowed some vertebrates to leave the oceans several hundred million years ago.

Skin is composed of two layers, the epidermis and, just beneath it, the dermis (see Fig. 15-2). The upper portion of the epidermis is made up of flattened, somewhat overlapping squamous (scalelike) cells. Beneath these cells, near the base of the epidermis, are several layers of round basal cells. Interspersed within the basal cells are still two other cell types: melanocytes, which produce melanin, and keratinocytes, which are involved in vitamin D synthesis.

Skin cells are continuously produced at the base of the epidermis through mitosis. As they mature, they migrate to the surface, becoming flattened and avascular; that is, they have no direct blood supply. Approximately one month after forming, skin cells die in a process of genetically directed cellular suicide. The results of this suicidal act are the little white flakes people with dry skin are uncomfortably aware of. (Incidentally, dead skin cells are a major component of common household dust.)

The dermis is composed of connective tissue and many structures, including blood vessels, lymphatic vessels, sweat glands, oil glands, and hair follicles. Together, the epidermis and dermis allow the body to retain fluid, help regulate body temperature, synthesize a number of essential substances, and provide protection from ultraviolet (UV) radiation.

There are three main types of UV radiation, but here we're concerned with only two: UVA and UVB. UVA has the longest wavelength and can penetrate through to the bottom of the dermis, while the medium-length UVB waves usually penetrate only to the basal layer of the epidermis (see Fig. 15-2).

The stimulation of vitamin D production by UVB waves is the only benefit we get from exposure to UV radiation. Following a sunburn, both UVB and UVA rays cause short-term suppression of the immune system. But because UVB is directly absorbed by the DNA within cells, it can potentially cause genetic damage, and this damage can lead to skin cancer.

You know that cancers are tumorous growths that invade organs, a process that often results in death, even after treatment. But you may not know that a cell becomes cancerous when a carcinogenic agent, such as UV radiation, damages its DNA, and some DNA segments are more susceptible than others. This damage allows the affected cell to divide uncontrollably. Each subsequent generation of cells receives the mutant DNA, and with it, the potential to divide indefinitely. Eventually, cancer cells form a mass that invades other tissues. They can also break away from the original tumor and travel through the circulatory or lymphatic system to other parts of the body, where they establish themselves and continue to divide. For example, cells from lung tumors (frequently caused by carcinogenic agents in tobacco) can travel to the brain or parts of the skeleton and develop tumors in these new sites before the lung tumor is even detectable. (Former Beatle George Harrison died of brain cancer that had spread from his lungs. It's probably no coincidence that he was a heavy smoker when he was young.)

All three types of cells in the epidermis are susceptible to cancerous changes. The most common form of skin cancer is basal cell carcinoma (BCC), which affects about 800,000 people per year in the United States. Fortunately BCCs are slow growing and, if detected early, can be successfully removed before they spread. They can appear as a raised lump and be uncolored, red-brown, or black (Fig. 1a).

Two rules that pertain to the relationship between body size, body proportions, and climate are *Bergmann's rule* and *Allen's rule*.

1. *Bergmann's rule concerns the relationship of body mass or volume to surface area.* Among mammals, body size tends to be greater in populations that live in colder climates. This is because as mass increases, the relative amount of surface area decreases proportionately. Since heat is lost at the surface, it follows that increased mass allows for greater heat retention and reduced heat loss. (Remember our discussion of basal metabolic rate and body size in Chapter 7.)
2. *Allen's rule concerns the shape of the body, especially appendages.* In colder climates, shorter appendages, with increased mass-to-surface ratios, are adaptive because they're more effective at preventing heat loss. Conversely, longer

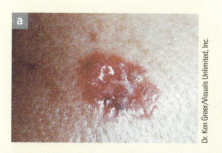
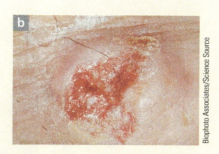
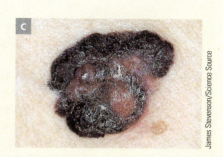

▲ **Figure 1**

(**a**) Basal cell carcinoma. (**b**) Squamous cell carcinoma. (**c**) Malignant melanoma.

Squamous cell carcinoma (SCC) is the second most common skin cancer (Fig. 1b). These cancers grow faster than BCCs, but they're also amenable to treatment if detected reasonably early. They usually appear as firm pinkish lesions and may spread rapidly on skin exposed to sunlight.

The third form is malignant melanoma, a cancer of the melanocytes. Melanoma is thought to be caused by UVA radiation and accounts for only about 4 percent of all skin cancers. But while it's the least common of the three, melanoma is the fastest growing and the deadliest, killing 30 to 40 percent of affected people. Melanoma looks like an irregularly shaped, very dark or black mole (Fig. 1c). In fact, it may be a mole that has changed because some of its cells have been damaged. It's extremely important to notice any changes in a mole or the appearance of a new dark, perhaps roughened spot on the skin and have it examined as soon as possible. If a melanoma is less than a millimeter deep, it can be removed before it spreads. But if it has progressed into the dermis, it's likely that it has already spread to other tissues.

Brash and colleagues (1991) and Ziegler and colleagues (1994) determined that the underlying genetic factor in most nonmelanoma skin cancers is a mutation of a gene called *p53* located on chromosome 17. This gene produces the protein *p53*, which prevents any cell (not just skin cells) with damaged DNA from dividing until the damage is repaired. In addition, if the damage to a cell's DNA is too severe to repair, the *p53* protein can cause the cell to die. Thus, *p53* is what's known as a tumor suppressor gene (Vogelstein et al., 2000).

Unfortunately, the *p53* gene is itself susceptible to mutation, and when certain mutations occur, it can no longer prevent cancer cells from dividing. Luckily, there are other tumor suppressor genes. In fact, damaged *p53* genes don't appear to be involved in melanoma. Instead, a UV-induced mutation in another tumor suppressor gene on chromosome 9 appears to be the culprit.

BCCs and SCCs tend to appear in middle age, long after childhood and adolescence, when the underlying genetic damage occurred. If you've had even one serious sunburn in your life, your odds of developing one of the nonmelanoma skin cancers are dramatically increased. Malignant melanomas can occur at any age, although the DNA damage can precede the development of cancer by several years. The best advice is not to take the threat of skin cancer lightly and to avoid overexposing your skin to the sun. Wear a hat and a broad-based sun block that will filter out both UVA and UVB rays. In other words, do your best to protect your tumor suppressor genes—and yourself.

appendages, with increased surface area relative to mass, are more adaptive in warmer climates because they promote heat loss.

According to these rules, the most suitable body shape in hot climates is linear, with long arms and legs. Several studies have shown that human populations conform to these principles to some degree (Ruff, 1994; Katzmarzyk and Leonard, 1998). In cold climates, a stockier body with shorter limbs is more adaptive. Considerable data gathered from several human populations demonstrate that, in general, humans conform to these principles. In colder climates, body mass tends, on average, to be greater and to be characterized by a larger trunk relative to arms and legs. People living in the Arctic tend to be short and stocky, while many sub-Saharan Africans, especially East African pastoralists, are tall and linear (Fig. 15-6). However, there is

▲ **Figure 15-6**

(**a**) These Samburu women (and men in the background) have the linear proportions characteristic of many inhabitants of East Africa. The Samburu are cattle-herding people who live in northern Kenya. Here they are shown dancing. (**b**) By comparison, these Canadian Inuit women are shorter and stockier. Although the people in these two pictures don't typify everyone in their populations, they do serve as good examples of Bergmann's and Allen's rules.

a great deal of variation in human body proportions, and not all populations conform so obviously to Bergmann's and Allen's rules.

Response to Cold   There are two basic types of physiological responses to cold: those that retain heat and those that increase heat production. Of the two, heat retention is more efficient because it requires less energy. This is an important point, because energy is obtained from dietary sources. Unless food is abundant, and in winter it frequently is not, any factor that conserves energy can be beneficial.

Increases in metabolic rate and shivering are short-term responses that generate body heat. Increases in metabolic rate (the rate at which cells break up nutrients into their components) release energy in the form of heat. Shivering also generates muscle heat, as does voluntary exercise. But both these methods are costly because they require an increased intake of nutrients to provide needed energy. (Perhaps this explains why we tend to have a heartier appetite during the winter and why, during that season, we also tend to eat more fats and carbohydrates, the very sources of the energy we require.)

In general, people exposed to chronic cold (meaning much or most of the year) maintain higher metabolic rates than people who live in warmer climates. The Inuit (Eskimo) people living in the Arctic maintain metabolic rates between 13 and 45 percent higher than that observed in non-Inuit control subjects (Frisancho, 1993). What's more, the highest metabolic rates are seen in inland Inuit, who are exposed to even greater cold stress than coastal populations. Traditionally the Inuit had the highest animal protein and fat diet of any population in the world. Their diet was dictated by the available resource base, and it served to maintain the high metabolic rates required by exposure to chronic cold.

Vasoconstriction is another short-term response, but instead of producing heat, it minimizes heat loss and therefore is more energy efficient. Vasoconstriction restricts capillary blood flow to the surface of the skin, thus reducing heat loss at the body surface. Because retaining body heat is more economical than creating it, vasoconstriction is very efficient provided that temperatures don't drop below freezing. However, if temperatures do fall below freezing, continued vasoconstriction can lower skin temperature to the point of frostbite or worse.

Long-term responses to cold vary among human groups. For example, in the past, desert-dwelling native Australian populations experienced wide temperature fluctuations from day to night. Because they wore no clothing and didn't build shelters, they built sleeping fires to protect themselves from nighttime temperatures hovering only a few degrees above freezing. Also, they experienced continuous vasoconstriction throughout the night, which permitted a degree of skin cooling

vasoconstriction   Narrowing of blood vessels to reduce blood flow to the skin. Vasoconstriction is an involuntary response to cold and reduces heat loss at the skin's surface.

most people would find extremely uncomfortable. But since there was no threat of frostbite, continued vasoconstriction helped prevent excessive internal heat loss (Taylor, 2006).

By contrast, the Inuit experience intermittent periods of vasoconstriction and vasodilation. This compromise provides periodic warmth to the skin, which helps prevent frostbite in below-freezing temperatures. At the same time, because the vasodilation is intermittent, energy loss is restricted to retain more heat at the body's core.

Humans, and some other animals, also have a subcutaneous (beneath the skin) fat layer that provides insulation throughout the body. In populations with high levels of obesity today, this fat layer is an annoyance to many and a major health issue for others. However, in the not too distant past, our hunting and gathering ancestors relied on it not only for some protection against the cold but also as a source of nutrients when food was scarce.

These examples illustrate two of the ways in which adaptations to cold vary among human populations. Obviously winter conditions exceed our ability to adapt physiologically in many parts of the world. Consequently, if our ancestors hadn't developed cultural innovations, they would have remained in the tropics.

High Altitude

Studies of high-altitude residents have greatly contributed to our understanding of physiological adaptation. As you'd expect, altitude studies have focused on inhabitants of mountainous regions, particularly in the Himalayas, Andes, and Rocky Mountains. Of these three areas, the Himalayas probably have the longest history of permanent human habitation (Moore et al., 1998). Today perhaps as many as 25 million people live at altitudes above 10,000 feet. In Tibet, permanent settlements exist above 15,000 feet; in the Andes, they can be found as high as 17,000 feet (Fig. 15-7).

Because the mechanisms that maintain homeostasis in humans evolved at lower altitudes, we're compromised by the conditions at higher elevations. At high altitudes, many factors result in stress on the human body. These include **hypoxia**, more intense solar radiation, cold temperatures, aridity, wind (which amplifies cold stress), a reduced nutritional base, and rough terrain. Of these, hypoxia causes the greatest amount of physiological stress for humans, especially to the heart, lungs, and brain.

Hypoxia is caused by reduced barometric pressure. It's not that there's less oxygen in the atmosphere at high altitudes; rather, it's less concentrated. Therefore to obtain the same amount of oxygen at 9,000 feet as at sea level, people must make certain physiological alterations that increase the body's ability to transport and efficiently use the oxygen that's available.

Reproduction in particular is affected through increased infant mortality rates, miscarriage, low birth weights, and premature births. One cause of fetal and maternal death is preeclampsia, a severe elevation of blood pressure in pregnant women after the 20th gestational week. In another study of Colorado residents, Palmer and colleagues (1999) reported that among pregnant women living at elevations over 10,000 feet, the prevalence of preeclampsia was 16 percent, compared with 3 percent at around 4,000 feet. In general, the problems related to childbearing are attributed to issues that compromise the vascular supply (and thus oxygen transport) to the fetus.

People born at lower altitudes and high-altitude natives differ somewhat in how they adapt to insufficient amounts of available oxygen. When people born at low elevations travel to higher ones, the process of acclimatization begins within a day or two. These changes include increases in metabolic rate, respiration, heart rate,

hypoxia Insufficient levels of oxygen in body tissues; oxygen deficiency.

▲ **Figure 15-7**

(**a**) Namche Bazaar, Tibet, situated at an elevation of over 12,000 feet above sea level. (**b**) La Paz, Bolivia, at just over 12,000 feet, is home to more than 1 million people.

and the production of red blood cells. (Red blood cells contain hemoglobin, the protein responsible for transporting oxygen to organs and tissues.)

In high-altitude natives, acclimatization occurs during growth and development. This type of developmental acclimatization is present only in people who grow up in high-altitude areas, not in those who moved there as adults. Lifelong residents of high elevations have larger hearts and greater lung capacity compared with people from lower elevations. They are also more efficient than migrants at diffusing oxygen from their blood to their body tissues, and geneticists are beginning to identify the genes that regulate this ability. Developmental acclimatization to high altitude serves as a good example of physiological flexibility by illustrating how, within the limits set by genetic factors, development can be influenced by environmental factors.

But the best evidence for permanent high-altitude adaptation is provided by the indigenous peoples of Tibet, who have inhabited regions higher than 12,000 feet for at least 7,000 (Simonson et al., 2010) and perhaps as long as 25,000 years. For this reason, these populations have been the subject of many studies. Altitude does not negatively affect reproduction in highland Tibetans to the degree it does in other populations. Infants have birth weights as high as those of lowland Tibetan groups and higher than those of recent (20 to 30 years) Chinese immigrants. This fact may be the result of alterations in maternal blood flow to the uterus during pregnancy (Moore et al., 2006).

Another line of evidence concerns how the body processes glucose (blood sugar). Glucose is critical because it's the only source of energy used by the brain, and it's also used, although not exclusively, by the heart. Both highland Tibetans and the Quechua (inhabitants of high-altitude regions of the Peruvian Andes) burn glucose in a way that permits more efficient oxygen use. This implies the presence of genetic mutations in the mitochondrial DNA, because mtDNA directs how cells process glucose. It also indicates that natural selection has acted to increase the frequency of these advantageous mutations in these groups.

We now have solid evidence that natural selection has acted strongly and rapidly to increase the frequency of certain alleles that have produced adaptive responses to altitude in Tibetans. Ninety percent of Tibetan highlanders possess a point mutation in a gene called *EPAS1*, which is involved in red blood cell production. In effect, the *EPAS1* mutation inhibits the increased red blood cell production we would expect to see in people living at high altitude. Thus Tibetans have red cell counts similar to those of populations living at sea level. Interestingly, the Quechua and other high-altitude residents of the Andes do not have this mutation and have elevated red cell counts compared with lowland inhabitants. But if increased red blood cell production is advantageous at high altitude, why would selection favor a mutation that acts against it in Tibetans? The answer is that beyond certain levels, elevated numbers of red cells can actually "thicken" the blood and lead to increased risk of stroke, blood clots, and heart attack. In pregnant women, they can also lead to impaired fetal growth and even fetal death. Thus, although the mechanisms aren't yet understood, Tibetans have acquired a number of genetically influenced adaptations to hypoxic conditions while still producing the same amount of hemoglobin we would expect at sea level. This mutation is believed to have appeared only around 4,000 ya, yet it is present throughout most highland Tibetan populations. The fact that it has spread so rapidly indicates that it is extremely advantageous and that natural selection has acted very powerfully and quickly to increase its frequency (Yi et al., 2010).

Infectious Disease

Infection, as opposed to other disease categories such as degenerative or genetic disease, includes pathological conditions caused by microorganisms (viruses, bacteria, fungi, and other one-celled organisms). Throughout the course of human evolution, infectious disease has exerted enormous selective pressures on populations, influencing the frequency of alleles that affect the immune response. Indeed the importance of infectious disease as an agent of natural selection in human populations cannot be overemphasized. But as important as infectious disease has been, its role in this regard isn't very well documented.

The effects of infectious disease on humans are mediated culturally as well as biologically. Innumerable cultural factors, such as architectural styles, subsistence techniques, exposure to domesticated animals, transportation, and even religious practices, affect how infectious disease develops and persists within and between populations.

Until about 15,000 years ago, all humans lived in small nomadic hunting and gathering groups. These groups rarely stayed in one location more than a few days or weeks at a time, so they had little contact with refuse heaps that house disease **vectors**. But with the domestication of plants and animals, people became more sedentary and began living in small villages. Gradually, villages became towns; and towns, in turn, developed into densely crowded, unsanitary cities.

As long as humans lived in small bands, there was little opportunity for infectious disease to affect large numbers of people. Certainly people were sometimes infected with various **pathogens** through contact with animals they killed and

vectors Agents that transmit disease from one carrier to another. Mosquitoes are vectors for malaria, just as fleas are vectors for bubonic plague.

pathogens Substances or microorganisms, such as bacteria, fungi, or viruses, that cause disease.

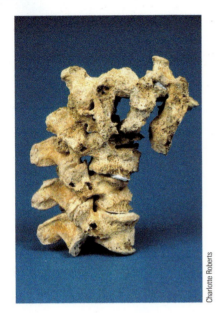

Charlotte Roberts

▲ **Figure 15-8**

Portion of a vertebral column from a 17- to 25-year-old male infected with tuberculosis. Most of the bodies of three lower thoracic vertebrae (attached to the ribs) have been destroyed, and the spine has collapsed. This vertebral column is from a medieval burial site in England.

endemic Continuously present in a population.

zoonotic (zoh-oh-no´-tic) Pertaining to a zoonosis (*pl.*, zoonoses), a disease that's transmitted to humans through contact with nonhuman animals.

butchered; they were also exposed to infectious illness by drinking contaminated water, exposure to insects such as mosquitoes, and simply through association with each other. But even if an entire local group or band were wiped out, the effect on the overall population in a given area would have been negligible. Moreover, for a disease to become **endemic** in a population, there must be enough people to sustain it. Therefore small bands of hunter-gatherers weren't faced with continuous exposure to endemic disease.

With the advent of sedentary communities living in close proximity to domesticated animals, opportunities for exposure to disease increased. As sedentary life permitted larger group size, it became possible for several diseases to become permanently established in some populations. Moreover, exposure to domestic animals, such as cattle and fowl, provided an opportune environment for the spread of several **zoonotic** diseases. The crowded, unsanitary conditions that characterized parts of all cities until the late nineteenth century and that still persist in much of the world today further added to the disease burden borne by human populations. A recent study found strong evidence for a global increase in infectious disease since 1980, especially zoonotic diseases (Smith et al., 2014). The "At a Glance" outlines three examples of zoonotic diseases that affect humans.

Tuberculosis, discussed above, has been one of the most cited examples of zoonotic disease. It is believed to have been transmitted from cattle to humans after cattle were domesticated some 10,000 ya. In fact, TB is widely considered to be one of the many prices humans have paid for living in close association with domesticated animals. *Mycobacterium tuberculosis* usually infects the lungs. It's spread through sneezing and coughing, and symptoms include coughing, fatigue, and fever. Prior to the development of antibiotic therapies, the disease often proved fatal. In addition to the lungs, the bacterium can attack other tissues, including bone. The area of the skeleton most commonly involved is the spine and when this occurs, two or three vertebrae may be destroyed and eventually collapse (Fig. 15-8).

Malaria provides perhaps the best-documented example of how disease can act to change allele frequencies in human populations. In Chapter 4, you saw how, in some African and Mediterranean populations, malaria has altered allele frequencies at the locus that governs hemoglobin formation, leading to an increased prevalence of sickle-cell anemia. Despite extensive long-term eradication programs, malaria still poses a serious threat to human health. Indeed, the World Health Organization

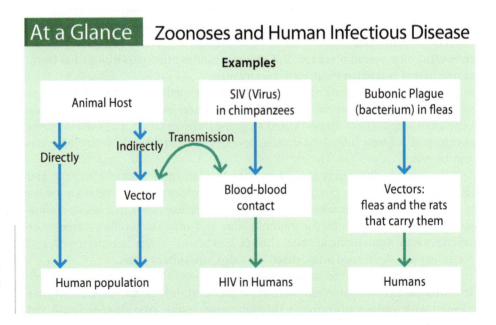

At a Glance **Zoonoses and Human Infectious Disease**

Examples

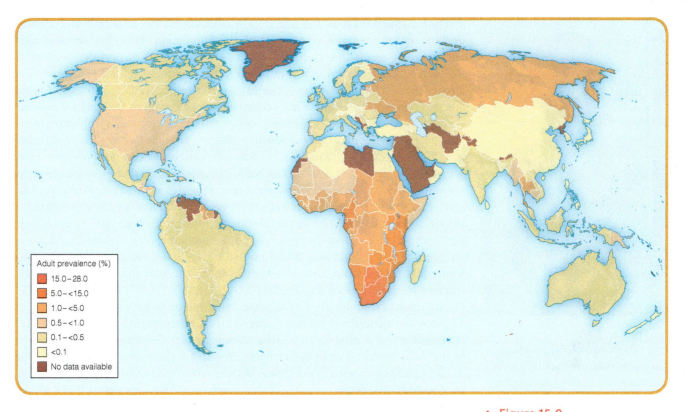

Adult prevalence (%)
- 15.0–28.0
- 5.0–<15.0
- 1.0–<5.0
- 0.5–<1.0
- 0.1–<0.5
- <0.1
- No data available

▲ **Figure 15-9**

Geographical distribution of HIV infection as of the end of 2009.

estimates the number of people currently infected with malaria to be between 300 and 500 million worldwide. And this number is increasing as drug-resistant strains of the disease-causing microorganism become more common (Olliaro et al., 1995).

Another example of the selective role of infectious disease is indirectly provided by AIDS (acquired immunodeficiency syndrome). In the United States, the first cases of AIDS were reported in 1981. Since then, perhaps as many as 1.5 million Americans have been infected by HIV (human immunodeficiency virus), the agent that causes AIDS. However, most of the burden of AIDS is borne by developing countries, where 95 percent of all HIV-infected people live (Fig. 15-9). According to World Health Organization estimates, globally an estimated 35 million people were living with HIV in 2012. This shows an increase from previous years, since more people were able to receive lifesaving medication. Approximately 2.3 million new HIV infections occurred globally in 2012, showing a 33 percent decline in the number of new infections from 3.4 million in 2001. Moreover, globally the number of AIDS deaths also declined with approximately 1.6 million AIDS deaths in 2012, down from 2.3 million in 2005 (UNAIDS Report on the Global AIDS Epidemic, 2013).

By the early 1990s, scientists were aware of some patients who had been HIV positive for 10 to 15 years but continued to show few if any symptoms, leading researchers to suspect that some individuals were naturally resistant to HIV. This was shown to be true in late 1996 with the publication of two independent studies that demonstrated a mechanism for HIV resistance (Dean et al., 1996; Samson et al., 1996).

These two reports describe a genetic mutation that involves a major receptor site on the surface of certain immune cells, including T4 cells. (Receptor sites are protein molecules that enable HIV and other viruses to invade cells.) As a result of the mutation, the receptor site doesn't function properly and the virus can't enter the cell. Current evidence strongly suggests that people who are homozygous for this allele may be completely resistant to many types of HIV infection. In heterozygotes, infection may still occur, but the course of HIV disease is significantly slowed.

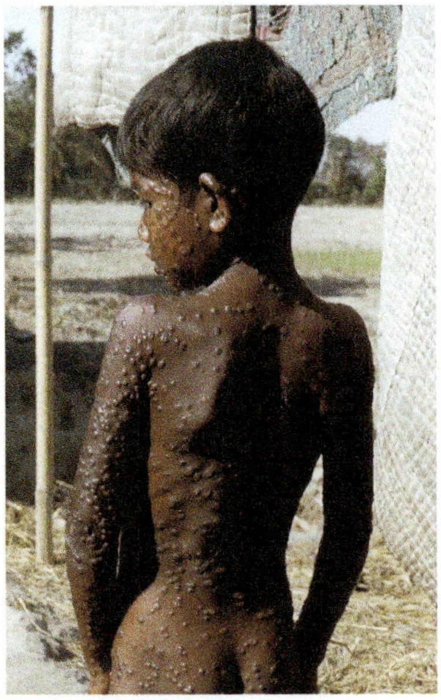

▲ **Figure 15-10**

This 1974 photo shows a young boy in Bangladesh with smallpox. His body is covered with the painful pustules that are typical of the disease. These lesions frequently leave severe scarring on the skin of survivors.

For unknown reasons, the mutant allele occurs mainly in people of European descent, found in about 10 percent of the population. However, the mutation appears to be absent in certain Japanese and West African groups that were studied (Samson et al., 1996). Another research team reported an allele frequency of about 2 percent among African Americans; they speculated that the presence of the allele in African Americans is due to genetic admixture (gene flow) with European Americans (Dean et al., 1996). They also suggested that this polymorphism exists in Europeans because of selective pressures favoring an allele that originally occurred as a rare mutation. But it's important to understand that the original selective agent was *not* HIV. Instead, it was some other as yet unidentified pathogen that requires the same receptor site as HIV, and some researchers have implicated the virus that causes smallpox. Lalani and colleagues (1999) reported that a poxvirus, related to the virus that causes smallpox, can use the same receptor site as HIV. Though there are other possible explanations, this hypothesis offers a very interesting avenue of research. It may reveal how a mutation that has been favored by selection because it provides protection against one type of infection (perhaps smallpox) can also increase resistance to another (AIDS).

Smallpox, once a deadly viral disease, is estimated to have accounted for 10 to 15 percent of all deaths in parts of Europe during the eighteenth century (Fig. 15-10). It's possible that during its long history, smallpox may have altered the frequency of the ABO blood types by selecting against the *A* allele. Smallpox had a higher incidence in people with blood type A or AB than in type O individuals, a fact that may be explained by the presence of an antigen on the smallpox virus that's similar to the A antigen. Thus, when some type A individuals were exposed to smallpox, their immune systems failed to recognize the virus as foreign and didn't mount an adequate immune response. This meant that people with the *A* allele died in greater numbers than those without it. So in regions where smallpox was common in the past, it could have altered allele frequencies at the ABO locus by selecting against the *A* allele.

Smallpox, once a devastating killer of millions, is the only condition to have been successfully eliminated by modern medical technology. By 1977, through massive vaccination programs, the World Health Organization was able to declare the smallpox virus extinct except for a few colonies in research labs in the United States and Russia.*

The Continuing Impact of Infectious Disease

It's important to understand that humans and pathogens exert selective pressures on each other, creating a dynamic relationship between disease organisms and their human (and nonhuman) hosts. Just as disease exerts selective pressures on host populations to adapt, microorganisms also evolve and adapt to various pressures exerted on them by their hosts.

Evolutionarily speaking, it's to the advantage of any pathogen not to be so deadly that it kills its host too quickly. If the host dies shortly after becoming

---

*Concern over the potential use of the smallpox virus by bioterrorists relates to these laboratory colonies. Although the virus is extinct outside these labs, some officials fear the possibility that samples of the virus could be stolen. Also, there are apparently some concerns that unknown colonies of the virus may exist in labs in countries other than Russia and the United States. Using disease organisms against enemies isn't new. In the Middle Ages, armies catapulted the corpses of smallpox and plague victims into towns under siege, and during the U.S. colonial period, British soldiers knowingly gave Native Americans blankets that had been used by smallpox victims.

infected, the virus or bacterium may not have time to reproduce and infect other hosts. Thus selection sometimes acts to produce resistance in host populations and/ or to reduce the virulence of disease organisms, to the benefit of both. However, members of populations exposed for the first time to a new disease frequently die in huge numbers. This type of exposure was a major factor in the decimation of indigenous New World populations after Europeans introduced smallpox into Native American groups. And it has also been the case with the current worldwide spread of HIV.

Of the known disease-causing organisms, HIV provides the best-documented example of evolution and adaptation in a pathogen. It's also one of several examples of interspecies transfer of infection. For these reasons, we focus much of this discussion of evolutionary factors and infectious disease on HIV.

The type of HIV responsible for the AIDS epidemic is HIV-1, which shows a very high degree of genetic variation. Since the late 1980s, researchers have been comparing the DNA sequences of HIV and a closely related virus called *simian immunodeficiency virus* (SIV), which is found in chimpanzees and several African monkey species. Like HIV, SIV is genetically variable, and each strain appears to be specific to a given primate species. SIV produces no symptoms in the African monkeys and chimpanzees that are its traditional hosts, but when injected into Asian monkeys, it eventually causes immune suppression, AIDS-like symptoms, and death. These findings indicate that the various forms of SIV have shared a long evolutionary history with a number of African primate species and that these primates have developed ways of accommodating this virus, which is deadly to their Asian relatives. These results also substantiate long-held hypotheses that SIV and HIV evolved in Africa. Furthermore, DNA comparisons have shown that HIV-1 almost certainly evolved from the form of SIV that infects chimpanzees indigenous to western central Africa (Gao et al., 1999).

As you read earlier, in parts of West Africa, chimpanzees are routinely hunted by humans for food. So the most probable explanation for the transmission of SIV from chimpanzees to humans is the hunting and butchering of chimpanzees (Gao et al., 1999; Weiss and Wrangham, 1999). Thus, HIV/AIDS is a zoonotic disease (Fig. 15-11). The DNA evidence further suggests that there were at least three separate human exposures to chimpanzee SIV, and at some point the virus was altered

◀ **Figure 15-11**
These people, selling butchered chimpanzees in West Africa, probably don't realize that by handling this meat they could be exposing themselves to HIV.

Karl Ammann

to the form we call HIV. Exactly when chimpanzee SIV was transmitted to humans is unknown. The oldest evidence of human infection is a frozen HIV-positive blood sample taken from a West African patient in 1959. Therefore, although human exposure to SIV/HIV probably occurred many times in the past, the virus didn't become firmly established in humans until the latter half of the twentieth century.

Influenza is a contagious respiratory disease caused by various strains of virus. It, too, is a zoonotic disease, and it has probably killed more humans than any other infectious disease. There were two flu pandemics in the twentieth century; the first of these killed an estimated 20 million people in 1918. Moreover, "seasonal flu," which comes around every year, killed approximately 36,000 people annually in the United States during the 1990s (Centers for Disease Control, 2009). Worldwide, it accounts for several hundred thousand deaths every year.

The influenza viruses that infect humans are initially acquired through contact with domestic pigs and fowl (Fig. 15-12). For this reason, influenza is frequently referred to as swine or avian (bird) flu, depending on which species transmitted it to humans. In 2009, a new swine flu virus called H1N1 caused great fear of another pandemic, partly because it caused more severe illness in younger people than most flu viruses.

Because swine flu epidemics are less frequent than the seasonal avian flu, people have less resistance when confronted with a "new" swine flu virus. Swine flu can also be more deadly, and health professionals are always mindful of, and haunted by, the memory of the catastrophic 1918 pandemic. For all these reasons, health professionals worldwide mobilized an enormous effort in 2009 to prepare for a new swine flu pandemic. Hundreds of millions of doses of vaccine were distributed, but the epidemic proved not to be as severe as originally feared. Still, health officials are always

▶ **Figure 15-12**
This woman, selling chickens in a Chinese market, is wearing a scarf over her nose and mouth in an attempt to protect herself from exposure to avian flu.

Hoang Dinh Nam/AFP/Getty Images

on the alert for the possibility of an influenza pandemic, partly because of the ever-present danger posed by close contact between humans, pigs, and domestic fowl.

Until the twentieth century, infectious disease was the number one cause of death in all human populations. Even today in many developing countries, as much as half of all mortality is due to infectious disease, compared with only about 10 percent in the United States. For example, there are an estimated 1 million deaths due to malaria every year. That figure computes to one malaria-related death every 30 seconds (Weiss, 2002)! Ninety percent of these deaths occur in sub-Saharan Africa, where 5 percent of children die of malaria before age 5 (Greenwood and Mutabingwa, 2002; Weiss, 2002). In the United States and other industrialized nations, with improved living conditions, better sanitation, and the widespread use of antibiotics since the 1940s, infectious disease has given way to heart disease and cancer as the leading causes of death.

Optimistic predictions held that infectious disease would one day be a thing of the past. You may be surprised to learn that in the United States mortality due to infectious disease has actually increased in recent years (Pinner et al., 1996). This increase may partly be due to the overuse of antibiotics. It's estimated that half of all antibiotics prescribed in the United States are used to treat viral conditions such as colds and flu. Because antibiotics are completely ineffective against viruses, antibiotic therapy in these cases is not only useless but also may actually have dangerous long-term consequences. There's considerable concern in the biomedical community over the indiscriminate use of antibiotics since the 1950s. Antibiotics have exerted selective pressures on bacterial species that have, over time, evolved antibiotic-resistant strains (an excellent example of natural selection). So in the past few years, we've seen the reemergence of many bacterial diseases, including, pneumonia, cholera, and TB in forms that are less responsive to treatment.

Tuberculosis (TB) is currently listed as the world's leading killer of adults by the World Health Organization (Centers for Disease Control and Prevention, 2015). Today, approximately one-third of the world's population is infected, with more than 9 million diagnosed cases and around 1.5 million deaths in 2013 alone. TB is also the leading killer of individuals affected by HIV. In the United States, nearly 9,500 new cases of TB were diagnosed in 2013, a slight decline from 2012 (Centers for Disease Control and Prevention, 2015). One very troubling aspect of the global increase in TB infection is that new strains of *Mycobacterium tuberculosis*, the bacterium that causes TB, are resistant to many antibiotics.

Various treatments for nonbacterial conditions have also become ineffective. One such example is the appearance of chloroquine-resistant malaria, which has rendered chloroquine (the traditional preventive medication) virtually useless in some parts of Africa. And many insect species have also developed resistance to commonly used pesticides.

In addition to threats posed by resistant strains of pathogens, there are other factors that may contribute to the emergence (or reemergence) of infectious disease. Political leaders in some (mostly European) countries and the overwhelming majority of scientists worldwide are becoming increasingly concerned over the potential for global warming to expand the geographical range of numerous tropical disease vectors, such as mosquitoes. In addition, the destruction of natural environments not only contributes to global warming; it also has the potential of causing disease vectors formerly restricted to local areas to spread to new habitats.

Fundamental to all these factors is human population size, which, as it continues to soar, causes more environmental disturbance and, through additional human activity, adds further to global warming. One could scarcely conceive of a better set of circumstances for the appearance and spread of communicable disease, and it remains to be seen if scientific innovation and medical technology are able to meet the challenge.

To make matters worse, the rise of an anti-vaccination movement within the United Kingdom and the United States has resulted in numerous outbreaks of infectious diseases, including a massive outbreak of measles at a Disneyland theme park in California in 2014 as well as the greatest surge in whooping cough (pertussis) within the U.S. school system in over 70 years. The anti-vaccination movement, which began in the 1990s, was stimulated by a now discredited medical study that proposed a link between vaccinations and autism. Although parents can often request an exemption from vaccinating their children due to religious or philosophical reasons, they are unnecessarily putting both their children and society at risk for acquiring numerous types of infectious disease.

Human Skeletal Biology: What Bones Can Tell Us about Ancient Diseases, Trauma, and Lifestyles

Many physical anthropologists concentrate on the study of human skeletons found in prehistoric and historic archaeological contexts. Similar expertise is also used in studies of very ancient remains dating back as far as several million years. Here we discuss investigations that focus on human remains dating to within the last 10,000 years. It's during this period that human populations began living in permanent settlements and burying their dead in concentrated areas (that is, cemeteries); as a result, there is far more available skeletal material to study than is true for any prior period.

Evidence of Prehistoric Diseases

Skeletal biologists who study disease and trauma in prehistoric and historic remains are called paleopathologists. In prehistoric skeletons, numerous kinds of conditions have been recognized, including dental problems, infectious disease, neoplasms (cancer and other tumors), metabolic disorders (which typically affect growth), and arthritis and related conditions. In addition, paleopathologists are also interested in trauma, which can be recognized in skeletons in the form of healed fractures or, occasionally, as weapon wounds.

Dental disease is the most common category of pathological conditions found in prehistoric remains. Commonly seen dental problems include extreme tooth wear (see Fig. 15-13), abscesses, and tooth loss. (For a very early example of antemortem tooth loss dating close to 2 mya, see Chapter 11, Fig. 11-7). Dental caries (cavities) were not common among hunter-gatherers prior to the adoption of agriculture, but with the introduction of new foods containing carbohydrates (especially grains such as corn or wheat), the frequency of caries increased dramatically. In fact, one "marker" of an agricultural lifestyle is the high frequency of caries (Larsen, 2015).

As we have discussed in this chapter, infectious disease became the leading cause of death in human populations during the past few thousand years and, consequently, a major adaptive challenge for our species. Paleopathologists have found numerous examples of severe infectious diseases such as TB and syphilis. In the New World there are a few cases of TB and several examples of fungal diseases including "valley fever," found in California and the American Southwest (Fig. 15-14).

▼ **Figure 15-13**
Severe wear in the maxillary dentition of a prehistoric Native Californian. Such extreme wear is typical in this population and is hypothesized to have been the result of grit in the diet and the use of teeth as tools.

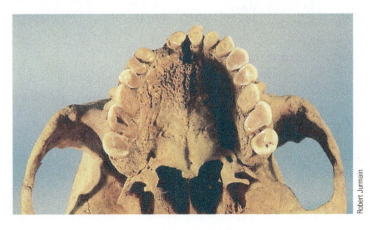

Robert Jurmain

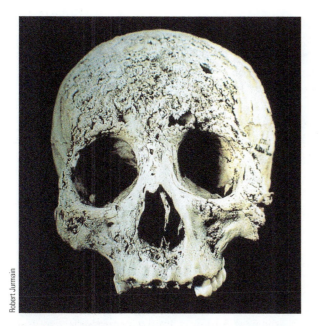

Robert Jurmain

▲ **Figure 15-14**

Extreme reaction in a cranium from an Alaskan Eskimo, diagnostic of syphilis (although other possibilities must be considered).

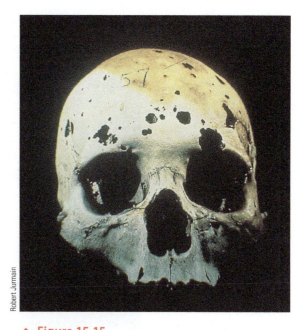

Robert Jurmain

▲ **Figure 15-15**

Numerous lesions of the cranium (such erosive lesions were also found in other bones), probably the result of a disseminated (metastasized) cancer, possibly originating from the breast, shown here in an Inuit (Eskimo) female.

Non-life-threatening benign bone tumors are quite common, but cases of severe cancer have only rarely been reported (Fig. 15-15). There are several possible explanations for the apparent rarity of cancer in the past: People died younger, on average, in prehistory, and cancer primarily affects older people. Also, many cancers don't affect bone or do so only in advanced cases. Thus many individuals who may have had cancer died before it progressed to their skeletons. Moreover, exposure to environmental carcinogens was less common in prehistory than it is today (Capasso, 2004).

Metabolic diseases such as rickets are most severe when they affect children during development (Fig. 15-16; also see Fig. 15-4, which shows rickets in a young child). Degenerative diseases include a wide variety of conditions, but those that directly affect the skeleton are colloquially referred to as "arthritis." The most common location is the spine, especially in older individuals. The joints of the limbs, particularly hips and knees, are also frequently affected (Fig. 15-17).

As mentioned, paleopathologists also study trauma, which is found most typically in the form of healed fractures (Fig. 15-18). Fractures that occur at or very near the time of death (that is, perimortem) exhibit no evidence of healing. Although these fractures have diagnostic characteristics, it can often be difficult to distinguish such perimortem traumatic lesions from damage that occurred perhaps centuries after the death of the individual. (Postmortem damage can occur any time burial sites are disturbed due to construction, agricultural activities, and many other factors.)

▼ **Figure 15-16**

These lower leg bones of a child from an archaeological site in England are bowed. Such bowing is typical of rickets.

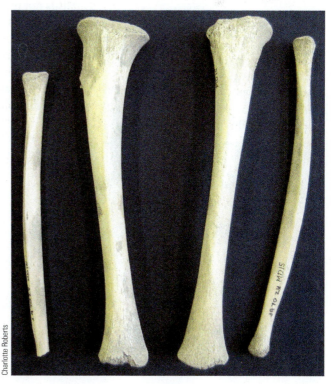

Charlotte Roberts

▲ **Figure 15-17**
Extreme degenerative arthritis in the knee of an adult female from Nubia (part of the modern country of Sudan, from about A.D. 700–1400).

▲ **Figure 15-18**
Fracture of a right femur (thigh bone) seen from the rear. (The normal left femur is shown for comparison.) Such an injury is extremely severe, even life-threatening, but in this individual the bone healed remarkably well.

▼ **Figure 15-19**
Embedded piece of an obsidian projectile point in a lumbar vertebra from a central California male, 25 to 40 years old. The portion being held was found with the burial and may have been retained during life in soft tissue (muscle?). The injury shows some evidence of healing.

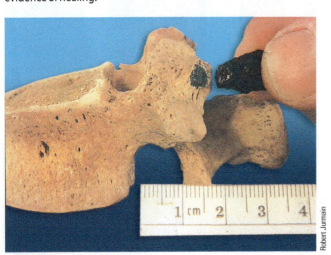

Wounds caused by weapons can be dramatic; even if they healed long before the person died, they are often still very obvious. Sometimes, if such injuries occurred shortly before or at death, it's possible to identify a likely cause of death, something that usually is not possible in archaeological material. For example, there are cases where arrow points have been found embedded in bones such as vertebrae (sometimes severing the spinal cord) or the skull, with no sign of healing. In such a situation, it's safe to assume that the person didn't die of natural causes (Fig. 15-19). In several Old World sites, burials with injuries caused by metal weapons have also been found, particularly in battlefield cemeteries. Not surprisingly, these skeletons display many fatal injuries (Fiorato et al., 2000).

In 2012, archaeologists excavated the skeletal remains of an adult male in Leicester, England. As of this writing, all evidence, including DNA testing, points to the remains belonging to that of King Richard III who died in battle in 1485 (Buckley et al., 2013; King et al., 2014). This is one of the most exciting archaeological discoveries in decades because it has the potential to answer questions about this infamous monarch that historians and others have been asking for 500 years. One near-contemporary account states that Richard III was killed by a blow to the back of the head. The rear portion of this newly discovered cranium exhibits several perimortem injuries, and additionally a barbed, metal projectile point was found in the "upper back" (Appleby et al., 2015). Last, the spine exhibits evidence of scoliosis and legend (strongly enhanced by Shakespeare) has always held that Richard III had a spinal deformity.

Reconstruction of Prehistoric Behavioral Patterns

Skeletal biologists are very much interested in learning how prehistoric peoples behaved and how various behaviors influenced their health. In the last two decades many skeletal experts have identified this approach with the term *bioarchaeology*, the use of which actually dates back to the late 1970s (Buikstra, 1977). In current practice, most bioarchaeologists use a broad-based approach (Buzon, 2012; Larsen, 2015).

Reconstructing Prehistoric Activities Understanding what sorts of activities ancient peoples practiced is obviously a fascinating area of research. Can we learn about specific activities from skeletons? The answer is that sometimes it's possible but frequently it isn't. The ways in which bone responds to activity (and other influences) involve complex physiological and biochemical processes and are best approached using rigorous scientific methods. Thus the study of evidence of activity in skeletons provides a good example of hypothesis testing and verification.

Three different types of skeletal changes have been especially popular with bioarchaeologists attempting to reconstruct prehistoric activity patterns: osteoarthritis, areas where muscles attach to bones (*entheses*), and bone geometry (that is, bone shape). Osteoarthritis (OA) is a very common condition seen in all human populations. A simple conclusion that is frequently made assumes that osteoarthritis results mainly from activity; following this logic, people who work harder should end up with more OA in their skeletons. Think about this interpretation as a hypothesis. Let's say we see more OA in the skeletons of some individuals than others in an ancient population. Did those with OA work harder? Did they participate in some particular activity that increased the amount of arthritic bone change?

The answer may be "yes," but most likely it's "no." The safest conclusion is that we really cannot say. The problem arises because we know from biomedical research (including thousands of published studies) that OA is caused by structural and biochemical changes to the cartilage at the ends of bones and that these changes are primarily caused by advancing age, genetic influences (varying considerably among individuals), and possibly previous injury (Jurmain, 1999). Because of the importance of age as a contributing factor to the development of OA, any comparison between groups must first consider age differences between them. If one group is primarily composed of younger individuals, then the prevalence of OA should be lower than it would be in a group composed mainly of older ones. Also, comparisons among groups require statistical testing, and this fact dictates that samples should be large enough for tests to be valid.

Many bioarchaeologists assume that OA (and other bone changes discussed below) results from regular adult activities such as climbing, carrying heavy loads, grinding grain, and so on. But once we consider particularly the influences of age and genes, there is little remaining evidence to suggest that activity was the primary cause of arthritic bone changes (Fig. 15-20). There are, however, a few exceptions. For example, elbow

▼ **Figure 15-20**

Bony lipping around the margins of two lumbar vertebrae. This condition is related to osteoarthritis and is caused by the same major factors (that is, age, genes, and prior acute injury). Although sometimes suggested by bioarchaeologists to be a result of activity, there are virtually no biomedical/clinical studies to substantiate this claim and much data to refute it. This is a very good example of how to confidently reject a hypothesis.

Lynn Kilgore

osteoarthritis in Alaskan Inuit skeletons likely reflects, at least in part, high functional stress on this joint resulting from intensive physical activity (Merbs, 1983; Jurmain, 1999).

Another type of skeletal change that has been related to specific activities is alterations to the areas where muscles attach to bones. In this type of research the basic assumption seems clear. That is, increased activity that repeatedly uses certain muscles produces changes to points of attachment. This certainly can be the case for acute injury (such as a torn muscle). But what can we say about more typical long-term adult activities? Once again, evidence from medical research indicates that the causes of such bone changes are numerous and include age and genetic influences (Milella et al., 2012). For example, the size of these muscle and ligament attachment sites has been shown to increase with age, and some individuals are genetically predisposed to form more bone than others at these attachment sites (Foster et al., 2014).

One very useful way to test hypotheses and help control for these various influences (which medical experts call "confounders") is through investigation of contemporary skeletal collections where age and sex are known.* Research of this kind has helped to standardize methods, test specific hypotheses, and demonstrate that the underlying biological influences on muscle attachment sites are complex (Alves Cardoso and Henderson, 2010; Jurmain et al., 2012; Milella et al., 2012).

Study of bone geometry is the third method that can potentially shed light on prehistoric activities. This approach has tended to be more biomedically oriented than the others discussed so far and has also been more successful in testing hypotheses. In particular, a study of student athletes at Cambridge University compared with a set of nonathletes provided strong confirmation that certain types of very strenuous activities can alter bone geometry (that is, the shape and strength of the bone) (Shaw and Stock, 2009a, b).

Reconstructing Prehistoric Diets Skeletal biologists also study prehistoric diets. Over the past four decades, chemical techniques have been developed that provide important insight on what people ate in the past. Stable isotope analysis has proven to be a very useful way to reconstruct the diets of ancient humans and has become widely used. As discussed in Chapter 9, stable isotopes are different versions of the same element that vary in their structure (that is, in their atomic weight). For example, carbon has two stable isotopes, ^{13}C and ^{12}C, which differ in atomic weight. Humans incorporate different amounts of these isotopes into their tissues from foods that vary in isotopic composition. Stable isotopes in tooth enamel and dentin specifically record childhood diet, and they do not change after they are formed; in adults, isotopic analyses of the organic (*collagen*) and mineral (*hydroxyapatite*) components of bone provide a record of diet over the last several years of life.

Stable carbon and nitrogen isotope analyses of human bone provide the most information about diet. Carbon isotope ratios in plants vary based on one of three possible chemical pathways (known as C3, C4, and CAM plants); these ratios are incorporated into the bones and teeth of people from their diet. In addition, marine organisms (for example, marine fish and marine mammals) have isotope ratios that differ from those of most terrestrial plants and animals. Stable nitrogen isotope ratios provide another source of information on diet. Plants typically have the lowest nitrogen isotope ratios, and these ratios increase in animals at each higher level in the food chain. Analysis of carbon and nitrogen isotopes together helps not

---

*Such collections can be found in museums in the United States (for example, at the Smithsonian Institution), Portugal, and Italy. These skeletons sometimes come from individuals whose bodies were unclaimed or from cemeteries that, by law, were required to be excavated.

only to identify the source of food (for example, marine or terrestrial), but can also indicate the general position of human societies within a local food web.

For example, stable carbon and nitrogen isotope analysis has revealed that early prehistoric Native Americans from the San Francisco Bay area consumed significant amounts of high trophic level marine resources, such as marine fish and marine mammals, which are near the top of the food chain. However, later in time, bone isotope ratios record a change in diet toward greater consumption of land animals and plant foods (for example, deer and acorns). These changes in diet may reflect increasing resource stress associated with population growth in the region (Bartelink, 2009).

How Do We Know?

Although humans can be seen as a highly successful species, we are not as "dominant" as we might think. Indeed, we are in an arms race with other species that could attack and kill millions of people. The most dangerous of these biological rivals include microorganisms, specifically bacteria and viruses.

In much of the world over the last 80 years, medical technology has reduced the dangers from bacterial infections, such as tuberculosis, through the use of antibiotics. However, the bacteria don't just disappear. What they do is to *evolve*, and they do it remarkably quickly. Bacteria can reproduce about every 20 minutes, compared with a human generational span of 20 years. What's more, they're far more numerous than any other life-form. One estimate suggests bacteria make up about 98 percent of all cells on earth.

We mentioned earlier that when bacteria are exposed to antibiotics, some of them (due to earlier random mutations) will probably be resistant. They will be the ones that reproduce, and in just a few years, resistant strains

could potentially spread around the world. Of course, this is an excellent example of natural selection. Humans certainly can't fight back simply by waiting for natural selection to make us immune to bacteria. We use technology instead and invent different and stronger antibiotics. The bacteria then evolve further through more natural selection, and the biological arms race continues.

Recently, our technology has seriously begun to lose ground to the microbes. The last 10 years have seen the appearance of at least two new mutations that make some bacteria resistant to even our most powerful antibiotics. One of these mutations apparently originated in southern Asia (India or Pakistan), and the other was first identified in U.S. hospitals. These bacterial strains now have spread to Europe, China, and South America.

With no antibiotics that can predictably combat these resistant strains, some hospital patients have died, despite the best efforts of doctors using the entire arsenal of drugs now available. Pharmaceutical companies could develop yet stronger and more creative antibiotics that would work—at least for

now. However, such new drugs require up to 10 years to develop, and there are none currently even in the early stages of such development.

So, in the absence of new antibiotics, there is a real danger of an increase in lethal infections caused by resistant bacterial strains. The war with microbes is one we can never completely win, and the next decade will certainly see increased threats to humans due to a lack of effective pharmaceutical weapons.

What Do You Think?

The overuse of antibiotics and antibacterial products today has created some unintended consequences. In our attempt to eradicate bacterial infection, we have created several antibiotic-resistant strains of microbes. What long-term challenges do you think society will face in the future if antibiotics are no longer effective? Is there anything that could be done to avoid serious pandemics of infectious disease? ■

Summary of Main Topics

- Variation in skin color has enormous adaptive value in response to conflicting selective pressures, all having to do with ultraviolet (UV) radiation. Heavily pigmented skin is adaptive in the tropics because it provides protection from UV radiation, which can cause skin cancer and also degrade the B vitamin folate. As people moved away from the tropics, dark skin became disadvantageous because a decrease in sunlight meant insufficient exposure to UV radiation for the adequate production of vitamin D. This is important because vitamin D is essential for the proper mineralization of bone and insufficient amounts of vitamin D causes rickets in children.

- Infectious disease has also played a critical role in human evolution, and the frequencies of certain alleles have changed in various populations in response to diseases such as malaria.

- Cultural innovations and contact with nonhuman animals have altered disease patterns and have increased the spread of infectious diseases. Examples of this type of spread are HIV/AIDS and malaria. We humans are still coping with infectious disease as we alter the environment and as global climate change facilitates the spread of disease vectors. Certainly without cultural adaptations, our species never

would have left the tropics. But as in the case of sickle-cell anemia, HIV, and many bacterial diseases, some of our cultural innovations themselves have become selective agents.

- Skeletal biologists diagnose diseases and other skeletal conditions on historic and prehistoric human remains to make interpretations of stress, behavior, diet, and health on past human populations.

Critical Thinking Questions

1. If a friend of yours said that skin color is a valuable tool to use in classifying humans, how would you explain that variations in human pigmentation are the result of natural selection in different environments?

2. Why is less pigmented skin advantageous in northern latitudes? There is now evidence that at least some Neandertals who lived in northern Europe also

had reduced melanin compared to populations in Africa. What is this evidence?

3. What are some examples of genetic adaptations of humans to high altitude environments? How is this different from the physiological changes experienced by people who visit high altitude locations?

4. How has infectious disease played an important role in human evolution? Do you think

it plays a current role in human adaptation? How have human cultural practices influenced the patterns of infectious disease seen today? List as many examples as you can, including some not discussed in this chapter.

5. What are the major kinds of pathological conditions paleopathologists study in skeletons from archaeological sites, and what information do they provide?

CONNECTIONS

Through natural selection, humans have and continue to adapt to environmental factors.

Human development and adaptation are best understood from an evolutionary perspective.

Humans have recently become disconnected from other life and are rapidly altering the planet.

Legacies of Human Evolutionary History: Effects on the Life Course

Evolved Biology and Contemporary Lifestyles—Is There a Mismatch?

Biocultural Evolution and the Life Course

Diet and Nutrition through the Life Course

Too Much and Too Little

Other Factors Influencing Growth and Development: Genes, Environment, and Hormones

Life History Theory and the Human Life Course

Pregnancy, Birth, Infancy, and Childhood

Onset of Reproductive Function in Humans

Decline in Reproductive Function

Aging and Longevity

Are We Still Evolving?

Student Learning Objectives After studying the material in this chapter, you should be able to:

▶ Describe the concept of evolutionary mismatch and explain why it is important to understanding modern diseases and health problems.

▶ Explain the importance of biocultural evolution in the expression of phenotypic traits.

▶ Explain the proposal that the human biology that evolved under dietary conditions of the past may be mismatched with the foods we consume today, resulting in a number of diseases and disorders such as hypertension, diabetes, and obesity.

▶ Describe life history theory and discuss key examples of life history characteristics in humans.

▶ Discuss three proposals for why humans age.

▶ Explain the ways in which human populations are still evolving.

Extended Asian family gathered for photo.

Antonia Tozer/AWL Images/Getty Images; Top Images: Robert Jurmain; Brian Seed/Alamy; iStockphoto.com /luoman

I n previous chapters, we have seen that modern humans are a highly generalized and a behaviorally flexible species. This means that we can live in a wide range of climates, eat a wide variety of foods, and respond to most environmental challenges in myriad ways. As the environments of our ancestors changed, those who were able to survive and reproduce in the new environments passed along advantageous characteristics to their offspring. The result is that today humans continue to survive and reproduce under a great variety of conditions, including high altitudes, extreme temperatures, high levels of environmental pollution, and dense urban populations, and with diets and lifestyles that differ greatly from those of our ancestors only a few generations ago. In fact, the human environment has changed more radically in the last few decades than it has at any point in the entire course of human evolutionary history. What are the consequences of these tremendous changes, some of which you have seen in your own lifetime? In this chapter and the next, we'll explore how the legacies of human evolution continue to have a profound impact on our biology and behavior throughout our lives and on the planet we inhabit, even in the face of ever-increasing rates of cultural and technological change.

Evolved Biology and Contemporary Lifestyles—Is There a Mismatch?

A frequently expressed concern today is that our evolved biology may not be well matched with our contemporary lives, resulting in poorer health and shorter lives than those of even our recent ancestors. This is referred to variously as a mismatch or discordance. Dozens of popular "paleo" books argue that if we could only return to the ways of living of our ancestors ("Stone -Age lives"), we would all become happier and healthier. (There are books on paleo diets, paleo parenting, paleo weight loss, paleo fitness training, paleo tooth health, and paleo love.) Certainly, there are aspects of ancestral life that would probably result in improved health if adopted (specifically, exercise and dietary changes), but with more than 7 billion people living on earth, returning to lifestyles like those of our ancestors is highly unlikely (Fig. 16-1).

◀ **Figure 16-1**
The lives of our ancestors differed in many ways from the lives of people today in nations like the United States and Japan.

Nigel Pavitt/AWL Images/Getty Images

iStockphoto.com/YinYang

For most of human history, individuals were born and grew up in environments not very different from those of their parents and grandparents. They faced few challenges in their lives that required significant cultural or biological adaptations. With the origin of food production approximately 10,000 ya, however, the pace of cultural change began to speed up. And since that time, there has been a veritable explosion of culture and technology, whereas biological change has been relatively slow (Pritchard, 2010). With so many changes occurring within a single lifetime, many people are stressed to their limits to adapt physically, emotionally, and materially. How far can our flexible and generalized biology take us in this rapidly changing world? These are some of the questions we will explore in this chapter as we consider the ways in which culture interacts with biology throughout the life course and in our everyday lives, paying particular attention to the challenges to our health and lifestyles and to the very planet that supports us.

Biocultural Evolution and the Life Course

A good place to explore the interaction of biology and culture and potential mismatches is the human life course. If we consider how a human develops from an embryo into an adult and examine the forces that operate on that process, we will have a better perspective of how both biology and culture influence our own lives and how our evolutionary history creates opportunities and sets limitations.

Of course, cultural factors interact with genetically based biological characteristics to widely varying degrees; these variable interactions influence how characteristics are expressed in individuals. Some genetically based characteristics will be exhibited no matter what the cultural context of a person's life happens to be. If a woman inherits two alleles for albinism, for example, she will be deficient in the production of the pigment melanin, resulting in lightly colored skin, hair, and eyes. This phenotype will emerge regardless of the woman's cultural or physical environment. Likewise, the sex-linked allele for hemophilia will be exhibited by all males who inherit it, no matter where they live.

Other characteristics, such as intelligence, body shape, and growth, reflect the interaction of environment and genes. We know, for example, that each of us is born with a genetic makeup that influences the maximum stature we can achieve in adulthood. But to reach that maximum stature, we must be properly nourished during growth (including during fetal development), and we must avoid many childhood diseases and other factors that inhibit growth. What factors determine whether we are well fed and receive good medical care? In the United States, socioeconomic status (a cultural factor) is probably the primary factor that influences diet and health. But in another culture, diet and health status might be influenced by whether the individual is male or female. In some cultures, males receive the best care in infancy and childhood and are thus often larger and healthier as adults than are females. If there's a cultural value on slimness in women, young girls may try to restrict their food intake in ways that affect their growth; but if the culture values plumpness, the effect on diet in adolescence will likely be different. These are all examples of how cultural values affect growth and development. The ability of the human body to develop in different ways under varying circumstances is a product of our evolutionary history.

Diet and Nutrition through the Life Course

Nutrition has an impact on human growth at every stage of the life cycle, and few aspects of the human environment have changed as much in the last 10,000 years as diet. It is therefore not surprising that there have also been changes in growth, development, maturation, and aging, all of which are directly or indirectly affected by diet. During pregnancy, for example, a woman's diet can have a profound effect on the development of her fetus and the eventual health of the child. Moreover, the effects are transgenerational, because a woman's own supply of eggs is developed while she herself is *in utero*. So if a woman is malnourished during pregnancy, the eggs that develop in her female fetus may be damaged in a way that affects her future grandchildren's health. And even if a baby girl whose mother was malnourished during pregnancy is well nourished from birth on (as often happens in adoptions), her growth, health, and future pregnancies appear to be compromised—a legacy that may extend for several generations (Kuzawa and Quinn, 2009; Kuzawa and Eisenberg, 2014). Furthermore, nutritional stress during pregnancy commonly results in low-birth-weight babies that are at great risk for developing hypertension, cardiovascular disease, and diabetes later in life (Barker, 2004; Gluckman and Hanson, 2006; Zhang et al., 2014). Low-birth-weight babies are particularly at risk if they are born into a world of abundant food resources (especially cheap fast food), and they gain weight rapidly in childhood (Kuzawa, 2005, 2008). These findings have clear implications for public health efforts to provide adequate nutritional support to pregnant women and infants throughout the world.

Another aspect of nutrition that has received a great deal of attention is the complex relationship between diet and the gut **microbiome**, the critters that live in our gut and affect digestion, immune function, and metabolism. At birth, the infant gut is sterile (Khan et al., 2015), but it is quickly populated by (mostly) beneficial bacteria from the birth canal, breast milk, and other environmental sources. This early colonization influences lifelong health, including risk for many chronic and degenerative diseases (Kau et al., 2011). It is notable that the bacteria with which the newborn gut is populated differ in infants born vaginally versus by cesarean section and in those fed by mother's milk versus formula (Hinde and Milligan, 2011; Trevathan and Rosenberg, 2014). Birth and breast-feeding are profoundly affected by culture, further demonstrating the effects of culture on a number of physiological processes, including growth and immune function.

Nutrients needed for growth, development, and body maintenance include proteins, carbohydrates, lipids (fats), vitamins, and minerals. The specific amount that we need of each of these nutrients coevolved with the types of foods that were available to human ancestors throughout our evolutionary history. For example, the specific pattern of amino acids required in human nutrition (the **essential amino acids**) reflects an ancestral diet high in animal protein. Unfortunately for modern humans, these coevolved nutritional requirements are often incompatible with the foods that are available and typically consumed today. To understand this mismatch of our nutritional needs and contemporary diets, we need to examine the impact on human evolutionary history of a relatively recent human innovation, food production, or agriculture.

The preagricultural diet, basically encompassing the entirety of our evolutionary history prior to 10,000 ya, was typically high in animal protein, but was probably low in fats, particularly saturated fats. That diet was also high in complex carbohydrates (including fiber), low in salt, and high in calcium. We don't need to be reminded that the contemporary diet that typifies many industrialized societies has the opposite configuration of the one just described. It's high in saturated fats and salt and low in complex carbohydrates, fiber, and calcium (Fig. 16-2). Although humans are notable for the great flexibility in their diets (Leonard, 2002; Turner and Thompson, 2013), there is very good evidence that many of today's diseases in industrialized countries are related to the lack of fit between our diet today and the one with which we evolved (Gluckman et al., 2009).

Along with agriculture and animal domestication came a number of "new" food types that are important and common today but were rare or nonexistent in

microbiome A collection of genomes of microbes in a system, such as the human body

essential amino acids The 9 (of 22) amino acids that must be obtained from the food we eat because they are not synthesized in the body in sufficient amounts.

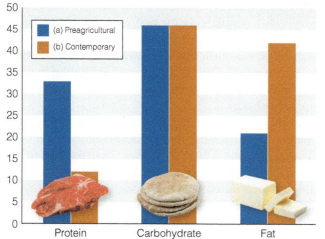

Percent of calories from protein, carbohydrates, and fats in preagricultural (a) and contemporary (b) diets.

Amount of sodium (mg) in preagricultural (a) and contemporary (b) diets.

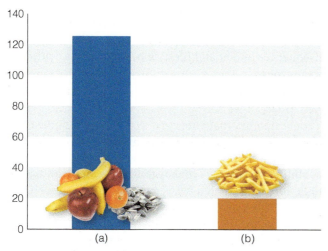

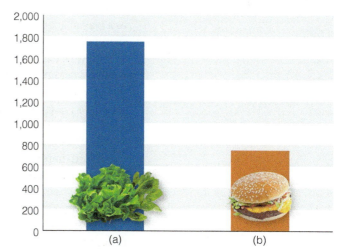

Amount of fiber (g) in preagricultural (a) and contemporary (b) diets.

Amount of calcium (mg) in preagricultural (a) and contemporary (b) diets.

▲ **Figure 16-2**

The photos show diets that were likely consumed by our ancestors (left) and those that are commonly consumed in nations such as the United States today (right). The graphs compare the composition of the two diets for selected nutrients. Human nutritional requirements coevolved with the foods consumed during the long period of human evolutionary history before agriculture, resulting in a mismatch between what we need to eat today and the composition of contemporary diets.

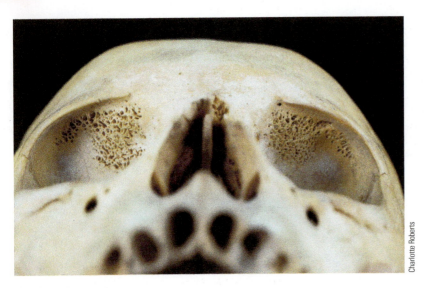

Charlotte Roberts

▲ **Figure 16-3**
Bone changes to the eye orbits that likely indicate anemia caused by a deficiency of vitamin B$_9$ (folic acid), vitamin B$_{12}$ (cobalamin), or vitamin C.

ancestral diets. Two examples include dairy products and cereal grains. In the previous chapter, we discussed the difficulty that some people have digesting dairy products because they lack the enzyme necessary for breaking down the milk sugar lactose. Others have difficulty digesting the gluten found in some cereal grains, most commonly wheat and its close relatives. Intolerance for both lactose and gluten is more common in populations that have only recently adopted milk products and cereal grains into their diets (Wiley, 2014). The introduction of cattle and grains into early agricultural populations may have increased food availability for many people, but for some people, specific foods that were not part of their ancestral diets are mismatched with their bodies in ways that lead to diarrhea and gastrointestinal upset. Unfortunately, food aid programs originating in parts of the world where milk and grains are staples sometimes have negative impacts on the malnourished populations they target.

Although we might reasonably expect that nutrition and health would have improved with the development of agriculture, human health actually declined in many parts of the world beginning about 10,000 ya. Some have referred to the changing patterns of disease that occurred with agriculture as an "epidemiological transition," marked by the rise of infectious and nutritional deficiency diseases. In many places, skeletal signs of malnutrition (for example, megaloblastic anemia; Fig. 16-3) appear for the first time with domesticated crops such as corn (Cohen and Armelagos, 1984; Larsen, 2002). Life expectancy also appears to have dropped. Clark Larsen refers to the adoption of agriculture as an "environmental catastrophe" (Larsen, 2006), and Jared Diamond has called it the worst mistake humans ever made (Diamond, 1987). Whether for better or worse, we're stuck with agriculture as a way of acquiring food because the planet couldn't possibly support the billions that live on it today without agriculture. The "At a Glance" on page 473 provides an overview of the health consequences of diet and lifestyle between preagricultural societies versus contemporary groups.

Too Much and Too Little

Many of our biological and behavioral characteristics evolved because in the past they contributed to adaptation, but today these same characteristics may be maladaptive. An example is our ability to store fat. This capability was an advantage in the past, when food availability often alternated between abundance and scarcity. Those who could store fat during times of abundance could draw on those stores during times of scarcity and remain healthy, resist disease, and, for women, maintain the ability to reproduce. Today, people with adequate economic resources spend much of their lives with a relative abundance of foods. Considering the number of disorders associated with obesity, the formerly positive ability to store extra fat has now turned into a liability. Our "feast or famine" biology is now incompatible with the constant feast many of us indulge in today.

Perhaps no disorder is as clearly linked with dietary and lifestyle behaviors as the form of diabetes mellitus that typically has its onset in later life, referred to variously as type 2 diabetes or NIDDM (non-insulin-dependent diabetes mellitus). A few years ago, type 2 diabetes was something that happened to older people

At a Glance   Diet, Lifestyle, and Consequences

PREAGRICULTURAL DIET
Low in fat and salt, high in complex carbohydrates and fiber

Active lifestyle

↓

Low body fat, little or no obesity

↓

Low incidence of diabetes, coronary artery disease, and stroke

CONTEMPORARY DIET
High in fat, low in complex carbohydrates, high in salt

Sedentary lifestyle

↓

High body fat and high obesity rates

↓

Diabetes, coronary artery disease, and stroke common

living primarily in the developed world. Sadly, this is no longer true. The World Diabetes Foundation estimates that 80 percent of the new cases of type 2 diabetes that appear between now and 2025 will be in developing nations, and the World Health Organization (WHO) predicts that more than 70 percent of *all* diabetes cases in the world will be in developing nations in 2025. Furthermore, type 2 diabetes is occurring in children as young as four (Pavkov et al., 2006), and the mean age of diagnosis in the United States dropped from 52 to 46 between 1988 and 2000 (Koopman et al., 2005). In fact, we would guess that almost everyone reading this book has a friend or family member who has diabetes. What's happened to make this former "disease of old age" and "disease of civilization" reach what some have described as epidemic proportions?

Although there appears to be a genetic link (type 2 diabetes tends to run in families), most fingers point to lifestyle factors. Two lifestyle factors that have been implicated in this epidemic are poor diet and inadequate exercise. Noting that our current diets and activity levels are very different from those of our ancestors, proponents of **evolutionary medicine** suggest that diabetes is the price we pay for consuming excessive sugars and other refined carbohydrates while spending our days in front of the TV or computer. The reason that the incidence of diabetes is increasing in developing nations is that these bad habits are spreading to those nations. In fact, we may soon see what can be called an "epidemiological collision" in countries such as Zimbabwe, Ecuador, and Haiti, where malnutrition and infectious diseases are rampant and obesity is on the rise, so that people are dying not only from diseases of poverty but also from those more characteristic of wealthier populations (Trevathan, 2010).

It's clear that both deficiencies and excesses of nutrients can cause health problems and interfere with childhood growth and adult health. Certainly, many people in all parts of the world, both industrialized and developing, suffer from inadequate supplies of food of any quality. We read daily of thousands dying from starvation due to drought, warfare, or political instability. The blame must be placed not only on the narrowed food base that resulted from the emergence of agriculture, but also on the increase in human population that occurred when people began to settle in permanent villages and have more children. Today, the crush of billions of humans almost completely dependent on cereal grains means that millions face **undernutrition**, **malnutrition**, and even starvation. Even with these huge

evolutionary medicine The application of principles of evolution to aspects of medical research and practice.

undernutrition A diet insufficient in quantity (calories) to support normal health.

malnutrition A diet insufficient in quality (i.e., lacking some essential component) to support normal health.

populations, however, food scarcity may not be as big a problem as food inequality. In other words, there may be enough food produced for all people on earth, but economic and political forces keep it from reaching those who need it most. Of increasing concern are the effects of globalization (including liberalization of trade and agricultural policies) on food security, especially in developing nations and what has become known as the "Global South." In particular, the adoption of Western diets and lifestyles has contributed to declining health in much of the world (Young, 2004).

Thirty years ago, the primary focus of international health and nutrition organizations, including the World Health Organization, was undernutrition and infectious diseases (Prentice, 2006). Today, more and more attention is focused on overnutrition and the diseases and disorders associated with obesity. By 2006, the number of people in the world who were overweight exceeded the number who were malnourished and underweight (Popkin, 2007). In many countries, including the United States, more than half of the population is overweight or obese (Fig. 16-4; CDC, 2015). Clearly, many people consume a diet that is mismatched with the nutrients required for a healthy body.

In summary, our nutritional adaptations were shaped in environments that included times of scarcity alternating with times of abundance. The variety of foods consumed was so great that nutritional deficiency diseases were rare. Small amounts of animal foods were probably an important part of the diet in many parts of the world. In northern latitudes, after about 1 mya, meat was an important part of the diet. But because meat from wild animals is low in saturated fats, the negative effects of high meat intake that we see today were rare. Additionally, meats consumed today often include additives such as antibiotics and growth hormones that were not part of ancestral diets. Our diet today is often *disc*onnected from the adaptations that evolved in the millions of years preceding the development of agriculture. The consequences of that mismatch include both starvation and obesity.

▼ **Figure 16-4**

Adult obesity rates in the United States.

Source: Center for Disease Control and Prevention (2015).

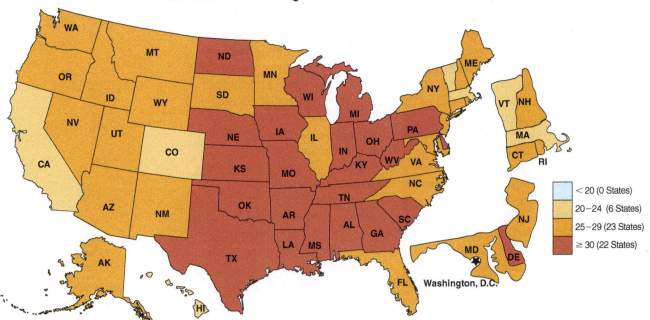

2014: Percent of Adults Aged 18 Years and Older Who are Obese †

< 20 (0 States)
20–24 (6 States)
25–29 (23 States)
≥ 30 (22 States)

† Obese is defined as body mass index (BMI) ≥ 30.0; BMI was calculated from self-reported weight and height (weight [kg]/ height [m²]).
Respondents reporting weight < 50 pounds or ≥ 650 pounds; height < 3 feet or ≥ 8 feet; or BMI: <12 or ≥ 100 were excluded. Pregnant respondents were also excluded.

Other Factors Influencing Growth and Development: Genes, Environment, and Hormones

Genetic factors set the underlying limitations and potentialities for growth and development, but the life experiences and environment of the organism determine how the body grows within those parameters. In fact, there is increasing evidence that environmental factors can change the ways in which genes are expressed without having an effect on the genes themselves and that people with identical genotypes—namely, identical twins—could have very different phenotypes. In other words, identical twins aren't really identical, and they become even more different as they age (Fraga et al., 2005; Gluckman et al., 2009). Phenotypic differences emerge in identical twins because of the "software" that provides instructions to the unfolding genotype. These instructions are known as the **epigenome**, and they are responsible for turning some genes on and some genes off. All of the cells in our body have the same genes (except the sex cells), but they do different things because of the epigenome. In different individuals, the epigenome may turn off some genes or turn on others, resulting in different phenotypes. This is one of the main ways in which the environment interacts with genes and helps explain why one member of a pair of identical twins may suffer from a genetically based cancer while the other is disease-free. Lifestyle factors are particularly important influences on the epigenome, especially diet and smoking.

The ongoing "nature-nurture debate" has pitted genetic factors against environmental factors in determining how an individual grows, develops, and behaves. The field of **epigenetics** helps to resolve this conflict by revealing that structural changes to DNA and associated proteins (without accompanying changes in the nucleotide sequence) can underlie gene expression. The changes are transmitted through mitosis, so that when they are established during development, they persist with further cell division. In this way, environmental factors (such as smoke or air pollution) can bring about changes during development that affect a person in adulthood, partially explaining differences in disease risk (Fig. 16-5). Although these changes in gene expression are not usually passed on to offspring, there is increasing evidence of epigenetic inheritance that transcends generations (Whitelaw and Whitelaw, 2006; but see Heard and Martienssen, 2014). In a classic example, Norwegian men whose grandfathers had been exposed as children to the famine known as the Dutch Hunger Winter during World War II had lower life expectancy due to epigenetic changes in genes associated with birth weight and cholesterol metabolism (Feinberg and Fallin, 2015).

Certainly, research in epigenetics calls into question the whole idea of genetic determinism for many traits. Of interest to social scientists is the suggestion that social factors may have an effect on the epigenetic programming of behavior throughout the life course (Szyf et al., 2008).

As discussed above, concerns about increasing rates of obesity in the world today indicate a need to develop interventions to prevent obesity; epigenetic research points to possible tools. Potential epigenetic markers at birth have been identified, allowing prediction of risks for obesity before adulthood. A search for modifiable factors *in utero*, childhood, and adulthood shows promise for interventions that could modify undesirable epigenetic effects (van Dijk et al., 2015).

One of the primary ways in which genes affect growth and development is through their effects on hormones. Hormones are substances produced in one cell that have an effect on another cell, and examples include estrogen, testosterone, cortisol, and insulin. Most hormones are produced by **endocrine glands**, such as the pituitary, thyroid, and adrenal glands, in addition to the ovaries and testes. Hormones are transported in the bloodstream, and almost all have an effect on

epigenome The instructions that determine which genes are expressed in cells and how.

epigenetics The study of changes in phenotype that are not related to changes in the DNA.

endocrine glands Glands responsible for the secretion of hormones into the bloodstream.

▶ **Figure 16-5**
The severe stress that often accompanies poverty can have an epigenetic effect on gene expression for some diseases and disorders.

Todd Gipstein/Getty Images

growth. The hypothalamus (located at the base of the forebrain) can be considered the relay station, control center, or central clearinghouse for most hormonal action. This control center receives messages from the brain and other glands and sends out messages that stimulate hormonal action. Most of the hormonal messages transmitted from the hypothalamus result in the inhibition or release of other hormones.

Growth hormone, secreted by the anterior pituitary, promotes growth and has an effect on just about every cell in the body. Tumors and other disorders can cause excessive or insufficient amounts of growth hormone secretion, which in turn can result in gigantism or dwarfism. One group of people who have notably short stature are African Efe pygmies (Fig. 16-6). Research suggests that altered levels of growth hormone and its controlling factors interact with nutritional factors and infectious diseases to produce the relatively short adult stature of these people (Shea and Bailey, 1996), providing another example of the interaction of biological and cultural forces.

▼ **Figure 16-6**
Charles Knowles of the Wildlife Conservation Network stands beside three Mbuti (Efe) staff members of the Okapi Conservation Project.

Wildlife Conservation Network/Charles Knowles

Another hormone that influences growth and development is cortisol, which is elevated during stress. Up to a point, cortisol elevation is adaptive, but if the response is prolonged or severe, there appear to be negative effects on health and behavior (Flinn, 1999; Flinn and England, 2003). Under conditions of chronic emotional and psychosocial stress, cortisol levels may remain high and suppress normal immune function. This means that a child living in a stressful situation is more vulnerable to infectious diseases and may experience periods of slowed growth if the stress is prolonged. A reasonable argument could be made that people today of all ages and in all parts of the world experience significantly higher levels of stress than our ancestors did, suggesting

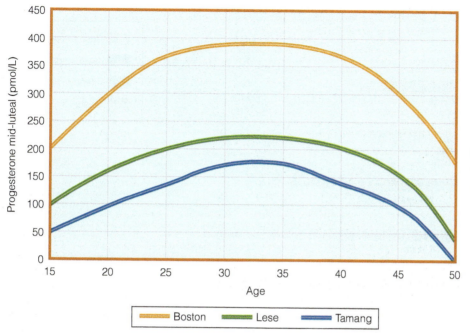

◀ Figure 16-7
Hormonal variation in three populations. (Redrawn from Ellison, 1994.)

that effects on growth may also be different. This is not to suggest that our ancestors didn't experience stress (few things are more stressful than a lion chasing you and your children), but the sources and duration of stressors were probably very different from those we experience today.

The levels of reproductive hormones in women from health-rich nations appear to be elevated over what is reported for women in traditional societies and what was probably the ancestral profile (Vitzthum, 2009; Fig. 16-7). Furthermore, women who use contraception and have few or no children and breast-feed for only a few months have more menstrual cycles (as many as 400) and the associated high levels of estrogen for the majority of their reproductive lives. Because reliable contraceptives were unavailable in the past, this high number of menstrual cycles is probably a relatively recent phenomenon. The result is a very different hormonal profile from ancestral women, who spent most of their adult years pregnant or nursing infants, yielding very few menstrual cycles (as few as 60 in their lifetimes). It's been suggested, in fact, that highly frequent menstrual cycling may be implicated in several cancers of the female reproductive organs, especially of the breast, uterus, and ovaries (Eaton et al., 1994; Strassmann, 1999; Greaves, 2008).

Life History Theory and the Human Life Course

As noted in earlier chapters, primatologists and other physical anthropologists view primate and human growth and development from an evolutionary perspective, with an interest in how natural selection has operated on the life cycle from conception to death, a perspective known as life history theory. Why, for example, do humans have longer periods of infancy and childhood compared with other primates (Fig. 16-8)? What accounts for differences seen in the life cycles of such closely related species as humans and chimpanzees? Life history research seeks to answer such questions (see Mace, 2000, for a review; Lawson and Mace, 2011).

Life history theory allows us to predict the timing of reproduction under favorable circumstances. It begins with the premise that there's only a certain amount of

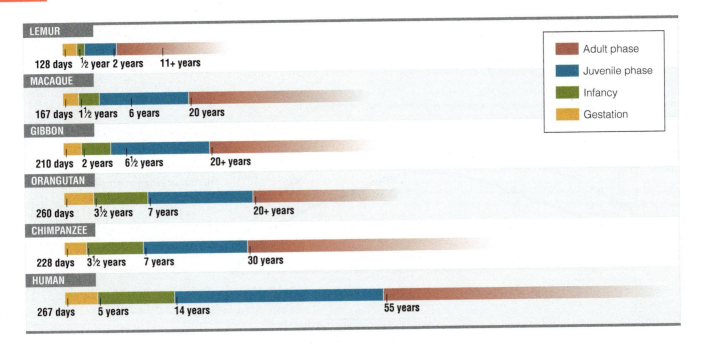

▲ **Figure 16-8**
Primate life-cycle stages.

energy available to an organism for growth, maintenance of life, and reproduction. Energy invested in one of these processes isn't available to another. Thus, the entire life course represents a series of trade-offs among various life history traits, such as length of gestation, age at weaning, time spent in growth to adulthood, adult body size, and length of life span. For example, life history theory provides the basis for understanding how fast an organism will grow and to what size, how many offspring can be produced, how long gestation will last, and how long an individual will live. Crucial to understanding life history theory is its link to the evolutionary process. It's the action of natural selection that shapes life history traits, determining which ones will succeed or fail in a given environment. Although it isn't clear how well life history theory works for contemporary human populations (Strassmann and Gillespie, 2002), it serves as a useful guide for examining the various life cycle phases from evolutionary and ecological perspectives (Low et al., 2013).

Most life cycle stages are well marked by biological transitions, such as those that occur at birth and puberty. Biological markers associated with life cycle changes are similar among higher primates, but for humans, there's an added complexity. They occur in cultural contexts that define and characterize them. Puberty, for example, has very different meanings in different cultures. A girl's first menstruation (**menarche**) is often marked with ritual and celebration, and a change in social status typically occurs with this biological transition. Likewise, **menopause** is often associated with a rise in status for women in non-Western societies, whereas it's commonly seen as a negative transition for women in many Western societies. As we shall see, collective and individual attitudes toward these life cycle transitions have an effect on growth, development, and health.

Pregnancy, Birth, Infancy, and Childhood

The biological aspects of conception and gestation can be discussed in a fairly straightforward way, drawing information from what is known about reproductive biology at the present time. A sperm fertilizes an egg; the resulting zygote travels through a uterine (fallopian) tube to become implanted in the uterine lining; and the embryo develops until it's mature enough to survive outside the womb, at which time birth occurs. But this is clearly not all there is to human pregnancy and birth.

menarche The first menstruation in girls, usually occurring in the early to midteens.

menopause The end of menstruation in women, usually occurring at around age 50.

Female reproductive biology may share similarities the world over, but cultural rules and practices are the primary determinants of who will get pregnant, as well as when, where, how, and by whom.

Once a pregnancy has begun, there's much variation in how a woman should behave, what she should eat, where she should and should not go, and how she should interact with other people. Almost every culture known imposes dietary restrictions on pregnant women. Many of these appear to serve an important biological function, particularly that of keeping the woman from ingesting toxins that would be dangerous for the fetus. Alcohol is a good example of a potential toxin whose consumption in pregnancy is discouraged in the United States (Fig. 16-9). The food aversions to coffee, alcohol, and other bitter substances that many women experience during pregnancy may be evolved adaptations to protect the embryo from toxins. The nausea of early pregnancy may also function to limit the intake of foods potentially harmful to the embryo at a critical stage of development (Profet, 1988; Williams and Nesse, 1991; but see Pike, 2000; Patil et al., 2012).

As already noted, there is increasing evidence that what happens during prenatal development has lifelong consequences, many of which are irreversible. Some researchers propose that conditions during pregnancy affect such factors as disease susceptibility and metabolism (Kuzawa, 2008; Barker, 2012); some go even further to suggest that prenatal factors can affect intelligence and temperament as well (Paul, 2010). The old adage "eating for two" can be expanded to "living for two," with evidence that stress, emotions, and pollution during pregnancy can have an effect on a developing fetus. Given the effects on metabolism, it may be that pregnancy is the best place to focus efforts to curb rising obesity rates worldwide.

Although they may seem small and helpless to us, the human newborn is huge at birth compared with the mother's body. Chimpanzee babies are only about 3 percent of their mother's size at birth; human babies are twice that percent (Fig. 16-10). The human newborn's head is especially large at birth, which accounts for some of the difficulties that women face giving birth compared with chimpanzees (Trevathan, 2015).

The continued growth of the brain after birth occurs at a rate far greater than that of any other part of the body, with the exception of the eyeball. At birth, the human brain is about 25 percent of its adult size, whereas for most mammalian species, at least 50 percent of adult brain size has been attained prior to birth. Human babies don't reach that 50 percent mark until 6 months of age, when the brain has doubled in size. Why do our babies have such undeveloped brains at birth? One reason may be that a pregnant woman's metabolism simply cannot keep up with the energetically hungry growing fetal brain and body, so she gives birth at the point when she can no longer meet the energy needs of her fetus (Ellison, 2001; Dunsworth et al., 2012). The size of the birth canal also provides limits to fetal head growth before birth (Trevathan, 2015). These metabolic and anatomical limitations, in addition to the value of having most brain growth occur in the more stimulating environment outside the womb, have resulted in human infants being born with far less of their total adult brain size than most other mammals. One by-product of this undeveloped brain is locomotor immaturity,

▲ **Figure 16-9**
Alcohol consumption in pregnancy is discouraged in many countries, including the United States.

▼ **Figure 16-10**
Toward the end of pregnancy, the human fetus is about 6 percent of the mother's body, whereas the monkey fetus is about half that, only 3 percent the mother's size.

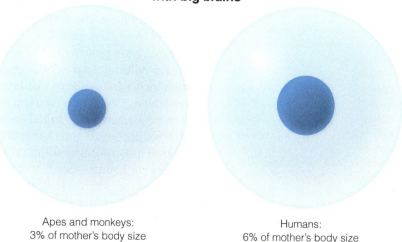

Humans gestate big-bodied babies with big brains

Apes and monkeys: 3% of mother's body size

Humans: 6% of mother's body size

meaning even greater dependence on adults for a longer time than is seen in other primates (Trevathan and Rosenberg, 2016).

Birth is an event that's celebrated with ritual in almost every culture studied. In fact, the relatively little fanfare associated with childbirth in the United States compared with many traditional societies is unusual by world standards. Because risk of death for both mother and child is so great at birth, it's not surprising that it's surrounded with ritual significance. Perhaps, because of the high risk of death, we tend to think that birth is far more difficult for humans than it is for other mammals. But since almost all primate infants have large heads relative to body size, birth is challenging to many primates.

Infancy is the period of nursing, and it typically lasts about two years in humans, with weaning occurring before infants are capable of moving independently of their mothers (Humphrey, 2010; van Noordwijk et al., 2013). When we consider how unusual it is for a mother to nurse her child for even a year in the United States or Canada, this figure may surprise us. However, considering that three or four years of nursing is the norm for the great apes and for women in some foraging societies, most anthropologists conclude that two to three years was the norm for most humans in the evolutionary past (Eaton et al., 1988; Dettwyler, 1995). On the other hand, mother's milk alone may not be sufficient to support the rapidly growing infant brain, so supplementation may have been important early in our evolutionary history, just as it is today (Kennedy, 2005; Humphrey, 2010; van Noordwijk et al., 2013).

Human milk, like that of other primates, is extremely low in fats and protein. Such a low-nutrient content is typical for species in which mothers are seldom or never separated from their infants and nurse in short, frequent bouts. Not coincidentally, prolonged, frequent nursing suppresses ovulation in marginally nourished women (Konner and Worthman, 1980), especially when coupled with high activity levels and few calorie reserves (Ellison, 2001). Under these circumstances, breast-feeding can help maintain a three-year birth interval, during which infants have no nutritional competition from siblings. Thus, nursing served as a natural (but not foolproof) birth control mechanism in the evolutionary past, as it does in some populations today.

The fact that infants born today can survive and grow without breast milk is further evidence of our species' flexibility and how cultural mechanisms have enabled us to transcend some of the biological limitations placed on our ancestors and on other mammalian species. Still, breast milk provides important antibodies and other biological factors that contribute to infant health and that are not available in formula and other milk substitutes (Hinde and Capitanio, 2010; Hinde and Milligan, 2011). Throughout the world, breast-fed infants have far greater survival rates than those who aren't breast-fed or who are weaned too early. The only exception is in societies where scientifically developed milk substitutes are readily available and appropriately used, and even then, infants don't get several important antibodies and other immune factors. The importance of adequate nutrients during this period of rapid brain growth can't be overestimated. Thus, it's not surprising that there are many cultural practices designed to ensure successful nursing. Furthermore, there is increasing evidence that breast-feeding may be protective against later-life obesity, types 1 and 2 diabetes, and hypertension (Pollard, 2008; Thompson, 2012). In fact, for women in the United States, obesity is associated with lower duration of breast-feeding (Hauff and Demerath, 2012). Like prenatal care, increasing rates of successful breast-feeding around the world is a worthy public health goal.

Caring for highly dependent infants involves more than breast-feeding. Unlike other primates, whose infants can cling to their mothers within days of birth, human infants must be carried for at least the first year of life. Even after they begin walking, they cannot do so very efficiently and must be carried when the family is traveling long distances. Carrying an infant in her arms is costly for the mother and can be even more energetically expensive than lactation (Wall-Scheffler et al., 2007). Sarah Hrdy and others have argued that the high degree of infant dependency in the first few years of life has led to a form of cooperative caregiving that involves the wider kin network, especially fathers and grandmothers (Hrdy, 2009; Bogin et al, 2014). In fact, our species is distinct from the other apes in the degree to which we share the raising of children, a phenomenon that likely led to an increase in infant survival, a decrease in the birth interval, and a resultant increase in human population, even before agriculture (Kramer, 2010). In fact, it has recently been suggested that the demands of caring for the highly dependent helpless human infant can account, in part, for many of the characteristics that make us human, such as language, food sharing, cooperative child care, prolonged female life span after menopause, and increased reliance on tools (Trevathan and Rosenberg, 2016).

Humans have an unusually long childhood, reflecting the importance of learning for our species (Bogin, 2006; Thompson and Nelson, 2011). Childhood is that time between weaning and puberty when the brain is completing its growth and the acquisition of technical and social skills is taking place. For most other mammals, once weaning has occurred, getting food is left to individual effort. Humans may be unique in the practice of providing food for juveniles (Lancaster and Lancaster, 1983). In the course of human evolution, it's possible that provisioning children between weaning and puberty may have doubled or even tripled the number of offspring that survived to adulthood (Table 16-1). This long period of extended child care by older children and adults probably enhanced the time for learning technological and social skills, also contributing to greater survival and reproductive success. Thus, the costs of extensive parental care were outweighed in human evolutionary history by the benefits of greater reproductive success. It is during childhood that the roles of fathers, older siblings, grandmothers, other kin, and even nonkin become very significant (Kramer and Russell, 2015). While mothers are highly involved with caring for infants, the socialization and child care of other children often fall to other family or community members. Clearly, family environment, stress, and other biosocial factors have a major impact on children's health (Flinn, 1999, 2008).

The major causes of childhood death worldwide today are infectious diseases exacerbated by poor nutrition (Pelletier et al., 1995; Caulfield et al., 2004; Liu et al., 2014). Noting how important it is to have sufficient caloric intake in infancy while the brain is developing, Christopher Eppig and his colleagues have suggested that infectious diseases and parasitic infections drain nutrients and energy necessary for brain development in ways that threaten cognitive development and may help explain variation in IQ scores seen across nations (Eppig et al., 2010). It's notable that the leading causes of childhood death in the United States and western Europe aren't typically related to malnutrition; for children under 5 years of age, accidents are the leading cause of death, followed by preterm births.

Table 16-1 | Providing for Juveniles

	Percent of Those Who Survive	
	Weaning	Adolescence
Lion	28	15
Baboon	45	33
Macaque	42	13
Chimpanzee	48	38
Provisioned macaque	82	58
Human populations		
!Kung*	80	58
Yanomamo[†]	73	50
Paleoindian[‡]	86	50

*Hunting and gathering population of southern Africa.
[†]Horticultural population of South America.
[‡]Preagricultural people of the Americas.
Source: Adapted from Lancaster and Lancaster, 1983.

Onset of Reproductive Function in Humans

For many animals, infancy ends with weaning as adulthood begins. For many social species, such as most primates, cetaceans, and carnivores, there's an additional life cycle stage called the juvenile stage (childhood in humans), when the young are weaned but not reproductively mature and are still dependent on adults for food.

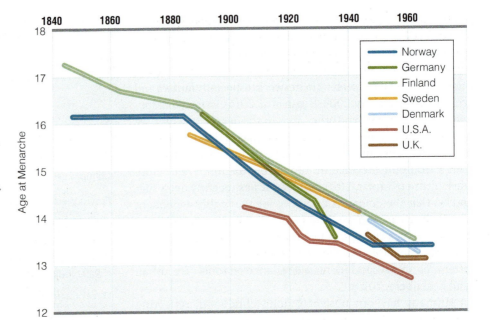

▶ **Figure 16-11**

The secular trend showing declining age of menarche in selected European nations.

Source: Wood, James W., 1994 *Dynamics of Human Reproduction*, New York: Aldine de Gruyter, original redrawn from Eveleth, P. B. and J. M. Tanner, 1976. *Worldwide Variation in Human Growth*, Cambridge: Cambridge University Press.

For humans there is yet another stage, adolescence, a period of extremely rapid growth, known as the **adolescent growth spurt**, that is not seen in other primates (Bogin, 1999, 2010).

A number of biological events mark the transition to adolescence for both males and females. These include increase in body size, change in body shape, and the increased development and enlargement of testes and penises in boys and breasts in girls. Hormonal changes are the driving forces behind all these physical alterations, especially increased testosterone production in boys and increased estrogen production in girls. As already noted, menarche is a clear sign of puberty in girls and is usually the marker of this transition in cultures where the event is ritually celebrated.

A number of factors affect the onset of puberty in humans, including genetics, gestational experience, nutrition, disease, activity levels, and stress. In humans and other primates, females reach sexual maturity before males do. An illustration of the "mismatch" effect of diet and other lifestyle factors on puberty is seen in the trend toward a lower age of menarche that has been noted in human populations in the last hundred years (Fig. 16-11) and the tendency for girls who are very active and thin to mature later than those who are heavier and less active. Socioeconomic factors are also implicated in this trend. In less industrialized nations, girls from higher social classes tend to mature earlier than girls from lower social classes. In general, physical development has accelerated in the past several decades along with worldwide improvements in public health and nutrition. Although we have emphasized the gradual decline in the age of maturity observed in the last century, there's a great range of variation within every population. An important lesson from life history theory is that maturation is sensitive to local environmental situations, including diet, health care, and parental care practices.

Decline in Reproductive Function

adolescent growth spurt The period during adolescence when well-nourished teens typically increase in stature at greater rates than at other times in the life cycle.

For women, menopause, or the end of menstruation, is a sign of entry into a new phase of the life cycle. Estrogen and progesterone production begins to decline toward the end of the reproductive years until ovulation (and thus menstruation) ceases altogether. This occurs at approximately age 50 in all parts of the world, although early life events seem to have an impact on the age of menopause;

malnutrition, for example, is related to earlier menopause (Sievert, 2014). As an example of the continuing effects of natural selection, there is evidence that women with a later age at menopause have more surviving offspring (Stearns et al., 2010). If this pattern continues, the authors suggest, the average age of menopause may increase by a year in the next 10 generations or 200 years.

Throughout human evolution, the majority of females (and males) did not survive to age 50; thus, few women lived much past menopause. But today, this event occurs when women have as much as one-third of their active and healthy lives ahead of them. There are a lot of theories about why humans have menopause and whether or not it is unique to our species, but one that seems to stand out is that menopause wasn't itself favored by natural selection; rather it's an artifact of the extension of the human life span that's occurred in the last several centuries. To put it another way, the long postreproductive years and associated menopause in women have been "uncovered" by an extended life expectancy because many causes of death are now reduced (Sievert, 2006).

Although many animals experience declines in fertility at later ages, the long and almost universal postreproductive period seen in humans is highly unusual, if not unique among primates (Hawkes and Coxworth, 2013; Levitis et al., 2013). Why do human females have such a long period during which they can no longer reproduce? One theory relates to parenting. Because it takes about 12 to 15 years before a child becomes independent, it's been argued that females are biologically "programmed" to live 12 to 15 years beyond the birth of their last child. This hypothesis assumes that the maximum human life span for preagricultural humans was about 65 years, a figure that corresponds to what is known for contemporary hunter-gatherers and for prehistoric populations.

Another theory about a long postreproductive life is known as the "grandmother hypothesis." This proposal argues that natural selection may have favored this long period in women's lives because by ceasing to bear and raise their own children, postmenopausal women would be freed to provide high-quality care for their grandchildren (Fig. 16-12). In other words, an older woman would be more likely to increase her reproductive fitness by enhancing the survival of her grandchildren (who share one-quarter of her genes) than by having her own, possibly low-quality infants (Hawkes et al., 1997; Lahdenperä et al., 2004; Hawkes and Coxworth, 2013). This is an example of the trade-offs considered by life history theory. In fact, one argument is that selection for grandmothering itself "drove" longevity in the human species (Kim et al., 2012).

University of Utah/James O'Connell

▲ **Figure 16-12**
Senior Hadza woman and grandchild.

Aging and Longevity

Postreproductive years are physiologically defined for women, but "old age" is a very ambiguous concept. In the United States, we tend to associate old age with physical ailments and decreased activity. Thus, a person who is vigorous and active at age 70 might not be regarded as "old," whereas another who is frail and debilitated at age 55 may be considered old.

One reason we're concerned with this definition is that old age is generally regarded negatively and is typically unwelcome in the United States, a culture noted

Table 16-2 | Maximum Life Spans for Selected Species

Organism	Approximate Maximum Life Span (in years)
Bristlecone pine	5,000
Tortoise	170
Rockfish	140
Human	120
Blue whale	80
Indian elephant	70
Gorilla	39
Domestic dog	34
Rabbit	13
Rat	5

Source: Stini, W. A. (1992). The Biology of Human Aging. In: *Applications of Biological Anthropology to Human Affairs*, C. G. N. Mascie-Taylor and G. W. Lasker (eds.), p. 215. Cambridge, UK: Cambridge University Press.

for its emphasis on youth. This attitude is quite different from that of many other societies, where old age brings with it wealth, higher status, and new freedoms, particularly for women. This is because high status is often correlated with knowledge, experience, and wisdom, which are themselves associated with greater age in most societies. Such has been the case throughout most of history, but today, in technologically developed countries, information is changing so rapidly that the old may no longer control the most relevant knowledge.

By and large, people are living longer today than they did in the past because, in part, they aren't dying from infectious disease. Currently, the top five killers in the United States, for example, are heart disease, cancer, stroke, chronic obstructive lung disease, and accidents. Together these account for almost 65 percent of deaths (CDC National Vital Statistics Report, 2015). All these conditions are considered "diseases of civilization" in that most can be accounted for by conditions in the modern environment that weren't present in the past, another example of the mismatch. Examples include cigarette smoke, air and water pollution, alcohol, automobiles, high-fat diets, and environmental carcinogens. It should be noted, however, that the high incidence of these diseases is also a result of people living to older ages because of factors such as improved hygiene, regular medical care, and new medical technologies.

Relative to most other animals, humans have a long life span (Table 16-2). The maximum life span potential, estimated to be about 120 years, has probably not changed in the last several thousand years, although life expectancy at birth (the average length of life) has increased significantly in the last 100 years, probably owing to increased standards of living and the decreased influence of infectious disease, which typically takes its toll on the young (Crews and Harper, 1998).

To some extent, aging is something we do throughout our lives. But we usually think of aging as **senescence**, the process of physiological decline in all systems of the body that occurs toward the end of the life course. Actually, throughout adulthood, there's a gradual decline in our cells' ability to synthesize proteins, in immune system function, in muscle mass (with a corresponding increase in fat mass) and strength, and in bone mineral density (Lamberts et al., 1997). This decline is associated with an increase in risk for the chronic degenerative diseases that are usually listed as the primary causes of death in industrialized nations.

Most causes of death that have their effects after the reproductive years won't necessarily be subjected to the forces of natural selection. In evolutionary terms, reproductive success isn't measured by how long we live; rather, as we've emphasized throughout this book, it's measured by how many offspring we produce. So organisms need to survive only long enough to produce offspring and rear them to maturity. Most wild animals die young of infection, starvation, predation, injury, and cold. Obviously, there are exceptions to this statement, especially in larger-bodied animals. Elephants, for example, may live over 50 years, and we know of several chimpanzees at Gombe that have survived into their 40s and even 50s.

One explanation for why we age and are affected by chronic degenerative diseases such as atherosclerosis, cancer, and hypertension is that genes that enhance reproductive success in earlier years (and thus were favored by natural selection) may have detrimental effects in later years. These are referred to as **pleiotropic genes**, meaning that they have multiple effects at different times in the life span or under different conditions (Williams, 1957). For example, genes that enhance the

senescence Decline in physiological function usually associated with aging.

pleiotropic genes Genes that have more than one effect; genes that have different effects at different times in the life cycle.

function of the immune system in the early years may also damage tissue so that cancer susceptibility increases in later life (Nesse and Williams, 1994). An example of this may be a gene responsible for lipid transport known as apolipoprotein E (apoE). One variant of this gene enhances immune function early in life but appears to be associated with increased risk of Alzheimer's and cardiovascular disease. In populations in which infectious agents are common, this variant is advantageous, but in populations where infectious diseases are rare and people live longer, the variant that protects against Alzheimer's and cardiovascular disease is more beneficial (Finch and Sapolsky, 1999).

Marcel Mooij/Fotolia

▲ **Figure 16-13**
Exercise throughout life may help prolong healthy mitochondrial function.

In another view of aging and pleiotropy, anticancer mechanisms operating in early life may have opposite effects in later life (Hornsby, 2010). What's more, epigenetic mechanisms affect not only aging itself but also the diseases associated with aging. Current research on these mechanisms points to possible epigenetic-based therapies and prevention strategies for dealing with the negative consequences of the aging process (Gravina and Vijg, 2010).

Pleiotropy may help us understand evolutionary reasons for aging, but what are the causes of senescence in the individual? Much attention has been focused recently on free radicals, highly reactive molecules that can damage cells. Protection against these by-products of normal metabolism is provided by antioxidants such as vitamins A, C, and E and by a number of enzymes (Kirkwood, 1997). Ultimately, damage to DNA can occur, which in turn contributes to the senescence of cells, the immune system, and other functional systems of the body. Additionally, there is evidence that programmed cell death is also a part of the normal process of development that can obviously contribute to senescence.

The mitochondrial theory of aging proposes that the free radicals produced by the normal action of the cell's mitochondria as by-products of daily living (for example, eating, breathing, walking) contribute to declining efficiency of energy production and accumulating mutations in mitochondrial DNA (mtDNA). When the mitochondria of an organ fail, there's a greater chance that the organ itself will fail. In this view, as mitochondria lose their ability to function, the body ages as well (Loeb et al., 2005; Kujoth et al., 2007). Two of the most promising strategies for enhancing health in later life are calorie reduction (Anderson and Weindruch, 2012) and aerobic exercise (Fig. 16-13), both of which appear to improve mitochondrial function in later life (Lanza and Nair, 2010).

Another hypothesis for senescence is known as the "telomere hypothesis." In this view, the DNA sequence at the end of a chromosome, known as the telomere, is shortened each time a cell divides (Fig. 16-14). Cells that have divided many times throughout the life course have short telomeres, eventually reaching the point at which they can no longer divide and are unable to maintain healthy tissues and organs. Short telomeres have been implicated in cancers and other diseases associated with aging (Oeseburg et al., 2010), but because the shortening process can remove cells before they become cancerous, they have also been described as anti-cancer defense mechanisms (Shay and Wright, 2007). Dan Eisenberg has proposed the "thrifty telomere hypothesis" to explain the mixed findings of both benefits and risks of short telomeres, suggesting that longer telomeres can be understood within life history theory as a way of maintaining healthy immune function at early ages,

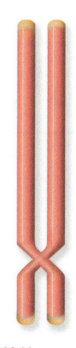

▲ **Figure 16-14**
Telomeres are repeated sequences of DNA at the ends of chromosomes, and the sequences appear to be the same in all animals. They stabilize and protect the ends of chromosomes; as they shorten with each cell division, the chromosomes eventually become unstable.

despite the costs later in life (Eisenberg, 2011). Humans have the shortest telomeres in the primate order, suggesting a partial explanation for human longevity, especially postmenopausal longevity (Tackney et al., 2014).

Far more important than genes and telomeres in the aging process, however, are lifestyle factors, such as smoking, physical activity, diet, and medical care. These factors extend even to the intestinal microbiota, which we know have an influence on health. The gut microbiota of the elderly differ from those of younger adults, reflecting activity levels and dietary factors and suggesting targets of health interventions in later life (O'Toole and Jeffery, 2015).

Life expectancy at birth varies considerably from country to country and among socioeconomic classes within a country. Throughout the world, women have higher life expectancies than men. A Japanese girl born in 2014, for example, can expect to live to age 87, a boy to age 85. Girls and boys born in that same year in the United States have life expectancies of 82 and 77, respectively. Unfortunately, gains in life expectancy in the United States appear to be slowing relative to other industrialized nations, primarily due to smoking, obesity, and sedentary habits (Seppa, 2011). In 2012, the latest year for which data were available, the United States ranked 36th in life expectancy among nations of the world (World Health Organization, 2014).

In contrast to children in industrialized nations, girls and boys in Malawi have life expectancies of only 46 and 42, respectively (data from World Health Organization, 2014). Many African nations have seen life expectancy drop to the low 40s due to deaths from AIDS. For example, before the AIDS epidemic, Botswanans had a life expectancy of almost 65 years; at the height of the AIDS epidemic, life expectancy in Botswana was slightly more than 40 (Fig. 16-15). In 1990, Zimbabweans could expect to live to 61, but by 2000 that figure had dropped to 45.

One consequence of improved health and longer life expectancy in conjunction with declining birth rates is an aging population, leading in some parts of the world to a shift toward older median ages and greater numbers of people older than 65 than younger than 20. In demographic terms, these two groups represent dependent categories, and there's increasing concern about the decline in the number

▼ **Figure 16-15**

Changes in life expectancy due to AIDS in seven African nations. (United Nations Population Division, 1998.)

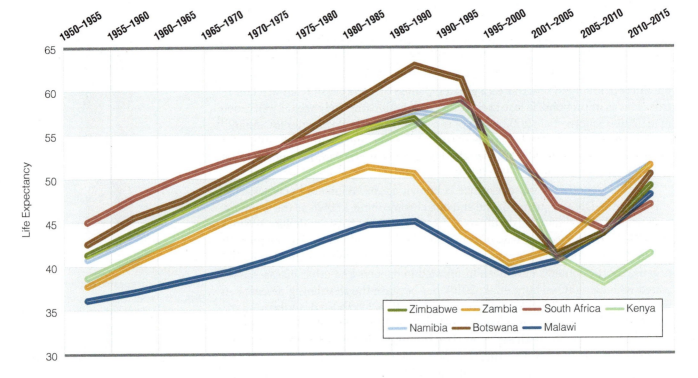

of working-aged adults available to support the younger and older segments of a population. In other words, the dependency ratio is increasing, with significant consequences for local and global economies. This phenomenon is of increasing concern in the United States and western Europe, where it is estimated that more than a third of the population will be older than age 65 and fewer than half will be in the workforce.

Are We Still Evolving?

In many ways, it seems that culture has enabled us to transcend most of the limitations our biology imposes on us. But that biology was shaped during millions of years of evolution in environments very different from those in which most of us live today. There is, to a great extent, a lack of fit, or a "mismatch," between our biology and our twenty-first-century cultural environments, resulting in health challenges at all ages. Our expectations that scientists can easily and quickly discover a "magic bullet" to enable us to resist any disease that arises have been painfully dashed as death tolls from AIDS reach catastrophic levels in many parts of the world. Moreover, obesity and related disorders are beginning to have a greater impact on human lives than undernutrition and infectious diseases.

Socioeconomic and political concerns also have powerful effects on our species today. Whether you die of starvation or succumb to disorders associated with overconsumption depends a great deal on where you live, what your socioeconomic status is, and how much power and control you have over your life—factors not related to biology. These factors also affect whether you'll be killed in a war or spend most of your life in a safe, comfortable community. Your chances of being exposed to pathogens such as HIV, Ebola, malaria, or Zika have a lot to do with where you live, your lifestyle, and other cultural factors. However, your chances of dying from the disease or failing to reproduce because of it still have a lot to do with your biology. The millions of children dying annually from respiratory infections and diarrheal disease are primarily those in the developing world, with limited access to adequate medical care—clearly a cultural factor. In those same areas, lacking that same medical care, are millions of other children who aren't getting the infections or aren't dying from them. Presumably, among the factors affecting this difference is resistance afforded by genes. It is clear that human gene frequencies are still changing from one generation to the next in response to selective agents such as disease; thus, our species is still evolving.

We can't predict whether we will become a different species or become extinct as a species (remember, that is the fate of almost every species that has ever existed). Will our brains get larger, or will our hands evolve solely to push buttons? Or will we change genetically so that we no longer have to eat food? This is the stuff of science fiction, not anthropology. But as long as new pathogens appear or new environments are introduced by technology, there's little doubt that just like every other species on earth, the human species will either continue to evolve or become extinct.

Has our evolutionary history prepared us for the twenty-first century? We have discussed a number of the disconnections between our evolved biologies and contemporary lives, but we have also emphasized that one of the most significant legacies from our evolutionary history is our biological and behavioral flexibility provided in part by the all-important phenomenon of culture. Culture has enabled us to transcend many limits imposed by our biology. Today, people who never would have been able to do so in the past are surviving and having children. This in itself means that we are adapting and evolving. How many of you would be reading this text if you had been born under the health and economic conditions prevalent 500 years ago?

How Do We Know?

A recent dietary fad, referred to as "the Paleolithic diet," "paleodiet," or "caveman diet," argues that there is a serious mismatch between our bodies and our modern diet and lifestyle. Citing literature on hunter-gatherer diets, nutritional science, and paleopathology, proponents of the Paleolithic diet argue that we should revert to an ancestral lifestyle, consuming only foodstuffs that predated the origins of agriculture (Cordain et al., 2002). Nutritional scientists have long argued that a diet of lean meat, fruits, vegetables, and nuts is key to a healthy lifestyle. Thus, much of what is argued for in the Paleolithic diet has been recommended by nutritionists for decades. However, proponents of the Paleolithic diet generally have stricter rules regarding consumption of certain types of resources, especially legumes, grains, and dairy. These resources are relatively new to the human diet, given the long span of human history as hunter-gatherers, and are commonly associated with digestive issues and food allergies. The low risk of cardiovascular disease, type 2 diabetes, and obesity among modern hunter-gatherer societies has been cited as further evidence for the benefits of the Paleolithic diet. Although drawn heavily from the anthropological literature, proponents of the Paleolithic diet have been criticized by academics who argue that it is an oversimplification of what earlier humans consumed. Bioarchaeologists and archaeologists who study preagricultural diets have noted significant regional and temporal dietary variation, indicating that there is no one "paleodiet" typical of all prehistoric hunter-gatherers. Further, there is evidence that many preagricultural societies did in fact consume legumes and grains.

Dietary fads, such as the Paleolithic diet, often have a basis in sound nutritional principles (for example, avoiding overly processed foods as well as foods high in sugars and fats). Clearly, the relationship between diet and health status is complex, making it especially difficult to make broad sweeping generalizations about the role of diet and nutrition in shaping human health in the past.

What Do You Think?

What role (if any) do you think anthropologists should play in making recommendations about modern human dietary practices? Do you think that we can learn valuable lessons about modern health by studying what our ancestors ate? ■

Summary of Main Topics

- Our biology, resulting from millions of years of evolution, may not be well matched with the diets and lifestyles we have today, perhaps contributing to many of the health problems we now face.
- The human life course is an excellent place to examine the interaction of culture and biology, given that patterns of human growth and nutritional requirements result from millions of years of biological evolution and thousands of years of cultural evolution.
- Nutrition has an impact on growth at every stage of the life cycle, and few aspects of the human environment have changed as much in the last 10,000 years as diet. In some ways, human health may have declined with the onset of agriculture and animal domestication approximately 10,000 years ago. One result of the mismatch between contemporary lifestyles and evolved biology may be a rise in the worldwide incidence of type 2 diabetes and obesity.
- Studies in epigenetics have revealed that structural changes to DNA and associated proteins caused by developmental and environmental factors can underlie gene expression, helping to resolve the age-old conflict between nature and nurture.
- There are three leading explanations that attempt to address why humans age. The pleiotropy hypothesis argues that genes that enhance reproductive success in earlier years (and thus were favored by natural selection) may have detrimental effects in later years. The mitochondrial hypothesis of aging argues that the free radicals produced by the normal action of the cell's mitochondria as by-products of daily living contribute to declining efficiency of energy production and accumulating mutations in mtDNA. As mitochondria lose their ability to function, the body ages as well. The telomere hypothesis argues that the DNA sequence at the end of a chromosome (known as a telomere) is shortened each time a cell divides, and eventually is no longer able to divide. This could result in loss of organ function and the development of certain diseases.
- Although it appears that culture has enabled us to transcend biological evolutionary processes, there is little doubt that our species continues to evolve.

Critical Thinking Questions

1. Do you think it's possible to study humans without studying culture? Can we study humans only as cultural animals, or do we need to know something about human biology to understand behavior?

2. Several times in this chapter the authors talk about a "mismatch" between our evolved biology and our contemporary lifestyles, and they suggest that this mismatch has negative consequences for health. Do you agree that many of our health problems result from this mismatch, or do you think that our health is generally much better than that of our ancestors?

3. Compare and contrast the human preagricultural diet with that seen today in places like the United States. Discuss at least one major health consequence of what has been termed the mismatch between the diet with which humans have evolved and that which many people now consume. Do you think our health would improve if we were to adopt a diet more like that of our ancestors?

4. Briefly discuss some of the theories for why humans age. Do you think it will be possible to extend the human life span to longer than 125 years? Why or why not?

5. The authors of this text claim that humans are still subjected to the forces of evolution. Do you agree? What is the evidence for or against that claim?

CONNECTIONS

Human development and adaptation are best understood from an evolutionary perspective.

Humans have recently become disconnected from other life and are rapidly altering the planet.

The Human Disconnection

Human Impacts on the Planet and on Other Life-Forms

Humans and the Impact of Culture

Global Climate Change

Public Perceptions of Climate Change

Earth's Shrinking Polar Ice

Impact on Biodiversity

Acceleration of Evolutionary Processes

Looking for Solutions

Is There Any Good News?

Student Learning Objectives After studying the material in this chapter, you should be able to:

▶ Discuss how human activities have led to a disconnect between ourselves and other species to which we are connected through our evolutionary past.

▶ Discuss some of the ways in which humans can limit their impact on the landscape.

▶ Explain how human societies have recently changed that may help alleviate their impact on the environment.

While reading this book, you have traveled through geological time to the present state of *Homo sapiens*: connecting us with earlier life through 225 million years of mammalian evolution, 65 million years of primate evolution, 6 million years of hominin evolution, and 2 million years of evolution of the genus *Homo*. So what do you think now? Are we just another mammal—or just another primate? In most ways, of course, we *are* like other mammals and primates. But as we have emphasized throughout this book, modern human beings are the result of *biocultural evolution*. In other words, modern human biology and behavior have been shaped by the biological and cultural forces that operated on our ancestors. In fact, it would be fruitless to attempt an understanding of modern human biology and diversity without considering that

A polar bear jumping between ice floes.

humans have evolved in the context of culture. It would be like trying to understand the biology of fish without considering that they live in water.

In the last few chapters, we saw how the choices we make as cultural animals have profound effects on human health. Although culture and technology have allowed us to adapt beyond our biological limits, they have also impacted other species and indeed the planet. We humans now have the ability to preserve or destroy a significant portion of the earth's life-forms—the results of millions of years of evolution. Here we will briefly discuss some of the challenges that have emerged as a result of our own actions. Many people refuse to believe that the earth's climate is changing, and of those who do, a large proportion think that this change is due to "natural" causes and not human activities. But the overwhelming consensus among climate scientists is that global warming is occurring, that the climate is changing more rapidly than anticipated, and that human activities are the cause. It is also a fact that the results of such rapid climate change are going to be more than simply "inconvenient."

Although physical anthropology textbooks don't usually dwell on the topics included here, we feel that it's important to consider them, however brief and simplified our treatment must be. We are living during a critical period in the earth's history. Indeed, the future of much of life as we know it will be decided in the next few decades, and these decisions will be irreversible. It's crucial that we, as individuals, cities, and nations, make wise decisions, and to do this we must be well informed. We also think that it's important to consider these problems from an anthropological perspective. This is something not usually done in the media and certainly not by politicians and heads of state. But if we are truly to comprehend the impact that human activities have had on the planet, then surely we must consider our biological and cultural evolution. We must also emphasize our place in nature and focus on how, from the time we began to domesticate plants and animals, we've altered the face of our planet while also shaping the destiny of thousands of species, including our own.

Human Impacts on the Planet and on Other Life-Forms

By most standards, *Homo sapiens* is a successful species. There are currently 7.4 billion humans living on this planet. Even so, we and all other multicellular organisms contribute only a small fraction of all the cells on earth—most of which are bacteria. So if we see life ultimately as a competition among reproducing organisms, bacteria are the winners, hands down.

Nevertheless, no matter what criterion for success is used, there is no question that humans have had an inordinate impact on the earth and its myriad forms of life. In the past, our ancestors had to respond primarily to challenges posed by nature. Today the greatest challenges for our species (and all others) are the vastly altered environments of our own making. Through our actions, which have caused widespread devastation of ecosystems all over the world, from the deep seas to the upper atmosphere, we have disconnected our species from its long evolutionary legacy. But at the same time we are still dependent on the ecosystems of which we remain a part. Can we survive as a species if we continue to challenge Mother Nature? Perhaps, but things will certainly be different, and the planet will be able to support far fewer humans.

Increasing population size is perhaps the single most important reason that our impact has been so great. As human population pressure increases, more and more land is converted to crops, pasture, construction, and human habitation,

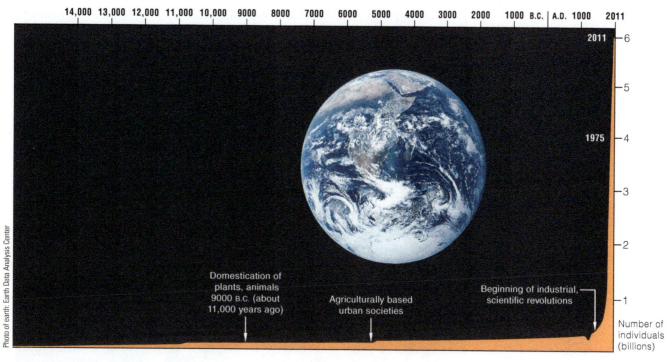

Photo of earth: Earth Data Analysis Center

Domestication of
plants, animals
9000 B.C. (about
11,000 years ago)

Agriculturally based
urban societies

Beginning of industrial,
scientific revolutions

Number of
individuals
(billions)

▲ **Figure 17-1**

Growth curve (orange) depicting the exponential growth of the world's human population. The vertical axis depicts world population size in billions. It wasn't until the mid-1800s that this figure reached 1 billion, but we now add 1 billion people every 13 years or so. Population increase occurs as a function of some percentage (in developing countries, the annual rate is over 3 percent). With advances in food production and medical technologies, humans are currently undergoing an unprecedented population explosion, as this figure illustrates.

providing more opportunities for still more humans and fewer (or no) habitats for most other species.

Scientists estimate that around 10,000 years ago, only about 5 million people inhabited the earth. By the year 1650, there were perhaps 500 million, and by 1800, around 1 billion (Fig. 17-1). Today, we add 1 billion people to the world's population approximately every 13 years (Barnosky et al., 2012). That comes out to about 77 million every year and roughly 200,000 every day—or just about 9,000 an hour.

The rate of population growth is not equally distributed among all nations. The most recent United Nations report on world population notes that 95 percent of this growth is occurring in the developing world. Likewise, resources are not distributed equally among all nations. Only a small percentage of the world's population, located in a few industrialized nations, controls and consumes most of the world's resources. A 2011 study estimated that 48 percent of the world's population survive on less than $2 per day (Population Reference Bureau, 2011).

Humans and the Impact of Culture

For most of human history, technology remained simple, and the rate of culture change was slow. From the archaeological record, it appears that around 15,000 ya, influenced in part by climate change (not induced by human activity) and the extinction of many large-bodied prey species, some cultures began to abandon their nomadic hunting and gathering lifestyles and adopt a settled way of life. Moreover, by about 10,000 ya (and probably earlier), some groups had learned that by keeping domestic animals and growing crops, they had more abundant and reliable food supplies. The domestication of plants and animals is seen as one of the most significant events in human history, one that was eventually to have far-reaching consequences for the entire planet. Human impact on local environments increased dramatically as soon as people began to live in permanent settlements.

Unfortunately humans began to exploit and increasingly depend on nonrenewable resources. Forests can be viewed as renewable resources provided they're

▶ **Figure 17-2**
Stumps of recently felled forest trees are still visible in this newly cleared field in the Amazon.

given the opportunity for regrowth. But in many areas forest clearing was virtually complete and was inevitably followed by soil erosion, frequent overgrazing, and overcultivation, which in turn led to further soil erosion (Fig. 17-2). In those areas, trees became a nonrenewable resource, perhaps the first resource to have this distinction.

Destruction of natural resources in the past has also had severe consequences for people living today. In 1990, a typhoon and subsequent flooding killed over 100,000 people in Bangladesh, and the flooding was at least partly due to previous deforestation in parts of the Himalayas of northern India. There is also evidence that deforestation has contributed to continued erosion and flooding in China. And millions of people in Pakistan were affected by flooding in 2010, 2011, and 2015 that resulted in part from deforestation and dam construction along tributaries of the Indus River. This flooding affected one-fifth of the country and set back years of infrastructure development.

Global Climate Change

There are several atmospheric substances that warm the earth by trapping heat. Collectively they are called greenhouse gases because as they accumulate in the atmosphere, they reduce the earth's ability to radiate heat produced by the sun back into space. They include water vapor, ozone, nitrous oxide, methane, chlorofluorocarbons, and carbon dioxide (CO_2). Without them the earth would freeze, but in abundance they can raise temperatures to dangerous levels, and that is what is currently happening. We can say this unequivocally because climate scientists are virtually unanimous in their view that the earth is heating up; moreover, it's happening more quickly than predicted, and it's due to human activities. Chief among these activities is the burning of fossil fuels (especially oil and coal) because they release CO_2 when burned, and CO_2 is the most significant contributor to global warming. Indeed, we currently release 35 billion tons of CO_2 into the atmosphere every year.

In 2012, scientists at the National Oceanic and Atmospheric Administration (NOAA) reported for the first time that CO_2 levels had reached 400 parts per million (ppm) in several northern locations. This figure vastly exceeds the natural range for the last 800,000 years of 180 to 300 ppm (Smol, 2012). This is highly significant because for several years climatologists have warned that if we are to keep average worldwide temperatures from increasing more than 2.5°F, the level of CO_2 must be kept at 350 ppm. In turn, keeping the increase below 2.5°F is important because many researchers consider that to be the maximum we can sustain without disastrous consequences for the environment and for thousands of species.

Public Perceptions of Climate Change

Currently, about 70 percent of Americans believe the climate is changing, and perhaps as many as 40 percent think this change is due to human activities. But this leaves around 50 to 60 percent (including many politicians and so-called "news commentators") who believe that the warming is part of a "normal" trend that has little, if anything, to do with human activities. At best, this is wishful thinking. But reversing the warming trend would be monumentally expensive and would require individual sacrifice as well as huge changes in business and industrial practices. Partly because of the sacrifices and expense, the topic of global warming is now as controversial in the United States as is evolution (Reardon, 2011). In fact, it is so controversial that in many school districts throughout the country, science teachers are strongly encouraged not to mention it.* Astonishingly, state officials in Florida have been instructed not to use the terms *climate change* or *global warming* in documents and policymaking discussions. The state of Wisconsin has implemented similar policies.

Several prominent people who deny that climate change is occurring or is the result of human activity call themselves "climate deniers" or "skeptics." Actually, skepticism is a necessary component of good science, but not when it's ideologically or financially based. As we discussed in Chapter 1, scientific research involves collecting data, evaluating the results, then publishing the findings in peer-reviewed journals. In this way, scientific claims are constantly being evaluated, critiqued, and revised. However, skepticism that is motivated primarily by ideology or financial gain is not only bad science; it's not science at all.

An important example of how scientifically based skepticism (unlike that shown by climate deniers) can add to our understanding of global climate change involves research carried out by Richard Muller, acclaimed physicist at the University of California, Berkeley. A few years ago, Professor Muller became dissatisfied with the way global warming was being evaluated. So he organized a highly regarded research team and founded the Berkeley Earth Surface Temperature Project. The team collected temperature data dating as far back as 1753 from hundreds of reporting sites around the globe, with most of the information coming from the United States and United Kingdom (ScienceInsider, *Science Magazine*, 2011). The initial results were announced in 2011. From this intensive scientific research,

---

*Sir David Attenborough, the much loved British producer of nature programs for more than 40 years, produced a highly acclaimed television series called *Frozen Planet*. When it aired in the United Kingdom in 2011, this beautifully filmed series consisted of seven parts, the last of which concerned global warming. (Unfortunately it was a tepid treatment.) Curiously, when the program aired on the Discovery Channel in the United States, it was only six episodes long. The global warming finale was not shown and most American viewers never knew about it. When questioned about this omission, spokespeople for the Discovery Channel explained that there had been a "scheduling conflict" that prevented them from showing the entire series.

Muller concluded that global warming is real and humans are almost entirely the cause.

This is a perfect example of how skepticism based in critical thinking can lead to a more accurate understanding of the world around us. However, the skeptics who were driven by ideology were not at all pleased with Muller's conclusions. These included many members of Congress as well as private individuals who helped fund the Berkeley research, believing that Muller's findings would support their denials of climate change.

One problem with climate science is that most people want definitive answers to complex questions, and they don't understand that scientific research doesn't necessarily provide definitive answers. Climate change is perhaps the most complex of phenomena because hundreds, if not thousands, of variables are involved. As more data are collected and analyzed, explanations are modified. This fact is something that most people, and apparently many politicians, do not understand. It is also a fact that climate change deniers take advantage of, because they can easily criticize what they see as contradictory results. When scientists publish results that appear to disagree with previous studies, they are reporting new conclusions based on more recent data analysis or more recently obtained evidence. While various studies may produce contradictory results, those contradictions often provide material for further study. But a great many people do not understand this, primarily because most people don't receive an adequate scientific education, if indeed they receive one at all.

In what can only be described as a cheap shot based on ignorance, U.S. Senator James Inhofe took a snowball onto the Senate floor in February 2015. This was an attempt to demonstrate (enhanced by what he no doubt considered humor) that it was very cold outside. The snowball was evidence that scientific reports stating that 2014 had been the warmest year on record worldwide were nothing more than alarmist propaganda. It is true that the winter of 2014–2015 was brutally cold in the northeastern United States, with record-breaking snowstorms and cold temperatures. But this does not mean that worldwide the climate isn't getting warmer. In fact, when annual land and oceanic temperatures are averaged, 2015 actually surpassed 2014 as the warmest year on record (National Climatic Data Center, 2016). Furthermore, 9 of the 10 warmest years on record (for the years 1880–2015) were in the twenty-first century. (The tenth was 1998.). Since 2001, we have seen 15 of the 16 warmest years on record (National Climatic Data Center, 2016). Unfortunately, 2016 is expected to break that record. Moreover, the cold experienced in the northeastern United States was consistent with predictions that as the global climate changes, we can expect much more severe weather and temperature extremes. The reason for the severe winter is the fact that the **jet stream** had changed from its normal course and was sending unusually cold temperatures farther south than normal. This change in the jet stream is believed to be due to warmer temperatures in the Arctic,* partially a result of global climate changes.

Earth's Shrinking Polar Ice

No one disputes that there have been dramatic climatic fluctuations throughout the earth's history that had nothing to do with human activity. (Indeed, human activity only became important about 250 years ago with the advent of the industrial revolution.) Consider, for example, that 50 mya there were no polar ice caps, and much of the planet was covered by tropical forests. Clearly, the climate has changed dramatically and often since then. And the Pleistocene epoch, which began around

jet stream A narrow band of strong winds that flow from west to east 6 to 8 miles above the earth. The northernmost, called the polar jet, is located in the northern part of the Northern Hemisphere. It can move farther south, causing cold temperatures and disrupting normal weather patterns.

*Arctic refers to the northern polar region, while Antarctic refers to the southern polar region.

2.6 mya, was characterized by intermittent periods of glacial advance and retreat throughout the Northern Hemisphere. These examples, based on scientific research, are the very ones climate change deniers refer to when they argue that earth's climate is constantly changing and has always done so. But even if the current warming were part of a natural cycle, scientists are convinced that human-produced greenhouse gases could tip the balance toward a catastrophic global climate change. One source of this concern is the study of ice core data, which show that there is significantly more carbon dioxide in the earth's atmosphere than at any time in the last 800,000 years. In view of this fact, consider this prediction from an international group of experts: "The mean [average] global temperature by 2070 (or possibly a few decades earlier) will be higher than it has been since the human species evolved" (Barnosky et al., 2012, p. 54). In 2007, scientists became alarmed at a sudden unexpected increase in the loss of Arctic sea ice. Unlike icebergs and glaciers that form on land, sea ice is frozen ocean water. The importance of sea ice to global climate systems can't be overemphasized because it reflects back into space about 80 percent of the sunlight (which contains heat) that hits it. But seawater absorbs approximately 90 percent of the sunlight that hits it. Therefore, as more ice melts, less sunlight is reflected and more heat is retained, resulting in yet more warming and more melting. Because of this, the polar regions are the most sensitive areas on earth to warming, and the loss of sea ice can accelerate climate change.

Since 1979, scientists have been tracking Arctic **sea ice maximum** and **sea ice minimum** data collected from satellites. In the first decade of this century, there was a sudden and alarming decline in the extent of sea ice during the summer months. Indeed, the six years between 2007 and 2012 (inclusive) saw the greatest declines in Arctic sea ice since the collection of satellite data began. The average minimum area covered by ice between 1979 and 2000 was 2.6 million square miles, but there was a significant change in 2005 when that figure was reduced to 2 million square miles. Just two years later, in 2007, the minimum was further reduced to less than 1.6 million square miles. Then, on September 16, the day that melting ceased in 2012, the extent of sea ice was 1.32 million square miles, 49 percent lower than the 1979–2000 average (Fig. 17-3). This difference of 1.28 million square miles represents an area nearly twice the size of the state of Alaska (National Snow and Ice Data Center, 2012).

The year 2015 marked another milestone in the Arctic. On February 25, the maximum extent of sea ice was reached, and at 5.61 million square miles, it was the lowest on record. The minimum sea ice extent for 2015 was reported on September 17 at 1.7 million square miles, the fourth lowest on record (see Fig. 17-3).

Scientists are now greatly concerned that the polar regions may have reached a "tipping point," a point beyond which the warming process cannot be reversed. In fact, the increase in warming is occurring faster than computer models were predicting just a few years ago. Recent estimates held that the Arctic could be ice-free for part of the summer perhaps as soon as 2030, but some scientists now fear that this could happen much sooner. It goes without saying that without sea ice in the summer, polar bears and several other species that depend on it may well become extinct in the foreseeable future.

However, there are more than a few who see financial opportunities in the melting sea ice. The absence of sea ice will drastically reduce the time it takes for ships to travel between Asia and Europe. Furthermore, it will make oil drilling possible and, in fact, Russia, Canada, and the United States already have oil exploration projects in progress.

Climate change is the result of the interactions of thousands of factors, and the consequences of these interactions aren't possible to predict with complete accuracy. But the overwhelming consensus among climate scientists points directly to

▲ **Figure 17-3**

The arctic sea ice extent for September, 17, 2015, was reported at 1.94 million square miles. The orange line indicates the average extent for that date from 1982 to 2010.

sea ice maximum In the Arctic, the greatest amount of sea ice that is present in one year. It occurs in March at the end of winter, just as the ice stops forming and begins to melt.

sea ice minimum The least amount of ice that is present in the Arctic in one year. Sea ice is at its minimum in September, just as the summer melting season ends but before the ice begins to form again.

"human-driven global change" (Barnosky et al., 2012), especially due to the burning of fossil fuels. They also agree that, as a consequence of such climate change, we are already experiencing severe fluctuations in weather patterns along with alterations in precipitation levels, and these will dramatically accelerate in the next few decades. For example, the extreme drought in the United States in the summer of 2012 (the worst in 50 years) forced many farmers to sell their farms and livestock and has caused dramatic increases in food prices. Ultimately this drought will cost at least a few billion dollars.

In late October 2012, Hurricane Sandy caused billions of dollars in damage along the northeastern coast of the United States. Streets in lower Manhattan and several subway tunnels were flooded, millions of households were without power, and thousands of homes were damaged or destroyed in New Jersey, New York, and several other states. Moreover, more than 200 people were killed.

In November 2013, another even more devastating typhoon (hurricane) struck the Philippines and other southeastern Asian countries. This Category 5 super storm, called Hurricane Haiyan, was the strongest storm to hit land ever recorded. Maximum sustained winds of 177 miles per hour were recorded, and in the Philippines alone more than 6,000 people died (not counting other affected countries, including Vietnam, southern China, and Micronesia). What's more, again just counting the Philippines, the United Nations estimated approximately 11 million people were directly affected (Fig. 17-4).

Scientists cannot state that global warming specifically caused any particular storm or severe weather pattern. However, they do say that weather will be increasingly unpredictable and that we can expect more extreme and destructive events as temperatures continue to rise. The destructive results of changing temperatures and precipitation patterns are incalculable. They include loss of agricultural lands due to desertification in some regions and flooding in others, rising sea levels inundating coastal areas throughout the world, increased human hunger, extinction of numerous plant and animal species, and altered patterns of infectious disease. Regarding the latter, health officials are particularly concerned about the spread of mosquito-borne diseases such as Zika, malaria, dengue fever, and yellow fever as warmer temperatures increase the geographical range of mosquitoes.

Another consequence of human-caused global climate change is increasing acidification of the oceans due to absorption of greater amounts of CO_2. The global

▶ **Figure 17-4**

Devastation from Typhoon Haiyan that struck the Philippines and other southeastern Asian countries in November 2013. This Category 5 super storm was the strongest storm to hit land that has ever been recorded.

dangers to ecosystems from ocean acidification are potentially as great as global warming, so much so, in fact, that some marine biologists have termed it "the other CO_2 problem" (Doney et al., 2009). Since the beginning of industrialization in the mid-1700s, ocean acidity has increased by 30 percent. If current CO_2 emission rates continue, it could increase a further 150 percent by the end of this century, reaching levels not seen in the oceans for more than 20 million years (Turley et al., 2007).

Tropical coral reefs are particularly vulnerable to acidification. Coral reefs constitute the most diverse marine ecosystems on earth, including an estimated 1 million species, which, in turn, represent up to 25 percent of all ocean-dwelling species. In addition to a tragic loss of biodiversity, there are direct economic effects of the destruction of coral reefs because more than 100 million people depend on them for food (Harrould-Kolieb and Savitz, 2009). As bad as this sounds, the longer-term effects of ocean acidification could be far more catastrophic, affecting tens of thousands of other species. Unless major action is taken soon to reduce CO_2 emissions, ocean ecosystems will probably be seriously affected by 2050 (Gruber et al., 2012). These changes could well be irreversible, or at best they will take generations to rebound. If you think this won't impact you and all of humanity, just consider that today, 20 to 25 percent of the animal protein consumed by humans comes from marine sources (Guinotte and Fabry, 2009) (Fig. 17-5).

▲ **Figure 17-5**
Coral reefs are the most biologically diverse habitats in the oceans—and also the most threatened.

There has been international recognition of the enormity of the problems associated with global climate change, and unprecedented international cooperation has begun. All this is happening because the governments of most nations understand the gravity of the impending crisis. But even though these governments recognize the problem, there is powerful opposition from industry to changes in existing policies.

In December 2009, the United Nations sponsored the International Convention on Climate Change in Copenhagen, Denmark; it was attended by representatives from nearly 200 countries. Leading up to this meeting, worldwide expectations ran high that earlier agreements (reached in 1997 at a prior international convention in Kyoto, Japan) would be expanded and strengthened with broader and more rigorous, binding agreements to cut carbon emissions.

The world looked especially to the United States for leadership and, even more, for signs of real commitment. Yet nothing substantive occurred in Copenhagen. Most world leaders indicated that they were fully prepared to commit to major cuts in carbon emissions. But widespread lack of trust in American willingness to make real political commitments (that is, effective legislation passed by Congress) as well as weak support from China led to no formal and certainly no binding agreements. Instead, only a broad statement of goals was made, with no mechanisms to ensure that even these would be met.

Another major international meeting, the United Nations Conference on Sustainable Development, again attended by representatives from almost 200 countries, was held in June 2012 in Rio de Janeiro, Brazil. This ambitious conference, also called the Earth Summit, was widely anticipated as another major opportunity to advance serious global action on climate change and related issues. However, no major initiatives were approved and most knowledgeable observers considered the conference a failure. This lack of progress has been frustrating and led many people to think that getting international cooperation was impossible. Nevertheless, *real* progress has been achieved during a huge international conference held in Paris late in 2015. This conference was attended by 40,000 people representing close to 200 nations. Although reaching agreement was complex, in the end, participants representing all these nations committed their counties to the following:

- To stop the rise of greenhouse gases as soon as possible.
- To keep the rise in worldwide temperatures during this century to less than 2 degrees C (3.6 degrees F)—and actually even by more, by holding it to 1.5°C (2.5°F).
- To have all nations submit detailed plans showing how they will reduce carbon emissions.
- To provide together 100 billion dollars yearly to poorer nations to assist them in rapidly moving away from fossil fuels to renewable ones by 2020. The wealthy countries together will provide these funds.

Such agreements are all noteworthy and, given the worldwide consensus, have been called, "historic." Yet, much remains to be done (for example, many of the initiatives are voluntary). Will the spirit of "Paris 2015" become the stimulus to truly deal with the damaging impacts of climate change? The future of our planet remains fragile.

In May 2015, Pope Francis issued a papal encyclical, or policy statement, to officials of the Catholic Church, in which he strongly condemned humanity's destruction and exploitation of the natural environment and loss of biodiversity in the name of profit. This unprecedented action has called international attention to the issue of climate change in a way that most other efforts have failed to do.

Impact on Biodiversity

According to biologist Stephen Palumbi (2001), humans are the "world's greatest evolutionary force." What Palumbi means is that we humans, like no other species before us, have had a profound effect on the evolutionary histories of almost all forms of life, including the potential to alter global ecology and destroy ourselves and much life on earth. Even massive geological events and mass extinctions did not wreak the havoc that may result from modern human technology.

The geological record indicates that in the last 570 million years, there have been at least 15 mass extinction events, two of which altered all of the earth's ecosystems (Ward, 1994). The first of these occurred some 250 mya and resulted from climate change that followed the merging of all the earth's landmasses into one supercontinent. The second event happened around 65 mya and eradicated tens of thousands of species, including most dinosaurs (recall from Chapter 5 that birds are their living descendants).

A third major extinction event, perhaps of the same magnitude, is occurring now, and according to some scientists, it may have begun in the late Pleistocene or early **Holocene** (Ward, 1994). Unlike all other mass extinctions, this one hasn't been caused by continental drift or collisions with asteroids. Today it's due to the activities of a single species, *Homo sapiens*.

The overall effects of human activities, particularly in the last 250 years, have had such a profound effect on the earth that many scientists are now recognizing these sudden and dramatic changes as marking a new geological era, called the Anthropocene (Vince, 2011). As an example of just how much our species has altered the planet, one current estimate suggests that as much as 43 percent of terrestrial habitats have been transformed to either agricultural or urban landscapes

Holocene The most recent epoch of the Cenozoic. Following the Pleistocene, it's estimated to have begun 10,500 years ago.

Tui De Roy/Minden Pictures/National Geographic Creative

◀ **Figure 17-6**
Feral goats, introduced into the Galápagos Islands, threaten the habitat of the giant Galápagos tortoise.

(and this does not include roads outside urban areas) (Barnosky et al., 2012). Like earlier major shifts in the earth's geology and biodiversity, the Anthropocene is comparable to the two planetary events mentioned earlier. These, however, were caused by gigantic asteroid collisions or super volcanoes; the Anthropocene ("the age of humans") is the result of human behavior.

For at least the past 15,000 years, human activities such as hunting and clearing land for cultivation have taken their toll on nonhuman species, but species are currently disappearing at an unprecedented rate. Hunting, which occurs for reasons other than acquiring food, is a major factor. This is particularly true for nonhuman primates, tigers, elephants, and rhinoceroses. As you saw in Chapter 6, aside from being hunted for food, nonhuman primate and tiger body parts are widely used in traditional medicines, mainly in Asia, and infant animals are commonly funneled into the exotic pet trade. Rhinoceros horns are also popular in parts of the Middle East, especially as knife handles, and in Asia for medicinal purposes. And there has been an enormous resurgence of elephant hunting in Africa for their ivory tusks. Competition with introduced nonnative species—such as pigs, goats, and rats—has also contributed enormously to the problems that wild animals face (Fig. 17-6). But in most cases the most important cause of extinction is habitat reduction.

Habitat loss is a direct result of the burgeoning human population and the resulting need for building materials, grazing and agricultural lands, and ever-expanding human habitations (Fig. 17-7). We're all aware of the risk to such highly visible species as elephants, pandas, rhinoceroses, tigers, and mountain gorillas, to name a few. These risks are real, and within your lifetime, some of these species will certainly become extinct. But the greatest threats to biodiversity are to the countless unknown species that live in the world's rain forests and in the oceans (particularly coral reefs).

Should we care about the loss of biodiversity? If so, why? In truth, many people don't seem to be very concerned, and this may be because these topics aren't extensively covered in most media. What's more, when people explain why we should care, they usually point out the benefits (known and unknown) that humans may derive from wild species of plants and animals. An example of such a benefit is the chemical taxol (derived from the Pacific yew tree), which may be an effective treatment for ovarian and breast cancer. These benefits are important, but preserving biodiversity for its own sake is every bit as crucial.

The United Nations recently organized a large international conference to address pressing issues concerning biodiversity. The conference (an extension of

▶ **Figure 17-7**

(**a**) Agricultural fields in China's Yunnan Province and (**b**) an aerial view of São Paulo, Brazil; with a population of about 19 million, it is one of the 10 largest cities in the world. The fields and city occupy land that once provided habitat for thousands of plants and animals.

the Convention on Biological Diversity) took place in October 2010 in Nagoya, Japan, and was attended by representatives from 193 countries. Unlike the lack of agreement that had until recently characterized the conferences focusing on global climate change, the results of the biodiversity meeting were quite encouraging. Conference members agreed to increase cooperation and to share financial benefits that come from the development of new drugs from wild plants and animals. What's more, they produced an impressive list of significant international goals to be reached by 2020, including an effort to reduce to half or bring close to zero the rate of loss of all natural habitats, to reduce pollution to levels that are not detrimental to ecosystems and biodiversity, to conserve at least 17 percent of terrestrial areas and 10 percent of coastal and marine areas in protected zones, to prevent the extinction of known threatened species, and to restore at least 15 percent of degraded ecosystems.

Acceleration of Evolutionary Processes

Another major impact of human activities is the acceleration of the evolutionary process for hundreds of bacteria and viruses. Many of these changes have occurred over a single human generation (that is, during the lifetime of many people living today), not the millions of years usually associated with evolution. As noted earlier, our use of antibiotics has dramatically altered the course of evolution of several bacterial diseases to the point where many bacteria have become resistant to antibiotics. Antibiotics have now become the most significant selective factors causing many bacteria to evolve into more virulent forms. It's even likely that human technology and lifestyles are responsible for the deadly nature of some of the so-called new diseases that have arisen in recent decades, such as HIV/AIDS, dengue hemorrhagic fever, Legionnaires' disease, Lyme disease, and resistant strains of *Mycobacterium tuberculosis*, *Staphylococcus*, and *Escherichia coli*. We could reach a point where we have no antibiotics capable of fighting dangerous bacteria that live and constantly mutate in our midst. For example, there are billions of beneficial bacteria in a person's digestive tract. We couldn't live without these bacteria, but some can and occasionally do mutate into varieties that cause serious illness and even death. Without antibiotics, these and many other bacteria in our environment would have the ability to drastically increase mortality due to infectious disease.

A similar phenomenon has occurred with the overuse and misuse of insecticides and pesticides on agricultural crops (Palumbi, 2001). DDT is perhaps the best known insecticide to have altered the course of a species' evolution. When this insecticide was first developed, it was hailed as the best way to reduce malaria by eliminating the mosquitoes that transmit the disease. DDT was highly effective when it was first applied to mosquito-ridden areas, but soon mosquitoes evolved resistance to the powerful agent, rendering it almost useless in the fight against malaria. Moreover, the use of DDT proved disastrous to many bird species, including the bald eagle (Fig. 17-8). In the 1970s, its use was curtailed and even banned in some countries, but the failure of other efforts to treat malaria has led to a recent call to begin using DDT again.

From these examples, it's clear that the human-caused accelerated process of microbial evolution is something that can lead to great harm to our species and the planet. Certainly, none of the scientists developing antibiotics, insecticides, pesticides, and other biological tools intend to cause harm. But unless they understand the evolutionary process, they may not be able to foresee the long-term consequences of their work. As the great geneticist Theodosius Dobzhansky (1973) said, "Nothing in biology makes sense except in the light of evolution." Indeed, we can't afford to have even a single generation of scientists who are not fully informed about evolution. If human actions can cause an organism to evolve from a relatively benign state to a dangerously virulent one, there is no reason why we can't turn that process around. In other words, it is theoretically possible to direct the course of evolution of a dangerous virus such as HIV to a more benign, less harmful state (Ewald, 1999).

▲ Figure 17-8
DDT almost caused the extinction of the American bald eagle, the bird featured on the Great Seal of the United States.

U.S. Government

Looking for Solutions

The problems facing our planet reflect an adaptive strategy gone awry. Indeed, it's clear that we no longer enjoy the harmonious relationship we once had with culture or with the planet. Instead, culture has become an unintentional transformer of the environment. All we need to do is examine the very air we breathe to realize that we have overstepped our limits (Fig. 17-9).

Can the problems we've created be solved? Perhaps, but any objective assessment of the future fails to provide much optimism. Climate change, air pollution, depletion of the ozone layer, and loss of biodiversity are catastrophic problems in a world of 7.4 billion people. How do we cope *now* with feeding, housing, and educating all these inhabitants? What quality of life do the majority of the world's people enjoy right now? What kind of world have we wrought for the other organisms that share our planet, many of which are steadily isolated within fragments of what were once large habitats? If these concerns aren't overwhelming enough now, what kind of world will we see in the year 2050, when the human population could reach 10 billion? Among other consequences of this population growth, the world's food production would need to double in order for everyone to have enough to eat. (Millions are underfed and undernourished now.) Because our window of opportunity shrinks every year, industrialized nations must immediately help developing countries to adopt fuel-efficient technologies that will allow them to raise their standard of living without increasing their output of greenhouse gases. Furthermore, family planning must be adopted to slow population growth. In most societies, however, behavioral change is very difficult, and sacrifice on the part of the developing world alone wouldn't adequately stem the tide. It's entirely too easy for someone from North America to ask that the people of Bangladesh control their rate of reproduction (it runs two to three times that of the United States). But consider this: The average American uses an estimated 400 times the resources consumed by a resident of Bangladesh. The United States *alone* produces 25 to 30 percent of all carbon dioxide emissions that end up in the earth's atmosphere. In 2007, China caught up with the United States in this regard, but over 1.3 billion people live in China, compared with 300 million in the United States. In his book *The Future of Life* (2002), E. O. Wilson discussed the issue in terms of "ecological footprints," or the average amount of land and sea required for each person to support his or her lifestyle. This includes all resources consumed for energy, housing, transportation, food, water, and waste disposal. In nonindustrialized nations,

▼ **Figure 17-9**

Today, air pollution is a worldwide problem. (**a**) Two Vietnamese girls using scarves as protective masks. (**b**) Sunrise over Delhi, India. (**c**) Toronto, Canada, in the gloom. (**d**) Sunset over Beijing, China. (**e**) A smoggy day in Los Angeles.

the ecological footprint per capita is about 2.5 acres, but in the United States it's 24 acres! Wilson went on to point out that four additional planet earths would be needed for every person on the planet to reach the current levels of consumption in the United States. Clearly, much of the responsibility for the world's problems rests squarely on the shoulders of the industrialized West.

Is There Any Good News?

Although world population growth continues, it appears that the rate of growth has slowed somewhat. It's common knowledge among economists that as income and education increase, family size decreases, and as infant and childhood mortality rates decrease, families have fewer children. In fact, one of the best strategies for reducing family size and thus world population is to educate girls and women. Educated women are more likely to be in the labor force and are better able to provide food for their families, seek health care for themselves and their children, and practice family planning.

With decreases in family size and improvements in education and employment opportunities for both men and women throughout the world, we are also likely to see improvements in environmental conservation and habitat preservation. The small Central American country of Costa Rica has recognized the economic importance of its abundant and beautiful natural resources. By developing ecotourism as a means of generating income, Costa Rica has been able, for the present, to preserve much of its forests and wildlife. In fact, ecotourism has become its primary industry, and Costa Rica's poverty levels are the lowest in Central America. Habitat destruction and poverty often go hand in hand. Although successes like those accomplished in Costa Rica can't be replicated everywhere, this small nation has been a model for making environmental concerns integral to social and economic development.

Annually since 2005, leaders from both developing and developed countries have come together to discuss new ways of reducing global poverty, especially in sub-Saharan Africa. Additionally, some of the wealthiest people in the world (including Bill and Melinda Gates, George Soros, Warren Buffet, Richard Branson, and Ted Turner) have begun to invest their personal fortunes to help reduce poverty and poor health and thus to promote global peace and prosperity. Lastly, the degree of international cooperation shown at the 2010 conference on biodiversity is a hopeful development that could be a foundation for slowing species extinctions and maintaining natural habitats.

What should be obvious is that only by working together can nations and individuals hope to develop solutions to the world's problems. As we discussed in Chapter 7, cooperation is important to survival in nonhuman primates, and this was no doubt true for our ancestors as well. The question now is whether or not we have the collective will to see that our admirable goals are met. Many people believe that it's our only hope.

Studies of human evolution have much to contribute to our understanding of how we, as a single species, came to exert such control over the destiny of our planet. It's a truly phenomenal story of how a small apelike creature walking on two feet across the African savanna challenged nature by learning to make stone tools. From these humble beginnings came large-brained humans who, instead of stone tools, now have telecommunications satellites, computers, and nuclear arsenals at their fingertips. The human story is indeed unique and wonderful. Our two feet have carried us not only across the plains of Africa but onto the polar caps, the ocean floor, and even on the surface of the moon! Surely, if we can accomplish so much in so short a time, we can act responsibly to preserve our home and the wondrous creatures that share it with us.

How Do We Know?

In this chapter, we discussed many of the negative effects humans have had on our planet. Human impacts on the environment have become increasingly dramatic over time, especially during the last two centuries. This period, labeled the "Anthropocene" by some researchers, marks a time when humans have had a more profound impact on the planet than any other force of nature. Although humans have had a significant, and often negative, impact on the earth's environments for at least the last 12,000 years (since the origin of farming), the Anthropocene best captures anthropogenic impacts on the landscape, including species extinction, deforestation, land degradation, pollution, urbanization, loss of polar ice, and global warming. Massive population growth during this period has only served to exacerbate global environmental problems. But is the Anthropocene a meaningful geological period? Yes and no. Some researchers have argued that human impacts, beginning with the first farmers around 11,500 years ago, mark the beginning of the Anthropocene. For example, the earliest agricultural societies deforested the landscape to create arable land for growing crops and for developing cities. Other researchers have argued that the Anthropocene should be used more as an informal term to refer to the past 250 years of human impacts on the landscape. Despite these arguments, one thing is clear. Humans have never had as significant an impact on local environments as they do today, and our degrading environment will introduce an array of exceedingly significant challenges to future generations.

What Do You Think?

The concept of the Anthropocene is largely discussed within academic circles and is not well known to the public. Do you think this concept could be useful in promoting public understanding of the impact of humans on the landscape? Why or why not? ■

Summary of Main Topics

- Humans are the product of millions of years of biocultural evolution; but in just the last few hundred years we have exerted a huge influence on other life-forms and the planet itself. No other organism in the earth's history has had such an impact. A major contributor to the scope of recent human disruptions of the earth's ecosystems is population growth. Probably the most immediate and crucial challenge we face is to reduce our influence on global climate change. Public perceptions of climate change have influenced politicians and others who try to discredit the evidence to serve political purposes. Despite these challenges, scientific evidence strongly demonstrates that climate change is largely driven by human activities. Climate change has resulted in the loss of biodiversity on planet earth, including habitat loss, overhunting, and forest clearing. Many organisms are directly or indirectly threatened with extinction.

- Solutions for the impacts of climate change are difficult to implement. The move toward more fuel-efficient technologies, new approaches to growing more food in a sustainable way, and reducing global population growth can all help to reduce the human footprint on the environment.

- Some promising signs are that the rate of human population growth is diminishing somewhat, more women are entering the workforce and are therefore having fewer children, and infant mortality rates are lower. Improvements in economic and education circumstances may help promote a higher level of conservation within developing nations.

Critical Thinking Questions

1. What do you think will happen in your local area, to the country, and to the planet if population growth continues?

2. Why do most scientists support the conclusion that CO_2 emissions are the primary cause of global climate change? If you think this conclusion is not correct, can you point to scientific evidence that supports your view?

3. What do you personally think individuals, large corporations, and world leaders should do to address the world's environmental problems?

4. What are some benefits of preserving biodiversity? Why do you think biodiversity is important for the overall health of the planet?

Appendix A
Atlas of Primate Skeletal Anatomy

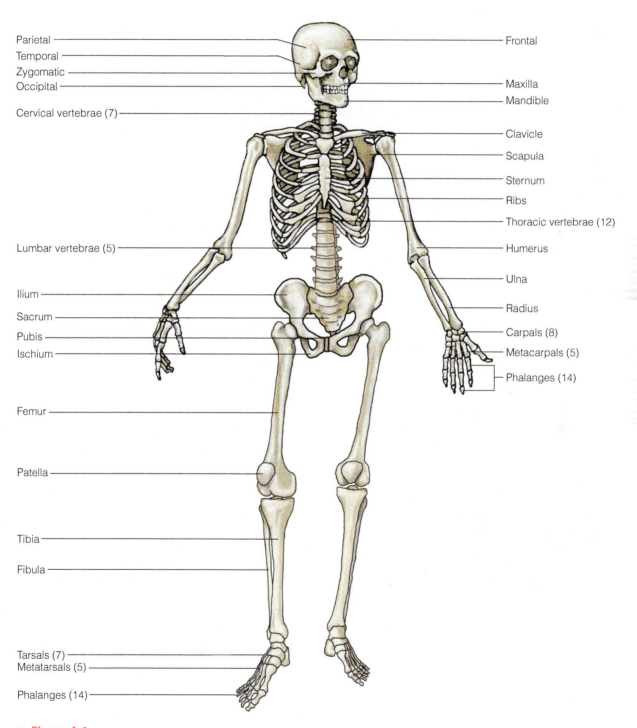

Parietal

Temporal

Zygomatic

Occipital

Cervical vertebrae (7)

Lumbar vertebrae (5)

Ilium

Sacrum

Pubis

Ischium

Femur

Patella

Tibia

Fibula

Tarsals (7)

Metatarsals (5)

Phalanges (14)

Frontal

Maxilla

Mandible

Clavicle

Scapula

Sternum

Ribs

Thoracic vertebrae (12)

Humerus

Ulna

Radius

Carpals (8)

Metacarpals (5)

Phalanges (14)

▲ **Figure A-1**

Human skeleton (*Homo sapiens*)—
bipedal hominin.

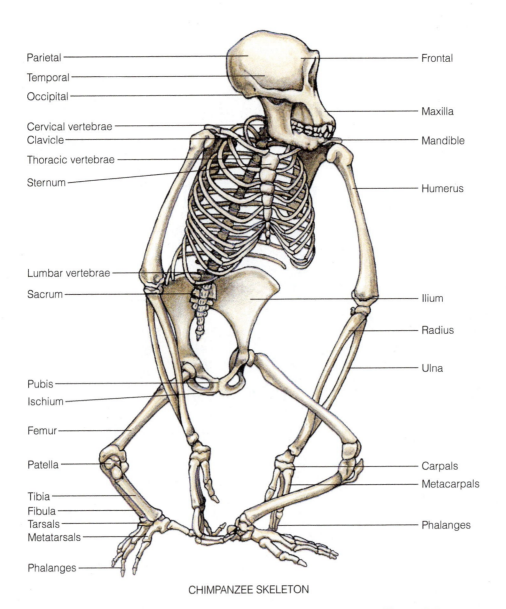

Parietal

Temporal

Occipital

Cervical vertebrae

Clavicle

Thoracic vertebrae

Sternum

Lumbar vertebrae

Sacrum

Pubis

Ischium

Femur

Patella

Tibia

Fibula

Tarsals

Metatarsals

Phalanges

Frontal

Maxilla

Mandible

Humerus

Ilium

Radius

Ulna

Carpals

Metacarpals

Phalanges

CHIMPANZEE SKELETON

▲ **Figure A-2**
Chimpanzee skeleton (*Pan troglodytes*)—
knuckle-walking ape.

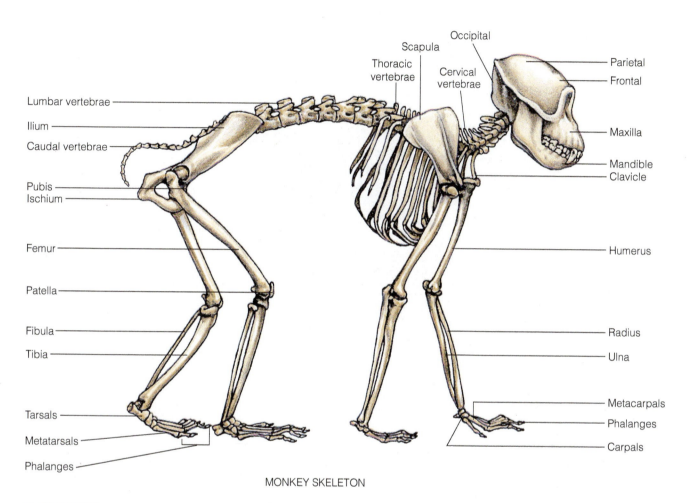

MONKEY SKELETON

▲ **Figure A-3**

Monkey skeleton (rhesus macaque; *Macaca mulatta*)—a typical quadrupedal primate.

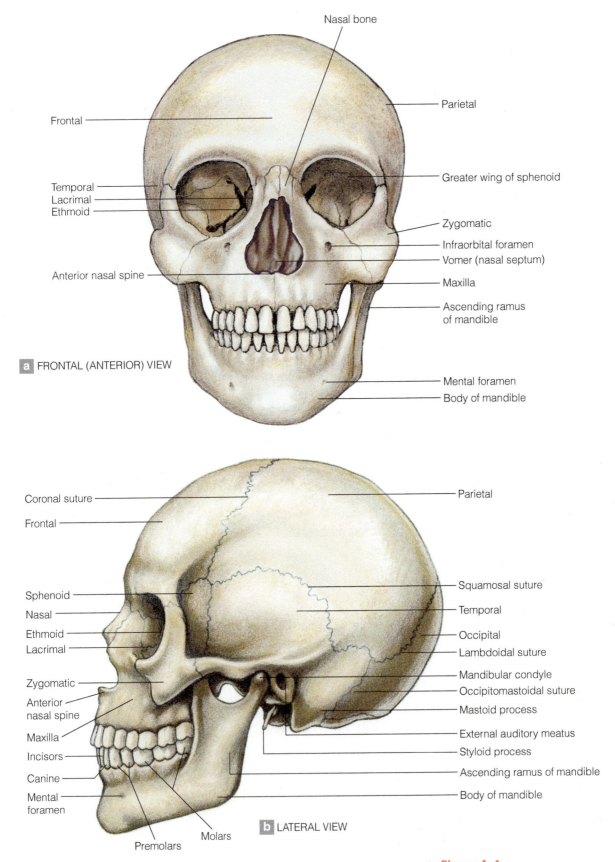

Nasal bone

Parietal

Frontal

Greater wing of sphenoid

Temporal
Lacrimal
Ethmoid

Zygomatic

Infraorbital foramen

Vomer (nasal septum)

Anterior nasal spine

Maxilla

Ascending ramus
of mandible

a FRONTAL (ANTERIOR) VIEW

Mental foramen

Body of mandible

Coronal suture

Parietal

Frontal

Squamosal suture

Sphenoid

Temporal

Nasal

Occipital

Ethmoid

Lambdoidal suture

Lacrimal

Mandibular condyle

Occipitomastoidal suture

Zygomatic

Mastoid process

Anterior
nasal spine

External auditory meatus

Maxilla

Styloid process

Incisors

Ascending ramus of mandible

Canine

Body of mandible

Mental
foramen

b LATERAL VIEW

Premolars

Molars

▲ **Figure A-4**

Human cranium.

(continued on next page)

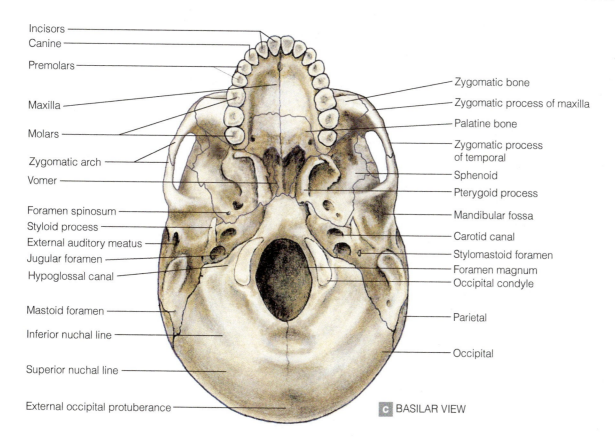

Incisors
Canine
Premolars
Maxilla
Molars
Zygomatic arch
Vomer
Foramen spinosum
Styloid process
External auditory meatus
Jugular foramen
Hypoglossal canal
Mastoid foramen
Inferior nuchal line
Superior nuchal line
External occipital protuberance

Zygomatic bone
Zygomatic process of maxilla
Palatine bone
Zygomatic process of temporal
Sphenoid
Pterygoid process
Mandibular fossa
Carotid canal
Stylomastoid foramen
Foramen magnum
Occipital condyle
Parietal
Occipital

c BASILAR VIEW

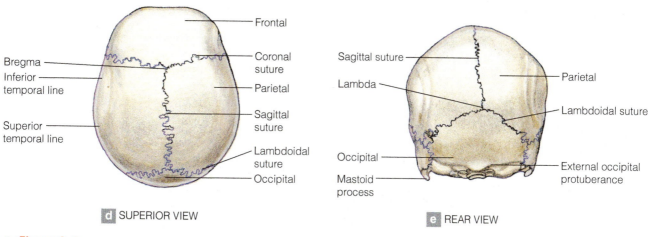

Frontal
Bregma
Inferior temporal line
Superior temporal line
Coronal suture
Parietal
Sagittal suture
Lambdoidal suture
Occipital

d SUPERIOR VIEW

Sagittal suture
Lambda
Occipital
Mastoid process
Parietal
Lambdoidal suture
External occipital protuberance

e REAR VIEW

▲ **Figure A-4**
Human cranium.

(continued)

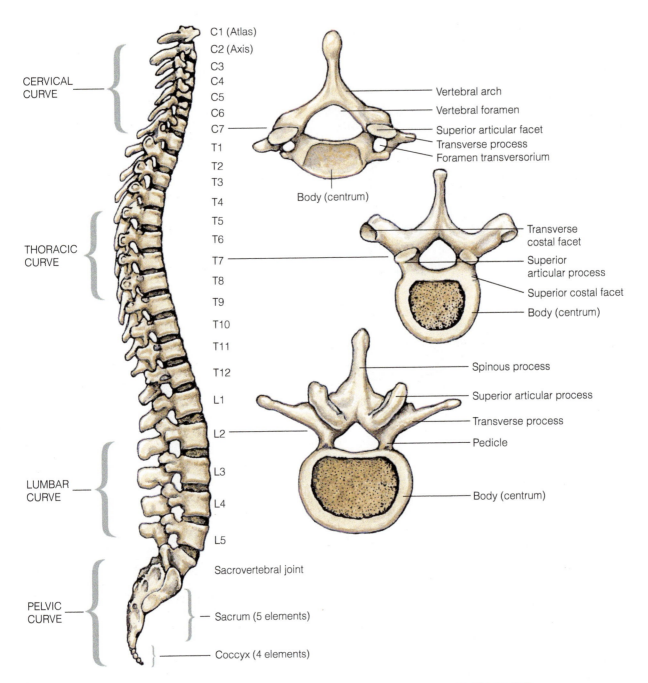

CERVICAL
CURVE

C1 (Atlas)
C2 (Axis)
C3
C4
C5
C6
C7
T1
T2
T3
T4

Vertebral arch
Vertebral foramen
Superior articular facet
Transverse process
Foramen transversorium

Body (centrum)

THORACIC
CURVE

T5
T6
T7
T8
T9
T10
T11
T12
L1

Transverse
costal facet

Superior
articular process

Superior costal facet

Body (centrum)

Spinous process

Superior articular process

Transverse process

Pedicle

LUMBAR
CURVE

L2
L3
L4
L5

Body (centrum)

Sacrovertebral joint

PELVIC
CURVE

Sacrum (5 elements)

Coccyx (4 elements)

▲ **Figure A-5**
Human vertebral column (lateral view)
and representative cervical, thoracic, and
lumbar vertebrae (superior views).

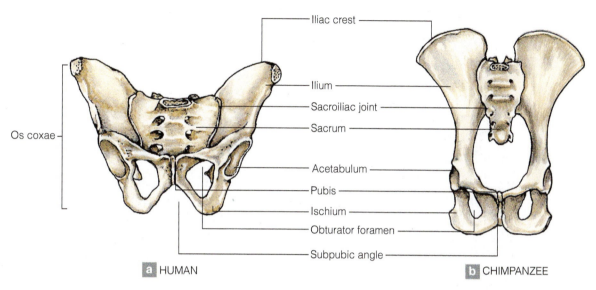

Iliac crest

Ilium

Sacroiliac joint

Sacrum

Acetabulum

Pubis

Ischium

Obturator foramen

Subpubic angle

Os coxae

a HUMAN

b CHIMPANZEE

▲ **Figure A-6**
Pelvic girdles.

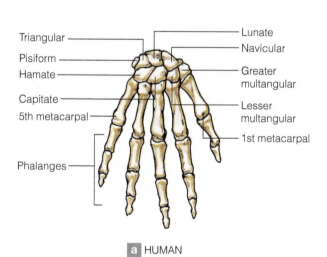

Triangular

Pisiform

Hamate

Capitate

5th metacarpal

Phalanges

Lunate

Navicular

Greater
multangular

Lesser
multangular

1st metacarpal

a HUMAN

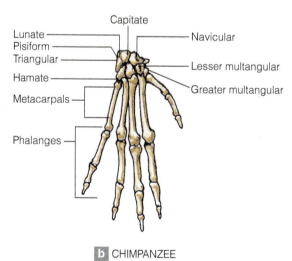

Capitate

Lunate

Pisiform

Triangular

Hamate

Metacarpals

Phalanges

Navicular

Lesser multangular

Greater multangular

b CHIMPANZEE

▲ **Figure A-7**
Hand anatomy.

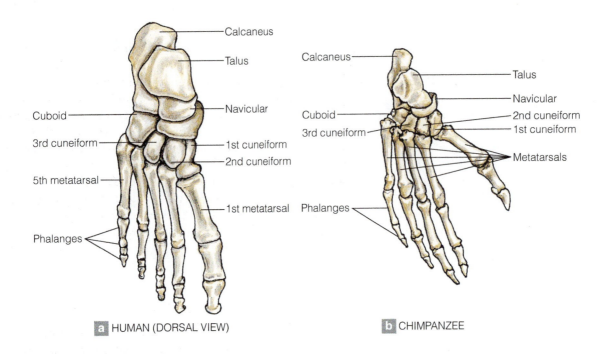

a HUMAN (DORSAL VIEW)

b CHIMPANZEE

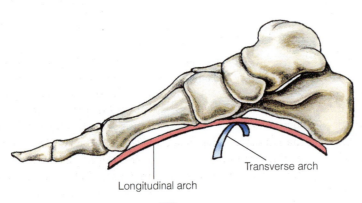

c HUMAN (MEDIAL VIEW)

▲ **Figure A-8**
Foot (pedal) anatomy.

Appendix B
Sexing and Aging the Skeleton

The field of physical anthropology that is directly concerned with the analysis of skeletal remains is called *osteology*. Using an osteological perspective allows researchers to study skeletons of both human and nonhuman primates to understand the ways in which hominins are similar to, and distinct from, other primates. Moreover, paleoanthropologists also use many of the same techniques to analyze the remains of fossil hominins (which mostly consist of teeth and bones). In more recent contexts, encompassing the last few thousand years, skeletal remains of *Homo sapiens* have been investigated by osteologists to learn about the size, nutritional status, and diseases present in prior human populations.

Two very important questions that osteologists ask when analyzing a skeleton are the sex and age of the individual. Such basic demographic variables as sex and age are crucial in any comprehensive osteological analysis, especially of human remains.

Sexing the Skeleton

During infancy and childhood, male and female skeletons do not differ much. Consequently, osteologists usually cannot determine the sex of a skeleton of someone who died before 13 to 15 years of age. However, during development, *sexual dimorphism* is increasingly manifested in the skeleton, making sex determination feasible in adult remains, provided enough of the skeleton is present. We should mention that molecular techniques are sometimes able to detect the presence of the Y chromosome from bone or dental tissue (thus determining that a skeleton is that of a male). Though not yet used widely, molecularly based sexing is becoming more common in osteological analyses.

The differences between male and female skeletons are most clearly expressed in the pelvis (*pl.*, pelves), and this variation is due to the requirements of childbirth in females. In particular, during hominin evolution, the dual influences of bipedal locomotion and relatively large-brained newborns placed adaptive constraints on pelvic anatomy. As a result, in females the pelvis is generally broader and more splayed out than in males. The most useful criteria for sex determination are listed in Table B-1 and illustrated in Figure B-1. Although these criteria, taken together, are good indicators of sex, you should be aware that none, taken in isolation, is accurate in all cases. Moreover, this is not a complete listing of all traits used in sexing skeletons, although it does include those most commonly used.

There are also sex differences in cranial dimensions, most especially relating to facial proportions. However, these differences are not as consistent as those in the pelvis. Therefore, it is important to recognize patterns of cranial variation as they are expressed in different populations. The cranial features most commonly used for sex determination are listed in Table B-2 (see also Fig. B-2). These differences reflect the fact that in males, the skeleton is larger than in females. The bones are denser, and areas of muscle attachment are frequently more robust. However, such differences are not consistently expressed across various populations, and knowledge of relevant population variation is thus important in drawing reasonable determinations of sex.

Table B-1 | Differences between the Male and Female Pelvis

Pelvic Characteristic	Female	Male
General	Muscle attachments less robust; overall appearance sometimes less massive	Muscle attachments more robust; overall appearance sometimes more massive
Subpubic angle	Wider (more than 90°)	Narrower (less than 90°)
Greater sciatic notch	Wider—more open (more than 68°)	Narrower—more closed (less than 68°)
Ischiopubic ramus (medial view)	Thinner	Thicker
Ventral arc (elevated ridge on ventral surface of pubis)	Frequently present	Absent
Sacrum	Wider and straighter	Narrower and more curved

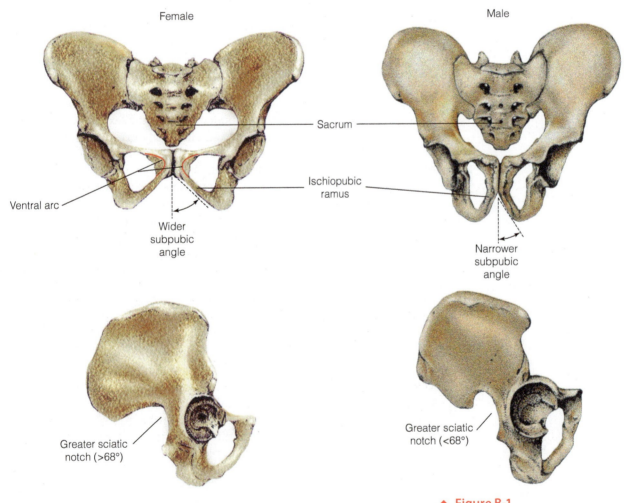

▲ **Figure B-1**
Male and female pelves compared.

Table B-2	Differences between the Male and Female Cranium	
Cranial Feature	**Female**	**Male**
Points of muscle attachment (e.g., mastoid process)	Less pronounced	Larger, more pronounced
Supraorbital torus (browridge)	Less pronounced or absent	More pronounced
Supraorbital rim (upper margin of eye orbit)	Sharper	More rounded
Palate	More shallow	Deeper

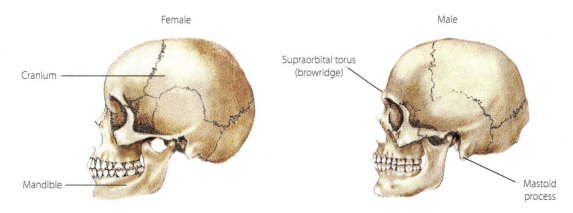

▲ **Figure B-2**
Male and female cranium and mandible.

Determining Age

During growth, the skeleton and dentition undergo developmental changes that occur within known age ranges. Thus, estimating age in individuals who were younger than 20 when they died is based primarily on the presence of deciduous (baby) and permanent teeth, the appearance of ossification centers of bones, and the fusion of the ends of long bones to bone shafts.

Dental Eruption

Age estimation based on dental eruption is useful in individuals up to approximately 15 years of age. The third molar (wisdom tooth) erupts after this time, but the age of eruption of this tooth (if it forms at all) is highly variable. Thus, the third molar is not a very reliable indicator of age except that its presence indicates that the individual was at least a young adult (Fig. B-3).

Bone Growth

The size of the long bones, the development of secondary ossification centers (epiphyses), and the degree of fusion of epiphyses (ends of the bones) to diaphyses (bone shafts) are just as important as dental eruption. Postcranial bones are preceded by a cartilage model that is gradually replaced by bone, both in the diaphyses and the secondary centers (epiphyses). In children and adolescents, bones continue to grow until the epiphyses fuse to the diaphyses. Because this fusion occurs within different age ranges in different bones, the age of an individual can be estimated by determining which epiphyses have fused and which have not (Fig. B-4). The characteristic undulating appearance of the unfused surfaces helps differentiate immature elements from the broken end of a mature bone.

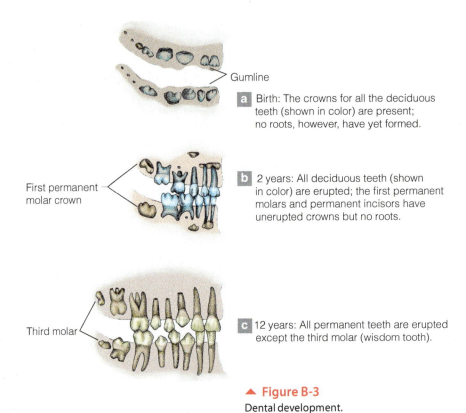

Gumline

a Birth: The crowns for all the deciduous teeth (shown in color) are present; no roots, however, have yet formed.

First permanent molar crown

b 2 years: All deciduous teeth (shown in color) are erupted; the first permanent molars and permanent incisors have unerupted crowns but no roots.

Third molar

c 12 years: All permanent teeth are erupted except the third molar (wisdom tooth).

▲ **Figure B-3**
Dental development.

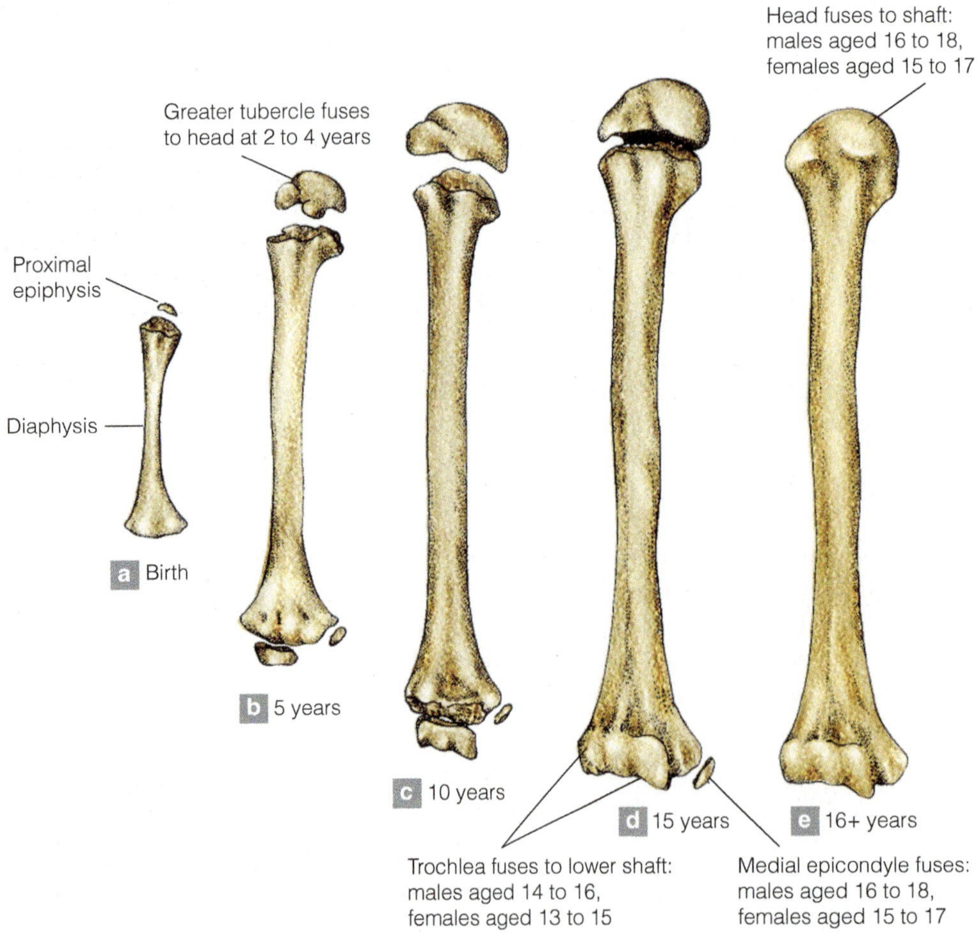

Head fuses to shaft: males aged 16 to 18, females aged 15 to 17

Greater tubercle fuses to head at 2 to 4 years

Proximal epiphysis

Diaphysis

a Birth

b 5 years

c 10 years

d 15 years

e 16+ years

Trochlea fuses to lower shaft: males aged 14 to 16, females aged 13 to 15

Medial epicondyle fuses: males aged 16 to 18, females aged 15 to 17

◀ **Figure B-4**
Skeletal age: epiphyseal union in the humerus. Some regions of the humerus exhibit some of the earliest fusion centers in the body, while others are among the latest to complete fusion (not until late adolescence).

Other Skeletal Changes

Once a person has reached physiological maturity (by the early 20s), determinations of age become more difficult and less precise. Several techniques are used, and these are based on the occurrence of progressive, regular changes in the face of the pubic symphysis (the most common technique), in the sternal ends of the ribs, and in the auricular surface of the ilium (where the ilium articulates with the sacrum). Other indicators are closure of the cranial sutures and cellular changes that are determined by microscopic examination of cross sections of long bones. Degenerative changes, such as arthritis, osteoporosis, and wear of dental enamel, can also aid in the determination of relative age (older versus younger), but they provide imprecise estimates. In fact, it is very difficult to age the skeletons of adults accurately. For example, the presence of severe tooth wear would imply that the individual was not young, but enamel attrition varies between populations and depends on many factors, including diet. Moreover, the appearance of many degenerative changes is influenced by disease, trauma, and the biological makeup of individuals. Thus, at present, osteologists must be content to use broad age ranges when estimating age at death in mature skeletons.

Pubic Symphyseal Face   The face of the pubic symphysis in young individuals is characterized by a billowing surface (with ridges and furrows) such as that seen on the surface of an epiphysis (Fig. B-5). The symphyseal face undergoes regular age-related changes from the age of about 18 onward.

The first aging technique based on alterations of the pubic symphysis was developed by T. W. Todd (1920, 1921), utilizing dissection room cadavers. McKern and Stewart (1957) developed a technique by analyzing a sample of American males killed in the Korean War. Both of the samples from which these systems were derived, however, had limitations. The dissection room sample used by Todd contained some individuals of uncertain age, and the Korean War sample was predominantly made up of young white males, with few being older than 35.

More recently, a system has been developed by Judy Suchey and colleagues (Katz and Suchey, 1986) based on very well-documented autopsy samples of males and females. These samples have proved more representative of the general population than the earlier samples. Because this technique is derived from data collected from a large sample of people of known age at death, it is currently the most accurate method available for estimating age in adult human skeletal remains.

▼ **Figure B-5**
Skeletal age: remodeling of the pubic symphysis. This area of the pelvis shows systematic changes progressively throughout adult life. Two of these stages are shown in (**b**) and (**c**).

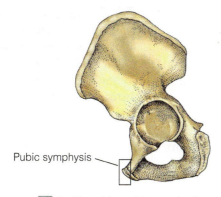

a Position of the pubic symphysis.

b Age 21. The face of the symphysis shows the typical "billowed" appearance of a young joint; no rim present.

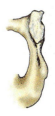

c Age mid-50s. The face is mostly flat, with a distinct rim formed around most of the periphery.

Glossary

acclimatization Physiological responses to changes in the environment that occur during an individual's lifetime. Such responses may be temporary or permanent, depending on the duration of the environmental change and when in the individual's life it occurs. The capacity for acclimatization may typify an entire population or species, and because it's under genetic influence, it's subject to evolutionary factors such as natural selection and genetic drift.

Acheulian (ash´-oo-lay-en) Pertaining to a stone tool industry from the Early and Middle Pleistocene; characterized by a large proportion of bifacial tools (flaked on both sides). Acheulian tool kits are common in Africa, Southwest Asia, and western Europe, but they're thought to be less common elsewhere. Also spelled Acheulean.

adaptation An anatomical, physiological, or behavioral response of organisms or populations to the environment. Adaptations result from evolutionary change (specifically as a result of natural selection).

adaptive niche An organism's entire way of life: where it lives, what it eats, how it gets food, how it avoids predators, and so on.

adaptive radiation The relatively rapid expansion and diversification of life-forms into new ecological niches.

adaptive zone A general ecological lifestyle more basic than the narrower ecological niche characteristic of an individual species.

adolescent growth spurt The period during adolescence when well-nourished teens typically increase in stature at greater rates than at other times in the life cycle.

affiliative behaviors Amicable associations between individuals. Affiliative behaviors, such as grooming, reinforce social bonds and promote group cohesion.

allele frequency In a population, the percentage of all the alleles at a locus accounted for by one specific allele.

alleles Alternate forms of a gene. Alleles occur at the same locus on paired chromosomes and thus govern the same trait, but because they're different, their action may result in different expressions of that trait.

altruism Actions that benefit another individual but at some potential risk or cost to oneself.

amino acids Small molecules that are the components of proteins.

analogies Similarities between organisms based strictly on common function, with no assumed common evolutionary descent.

ancestral Referring to characters inherited by a group of organisms from a remote ancestor and thus not diagnostic of groups (lineages) that diverged after the character first appeared; also called primitive.

anthropocentric Viewing nonhuman organisms in terms of human experience and capabilities; emphasizing the importance of humans over everything else.

anthropoids Members of the primate infraorder Anthropoidea (pronounced "an-throw-poid´-ee-uh"), which includes monkeys, apes, and humans.

anthropology The field of inquiry that studies human culture and evolutionary aspects of human biology; includes cultural anthropology, archaeology, linguistics, and physical, or biological, anthropology.

antigens Large molecules found on the surface of cells. Several different loci govern various antigens on red and white blood cells. (Foreign antigens provoke an immune response.)

applied anthropology The practical application of anthropological and archaeological theories and techniques. For example, many biological anthropologists work in the public health sector.

arboreal Tree living; adapted to life in the trees.

artifacts Objects or materials made or modified for use by hominins. The earliest artifacts are usually tools made of stone or occasionally bone.

Aurignacian Pertaining to an Upper Paleolithic stone tool industry in Europe beginning at about 40,000 ya.

australopiths A colloquial name referring to a diverse group of Plio-Pleistocene African hominins. Australopiths are the most abundant and widely distributed of all early hominins and are also the most completely studied.

autonomic Pertaining to physiological responses not under voluntary control. An example in chimpanzees would be the erection of body hair during excitement. Blushing is a human example. Both convey information regarding emotional states, but neither is deliberate, and communication isn't intended.

autosomes All chromosomes except the sex chromosomes.

balanced polymorphism The maintenance of two or more alleles in a population due to the selective advantage of the heterozygote.

behavior Anything organisms do that involves action in response to internal or external stimuli; the response of an individual, group, or species to its environment. Such responses may or may not be deliberate and they aren't necessarily the results of conscious decision making.

behavioral ecology The study of the evolution of behavior, emphasizing the role of ecological factors as agents of natural selection. Behaviors and behavioral patterns have been favored because they increase the reproductive fitness of individuals (i.e., they are adaptive) in specific environmental contexts.

bilophodont Referring to molars that have four cusps oriented in two parallel rows, resembling ridges, or "lophs." This trait is characteristic of Old World monkeys.

binocular vision Vision characterized by overlapping visual fields provided by forward-facing eyes. Binocular vision is essential to depth perception.

binomial nomenclature (*binomial*, meaning "two names") In taxonomy, the convention established by Carolus Linnaeus whereby genus and species names are used to refer to living things. For example, *Homo sapiens* refers to human beings.

bioarchaeology The study of skeletal remains and their archaeological context.

biocultural evolution The mutual interactive evolution of human biology and culture; the concept that biology (anatomy, neurological attributes, etc.) makes culture possible and that developing culture further influences the direction of biological evolution; this is a basic concept in understanding the unique components of human evolution.

biological continuity A biological continuum. When expressions of a phenomenon continuously grade into one another so that there are no discrete categories, they exist on a continuum. Color is one such phenomenon, and life-forms are another.

biological continuum Refers to the fact that organisms are related through common ancestry and that

behaviors and traits seen in one species are also seen in others to varying degrees. (When expressions of a phenomenon continuously grade into one another so that there are no discrete categories, they are said to exist on a continuum. Color is one such phenomenon.)

biological determinism The concept that phenomena, including various aspects of behavior (e.g., intelligence, values, morals) are governed by biological (genetic) factors; the inaccurate association of various behavioral attributes with certain biological traits, such as skin color.

biological species concept A depiction of a species as a group of individuals capable of fertile interbreeding but reproductively isolated from other such groups.

biostratigraphy A relative dating technique based on the regular changes seen in evolving groups of animals as well as the presence or absence of particular species.

bipedally On two feet; walking habitually on two legs.

blanks In archaeology, stones suitably sized and shaped to be further worked into tools.

brachiation Arm swinging, a form of locomotion used by some primates. Brachiation involves hanging from a branch and moving by alternately swinging from one arm to the other.

breeding isolates Populations that are clearly isolated geographically and/or socially from other breeding groups.

burins Small, chisel-like tools with a pointed end; thought to have been used to engrave bone, antler, ivory, or wood.

catarrhine Member of Catarrhini, a parvorder of Primates, one of the three major divisions of the suborder Haplorhini. It contains the Old World monkeys, apes, and humans.

catastrophism The view that the earth's geological landscape is the result of violent cataclysmic events.

Cuvier promoted this view, especially in opposition to Lamarck.

Cercopithecidae (serk-oh-pith´-eh-see-dee) The taxonomic family that includes all Old World monkeys.

cercopithecines (serk-oh-pith'-eh-seens) Common name for members of the subfamily of Old World monkeys that includes baboons, macaques, and guenons.

Cercopithicinae (serk-oh-pith'-eh-see-nee) Taxonomic subfamily of Old World monkeys that have cheek pouches for storing food. Includes macaques, baboons, and several other species of monkey that use both arboreal and terrestrial habitats.

Chatelperronian Pertaining to an Upper Paleolithic industry found in France and Spain, containing blade tools and associated with Neandertals.

Chordata The phylum of the animal kingdom that includes vertebrates.

Christian fundamentalists Adherents to a movement in American Protestantism that began in the early twentieth century. This group holds that the teachings of the Bible are infallible and should be taken literally.

chromosomes Discrete structures composed of DNA and proteins found only in the nuclei of cells. Chromosomes are visible under magnification only during certain phases of cell division.

chronometric dating (*chrono*, meaning "time," and *metric*, meaning "measure") A dating technique that gives an estimate in actual numbers of years; also known as absolute dating.

clade A group of organisms sharing a common ancestor. The group includes the common ancestor and all descendants.

cladistics An approach to classification that attempts to make rigorous evolutionary interpretations based solely on analysis of certain types of homologous characters (those considered to be derived characters).

cladogram A chart showing evolutionary relationships as determined by cladistic analysis. It's based solely on interpretation of shared derived characters. It contains no time component and does not imply ancestor-descendant relationships.

classification In biology, the ordering of organisms into categories, such as orders, families, and genera, to show evolutionary relationships.

clones Organisms that are genetically identical to another organism. The term may also be used to refer to genetically identical DNA segments, molecules, or cells.

codominance The expression of two alleles in heterozygotes. In this situation, neither allele is dominant or recessive, so they both influence the phenotype.

codons Triplets of messenger RNA bases that code for specific amino acids during protein synthesis.

Colobinae (kole'-uh-bi-nay) Taxonomic subfamily of Old World leaf-eating monkeys that have reduced thumbs and multi-chambered stomachs. Includes colobus monkeys, proboscis monkeys, and langurs.

colobines (kole'-uh-bines) Common name for members of the subfamily of Old World monkeys that includes the African colobus monkeys and Asian langurs.

communication Any act that conveys information to another individual. Frequently, the result of communication is a change in the behavior of the recipient. Communication may not be deliberate but may instead be the result of involuntary processes or a secondary consequence of an intentional action.

complementary In genetics, referring to the fact that DNA bases form pairs (called base pairs) in a precise manner. For example, adenine can bond only to thymine. These two bases are said to be complementary because one requires the other to form a complete DNA base pair.

context The environmental setting where an archaeological trace is found. Primary context is the setting in which the archaeological trace was originally deposited. A secondary context is one to which it has been moved (such as by the action of a stream).

continental drift The movement of continents on sliding plates of the earth's surface. As a result, the positions of large landmasses have shifted drastically during the earth's history.

continuum A set of relationships in which all components fall along a single integrated spectrum (e.g., color). All life reflects a single biological continuum.

core A stone reduced by flake removal. A core may or may not itself be used as a tool.

core area The portion of a home range containing the highest concentration and most reliable supplies of food and water. The core area is defended.

crown group All of the taxa that come after a major speciation event. Crown groups are easier to identify than stem groups because the members possess the clade's shared derived traits.

culture Behavioral aspects of human adaptation, including technology, traditions, language, religion, marriage patterns, and social roles. Culture is a set of learned behaviors transmitted from one generation to the next by nonbiological (i.e., nongenetic) means.

cusps The bumps on the chewing surface of premolars and molars.

cytoplasm The semifluid, gel-like substance contained within the cell membrane. The nucleus and numerous structures involved with cell function are found within the cytoplasm.

data (*sing.*, datum) Facts from which conclusions can be drawn; scientific information.

dental formula Numerical device that indicates the number of each type of tooth in each quadrant of the upper and lower jaws.

derived (modified) Referring to characters that are modified from the ancestral condition and thus diagnostic of particular evolutionary lineages.

direct percussion Striking a core or flake with a hammerstone.

displays Sequences of repetitious behaviors that serve to communicate emotional states. Nonhuman primate displays are most frequently associated with reproductive or agonistic behavior. Examples include chest slapping in gorillas and, in male chimpanzees, dragging and waving branches while charging and threatening other animals.

diurnal Active during the day.

DNA (deoxyribonucleic acid) The double-stranded molecule that contains the genetic code. DNA is a main component of chromosomes.

dominance hierarchies Systems of social organization wherein individuals within a group are ranked relative to one another. Higher-ranking animals have greater access to preferred food items and mating partners than lower-ranking individuals. Dominance hierarchies are sometimes called "pecking orders."

dominant In genetics, describing a trait governed by an allele that's expressed in the presence of another allele (i.e., in heterozygotes). Dominant alleles prevent the expression of recessive alleles in heterozygotes. (This is the definition of *complete* dominance.)

ecological Pertaining to the relationships between organisms and all aspects of their environment (temperature, predators, nonpredators, vegetation, availability of food and water, types of food, disease organisms, parasites, etc.).

ecological niche The position of a species within its physical and biological environments. A species' ecological niche is defined by such components as diet, terrain, vegetation, type of predators, relationships with other species, and activity patterns, and each niche is unique to a given species.

Together, ecological niches make up an ecosystem.

ecological species concept The concept that a species is a group of organisms exploiting a single niche. This view emphasizes the role of natural selection in separating species from one another.

empathy The ability to identify with the feelings and thoughts of another individual.

empirical Relying on experiment or observation; from the Latin *empiricus*, meaning "experienced."

encephalization The proportional size of the brain relative to some estimate of overall body size, such as weight. More precisely, the term refers to increases in brain size beyond what would be expected given the body size of a particular species.

endemic Continuously present in a population.

endocast A solid impression of the inside of the skull vault, often preserving details relating to the size and surface features of the brain.

endocrine glands Glands responsible for the secretion of hormones into the bloodstream.

endogamy Mating with individuals from the same group.

endothermic (*endo*, meaning "within" or "internal," and *thermic*, meaning "heat") Able to maintain internal body temperature by producing energy through metabolic processes within cells; characteristic of mammals, birds, and perhaps some dinosaurs.

enzymes Specialized proteins that initiate and direct chemical reactions in the body.

epigenetics The study of changes in phenotype that are not related to changes in the DNA.

epigenome The instructions that determine which genes are expressed in cells and how.

epochs Categories of the geological time scale; subdivisions of periods. In the Cenozoic era, epochs include the Paleocene, Eocene, Oligocene, Miocene, and Pliocene (from the

Tertiary Period) and the Pleistocene and Holocene (from the Quaternary Period).

essential amino acids The 9 (of 22) amino acids that must be obtained from the food we eat because they are not synthesized in the body in sufficient amounts.

ethnocentric Viewing other cultures from the inherently biased perspective of one's own culture. Ethnocentrism often causes other cultures to be seen as inferior to one's own.

ethnographies Detailed descriptive studies of human societies. In cultural anthropology, an ethnography is traditionally the study of a non-Western society.

eugenics The philosophy of "race improvement" through the forced sterilization of members of some groups and increased reproduction among others; an overly simplified, often racist view that's now discredited.

euprimates "True primates." This term was coined by Elwyn Simons in 1972.

evaporative cooling A physiological mechanism that helps prevent the body from overheating. It occurs when perspiration is produced from sweat glands and then evaporates from the surface of the skin.

evolution A change in the genetic structure of a population. The term is also frequently used to refer to the appearance of a new species.

evolutionary medicine The application of principles of evolution to aspects of medical research and practice.

evolutionary systematics A traditional approach to classification (and evolutionary interpretation) in which presumed ancestors and descendants are traced in time by analysis of homologous characters.

exogamy Mating pattern whereby individuals obtain mating partners from groups other than their own.

exons Segments of genes that are transcribed and are involved in protein synthesis. (The prefix *ex*

denotes that these segments are expressed.)

fertility The ability to conceive and produce healthy offspring.

fitness Pertaining to natural selection, a measure of the relative reproductive success of individuals. Fitness can be measured by an individual's genetic contribution to the next generation compared with that of other individuals. The terms *genetic fitness*, *reproductive fitness*, and *differential net reproductive success* are also used.

fixity of species The notion that species, once created, can never change is diametrically opposed to theories of biological evolution.

flake A thin-edged fragment removed from a core.

flexed The position of the body in a bent orientation, with arms and legs drawn up to the chest.

forensic anthropology An applied anthropological approach focused on the application of osteology and archaeology to legal matters. Forensic anthropologists work with coroners and others in identifying and analyzing human remains.

fossils Traces or remnants of organisms found in geological beds on the earth's surface.

founder effect A type of genetic drift in which allele frequencies are altered in small populations that are taken from larger populations or are remnants of the latter.

frugivorous Having a diet composed primarily of fruits.

gametes Reproductive cells (eggs and sperm in animals) developed from precursor cells in ovaries and testes.

gene A sequence of DNA bases that specifies the order of amino acids in an entire protein, a portion of a protein, or any functional product, such as RNA. A gene may be composed of thousands of DNA bases.

gene flow Exchange of genes between populations.

gene pool The total complement of genes shared by the reproductive members of a population.

genetic Having to do with the study of gene structure and action, and the patterns of inheritance of traits from parent to offspring. Genetic mechanisms are the foundation of evolutionary change.

genetic drift Evolutionary changes, or changes in allele frequencies, produced by random factors in small populations. Genetic drift is a result of small population size.

genome The entire genetic makeup of an individual or species. In humans, it's estimated that the human genome comprises about 3 billion DNA bases.

genotype The genetic makeup of an individual. Genotype usually refers to an organism's genetic makeup (or alleles) at a particular locus.

genus (*pl.*, genera) A group of closely related species.

geological time scale The organization of earth history into eras, periods, and epochs; commonly used by geologists and paleoanthropologists.

glaciations Climatic intervals when continental ice sheets cover much of the northern continents. Glaciations are associated with colder temperatures in northern latitudes and more arid conditions in southern latitudes, most notably in Africa.

grooming Picking through fur to remove dirt, parasites, and other materials that may be present. Social grooming is common among primates and reinforces social relationships.

habitual bipedalism Bipedal locomotion as the form of locomotion shown by hominins most of the time.

half-life The time period in which one-half the amount of a radioactive isotope is converted chemically to a daughter product. For example, after 1.25 billion years, half the potassium-40 (^{40}K) remains; after 2.5 billion years, one-fourth remains.

haplorhines (hap-lore´-ines) Members of the primate suborder Haplorhini, which includes tarsiers, monkeys, apes, and humans.

Haplorhini (hap'-lo-rin-ee) The primate suborder that includes tarsiers, monkeys, apes, and humans. (Colloquial form: haplorhine.)

Hardy-Weinberg theory of genetic equilibrium The mathematical relationship expressing—under conditions in which no evolution is occurring—the predicted distribution of alleles in populations; the central theorem of population genetics.

hemisphere One of the two halves of the cerebrum, which are connected by a dense mass of fibers. (The cerebrum is the large rounded outer portion of the brain.)

hemoglobin A protein molecule that occurs in red blood cells and binds to oxygen molecules.

heterodont Having different kinds of teeth; characteristic of mammals, whose teeth consist of incisors, canines, premolars, and molars.

heterozygous Having different alleles at the same locus on members of a pair of chromosomes.

Holocene The most recent epoch of the Cenozoic. Following the Pleistocene, it's estimated to have begun 10,500 years ago.

homeobox genes An evolutionarily ancient family of regulatory genes that directs the development of the overall body plan and the segmentation of body tissues. There are at least 20 families of homeobox genes.

homeostasis A condition of balance, or stability, within a biological system, maintained by the interaction of physiological mechanisms that compensate for changes (both external and internal).

hominins Colloquial term for members of the evolutionary group that includes modern humans and all extinct bipedal relatives.

Hominoidea Taxonomic superfamily that includes all apes and humans (tailless primates).

hominoids Members of the primate superfamily (Hominoidea), which includes apes and humans.

homologies Similarities between organisms based on descent from a common ancestor.

homoplasy (*homo*, meaning "same," and *plasy*, meaning "growth") The separate evolutionary development of similar characteristics in different groups of organisms.

homozygous Having the same allele at the same locus on both members of a pair of chromosomes.

honing complex The shearing of a large upper canine with the first lower premolar, with the wear leading to honing of the surfaces of both teeth. This anatomical pattern is typical of most Old World anthropoids but is mostly absent in hominins.

hormones Substances (usually proteins) that are produced by specialized cells and that travel to other parts of the body, where they influence chemical reactions and regulate various cellular functions.

Human Genome Project An international effort aimed at sequencing and mapping the entire human genome, completed in 2003.

hybrids Offspring of parents who differ from each other with regard to certain traits or certain aspects of genetic makeup; also known as heterozygotes.

hypotheses (*sing.*, hypothesis) Provisional explanations of phenomenon. Hypotheses require verification or falsification through testing.

hypoxia Insufficient levels of oxygen in body tissues; oxygen deficiency.

inbreeding A type of nonrandom mating in which relatives mate more often than predicted under random mating conditions.

incest avoidance In animals, the tendency not to mate with close relatives. This tendency may be due to various social and ecological factors that keep the individuals apart. There may also be innate factors that lead to incest avoidance, but these aren't well understood.

intelligence Mental capacity; ability to learn, reason, or comprehend and interpret information, facts, relationships, and meanings; the capacity to solve problems, whether through the application of previously acquired knowledge or through insight.

interglacials Climatic intervals when continental ice sheets are retreating, eventually becoming much reduced in size. Interglacials in northern latitudes are associated with warmer temperatures, while in southern latitudes the climate becomes wetter.

interspecific Between species; refers to variation beyond that seen within the same species to include additional aspects seen between two different species.

introns Segments of genes that are initially transcribed and then deleted. Because introns are not expressed, they aren't involved in protein synthesis.

island hopping Traveling from one island to the next.

jet stream A narrow band of strong winds that flow from west to east 6 to 8 miles above the earth. The northernmost, called the polar jet, is located in the northern part of the Northern Hemisphere. It can move farther south, causing cold temperatures and disrupting normal weather patterns.

karyotype The chromosomes of an individual, or what is typical of a species, viewed microscopically and displayed in a photograph. The chromosomes are arranged in pairs and according to size and position of the centromere.

knappers People (frequently archaeologists) who make stone tools.

K-selected Pertaining to K-selection, an adaptive strategy whereby individuals produce relatively few offspring, in whom they invest increased parental care. Although only a few infants are born, chances of survival are increased for each one because of parental investments of time and energy (compared with r-selected species). Birds, elephants, and canids (wolves, coyotes, and dogs) are examples of K-selected nonprimate species.

lactase persistence In adults, the continued production of lactase, the enzyme that breaks down lactose (milk sugar). This allows adults in some human populations to digest fresh milk products. The discontinued production of lactase in adults leads to lactose intolerance and the inability to digest fresh milk.

language A standardized system of arbitrary vocal sounds, written symbols, and gestures used in communication.

last common ancestor (LCA) The final evolutionary link between two related groups.

Late Pleistocene The portion of the Pleistocene epoch beginning 125,000 ya and ending approximately 10,500 ya.

life history traits Characteristics and developmental stages that influence reproductive rates. Examples include longevity, age at sexual maturity, and length of time between births.

lithic (*lith*, meaning "stone") Referring to stone tools.

locus (*pl.*, loci) (lo'-kus, lo-sigh') The position or location on a chromosome where a given gene occurs. The term is sometimes used interchangeably with *gene*.

macroevolution Changes produced only after many generations, such as the appearance of a new species.

Magdalenian Pertaining to the final phase of the Upper Paleolithic stone tool industry in Europe.

malnutrition A diet insufficient in quality (i.e., lacking some essential component) to support normal health.

matrilines Groups that consist of a female, her daughters, and their offspring. Matrilines are common among macaques.

meiosis Cell division in specialized cells in ovaries and testes. Meiosis involves two divisions and results in four daughter cells, each containing only half the original number of chromosomes. These cells can develop into gametes.

menarche The first menstruation in girls, usually occurring in the early to midteens.

Mendelian traits Characteristics that are influenced by alleles at only one genetic locus. Examples include many blood types, such as ABO. Many genetic disorders, including sickle-cell anemia and Tay-Sachs disease, are also Mendelian traits.

menopause The end of menstruation in women, usually occurring at around age 50.

messenger RNA (mRNA) A form of RNA that's assembled on a sequence of DNA bases. It carries the DNA code to the ribosome during protein synthesis.

metabolism The chemical processes within cells that break down nutrients and release energy for the body to use. (When nutrients are broken down into their component parts, such as amino acids, energy is released and made available for the cells to use.)

microbiome A collection of genomes of microbes in a system, such as the human body.

microevolution Small changes occurring within species, such as changes in allele frequencies.

microliths (*micro*, meaning "small," and *lith*, meaning "stone") Small stone tools usually produced from narrow blades punched from a core; found especially in Africa during the latter part of the Pleistocene.

microwear Polishes, striations, and other diagnostic microscopic changes on the edges of stone tools.

Middle Pleistocene The portion of the Pleistocene epoch beginning 780,000 ya and ending 125,000 ya.

mineralization The process in which parts of animals (or some plants) become transformed into stone-like structures. Mineralization usually occurs very slowly, as water carrying minerals—such as silica or iron—seeps into the tiny spaces within a bone. In some cases, the original minerals within the bone or tooth can be completely replaced, molecule by molecule, with other minerals.

mitochondria (*sing.*, mitochondrion) Structures contained within the cytoplasm of eukaryotic cells that convert energy, derived from nutrients, to a form that can be used by the cell.

mitochondrial DNA (mtDNA) DNA found in the mitochondria. Mitochondrial DNA is inherited only from the mother.

mitosis Simple cell division; the process by which somatic cells divide to produce two identical daughter cells.

Modern Synthesis A synthesis of multiple lines of evidence to integrate Mendelian genetics and natural selection within evolutionary theory.

molecules Structures made up of two or more atoms. Molecules can combine with other molecules to form more complex structures.

monophyletic Referring to an evolutionary group (clade) composed of descendants all sharing a common ancestor.

morphological Pertaining to the form and structure of organisms.

morphology The form (shape, size) of anatomical structures; can also refer to the entire organism.

mosaic evolution A pattern of evolution in which the rate of evolution in one functional system varies from that in other systems. For example, in hominin evolution, the dental system, locomotor system, and neurological system (especially the brain) all evolved at markedly different rates.

Mousterian Pertaining to the stone tool industry associated with Neandertals and some modern *H. sapiens* groups; also called Middle Paleolithic. This industry is characterized by a larger proportion of flake tools than is found in Acheulian tool kits.

multidisciplinary Pertaining to research involving mutual contributions and the cooperation of experts from various scientific fields, or disciplines.

mutation A change in DNA. The term can refer to changes in DNA bases (specifically called point mutations) as well as to changes in chromosome number and/or structure.

natal group The group in which animals are born and raised. (*Natal* pertains to birth.)

natural selection The most critical mechanism of evolutionary change, first described by Charles Darwin; the term refers to genetic change or changes in the frequencies of certain traits in populations due to differential reproductive success between individuals.

neocortex The more recently evolved portions of the cortex (outer layer) of the brain that are involved with higher mental functions and composed of areas that integrate incoming information from different sensory organs.

neural tube In early embryonic development, the anatomical structure that develops to form the brain and spinal cord.

nocturnal Active during the night.

noncoding DNA DNA that does not direct the production of proteins. However, such DNA segments produce thousands of molecules (e.g., RNA) that are involved in gene regulation. Thus the term noncoding DNA is misleading.

nonrandom mating Pattern of mating in which individuals choose mating partners preferentially, with mate choice based on criteria such as social status, ethnicity, or biological relationship. In nonrandom mating, an individual doesn't have an equal chance of mating with all other individuals in the group.

nuchal torus (nuke´-ul) (*nucha*, meaning "neck") A projection of bone in the back of the cranium where neck muscles attach. These muscles hold up the head.

nucleotides Basic units of the DNA molecule, composed of a sugar, a phosphate, and one of four DNA bases.

nucleus A structure (organelle) found in all eukaryotic cells. The nucleus contains DNA and RNA, among other things.

obligate bipedalism Bipedalism as the *only* form of hominin terrestrial locomotion. Since major anatomical changes in the spine, pelvis, and lower limbs are required for bipedal locomotion, once hominins adopted this mode of locomotion, other forms of locomotion on the ground became impossible.

olfaction The sense of smell.

omnivorous Having a diet consisting of many food types, such as plant materials, meat, and insects.

orthograde Referring to an upright body position. This term relates to the position of the head and torso during sitting, climbing, etc., and doesn't necessarily mean that an animal is bipedal.

osteology The study of skeletal material. Human osteology focuses on the interpretation of skeletal remains from archaeological sites, skeletal anatomy, bone physiology, and growth and development. Some of the same techniques are used in paleoanthropology to study early hominins.

paleoanthropology The interdisciplinary approach to the study of earlier hominins—their chronology, physical structure, archaeological remains, habitats, and so on.

paleomagnetism Dating method based on the earth's shifting magnetic pole.

paleopathology The branch of osteology that studies the evidence of disease and injury in human skeletal (or, occasionally, mummified) remains from archaeological sites.

paleoprimatologists Anthropologists specializing in the study of the nonhuman primate fossil record.

paleospecies Species defined from fossil evidence, often covering a long time span.

paradigm shift A transition from one conceptual framework or prevailing and widely accepted viewpoint to another. The acceptance of the discovery that the sun is the center of our solar system is an example of a paradigm shift.

parvorder A taxonomic group below infraorder.

pathogens Substances or microorganisms, such as bacteria, fungi, or viruses, that cause disease.

pedigree chart A diagram showing family relationships. It's used to trace the hereditary pattern of particular genetic (usually Mendelian) traits.

phenotypes The observable or detectable physical characteristics of an organism; the detectable expressions of genotypes, frequently influenced by environmental factors.

phylogenetic tree A chart showing evolutionary relationships as determined by evolutionary systematics. It contains a time component and implies ancestor-descendant relationships.

phytoliths (*phyto*, meaning "hidden," and *lith*, meaning "stone") Microscopic silica structures formed in the cells of many plants, particularly grasses.

pigment In this context, molecules that influence the color of skin, hair, and eyes.

placental A type (subclass) of mammal. During the Cenozoic, placentals became the most widespread and numerous mammals and today are represented by upward of 20 orders, including the primates.

platyrrhines Members of Platyrrhini, a parvorder of Primates, one of the three major divisions of the suborder Haplorhini. These include only the New World monkeys.

pleiotropic genes Genes that have more than one effect; genes that have different effects at different times in the life cycle.

pleiotropy A situation where the action of one gene affects several different traits.

Pleistocene The epoch of the Cenozoic from 2.6 mya until 10,500 ya. Frequently referred to as the Ice Age, this epoch is associated with continental glaciations in northern latitudes.

Plio-Pleistocene Pertaining to the Pliocene and first half of the Pleistocene, a time range of 5 to 1 mya. For this time period, numerous fossil hominins have been found in Africa.

point mutation A change in one of the four DNA bases.

polyandry A mating system wherein a female continuously associates with more than one male (usually two or three) with whom she mates. Among nonhuman primates, polyandry is seen only in marmosets and tamarins. It also occurs in a few human societies.

polygenic Referring to traits influenced by genes at two or more loci. Examples include stature, skin color, eye color, and hair color. Many polygenic traits are influenced by environmental factors such as nutrition and exposure to sunlight.

polygynous Pertaining to polygyny; a mating system in which a male mates with more than one female. This is the most common mating pattern found in mammals, including most primates.

polymerase chain reaction (PCR) A method of producing thousands of copies of a DNA sample.

polymorphisms Loci with more than one allele. Polymorphisms can be expressed in the phenotype as the result of gene action (as in ABO), or they can exist solely at the DNA level within noncoding regions.

polyphyletic Referring to an evolutionary group composed of descendants with more than one common ancestor (and thus not a true clade).

polytypic Referring to species composed of populations that differ in the expression of one or more traits.

population Within a species, a group of individuals where mates are usually found.

population genetics The study of the frequency of alleles, genotypes, and phenotypes in populations from a microevolutionary perspective.

postcranial Referring to all or part of the skeleton not including the skull. The term originates from the fact that in quadrupeds the body is posterior to the head; the term literally means "behind the head."

pressure flaking A method of removing flakes from a core by pressing a pointed implement (e.g., bone or antler) against the stone.

primate paleontology The study of fossil primates, especially those that lived before the appearance of hominins.

primates Members of the mammalian order Primates (pronounced "pry-may´-tees"), which includes lemurs, lorises, tarsiers, monkeys, apes, and humans.

primatology The study of the biology and behavior of nonhuman primates (lemurs, lorises, tarsiers, monkeys, and apes).

principle of independent assortment The distribution of one pair of alleles into gametes does not influence the distribution of another pair. The genes controlling different traits are inherited independently of one another.

principle of segregation Genes (alleles) occur in pairs because chromosomes occur in pairs. During gamete formation, the members of each pair of alleles separate, so that each gamete contains one member of each pair.

principle of superposition In a stratigraphic sequence, the lower layers were deposited before the upper layers. Or, simply put, the stuff on top of a heap was put there last.

prosocial behaviors Actions that benefit other individuals and/or a society as a whole. Loosely speaking, the term "prosocial" is the opposite of "antisocial."

protein synthesis The manufacture of proteins; that is, the assembly of chains of amino acids into functional protein molecules. Protein synthesis is directed by DNA.

proteins Three-dimensional molecules that serve a wide variety of functions through their ability to bind to other molecules.

quadrupedal Using all four limbs to support the body during locomotion; the basic mammalian (and primate) form of locomotion.

quantitatively Pertaining to measurements of quantity and including such properties as size, number, and capacity. When data are quantified, they're expressed numerically and can be tested statistically.

random assortment The chance distribution of chromosomes to daughter cells during meiosis. Along with recombination, random assortment is an important source of genetic variation (but not new alleles).

recessive Describing a trait that isn't expressed in heterozygotes; it also refers to the allele that governs the trait. For a recessive allele to be expressed, an individual must have two copies of it (i.e., the individual must be homozygous).

recognition species concept A depiction of species in which the key aspect is the ability of individuals to identify members of their own species for purposes of mating (and to avoid mating with members of other species). In theory, this type of selective mating is a component of a species concept emphasizing mating and is therefore compatible with the biological species concept.

recombination The exchange of genetic material between paired chromosomes during meiosis; also called *crossing over.*

regulatory genes Genes that influence the activity of other genes. Regulatory genes direct embryonic development and are involved in physiological processes throughout life. They are critically important to the evolutionary process.

relativistic Viewing entities as they relate to something else. Cultural relativism is the view that cultures have merits within their own historical and environmental contexts.

replicate To duplicate. The DNA molecule is able to make copies of itself.

reproductive strategies Behaviors or behavioral complexes that have been favored by natural selection to increase individual reproductive success. The behaviors need not be deliberate, and they often vary considerably between males and females.

reproductive success The number of offspring an individual produces and rears to reproductive age, or an individual's genetic contribution to the next generation.

reproductively isolated Pertaining to groups of organisms that, mainly because of genetic differences, are prevented from mating and producing offspring with members of other such groups. For example, dogs cannot mate and produce offspring with cats.

rhinarium (rine-air´-ee-um) The moist, hairless pad at the end of the nose seen in most mammalian species. The rhinarium enhances an animal's ability to smell.

ribosomes Structures composed of a form of RNA called ribosomal RNA (rRNA) and protein. Ribosomes are found in a cell's cytoplasm and are essential to the manufacture of proteins.

RNA (ribonucleic acid) A single-stranded molecule similar in structure to DNA. Three forms of RNA are essential to protein synthesis: messenger RNA (mRNA), transfer RNA (tRNA), and ribosomal RNA (rRNA).

r-selected Pertaining to r-selection, a reproductive strategy that emphasizes relatively large numbers of offspring and reduced parental care (compared with K-selected species). *K-selection* and *r-selection* are relative terms; for example, mice are r-selected compared with primates but K-selected compared with insects.

sagittal crest A ridge of bone that runs down the middle of the cranium like a short Mohawk. This serves as the attachment for the large temporal muscles, indicating strong chewing.

savanna (also spelled savannah) A large flat grassland with scattered trees and shrubs. Savannas are found in many regions of the world with dry and warm-to-hot climates.

science A body of knowledge gained through observation and experimentation; from the Latin *scientia,* meaning "knowledge."

scientific method An approach to research whereby a problem is identified, a hypothesis (provisional explanation) is stated, and that hypothesis is tested by collecting and analyzing data.

scientific testing The precise repetition of an experiment or expansion of observed data to provide verification; the procedure by which hypotheses and theories are verified, modified, or discarded.

sea ice maximum In the Arctic, the greatest amount of sea ice that is present in one year. It occurs in March at the end of winter, just as the ice stops forming and begins to melt.

sea ice minimum The least amount of ice that is present in the Arctic in one year. Sea ice is at its minimum in September, just as the summer melting season ends but before the ice begins to form again.

sectorial Adapted for cutting or shearing; among primates, this term refers to the compressed (side-to-side) first lower premolar, which functions as a shearing surface with the upper canine.

selective breeding A practice whereby animal or plant breeders choose which individual animals or plants will be allowed to mate based on the traits (such as coat color or body size) they hope to produce in the offspring. Animals or plants that don't have the desirable traits aren't allowed to breed.

selective pressures Forces in the environment that influence reproductive success in individuals.

semiorder The taxonomic category above suborder and below order.

senescence Decline in physiological function usually associated with aging.

sensory modalities Different forms of sensation (e.g., touch, pain, pressure, heat, cold, vision, taste, hearing, and smell).

sex chromosomes In mammals, the X and Y chromosomes.

sexual dimorphism Differences in physical characteristics between males and females of the same species. For example, humans are slightly sexually dimorphic for body size, with males being taller, on average, than females of the same population. Sexual dimorphism is very pronounced in many species, such as gorillas.

sexual selection A type of natural selection that operates on only one sex within a species. It's the result of competition for mates, and it can lead to sexual dimorphism with regard to one or more traits.

shared derived Relating to specific character traits shared in common between two life-forms and considered the most useful for making evolutionary interpretations.

sickle-cell anemia A severe inherited hemoglobin disorder in which red blood cells collapse when deprived of oxygen. It results from inheriting two copies of a mutant allele. The type of mutation that produces the sickle-cell allele is a point mutation.

sickle-cell trait Heterozygous condition where a person has one Hb^A allele and one Hb^S allele. Thus they have some normal hemoglobin.

sister groups The relationship of new clades that result from the splitting of a single common lineage.

slash-and-burn agriculture A traditional land-clearing practice involving the cutting and burning of trees and vegetation. In many areas, fields are abandoned after a few years and clearing occurs elsewhere.

social structure The composition, size, and sex ratio of a group of animals. The social structure of a species is, in part, the result of natural selection in a specific habitat, and it guides individual interactions and social relationships.

somatic cells Basically, all the cells in the body except those involved with reproduction.

speciation The process by which a new species evolves from an earlier species. Speciation is the most basic process in macroevolution.

species A group of organisms that can interbreed to produce fertile offspring. Members of one species are reproductively isolated from members of all other species (i.e., they cannot mate with them to produce fertile offspring).

spina bifida A condition in which one or more of the vertebral arches fail to fuse and form a protective barrier around the spinal cord.

stable carbon isotopes Isotopes of carbon that are produced in plants in differing proportions, depending on environmental conditions. By analyzing the proportions of the isotopes contained in fossil remains of animals (who ate the plants), it's possible to reconstruct aspects of ancient diet and environments (particularly temperature and aridity).

stem group All of the taxa in a clade before a major speciation event. Stem groups are often difficult to recognize in the fossil record since they don't often have the shared derived traits found in the crown group.

stereoscopic vision The condition whereby visual images are, to varying degrees, superimposed. This provides for depth perception, or viewing the external environment in three dimensions. Stereoscopic vision is partly a function of structures in the brain.

stratigraphy Study of the sequential layering of deposits.

strepsirrhines (strep-sir´-rines) Members of the primate suborder Strepsirrhini, which includes lemurs and lorises.

Strepsirrhini (strep'-sir-in-ee) The primate suborder that includes lemurs and lorises. (Colloquial form: strepsirrhine.)

stress In a physiological context, any factor that acts to disrupt homeostasis; more precisely, the body's response to any factor that threatens its ability to maintain homeostasis.

subfossil Bone not old enough to have become completely mineralized as a fossil.

superorder A taxonomic group ranking above an order and below a class or subclass.

tandem repeats Short, adjacent segments of DNA within a gene that are repeated several times.

taphonomy (*taphos*, meaning "tomb") The study of how bones and other materials came to be buried in the earth and preserved as fossils. Taphonomists study the processes of sedimentation, the action of streams, preservation properties of bone, and carnivore disturbance factors.

taxa (*sing.* taxon) A taxonomic group of any rank (e.g., species, family, or class).

taxonomy The branch of science concerned with the rules of classifying organisms on the basis of evolutionary relationships.

terrestrial Living and locomoting primarily on the ground.

territorial Pertaining to the protection of all or a part of the area occupied by an animal or group of animals. Territorial behaviors range from scent marking to outright attacks on intruders.

territories Portions of an individual's or group's home range that are actively defended against intrusion, especially by members of the same species.

theory A broad statement of scientific relationships or underlying principles that has been substantially verified through the testing of hypotheses.

thermoluminescence (TL) (thermo-loo-min-ess´-ence) A technique for dating certain archaeological materials (such as stone tools) that were heated in the past and that, upon reheating, release the stored energy of radioactive decay as light.

theropods Small- to medium-sized ground-living dinosaurs, dated to approximately 150 mya and thought to be related to birds.

transfer RNA (tRNA) A type of RNA that binds to specific amino acids and transports them to the ribosome during protein synthesis.

undernutrition A diet insufficient in quantity (calories) to support normal health.

uniformitarianism The theory that the earth's features are the result of long-term processes that continue to operate in the present just as they did in the past. Elaborated on by Lyell, this theory opposed catastrophism and greatly contributed to the concept of deep geological time.

Upper Paleolithic A cultural period usually associated with modern humans and also found with some Neandertals and distinguished by technological innovation in various stone tool industries. Best known from western Europe, similar industries are also known from central and eastern Europe and Africa.

variation In genetics, inherited differences among individuals; the basis of all evolutionary change.

vasoconstriction Narrowing of blood vessels to reduce blood flow to the skin. Vasoconstriction is an involuntary response to cold and reduces heat loss at the skin's surface.

vasodilation Expansion of blood vessels, permitting increased blood flow to the skin. Vasodilation permits warming of the skin and facilitates radiation of warmth as a means of cooling. Vasodilation is an involuntary response to warm temperatures, various drugs, and even emotional states (blushing).

vectors Agents that transmit disease from one carrier to another. Mosquitoes are vectors for malaria, just as fleas are vectors for bubonic plague.

vertebrates Animals with segmented, bony spinal columns. Vertebrates include fishes, amphibians, reptiles (including birds), and mammals.

worldview General cultural orientation or perspective shared by the members of a society.

Y-5 molar Molar that has five cusps with grooves running between them, forming a Y shape. This is characteristic of hominoids.

zoonotic (zoh-oh-no´-tic) Pertaining to a zoonosis (*pl.*, zoonoses), a disease that's transmitted to humans through contact with nonhuman animals.

zygomatics Cheekbones.

zygote A cell formed by the union of an egg cell and a sperm cell. It contains the full complement of chromosomes (in humans, 46) and has the potential of developing into an entire organism.

References

Abzhanov, A., W. Kuo, C. Hartmann, et al.
2006   The calmodulin pathway and the evolution of elongated beak morphology in Darwin's finches. *Nature* 442:563–567.

Abzhanov, A., M. Protas, B. R. Grant, et al.
2004   *Bmp4* and morphological variation of beaks in Darwin's finches. *Science* 305:1462–1465.

Aiello, L. C.
1992   Body size and energy requirements. In: *The Cambridge Encyclopedia of Human Evolution*, J. Jones, R. Martin, and D. Pilbeam (eds.), pp. 41–45. Cambridge, UK: Cambridge University Press.

Aiello, L. C., and P. Wheeler
1995   The expensive tissue hypothesis. *Current Anthropology* 36:184–193.

Alba, D. M., S. Almécija, D. DeMiguel, et al.
2015   Miocene small-bodied ape from Eurasia sheds light on hominoid evolution. *Science* 350:aab2625. doi:10.1126/science.aab2625.

Alba, D. M., J. Fortuny, and S. Moyà-Solà
2010   Enamel thickness in the Middle Miocene great apes *Anoiapithecus*, *Pierolapithecus* and *Dryopithecus*. *Proceedings of the Royal Society B* 277:2237–2245.

Alba, D. M., S. Moyà-Solà, A. Malgosa, et al.
2010   A new species of *Pliopithecus gervais*, 1849 (Primates: Pliopithecidae) from the Middle Miocene (MN8) of Abocador de Can Mata (els Hostalets de Pierola, Catalonia, Spain). *American Journal of Physical Anthropology* 141:52–75.

Alemseged, Z., F. Spoor, W. H. Kimbel, et al.
2006   A juvenile early hominin skeleton from Dikika, Ethiopia. *Nature* 443:296–301.

Ali, J. R., and M. Huber
2010   Mammalian biodiversity on Madagascar controlled by ocean currents. *Nature* 463:653–656.

Alves Cardoso, F., and C. Y. Henderson
2010   Enthesopathy formation in the humerus: Data from known age-at-death and known occupation skeletal collections. *American Journal of Physical Anthropology* 141:550–560.

Anderson, R. M., and R. Weindruch
2012   The caloric restriction paradigm: Implications for healthy human aging. *American Journal of Human Biology* 24:101–106.

Andrews, P.
1984   An alternative interpretation of the characters used to define *Homo erectus*. *Cour Forschungist Senckenb* 69:167–175.

Andrews, P. J., and L. Martin
1987   Cladistic relationships of extant and fossil hominoids. *Journal of Human Evolution* 16:101–118.

Antón, S. C.
2013   *Homo erectus* and related taxa. In: *A Companion to Paleoanthropology*, D. R. Begun (ed.). Hoboken: Wiley-Blackwell.

Appleby, J., G. N. Rutty, S. V. Hainsworth, et al.
2015   Perimortem trauma in King Richard III: A skeletal analysis. *The Lancet* 385:253–259.

Arnason, U., A. Gullberg, A. S. Burguete, et al.
2000   Molecular estimates of primate divergences and new hypotheses for primate dispersal and the origin of modern humans. *Hereditas* 133:217–228.

Arnold, L. J., M. Demuro, J. M. Pares, et al.
2014   Luminescence dating and palaeomagnetic age constraint on hominins from Sima de los Huesos, Atapuerca, Spain. *Journal of Human Evolution* 67:85–107.

Arsuaga, J.-L., C. Lorenzo, A. Gracia, et al.
1999   The human cranial remains from Gran Dolina Lower Pleistocene site (Sierra de Atapuerca, Spain). *Journal of Human Evolution* 37:431–457.

Arsuaga, J.-L., I. Martinez, L. J. Arnold, et al.
2014   Neandertal roots: Cranial and chronological evidence from Sima de los Huesos. *Science* 344:1358–1363.

Arsuaga, J.-L., I. Martinez, A. Gracia, et al.
1997   Sima de los Huesos (Sierra de Atapuerca, Spain): The site. *Journal of Human Evolution* 33:109–127.

Ascenzi, A., I. Biddittu, P. F. Cassoli, et al.
1996   A calvarium of late *Homo erectus* from Ceprano, Italy. *Journal of Human Evolution* 31:409–423.

Asfaw, B., W. H. Gilbert, Y. Beyene, et al.
2002   Remains of *Homo erectus* from Bouri, Middle Awash, Ethiopia. *Nature* 416:317–320.

Ashley-Koch, A., Q. Yang, and R. S. Olney
2000   Sickle hemoglobin (HbS) alleles and sickle celldisease: A HuGE review. *American Journal of Epidemiology* 151:839–845.

Ashraf, S., and M. Z. Mughal
2002   The prevalence of rickets among non-Caucasian children. *Archives of Disease in Childhood* 87(3):263–264.

Aubert, M., A. Brumm, M. Ramli, et al.
2014   Pleistocene cave art from Sulawesi, Indonesia. *Nature* 514: 223-227.

Aureli, F., C. M. Schaffner, J. Verpooten, et al.
2006   Raiding parties of male spider monkeys: Insights into human warfare? *American Journal of Physical Anthropology* 131:486–497.

Ayala, F. J., and A. Rzhetskydagger
1998   Origin of the Metazoan phyla: Molecular clocks confirm paleontological estimates. *Proceedings of the National Academy of Sciences USA* 95(2):606–611.

Baab, K. L., K. P. McNulty, and K. Harvati
2013 *Homo floresiensis* contextualized: A geometric morphometric comparative analysis of fossil and pathological human samples. *PLoS ONE* 8:e69119.

Badrian, A., and N. Badrian
1984 Social organization of *Pan paniscus* in the Lomako Forest, Zaire. In: *The Pygmy Chimpanzee*, R. L. Susman (ed.), pp. 325–346. New York: Plenum Press.

Badrian, N., and R. K. Malenky
1984 Feeding ecology of *Pan paniscus* in the Lomako Forest, Zaire. In: *The Pygmy Chimpanzee*, R. L. Susman (ed.), pp. 275–299. New York: Plenum Press.

Bajpai, S., R. F. Kay, B. A. Williams, et al.
2008 The oldest Asian record of Anthropoidea. *Proceedings of the National Academy of Sciences USA* 105:11093–11098.

Balter, M.
2006 Radiocarbon dating's final frontier. *Science* 313:1560–1563.

Balter, M.
2007 Zebrafish researchers hook gene for human skin color. *Science* 310:1754–1755.

Balter, M.
2010 Candidate human ancestor from South Africa sparks praise and debate. *Science* 328:154–155.

Bamshad, M. J., and S. E. Olson
2003 Does race exist? *Scientific American* 289:78–85.

Bamshad, M. J., S. Wooding, W. S. Watkins, et al.
2003 Human population genetic structure and inference of group membership. *American Journal of Human Genetics* 72:578–589.

Barker, D. J. P.
2004 The developmental origins of adult disease. *Journal of the American College of Nutrition* 23(Suppl. 6): 588S–595S.

Barker, D. J. P.
2012 Developmental origins of chronic disease. *Public Health* 126:85–189.

Barker, G., H. Barton, M. Bird, et al.
2007 The human revolution in lowland tropical Southeast Asia: The antiquity and behavior of anatomically modern humans at Niah Cave (Sarawak, Borneo). *Journal of Human Evolution* 52:243–261.

Barnosky, A. D., E. A. Hadly, J. Bascompte, et al.
2012 Approaching a state shift in Earth's biosphere. *Nature* 486:52–58.

Bartelink, E. J.
2009 Late holocene dietary change in the San Francisco Bay Area: Stable isotope evidence for an expansion in diet breadth. *California Archaeology* 1:227–252.

Bartlett, T. Q., R. W. Sussman, and J. M. Cheverud
1993 Infant killing in primates: A review of observed cases with specific references to the sexual selection hypothesis. *American Anthropologist* 95:958–990.

Barton, R. A., and R. L. M. Dunbar
1997 Evolution of the social brain. In: *Machiavellian Intelligence*, A. Whiten and R. Byrne (eds.). Cambridge, UK: Cambridge University Press.

Bearder, S. K.
1987 Lorises, bush babies & tarsiers: Diverse societies in solitary foragers. In: *Primate Societies*, B. B. Smuts, D. L. Cheney, and R. M. Seyfath (eds.), pp. 11–24. Chicago: University of Chicago Press.

Begun, D., and A. Walker
1993 The Endocast. In: *The Nariokotome* Homo erectus *Skeleton*, A. Walker and R. E. Leakey (eds.), pp. 326–358. Cambridge, MA: Harvard University Press.

Begun, D. R.
1994 Relations among the great apes and humans: New interpretations based on the fossil great ape *Dryopithecus. Yearbook of Physical Anthropology* 37:11–63.

Begun, D. R.
2002 The Pliopithecoidea. In: *The Primate Fossil Record*, W. C. Hartwig (ed.), pp. 221–240. Cambridge, UK: Cambridge University Press.

Begun, D. R.
2003 Planet of the apes. *Scientific American* 289:74–83.

Begun, D. R.
2010 Miocene hominids and the origins of the African apes. *Annual Review of Anthropology* 39:67–84.

Begun, D. R., M. C. Nargolwalla, and L. Kordos
2012 European Miocene Hominids and the origin of the African ape and human clade. *Evolutionary Anthropology* 21:10–23.

Behrensmeyer, A. K., D. Western, and D. E. D. Boaz
1979 New perspectives in vertebrate paleoecology from a recent bone assemblage. *Paleobiology* 5(1):12–21.

Beja-Pereira, A., G. Luikart, P. R. England, et al.
2003 Gene-culture coevolution between cattle milk protein genes and human lactase genes. *Nature Genetics* 35:311–313.

Benefit, B. R., and M. L. McCrossin
1997 Earliest known Old World monkey skull. *Nature* 388:368–371.

Benefit, B. R., and M. L. McCrossin
2015 A window into ape evolution: A fossil of an ape ancestor helps to explain gibbon evolution. *Science* 350:515–516.

Berger, L. R., D. J. de Ruiter, S. E. Churchill, et al.
2010 *Australopithecus sediba*: A new species of *Homo*-like australopith from South Africa. *Science* 328:195–204.

Berger, L. R., J. Hawks, D. J. de Ruiter, et al.
2015 *Homo naledi*, a new species of the genus *Homo* from the Dinaledi Chamber, South Africa. *Elife* 4:e09560.

Berger, T. D., and E. Trinkaus
1995 Patterns of trauma among the Neandertals. *Journal of Archaeological Science* 22(6):841–852.

Bermúdez de Castro, J. M., J. Arsuaga, E. Carbonell, et al.
1997 A hominid from the Lower Pleistocene of Atapuerca, Spain. Possible ancestor to Neandertals and modern humans. *Science* 276:1392–1395.

Bermúdez de Castro, J. M., M. Martinon-Torres, E. Carbonell, et al.
2004 The Atapuerca sites and their contribution to the knowledge of human evolution in Europe. *Evolutionary Anthropology* 13:25–41.

Bermúdez de Castro, J. M., M. Martinon-Torres, A. Gómez-Robles, et al.
2011 The Gran Dolina-TD6 human fossil remains and the origin of Neanderthals. In: *Vertebrate Paleobiology and Paleoanthropology* 67–75[RJ1].

Berna, F., P. Goldberg, L. K. Horwitz, et al.
2012 Microstratigraphic evidence of in situ fire in the Acheulean strata of Wonderwerk Cave, Northern Cape province South Africa. *Proceedings of the National Academy of Sciences* 109:E1215e–E1220.

Biasutti, R.
1959 Razze e popoli della terra. *Turin: Unione-Tipografico-Editrice.*

Binford, L. R.
1981 *Bones. Ancient Men and Modern Myths.* New York: Academic Press.

Binford, L. R.
1983 *In Pursuit of the Past.* New York: Thames and Hudson.

Binford, L. R., and C. K. Ho
1985 Taphonomy at a distance: Zhoukoudian, "the cave home of Beijing Man." *Current Anthropology* 26:413–442.

Binford, L. R., and N. M. Stone
1986a The Chinese Paleolithic: An outsider's view. *AnthroQuest* 1:14–20.

Binford, L. R., and N. M. Stone
1986b Zhoukoudian: A closer look. *Current Anthropology* 27:453–475.

Bininda-Emonds, R. P. Olaf, M. Cordillo, et al.
2007 The delayed rise of present-day mammals. *Nature* 446:507–512.

Bird, M. I., L. K. Fifield, G. M. Santos, et al.
2003 Radiocarbon dating from 40 to 60 ka BP at Border Cave, South Africa. *Quaternary Science Reviews* 22:943–947.

Bischoff, J. L., R. W. Williams, R. J. Rosebauer, et al.
2007 High-resolution U-series dates from the Sima de los Huesos hominids yields 600+/−66 kyrs: Implications for the evolution of the early Neanderthal lineage. *Journal of Archaeological Science* 34:763–770.

Bloch, J. I., and D. M. Boyer
2002 Grasping primate origins. *Science* 298:1606–1610.

Bloch, J. I., and M. T. Silcox
2001 New basicrania of Paleocene-Eocene Ignacius: Re-evaluation of the plesiadapiform-dermopteran link. *American Journal of Physical Anthropology* 116:184–198.

Bloch, J. I., M. T. Silcox, D. M. Boyer, et al.
2007 New Paleocene skeletons and the relationship of plesiadapiforms to crown-clade primates. *Proceedings of the National Academy of Sciences USA* 104(4):1159–1164.

Bloch, J. I., E. D. Woodruff, A. R. Wood, et al.
2016 First North American fossil monkey and early Miocene tropical biotic interchange. *Nature* 533:243–246.

Blumenschine, R. J.
1995 Percussion marks, tooth marks, and experimental determinants of the timing of hominid and carnivore access to long bones at FLK *Zinjanthropus*, Olduvai Gorge, Tanzania. *Journal of Human Evolution* 29:21–51.

Blumenschine, R. J., and J. A. Cavallo
1992 Scavenging and human evolution. *Scientific American* 267:90–96.

Blumenschine, R. J., and C. R. Peters
1998 Archaeological predictions for hominid land use in the paleo-Olduvai Basin, Tanzania, during lowermost Bed II times. *Journal of Human Evolution* 34:565–607.

Boag, P. T., and P. R. Grant
1981 Intense natural selection in a population of Darwin's finches (Geospizinae) in the Galapagos. *Science* 214:82–85.

Boaz, N. T., and A. K. Behrensmeyer
1976 Hominid taphonomy: Transport of human skeletal parts in an artificial fluviatile environment. *American Journal of Physical Anthropology* 45:56–60.

Boaz, N. T., and R. L. Ciochon
2001 The scavenging of *Homo erectus pekinensis. Natural History* 110(2):46–51.

Bocherens, H.
2009 Neanderthal dietary habits: Review of the isotopic evidence. In: *The Evolution of Hominin Diets: Integrating Approaches to the Study of Paleolithic Subsistence,* J. J. Hublin and M. P. Richards (eds.), pp. 241–250. New York: Springer.

Bocherens, H., F. Schrenk, Y. Chaimanee, et al.
2015 Flexibility of diet and habitat in Pleistocene South Asian mammals: Implications for the fate of the giant ape *Gigantopithecus. Quaternary International* (online December 19, 2015). doi:10.1016/j.quaint.2015.11.059.

Boesch, C.
1996 Social grouping Tai chimpanzees. In: *Great Ape Societies,* W. C. McGrew, L. Marchant, and T. Nishida (eds.), pp. 101–113. Cambridge, UK: Cambridge University Press.

Boesch, C., and H. Boesch-Achermann
2000 *The Chimpanzees of the Tai Forest.* New York: Oxford University Press.

Boesch, C., P. Marchesi, B. Fruth, et al.
1994 Is nut cracking in wild chimpanzees a cultural behaviour? *Journal of Human Evolution* 26:325–338.

Boesch, C., and M. Tomasello
1998 Chimpanzee and human cultures. *Current Anthropology* 39:591–614.

Bogin, B.
1999 *Patterns of Human Growth*, 2nd ed. Cambridge, UK: Cambridge University Press.

Bogin, B.
2006 Modern human life history: The evolution of human childhood and fertility. In: *The Evolution of Human Life History,* K. Hawkes and R. R. Paine (eds.). Santa Fe, NM: SAR Press.

Bogin, B.
2010 Evolution of human growth. In: *Human Evolutionary Biology,* Muehlenbein, Michael (ed.), pp. 379–395. Cambridge, UK: Cambridge University Press.

Bogin, B., J. Bragg, and C. Kuzawa
2014 Humans are not cooperative breeders but practice biocultural reproduction. *Annals of Human Biology* 41:368–380.

Böhme, M., H. A. Aziz, J. Prieto, et al.
2011 Bio-magnetostratigraphy and environment of the oldest Eurasian hominoid from the Early Miocene of Engelwies (Germany). *Journal of Human Evolution* 61:331–339.

Bond, M., M. F. Tejedor, K. E. Campbell, Jr., et al.
2015 Eocene primates of South America and the African origins of New World monkeys. *Nature* 520:538–541.

Borries, C., K. Launhardt, C. Epplen, et al.
1999 DNA analyses support the hypothesis that infanticide is adaptive in langur monkeys. *Proceedings of the Royal Society of London Series B: Biological Sciences* 266:901–904.

Brace, C. L., H. Nelson, and N. Korn
1979 *Atlas of Human Evolution*, 2nd ed. New York: Holt, Rinehart & Winston.

Brain, C. K.
1981 *The Hunters or the Hunted? An Introduction to African Cave Taphonomy*. Chicago: University of Chicago Press.

Brash, D. E., J. A. Rudolph, J. A. Simon, et al.
1991 A role for sunlight in skin cancer: UV-induced P53 mutations in squamous cell carcinoma. *Proceedings of the National Academy of Sciences USA* 88:10124–10128.

Breuer, T., M. Ndoundou-Hockemba, V. Fishlock, et al.
2005 First observations of tool use in wild gorillas. *PloS Biology* 3(11):e380. doi:10.1371/journal .pbio.0030380.

Briggs, A., J. M. Good, R. E. Green, et al.
2009 Targeted retrieval and analysis of five Neandertal mtDNA genomes. *Science* 325:318–320.

Bromage, T. G., and C. Dean
1985 Re-evaluation of the age at death of immature fossil hominids. *Nature* 317:525–527.

Brown, K. S., C. W. Marean, A. I. R. Herries, et al.
2009 Fire as an engineering tool of early modern humans. *Science* 325:859–862.

Brown, K. S., C. W. Marean, Z. Jacobs, et al.
2012 An early and enduring advanced technology originating 71,000 years ago in South Africa. *Nature* 491:590–593.

Brown, P., T. Sutikna, M. K. Morwood, et al.
2004 A new small-bodied hominin from the Late Pleistocene of Flores, Indonesia. *Nature* 431:1055–1061.

Brumm, A., G. M. Jensen, G. D. van den Bergh, et al.
2010 Hominins on Flores, Indonesia, by one million years ago. *Nature* 464:748–752.

Brumm, A., G. D. van den Bergh, M. Storey, et al.
2016 Age and context of the oldest known hominin fossils from Flores. *Nature* 534:249–253.

Brunet, M., F. Guy, D. Pilbeam, et al.
2002 A new hominid from the Upper Miocene of Chad, Central Africa. *Nature* 418:145–151.

Buchan, J. C., S. C. Alberts, J. B. Silk, et al.
2003 True paternal care in a multi-male primate society. *Nature* 425:179–180.

Buckley, R., M. Morris., J. Appleby, et al.
2013 'The king in the car park': New light on the death and burial of Richard III in the Grey Friars church, Leicester, in 1485. *Antiquity* 87:519–538.

Buikstra, J. E.
1977 Biocultural dimensions of archeological study. In: *Biocultural Adaptation in Prehistoric America*. R. L. Blakely (ed.), pp. 67–84. Athens: University of Georgia Press.

Bunn, H. T.
1981 Archaeological evidence for meat-eating by Plio-Pleistocene hominids from Koobi Fora and Olduvai Gorge. *Nature* 291:574–577.

Burchard, E. G., E. Ziv, N. Coyle, et al.
2003 The importance of race and ethnic background in biomedical research and clinical practice. *New England Journal of Medicine* 348:1170–1175.

Buzon, M. R.
2012 The bioarchaeological approach to paleopathology. In: *A Companion to Paleopathology*, A. L. Grauer (ed.), pp. 58–75. Oxford, UK: Wiley-Blackwell.

Campbell, M. C., and S. A. Tishkoff
2010 The evolution of human genetic and phenotypic variation in Africa. *Current Biology* 20:R166–R173.

Cann, R. L., M. Stoneking, and A. C. Wilson
1987 Mitochondrial DNA and human evolution. *Nature* 325:31–36.

Cantalupo, C., and W. D. Hopkins
2001 Asymmetric Broca's area in great apes: A region of the ape brain is uncannily similar to one linked with speech in humans. *Nature* 414:505–505.

Capasso, L. L.
2004 Antiquity of cancer. *International Journal of Cancer* 113:2–13.

Caramelli, D., C. Lalueza-Fox, C. Vernesi, et al.
2003 Evidence for genetic discontinuity between Neandertals and 24,000-year-old anatomically modern humans. *Proceedings of the National Academy of Sciences USA* 100:6593–6597.

Carbonell, E., J. M. Bermuda de Castro, J. M. Pares, et al.
2008 The first hominin of Europe. *Nature* 452:465–469.

Carbonell, E., I. Cáceres, M. Lozano, et al.
2010 Cultural cannibalism as a paleoeconomic system in the European Lower Pleistocene. *Current Anthropology*, 51:539–549.

Carroll, S.B.
2003 Genetics and the making of *Homo sapiens. Nature* 422:849–857.

Carroll, S. B., J. K. Grenier, and S. D. Weatherbee
2001 *From DNA to Diversity. Molecular Genetics and the Evolution of Animal Design*. Malden, MA: Blackwell Science.

Carroll, S. B., B. Prud'homme, and N. Gompel
2008 Regulating evolution. *Scientific American* 298(5):61–67.

Cartmill, M.
1972 Arboreal adaptations and the origin of the order Primates. In: *The Functional and Evolutionary Biology of Primates*, R. H. Tuttle (ed.), pp. 97–122. Chicago: Aldine-Atherton.

Cartmill, M.
1992 New views on primate origins. *Evolutionary Anthropology* 1:105–111.

Catlett, K. K., G. T. Schwartz, L. R. Godfrey, et al.
2010 "Life history space": A multivariate analysis of life history variation in extant and extinct Malagasy lemurs. *American Journal of Physical Anthropology* 142:391–404.

Caulfield, L. E., M. de Onis, M. Blössner, et al.
2004 Undernutrition as an underlying cause of child deaths associated with diarrhea, pneumonia, malaria, and measles. *American Journal of Clinical Nutrition* 80:193–198.

Centers for Disease Control
2009 www.cdc.gov/flu/about/disease

Centers for Disease Control and Prevention (CDC)
2015 Nutrition, Physical Activity and Obesity Data, Trends and Maps website. U.S. Department of Health and Human Services, Centers for Disease

Control and Prevention (CDC), National Center for Chronic Disease Prevention and Health Promotion, Division of Nutrition, Physical Activity and Obesity, Atlanta, GA.

Chaimanee, Y., O. Chavasseau, K. C. Beard, et al.
2012   Late Middle Eocene primate from Myanmar and the initial anthropoid colonization of Africa. *Proceedings of the National Academy of Sciences* 109:1956–1963.

Chaimanee, Y., R. Lebrun, C. Yamee, et al.
2011   A new Middle Miocene tarsier from Thailand and the reconstruction of its orbital morphology using a geometric-morphometric method. *Proceedings of the Royal Society B* 278:1956–1963.

Chaimanee, Y., V. Suteethorn, P. Jintasakul, et al.
2004   A new orangutan relative from the Late Miocene of Thailand. *Nature* 427:439–441.

Chaimanee, Y., C. Yamee, P. Tian, et al.
2006   *Khoratpithecus piriyai*, a Late Miocene hominoid of Thailand. *American Journal of Physical Anthropology* 131:311–323.

Chatterjee, H. J.
2006   Phylogeny and biogeography of gibbons: A dispersal-vicariance analysis. *International Journal of Primatology* 27:699–712.

Chen, F. C., and W.-H. Li
2001   Genomic divergences between humans and other hominoids and the effective population size of the common ancestor of humans and chimpanzees. *American Journal of Human Genetics* 68:444–456.

Cheng, Z., M. Ventura, X. She, et al.
2005   A Genome-wide comparison of recent chimpanzee and human segmental duplications. *Nature* 437:88–93.

Chester, S. G. B., J. I. Bloch, D. M. Boyer, et al.
2015   Oldest known euarchontan tarsals and affinities of Paleocene *Purgatorius* to Primates. *Proceedings of the National Academy of Sciences USA* 112:1487–1492.

Chimpanzee Sequencing and Analysis Consortium
2005   Initial sequence of the chimpanzee genome and comparison with the human genome. *Nature* 437:69–87.

Churchill, S. E.
2014   *Thin on the Ground: Neandertal Biology, Archeology and Ecology.* Hoboken: Wiley-Blackwell.

Churchill, S. E., T. W. Holliday, K. J. Carlson, et al.
2013   The upper limb of *Australopithecus sediba. Science* 340:1233477.

Ciochon, R. L.
2009   The mystery ape of Pleistocene Asia. *Nature* 459:910–911.

Ciochon, R. L., and E. A. Bettis
2009   Asian *Homo erectus* converges in time. *Nature* 458:153–154.

Ciochon, R. L., and A. B. Chiarelli
1980a   Paleobiogeographic perspectives on the origin of Platyrrhini. In: *Evolutionary Biology of the New World Monkeys and Continental Drift*, R. L. Ciochon and A. B. Chiarelli (eds.), pp. 459–493. New York: Plenum Press.

Ciochon, R. L., and A. B. Chiarelli
1980b   *Evolutionary Biology of the New World Monkeys and Continental Drift.* New York: Plenum Press.

Ciochon, R. L., O. F. Huffman, E. A. Bettis, III, et al.
2009   Rediscovery of the *Homo erectus* bed at Ngandong: Site formation of a Late Pleistocene hominin site in Asia. *American Journal of Physical Anthropology, Supplement* 48:110.

Ciochon, R. L., J. J. Olsen, and J. James
1990   *Other Origins: The Search for the Giant Ape in Human Prehistory.* New York: Bantam.

Clark, A. G., S. Glanowski, R. Nielsen, et al.
2003   Inferring nonneutral evolution from human-chimp-mouse orthologous gene trios. *Science* 302:1960–1963.

Clark, J. D., J. de Heinzelin. K. D. Schick, et al.
1994   African *Homo erectus*: Old radiometric ages and young Oldowan assemblages in the Middle Awash Valley, Ethiopia. *Science* 264:1907–1910.

Clarke, R. J., and P. V. Tobias
1995   Sterkfontein Member 2 foot bones of the oldest South African hominid. *Science* 269:521–524.

Clemens, W.
1974   *Purgatorius*, an early paromomyid primate. *Science* 184 (4139):903–905.

Clemens, W. A.
2004   *Purgatorius* (Plesiadapiformes, Primates?, Mammalia), A Paleocene immigrant into Northeastern Montana: Stratigraphic occurrences and incisor proportions. *Bulletin of Carnegie Museum of Natural History* 36.

Cohen, M. L., and G. Armelagos
1984   *Paleopathology at the Origins of Agriculture.* New York: Academic Press.

Conroy, G. C.
1997   *Reconstructing Human Origins: A Modern Synthesis.* New York: Norton.

Constable, J. L., M. V. Ashley, J. Goodall, et al.
2001   Noninvasive paternity assignment in Gombe chimpanzees. *Molecular Ecology* 10:1279–1300.

Cook, L. M., B. S. Grant, I. J. Saccheri, et al.
2012   Selective bird predation on the peppered moth: The last experiment of Michael Majerus. *Biology Letters* 8:609–612.

Cooper, R. S., J. S. Kaufman, and R. Ward
2003   Race and genomics. *New England Journal of Medicine* 348:1166–1170.

Cordain, L.
2002   *The Paleo Diet: Lose Weight and Get Healthy by Eating the Food You Were Designed to Eat.* New York: Wiley.

Cordain, L., S. B. Eaton, J. B. Miller, et al.
2002   The paradoxical nature of hunter-gatherer diets: Meat-based, yet non-atherogenic. *European Journal of Clinical Nutrition* 56 (Suppl. 1):S42–S52.

Cortés-Sánchez, M., A. Morales-Muniz, M. D. Simon-Vallejo, et al.
2011   Earliest known use of marine resources by Neanderthals. *PLoS ONE* 6(9):e24026.

Crevecoeur, I. E., H. Rougier, F. Grine, et al.
2009   Modern human cranial diversity in the Late Pleistocene of Africa and Eurasia: Evidence from Nazlet Khater, Peştera cu Oase, and Hofmeyr. *American Journal of Physical Anthropology* 140:347–358.

Crews, D. E., and G. J. Harper
1998   Ageing as part of the developmental process. In: *The Cambridge Encyclopedia of Human Growth and Development*, S. J. Ulijaszek (ed.), pp. 425–427. Cambridge, UK: Cambridge University Press.

Cummings, M.
2000   *Human Heredity. Principles and Issues*, 5th ed. St. Paul, MN: Wadsworth/West.

Cunningham, D., and D. Wescott
2002   Within-group human variation in the Asian Pleistocene: The three Upper Cave crania. *Journal of Human Evolution* 42:627–638.

Currat, M., G. Trabuchet, D. Rees, et al.
2002   Molecular analysis of the beta-globin gene cluster in the Niokholo Mandenka population reveals a recent origin of the beta(S) Senegal mutation. *American Journal of Human Genetics* 70:207–223.

Curtin, R., and P. Dolhinow
1978   Primate social behavior in a changing world. *American Scientist* 66:468–475.

Daeschler, E. B., N. H. Shubin, and F. A. Jenkins Jr.
2006   A Darwinian tetrapod-like fish and the evolution of the tetrapod body plan. *Nature* 440:757–763.

D'Anastasio, R., S. Wroe, C. Tuniz, et al.
2013   Micro-biomechanics of the Kebara 2 hyoid and its implications for speech in Neanderthals. *PLoS ONE* 8:e82261.

Darwin, F.
1950   *The Life and Letters of Charles Darwin*. New York: Henry Schuman.

Dat, L. T., F. Pengfei, Y. Lu, et al.
2008   Census report for the global Cao Vit gibbon (*Nomascus nasutus*) population. Report Fauna and Flora International, Vietnam and China Programmes.

Day, M. H., and E. H. Wickens
1980   Laetoli Pliocene hominid footprints and bipedalism. *Nature* 286:385–387.

de Heinzelin, J., J. D. Clark, T. White, et al.
1999   Environment and behavior of 2.5-million-year-old Bouri hominids. *Science* 284:625–629.

d'Errico F., L. Backwell, P. Villa, et al.
2012   Early evidence of San material culture represented by organic artifacts from Border Cave, South Africa. *Proceedings of the National Academy of Sciences USA* 109:13214–13219.

de Ruiter, D. J., T. J. DeWitt, K. B. Carlson, et al.
2013   Mandibular remains support taxonomic validity of *Australopithecus sediba*. *Science* 340:1232997.

de Ruiter, D. J., R. Pickering, C. M. Steininger, et al.
2009   New *Australopithecus robustus* fossils and associated U-Pb dates from Cooper's Cave (Gauteng, South Africa). *Journal of Human Evolution* 56:497–513.

DeSilva, J. M.
2011   A shift toward birthing relatively large infants early in human evolution. *Proceedings of the National Academy of Sciences*, 108:1022–1027.

DeSilva, J. M., K. G. Holt, S. E. Churchill, et al.
2013   The lower limb and mechanics of walking in *Australopithecus sediba*. *Science* 340:1232999.

Dettwyler, K. A.
1995   A Time to wean: The hominid blueprint for the natural age of weaning in modern human populations. In: *Breastfeeding: Biocultural Perspectives*, P. Stuart-Macadam and K. A. Dettwyler (eds.), pp. 39–73. New York: Aldine de Gruyter.

de Waal, F.
1996   *Good Natured: The Origins of Right and Wrong in Humans and Other Animals*. Cambridge, MA: Harvard University Press.

de Waal, F.
1999   Cultural primatology comes of age. *Nature* 399:635–636.

de Waal, F. B. M.
2007   With a little help from a friend. *PLoS Biology* 5:1406–1408.

de Waal, F., and F. Lanting
1997   *Bonobo: The Forgotten Ape*. Berkeley: University of California Press.

Deacon, T. W.
1992   The human brain. In: *The Cambridge Encyclopedia of Human Evolution*, S. Jones, R. Martin, and D. Pilbeam (eds.), pp. 115–123. Cambridge, UK: Cambridge University Press.

Dean, C., M. G. Leakey, D. Reid, et al.
2001   Growth processes in teeth distinguishing modern humans from *Homo erectus* and earlier hominins. *Nature* 414:628–631.

Dean, M., M. Carring, C. Winkler, et al.
1996   Genetic restriction of HIV-1 infection and progression to AIDS by a deletion allele of the CKR5 structural gene. *Science* 273:1856–1862.

Dean, M. C., and B. H. Smith
2009   Growth and development of the Nariokotome youth, KNM-ER-15000. In: *The First Humans. Origin and Evolution of the Genus* Homo, F. E. Grine, J. J. Fleagle, and R. E. Leakey (eds.), pp. 101–120. New York: Springer.

Delson, E., I. Tattersall, and J. V. Couvering (eds.)
2000   *Encyclopedia of Human Evolution and Prehistory*, 2nd ed. New York: Garland.

Dembo, M., D. Radovčić, H. M. Garvin, et al.
2016   The evolutionary relationships and age of *Homo naledi*: An assessment using dated Bayesian phylogenetic methods. *Journal of Human Evolution* 97:17–26.

Demuth, J. P., T. De Bie, J. E. Stajich, et al.
2006   The evolution of mammalian gene families. *PLoS ONE* 1(1): e85. doi: 10.1371/journal.pone.0000085.

Denys, C.
2002   Taphonomy and experimentation. *Archaeometry* 44:469–484.

Deragon, J. M., and P. Capy
2000   Impact of transposable elements on the human genome. *Annals of Medicine* 32:264–273.

Desmond, A., and J. Moore
1991   *Darwin*. New York: Warner Books.

Diamond, J.
1987   The worst mistake in the history of the human race. *Discover* May, 64–66.

DiMaggio, E. N., C. J. Campisano, J. Rowan, et al.
2015   Late Pliocene fossiliferous sedimentary record and the environmental context of early *Homo* from Afar, Ethiopia. *Science* 347:1355–1359.

Ding, Q., Y. Hu, S. Xu, et al.
2014   Neanderthal origin of the haplotypes carrying the functional variant Val92Met in the MC1R in

modern humans. *Molecular Biology and Evolution* 31:1994–2003.

Dirks, P. H., L. R. Berger, E. M. Roberts, et al.
2015   Geological and taphonomic context for the new hominin species *Homo naledi* from the Dinaledi Chamber, South Africa. *eLife* 4:e09561.

Dirks, P. H. G. M., J. M. Kibii, B. F. Kuhn, et al.
2010   Geological setting and age of *Australopithecus sediba* from southern Africa. *Science* 328:205–208.

Dobzhansky, T.
1973   Nothing in biology makes sense except in the light of evolution. *American Biology Teacher* 35:125–129.

Domínguez-Rodrigo, M., and L. Alcalá
2016   3.3-Million-year-old stone tools and butchery traces? More evidence needed. *PaleoAnthropology* 46–53.

Domínguez-Rodrigo, M., T. R. Pickering, and H. T. Bunn
2010   Configurational approach to identifying the earliest hominin butchers. *Proceedings of the National Academy of Sciences USA* 107:20929–20934.

Dominy, N. J., and P. W. Lucas
2001   Ecological importance of trichromatic vision to primates. *Nature* 410:363–366.

Doney, S. C., V. J. Fabry, R. A. Feely, et al.
2009   Ocean acidification: The other CO_2 problem. *Annual Review of Marine Science*, online journal; doi:10.1146/annurev.marine.010908.163834.

Doran, D. M., and A. McNeilage
1998   Gorilla ecology and behavior. *Evolutionary Anthropology* 6:120–131.

Duarte, C., J. Mauricio, P. B. Pettitt, et al.
1999   The early Upper Paleolithic human skeleton from the Abrigo do Lagar Velho (Portugal) and modern human emergence in Iberia. *Proceedings of the National Academy of Sciences USA* 96:7604–7609.

Dunbar, R. I. M.
1998   The social brain hypothesis. *Evolutionary Anthropology* 6:178–190.

Dunsworth, H. M., A. G. Warrener, T. Deacon, et al.
2012   Metabolic hypothesis for human altriciality. *Proceedings of the National Academy of Sciences* 109:15212–15216.

Durbin, R. M.
2010   A map of human genome variation from population scale sequencing. *Nature* 467:1061–1073.

Eaton, S. B., M. C. Pike, R. V. Short, et al.
1994   Women's reproductive cancers in evolutionary context. *Quarterly Review of Biology* 69:353–367.

Eaton, S. B., M. Shostak, and M. Konner
1988   *The Paleolithic Prescription*. New York: Harper and Row.

Ecker, M., H. Bocherens, M. A. Julien, et al.
2013   Middle Pleistocene ecology and Neanderthal subsistence: Insights from stable isotope analyses in Payre (Ardeche, southeastern France). *Journal of Human Evolution* 65:363–373.

Eiberg, H., J. Troelsen., M. Nielsen, et al.
2008   Blue eye color in humans may be caused by a perfectly associated founder mutation in a regulatory element located within the HERC2 gene inhibiting OCA2 expression. *Human Genetics* 123:177–187.

Eisenberg, D. T.
2011   An evolutionary review of human telomere biology: The thrifty telomere hypothesis and notes on potential adaptive paternal effects. *American Journal of Human Biology* 23:149–167.

Ellison, P. T.
2001   *On Fertile Ground: A Natural History of Human Reproduction*. Cambridge, MA: Harvard University Press.

Enard, W., M. Przeworski, S. E. Fisher, et al.
2002   Molecular evolution of FOXP2, a gene involved in speech and language. *Nature* 418:869–872.

ENCODE Project Consortium
2012   An integrated encyclopedia of DNA elements in the human genome. *Nature* 489:57–74.

Eppig, C., C. L. Fincher, and R. Thornhill
2010   Parasite prevalence and the worldwide distribution of cognitive ability. *Proceedings of the Royal Society of London B* 277:3801–3808.

Ewald, P. W.
1999   Evolutionary control of HIV and other sexually transmitted viruses. In: *Evolutionary Medicine*, W. R. Trevathan, E. O. Smith, and J. J. McKenna (eds.). New York: Oxford University Press.

Falguères, C., J. J. Bahain, Y. Yokoyama, et al.
1999   Earliest humans in Europe: The age of TD6 Gran Dolina, Atapuerca, Spain. *Journal of Human Evolution* 37:343–352.

Falk, D.
1990   Brain evolution in *Homo*: The "Radiator" Theory. *Behavioral and Brain Sciences* 13:333–344.

Falk, D.
2012   Hominin brain evolution, 1925–2011: An emerging overview. In: *African Genesis: Perspectives on Hominin Evolution*, S. C. Reynolds and A. Gallagher (eds.), pp. 145–162. Cambridge: Cambridge University Press.

Falk, D., C. Hildebolt, K. Smith, et al.
2005   The brain of LB1, *Homo floresiensis*. *Science* 308:242–245.

Falk, D., C. Hildebolt, K. Smith, et al.
2008   LB1 did not have Laron syndrome. *American Journal of Physical Anthropology, Supplement* 43:95 (abstract).

Falk, D., C. Hildebolt, K. Smith, et al.
2009   LM1's virtual endocast, microcephaly, and hominin brain evolution. *Journal of Human Evolution* 57:597–607.

Falk, D., C. P. E. Zollikofer, N. Morimoto, et al.
2012   Metopic suture of Taung (*Australopithecus africanus*) and its implications for hominin brain evolution. *Proceedings of the National Academy of Sciences* 109:8467–8470.

Feathers, J. K., and E. Migliorini
2001   Luminescence dating at Katanda: A reassessment. *Quaternary Science Reviews* 20:961–966.

Fedigan, L. M.
1983   Dominance and reproductive success in primates. *Yearbook of Physical Anthropology* 26:91–129.

Feinberg, A. P., and M. D. Fallin
2015   Epigenetics at the crossroads of genes and the environment. *Jama* 314:1129–1130.

Ferring, R., O. Oms, J. Agustí, et al.
2011   Earliest human occupations at Dmanisi (Georgian Caucasus) dated to 1.85–1.78 Ma. *Proceedings of the National Academy of Science USA* 108(26):10432–10436.

Finch, C. E., and R. M. Sapolsky
1999   The evolution of Alzheimer disease, the reproductive schedule, and apoE isoforms. *Neurobiology of Aging* 20:407–428.

Fiorato, V., A. Boylston, and C. Knüsel (eds.)
2000   *Blood Red Roses: The Archaeology of a Mass Grave from the Battle of Towton AD 1461.* Oxford, UK: Oxbow Books.

Fisher, S. E., and C. Scharff
2009   FOXP2 as a molecular window into speech and language. *Trends in Genetics* 25:166–177.

Fleagle, J.
1999   *Primate Adaptation and Evolution*, 2nd ed. New York: Academic Press.

Fleagle, J.
2013   *Primate Adaptation and Evolution*, 3rd ed. New York: Academic Press.

Flinn, M.
2008   Why words can hurt us: Social relationships, stress and health. In: *Evolutionary Medicine and Health*, W. R. Trevathan, E. O. Smith, and J. J. McKenna (eds.), pp. 242–258. New York: Oxford University Press.

Flinn, M. V.
1999   Family environment, stress, and health during childhood. In: *Hormones, Health, and Behavior*, C. Panter-Brick and C. M. Worthman (eds.), pp. 105–138. Cambridge, UK: Cambridge University Press.

Flinn, M. V., and B. G. England
2003   Childhood stress: Endocrine and immune responses to psychosocial events. In: *Social and Cultural Lives of Immune Systems*, James MacLynn Wilce (ed.), pp. 107–147. London: Routledge Press.

Foley, R. A.
1991   How many hominid species should there be? *Journal of Human Evolution* 20:413–427.

Foley, R. A.
2002   Adaptive radiations and dispersals in hominin evolutionary ecology. *Evolutionary Anthropology* 11(Suppl. 1):32–37.

Fondon, J. W., and H. R. Garner
2004   Molecular origins of rapid and continuous morphological evolution. *Proceedings of the National Academy of Sciences USA* 101:18058–18063

Formicola, V., and A. P. Buzhilova
2004   Double child burial from Sunghir (Russia): Pathology and inferences for Upper Paleolithic funerary practices. *American Journal of Physical Anthropology* 124:189–198.

Foster, A., H. Buckley, and N. Tayles
2014   Using enthesis robusticity to infer activity in the past: A review. *Journal of Archaeological Method and Theory* 21:511–533.

Fouts, R. S., D. H. Fouts, and T. T. van Cantfort
1989   The infant Loulis learns signs from cross-fostered chimpanzees. In: *Teaching Sign Language to Chimpanzees*, R. A. Gardner (ed.), pp. 280–292. Albany: State University of New York Press.

Fraga, M. F., E. Ballestar, M. F. Paz, et al.
2005   Epigenetic differences arise during the lifetime of monozygotic twins. *Proceedings of the National Academy of Sciences USA* 102:10604–10609.

Fragaszy, D., P. Izar, E. Visalberghi, et al.
2004   Wild capuchin monkeys (*Cebus libidinosus*) use anvils and stone pounding tools. *American Journal of Primatology* 64:359–366.

Franzen, J. L., P. D. Gingerich, J. Habensetzer, et al.
2009   Complete primate skeleton from the Early Eocene of Messel in Germany: Morphology and paleobiology. *PLoS ONE* 4:e5723.

Freundlich, J. C., H. Schwabedissen, and E. Wendt
1980   Köln radiocarbon measurements II. *Radiocarbon* 22:68–81.

Frisancho, A. R.
1993   *Human Adaptation and Accommodation.* Ann Arbor: University of Michigan Press.

Fruth, B., J. M. Benishay, I. Bila-Isia, et al.
2008   *Pan paniscus:* The IUCN red list of threatened species 2008:e.T15932A5321906.

Fu, Q., M. Hajdinjakm, O. Teodora, et al.
2015   An early modern human from Romania with a recent Neanderthal ancestor. *Nature* 524:216–219.

Fu, Q., H. Li, P. Moorjani, et al.
2014   Genome sequence of a 45,000-year-old modern human from western Siberia. *Nature* 514:445–450.

Fu, Q., M. Meyer, X. Gao, et al.
2013   DNA analysis of an early modern human from Tianyuan Cave, China. *Proceedings of the National Academy of Sciences* 110:2223–2227.

Galik, K., B. Senut, M. Pickford, et al.
2004   External and internal morphology of the bar, 1002'00 *Orrorin tugenensis* femur. *Science* 305:1450–1453.

Gao, F., E. Bailes, D. L. Robertson, et al.
1999   Origin of HIV-1 in the chimpanzee *Pan troglodytes troglodytes. Nature* 397:436–441.

Garcia, T., G. Féraud, C. Falguères, et al.
2010   Earliest human remains in Eurasia: New ^{40}Ar/^{39}Ar dating of the Dmanisi hominid-bearing levels, Georgia. *Quaternary Geochronology* 5:443–451.

Gardner, R. A., B. T. Gardner, and T. T. van Cantfort (eds.)
1989   *Teaching Sign Language to Chimpanzees.* Albany: State University of New York Press.

Gebo, D. L., et al.
1997   A hominoid genus from the early Miocene of Uganda. *Science* 276:401–404.

Gibbons, A.
2011a   Skeletons present an exquisite paleo-puzzle. News Focus. *Science* 333:1370–1372.

Gibbons, A.
2011b   A new view of the birth of *Homo sapiens. Science* 331:392–394.

Gibson, D., J. Glass, C. Lartique, et al.
2010   Creation of a bacterial cell controlled by a chemically synthesized genome. *Science Express:* www.sciencemag.org/cgi/content/abstract/science.1190719

Gilbert, W. H.
2008   Hominid systematics. In: *Homo erectus: Pleistocene Evidence from the Middle Awash, Ethiopia.* W. H.

Gilbert and B. Asfaw (eds.). Berkeley: University of California Press.

Gilbert, W. H., and B. Asfaw (eds.)
2008 *Homo erectus: Pleistocene Evidence from the Middle Awash, Ethiopia.* Berkeley: University of California Press.

Gilbert, W. H., T. D. White, and B. Asfaw
2003 *Homo erectus, Homo ergaster, Homo "cepranensis,"* and the Daka cranium. *Journal of Human Evolution* 45:255–259

Gluckman, P., A. Beedle, and M. Hanson
2009 *Principles of Evolutionary Medicine.* Oxford, UK: Oxford University Press.

Gluckman, P. D., and M. A. Hanson
2006 *Developmental Origins of Health and Disease.* Cambridge, UK: Cambridge University Press.

Goodall, J.
1986 *The Chimpanzees of Gombe.* Cambridge, MA: Harvard University Press.

Goodman, C. S., and B. C. Coughlin
2000 The evolution of evo-devo biology. *Proceedings of the National Academy of Sciences USA* 97(9):4424–4425.

Goodman, S., and H. Schütz
2000 The lemurs of the northeastern slopes of the Réserve Spéciale de Manongarivo. *Lemur News* 5:30–33.

Gossett, T. F.
1963 *Race: The History of an Idea in America.* Dallas: Southern Methodist University Press.

Gould, S. J.
1981 *The Mismeasure of Man.* New York: Norton.

Gould, S. J.
1985 Darwin at sea—and the virtues of port. In: *The Flamingo's Smile: Reflections in Natural History,* S. J. Gould (ed.), pp. 347–359. New York: Norton.

Granger, D. E., R. J. Gibbon, K. Kuman, et al.
2015 New cosmogenic burial ages for Sterkfontein Member 2 *Australopithecus* and Member 5 Oldowan. *Nature* 522:85–88.

Graves, R. R., A. C. Lupo, R. C. McCarthy, et al.
2010 Just how strapping was KNM-WT 15000? *Journal of Human Evolution* 59: 542–554.

Gravina, S., and J. Vijg
2010 Epigenetic factors in aging and longevity. *European Journal of Physiology* 459:247–258.

Gravlee, C. C.
2009 How race becomes biology: Embodiment of social inequality. *American Journal of Physical Anthropology* 139:47–57.

Greaves, M.
2008 Cancer: Evolutionary origins of vulnerability. In: *Evolution in Health and Disease,* 2nd ed., S. C. Stearns and J. C. Koella (eds.). Oxford, UK: Oxford University Press, pp. 277–287.

Green, D. J., and Z. Alemseged
2012 *Australopithecus afarensis:* Scapular ontogeny, function, and the role of climbing in human evolution. *Science,* 338:514–517.

Green, R. E., J. Krause, A. W. Briggs, et al.
2010 A draft sequence of the Neandertal genome. *Science* 328:710–722.

Green, R. E., J. Krause, E. Ptak, et al.
2006 Analysis of one million base pairs of Neanderthal DNA. *Nature* 444:330–336.

Greene, J. C.
1981 *Science, Ideology, and World View.* Berkeley: University of California Press.

Greenwood, B., and T. Mutabingwa
2002 Malaria in 2000. *Nature* 415:670–672.

Gros-Louis, J., H. Perry, and J. H. Manson
2003 Violent coalitionary attacks and intraspecific killing in wild white-faced capuchin monkeys (*Cebus capucinus*). *Primates* 44:341–346.

Gruber, N., C. Hauri, Z. Lachkar, et al.
2012 Rapid progression of ocean acidification in the California current system. *Science* 337:220–223.

Grueter, C. C., D. Li, B. Ren, et al.
2009 Choice of analytical method can have dramatic effects on primate home range estimates. *Primates* 50:81–84.

Grün, R., and C. B. Stringer
1991 ESR dating and the evolution of modern humans. *Archaeometry* 33:153–199.

Grün, R., C. B. Stringer, F. McDermott, et al.
2005 U-series and ESR analysis of bones and teeth relating to the human burials from Skhūl. *Journal of Human Evolution* 49:316–334.

Guinotte, J., and V. J. Fabry
2009 The threat of acidification to ocean ecosystems. *The Journal of Marine Education* 25:2–7.

Gursky, S.
2003 Predation experiments on infant spectral tarsiers (Tarsius spectrum). *Folia Primatologica* 74:272–284.

Gutiérrez, M.
2011 Taxonomic and Ecological Characterization of a Late Oligocene Mammalian Fauna from Kenya. Unpublished Ph.D. dissertation, Washington University in St. Louis, *Electronic Theses and Dissertations.* Paper 139. http://openscholarship.wustl.edu/etd/139

Haeusler, M., R. Schiess, and T. Boeni
2011 New vertebral and rib material point to modern bauplan of the Nariokotome *Homo erectus* skeleton. *Journal of Human Evolution* 61:575-582.

Haile-Selassie, Y., L. Gibert, S. M. Melillo, et al.
2015 New species from Ethiopia further expands Middle Pliocene hominin diversity. *Nature* 521:483–488.

Haile-Selassie, Y., B. M. Latimer, M. Alene, et al.
2010 An early *Australopithecus afarensis* postcranium from Woranso-Mille, Ethiopia. *Proceedings of the National Academy of Sciences USA* 107:12121–12126.

Haile-Sellassie, Y., B. Z. Saylor, A. Deino, et al.
2012 A new hominin foot from Ethiopia shows multiple Pliocene bipedal adaptations. News and Views. *Nature* 483:565–569.

Haile-Selassie, Y., G. Suwa, and T. D. White
2004 Late Miocene teeth from Middle Awash, Ethiopia, and early hominid dental evolution. *Science* 303:1503–1505.

Hare, B., and S. Kwetuenda
2010 Bonobos voluntarily share their own food with others. *Current Biology* 20(5):R230–R231.

Harmand, S., J. E. Lewis, C. S. Feibel, et al.
2015 3.3-million-year-old stone tools from Lomekwi 3, West Turkana, Kenya. *Nature* 521:310–315.

Harrison, T.
2002   Late Oligocene to middle Miocene catarrhines from Afro-Arabia. In: *Primate Fossil Record,* W. Hartwig (ed.), pp. 311–338. Cambridge, UK: Cambridge University Press.

Harrison, T.
2010a   Apes among the tangled branches of human origins. *Science* 327:532–534.

Harrison, T.
2010b   Dendropithecoidea, Proconsuloidea and Hominoidea (Catarrhini, Primates). In: *Cenozoic Mammals of Africa,* L. Werdelin and W. J. Sanders (eds.), pp. 429–469. Berkeley: University of California Press.

Harrison, T., X. Ji, and L. Zheng
2008   Renewed investigations at the late Miocene hominoid locality of Leilao, Yunnan, China. *American Journal of Physical Anthropology* 135(S46):113.

Harrould-Kolieb, E., and J. Savitz
2009   Can we save our oceans from CO_2? In: *Oceana: Protecting the World's Oceans,* 2nd ed. Online publication, June 2009, available at na.oceana.org/sites/default/files/o/.../Acid.../Acidification_Report.pdf

Hart, W. K., G. WoldeGabriel, S. Katoh, et al.
2003   Dating of the Herto hominin fossils. *Nature* 426:622.

Hauff, L. E., and E. W. Demerath
2012   Body image concerns and reduced breastfeeding duration in primiparous overweight and obese women. *American Journal of Human Biology* 24:339–349.

Hawkes, K., and J. E. Coxworth
2013   Grandmothers and the evolution of human longevity: a review of findings and future directions. *Evolutionary Anthropology: Issues, News, and Reviews* 22:294–302.

Hawkes, K., J. F. O'Connell, and N. G. Blurton Jones
1997   Hadza women's time allocation, offspring provisioning, and the evolution of long postmenopausal life spans. *Current Anthropology* 38:551–577.

Hawks, J., and L. R. Berger
2016   The impact of a date for understanding the importance of *Homo naledi. Transactions of the Royal Society of South Africa* 13:1–4.

Hawks, J., D. J. de Ruiter, L. R. Berger
2015   Comment on "Early *Homo* at 2.8 Ma from Ledi-Geraru, Afar, Ethiopia." *Science* 348:1326–1326.

Heard, E., and R. A. Martienssen
2014   Transgenerational epigenetic inheritance: Myths and mechanisms. *Cell* 157:95–109.

Heizmann, E., and D. R. Begun
2001   The oldest European hominoid. *Journal of Human Evolution* 41:465–481.

Henry, A. G., A. S. Brooks, and D. R. Piperno
2011   Microfossils in calculus demonstrate consumption of plants and cooked foods in Neanderthal diets (Shanidar III, Iraq; Spy I and II, Belgium). *Proceedings of the National Academy of Sciences USA* 108:486–491.

Henry, A. G., P. S. Ungar, B. H. Passey, et al.
2012   The diet of Australopithecus sediba. *Nature* 487:90–93.

Henshilwood, C. S., F. d'Errico, M. Vanhaeren, et al.
2004   Middle stone age shell beads from South Africa. *Science* 304:404.

Henshilwood, C. S., F. d'Errico, K. L. Van Niekerk, et al.
2011   A 100,000-year-old ochre-processing workshop at Blombos Cave, South Africa. *Science* 334:219–222.

Henzi, P., and L. Barrett
2003   Evolutionary ecology, sexual conflict, and behavioral differentiation among baboon populations. *Evolutionary Anthropology* 12:217–230.

Hershkovitz, P.
1977   *Living New World Monkeys (Platyrrhini): With an Introduction to Primates.* Chicago and London: University of Chicago Press.

Higham, T., L. Basell, R. Jacobi, et al.
2012   Testing models for the beginnings of the Aurignacian and the advent of figurative art and music: The radiocarbon chronology of Geissenklösterle. *Journal of Human Evolution* 62:664–676.

Higham, T., C. B. Ramsey, I. Karavanic, et al.
2006   Revised direct radiocarbon dating of the Vindija G1 Upper Paleolithic Neandertals. *Proceedings of the National Academy of Sciences USA* 103:553–557.

Hill, A.
2007   Introduction. In: *Hominin Environments in the East African Pliocene: An Assessment of the Faunal Evidence,* R. Bobe, Z. Alemseged, and A. K. Behrensmeyer (eds.), pp. xvii–xx. Dordrecht, The Netherlands: Springer.

Hinde, K., and J. P. Capitanio
2010   Lactational programming? Mother's milk predicts infant temperament and behavior. *American Journal of Primatology* 72:522–529.

Hinde, K., and L. M. Milligan
2011   Primate milk synthesis: Proximate mechanisms and ultimate perspectives. *Evolutionary Anthropology* 20:9–23.

Hoffstetter, R.
1972   Relationships, origins, and history of the ceboid monkeys and the caviomorph rodents: A modern reinterpretation. In: *Evolutionary Biology,* T. Dobzhansky, T. M. K. Hecht, and W. C. Steere (eds.), pp. 323–347. New York: Appleton-Century-Crofts.

Holliday, T. W.
2003   Species concepts, reticulation, and human evolution. *Current Anthropology* 44: 653–673.

Holloway, R. L.
1983   Cerebral brain endocast pattern of *Australopithecus afarensis* hominid. *Nature* 303:420–422.

Holloway, R. L.
1985   The poor brain of *Homo sapiens neanderthalensis.* In: *Ancestors: The Hard Evidence,* E. Delson (ed.), pp. 319–324. New York: Alan R. Liss.

Hornsby, P. J.
2010   Senescence and life span. *European Journal of Physiology* 459:291–299.

Horvath, J. E., D. W. Weisrock, S. L. Embry, et al.
2008   Development and application of a phylogenetic toolkit: Resolving the evolutionary history of Madagascar's lemurs. *Genome Research* 18:489–499.

Horvath, J. E., and H. F. Willard
2007   Primate comparative genomics: Lemur biology and evolution. *Trends in Genetics* 23:173–182.

Hou, Y., R. Potts, Y. Baoyin, et al.
2000   Mid-Pleistocene Acheulean-like stone technology of the Bose Basin, South China. *Science* 287:1622–1626.

Houle, A.
1998   Floating islands: A mode of long-distance dispersal for small and medium-sized terrestrial vertebrates. *Diversity and Distribution* 4:201–219.

Houle, A.
1999   The origin of platyrrhines: An evaluation of the Antarctic scenario and the floating island model. *American Journal of Physical Anthropology* 109:541–559.

Hrdy, S. B.
1977   *The Langurs of Abu*. Cambridge, MA: Harvard University Press.

Hrdy, S. B.
2009   *Mothers and Others: The Evolutionary Origins of Mutual Understanding*. Cambridge, MA: Harvard University Press.

Hrdy, S. B., C. Janson, and C. van Schaik
1995   Infanticide: Let's not throw out the baby with the bath water. *Evolutionary Anthropology* 3:151–154.

Hublin, J. J., S. Talamo, M. Julien, et al.
2012   Radiocarbon dates from the Grotte du Renne and Saint-Cesaire support a Neandertal origin for the Chatelperronian. *Proceedings of the National Academy of Sciences USA* 109:18743–18748.

Hudjashou, G., T. Kivisid, P. A. Underhill, et al.
2007   Revealing the prehistoric settlement of Australia by Y chromosome and mtDNA analysis. *Proceedings of the National Academy of Sciences USA* 104:8726–8730.

Humphrey, L. T.
2010   Weaning behaviour in human evolution. *Seminars in Cell & Developmental Biology* 21:453–461.

Hunt, G. R.
1996   Manufacture and use of hook-tools by New Caledonian crows. *Nature* 379:249–251.

International Human Genome Sequencing Consortium
2001   Initial sequencing and analysis of the human genome. *Nature* 409:860–921.

International SNP Map Working Group
2001   A map of human genome sequence variation containing 1.42 million single nucleotide polymorphisms. *Nature* 409:928–933.

Irish, J. D., D. Guatelli-Steinberg, S. S. Legge, et al.
2013   Dental morphology and the phylogenetic "place" of *Australopithecus sediba*. *Science* 340:1233062.

Jablonski, N. G.
1992   Sun, skin colour, and spina bifida: An exploration of the relationship between ultraviolet light and neural tube defects. *Proceedings of the Australian Society of Human Biology* 5:455–462.

Jablonski, N. G., and G. Chaplin
2000   The evolution of human skin coloration. *Journal of Human Evolution* 39:57–106.

Jablonski, N. G., and G. Chaplin
2010   Human skin pigmentation as an adaptation to UV radiation. *Proceedings of the National Academy of Sciences* 107:8962–8968.

Jablonski, N. J., and S. R. Frost
2010   Cercopithecoidea. In: *Cenozoic Mammals of Africa*, L. Werdelin and W. J. Sanders (eds.), pp. 393–428. Berkeley: University of California Press.

Jacob, T., E. Indriati, R. P. Soejono, et al.
2006   Pygmoid Australomelonesian *Homo sapiens* skeletal remains from Liang Bua, Flores: Population affinities and pathological anomalies. *Proceedings of the National Academy of Sciences USA* 103:13421–13426.

Jacobs, Z., G.A.T. Duller, A. G. Wintle, et al.
2006   Extending the chronology of deposits at Blombos Cave, South Africa, back to 140 ka using optical dating of single and multiple grains of quartz. *Journal of Human Evolution* 51:255–273.

Jaeger, J.-J., K. C. Beard, Y. Chaimanee, et al.
2010   Late middle Eocene epoch of Libya yields earliest known radiation of African anthropoids. *Nature* 467:1095–1098.

Jaeger, J.-J., A. N. Soe, O. Chavasseau, et al.
2011   First hominoid from the Late Miocene of the Irrawaddy Formation (Myanmar). *PLoS ONE* 6:e17065. doi:10.1371/journal.pone.0017065.

Jakobsson, M., S. W. Scholz, P. Scheet, et al.
2008   Genotype, haplotype and copy-number variation in worldwide human populations. *Nature* 451:998–1003.

Jameson, N. M., Z.-C. Hou, K. N. Sterner, et al.
2011   Genomic data reject the hypothesis of a prosimian primate clade. *Journal of Human Evolution* 61:295–305.

Jantz, R. L., and S. D. Ousley
2005   FORDISC 3: Computerized forensic discriminant functions. Version 3.

Jerison, H. J.
1973   *Evolution of the Brain and Behavior*. New York: Academic Press.

Ji, X. P., N. G. Jablonski, D. F. Fue, et al.
2013   Juvenile hominoid cranium from the terminal Miocene of Yunnan, China. *Chinese Science Bulletin* 58:3771–3779.

Jia, L., and W. Huang
1990   *The Story of Peking Man*. New York: Oxford University Press.

Jobling, M., E. Hollox, M. Hurles, et al.
2013   *Human Evolutionary Genetics*, 2nd ed. New York: Garland Science.

Jolly, C. J.
1970   The seed-eaters: A new model of hominid differentiation based on a baboon analogy. *Man, New Series* 5:5–26.

Jungers, W. L.
2013   *Homo floresiensis*. In: *A Companion to Paleoanthropology*. D. R. Begun (ed.), pp. 582–598. Chichester: Wiley-Blackwell,

Jungers, W. L., W. E. H. Harcourt-Smith, R. E. Wunderlich, et al.
2009   The foot of *Homo floresiensis*. *Nature* 459:81–84.

Jurmain, R.
1999   *Stories from the Skeleton: Behavioral Reconstruction in Human Osteology*. Oxford, UK: Taylor and Francis.

Jurmain, R., F. A. Cardosa, C. Henderson, et al.
2012   Bioarchaeology's Holy Grail: The reconstruction of activity. In: *Companion to Paleopathology*, A. L. Grauer (ed.), pp. 532–552. Oxford: Wiley-Blackwell.

Kaback, M. M.
2000   Population-based genetic screening for reproductive counseling: The Tay-Sachs disease model. *European Journal of Pediatrics* 159:S192–S195.

Kaifu, Y., H. Baba, T. Sutikna, et al.
2011   Craniofacial morphology of *Homo floresiensis*: Description, taxonomic affinities, and evolutionary implication. *Journal of Human Evolution* 61:644–682.

Kano, T.
1992   *The Last Ape: Pygmy Chimpanzee Behavior and Ecology*. Stanford, CA: Stanford University Press.

Kappeler, P. M.
2000   Lemur origins: Rafting by groups of hibernators? *Folia Primatologica* 71:422–425.

Katz, D., and J. M. Suchey
1986   Age determination of the male os pubis. *American Journal of Physical Anthropology* 69:427–435.

Katzmarzyk, P. T., and W. R. Leonard
1998   Climatic influences on human body size and proportions: Ecological adaptations and secular trends. *American Journal of Physical Anthropology* 106:483–503.

Kau, A. L., P. P. Ahern, N. W. Griffin, et al.
2011   Human nutrition, the gut microbiome and the immune system. *Nature* 474:327–336.

Kay, R. F., D. Schmitt, C. J. Vinyard, et al.
2004   The paleobiology of Amphipithecidae, South Asian late Eocene primates. *Journal of Human Evolution* 46:3–25.

Kayser, M.
2010   The human genetic history of Oceania: Near and remote views of dispersal. *Current Biology* 20:R194–R201.

Keeley, L. H., and N. Toth
1981   Microwear polishes on early stone tools from Koobi-Fora, Kenya. *Nature* 293:464–465.

Keller, A., A. Graefen, M. Ball, et al.
2012   New insights into the Tyrolean Iceman's origin and phenotype as inferred by whole-genome sequencing. *Nature Communications* 3:698. doi: 10.1038/ncomms1701.

Kelley, J., and F. Gao
2012   Juvenile hominoid cranium from the late Miocene of southern China and hominoid diversity in Asia. *Proceedings of the National Academy of Sciences USA* 109:6882–6885.

Kelley, R. I., D. Robinson, E. G. Puffenberger, et al.
2002   Amish lethal microcephaly: A new metabolic disorder with severe congenital microcephaly and 2-ketoglutaric aciduria. *American Journal of Medical Genetics* 112:318–326.

Kennedy, G. E.
2005   From the ape's dilemma to the weanling's dilemma: Early weaning and its evolutionary context. *Journal of Human Evolution* 48:123–145.

Keynes, R.
2002   *Darwin, His Daughter and Human Evolution*. New York: Riverhead Books.

Khan, S., R. Hansen, K. P. Scott, et al.
2015   G116 (P) The human gut is probably sterile at birth. *Archives of Disease in Childhood* 100(Suppl. 3): A50–A51.

Kim, P. S., J. E. Coxworth, and K. Hawkes
2012   Increased longevity evolves from grandmothering. *Proceedings of the Royal Society B: Biological Sciences* 279:4880–4884.

Kimbel, W. H.
2013   Palaeoanthropology: Hesitation on hominin history. *Nature* 497:573–574.

Kimbel, W. H., R. C. Walter, D. C. Johanson, et al.
1996   Late Pliocene *Homo* and Oldowan tools from the Hadar Formation (Kada Hadar member), Ethiopia. *Journal of Human Evolution* 31:549–561.

Kimbel, W. H., T. D. White, and D. C. Johanson
1988   Implications of KNM-WT-17000 for the evolution of 'robust' *Australopithecus*. In: *Evolutionary History of the Robust Australopithecines* (Foundations of Human Behavior), F. E. Grine (ed.), pp. 259–268. Somerset, NJ: Aldine Transaction.

King, B. J.
1994   *The Information Continuum*. Santa Fe, NM: School of American Research.

King, B. J.
2004   *Dynamic Dance: Nonvocal Communication in the African Great Apes*. Cambridge, MA: Harvard University Press.

King, M. C., and A. G. Motulsky
2002   Mapping human history. *Science* 298: 2342–2343.

King, T. E., G. G. Fortes, P. Balaresque, et al.
2014   Identification of the remains of King Richard III. *Nature Communications* 5:1–8.

Kirkwood, T. B. L.
1997   The origins of human ageing. *Philosophical Transactions of the Royal Society of London B* 352:1765–1772.

Klein, R. G.
1999   *The Human Career. Human Biological and Cultural Origins*, 2nd ed. Chicago: University of Chicago Press.

Klein, R. G.
2009   *The Human Career: Human Biological and Cultural Origins*, 3rd ed. Chicago: University of Chicago Press.

Klein, R. G., and B. Edgar
2002   *The Dawn of Human Culture*. New York: Wiley.

Konner, M. J., and C. M. Worthman
1980   Nursing frequency, gonadal functioning, and birth spacing among !Kung hunter-gartherers. *Science* 207:788–791.

Koopman, R. J., A. G. Mainous, V. A. Diaz, et al.
2005   Changes in age at diagnosis of type 2 diabetes mellitus in the United States, 1988 to 2000. *Annals of Family Medicine* 3(1):60–69.

Kramer, A.
1993   Human taxonomic diversity in the Pleistocene: Does *Homo erectus* represent multiple hominid species? *American Journal of Physical Anthropology* 91:161–171.

Kramer, K. L.
2010   Cooperative breeding and its significance to the demographic success of humans. *Annual Review of Anthropology* 39:417–436.

Kramer, K. L., and A. F. Russell
2015   Was monogamy a key step on the hominin road? Reevaluating the monogamy hypothesis in the evolution of cooperative breeding. *Evolutionary Anthropology: Issues, News, and Reviews* 24:73–83.

Krause, J., L. Orlando, D. Serre, et al.
2007a   Neanderthals in central Asia and Siberia. *Nature* 449:902–904.

Krause, J., C. Lalueza-Fox, L. Orlando, et al.
2007b   The derived FOXP2 variant of modern humans was shared with Neandertals. *Current Biology* 17:1908–1912.

Krause, J., Q. Fu, J. M. Good, et al.
2010   The complete mitochondrial DNA genome of an unknown hominin from southern Siberia. *Nature* 464:894–896.

Krings, M., C. Capelli, F. Tschentscher, et al.
2000   A view of Neandertal genetic diversity. *Nature Genetics* 26(2):144–146.

Krings, M., A. Stone, R. W. Schmitz, et al.
1997   Neandertal DNA sequences and the origin of modern humans. *Cell* 90(1):19–30.

Kujoth, G. C., P. Bradshaw, S. Haroon, et al.
2007   The role of mitochondrial DNA mutations in mammalian aging. *PLoS Genetics* 3:e24.

Kulikov, E. E., A. B. Poltaraus, and I. A. Lebedeva.
2004   DNA analysis of Sunghir remains: Problems and perspectives. Poster presentation. European Paleopathology Association Meetings, Durham, UK, August 2004.

Kunimatsu, Y., M. Nakatsukasa, Y. Sawada, et al.
2007   A new Late Miocene great ape from Kenya and its implications for the origins of African great apes and humans. *Proceedings of the National Academy of Sciences USA* 104:19220–19225.

Kuzawa, C. W.
2005   The fetal origins of developmental plasticity: Are fetal cues reliable predictors of future nutritional environments? *American Journal of Human Biology* 17:5–21.

Kuzawa, C. W.
2008   The developmental origins of adult health: Intergenerational inertia in adaptation and disease. *Evolutionary Medicine and Health: New Perspectives*, W. R. Trevathan, E. O. Smith, and J. J. McKenna (eds.), pp. 325–349. New York: Oxford University Press.

Kuzawa C.W., and D. T. A. Eisenberg
2014   The long reach of history: Intergenerational pathways to plasticity in human lifespan. In: *Society, Hierarchy, Health: Comparative Biodemography*, M. Weinstein and M. A. Lane (eds.). Washington, DC: The National Academies Press.

Kuzawa, C. W., and E. A. Quinn
2009   Developmental origins of adult function and health: Evolutionary hypotheses. *Annual Review of Anthropology* 38:131–147.

L'Abbé, E. N., S. A. Symes, J. T. Pokines., et al.
2015   Evidence of fatal skeletal injuries on Malapa Hominins 1 and 2. *Scientific Reports* 5:15120.

Lachance, J., B. Vernot, C. C. Elbers, et al.
2012   Evolutionary history and adaptation from high-coverage whole-genome sequences of diverse African hunter-gatherers. *Cell* 150:457–469.

Lack, D.
1966   *Population Studies of Birds*. Oxford, UK: Clarendon.

Lahdenperä, M., V. Lummaa, S. Helle, et al.
2004   Fitness benefits of prolonged post-reproductive lifespan in women. *Nature* 428:178–181.

Lahr, M. M., and R. A. Foley
1998   Towards a theory of modern human origins: Geography, demography, and diversity in recent human evolution. *Yearbook of Physical Anthropology* 41:137–176.

Lai, C. S. L., S. E, Fisher, J. A. Hurst, et al.
2001   A forkhead-domain gene is mutated in a severe speech and language disorder. *Nature* 413:519–523.

Lakshminarayan, V. R., and L. R. Santos
2008   Capuchin monkeys are sensitive to others' welfare. *Current Biology* 20(5):R230–R231.

Lalani, A. S., J. Masters, W. Zheng, et al.
1999   Use of chemokine receptors by poxviruses. *Science* 286:1968–1971.

Lalueza-Fox, C., H. Römpler, D. Caramelli, et al.
2007   A melanocortin receptor allele suggests varying pigmentation among Neanderthals. *Science Express* October 25, 2007.

Lalueza-Fox, C., A. Rosas, A. Estalrrich, et al.
2011   Genetic evidence for patrilocal mating behavior among Neandertal groups. *Proceedings of the National Academy of Sciences USA* 108:250–253.

Lamason, R. L., M.-A. P. K. Mohideen, J. R. Mest, et al.
2005   SLC24A5, a putative cation exchanger, affects pigmentation in zebrafish and humans. *Science* 310:1782–1786.

Lamberts, S. W. J., A. W. van den Beld, and A. J. van der Lely
1997   The endocrinology of aging. *Science* 278:419–424.

Lamichhaney, S., F. Han, J. Berglund, et al.
2016   A beak size locus in Darwin's finches facilitated character displacement during a drought. *Science* 352:470–474.

Lancaster, J. B., and C. S. Lancaster
1983   Parental investment: The hominid adaptation. In: *How Humans Adapt: A Biocultural Odyssey*, D. J. Ortner (ed.), pp. 33–66. Washington, DC: Smithsonian Institution Press.

Lanza, I. R., and K. S. Nair
2010   Mitochondrial function as a determinant of life span. *European Journal of Physiology* 459:277–289.

Larick, R., and R. L. Ciochon
2015   Early hominin biogeography in Island Southeast Asia. *Evolutionary Anthropology: Issues, News, and Reviews* 24:185–213.

Larsen, C. S.
2002   *Skeletons in Our Closet: Revealing Our Past through Bioarchaeology.* Princeton, NJ: Princeton University Press.

Larsen, C. S.
2006   The agricultural revolution as environmental catastrophe: Implications for health and lifestyle in the Holocene. *Quaternary International* 150:12–20.

Larsen, C. S.
2015   *Bioarchaeology: Interpreting Behavior from the Human Skeleton.* Cambridge, UK: Cambridge University Press.

Lawson, D. W., and R. Mace
2011   Parental investment and the optimization of human family size. *Philosophical Transactions of the Royal Society of London B Biological Sciences* 366:333–343

Leakey, M. D., and R. L. Hay
1979   Pliocene footprints in Laetolil beds at Laetoli, Northern Tanzania. *Nature* 278:317–323.

Leakey, R. E., M. G. Leakey, A. C. Walker
1988   Morphology of *Afropithecus turkanensis* from Kenya. *American Journal of Physical Anthropology* 76:289–307.

Leonard, W. R.
2002   Dietary change was a driving force in human evolution. *Scientific American* 287:106–116.

Lepre, C. J., and D. V. Kent
2010   New magnetostratigraphy for the Olduvai Subchron in the Koobi Fora Formation, northwest Kenya, with implications for early *Homo*. *Earth and Planetary Science Letters* 290:362–374.

Lerner, I. M., and W. J. Libby
1976   *Heredity, Evolution, and Society.* San Francisco: W. H. Freeman.

Levitis, D. A., O. Burger, and L. B. Lackey
2013   The human post-fertile lifespan in comparative evolutionary context. *Evolutionary Anthropology: Issues, News, and Reviews* 22:66–79.

Lewontin, R. C.
1972   The apportionment of human diversity. In: *Evolutionary Biology*, T. Dobzhansky (ed.), pp. 381–398. New York: Plenum.

Li, J. Z., D. M. Assher, H. Tang, et al.
2008   Worldwide human relationships inferred from genome-wide patterns of variation. *Science* 319:1100–1104.

Li, T. Y., and D. A. Etler
1992   New middle Pleistocene hominid crania from Yunxian in China. *Nature* 357:404–407.

Lieberman, D. L.
2012   Those feet in ancient times. News and Views. *Nature* 483:550–551.

Lin, D. R., and J. H. White
2004   Pleiotropic actions of vitamin D. *BioEssays* 26(1):21–28.

Lin, J. Y., and D. E. Fisher
2007   Melanocyte biology and skin pigmentation. *Nature* 445:843–850.

Liu, L., S. Oza, D. Hogan, J. Perin, et al.
2014   Global, regional, and national causes of child mortality in 2000–13, with projections to inform post-2015 priorities: An updated systematic analysis. *The Lancet* 385:430–440.

Liu, P. T., S. Stenger, H. Li, et al.
2006   Toll-like receptor triggering of a vitamin D–mediated human antimicrobial response. *Science* 311:1770–1773.

Locke, D. P., L. W. Hillier, W. C. Warren, et al.
2011   Comparative and demographic analysis of orangutan genomes. *Nature* 469:529–533.

Loeb, L. A., D. C. Wallace, and G. M. Martin
2005   The mitochondrial theory of aging and its relationship to reactive oxygen species damage and somatic mtDNA mutations. *Proceedings of the National Academy of Sciences (PNAS)* 102:18769–18770.

Lofgren, D. L.
1995   The bug creek problem and the Cretaceous-Tertiary transition at McGuire Creek, Montana. *University of California Publications in Geological Sciences* 140:1–185.

Lohmueller, K. E., A. R. Indap, S. Schmidt, et al.
2008   Proportionally more deleterious genetic variation in European than in African populations. *Nature* 451:994–997.

Lordkipanidze, D., M. S. P. de León, A. Margvelashvili, et al.
2013   A complete skull from Dmanisi, Georgia, and the evolutionary biology of early *Homo*. *Science* 342:326-331.

Lordkipanidze, D., T. Jashashuil, A. Vekua, et al.
2007   Postcranial evidence from early *Homo* from Dmanisi, Georgia. *Nature* 449:305–310.

Lordkipanidze D., A. Vekua, R. Ferring, et al.
2006   A fourth hominid skull from Dmanisi, Georgia. *The Anatomical Record: Part A* 288:1146–1157.

Lovejoy, C. O.
1981   The origin of man. *Science* 211:341–350.

Lovejoy, C. O.
2009   Reexamining human origins in light of *Ardipithecus ramidus*. *Science* 326:74e1–74e8.

Lovejoy, C. O., B. Latimer, G. Suwa, et al.
2009a   Combining prehension and propulsion: The foot of *Ardipithecus ramidus*. *Science* 72e1–72e8.

Lovejoy, C. O., G. Suwa, S. W. Simpson, et al.
2009b   The great divides: *Ardipithecus ramidus* reveals the postcrania of our last common ancestors with African great apes. *Science* 326:100–106.

Low, B. S., N. Parker, A. Hazel, et al.
2013   Life expectancy, fertility, and women's lives: A life-history perspective. *Cross-Cultural Research* 47:198–225.

Mace, R.
2000   Evolutionary ecology of human life history. *Animal Behaviour* 59:1–10.

MacKinnon, J., and K. MacKinnon
1980   The behavior of wild spectral tarsiers. *International Journal of Primatology* 1:361–379.

Maher, B.
2012   ENCODE: The human encyclopaedia. *Nature* 489:46.

Majerus, M. E. N.
2009   Industrial melanism in the peppered moth, *Biston betularia*: An excellent teaching example of Darwinian evolution in action. *Evolution Education and Outreach* 2:63–74.

Majumder, P. P.
2010   The human genetic history of South Asia. *Current Biology* 20:R184–R187.

Manson, J. H., and R. W. Wrangham
1991   Intergroup aggression in chimpanzees and humans. *Current Anthropology* 32:369–390.

Marean, C. M.
2010   When the sea saved humanity. *Scientific American* 303:54–61.

Marean, C. W., M. Bar-Matthews, J. Bernatchez, et al.
2007   Early human use of marine resources and pigment in South Africa during the Middle Pleistocene. *Nature* 449:905–908.

Marris, E.
2006   Bushmeat surveyed in Western cities. Illegally hunted animals turn up in markets from New York to London. *News@Nature.com.* doi:10.1038/news060626-10.

Martin, R. D.
1990   *Primate Origins and Evolution: A Phylogenetic Reconstruction.* Princeton, NJ: Princeton University Press.

Martin, R. D., A. M. Maclaranon, J. C. Phillips, et al.
2006   Flores hominid: New species or microcephalic dwarf? *The Anatomical Record: Part A* 288A:1123–1145.

Matsuzawa, T., T. Humle, and Y. Sugiyama (eds.)
2011   *The Chimpanzees of Bossou and Nimba.* Tokyo: Springer Press.

Maurano, M. T., R. Humbert, E. Rynes, et al.
2012   Systematic localization of common disease-associated variation in regulatory DNA. *Science* 337:1190–1195.

Mayr, E.
1970   *Population, Species, and Evolution.* Cambridge, MA: Harvard University Press.

Mayr, E.
1981   *The Growth of Biological Thought.* Cambridge, MA: Harvard University Press.

Mbua, E., S. Kusaka, Y. Kunimatsu, et al.
2016   Kantis: A new Australopithecus site on the shoulders of the Rift Valley near Nairobi, Kenya. *Journal of human evolution* 94:28–44.

McBrearty, S., and N. G. Jablonski
2005   First fossil chimpanzee. *Nature* 437:105–108.

McCall, R. A.
1997   Implications of recent geological investigations of the Mozambique channel for the mammalian colonization of Madagascar. *Proceedings of the Royal Society of London Series B: Biological Sciences* 264:663–665.

McCarthy, R. C., and L. Lucas
2014   A morphometric re-assessment of BOU-VP-16/1 from Herto, Ethiopia. *Journal of Human Evolution* 74:114–117.

McCollum, M. A., B. A. Rosenman, G. Suwa, et al.
2010   The vertebral formula of the last common ancestor of African apes and humans. *Journal of Experimental Zoology Part B: Molecular and Developmental Evolution* 314B:123–134.

McDougall, I., F. H. Brown, and J. G. Fleagle
2005   Stratigraphic placement and age of modern humans from Kibish, Ethiopia. *Nature* 433:733–736.

McDowell, G., E. Mules, P. Fabacher, et al.
1992   The presence of two different infantile Tay-Sachs disease mutations in a Cajun population. *American Journal of Human Genetics* 51:1071–1077.

McGrew, W. C.
1992   *Chimpanzee Material Culture: Implications for Human Evolution.* New York: Cambridge University Press.

McGrew, W. C.
1998   Culture in nonhuman primates? *Annual Review of Anthropology* 27:301–328.

McHenry, H.
1988   New estimates of body weight in early hominids and their significance to encephalization and megadontia in "robust" australopithecines. In: *Evolutionary History of the Robust Australopithecines* (Foundations of Human Behavior), F. E. Grine (ed.), pp. 133–148. Somerset, NJ: Aldine Transaction.

McHenry, H.
1992   Body size and proportions in early hominids. *American Journal of Physical Anthropology* 87:407–431.

McKern, T. W., and T. D. Stewart
1957   *Skeletal Age Changes in Young American Males.* Natick, MA: Quartermaster Research and Development Command, Technical Report EP-45.

McKusick, V. A.
2000   Ellis-van Creveld syndrome and the Amish. *Nature Genetics* 24:203–204.

McPherron, S. P., Z. Alemseged, C. W. Marean, et al.
2010   Evidence of stone-tool-assisted consumption of animal tissue before 3.39 million years ago at Dikika, Ethiopia. *Nature* 466:857–860.

Merbs, C. F.
1983   Patterns of activity-induced pathology in a Canadian Inuit population. Archaeological Survey of Canada, Paper 119. Ottawa: National Museums of Canada.

Meyer, M., J.-L. Arsuaga, C. de Filipp, et al.
2015   Nuclear DNA sequences from the Middle Pleistocene Sima de los Huesos hominins. *Nature* 531:504–507.

Meyer, M., Q. Fu, A. Aximu-Petri, et al.
2014   A mitochondrial genome sequence of a hominin from Sima de los Huesos. *Nature* 505:403–406.

Meyer, M., M. Kircher, M.-T. Gansauge, et al.
2012   A high-coverage genome sequence from an archaic Denisovan individual. *Science* 338:222–226.

Milella, M., M. G. Belcastro, C. P. E. Zollikofer, et al.
2012   The effect of age, sex, and physical activity on entheseal morphology in a contemporary Italian skeletal collection. *American Journal of Physical Anthropology*, 148:379–388.

Miles, H. L. W.
1990   The cognitive foundations for reference in a signing orangutan. In: *Language and Intelligence in Monkeys and Apes: Comparative Developmental Perspectives*, S. T. Parker and K. R. Gibson (eds.), pp. 511–539. New York: Cambridge University Press.

Miller, E. R., B. R. Benefit, M. L. McCrossin, et al.
2009   Systematics of early and middle Miocene Old World monkeys. *Journal of Human Evolution* 57:195–211.

Miller, E. R., G. F. Gunnell, and R. D. Martin
2005   Deep time and the search for anthropoid origins. *Yearbook of Physical Anthropology* 48:60–95.

Mitani, J. C., D. P. Watts, and S. J. Amsler
2010 Lethal intergroup aggression leads to territorial expansion in wild chimpanzees. *Current Biology* 20(12):R507–R508.

Mittermeier , R. A., C. Schwitzer, A. B. Rylands, et al. (eds.)
2009 Primates in peril: The world's 25 most endangered primates, 2008–2010. Arlington, VA: IUCN/SSC Primate Specialist Group (PSG), International Primatological Society (IPS), and Conservation International (CI).

Mittermeier , R. A., C. Schwitzer, A. B. Rylands, et al.
2014 Primates in peril: The world's top 25 most endangered primates, 2012–2014. Washington, DC: IUCN/SCC Primate Specialist Group (PSG), Conservation International (CI), and International Primatological Society (IPS).

Molnar, S.
1983 *Human Variation. Races, Types, and Ethnic Groups*, 2nd ed. Englewood Cliffs, NJ: Prentice-Hall.

Moore, L. G., S. Niermeyer, and S. Zamudio
1998 Human adaptation to high altitude: Regional and life-cycle perspectives. *Yearbook of Physical Anthropology* (Suppl.)27:25–64.

Moore, L. G., M. Shriver, L. Bemis, et al.
2006 An evolutionary model for identifying genetic adaptation to high altitude. *Advances in Experimental Medicine and Biology* 588:101–118.

Morwood, M. J., P. Brown, T. Jatmiko, et al.
2005 Further evidence for small-bodied hominins from the Late Pleistocene of Flores, Indonesia. *Nature* 437:1012–1017.

Morwood, M. J., R. P. Suejono, R. G. Roberts, et al.
2004 Archaeology and age of a new hominin from Flores in eastern Indonesia. *Nature* 431:1087–1091.

Moura, A. C. A., and P. C. Lee
2004 Capuchin tool use in Caatinga dry forest. *Science* 306:1909.

Mouse Genome Sequencing Consortium
2002 Initial sequencing and comparative analysis of the mouse genome. *Nature* 420:520–562.

Murray, R. D.
1980 The evolution and functional significance of incest avoidance. *Journal of Human Evolution* 9:173–178.

Nakatsukasa, M., and Y. Kunimatsu
2009 *Nacholapithecus* and its importance for understanding hominoid evolution. *Evolutionary Anthropology* 18:103–119.

Nakatsukasa, M., C. V. Ward, A. Walker, et al.
2004 Tail loss in *Proconsul heseloni*. *Journal of Human Evolution* 46:777–784.

Napier, J.
1967 The antiquity of human walking. *Scientific American* 216:56–66.

National Climatic Data Center
2016 State of the climate in 2016. http://www.ncdc.noaa.gov/sotc/global/201606

National Snow and Ice Data Center
2012 Arctic Sea Ice News and Analysis. Arctic sea ice extent settles at record seasonal minimum. Nsdic.org/arcticseaicenews/

Neme, L.
2014 Endangered orangutans gain from eco-friendly shifts in palm oil market. *National Geographic*. www.news.nationalgeographic.com

Nesse, R. M., and G. C. Williams
1994 *Why We Get Sick: The New Science of Darwinian Medicine*. New York: Vintage Books.

Nevell, L., A. Gordon, and B. Wood
2007 *Homo floresiensis* and *Homo sapiens* size-adjusted cranial shape variations. *American Journal of Physical Anthropology, Supplement* 14:177–178 (abstract).

Newport, F.
2014 In U.S., 42% believe creationist view of human origins. Values and Beliefs Gallup Poll, May 8–11, 2014. http:// www.gallup.com/poll/

News in Brief
2007 Congolese government creates bonobo reserve. *Nature* 450:470. doi:10.1038450470f.

Ni, X., D. L. Gebo, M. Dagosto, et al.
2013 The oldest known primate skeleton and early haplorhine evolution. *Nature* 498:60–64.

Ni, X., Q. Li, L. Lüzhou, et al.
2016 Oligocene primates from China reveal divergence between African and Asian primate evolution. *Science* 353:673–677.

Nishida, T.
1991 Comments: Intergroup aggression in chimpanzees and humans, by J. H. Manson and R. Wrangham. *Current Anthropology* 32:369–390, 381–382.

Nishida, T., N. Corp, M. Hamai, et al.
2003 Demography, female life history, and reproductive profiles among the chimpanzees of Mahale. *American Journal of Primatology* 59:99–121.

Nishida, T., M. Hiraiwa-Hasegawa, T. Hasegawa, et al.
1985 Group extinction and female transfer in wild chimpanzees in the Mahale National Park, Tanzania. *Zeitschrift Tierpsychologie—Journal of Comparative Ethology* 67:284–301.

Nishida, T., H. Takasaki, and Y. Takahata
1990 Demography and reproductive profiles. In: *The Chimpanzees of the Mahale Mountains*, T. Nishida (ed.), pp. 63–97. Tokyo: University of Tokyo Press.

Nishida, T., R. W. Wrangham, J. Goodall, et al.
1983 Local differences in plant-feeding habits of chimpanzees between the Mahale Mountains and Gombe National Park, Tanzania. *Journal of Human Evolution* 12:467–480.

Nomade, S., G. Muttoni, H. Guillou, et al.
2011 First ^{40}Ar/^{39}Ar age of the Ceprano man (central Italy). *Quaternary Geochronology* 6:453–457.

Nowak, R. M.
1999 *Walker's Primates of the World*. Baltimore, MD: Johns Hopkins University Press.

Oakley, K.
1963 Analytical methods of dating bones. In: *Science in Archaeology*, D. Brothwell and E. Higgs (eds.). New York: Basic Books.

Oates, J. F., M. Abedi-Lartey, W. S. McGraw, et al.
2000 Extinction of a West African red colobus monkey. *Conservation Biology* 14:1526–1532.

Oates, J. F., R. A. Bergl, J. Sunderland-Groves, et al.
  2007   *Gorilla gorilla* ssp. Diehli. *2007 IUCN Red List of Threatened Species.*

O'Connell, J. F., and J. Allen
  2015   The process, biotic impact, and global implications of the human colonization of Sahul about 47,000 years ago. *Journal of Archaeological Science* 56:73–84.

Oeseburg, H., R. A. de Boer, W. H. van Gilst, et al.
  2010   Telomere biology in health aging and disease. *European Journal of Physiology* 459:259–268.

Olliaro, P., J. Cattani, and D. Wirth
  1995   Malaria, the submerged disease. *Journal of the American Medical Association* 275:230–233.

Orr, C. M., M. W. Tocheri, S. E. Burnett, et al.
  2013   New wrist bones of *Homo floresiensis* from Liang Bua (Flores, Indonesia). *Journal of Human Evolution* 64:109–129

O'Toole, P. W., and I. B. Jeffery
  2015   Gut microbiota and aging. *Science* 350:1214–1215.

Ottoni, E. B., and P. Izar
  2008   Capuchin monkey tool use: Overview and implications. *Evolutionary Anthropology* 17: 171–178.

Ousley, S., R. Jantz, and D. Freid
  2009   Understanding race and human variation: Why forensic anthropologists are good at identifying race. *American Journal of Physical Anthropology* 139:68–76.

Ovchinnikov, I. V., A. Gotherstrom, G. P. Romanova, et al.
  2000   Molecular analysis of Neanderthal DNA from the northern Caucasus. *Nature* 404:490–493.

Padian, K., and L. M. Chiappe
  1998   The origin of birds and their flight. *Scientific American* 278:38–47.

Pagani, L., S. Schiffels, D. Gurdasani, et al.
  2015   Tracing the route of modern humans out of Africa by using 225 human genome sequences from Ethiopians and Egyptians. *American Journal of Human Genetics* 96:986–991.

Pagel, M., C. Venditti, and A. Meade
  2006   Large punctuational contribution of speciation to evolutionary divergence at the molecular level. *Science* 314:119–121.

Palmer, S. K., L. G. Moore, D. Young, et al.
  1999   Altered blood pressure course during normal pregnancy and increased preeclampsia at high altitude (3100 meters) in Colorado. *American Journal of Obstetrics and Gynecology* 180:1161–1168.

Palumbi, S. R.
  2001   *The Evolution Explosion: How Humans Cause Rapid Evolutionary Change.* New York: Norton.

Pappu, S., Y. Gunnell, K. Akhilesh, et al.
  2011   Early Pleistocene presence of Acheulian hominins in South India. *Science* 331:1596–1599.

Parés, J. M., and A. Pérez-González
  1995   Paleomagnetic age for hominid fossils at Atapuerca archaeological site, Spain. *Science* 269:830–832.

Park, E.
  1978   The Ginsberg caper: Hacking it as in Stone Age. *Smithsonian* 9:85–96.

Patil, C. L., E. T. Abrams, A. R. Steinmetz, et al.
  2012   Appetite sensations and nausea and vomiting in pregnancy: An overview of the explanations. *Ecology of Food and Nutrition* 51:394–417.

Paul, A. M.
  2010   *Origins: How the Nine Months before Birth Shape the Rest of Our Lives.* New York: Free Press.

Pavkov, M. E., P. H. Bennett, W. C. Knowler, et al.
  2006   Effect of young-onset type 2 diabetes mellitus on incidence of end-stage renal disease and mortality in young and middle-aged Pima Indians. *Journal of the American Medical Association* 296:421–426.

Pelletier, D. L., E. A. Frongillo, D. G. Schroeder, et al.
  1995   The effects of malnutrition on child mortality in developing countries. *Bulletin of the World Health Organization* 73:443–448.

Pennisi, E.
  2005   Why do humans have so few genes? *Science* 309:80.

Perelman, P., W. E. Johnson, C. Roos, et al.
  2011   A molecular phylogeny of living primates. *PLOS Genetics* 7:e1001342.

Peres, C. A.
  1990   Effects of hunting on western Amazonian primate communities. *Biological Conservation* 54(1):47–59.

Perkins, S.
  2003   Learning from the present. *Science News* 164:42–44.

Phillips, K. A.
  1998   Tool use in wild capuchin monkeys (*Cebus albifrons trinitatis*). *American Journal of Primatology* 46:259–261.

Pickering, R., P. H. G. M. Dirks, Z. Jinnah, et al.
  2011   *Australopithecus sediba* at 1.977 Ma and implications for the origins of the genus *Homo*. *Science* 333:1421–1423.

Pickford, M., and B. Senut
  2001   The geological and faunal context of late Miocene hominid remains from Lukeino, Kenya. *Comptes Rendus de l'Académie des Sciences, Ser. 11A,* Earth and Planetary Science 332:145–152.

Pike, A. W. G., D. L. Hoffmann, M. García-Diez, et al.
  2012   U-Series dating of Paleolithic art in 11 caves in Spain. *Science* 336:1409–1413.

Pike, I. L.
  2000   The nutritional consequences of pregnancy sickness: A critique of a hypothesis. *Human Nature* 11:207–232.

Pilbeam, D.
  1982   New hominoid skull material from the Miocene of Pakistan. *Nature* 295:232–234.

Pilbeam, D.
  1996   Genetic and morphological records of the Hominoidea and hominid origins: A synthesis. *Molecular Phylogenetics and Evolution* 5(1):155–168.

Pilbeam, D., M. D. Rose, J. C. Barry, et al.
  1990   New *Sivapithecus* humeri from Pakistan and the relationship of *Sivapithecus* and *Pongo*. *Nature* 348:237–239.

Pinner, R. W., S. M. Teutsch, L. Simonson, et al.
  1996   Trends in infectious diseases mortality in the United States. *Journal of the American Medical Association* 275:189–193.

Pokines, J., and S. A. Symes (eds.)
2013   *Manual of Forensic Taphonomy.* Boca Raton, FL: CRC Press.

Pollard, T. M.
2008   *Western Diseases: An Evolutionary Perspective.* Cambridge, UK: Cambridge University Press.

Popkin, B. M.
2007   The world is fat. *Scientific American,* 297(3):88–95.

Population Reference Bureau
2011   World Population Data Sheet. http://www.prb.org /pdf11/2011population-data-sheet_eng.pdf

Poremba, A., M. Malloy, R. C. Saunders, et al.
2004   Species-specific calls evoke asymmetric activity in the monkey's temporal poles. *Nature* 427:448–451.

Potts, R.
1991   Why the Oldowan? Plio-Pleistocene toolmaking and the transport of resources. *Journal of Anthropological Research* 47:153–176.

Potts, R.
1993   Archeological interpretations of early hominid behavior and ecology. In: *The Origin and Evolution of Humans and Humanness,* D. T. Rasmussen (ed.), pp. 49–74. Boston: Jones and Bartlett.

Potts, R., and P. Shipman
1981   Cutmarks made by stone tools on bones from Olduvai Gorge, Tanzania. *Nature* 291:577–580.

Poux, C., P. Chevret, D. Huchon, et al.
2006   Arrival and diversification of caviomorph rodents and platyrrhine primates in South America. *Systematic Biology* 55:228–244.

Poux, C., and E. J. Douzery
2004   Primate phylogeny, evolutionary rate variations, and divergence times: A contribution from the nuclear gene IRBP. *American Journal of Physical Anthropology* 124:1–16.

Powell, K. B., and S. A. Tishkoff
2003   The evolution or lactase persistence in African populations. *American Journal of Physical Anthropology. Supplement* 36:170.

Pozzi L., J. A. Hodgson, A. S. Burrell, et al.
2011   The stem catarrhine *Saadanius* does not inform the timing of the origin of crown catarrhines. *Journal of Human Evolution* 61:209–210.

Prentice, A. M.
2006   The emerging epidemic of obesity in developing countries. *International Journal of Epidemiology* 35:93–99.

Pritchard, J. K.
2010   How we are evolving. *Scientific American* 303:41–47.

Proctor, R.
1988   From anthropologie to rassenkunde. In: *Bones, Bodies, Behavior: History of Anthropology* (Vol. 5), W. J. Stocking, Jr. (ed.), pp. 138–179. Madison: University of Wisconsin Press.

Profet, M.
1988   The evolution of pregnancy sickness as a protection to the embryo against Pleistocene teratogens. *Evolutionary Theory* 8:177–190.

Profico, A., F. D. Vincenzo, L. Gagliard, et al.
2016   Filling the gap: Human cranial remains from Gambore II (Melka Kunture, Ethiopia ca. 850 ka) and the origin of *Homo heidelbergensis. Journal of Anthropological Sciences* 94:1–24.

Pruetz, J. D., and P. Bertolani
2007   Savanna chimpanzees, *Pan troglodytes verus,* hunt with tools. *Current Biology* 17:412–417.

Prüfer, K., K. Munch, I. Hellman, et al.
2012   The bonobo genome compared with the chimpanzee and human genomes. *Nature* 486:527–531.

Prufer, K., F. Racimo, N. Patterson, et al.
2014   The complete genome sequence of a Neanderthal from the Altai Mountains. *Nature* 505:43–49.

Pusey, A., J. Williams, and J. Goodall
1997   The influence of dominance rank on the reproductive success of female chimpanzees. *Science* 277:828–831.

Rak, Y., A. Ginzburg, and E. Geffen
2007   Gorilla-like anatomy on *Australopithecus afarensis* mandibles suggests *Au. afarensis* link to robust australopiths. *Proceedings of the National Academy of Sciences USA* 104:6568–6572.

Rasmussen, M., X. Guo, Y. Wang, et al.
2011   An Aboriginal Australian genome reveals separate human dispersals into Asia. *Science* 334:94–98.

Rasmussen, M., Y. Li, S. Lindgreen, et al.
2010   Ancient human genome sequence of an extinct Palaeo-Eskimo. *Nature* 463:757–762.

Reardon, S.
2011   Climate change sparks battles in classroom. *Science* 333:688–689.

Reich, D., R. E. Green, and M. Kircher
2010   Genetic history of an archaic hominin group from Denisova Cave in Siberia. *Nature* 468:1053–1060.

Reich, D., N. Patterson, M. Kircher, et al.
2011   Denisova admixture and the first modern human dispersals into Southeast Asia and Oceania. *American Journal of Human Genetics* 89:1–13.

Reich, D., N. Patterson, D. Campbell, et al.
2012   Reconstructing Native American population history. *Nature.* doi:10.1038/nature11258.

Relethford, J. H.
2001   *Genetics and the Search for Modern Human Origins.* New York: Wiley-Liss.

Rendu, W., C. Beauval, I. Crevecoeur, et al.
2014   Evidence supporting an intentional Neandertal burial at La Chapelle-aux-Saints. *Proceedings of the National Academy of Sciences USA* 108:3888–3893.

Renne, P. R., W. D. Sharp, A. L. Deino, et al.
1997 ^{40}Ar/^{39}Ar dating into the historic realm: Calibration against Pliny the younger. *Science* 277:1279–1280.

Reno, P. L., and C. O. Lovejoy
2015   From Lucy to Kadanuumuu: Balanced analyses of *Australopithecus afarensis* assemblages confirm only moderate skeletal dimorphism. *PeerJ* 3:e925.

Reno, P. L., R. S. Meindl, M. A. McCollum, et al.
2003   Sexual dimorphism in *Australopithecus afarensis* was similar to that of modern humans. *Proceedings of the National Academy of Sciences USA* 100:9404–9409.

Reno, P. L., R. S. Meindl, M. A. McCollum, et al.
2005   The case is unchanged and remains robust: *Australopithecus afarensis* exhibits only moderate skeletal dimorphism: A reply to Plavcan et al., 2005. *Journal of Human Evolution* 49:279–288.

Rhesus Macaque Genome Sequencing and Analysis Consortium
2007 Evolutionary and biomedical insights from the rhesus macaque genome. *Science* 316:222–234.

Richards, M. P., and E. Trinkaus
2009 Isotopic evidence for the diets of European Neanderthal and early modern humans. *Proceedings of the National Academy of Sciences USA* 106:16034–16039.

Richmond, B. G., and W. L. Jungers
2008 *Orrorin tugenensis* femoral morphology and the evolution of hominin bipedalism. *Science* 319:1662–1665.

Richter, D., and M. Krbetschek
2015 Luminescence dating of the Lower Palaeolithic occupation at Schoningen. *Journal of Human Evolution* 89:46–56.

Riddle, R. D., and C. J. Tabin
1999 How limbs develop. *Scientific American* 280:74–79.

Ridley, M.
1993 *Evolution.* Boston: Blackwell Scientific Publications.

Rightmire, G. P.
1998 Human evolution in the Middle Pleistocene: The role of *Homo heidelbergensis. Evolutionary Anthropology* 6:218–227.

Rightmire, G. P.
2004 Affinities of the Middle Pleistocene cranium from Dali and Jinniushan. *American Journal of Physical Anthropology, Supplement* 38:167 (abstract).

Robins, A. H.
1991 *Biological Perspectives on Human Pigmentation.* Cambridge, UK: Cambridge University Press.

Roebroeks, W., and M. Soressi
2016 Neandertals revised. *Proceedings of the National Academy of Sciences USA* 113:6372–6379.

Rose, K. D., S. G. B. Chester, R. H. Dunn, et al.
2011 New fossil of the oldest North American euprimates *Teilhardina brandti* (Omomyidae) from the Paleocene-Eocene Thermal Maximum. *American Journal of Physical Anthropology* 146:281–305.

Rose, M. D.
1993 Locomotor anatomy of Miocene hominids. In: *Postcranial Adaptation in Nonhuman Primates,* D. L. Gebo (ed.), pp. 252–272. DeKalb, IL: NIU Press.

Rosenberg, N. A., J. K. Pritchard, J. L. Weber, et al.
2002 Genetic structure of human populations. *Science* 298:2381–2385.

Ross, C. F.
2000 Into the light: The origin of Anthropoidea. *Annual Review of Anthropology* 29:147–194.

Ross, C. F., M. Henneberg, M. J. Ravosa, et al.
2004 Curvilinear, geometric and phylogenetic modeling of basicranial flexion: Is it adaptive, is it constrained? *Journal of Human Evolution* 46:185–213.

Rossie, J. B., and L. MacLatchy
2006 A new pliopithecoid genus from the early Miocene of Uganda. *Journal of Human Evolution* 50:568–586.

Rossie, J. B., X. Ni, and K. C. Beard
2006 Cranial remains of an Eocene tarsier. *Proceedings of the National Academy of Sciences USA* 103:4381–4385.

Rovner, I.
1983 Plant opal phytolith analysis: Major advances in archaeobotanical research. In: *Advances in Archaeological Method and Theory,* M. B. Schiffer (ed.), pp. 225–266. New York: Academic Press.

Rudran, R.
1973 Adult male replacement in one-male troops of purple-faced langurs (*Presbytis senex senex*) and its effect on population structure. *Folia Primatologica* 19:166–192.

Ruff, C.
2010 Body size and body shape in early hominins—implications of the Gona pelvis. *American Journal of Physical Anthropology, Supplement* 50:203 (abstract).

Ruff, C. B.
1994 Morphological adaptation to climate in modern and fossil hominids. *American Journal of Physical Anthropology* 37(S19):65–107.

Ruff, C. B., and A. Walker
1993 The body size and shape of KNM-WT 15000. In: *The Nariokotome* Homo erectus *Skeleton,* A. Walker and R. E. Leakey (eds.), pp. 234–265. Cambridge, MA: Harvard University Press.

Ruxton, G. D., and D. M. Wilkinson
2012 Population trajectories for accidental versus planned colonization of islands. *Journal of Human Evolution,* 63:507–511.

Rylands, A. B., and R. A. Mittermeier
2014 Primate taxonomy: Species and conservation. *Evolutionary Anthropology: Issues, News, and Reviews* 23:8–10.

Sagan, C.
1977 *The Dragons of Eden: Speculations on the Evolution of Human Intelligence.* New York: Random House.

Salazar- García, D. C., R. C. Power, A. S. Serra, et al.
2013 Neanderthal diets in central and southeastern Mediterranean Iberia. *Quaternary International* 318:3–18.

Samonds, K. E., L. R. Godfrey, J. R. Ali, et al.
2012 Spatial and temporal arrival patterns of Madagascar's vertebrate fauna explained by distance, ocean currents, and ancestor type. *Proceedings of the National Academy of Sciences* 109: 5352–5357.

Samson, M., F. Libert, B. J. Doranz, et al.
1996 Resistance to HIV-1 infection in Caucasian individuals bearing mutant alleles of the CCR-5 chemokine receptor gene. *Nature* 382:722–725.

Sánchez-Quinto, F., H. Schroeder, O. Ramirez, et al.
2012 Genomic affinities of two 7,000-year-old Iberian hunter-gatherers. *Current Biology* 22:R631–R633.

Sankararaman, S., S. Mallick, M. Dannemann, et al.
2014 The genomic landscape of Neandertal ancestry in present-day humans. *Nature* 507:354–357.

Sargis, E. J., D. M. Boyer, J. J. Bloch, et al.
2007 Evolution of pedal grasping in Primates. *Journal of Human Evolution* 53(1):103–107

Sarmiento, E. E.
2010 Comment on the paleobiology and classification of *Ardipithecus ramidus. Science* 328:1105.

Sarmiento, E. E., and J. F. Oates
2000 The Cross River gorilla: A distinct subspecies *Gorilla gorilla diehli* Matschie 1904. *American Museum Novitates* 3304:1–55.

Savage-Rumbaugh, S.
1986 *Ape Language: From Conditioned Responses to Symbols.* New York: Columbia University Press.

Savage-Rumbaugh, S., and R. Lewin
1994   *Kanzi: The Ape at the Brink of the Human Mind.*
New York: Wiley.

Savage-Rumbaugh, S., K. McDonald, R. A. Sevic, et al.
1986   Spontaneous symbol acquisition and communicative
use by pygmy chimpanzees (*Pan paniscus*). *Journal
of Experimental Psychology: General* 115:211–235.

Scally, A., J. Y. Dutheil, L. W. Hillier, et al.
2012   Insights into hominid evolution from the gorilla
genome sequence. *Nature* 483:169–175.

Schauber, A. D., and D. Falk
2008   Proportional dwarfism in foxes, mice, and humans:
Implications for relative brain size in *Homo
floresiensis. American Journal of Physical
Anthropology, Supplement* 43:185 (abstract).

Schmid, P., S. E. Churchill, S. Nalla, et al.
2013   Mosaic morphology in the thorax of
Australopithecus sediba. Science 341:1234598.

Schmitz, R. W., D. Serre, G. Bonani, et al.
2002   The Neandertal type site revisited: Interdisciplinary
investigations of skeletal remains from the Neander
Valley, Germany. *Proceedings of the National
Academy of Sciences USA* 99:13342–13347.

Schoch, W. H., B. G. Bigga, U. Böhner, et al.
2015   New insights on the wooden weapons from the
Paleolithic site of Schöningen. *Journal of Human
Evolution* 89:214–225.

Schuster, S. C., W. Miller, A. Ratan, et al.
2010   Complete Khoisan and Bantu genomes from
southern Africa. *Nature* 463:943–947.

ScienceInsider
2011   *Science.* http://news.sciencemag.org/policy/2011/04
/qa-richard-muller-physicist-and-his-surprisingclimate
-data

Seiffert, E. R., E. L. Simons, and Y. Attia
2003   Fossil evidence for an ancient divergence of lorises
and galagos. *Nature* 422:421–424.

Seiffert, E. R., E. L. Simons, T. M. Ryan, et al.
2005a   Additional remains of *Wadilemur elegans*, a
primitive stem galagid from the late Eocene of Egypt.
Proceedings of the National Academy of Science USA
102:11396–11401.

Seiffert, E. R., E. L. Simons, W. C. Clyde, et al.
2005b   Basil anthropoids from Egypt and the antiquity
of Africa's higher primate radiation. *Science*
310:300–304.

Seiffert, E. R., J. M. G. Perry, E. L. Simons, et al.
2009   Convergent evolution of anthropoid-like adaptations
in Eocene adapiform primates. *Nature* 461:1118–1121.

Seiffert, E. R., E. L. Simons, D. M. Boyer, et al.
2010   A fossil primate of uncertain affinities from the
earliest late Eocene of Egypt. *Proceedings of the
National Academy of Sciences USA* 107:9712–9717.

Semaw, S., M. J. Rogers, J. Quade, et al.
2003   2.6-million-year-old stone tools and associated
bones from OGS-6 and OGS-7, Gona, Afar,
Ethiopia. *Journal of Human Evolution* 45:169–177.

Senut, B., M. Pickford, D. Grommercy, et al.
2001   First hominid from the Miocene (Lukeino
Formation, Kenya). *Comptes Rendus de l'Académie
des Sciences, Ser. 11A, Earth and Planetary Science*
332:137–144.

Seppa, N.
2011   U.S. falters in life expectancy gains. *Science News,*
February 26, p. 10.

Serre, D., A. Langaney, M. Chech, et al.
2004   No evidence of Neandertal mtDNA contribution to
early modern humans. *PloS Biology* 2:313–317.

Seyfarth, R. M., D. L. Cheney, and P. Marler
1980a   Monkey responses to three different alarm calls.
Science 210:801–803.

Seyfarth, R. M., D. L. Cheney, and P. Marler
1980b   Vervet monkey alarm calls: Semantic communication
in a free-ranging primate. *Animal Behaviour*
28:1070–1094.

Shang, H., H. Tong, S. Zhang, et al.
2007   An early modern human from Tianyuan Cave,
Zhoukoudian, China. *Proceedings of the National
Academy of Sciences USA* 104:6573–6578.

Shaw, C. N., and J. T. Stock
2009a   Habitual throwing and swimming correspond with
upper limb diaphyseal strength and shape in modern
athletes. *American Journal of Physical Anthropology*
140:160–172.

Shaw, C. N., and J. T. Stock
2009b   Intensity, repetitiveness, and directionality of
habitual adolescent mobility patterns influence the
tibial diaphysis morphology of athletes. *American
Journal of Physical Anthropology* 140:149–159.

Shay, J. W., and W. E. Wright
2007   Hallmarks of telomeres in ageing research. *The
Journal of Pathology* 211:114–123.

Shea, B. T., and R. C. Baily
1996   Allometry and adaptation of body proportions and
stature in African pygmies. *American Journal of
Physical Anthropology* 100:311–340.

Shen, G., X. Gao, B. Gao, and D. E. Granger
2009   Age of Zhoukoudian *Homo erectus* with $^{26}Ar/^{10}Be$
burial dating. *Nature* 458:198–200.

Shipman, P.
1983   Early hominid lifestyle: Hunting and gathering
or foraging and scavenging? In: *Animals and
Archaeology,* J. Clutton-Brock and C. Grigson (eds.),
pp. 31–51. Vol. I: Hunters and Their Prey. London:
Brit. Arch. Rpts.

Shreeve, J.
2009   Oldest skeleton of human ancestor found. *National
Geographic News,* October 1, 2009. http://news
.nationalgeographic.com/news/2009/10/091001
-oldest-human-skeleton-ardi-missing-link-chimps
-ardipithecus-ramidus.html

Shubin, N. H., E. B. Daeschler, and F. A. Jenkins, Jr.
2006   The pectoral fin of *Tiktaalik roseae* and the origin of
the tetrapod limb. *Nature* 440:764–771.

Shubin, N., C. Tabin, and S. Carroll
1997   Fossils, genes, and the evolution of animal limbs.
Nature 388:639–648.

Sievert, L. L.
2006   *Menopause: A Biocultural Perspective.*
New Brunswick, NJ: Rutgers University Press.

Sievert, L. L.
2014   Anthropology and the study of menopause:
Evolutionary, developmental, and comparative
perspectives. *Menopause* 21:1151–1159.

Silcox, M. T.
2001   *A Phylogenetic Analysis of Plesiadapiformes and Their Relationship to Euprimates and Other Archontans.* Unpublished PhD dissertation, Johns Hopkins University School of Medicine, Baltimore, MD.

Silcox, M. T.
2007   Primate taxonomy, plesiadapiforms, and approaches to primate origins. In: *Primate Origins: Adaptations and Evolution*, M. J. Ravosa and M. Dagosto (eds.), pp. 143–178. New York: Plenum Press.

Silk, J. B., S. C. Alberts, and J. Altman
2003   Social bonds of female baboons enhance infant survival. *Science* 302:1231–1234.

Silk, J. B., S. F. Brosman, J. Vonk, et al.
2005   Chimpanzees are indifferent to the welfare of unrelated group members. *Nature* 437:1357–1359.

Simons, E. L.
1976   The fossil record of primate phylogeny. In: *Molecular Anthropology: Genes and Proteins in the Evolutionary Ascent of the Primates*, M. Goodman (ed.), pp. 35–62. New York: Plenum Press.

Simons, E. L., E. R. Seiffert, T. M. Ryan, et al.
2007   A remarkable female cranium of the early Oligocene anthropoid *Aegyptopithecus zeuxis* (Catarrhini, Propliopithecidae). *Proceedings of the National Academy of Sciences* 104:8731–8736.

Simonson, T. S., Y. Yang, C. D. Huff, et al.
2010   Genetic evidence for high-altitude adaptation in Tibet. *Science* 329:72–75.

Simpson, S. W., J. Quade, N. E. Levin, et al.
2008   A female *Homo erectus* pelvis from Gona, Ethiopia. *Science* 322:1089–1092.

Singleton, I., J. Supriatna, and S. Wich
2009   Sumatran Orangutan. In: Mittermeier, R.A., et al. (Eds.), *Primates in Peril. The World's 25 Most Endangered Primates 2008–2010.* Arlington, VA: IUCN/SSC Primate Specialist Group (PSG), International Primatological Society (IPS), and Conservation International (CI).

Smith, F. H.
1984   Fossil hominids from the Upper Pleistocene of central Europe and the origin of modern Europeans. In: *The Origins of Modern Humans*, F. H. Smith and F. Spencer (eds.), pp. 187–209. New York: Alan R. Liss.

Smith, F. H.
2002   Migrations, radiations and continuity: Patterns in the evolution of Late Pleistocene humans. In: *The Primate Fossil Record*, W. Hartwig (ed.), pp. 437–456. New York: Cambridge University Press.

Smith, F. H., A. B. Falsetti, and S. M. Donnelly
1989   Modern human origins. *Yearbook of Physical Anthropology* 32:35–68.

Smith, K. F., M. Goldberg, S. Rosenthal, et al.
2014   Global rise in human infectious disease outbreaks. *Journal of the Royal Society Interface* 11:20140950.

Smith, T., K. D. Rose, and P. Gingerich
2006   Rapid Asia-Europe-North America geographic dispersal of earliest Eocene primate *Teilhardina* during the Paleocene-Eocene thermal maximum. *Proceedings of the National Academy of Sciences USA* 103:11223–11227.

Smith, T. M.
2008   Incremental dental development: Methods and applications in hominoid evolutionary studies. *Journal of Human Evolution* 54:205–224.

Smith, T. M., P. Tafforeau, A. Le Cabec, et al.
2015   Dental ontogeny in Pliocene and early Pleistocene hominins. *PloS ONE* 10:e0118118.

Smol, J.
2012   A planet in flux. How is life on Earth reacting to climate change? *Nature* 483:S12–S15.

Snyder, M., and M. Gerstein
2003   Genomics. Defining genes in the genomics era. *Science* 300:258–260.

Soares, P., A. Achilli, O. Semino, et al.
2010   The archaeogenetics of Europe. *Current Biology* 20:R174–R183.

Sponheimer, M., and J. A. Lee-Thorp
1999   Isotopic evidence for the diet of an early hominid. *Australopithecus africanus. Science* 283:368–370.

Sponheimer, M., B. H. Passey, D. J. de Ruiter, et al.
2006   Isotopic evidence for dietary variability in the early hominin *Paranthropus robustus. Science* 314:980–982.

Spoor, F, P. Gunz, S. Neubauer, et al.
2015   Reconstructed *Homo habilis* type OH 7 suggests deep-rooted species diversity in early *Homo. Nature* 519:83–86.

Spoor, F., M. G. Leakey, P. N. Gathago, et al.
2007   Implications of new early *Homo* fossils from Ileret, East of Lake Turkana, Kenya. *Nature* 448:688–691.

Srivastava, M., O. Simakov, J. Chapman, et al.
2010   The *Amphimedon queenslandica* genome and the evolution of complexity. *Nature* 466:720–726.

Stearns, S. C., S. G. Byars, D. R. Govindaraju, et al.
2010   Measuring selection in contemporary human populations. *Nature Reviews: Genetics* 11:611–622.

Steiper, M. E., and E. R. Seiffert
2012   Evidence for a convergent slowdown in primate molecular rates and its implications for the timing of early primate evolution. *Proceedings of the National Academy of Sciences* 109:6006–6011.

Steiper, M. E., and N. M. Young
2006   Primate molecular divergence dates. *Molecular Phylogenetics and Evolution* 41:384–394.

Steiper, M. E., and N. M. Young
2008   Timing primate evolution: Lessons from the discordance between molecular and paleontological estimates. *Evolutionary Anthropology* 17:179–188.

Steklis, H. D.
1985   Primate communication, comparative neurology, and the origin of language reexamined. *Journal of Human Evolution* 14:157–173.

Stelzner, J., and K. Strier
1981   Hyena predation on an adult male baboon. *Mammalia* 45:259–260.

Stevens, N. J., and C. P. Heesy
2006   Malagasy primate origins: Phylogenies, fossils, and biogeographic reconstructions. *Folia Primatologica* 77:419–433.

Stevens, N. J., E. R. Seiffert, P. M. O'Connor, et al.
2013   Paleontological evidence for an Oligocene divergence between Old World monkeys and apes. *Nature* 497:611–614.

Stewart, J. R., and C. B. Stringer
2012 Human evolution out of Africa: The role of refugia and climate change. *Science* 335:1317–1321.

Stoneking, M., and F. Delfin
2010 The human genetic history of East Asia: Weaving a complex tapestry. *Current Biology* 20:R188–R193.

Strassmann, B. I.
1999 Menstrual cycling and breast cancer: An evolutionary perspective. *Journal of Women's Health* 8(2):193–202.

Strassmann, B. I., and B. Gillespie
2002 Life-history theory, fertility and reproductive success in humans. *Proceedings of the Royal Society of London Series B: Biological Sciences* 269(1491):553–562.

Strier, K. B.
2003 *Primate Behavioral Ecology*. Boston: Allyn and Bacon.

Stringer, C.
2014 Why we are not all multiregionalists now. *Trends in Ecology and Evolution* 29:248–251.

Stringer, C.
2016 The origin and evolution of Homo sapiens. *Philosophical Transactions of the Royal Society B* 371:20150237.

Stringer, C. B.
2012 The status of *Homo heidelbergensis* (Schoentensack, 1908). *Evolutionary Anthropology* 21:101–107.

Stringer, C. B., and P. Andrews
1988 Genetic and fossil evidence for the origin of modern humans. *Science* 239:1263–1268.

Stringer, C. B., J. C. Finlayson, R. N. E. Barton, et al.
2008 Neanderthal exploitation of marine mammals in Gibralter. *Proceedings of the National Academy of Sciences USA* 105:14319–14324.

Struhsaker, T. T.
1967 Auditory communication among vervet monkeys (*Cercopithecus aethiops*). In: *Social Communication Among Primates*, S. A. Altmann (ed.). Chicago: University of Chicago Press.

Struhsaker, T. T., and L. Leland
1987 Colobines: Infanticide by adult males. In: *Primate Societies*, B. Smuts, D. L. Cheney, R. M. Seyfarth, et al. (eds.), pp. 83–97. Chicago: University of Chicago Press.

Sturm, R. A., D. L. Duffy, Z. Z. Zhao, et al.
2008 A single SNP in an evolutionary conserved region within intron 86 of the HERC2 gene determines human blue-brown eye color. *American Journal of Human Genetics* 82:424–431.

Sumner, D. R., M. E. Morbeck, and J. Lobick
1989 Age-related bone loss in female Gombe chimpanzees. *American Journal of Physical Anthropology* 72:259.

Susman, R. L. (ed.)
1984 *The Pygmy Chimpanzee: Evolutionary Biology and Behavior*. New York: Plenum.

Susman, R. L., J. T. Stern, and W. L. Jungers
1985 Locomotor adaptations in the Hadar hominids. In: *Ancestors: The Hard Evidence*, E. Delson (ed.), pp. 184–192. New York: Alan R. Liss.

Sussman, R. W.
1991 Primate origins and the evolution of angiosperms. *American Journal of Primatology* 23:209–223.

Sutikna, T., M. W. Tocheri, M. J. Morwood, et al.
2016 Revised stratigraphy and chronology for *Homo floresiensis* at Liang Bua in Indonesia. *Nature* 532:366–369.

Szyf, M., P. McGowan, and M. J. Meaney
2008 The social environment and the epigenome. *Environmental and Molecular Mutagenesis* 49:46–60.

Tackney, J., R. M. Cawthon, J. E. Coxworth, et al.
2014 Blood cell telomere lengths and shortening rates of chimpanzee and human females. *American Journal of Human Biology* 26(4):452–460.

Tattersall, I.
1982 *The Primates of Madagascar*. New York: Columbia University Press.

Tavera-Mendoza, L. E., and J. H. White
2007 Cell defenses and the sunshine vitamin. *Scientific American* 297(5): 62–72.

Taylor, N. A.
2006 Ethnic differences in thermoregulation: Genotypic versus phenotypic heat adaptation. *Journal of Thermal Biology* 31:90–104.

Teresi, D.
2002 *Lost Discoveries: The Ancient Roots of Modern Science—from the Babylonians to the Maya*. New York: Simon and Schuster.

Thieme, H.
1997 Lower Palaeolithic hunting spears from Germany. *Nature* 385:807–810.

Thinh, V. N., A. R. Mootnick, T. Geissmann, et al.
2010 Mitochondrial evidence for multiple radiations in the evolutionary history of small apes. *BMC Evolutionary Biology* 10:74. http://www.biomedcentral.com/1471-2148/10/74

Thompson, A. L.
2012 Developmental origins of obesity: Early feeding environments, infant growth, and the intestinal microbiome. *American Journal of Human Biology* 24:350–360.

Thompson, J. L., and A. J. Nelson
2011 Middle childhood and modern human origins. *Human Nature* 22:249–280.

Tiemel, C., Y. Quan, and W. En
1994 Antiquity of *Homo sapiens* in China. *Nature* 368:55–56.

Tishkoff, S. A., F. A. Reed, A. Ranciaro, et al.
2007 Convergent adaptation of human lactase persistence in Africa and Europe. *Nature Genetics* 39(1):31–40.

Tobias, P.
1971 *The Brain in Hominid Evolution*. New York: Columbia University Press.

Tobias, P.
1983 Recent advances in the evolution of the hominids with especial reference to brain and speech. Pontifical Academy of Sciences. *Scrita Varia* 50:85–140.

Tocheri, M. W., C. M. Orr, S. G. Larson, et al.
2007 The primitive wrist of *Homo floresiensis* and its implications for hominin evolution. *Science* 317:1743–1745.

Todd, T. W.
1920 Age changes in the pubic bone. I. The male white pubis. *American Journal of Physical Anthropology* 3:285–339.

Todd, T. W.
  1921   Age changes in the pubic bone. III. The pubis of the white female. *American Journal of Physical Anthropology* 4:26–39.

Tollefson, J.
  2008   Brazil goes to war against logging. *Nature* 452:134–135.

Tollefson, J.
  2012   President prunes forest reforms. *Nature* 486:13.

Tornow, M. A.
  2008   Systematic analysis of the Eocene primate family Omomyidae using gnathic and postcranial data. *Bulletin of the Peabody Museum of Natural History* 49:43–129.

Trevathan, W.
  2010   *Ancient Bodies, Modern Lives: How Evolution Has Shaped Women's Health*. New York: Oxford University Press.

Trevathan, W. R.
  2015   Primate pelvic anatomy and implications for birth. *Philosophical Transactions of the Royal Society B: Biological Sciences* 370:20140065.

Trevathan, W. R., and K. R. Rosenberg
  2014   Caesarean section. *Evolution, Medicine, and Public Health* 2014:164.

Trevathan, W. R., and K. R. Rosenberg (eds.).
  2016   *Costly and Cute: The Helpless Infant and Human Evolution*. Albuquerque, NM: SAR/UNM Press.

Trinkaus, E.
  1983   *The Shanidar Neandertals*. New York: Academic Press.

Trinkaus, E.
  2005   Early modern humans. *Annual Review of Anthropology* 34:207–230.

Trinkaus, E., S. Milota, R. Rodrigo, et al.
  2003   Early modern human cranial remains from Pestera cu Oase, Romania. *Journal of Human Evolution* 45:245–253.

Trinkaus, E., C. B. Ruff, S. E. Churchill, et al.
  1998   Locomotion and body proportions of the Saint-Cesaire 1 Chatelperronian Neandertal. *Proceedings of the National Academy of Sciences USA* 95:5836–5840.

Trinkaus, E., and P. Shipman
  1992   *The Neandertals*. New York: Knopf.

Turley, C. M., J. M. Roberts, and J. M. Guinotte
  2007   Corals in deepwater: Will the unseen hand of ocean acidification destroy cold-water ecosystems? *Coral Reefs* 26:445–448.

Turner, B. L., and A. L. Thompson
  2013   Beyond the Paleolithic prescription: Incorporating diversity and flexibility in the study of human diet evolution. *Nutrition Reviews* 71:501–510.

UNAIDS Report on the Global AIDS Epidemic
  2013   http://www.unaids.org/sites/default/files/media_asset/UNAIDS_Global_Report_2013_en_1.pdf

Ungar, P.
  2002   Reconstructing the diets of fossil primates. In: *Reconstructing Behavior in the Primate Fossil Record*, J. M. Plavcan, R. F. Kay, W. L. Jungers, et al. (eds.), pp. 261–296. New York: Springer Press.

Ungar, P. S., and R. F. Kay
  1995   The dietary adaptations of European Miocene catarrhines. *Proceedings of the National Academy of Sciences USA* 92:5479–5481.

United Nations Population Division
  1998   *World Population Prospects: The 1998 Revision.*

van den Bergh, G. D., Y. Kaifu, I. Kurniawan, et al.
  2016   *Homo floresiensis*-like fossils from the early Middle Pleistocene of Flores. *Nature* 534:245–248.

van den Bergh, G. D., B. Li, A. Brumm, et al.
  2016   Earliest hominin occupation of Sulawesi, Indonesia. *Nature* 529:208–211.

van der Ven, K, R, Fimmers, G. Engels, et al.
  2000   Evidence for major histocompatability complex-mediated effects on spermatogenesis in humans. *Human Reproduction* 15:189–196.

van Dijk, S. J., P. L. Molloy, H. Varinli, et al.
  2015   Epigenetics and human obesity. *International Journal of Obesity* 39:85–97.

van Noordwijk, M. A., C. W. Kuzawa, and C. P. Schaik
  2013   The evolution of the patterning of human lactation: A comparative perspective. *Evolutionary Anthropology: Issues, News, and Reviews* 22:202–212.

van Schaik, C. P., M. Ancrenaz, G. Bogen, et al.
  2003   Orangutan cultures and the evolution of material culture. *Science* 299:102–105.

van't Hof, A. E., P. Campagne, D. J. Rigden, et al.
  2016   The industrial melanism mutation in British peppered moths is a transposable element. *Nature* 534:102–105.

Venter, J. C., M. D. Adams, E. W. Myers, et al.
  2001   The sequence of the human genome. *Science* 291:1304–1351.

Vernot, B., and J. M. Akey
  2014   Resurrecting surviving Neandertal lineages from modern human genomes. *Science* 343:1017–1021.

Vialet, A., L. Tianyuan, D. Grimaud-Herve, et al.
  2005   Proposition de reconstitution du deuxième crâne d'*Homo erectus* de Yunxian (Chine). *Comptes rendus. Palévol* 4:265–274.

Vigilant, L., M. Hofreiter, H. Siedel, et al.
  2001   Paternity and relatedness in wild chimpanzee communities. *Proceedings of the National Academy of Sciences USA* 98:12890–12895.

Vignaud, P., P. Duringer, H. MacKaye, et al.
  2002   Geology and palaeontology of the Upper Miocene Toros-Menalla hominid locality, Chad. *Nature* 418:152–155.

Villmoare, B., W. H. Kimbel, C. Seyoum, et al.
  2015   Early *Homo* at 2.8 Ma from Ledi-Geraru, Afar, Ethiopia. *Science* 347:1352–1355.

Vince, G.
  2011   An epoch debate. News Focus. *Science* 334:33–37.

Visalberghi, E.
  1990   Tool use in *Cebus*. *Folia Primatologica* 54:146–154.

Visalberghi, E., D. Fragaszy, E. Ottoni, et al.
  2007   Characteristics of hammer stones and anvils used by wild bearded capuchin monkeys (*Cebus libidinosus*) to crack open palm nuts. *American Journal of Physical Anthropology* 132:426–444.

Vitzthum, V.
2009   The ecology and evolutionary endocrinology of reproduction in the human female. *Yearbook of Physical Anthropology* 52:95–136.

Vogelsang, R.
1998   *The Middle Stone Age Fundstellen in Süd-west Namibia*. Köln: Heinrich Barth Institut.

Vogelstein, B., D. Lane, and A. J. Levine
2000   Surfing the p53 network. *Nature* 408:307–310.

Wadley, L.
2009   Were snares and traps used in the Middle Stone Age and does it matter? A review and a case study from Sibudu, South Africa. *Journal of Human Evolution* 58:179–92.

Wadley, L., T. Hodgkiss, and M. Grant
2009   Implications for complex cognition from the hafting of tools with compound adhesives in the Middle Stone Age, South Africa. *Proceedings of the National Academy of Sciences USA* 106:9590–9594.

Wakayama, S., H. Ohta, T. Hikichi, et al.
2008   Production of healthy cloned mice from bodies frozen at –20°C for 16 years. *Proceedings of the National Academy of Sciences* 105:17318–17322.

Walker, A.
1991   The origin of the genus *Homo*. In: *Evolution of Life*, S. Osawa and T. Honjo (eds.), pp. 379–389. Tokyo: Springer-Verlag.

Walker, A., and R. E. Leakey
1993   *The Nariokotome* Homo erectus *Skeleton*. Cambridge, MA: Harvard University Press.

Walker, A.
1976   Remains attributable to *Australopithecus* from East Rudolf. In: *Earliest Man and Environments in the Lake Rudolf Basin*, Y. Coppens (ed.), pp. 484–489. Chicago: University of Chicago Press.

Walker, J., R. A. Cliff, and A. G. Latham
2006   U-Pb isoptoic age of the Stw 573 hominid from Sterkfontein, South Africa. *Science* 314:1592–1594.

Wall-Scheffler, C. M., K. Geiger, and K. L. Steudel-Numbers
2007   Infant carrying: The role of increased locomotory costs in early tool development. *American Journal of Physical Anthropology* 133:841–846.

Walsh, P. D., et al.
2003   Catastrophic ape decline in western equatorial Africa. *Nature* 422:611–614.

Ward, C. V.
2005   Torso morphology and locomotion in *Proconsul nyanzae*. *American Journal of Physical Anthropology* 92:321–328.

Ward, P.
1994   *The End of Evolution*. New York: Bantam.

Warinner, C., J. Hendy, C. Speller, et al.
2014   Direct evidence of milk consumption from ancient human dental calculus. *Scientific Reports* 4:7104.

Warren, W. C., L. W. Hillier, J. A. Marshall, et al.
2008   Genome analysis of the platypus reveals unique signatures of evolution. *Nature* 453:175–183.

Watson, J. D., and F. H. C. Crick
1953a   Genetical implications of the structure of the deoxyribonucleic acid. *Nature* 171:964–967.

Watson, J. D., and F. H. C. Crick
1953b   A structure for deoxyribonucleic acid. *Nature* 171:737–738.

Weiner, J. S.
1955   *The Piltdown Forgery*. London: Oxford University Press.

Weiner, S., Q. Xu, P. Goldberg, et al.
1998   Evidence for the use of fire at Zhoukoudian, China. *Science* 281:251–253.

Weir, A. A. S., J. Chappell, and A. Kacelnik
2008   Shaping of hooks in New Caledonian crows. *Science* 297: 981.

Weiss, R. A., and R. W. Wrangham
1999   From *Pan* to pandemic. *Nature* 397:385–386.

Weiss, U.
2002   Nature insight: Malaria. *Nature* 415:669.

Westaway, M. C., A. C. Durband, C. P. Groves, et al.
2015   Mandibular evidence supports *Homo floresiensis* as a distinct species. *Proceedings of the National Academy of Sciences* 112:E604–E605.

Westergaard, G. C., and D. M. Fragaszy
1987   The manufacture and use of tools by capuchin monkeys (*Cebus apella*). *Journal of Comparative Psychology* 101:159–168.

White, T. D.
1986   Cut marks on the Bodo cranium: A case of prehistoric defleshing. *American Journal of Physical Anthropology* 69:503–509.

White, T. D., B. Asfaw, Y. Beyene, et al.
2009   *Ardipithecus ramidus* and the paleobiology of early hominids. *Science* 326:75–86.

White, T. D., B. Asfaw, D. DeGusta, et al.
2003   Pleistocene *Homo sapiens* from Middle Awash, Ethiopia. *Nature* 423:742–747.

White, T. D., G. Suwa, and C. O. Lovejoy
2010   Response to comment on the paleobiology and classification of *Ardipithecus ramidus*. *Science* 328:5982.

White, T. D., G. WoldeGabriel, B. Asfaw, et al.
2006   Asa Issie, Aramis and the origin of *Australopithecus*. *Nature* 440:883–889.

Whitelaw, N. C., and E. Whitelaw
2006   How lifetimes shape epigenotype within and across generations. *Human Molecular Genetics* 15:R131–R137.

Whiten, A., J. Goodall, W. C. McGrew, et al.
1999   Cultures in chimpanzees. *Nature* 399:682–685.

Wildman, D. E., M. Uddin, G. Liu, et al.
2003   Implications of natural selection in shaping 99.4% nonsynonymous DNA identity between humans and chimpanzees: Enlarging genus *Homo*. *Proceedings of the National Academy of Sciences USA* 100:7181–7188.

Wiley, A. S.
2014   *Cultures of Milk: The Biology and Culture of Dairy Consumption in India and the United States*. Cambridge: Harvard University Press.

Wilkinson, R. D., M. E. Steiper, C. Soligo, et al.
2011   Dating primate divergences through an integrated analysis of palaeontological and molecular data. *Systematic Biology* 60: 16–31.

Williams, B. A., R. F. Kay, and E. C. Kirk
2010   New perspectives on anthropoid origins. *Proceedings of the National Academy of Sciences USA* 107:4797–4804.

Williams, G. C.
1957   Pleiotropy, natural selection, and the evolution of senescence. *Evolution* 11:398–411.

Williams, G. C., and R. M. Nesse
  1991   The dawn of Darwinian medicine. *Quarterly Review of Biology* 66:1–22.
Williams, J. M.
  1999   *Female Strategies and the Reasons for Territoriality in Chimpanzees. Lessons from Three Decades of Research at Gombe.* Unpublished Ph.D. Thesis, University of Minnesota.
Williams, S. A., K. R. Ostrofsky, N. Frater, et al.
  2013   The vertebral column of *Australopithecus sediba*. *Science* 340:1232996.
Wilson, E. O.
  1992   *The Diversity of Life.* Cambridge, MA: Belknap Press of Harvard University Press.
Wilson, M. L., W. R. Wallauer, and A. E. Pusey
  2004   New cases of intergroup violence among Chimpanzees in Gombe National Park, Tanzania. *International Journal of Primatology* 25:523–549.
Wolpoff, M. H., J. Hawks, D. Frayer, and K. Hunley
  2001   Modern human ancestry at the peripheries: A test of the replacement theory. *Science* 291:293–297.
Wolpoff, M. H., B. Senut, M. Pickford, and J. Hawks
  2002   Paleoanthropology (communication arising): *Sahelanthropus* or '*Sahelpithecus*'? *Nature* 419:581–582.
Wolpoff, M. H., A. G. Thorne, F. H. Smith, et al.
  1994   Multiregional evolutions: A world-wide source for modern human populations. In: *Origins of Anatomically Modern Humans*, M. H. Nitecki and D. V. Nitecki (eds.), pp. 175–199. New York: Plenum Press.
Wong, K.
  2009   Rethinking the hobbits of Indonesia. *Scientific American* 301 (November):66–73.
Woo, J. K.
  1966   The skull of Lantian Man. *Current Anthropology* 7:83–86.
Wood, B.
  1991   *Koobi Fora Research Project IV: Hominid Cranial Remains from Koobi Fora.* Oxford, UK: Clarendon Press.
Wood, B.
  2010   Reconstructing human evolution: Achievements, challenges, and opportunities. *Proceedings of the National Academy of Sciences USA* 107(Suppl. 2):8902–8909.
Wood, B., and M. Collard
  1999a   The human genus. *Science* 284:65–71.
Wood, B., and M. Collard
  1999b   The changing face of genus *Homo*. *Evolutionary Anthropology* 8:195–207.
Wood, B., and T. Harrison
  2011   The evolutionary context of the first hominins. *Nature*, 470:347–352.
World Health Organization (WHO)
  2014   *World Health Statistics 2014.* Geneva, Switzerland: World Health Organization.
Wrangham, R., A. Clark, and G. Isabiryre-Basita
  1992   Female social relationships and social organization of Kibale forest chimps. In: *Topics in Primatology*, W. McGrew, T. Nishida, P. Marler, et al. (eds.), pp. 81–98. Tokyo: Tokyo University Press.

Wrangham, R. W.
  1980   An ecological model of female-bonded primate groups. *Behaviour*, 75:262–300.
Wrangham, R. W.
  1999   The evolution of coalitionary killing. *Yearbook of Physical Anthropology* 42:1–30.
Wright, P. C., E. L. Simons, and S. Gursky (eds.)
  2003   *Tarsiers: Past, Present, and Future.* New Brunswick, NJ: Rutgers University Press.
Wu, R., and X. Dong
  1985   *Homo erectus* in China. In: *Palaeoanthropology and Palaeolithic Archaeology in the People's Republic of China*, R. Wu and J. W. Olsen (eds.), pp. 79–89. New York: Academic Press.
Wu, R., and J. W. Olsen (eds.)
  1985   *Palaeoanthropology and Palaeolithic Archaeology in the People's Republic of China.* Orlando, FL: Academic Press.
Wu, X., and F. E. Poirier
  1995   *Human Evolution in China.* New York: Oxford University Press.
Wuethrich, B.
  1998   Geological analysis damps ancient Chinese fires. *Science* 281:165–166.
Xu, Q., and Q. Lu
  2007   *Series monograph III:* Lufengpithecus—*An Early Member of Hominidae.* Beijing: Science Press.
Yellen, J. E., A. S. Brooks, E. Cornelissen, et al.
  1995   A Middle Stone-Age worked bone industry from Katanda, Upper Semliki Valley, Zaire. *Science* 268:553–556.
Yi, X., Y. Liang, E. Huerta-Sanchez, et al.
  2010   Sequencing of 50 human exomes reveals adaptation to high altitude. *Science* 329:75–78.
Yoder, A. D., M. Cartmill, M. Ruvolo, et al.
  1996   Ancient single origin for Malagasy primates. *Proceedings of the National Academy of Sciences* 93:5122–5126.
Yokoyama, Y., C. Falguères, F. Sémah, et al.
  2008   Gamma-ray spectrometric dating of late *Homo erectus* skulls from Ngandong and Sambungmacan, Central Java, Indonesia. *Journal of Human Evolution* 55:274–277.
Young, E. M.
  2004   Globalization and food security: Novel questions in a novel context? *Progress in Development Studies* 4:1–21.
Zaim, Y., R. L. Ciochon, J. M. Polanski, et al.
  2011   New 1.5 million-year-old *Homo erectus* maxilla from Sangiran (Central Java, Indonesia). *Journal of Human Evolution*, 61:363–376.
Zalmout, I. S., W. J. Sanders, L. M. MacLatchy, et al.
  2010   New Oligocene primate from Saudi Arabia and the divergence of apes and Old World monkeys. *Nature* 466:360–365.
Zhang, F., S. L. Kearns, P. J. Orr, et al.
  2010   Fossilized melanosomes and the colour of Cretaceous dinosaurs and birds. *Nature* 463:1075–1078.
Zhang, Z., P. M. Kris-Etherton, and T. J. Hartman
  2014   Birth weight and risk factors for cardiovascular disease and type 2 diabetes in US children and adolescents: 10 year results from NHANES. *Maternal and Child Health Journal* 18:d1423–1432.

Zhao, L. X., and L. Z. Zhang
    2013   New fossil evidence and diet analysis of *Gigantopithecus blacki* and its distribution and extinction in South China. *Quaternary International* 286:69–74.

Zhu, R. X., Z. S. An, R. Potts, et al.
    2003   Magnetostratigraphic dating of early humans in China. *Earth Science Reviews* 61:341–359.

Zhu, Z. Y., R. Dennell, W. W. Huang, et al.
    2015   New dating of the Homo erectus cranium from Lantian (Gongwangling), China. *Journal of Human Evolution* 78:144–157.

Ziegler, A., A. S. Jonason, D. J. Leffellt, et al.
    1994   Sunburn and P53 in the onset of skin-cancer. *Nature* 372:773–776.

Zilhão, J., D. E. Angelucci, E. Badal-García, et al.
    2010   Symbolic use of marine shells and mineral pigments by Iberian Neandertals. *Proceedings of the National Academy of Sciences* 107:1023–1028.

Index

Abrigo do Lagar Velho site, 400
Absolute dating, 273
Acclimatization, 438–439
Acheulian tool industry, 330, 340, 345, 357, 359, 379
Achondroplasia, 88, 90–91
Acquired characteristics, 30–31
Adapis, 233–234
Adapoids, 233–234
Adaptation, 5, 14, 40, 436–464
    allele frequencies, shifts in, 105
    basic concepts, 438–439
    bipedal adaptation, 288–293
    endothermic capability and, 136
    to environment, 14, 40, 148–149
    generalized characteristics and, 137–138
    morphological adaptations, 288
    paleoanthropology and, 13–14
    specialized characteristics and, 137–138
    See also Human adaptation; Primate adaptations
Adaptive niches, 149
Adaptive radiation, 136–137, 231
Adaptive significance, 13–14
Adaptive zone, 128
Adenine, 53
Adolescence, 482
Aegyptopithecus, 241–242
Affiliative behaviors, 196–197, 223
Afradapis, 233
Africa:
    changing Pleistocene environments in, 349
    early genus *Homo* in, 310–311
    early hominin fossils in, 293–309
    endangered primates and, 176
    first *Homo sapiens* in, 384
    fossil site locations in, 295, 298, 312, 322
    hominin origins in, 287–316
    Homo heidelbergensis in, 351–352, 357, 384
    life expectancies in (human), 486
    malaria and, 106
    modern human origins in, 389–392
    NASA satellite image, 262
    "out of Africa" scenario, 387, 423
    premodern humans and, 351–352
    sickle-cell anemia and, 431
    Upper Paleolithic art and, 405–407
    Upper Paleolithic industry and, 405–407
    See also Hominin origins
African Americans:
    gene flow and, 101
    rickets and, 442
Afropithecus, 250–251, 253, 254
Aggressive behaviors, 196, 216–218
Aging, 483–487, 488
    life spans, maximum, 484

lifestyle factors and, 486
    mitochondrial theory of, 485, 488
    telomere hypothesis, 485–486, 488
Agriculture, 12, 470–472, 493
    declining human health and, 472
    dietary changes and, 470–472
    domesticated animals and, 493
    epidemiological transition and, 472
    slash-and-burn agriculture, 431
    subsistence agriculture, 12
Air pollution, 10, 503, 504
Albinism, 88, 91–93, 441
Alleles, 66, 99
    allele frequency, adaptation and, 105, 452–453, 464
    allele frequency, calculation of, 428–429
    allele frequency, evolution and, 99, 100, 108, 426–429
    allele frequency in populations, 99, 100, 124
    dominant/recessive alleles, 85–86
    heterozygous individuals, 85
    homozygous individuals, 85
    Mendelian traits/discrete traits and, 84, 87
    recessive alleles, 85
    See also Population genetics
Allen's rule, 446–447
Altamira site, 403, 404
Altitude, 14, 449–451
    acclimatization process and, 450
    glucose processing and, 451
    hemoglobin production and, 450
    high altitude stressors and, 449–451
    human adaptation to, 449–451
    hypoxia and, 449
    mutations and, 451
    See also Human adaptation
Altruism, 219–220, 223
Alzheimer's disease, 485
Amber, 128, 129
Amino acids, 55, 56, 57
    essential, 55, 470
    mutation and, 62–63
    See also DNA (deoxyribonucleic acid); Protein synthesis; RNA (ribonucleic acid)
Amish microcephaly, 104
Amud site, 361, 362
Analogies, 117
Anatomy, 18
    argument from design and, 28
    brachiation and, 154
    catarrhine characteristic, 240
    comparative, 144
    endocasts and, 307
    foramen magnum repositioning and, 290, 294

habitual bipedal locomotion and, 292
    hyoid bone and, 371
    nuchal torus and, 324
    occipital bun and, 361, 362
    pelvic/hip modifications and, 288, 289, 290–291
    platyrrhine characteristic, 241
    primate cranial anatomy, 148–149
    sagittal crest and, 304, 305
    sagittal keel and, 325
    sagittal ridge and, 324
    soft tissue anatomy and, 18
    zygomatics and, 255
    See also Bones; Brain size; Dentition; Skeletal remains
Ancestral characters, 120, 137–138, 145
Anemia, 472
    See also Sickle-cell anemia
Animals, 114–116
Anning, Mary, 33
Anthropocene epoch, 500–501, 506
Anthropocentric perspective, 216
Anthropoids, 144, 160–166
    characteristics/traits of, 160–161
    Eocene/Oligocene early anthropoids, 237–240
    New World anthropoids, 242–245
    New World monkeys and, 161–164, 243
    Old World monkeys and, 245–246, 261
    true anthropoids, emergence of, 240–242
    See also Apes; Fossil primates; Modern humans; Monkeys; Primates
Anthropological perspective, 21–23
Anthropology, 4, 5, 10–11
    applied anthropology and, 11, 18–19, 22
    archaeology and, 12
    cultural anthropology and, 11
    forensic anthropology and, 16–18, 22
    four-field approach to, 11
    linguistic anthropology and, 11–12
    medical anthropology and, 20
    molecular anthropology, 15
    nutritional anthropologists and, 14, 15
    paleopathology and, 12–13, 16
    primatology and, 18, 19
    subfields of, 11, 23
    See also Paleoanthropology; Physical anthropology
Antibiotic overuse, 10, 457
Antibiotic resistance, 10, 41, 457, 463, 503
Antigens, 89
Apes, 26, 143, 252
    African great apes, evolution of, 258–259
    Asian apes, 167, 259–260
    Asian true apes, 255–257
    bonobos, 172–173

Apes (*Continued*)
characteristics of, 160–161, 166–167
chimpanzees, 171–172
endangered primates, 176
European true apes, 253–257
geographical distribution of, 167
gibbons, 167–168
gorillas, 169–171
humans, differences from, 166–167
hylobatids/lesser apes, evolution of, 258
knuckle walking and, 154
language capabilities, 209, 266
Miocene, evolution and dispersal of, 254
orangutans, 168
proconsuloids and, 248–251
siamangs, 167–168
true apes, emergence of, 253–257, 261
See also Anthropoids; Fossil primates
Apidium, 239, 241
Apolipoprotein E (apoE), 485
Apollo 11 rock shelter site, 404, 405
Applied anthropology, 11, 18–19, 22
See also Anthropology; Physical
anthropology; Scientific method
Arago cave site, 354
Aramis site, 296, 297, 298
Arboreal hypothesis, 150
Arboreal living, 149–150, 230, 314
Archaeolemur, 234, 235
Archaeology, 12
artifacts and, 12, 270
bioarchaeology, 16
experimental archaeology and, 276–279,
284
human behavior, evidence of, 12
stone knappers and, 277
See also Anthropology; Paleoanthropology
Arctic polar ice, shrinking of, 496–497
Ardi. See *Ardipithecus*
Ardipithecus, 259, 294–297, 298, 314
Ardipithecus ramidus, 298, 309
Aristotle, 28
Art:
cave art, 382, 402–405
European Upper Paleolithic art, 400–405
female figurines and, 403
portable, 403
rock art, 406–407
shell/bone ornament, 406
Upper Paleolithic art, 400–408
Arthropods, 118
Artifacts, 12, 270
Artificial organisms, 75–76
Asia:
Central Asian Neandertals, 366
Chinese *Homo erectus*, 331–337
Denisovans and, 366–367, 372–373
endangered primates and, 176
fossil site locations in, 323, 355
great ape of, 259–260
Homo erectus, 323, 336–337, 338, 340
Homo floresiensis, 342–344, 345
Indonesian *Homo erectus*, 325, 330–331
modern human localities in, 394–396
Neandertals and, 365–366
premodern humans and, 353–356

Assimilation model, 388
Atapuerca region, 338, 352, 354
Atlatls, 402, 407
Aurignacian tool industry, 359, 399, 400
Australia, modern human fossils and, 395,
396, 400
Australopithecus afarensis, 4, 299–303, 309
as ancestor of later hominins, 303, 314
bipedalism and, 300
brain size, 375
cranial capacity of, 301, 302
habitual bipedalism and, 303
hominin characteristics of, 303
in hominin phylogeny, 314
jaws of, 301
juvenile skeletal remains of, 302–303
Laetoli footprints and, 3, 4, 299
locomotor behavior and, 303
Lucy skeleton and, 295, 300, 302
obligate bipedalism and, 303
postcranial material of, 301–302
primitive characteristics of, 301
sexual dimorphism and, 302
teeth of, 301
See also Australopiths; Hominin origins
Australopithecus africanus, 307, 308, 309, 314
Australopithecus anamensis, 298, 299, 309, 314
Australopithecus deyiremeda, 304
Australopithecus sediba, 295, 308–309, 310, 314
Australopiths, 293, 296, 297–303, 316
Australopithecus afarensis and, 299–303,
309, 314
Australopithecus africanus and, 307, 308,
309, 314
Australopithecus anamensis and, 298, 299,
309, 314
Australopithecus deyiremeda, 304
Australopithecus sediba, 295, 308–309,
310, 314
characteristics of, 298, 300–302
cranial capacity of, 301, 302
dentition in, 298, 304, 305
derived australopiths, 304–307
later australopiths, 304–307
locomotor behavior of, 298, 300
Lucy skeleton and, 295, 300, 302
major features, 298
Paranthropus and, 297, 304–306, 309, 314
Paranthropus aethiopicus and, 306, 309
Paranthropus boisei and, 306, 309
Paranthropus robustus and, 306, 309
sectorial premolars and, 298
Taung child and, 286, 295, 307
timeline of, 309
toe, divergent and opposable, 304
transitional australopiths and, 307–309
See also Early *Homo*; Hominin origins;
Pre-Australopiths
Autosomal dominant traits, 90–91
Autosomal recessive traits, 91–93
Autosomes, 66
Avian influenza, 456
Aye-ayes, 137, 175

Baboons, 19, 142, 165, 246
behavioral patterns, 191–192, 194, 195, 197

infanticide and, 200–201
mating consortships, 198
multi-male/multi-female groups and,
191–192
sexual dimorphism and, 165
skull of, 149
See also Apes
Bacteria, 50
accelerated evolution due to human
activities, 502–503
antibiotic resistance of, 10, 41, 457, 463, 503
self-replicating synthetic bacteria, 75, 76
synthetic bacterial genome, 75
See also Infectious disease
Bald eagle, 503
Basal metabolic rate (BMR), 188
Beagle voyage, 34, 35
Begun, David, 253
Behavior, 6, 186
comparative, 144
evolution of, 186–191
genetic influences on, 186
See also Behavioral patterns; Human
behavior; Primate behavior
Behavioral ecology, 186–187, 222–223
Behavioral genetics, 187, 222
Behavioral isolation, 125
Behavioral patterns, 6
affiliative behaviors, 196–197, 223
aggressive behaviors, 196, 216–218
altruism and, 219–220, 223
conflict behaviors, 216–218
culture, learned behaviors and, 6
empathy and, 219–220
primate paleontological studies and, 13
primatology and, 18, 19
prosocial behaviors, 218–220
territoriality, 166, 216
See also Human behavior; Primate behavior
Berger, Lee, 327
Berger, Thomas, 368
Bergmann's rule, 446
Bible, literal interpretation of, 43
Big Bang, 133
Bilophodont molars, 235, 250
Binford, Lewis, 268, 334
Binocular vision, 147
Binomial nomenclature, 29–30
Bioarchaeology, 16, 461–463
Biocultural evolution, 6–10, 23, 266–267, 284,
431–434, 435
biology-culture interactions and, 6, 10
culture, human capacity for, 6
health/disease incidence and, 10, 431–434
human biocultural evolution, 10, 431–434,
491–492
human life course and, 469
lactase persistence and, 432–433
worldview and, 6
See also Anthropology; Human
adaptation; Physical anthropology
Biodiversity, 500–502
Biological anthropology, 5, 12
See also Physical anthropology
Biological continuity, 43
Biological continuum, 6, 43, 221–222

Biological determinism, 413
Biological profile, 22
Biological species concept, 123–124
Biology, 31, 49–78
    cell division, 64–72
    cells, structure/function of, 50–51
    chromosomes, 64–66
    DNA replication, 53–54
    DNA structure, 52–53
    embryonic development, 60–61, 118
    genes, 57–60
    mutation, 62–64, 71
    new frontiers in, 72–77
    protein synthesis, 54–56
    See also DNA (deoxyribonucleic acid);
        Genetics; Heredity; Human adaptation;
        Mendelian inheritance; RNA
        (ribonucleic acid)
Biomedical research, 19
Biosocial perspective, 136
Biostratigraphic correlation, 276
Bipedal locomotion, 4, 21, 173, 174, 265,
    279–283, 288–293
    balance, maintaining, 288–289
    behavioral stimuli for, 292
    factors influencing, 279–283, 284
    habitual bipedalism, 292, 303, 316
    hominins and, 292, 303, 316
    major features of, 290–291
    mechanics of, 288–293
    obligate bipedalism, 292, 303, 316
    See also Locomotion
Bird evolution, 121–123
Biretia, 239–240, 250
Black, Davidson, 256
Black Skull, 304–306
Blanks, 277
Blending theory of inheritance, 42, 82
Blombos Cave site, 404, 405
Blood types, 89, 100
    ABO system, 89, 98, 99, 419–420
    allele frequency and, 100
    antigens and, 89
    environmental factors and, 98
    human polymorphisms and, 419–420
    human variation and, 419–420
    Mendelian inheritance and, 89, 98
    MN system and, 420
    smallpox and, 454
    See also Hemoglobin
Blumenbach, Johann Friedrich, 412–413
Blumenschine, Robert, 268
Bodo site, 351, 352, 354
Body size, 188
    brain and, 204–206
    and proportions, climate adaptations and,
        445–448
    social structure and, 188
Body temperature, optimal, 444
Bones:
    analysis of bone, 16, 278–279, 434–435
    bone geometry, 462
    fluorine analysis, 273–274
    forensic anthropology and, 16–18
    osteology, 16
    skeletal biology, 458–463

    stone tool/lithic industry and, 277–278
    tuberculosis and, 442–443
    vitamin D and, 442
    See also Anatomy; Archaeology;
        Paleoanthropology; Skeletal remains
Bonobo Conservation Initiative, 181
Bonobos, 172–173, 265
    behavioral patterns of, 198
    cranial capacity of, 302
    geographical distribution of, 172
    knuckle walking and, 154
    language and, 209
    mating consortships, 198
    sexual activity of, 173
    social organization of, 173
    See also Apes
Border Cave site, 390, 393
Boule, Marcellin, 360
Bouri Peninsula site, 269
Brace, C. Loring, 402
Brachiation, 154, 172
Brain, C. K., 278
Brain:
    body size and, 204
    comparison of mammalian, 205
    encephalization index, 204
    growth after birth (human), 479–480,
        481
    growth, timing of, 204–205
    hemispheres of, 147, 210
    increased complexity in primates, 147
Brain function:
    binocular vision and, 147
    bipedalism, brain-cooling/radiator theory
        and, 282–283
    brain/body size, encephalization and, 204
    Broca's area and, 210
    hemispheres and, 147, 210
    language areas, 210–211
    neocortex and, 134, 147, 204, 205
    speech production mechanisms and,
        369–370, 371
    visual centers and, 147
    Wernicke's area, 210
Brain size:
    Australopithecus afarensis and, 301
    bipedalism and, 282
    body size and, encephalization, 204–206
    cerebrum and neocortex, 134, 204, 205
    comparison of hominoid, hominin, and
        early *Homo*, 265
    comparison of mammalian brains, 205
    comparison of vertebrate brains, 134
    cranial capacity comparison, 302
    diet and, 269
    early *Homo*, 265, 302, 310, 314–315
    in hominins, 375
    Homo erectus and, 321, 341, 344
    humans and, 221, 269, 302, 479–480
    language, evolution of, 209–211
    large brains, metabolic costs of, 206
    mammalian evolution and, 134–135
    radiator theory, brain-cooling effect and,
        282–283
    Sahelanthropus and, 314, 375
    social brain hypothesis and, 206

Brassempouy site, 404
Breeding isolates, 425
Breeding process:
    breeding isolates and, 425
    hybrids and, 83, 125
    selective breeding, 36–37, 47, 82, 100, 101,
        125
Broca's area, 210
Broken Hill site, 351, 352
Buffon, G.-L. L. de, 30
Burial practices:
    flexed position and, 360, 372
    grave goods and, 401, 406–407
    Neandertal burials, 370–372, 406, 407
    Sungir site, 401, 404, 406
    Upper Paleolithic burial sites and, 401
Bushmeat trade, 179–181
Butchering practices, 341

Capuchin monkeys, 215
Carbon-14 dating method, 274–275
Carbon dioxide, 494–495, 504
Carbon isotope ratios, 462–463
Carpolestes, 230, 231, 234
Carpolestidae, 230
Carriers, 89, 93
Cars and trucks, cladistic analysis of, 120–121
Catarrhines, 163, 240, 245, 249
Catastrophism, 32
Catopithecus, 240
Cave art, 382, 402–405
Cell division, 48, 64–72, 78
    chromosomes and, 64–66
    DNA replication and, 53–54
    evolutionary significance of meiosis, 71
    meiosis and, 67, 69–72
    mitosis and, 67–69
    recombination process and, 69, 93
    reduction division and, 69, 70, 71
    See also Biology; Cells; Chromosomes
Cells, 50–51, 78
    cytoplasm and, 50, 51, 55
    eukaryotic cells and, 50
    gametes and, 51, 69, 78
    mitochondria and, 50, 51
    molecules and, 50
    multicellular forms and, 50, 114
    nuclear membrane and, 50, 51
    nucleus in, 50, 51, 55
    organelles in, 50, 51
    protein synthesis and, 50, 54–56
    regulatory genes and, 60–61
    ribosomes and, 50, 51
    somatic cells, 51, 67–69, 78
    stem cell research, 49
    See also Biology; Cell division; DNA
        (deoxyribonucleic acid); Mitochondrial
        DNA (mtDNA); Protein synthesis;
        RNA (ribonucleic acid)
Cenozoic era, 130, 133
    Age of Mammals and, 134
    continental drift and, 131
    epochs of, 131, 133
    mammalian radiation and, 137
    periods of, 133
    primate origins and, 226, 227–229

Centromeres, 64
Ceprano site, 338–339, 340
Cercopithecidae, 164, 246
Cercopithecines, 164, 246
Characters, 117
Chatelperronian tool industry, 359, 364, 400
Cheetah genetics, 104
Chimpanzees, 19, 143, 171–172, 478
    aggressive behavior and, 196, 216–218
    altruism/empathy and, 219–220
    babies, size of, 479
    behavioral patterns of, 195, 197, 203
    brachiation and, 172
    bushmeat trade in, 455
    Chimpanzee Politics, 197
    chromosomes of, 46, 65
    comparative genomics and, 46
    cranial capacity and, 149, 302
    cultural behaviors and, 222
    culture, predisposition for, 10
    diet of, 172
    displays by, 195
    facial expressions of, 195
    fossil, 259
    genome sequencing and, 43, 75
    geographical distribution of, 172
    humans, differences from, 46–47
    humans, similarities to, 128, 155–157,
        265, 284
    knuckle walking and, 155, 172
    language and, 208–209
    locomotion of, 155, 172
    sexual dimorphism and, 172
    skull of, 149, 256
    social organization of, 172
    territoriality and, 216–218
    tool use by, 213, 214, 215, 222
    See also Apes; Primate behavior; Primates
Chimpanzee Sequencing and Analysis
    Consortium, 75
China:
    carbon dioxide production of, 504
    Dragon Bone Hill cave and, 336–337
    Hexian County site, 323, 335
    Homo erectus in, 331–337
    Lantian County sites, 323, 335
    Yunxian County site and, 335
    Zhoukoudian Cave *Homo erectus*, 323,
        324, 331–335, 338
Chordata (phylum), 114, 115
Christian fundamentalists, 43, 44, 47
Christianity, 27, 28, 43
Chromosomes, 64–66
    abnormal number of, 71–72, 73
    alleles and, 66
    autosomes, 66
    centromeres and, 64
    DNA and, 64–66
    gene locus and, 66
    karyotyping, 66–67
    meiosis and, 67, 69–71
    mitosis and, 67–69
    mutation and, 93, 105, 108
    numbers of, 64–66, 71–72
    pairs of, 66, 69, 105
    random assortment of, 71, 86–87

    sex chromosomes, 66
    somatic cells and, 67–69
    types of, 66
Chronometric dating, 273, 274, 275
Ciochon, Russell L., 13
Clades, 120
Cladistics, 117–123, 139
    clades and, 120
    cladistic analysis, example of (cars and
        trucks), 120–121
    cladogram and, 123
    crown group and, 228
    derived/modified characters and, 120
    evolutionary systematics compared with,
        117–120, 124
    homologies and, 117, 120, 139
    homoplasy and, 117
    monophyletic groups and, 120
    phylogenetic trees and, 123
    polyphyletic groups and, 120
    shared derived characters and, 122
    using to interpret organisms, 121–123
    See also Classification
Cladogenesis, 125
Cladograms, 123
Classification, 29–30, 114–123, 139
    analogies and, 117
    ancestral/primitive characters and, 120
    animals and, 114–116
    chordata phylum, 114, 115
    clades and, 120
    cladistics and, 117–123, 139
    derived/modified characters and, 120, 294
    evolutionary systematics and, 117–120,
        124, 139
    fossil genera, 127–128
    fossil species, 126–127
    hominins and, 265–266
    homologies and, 116–117, 120, 139
    human variation and, 412–413
    Linnean, 29–30, 115, 127, 412
    monophyletic groups and, 120, 265
    phyla within, 114, 115
    phylogenetic trees and, 123, 314
    polyphyletic groups and, 120
    primate classification, 155–157
    principles of, 116–117
    shared derived characters and, 122
    vertebrates and, 114, 115
    See also Macroevolution
Climate change, 494–500, 506
    Anthropocene epoch and, 500–501, 506
    anti-scientific positions and, 495–496
    biodiversity, impacts on, 500–502
    carbon dioxide and, 494–495, 504
    "climate deniers" and skeptics, 495–496
    coral reefs and, 499
    diseases and, 498
    extreme storms and, 498
    glaciations and, 348
    global climate change, 494–495
    goals for future, 495, 500
    human disconnect and, 492
    human population growth and, 492–493,
        503, 506
    humans as cause of, 496, 497–498

    interglacials and, 348, 359
    international conferences and agreements
        on, 499–500
    jet stream change and, 496
    ocean acidification and, 498–499
    polar ice, shrinking of, 496–497
    public perceptions of, 495–496
    scientific consensus on, 492, 495–496,
        497–498
    sea ice maximum/minimum, 497
    tipping points and, 497
    in Upper Paleolithic, 400, 401, 407–408
    See also Human disconnection
Climatic conditions:
    acclimatization and, 438–439
    Upper Paleolithic, 400, 401
    See also Climate change; Cold climates;
        Hot climates
Clones, 71
Cloning, 71, 73–75
Codominance, 89
Codons, 56, 57
Coevolution, 433
Cold climates, 14, 448–449
    body size/proportions and, 445–448
    responses to cold, 448–449
    vasoconstriction and, 448
    See also Hot climates; Human adaptation
Colobines, 164, 165, 188, 246
Colobus monkeys, 165, 174–175
Color vision, 146, 150
Common ancestors, 26
Communication, 194–196, 223
    autonomic responses and, 194
    grooming behavior and, 194
    language, evolution of, 209–211
    submissive stance and, 194
    vocalizations and, 207
    See also Language; Primate behavior
Communications technology, 7
Comparative genomics, 46, 72, 75, 76, 155, 435
Comparative studies, 144, 181
Complementary bases, 54
Complete replacement model, 386–387, 409
Conflict behaviors, 216–218
Conserved genes, 61, 95, 118–119
Context, 272
Continental drift, 131, 132
Continuous traits, 94, 96
Continuum, 6, 43, 221–222
Copernicus, 28
Copy number variants (CNVs), 59, 100, 421, 424
Core area, 216
Core (stone tools), 277
Cortisol, 476–477
Cosmic calendar, 133
Costa Rica, 505
Creation science movement, 44–45
Crick, Francis, 52, 53
Crime investigations, 16–17, 22, 77
Cro-Magnon site, 393, 397–400, 406
Crown group, 227, 228
Cultural anthropology, 11
    ethnographies and, 11
    subcultures, interactions of, 11
    traditional societies, study of, 11

Cultural behavior, 6, 211–218
Cultural relativism, 22–23
Cultural tradition, 212
Culture, 6–10, 211, 266
    components of, 6, 7
    human capacity for, 266
    human evolution and, 10
    impact on world's resources, 493–494
    learned nature of, 6, 212
    material culture, 266
    primate cultural behavior, 6, 211–218, 222,
        223, 266
    relativistic view of, 22–23
    transmission of, 6, 222
    worldview and, 6
    See also Biocultural evolution
Cusps, 151
Cuvier, Georges, 31–32, 233–234, 413
Cystic fibrosis, 88
Cytoplasm, 50, 51, 55
Cytosine, 53

Dali skull, 353, 355, 356
Dart, Raymond, 307
Darwin, Charles, 12, 27, 30, 33–38, 39, 47, 61,
    82, 98, 119, 199, 413
Darwin, Erasmus, 30
Darwinius, 223, 234
Data, 20
Dating techniques, 272–276, 284
    See also Paleoanthropology
DDT spraying, 431, 432, 503
de Merode, Dr. Emmanuel, 178
de Waal, F., 220
Deep time, 33, 132–133, 138
Deforestation, 167–168, 176, 177, 179, 180,
    493–494
Democratic Republic of the Congo (DRC),
    169, 177–178, 181
Denisova Cave site, 355, 366, 372
Denisovans, 357, 366–367, 372–373, 377,
    388
    genome sequencing of, 76
Dental formula, 151, 154
Dentition:
    bilophodont molars, 235, 250
    canine teeth, 194, 294
    caries and, 458
    cusps and, 151
    dental formula and, 151, 154
    diet and, 458
    fossil record, disproportionate
        representation of teeth in, 135
    fossil teeth, ecological inferences from,
        260–261
    generalized, 146
    heterodont dentition, 135, 144, 182
    hominin, compared with hominoids and
        modern *Homo*, 265
    homodont dentition, 135
    honing complex and, 294
    mammalian evolution and, 135
    omnivorous diet and, 146, 149, 150–151
    primate dentition, 144, 146, 150–151, 182
    sectorial premolars and, 298
    Y-5 molar and, 248, 250

Derived characters, 120, 226, 294
Development:
    embryonic development, 60–61, 118–119
    evo-devo (evolutionary developmental
        biology), 43, 118–119
Developmental acclimatization, 439
Diabetes, 472–473
Diamond, Jared, 472
Diet:
    agriculture and, 470–472
    ancient hominin, 379
    brain size and, 269, 344
    contemporary human diet, 472–473
    dental health and, 458
    diabetes and, 472–473
    expensive-tissue hypothesis, 344
    fat storage and, 472
    food scarcity, 474
    frugivorous diet, 168
    globalization and, 474
    life course and, 469–474
    lifestyles and consequences for, 473
    male-provisioning scenario and, 281, 282
    microbiome and, 470
    mismatched diets/dietary needs and,
        482, 488
    nutritional anthropologists and, 14, 15
    nutritional deficiencies and, 470, 473
    obesity and, 474, 475
    omnivorous diet, 146, 149, 150–151, 182
    Paleolithic ("caveman") diet, 401, 488
    preagricultural diet, 470, 471, 473
    pregnancy and, 470, 479
    prehistoric diet, reconstructing, 462–463
    primate diet, 146, 149, 150–151, 182
    scavenging and, 268–269
    seed-eating hypothesis and, 280–282
    social structure and, 188–189
    undernutrition/malnutrition and, 473–474
    in Upper Paleolithic, 401
    vegetarian diet, 171
    See also Human growth/development;
        Hunting; Subsistence patterns
Differential net reproductive success, 42
Digits, extra, 81–82
Dikika site, 270, 302
Dinosaurs, 121–123
    Age of Dinosaurs, 135
    birds, links with, 121–123
    extinction of, 131, 135
    feathers and, 122, 128
    fossils of, 113, 114
    theropods and, 122
    warm-bloodedness and, 133
    See also Vertebrate evolution
Direct percussion method, 277
Disconnection. *See* Human disconnection
Discontinuous traits, 94
Discrete traits, 84, 87
Disease, 10, 88, 487
    aging and, 483–487
    agriculture, epidemiological transition
        and, 472
    air pollution and, 10, 504
    air travel and, 10
    biocultural evolution and, 10, 431–434

    cancers and, 459
    climate change and, 498
    diabetes, 472–473
    diseases of civilization, 484
    free radicals, oxidation and, 485
    gene variants and, 10
    genetic disorders, 88–89
    genetic risk factors, 424
    new diseases, human activity and,
        502–503
    obesity/overnutrition and, 474, 475
    osteoarthritis and, 459, 460, 461–462
    paleopathology and, 16
    pathogens, 451–452, 487
    prehistoric, evidence of, 458–460
    rickets, 442, 459
    sickle-cell anemia and, 62–63, 78
    skin cancer, 440, 441, 446–447
    vectors of, 10, 451–452, 457, 498
    Vitamin D and, 442
    See also Health; Infectious disease
Dispersal, 190, 319
    See also Homo erectus; Migrations;
        Modern human origins/dispersal
Displays, 195–196
Diurnal habit, 146, 148
Dmanisi site, 318, 322, 329–330, 338, 340,
    341, 345
DNA (deoxyribonucleic acid), 6, 15, 42, 50,
    52–61, 78, 120
    ancient DNA, 386
    ancient human migrations, DNA evidence
        for, 422–423
    base substitution/point mutation and, 64
    bases and, 52–53, 54
    coding sequences and, 56, 58, 61
    complementary bases and, 54
    copy number variants and, 59, 100,
        421, 424
    double helix, 52–54
    ENCODE project, 76–77
    enzymes, role of, 54
    exons/introns and, 58
    from fossils, 15
    genes and, 56, 57–60
    genetic code, 56, 59–60
    heredity and, 48, 78
    infanticide studies and, 21
    mitochondrial DNA, 50–51, 97
    molecular anthropology and, 15, 228
    mutations and, 56, 62–64, 93, 105
    noncoding/junk DNA, 58, 59, 61, 77, 421
    nuclear DNA, 50
    nucleotides and, 52
    polymerase chain reaction and, 72
    polymorphisms and, 421–425
    recombinant DNA technology and, 73
    regulatory genes, embryonic development
        and, 60–61
    replication and, 53–54
    single nucleotide polymorphisms and,
        421, 438
    structure of, 52–53
    synthetic, 75
    telomere hypothesis and, 485–486
    transcription and, 55–56, 57

DNA (deoxyribonucleic acid) (*Continued*)
transposable elements (TEs), 59
triplet, 55, 56
See also Biology; Cell division;
Chromosomes; Genetics; Protein
synthesis; RNA (ribonucleic acid)
DNA fingerprints, 72–73, 74
Dobzhansky, T., 503
Dogs, 37, 100, 101
Dolní Věstonice site, 403, 404
Domesticated animals, 10, 37, 493
Dominance, 83, 85–86
autosomal dominant traits and, 90–91
codominance and, 89
genetic disorders and, 88
Mendelian traits in humans, 88–89
misconceptions about, 89–90
See also Heredity; Mendelian inheritance
Dominance (behavior)/dominance hierarchies,
192–194, 223
Down syndrome, 72
Dragon Bone Hill cave, 336–337
Drimolen site, 13, 295
Drought, 498
Dryopithecus, 254, 255, 259
Dubois, Eugene, 330–331
Dwarfism, achondroplasia and, 88, 90–91

Early *Homo*, 310–311, 316
brain size and, 265, 302, 310, 314–315, 375
coexistence of early forms, 311, 312
cranial capacity of, 302, 310
fossil sites, 311, 312
hominin phylogeny, tentative, 314
Homo erectus, coexistence with, 311
Homo habilis and, 310, 314
interbreeding with Neandertals, 75, 364,
373–374, 409
Plio-Pleistocene hominins and, 227, 304,
310–311
See also Australopiths; Hominin origins;
Homo erectus
Earth, age of, 46
East Lake Turkana site, 311, 312, 325, 327
Ebola, 10
Ecological footprints, 504–505
Ecological niches, 125, 131
primates, adaptive niches of, 149
Ecological species concept, 125–126
El Castillo site, 382, 403
El Sidrón site, 362, 364
Elandsfontein site, 354
Electron spin resonance (ESR) dating
method, 275
Embryonic development, 60–61, 118–119
Hox genes and, 119
Empathy, 219–220
Empirical approach, 20
Encephalization, 204
ENCODE (Encyclopedia of DNA Elements)
project, 76–77
Endangered species, 174–181, 182
in Africa, 176
in Asia, 176
aye-ayes and, 175
bushmeat trade and, 179–181

conservation efforts, 169, 179, 181
deforestation and, 167–168, 176, 177,
179, 180
gibbons and, 167
gorillas and, 169, 176, 178
habitat loss and, 167–168, 176, 177, 178, 501
human hunting activities and, 177
live capture/illegal trade and, 177, 179
in Madagascar, 176
New World, 176
nonhuman primates, most highly
endangered, 176
orangutans and, 168, 178–179
Endemic disease, 452
Endocasts, 307
Endocrine glands, 475–476
Endogamy, 425
Endothermy, 136, 144
Environment:
adaptation to, 14, 40, 148–149
environmental factors, interactions with
genetic factors, 98, 469
Environmental degradation:
air pollution and, 10, 503, 504
biodiversity, 500–502
deforestation, 167–168, 176, 177, 179, 180,
493–494
flood events and, 494
Francis, Pope, encyclical on, 500
human impact and, 492–503
human population growth and, 492–493
See also Climate change; Endangered
species; Human disconnection
Enzymes, 54
Eocene euprimates, 227, 230, 231–240
Epidemiological transition, 472
Epigenetics, 475–477, 488
Epigenome, 475
Epochs, 133, 500
Eppig, Christopher, 481
An Essay on the Principle of Population, 32
Essential amino acids, 55, 470
Establishment clause, 45
Ethnocentrism, 22
Ethnographies, 11
Eugenics, 413
Eukaryotic cells, 50
Euprimates, 230, 231–240
Europe:
Central European modern human fossils,
396–397
Central European Neandertals, 363–364
Homo heidelbergensis and, 350, 352–353,
357
later *Homo erectus* and, 338–339, 340
Neandertal fossil finds, 359, 359–364,
360, 363–364
premodern humans and, 352–353
true apes and, 253–255
Upper Paleolithic art and, 400–405
Upper Paleolithic technology and,
401–403, 404
UV radiation, skin pigmentation and, 442
vitamin D hypothesis and, 442
Western European modern humans,
397–400

See also Neandertals; Premodern humans
Evaporative cooling, 445
Evo-devo (evolutionary developmental
biology), 43, 118–119
Evolution, 5, 47, 98–109
acceleration of, by human activities,
502–503
of behavior, 186–191
biological continuum and, 6, 43, 221–222
conserved genes and, 61
current definition of, 99
factors in, 98, 100–105, 108–109
levels of organization in process of, 93, 105
life course, effects on, 466–489
macroevolution, 5, 99, 113–140
meiosis, evolutionary significance of, 71
microevolution, 5, 26, 99, 101
mosaic evolution, 264, 265
mutation and, 64, 71, 100
opposition to, today, 43–46
population genetics, changes in, 5
primatology and, 18, 19
rate of, 138, 139
regulatory genes and, 61, 100, 118–119
teaching of, 26, 44–45, 47
variation, role in, 99, 100–105
See also Biocultural evolution;
Evolutionary theory; Heredity; Human
evolution; Modern evolutionary
theory; Natural selection
Evolutionary medicine, 19, 473
Evolutionary systematics, 117–120, 124, 139
See also Classification
Evolutionary theory, 2, 25–47
acquired characteristics, inheritance of,
30–31
argument from design and, 28
biological continuum concept, 43, 221
blending theory of inheritance and, 42, 82
brief history of, 26–38
catastrophism and, 32
common ancestor concept and, 26
constraints on, 42–43
creation science movement and, 44–45
in Darwin's shadow, 38
deep time concept and, 33, 132–133, 138
development of, 24–47
environment-organism (evo-devo)
relationship and, 43, 118–119
evo-devo approach and, 43, 118–119
examples and support for, 39–41, 46
fixity of species concept and, 27, 30
microevolutionary changes and, 26
natural selection, discovery/development
of, 33–38
opposition to, 43–46
paradigm shifts and, 28–29
population evolution and, 39
precursors of, 29–33
religious beliefs, anti-scientific positions
and, 27–28, 34, 43, 47
reproductively isolated organisms and,
29, 47
scientific revolution and, 28–29
teaching of, 26, 44–45, 47
uniformitarianism and, 32–33

See also Evolution; Human evolution; Modern evolutionary theory; Natural selection

Exogamy, 425

Exons, 58

Expensive-tissue hypothesis, 344

Experimental archaeology, 276–279, 284
    bone, analysis of, 278–279
    stone tool/lithic technology and, 277–278
    See also Archaeology; Paleoanthropology

Extinction, 31–32, 181
    catastrophism doctrine and, 32
    climate change and, 500–501
    cloning of extinct animals, 75
    colobus monkeys and, 174–175
    current extinction event, 500–501
    dinosaur extinction, 131, 135
    human activities and, 500–501
    major extinction events, 131, 135, 500
    primate species, 174–175, 181

Eye color, 95, 96

Eye contact, 194

Facial expressions, 195

Falk, Dean, 282–283

Falsification, 20, 21, 44, 279

Family tree, 228

Fat storage, 472

Fathers, 203

Faunal correlation, 276

Fayum Depression, 239, 241, 261

Fertility, 41–42

Finches. *See* Galápagos finches

Fire, control and use of, 334, 357–358, 402

First Amendment, 45

First dispersal. *See Homo erectus*; Modern human origins/dispersal

Fitness, 39, 41
    reproductive, 187, 441

Fixity of species concept, 27, 30

Flake tools, 277

Flexed position burial, 360, 372

Flood events, 494

Florisbad site, 354

Flourine analysis, 273–274

Folate, 441, 463–464

Foot structure, 292–293
    early hominins, 292

Footprints:
    ecological footprint, 504–505
    Laetoli footprints, 3, 4, 299
    lunar footprints, 4, 5

Foramen magnum, 290, 294

Forensic anthropology, 16–18, 22, 417, 434–435

Fossil primates, 13, 225–261
    Adapis and, 233–234
    Adapoids and, 223–224
    adaptive radiation and, 231, 261
    Aegyptopithecus and, 241–242
    Afradapis and, 233
    African great apes, evolution of, 258–259
    Afropithecus and, 250–251, 253, 254
    anthropoids and, 237–245
    ape gap and, 258
    apelike proconsuloids, 248–251

apes and, 252, 253–259, 261

Apidium and, 239, 241

arboreal adaptation, primate evolution and, 230

Archaeolemur and, 234, 235

archaic primates and, 229–230

Asian great ape and, 255–257, 259–260

bilophodont molars and, 235, 250

biostratigraphic/faunal correlation and, 276

Biretia and, 239–240, 250

Cantius and, 233

Carpolestes and, 230, 231, 234

Carpolestidae and, 230

catarrhines and, 240, 245, 249

Catopithecus and, 240

Cenozoic era, 226, 227–229

crown group and, 227, 228

Darwinius and, 223, 234

derived skeletal traits and, 226

Dryopithecus and, 254, 255, 259

euprimates, Eocene epoch and, 227, 230, 231–240

European true apes and, 253–255

Fayum Depression and, 239, 241, 261

Gigantopithecus and, 253, 254, 255–257, 260

Griphopithecus and, 253, 254, 259, 259–260, 261

haplorhines and, 226, 232

Homininae, cladogram of, 259

hominoid evolution and, 258–260

homologies and, 233

homoplasy and, 233

island hopping and, 235, 243, 244

Khoratpithecus and, 253, 260, 261

last common ancestor and, 227, 228

late Mesozoic era and, 226–229

lemuriforms and, 223–224, 238

Lomorupithecus and, 251

Lufengpithecus and, 254, 257

Miocene primates and, 227, 245–257

molecular primate family tree and, 228, 229, 232

Nakalipithecus and, 254, 258, 259, 261

New World anthropoids and, 242–245, 261

Nsungwepithecus and, 245

Old World monkeys and, 245–246, 252, 261

Oligocene primates and, 227, 240–245

omomyoids and, 236–237

Ouranopithecus and, 253, 254, 255, 258, 259, 261

Panamacebus and, 242–243, 245, 250

Parapithecus and, 241

Perupithecus and, 242, 250

Pilobates and, 224

platyrrhines and, 241, 242–245

plesiadapiforms and, 229, 230

Plesiadapis and, 230

Pliobates and, 251, 253

Pliocene and, 227

Pliopithecoidea and, 251

Pongo and, 257

Proconsul and, 250, 254

Purgatorius and, 230, 234

Saadanius and, 242, 249, 250, 251

semiorders and, 230

Sivapithecus and, 254, 255, 256, 260

stem group and, 227, 228

strepsirrhines and, 226, 232, 238

subfossil lemurs and, 235

tarsier-like omomyoids and, 236–237

taxon/taxa and, 227

Teilhardina and, 234, 236

Theropithecus and, 248

true anthropoids and, 240–242

true apes and, 253–257, 261

true lemurs/lorises, evolution of, 234–236

true tarsiers, evolution of, 237

Victoriapithecus and, 246, 250

Y-5 molar and, 248, 250

Yuanmoupithecus and, 258, 261

See also Fossils; Primate adaptation; Primates

Fossils, 33, 112–114, 126–128, 139
    amber and, 128, 129
    catastrophism doctrine and, 32
    DNA extraction and, 15
    early hominins, 293–309
    examples of, 129
    formation of, 128–130, 139
    fossil genera, recognition of, 127–128
    fossil record, disproportionate representation in, 135
    fossil record, incompleteness of, 138–139
    fossil record, interpretation of, 126–128, 138–139, 311–313
    fossil species, recognition of, 126–127
    interspecific variation and, 127
    intraspecific variation and, 127
    Laetoli footprints and, 3, 4, 299
    locations of fossil sites, 295, 298, 312
    microfossils and, 128
    mineralization and, 128, 129
    molecular clock and, 228
    paleoanthropology and, 13
    paleospecies, variation in, 127
    primate paleontology and, 13
    sexual dimorphism and, 126
    soft tissue and, 128, 130
    species, interpretation of, 126
    species, recognition of, 126–127
    splitters vs. lumpers and, 127, 375–376
    taphonomy and, 130, 139, 272, 278
    taxonomic labels, 126
    teeth, prevalence of, 135
    variations in, 126
    See also Fossil primates; Macroevolution; Mammalian evolution; Skeletal remains; Vertebrate evolution

Founder effect, 102–105
    colonization and, 102–103
    See also Modern evolutionary theory

FOXP2 gene, 211, 369

Franklin, Rosalind, 52, 53

Free radicals, 485

Frugivorous diet, 168

Galagos, 158–159, 176

Galápagos finches, 24, 34–36, 39, 40–41, 61

Galápagos Islands, 34, 35
Galileo, 28
Galton, Francis, 413
Gametes, 51, 69, 78
    egg cells, 51
    heredity and, 51
    recombination and, 69, 93, 105
    sperm cells, 51
    zygotes, formation of, 51
    See also Biology; Cells; Meiosis
Gene duplication, 188–189
Gene flow, 93, 100–102
Gene pools, 99, 105
Generalized characteristics, 137–138,
    144–145, 182
Genes, 6, 56, 57–60, 78
    cloning and, 71, 73–75
    coding sequences and, 56, 58, 61
    conserved, 61, 95, 118–119
    definition of, 57–58
    exons and, 58
    function, shifting view of, 58
    gene locus, 66
    homeobox/hox genes, 60–61, 119
    introns and, 58
    jumping genes, 59
    language and (*FOXP2*), 211, 369
    mutation and, 56, 62–64, 100
    new, mutation and, 100
    noncoding/junk DNA and, 58, 59, 61, 77
    pairs of, 84
    pleiotropic genes, 484–485
    point mutation and, 64
    recombinant DNA technology and, 73
    regulatory genes and, 60–61, 100
    transcription and, 57
    See also DNA (deoxyribonucleic acid);
        Genetic code; Genetics; Protein
        synthesis; RNA (ribonucleic acid)
Genetic, defined, 5
Genetic bottlenecks, 103–104, 408
Genetic code, 56, 59–60
Genetic drift, 93, 102–105, 108, 124
    as random, 124
Genetic equilibrium, Hardy-Weinberg theory
    of, 425–426, 435
Genetic tool kit, 118–119
Genetic variation, 13–14, 61
Genetically closed system, 425
Genetics, 50, 78, 108–109
    behavior, influence on, 186
    behavioral genetics, 187, 222
    comparative genomics and, 46, 72, 75, 76,
        155, 435
    disease and, 10
    environment, interaction with, 98
    evo-devo approach and, 43
    genetic variation and, 13–14
    macroevolutionary processes and, 5
    microevolutionary processes and, 5
    molecular anthropology and, 15
    new frontiers in, 72–77
    polymorphisms, study of, 419–421
    populations, evolutionary changes in, 5, 39
    See also DNA (deoxyribonucleic acid);
        Heredity; Human variation; Mendelian

inheritance; Mendelian inheritance in
    humans; Population genetics
Genocide, 17
Genomes, 43, 58, 118
    comparative genomics, 46, 72, 75, 76, 155,
        435
    Neanderthal, 373–374
    whole-genome analysis, 422–423
    See also Genome sequencing; Human
        Genome Project
Genome sequencing, 43, 58, 75, 228
Genotypes, 85, 86, 87, 98
Genus/genera, 29–30, 127–128
Geographical distribution:
    apes and, 167
    gorillas and, 169
    HIV/AIDS and, 453
    malaria and, 106–107
    New World monkeys and, 152, 161
    Old World monkeys and, 153, 164
    Old World sickle-cell allele, 106, 107
    primate groups and, 150, 152–153
    skin color, indigenous human populations
        and, 439
    See also Fossil primates; Hominin origins;
        Homo erectus
Geographical isolation, 14, 124
    continental drift and, 131
    See also Geographical distribution
Geological time scale, 32–33, 130, 131
Geology, 32–33, 132, 267–268
    catastrophism doctrine and, 32
    continental drift/plate tectonics and,
        131, 132
    deep time and, 3, 33, 132–133, 138
    stratigraphy and, 273
Gibbons, 167–168, 478
    endangered status of, 167
    geographical distribution of, 167
    skull of, 148
    territoriality and, 167
    See also Apes
Gibraltar site, 361, 362
Gigantopithecus, 13, 253, 254, 255–257, 260
Giraffe, neck of, 31
Glaciations, 348
Global climate change. *See* Climate change
Globalization, 474
Glucose processing, 451
Gluteus maximus, 289
Gombe National Park, 172, 193
Gona site, 326–327
Gondwanaland, 131, 132
Goodall, Jane, 217
Gorilla gorilla, 169
Gorillas, 169–171, 259
    behavioral patterns of, 171
    chromosome number and, 65
    conservation efforts and, 169
    cranial capacity and, 302
    Cross River gorillas and, 169
    in Democratic Republic of the Congo
        (DRC), 169, 177–178
    diet of, 171, 188
    endangered status of, 169, 176, 178
    genome sequencing and, 75

geographical distribution of, 169
    infants, care of, 203
    knuckle walking and, 154
    language and, 208
    lowland gorillas and, 169, 170–171
    mountain gorillas and, 170–171
    natal groups and, 170
    silverback males and, 170, 171, 177, 203
    tool use by, 213, 214
    Virunga Volcanoes Conservation Area
        and, 177–178
    See also Apes; Lowland gorillas; Mountain
        gorillas; Primate adaptations; Primate
        behavior; Primates
Gould, John, 35–36
Gould, Steven Jay, 132
Gran Dolina site, 322, 338, 341, 352
Grand Designer, 28
Grandmother hypothesis, 483
Gravettian tool industry, 359, 400
Gravlee, Clarence, 424
Griphopithecus, 253, 254, 259, 259–260, 261
Grooming behavior, 194, 197, 223
Grotte Chauvet Cave site, 403–405
Growth. *See* Human growth/development
Guanine, 53

H1N1 (swine flu) virus, 10, 456–457
Habitat loss, 167–168, 176, 177, 178, 501
Habitual bipedalism, 4, 173, 292, 303, 316
Hadar region, 295, 298, 299, 303, 312
Hailie-Selassie, Y., 294–295, 304
Half-life, 274
Haplorhini, 155, 182, 226, 232
Hardy-Weinberg theory of genetic equilib-
    rium, 425–426, 435
Harmand, Sonia, 270
Health:
    evolutionary medicine and, 19, 473
    See also Disease; Infectious disease
Heat:
    body size and proportion and, 445–448
    body temperature, optimal, 444
    human responses to, 445–448
    See also Climate change; Hot climates
Hemisphere, 147
Hemoglobin, 54, 55, 66, 108
    high-altitude environment and, 450
    malaria-sickle-cell correlation and,
        106–107
    sickle-cell anemia and, 62–63, 78, 105–107
    See also Blood types
Hemophilia, 93–94, 469
Henry, Amanada, 309
Heredity, 81–98
    acquired characteristics, use-disuse theory
        and, 30–31
    blending theory of inheritance and, 42, 82
    conserved genes and, 61, 95
    DNA and, 48, 78
    environmental factors and, 98
    gametes, role of, 51
    homeobox/hox genes and, 60–61
    Mendelian inheritance, 83–87
    modern evolutionary theory and, 98–99
    mutation and, 62–64, 100

natural selection and, 39, 41
non-Mendelian inheritance, 94–97
point mutation and, 64
sickle-cell anemia and, 62–63, 78
See also Genes; Genetics; Mendelian
inheritance; Mendelian inheritance
in humans; Natural selection;
Non-Mendelian inheritance
Herto site, 389–390, 393, 394, 409
Heterodont dentition, 135, 144, 182
Heterozygous individuals, 85
Hexian County site, 323, 335
Hip bones, 289
HIV/AIDS, 453–454, 455–456
life expectancies and, 486
simian immunodeficiency virus (SIV) and,
455–456
HMS *Beagle*, 34, 35
Holocene epoch, 227, 500
Homeobox genes, 60–61, 116
embryonic development and, 119
Homeostasis, 438
Hominin behavior/ecology, 203, 263–284
adaptive patterns of, 313–315
biocultural evolution and, 266–267
bipedal locomotion and, 265, 279–283,
288–293
butchering practice and, 341
diet, 268–269
encephalization index, 204
hominoid classification and, 265–266
male-provisioning scenario and, 281, 282
material culture and, 266
mosaic evolution and, 264, 265
paleoecological settings and, 272
radiator theory and, 282–283
reconstruction/interpretation of, 263–264,
279–283
scavenging strategy and, 268–269
seed-eating hypothesis and, 280–282
stable carbon isotope analysis and, 269
stone tools/lithic technology and, 277–278
toolmaking, 265
See also Hominin origins; Hominins;
Paleoanthropology
Hominin origins, 284, 287–316
adaptive patterns of, 313–315
australopiths and, 293, 296, 297–303, 316
big picture of, 313–315
bipedal adaptation and, 288–293, 296, 303
bipedal adaptation, brain cooling and, 282
body weights and stature and, 297
contemporaneous lineages, coexistence of,
304–307
cranial capacity and, 302
dating methods and, 272–276
dispersal out of Africa, 319–320, 422–423
early Homo and, 310–311, 314, 316,
320–321
evolutionary groups and, 293
hominin characteristics, compared with
hominoid and modern *Homo*, 265
hominoids, extant, evolution of, 258–260
interpretations of, 311–313
later, more derived australopiths and,
304–307

locations of fossil sites, 295, 298, 310, 312
Pleistocene subdivisions and, 359
pre-australopiths and, 293–297, 316
tentative hominin phylogeny and, 314
timeline of, 309
See also Australopiths; Hominin behavior/
ecology; Hominins; *Homo erectus*;
Pre-australopiths
Hominins, 3–4, 264–266
bipedal locomotion and, 21, 279–283, 284,
288–293, 316
bipedalism, behavioral stimuli for, 292
body weight/stature table, 297
brain and, 265, 375
characteristics, compared with hominoid
and modern *Homo*, 265
classification of, 265–266
culture, predisposition for, 10
definition of, 264–266
dentition and, 265
evolution of, 293–309
foramen magnum repositioning and,
290, 294
habitual bipedalism and, 292
locomotion and, 265
naming/terminology of, 265–266, 316, 350
obligate bipedalism and, 292
pelvic/hip modifications and, 288, 289,
290–291
phylogeny of, 314
pre-australopiths and, 293–297
tool use and, 4, 265
toolmaking and, 265
See also Hominin behavior/ecology;
Hominin origins; Prehominins;
Premodern humans
Hominoidea, 166, 253
Hominoids, 166–174
characteristics of, 166–167, 265
classification of, 265–266
extant hominoids, evolution of, 258–260
first true apes and, 253–257
See also Anthropoids; Apes; Modern
humans
Homo, 30, 269, 310–311
first dispersal of, 319–345
phylogeny of, 377
See also Early *Homo*; Hominin origins
Homo erectus, 311, 319–345
Acheulian tool industry and, 330, 340, 341,
345, 379
in Africa, 325–327, 336–337, 345
African emigration, first dispersal and,
319–320, 328–330, 341, 345, 387
African origin of, 387
Asian *Homo erectus* and, 329, 331–337,
338, 340, 345
Asian *Homo erectus*, compared to African,
336–337
body size of, 321, 345
brain growth and, 327
brain size of, 321, 341, 344, 375
characteristics of, 321–325, 345
Chinese *Homo erectus* and, 331–336
cranial capacity of, 321, 325
cranial shape of, 324–325

Dragon Bone Hill/Zhoukoudian cave and,
323, 324, 331–337, 338
European *Homo erectus* and, 338–339,
340, 345
fire, control/use of, 334
fossil sites for, 311, 322–323
geographic range of, 325–340
Homo floresiensis and, 342–344, 345
Homo naledi and, 327–328
hunting, debate about, 336–337
Indonesian/Javan *Homo erectus* and, 325,
330–331, 332, 338
interpretations of, 341–342
key discoveries of, 327
modern humans and, 387
Nariokotome boy and, 326, 327
Oldowan tool industry and, 340
pelvis of, 326–327
phylogeny of, 314
premodern humans and, 250
technological trends and, 340–341
time line for discoveries of, 339
tool construction/use and, 330
Trinil skullcap and, 323, 331
variation in, 324
See also Early *Homo*; Neandertals;
Premodern humans
Homo ergaster, 320, 341
Homo floresiensis, 342–344, 345
Homo habilis, 310, 314
Homo heidelbergensis, 350, 359, 374–375, 379
in Africa, 351–352, 357, 384
in Asia, 356, 357
in Europe, 352–353, 357
Homo naledi, 327–328
Homo neanderthalensis, 386
Homo sapiens, 5, 30, 173–174, 384
archaic *Homo sapiens* and, 350, 376
characteristics of, 173–174
classification of, 385
earliest finds, in Africa, 409
early, dispersal of, 383–409
first populations, appearance in Africa,
384
morphology and variation in, 391
Neandertals, coexistence/interbreeding
with, 363–364, 373–374, 377, 380,
387–388, 409
time line of modern discoveries, 393
See also Anthropoids; Modern human
origins/dispersal; Modern humans;
Upper Paleolithic
Homo sapiens idaltu, 392, 394
Homo sapiens sapiens, 392, 394, 400
Homodont dentition, 135
Homologies, 116–117, 120, 139, 145, 233
Homoplasy, 117, 122, 166, 233
Homozygous individuals, 85
Honing complex, 294
Hormones, 55, 475–477
in adolescence/puberty, 482
endocrine glands and, 475–476
stress response and, 476–477
Hot climates, 14, 444–449
Allen's rule and, 446–447
Bergmann's rule and, 446

Hot climates (*Continued*)
  body size/proportion and, 445–448
  evaporative cooling and, 445
  human adaptations to, 444–449
  most suitable body shape, 447, 448
  sweating response and, 445
  vasodilation and, 445
  See also Cold climates; Human adaptation
Hox genes, 60–61, 116, 119
  mutations in, 119
  numbers of, in vertebrates vs. invertebrates, 119
Hubble Space Telescope, 7, 133
Human adaptation, 5, 436–464
  acclimatization and, 438–439
  Allen's rule and, 446–447
  Bergmann's rule and, 446
  biocultural forces in, 464
  body size/proportion and, 445–448
  cold, responses to, 448–449
  culture and, 451–458, 464
  dental formula and, 154
  developmental acclimatization and, 439
  dietary practices and, 438
  endemic disease and, 452
  environmental factors and, 14
  evaporative cooling and, 445
  folate degradation, neural tube defects/
    spina bifida and, 441, 463–464
  glucose processing and, 451
  heat, responses to, 445–448
  high-altitude settlements and, 449–451
  homeostasis and, 438
  hypoxia and, 449
  infectious disease and, 451–458, 464
  long-term adaptations and, 438, 448–449
  maladaptive characteristics for life
    course, 472
  metabolic rate and, 448
  molecular anthropology and, 15
  single nucleotide polymorphisms and, 438
  skeletal biology and, 458–463
  skeletal evidence, disease/trauma/lifestyle
    and, 458–463
  skin cancer, UV radiation and, 440, 441
  skin color, solar radiation and, 439–444, 463
  stress on physiological mechanisms and, 438
  temporary/rapid adjustments and,
    438–439
  thermal environment and, 444–449
  UV radiation, pigmented skin and, 438,
    438–444
  vasoconstriction and, 448
  vasodilation and, 445
  vitamin D hypothesis and, 442–444
  zoonotic diseases and, 452, 455–456
Human behavior, 5, 220
  archaeological excavations and, 12
  brain and body size and, 204–206
  culture, learned behaviors and, 6
  genetic influences and, 186
  language acquisition/use and, 174,
    206–208, 212
  primate behavior models of, 203–206, 223
  See also Anthropology; Human
    adaptation; Modern humans

Human connections, 2, 6, 8–9, 23
Human disconnection, 487
  accelerated disease emergence, human
    activity and, 502–503
  air pollution and, 503, 504
  Arctic sea ice, loss of, 496–497
  biodiversity, impact on, 500–502
  climate change and, 492, 494–500, 506
  climate crisis, international policy
    initiatives on, 499–500
  deforestation and, 493–494
  drought and, 498
  ecological footprints and, 504–505
  environmental degradation and, 493–494
  evolutionary processes, acceleration of,
    502–503
  extinctions and, 500–501
  flood events and, 494
  fossil site locations, 390
  habitat loss and, 501
  human-created problems, solutions for,
    503–505, 506
  morphology and variation, 391
  natural resources, destruction of, 493–494
  planet/life forms, impact on, 492–503
  population growth and, 492–493, 503, 506
  sea ice maximum/minimum data and, 497
  severe weather events and, 498
  soil erosion and, 494
  solutions, looking for, 503–505, 506
  weather patterns, severe fluctuations in,
    496, 498
  See also Climate change; Endangered
    species; Environmental degradation
Human evolution, 5
  anthropoid characteristics and, 160–161
  biocultural evolution and, 431–434
  biological continuum and, 6, 43, 221–222
  breeding isolates and, 425
  culture, predisposition for, 10
  fossil apes, cladogram of, 259
  genetic drift and, 108, 124
  geological time scale and, 130–134
  language, development of, 11–12, 174,
    206–208, 212
  last common ancestor and, 26
  lineage divergence from chimpanzee, 155
  mammalian evolution and, 134–136
  molecular anthropology and, 15
  primate heritage and, 173–174
  religious perspective on, 27–28, 43, 47
  vertebrate evolution and, 130–138
  See also Biocultural evolution; *Homo
    erectus*; Human variation; Modern
    evolutionary theory; Modern humans
Human genome, 43, 58
Human Genome Project, 58, 75, 421
Human growth/development, 469–474
  adolescent growth spurt and, 482
  agriculture, epidemiological transition
    and, 472
  brain growth and, 479–480, 481
  contemporary diet, deficiencies in,
    472–473
  diet and, 470–472
  epigenetics and, 475–477, 488

epigenome and, 475
  essential amino acids and, 470
  evolutionary perspective on, 477
  food insecurity, 474
  genetic factors in, 475–477
  hormones, action of, 475–477
  life cycle stages and, 478
  life expectancy, declines in, 486–487
  lifestyle factors in, 473, 486
  malnutrition and, 473–474
  microbiome and, 470
  mismatched diets/dietary needs and,
    482, 488
  nature-nurture debate and, 475
  nutrition, effects of, 469–474
  obesity/overnutrition and, 474, 475
  preagricultural diet and, 470, 471, 473
  pregnancy, 478–479
  pregnancy, diet during, 470, 479
  puberty and, 478
  stress response, cortisol elevation and,
    476–477
  undernutrition and, 473–474
  See also Life history theory; Modern
    humans
Human life course. *See* Life course
Human variation, 13, 23, 410–435
  adaptive significance of, 13–14, 438–451
  allele frequencies and, 426–427
  ancient migration patterns, DNA evidence
    for, 422–423
  biocultural evolution and, 431–434, 435
  biological determinism and, 413–414
  contemporary interpretations of, 418–425
  DNA-level polymorphisms and, 419–421
  environmental stressors and, 14, 438
  eugenics and, 413
  evolution in modern human populations,
    430–431
  genetic ancestry data and, 422–424
  genetic polymorphisms and, 421–425
  genetic variation and, 13–14, 61
  genomic studies and, 76
  geographically patterned variation and,
    416–417
  historical views of, 412–413
  lactase persistence and, 432–433
  phenotypic variation, 416–417, 418–419,
    435
  physical variation and, 13–14
  point mutation and, 64
  polygenic characteristics and, 417, 418
  polymorphisms and, 419–425
  polytypic species and, 413
  population genetics and, 422–424,
    425–431, 435
  race, concept of, 413–418
  racial purity ideology and, 414–415
  single nucleotide polymorphisms and, 421,
    438
  skin color and, 412–413
  skin color, ranking by, 415
  whole-genome analysis and, 422–423
  See also Human evolution; Modern
    evolutionary theory; Modern humans;
    Population genetics; Variation

Humans, 173–174
  apes, differences from, 166–167
  characteristics of, 139, 160–161, 173–174
  chimpanzees, closeness to, 155–157, 265
  chromosome number and, 65
  impacts on planet and life-forms, 492–503
  as mammals, 134–136
  mating patterns and, 101
  Mendelian inheritance in, 87–94
  place in natural world, 114–117
  as primates, 173–174
  as vertebrates, 130–134, 139
  as "world's greatest evolutionary force," 500
  See also Homo sapiens
Hunter/gatherers, 368–369, 422
Hunting:
  bow and arrow hunting, 407
  butchering practice and, 341
  Homo erectus, debate about, 336–337
  premodern humans and, 358
  species extinctions and, 501
Huntington disease, 88
Hurricane Sandy, 498
Hussein, Sadam, 17
Hybrids, 83, 84, 125
Hylobates, 258
Hypotheses, 19–21, 23
Hypothesis testing, 20–21, 23, 43
Hypoxia, 449

Ice Man, 386
Ichthyosaurus fossil, 33
Inbreeding, 430–431
Incest avoidance behavior, 431
Incest taboos, 430
Independent assortment principle, 86–87
Indonesia:
  Homo erectus, 325, 330–331
  Homo floresiensis, 342–344, 345
  rock art, 406–407
Infancy (human), 480–481
Infanticide, 20–21, 200–201
Infectious disease, 10, 451–458, 464
  accelerated disease emergence, human activity and, 502–503
  antibiotic resistance and, 10, 457
  domesticated animals/plants, contact with, 10
  endemic diseases and, 452
  HIV/AIDS and, 453–454, 455–456
  human adaptation and, 451–454
  influenza and, 10, 456–457
  malaria and, 106–107, 431–432, 452–453, 464
  microorganisms, altered genetic makeup of, 10
  paleopathology and, 16
  pathogens and, 451–452
  resistance, development of, 41
  smallpox and, 454
  swine flu and, 10, 456–457
  syphilis and, 458, 459
  treatment-resistant microorganisms and, 41
  tuberculosis, 41, 442–443, 452

  vectors of, 10, 451–452, 457, 498
  zoonotic diseases and, 452, 455–456
  See also Disease
Influenza, 10, 456–457
Inheritance. *See* Genetics; Heredity; Mendelian inheritance; Mendelian inheritance in humans; Non-Mendelian inheritance
Insects:
  in amber, 128, 129
  molecular body plan, 118
Intelligence, 174, 182, 469
Intelligent design (ID) argument, 44–45
Interglacials, 348, 359
International Human Genome Sequencing Consortium, 75
Interspecific variation, 127
Intraspecific variation, 127
Introns, 58
Iraqi Neandertals, 366
Island hopping, 235, 243, 244
Isolation. *See* Geographical isolation; Reproductive isolation
Israel:
  modern humans fossils and, 392–393
  Neandertals and, 365

Java:
  Homo erectus and, 331, 332, 338
  Homo floresiensis and, 342–344, 345
Jebel Qafzeh site, 390, 393
Jet stream, 496
Jinniushan site, 355, 356–357
Johanson, Don, 300
Jolly, Clifford, 280, 282

Kabwe site, 351, 352, 354
Kanapoi site, 295
Kanzi, 209
Karyotyping chromosomes, 66–67
Katanda region, 404
Keeley, Lawrence, 278
Khoratpithecus, 253, 260, 261
Kimeu, Kamoya, 325–326
Kin selection hypothesis, 220
Klasies River Mouth site, 389, 390, 393
Knappers, 277, 401
Knowles, Charles, 476
Knuckle walking, 154, 155, 172
Koko, 208
Koobi Fora site, 295, 305
Kow Swamp site, 393, 395, 396
Krapina site, 362, 363, 364
K-selected species, 198, 282
Ku Klux Klan, 415

La Chapelle site, 360, 361, 362, 363, 367, 370
La Ferrassie site, 361, 362
Lactase, 55
Lactase persistence, 432–433, 435
Lactose intolerance, 432–433, 438
Laetoli site, 3–4, 295, 298–300
Lagar Velho site, 393, 399
Lake Mungo site, 393, 395, 396
Lake Turkana. *See* East Lake Turkana; West Lake Turkana

Lamarck, Jean-Baptiste, 30–31, 34
Language, 11, 195, 206–211, 370–371
  brain and, 209–211
  chimpanzees, apes and, 208–209, 266
  evolution of, 209–211, 212, 370–371
  genes (*FOXP2*), 211, 369
  human predisposition for, 11, 174, 207–208, 266
  hyoid bone and, 371
  Neandertals, speech/symbolic behavior and, 369–370
  primate communication and, 206–211
  speech production and, 369–370, 371
  symbolic language, 207–208, 209
  See also Linguistic anthropology
Langur species, 200
Lantian County sites, 323, 335
Larsen, Clark, 472
Lascaux Cave site, 403–405
Last common ancestor (LCA), 26, 227, 228
Late Pleistocene, 348, 359
  premodern humans of, 358–367
  tool industries of, 359
  See also Neandertals; Premodern humans
Laurasia, 131, 132
Leakey, Louis, 310
Leakey, Richard, 325
Learning:
  culture and, 6, 212
  primate dependence on, 147–148, 221
Lee-Thorp, Julia, 269
Lemurs, 144, 157–158, 202
  adaptive level of, 159
  aye-ayes and, 137, 175
  behavioral patterns of, 158
  evolution of, 234–236, 238
  fossil primates and, 223–224, 238
  geographical distribution of, 158
  locomotion of, 158
  olfaction, reliance on, 157
  rhinarium of, 157
  See also Fossil primates; Primate adaptations; Primates
Lewontin, Richard, 424
Liang Bua Cave site, 343
Life course, 466–489
  biocultural evolution and, 469
  diet and nutrition through, 469–474, 488
  diet, lifestyle, and consequences, 473
  evolution, continuation of, 487, 488
  evolved biology and contemporary lifestyles, mismatch, 467–469, 487
  growth and development, factors influencing, 469–477
  human adaptation and maladaptive characteristics, 472
  life history theory and, 477–483
  maladaptive characteristics and, 472
  See also Diet; Life history theory
Life history theory, 477–483
  adolescence and, 482
  aging/longevity and, 483–487, 488
  birth and, 480
  child care and, 480–481
  childhood stage and, 480–481

Life history theory (*Continued*)
  dependency of infants and children and, 480–481
  diseases of civilization and, 484
  epigenetic mechanisms and, 488
  free-radicals, oxidation and, 485
  grandmother hypothesis and, 483
  HIV/AIDS, impact of, 486
  infancy and, 480–481
  life cycle stages and, 478
  life spans/life expectancies and, 484, 486–487
  lifestyle factors, aging and, 486
  menarche and, 478, 482
  menopause and, 478, 482–483
  mismatched diets/dietary needs and, 482, 488
  mitochondrial theory of aging and, 485, 488
  nursing infants and, 480
  pregnancy and, 478–479
  puberty, onset of, 478, 482
  reproductive functioning, decline in, 482–483
  reproductive functioning, onset of, 481–482
  senescence and, 484–486
  telomere hypothesis and, 485–486, 488
  See also Human growth/development; Modern humans
Life history traits, 190–191, 223
Life on earth, time of beginning of, 50
Limb structures, 116–117, 146
Linguistic anthropology, 11–12
  language acquisition/use, study of, 11–12
Linnaeus, Carolus, 29–30
Linnean classification, 29–30, 115, 127, 412
Lithic assemblage, 277
Lithic tool industry, 277–278
Locomotion:
  bipedal adaptation, skeletal and muscle modifications and, 288–293
  bipedal locomotion and, 4, 21, 174, 265, 279–283, 284, 316
  bipedal locomotion, mechanics of, 288–293
  brachiation and, 154, 172
  brain-cooling/radiator theory and, 282–283
  habitual bipedalism and, 4, 173, 292, 316
  knuckle walking and, 154, 155, 172
  male-provisioning scenario and, 281, 282
  obligate bipedalism and, 292, 316
  prehensile tails and, 154
  primate locomotion and, 146, 151–154
  quadrupedal locomotion, 21, 151
  seed-eating hypothesis and, 280–282
  soft tissue anatomy and, 18
  vertical clinging/leaping and, 151
Locus, 66
Lomorupithecus, 251
Lorises, 157, 158–159
  adaptive level of, 159
  evolution of, 234–236
  locomotion of, 158–159
  rhinarium of, 157

  See also Fossil primates; Primate adaptations; Primates
Lovejoy, Owen, 280, 282
Lowland gorillas, 169, 170–171
  See also Gorillas; Mountain gorillas
Lucy skeleton, 295, 300, 302
Lufengpithecus, 254, 257
Lumpers, 127, 376
Lyell, Charles, 32–33, 413

Maasai cattle herders, 15
Macaque species, 165, 211, 212, 246, 478
Macroevolution, 5, 99, 113–140, 138, 139
  adaptive radiation and, 136–137
  cladistics and, 117–123
  classification, need for, 114–116, 117
  conserved genes and, 118–119
  continental drift/plate tectonics and, 131, 132
  evo-devo approach and, 43, 118–119
  evolutionary systematics and, 117–120, 124
  fossil record, interpretation of, 126–128, 139
  generalized characteristics and, 137–138
  genetic tool kit and, 118–119
  geological time scale and, 130, 131
  hox genes and, 119
  microevolution, working with, 138
  principles of classification, 116–117
  processes of, 136–138
  rate/pace of change and, 138, 139
  specialized characteristics and, 137–138
  speciation process and, 124–125, 139
  species, definition of, 123–128
  See also Fossils; Mammalian evolution; Vertebrate evolution
Madagascar:
  aye-ayes and, 137, 175
  endangered primates and, 176
  lemurs and, 158
  primitive birds and, 122
  subfossil lemurs and, 235
  See also Africa
Magdalenian tool industry, 359, 400, 401–402
Malapa Cave site, 295, 308, 309, 310
Malaria, 106–107, 431–432, 452–453, 464
  chloroquine-resistant, 457
  DDT spraying and, 431, 432
  geographical distribution of, 106, 107
  human adaptation, allele frequencies and, 452–453, 464
  plasmodial parasites and, 106, 107
  sickle-cell trait, correlation between, 106–107
  slash-and-burn agriculture and, 431
  See also Infectious disease
Male-provisioning scenario, 281, 282
Malnutrition, 473–474
Malthus, Thomas, 32, 37
Mammalian evolution, 134–136, 226
  adaptive radiation and, 136–137
  Age of Mammals and, 134, 226
  brain development and, 134–135
  brain size/complexity and, 134, 205
  dependency, period of, 136, 199

  diversification and, 231
  DNA of living mammalian species, 134
  endothermic capability and, 136
  fossil evidence and, 134
  generalized characteristics and, 137, 144–145
  heterodont dentition and, 135
  internal fertilization and development, 135
  learning, capacity for, 147–148
  marsupial mammals and, 135, 136
  neocortex and, 134, 147, 205
  number of species, today, 134
  placental mammals and, 135, 136
  slower development and, 135
  specialized characteristics and, 137–138
  warmbloodedness and, 135–136
  See also Fossil primates; Fossils; Macroevolution; Speciation; Species; Vertebrate evolution
Marfan syndrome, 88
Marmosets, 163
Marsupial mammals, 135, 136
Material culture, 266
Matrilines, 189
Mauer site, 354
Mayr, Ernst, 30
MC1R gene, 443
Measurement:
  of polygenic traits, 96
  quantitative, 20
Medical anthropology, 20
Megaladapis, 235–236
Meiosis, 67, 69–72
  compared to mitosis, 71
  evolutionary significance of, 71
  genetic recombination and, 105
  independent assortment and, 86–87
  nondisjunction and, 71–72, 73
  principle of segregation and, 85
  problems with, 71–72
  trisomy and, 72, 73
Melanin, 95, 440–441, 442
Menarche, 478, 482
Mendel, Gregor, 42, 82, 83, 109
Mendelian inheritance, 83–87, 109
  discontinuous traits and, 94
  discrete traits and, 84, 87, 94
  dominance and, 83, 85–86
  F-1 generation and, 84, 87
  F-2 generation and, 84, 87
  genotypes and, 85, 86, 87
  heterozygous individuals and, 85
  homozygous individuals and, 85
  hybrids and, 83, 84
  independent assortment principle and, 86–87
  parent generation and, 84
  phenotypes and, 85–86, 87, 110
  polydactyly and, 81–82
  polygenic inheritance and, 94
  random assortment and, 86–87
  recessiveness and, 83, 85–86, 89
  segregation principle and, 84–85, 93
  See also Heredity; Mendelian inheritance in humans

Mendelian inheritance in humans, 87–94
    autosomal dominant traits and, 90–91
    autosomal recessive traits and, 91–93
    carriers and, 89, 93
    codominance and, 89
    dominance/recessiveness, misconceptions
        about, 89–90
    genetic disorders and, 88–89
    modes of, 90
    patterns of, 90–97
    See also Mendelian traits in humans;
        Non-Mendelian inheritance
Mendelian traits, 87, 96, 97, 110
    vs. polygenic traits, 96
Mendelian traits in humans, 87–94
    diseases/syndromes and, 88
    patterns of Mendelian inheritance, 90–97
    pedigree charts and, 90, 91, 92, 94
    segregation principle and, 93
    sex-linked traits and, 93–94
    See also Heredity; Mendelian inheritance;
        Non-Mendelian inheritance
Menopause, 478, 482–483
Mesozoic era, 130, 131–133
    continental drift and, 131, 132
    land vertebrates and, 131–133
    mammalian radiation and, 136–137
    primate evolution and, 226–229
    reptiles in, 131
Messenger RNA (mRNA), 55–56, 57, 78
Metabolism, 188, 448
Microbiome, 470, 486
Microevolution, 5, 26, 99
    allele frequencies and, 426–428
    gene flow, modern human populations
        and, 101
    genetic drift and, 104, 124
    macroevolution, working with, 138
Microliths, 277–278, 405–406
Microwear, 278
Middle Awash area, 269, 294, 295, 297,
    298, 299
Middle Pleistocene, 348, 359, 376, 379
    Acheulian tool industry and, 357, 359, 379
    African premodern humans and, 351–352
    culture of, 357–358, 359
    Dali skull and, 353, 355, 356
    dispersal of premodern humans, 349–350
    European premodern humans and,
        352–353
    evolutionary trajectory in, 356–357
    fire, deliberate control/use of, 357–358
    Homo heidelbergensis and, 350, 351–353,
        357, 359, 379
    Javanese Homo erectus and, 331
    main fossil sites, 354–355
    premodern humans of, 351–357
    terminology for hominins in, 350
    time line of hominin evolution in, 357
    See also Late Pleistocene; Neandertals;
        Premodern humans
Migration of genes. See Gene flow
Migrations, 100–101
    DNA evidence of ancient migrations,
        422–423
    island hopping and, 235, 243, 244

Neandertal-Homo sapiens interbreeding
        and, 364, 373–374
    rafting and, 243–245
    See also Homo erectus; Modern human
        origins/dispersal; Premodern humans
Mineralization process, 128, 129
Miocene primates, 227, 245–257
Mitochondria, 50, 51, 97
Mitochondrial DNA (mtDNA), 50–51, 97,
    366, 386–387, 485
    mitochondrial DNA clock, 409
Mitochondrial inheritance, 97
Mitochondrial theory of aging, 485, 488
Mitosis, 67–69, 71
Mladeč site, 393, 397, 398, 399
Modern evolutionary theory, 98–99, 110
    allele frequency in populations and, 99,
        100, 108
    evo-devo approach and, 43, 118–119
    evolution, current definition of, 99
    founder effect and, 102–105
    gene flow and, 93, 100–102
    gene pools and, 99
    genetic bottlenecks and, 103–104
    genetic drift and, 93, 102–105, 108
    genetic-environmental interaction and, 98
    Modern Synthesis and, 98–99, 138
    multiregional evolution and, 385
    mutation and, 100, 110
    natural selection and, 99, 105, 110
    natural selection, directional nature of,
        105–107
    organizational levels in evolutionary
        process and, 93, 105
    recombination and, 105
    sickle-cell trait, malaria resistance and,
        106–107
    tandem repeats and, 100
    See also Evolutionary theory; Human
        variation
Modern human origins/dispersal, 383–409
    African modern humans, 389–392, 394,
        409
    approaches to understanding, 385–389,
        409
    Asian early modern humans, 394–396
    Australian early modern humans, 395,
        396
    Central European early modern humans,
        396–397
    complete replacement model and,
        386–387, 409
    Cro-Magnon site and, 393, 397–400
    Denisovans and, 372–373, 388
    diversity in African populations, 386
    DNA analysis and, 386–387
    earliest discoveries of modern humans,
        389–400
    genetic bottleneck and, 104, 408
    genetic relationships with Denisovans and
        Neandertals, 388, 397
    Homo erectus, African origin and, 387
    Homo erectus and contemporaries, 319–345
    hunting and, 402, 407
    interbreeding and, 386, 387–389, 409
    interbreeding, assimilation model and, 388

mitochondrial DNA and, 386–387
    Neandertal DNA and, 386–387, 397
    Neandertal-human interbreeding and,
        364, 373–374, 380, 388–389, 409
    Near Eastern early modern humans and,
        392–393, 394
    out of Africa, 387, 422–423
    partial replacement models and, 387–389,
        409
    radiometric dating and, 392
    regional continuity model: multiregional
        evolution, 385, 387, 409
    replacement models, 385–389, 409
    scenarios for, 387
    technology and art, 400–408
    time line of discoveries, 393
    Western European early modern humans,
        397–400
    See also Homo sapiens; Modern humans;
        Premodern humans; Upper Paleolithic
Modern humans, 383–409
    biocultural evolution and, 431–434, 435
    biological continuum and, 6
    brain/body size, index of encephalization
        and, 204–206
    brain size/complexity and, 265, 375
    culture and, 6, 7
    habitual bipedal locomotion and, 174,
        265, 288
    intelligence and, 174
    language acquisition/use and, 174,
        207–208
    Neandertal genes, human-Neandertal
        interbreeding and, 364, 373–374, 380,
        387–389, 409
    pelvis of, 288, 289
    See also Anthropoids; Biocultural
        evolution; Homo sapiens; Human
        evolution; Human growth/
        development; Life history theory;
        Mendelian inheritance in humans;
        Modern human origins/dispersal;
        Premodern humans
Modern Synthesis, 98–99, 138
Molecular anthropology, 15, 228
Molecular clock, 228
Molecules, 50
    See also Biology; Cells
Monkeys, 26, 160–166
    characteristics of, 160–161
    diet of, 164, 188–189
    encephalization index and, 204
    endangered species of, 174–175
    locomotion of, 154, 163, 164, 165
    tool use by, 215
    vocalizations of, 207
    See also Anthropoids; Fossil primates;
        New World monkeys; Old World
        monkeys; Primates
Monophyletic groups, 120, 265
Moon, footprints on, 4, 5
Morphological adaptations, 288
Morphology, 146
Mosaic evolution, 264, 265
Mosquitos. See Malaria
Mothers, 201–203

Mountain gorillas, 170–171
 silverback males and, 170, 171, 177
 See also Gorillas; Lowland gorillas
Mousterian tool industry, 359, 367–368, 380
Movement. *See* Locomotion
Muller, Richard, 495–496
Multidisciplinary approach, 267
Multiregional evolution, 385, 409
Mutation, 56, 62–64, 71, 100, 105
 evolution and, 93, 98, 108, 110
 Hox genes and, 119
 passed from one generation to the next,
  100, 108
 peppered moth and, 40
 point mutation, 64
 tandem repeats and, 100
 variation, production/redistribution
  of, 100

Nakalipithecus, 254, 258, 259, 261
Nariokotome boy, 326, 327
Nariokotome site, 322, 326, 327
Natal groups, 170
Natural selection, 27, 33–42, 93, 98, 105–107
 in action, 39–41
 basic principles of, 39–42
 basic processes of, 39
 Beagle voyage and, 34, 35
 of behavior, 186–187
 biological variation within species and, 37
 differential net reproductive success
  and, 42
 directional nature of, 105–107
 discovery/development of, 33–38
 disease-causing microorganisms, resistant
  strains of, 41
 environment-organism relationship and,
  43, 118–119
 examples of, 39–41
 favorable variations, preservation of,
  39, 47
 fertility and, 41–42
 fitness criterion and, 39, 41
 fixity of species and, 27, 30
 Galápagos finches and, 34–36, 39, 40–41
 heritable traits and, 39, 41
 individual organisms and, 39, 45
 mechanisms of, 45
 peppered moth example and, 39–41
 point mutation and, 64
 populations, evolution of, 39
 religion, anti-scientific position and, 28,
  34, 43, 47
 reproductive success and, 39, 41–42, 45,
  124–125, 484
 role in evolution, 98, 99, 108–109, 110
 selective agents and, 40, 45, 199
 selective pressures and, 39, 40
 sickle-cell anemia and, 105–107, 110
 speciation process and, 36–38, 45,
  124–125
 variation and, 42, 99
 See also Evolutionary theory
Nature-nurture debate and, 475
Nazis, 413, 414–415
Neander Valley, 362

Neandertals, 347–348, 358–367, 392
 Asian fossil finds and, 366
 burial practices of, 370–372, 406, 407
 Central European Neandertals, 363–364
 characteristics of, 360
 Chatelperronian tool industry and, 364
 classification of, 359, 386
 coexistence with *Homo sapiens*, 363–364,
  369–370
 cranial shape/size and, 360, 362
 culture of, 367–372
 Denisovans, contemporary existence of,
  366–367, 372–373, 377
 DNA, 15, 366, 372, 373–375, 386–387, 397
 European fossil finds and, 359, 360–363
 flexed position burial and, 360, 372
 fossil locations, 361–362
 genetic evidence, molecular connections
  and, 372–375
 genome sequencing and, 75, 387
 Homo heidelbergensis and, 353, 357,
  374–375, 379–380
 Homo sapiens, coexistence/ interbreeding
  with, 363–364, 373–374, 377, 380,
  387–389, 409
 hunter-gatherer behavior and, 368–369
 hyoid bone and, 371
 language, evolution of, 370–371
 modern Europeans/Asians, genetic
  inheritance of, 397
 modern humans and, DNA, 366
 morphology and variation in, 361
 Mousterian tool industry and, 359,
  367–368, 380
 occipital bun and, 361, 362
 speech and symbolic behavior, 369–370
 subsistence strategies and, 368–369
 symbolic behavior and, 369–370, 380
 technology and, 368
 time line for fossil discoveries, 365
 Western Asian Neandertals, 365–366
 Western European Neandertals, 360, 361
 See also Late Pleistocene; Middle
  Pleistocene; Modern human origins/
  dispersal; Modern humans; Premodern
  humans; Upper Paleolithic
Neocortex, 134, 147, 204, 205
Neural tube defects, 441
New World monkeys, 161–164
 arboreal adaptations and, 163
 behavioral patterns of, 163
 cladogram of extant, 243
 diet of, 164
 endangered status and, 176
 fossil primates and, 242–245, 261
 geographical distribution of, 152, 161
 locomotion of, 163
 nose of, 163
 Old World monkeys, differences from,
  163, 247
 Old World monkeys, homoplasy and, 166
 platyrrhine characteristic of, 163
 prehensile tails and, 154
 rafting and, 243–245
 See also Anthropoids; Monkeys; Old
  World monkeys; Primates

Ngandong site, 323, 324, 331, 338
Niah Cave site, 393, 394–396, 400
Nocturnal habit, 146
Non-Mendelian inheritance, 94–97
 continuous variation and, 94
 genetic-environmental factors, interaction
  of, 98
 mitochondrial inheritance and, 97
 pleiotropy and, 97
 polygenic inheritance and, 94–97
 skin/hair/eye color and, 94–96
 See also Heredity; Mendelian inheritance;
  Mendelian inheritance in humans
Noncoding DNA, 58, 59, 61, 77
Nondisjunction, 71–72, 73
Nonrandom mating, 430–431
Nsungwepithecus, 245
Nucleotides, 52
Nucleus, 50, 51
Nutrition, life course and, 469–474
Nutritional anthropologists, 14, 15
Nye, Bill, 45–46

Oakley, Kenneth, 273–274
Oase Cave site, 393, 397, 398
Obesity, 474, 475
Obligate bipedalism, 292, 303, 316
Ocean acidification, 498–499
Old World monkeys, 161, 164–166
 apes, compared, 252
 catarrhine characteristic of, 163, 245
 cercopithecines and, 164, 246
 colobines and, 164, 165, 246
 fossil primates and, 245–246, 261
 geographical distribution of, 153, 164
 locomotion of, 164, 165
 New World monkeys, differences from,
  163, 247
 New World monkeys, homoplasy and, 166
 nose of, 163
 sexual dimorphism and, 165, 166
 See also Monkeys; New World monkeys;
  Primates
Oldowan tool industry, 277, 340, 359
Olduvai Gorge site, 270, 273, 295, 305, 310,
  312
 bone accumulations, analysis of, 268
 Homo erectus and, 322, 326, 327
 Homo habilis and, 310
 Zinjanthropus cranium and, 274, 275
Olfaction, 146, 147, 157
Oligocene euprimates, 227
Oligocene primates, 240–245
Omnivorous diet, 146, 149, 150–151, 182
Omo Kibish site, 295, 389, 390, 393, 394
Omomyoids, 236–237
On the Origin of Species, 12, 36, 38, 43, 119
Opposable thumb/toe, 146
Orangutans, 168, 260, 478
 behavior of, 184
 cranial capacity of, 302
 diet of, 168
 endangered status of, 168, 178–179
 geographical distribution of, 167
 locomotion of, 168
 See also Apes; Primate behavior; Primates

Ordos site, 393, 394
Orrorin, 294, 309, 314
Orrorin tugenensis, 298, 309
Osteology, 16
Ouranopithecus, 253, 254, 255, 258, 259, 261

Paleoanthropology, 12–13, 263–284
  absolute dating and, 273
  artifacts and, 270
  biostratigraphic correlation and, 276
  bone, analysis of, 278–279
  carbon-14 dating method and, 274–275
  chronometric dating and, 273, 274, 275
  context/environmental settings and, 272
  dating methods and, 272–276, 284
  electron spin resonance dating method
    and, 275
  experimental archaeology and, 276–279,
    284
  faunal correlation and, 276
  fieldwork in, 267–272
  fieldwork, steps in, 313
  fluorine analysis and, 273–274
  half-life and, 274
  hominin behavior/ecology, reconstruction
    of, 263–264, 279–283
  hominoid classification and, 265–266
  knappers and, 277
  multidisciplinary approach of, 267
  paleomagnetism and, 276
  potassium-argon dating method and, 274
  primary contexts and, 272
  secondary contexts and, 272
  splitters vs. lumpers and, 127
  stable carbon isotope analysis and, 269,
    462–463
  stone tool/lithic technology and, 277–278
  stratigraphic dating and, 273
  subdisciplines of, 267, 284
  superposition principle and, 273
  taphonomy and, 130, 272, 278
  thermoluminescence dating method
    and, 275
  See also Archaeology; Geology; Physical
    anthropology
Paleolothic, 359
Paleolithic ("caveman") diet, 401, 488
Paleomagnetism, 276
Paleontology, 112–114
Paleopathology, 16
Paleoprimatologists, 236
Paleospecies, 127
Paleozoic era, 130–131, 136
  continental drift and, 131
  periods of, 131
Pan paniscus, 172, 259
Pan troglodytes, 171, 259
  See also Chimpanzees
Panamacebus, 242–243, 245, 250
Pangea, 131, 132
Paradigm shifts, 28–29
Paranthropus, 297, 304–306, 309
  arboreal habitats and, 314
  Black Skull find and, 304–306
  dentition of, 305
  in hominin phylogeny, 314

  morphological characteristics of, 304–306
  sagittal crest and, 304, 305
  sexual dimorphism and, 306
  See also Australopiths
Paranthropus aethiopicus, 306, 309
Paranthropus boisei, 306, 309
Paranthropus robustus, 306, 309
Parapithecus, 241
Partial replacement models, 387–389, 409
Parvorders, 241
Pathogens, 451–452
Pedigree charts, 90, 91, 92, 94
Peppered moths, 39–41
Perupithecus, 242, 250
Petralona site, 354
Phenotypes, 85–86, 87, 96, 98, 110
  phenotypic polymorphisms and, 421
  phenotypic variation and, 96, 416–417,
    418, 435
Phenylkentonuria (PKU), 88, 97
Phylogenetic trees, 123, 314
Phylogeny, 123
Phylum, 114, 115
Physical anthropology, 2, 5, 12–18, 23
  anatomy and, 18
  anthropological perspective and, 21–23
  applied anthropology and, 11, 18–19, 22
  bioarchaeology and, 16
  forensic anthropology and, 16–18, 22
  human variation, adaptive significance of,
    13–14
  human variation, explanation of, 417
  introduction to, 3–23
  language acquisition/use, study of, 11–12
  nutritional anthropology and, 14, 15
  osteology and, 16
  paleoanthropology and, 12–13
  paleopathology and, 16
  primate paleontology and, 13
  primatology and, 18, 19
  scientific method and, 19–21
  See also Anthropology; Biocultural
    evolution; Evolution; Human evolution
Phytoliths, 278
Pigment:
  art applications, 369
  melanin, 95, 440–441, 442
  See also Skin color
Pilobates, 224
Piltdown Man, 273–274
Pinnacle Point site, 404, 405
PKU (phenylkentonuria), 88, 97
Placental mammals, 135, 136
Plate tectonics, 131
Platyrrhines, 163, 241, 242–245
Pleiotropic genes, 484–485
Pleiotropy, 97
Pleistocene, 227, 331, 348–349
  correlation with archeological industries
    and hominins, 359
  glaciations and, 348
  interglacials and, 348, 359
  See also Late Pleistocene; Middle
    Pleistocene; Premodern humans
Plesiadapiforms, 229, 230
Plesiadapis, 230

Plesiosaurus, 33
Plio-Pleistocene hominins, 227, 304, 310–311
Pliobates, 251, 253
Pliopithecoidea, 251
Point mutation, 64
Polar ice, shrinking of, 496–497
Pollution. *See* Environmental degradation;
    Human disconnection
Polyandry, 190, 201
Polydactyly, 81–82
Polygenic inheritance, 94–97
  polygenic traits, vs. Mendelian traits, 96
Polygynous mating, 199
Polymerase chain reaction (PCR) technique, 72
Polymorphisms, 419–425
  balanced polymorphism and, 431–432
  DNA-level polymorphisms, 421–425
  single nucleotide polymorphisms and,
    421, 438
  See also Human variation
Polyphyletic groups, 120
Polytypic species, 413
Pongo, 168, 257, 260
Population genetics, 422–424, 425–431, 435
  allele frequencies and, 426–428
  allele frequencies, calculation of, 428–429
  breeding isolates and, 425
  endogamy and, 425
  exogamy and, 425
  gene pools and, 425
  Hardy-Weinberg theory of genetic
    equilibrium and, 425–426, 435
  inbreeding and, 430–431
  incest avoidance behavior and, 430–431
  modern human populations and, 430–431
  nonrandom mating and, 430–431
  See also Human variation; Populations;
    Reproduction
Population growth, human, 492–493, 503, 506
  family planning and, 504, 505
  female education and, 505
  slight slowing of, 505, 506
Populations, 99
  adaptive radiation process and, 136–137
  allele frequency in, 99, 100, 108, 124,
    426–427
  biological adaptations, environmental
    influences on, 13–14
  environmental stressors and, 14
  evolutionary processes and, 5, 124–125
  founder populations and, 102
  gene pools of, 99, 425
  human population growth, 492–493, 503
  human population movements, 101
  macroevolutionary processes and, 5
  Malthus on, 32
  microevolutionary processes and, 5
  molecular anthropology and, 15
  point mutation and, 64
  See also Human adaptation; Human
    variation; Migrations; Natural
    selection; Physical anthropology;
    Population genetics
Postcranial material, 230
Potassium-argon (K/Ar) dating method, 274
Pottery, 403

Potts, Richard, 266–267
Poverty, 476
Pre-australopiths, 293–297, 316
   Ardipithecus and, 294–297, 298, 314
   bipedal locomotion, 296
   foramen magnum repositioning and, 294
   honing complex and, 294
   key discoveries of, 298
   Orrorin and, 294, 298, 309, 314
   Sahelanthropus and, 293, 294, 295, 298,
     309, 314
   See also Australopiths; Hominin origins
Predation, social structure and, 189
Předmostí site, 403, 404
Pregnancy (in humans), 470, 478–479
Prehensile hands, 146
Prehensile tails, 154
Prehominins, 288
   See also Hominin origins; Hominins
Premodern humans, 347–380
   Acheulian tool industry and, 357, 359
   in Africa, 351–352
   in Asia, 353–356
   brain size of, 375
   classification/terminology for, 350, 376
   culture of, 357–358
   Denisovans and, 357, 372–373, 377
   dispersal of, 349–350
   diversity among, 376–378
   ecological niches, refugia and, 376
   in Europe, 352–353
   evolution in Middle Pleistocene and,
     356–357
   fire, deliberate control/use of, 357–358
   fossil site locations, 354–355, 356
   glaciations and, 348–349
   Homo erectus and, 379
   Homo heidelbergensis and, 350, 351–353,
     356, 357, 359, 374–375, 379, 384
   hunting capabilities and, 358
   interglacials and, 348–349
   Late Pleistocene and, 348–349, 358–367
   Middle Pleistocene and, 348–349,
     351–358, 379
   mitochondrial DNA from, 353
   Neandertals and, 347–348, 358–367
   Neanderthal DNA and, 373–375
   time line of hominin evolution, 357
   See also Homo erectus; Human evolution;
     Modern human origins/ dispersal;
     Modern humans; Neandertals
Pressure flaking method, 278
Primate adaptations, 148–154
   adaptive niches and, 149
   arboreal hypothesis and, 150
   arboreal living and, 149–150, 230, 314
   brachiation and, 154
   dentition and, 144, 146, 149, 150–151
   diet and teeth and, 150–151
   environmental circumstances and, 148–149
   evolutionary factors and, 149–150
   geographical distribution and habitats,
     150, 152–153
   locomotion and, 146, 151–154
   omnivorous diet and, 146, 149, 150–151,
     182

visual predation hypothesis and, 150
   See also Fossil primates; Primate behavior;
     Primates
Primate behavior, 18, 185–223
   activity patterns and, 191
   affiliative behavior and, 196–197, 223
   aggressive behaviors and, 196, 216–218
   altruism and, 219–220, 223
   autonomic responses and, 194
   behavioral ecology and, 186–187, 222–223
   behavioral genetics and, 187, 222
   brain and body size and, 204–206
   communication and, 194–196, 223
   conflict behaviors and, 216–218
   cultural behavior and, 6, 211–218, 222, 223
   displays and, 195–196
   dominance and, 192–194, 223
   empathy and, 219–220
   evolution of, 186–191, 212, 222
   eye contact and, 194
   facial expressions and, 195
   genetic influences and, 186, 222
   grooming behavior and, 194, 197, 223
   human activities, impact of, 191
   infanticide and, 20–21, 200–201
   kin selection hypothesis and, 220
   language and, 195, 206–211
   learned behaviors, dependence on,
     147–148, 212, 221
   life history traits and, 190–191, 223
   as models for human behavior, 203–206,
     223
   mother-infant bond, 201–203
   mothers, fathers, and infants, 201–203
   polygynous mating and, 199
   predation and, 189, 191–192
   prosocial behaviors and, 218–220
   reproductive behaviors and, 198–203
   reproductive strategies and, 198–199
   sexual dimorphism and, 199–200
   sexual selection and, 199
   sleeping sites, distribution/types of,
     181, 280
   social behavior and, 191–206
   social brain hypothesis and, 206
   social groups and, 190, 223
   social strategies and, 193
   social structure, factors in, 187–191
   strategies of behavior and, 191, 193
   territoriality and, 166, 216–218
   tool use and, 212–215, 222
   vocalizations and, 207
   young dependent primates, parental
     investment in, 199
   See also Primate adaptations; Primates;
     Social organization
Primate paleontology, 13
Primates, 5, 13, 143–182
   ancestral mammalian traits and, 145
   binocular vision and, 147
   biological continuum and, 221–222
   brain/body size, index of encephalization
     and, 204–206
   brain size/complexity and, 147, 210–211
   bushmeat trade and, 179–181
   characteristics of, 144–148

classification of, 155–157
color vision and, 146, 150
cranial anatomy of, 148–149
dental formula and, 151, 154
dentition of, 144, 146, 149, 150–151, 182
depth perception and, 147
digits, number of, 146
diurnal habit and, 146, 148
endangered, conservation efforts, 169
endangered primates and, 174–181, 182
evolution of, 225–261
fossils of, 13, 225–261
generalized traits of, 144–145, 182
gestation, length of, 144
Haplorhini, 155, 182, 226, 232
hominoids and, 166–174
humans and, 173–174
learning, dependence on, 147–148, 221
lemurs and lorises and, 157–159
life cycle stages and, 478
limb structure and, 146
locomotion of, 146, 151–154
maturation, learning, and behavior,
   147–148, 199
monkeys and, 160–166
morphology, generalized locomotor
   anatomy and, 146
nails vs. claws and, 146
neocortex of, 147, 204, 205
New World primates and, 152, 161–164
nocturnal habit and, 146
nonhuman, geographical distribution of
   living, 152–153, 158
nonhuman, number of species of, 144
nonhuman, survey of living, 157–166
Old World primates and, 153, 164–166
olfaction, decreased reliance on, 146, 147
omnivorous diet and, 146, 149, 150–151
opposable thumb/toe and, 146
prehensile hands/feet and, 146, 154
sensory modalities and, 146, 147
social grouping of, 148, 223
stereoscopic vision and, 147
Strepsirrhini and, 155, 157, 182, 226,
   232, 238
tactile pads and, 146
tarsiers and, 159–160
taxonomy and, 155, 156
vocalizations and language capabilities
   and, 206–211
   See also Anthropoids; Apes; Fossil
     primates; Modern humans; Monkeys;
     Primate adaptations; Primate behavior
Primatology, 18, 19, 187
Principle of independent assortment, 86–87
Principle of segregation, 84–85, 93
Principles of Geology, 32
Proboscis monkey, 165, 187
Proconsul, 250, 254
Proconsuloids, 248–251
Protein synthesis, 50, 54–56
   amino acids and, 55, 56
   codons, 56, 57
   hormones and, 55
   messenger RNA and, 55–56
   regulatory genes and, 60–61

ribosomes and, 55
transcription and, 55–56, 57
See also Biology; Proteins
Proteins, 50, 119
amino acids and, 55, 56
functions of, 55
hormones and, 55
See also Biology; Protein synthesis
PTC (phenylthiocarbamide) tasting, 420–421, 429
Punch blade technique, 402
Purgatorius, 230, 234
Pygmies, 422, 476

Qafzeh Cave site, 392–393, 394
Quadrupedal locomotion, 21, 151
Quantitative measurement, 20
Queen Victoria, 93, 94

R-selected species, 198–199
Race:
Aryan race myth and, 414
biological determinism and, 413
California ballot measure on data, 424
concept of, 413–418
eugenics and, 413
genetic ancestry data and, 422–424
genocide and, 414–415
geographically patterned phenotypic variation and, 416–417
historical views of, 412–413
physically visible traits, classification by, 435
as polygenic, 417, 418
racial purity ideology and, 414–415
skin color, racial categorization and, 412–413, 415
stereotypes and, 417
See also Human variation
Radiator theory, 282–283
Rafting, 243–245
Random assortment, 71, 86–87
Ray, John, 29
Recessiveness, 83, 85–86, 89
autosomal recessive traits and, 91–93
carriers and, 89, 93
Mendelian traits in humans and, 88–89
misconceptions about, 89–90
See also Heredity; Mendelian inheritance
Recognition species concept, 125
Recombinant DNA technology, 73
Recombination process, 69, 93, 105
Reduction division, 69, 70, 71
Regional continuity model, 385, 409
Regulatory genes, 60–61, 100
embryonic development and, 60–61, 118
evolution and, 61, 100, 118–119
genetic tool kit and, 118–119
homeobox/hox genes, 60–61, 116, 119
tandem repeats and, 100
See also Genes
Relativistic perspective, 22–23
Religion, 43, 47
anti-scientific positions and, 27–28, 34, 43
argument from design and, 28
biblical accounts of creation and, 43

Christian fundamentalists and, 43, 44, 47
Christianity and, 27, 28, 43
creation science and, 44–45
earth-centered planetary system and, 28–29
evolutionary theory, opposition to, 27–28, 34, 43, 47
First Amendment, establishment clause and, 45
fixity of species concept and, 27
fundamentalism and, 44
intelligent design argument and, 44–45
Muslims and, 43, 47
natural selection and, 28, 34, 43, 47
separation of church and state, 45
Replacement models, 385–389, 409
complete replacement model and, 386–387
interbreeding, assimilation model and, 388
partial replacement models and, 387–389
See also Modern human origins/ dispersal
Replication, 53
DNA replication, 53–54
Reproduction, 198–203
breeding isolates and, 425
clones and, 71, 73–75
competition for mates and, 196
differential net reproductive success and, 42
estrus and, 198
female cycle and, 198
female investment in, 199
fertility and, 41–42
folate, role of, 441
gametes and, 51
hormones in, 477
human reproductive functioning, onset of, 481–482
hypoxia and, 449
infanticide, role of, 20–21, 200–201
K-selected species and, 198
life history traits and, 190–191, 223
male strategies for, 199
mating consortships and, 198
meiosis, impacts of, 71, 105
menopause and, 478, 482–483
mothers, fathers, and infants and, 201–203
neural tube defects/spina bifida and, 441
nondisjunction problem and, 71–72
nonrandom mating and, 430–431
r-selected species and, 198–199
random assortment of chromosomes and, 71
regulatory genes, embryonic development and, 60–61, 118
sexual dimorphism and, 199–200
sexual reproduction, genetic variation and, 71, 105
sexual selection and, 199
trisomy and, 72, 73
See also Human growth/development; Population genetics; Primate behavior; Reproductive success; Speciation
Reproductive fitness, 187, 441
Reproductive isolation, 29, 47, 123
Reproductive strategies, 198–199

Reproductive success, 39, 41–42, 45, 484
differential net reproductive success, 42
dominance hierarchies and, 192–193
fitness and, 39, 41, 187
hybrids and, 125
See also Natural selection; Reproduction
Reptiles, 137
adaptive radiation of, 137
bird-dinosaur links and, 121–123
ecological niches of, 131
ectothermic capability and, 136
homodont dentition and, 135
Mesozoic era and, 137
terrestrial reptiles, 137
Resource distribution, 189
Rhesus Macaque Genome Sequencing and Analysis Consortium, 75
Rhinarium, 157
Ribosomes, 50, 51, 55, 57
Rickets, 442, 459
Rightmire, Philip, 339
RNA (ribonucleic acid), 50, 78
codons and, 56, 57
exons/introns and, 58
messenger RNA and, 55–56
ribosomes and, 51
transcription and, 55–56, 57
transfer RNA and, 56
See also Biology; DNA (deoxyribonucleic acid); Genetics; Protein synthesis
Rock art, 406–407
Russian imperial family, remains of, 18

Saadanius, 242, 249, 250, 251
Sagan, Carl, 133
Sagittal crest, 304, 305
Sagittal keel, 325
Sahelanthropus, 293, 294, 295, 298, 309, 314, 375
Sahelanthropus tchadensis, 294, 298, 309
Sangiran site, 323, 338
Savage-Rumbaugh, S., 208–209
Savanna, 3
Scanning electron microscopy (SEM), 278, 279
Scavenging, 268–269
Schöningen site, 354, 358
Science, 19
religion and, 43
Scientific method, 19–21
anti-scientific positions and, 21, 27–28, 34
critical thinking skills, development of, 21
data and, 20
empirical approach and, 20
falsification and, 20, 21, 44, 279
hypotheses and, 19–21, 23
hypothesis testing and, 20–21, 23, 43
quantitative measurement and, 20
theory and, 20–21
See also Climate change; Physical anthropology
Scientific revolution, 28–29
Scientific testing, 20–21, 43
SCL gene, 443
Scopes monkey trial, 44
Sea ice maximum/minimum, 497
Sea ice, shrinking of, 496–497

Sectorial premolar, 298
Seed-eating hypothesis, 280–282
Segregation principle, 84–85, 93
Selective agents, 40, 45, 199
Selective breeding, 36–37, 47, 82, 100, 101, 125
Selective pressures, 39, 40
Semiorders, 230
Senescence, 484–486
Sensory modalities, 146, 147
Sex cells. *See* Gametes
Sex chromosomes, 66
    abnormal number of, 71–72, 73
    nondisjunction problem and, 71–72, 73
    sex-linked traits and, 93–94
    See also Chromosomes; Reproduction;
      Zygotes
Sexual activity, *See also* Human growth/
    development; Reproduction
Sexual dimorphism, 126, 165, 166, 199–200, 282
Sexual selection, 199
Shanidar site, 361, 362, 366, 370
Shared derived characters, 122
Siamangs, 167–168
    behavioral patterns of, 203
    territoriality and, 167
    See also Apes
Sibudu, 406
Sickle-cell anemia, 62–63, 78, 88, 105–107,
    431–432
    DDT spraying and, 431, 432
    malaria, correlation with, 106–107, 431
    natural selection, demonstration of,
      105–107, 110
    Old World distribution of, 106, 107
Sickle-cell trait, 62, 106–107
Sifakas, 159
Signaling molecules, 119
Silverback gorillas, 170, 171, 177
Sima del Elefante site, 322, 338, 340, 341
Sima del los Huesos site, 347, 352–353, 371
Simian immunodeficiency virus (SIV),
    455–456
Simons, Elwyn, 239
Single nucleotide polymorphisms (SNPs),
    421, 438
Sister groups, 226, 237
Sivapithecus, 254, 255, 256, 260
Skeletal biology, 458–463
Skeletal remains:
    bioarchaeology and, 16, 461–463
    cancers and, 459
    dental disease evidence and, 458
    derived skeletal traits and, 226
    forensic anthropology and, 16–18, 22
    fractures and, 459, 460
    metabolic diseases and, 459
    osteoarthritis and, 459, 460, 461–462
    osteology and, 16
    prehistoric behavior/diet, skeletal
      evidence of, 461–463
    prehistoric diseases, skeletal evidence of,
      458–460
    preservation of, 128–130, 139
    scoliosis and, 460
    wounds caused by weapons and, 460
    See also Anatomy; Bones; Fossils

Skhūl Cave site, 390, 392–393, 394
Skin cancer, 440, 441, 446–447
Skin color, 95–96, 439–444, 463
    carotene and, 440
    early hominins and, 441
    genes involved in, 443
    geographical distribution in indigenous
      human populations, 439
    hemoglobin and, 440
    melanin and, 440–441, 442
    racial categories and, 412–413, 415
    skin cancer, protection from, 440, 441,
      446–447
    solar radiation and, 439–444, 463
    UV radiation, pigmented skin and, 438,
      439–444
    vitamin D hypothesis and, 442–444, 464
Slash-and-burn agriculture, 431
Smallpox, 454
Smith, Fred, 388, 397
Social behavior, primates, 192–206, 218–220
Social brain hypothesis, 206
Social hierarchies/rank, 192–194
Social organization, 190
    bonobos and, 173
    chimpanzees and, 172
    gibbons/siamangs and, 167
    primate social groupings and, 148,
      190, 223
    tarsiers and, 159–160
    See also Primate behavior; Social structure
Social structure, 187–191
    activity patterns and, 191
    basal metabolic rate and, 188
    body size and, 188
    diet/nutritional requirements and,
      188–189
    dispersal patterns and, 190
    human activities, impact of, 191
    life history traits and, 190–191, 223
    matrilines and, 189
    monogamous paring, 190
    multi-male/multi-female groups and,
      190, 191
    one-male/multi-female groups and, 190
    polyandrous group and, 190, 201
    predation and, 189, 191–192
    resource distribution and, 289
    sleeping sites, distribution/types of, 191
    social groupings and, 190, 223
    solitary individuals and, 190
    strategies of behavior and, 191, 193
    See also Primate behavior; Social
      organization
Solar radiation:
    folate, degradation of, 441, 463–464
    skin cancer and, 446–447
    skin color and, 438, 438–444
    tuberculosis and, 442–443
    vitamin D hypothesis and, 442–444
    vitamin D synthesis and, 464
    See also Human adaptation
Solutrean tool industry, 359, 400, 401
Somatic cells, 51, 78
    chromosomes in, 67–69
    mitosis and, 67–69

Space exploration, 4, 5, 7
Spear-throwers (atlatls), 402, 407
Specialized characteristics, 137–138
Speciation, 5, 29–30, 38, 124–125, 139
    behavioral isolation and, 125
    biological species concept and, 123–124
    branching evolution/cladogenesis and, 125
    crown group and, 227
    ecological species concept and, 125–126
    genetic drift/natural selection, cumulative
      effects of, 124–125
    geographical isolation and, 124
    natural selection processes and, 36–38, 45,
      124–125
    pace of, 138
    polytypic species and, 413
    recognition species concept and, 125
    reproductive isolation and, 123
    speed of, 46
    splitters vs. lumpers and, 127, 375–376
    taxon/taxa and, 227
    time for, 26
    See also Fossil primates; Fossils;
      Macroevolution; Species
Species, 5, 29, 123–128
    acquired characteristics, use-disuse theory
      and, 30–31
    binomial nomenclature and, 29–30
    biological variation within, 37
    catastrophism doctrine and, 32
    definition of, 123–128
    derived traits and, 120
    diversity of, 118
    environment-organism relationship and,
      118–119
    fixity of species concept, 27, 30
    fossils and, 126–127
    founder effect and, 102
    genetic bottlenecks and, 103–104
    genetic drift and, 124
    genus/genera and, 29–30
    geographical isolation and, 124
    interbreeding and, 123, 425
    last common ancestor and, 26, 227
    microevolutionary changes and, 26
    number of, 114
    number of nonhuman primate species,
      144
    paleospecies and, 127
    polytypic species and, 413
    reproductive isolation and, 29, 47, 123
    speciation and, 5
    See also Endangered species; Fossils;
      Modern evolutionary theory; Natural
      selection; Speciation
Spider monkeys, 164
Spina bifida, 441
Splitters, 127, 376
Sponheimer, Matt, 269
Spy site, 362
St. Césaire site, 361, 362, 364
Stable carbon isotope analysis, 269, 462–463
Standard deviation, 96
Steinheim site, 353, 354
Stem cell research, 49
Stem group, 227, 228

Stereoscopic vision, 147
Sterkfontein site, 208, 292, 295, 311, 312
Stewart, John, 376
Stone tools. *See* Tools
Stratigraphic dating, 273
Strepsirrhini, 155, 157, 182, 226, 232, 238
Stress, 438, 476
Stringer, Chris, 376
Struggle for existence, 37
Subfossils, 235
Subsistence patterns, 12, 368–369
Sungir site, 401, 404, 406
Superorder, 226
Superposition principle, 273
Swanscombe site, 353, 354
Swartkrans site, 208, 295, 305, 311, 312, 322
Sweating, 445
Swine flu, 10, 456–457
Symbolic behavior, 369–370, 380
Symbolic language, 207–208, 209, 223
Symbolic representation. *See* Art
Synthetic bacteria, 75, 76
Syphilis, 458, 459

Tabun Cave site, 362, 365
Tamarins, 163
Tandem repeats, 100
Taphonomy, 130, 139, 272, 278
Tarsiers, 159–160
    anthropoid characteristics of, 160
    behavioral patterns of, 159–160
    evolution of, 236–237
    eyes of, 160
    geographical distribution of, 160
    vocalizations of, 207
    See also Fossil primates; Primate
        adaptations; Primates
Tasters and nontasters, 420–421, 429
Taung child, 286, 295, 307
Taxon/taxa, 227
Taxonomy, 30, 116
    of primates, 155, 156
    See also Classification
Tay-Sachs disease, 88, 109
Technology, 6, 7, 400–408
    communications technology, 7
    skyscrapers and, 7
    See also Tools
Teeth. *See* Dentition
Teilhardina, 234, 236
Telomere hypothesis, 485–486
Terra Amata site, 354
Terrestrial lifestyle, 258
Territoriality, 166, 167, 216–218
Teshik Tash site, 362, 366
Thalassemia, 88
Theory, 20–21
    falsification and, 20, 21, 44, 279
    verification of, 20–21
    See also Evolutionary theory; Scientific
        method
Thermal environment. *See* Climate change;
        Cold climates; Hot climates; Human
        adaptation
Thermoluminescence (TL) dating method, 275
Theropithecus, 248

Theropods, 122
Thymine, 53
Tianyuan Cave site, 393, 394, 400
Tibetans, 450, 451
Time. *See* Cosmic calendar; Deep time;
        Geological time scale
Timpuseng site, 407
Tools:
    Acheulian tool industry and, 330, 340, 341,
        345, 357, 359, 379
    Aurignacian tool industry and, 359,
        399, 400
    blanks and, 277
    burins and, 402
    butchering and, 341
    Chatelperronian tool industry and, 359,
        364, 400
    cores and, 277
    direct percussion method and, 277
    flake tools and, 277
    Gravettian tool industry and, 359, 400
    hominin toolmaking and, 265
    knappers and, 277, 401
    lithic assemblage and, 277
    Magdalenian tool industry and, 359, 400,
        401–402
    microliths and, 277–278, 405–406
    microwear and, 278
    Mousterian tool industry and, 359,
        367–368, 380
    Oldowan tool industry and, 277, 340, 359
    pressure flaking method and, 278
    primate tool use, 212–215, 222
    punch blade technique and, 402
    Solutrean tool industry and, 359, 400, 401
    spear-throwers (atlatls) and, 402, 407
    stone tool/lithic technology and, 277–278
    stone tools and, 4, 7, 265
    stone tools, location of sites in Africa, 271
    thrust spear hunting and, 358
    See also Technology
Toros-Menalla site, 293, 295, 297, 298
Toxin exposure, 98
Transcription, 55–56, 57
Transcription factors, 119
Transfer RNA (tRNA), 56
Transposable elements (TEs), 59
Trinil site, 323, 331
Trinil skullcap, 331
Trinkaus, Eric, 368, 399
Trisomy, 72, 73
Tuberculosis, 41, 442–443, 452
    antibiotic-resistant, 457
Tugen Hills site, 294, 295, 297, 298
Tutu, Desmond, 422
Tyrannosaurus rex, 113, 114

Ultraviolet light, 440–441
    See also Solar radiation
Undernutrition, 473–474
Uniformitarianism, 32–33
United States:
    adult obesity rates in, 474
    carbon dioxide production of, 504
    Christian fundamentalist beliefs and, 43,
        44, 47

    extreme drought in, 498
    extreme storms in, 498
    First Amendment, establishment clause
        and, 45
    life expectancy in, 484, 486
    teaching evolution in public schools in, 26,
        44–45, 47
    top five killers in, 484
Upper Paleolithic, 359, 363, 370, 409
    art and, 400–405
    Aurignacian tool industry and, 399, 400
    bow and arrow hunting and, 407
    burial practices and, 401
    burins and, 402
    Chatelperronian tool industry and, 364, 400
    climate change and, 400, 401, 407–408
    cultural periods of, 400
    culture of, 400–408
    fire, deliberate control/use of, 402
    Gravettian tool industry and, 359, 400
    knapping and, 401
    Magdalenian tool industry and, 359, 400,
        401–402
    Neanderthals and, 369
    pottery, 403
    punch blade technique and, 402
    Solutrean tool industry and, 400, 401
    See also Modern human origins/dispersal;
        Modern humans
Use-disuse theory, 30–31
Ust'-Ishim site, 395, 396
UV radiation. *See* Solar radiation

Vaccination: anti-vaccination movement, 457
Valley fever, 458
Variation, 5, 23, 37, 99, 100–105, 410–435
    adaptive significance and, 13–14
    biological significance of, 126–127
    continuous variation, 94, 96
    in fossils, 126
    founder effect and, 102–105
    gene flow and, 100–102
    genetic bottlenecks and, 103–104
    genetic drift and, 102–105
    genetic variation and, 13–14, 61
    homeobox/hox genes and, 60–61
    interspecific variation and, 127
    intraspecific variation and, 127
    in modern humans, 410–435
    mutation and, 100
    natural selection and, 42, 99
    paleospecies, variation in, 127
    phenotypic variation and, 96, 416–417,
        418, 435
    physical variation, 13–14
    production and redistribution of, 99,
        100–101
    recombination and, 69, 105
    selective pressures and, 39
    sexual dimorphism and, 126
    sexual reproduction and, 37
    species, biological variation within, 37
    See also Fossils; Human variation; Modern
        evolutionary theory; Natural selection
Vasoconstriction, 448
Vasodilation, 445

Vectors of disease, 10, 451–452, 457, 498
Velociraptor, 122
Vertebral column, curves in, 292
Vertebrate evolution, 130–138
    Age of Dinosaurs and, 135
    Age of Fishes and, 134
    Age of Mammals and, 134, 226
    analogies and, 117
    ancestral/primitive characters and, 120, 137–138, 145
    biological continuum and, 221–222
    cladistics and, 117–123
    cladogram of relationships, 123
    common land vertebrate ancestor and, 122
    conserved genes and, 118–119
    continental drift, impact of, 131, 132
    derived/modified characters and, 120
    evo-devo approach and, 118–119
    evolutionary systematics and, 117–120, 124
    first fishes, 134
    first reptiles, 134
    genetic tool kit and, 118–119
    geological time scale and, 130–134
    homologies and, 116–117, 120, 145
    homoplasy and, 117, 122, 166
    hox genes and, 119
    major extinction events and, 131, 135, 500
    monophyletic groups and, 120
    placental and marsupial mammals and, 135, 136
    polyphyletic groups and, 120
    reptile radiation and, 135
    shared derived characters and, 122
    time line of, 134–135
    See also Dinosaurs; Fossils; Macroevolution; Mammalian evolution; Species
Vertebrates, 114–116, 139
    characteristics of, 114, 118, 139
    classes of, 114
    classification of, 114–116
    number of *Hox* genes in, 119
Victoria, Queen of England, 93, 94
Victoriapithecus, 246, 250
Vindija site, 367
Virunga Volcanoes Conservation Area, 177–178
Vision:
    binocular vision and, 147
    color vision and, 146, 150
    depth perception and, 147
    stereoscopic vision and, 147
Visual predation hypothesis, 150
Vitamin D hypothesis, 442–444
Vitamin D synthesis, 444, 464
Vocalizations, 207
Volcanoes:
    fossil footprints and, 3
    fossil preservation and, 3
von Koenigswald, Ralph, 255

Wadley, Lyn, 406
Wallace, Alfred Russel, 27, 38, 47, 98
Warmbloodedness, 135–136, 144
Watson, John, 52, 53
Wenzhong, Pei, 336
Wernicke's area, 210
West Lake Turkana site, 305, 326
White, Tim, 296, 389
Whole-genome analysis, 422–423
Wilkins, Maurice, 52, 53
Wilson, E. O., 504
Wolpoff, Milford, 385
Woranso-Mille area, 303
Worldview, 6

X chromosome, 72, 73

Y-5 molar, 248, 250
Y chromosome, 72, 73
Yuanmoupithecus, 258, 261
Yunxian County site finds, 335

Zagros Mountains, 366
Zhoukoudian Cave site, 323, 324, 331–335
    cultural remains from, 333–335
    Dragon Bone Hill cave and, 336–337
    fire, deliberate control/use of, 334
    Homo erectus skeletal remains and, 323, 324, 331–335, 338
    tool construction/use and, 331
    See also Homo erectus
Zhoukoudian Upper Cave site, 393, 394, 395
Zinjanthropus, 274, 275
Zoonotic diseases, 452, 455–456
Zygomatics, 255, 305
Zygotes, 51, 478
    See also Reproduction